CULINARY ARTS INSTITUTE

encyclopedic
COOKBOOK

• new revised edition

edited by RUTH BEROLZHEIMER

associate editors   EDNA L. GAUL   MADELEINE JASPER   DOROTHY L. HEALD
ANN HEIBERG   CAROLINE SCHOETTKER   ANNIS R. GROSS   HELEN LUCY KINNEY
LOUISE WILLEY   JEANNE R. HOMM   HENRIETTA DUNLOP   ETHEL J. GANS
JANE C. MORELAND   ELLEN V. LITTLEJOHN   DOROTHY SHAUGER   ELLEN LEVIN
ELIZABETH TYNE   DORCAS LAUGHLIN   ETHEL MCDONALD   DOROTHY CANFIELD

A Perigee Book

Perigee Books
are published by
The Putnam Publishing Group
200 Madison Avenue
New York, NY 10016

1988 Edition

Library of Congress Cataloging-in-Publication Data

Culinary Arts Institute encyclopedic cookbook.

Reprint. Originally published: New York :
Putnam, 1986.
Includes index.
1. Cookery, American.   2. Menus.   I. Berolzheimer, Ruth.
II. Culinary Arts Institute.
[TX715.C96256   1987]   641   87-2522
ISBN 0-399-51388-4

Printed in the United States of America
3 4 5 6 7 8 9 10

Contents

(In many cases variations of recipes follow cooking instructions)

The Personality of a Cookbook is as apparent as it is important. It is composed of known and stable ingredients with unknown and elusive ones to make a mixture as familiar, friendly and exhilarating as a pine woods early on a summer morn.

The Stable Ingredients are compounded of a sound knowledge of what the homemaker needs for herself and her family; an easy handling of all fundamental facts on preparing and serving foods, based on the science of nutrition up to the date of publication, and on the presentation of those facts in a simple, concise, explicit, well organized, specific, easy-to-follow, step-by-step procedure that gives a comforting feeling of confidence in the final product.

The Elusive Charm of this personality stems from clear overtones: a light touch —a sense of humor—a flair for the clever idea in cooking and serving that results in something called style, but above all a feeling for the kind of beauty that women want about them in their work-a-day world.

Most of This Beauty has been made possible by the cooperation and confidence of colleagues in the food and equipment industry, whose constant flow of inspiring ideas has resulted in illustrations of glorious usefulness. For these the editors are deeply indebted to:

Aluminum Cooking Utensil Company, American Can Company, American Cranberry Exchange, American Dairy Association, American Fruit Growers, Inc., American Gas Association, American Institute of Baking, American Meat Institute, American Molasses Company, American Spice Trade Association, Angelus-Campfire Company, Appalachian Apple Service, Inc., Armour and Company, Ball Brothers Company, Biscuit and Cracker Manufacturers Association, Blueberry Cooperative Association, Booth Fisheries Corporation, Brazil Nut Advertising Fund, Brown County Pottery, Bureau of Industrial Service, Inc., California Extension Service, California Fig Institute, California Food Research Institute, California Fruit Growers Exchange, California Lima Bean Growers Associaton, Campbell Soup Company, Canned Salmon Industry, Carnation Company, Cookware Associates, Corning Glass Works, Corn Products Refining Company, Cranberry Canners, Inc., Cranberry Growers, Inc., Cudahy Packing Company, Cultivated Mushroom Institute of America, Inc., Dixie Vortex Company, Dow Chemical Company, Florida Citrus Commission, Foley Manufacturing Company, Fostoria Glass Company, Frosted Food Sales Co., Gaper Catering Company, Gebhardt Chili Powder Company, General Foods Corporation, Hawaiian Pineapple Company, Hecker Products Corporation, H. J. Heinz Company, Hershey Estates, Hotpoint, Idaho Potato Growers, International Harvester Company, International Silver Company, Evaporated Milk Association, John F. Jelke Company, Kalamazoo Vegetable Parchment Company, Kerr Glass Manufacturing Company, Kraft Foods Company, Land O' Lakes Creameries, Inc., Lenox, Inc., Louisiana State University, Lunt Silversmiths, McGraw Electric Company, Maine Development Commission, Beatrice Foods Co., Miami Beach Gas Company, Milk Foundation, Mirro Aluminum, John Morrell and Company, Muench Kreuzer Candle Company, Inc., National Association Service, National Biscuit Company, National Dairy Council, National Kraut Packers Association, Inc., National Live Stock and Meat Board, National Peach Council, National Peanut Council, National Presto Industries, Inc., National Shrimp Canners Association, New Mexico College of Agriculture and Mechanical Arts, Northwestern Yeast Company, Ohio State University, Oklahoma Agricultural and Mechanical College, Oneida Community, The Palmer House, Pendleton and Dudley, Pennsylvania State College, Peoples Gas Light and Coke Company, Pet Milk Company, Pillsbury Flour Mills, Poultry and Egg National Board, Publicity Associates, Purdue University, Quaker Oats Company, Reed and Barton, Reynolds Metals Company, Robertshaw Thermostat Company, Rumford Chemical Works, St. Charles Custom Kitchens, San Antonio Public Service Company, Sealtest Laboratory Kitchen, South Dakota State College, Standard Brands, Inc., State of Wisconsin, Wisconsin Department of Agriculture, Sunsweet, The Best Foods, Inc., The Borden Company, The Junket Folks, The Kellogg Company, 3-Squares-a-Day Cooking School, United Brewers Industrial Foundation, U. S. Bureau of Human Nutrition and Home Economics, U. S. Bureau of Fisheries, University of Georgia, University of Illinois, University of Minnesota, University of Wisconsin, Utah State Agricultural College, VanCamp Sea Food Company, Vernon Kilns, Washington State Apple Commission, Wesson Oil & Snowdrift Sales Co., West Bend Aluminum Company, Wheat Flour Institute, Wine Institute, Winter Pear Bureau.

Ruth Berolzheimer

The American Family and the American Community have always been food conscious . . . In every section of the country there are special food festivals . . . Fish Frys in the South, Barbecues and Chuck Wagon days in the West, Clambakes in the East and Steak Frys and Weiner Roasts in the North . . . All happy occasions are celebrated with food . . . often very colorfully . . . The etched inserts on the Chapter Title Pages are a salute to many of these occasions. They are warm-hearted reminders of the richness of the American scene.

APPETIZER—A small serving of food or beverage served before or as the first course of a meal.

ARTICHOKE—A vegetable. The Jerusalem artichoke looks like a potato. The globe artichoke is cylindrical in shape, with a tapering "heart" covered with fibrous green leaves.

ASPIC—A transparent jelly, usually made of meat stock, which has been boiled down sufficiently to become firm when cold. Also applies to meat, fish or vegetable stock which has been thickened with gelatin.

BATTER—A mixture of liquid, flour, etc., that can be beaten or stirred.

BISQUE—A rich thick cream soup usually made from fish. Also a rich frozen dessert, usually containing powdered nuts or macaroons.

BONBON—A sweet made of or dipped into fondant.

BOUILLABAISE—A chowder made of several varieties of fish and white wine.

Meat, fish or vegetables molded in aspic and served on chicory are found on many a luncheon plate

BOUILLON—Clear delicately seasoned soup usually made from lean beef stock.

CAFFEINE—An alkaloidal substance found in the coffee bean, coffee leaf, tea leaf, yerba mate, cacao bean, etc. The content in a cup of coffee is 1.5 grains; in tea less than 1 grain.

CANAPÉ—An appetizer made of a small piece of bread spread with a highly seasoned food.

CARAMEL—Burnt sugar sirup used for coloring and flavoring. Also a chewy candy.

CAVIAR—Salted roe (fish eggs). Originally from sturgeon.

CAPON—A castrated male chicken. Grows large and has tender meat.

CHARLOTTE OR CHARLOTTE RUSSE—Usually a gelatin dessert with flavored whipped cream molded in a form lined with cake or ladyfingers.

CHICORY—The root of a plant that is cut into slices, dried and roasted as coffee. Leaves of plant are used for salad and sometimes called curly endive.

CHOWDER—A dish made of fresh fish, or clams, pork, crackers, onions, etc., stewed together.

CIDER—The juice pressed from apples used as a beverage or to make vinegar.

COBBLER—A deep-dish fruit pie with a rich biscuit dough used instead of pastry.

COCKTAIL—(a) An appetizer served before or as the first course of a meal. (b) An alcoholic beverage usually served before dinner. (c) Fruit or vegetable juice. (d) Cut fruit or shellfish with tart sauce served as first course.

COMPOTE—Sweetened stewed fruit, cooked to keep the fruit as whole as possible.

CONDIMENTS—Food seasonings such as salt, vinegar, herbs and spices.

CONSOMMÉ—A highly seasoned clear soup made from one or a combination of meats.

CRACKLINGS—Crisp particles left after fat has been fried out.

CREAM SAUCE—A white sauce made with cream.

CROQUETTES—A mixture of chopped or ground cooked food held together by eggs on a thick sauce, shaped, dipped into egg and crumbs and fried.

CROUTONS—Cubes of toasted or fried bread served with soup.

CUSTARD—A cooked or baked mixture mainly of eggs and milk. It may be sweetened to use as a dessert or flavored with cheese, fish, etc., as an entrée.

CUTLET—A small piece of meat cut from the leg or rib of veal or pork, or a croquette mixture made into the shape of a cutlet.

DEEP-DISH PIE—A fruit pie with top crust only, baked in a deep dish.

DOUGH—A mixture of liquid, flour, etc., that is stiff enough to be handled or kneaded.

DRIPPINGS—Fat and liquid resulting from cooking meat.

ENTRÉE—The main dish of an informal meal or a subordinate dish served between main courses.

FONDANT—A sugar and water mixture cooked to the soft-ball stage (234°F.), cooled and kneaded.

FONDUE—A baked food similar to a soufflé but including bread or cracker crumbs.

FRAPPÉ—Sweetened fruit juice frozen until of mushy consistency.

FRITTERS—Fruit, meat, vegetables or fish covered with batter or chopped and mixed with batter. Usually fried in deep fat.

FROSTING—A cooked or uncooked sugar mixture used to cover and decorate cakes, cookies and other foods.

GELATIN—A purified protein found in connective tissues and bones of animals.

GIBLETS—The heart, liver and gizzard of poultry.

GOULASH—A thick meat stew originating in Hungary.

HOLLANDAISE—A rich sauce made of eggs and butter, served hot with vegetables and fish.

HORS D'OEUVRES—Salty, tart or crisp foods served as appetizers, such as canapés, fish, pickles, olives, celery, sausages, etc.

ICE—A frozen mixture of fruit juice, sugar and water.

INFUSION—Liquid extracted from coffee, tea or herbs.

JULIENNE—Food cut into match-like strips.

MACEDOINE—A mixture of vegetables or fruits.

MARINADE—An oil and acid mixture as French dressing in which food is allowed to stand to give flavor to meats and salads.

MARZIPAN—A paste of sweet almonds and sugar.

MERINGUE—A mixture of stiffly beaten egg whites, flavoring and sugar. Used on pies, etc.

MINESTRONE—A thick Italian vegetable soup.

MOCHA—A flavoring made with coffee infusion or with coffee infusion and chocolate.

MOUSSE—A mixture of whipped cream, sugar and flavoring frozen without stirring. Or flavored thin cream and gelatin combined with meat, fruits or vegetables.

MUFFIN—A drop batter baked in individual pans and served as a quick bread.

PARFAIT—A frozen dessert made of a foundation of beaten egg whites or yolks cooked with hot sirup, sometimes with whipped cream added. Also applied to ice cream and sirup served in parfait glasses.

PURÉE—A smooth thick liquid made by pressing cooked fruit or vegetables through a sieve.

RAGOUT—A thick highly seasoned stew.

RELISH—A highly seasoned food used as an accompaniment.

ROE—Eggs of fish.

SHERBET—Frozen mixture of fruit juice, sugar, egg whites and milk or water.

SKEWER—A long strong pin of wood or metal used to hold food in shape while cooking.

STOCK—A rich extract of soluble parts of meat, fish, poultry, etc. A basis for soups or gravies.

VEGETABLE MARROW—An egg-shaped gourd about 8 to 10 inches long. A vegetable.

PROCESSES

BAKE—To cook by dry heat, usually in an oven.

BARBECUE—To roast or broil whole, as a hog, fowl, etc. Usually done on a revolving frame over coals or upright in front of coals. To cook thin slices of meat in a highly seasoned vinegar sauce.

BASTE—To moisten roasting meat or other food while baking by pouring melted fat, drippings or sauces over it.

BEAT—To make a mixture smooth and introduce air by a brisk regular motion that lifts mixture over and over.

BLANCH—To pour boiling water over a food, then drain and rinse with cold water. Used to

Hollandaise sauce is decorative and delicious on vegetables and fish

whiten or to remove skins as from almonds.

BLEND—To mix two or more ingredients so that each loses its identity.

BOIL—To cook in liquid, usually water, in which large bubbles rise rapidly and continually so that all of the liquid is agitated.

BRAISE—To cook meat by searing in fat, then simmering in a covered dish in small amount of moisture.

BREW—To steep or let stand in hot water to extract the essence or flavor, as in tea.

BROIL—To cook by exposing the food directly to the heat.

CANDY—To conserve or preserve by boiling with sugar. To incrust or coat with sugar.

CARAMELIZE—To heat dry sugar or foods containing sugar until light brown and of caramel flavor.

CHOP—To cut into pieces.

COMBINE—To mix ingredients.

CREAM—To work foods until soft and fluffy. Usually applied to shortening and sugar.

CRUMB—To dip food into or roll in cracker or bread crumbs.

CUT—(a) To divide foods with a knife or scissors. (b) To incorporate solid fat into dry ingredients with the least amount of blending, so the fat remains in small particles.

DEVIL—To make a food hot or spicy by adding condiments.

DICE—To cut into small cubes.

DISSOLVE—To pass into solution.

DREDGE—To coat with flour.

FOLD IN—To mix food without releasing air bubbles by lifting a part of the liquid from the very bottom of the bowl through the rest of the mixture to the top till the foods are blended.

FRICASSEE—To cook meat by stewing in gravy.

FRY—To cook in fat.

(a) PAN-FRY—To cook in small amount of fat.

(b) DEEP-FAT FRY—To cook in enough fat to completely cover food while cooking.

GARNISH—To ornament with something bright and savory. Something added for decoration.

GLACÉ—To coat with a thin sugar sirup that has been cooked to crack stage.

GRATE—To reduce to small particles by rubbing with anything rough and indented.

GRILL—To cook by direct heat on a gridiron.

GRIND—To reduce food to particles by using a food chopper. .

KNEAD—To manipulate with a pressing motion plus folding and stretching. Usually applied to bread dough.

LARD—To place strips of fat into or on top of lean meat or fish.

LEAVEN—To cause baked foods to rise by adding a leavening agent.

MARINATE—To treat with a marinade.

MASK—To completely cover with a thick sauce, jelly or mayonnaise.

MELT—To liquefy by heat.

MINCE—To chop very fine.

MIX—To combine in any manner that effects distribution.

MOLD—To shape food, usually by pouring the liquified food into a mold. When the liquid is cooled it will retain the shape of the mold.

PAN-BROIL—To cook meat on a hot surface, pouring off fat as it accumulates.

PARBOIL—To boil raw food until partially cooked.

PARCH—To brown by means of dry heat. Applied to grains.

PARE—To cut off the outside covering. Applied to potatoes, apples, etc.

PASTEURIZE—To preserve food by heating sufficiently to destroy micro-organisms and arrest fermentation. Applied to liquids such as milk and fruit juices.

PEEL—To strip off the outer covering. Applied to oranges, grapefruit, etc.

POACH—To cook slowly in hot liquid to cover.

RENDER—To free fat from connective tissue by heating until fat melts and can be drained off.

ROAST—To cook by dry heat, usually in an oven.

SAUTÉ—To cook in a small quantity of fat, shifting the food from side to side.

SCALD—To heat liquid to temperature just below the boiling point. A thin skin forming over milk indicates sufficient heating.

SCORE—To cut lightly so as to mark with lines.

SHIRR—To break eggs into a dish with cream or crumbs and bake in oven.

SIMMER—To cook in liquid usually water, at a temperature below boiling. Small bubbles are formed and rise slowly but the liquid is practically motionless.

SKEWER—To pierce or fasten with skewers—as a piece of meat.

STEAM—To cook in the steam generated by boiling water.

STEW—To cook in a small amount of water. The water may boil or simmer.

SPICES AND HERBS

ALLSPICE—The dried berry of pimento tree of the West Indies. Used as a condiment. The name is due to the flavor which resembles a combination of cloves, cinnamon and nutmeg.

ANISE—The fruit of a small annual plant which dries into the form of a seed. The best is grown in Spain, Mexico and India. Used on breads, cakes and cookies and as a flavoring for medicine and licorice products.

BALM—A perennial garden herb with a sharp lemon scent. Use fresh or dried in soups and salads.

BASIL—An annual plant cultivated in Western Europe. Leaves are dried, ground and powdered. Used to flavor soups, sauces, sausages and stews. The flavor combines well with tomatoes.

BAY LEAF—The aromatic leaf of the sweet-bay or laurel tree. Dried whole and used to flavor soups, meats and pickles.

CAPERS—The flower buds of Capparis spinosa grown in Mediterranean countries. Pickled and used as a condiment.

CARAWAY—A biennial herb with an aromatic fruit usually known as caraway seeds. Used in breads, cookies, cakes, candies, salads and cheese. Marketed whole or ground.

CARDAMOM—An aromatic fruit of a number of zinziberaceous plants grown in Ceylon, India and Central America. The fruit is in the shape of a pod with seeds inside. Sold in the whole pod, as whole seeds or as ground seeds. Used as a condiment.

CAYENNE PEPPER—Powdered pod and seeds of various capsicums yielding a hot, savory flavor used in meat dishes and gravies and sometimes called red pepper. Grown mainly in Africa.

CELERY SEED—Seed of a small plant similar in appearance and taste to celery. Used whole or ground to flavor soups, stews, cheese, pickles and some salads. Southern France, India and the United States are producers.

CELERY SALT—Mixture of ground celery seed and fine white salt. Used in meats, salads and many other dishes.

CHERVIL—An apiaceous plant with aromatic leaves used to flavor soups and salads.

CHILI—A hot pepper. Used as a base for chili sauce and other spicy dishes.

CHILI POWDER—A mixture of ground red peppers, cuminseed and other spices. Used to flavor omelettes, sea food cocktails, etc.

CHIVES—Similar to green onions though smaller and milder.

CHUTNEY—A spicy pickle of compound fruit and seasonings.

CINNAMON—True cinnamon is the inner bark of Cinnamon zeylancium which grows only in Ceylon. It has a very mild flavor. Cassia cinnamon grown also in the Far East is most generally used and has a more full-bodied flavor. The dried bark is sold in sticks or ground.

CLOVES—The flower buds of a tree which is grown in the Netherlands East Indies, Zanzibar and Madagascar. Sold whole or ground.

CORIANDER—An herb with aromatic seeds. Used for confections, cookies, pickles and meat products.

CUMINSEED—Dried fruit of Cuminum cyninum. Has a slightly bitter flavor. Used for flavoring meats, sausages, pickles and as an ingredient of curry powder.

CURRY POWDER—A yellow condiment from India containing various spices.

DILL—An annual herb grown for its aromatic seed. Used in pickles and sauces. Grown mostly in India.

FENNEL—An herb, seeds of which are ground and used to flavor fish sauces and apple pie. It resembles celery in appearance and has a fragrance and taste suggestive of anise. The young stalks are used as a salad green or served like celery in Latin countries.

Here are cinnamon sticks, whole mace, nutmegs and cloves with ground cinnamon and nutmeg

GARLIC—A strong flavored plant of the lily family, cloves of which are used to flavor meats, salads, etc.

GARLIC SALT—Mixture of garlic and fine white salt used in meats, salads, etc.

GINGER—The root of an herbaceous perennial grown in semi-tropical countries.
Black ginger—Unscraped rootstock.
White ginger—Scraped and peeled rootstock. Often candied.

LEEKS—Strong flavored plant similar to onion.

MACE—The network around the nutmeg kernel. It is a vivid red when fresh and dries to a light orange. It is sold whole as "blades" or ground and is used to flavor sauces, gravies, cakes and pies. The aroma is similar to nutmeg but it has a different flavor.

MARJORAM—A fragrant annual of the mint family. Leaves are dried and used whole or powdered to flavor soups, salads, stuffings, meats and sausages. The best grade comes from France, though grown also in Northern Africa and Chile.

MINCEMEAT SPICE—A mixture of spices such as cloves, allspice, cinnamon, etc. Used to flavor mincemeat, cakes, cookies and sauces.

MINT—A fragrant plant, the leaves of which are used (either fresh or dried) to flavor certain soups, vegetables, fruits and beverages.

MUSTARD—A plant, the seeds of which are used either whole or ground. Also combined with spices and vinegar to make a moist product known as prepared mustard. Used in pickles, meats, salads, etc.

NUTMEG—The kernel of fruit of the Myristica tree grown in the Netherlands East Indies and British West Indies. The whole fruit resembles an apricot in shape and size. It has four parts: the outer husk, the mace, the inner shell and the seed or nutmeg. Sold whole or ground.

ONION—A strong flavored plant of the lily family. Used to flavor meats, salads, etc.

ONION SALT—A dried mixture of onion and fine white salt used to flavor meats, soups and salads.

PAPRIKA—A sweet red pepper which is dried and ground after seeds and stem are removed. Its mild flavor is good with shellfish, fish and salad dressings. The best brands are made of Spanish and Hungarian paprikas.

PARSLEY—A biennial herb used to flavor meats, vegetables and salads. Used also as a garnish

PEPPER—Made from peppercorns which are the dried berries of a vine, Piper Nigrum.
Black pepper—Made from the whole berry.
White pepper—Made from what is left of the fully ripened berry after the outer coat has been removed.

PIMIENTO—The fleshy fruit of the Spanish paprika. Canned and used in meat and vegetable dishes and salads.

POPPY SEED—Seed of one variety of the poppy plant, but not the opium poppy. Used for breads, rolls, cakes and cookies. Oil may be extracted and used in a salad oil. Mostly imported from central Europe.

POULTRY SEASONING—A mixture of spices such as sage, thyme, marjoram, etc. Used as a flavoring.

PUMPKIN PIE SPICE—A mixture of spices such as cinnamon, cloves, ginger, etc. Used to flavor pumpkin pie.

ROSEMARY—An evergreen plant, the leaves and flowers of which are used to flavor and garnish fish, stews and sauces.

SAFFRON—The stigma of a flower similar to a crocus, Crocus sativus. Dried and used to flavor breads and meats. Has a rich orange-yellow color.

SAGE—A perennial mint, the leaves of which are dried and used in stuffings and meats.

SAUSAGE SEASONING—A mixture of spices such as white pepper, coriander and nutmeg.

SAVORY OR SUMMER SAVORY—An annual mint. May be used fresh or dried in sauces, stuffings, croquettes and stews. It is generally an important ingredient in prepared poultry seasonings.

SCALLIONS—Small onions.

SESAME—An herb, the seeds of which are used to flavor rolls and cookies, and after baking the flavor resembles toasted almonds. Marketed in unhulled and hulled form, the latter being preferable. The best grade of unhulled seed is a fancy orange variety from Turkey.

SOY SAUCE—A sauce made from fermented soybeans.

TABASCO SAUCE—A highly seasoned sauce made with cayenne peppers and other ingredients.

TARRAGON—A perennial herb the fresh or dried leaves of which are used to flavor salads pickles and vinegar.

THYME—An herb, the powdered leaves of which are used to season meat, poultry and clams.

These cacao pods are the beginning of all your chocolate favorites

FOOD INGREDIENTS
COCOA AND CHOCOLATE

CHOCOLATE—The plastic or solid product derived from grinding cacao nibs.

COCOA—Pulverized chocolate from which part of cacao butter has been removed.

DUTCH COCOA—Has a rich dark color due to the alkalies or carbonates used in processing.

FATS AND OILS

BUTTER—Fat from sour or ripened cream gathered in a mass, sometimes salted and colored. It contains not less than 80% by weight of milk fat.

COMPOUND—A mixture of animal fats, a mixture of vegetable fats or a mixture of both.

CORN OIL—Refined oil from the dried, crushed corn germ.

COTTONSEED OIL—Refined oil from the crushed seed of the cotton plant.

CRACKLINGS—The residue from rendered fat of meat or poultry.

CREAM—The fat of milk that rises to the top when it stands.

DRIPPINGS—The fat obtained from cooking meats.

HYDROGENATED FATS—Oils or soft fats changed to solid fat by treatment with hydrogen.

LARD—Fat rendered from the fatty tissues of the hog.

NUT MARGARINE—Made from nut oils; coconut, peanut or palm oil.

OLEOMARGARINE—Made by churning a mixture of oils, milk and salt to a consistency similar to butter. It is used as a substitute for butter.

OLIVE OIL—Oil from flesh of ripe olives. Virgin olive oil is that which is first extracted and is better in flavor and appearance than the oil produced by the second or third pressing.

PEANUT OIL—The oil extracted from peanuts. A by-product of peanut butter.

SUET—Clear, white fat of beef and mutton, usually from around the heart or kidney.

SWEET BUTTER—Made from sweet cream. Unsalted.

WHIPPED BUTTER—Butter into which air has been whipped.

FLOUR

ALL-PURPOSE FLOUR—A blend of hard or soft wheat flours, which is lower in protein than bread flour but higher than cake flour. It can be used with good results for all types of home-baked products.

BRAN—A by-product of whole wheat flour. It contains some of the outer husk and some of the endosperm.

BREAD FLOUR—Milled from inner part of hard or spring wheat.

BUCKWHEAT FLOUR—Milled from the finely ground buckwheat kernel.

Vegetable oils are quickly available for making your mayonnaise

CAKE FLOUR—Milled from soft wheat, the most highly refined flour milled; granulation uniform; protein content very low and also very delicate in quality.

CORN MEAL—Milled from corn

WHOLE-WHEAT FLOUR—Milled from cleaned whole-wheat grain.

PASTRY FLOUR—Usually made of soft wheat; low in protein and finely milled, though not as fine as cake flour.

RICE FLOUR—Milled from rice.

RYE FLOUR—Milled from rye grain. More like wheat flour in breadmaking qualities than any other grain.

SELF-RISING FLOUR—Milled from soft or winter wheat and has salt and leavening added.

SOYBEAN FLOUR—Milled from the soybean.

MILK

BUTTERMILK—Was once a by-product in the "churning" of milk or cream in making butter. Buttermilk is now made by adding a lactic acid bacteria "culture" to fresh skim milk giving it a characteristic flavor and consistency. It may be used like soured milk in cooking.

CERTIFIED MILK—Milk produced under carefully controlled hygienic conditions so it has a low bacteria count. It is usually pasteurized.

DRY MILK—Milk from which all the water has been removed. Sold in powdered form.

EVAPORATED MILK—Milk from which more than half of the water has been removed by heating in a vacuum. It is hermetically sealed in cans and then sterilized.

FORTIFICATION OF EVAPORATED MILK—Evaporated milk is now fortified with 400 USP units of Vitamin D per reconstituted quart. This procedure has replaced irradiation.

HOMOGENIZING PROCESS—Mechanical treatment of milk reducing the size and increasing the number of fat globules. Cream does not rise to the surface after this treatment but remains dispersed throughout the milk.

MALTED MILK—Product made by drying a combination of whole milk and liquid separated from a mash of ground barley malt and wheat flour. It may contain sodium chloride, sodium bicarbonate or potassium bicarbonate.

PASTEURIZED MILK—Milk that has been heated to a temperature not lower than 142°F. for 30 minutes to destroy bacteria, then cooled at once to 50° or lower.

SKIM MILK—Portion of milk remaining after part or all of cream has been removed.

DAIRY SOUR CREAM—Made by adding a "culture" to pasteurized, homogenized sweet cream. Product is thick, smooth, creamy-white, and delicately acid in flavor.

SOUR MILK—Sweet milk soured artificially by adding lemon juice or vinegar.

SWEETENED CONDENSED MILK—Sweetened whole milk from which a large amount of water has been evaporated.

VITAMIN D MILK—Milk with increased vitamin D content.

SIRUPS

CANE SIRUP—The concentrated sap of sugar cane.

CORN SIRUP—Made from corn.

CRYSTAL WHITE SIRUP—Corn sirup, granulated sugar and vanilla.

GOLDEN SIRUP—Corn sirup and refiners' sirup.

FLAVORED SIRUP—Corn sirup with one or more of the following flavorings: maple, honey, sorghum and butterscotch.

HONEY—A sirupy sweet material out of nectar of flowers, elaborated in honey sac of the honey bee and stored in their nests.

MAPLE SIRUP—The concentrated sap of the maple tree.

MOLASSES—The reduced liquor from which raw sugar has crystallized.

REFINERS' SIRUP—The liquor obtained in the process of refining sugar.

SORGHUM SIRUP—Obtained by clarification and concentration of juice of the sugar sorghum. Not to be confused with molasses.

SUGAR

BROWN SUGAR—Contains some of the molasses found in the juices from the sugar cane.

CONFECTIONERS' SUGAR—Powdered sugar which has been sifted and made into a very fine powder.

CORN SUGAR—Sugar manufactured from corn.

CUBE SUGAR—Crystals of granulated sugar pressed together into molds and cut into cubes.

GRANULATED SUGAR—Refined into crystals or granulated form from either sugar cane or beets.

LOAF SUGAR—Same as cube sugar except cut into different shapes.

MAPLE SUGAR—Crystallized maple sirup.

POWDERED SUGAR—Granulated sugar powdered by pressure.

Here is an array of tasty cheeses made in America

CHEESE

AMERICAN

BRICK—Rennet cheese, with strong sweetish flavor, an elastic texture and many small round eyes or holes.

CHEDDAR—Similar to English-made Cheddar.

COTTAGE—Soft curds. Made commercially from pasteurized sour milk with or without rennet. Also known as smierkase.

CREAM—A soft rich cheese with mild flavor. Genuine cream cheese is made from pasteurized rich cream thickened by souring or from sweet cream thickened with rennet. It is also made from thin cream thickened with rennet and from whole milk.

HAND—Soft; sharp pungent taste and odor. Made from sour milk and shaped by hand. Caraway seeds are sometimes added.

HERKIMER—Aged Cheddar.

LIEDERKRANZ—Highly flavored soft cheese; milder than Limburger. Made in Ohio from milk set with rennet. Turns tawny yellow as it ripens.

PINEAPPLE—Hard, highly colored Cheddar made in pineapple shape, then hung and dried in a net, making diamond-shaped corrugations on surface.

PROCESS CHEESE—Cheese is blended with an emulsifying agent and pasteurized.

SAGE—A Cheddar cheese formerly made by adding sage leaves to the curd. Now a sage extract is usually used.

SWISS—Similar to Swiss-made Emmenthaler.

FOREIGN TYPES—Most of the cheeses formerly imported from Europe are now successfully produced in America.

ENGLISH-MADE

CHEDDAR—Hard, sharp, white or yellow color. Made from sweet milk and sold as "full cream" (when whole milk is used), "part skim" or "skim", depending on the type of milk used.

CHESHIRE—Hard rennet cheese somewhat like Cheddar.

STILTON—Hard rennet cheese with green or blue mold and wrinkled or ridged skin or rind.

FRENCH-MADE

BRIE—Soft, rennet cheese, definite odor, sharp flavor with a red color on the surface. Made from whole or partly skimmed milk.

CAMEMBERT—Soft, rennet cheese covered with a firm rind of molds and dried cheese.

COULOMMIERS—Soft rennet cheese, somewhat like Brie.

LIVEROT—Soft rennet cheese, somewhat like Brie. Made from partially skimmed milk. Has a strong piquant flavor.

NEUFCHÂTEL—Very soft rennet cheese, made from whole or skimmed milk.

PONT L'ÉVÊQUE—Soft rennet cheese, somewhat like Brie.

ROQUEFORT—Semihard rennet cheese with blue and green mold.

GERMAN-MADE

LIMBURGER—Soft rennet cheese with strong, characteristic odor.

MÜNSTER—Semihard rennet cheese, caraway seeds or aniseed added. Made of whole milk.

HOLLAND-MADE

EDAM—Hard rennet cheese, round with a red rind.

GOUDA—Hard rennet cheese, slightly round and flat.

LEYDEN—Hard rennet cheese. Cuminseed and cloves are added to the middle of 3 layers.

ITALIAN-MADE

CACIOCAVALLO—A hard, beet-shaped rennet cheese.

GORGONZOLA—Semihard rennet cheese with streaks of mold.

PARMESAN—Hard, rennet cheese made from partly skimmed milk. Green or black rind.

PROVOLI or PROVOLONI—Made from cows' or buffaloes' milk. Hard, round, smoked and held by a net.

CHEESE—Cont.

REGGIANO—The best variety of Parmesan cheese.

SCANDINAVIAN-MADE

APPETITOST—Semihard, made from sour buttermilk.

GAMMELOST—Hard, made from skimmed sour milk, definite odor.

GJEDOST—Hard, made from goats' milk, chocolate-colored, sweet taste.

MYSOST—Semisoft whey cheese of mild sweetish flavor.

NOKKELOST—Hard, made from skimmed milk with spices.

SWISS-MADE

EMMENTHALER—Hard rennet cheese with large holes and a mild, somewhat sweetish flavor.

GRUYÈRE—Hard blended rennet cheese. Nut-like flavor.

SAP SAGO—Small, hard and green in color. Used grated.

COFFEE

There are more than 100 different kinds of coffee bought and sold in the United States. They may be divided into two general groups—Brazils and Milds. Brazils are classified into groups bearing the names of the ports through which they are exported. Following is a list of the Brazils in order considered best:

SANTOS—Bourbon is the best of the Santos; it is often used as a blend with higher priced coffee.

MINAS—In the Rio group.

PARANÀ—From Paranagua.

BAHIAS

PERNAMBUCO—From Recife.

RIOS—Have a peculiar strong flavor and a heavy taste but are used as a blend in the popular-priced packaged blends.

VICTORIAS

Milds include coffees grown in

There are many varieties of coffee; select the blend that pleases your family

all districts other than the Brazilian States.

Mexicans, Guatemalas, Haiti's Coffee, Puerto Rican Coffee, Colombians, Venezuelan Coffee, Mochas, Indian Coffee.

TEA

BLACK TEA—Made by fermentation of leaves.

Standards

Formosa Black, Congou

Java (used for all fully fermented teas except China, Japan and Formosa)

Japan Black

Kinds

North China Congous—Strong, full-bodied and fragrant, leaves are hard, black and aromatic, "the Burgundies of China teas."

South China Congous—Light in cup, leaves reddish, "the clarets of China teas."

India, Ceylon and Java—Grades according to leaf size: Broken Orange Pekoe, Orange Pekoe, Broken Pekoe, Pekoe, Pekoe Souchong, Souchong, Fannings, Dust. India teas are named after the districts in which they are grown.

Darjeiling—Finest and mo delicately flavored.

Assam—A hard flinty lea makes a strong, pungent, co orful liquid.

Travancore—Resembles Ceylo tea.

Dovars—A tea used for blend ing because of the soft, me low liquor which it makes. Ceylon teas are: High-grown— fine flavor and aroma. Low grown—lacking in flavor; mak a common liquid.

Java and Sumatra teas a named from the estates pro ducing them. They are mediu strength.

GREEN TEA—Made by steamin and drying leaves while fresh.

Standards

Japan Green, Japan Dust

Gunpowder (used for all Chin green teas)

Scented Orange Pekoe

Kinds

Japan Teas—Styles of prepar ing leaf: Pan-fried—straigh Guri—curled; Basket-fired— long spider-leg leaf; Natural— formerly called "porcelair fired." Also graded in distric types.

China Green Teas—Country Greens—makes a rich, clear cup; Hoochows—light in flavor, good appearance; Pingsueys— poorer cup, slightly metallic. Prepared in the following styles:

Gunpowder—a round rolled leaf, fine to medium; Pea-leaf—a bold round rolled leaf; Imperial —large size round rolled; Young Hyson — long rough twisted leaf; Hyson — small well-made curly leaf.

India, Ceylon and Java Green Teas are usually made up into Hyson and Young Hyson styles and produce a pungent light cup.

OOLONG TEA—Made by partial fermentation of leaves.

Standards

Canton Oolong (used for Scented Canton and all China Oolongs)

Formosa Oolong

Kinds

Formosa Oolong—Fine flavor and very fragrant; leaf is greenish-brown; known by district names.

Foochow Oolongs—A thin, medium flavor; leaf is long, blackish and coarse looking. Formosas are sometimes blended with Gunpowders and Japans to make a mixed tea.

FRUITS

ORANGES

Name	Grove	Season	Size	Seed	Skin	Color
id Gloves	Gulf States	Oct.-March	2½-3	Seeded	Thin	Golden
ing (of Siam)	Gulf States	Oct.-March	2½-3	Seeded	Thin	Golden
Mandarin	Gulf States	Nov.-April	2-2½	Seeded	Thin	Golden yellow
Navel	California	Nov.-May	2½-3½	Seedless	Medium	Deep yellow
arson Brown	Florida	Oct.-Nov.	2½-3½	Seeded	Thin	Light yellow
ineapple	Florida	Jan.-March	2½-3	Seeded	Medium	Golden brown
atsumas	Gulf States	Nov.-Feb. ·	2½-3½	Seeded	Thin	Golden
eedling	Florida	Nov.-March	2½-3	Small	Thin	Golden
angelo	Florida	Nov.-Feb.	2½-3	Seeded	Medium	Golden
angerine (Dancy)	Florida	Spring	2-2½	Seeded	Thin	Golden brown
angerine, King	Florida	Spring	2½-3	Seeded	Thin	Golden (light)
emple	Florida	Nov.-March	2½-3	Seeded	Rough	Reddish
alencia (1)	California	May-Nov.	2-3	Seeded	Thin	Light yellow
alencia (2)	Florida	March-May	2-3	Seeded	Thin	Light Yellow

LEMONS

emons	California	All year	2¾-3¼	Seeded	Smooth	Yellow
emons	Florida	All year	2¾-3¼	Seeded	Smooth	Yellow

LIMES

imes	Mexico	All year	1-1¼	Seedless	Smooth	Green to
.imes	W. Indies					yellowish

KUMQUATS

umquats	California, Florida	Dec.-Jan.	2-2½	Seedless	Smooth	Deep orange

PEARS

Varieties	Season	Use	
artlett	Aug.-Nov.	Uncooked	Canned
ieffer	Sept.-Nov.	Pickles	Canned in sirup
osc	Sept.-Jan.	Baking	Salads
D'Anjou	Oct.-April	Baking	Salads
omice	Oct.-Feb.	Baking	Salads
Winter Nelis	Dec.-June	Baking	Salads

APPLES

Variety	Season	Eating	Cooking	Baking	General
Yellow Transparent	July, August	X	X		
Gravenstein	July through Sept.	X	X		X
Oldenburg	July through Oct.		X	X	
Williams	Aug., Sept.	X			X
Maiden Blush	Aug. through Nov.		X		X
Wealthy	Aug. through Dec.		X		X
Twenty Ounce	Sept. through Nov.		X		
King David	Oct., Nov.	X			X
Winter Banana	Oct. through Dec.	X			X
Fameuse (Snow)	Oct. through Dec.	X			
McIntosh	Oct. through Jan.	X		X	X
Grimes Golden	Oct. through Jan.	X			X
Spitzenburg	Oct. through Feb.	X			X
York Imperial	Oct. through Feb.	X			X
Jonathan	Oct. through Feb.	X			X
Rhode Island Greening	Oct. through March		X		X
Northwestern Greening	Oct. through March		X		
Northern Spy	Oct. through March	X			X
Tolman Sweet	Oct. through March	X		X	
Delicious	Oct. through April	X			
Wagener	Nov. through Jan.	X			X
Thompkins King	Nov. through Feb.	X			X
Stayman Winesap	Nov. through April	X		X	X
Baldwin	Nov. through April	X			X
Rome Beauty	Nov. through May		X	X	
Ben Davis	Nov. through May		X		
Arkansas (Mammoth Black Twig)	Nov. through May		X	X	
White Pearmain	Dec. through March	X			X
Stark	Dec. through May		X		
Winesap	Jan. through May	X			X
Wolf River	Sept. through Dec.		X	X	
Yellow Newton (Albemarle Pippin)	Jan. through May	X			X
Missouri Pippin	Jan. through May		X		
Ingram	Jan. through May				X

Vegetables

VEGETABLE	AMOUNT FOR 5	PREPARATION	METHOD OF COOKING	TIME, MINUTES
Artichokes	5	Wash; drain, bottoms up. Cut off stems.	Cover head and stem with boiling water; add 1 teaspoon salt. Cook uncovered until leaf will pull out.	20-30
Asparagus	1-1½ pounds	Cut off where stalk begins to be woody. Remove large scales and skins of woody ends. Wash.	Place upright in bottom of double boiler, half fill with water, add salt, invert top of double boiler as cover.	15-25
Beans, green	1-1½ pounds	Wash. Remove stem ends. Leave whole, slice or break.	Boil in small amount boiling salted water uncovered.	15-30
Lima	3½ pounds	Wash and shell.	Same as green beans.	20-30
Beets	1-1½ pounds	Wash, cut off tops 1 inch from beets.	Boil in water to cover. Cover closely. Rub off skins when done.	30-50
Broccoli	2½ pounds	Trim off woody part of stalks. Wash.	Boil in small amount of boiling salted water like asparagus. Do not cover.	15-25
Brussels sprouts	1 quart	Remove injured leaves. Let stand 30 minutes in cold salted water; drain.	Cook in small amount boiling salted water uncovered.	10-15
Cabbage	2 pounds	Discard injured leaves, chop or cut into wedges.	Same as Brussels sprouts.	5-15
Carrots	2½ pounds	Cut off tops, scrub. Scrape old carrots, leave skins on young ones. Slice or dice.	Boil in small amount salted water, closely covered.	15-25
Cauliflower	1 large head (2 pounds)	Discard injured leaves. Leave whole or break into flowerettes.	Same as broccoli.	10-15
Celery root or Celeriac	1½ pounds	Remove top. Wash.	Boil in ¼ to ½ cup boiling salted water, closely covered Rub off skins when cool.	20-30
Corn	10 ears	Remove silk and all but last husk.	Cook in boiling water to cover. Keep covered.	6-10

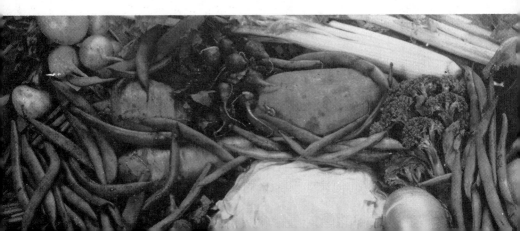

VEGETABLE	AMOUNT FOR 5	PREPARATION	METHOD OF COOKING	TIME, MINUTES
Greens Beet tops Spinach	1½ pounds	Cut off roots and discard. Wash thoroughly, several times. Lift out of last water.	Cook in water which clings to leaves, uncovered over low heat. Stir occasionally. Season.	8-10
Collards Dandelions Kale Mustard Turnip tops	1½ pounds	Same as spinach.	Boil in 2 cups boiling salted water. If very tender, same as spinach.	15-30
Kohlrabi	1½ pounds	Wash, pare and dice or slice.	Cook in small amount boiling salted water, uncovered.	20-30
Leeks	4 bunches	Wash, cut off roots and discard. Cut tops in long pieces.	Cook like onions.	15-20
Onions	10 medium	Peel and wash.	Boil in small amount of salted water uncovered. Add small slice of lemon.	20-40
Parsnips	10 medium	Wash and scrape. Cut into halves, quarters or slices.	Boil in small amount of salted water.	15-30
Peas	2½ pounds	Shell and wash.	Simmer in small amount boiling salted water, uncovered. Add few grains sugar.	10-15
Rutabagas and Turnips	2 pounds	Scrub; cut off roots and tops; cut into slices or cubes.	Boil in small amount water, covered; add salt, mash.	20-40
Salsify	1½-2 pounds	Scrub, scrape and drop at once into acidulated water (1 tablespoon vinegar for 1 quart water). Drain and slice.	Boil in salted water to cover.	20-30
Summer squash	1½-2 pounds	Use small squash. Wash, pare, remove seeds and slice.	Cook in ½ cup boiling salted water, closely covered. Drain and mash.	10-20

EGGS

Color of shell is determined by the breed of the bird and has nothing to do with the quality of the egg.

Color of the yolk is determined by the diet of hens and there is no relation between the color of yolk and color of shell.

CARE OF EGGS

Store eggs in closed container in refrigerator, small end down. To keep whites after eggs have been broken and separated, store in covered container in refrigerator or freezer.

To keep separated yolks, put in container, cover with water; cover tightly and store in refrigerator. Use within three days. For longer periods, follow directions for freezing them. Remove eggs from refrigerator long enough before using so they will become warmed at room temperature. Eggs are most easily separated as soon as they are removed from refrigerator.

CARE OF FRESH AND FROZEN FISH

Remove any scales neglected at market. Rinse body cavity with cold water; drain, and pat dry. Cook fresh fish as soon as possible after purchasing. If stored, wrap in freezer material or foil and place in freezer. Frozen fish (steaks, fillets and sticks) should be kept solidly frozen. Never refreeze after thawing.

CARE OF FRESH FRUITS

Highly perishable fruits such as berries, cherries and plums should be placed in the refrigerator without washing and as soon as received from market.

Place fruit in a colander and wash with a spray.

The more firm fruit such as peaches, apples, pears, etc., may be washed by light rubbing in water.

CARE OF MEAT

Remove fresh, uncooked meat from market wrap; rewrap loosely in waxed paper and store in meat compartment of refrigerator. For longer storage periods, wrap meat closely in freezer material and store in freezer.

Pre-packaged, table-ready sliced meats and frankfurters keep best if stored in original moisture-proof wrappings.

CARE OF MILK IN THE HOME

Take milk into the house as soon after delivery as possible. Wash the top of bottle and cap in cold running water before opening or putting away.

Place the milk in the coldest part of the refrigerator at once. Return milk to refrigerator as soon as the amount needed has been removed.

Keep milk closely covered as it absorbs odors from other foods readily.

Wash the bottle in cold water as soon as empty, then scald. Do not use milk bottles for any other purpose.

Return bottles to dairy promptly.

CARE OF POULTRY

Poultry, a highly perishable food, should be purchased only where the birds are kept refrigerated or are frozen.

To store fresh, chilled poultry remove from market wrap and re-

wrap loosely; then store in coldest part of refrigerator.

Whole birds with giblets wrapped separately, may be stored up to two days. Cut-up birds should be held no longer than twenty-four hours.

Quick frozen poultry must be kept frozen until ready to use. To thaw before cooking, follow directions on the label. Once thawed never refreeze.

Ready-to-cook poultry, whole or in pieces, should be rinsed in cold water, drained and patted dry. Do not soak in water, as flavor is dissipated.

Dressed birds should be drawn immediately, preferably at market.

Remove pinfeathers with sharp-pointed knife or strawberry huller. Singe bird over direct heat to remove fine hairs. Remove oil sack from tail. Wash inside and out; pat dry. Never stuff bird until ready to roast.

CARE OF FRESH VEGETABLES

Wash vegetables such as greens, carrots, radishes, and green beans when received from market. Drain; pat dry with towel or absorbent paper. Store in refrigerator vegetable drawers or plastic bags. Never soak vegetables when washing. If wilted, put in cold water for only a few minutes, shake off moisture and gently pat dry.

Store vegetables such as potatoes, dry onions, cabbage, rutabega and squash in a cool, dark, well ventilated place without previously washing them.

Keep onions separated from other vegetables.

MILK
quart daily for each child
pint daily for each adult

VEGETABLES AND FRUITS
1/2 to 5 or more servings per person daily
1 serving daily of potatoes
1 serving daily of tomatoes or citrus fruits

1 serving daily of leafy, green or yellow vegetables
3 to 5 servings a week of other vegetables
1 serving daily of fruit

EGGS
2 to 3 a week for adults, 4 to 5 for young children
A few for cooking

MEAT, FISH OR POULTRY
About 5 times a week or daily if prepared in combination with cereals or vegetables

CEREALS
Daily, preferably at least half made from whole grain

BREAD AND BUTTER
At every meal.

THE VITAMINS IN IMPORTANT FOODS

Food	Vitamin A	Vitamin B	Vitamin C	Vitamin B₂
Almonds	A	BB	—	B_2B_2
Apples	A	B to BB	CC	B_2B_2
Apricots	AA	—	CC	B_2B_2
Asparagus	A	—	CC	—
Avocado	AA	BBB	C	B_2B_2
Bacon	— to A	B to BB	—	B_2B_2
Bananas	A to AA	B to BB	CC	B_2B_2
Barley, whole	A	BB	—	B_2
Beans, dry or canned	A	BB	—	B_2
Beans, string	AA	BB	CC	B_2B_2
Beef	A	BB	— to C	B_2B_2
Beef, fat	AA	—	—	—
Beets (roots)	A	B	C	B_2
Beet leaves	AA	BB	—	$B_2B_2B_2$
Blackberries	AA	B	—	—
Grains	A	BB	—	—
Brazil nuts	A	BB	—	B_2B_2
Bread, white, water†	—	B	—	—
Bread, white, milk†	A	B	— to C	B_2
Bread, whole wheat, water†.	A	BBB	—	B_2
Bread, whole wheat, milk†.	AA	BBB	— to C	B_2B_2
Broccoli	AAAA	BB	C	$B_2B_2B_2$
Butter*	AAA	—	—	—

*Supplies a small amount of Vitamin D
†When irradiated, an excellent source of Vitamin D

CALCIUM

The following foods are arranged in the order of importance as source of calcium calculated on an average serving portion.

Milk
Cheese, American or Cheddar
  Swiss

Vegetables, fresh (group A)
  Turnip tops
  Mustard greens
  Collards, Kale
  Watercress
  Broccoli
  Swiss chard
  Dandelion greens

Oysters

Molasses

Vegetables, fresh (group B)
  Cauliflower
  Kohlrabi, Rutabagas
  Turnips, Parsnips
  Leek

These foods are rich in Vitamin A; use some of them each day

Food	Vitamin A	Vitamin B	Vitamin C	Vitamin B₂
Buttermilk..............	A	BB	C	$B_2B_2B_2$
Cabbage, green, raw......	AA	BB	CCC	B_2B_2
Cabbage, head, cooked.....	A	BB	C	B_2B_2
Cantaloupe..............	AA	BB	CCC	B_2B_2
Carrots................	AAA	BB	CC	B_2B_2
Cauliflower.............	A	BB	C	B_2B_2
Celery, bleached stems....	— to A	BB	CC	—
Celery, green leaves......	AA	BB	—	—
Chard..................	AA	B to BB	—	—
Cheese, whole milk*......	AA to AAA	—	—	B_2
Cheese, cottage..........	A	—	—	B_2
Cherries...............	AA	B	CC	—
Chestnuts..............	—	B	—	B_2
Chicken................	—	BBB	—	$B_2B_2B_2$
Chinese cabbage.........	AA	BB	CCC	B_2
Coconut................	A	BB	—	B_2B_2
Cod-liver oil††..........	AAA	—	—	—
Collards...............	AAA	BB	CC	B_2B_2
Corn, yellow............	AA	BB	—	B_2
Corn meal, yellow.......	A to AA	B	—	—
Corn oil...............	A	—	—	—
Cranberries (or juice).....	A	—	CC	—
Cream.................	AAA	BB	C	$B_2B_2B_2$
Cucumber..............	— to A	B	CC	B_2
Dandelion greens........	AAA	BB	C	B_2B_2
Dasheens..............	A	B	C	—
Dates.................	A	BB	—	B_2
Eggs or egg yolk*.......	AAA	B to BB	—	$B_2B_2B_2$
Egg white..............	—	—	—	B_2B_2
Eggplant...............	A	B	C	B_2B_2
Endive.................	AA	—	C	—
Escarole...............	AAA	—	C	B_2B_2
Figs..................	A	—	C to—	B_2
Filberts...............	—	BB	—	B_2B_2
Fish, fat*..............	A	B	—	B_2
Fish, lean.............	— to A	B	—	B_2

*Supplies a small amount of Vitamin D
††An excellent source of Vitamins A and D

CALCIUM—Cont.

String beans
Cabbage
Carrots
Lettuce
Celery
Cheese, Cottage
Beans, Peas, dried
Figs, Dates
Raisins, Prunes
Eggs
Bread
Fish
Strawberries, Oranges
Raspberries, Blackberries
Filberts, Almonds
Potatoes
Poultry
Meat
Cereals

IRON AND COPPER

The following foods are arrange
in the order of importance
source of iron and copper calcu
lated on an average serving po
tion:

Liver, beef
Heart, Oysters
Beef, Veal
Vegetables (group A)
    Mustard greens
    Turnip greens
    Beet greens
    Swiss chard
    Dandelion greens

To avoid Vitamin B deficiency use generous amounts of these

Food	Vitamin A	Vitamin B	Vitamin C	Vitamin B₂
rapefruit (or juice fresh canned)	A	BB	CCC	B₂B₂
rapes	A	B	C to —	B₂
rape juice	—	B to —	—	— to B₂
am	— to A	BB	—	B₂B₂
eart	A	BB	C	B₂B₂B₂
ickory nuts	—	BB	—	B₂B₂
e cream (regular)	AA	BB	C	B₂B₂B₂
ale	AAA	B	CC	B₂B₂B₂
idney	AA	BB	C	B₂B₂B₂
ohlrabi	—	B	C	—
amb	— to A	B	— to C	B₂B₂
emon juice	A	BB	CCC	B₂B₂
ettuce	A to AA	BB	CC	B₂B₂
imes (or juice)	—	—	CC	—
ver	AA to AAA	BB	C	B₂B₂B₂
ilk, whole† "scalded"	AAA	BB	C	B₂B₂B₂
ilk, condensed†	AAA	BB	C	B₂B₂B₂
ilk, evaporated†	AAA	BB	—	B₂B₂B₂
ilk, skim, dried or fresh	A	BB	C	B₂B₂B₂
olasses	—	B	—	—
ustard greens	AAA	—	CCC	B₂B₂B₂
atmeal	— to A	BB	—	B₂
kra	AA	BB	—	—
nions, raw	— to A	B	CC	B₂
nions, cooked	— to A	B	C	B₂
range (or juice)	A	BB	CCC	B₂B₂
range peel	A	B	CC	—
ysters	AA	BB	C	B₂B₂
arsley	AAA	BB	CCC	—
arsnips	— to A	BB	—	—
eaches, raw	A to AA	B to BB	CC	B₂ to B₂B₂
eanuts, Peanut butter	A	BB	—	B₂
ears	—	BB	C	B₂B₂
eas, green	AA	BB	CCC	B₂B₂
eas, dry	A	BB	—	B₂B₂
ecans	A	BB	—	—
eppers, green	AA	BB	CCC	—
mientos	AAA	—	CCC	—
ineapple, raw, canned	A	BB	CC	B₂

†When irradiated, an excellent source of Vitamin D

IRON AND COPPER— Cont.

Vegetables (group A)
  Spinach
  Kale
  Broccoli
Beans, Peas, Lentils, dried
Lamb
Pork
Fowl
Eggs
Molasses
Fruit, dried
Apricots
Peaches
Currants
Dates
Prunes
Raisins
Figs
Vegetables (group B)
  Escarole
  Brussels sprouts
  String Beans
  Potatoes, white
  Pumpkin
  Beets, Carrots
  Cabbage
Fish
Almonds
Brazil nuts
Black walnuts
Oatmeal
Fresh fruit
  Grapes
  Strawberries
  Bananas, Apricots
  Oranges
  Peaches

Your daily Vitamin C is in these fruits and vegetables

Food	Vitamin A	Vitamin B	Vitamin C	Vitamin B₂
Pork	— to A	BB	—	B₂B₂
Potatoes, white	A	BB	CC	B₂
Prunes	AA	BB	—	B₂B₂
Pumpkin	AA	B	C	B₂
Radish	— to A	BB	CC	—
Raisins	—	B	—	B₂
Raspberries	AA	B	CCC	—•
Rhubarb	—	—	C	—
Rice, white	—	—	—	—
Rice, whole grain or brown	A	BB	—	B₂
Roe, fish	AA	BB	—	—
Romaine	AA	BB	—	B₂B₂
Rutabaga	— to A	BB	CCC	—
Rye, whole	A	BB	—	B₂
Salmon, canned	A	—	—	B₂B₂
Sauerkraut	A	B	C to CC	—
Shrimp	A	—	—	—
Spinach	AAA	B	CC	B₂B₂
Squash, Hubbard	AAA	B	—	B₂
Squash, summer	A	B	—	B₂
Strawberries	A	B	CCC	—
Sweetbreads	A	B	—	—
Sweetpotatoes	AAA	BB	CC	B₂
Tomato, raw or canned	AA	BB	CCC	B₂
Turnip	— to A	B	CC	B₂
Turnip greens	AAA	BB	CCC	B₂B₂
Veal	— to A	B	—	B₂B₂
Walnuts	A	BB	—	—
Watercress	AAA	BB	CCC	B₂B₂
Watermelon	A	B	CCC	B₂
Wheat, bran or whole	A	BB	—	B₂
Wheat embryo	AA	BBB	—	B₂B₂
Yeast†	—	BBB	—	B₂B₂B₂
Yeast bouillon†	—	BBB	—	B₂B₂B₂

†When irradiated an excellent source of Vitamin D

PHOSPHORUS

The following foods are arrange in the order of importance a source of phosphorus calculate on an average serving portion.

Liver, Lean meat
Veal, Fowl, Fish
Lamb, Pork, Beef
Glandular meats
   Sweetbreads
   Kidney
   Heart, Brains
Milk, Oysters, Cheese
Beans, Peas, Lentils, dried
Eggs, Oatmeal
Fresh vegetables (group A)
   Cauliflower
   Pumpkin, Peas
   Mustard greens
   Potatoes, white
   Turnip greens
   String beans
   Turnips
Brazil nuts, Cashew nuts
Almonds, Peanuts, Walnuts
Filberts, Bread
Vegetables (group B)
   Kale
   Brussels sprouts
   Corn, Collards
   Parsnips, Broccoli
   Beets, Carrots
   Cabbage, Tomatoes
Raisins

These foods as well as irradiated products provide Vitamin D

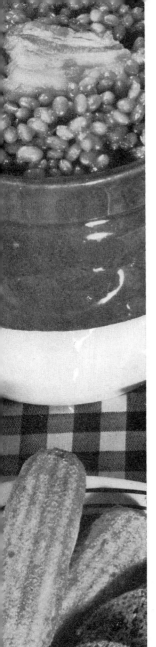

In blustery weather, these high calorie foods provide warmth and energy

THE CALORIE

A calorie is a measure of the heat and energy produced by foods when used in the body. Work and play use up the energy and cold weather increases the need for heat, but even so, increasing the food of high calories eaten each day causes a gain in weight, while a reduction should cause loss. Calorie requirements vary with types of work, age, climate and other factors.

VITAMINS

Vitamins are chemical compounds of definite composition found in natural foods. Since each has a definite function in promoting good health an adequate daily amount of each is essential. An insufficient amount of any one vitamin over a period of time results in definite diseases which can be cured only by supplying the vitamin or vitamins lacking.

THE NUMBER OF CALORIES IN AVERAGE SERVINGS

FOOD	CALORIES
Almonds, 12, shelled	100
Almonds, chocolate, 5	100
Almonds, chopped, 1 cup	550
Apple, 1 large	100
Apple, baked, 2 tablespoons sugar	200
Apple, baked, 1 tablespoon sugar	150
Apple brown Betty, ½ cup	250
Apple pie, ⅙ of 9-inch pie	300-350
Applesauce, ⅜ cup	100
Apple tapioca, ½ cup	205
Apricots, cooked. 3 large halves with 2 tablespoons juice	100
Apricots, dried, 9 halves	100
Apricots, fresh, 5	100
Artichoke, French, 1	158
Asparagus, 10 large stalks, no butter	50
Asparagus, 10 large stalks with butter	150
Asparagus, 10 large stalks with hollandaise sauce	240
Asparagus soup, cream of, ½ cup	100
Avocado, ½ fruit	120-300
Bacon, broiled. 4 small slices	100
Bacon fat, 1 tablespoon	100
Baking powder biscuits. 4 small biscuits	200
Bananas, average size	100
Beans, Lima. dried, ½ cup uncooked	273
Beans, Lima, fresh or canned, ½ cup	100
Beans, navy. canned baked, ⅓ cup	100
Beans, navy, dried, ½ cup uncooked	342
Beans, soy, dried, 3½ tablespoons	200
Beans, string, ½ cup	22
Beef, corned. boiled lean, 3 ounces	100
Beef, dried, 4 thin slices	100
Beef, Hamburg steak, broiled, cake 2½ inches diameter, ⅞ inch	100
Beef loaf, slice, 4x6x⅛ inches	100
Beef rib. roasted, lean, slice, 5x2½x¼ inches	100
Beef, round steak, lean, 4-ounces	170-220
Beef steak. lean, broiled, slice 2x1½x¾ inches	100
Beef stew, 1 cup	250
Beet greens, ½ cup	22
Beets, 2, 2 inches in diameter	50
Blackberries, fresh, 25	50
Blackberries, cooked, with sugar, ½ cup	200
Blueberries, fresh, ½ cup	50
Bluefish, broiled, small serving	100

FOOD	CALORIES
Bologna sausage, slice 2⅛ inches diameter, ½ inch thick	100
Bouillon, 1 cup	25
Brazil nuts, 2	100
Bread, Boston brown, slice ½ inch thick	52
Bread, rye, slice ½ inch thick	70
Bread, white, slice ½ inch thick	50
Bread, 50% whole-wheat, slice ½ inch thick	75
Bread crumbs, dry, 1 cup	400
Bread crumbs, soft, 1 cup	150
Broccoli, 1 cup	45
Brussels sprouts, 6	50
Butter, 1 tablespoon	100
Buttermilk, 1 cup	84
Cabbage, cooked, ½ cup	32
Cabbage, raw, shredded, ½ cup	13
Cake, 2 egg, 1 ¾-inch cube	100
Cantaloupe, ½	50
Carrots, cooked, ½ cup	30-40
Cauliflower, ½ cup	25
Celery, ⅔ cup	15
Celery soup, cream of, per cup	200
Chard, cooked, ½ cup	36
Cheese, American, grated, 1 tablespoon	33
Cheese, 1-inch cube	70
Cheese, cottage, 5 tablespoons	100
Cheese, full cream, 2x1x⅜ inch piece	100
Cheese soufflé, ½ cup	100
Cherries, 10 large	50
Chestnuts, 7 average	100
Chicken, roast, slice 4x2½x¼ inch slice	100
Chicken salad, ½ cup	200
Chocolate, bitter, 1 ounce	173
Chocolate, bitter, 1 tablespoon grated	29
Chocolate cake, 1 small piece	200
Chocolate cream candy, average piece	80-100
Chocolate cream mint, 1½-inch diameter	100
Chocolate drop cookie, 2-inch diameter	60
Chocolate éclair	260-400
Chocolate fudge, 1-inch cube	80-90
Chocolate malted milk, large glass	465
Chocolate, milk, sweet, 2½x1x⅛ inch slice	100
Chocolate nut caramel, 1 cube	100
Clams, 6	50
Cocoa, powder, 1 tablespoon	40
Coconut, shredded, 1 tablespoon	34
Codfish, creamed, ½ cup	100
Cod-liver oil, 1 tablespoon	100
Coleslaw, ½ cup	50
Collards, cooked, ½ cup	50
Consommé, 1 cup	25
Corn bread, average piece	120
Corn, canned, ⅓ cup	100
Corn flakes, ¾ cup	100
Corn, fresh, on cob, 1 ear, 6 inches long	50
Corn meal, cooked, ⅓ cup	50
Corn meal, uncooked, ½ cup	252
Corn sirup, 1 tablespoon	75
Crackers, graham, 2½	100
Crackers, soda, 2	50
Cream, heavy, 40%, 1 tablespoon	60
Cream, whipped, 1 tablespoon	35
Cream, thin, 18%, 1 tablespoon	30
Cucumber, 10 inches long	50
Cup custard, ½ cup	100

Leafy vegetables are low i[n] calories but high in vitamin[s] and mineral salts

*ilk drinks in attractive
riety help with Vitamin A
d calcium*

FOOD	CALORIES
Currants, dry, ¼ cup	126
Currants, fresh, ½ cup	34
Dates, 3 or 4	100
Doughnut	200
Duck, 4 ounces	234
Egg	70-75
Eggs, scrambled, ¼ cup	100
Eggnog, 1 cup	200
Farina, cooked, ¾ cup	100
Figs, dried, 1½	100
Filberts, 8 to 10	100
Frankfurters, 1	100
French dressing, 1 tablespoon	67
Fruitcake, 1 (⅞x1⅞x⅜ inch) slice	100
Ginger ale, 1 cup	72
Grapefruit, ½, average size	100
Grapefruit, ½, average size with 2 teaspoons sugar	134
Grapefruit juice, 1 cup	100
Grape juice, ½ cup	100
Grapes, large bunch	100
Grapes, Malaga, 20 to 25	100
Griddlecake, 1 (4 to 5 inch) cake	100
Halibut, cooked, 3 ounces	85-110
Ham, ¼ pound	270-400
Hard sauce, 1 tablespoon	100
Hickory nuts, chopped, ½ cup	607
Hominy grits, cooked, ½ cup	62
Honey, 1 teaspoon	25
Ice cream, commercial, vanilla, ⅜ cup	100
Kale, cooked without fat, ½ cup	20
Kohlrabi, creamed, ½ cup	100
Lamb chops, broiled, 1 (2 inches thick)	100
Lamb, roast leg, 4 ounces	225
Leeks, 3 (5 inches long)	45
Lemon, 1	30
Lemon juice, 1 tablespoon	5
Lemon meringue pie, ⅙ of 9-inch pie	450
Lettuce, ¼ head	12
Lettuce, ¼ head with salad dressing	100-150
Liver, ¼ pound	145-220
Macaroni, cooked, ½ cup	67
Macaroni with cheese, ⅔ cup	200
Macaroons, each	50
Mackerel, ¼ pound	85-100
Maple sirup, 1 tablespoon	67
Marshmallows, 5	100
Mayonnaise, 1 tablespoon	100
Milk, irradiated evaporated, ½ cup undiluted	175
Milk, skim, 1 cup	88
Milk, whole, 1 cup	170
Mince pie, ⅙ of 9-inch pie	450
Muffin, 1	125-150
Mutton, ¼ pound	225-500
Napoleon, average size	453
Oats, rolled, cooked, ½ to ¾ cup	100
Olives, each	15
Onions, cooked, 3 to 4, small	50-60
Orange, large	100
Orange juice, 1 cup	133
Oysters, according to size, each	6-16
Parsnips, 1 (7 inches long)	100
Peaches, canned, 1 large half with 1½ tablespoons juice	50
Peaches, fresh, 1 small	35
Peanuts, ¼ pound, shelled	620

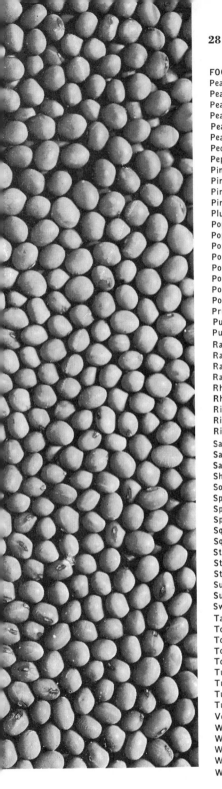

FOOD	CALORIE
Peanut butter, 1 tablespoon	1(
Pears, canned, 1 half with 1 tablespoon juice	
Pears, fresh, 1 medium	
Peas, dried, ¼ pound	4(
Peas, fresh, cooked, ⅜ cup	
Pea soup, cream of, 1 cup	1
Pecans, 6 nuts, shelled	1
Peppers green average size	
Pineapple, canned, 1 slice, 3 tablespoons juice	1
Pineapple, canned, shredded, ¼ cup	1
Pineapple, fresh, 1 slice, ¾ inch thick	
Pineapple juice, 1 cup	1
Plums, 3 or 4 large, fresh	1
Popcorn, popped, 1½ cups	1
Popover, 1	1
Pork ¼ pound	300-6
Pork chops, broiled, 1, fat not included	2
Pork sausage, cooked, 2 sausages 3 inches long, ½ inch in diameter.	1
Potato, 1, average size, white	1
Potato chips, 8 to 10	1
Potato salad, ½ cup	2
Prunes, average size, 1	
Pumpkin, cooked, ½ cup	
Pumpkin pie, ⅙ of 9-inch pie	2
Radish, average size, 1	
Raisin pie, ⅙ of 9-inch pie	4
Raisins, ¼ cup	1
Raspberries, fresh, ½ cup	
Rhubarb, stewed and sweetened, ½ cup	1
Rhubarb pie, ⅙ of 9-inch pie	2
Rice, steamed, ½ cup	
Rice pudding, plain, ½ cup	2
Rice pudding, with egg, ½ cup	1
Salmon, canned, ½ cup	1
Sardines, canned, 2 (3 inches long)	
Sauerkraut, ¾ cup	
Shrimp, without oil, each	
Soda, chocolate	4
Spinach, ¾ cup	
Spinach soup, cream of, 1 cup	1
Spongecake, hot water, 2x2¾x⅞ inches	1
Squash, Hubbard, cooked, ½ cup	
Squash pie, ⅙ of 9-inch pie	2
Strawberries, fresh, ½ cup	
Strawberry shortcake	4
Strawberry shortcake with whipped cream	5
Sugar, 1 teaspoon	
Sundae, chocolate	3
Sweetpotato, 1 medium	
Tapioca cream, ½ cup	
Tomatoes, canned, ½ cup	
Tomatoes, fresh, 1 large	
Tomato juice, 1 cup	
Tomato soup, cream of	2
Tuna, canned with oil, ¼ pound	3
Tuna, canned, without oil, ¼ pound	1
Turnips, ½ cup	
Turnip greens, ½ cup	
Veal, ¼ pound	115-2
Waffles, 1 (6 inches in diameter)	2
Walnuts, English, 16 halves	1
Watercress, ½ bunch	
Watermelon, ¾-inch slice, 6 inches in diameter	1
Wheat breakfast food, dry, 1 ounce	

BEVERAGES

1 pound medium grind coffee................makes about 45 cups
1 pound tea.............................makes about 60 cups

CEREALS

1 pound all-purpose flour.........................4 cups sifted
1 pound arrowroot.................................about 4 cups
1 pound barley flour...................................2 cups
1 pound buckwheat flour.........................about 4½ cups
1 pound cake flour............................4¼ cups sifted
1 pound corn flakes..................................18 cups
1 pound corn meal................................about 3 cups
1 pound cornstarch...............................about 3 cups
1 pound cracked wheat...........................about 2¼ cups
1 pound cream of wheat..........................about 2½ cups
1 pound graham flour............................about 3½ cups
1 pound hominy grits............................about 2½ cups
1 pound macaroni, broken............5 cups; about 12 cups, cooked
1 pound noodles, broken.........5½ cups; about 10 cups, cooked
1 pound pearl barley..............................about 2 cups
1 pound rice.....................2¼ cups; about 8 cups, cooked
1 pound rice flour...............................about 4 cups
1 pound rolled oats...............5 cups; about 10 cups, cooked
1 pound rye flour...............................about 4½ cups
1 pound soybean flour..........................about 7½ cups
1 pound spaghetti, broken........5½ cups; about 11 cups, cooked
1 pound tapioca ....about 2½ cups

DAIRY PRODUCTS

1 pound cheese, grated............................4 to 5 cups
1 (15-ounce) can condensed milk.....................1⅓ cups
1 pint cream...2 cups
1 (14½-ounce) can evaporated milk...................1¾ cups
1 pint fresh milk....................................2 cups
1 pound powdered milk................................3 cups

DRIED FRUITS

1 pound currants...............................about 3½ cups
1 pound dates.............about 2½ cups, pitted; 3 cups, chopped
1 pound dried apples.....................about 10 cups, cooked
1 pound dried apricots...................about 4½ cups, cooked
1 pound dried peaches.....................about 6 cups, cooked
1 pound dried prunes, 2 cups pitted..........about 4 cups, cooked
1 pound figs.............................about 3 cups, chopped
1 pound raisins (seeded)......................about 2½ cups
              (seedless).........................about 3 cups

MIISCELLANEOUS

1 pound chocolate, grated.......................about 3 cups
1 ounce chocolate, grated...................about 3 tablespoons
1 pound cocoa...................................about 4 cups
1 pound fat..2 cups

NUTS

1 pound coconut....................about 5½ cups, shredded
                        about 2½ cups, fresh shredded

FRESH FRUIT

1 pound apples.....2 to 6 apples; 3 cups, diced; 1½ cups sauce
1 pound apricots......8 to 14 apricots; about 2½ cups, cooked
1 medium avocado......................about 2 cups, cubed
1 pound bananas........about 3 bananas; about 2 cups, sliced
1 pint berries....................................about 2 cups
1 pound cherries......3 cups, stemmed; about 2½ cups, pitted
1 pound cranberries..........about 4 cups; about 4 cups sauce
1 medium grapefruit...about 1⅓ cups pulp, about 1 cup juice
1 pound grapes...........about 1 bunch; about 2 cups, halved
1 dozen lemons........................about 2½ cups juice
1 dozen oranges.......................3 to 5 cups juice
1 pound peaches.......4 to 6 peaches; about 2½ cups, sliced
1 pound pears...........3 to 5 pears; about 2½ cups, cooked
1 pineapple..........................about 2½ cups, cubed
1 pound plums...........12 to 20 plums; about 2 cups, cooked
1 pound rhubarb. 4 to 8 stalks; 3½ cups, diced; 2 cups, cooked

MELONS

2-pound cantaloupe.........................2 or 3 portions
6- to 10-pound casaba......................6 to 8 portions
5-pound honeydew..........................5 or 6 portions
5- to 50-pound watermelon.................3 to 20 portions

Milk and eggs are heartily welcomed when served a simple but attractive custard.

VEGETABLES

1 pound dried beans..about 2½ cups, 5-7½ cups cooked
1 pound split peas..about 2 cups, 4 cups cooked
1 pound Jerusalem artichokes..serve 3 or
1 pound asparagus, 15-22 stalks.................................2 cups cooked, cut, serves 3 or
1 pound beets...2 cups cooked, diced, serves 3 or
1 bunch broccoli...1½ to 2½ pounds, serves 4 to
1 pound Brussels sprouts.......................................3 cups cooked, serves 4 or
1 pound cabbage.................3½ cups shredded, 2½ cups cooked, cut, serves 3 (cooked
1 pound carrots.....................2¼ cups diced uncooked, 2 cups cooked, serves 3 or
2-pound head cauliflower...................................3 cups cooked, cut, serves 4 or
1¼-pound bunch celery.......................3 cups diced uncooked, 2 cups, serves 4 (cooked
4 medium ears corn...1 cup cu
1-pound eggplant...............11 (½-inch) slices; 4½ cups, diced, uncooked; 1¾ cups diced, cooked
1 pound green or wax beans......................................3 cups cooked, serves 4 or
1 pound kohlrabi........................4 medium kohlrabi, cups cooked, diced, serves
1 pound fresh Lima beans.................................⅔ cup shelled, uncooked, serves
1 pound mushrooms............35 to 45 medium mushrooms, serves 4, broiled; serves 5 or 6, creamed
1 pound dry onions..3 large onions, serves
1 pound parsnips.....................4 medium parsnips, 2½ cups cooked, diced; serves 4 or
1 pound peas..1 cup cooked, serves
1 pound spinach or other greens, 2 quarts......................1½ to 2 cups cooked, serves 3 or
2-pound summer squash.....................................2 cups cooked, mashed
5-pound Hubbard squash.................................5 cups cooked, mashed; 1 cup serves
1¼ pounds sweetpotatoes................................2¾ cups cooked, mashed; serves 3 or
1 pound tomatoes..................................4 small to medium, 4 slices to each tomato
1 pound white turnips.....................................3 or 4 medium, serves
1 pound rutabaga...........................2⅔ cups cooked, diced; 2 cups mashed; serves 3 or
1 pound white potatoes.....................3 medium potatoes, 2½ cups diced cooked, serves 3 or

FISH—See pages 310-311

FRUITS

PPLES—Choose firm apples of ood color and flavor. Immature pples are poor in color and flavor nd shrivel after storage. Overpe apples are mealy and poor in avor. Brown-tinted irregular rea on surface is called scald. It caused by gases given off by pples during storage. If slight, it ffects quality very little.

PRICOTS—Are usually picked ightly immature. Best quality, ee-ripened cannot be shipped, they are found only near growg area. Select plump, firm, unirmly colored fruit. Immature uit is greenish-yellow, hard and ightly shriveled; lacks flavor. ipe fruit very perishable; avoid ruised fruit.

VOCADOS—May vary from pherical to pear-shaped, 5 ounces 3 pounds, thin smooth skin to nick rough skin, green to almost ack. Shape, size and skin do ot indicate quality. Select bright esh-looking fruit just beginning soften; avoid bruised fruit. ght brown irregular marking oes not affect quality. Decay incated by dark sunken spots.

ANANAS—Have the best flaor if harvested green. Buy yelw-ripe or full-ripe fruit. Good eating quality indicated by a full yellow or red color flecked with brown. Avoid soft, mushy fruit, blackened areas or mold. Bananas that have become too cold will not ripen properly and will be of poor flavor.

BLACKBERRIES DEWBERRIES, LOGANBERRIES, RASPBERRIES —Should have a bright, clean, fresh plump appearance and solid full color. Overripe berries are dull in color, soft, leaky. Leaky berries stain inside of container. Adhering caps indicate unripe fruit.

BLUEBERRIES AND HUCKLE-BERRIES—Select plump, fresh looking, clean and dry berries that are free from trash. Deep full color indicates good quality; mold indicates decay. Moisture indicates breakdown of fruit. Overripe fruit is dull and lifeless. Berries held long after picking are dull and shriveled.

CHERRIES—Select sweet cherries for eating and tart cherries for cooking. Bright fresh appear-ance, plumpness and good color indicate good quality. Unripe fruit is small, hard, poor in color, usually acid. Overripe fruit is soft, dull in color, shriveled and leaky. Avoid bruised fruit and fruit with small brown circular spots.

Fruits vary greatly in quality; choose them carefully and you will be well rewarded

CRANBERRIES—Should have fresh, plump appearance, firmness and luster to indicate good quality. Avoid shriveled, dull, soft or moist berries.

FRESH FIGS—Choose fully ripe and soft figs. Color and size depend upon variety. Ripe figs sour and ferment quickly. Odor indicates souring. Avoid bruised fruit.

GRAPEFRUIT—Russet on fruit does not affect flavor. Should be firm and springy, not soft or flabby. Should be heavy for their size. Decay indicated by soft discolored area at button end.

GRAPES—Grapes to be served on the stem should be firm, highly-colored and should adhere to stem. For juice, ripeness is essential but compactness or shattering from stem are not important. Frozen grapes have poor flavor; indicated by dullness, stickiness, shattering from stem. Decay indicated by mold, wet berries and stained containers.

LEMONS—Select heavy ones with smooth-textured skins. Avoid decay at stem end or soft, spongy fruit.

LIMES—Select green, heavy fruit. Surface blemishes do not indicate poor fruit. Yellow fruit is not acid enough.

ORANGES—Select firm, heavy fruit. Surface blemishes do not affect fruit. Avoid light, puffy fruit with badly creased skins.

PEACHES—Should be free from blemishes, firm, fresh-appearing with whitish or yellowish ground color. Green ground color indicates fruit was picked too soon to allow ripening. Select overripe fruit only for immediate consumption. Worminess is shown by small holes from which gum exudes. Decay (brown circular spots) spreads rapidly.

PEARS—Firm, not hard, free from blemish, clean, not misshapen, wilted or shriveled. Soft at base of stem, for immediate consumption. Wilted or shriveled fruits have been picked too early and will never ripen or have good flavor. Avoid fruit with water-soaked appearance.

PINEAPPLES—Are picked in slightly immature state. Ripe pineapple has a dark orange-yellow color and a fragrant odor and the eyes are flat. Select fruit relatively heavy for its size. If picked when too immature fruit will not ripen, will be dull and lifeless, often yellow, eyes poorly developed, pointed. Avoid bruised fruit. Fruit loses moisture if held a long time, shrinks in size, color darkens. Decays rapidly; look for dark areas at base or around eyes, sour odor, mold, moisture. Light-colored area on side indicates sunburn; fruit will be hard, dry and pithy.

PLUMS AND PRUNES—Ripe fruit is plump and yields to slight pressure. Immature fruit is hard, shriveled, poor in color and flavor. Overmature fruit is soft, leaky and insipid. Brownish color on side indicates sunburn and the flavor is likely to be poor.

QUINCES—Good fruit is hard, free from blemish, greenish-yellow. Immature fruit is green and lacks flavor.

RHUBARB—Choose fresh, firm, crisp, tender, thick stalks (red or pink).

STRAWBERRIES—Choose bright, clean berries of solid red color and with caps attached. Small, misshapen berries have poor flavor and often have small hard green area.

MELONS

CANTALOUPES—Scar at stem end should be slightly sunken and calloused. Do not depend on softening at stem end; repeated pressure will produce this on immature fruit. Pronounced yellowing indicates overripeness. Netting should be coarse, corky and greyish. Avoid bruised or flabby fruit. Decay shows as soft sunken spots, mold or moisture at stem end.

CASABA—Select melon of yellow-colored rind, softening at blossom end. Immaturity is shown by firmness and greenish-white color; decay by dark sunken areas.

HONEY BALL OR HONEYDEW—Choose a melon with rind of light yellow which yields slightly to pressure. Dark sunken spots show decay. Flavor will be good if spots have not penetrated rind. Greenish-white color and hardness show immaturity.

WATERMELONS—Should be firm, symmetrical, fresh, good color, a bloom on surface, lower side yellowish. Immature melons are hard, unripe in appearance, underside is white or pale green. Overmature melons are dull, lifeless and feel springy to touch. Misshapen melons are usually of poor quality. Worm injury is shown as healed punctures or burrows. Decay occurs at stem and spreads rapidly. Fresh-cut stems are often painted with copper sulphate paste to prevent decay. Decay at blossom end is shown by a flat, dry, leathery spot. Dark, sunken, watery spots on body of melon do not affect quality if flesh is not penetrated.

VEGETABLES

GLOBE ARTICHOKES—Select compact, heavy, plump globes, large, clinging, fleshy leaf scales, good green color. Age or injury produces brown color. Overmature artichokes are open, centers may be fuzzy or purple, tips of scales hard and woody. Flavor will be strong, scales woody. Look for worm injury at base of bud.

ASPARAGUS—Select fresh, tender and firm with close compact tips. Wilted stalks with spreading tips indicate long time has elapsed since cutting. Angular stalks are likely to be woody.

LIMA BEANS—Pods should be well-filled, bright and dark green. Shelled beans should be plump, tender-skinned, greenish-white. Avoid dried, shriveled, spotted, yellow or flabby pods. Test shelled beans for tenderness.

BEETS—Should be smooth and free from blemish. Avoid shriveled beets. Beets which have been left too long in the field will have short necks covered with leaf scars.

BROCCOLI—Should be fresh, clean and not overmature. Select stalks that are tender and firm and heads compact with no evidence of flowering. Yellowish leaves may indicate woodiness. An occasional opened blossom does not indicate overmaturity.

Select firm sound pears like those shown on page 33

BRUSSELS SPROUTS—Select sprouts that are firm and compact and have a fresh green color. Puffy sprouts are of poor quality. Worm injury may cause considerable waste. Smudgy dirty appearance may indicate the presence of plant lice.

CABBAGE—Select reasonably solid heads with all but 3 or 4 wrapper leaves removed and stem cut close to head. Early cabbage will not be as firm as winter cabbage. Avoid worm injury, decay, yellowing of leaves, bursting heads. Cabbage only slightly affected can be trimmed and used to advantage. If base of some of outer leaves have separated from stem, cabbage may be strong flavored and coarse.

CARROTS—Select firm, fresh, smooth and well-shaped carrots with good color. Avoid wilted, shriveled, cracked, excessively forked carrots. Excessive masses of leaf stems indicate large cores.

CAULIFLOWER—Choose white, clean, firm, compact heads. Avoid spreading flower clusters, spotted or bruised curd.

CELERY—Should be brittle enough to snap easily. Avoid pithy, stringy stalks; detect by pressure. Open head to detect rot, insect injury and seed stem formation.

CHARD—Leaves should be crisp, tender and free from insect injury.

CHAYOTE—Varies greatly in size and shape. Select firm chayote.

CHICORY, ENDIVE, ESCAROLE —Should be crisp, fresh and tender. Tough coarse-leaved plants may be bitter.

COLLARDS—Are similar to kale. Leaves should be large and curled at edges.

CORN — Field corn may be as tender as sweet corn but not as sweet. Sweet corn is usually smaller, husks are darker green, ribbonlike ends hang free. Dry, straw-colored husks are an indication of age or damage. Immature corn lacks flavor. Worm injury confined to tips can be cut out with little waste.

CUCUMBERS—Should be firm, fresh, well-shaped and a deep green color. Shriveled, withered cucumbers are rubbery and bitter. Overmaturity is shown by puffiness, yellowing; flesh rubbery and seeds hard. These are not suitable for slicing but excellent for some kinds of pickles.

DANDELIONS—Select large, tender, fresh green plants before the plant begins to flower.

DASHEENS—Tubers are small; scars are natural, not blemishes.

EGGPLANT—Should be heavy, firm, free from blemish and a uniform dark color. Wilted, shriveled, soft or flabby eggplants are often bitter.

FENNEL—Select crisp bulbs and stalks.

GARLIC—Should be dry and not soft or spongy, outer covering unbroken. Avoid dirty bulbs.

KALE—Should be dark or bluish-green color, clean and fresh. Avoid wilted or yellow leaves.

KOHLRABI—Select small bulbs without woody tops.

LETTUCE—Head lettuce should be fresh, crisp, tender, firm, free from decay and should not have excess covering leaves. Seed stem (knob-like swelling beyond normal contours) indicates bitter flavor. Dead or discolored areas may indicate decay. Wilted outer leaves do not affect interior. Leaf lettuce should be crisp.

MUSHROOMS—Select firm mushrooms with no mold or softness.

MUSTARD GREENS—Should be fresh, tender, crisp and a full green color. Wilted, dirty, spotted leaves show age. Do not select those with seed stems.

OKRA—Choose fresh, tender pods that will snap easily. Dull dry appearance shows hard, woody fibrous texture with hard seeds. If shriveled or discolored, okra will lack flavor.

DRY ONIONS—Should be bright, clean, hard and well-shaped with dry skins. Avoid developed seed stem or sprouts. Moisture at neck indicates decay.

GREEN ONIONS—Should have green fresh tops, well blanched 2 to 3 inches from root. They should be young, crisp and tender. Wilting and yellowing of top may indicate age or too long a period since pulling.

PARSLEY—Select bright, green fresh parsley free from yellowed leaves. Slightly wilted stock may be revived in ice water or in a covered container in the refrigerator.

PARSNIPS—Select smooth, firm parsnips of medium size. Soft flabby roots are pithy and fibrous. Large roots will have woody cores. Softness may mean decay.

PEAS—Should be young, fresh, tender and sweet. Pod should be bright green, slightly velvety, fresh-picked. Flat, dark green pods indicate immature peas. Swollen pods of poor color flecked with grey specks indicate an advanced stage of maturity. Peas will be tough, flavor poor. Avoid wet and mildewed pods.

PEPPERS—Select firm, thick-fleshed, well-shaped peppers of fresh appearance. Immature pepers are soft, pliable, thin-fleshed, pale. Avoid shriveled, limp or pliable peppers or those with surface blemishes.

POTATOES—Should be sound, smooth, shallow-eyed and reasonably clean. Select size according to use intended. Avoid leathery, wilted, discolored potatoes. Green color is sunburn and gives bitter taste. Hollow heart or blackheart can be found only by cutting. It is more likely to be found in very large potatoes. Frozen potatoes may be wet, have dark rings below surface and turn black on cooking. If a quantity is bought sort into similar sizes to insure uniform cooking.

RUTABAGAS—Often coated with wax to preserve freshness. If not coated, select rutabagas that are firm and unwrinkled.

RADISHES—Select smooth, tender, crisp radishes, mild in flavor. Leaves are not indication of quality. Avoid pithy, spongy radishes.

SALSIFY (OYSTER PLANT)—Choose smooth firm roots of medium size. Soft, flabby roots will be pithy and fibrous. Woody cores will be found in large roots.

SPINACH—Should be well-developed stocky plants with fresh, crisp and clean leaves. Small, straggly or overgrown stalky plants are often tough. Watch for seed stems and soft slimy rot.

SQUASH—Summer squash should be fresh, heavy for size, free from blemish, rind easily punctured. Winter squash should be heavy, free from blemish, rind hard.

SWEETPOTATOES—Should be smooth, well-shaped and unblemished. Misshapen, cracked potatoes are undesirable only because of waste. Decay may be a soft wet or a dry shriveled sunken discolored area. Small dark clay-colored spots uniting to form large dark blotches are only skin deep. Damp potatoes may have been badly frozen.

TOMATOES—Should be mature, firm, plump, smooth, good color and free from blemishes. Cracked tomatoes must be used at once.

TURNIP TOPS—Be sure they are fresh, clean, crisp and tender.

Examine for plant lice.

TURNIPS—Select smooth, firm turnips with only a few leaf scars around crown. Tops should be fresh, green and young.

ZUCCHINI—Select small crisp zucchini. Wilted zucchini will have poor flavor.

PURCHASING GUIDE FOR MEAT

1 pound boneless meat, serves 4
  Boned meats, Ground meats
  Flank steaks
  Liver, Heart, Kidneys
  Sausages, Brains, Sweetbreads
  Most canned meats
1 pound meat with small amount of bone, serves 3
  Round steak, Pot roasts
  Ham slices, Rib roasts
1 pound meat with large amount of bone or fat, serves 2
  Most steaks, Poultry
  Shoulder cuts, Short ribs, Neck
  Chops, Breasts, Plate, Brisket

Choose vegetables personally and prepare them so as to retain the vitamins and minerals

EGG

8 to 10 egg whites........1 cup
10 to 14 egg yolks........1 cup
4 to 6 whole eggs........1 cup
10 average eggs without
   shell ....1 pound
7 to 8 large eggs with
   shell ....1 pound
9 to 10 medium eggs with
   shell ....1 pound
11 to 12 small eggs with
   shell ....1 pound

FLOUR

For 1 cup sifted all-purpose flour
use any one of the following
(sifted if possible):
1 cup cake flour+2 tablespoons
flour
$\frac{1}{3}$ cup corn meal+$\frac{2}{3}$ cup all-purpose flour
$\frac{1}{2}$ cup corn meal+$\frac{1}{2}$ cup all-purpose flour
$\frac{3}{4}$ cup bran+$\frac{1}{4}$ cup all-purpose flour
$\frac{1}{2}$ cup bran+$\frac{1}{2}$ cup all-purpose flour
$\frac{1}{2}$ cup rice flour+$\frac{1}{2}$ cup all-purpose flour
1 cup rice flour
$\frac{1}{2}$ cup rye flour+$\frac{1}{2}$ cup all-purpose flour
1 cup rye flour
$\frac{1}{4}$ cup soybean flour+$\frac{3}{4}$ cup all-purpose flour
$\frac{1}{3}$ cup soybean flour+$\frac{2}{3}$ cup all-purpose flour
$\frac{1}{2}$ cup whole-wheat flour+$\frac{1}{2}$ cup all-purpose flour
$\frac{3}{4}$ cup whole-wheat flour+$\frac{1}{4}$ cup all-purpose flour

MILK

For 1 cup fresh sweet milk in
batters use: $\frac{1}{2}$ cup evaporated
milk and $\frac{1}{2}$ cup water.
1 cup sour milk with $\frac{1}{2}$ teaspoon
soda as leavening. Omit 2 teaspoons tartrate or 1 teaspoon
double-action baking powder.
1 cup buttermilk with $\frac{1}{2}$ teaspoon
soda as leavening. Omit 2 tea-
spoons tartrate or 1 teaspoon
double-action baking powder.
1 cup skim milk and 2 tablespoons
fat.

COCOA AND CHOCOLATE

For 1 ounce (square) chocolate
use 4 tablespoons cocoa and
$\frac{1}{2}$ tablespoon fat.
For $\frac{1}{4}$ cup or 4 tablespoons cocoa
use 1 ounce (square) chocolate
and omit $\frac{1}{2}$ tablespoon fat.

SUGAR

For 1 cup granulated sugar use:
1 cup brown sugar, well packed.
$\frac{3}{4}$ cup honey and reduce liquid.
$1\frac{1}{2}$ cups molasses and reduce liquid.
$1\frac{1}{2}$ cups sorghum and reduce liquid.
2 cups corn sirup and reduce liquid.
$1\frac{1}{2}$ cups maple sirup and reduce liquid.

GENERAL EQUIVALENTS

2 cups solid butter = 1 pound
1 bouillon cube=1 teaspoon beef extract
1 tablespoon cornstarch=$\frac{2}{3}$ tablespoon arrowroot or $1\frac{3}{4}$ tablespoons wheat or rice flour
1 tablespoon unflavored gelatin= $\frac{1}{4}$ ounce (or $2\frac{2}{3}$ leaves leaf or French gelatin)
Horse-radish (1 tablespoon fresh grated)=2 tablespoons bottled
$1\frac{1}{2}$ cups molasses=1 cup sugar
1 tablet rennet=1 tablespoon liquid rennet
$1\frac{1}{2}$ tablespoons quick-cooking tapioca=$\frac{1}{4}$ cup pearl tapioca (soaked at least 1 hour)

STANDARD CAN SIZES

8 Z	1 cup
Picnic No. 1-East.......	$1\frac{1}{4}$ cups
12 ounce	$1\frac{2}{3}$ cups
No. 300	$1\frac{3}{4}$ cups
No. 1 tall	2 cups
No. 2	$2\frac{1}{2}$ cups
No. $2\frac{1}{2}$	$3\frac{1}{2}$ cups
No. 3	4 cups
No. 3 squat	$2\frac{3}{4}$ cups
No. 5	$7\frac{1}{3}$ cups
No. 10	13 cups
No. 1 square	1 pound
No. $2\frac{1}{2}$ square........	31 ounces

PROPORTIONS FOR LEAVENING AGENTS

Baking powder—$1\frac{1}{2}$ teaspoons to each cup of flour or $1\frac{3}{4}$ to 2 teaspoons tartrate powder
1 to $1\frac{1}{2}$ teaspoons phosphate powder
1 teaspoon S. A. S. phosphate (double-action powder)
Baking soda—$\frac{1}{2}$ teaspoon to 1 cup sour milk
$\frac{1}{2}$ teaspoon to 1 cup molasses
$\frac{1}{5}$ teaspoon to 1 ounce (square) chocolate
$\frac{1}{2}$ teaspoon with 1 teaspoon cream of tartar is equal to 2 teaspoon tartrate baking powder
Yeast—$\frac{1}{4}$ to 1 cake with 1 cup liquid depending upon the kind of flour used and the speed of rising desired

CAKES AND PAN SIZES

For any plain 1 or 2 egg cake with
   1 to 2 cups flour, use......8x8 inch pan or 2 (8-inch) layers
   If more than $\frac{1}{2}$ cup of fruit and nuts are added, use... 9x9, 10x10 or 8x12 inch pan
For 2 eggs and $2\frac{1}{2}$ cups flour use........9x9 or 10x10 inch pan or 2 (9-inch) layers
For 4 eggs and 2 to 3 cups flour use.....9x13 or 10x12 inch pan, 2 (9-inch) layers or 3 (8-inch) layers
For 6 egg whites and $2\frac{1}{2}$ cups flour use......10x14 inch pan or 3 (9-inch) layers
For 6 or more egg whites and 3 to $3\frac{1}{2}$ cups of flour, use..... 9x13 or 9x14 inch pan or 3 (9-inch) layers
For 8 or more egg whites and $2\frac{1}{2}$ cups flour, use.........10x14 inch pan
For 2 (8-inch) layers, use..... 8x8 or 9x9 inch pan
For 3 (8-inch) layers, use..... 10x10 or 8x12 inch pan
For 2 (9-inch) layers, use..... 9x13 inch pan

ONE POUND SHELLED NUTS EQUALS

Pounds Unshelled	Cups, Chopped
3½ pounds almonds	4½ cups
2¼ pounds filberts	3½ cups
1½ pounds peanuts	3 cups
2½ pounds pecans	3 cups
5½ pounds (black) walnuts	3 cups
2½ pounds (English) walnuts	4 cups

SUGARS

1 pound berry or fruit sugar	about 2¼ cups
1 pound brown sugar	2 cups, firmly packed
1 pound cane sirup	about 1½ cups
1 pound confectioners' sugar	about 2½ cups
1 pound corn sirup	about 1½ cups
1 pound cube sugar	180 to 220 pieces
1 pound granulated sugar	about 2 cups
1 pound honey, strained	about 1½ cups
1 pound maple sirup	about 1½ cups
1 pound molasses	about 1½ cups
1 pound sorghum	about 1½ cups

METRIC EQUIVALENTS

1 teaspoon	4.9 cubic centimeters
1 tablespoon	14.8 cubic centimeters
1 cup	236.6 cubic centimeters

TABLE OF PROPORTIONS

BATTERS

Pour batter ......1 cup liquid to 1 cup flour
Drop batter or sponge....1 cup liquid to 2 cups flour
Soft dough ....1 cup liquid to 3 cups flour
Stiff dough ....1 cup liquid to 4 cups flour

GELATIN (Unflavored)

1 tablespoon thickens 2 cups liquid

SALT

Soups and sauces....1 teaspoon salt to 1 quart sauce
Dough ....1 teaspoon salt to 4 cups flour
Cereals ....1 teaspoon salt to 2 cups liquid
Meat ....1 teaspoon salt to 1 pound meat
Vegetables ...½ teaspoon salt to 1 pound, using ¼ cup water
Vegetables ....½ teaspoon salt using 1 quart water

WEIGHTS AND MEASURES

60 drops	1 teaspoon
3 teaspoons	1 tablespoon
2 tablespoons	1 liquid ounce
4 tablespoons	¼ cup
16 tablespoons	1 cup
2 cups	1 pint
2 pints	1 quart
4 quarts	1 gallon
8 quarts	1 peck
4 pecks	1 bushel
16 ounces	1 pound

1 peck potatoes	15 pounds
1 bushel plums	50 pounds
1 bushel pears	48 pounds
1 bushel peaches	48 pounds
1 bushel apples	44 pounds

An experienced cook knows the "feel" of a soft dough and a stiff dough

CARE OF KITCHEN UTENSILS

ALUMINUM—Wash with soap and water and scour to remove spots. Dry thoroughly after washing.

CHROME—Wash with soap and water and polish with a dry soft cloth.

COPPER—Wash lacquered copper with soap and water and dry thoroughly. Polish unlacquered copper with a copper polish, wash with soap and water and dry thoroughly.

ENAMEL—Treat as glassware.

GLASS—Glass made especially for cooking and baking needs little care except washing with soap and water. When spots are hard to remove rub with scouring pads or a fine cleansing powder.

IRON—Wash with soap and water. Avoid scouring. Dry thoroughly after washing.

MONEL METAL—Wash with cloth wrung out of soapy water. Do not scour but polish occasionally with a fine cleansing powder.

NICKEL—Wash with soap and water. Polish with dry cloth.

STEEL—Wash with soap and water and scour to remove spots. Dry thoroughly after washing.

TIN—Wash with soap and water and scour with mild cleansing powders. Tin rusts easily so dry thoroughly after washing.

WOOD—Scrape with dull blade and wash with lukewarm water. After removing cooked food from utensils pour hot water into them, cover and set aside to loosen any food that adheres to pan. Do not soak wooden utensils.

TEAKETTLES

Fill with equal parts vinegar and water and heat to boiling. Let stand several hours; scrape off lime deposit.

TYPES OF TEAPOTS

Enamelware
Earthenware
China, Glass
Pottery

CARE OF TEAPOTS

Use a mild scouring material to remove stains from inside of pot. Wash with hot soapy water, rinse with boiling water, drain and dry thoroughly.

Avoid keeping tea in pot for any length of time.

TYPES OF COFFEEPOTS

Enamel pot, used to boil or steep coffee.

Percolator, valve or valveless types.

Electric with heating element at the base.

Those for use on range.

Drip pot with metal or paper filter.

French coffee biggin. (Earthenware drip with filter)

Glass coffee maker—siphon or vacuum.

Choose a coffeepot that is easy to clean.

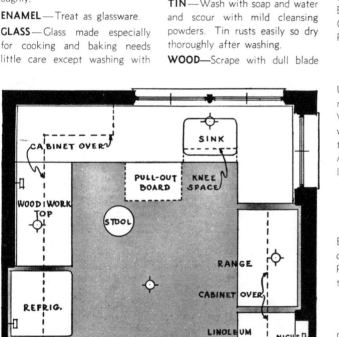

CABINET OVER
SINK
PULL-OUT BOARD
KNEE SPACE
WOOD WORK TOP
STOOL
RANGE
CABINET OVER
REFRIG.
LINOLEUM COUNTER
NICHE
SERVICE DOOR
UTILITY CLOSET
DINING ROOM DOOR
0 1 2 3 4 5
SCALE IN FEET

Plan your kitchen to save steps and to avoid congestion at any point

CARE OF COFFEEPOTS

Use a mild scouring material to remove stains from inside of pot. Wash with hot soapy water, rinse with boiling water, drain and dry thoroughly or boil a solution of baking soda and water in the pot 5 minutes, then rinse in boiling water.

Wash cloth filters in a solution of baking soda and water. Rinse well. If used each day, filters may be kept in a covered glass of cold water. Rinse new filters thoroughly in cold water before using.

CARE OF AUTOMATIC REFRIGERATOR

Defrost and clean refrigerator once every week or 10 days.

Turn temperature control to defrost. Remove ice trays. (Ice cubes may be kept in a vacuum jar for several hours.)

Remove food from refrigerator. Leave door open. Ice trays may be filled with tepid water to hasten defrosting. Do not chip ice from freezing unit with any sharp instrument.

Wash inside of box and inside and outside of freezing unit with a solution of soda and warm water. Remove shelves and wash. Rinse with clear warm water.

When defrosted, empty water collected in drip tray.

Turn control to normal operation (if not automatic).

Wash drip tray in solution of soda and warm water, rinse in clear lukewarm water and return to refrigerator.

Cover most foods.

Replace food in refrigerator, leaving space around each article for proper circulation of cold air.

CARE OF HOME FREEZER

Keep enameled surfaces of freezer spotlessly clean and protect finish using a creamy wax polish. DEFROSTING is necessary about once a year. However, in a warm, humid climate it is sometimes necessary to defrost as often as three times a year. (Do not allow more than half an inch of frost to collect on refrigerated areas of cabinet.) Defrost when food supply is low, moving packages from one part of freezer to the other. Remove dry frost with a dull spatula, wooden paddle or scraper provided for the purpose. Catch frost on a cardboard or .newspaper.

If cabinet has a slight odor and food has been spilled, a more thorough cleaning is needed. In this case, disconnect freezer, remove food packages and wrap them in newspapers and blankets to keep cold. Scrape frost from sides and bottom of cabinet. Wash cabinet with warm water to which a little baking soda has been added. Dry thoroughly before replacing food.

In case of a power failure, a well-insulated freezer keeps food frozen for about 48 hours providing lid is not lifted frequently. To prevent food from thawing for a longer period, obtain 25 pounds of dry ice from a locker plant and scatter it on top of food.

TO CLEAN WAFFLE IRONS EASILY use a small stiff brush.

TO CLEAN A BURNT OR GREASY PAN EASILY pour 1 inch water into pan, add about 1 teaspoon washing soda, cover, and heat to boiling.

The modern refrigerators are a joy to keep spotless and neatly arranged

CARE OF EGG BEATER

Wash beater in cold water to remove all food, then wash with other dishes. Never immerse the cogs in the water. If an electric beater is used detach the beaters to wash them so that no water gets into the motor.

CARE OF FOOD CHOPPER

Take chopper apart and wash each part thoroughly. Dry each part very carefully before assembling chopper. If chopper is not used frequently, rub contact parts with unsalted fat and keep in a paper bag. Wipe off the fat before using.

CARE OF FLOUR SIFTER

Keep sifter in flour bin. If a bin is not available keep sifter in a paper sack or any other kind of container so that it will not collect grease and dust but will be ready to use when needed.

Store small equipment in drawers and cupboards and keep your work surfaces uncluttered

CARE OF THE RANGE

The modern range is as easy to take care of as a set of mixing bowls. The parts are easily dissembled making it a simple matter to keep each part scrupulously clean. Most ranges have an enamel finish which requires the same attention that one would give to a bowl made of the same material. Clean with mild soap and lukewarm water. To remove spots, rub lightly with a fine cleansing powder, one which does not scratch the surface of the enamel. Polish with a clean dry cloth. Wash the interior of the oven each time it is used. The broiler may require special attention with a scouring pad to remove all stubborn spots. Be sure that the oven is cool or cold before washing as too abrupt changes in temperature may check the enamel. Wash the cooking surface daily so that any food particles and grease may be removed before they burn and become difficult to remove. Also remember to keep acids away from the enamel as they are apt to destroy the luster.

ESSENTIALS

NEAR FOOD PREPARATION CENTER

Rolling pin
Mixing spoons—2 wooden (large and small)—2 metal
Teaspoons
Measuring spoons
Measuring cups
Lemon reamer
Grater
Cookie cutter
Doughnut cutter
Corkscrew
Knife sharpener
Long-handled rubber scraper
Knives—2 case—2 paring—
    1 butcher—1 chopping—1 bread
Forks—1 (2-tine)—2 small
Spatula
Sieve
Egg whisk
Egg beater
Can opener
Flour sifter
Mixing bowls (3 sizes)
Custard cups
Piepans
Bread pans
Cake pans—3 layers—1 loaf
Muffin pans
Baking sheet
Casseroles
Breadbox, Cakebox
Roasting pan
Saucepans with covers
Food chopper
Potato masher

NEAR RANGE

Frying pans (2 sizes)
Teapot, Coffeepot
Salt and pepper shakers
Double boiler
Oven thermometer (if range is not equipped with one)
Ladle, Pancake turner
Large 2-tine fork
Basting spoons
Draining spoon

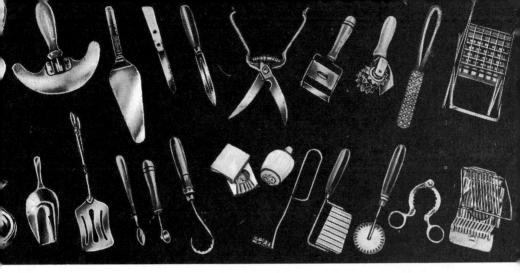

AT THE SINK

Soap dish
Scouring materials
Strainers (2 sizes)
Colander
Dishpan
Dish drainer
Vegetable brushes
Garbage pail

NEAR REFRIGERATOR

Covered refrigerator dishes
Bottle opener

EXTRAS FOR EFFICIENCY

Additional frying pans, bowls,
baking pans, small utensils, etc.,
according to size of family and
amount of entertaining.
Spatulas, 3 sizes
Pastry brush
Pastry board
Chopping bowl
Fish and steak planks
Shears
Meat cleaver
Pastry blender
Skewers
Tube pan
Cake coolers
Cake tester
Canister set
Funnel
Apple corer
Individual molds
Ring mold
Pudding mold

Butter molds
Cookie press
Pastry bag and tubes
Wire whisk
Griddle
Timbale iron
Dutch oven
Meat thermometer
Candy and jelly thermometer
Deep-fat frying thermometer
Potato ricer
Electric timer
Sink mat
Brushes—Bottle, Vegetable
Paper towel rack
Short-handled rubber scraper
Parchment paper
Wire baskets
Cellophane or oiled silk bags
Refrigerator thermometer
Water bottle

MISCELLANEOUS STORAGE COMPARTMENT

Preserving kettle
Sizzling steak platter
Deep-fat frying kettle
Sink garbage container
Electric mixer
Waffle iron
Electric roaster
Waterless cooker
Pressure cooker
Ice cream freezer
Ice bag and mallet
Scales
Toaster

Few of us can resist these little articles that make food preparation such fun

GADGETS

Egg slicer
Onion chopper
Nut mill
Glass fruit knife
French ball cutter
Cheese slicer
Cake breaker
Canvas pastry cloth
Fowl shears
Tomato or fruit slicer
French butter curler
Grapefruit knife
Refrigerator cookie molds
Checkerboard cake pans
Pea sheller
Wall can opener
Poultry pins
Jar opener, Pie crimper
Tongs, Garnish cutters
Ice cube crusher
Egg timer
Cherry pitter, Bean slicer
Strawberry huller
Pineapple eyer
Muddlers, Fish rack
Egg opener and separator
Birds'-nest fryer
Nutcracker
Milk-cap opener
Cream separator
Mortar and pestle

TIME, TEMPERATURE AND TESTS

BAKING TIMES AT PREHEATED OVEN TEMPERATURES

	TEMPERATURE FAHRENHEIT	TIME MINUTES (APPROXIMATE)
BREADS		
Baking powder biscuits.........................	450°	12 to 15
Bread	400° then 350°	20 then 40 to 50
Coffee bread	375-400°	20 to 25
Coffee cake...................................	400°	30
Corn bread	400°	30
Fruit or nut bread	350°	60
Muffins	425°	20 to 30
Popovers	450° then 350°	20 then 15 to 20
Rolls	400-425°	15 to 20
Spoon.......................................	350°	35 to 45
CAKES		
Angel Food	325°-350°	50 to 75
Chocolate		
Layer	350°	25 to 35
Square	350°	35 to 45
Cup	375°	20 to 25
Fruitcake		
Steamed 1 hour, then baked		
light	250°	1 hour
rich	250°	3 hours
Entirely baked	275-300°	1½ to 4 hours
Gingerbread	350°	45 to 50
Jelly roll	350°	15 to 20
Layer	350°-375°	25 to 35
Loaf (deep)	325-350°	50 to 75
Poundcake	275-325°	1 to 2 hours
Spongecake	325°	60
Square (shallow loaf)	350°	45 to 55
Tortes	350°	20 to 40
Upside-down cake	350°	40 to 50
COOKIES		
Fruit, molasses or chocolate..................	325-350°	10 to 15
Other drop and rolled.......................	375-400°	8 to 12
Other refrigerator (sliced)	400°	8 to 10
Bar	325°-350°	25 to 40
Macaroons	300°-325°	20 to 30
MEATS....Braising—page 349. Broiling—page 351		
MERINGUES	275°	45 to 60
PASTRY		
Pie shells	450°	10 to 12
Puff pastry	450-500°	5 to 8
Puff shells		
Cream puffs and éclairs	450° then 350°	15 then 20 to 25
Tarts	450°	10 to 15
Turnovers	450°	15
POULTRY AND GAME................page 409		

PIES

Deep-dish pies	450°	10
	then 350°	30 to 35
Meat pies		
Biscuit top	450°	15 to 20
Pastry	450°	15
	then 350°	30
Meringues on cooked fillings	350°	10 to 15
One-crust (unbaked)	450°	10
	then 350°	25 to 30

TIME AND TEMPERATURES FOR PASTRY

When temperature is too high:

Crust may be too dark.

Pie may not be evenly baked.

When temperature is too low:

Crust may be pale.

Crust may be doughy.

Filling may not be thoroughly cooked.

When pie is not baked long enough:

Crust may be pale.

Lower crust may be doughy.

TESTS FOR CAKES

Cakes are baked if: Cake tester or toothpick inserted in center of cake comes out clean.

Cake shrinks from edges of pan.

Cake springs back when touched lightly with finger.

Small cakes and cookies are baked if: They spring back from the finger touch and are brown.

A spacious oven in your range is a convenience when cooking complete oven meals.

DEEP-FAT FRYING

Cooking fats used for deep-fat frying are all-purpose shortenings and oils. Butter, margarine, drippings and chicken fat are suitable for pan-frying but are generally not used for deep-fat frying as they break down and scorch at a temperature of about 350°F. For deep-fat frying fats are best which have a higher smoking point. These include vegetable shortenings, regular and new improved lard, and salad oil (except olive oil) which break down at a temperature above 350°F.

The electric deep-fat fryer has almost taken the guesswork out of deep-fat frying but if you do not have one a heavy saucepan will do. For accurate results a deep-fat frying thermometer is essential. Without a thermometer, test the fat with an inch cube of day-old bread which will brown in fat at 365-375°F. in 60 seconds.

This is a good frying temperature and when in doubt use it. For previously cooked foods, fish balls, croquettes, etc. use 375-385°F. (Bread cube browns in 40 seconds.) For doughnuts, fritters, and raw dough mixtures use 365-370°F. For French fried potatoes use 385-390°F. (Bread cube browns in 20 seconds.)

EGGS

Since eggs are toughened by high heat they should be cooked at low temperatures. Place custards, soufflés and similar egg dishes in a pan of water when baking to prevent overheating of the egg mixture. Cook egg sauces over hot water.

COOKING EGGS IN SHELL

Eggs in the shell should **NOT** be cooked in boiling water. When eggs are hard-cooked in boiling water they are likely to be tough and leathery, while soft-cooked eggs are unevenly cooked.

METHOD 1 — Place eggs in saucepan, cover with cold water and heat slowly to boiling.

FOR SOFT-COOKED EGGS— Remove when water starts to boil.

FOR HARD-COOKED EGGS— Reduce heat and simmer 5 to 8 minutes.

METHOD II—Heat to boiling enough water to cover eggs 1 inch deep. Lower eggs into water and remove pan from heat.

FOR SOFT-COOKED EGGS—Allow to remain in water 6 minutes.

FOR HARD-COOKED EGGS— Allow to remain in water 25 minutes.

METHOD III—Pour hot water into both parts of a double boiler. When water in the lower part boils, place eggs in top. (When cooked by this method the temperature cannot reach the boiling point and eggs are cooked evenly.)

FOR SOFT COOKED EGGS— Cook 12 to 15 minutes.

FOR HARD-COOKED EGGS— Cook 25 to 30 minutes.

TEMPERATURES FOR BAKING FISH

Fish such as whitefish, lake trout, shad, or bass, weighing from 4 to 5 pounds, may be baked on heavy paper or foil in a shallow pan. The backbone may be removed, if you wish, and body cavity filled with a flavorsome stuffing. Bake fish at 350°F. 45 to 50 minutes, or until it flakes easily.

TEMPERATURES AND TESTS FOR CANDY AND FROSTINGS

Sirup, Thread stage 228° to 234° F. Spins a 2-inch thread, when dropped from spoon.

Fudge, Penuche, Frosting, Fondant, Soft-ball stage, 234° to 240° F. When a small amount is dropped into cold water it forms a soft ball which flattens when removed.

Caramels, Firm-ball stage, 244° to 248° F. When a small amount is dropped into cold water it forms a firm ball which does not flatten when removed.

Divinity, Nougat, Popcorn balls, Salt-water taffy, Hard-ball stage, 250° to 265° F. When a small amount is dropped into cold water it forms a ball which holds its shape.

Butterscotch taffy, Pulled candies, Crack stage, 270° to 290° F. When a small amount is dropped into cold water it separates into threads but is not brittle.

Brittle, Glacé, Hard-crack stage, 295° to 310° F. When a small amount is dropped into cold water it separates into hard brittle threads.

Caramel Burnt sugar, Clear to brown liquid, 310° F., becomes hard when cool.

A meat thermometer is almost a "must" in determining when the roast is done to a turn

TEMPERATURES FOR ROASTING MEATS

Roasting meat at a constant low temperature 300° F. (or 350° F. for pork) gives better results than the old method by which the meat was first seared at a high temperature and the roasting finished at a low temperature. The searing does not retain the juices as was once thought and causes excessive shrinkage. Use any shallow pan large enough to hold the meat and place a wire rack in bottom to hold the meat up out of the juices and to allow the heat to penetrate evenly from all sides. See Page 348 for full chart of time and temperature for various cuts, weights of meat, including internal temperatures.

CREAM AND MILK

TO MAKE SWEET MILK SOUR measure one tablespoon vinegar or lemon juice into a measuring cup. Add sweet milk up to one cup level and stir well. (The process of pasteurization prevents milk from souring naturally as raw milk did in Grandmother's day.)

TO WHIP CREAM READILY add a few drops of lemon juice and chill thoroughly before whipping.

TO KEEP SCALDING MILK FROM SCORCHING rinse pan with hot water before using.

TO WHIP EVAPORATED MILK place a can of milk in freezing unit of refrigerator until partially frozen. Pour contents into a very cold bowl, add 1 tablespoon lemon juice to 2/3 cup milk and whip as cream.

EGGS

TO HARD-COOK EGG YOLKS drop into simmering water and keep below boiling until firm.

TO DIVIDE AN EGG beat slightly and measure with tablespoon.

TO HOLD EGGS TOGETHER WHILE POACHING add a few drops of vinegar or lemon juice to the cooking water.

TO CUT HARD-COOKED EGGS WITHOUT BREAKING THE YOLK dip the knife into water.

TO PREVENT MERINGUE ON PIES FROM SHRINKING spread meringue on filling so that it touches the sides of pastry all around the edge. Bake 10 to 15 minutes in a 350°F. oven.

TO GLAZE TOP OF ROLLS, PASTRY, ETC., brush before baking with slightly beaten egg white and 1 tablespoon milk or water; use whole egg for yellow glaze.

BUTTER, SHORTENING AND FAT

TO CUT BUTTER CLEANLY cover blade of knife with waxed paper or heat in hot water.

TO MEASURE LESS THAN 1 CUP OF SHORTENING pour cold water (the amount being the difference between the amount of shortening called for in recipe and 1 cup) into measuring cup and add shortening until water reaches the top of cup. For example, if 1/4 cup shortening is desired, pour 3/4 cup cold water into cup, add shortening until water reaches top and pour off water before using shortening.

TO CLARIFY FAT strain slightly cooled fat through several thicknesses of cheesecloth to remove foreign materials. Put slices of raw potato in cooled fat; heat slowly until slices are well browned. Strain again and store in covered container in a cool place.

TO MAKE BUTTER BALLS scald a pair of wooden butter paddles and place in ice water about 1 hour. Measure butter by tablespoons to make balls uniform in size. Have butter firm but not hard and roll lightly between paddles with circular motion to form balls. Drop onto a chilled plate, onto cracked ice or into ice water.

ROLLS—Proceed as for butter balls and flatten balls into cylinders. Chill as above.

CURLS—Have butter firm but not hard. Dip butter curler into hot water each time. Begin at far end of pound print of butter, draw curler lightly and quickly toward you to make a thin shaving which curls up. Chill.

MOLDS—Scald fancy butter molds, then place in ice water for 1 hour. Pack solidly with butter and level off top surface. Press out butter and chill.

Evaporated milk will whip beautifully for frozen desserts, cakes and frostings

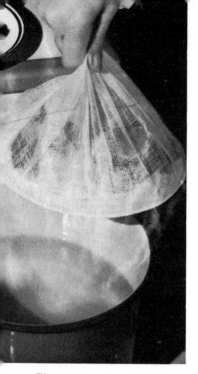

This trick keeps fish from dissolving into the broth

MISCELLANEOUS

TO MAKE SWEET PICKLE FANS cut pickles into thin parallel slices almost to the end. Spread and press uncut end carefully to hold fan in place.

TO PREPARE A QUICK FRENCH DRESSING heat 1 cup vinegar and 1 peeled, crushed clove of garlic to boiling. Strain, add salt, pepper and dry mustard and store in corked bottle. Add to oil whenever dressing is needed.

TO SAVE TIME prepare a quantity of white sauce at one time, pour into quart jar, cover, store in refrigerator and use as needed.

TO SAVE TIME when serving hot biscuits for dinner prepare them in the morning, (using double-action baking powder). Cut into shapes, place on baking sheet and place in refrigerator. "Pop" into oven to bake about 20 minutes before serving.

FISH AND MEAT

TO MAKE FISH FIRM AND WHITE add a little lemon juice to water while boiling.

TO AVOID UNPLEASANT ODORS WHILE COOKING FISH cover with browned butter or lemon juice.

TO REMOVE FISH ODORS FROM COOKING UTENSILS add 2 tablespoons ammonia to the dish water.

TO KEEP SALMON AND OTHER FRAGILE FOODS FROM BREAKING WHILE BEING BOILED place food on a plate, tie in a square of cheesecloth and lower all into water.

MEAT OR CHICKEN MAY BE FLOURED EASILY by placing in a paper bag with flour and shaking well.

TO KEEP BACON FROM CURLING snip edges with shears before cooking or broil between racks.

TO KEEP BONES ON CROWN ROASTS FROM BURNING place in pan with bones down or spear ends of bones with fat meat

WHEN PREPARING SMALL BITS OF MEAT place them on skewers.

SUGAR

TO KEEP BROWN SUGAR FROM BECOMING HARD place it in a glass jar and cover tightly.

TO MOISTEN BROWN SUGAR WHICH HAS ALREADY HARDENED place a slashed apple or ½ apple in jar with sugar or place sugar to one side in a container, arrange slice of very moist bread on other side; cover tightly.

TO SPRINKLE SUGAR OR SUGAR MIXTURES such as sugar and spices, sugar and flour, use a salt shaker.

FRUITS

TO MAKE ORANGE OR GRAPEFRUIT SEGMENTS pare with a sharp knife, slide knife blade along each segment wall to center and turn out segment with a slight twist of the knife.

TO PEEL GRAPEFRUIT AND ORANGES EASILY let them stand in boiling water about 8 minutes before peeling.

TO KEEP LEMONS FRESH place in glass jar, fill with water and cover tightly.

TO OBTAIN MOST JUICE FROM LEMONS heat before squeezing.

TO EXTRACT JUICE FROM LEMON WHEN A SMALL AMOUNT IS NEEDED puncture the skin with a fork and gently squeeze out the amount required

TO KEEP LIMES FRESH place them in a jar, cover and store in refrigerator.

TO REMOVE PITS FROM CHERRIES EASILY insert a new pen point into penholder, pointed end in, and take out pits with the round end, or with hump of unused hairpin.

TO AVOID WRINKLED SKINS ON BAKED APPLES slit in a few places before baking.

TO KEEP CUT FRUITS FROM DISCOLORING sprinkle lemon or pineapple juice over them.

TO PREVENT DRIED FRUITS FROM CLOGGING THE FOOD CHOPPER add a few drops of lemon juice before grinding.

TO KEEP JUICE IN FRUIT WHICH HAS BEEN CUT cover exposed part with waxed paper and place fruit cut-side down on a dish, or fit with a transparent bowl cover and leave cut side up.

WASH BERRIES BEFORE hulling to retain juice.

Bread croustades are very simple to make and effective for serving entrées

BREAD

TO CUT FRESH BREAD EASILY cut with a hot knife.

TO MAKE A LARGE CROUSTADE for serving creamed food, cut crusts from a loaf of bread and remove center, leaving walls and bottom ¾ inch thick. Brush with butter. Toast. Make small croustades from sections of loaf.

TO BUTTER BREAD FOR THIN SANDWICHES, spread end of loaf with softened butter and cut as thin as possible. Repeat.

TO FRESHEN ROLLS place in a paper bag. Twist top of bag closed and heat in hot oven (400° F.) 15 minutes.

TO PREVENT TOAST FROM BECOMING SOGGY when used as base for poached egg, use a pierced pancake turner to remove egg from water and let drain thoroughly.

TO PREPARE CRUMBS FROM DRY BREAD force through a food chopper or place dry bread in a small cloth sack and crush with a rolling pin.

TO KEEP BREAD CRUMBS FROM SCATTERING tie a paper bag onto end of food chopper when preparing crumbs.

TO MAKE ATTRACTIVE DESIGNS ON CRACKERS press cheese and smooth spreads through pastry tube or a funnel made of heavy white paper.

TO REMOVE PIE, CAKE OR BREAD PANS FROM OVEN use a large pancake turner or a pair of strong tongs.

These toast timbales can be made in the twinkling of an eye

TO PREPARE QUICK TIMBALES
press squares of fresh bread into muffin pans and toast. The corners will turn up.

PIES, CAKES, ETC.

TO PREVENT JUICES FROM COOKING OUT OF PIES INTO OVEN place a strip of dampened cloth or pastry tape around edge of pie; or place a tiny funnel or 4-inch stick of uncooked macaroni upright in center of pie.

TO AVOID SHRINKAGE OF PIE CRUST roll pastry, place in pie-pan without stretching and set aside 5 minutes before fluting the edge. Or place another pie-pan on pastry before baking. Remove after 15 minutes of baking.

LINE CAKE PANS WITH PLAIN OR WAXED PAPER instead of greasing. Cut several pieces at one time to fit the bottom of pans and keep them on hand.

TO GREASE PANS EASILY mix ½ cup shortening and ¼ cup flour to a smooth paste. Spread thinly on pans. Keep a supply of the mix in a covered dish to use when needed.

VEGETABLES

TO SCORE CUCUMBERS mark lengthwise with tines of fork and cut slices crosswise. Flute peeled bananas in the same way.

GREASE POTATO SKINS BEFORE BAKING to keep them soft and tender.

TO KEEP SWEET POTATOES AND APPLES FROM TURNING BLACK place them in salted water at once after paring.

PEEL ONIONS under water to keep them from affecting eyes.

TO PREVENT ODOR OF COOKING ONIONS AND CABBAGE add 1 tablespoon lemon juice or wedge of lemon with skin on.

TO EXTRACT JUICE FROM ONION cut a slice from root end and scrape juice from center with edge of a teaspoon.

TO MINCE ONION AND OTHER VEGETABLES, peel, cut off a slice, cut exposed surface of onion into ⅛-inch squares and as deep as needed. Slice thinly.

TO KEEP FRESH PARSLEY, MINT, AND WATERCRESS wash thoroughly, shake off excess water, place in a glass jar, cover and place in refrigerator.

TO REMOVE VEGETABLE STAINS FROM HANDS rub them with a slice of lemon.

TO MAKE CELERY CURLS cut stalks lengthwise into thin strips to within 1 inch of end and place in ice water. Longer stalks may be curled at both ends.

FOR DELICIOUS AND CRISP CELERY let stand in cold water to which 1 teaspoon sugar per quart has been added.

TO SEPARATE LETTUCE LEAVES EASILY cut out core and place lettuce head under running water so that it runs into cavity. Drain and dry leaves before using.

TO GARNISH LETTUCE LEAVES place paprika on waxed paper and dip edges of leaves into it.

TO FRESHEN ASPARAGUS set stems in cold water.

TO FRESHEN WITHERED PARSNIPS, CARROTS, POTATOES, CABBAGE, LETTUCE, etc., let stand in very cold salted water.

TO REMOVE THE SKINS FROM CARROTS EASILY, drop into boiling water and let stand for a few minutes.

TO KEEP CAULIFLOWER WHITE WHILE COOKING use ½ milk and ½ water and cook without covering, until just tender.

TO RESTORE SWEETNESS IN OLD VEGETABLES add a little sugar to water while cooking.

TO SKIN A TOMATO EASILY place a fork through the stem end, plunge into boiling water and then into cold water. Or hold over direct heat. Break skin at blossom end and peel skin back.

TO KEEP LEFTOVER CANNED PIMIENTOS FROM SPOILING, place in small dish and cover with cooking oil.

MISCELLANEOUS

DRAIN DEEP FAT FRIED FOODS on absorbent paper.

TO MELT CHOCOLATE place on waxed paper in top of double boiler and heat until melted.

TO SHELL POPCORN use a large grater.

TO AVOID "BOIL OVERS" WHILE COOKING MACARONI OR SPAGHETTI add 1 tablespoon cooking oil or shortening to the water.

TO AVOID STICKING WHILE COOKING MACARONI OR SPAGHETTI place in a colander or sieve and place in boiling water.

TO MAKE RICE WHITER AND MORE FLUFFY add 1 teaspoon lemon juice to each quart of water while cooking.

TO KEEP CORN MEAL FROM LUMPING moisten it with cold water before adding to boiling water.

TO MAKE A SMOOTH THICKENING OF FLOUR AND WATER place in a small jar, cover tightly and shake well.

TO KEEP COOKED SALAD DRESSING FROM CURDLING stir the beaten eggs into the cold vinegar before cooking and cook slowly in double boiler.

TO FRESHEN SHREDDED COCONUT soak in fresh milk with a dash of sugar a few minutes before using, or place in a sieve, set over boiling water and steam until moist.

TO KEEP CHEESE FRESH wrap in a cloth dampened with vinegar and store in a cool place (not in refrigerator).

TO GIVE DOUGHNUTS ADDED FLAVOR place a few whole cloves or stick of cinnamon in fat while frying.

WHEN COVERING JELLY WITH PARAFFIN pour a thin layer over top of jelly, place a strong piece of string on top with end over edge of glass and pour another layer of paraffin over top. Remove paraffin with string when jelly is to be used.

TO OPEN FRUIT JARS EASILY set them upside down in hot water for a few minutes.

TO REMOVE ODORS FROM JARS AND BOTTLES pour a solution of water and dry mustard into them and let stand for several hours or use a dilute chlorine solution, then rinse in hot water.

KEEP GLASS JARS AND COVERS IN WHICH SALAD DRESSING is purchased. Remove pasteboard insert, wash, dry and use as containers for leftovers or for spices, cut onion, garlic, sugars, etc., on shelf.

TO KEEP A BOWL FROM SLIPPING on WORKING SURFACE place it on a folded wet towel.

AVOID POURING COLD WATER INTO HOT PANS; the sudden change of temperature will cause metals to warp.

TO TEST HEAT OF A GRIDDLE place a few drops of water on griddle and if water scatters it is hot enough to brown food.

USE KITCHEN SHEARS to cut parsley, diced cooked meats, dice giblets, cut crusts from bread, cut marshmallows, rhubarb, celery, etc.

WHEN FREEZING A MOUSSE OR PARFAIT IN THE REFRIGERATOR line tray with waxed paper, then pour in mixture to be frozen. Allow slightly more time for freezing. Or, fill paper soufflé cups with mixture, place in freezing tray. When firmly frozen pull out at the edge, removing plaits in cup and lift out onto serving plate. Garnish before or after freezing.

It's fun to watch the drop of water bounce around on a "just right" griddle

PASTRY

When pastry is rolled too thin:
  It absorbs juices easily.
  It may not brown well.
  Top crust softens when pie cools.
  Crust breaks easily.
When pastry is rolled too thick:
  It may not bake thoroughly.
When pastry is not properly fitted:
  It may not brown evenly on bottom.
  Air under crust causes bubbles, making crust uneven.
  It may shrink during baking if stretched too much.
  Edge may become too brown if pastry is too far above pan.

FILLING

When too much filling is used:
  Juice may cook out into oven.
  Filling may not be thoroughly cooked.
When too much sugar is used:
  It may be too sweet.
  It may be too sirupy, possibly cooking out into oven.
When too much thickening is used:
  Filling may be pasty.
When not enough filling is used.
  Pie may be uneven in shape; lower in center than at sides.
When not enough sugar is used
  Filling may be sour.
  May be too thin to serve nicely.
When not enough thickening is used:
  Filling may be too juicy.
  Crust may soak.
  Pie is hard to serve.

CAKES

Measure ingredients accurately with standard measuring equipment, mix ingredients carefully, use correct size of pan and bake using the correct baking time and oven temperature and you will never experience any difficulties.

RULES FOR MAKING HOT TEA

Have all equipment perfectly clean.
Scald teapot.
Measure water and tea with standard measuring equipment.
Use freshly drawn water.
Have water boiling vigorously.
Add tea leaves at once and remove from heat.
Steep tea for desired length of time, then strain at once into hot teapot.
Provide a pot of freshly boiled water to weaken tea for those who do not like it strong.
Do not use tea leaves more than once.

RULES FOR MAKING ICED TEA

Prepare as for hot tea using only half the amount of water.
Steep the same length of time as for hot tea and strain at once over ice.
Hot tea may be safely poured into glasses filled with ice.

Serving a cup of perfectly brewed tea in the afternoon is a gracious custom

RULES FOR MAKING COFFEE

Have all equipment perfectly clean.
If a cloth filter is used, boil after each use or keep filter in water.
Use freshly drawn water.
Always use standard measuring cup and spoon.
Remove grounds as soon as coffee is made.
Serve at once.
Do not reheat coffee or reuse grounds.
Unless coffee is ground at home purchase only 1 week's supply at a time. Coffee begins to deteriorate somewhat after it is roasted and loses flavor rapidly after it is ground.
Flavor is best preserved by storing coffee in a covered container

RULES FOR MAKING ICED COFFEE

Prepare as for hot coffee using only half the amount of water.
Pour at once over ice.
Hot coffee may be safely poured into glasses filled with ice.

ICED COFFEE AND TEA CUBES

—Make regular brew for coffee or tea and freeze in cube form. Pour normal brew over cubes.

MENUS

700 Menus
for Every Day
in the Year

January Dinners

NEW YEAR'S DINNER

Pâté de Fois Gras
Roast Goose with Apple Stuffing, 436, 406
Orange Sweetpotatoes
Glazed Onions
Chicory with French Dressing
Cranberry Refrigerator Cake
Coffee   Milk

∨ ∨ ∨

Tamale Pie, 256
Apple Fritters
Butter Peas
Coleslaw
Apricot Upside-down Gingerbread
Coffee   Milk

∨ ∨ ∨

Shrimp Canapés
Broiled Lamb Chops, 369, 902
Mashed Rutabaga
Spiced Beets
Apple and Nut Salad
Filled Cookies
Coffee   Milk

∨ ∨ ∨

Pineapple Juice
Ham Omelet, 278, 282
Kidney Bean Salad
Bran Muffins
Ginger Parfait
Coffee   Milk

Roast Leg of Lamb, 368
With Mint Jelly
Franconia Potatoes
Broccoli with Hollandaise Sauce
Whole-wheat Rolls
Plum Fluff
Coffee   Milk

∨ ∨ ∨

Fruit Cocktail
Broiled Whitefish, 320
With Tartare Sauce
Shoestring Potatoes
Creamed Spinach
Lemon Chiffon Pie
Coffee   Milk

∨ ∨ ∨

Vegetable Juice
Pot Roast of Beef, 353
Brabant Potatoes, Carrots and Onions
Cabbage Filled Peppers
Orange Bavarian Cream

∨ ∨ ∨

Frozen Fruit Juices
Breast of Veal with Celery Stuffing, 392, 406
Green Beans in Onion Sauce
Brazil-nut Pudding
Coffee   Milk

∨ ∨ ∨

Vegetable Soup
Roast Loin of Pork, 374
Mashed Parsnips
Hot Chicory Salad Bowl
Deep-dish Apple Pie
Coffee   Milk

Swiss Steak in Sour Cream, 360
Baked Potatoes
Brussels Sprouts
Winter Vegetable Salad Bowl
Coconut Nut Kisses
Coffee   Milk

∨ ∨ ∨

Cod Steaks with Mushroom Sauce, 315
Baked Stuffed Potatoes
Buttered Beets Julienne
Fresh Spinach Salad
Cherry Cottage Pudding with Hot Cherry Sauce
Coffee   Milk

∨ ∨ ∨

Cream of Mushroom Soup
Baked Liver Rolls, 399
Baked Potatoes
Vegetable Soufflé
Frosted Orange Pie
Coffee   Milk

∨ ∨ ∨

Pork Tenderloin Piquante, 378
Mashed Potatoes
Parsnip Fritters
Chicory Salad Bowl
Baked Apples with Cranberries
Coffee   Milk

Start the New Year right by garnishing the roast goose with baked oranges

oiled Steak, 352, 901
ashed Potatoes
ench Fried Onions
ixed Vegetable Salad Bowl with
　Garlic French Dressing
icecake with Fig Filling and
　Seven Minute Icing
offee　　　　　　Milk

∨ ∨ ∨

egetable Soup
uffed Pork Chops, 378
aked Sweetpotatoes
reamed Celery
range Pineapple Pie
offee　　　　　　Milk

∨ ∨ ∨

**eal Loaf with Mushroom Tomato
　Sauce, 394**
aked Potatoes
reen Beans
aked Raisin Honey
　Bread Pudding with Cream
offee　　　　　　Milk

∨ ∨ ∨

**iver Dumplings in Beef Broth,
　98, 402**
un Glow Salad
offee　　　　　　Milk

∨ ∨ ∨

lot Crab-meat Canapés
**egetable Plate (Mashed Pota-
　toes, Asparagus, Diced Beets
　and Turnips), 518**
anana Spicecake
offee　　　　　　Milk

'romote the idea of eating
egetables by serving them
ften and attractively

SUNDAY DINNER
Avocado Cocktail Salad
Duck with Sauerkraut, 434
Carrot and Celery Soufflé
Hot Mince Pie with Rum Sauce
Coffee　　　　　　Milk

∨ ∨ ∨

Dinner-in-a-Dish, 356
Fruit Salad
Cheese
Toasted Crackers
Coffee　　　　　　Milk

∨ ∨ ∨

Onion Soup
**Baked Herring with Tomato
　Sauce, 314, 490**
Mashed Potatoes
Breaded Brussels Sprouts
Apple Gingerbread Upside-down
　Cake
Coffee　　　　　　Milk

∨ ∨ ∨

**Baked Ham with Orange Glaze,
　379, 858**
Yam Puff
Creamed Cabbage
Pickled Crab Apples
Sherry Chiffon Pie
Coffee　　　　　　Milk

∨ ∨ ∨

Tomato Consommé de luxe
Liver Pot Roast, 402
Whipped Mashed Potatoes
Buttered Green Beans
Mince Custard Pie
Coffee　　　　　　Milk

Vegetable Soup
Deviled Scallops, 341
American Fried Potatoes
Fresh Spinach Salad
Cream Cheese Cake
Coffee　　　　　　Milk

∨ ∨ ∨

Chicken Liver Canapés
Roast Chicken, 412
Mashed Potatoes
Creamed Peas and Onions
Orange and Avocado Salad
Frozen Pudding

∨ ∨ ∨

Fruit Cocktail
Stuffed Lamb Shoulder, 367
Franconia Potatoes
Broccoli with Hollandaise Sauce
Watercress Salad
Peppermint Mousse

∨ ∨ ∨

Tomato Juice
Hungarian Beef Stew, 356
Buttered Noodles
Pea and Cauliflower Salad Bowl
Molasses Fruit Pudding
Coffee　　　　　　Milk

∨ ∨ ∨

Oyster Cocktail
Cranberry Ham Slice, 380
Baked Stuffed Sweetpotatoes
French Fried Cauliflower
Wax Bean Salad with Vinaigrette
　Dressing
Chocolate Caramel Sandwiches
Coffee　　　　　　Milk

∨ ∨ ∨

Chicken Liver Canapés
Stewed Chicken, 416, 417
Drop Dumplings
Baked Acorn Squash
Mixed Vegetable Salad
　(Cauliflower, Green Beans, Car-
　rots)
Cranberry Pineapple Sherbet
Coffee　　　　　　Milk

∨ ∨ ∨

Hawaiian Baked Pork, 378
Baked Sweetpotatoes
Creamed Celery
Green Beans
Cranberry Nut Cobbler
Coffee　　　　　　Milk

∨ ∨ ∨

**Stuffed Hearts with Prune Dress-
　ing, 398, 406**
Mashed Rutabagas
Chicory with Hollandaise Sauce
Scalloped Apples

Luncheons

Pickled Tongue with Ginger
  Sauce, 844, 865
Potato Cakes
Coleslaw
Scalloped Apples

∨ ∨ ∨

Chicken Dressing Ring with
  Creamed Chicken, 448, 255
Jellied Cranberry Salad
Raisin-filled Cookies

∨ ∨ ∨

Cream of Vegetable Soup, 116
Croutons
Lettuce Salad with Roquefort
  Dressing
Hot Date Loaf

∨ ∨ ∨

Black Soybean Soup, 121
Rye Toast
Apricot Rice Mold

∨ ∨ ∨

Welsh Rarebit on Toast, 231, 802
Cabbage Salad
Baked Apple
Pfeffernüsse

∨ ∨ ∨

Planked Eggs, 250
Black Cherry Salad
Cereal-flake Macaroons

∨ ∨ ∨

Liver Patties, 232, 240
French Fried Potato Chains
Wilted Lettuce Bowl
Fig Nut Whip

∨ ∨ ∨

Oyster Pie, 806
Cranberry Orange Mold
Buttered Broccoli
Prune Soufflé

∨ ∨ ∨

Baked Lima Beans, 457
Tomato Relish
Corn Bread
Apple Butter

∨ ∨ ∨

Veal Scallopine, 394
Mashed Rutabagas
Broiled Grapefruit
Tea   Milk

∨ ∨ ∨

Noodle Ring with Meat Balls, 804
Buttered Broccoli
Broiled Mushrooms on Tomato
  Slices
Orange Ice

Lamb Casserole, 366, 371
Vegetable Salad
Canned Red Raspberries
Graham Crackers

∨ ∨ ∨

Corned Beef Loaf, 358
Kale with Sour Cream
Corn Bread
Ambrosia

∨ ∨ ∨

Cream of Celery Soup, 112
Croutons
Honey Chocolate Cake

∨ ∨ ∨

Hot Baked Cheese Sandwiches,
  187
Waldorf Salad
Hot Cocoa

∨ ∨ ∨

Creamed Egg and Asparagus Sandwiches, 298
Grapefruit and Almond Salad

∨ ∨ ∨

Corn Tomato Chowder, 109
Saltines
Apricot Upside-down Cake

∨ ∨ ∨

Chicken Mushroom Soup, 117
Toasted Bran Muffins
Hot Cabbage Salad Bowl
Tokay Grapes

∨ ∨ ∨

Meat Pasties, 372
Broccoli with Cheese Sauce
Peach Chutney
Molasses Fruit Pudding

Sautéed Oysters and Ham o
  Toasted English Muffins wit
  Hollandaise Sauce, 331, 38
  175, 861
Buttered Green Beans
Grapefruit Sections with Ginge
  and Coconut

∨ ∨ ∨

Stuffed Pimientos, 233
Oatmeal Muffins
Pineapple Coleslaw

∨ ∨ ∨

Squash in Casserole, 512
Chicory Crown Salad
Glazed Peaches

∨ ∨ ∨

American Chop Suey, 378
Steamed Rice
Almond Cookies

∨ ∨ ∨

Beef Bouillon
Croutons
Ham, Egg and Mushroom San
  wiches, 196
Fruit Whip

∨ ∨ ∨

Lobster Stew, 106
Pilot Crackers
Celery
Fruitcake
Tea   Milk

*Serving the whole luncheo
on a large platter is an a
tractive and labor-savin
idea*

WASHINGTON'S BIRTHDAY DINNER

Flag Canapés ·
(Cheese and Caviar)
Baked Ham with Fruit Sauce, 379, 850
Scalloped Potatoes
Buttered Corn
Ripe Cucumber Pickles
Red Cabbage Salad
Cherry Pie
Coffee   Milk

∨ ∨ ∨

French Onion Soup
Fried Scallops with Lemon Butter, 341, 344
Baked Potatoes
Stewed Tomatoes
Spinach and Lettuce Salad Bowl
Pineapple Sherbet
Coffee   Milk

∨ ∨ ∨

Hot Tomato Juice
Veal Birds, 391
Mashed Potatoes
Gravy
Cauliflower with Egg Sauce
Pickled Beets
Blueberry Betty
Coffee   Milk

Remember to serve liver once a week; there are many ways of preparing it

SUNDAY DINNER

Consommé à la Royal
Candle Roast of Pork, 374
Baked Potatoes
Cauliflower with Browned Crumbs
Cranberry Orange Relish
Orange Chiffon Pie

∨ ∨ ∨

Cream of Spinach Soup
Baked Pompano with Shrimp Sauce, 314, 852
French Puffed Potato Slices
Pea, Carrot and Cauliflower Salad Bowl
Plum Pudding with Lemon Sauce
Coffee   Milk

∨ ∨ ∨

Sauerbraten, 266
Potato Dumplings
Brussels Sprouts
Celery
Carrot Sticks
Linzer Torte
Coffee   Milk

∨ ∨ ∨

Black Bean Soup
Roast Beef, 352
Franconia Potatoes
Buttered Green Beans
Lettuce with Horse-radish Mayonnaise
Peppermint Ice Cream with Chocolate Sauce
Coffee   Milk

LINCOLN'S BIRTHDAY DINNER

Grapefruit, Pomegranate and Blueberry Appetizer Salad
Fried Chicken, 422
Buttered Steamed Rice
Harvard Beets
Pumpkin Pie
Coffee   Milk

∨ ∨ ∨

Egg Canapés
Crown of Frankfurters, 387
Hot Potato Salad
Braised Celery
Piccalilli
Plum Pie
Coffee   Milk

∨ ∨ ∨

Roast Duck with Sauerkraut, 434
Mashed Potatoes
Pickled Watermelon Rind
Waldorf Salad
Lemon Chiffon Pie
Coffee   Milk

∨ ∨ ∨

Sardine Canapés
Kidney Stew with Sherry, 403
Buttered Carrots
Steamed Fig Puddings
Coffee   Milk

∨ ∨ ∨

Roast Pork and Sage Stuffing, 374, 406
Spinach Ring
Apple Frappé
Celery
Frosted Gingerbread
Coffee   Milk

∨ ∨ ∨

Fried Oysters with Tartare Sauce, 331, 863
Buttered Carrots with Onion
Whole-wheat Muffins
Fresh Cauliflower Salad
Devil's Food Cake
Coffee   Milk

∨ ∨ ∨

Hot Vegetable Broth with Noodles
Braised Liver with Vegetables, 400
Boiled Potatoes
Grapefruit and Banana Salad
Chocolate Cookies
Coffee   Milk

ST. VALENTINE'S DAY DINNER

Consommé Madrilene with Heart-shaped Noodles
Celery
Carrot Sticks
Pork Tenderloin Piquante, 378
Brussels Sprouts
Heart-shaped Beet Salad
Cranberry Meringue Pie

∨ ∨ ∨

Chicken Soup
Meat Loaf with Tomato Sauce, 354, 490
Buttered Shoestring Carrots
Creamed Broccoli
Celery
Cherry Cottage Pudding
Coffee   Milk

∨ ∨ ∨

Grapefruit Juice
Sausage and Corn Casserole, 385
Lyonnaise Potatoes
Endive with French Dressing
Baked Apples with Ginger Whipped Cream

∨ ∨ ∨

Smoked Whitefish with Vinaigrette Sauce, 310, 864
Parsley Potatoes
Scalloped Tomatoes
Pear and Grape Salad
Coconut Balls

∨ ∨ ∨

Baked Corned Beef with Horse-radish Sauce, 358, 344
American Fried Potatoes
Creamed Spinach
Orange Luncheon Salad
Coconut Cake
Coffee   Milk

SUNDAY DINNER

Hot Cheese Appetizers
Baked Ham with Lemon Currant Sauce, 379, 853, 857
Sherried Sweetpotato Soufflé
Buttered Green Beans
Corn Relish
Glacéed Fruits and Nuts
Coffee   Milk

∨ ∨ ∨

Chicken Fricassee with Dumplings, 417, 406, 416
Buttered Cauliflower
Pickled Beets
Cranberry Molded Salad
Baked Custard

∨ ∨ ∨

Broiled Lamb Chops, 369, 902
Buttered Peas in Carrot Ring
Celery
Mint Jelly
Old-fashioned Steamed Pudding with Butterscotch Sauce

∨ ∨ ∨

Consommé Julienne
Pan-broiled Calf's Liver and Bacon, 401
Creamed Potatoes
French Fried Onions
Corn Bread
Grapefruit and Cherry Salad
Coffee   Milk

∨ ∨ ∨

Slavic Oven Stew, 384
Baked Potatoes
Buttered Broccoli
Pickled Crab Apples
Lettuce with Roquefort Dressing
Ambrosia

Valentine desserts follow th[e] heart motif in decoratio[n] and accompaniment

Tangerine Appetizer
Corned Beef with Mustard Sauc[e] 843, 289
Buttered Cabbage
Boiled Potatoes
Pickled Beet and Onion Salad
Rice Pudding with Chocolate Sauce
Coffee   Milk

A hearty New England boil[ed] dinner will support the i[n-] ner man during bluste[ry] February weather

Luncheons

egetable Chowder, 110
asted Cheese Sticks
osted Jelly Roll with Cherries

∨ ∨ ∨

dividual Ham and Egg
Soufflés, 306
atmeal Muffins
neapple and Banana Salad

∨ ∨ ∨

egetable and Smoked Herring
Salad Bowl, 534
t Graham Biscuits
ked Custard

∨ ∨ ∨,

sh Mulligan, 104
elba Toast
ple Gingerbread Upside-down
Cake

∨ ∨ ∨

rbecued Beef Patties, 362
ttered Spinach
een Onions
ange Charlotte Russe

osted jelly roll with cher-
es and hatchets will delight
e children on Washing-
n's Birthday

VALENTINE LUNCHEON

Hearts of Jellied Tomato Bouillon
Whole-wheat Croutons
**Salmon in Rice Hearts, 325
with Sour Beets, 458** '
Strawberry Mousse in Heart
Molds
Caramel Sugar Cookies

∨ ∨ ∨

Salmon and Pea Chowder, 108
Lettuce Sandwiches
Filled Cookies

∨ ∨ ∨

Baked Stuffed Onions, 256, 472
Spiced Beets
Peanut-butter Bread

∨ ∨ ∨

BRIDGE LUNCHEON

Broiled Lamb Chops, 369, 902
Buttered Peas in French Fried
Potato Baskets
Olives and Pickles
Bran Muffins
Orange Shortcake
Coffee   Tea

**Chicken Turnovers with Mush-
room Sauce, 427, 278**
Buttered Carrots
Sparkling Fruit Mold

∨ ∨ ∨

Liver and Ham Loaf, 402
Shoestring Potatoes
Orange Cranberry Upside-down
Cake

∨ ∨ ∨

**Corn and Cheese Soufflé with
Tomato Sauce, 800, 490**
Whole-wheat Toast Sticks
Banbury Tarts

∨ ∨ ∨

Oyster Stew, 330, 900
Croutons
Celery Stuffed with Snappy
Cheese
Nut Loaf Cake

∨ ∨ ∨

Veal and Pork en Brochette, 389
Fried Parsnips
Spiced Raspberries
Molasses Cookies

∨ ∨ ∨

Split Pea Soup, 122
Toasted Soup Rings
Orange Bavarian Cream

∨ ∨ ∨

Fish Hash, 322
Pickled Baby Beets
Corn Bread
Head Lettuce
with French Dressing
Chocolate Cookies

∨ ∨ ∨

SUNDAY NIGHT SNACKS

**Baked Potatoes Stuffed with
Cocktail Sausages, 387, 489**
Glazed Apple Slices
with Cranberries
Toasted Rye Wafers

∨ ∨ ∨

**Rice Waffles, 171, 244
with Pork Sausages, 387**
Maple Sirup
**French Fried Sandwiches with
Deviled Ham Filling, 194, 184**
Apple Nut Salad
Coffee

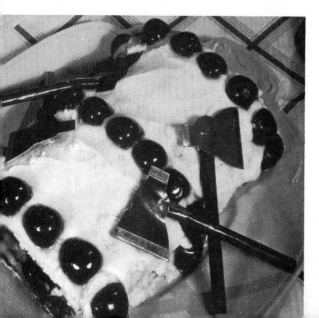

March Dinners

EASTER SUNDAY DINNER

Fruit Cup
Baked Ham, 379
Potatoes and Peas in Cream
Cucumber Pineapple Aspic Salad
Frozen Apricot Shortcake
Coffee   Milk

∨ ∨ ∨

Consommé Madrilene
**Roast Chicken with Mushroom
Stuffing, 412, 448**
Hominy Grits
Buttered Peas
Vanilla Ice Cream with Butter-
scotch Sauce

∨ ∨ ∨

Tomato Juice
Broiled Fish Fillets, 320
Scalloped Cabbage with Pimiento
Lima Bean Casserole
Devil's Food Cake

*Tie the stuffed flank steak
at the corners and you have
an amusing turtle*

Fruit Cocktail
Fillet of Sole Marguéry, 316
Mashed Potatoes
Buttered Green Beans
Celery
Chocolate Pie with Whipped
Cream

∨ ∨ ∨

Grapefruit Juice
Stuffed Lamb Shoulder, 367
Corn O'Brien
Julienne Carrots
Butterscotch Pudding

∨ ∨ ∨

Vegetable Juice
Pan-broiled Liver and Bacon, 401
Duchess Potato Puffs
Julienne Green Beans
Coleslaw with Sour Cream
Dressing
Maple Parfait
Coffee   Milk

∨ ∨ ∨

Fruit Cocktail
Hot Chicken Loaf, 428
Cauliflower Fritters
Creamed Peas
Lettuce with Caper French
Dressing
Fig Pudding
Coffee   Milk

Grapefruit and Orange Appetizer
Salad
Barbecued Lamb, 368
Baked Potatoes
Buttered Spinach with Egg
Fig Cake, Coffee, Milk

∨ ∨ ∨

Bouillon
Kidney Veal Chops, 392
Mashed Potatoes
Buttered Carrots
Fruit Compote
Vanilla Wafers

∨ ∨ ∨

Bouillon with Egg Balls
Beef Pot Roast with Prunes, 3.
Cabbage with Carrots
Lettuce and Tomatoes with
Roquefort Dressing
Banana Shortcake

∨ ∨ ∨

Tomato Juice
Stuffed Flank Steak, 353
Corn Fritters
Creamed Cabbage
Lettuce with Garlic Dressing
Butterscotch Pudding

*Your favorite lamb chops with
peas in potato cups*

→

Consommé Royal
Rolled Flank Steak, 363
Potato Charlotte
Baked Tomatoes
Escarole with French Dressing
Orange Cake Custard

∨ ∨ ∨

Pineapple Juice
Sausage Balls, 387
Mashed Potatoes
Buttered Green Beans
Pickled Watermelon Rind
Lemon Meringue Pie
Coffee   Milk

∨ ∨ ∨

Tomato Juice
Baked Chicken in Cream, 413
Baking Powder Biscuits
Harvard Beets
Sliced Oranges
Angel Food Cake
Coffee   Milk

∨ ∨ ∨

Pot Roast of Beef, 353
Brabant Potatoes
Browned Carrots and Onions
Cabbage Salad
Prune Whip Pie
Coffee   Milk

∨ ∨ ∨

Chicken Bouillon
**Crown Roast of Frankfurters
Stuffed with Bread Stuffing,
387, 406**
Braised Celery
Grated Carrot Salad
Date Pudding
Coffee   Milk

∨ ∨ ∨

Sardine Canapés
Stuffed Heart, 399
Baked Potatoes
Buttered Cauliflower
Lettuce with Russian Dressing
Orange Marmalade Layer Cake
Coffee   Milk

∨ ∨ ∨

Grapefruit and Chives Appetizer
Broiled Sirloin Steak, 352
French Fried Potatoes
Lyonnaise Carrots
Rhubarb Pie
Coffee   Milk

∨ ∨ ∨

Grapefruit Juice Cocktail
Roast Loin of Pork, 374
Mashed Sweetpotato Caramel
Cabbage and Celery Casserole
Sliced Oranges on Chicory
Coffee   Milk

Swiss Steak in Sour Cream, 360
Green Beans
Baked Potatoes
Lettuce Salad, French Dressing
Coconut Soufflé

∨ ∨ ∨

Liver Birds, 400
Stewed Tomatoes with Green
   Pepper
Scalloped Potatoes
Radishes and Celery
Plum Fluff

∨ ∨ ∨

Fresh Fruit Cocktail with Orange
   Ice
Roast Stuffed Chicken, 412
Mashed Potatoes
Corn O'Brien
Maple Nut Pudding

∨ ∨ ∨

Vegetable Soup
Broiled Finnan Haddie, 320
Buttered Asparagus on Toast
Grapefruit and Pimiento Salad
Burnt Sugar Dumplings
Coffee   Milk

*Rolled flank steak with
baked stuffed tomatoes —
a delicious budget dinner*

∨ ∨ ∨

Simple Appetizers
Spiced Tongue Mold, 405
Deviled Green Beans
Mashed Potatoes
Cabbage Pimiento Salad
Apricot Whip
Almond Cookies
Coffee   Milk

∨ ∨ ∨

Jellied Egg Canapés
Paprika Cream Schnitzel, 390
Julienne Green Beans
French Fried Onion Rings
Lettuce, Roquefort Dressing
Bran Muffins
Pineapple Tapioca Cream
Coffee   Milk

*Sliced oranges on chicory
make a salad easy to pre-
pare and most welcome
when Spring is just around
the corner*

Luncheons

Shrimp Omelet, 285
Wilted Lettuce Salad Bowl
Frozen Marshmallow Sponge
  with Bananas

∨ ∨ ∨

Cottage Cheese Omelet, 282
Bran Bread Sandwiches
Strawberry Jam
Coffee   Milk

∨ ∨ ∨

Egg Timbales with Tomato Sauce,
  306, 490
Chopped Buttered Spinach
Corn-meal Muffins
Caramel Banana Ice Cream

∨ ∨ ∨

Jellied Calf's Liver, 229
Parsnip Fritters
Dilled Dills
Sliced Oranges

∨ ∨ ∨

Jellied Bouillon with Frankfurters,
  229
Whole-wheat Snacks
Rhubarb Pie

*Hot cross buns for Lenten
menus are equally good
throughout the year*

ST. PATRICK'S LUNCHEON

Spinach Purée
Croutons
Chicken in Nest, 424
Buttered Green Beans
St. Patrick's Salad
Hot Cross Buns

∨ ∨ ∨

Carrot Soup
Salami Tidbits, 191
Buttered Asparagus Tips
Sponge Drop Cookies

∨ ∨ ∨

Bacon and Cheese Toast, 188
Celery Hearts
Plum Fluff
Cocoa

∨ ∨ ∨

Stuffed Cabbage, 552
Broiled Bacon
Rye Toast
Grape-nut Rennet-Custard

∨ ∨ ∨

Beef Miroton, 250
Carrot and Celery Salad
Orange Nut Bread

∨ ∨ ∨

French Onion Soup, 102
Rye Toast Sticks
Chocolate Cream Roll

**Poached Eggs in Rice Nests with
  Cheese and Olive Sauce, 296**
Lettuce with French Dressing
Hawaiian Wedges

∨ ∨ ∨

Vegetable Soup, 101
Tongue and Lettuce Sandwiches
Lemon Refrigerator Cake

∨ ∨ ∨

**Baked Potatoes Stuffed with
  Salmon, 326**
Creamed Peas
Caramel Custards

∨ ∨ ∨

Oyster Stew, 330, 900
Crackers
Celery
Apple Upside-down Gingerbread

∨ ∨ ∨

Goldenrod Eggs, 302
Vienna Sausages
Toast
Spiced Pineapple
Individual Angel Food Cakes

∨ ∨ ∨

Macaroni and Cheese, 874
Carrot and Celery Salad
Broiled Grapefruit

∨ ∨ ∨

Polish Pancakes, 286
Link Sausages
Applesauce
Almond Butter Coffee Cake

∨ ∨ ∨

Nut Vegetable Loaf, 231
Radish Roses
Caramel Custard

∨ ∨ ∨

Barbecued Lamb Hash, 369
Prune Bread
Crowned Cherry Tarts

∨ ∨ ∨

**Broccoli Ring with Creamed
  Mushrooms, 459, 470**
Peanut-butter Bread
Rhubarb Crisp

∨ ∨ ∨

SUNDAY NIGHT SUPPER

Cambrisson Salad, 551
Brioche
Coffee   Milk

April Dinners

Tomato Juice
Braised Short Ribs of Beef, 360
Baked Potatoes
Baked Stuffed Onions with
   Pimientos
Lettuce with Herb Dressing
Strawberry Meringues

∨ ∨ ∨

Cream of Spinach Soup
Baked Stuffed Fish, 316
Tomatoes Stuffed with Corn
Lettuce with French Dressing
Hot Frosted Gingerbread

∨ ∨ ∨

**Deviled Chicken Backs, Legs and
   Wings, 419**
Baked Potatoes
Buttered Green Lima Beans
Radishes
Olives
Butterscotch Pudding
Old-fashioned Sugar Cookies

∨ ∨ ∨

SUNDAY DINNER
Vegetable Soup
**Roast Leg of Lamb with Mint
   Sauce, 368, 855**
Baked Stuffed Potatoes
Buttered Cauliflower
Green Salad Bowl with Claret
   Dressing
Cranberry Mousse
Coffee   Milk

Chicken Liver Canapés
Casserole Roasting Chicken, 419
Hominy Grits
Buttered Peas
Strawberries and Cream

∨ ∨ ∨

Vegetable Juice
Breaded Veal Cutlets, 390, 902
Mashed Carrots
Glazed Onions
Lettuce with Herb Mayonnaise
Chocolate Bread Pudding
Coffee   Milk

∨ ∨ ∨

Chicken Bouillon
Roast Beef, 352
Yorkshire Pudding
Buttered Spinach
Buttered Rutabagas
Orange Shortcake
Coffee   Milk

∨ ∨ ∨

Grapefruit Juice
Savory Salmon Loaf, 326
Buttered Peas
Lettuce, Roquefort Dressing
Peaches in Meringue

∨ ∨ ∨

Antipasto
Minestrone
Ravioli
Chicken Cacciatori, 422
Zabaglione
Assorted Fresh Fruit

Chive Butter Canapés
Fish Croquettes, 806
Chopped Dandelion Greens with
   Lemon Butter Sauce
Toasted Rice Muffins
Floating Island Pudding

∨ ∨ ∨

Anchovy Appetizer Salad
Stuffed Pork Chops, 378, 901
Applesauce
Braised Celery
Pineapple Upside-down Cake
Coffee   Milk

∨ ∨ ∨

Vegetable Juice
Radishes
Celery
**Tuna and Mushroom Casserole
   327**
Sautéed Rice Cakes
Stewed Pineapple and Grapefruit
Pinwheel Cookies

∨ ∨ ∨

Tomato Juice
Salisbury Steak, 361
Buttered Asparagus
Mashed Potatoes
Strawberries and Cream
Coffee

*When roast lamb appears on
the dinner table, can Spring
be far behind?*

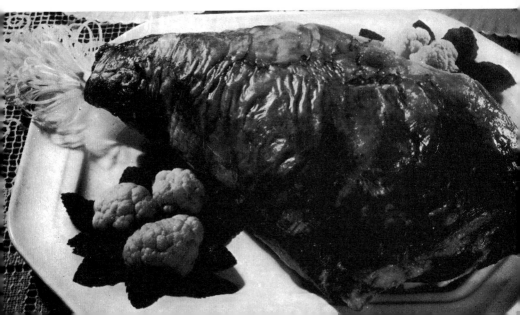

sorted Canapés
zed Ham Slice, 380
eamed Potatoes
a Croquettes
ing Onions
lery, Radishes
eapple Chiffon Pie
ffee   Milk
          ∨ ∨ ∨

mato Appetizer Salad
oiled Steak, 352
nch Fried Potatoes
een Beans in Onion Sauce
awberry Shortcake
ffee   Milk
          ∨ ∨ ∨

ster Cocktail
**aised Chicken with Sour Cream,
425**
eamed Rice
onnaise Carrots
ttuce with Herb Mayonnaise
gel Food Cake with Ice
Cream and Chocolate Sauce
          ∨ ∨ ∨

adrilene Soup
ndle Roast of Pork, 374
tato Dumplings
ckled Peaches
egetable Salad
uffed Oranges
offee   Milk
          ∨ ∨ ∨

ked Tongue and Noodles, 405
owned Carrots and Onions
uit Salad Bowl
uit Bread

*atch the smelt run at its
eight and serve these de-
cious little fish often*

Chicken Liver Appetizers
**Chicken à la King in Patty Shells,
424, 568**
Buttered Peas
Celery Curls
Gingerbread and Whipped Cream
          ∨ ∨ ∨

Apricot Juice
Ham Loaf, 380
Spinach Ring with Creamed Cau-
liflower
Grated Carrot and Peanut Salad
Cherry Pie
          ∨ ∨ ∨

Ham and Asparagus Rolls
Broiled Halibut Steak, 320
French Fried Potatoes
Pepper Relish
Hot Cabbage Salad
Chocolate Refrigerator Cookies
Coffee   Milk
          ∨ ∨ ∨

Vegetable Juice
Sautéed Liver with Onions, 908
Buttered Carrots
Lettuce with Anchovy Mayonnaise
Mocha Cake
Coffee   Milk .
          ∨ ∨ ∨

Shrimp Cocktail
Smothered Meat Balls, 360
Baked Potatoes
Cauliflower with Pimiento
Egg and Onion Salad Bowl
Apple Pie with Cheese
          ∨ ∨ ∨

Grapefruit Appetizer
Pan-fried Smelt, 321
French Puffed Potato Slices
Spinach and Tomatoes au Gratin
Coconut Snowball Sundae

Consommé Julienne
Swiss Steak in Sour Cream, 360
Hashed Brown Potatoes
Spinach Balls
Radish Roses
Strawberry Ice Cream Pie
Coffee   Milk
          ∨ ∨ ∨

Herring on Picks
Lamb en Brochette, 369
Supreme Stuffed Potatoes
Braised Celery
Baked Alaska
Coffee   Milk
          ∨ ∨ ∨

Jellied Veal Consommé
Barbecued Hamburger, 356
Parsley Buttered Potatoes
Dandelion Greens
Green Onions
Rhubarb Upside-down Cake
Coffee   Milk
          ∨ ∨ ∨

Pineapple Juice
Baked Chicken in Cream, 413
Baked Stuffed Potatoes
Fried Zucchini
Lettuce with Russian Dressing
Oatmeal Muffins
Toasty Prune Betty
Coffee   Milk
          ∨ ∨ ∨

Jellied Tomato Bouillon
Wiener Schnitzel, 390
Parsley New Potatoes
Buttered Fresh Asparagus
Spring Onions
Radishes
Rhubarb Pie
Coffee   Milk

Scrambled Eggs in Sautéed Bo-
logna Cups, 288
Wilted Lettuce Salad
Rhubarb Cream Sherbet

∨ ∨ ∨

Egg and Spring Onion Salad, 531
Cucumber Tomato Rye
Sandwiches
Peach Bavarian Cream

∨ ∨ ∨

Sliced Pickled Tongue, 404
Julienne Green Beans
Hot Lettuce Bowl with Sour
Cream Dressing
Banana Fritters with Lemon Sauce

∨ ∨ ∨

Scalloped Potatoes with Peas, 486
Celery   Radishes
Cracked Wheat Muffins
Stewed Rhubarb

∨ ∨ ∨

Veal Birds, 391
Cheese Stuffed Prunes
on Orange Slices
Strawberry Ice

∨ ∨ ∨

Liver Patties Wrapped in Bacon,
232, 240
Macedoine Luncheon Salad
with Horse-radish Dressing
Meringue Spongecake with
Banana Custard Filling

∨ ∨ ∨

Club Sandwiches, 207, 210
Berry Fluff
Tea   Milk

∨ ∨ ∨

Oysters Louisiana, 924
in Potato Nests, 489
Spiced Beets
Grapefruit and Orange Salad
Cheese Sticks

∨ ∨ ∨

Stuffed Hard-cooked Eggs, 307
Toasted Whole-wheat Rolls
Lettuce with Thousand Island
Dressing
Strawberry Milk Mallobet
Tea   Milk

∨ ∨ ∨

Ham Asparagus Rolls with Cheese
Sauce, 223, 278
Celery
Spring Onions
Coconut Cake

APRIL FOOL'S LUNCHEON

Hard-cooked Eggs in Jellied
Bouillon
Meat Loaf in Blanket, 355
with Mushroom Sauce, 278
Vegetable Salad
Fresh Strawberry Tarts

∨ ∨ ∨

Cottage Cheese and Olive Sand-
wiches, 179
Celery   Pickle Slices
Fruit Soufflé

∨ ∨ ∨

Sliced Cold Meats, 552
Hot Potato Salad
Stuffed Celery
Orange Nut Bread

∨ ∨ ∨

Crab-meat Salad Sandwiches, 182
Sweet Pickles   Celery
Frozen Pear and Cheese Salad

∨ ∨ ∨

Swiss Chard Ring, 260
with Creamed Eggs, 298
Celery Curls   Pickle Fans
Hot Bran Muffins
Fresh Pineapple Wedges

∨ ∨ ∨

Cream of Asparagus Soup, 111
Lettuce and Egg Salad
Strawberries
Hot Cross Buns

SMÖRGÅSBORD

Pickled Herring
Ripe Olives   Filled Celery
Herring Salad, 553
Jellied Veal Loaf, 389
Swedish Meat Balls, 362
Braised Liver
Red Cabbage Salad
Potato Salad, 538, 540
Apple Salad, 525
Molded Fruit Salad
Assorted Cheese
Swedish Hardtack, 147
Limpa, 137
Continental Soup   Calla Lilie
Coffee

∨ ∨ ∨

SUNDAY NIGHT SUPPERS

Jellied Salmon Ring with Cucum
ber Dressing, 545, 865
Potato Chips
Lemon Mallobet
Hot Coffee   Milk

∨ ∨ ∨

Fresh Asparagus Tips and Poache
Eggs on Toast with Crear
Sauce, 294, 852
Chocolate Refrigerator Cake
Coffee   Milk

*Hail the opening of th
berry season with lusciou
shortcake*

Tomato Juice
Spiced Ham Loaf, 380
Mustard Greens
Buttered Beets
Lettuce with Russian Dressing
Glazed Strawberry Tarts
∨ ∨ ∨

Planked Shad with Duchess Potatoes, 315, 494
Green Beans Cooked with Bacon
Jellied Apricot Salad
Cheese Cake
Coffee   Milk
∨ ∨ ∨

Lamb en Brochette with Grilled Tomato and Bacon, 369, 513
Buttered New Peas
Pineapple Celery Salad with Mint French Dressing
Chocolate Bread Pudding
Iced Coffee
∨ ∨ ∨

Vegetable Juice Cocktail
Shrimp Asparagus Casserole, 340
Garlic Bread
Lettuce Salad
Banana Butterscotch Pie
Coffee   Milk
∨ ∨ ∨

Pineapple Juice
Charcoal Broiled Steak, 352
Grilled Tomato Halves
Creamed New Potatoes
Mashed Turnips
Strawberry Ice Cream

Fish on the menu at least once a week should be garnished and served attractively

Pineapple and Strawberry Juice
Roast Beef, 352
Franconia Potatoes
Cooked Cabbage
Molded Tomato Salad
Jellied Apricot Pie
Coffee   Milk
∨ ∨ ∨

Fresh Fruit Cup
Chicken Fricassee, 417
Hominy
Buttered Peas
Hot Biscuits
Rhubarb Upside-down Cake
Coffee   Milk
∨ ∨ ∨

Breaded Fillets of Whitefish with Bacon, 320, 374
Parsley Potato Balls
Green Beans with Egg Sauce
Marinated Tomato Slices
Spring Onions
Chocolate Mallow Pie
Coffee   Milk
∨ ∨ ∨

Braised Veal, 393
Fried Potatoes
Asparagus Tips with Hollandaise Sauce
Lettuce Cucumber Salad Bowl
Strawberry Shortcake
Coffee   Milk
∨ ∨ ∨

Apricot Juice
Baked Ham and Pineapple, 379
Baked Potatoes
Chopped Spinach
Sliced Tomatoes, French Dressing
Rhubarb and Banana Pudding
Coffee   Milk

Tomato Consommé de Luxe
Baked Stuffed Fish, 316
Baked Potatoes
Chopped Spinach
Grated Carrots and Cucumbers in Sour Cream
Pineapple Marlow
∨ ∨ ∨

Apple Juice
Salisbury Steak with Onions, 361
Mashed Potatoes
Buttered Green Beans
Floating Island
∨ ∨ ∨

Cream of Tomato Soup
Pan-broiled Liver and Bacon, 401, 513
Mashed.Potatoes
Buttered Beets
Green Pepper and Cottage Cheese Salad
Rhubarb Cream Pie
∨ ∨ ∨

Pineapple Juice
Chicken and Dumplings, 416
Buttered Asparagus
Tomato and Cucumber Salad
Peaches
Daffodil Cake
Coffee   Milk
∨ ∨ ∨

Jellied Fruit Cocktail Salad
Veal Fricassee, Jardinière, 389
Curried Rice
Sliced Tomatoes
Burnt Almond Parfait
Coffee   Milk
∨ ∨ ∨

Sauerkraut Juice
Stuffed Pork Chops, 378
Mustard Greens
Baked Tomatoes
Strawberries and Cream

Fruit Cocktail
Stuffed Cubed Steaks, 360
Au Gratin Stuffed Potatoes
Creamed Onions
Radish Roses, Celery Curls
Chantilly Sponge
Coffee   Milk

∨ ∨ ∨

Mackerel Grill with Bacon and Tomatoes, 320
Russian Style Potatoes
Green Pepper Rings Filled with Cabbage Slaw
Strawberry Pineapple Delicious
Coffee   Milk

∨ ∨ ∨

Grapefruit Juice
Liver Ring with Spinach, 402, 510
Baked Potatoes
Radishes, Green Onions
Apple Gingerbread Upside-down Cake
Coffee   Milk

∨ ∨ ∨

Consommé Jardinière
Braised Pork Chops, 378
Baked Hominy Grits
Zucchini and Tomatoes au Gratin
Applesauce Relish
Royal Pineapple Cream
Coffee   Milk

Tomato Juice
Pork Shoulder with Prune Apple Stuffing, 376
Turnip Greens
Browned Carrots
Strawberry Shortcake

∨ ∨ ∨

Tomato Juice
Peppers Stuffed with Hamburger and Rice, 252
Glazed Onions
Celery
Rhubarb Brown Betty

∨ ∨ ∨

Apricot Juice
Chili Con Carne with Kidney Beans, 361
Lettuce with Russian Dressing
Strawberries and Cream

∨ ∨ ∨

Tomato Consommé de luxe
Pot Roast with Prunes, 357
Buttered Carrots and Peas
Green Onions
Cherry Cottage Pudding with Hot Cherry Sauce

∨ ∨ ∨

Liver Sausage Canapés
Roast Stuffed Chicken, 412
Baked Potatoes
Buttered Asparagus
Orange and Avocado Salad
Strawberry Parfait

SUNDAY DINNERS

Fresh Pineapple Strawberry Cocktail
Boiled Beef Tongue, 405
Creamed Potatoes
Chopped Spinach
Spring Salad Bowl
Caramel Bavarian Cream
Coffee   Milk

∨ ∨ ∨

Jellied Consommé Madrilene
Celery   Radishes
Spring Onions
Veal Steaks with Madeira Sauce 392, 867
French Puffed Potato Slices
Buttered New Peas
Strawberry Ice Cream Pie
Coffee   Milk

∨ ∨ ∨

Celery Cheese Salad
Barbecued Lamb, 368
Toasted Potato Balls
Parsley New Carrots Julienne
Fresh Pineapple and Strawberries
Coconut Ginger Cupcakes
Coffee   Milk

The humble pot roast comes up in the world when escorted by prunes and apricots

Luncheons

Chicken Livers in Noodle Ring, 431, 305
Buttered Turnip Greens
Banana Sherbet
∨ ∨ ∨

Broiled Shad Roe on Toast with Bacon, 320
Grilled Onion and Tomato Slices
Rhubarb Crisp
∨ ∨ ∨

Veal à la King in Rice Nests, 394, 325
Wilted Lettuce
Strawberry Sherbet
Butter Cookies
∨ ∨ ∨

Eggs with Corned Beef Hash, 247, 359
Creamed New Peas
Vanilla Bavarian Cream with Fresh Strawberries
∨ ∨ ∨

Vienna Sausages, 386, 387
Cabbage with Cheese
Black Cherry Salad
Chocolate Meringue Pie
∨ ∨ ∨

Cream of Lima Bean Soup, 115
Julienne Toast
Rhubarb Salad Ring, filled with Cottage Cheese

Fruit salad is an adventure when it is served in these stunning pineapple baskets

BRIDE'S LUNCHEON
Spring Flower Salads
Creamed Chicken and Sweetbreads in French Fried Potato Nests, 425, 489
Buttered New Peas
Baked Alaskas with Slivered Toasted Almonds
Iced Coffee
∨ ∨ ∨

Tomatoes Stuffed with Coleslaw, 541, 535
Braised Celery and Green Beans
Marshmallow Chocolate Roll
∨ ∨ ∨

Dandelion Lettuce Salad Bowl with Swiss Cheese, Tomatoes, Eggs and Spring Onions, 530
Buttered Rye Toast
Sliced Bananas with Strawberries
∨ ∨ ∨

SUNDAY NIGHT SUPPERS
Welsh Rarebit, 231, 802
Buttered Asparagus Tips
Sliced Tomatoes
Fruit Salad Bowl
∨ ∨ ∨

Egg and Asparagus Casserole, 300
Pickled Baby Beets
Cheese Biscuits
Fruit Compote

Spanish Omelet, 284
Bran Muffins
Frozen Summer Fruit Salad
∨ ∨ ∨

Creamed Egg and Asparagus Sandwiches, 189, 298
Coleslaw
Party Roll
∨ ∨ ∨

Cream of Tomato Soup
Toasted Cheese Sticks
Stuffed Zucchini with Bacon, 519
Strawberry Fluff Pie
∨ ∨ ∨

Kedgeree in Potato Twirls, 258, 488, 491
Vegetable Salad Bowl
Rhubarb Sauce
Applesauce Cake
∨ ∨ ∨

Cream of Pea Soup
Pimiento Soup Cream
Pineapple Basket Salad, 529
Baking Powder Biscuits
Chocolate Angel Food Cake
Banana Milk Shake
∨ ∨ ∨

Sliced Cold Meats, 552
Potato Salad in Green Pepper Cups
Bread Sticks
Chocolate Waffles with Ice Cream
∨ ∨ ∨

Barbecued Beef Sandwiches, 190
Fresh Cauliflower Salad
Ribbon Fudge
Hot Chocolate
∨ ∨ ∨

Cream of Celery Soup, 112
Parsley Cream Garnish
Frozen Pineapple Salad
Cinnamon Toast
One-Egg Cake, Caramel Pecan Icing
∨ ∨ ∨

Asparagus Crowns, 193
Fruit and Cottage Cheese Mold
Rice and Apricot Pudding
∨ ∨ ∨

Eggs Baked in Bacon-lined Tomato Cups, 293
Toasted English Muffins
Orange Marmalade
Strawberry Ice Cream

June Dinners

SUNDAY DINNER

Cherry Juice Cocktail
Braised Veal with Spiced Pumpkin, 393, 838
Creamed New Peas, in French Fried Potato Nests
Lettuce Salad with Avocado Dressing
Strawberry Parfait
Iced Coffee

∨ ∨ ∨

Broiled Steak, 352
Duchess Potatoes
Peas Cooked in Lettuce
Hot Rolls
Frozen Fruit Ginger Salad with Whipped Cream Dressing

∨ ∨ ∨

Cream of Pea Soup
Stuffed Lamb Roll, 367
Brabant Potatoes
Cauliflower with Browned Crumbs
Watermelon Balls
Iced Tea

∨ ∨ ∨

Tomato Caviar Salad
Broiled Squab Chicken with Broiled Pineapple, 415
Steamed Wild Rice
Fried Spinach Balls
Strawberry Chiffon Pie

Broiled Lamb Chops Wrapped in Bacon, 369
New Potatoes in Cream
Buttered Turnip Greens
New Carrot Sticks
Red Raspberry Shortcake

∨ ∨ ∨

Spiced Fresh Tongue, 405
Shoestring Potatoes
Fresh Spinach with Horse-radish Butter Sauce
Radishes and Spring Onions
Rhubarb Crisp

∨ ∨ ∨

Assorted Cold Meats, 552
French Potato Salad Bowl
Buttered New Peas
Ice Cream Roll with Red Raspberries

∨ ∨ ∨

Perch with Wine Sauce, 319
French Fried Lattice Potatoes
Crumbed Green Beans
Fresh Pineapple Shortcake

∨ ∨ ∨

Lamb Kidneys and Bacon en Brochette, 371
Scalloped Potatoes
Summer Squash
Sliced Tomatoes
Individual Baked Alaskas

Brazil-nut Jellied Veal Loaf, 38
Buttered Baby Beets
Julienne Vegetable Salad Bowl
Black Raspberry Pie
Iced Tea

∨ ∨ ∨

Melon Cup with Lime Juice
Baked Swordfish with Tartare Sauce, 314, 863
Creamed New Potatoes with Pimiento Buttered Swiss Chard
Cupcakes with Banana Custard Filling
Iced Coffee

∨ ∨ ∨

Plum Tomato and Egg Appetizer
Liver à la Bourgeoise, 401
Boiled Potatoes
Sparkling Fruit Mold
Coconut Soufflé

∨ ∨ ∨

Chilled Court Bouillon
Spring Chicken Marvland, 423
Hominy Grits and Gravy
Buttered Green Lima Beans
Sliced Cucumbers
Cherry Pie

Watch the cheering section when Maryland chicken is on the bill of fare

Vegetable salads are especially attractive if each vegetable is in a separate lettuce cup

Fresh Fruit Juice Cocktail
Crown Roast of Lamb with Mushroom Stuffing, 367, 406
Baked Potatoes
Cauliflower, Peas and Carrot
  Salad Bowl
Angel Food Cake
  with Lemon Butter Filling
Iced Coffee

∨ ∨ ∨

Sliced Cold Meats, 552
Braised Fennel
Avocado Salad with Frozen Tomato Mayonnaise
Cantaloupe

∨ ∨ ∨

SUNDAY DINNER
Green Bean, Pearl Onion Salad
Old-fashioned Fried Chicken with Cream Gravy, 423, 278
Whipped Mashed Potatoes
Cut Corn
Strawberry Shortcake
Iced Coffee

∨ ∨ ∨

Fruited Meat Roll, 364
Creamed New Potatoes
Buttered Mustard Greens
Dewberries and Cream
Coffee   Milk

∨ ∨ ∨

Ham and Rice Scallop, 379
Spinach with Peppers
Lettuce with Lemon Cream
  Mayonnaise
Baked Chocolate Custard

Endive Cheese Appetizer Salad
Spinach Ring with Mushrooms, 260, 470, 474, Bordered with Baked Tomatoes
Cherry Cottage Pudding
Coffee

∨ ∨ ∨

Jellied Consommé
Stewed Kidney, 403
Hashed Brown Potatoes
Pea Croquettes
Lettuce Salad, French Dressing
Rhubarb Brown Betty
Iced Coffee

∨ ∨ ∨

Beef Pot Roast with Peas, Onions and Carrots, 353
Potato Charlotte
Applesauce
Mint Meringues with Chocolate
  Ice Cream
Coffee   Milk

∨ ∨ ∨

Tomato Juice
Baked Stuffed Fish, 316
Cottage Fried Potatoes
Cauliflower with Cheese Sauce
Grated Carrots and Cabbage in
  Molded Salad
Raspberry Chiffon Pie
Coffee

∨ ∨ ∨

Grilled English Lamb Chops Wrapped in Bacon, 369
New Potato Balls in Minted
  Butter
Grilled Tomato Slices
Pineapple Basket Salads with
  Pineapple and Strawberries
Iced Tea

Vegetable Juice Cocktail
Broiled Scallops Hawaiian, 341
Shoestring Potatoes
Vegetable Soufflé
Jellied Cucumber Salad
Old-fashioned Strawberry Shortcake

∨ ∨ ∨

Jellied Consommé
Veal Paprika Schnitzel, 390
Parsley Potato Balls
New Peas with Onion Butter
Lettuce Salad with Frozen Tomato Mayonnaise
Fresh Pineapple with Kirsch

∨ ∨ ∨

Savory Meat Loaf, 361
Baked Stuffed Potatoes
Fried Zucchini
Spiced Beet and Onion Salad
Blackberries and Cream

∨ ∨ ∨

Avocado Cocktail Salad
Lamb en Brochette, 369
Carrot Ring with Creamed Peas
Hot Rolls
Raspberry Ice Cream

∨ ∨ ∨

Veal Stew with Dumplings, 393
Mashed Potatoes
Summer Squash
Rhubarb Cream Pie

∨ ∨ ∨

Old-fashioned Potato Soup
Egg Noodle Ring, 305, with Ham à la King
Vegetable Salad Bowl
Cheese Platter with Bar-le-Duc

∨ ∨ ∨

Boiled Beef Tongue, 405
Horse-radish Sauce
Tomatoes Stuffed with Spinach
Scalloped Potatoes
Pineapple Cream Pudding
Caramel Sugar Cookies

∨ ∨ ∨

Stewed Chicken and Drop Dumplings, 416
Mashed Potatoes
Green Beans
Pickled Crab Apples
Sliced Tomatoes
Chocolate Parfait

∨ ∨ ∨

Jellied Chicken Bouillon
Creole Liver, 401
Globe Artichokes with Drawn
  Butter
Radishes
Strawberry Shortcake

Luncheons

SHOWER LUNCHEON

Jellied Tomato Ring with Shrimp, Pea and Cucumber Salad, 545, 542
French Fried Potato Chips
Little Angel Food Cakes, Filled with Crushed Strawberries
∨ ∨ ∨

Summer Squash Stuffed with Ham à la King, 512
Broiled Tomatoes
Glazed Strawberry Tarts
∨ ∨ ∨

Sliced Cold Picnic Ham, 379
Summer Squash in Sour Cream
Pickled Beets
Orange Cake Custard
∨ ∨ ∨

Cream of Pea Soup, 115
Lettuce Sandwiches
Pineapple Basket with Fresh Fruit
∨ ∨ ∨

Chicken Livers with Bacon en Brochette, 431
Zucchini in Tomato Sauce
Coffee Rennet-Custard
∨ ∨ ∨

Creamed Mushrooms in Croustades, 470, 227
Bacon Curls
Asparagus Salad
Cherry Roly-Poly
∨ ∨ ∨

Pineapple Juice
Barbecued Lamb Hash, 369
Buttered Peas
Strawberry and Rhubarb Pie
∨ ∨ ∨

Spinach Soufflé, 510
Broiled Bacon
Plum Tomato and Cucumber Salad
Black Raspberries with Cream
∨ ∨ ∨

Double-decked Canapés
Goldenrod Asparagus, 805
Hot Cheese Biscuits
Rhubarb and Banana Pudding
Coffee   Milk
∨ ∨ ∨

Fruit and Cottage Cheese Mold, 547
Butterscotch Bread
Celery and Radishes
Coconut Cream Pie

Consommé à la Royale
Party Sandwich Loaf, 208
Pickle Fans   Celery Curls
Maple Nut Parfait
∨ ∨ ∨

Cantaloupe Cherry Salad Bowl, 525
Rice Muffins
Mocha Fluff, Coffee
∨ ∨ ∨

Cream of Vegetable Soup, 116
Bacon Cheese Rolls
Strawberry Sundae
∨ ∨ ∨

Sour Cream Potato Salad, 540
Bran Muffins
Cherry Pecan Upside-down Cake
∨ ∨ ∨

Tuna Supreme, 327
Green Salad Bowl
Burnt Almond Parfait
Chocolate Sauce
∨ ∨ ∨

French Fried Liver Sandwiches, 194
Chicory Salad Bowl
Fruit Whip
∨ ∨ ∨

Eggs Florentine, 292
Tomato and Cucumber Salad
Melba Toast
Banana Layer Cake

SUNDAY NIGHT SUPPER

Cheese Soufflé, 231
Tomatoes Stuffed with Dutch Slaw
Crisp Rye Wafers
Iced Tea
∨ ∨ ∨

Tomato Juice
Salmon Club Sandwiches, 195
Rhubarb Brown Betty
∨ ∨ ∨

Peppers Stuffed with Macaroni, 476
Pineapple and Banana Salad
Cheese Sticks
Caramel Tapioca Cream
Chocolate Walnut Cookies
∨ ∨ ∨

Ham and Egg Croquettes, 280
Creamed Beet Greens
Toasted Crackers
Cherry Pie
∨ ∨ ∨

Lima Bean Chowder, 109
Cheese Puffs
Strawberry Melon Salad Bowl
Iced Tea   Milk

It takes a little time to mold the cheese into a ring but the result is worth it

Pineapple Juice Cocktail
Baked Pickerel, 314
Shoestring Potatoes
Carrot Soufflé
Lettuce Salad with Thousand
 Island Dressing
Honeydew Melon Rings with Mel-
 on Balls   Iced Tea

∨ ∨ ∨

Stuffed Lamb Shoulder, 367
Franconia Potatoes
Summer Squash Tomato Casserole
Carrot Raisin Salad
Maple Nut Pudding

∨ ∨ ∨

Filled Beets
**Planked Ham Loaf with Duchess
 Potatoes, Baked Onions and
 Tomatoes, 380, 494, 472, 513**
Royal Salad
Brazil-nut Marshmallow Cream

∨ ∨ ∨

Apricot Juice
Rump Roast of Beef, 352
Mashed Potatoes
Gravy
Kohlrabi
Lettuce with French Dressing
Red Raspberry Sundae

*Plan a casserole dinner and
give yourself more time to
enjoy the summer weather*

Pineapple Appetizer Salad
**Baked Chicken with Sage Stuff-
 ing, 406, 413**
Mashed Sweetpotatoes
Buttered Broccoli
Peppermint Stick Parfait with
 Chocolate Sauce
Coffee   Milk

∨ ∨ ∨

Sweetbreads with Mushrooms, 397
Broiled Tomato Slices
Buttered Beet Greens
Cottage Cheese Salad with Thou-
 sand Island Dressing
Gooseberry Date Pie

Fried Perch with Lemon, 321
Parsley Potatoes
Buttered Beets Julienne
Green Salad Bowl with Hot Bacon
 Sauce
Huckleberry Upside-down Cake
Coffee

∨ ∨ ∨

Breaded Veal Cutlets, 390, 902
Swiss Chard Hollandaise Sauce
O'Brien Potatoes
Pickled Beet Salad
Cantaloupe Basket with Ice Cream

∨ ∨ ∨

Pan-broiled Liver with Bacon, 401
Green Peppers Stuffed with Rice
 au Gratin
Buttered Carrots
Red Cabbage Salad
Black Raspberries and Cream

Baked Stuffed Lobster, 338
Shoestring Potatoes
Pea Timbales
Tomato Cups on Lettuce with
 Cucumber Mayonnaise
Lemon Roll
Iced Tea

∨ ∨ ∨

Hot Swiss Cheese, Canapés
Vegetable Plate, 518
(Zucchini and Tomatoes au Grat-
 in, Harvard Beets, Corn and
 Pepper Fritters, Green Beans)
Graham Biscuits
Cottage Cheese and Chive Salad
Baked Caramel Custard
Coffee   Milk

∨ ∨ ∨

Steak and Kidney Pie, 404
Mustard Greens
Harvard Beets
Plum Compote

∨ ∨ ∨

**Meat Loaf Ring with Creamed
 Spinach, 364, 510**
Buttered New Lima Beans
Beet Horse-radish Relish
Black Raspberry Shortcake
Coffee

∨ ∨ ∨

Vegetable Juice Cocktail
Marinated Broiled Chicken, 414
Corn on the Cob
Asparagus Soufflé
Garden Salad
Frozen Roll
Iced Coffee

∨ ∨ ∨

Smoked Salmon Canapés
**Scalloped Potatoes with Pork
 Chops, 486, 378**
Deviled Green Beans
Garden Salad Bowl
Raspberry Bavarian Cake
Coffee   Milk

∨ ∨ ∨

Lamb Curry Pie, 366
Steamed Rice   Swiss Chard
Spiced Peaches
Iced Watermelon

∨ ∨ ∨

Broiled Steak, 352
Baked Tomatoes Stuffed with
 Mushrooms
Sautéed Potato Balls
Lettuce and Chives Salad Bowl
Fig Cake   Coffee

FOURTH OF JULY DINNER

Jellied Consommé
Broiled Half Chicken, Rolled in Crumbs and Parsley, 414
Corn on the Cob
Asparagus Tips in Tomato Cups
Mashed Potatoes
Small Hot Rolls
Summer Salad Bowl
(Cucumbers, Radishes, Spring
Onions with Watercress,
French Dressing)
Strawberry Tarts with Ice Cream
∨ ∨ ∨

Grapefruit Juice
Roast Beef, 352
Potato Soufflé
Baked Corn and Tomatoes
Molded Cucumber Salad
Chocolate Filled Angel Food
∨ ∨ ∨

Baked Ham with Pineapple, 379
Stewed Potatoes
Golden Mountain
Waldorf Salad
Cherry Cream
∨ ∨ ∨

Brazil-nut Cheese Canapés
Tuna Loaf, 327
Baked Potatoes
Creamed Peas
Carrot Raisin Salad
Plum Pie
∨ ∨ ∨

Broiled Sweetbreads with Bacon, 397
Shoestring Potatoes
Buttered Green Beans
Combination Salad Bowl
Chilled Cantaloupe
Iced Coffee
∨ ∨ ∨

Kidney Veal Chops, 392
Creamed New Potatoes with
Parsley
Buttered Cauliflower
Frozen Tomato Appetizers
Refrigerator Cheese Pies
∨ ∨ ∨

Iced Orange Bouillon
Liver Birds, 400
Vegetable Casserole
Bread Sticks
Pickled Crab Apples
Coconut Delight
∨ ∨ ∨

Baked Black Bass, 314
Buttered New Carrots
Beet Greens with Lemon Butter
Cucumber Salad Bowl
Raspberry Tarts
Iced Coffee

Tomato Juice
Tongue with Raisin Sauce, 405, 854
Spinach and Cheese Casserole
Buttered Rice
Pickled Beet and Onion Salad
Blackberries and Cream
∨ ∨ ∨

Baked Swordfish with Tartare Sauce, 314, 863
French Fried Lattice Potatoes
Buttered New Peas
Garden Salad Bowl
(Tomatoes, Cucumbers, Green
Onions)
Cherry Roly-Poly
Iced Coffee
∨ ∨ ∨

SUNDAY DINNER

Anchovy Appetizer Salad
Broiled Chicken with Tomatoes, 415
Corn on the Cob
Steamed Rice
Peach Banana Sundae
Iced Coffee
∨ ∨ ∨

Rumanian Meat and Vegetable Casserole, 392
Toasted Potato Balls
Mixed Greens Salad, Chive
French Dressing
Chocolate Upside-down Cake
∨ ∨ ∨

Cold Sliced Smoked Tongue, 405
Vegetable Soufflé
Fresh Spinach Salad Bowl with
Horse-radish French Dressing
Blueberry Pie

Jellied Consommé
Crown Roast of Lamb, 367
Browned Potato Balls
Minted New Peas
Fresh Spinach Salad
Pineapple Cherry Chiffon Pie
∨ ∨ ∨

Fruit Cup
Baked Veal with Fruit Stuffing 392, 406
Corn on the Cob
Buttered Green Beans
Garden Salad Bowl
Frozen Peach Mousse
Iced Coffee
∨ ∨ ∨

Salisbury Steak, 361
Lemon Rice Croquettes
Creamed Spinach
Mixed Vegetable Salad Bowl
Heavenly Hash
∨ ∨ ∨

Pan-broiled Liver with Onions 401, 874
Potatoes O'Brien
Carrot and Celery Soufflé
Wilted Lettuce Bowl
Butterscotch Parfait
∨ ∨ ∨

Sliced Cold Lamb, 368
Duchess Potato Ring with Mintec
Peas
Tomato Cucumber Salad Bowl
Gooseberry Pie
Iced Coffee

As summer advances, the price of lamb goes down and a crown roast comes within the range of modest budgets

Luncheons

almon Salad, 545, 549
anana Bran Nut Bread
lum Cobbler
Milk

∨ ∨ ∨

resh Vegetable Soup
Veal and Liver Sausage Sandwiches, 184
Milk

∨ ∨ ∨

aked Tomatoes Stuffed with Fresh Corn, 514
roiled Bacon
Cherry Tarts

∨ ∨ ∨

Cottage Cheese Salad Ring with Mixed Fresh Fruit, 547
Quick Nut Bread
Chocolate Soufflé

∨ ∨ ∨

illed Potato Croquettes, 491
ummer Squash in Sour Cream
weet Beets
erry Marlow

*ce cream is a "must" for
children's summer parties;
he circus parade adds en-
chantment*

Sautéed Fresh Corn, 466
Broiled Bacon
Broiled Tomato Slices
Cantaloupe and Watermelon Balls
Iced Tea   Milk

∨ ∨ ∨

SUNDAY NIGHT SUPPER

Honeydew Melon Ring with Sweetened Red Raspberries, 529
Cream Cheese Nut Bread Sandwiches
Iced Coffee with Whipped Cream

∨ ∨ ∨

Sliced Egg, Tomato and Lettuce Salad with Chicken Liver French Dressing, 532, 866
French Fried Potato Chips
Individual Blueberry Shortcakes
Milk

∨ ∨ ∨

Citrus Juice
Chicken Curry Sandwiches, 195
Mocha Fluff
Coffee

Tomatoes Stuffed with Tuna Salad, 541, 547
French Fried Shoestring Potatoes
Cherry Roly-Poly

∨ ∨ ∨

Cream of Pea Soup
Hawaiian Fruit Plate, 548
Bran Muffins

∨ ∨ ∨

Bologna Cups with Peas and Rice, 386
Rolls-in-Loaf
Cherry Pie with Cottage Cheese Lattice

∨ ∨ ∨

Calf's Liver Club Sandwiches, 210
Pickle Fans
Biscuit Tortoni

∨ ∨ ∨

Corn Oysters, 260
Stewed Fresh Tomatoes
Wilted Lettuce Bowl
Baked Custard

∨ ∨ ∨

Melon Salad Luncheon Plate, 549
Orange Marmalade Rolls
Butterscotch Rice Mold
Coffee   Milk

∨ ∨ ∨

Creamed Shrimp in Potato Nests, 489, 340
Cheese-leaf Rolls
Celery and Radishes
Sunshine Cake, Hot Chocolate Sauce, and Nuts

∨ ∨ ∨

Cream of Corn Soup, 247
Green Salad Bowl
Bran Muffins
Crab Apple Jelly
Honeydew Melon

∨ ∨ ∨

Meat Platter on Watercress, 552
Cucumber Rye Sandwiches
Blackberry Pie

∨ ∨ ∨

OUTDOOR LUNCHEON

Baked Trout for Campers, 314
Roast Corn on the Cob
Cucumber Wedges
Baked Johnnycake
Fresh Black Raspberries and Cream

Meat Loaf, 354
Browned Rice
Sautéed Pineapple Rings
Cucumber, Peas and Watercress
  Salad Bowl with Horse-radish
  French Dressing
Chilled Melon
Hot Tea

∨ ∨ ∨

Liver Birds, 400
Baked Potatoes and Carrots
Cucumber Salad
Spiced Pear Pie
Coffee   Milk

∨ ∨ ∨

**Planked Salmon with Glazed
Beets, Buttered Spinach,
Mashed Potatoes and Hard-
Cooked Eggs, 315, 494, 510**
Hot Rolls
Apple and Nut Salad
Peppermint Stick Ice Cream
  with Chocolate Sauce
Coffee   Milk

∨ ∨ ∨

Burning Bush Hors d'Oeuvres
Lettuce Roll Hors d'Oeuvres
**Braised Short Ribs of Beef with
Vegetables, 360**
Jellied Fruit Salad
Lemon Custard in Meringue Cups
Coffee   Milk

∨ ∨ ∨

Veal Fricassee Jardinière, 389
Steamed Rice
Wax Bean Salad
  with Vinaigrette Dressing
Melon Balls with Lime Ice
Iced Coffee

∨ ∨ ∨

Broiled Steak, 352
Hashed Brown Potatoes
Creamed Fresh Corn
Mixed Green Salad, Roquefort
  Cheese Dressing
Fresh Fruit Platter with Crackers
Coffee   Milk

∨ ∨ ∨

Shrimp Cocktail
**Vegetable Plate (Broccoli Ring
Filled with Creamed Eggs,
Baked Squash, Grilled Toma-
toes), 459, 298, 512, 513**
Cottage Cheese and Chive Salad
Seven-layer Cake
Coffee

Melon Balls with Lime Juice
Rolled Stuffed Veal Shoulder, 392
Baked Potatoes   Swiss Chard
Lettuce with French Dressing
Plum Pie
Coffee   Milk

∨ ∨ ∨

Glazed Lamb Roast, 368
Parsley Carrots
Hot Rolls
Hominy Grits
Mint Grapefruit Ice
Sponge Cupcakes
Coffee   Milk

∨ ∨ ∨

Cantaloupe Balls with Lime
Scalloped Potatoes with Ham, 486
Sweet-sour Spinach
Cinnamon Apple Salad
Date Pudding with
  Whipped Cream
Tea   Milk

∨ ∨ ∨

Cream of Cauliflower Soup
Cheese Straws
Barbecued Beef Patties, 362
Scalloped Potatoes
Green Beans   Coleslaw
Compote of Peaches and Nec-
  tarines
Coffee   Milk

**Baked Lobster and Shrimp Cas-
serole, 340**
French Fried Shoestring Potatoes
Okra in Lemon Butter
Cucumber Salad
Peach Pie
Coffee   Milk

∨ ∨ ∨

FISHERMAN'S PRIDE

Broiled Brook Trout, 320
Chopped Spinach
  with Lemon Butter
Mashed Potatoes
Sliced Tomatoes
Chocolate Refrigerator Cake
  with Marshmallow Cream
Coffee   Milk

∨ ∨ ∨

SUNDAY DINNER

Honeydew Melon
French Fried Chicken, 422
Potato Soufflé
Green Beans
Lettuce Salad
  with Chive French Dressing
Butterscotch Parfait
Coffee   Milk

*Ice cream is doubly welcome
in a crunchy ring of caramel cereal flakes*

Shredded vegetables look twice as cool in a mold of shimmering aspic

Planked Whitefish with Duchess Potatoes and Buttered Peas, 315, 494, 474
Lettuce and Tomato Salad Bowl
Peach Shortcake
Iced Tea

∨ ∨ ∨

Baked Liver Rolls, 399
Mashed Potatoes
Baked Whole Tomatoes
Lettuce Salad
  with French Dressing
Plum Pie
Coffee

∨ ∨ ∨

Fried Soft-shelled Crabs with Tartare Sauce, 333, 863
Grilled Tomato Slices
Buttered New Peas
Coleslaw
Chilled Baked Rice Custard

∨ ∨ ∨

Apricot Juice
Barbecued Chicken, 415
Riced Potatoes
Corn Fritters
Peach Bavarian Cream
Coffee or Tea

∨ ∨ ∨

Dill Pickle Hors d'Oeuvres
Ham Cheese Savory, 379
French Fried Potato Twirls
Baked Summer Squash and To-
  matoes
Grape and Pear Salad
Peppermint Mousse
Coffee

Roast Beef, 352
Brabant Potatoes
Zucchini in Tomato Sauce
Head Lettuce
  with Russian Dressing
Cheese and Fresh Fruit Platter
Iced Coffee

∨ ∨ ∨

Honeydew Melon with Lime Juice
Lobster Thermidor, 337
French Fried Potatoes
Buttered Swiss Chard
Tomato and Watercress Salad
Grape Sherbet

∨ ∨ ∨

Shrimp Cocktail
Planked Stuffed Eggplant, 468
Watercress and Egg Salad
Hot Biscuits
Chocolate Butterscotch Pie

∨ ∨ ∨

TEEN-AGE PARTY

Jellied Veal Loaf, 229, 389
Sun Glow Salad (Peach and
  Pineapple)
French Fried Saratoga Chips
Beets in Orange Sauce
Baked Alaska

∨ ∨ ∨

Jellied Bouillon
Spanish Omelet, 284
Creamed Spinach
Bologna Cups with Peas
Party Roll
Coffee   Milk

∨ ∨ ∨

Tomato Juice
Hungarian Goulash, 393
Carrot Croquettes
Hot Biscuits
Chicory Crown Salad
Honey Pie

Pomegranate Juice
Baked Ham, 379
Glazed Pineapple
Potatoes au Gratin
Hot Biscuits
Green Bean Salad Bowl
Iced Watermelon
Coffee   Milk

∨ ∨ ∨

Melon Cup
Roast Leg of Lamb with Grape Jelly and Mint, 368
Potato Puff Balls
Buttered Baby Lima Beans
Fresh Spinach Salad Bowl
Orange Refrigerator Pudding
Iced Coffee

∨ ∨ ∨

Baked Stuffed Fish, 316
Creamed New Potatoes
  with Parsley
Peas with Onion Butter
Mixed Salad Greens
Pear Upside-down Cake

∨ ∨ ∨

Stuffed Celery Appetizer Salad
Creole Liver, 401
Curried Rice
Buttered Green Beans
English Toffee Ice Cream
Coffee

∨ ∨ ∨

Grapefruit Juice
Chicken à la King, 424
Stuffed Vegetable Marrow
Jellied Vegetable Salad
Boston Cream Pie

∨ ∨ ∨

Oxtail Soup, 125
Whole Wheat Rolls
Peanut and Carrot Salad
Orange Cake Custard

Luncheons

BRIDGE LUNCHEON

Jellied Madrilene
Melba Toast
**Sliced Cold Chicken and Ham
With Watercress, 412, 379**
Fruit Salad
in Orange Ice Rings
Petits Fours
Mint Iced Tea

v v v

Cheese and Tomato Crown, 547
Sardine and Watercress Sand-
wiches
Peach Shortcake

v v v

Shrimp Fritters, 257, 321
Cucumbers
with Hollandaise Sauce
Frozen Pineapple Rice Pudding

v v v

Continental Soup
Chicken Club Sandwiches, 210
Rum Custard
Hot Tea or Coffee

v v v

Brazil-nut Jellied Veal Loaf, 389
Prune Bread
Baked Oranges
Iced Tea or Coffee

v v v

**Baked Salmon Ring with Creamed
Carrots and Pimiento, 325, 516**
Green Onions and Radishes
Honeydew Melon Basket
with Fresh Fruit

v v v

**Crab-flake Salad in Cucumber
Boats, 551, 535**
Buttered Peas
French Fried Potato Chips
Cream Cheese Cake

v v v

Corn and Celery Casserole, 516
Graham Biscuits
Pickled Watermelon Rind
Dream Pie

v v v

Cheese Eggs, 294
Pimiento, Lettuce and Mayonnaise Sandwiches with Whole-
wheat Bread
Grape and Pear Salad

Tomato Consommé de luxe
Fish Salad Bowl, 554
Watercress Sandwiches
Chilled Watermelon

v v v

Avocado Fruit Salad Bowl, 527, 532
Toasted Cheese Sandwiches
Grape Sherbet
Haystacks

v v v

**Frosted Fruit Platter of Plums,
Peaches, Pears, Grapes, Nec-
tarines, 526, 527**
Cottage Cheese   Crackers
Butterscotch Pie

v v v

**Baked Eggs and Canadian Bacon
on Toasted English Muffins
with Hollandaise Sauce, 290,
861, 175**
Orange Meringue Ring with
Butter Pecan Ice Cream

v v v

**Corned Beef Loaf with Tomato
Sauce, 358, 490**
Carrots and Peas
Banana Lime Dessert

ALFRESCO LUNCHEONS

Scalloped Corn and Sausages, 466
Pepper Relish Sandwiches
Hawaiian Wedges
Gingersnaps

v v v

Potato Aspic Salad, 539
Stuffed Eggs
Sweet Pickles
Raspberry Purée

v v v

Pineapple Juice
Liver Sausage Sandwiches, 210
Stuffed Tomato Salads
Cantaloupe with Ice Cream

v v v

SUNDAY NIGHT SUPPER

Swiss Salad Bowl, 554
Cucumber Rye Sandwiches
Ginger Ale

*Cantaloupe with ice cream
deserves its popularity but
peaches and blackberries
add to its luster*

September Dinners

LABOR DAY PICNIC

Tomato Juice
Savory Meat Loaf, 361
Green Onions, Carrot Sticks, Cu-
cumber Wedges
Cheese and Dill Sandwiches
Garden Salad Sandwiches
Oatmeal Cookies
Lemonade

∨ ∨ ∨

Chicken Broth
Paprika Cream Schnitzel, 390
Brabant Potatoes
Buttered Green Beans
Pineapple Mallobet
with Whipped Cream

∨ ∨ ∨

**Baked Cod with Oyster Sauce,
314, 852**
Parsley Potato Balls
Mustard Greens
Beet Horse-radish Relish
Apple Frappé
Coffee   Milk

∨ ∨ ∨

Garden Soup
Liver Dumplings, 402
Sauerkraut
Banana and Cherry Salad
Linzer Torte

*Even those who care little
for liver often enjoy liver
dumplings with sauerkraut*

Melon Balls
**Codfish Puffs with Tomato Sauce,
321, 490**
Mustard Greens
Spiced Currants
Cabbage and Carrot Salad
Quick Maple Pudding
Coffee   Milk

∨ ∨ ∨

Apricot Juice
Stuffed Lamb Shoulder, 367
Potato Puff Balls
Peas and Onions
Lettuce Salad
   with Mint French Dressing
Banana Cream Pie

∨ ∨ ∨

Grapefruit Juice
Stuffed Heart, 398
Stuffed Potatoes au Gratin
Carrot-Green Bean Casserole
Orange Bavarian Cream

∨ ∨ ∨

Tomato Chicken Bouillon
**Roast Chicken, Sage Stuffing,
412, 406**
Mashed Potatoes   Corn Oysters
Cauliflower, Beet and Green
   Bean Salad Bowl
Pumpkin Pie
Coffee   Milk

Veal and Pork en Brochette, 389
Baked Sweetpotatoes
Creamed Fresh Peas
Cinnamon Apple Salad
Grape Pie

∨ ∨ ∨

Pomegranate Juice
Rump Roast of Beef, 352
Franconia Potatoes
Green Beans with Egg Sauce
Mixed Vegetable in Tomato Aspic
Apple Charlotte

∨ ∨ ∨

Grapefruit Cocktail
Veal Scallopine, 394
Whipped Mashed Potatoes
Peas in Turnip Cups
Old-fashioned Tarts
Coffee   Milk

∨ ∨ ∨

**Lamb and Lima Bean Casserole,
371**
Stewed Tomatoes with Peppers
Cabbage Slaw
Date Walnut Torte
Coffee   Milk

∨ ∨ ∨

Cream of Spinach Soup
Breaded Oxtails, 356
Lyonnaise Potatoes
Green Bean Radish Salad Bowl
Baked Peaches Hawaiian
Coffee   Milk

Grape Juice
Broiled Lamb Chops, 369
Creamed Potatoes
Fried Summer Squash
Pickled Watermelon Rind
Jellied Mint and Celery Salad
Banana Tapioca Cream

∨ ∨ ∨

Tomato Juice
**Baked Eggplant Stuffed with Ham
and Rice, 252**
Corn Fritters
Pepper Relish
Lettuce with French Dressing
Glazed Apple Ring
  with Butterscotch Sauce

∨ ∨ ∨

Shrimp and Green Bean Curry, 258
Steamed Rice, Buttered Carrots
Apple Chutney
Celery
Baked Ginger Pears with Coconut

∨ ∨ ∨

**Braised Pork Steaks with Grape
Apples, 374**
Stuffed Baked Potatoes
Baked Summer Squash
  with Tomatoes
Chilled Honeydew Melon

∨ ∨ ∨

Oyster Cocktail
**Eggs à la King in Patty Shells,
298, 565**
Buttered Peas
Pear Salad with French Dressing
Hot Biscuits
Apple Pie

∨ ∨ ∨

Melon Ball Cocktail
**Chicken Fricassee with Dump-
lings, 417, 406**
Mashed Potatoes
Swiss Chard Greens
Spiced Beets
Chocolate Mint Mousse

∨ ∨ ∨

Tomato Onion Salad
Stuffed Flank Steak, 353
American Fried Potatoes
Green Beans with Sour Cream
Devil's Food Pudding
  with a Dessert Sauce
Coffee   Milk

∨ ∨ ∨

Tomato Consommé de Luxe
Braised Liver Casserole, 400
Carrots
Baked Stuffed Onions
Baked Potatoes
Sparkling Fruit Mold
Apricot Upside-down Gingerbread

Claret Consommé
**Planked Steak with Duchess Po-
tatoes, 352, 494**
Baked Tomatoes with Mushrooms
Wax Bean Salad
  with Vinaigrette Dressing
Black Walnut Pie
Coffee   Milk

∨ ∨ ∨

Sweet Cider
Mock Chicken Legs, 389
Orange Candied Sweetpotatoes
Breaded Eggplant
Lettuce and Tomato Salad
Burnt Almond Parfait

∨ ∨ ∨

Cream of Green Pea Soup
Spicy Lamb Shanks, 369
Stuffed Potatoes
Chapeau Vegetable Plate
Tomato Cheese Crown
Grapefruit Cake

∨ ∨ ∨

Chicken Bouillon
Country Chicken Loaf, 428
Frozen Pear and Cheese Salad
Orange Purée
Butterscotch Bars

∨ ∨ ∨

Apricot Juice
**Rolled Veal Roast with Frank-
furters, 350, 392, 230**
Peach and Prune Garnish
Turnips with Pepper Sauce
Grated Carrot Salad
Cola Marsh Sherbet

Glazed Lamb Roast, 368
Parsley Buttered Potatoes
Creamed Swiss Chard Greens
Biscuits
Currant Jelly
Lettuce Salad
  with Roquefort Dressing
Maple Nut Pudding

∨ ∨ ∨

Tomato Juice
Sea Food Grill, 320
Baked Stuffed Potatoes
Buttered Spinach
Pickled Beet and Onion Salad
Coconut Cream Pie

∨ ∨ ∨

Smothered Meat Balls, 360
Mashed Potato Casserole
Crumbed Green Beans
Marinated Tomato Slices on
  Chicory
Fresh Plum Pie

∨ ∨ ∨

SUNDAY DINNER

Vegetable Soup
**Roast Tenderloin of Beef with
Mushroom Sauce, 352, 233**
Stuffed Baked Potatoes
Breaded Eggplant
Waldorf Salad
Pumpkin Chiffon Pie

*Here is a time saver: roll
sausages into the veal roast
instead of making a stuffing*

Luncheons

Grilled Hamburger on Grilled Tomato Halves, 356
Escarole Onion Salad Bowl
Plum Jam Pastry Roll
Coffee   Milk

∨ ∨ ∨

Grilled Cheese Sandwiches with Bacon, 188
Braised Celery
Jellied Fruit

∨ ∨ ∨

Baked Noodle Ring with Creole Liver, 305, 802, 401
Pickled Baby Beets
Apple Betty

∨ ∨ ∨

French Toast Sandwiches with Deviled Ham Filling, 194, 184
Cabbage and Pepper Relish in Tomato Cups
Maple Fluff

∨ ∨ ∨

Eggs Florentine, 292
Fried Tomatoes
Corn-meal Muffins
Fig Maple Puddings

The canny hostess plans a bridge luncheon dessert that can be prepared early like this frosted melon

Scalloped Tuna and Potatoes, 327
Deviled Green Beans
Lemon Mallobet

∨ ∨ ∨

Liver Soup, 100
Toasted Cheese Crackers
Fresh Spinach Salad Bowl
Pear Cake
    with Hard Sauce

∨ ∨ ∨

Scotch Broth with Spinach Dumplings, 99, 511
Crisp Toast Strips
Cauliflower and Carrot Salad
Pineapple Puffs

∨ ∨ ∨

Planked Eggs, 250
Sweet Pickles
Cherry Pie
Coffee

∨ ∨ ∨

Cheese Soufflé Sandwiches, 187
Spinach with Peppers
Honey Gingerbread
Coffee or Tea

∨ ∨ ∨

Hashed Lamb in Cabbage Leaves, 366
Lyonnaise Carrots
Whole-wheat Bread
Grape-nut Rennet-custard
Coffee or Tea

BRIDGE LUNCHEON

Assorted Canapés
Broccoli Ring with Creamed Sweetbreads and Mushrooms, 459, 397
French Fried Potato Chains
Orange Bran Muffins
Frosted Melon Mold

∨ ∨ ∨

Ham Banana Roll, 227
Stuffed Tomatoes in Frozen Dressing
Pineapple Nut Bread
Coffee Cream Pie

∨ ∨ ∨

Mushroom Omelet, 282
Tomato Avocado Salad
Melba Toast
Apricot Rice Mold

∨ ∨ ∨

Oyster Kebobs, 332
Baked Chinese Cabbage
Baking Powder Biscuits
Apricot Angel Cream
Coffee or Tea

∨ ∨ ∨

Tamale Pie, 256
Pickled Watermelon Rind
Fruit Salad
Floating Island Pudding

∨ ∨ ∨

Chicken Croquettes, 423
Creamed Peas
Crisp Bread Sticks
Orange Cranberry Upside-down Cake

∨ ∨ ∨

Deviled Eggs Creole, 308, 853
Fried Zucchini
Broiled Bacon
Scalloped Apples

∨ ∨ ∨

Ham and Corn Fritters, 381
Chopped Mustard Greens
Baked Apples with Whipped Cream and Butternuts

∨ ∨ ∨

SUNDAY NIGHT SUPPER

Peppers Stuffed with Shrimp, 252, 343
Baked Tomato Slices
Garlic Bread (Toasted)
Autumn Fruits

October Dinners

HALLOWEEN DINNER

Canapés of Egg and of Chicken
   Livers
Roast Stuffed Chicken, 412
Giblet Gravy
Mashed Potatoes
Buttered Broccoli
Spook Salad of Apples, Nuts and
   Marshmallows
Prune Pie with Pastry Witches

∨ ∨ ∨

SUNDAY DINNER

Pineapple Juice Cocktail
**Crown Roast of Pork with Cran-
berry Relish, 376, 837**
Browned Sweetpotatoes
Scalloped Celery Cabbage
Brazil-nut Tarts

∨ ∨ ∨

Roast Rabbit, 395
Baked Carrots
Creamed Celery
Green Salad Bowl with Grapefruit
Spice Pudding

∨ ∨ ∨

Vegetable Juice
Veal Loaf, 394
Creamed Potatoes
Corn and Pepper Fritters
Red Cabbage Salad
Baked Coffee Custard

Vegetable Bouillon
**Baked Ham with Cranberry
Glaze, 379, 858**
Lima Bean Casserole
Fried Spinach Balls
Chess Pies
Coffee   Milk

∨ ∨ ∨

Claret Consommé
**Chicken au Gratin with Oysters,
419**
Fall Asparagus Tips on Toast
Braised Celery
Tomato Cauliflower Salad
Plum Pudding
Coffee   Milk

∨ ∨ ∨

Black Bean Soup
Sauerbraten, 266, 357
Boiled Potatoes and Onions
Breaded Eggplant
Green Salad
Jelly Soufflé

∨ ∨ ∨

Sauerkraut Juice
Barbecued Spareribs, 384
Mashed Turnips
Green Beans
Baked Apples
Cookies   ∨ ∨ ∨

**Braised Lamb Neck Slices with
Vegetables, 366**
Baked Potatoes
Grapefruit Avocado Salad
Fresh Coconut Cake
Coffee

Prune Juice
**Breaded Veal Cutlets with Toma-
to Sauce, 390, 490**
Cottage Fried Potatoes
Buttered Celery Cabbage
Pickled Crab Apples
Chocolate Parfait

∨ ∨ ∨

Pineapple Cup
Lamb Curry Pie, 366
Potato Chips
Cauliflower, Carrot and Pea Salad
   Bowl
Mocha Baked Alaska
Iced Coffee

∨ ∨ ∨

Fruit Cocktail
**Smoked Tongue with Raisin
Sauce, 405, 854**
Potato Dumplings
Spinach
Lettuce with Herb Mayonnaise
Bavarian Cream in Orange Cups

∨ ∨ ∨

Grapefruit Appetizer Salad
**Fried Pork Chops with Onion
Rings, 378, 472**
Cottage Fried Potatoes
Mashed Parsnips
Peaches in Meringue

*Economy is practically pain-
less when it takes the form
of lamb neck slices with
vegetables*

Black-eyed Susans of pine-apple and ripe olives make a sparkling garnish for fish fillets

SUNDAY DINNER

Cranberry Juice
Broiled Venison Steak, 396
French Fried Cauliflower
Winter Vegetable Salad Bowl
Cheese, Toasted Crackers
ᵛ ᵛ ᵛ
Assorted Canapés
Roast Duck with Raisin and Apple Stuffing, 434, 406
Sweetpotato Casserole
 with Oranges
Buttered Peas
Green Salad Bowl
 with Claret Dressing
Cranberry Refrigerator Cake
Coffee   Milk
ᵛ ᵛ ᵛ
Stuffed Lamb Shoulder, 367
Baked Sweetpotatoes
Cauliflower with Cheese Sauce
Green Beans
Hot Biscuits
Mint Jelly
Banana Tapioca Cream
ᵛ ᵛ ᵛ

FOOTBALL SUPPER

Fried Rabbit with Cream Gravy, 395
Mashed Potatoes
Succotash
Wilted Lettuce
Cranberry Sherbet   Coffee

Consommé with Egg Balls
Roast Stuffed Chicken, 412
Grilled Peaches
Mashed Potatoes
Succotash
Bowl of Greens Salad
Pineapple Marlow

ᵛ ᵛ ᵛ

Tomato and Egg Canapés
Braised Short Ribs of Beef with Carrots, 360
Minted Potato Balls
Sliced Cucumbers
 with Horse-radish Dressing
Cherry Pie

ᵛ ᵛ ᵛ

Shrimp Canapés
Chicken and Mushroom Casserole, 413
Spinach, Celery, Olives
Gingerbread and Whipped Cream

ᵛ ᵛ ᵛ

Vegetable Juice Cocktail
Shrimp Soufflé, 231
French Fried Potatoes
Buttered Asparagus
Cucumber Salad
 with Sour Cream Dressing
Pineapple Tarts
Coffee

ᵛ ᵛ ᵛ

Roast Veal, 392, 348, 350
Cooked Rutabaga
Bowl of Mixed Greens
Ice Cream Roll
Hot Chocolate

Tomato and Egg Canapés
Stuffed Fish Fillets, 316
Buttered Beets and Celery
Chicory with Hollandaise Sauce
Melon Ball Salad
 with Lime French Dressing
Pecan Pie

ᵛ ᵛ ᵛ

Rhubarb and Pineapple Juice
 Cocktail
Lamb Loaf, 355
Duchess Potatoes
Minted Peas
Carrot Sticks
Celery Curls
Banana Sherbet
Coffee   Milk

ᵛ ᵛ ᵛ

Tomato Consommé de luxe
Beef à la Mode, 353
Cabbage and Potatoes
Fruit Salad in Orange Ice Rings
Damson Plum Pudding

ᵛ ᵛ ᵛ

Fish Purée
Nut Vegetable Loaf, 231
Orange and Grapefruit Salad
Apples Stuffed with Mincemeat

ᵛ ᵛ ᵛ

Grapefruit Juice
Salisbury Steak, 361
Chantilly Potatoes
Carrot Ring and Peas
Coronation Salad
Butterscotch Pudding

ᵛ ᵛ ᵛ

Bisque of Clam and Tomato
Broiled Lamb Chops, 369
Supreme Sweetpotatoes with
 Bananas
Peas with Onion Butter
Chicory Salad
Lemon Meringue Pie

ᵛ ᵛ ᵛ

Sauerkraut Juice
Liver Birds, 400
Potato Puff Balls
Baked Acorn Squash
Sweet Pickles
Orange Bavarian Cream
Coffee   Milk

ᵛ ᵛ ᵛ

Carrot Soup
Salmon Soufflé, 326
Delmonico Potatoes
Baked Parsnips
Coronation Salad
Glazed Caramel Custard
Curled Wafers
Coffee   Milk

Luncheons

Shepherd's Pie with Vegetables, 253, 373, 902
Pineapple Cabbage Slaw
Butterscotch Bars

∨ ∨ ∨

Cream of Cauliflower Soup, 112
Dry Whole-wheat Toast
Carrot Sticks, Celery
Cranberry Upside-down Cake

∨ ∨ ∨

Lima Beans Baked with Bacon and Tomatoes, 260, 371, 456, 457
Corn Bread
Hot Chicory Salad Bowl
Baked Custard

∨ ∨ ∨

MEXICAN SUPPER
Mexican Chile con Carne, 361, 909
Toasted Cheese Crackers
Chicory and Lettuce Salad Bowl
Snowy Baked Custard

∨ ∨ ∨

Broiled Canadian Bacon on Broiled Pineapple Slices, 374
Baked Acorn Squash
Apple Betty

Red Flannel Hash, 358
Piccalilli
Graham Muffins
Prune Whip

∨ ∨ ∨

Chinese Poached Eggs, 297
Cauliflower Fritters
Fruit Salad
Coffee Cream Pie
Tea, Milk, Coffee

∨ ∨ ∨

Chicken Vegetable Jiffy Soup
Spanish Potatoes, 490
Autumn Fruit Salad Bowl
Orange Marmalade Gingerbread
Coffee, Tea, Milk

∨ ∨ ∨

Anchovy Scrambled Eggs, 287
Hot Toast
Broccoli Parmesan
Stuffed Oranges

∨ ∨ ∨

Jiffy Lobster Supreme, 125
Bread Sticks
Waldorf Salad
Surprise Pie

Cabbage Rolls Stuffed with Corned Beef, 366
Crumbed Asparagus
Hot Spiced Applesauce

∨ ∨ ∨

Liver Cornish Pasties, 402
Wax Beans Creole
Boiled Pumpkin Custard

∨ ∨ ∨

Fried Apple Rings on Sausage Cakes, 646, 387
Mashed Turnips
Cranberry Roly-Poly

∨ ∨ ∨

AFTER-THE-GAME SUPPER
Creamed Chicken and Oysters on Waffles, 255, 170
Buttered Peas
Honeydew Melon
Tea

Witches, hobgoblins or ghostly cats decorate the tops of Halloween pies

November Dinners

aked Bluefish with Almonds, 316
arsley Potatoes
uttered Broccoli
rapefruit and Orange Salad
Coconut Cream Pie

∨ ∨ ∨

eef Stew with Vegetables, 356
uttered Beets
hredded Lettuce with Horse-
radish French Dressing
ruit and Cottage Cheese Mold

∨ ∨ ∨

eviled Chicken Backs, Legs and
Wings, 419
otato Soufflé
uttered Brussels Sprouts
Mixed Vegetable Salad
umpkin Pie

∨ ∨ ∨

eal Birds Wrapped in Bacon with
Cream Gravy, 391, 374, 278
Mashed Potatoes
piced Beets
oasty Prune Betty
Coffee   Milk

∨ ∨ ∨

calloped Ham and Sweetpotatoes, 501
uttered Green Beans
abbage Salad Bowl
with Mustard Dressing
aked Apples with Brazil-Nuts

*Slivered almonds over the
op of the baked fish dress
t up and add flavor as well*

Shrimp Cocktail
Barbecued Spareribs, 384
Baked Sweetpotatoes
Buttered Spinach
Grapefruit Segments on Escarole
with French Dressing
Baked Custard

∨ ∨ ∨

Stuffed Cubed Steak, 360
Cabbage and Celery Casserole
Bermuda Onion Salad Bowl
Relishes
Brazil-Nut Marshmallow Cream
Coffee   Milk

∨ ∨ ∨

Grapefruit Appetizer Salad
**Baked Ham and Raisin Sauce,
379, 854**
Whipped Mashed Sweetpotatoes
Buttered Broccoli
Spiced Cider Sherbet
Coffee   Milk

∨ ∨ ∨

Tomato Juice
Fried Fish, 321
French Fried Potatoes
Buttered Brussels Sprouts
Mixed Greens Salad
Mint Chocolate Chip Cake

∨ ∨ ∨

**Corned Beef Baked with Brown
Sugar and Cloves, 358**
Baked Sweetpotatoes
Creamed Cabbage
Spiced Peach Betty
Coffee   Milk

**Fresh Vegetable Platter, 518
(Baked Cauliflower, Glazed Car-
rots, Braised Celery, Buttered
Peas, Duchess Potatoes)**
Bran Muffins
Avocado, Grapefruit and Cheese
Salad
Apple Dumplings
Coffee   Milk

∨ ∨ ∨

Oyster Cocktail
**Salmon Vegetable Casserole,
900**
Buttered Cauliflower
Green Salad Bowl
with Sliced Eggs
Steamed Date Pudding
with Hot Wine Sauce
Coffee   Milk

∨ ∨ ∨

SUNDAY DINNER

Vegetable Bouillon, Croutons
**Pan Roast of Duck with Pecan
Stuffing, 438**
Fried Brussels Sprouts
Apple, Celery and Grape Salad
Cheese Cake
Coffee   Milk

STAG SUPPER

Simple Appetizers
Quail Baked in Wine, 439
Duchess Potatoes
Baked Broccoli with Cheese
Avocado Fruit Salad
Pumpkin Chiffon Pie

THANKSGIVING DINNER

Grapefruit Juice
Roast Turkey, 441, Giblet Gravy
Scalloped Oysters
Mashed Potatoes
Glazed Sweetpotatoes
Cooked Squash
Creamed Onions
Molded Cranberry and Orange on
   Watercress
Pumpkin Pie
Mince Pie
Nuts
Coffee

˅ ˅ ˅

Baked Liver Loaf with Bacon, 240
Stewed Tomatoes
Pickled Fruits
Persimmon Pie
Coffee

˅ ˅ ˅

**Stuffed Pork Chops with Sage
   Stuffing, 378, 406**
Grilled Sweetpotatoes
Broccoli
Celery Hearts
Steamed Cranberry Pudding
   with Hot Wine Sauce

Ham with Corn Fritters, 381
Sweetpotato and Bacon Crisp
Creamed Sliced Carrots
Tomato Relish
Prune Graham Cracker Pudding
   with Whipped Cream

˅ ˅ ˅

Tomato Juice
Barbecued Beef Patties, 362
Cauliflower Fritters
Baked Hubbard Squash
Hot Chicory Salad Bowl
Scalloped Apples

˅ ˅ ˅

Cranberry Juice
Fish Fillets Florentine, 315
Baked Potatoes
Grated Carrot and Raisin Salad
Baked Russet Pears

˅ ˅ ˅

**Noodle Ring with Turkey à la
   King, 305, 446**
Crumbed Autumn Asparagus
Baked Acorn Squash
Banana Cream Pie

˅ ˅ ˅

Heart en Casserole Italienne, 398
Onion Salad Bowl with Lemon
   French Dressing
Baked Oranges

Cream of Celery Soup
**Spareribs with Sweetpotato
   Stuffing, 384, 507**
Baked Spinach
Apple Dumplings
   with Hot Rum Sauce

˅ ˅ ˅

**Hashed Lamb in Cabbage Leaves,
   366**
Cottage Fried Potatoes
Browned Carrots
Cranberry Orange Relish
Lettuce with Cottage Cheese
   Mayonnaise
Apple Fritters
   with Maple Sirup

˅ ˅ ˅

**Deviled Salmon in Shoestring
   Potato Nests, 326**
Spinach Balls
Escarole with French Dressing
Almond Butter Coffee Cake
Coffee

˅ ˅ ˅

New England Boiled Dinner, 358
Pear Salad
Cranberry Sherbet

*The lordly turkey in all his
glory still seems the national
choice   for   Thanksgiving
dinner*

Luncheons

ixed Vegetable Salad Bowl, 534
an Muffins
ked Custard with Currant Jelly
∨ ∨ ∨

ked Apples Stuffed with
Sausage, 387
orn Bread
ut Soufflé
∨ ∨ ∨

calloped Oysters, 331
uttered Asparagus
elery, Olives
ut Kisses
∨ ∨ ∨

ked Ham and Egg Molds, 291
neapple Muffins
aldorf Salad
∨ ∨ ∨

usage Cups with Scrambled
Eggs, 288
basted English Muffins
pple Butter
∨ ∨ ∨

heese Soufflé, 231
picy Green Beans
atmeal Muffins
ranberry Mousse

*on't shy away from the
ore unusual vegetables;
y them once and you may
ant to have them often*

Creamed Tuna with Mushrooms
in Croustades, 327
Spinach and Potato Croquettes
Cranberry Steamed Pudding
∨ ∨ ∨

Cheese Blintzes, 263
Apple, Grape and Banana Salad
with Pineapple Cream Dressing
Coffee   Milk
∨ ∨ ∨

Corn Chowder, 109
Pilot Crackers
Chicory Lettuce Salad Bowl
Chocolate Pecan Squares
with Peppermint Spread
∨ ∨ ∨

Baked Potatoes with Creamed
Dried Beef, 478
Pickled Beets
Apples Stuffed with Mincemeat
∨ ∨ ∨

Cream of Pea Soup, 115
Grated Carrot Sandwich
Fruit Whip
Drop Hermits
∨ ∨ ∨

Baked Stuffed Onions, 472, 256
Bran Muffins
Mixed Greens and Grapefruit
Salad Bowl
Rice Baked Custard

Eggs à la King, 298
on Toast Squares
Black Cherry Salad
Chocolate Peppermint Cake
Coffee   Milk
∨ ∨ ∨

Fish Roll, 324
Spinach Ring
Celery   Pickles
Frozen Fig Pudding
∨ ∨ ∨

Tomato Aspic Ring Filled with
Vegetable Luncheon Salad,
547, 542
Potato Chips
Pumpkin Chiffon Pie
Coffee   Milk
∨ ∨ ∨

Vegetable Chowder de Luxe, 110
Molded Cheese Salad
Hot Rolls
Lazy Daisy Cake
Coffee   Milk
∨ ∨ ∨

Bologna Cups with Peas, 386
Buttered Rice
Beet and Horse-radish Relish
Banana Tapioca Cream
∨ ∨ ∨

Crab-meat Rarebit, 231, 227
in Croustades
Buttered Brussels Sprouts
Apricot Angel Cream
∨ ∨ ∨

Steak and Kidney Pie, 404
Wilted Lettuce Bowl
Cracker Pudding
∨ ∨ ∨

Broiled Trout, 320
Stuffed Baked Potato
Globe Artichoke
Peppermint Stick Ice Cream
Chocolate Crispies
∨ ∨ ∨

Ham Soufflé, 380
Baked Chinese Cabbage
Toasty Prune Betty
∨ ∨ ∨

SUNDAY NIGHT SUPPER

New England Clam Chowder, 104
Toasted Crackers
Spread with Cheese
Autumn Fruit Salad Bowl
Roasted Chestnuts
Coffee   Milk

December Dinners

SUNDAY DINNERS

Chicken Tomato Bouillon
Roast Ribs of Beef, 352
Yorkshire Pudding
Lyonnaise Carrots
Celery Cabbage Salad
Frozen Fruit Pudding
Coffee   Milk

∨ ∨ ∨

Grapefruit Cup
Curry of Chicken, 232
Steamed Rice
Buttered Peas
Buttermilk Muffins
Condiment Tray of:
    Apple Chutney, Fresh Coconut,
    Chopped Pimientos, Celery
Frozen Ginger Cream Pudding
Coffee   Milk

∨ ∨ ∨

Simple Appetizers
**Roast Duckling with Wild Rice
    Stuffing, 434, 448**
Glazed Kumquats
Broccoli with Hollandaise Sauce
Mixed Vegetable Salad Bowl
Frozen Christmas Puddings

Grapefruit Juice
Baked Stuffed Fish, 316
Carrot Ring with Creamed Peas
Lettuce with Anchovy Dressing
Apple Pie
Coffee   Milk

∨ ∨ ∨

Fillets of Turkey with Rice, 442
Cranberry Orange Mold
Buttered Rutabaga
Hot Chicory Salad Bowl
Spiced Rennet-Custard
Nut Butter Dainties

∨ ∨ ∨

Smoked Salmon Hors d'Oeuvres
Lamb Hot Pot, 366
Buttered Parsnips
Lettuce Chicory Salad Bowl
Individual Pineapple Upside-down
    Cakes

∨ ∨ ∨

Cranberry Juice
Steak and Kidney Pie, 404
Carrot Croquettes
Pepper Relish
Hot Applesauce with Nutmeg
Poundcake

Consommé à la Royal
**Baked Pork Tenderloin Slices
    Sour Cream, 378**
Cranberry Catchup
French Fried Cauliflower
Carrot and Celery Aspic
Sweetpotato Walnut Pudding
Coffee   Milk

∨ ∨ ∨

CHRISTMAS DINNER

Consommé
Melba Toast
Celery Curls
Olives
Roast Turkey, 441
Mushroom and Oyster Stuffing
Cranberry Relish
Sweetpotato Soufflé
Broccoli
Green Salad Bowl
    with French Dressing
Individual Plum Puddings
    with Brazil-nut Hard Sauce
Coffee   Milk

*When the north wind dot
blow, cheer the family wit
a bountiful rib roast*

ven the shepherd's pie can e served with a flourish

Pineapple Juice
Poached Fish with Egg Sauce, 318
Parsley Potatoes
Buttered Broccoli
Tomato and Celery Aspic
Chilled Peach Halves
Rolled Oatmeal Cookies
∨ ∨ ∨

Grapefruit Juice
Sweetpotato Ham Puffs, 380
Creamed Cauliflower
Lettuce with French Dressing
Pineapple Tarts
∨ ∨ ∨

Apricot Juice
Meat Pie with Vegetables and Biscuit Crust, 363, 251
Fresh Spinach Salad
  with Horse-radish Dressing
Banana Butterscotch Pudding
∨ ∨ ∨

Tomato Juice
Fried Scallops with Tartare Sauce, 341, 863
Baked Potatoes
Green Beans
Peach Betty
∨ ∨ ∨

Chicken Bouillon
Chicken and Noodle Scallop, 425
Baked Hubbard Squash
Celery Cabbage
  with French Dressing
Cranberry Nut Cobbler

Grapefruit Juice
Lamb Curry Pie, 366
Piccalilli
Baked Hubbard Squash
Apple Meringue Pudding
∨ ∨ ∨

Tomato Juice
Sliced Turkey in Gravy on Fried Corn-meal Mush, 445, 242
Broccoli with Lemon Butter
Pickled Beets
Orange Bavarian Cream
∨ ∨ ∨

Fresh Fruit Cup
Sliced Roast Beef in Gravy on Buttered Noodles, 352, 305
Tomato Relish
Buttered Carrots
Mocha Soufflé
∨ ∨ ∨

Vegetable Juice
Ham Patties on Pineapple Slices, 384
Sautéed Sweetpotatoes
Buttered Broccoli
Orange Chiffon Pie
∨ ∨ ∨

Meat Balls in Tomato Sauce, 360, 490
Mashed Turnips
Buttered Spinach
Corn Bread
Chocolate Mint Cake
∨ ∨ ∨

Curried Oysters and Shrimp, 258
Steamed Rice
Carrots and Peas
Baked Stuffed Apples
Butterscotch Bars

Tomato Juice
Browned Short Ribs of Beef, 360
Browned Carrots
Cauliflower Fritters
Piccalilli
Pumpkin Pie
∨ ∨ ∨

Consommé Julienne
Individual Chicken Shortcakes, 426
Celery Curls
Buttered Green Beans
Pineapple Tapioca Cream
∨ ∨ ∨

Grapefruit Juice
Scalloped Oysters, 331
Buttered Spinach
Carrot Salad
Deep-dish Apple Pudding
∨ ∨ ∨

Shrimp Cocktail
Eggplant Stuffed with Chopped Steak and Tomatoes, 252
Buttered Brussels Sprouts
Cranberry Muffins
Sweetpotato Pie
∨ ∨ ∨

Oxtail Soup
Shepherd's Pie, 373, 253
Baked Parsnips
Avocado Crescents with French
  Dressing
Chocolate Bread Pudding
∨ ∨ ∨

Braised Liver, 400
Creamed Potatoes
Onion Casserole
Cranberry Orange Molds
Apple Charlotte
∨ ∨ ∨

Broiled Grapefruit
Boiled Beef Tongue, 405, 344 with Horse-radish Sauce
Potatoes with Savory Sauce
Green Salad
Peanut Brittle Mousse
∨ ∨ ∨

Spiced Grape Juice
Braised Heart with Prune Stuffing, 398, 406
Baked Acorn Squash
Beet Salad with Chive
  French Dressing
Grapefruit Pie
∨ ∨ ∨

Irish Stew with Dumplings, 253
Fruit and Cottage Cheese Mold
Party Roll
∨ ∨ ∨

Two-Tone Meat Loaf, 389
Scalloped Potatoes
Braised Celery
Grated Carrot Salad
Butterscotch Rice Mold

Luncheons

Fish Chowder, 103-105
Pilot Crackers
Winter Vegetable Salad
Chocolate Brazil-Nut Tarts
∨ ∨ ∨

Oysters à la King in Croustades,
332, 227
Green Bean Salad
Hot Fruit Compote
∨ ∨ ∨

Lima Bean Soup, 121
Toasted Crackers
Glazed Apple Ring
    with Butterscotch Sauce
∨ ∨ ∨

Creamed Dried Beef with Olives
on French Toast, 196, 873
Grapefruit Chicory Salad
    with French Dressing
Date Bars
∨ ∨ ∨

Creole Gumbo, 119
Bread Sticks
Fruit Whip
∨ ∨ ∨

American Chop Suey, 378
Steamed Rice   Hot Rolls
Orange Marmalade   Tea
∨ ∨ ∨

Cabbage Soup with Marrow Balls,
101, 127
Toasted Water Crackers
Gingerbread with Orange Icing
∨ ∨ ∨

Grilled Chopped Steak with
Grilled Onion Ring on Toasted
Buns, 192, 472
Tomato Relish
Baked Pears
∨ ∨ ∨

Ham, Egg and Mushroom Sand-
wiches, 196
Cabbage Salad
Baked Apples with Cranberries
Coffee   Milk
∨ ∨ ∨

Vienna Potatoes, 478
Baked Squash
Brazil-nut Pudding
Chocolate Malted Milk
∨ ∨ ∨

Fruit Plate, 548
Cheese Sandwiches
Holiday Delight Pudding
Coffee   Milk

Crab Meat in Shells, 335
Cooked Chicory
Assorted Pickles and Relishes
Coconut Delight
∨ ∨ ∨

Poached Eggs in Rice Nests with
Cheese and Olive Sauce, 296
Waldorf Salad
Chocolate Pudding
Refrigerator Cookies

∨ ∨ ∨

Potato Carrot Mold, 482
Green Bean Salad Bowl
Butterscotch Pudding
Coffee

∨ ∨ ∨

Baked Noodles and Cheese, 799
Broccoli with Hollandaise Sauce
Baked Orange Fluff

∨ ∨ ∨

Creamed Shrimp, 340
in Potato Nests, 489
Tomato Aspic Ring
Raspberry Bavarian Cake

∨ ∨ ∨

Tamale Pie, 357, 256
Endive, Carrot Sticks and Grape-
fruit Salad with French Dressing
Gingerbread with Bananas

Scalloped Corn and Oysters, 8C
Pear Salad
Graham Cracker Cream Cake
Banana Milk Shake
∨ ∨ ∨

Celery Chowder
Fried Egg Sandwich, 190
Sliced Oranges
Butterscotch Bars
∨ ∨ ∨

Liver Sausage Cakes, 489
Harvard Beets
Floating Island Pudding
∨ ∨ ∨

NEW YEAR'S EVE SUPPER
Welsh Rarebit with Bacon Curl
231, 374
Fruit Salad Bowl
Assorted Wafers
Coffee

∨ ∨ ∨

*This funny snow man wil
bring hilarity to the servin
of baked eggs in brea
croustades with cream sauc*
→

*Fruit salad luncheon plate
with sandwich fingers ar
welcome through winte
drifts as well as summe
heat*

Breakfasts

BREAKFAST JUICES

(Canned or fresh)

Apple, Apricot
Cherry
Cranberry
Grapefruit
Mixed fruit
Orange
Pineapple
Pomegranate
Prune
Sauerkraut
Tangerine, Tomato

∨ ∨ ∨

COOKED FRUITS

Applesauce
Baked apples
Baked bananas
Baked or stewed blueberries

*A breath of the ol' South
for breakfast*

Baked or stewed grapes
Baked or stewed peaches
Baked or stewed pears
Baked or stewed rhubarb
Broiled, grapefruit
Canned blackberries
Canned cherries
Canned dewberries
Canned gooseberries
Canned grapefruit
Canned loganberries
Canned or stewed figs
Canned or stewed youngberries
Canned pineapple
Canned quinces
Canned raspberries
Stewed dried apricots
Stewed dried fruit compote
Stewed dried peaches
Stewed dried pears
Stewed nectarines
Stewed plums
Stewed prunes

UNCOOKED FRUITS

Apples, Apricots
Bananas
Blackberries, Blueberries
Cantaloupe
Cherries
Fresh Prunes
Grapefruit
Grapes
Honeydew melon
Kumquats
Nectarines
Oranges
Peaches
Pears
Persimmons
Pineapple
Plums
Pomegranates
Raspberries
Strawberries
Tangerines
Watermelon

Codfish balls aren't really hard to make and they add variety and good food value to the breakfast menu

FRUITS TO USE ON CEREALS

Applesauce
Baked apples
Bananas
Blackberries
Blueberries
Canned quinces
Dates
Peaches
Raspberries
Stewed dried apricots
Stewed dried peaches
Stewed prunes
Strawberries

∨ ∨ ∨

BREAKFAST CEREALS—Ready-to-serve cereals are prepared from almost all grains—flaked, puffed, shredded or rolled and cooked. These may be served just as they come from the package or they may be heated in the oven. Serve with milk or cream, adding fruit and sugar if desired. Cooked cereals are of 2 types, quick-cooking and those requiring a cooking period of 1 hour or more. The latter may be prepared ahead of time and reheated for serving. Serve with milk or cream and fruit. Hot cereals are particularly desirable during cold weather.

EGGS—Because eggs may be prepared in a great number of ways, they provide opportunity for variety and interest in the breakfast menu. Many people, however, prefer to cook their breakfast eggs in the same way every morning.

The simplest methods of cooking eggs are frying, scrambling, soft cooking and poaching. Fried eggs are often served with bacon or ham. Scrambled eggs may have tomatoes, chopped cooked bacon or ham, cheese, pimientos or other foods mixed with them.

Additional egg dishes are shirred eggs, creamed eggs, omelets and fluffy egg nests. These are especially suitable for Sunday breakfasts when one usually has more leisure for the preparation and enjoyment of the meal.

BREADS—Breakfast breads are usually hot and freshly made. Sweet rolls and coffee cakes, however, are as often served cold as hot. Toast, dry or buttered, is the simplest breakfast bread. Others are biscuits, hot rolls, waffles, pancakes, doughnuts, fruit turnovers, muffins and popovers. These are made of a variety of flours: wheat, whole-wheat, graham, corn, rye, bran, oats and rice. Fruit and meat are often added: blueberries, cranberries, bananas, apples, blackberries, raisins, currants, dried

prunes and apricots, cheese, crisp bacon, cracklings and jelly.

SWEETS—Jams, jellies, marmalades, sirups and honey are often served at breakfast, particularly with hot breads.

BEVERAGES—A hot beverage is a valuable stimulant at breakfast time. For children, this is usually a drink made almost entirely of milk. Adults often prefer coffee, tea or a cereal beverage.

∨ ∨ ∨

LIGHT SUMMER BREAKFASTS

Strawberries and Cream
Ready-to-serve Cereal
Rye Bread Toast
Coffee   Milk
∨ ∨ ∨

Fresh Pineapple
Creamed Dried Beef on Toast, 196
Coffee   Milk
∨ ∨ ∨

Cantaloupe
Poached Egg, 294-297
Melba Toast
Coffee   Milk
∨ ∨ ∨

Ready-to-serve Cereal with Sliced Fresh Peaches
Blueberry Muffins
Coffee   Milk
∨ ∨ ∨

Orange Juice
Puffed Cereal with Cream
Hot Buttered Toast
Coffee   Milk
∨ ∨ ∨

Grapefruit Juice
Scrambled Eggs in Toasted Buns, 287, 288
Coffee   Milk

HEAVY SUMMER BREAKFASTS
Prune Juice
Ready-to-serve Cereal with Cream
  and Blueberries
Poached Eggs on Toast, 294-297
Buttered Toast
Orange Marmalade
Coffee   Milk
            √ √ √

Broiled Grapefruit
Ready-to-serve Cereal with
  Cream
Scrambled Eggs, 287, 288
Bacon
Popovers
Blackberry Jelly
Coffee   Milk
            √ √ √

Pineapple Juice
Ready-to-serve Cereal with Blue-
  berries
**Creamed Dried Beef in Popovers,
  196, 174-176**
Coffee Cake
Coffee   Milk
            √ √ √

Raspberries and Cream
Fluffy Egg Nests, 289
Hot Melba Toast
Apple Butter
Coffee   Milk
            √ √ √

Applesauce
Fish Omelet, 282-285
Jelly Corn Muffins
Coffee   Milk
            √ √ √

Orange Sections and Strawberries
  with Sugar
Shredded Cereal with Cream
Egg Frizzle, 287
Whole-wheat Toast
Coffee   Milk

LIGHT WINTER BREAKFASTS
Broiled Grapefruit
Scrambled Eggs with Bacon, 287
Whole-wheat Toast
Marmalade
Coffee   Hot Milk
            √ √ √

Stewed Dried Apricots
Cooked Wheat Cereal, 872
Bran Muffins
Coffee   Hot Milk
            √ √ √

Baked Apples
Oatmeal and Cream, 872
Toast and Orange Marmalade
Coffee   Hot Milk
            √ √ √

Stewed Prunes
**Poached Egg on Whole-wheat
  Toast, 294-297**
Strawberry Preserves
Coffee   Hot Milk
            √ √ √

Stewed Pears
Codfish Balls, 321
Cracked Wheat Toast
Coffee   Milk
            √ √ √

Orange Juice
Sweetpotato Waffles
Link Sausages, 387
Coffee   Milk
            √ √ √

**Oatmeal and Cream with Stewed
  Prunes, 872**
Baking Powder Biscuits
Orange Marmalade
Coffee   Milk
            √ √ √

Wheat Cereal Cooked with Dates
Broiled Bacon, 374
Cinnamon Toast

HEAVY WINTER BREAKFASTS
Orange Juice
Oatmeal with Cream
Fried Eggs and Bacon, 280, 374
Cranberry Muffins
Coffee   Hot Milk
            √ √ √

Cooked Whole-wheat Cereal with
  Baked Sliced Apples and Cream
**Eggs Scrambled with Bacon, 287,
  288**
Hot Biscuits
Strawberry Jam
Coffee   Hot Milk
            √ √ √

Applesauce
**Fried Eggs with Fried Hominy
  Grits, 280, 242**
Bacon
Waffles and Maple Sirup
Coffee   Hot Milk
            √ √ √

Orange Juice
Cooked Wheat Cereal with Ba-
  nanas
Soft-cooked Eggs, 303
Buttered Toast
Doughnuts
Coffee   Hot Milk
            √ √ √

Prune Juice
Oyster Omelet, 282
Oatmeal Muffins
Coffee   Hot Milk
            √ √ √

Cherry Juice
Cooked Hominy Grits and Cream
Eggs with Shrimp, 288
Toast with Peach Jam
Coffee   Hot Milk

*White or whole-wheat bread
may be toasted in this form
with a coating of cheese for
breakfast or brunch*

Brunch as informal enter-
tainment is riding to fame
in such dishes as this

BRUNCHES

Pomegranate Juice
Fried Apple Rings
Sautéed Link Sausages, 387
Rye Pancakes
Hot Maple Sirup
Coffee Milk
√ √ √

Persimmons and Blackberries
Puffed Cereal with Cream
**Poached Eggs on Shepherd's Pie,
294, 373**
Sliced Tomatoes
Honey Twist
Coffee Milk
√ √ √

Apple Juice
Oyster Kebobs, 332
Broiled Bacon
Rice Muffins
Orange Marmalade
Coffee Milk
√ √ √

P.T.A. BRUNCH

Cranberry Juice
**Poached Eggs with Cheese Sauce
in Croustades, 294-297, 227**
Canadian Bacon
Orange Marmalade Rolls
Coffee Milk
√ √ √

Prunes in Orange Juice
Goldenrod Eggs, 302
Sausages, 387
Hot Buns
Coffee Milk

Strawberries and Orange
Sections with Sugar
Puffy Omelet, 282
Sausages
Hot Biscuits Plum Jam
Swedish Tea Ring
Coffee Milk
√ √ √

Red Raspberries in Cantaloupe
Baskets
**Scrambled Eggs with Mushrooms,
288**
Canadian Bacon
Hot Biscuits Strawberry Jam
Pineapple Coffee Cake
Coffee Milk
√ √ √

Cantaloupe and Watermelon Balls
Sausage Omelet, 283
Popovers
Blackberry Jam
Sweet Rolls
Coffee Milk
√ √ √

Blackberries and Cream
**Eggs Baked with Chicken Livers,
289, 293**
Brioche Coffee Milk
√ √ √

EASTER BREAKFAST

Orange and Pineapple Juice
Puffed Cereal with Strawberries
and Cream
**Broiled Sweetbreads with Bacon
and Sherry, 397**
Buttermilk Muffins
Blackberry Jelly
Coffee Milk

HUNT BREAKFAST

Cherry Juice
Eggs with Black Butter, 280
Potato Pancakes
Broiled Bacon Applesauce
Moravian Bread
Coffee Milk
√ √ √

Strawberries and Rhubarb Sauce
Mushroom Omelet, 282
Coffee Nut Muffins
Currant Jelly
Coffee Milk
√ √ √

Pears, Plums, Cherries
Chicken Livers en Brochette, 431
Corn Cakes
Broiled Tomato Slices
Prune Ladder
Coffee Milk
√ √ √

Stewed Figs and Rhubarb
**Codfish Balls and Tomato Sauce,
321, 490**
Broiled Bacon
Baked Hominy Grits
Pineapple Coffee Cake
Coffee Milk
√ √ √

Sliced Oranges
Fried Chicken, 422-423
Batter Bread
Currant Jelly
Sweet Rolls
Coffee Milk
√ √ √

Pineapple Juice
Shirred Eggs with Sausage, 293
Melba Toast
Gooseberry Jam
Honey Twist
Coffee Milk
√ √ √

Strawberries and Cream
**Scrambled Eggs in Sausage Cups,
288**
Buttermilk Waffles
Maple Sirup
Coffee Milk
√ √ √

Peaches and Cream
Lobster Omelet, 282
Asparagus
Sour Cream Biscuits
Crab Apple Jelly
Brioche
Coffee Milk
√ √ √

Baked Apples and Cream
Eggs in Bacon Rings, 290
Banana Bran Muffins
Coffee Milk

Cranberry Juice
Sweetpotato Ham Puffs, 380
Broiled Pineapple
Toasted White Bread
Toasted Cracked Wheat Bread
Cider Apple Butter
Coffee   Milk

∨ ∨ ∨

Stewed Prunes, Apricots and
   Pears
**Fried Eggs with Sautéed Breaded
   Eggplant and Grilled Toma-
   toes, 280, 468**
Oatmeal Muffins
Grape Jelly
Coffee Cake
Coffee   Milk

∨ ∨ ∨

Fresh Figs and Cream
Chicken Livers with Anchovy, 431
Crackling Bread
Blackberry Jelly
Fruit Bread
Coffee   Milk

∨ ∨ ∨

Prune and Apricot Juice
Sausage Balls, 387
Orange Waffles
Honey, Jelly
Frosted Molasses Cookies
Coffee   Milk

∨ ∨ ∨

Pear and Raspberry Sauce
Eggs with Herbs in Ramekins, 293
Broiled Bacon
Cream Biscuits
Currant Jelly
Napfkuchen
Coffee   Milk

Blueberries and Cream
Puffed Cereal
Broiled Ham, 381
Fried Eggs, 280
Flapjacks
Maple Sirup
Swedish Tea Ring
Coffee   Milk

∨ ∨ ∨

Grapefruit Juice
Chicken Yorkshire, 427
Mushroom Sauce
Quince Jelly
Quick Coffee Cake
Coffee   Milk

∨ ∨ ∨

Baked Oranges
Sausage Omelet, 282, 283
Fried Green Tomatoes
Cheese Gems
Plum Jam
Coffee   Milk

*Your next conference break
fast will do more work o
batter bread*

CLASS DAY BRUNCH

Honeydew Melon
Fish in Ramekins, 257
Buttermilk Muffins
Peach Jam
Brioche
Coffee   Milk

∨ ∨ ∨

Apples Sliced and Baked with
   Honey
Broiled Bacon, 374
Egg Bread
Honey or Maple Sirup
Coffee   Milk

*A platter of Polish pancake
and pork sausages can b
refilled many times durin
brunch*

WEDDING BREAKFASTS

Sliced Bananas in Orange Juice
Lobster à la Newburg in Timbale Cases, 337, 601
Asparagus
Parker House Rolls
Raspberry Jelly
Salted Nuts, Mints
Wedding Cake
Coffee

∨ ∨ ∨

Fruit Cocktail
Chicken and Sweetbread Salad, 429
Sliced Tomatoes and Cucumbers
Clover-leaf Rolls
Kumquat Preserves
Jordan Almonds
Wedding Cake
Coffee

∨ ∨ ∨

Avocado Cranberry Sherbet, in Lemon Cups
Lobster Thermidor, 337
Cauliflower Fritters
Celery   Stuffed Olives
Butterleaf Rolls
Currant Jelly
Jordan Almonds
Frosted Fruits
Mocha Ice Cream and Black Walnut Parfait Bombe
Wedding Cake
Coffee

Savory eggs are a gala touch at any breakfast

Fruit in Pineapple Baskets
Oysters Rockefeller, 332
Parsley Paprika Lima Beans
Poppy Seed Rolls
Rose Geranium Jelly
Plum Conserve
Chocolate Chip Ice Cream and Butter Pecan Mousse Bombe
Wedding Cake

∨ ∨ ∨

Stuffed Cantaloupe
Capon Terrapin in Potato Nests, 425, 489
Green Peas with Pimientos
Buttermilk Biscuits
Cream Cheese   Bar-le-Duc
Apple Jelly
Salted Nuts   Mints
Brick Ice Cream
Wedding Cake
Coffee

∨ ∨ ∨

Honeydew Melon Rings with Raspberry Sherbet
Baked Ham with Currant Jelly Glaze, 379
Sweetpotatoes in Orange Baskets
Butterleaf Rolls
Wedding Cake

∨ ∨ ∨

Fruit Punch
Chicken and Fruit Salad, 429
Hot Rolls
Honey Jelly
Salted Nuts   Mints
Maple Ice Cream
Wedding Cake

Broiled Grapefruit
Scrambled Eggs with Vienna Sausage in Timbale Cases, 288, 601
Baked Tomatoes
Buttermilk Biscuits
Cherry Preserves
Dewberry Jelly
Caramel Ice Cream
Wedding Cake
Coffee

∨ ∨ ∨

Blackberries in Orange Baskets
Crab Thermidor in Shells, 336
Artichokes with Hollandaise Sauce
Beaten Biscuits
Strawberry Jam
Peach Ice Cream
Salted Nuts   Mints
Wedding Cake
Coffee

∨ ∨ ∨

Baked Stuffed Pears
Roast Wild Duck, 434
Brown Rice
Fried Zucchini
Currant Jelly
Clover-leaf Rolls
Grapefruit, Avocado and Japanese Persimmon Salad
Wedding Cake
Glacéed Fruits and Nuts
Coffee

∨ ∨ ∨

Melon Balls in Grapefruit Baskets
Turkey Shortcake, 426
Celery Curls   Pickle Fans
Radish Roses
Stuffed Artichoke Salad
Butterleaf Rolls
Individual Hearts of Loganberry Cream Sherbert on Spun Sugar
Wedding Cake
Pistachio Nuts
Coffee

∨ ∨ ∨

Sugared Strawberries
Savory Eggs, 308
Link Sausages, 387
Broiled Tomato Halves
Baking Powder Biscuits
Orange Marmalade
Damson Plum Jam
Salted Nuts, Mints
Wedding Cake
Coffee

If there are many guests, the wedding breakfast may be served buffet style

Raspberries and Cream
Planked Lamb Chops, 369
Asparagus
Honey Mint Jelly
Parker House Rolls
Toasted Almonds
Peppermint Stick Parfait
Wedding Cake
Coffee

∨ ∨ ∨

Sliced Oranges with Strawberries
Smoked Turkey, 437
Cantaloupe Slices
Molded Salad
Pea and Mushroom Casserole
Hot Rolls
Gooseberry Jam
Salted Nuts   Mints
Vanilla Ice Cream
Wedding Cake
Coffee

∨ ∨ ∨

Melon Ball and Orange Fruit
   Cocktail
Eggs à la Benedictine, 291
Crumbed Asparagus
Baking Powder Biscuits
Orange Marmalade
Raspberry and Cherry Conserve
Salted Nuts
Peppermint Creams
Vanilla Mousse
Wedding Cake
Coffee

Fruit Punch
**Avocados Filled with Lobster and
   Grapefruit Salad, 551**
Celery Curls   Ripe Olives
Oven-toasted Bread
Rose Geranium Jelly
Salted Nuts   Fruit Creams
Peach Mousse
Wedding Cake
Coffee

∨ ∨ ∨

Fruit in Orange Baskets
**Stuffed Eggs in Jellied Bouillon
   on Summer Sausage, 224**
Crisped Cucumbers, Olives
Hot Rolls
Rose Geranium Jelly
Coffee

Peaches and Cream
**Individual Chicken Salads in
   Aspic, 546, 430**
Sliced Tomatoes
Olives   Celery Curls
Mushrooms Stuffed with Brazil
   Nuts
Crescent Rolls
Orange Marmalade
Toasted Nuts   Candy Acorns
Eggnog Ice Cream
Wedding Cake
Coffee

*Planked lamb chops with a
frill of creamy mashed potatoes will delight every
guest at the wedding breakfast*

Soups and Chowder

250 SOUPS AND CHOWDERS

BOUILLON

2 pounds beef and soupbone
1¼ quarts cold water
4 peppercorns, 2 cloves
1 bay leaf, 1 blade mace
1 teaspoon sweet herbs
1 tablespoon diced carrot
1 tablespoon diced onion
1 tablespoon diced celery
1 tablespoon diced turnip
Sprig parsley, 1 teaspoon salt

Cut meat into small pieces Combine with other ingredients in a kettle. Heat to boiling slowly and simmer 3 to 4 hours. Strain stock through several thicknesses of cheesecloth and cool quickly When cold remove fat from the top. Reheat and serve hot. Makes 1 quart stock. If a darker colored stock is desired, brown the meat in 2 tablespoons shortening before adding water and other ingredients.

VEGETABLE SOUP—Add 1 cup diced vegetables, uncooked or cooked. If uncooked vegetables are used, simmer in bouillon until tender. It may be necessary to add more salt.

BARLEY, RICE OR SAGO SOUP

—Add 2 tablespoons barley, rice or sago. Soak rice or sago ½ hour in water to cover, before adding to bouillon. Barley should be soaked overnight. Add to bouillon and simmer ½ hour.

CONSOMMÉ

1 pound lean beef
1 veal knuckle
1½ quarts cold water or 1 pint cold water and 1 pint chicken stock
2 peppercorns, 1 clove
½ teaspoon sweet herbs
1 tablespoon diced celery
1 tablespoon diced carrot
1 tablespoon diced onion
Sprig parsley, 1 teaspoon salt

Cut meat into small pieces. Combine all ingredients in a kettle, heat slowly to boiling and simmer 3 to 4 hours. Strain consommé through several thicknesses of cheesecloth and cool quickly. When cold remove fat from the top. Reheat and serve hot. Makes 1 quart consommé.

CONSOMMÉ PRINCESSE—Consommé served with shreds or small dice of cooked chicken and green peas.

CONSOMMÉ À LA ROYALE — Consommé served with tiny cubes of Custard Royale.

CONSOMMÉ JULIENNE OR JULIENNE SOUP — Consommé served with cooked carrot, onions, turnips and celery which have been cut into shreds about as thick as a match. The vegetables should be boiled in clear water before being added to the consommé.

CONSOMMÉ JARDINIÈRE—Consommé served with cooked vegetables which have been cut into attractive shapes with vegetable cutters. Allow ¾ cup vegetables to 4 cups consommé.

CLARET—Cook ½-inch stick cinnamon in consommé for 5 minutes, then remove. Add 1 cup each claret and hot water. Pour into 1 beaten egg-yolk, stirring constantly. Fold in stiffly beaten egg white and serve immediately.

The intriguing aroma of clear hot consommé forecasts a fine dinner

WHITE STOCK

2 pounds chicken or knuckle of
    veal
1¼ quarts cold water
2 peppercorns, 1 clove
½ teaspoon sweet herbs
1 tablespoon diced onion
1 tablespoon diced celery
1 teaspoon salt

Cut chicken into small pieces, add remaining ingredients and simmer 2 to 3 hours. Strain through several thicknesses of cheesecloth. Cool quickly and remove fat from surface. Reheat and serve hot. Makes 1 quart.

BROWN STOCK

5 pounds beef soupbone
3 quarts cold water
8 peppercorns, 5 cloves
1 bay leaf, 2 sprigs parsley
3 sprigs thyme, 1 tablespoon salt
1 stalk celery
½ cup diced carrots
½ cup diced turnips
2 large onions, sliced

Cut lean meat from the bones and brown ⅓ of it in the marrow taken from the bones. Put the rest of the meat and bones in a large kettle, cover with water and let stand 1 hour. Add browned meat and seasonings and bring to a boil. Reduce heat and simmer for 5 hours. Add the vegetables and cook 1½ hours longer. Strain through a cheesecloth and cool. When cold remove layer of fat which forms on top. Serve hot for 10 persons.

MUTTON, HAM, OR LAMB STOCK OR BROTH—Use mutton, ham, or lamb instead of beef, removing most of the fat from the meat.
Add 2 tablespoons pearl barley which has been soaked overnight in cold water. Drain and add to stock and simmer about ½ hour.

MACARONI, NOODLE, SPA-GHETTI OR VERMICELLI SOUP —Add ¼ cup macaroni, noodles, spaghetti or vermicelli (broken into small pieces) to stock, simmer until tender.

TO CLEAR SOUP STOCK

Remove layer of fat which has formed on cold stock. Measure amount to be cleared and to every quart of stock use 1 egg white and shell (which has been washed before breaking egg) Beat egg white slightly and add broken shell. Add to stock and boil for 5 minutes. Remove to a warm place and add ½ cup cold water and let stand 15 minutes. Strain through cheesecloth.

BEEF TEA

1 pound lean beef, 1 cup water
½ teaspoon salt

METHOD 1—Put beef through a food grinder, using a coarse knife. Place in top of double boiler and add the water. Simmer over very low heat about 3½ hours. Add salt. Remove all fat. Strain and keep liquid in a cool place. It may be diluted with some boiling water to the strength desired. Makes 1 cup broth.

METHOD 2—Place ground meat in a fruit jar, add 2 cups cold water and let stand 1 hour. Place jar on a cloth in a saucepan of cold water and heat slowly to 140°F. Do not allow to boil. Keep at this temperature 2 hours.

BEEF JUICE

1 pound round steak

Have meat cut 1 inch thick. Place under the broiler and broil on both sides until meat is warm and the juice has started to flow; about 2 minutes. Remove meat, sprinkle with salt, cut into small pieces, place in a small piece of cheesecloth, a presser, lemon squeezer or a potato ricer and squeeze out all the juice. Serve cold or heat very carefully over water, stirring constantly to prevent overheating and coagulation of protein. Beef juice is rich in phosphorous and iron and is used generally under doctor's direction. 1 pound beef makes 4 ounces or ½ cup juice.

SWEETBREAD SOUP

2 pairs sweetbreads
Cold water
2 tablespoons butter
2 onions, sliced
3 carrots, diced
1 small head cabbage, shredded
3 tablespoons flour
4 cups stock, boiling
1 teaspoon salt
⅛ teaspoon pepper
1 cup cooked asparagus tips

Cover sweetbreads with cold water and let soak for 3 to 4 hours, changing the water 2 or 3 times during that period. Drain and cover with fresh cold water; heat to boiling and cook for 2 minutes. Remove from water and place on a clean towel to drain. Cut away bits of skin and veins with a knife, being careful not to break the sweetbreads, then cut them into 2-inch pieces. Melt butter in a saucepan and add onions, carrots and cabbage and simmer about 10 minutes; add flour and stir until blended, then add stock. Stir until mixture is well blended. Season with salt and pepper. Cover pan and simmer about 45 minutes. Add sweetbreads and continue cooking for 30 minutes or until tender. When ready to serve remove sweetbreads to a soup tureen and strain soup over them. Garnish with asparagus tips. Serves 4.

BORSCH

1 cup tomatoes, fresh or canned
2 cups shredded beets
4 cups water, 1 small onion
½ pound lean beef
1 tablespoon lemon juice
¼ cup sugar
¼ teaspoon salt, 4 eggs

Strain tomatoes through a fine sieve over beets. Add water, onion and meat, cut into small pieces, and simmer 30 minutes. Add lemon juice, sugar and salt. Boil 30 minutes longer. Beat eggs. Add the hot borsch to them a little at a time, stirring well during each addition. Serve at once, while very hot. Serves 4.

LIVER SOUP

½ pound beef liver
1 cup chopped mushrooms
2 teaspoons minced parsley
3 tablespoons fat, 1 teaspoon salt
4 cups brown stock or bouillon
1 tablespoon flour
1 cup cream or evaporated milk

Cut liver into very fine pieces. Sauté liver, mushrooms and parsley in 2 tablespoons fat for 5 minutes. Add salt and brown stock or bouillon and simmer, covered, for ½ hour, or until liver is tender. Combine remaining 1 tablespoon fat with flour and brown, add liver mixture gradually and cook 5 minutes. Add cream or evaporated milk, reheat and serve immediately, garnished with croutons. Serves 6.

PEPPER POT

1 pound honeycomb tripe, cubed
1 pound stewing beef, cubed
2 quarts water
1 medium onion, diced
⅓ cup diced celery
¼ cup diced green pepper
4 tablespoons fat
4 tablespoons flour
2 medium potatoes, diced
1 tablespoon salt

Cover meat with cold water, heat to boiling and simmer until meat is tender. Combine onion, celery and green pepper and simmer in fat for about 15 minutes. Add flour and stir until blended, add meat, stock, potatoes and seasoning. Cover and simmer for 1 hour. Serve hot. Serves 6 to 8.

PETITE MARMITE

2 pounds lean beef
1 2½-pound chicken
6 quarts consommé
3 carrots, diced
2 turnips, diced
2 stalks celery, diced
3 leeks, sliced
¼ head cabbage, sliced
Salt and pepper
1 marrowbone, cooked
1 teaspoon chopped chervil
1 teaspoon chopped parsley

Cover beef and chicken with cold water and heat to boiling. Drain water thoroughly. Then cover beef and chicken with consommé and heat to boiling. Skim. Add vegetables and cook until meat and vegetables are tender. Salt and pepper to taste. Remove beef and chicken, cut into small squares, add to soup. Add cooked sliced marrow, also chervil and parsley. Serve Toasted Cheese Sticks separately. Serves 12.

Liver soup with its square crouton is a delicious way to secure more of these rare nutritive qualities

CABBAGE AND BEET SOUP

1 small head cabbage, shredded
2½ cups diced cooked beets
1 small onion, diced
2 quarts soup stock
1 teaspoon salt
¼ teaspoon pepper
8 thick slices bread
½ cup grated cheese

Combine cabbage, beets, onion, stock, salt and pepper and cook until cabbage is tender. Pour soup over bread, allowing 1 slice to each serving. Sprinkle with cheese. Serves 8. For variety cook 1 cup cranberries, strain and add. Omit bread and cheese.

CARROT SOUP

2 tablespoons fat
1 large onion, sliced
1 tablespoon flour
4 cups beef or veal stock
3½ cups sliced carrots
1 cup minced celery
2 teaspoons salt
¼ teaspoon pepper

Melt fat in a large soup kettle and brown the onion, stir in flour and add broth. Stir while heating to boiling; cook 2 minutes. Add remaining ingredients and let simmer 1 hour. Rub through a sieve and serve hot. Serves 6.

GARDEN SOUP

1 carrot, diced
½ small turnip, diced
⅓ cup shredded cabbage
1 tablespoon butter
3 cups soup stock
½ leek, sliced
½ cup shelled peas
Salt
½ potato, diced
1 teaspoon minced parsley

Sauté carrot, turnip and cabbage in butter. Add soup stock leek, peas, salt, potato and parsley. Cover and simmer for 40 minutes. Serves 4.

Vegetables of every size and kind are welcome ingredients for your soup making

BROWN CABBAGE SOUP

Soupbone (3 to 4 pounds)
2 quarts cold water
2 teaspoons salt
¼ teaspoon pepper
1 bay leaf
½ medium head cabbage
2 medium onions, sliced
1 cup chopped celery
1 cup chopped beet tops
1 tablespoon fat or oil

Cover bone with water and add salt, pepper and bay leaf. Heat to boiling and cook 1½ hours. Cut cabbage into eighths and cook with remaining vegetables in fat or oil. Brown well. Add to stock and bone and continue cooking for ¾ hour. Remove meat from bone and add to soup. Serve, if desired, with 1 tablespoon salted whipped cream or clotted sour cream. Serves 8.

LETTUCE SOUP—Omit cabbage and fat. Add 1½ cups shredded lettuce and ½ cup tomatoes. Do not brown vegetables. Add 2 tablespoons rice if desired.

RUSSIAN CABBAGE SOUP

½ pound lean beef
½ pound fat pork
1 large head white cabbage, shredded
1 large tomato, quartered
1 onion, sliced
5 cups stock or water
1 bay leaf
2 teaspoons salt
¼ teaspoon pepper
Sour cream

Combine meats and vegetables and add stock or water. Add seasonings and simmer slowly for several hours or until meat is tender. Remove meat from soup, cut into slices and serve with soup. Garnish soup with sour cream. Serves 4.

DUTCH VEGETABLE SOUP

2 cups dried Lima beans
1 large soupbone
2 cups tomatoes
2 cups grated corn
2 cups chopped cabbage
1 large turnip, diced
1 carrot, diced; 1 onion, sliced
Salt and pepper
1 teaspoon flour, ½ cup milk

Soak Lima beans in water for several hours. Wash soupbone thoroughly, cover with cold water and boil slowly for several hours. Skim off fat and add vegetables and drained beans. Season to taste. Cook until vegetables are tender, 1 hour. Mix flour with milk and stir into soup. Cook 15 minutes and serve hot. Serves 10.

Add ¼ pound liver, cut into small pieces, with soupbone.

OLD-FASHIONED VEGETABLE SOUP

2 pounds shin of beef with meat
¼ pound beef liver, diced
2 quarts cold water
2 teaspoons salt
½ cup shredded cabbage
½ cup diced carrots
½ cup diced celery root
2 tablespoons green pepper
1 small onion, diced
2 sprigs parsley, chopped
½ cup peas
½ cup diced potatoes
¼ pound spinach, chopped
1 cup tomatoes
½ cup diced turnip

Wash meat in running water and cut into small pieces. Add liver and water, heat to boiling and simmer 3 hours or until meat is tender. Add remaining ingredients and cook 1 hour longer or until vegetables are tender. Remove bone. Cool, remove fat. Reheat and serve for 6.

MINESTRONE

¼ pound bacon, chopped
¼ pound ham, chopped
¼ pound Italian sausage, chopped
2 onions, chopped
2 tomatoes, chopped
½ cup rice
½ cup dried beans or marrowfat
    peas (soaked in water 2 to 3
    hours)
¼ cup diced celery
6 cups meat stock
¼ head cabbage, shredded
1 cup mixed green vegetables
1½ teaspoons salt
⅛ teaspoon pepper
Grated Parmesan cheese

Fry bacon, ham, sausage and onions together until slightly browned. Add tomatoes, rice, soaked beans or peas, celery and stock and simmer until beans are tender, skimming off fat frequently. Add shredded cabbage and mixed green vegetables (peas, Lima beans, string beans) and simmer until soup is thick and vegetables are soft. Season with salt and pepper. Serve with grated cheese. Serves 4 to 6.

FRENCH ONION SOUP

4 medium onions
1 tablespoon butter
1 quart Brown Stock
½ teaspoon Worcestershire sauce
Salt and pepper
Rounds of toast
Grated Parmesan cheese

Slice onions thin and brown in butter. Add broth, Worcestershire sauce, salt and pepper and simmer until onions are tender. Pour soup into an earthen jar or casserole. Arrange toast on top of soup, sprinkle with grated cheese and place under broiler until cheese melts and browns. Serves 4
Rub casserole or toast with cut clove of garlic.

GREEN PEA SOUP

2 cups Brown Stock
1 quart water
4 cups green peas
¼ cup diced celery
1 onion
1 turnip, diced
2 sprigs mint
1 tablespoon flour
1 tablespoon fat
1 teaspoon salt
⅛ teaspoon pepper
½ teaspoon sugar

Combine brown stock, water, 3½ cups peas, celery, onion, turnip and mint. Cook until vegetables are tender. Rub through a sieve. Thin with stock or water, if necessary. Blend flour and fat and season with salt, pepper and sugar. Add to puréed vegetables gradually and heat to boiling, stirring constantly. Add remaining whole peas, cook until tender and serve. Serves 6.

Use 5 cups White Stock instead of brown stock and water. Use 1½ heads lettuce, shredded, instead of turnips and mint.

POLISH BARLEY SOUP

¾ cup pearl barley
8 cups soup stock
½ cup butter or other fat
2 onions, chopped
2 carrots, diced
1 turnip, diced
1 leek, chopped
½ cup chopped celery
⅔ cup sliced mushrooms
1 teaspoon salt
⅛ teaspoon pepper
4 tablespoons sour cream

Simmer barley in 1½ cups of stock until tender; add butter gradually. Boil chopped vegetables until tender in the remainder of the stock, then add the cooked barley and seasoning. When ready to serve add sour cream. Serves 6.

FISH SOUPS, CHOWDERS AND BISQUES

COURT BOUILLON

1⅓ tablespoons fat
1⅓ tablespoons flour
1 pound fish, sliced
2 cups tomatoes, 4 cups water
1 green pepper, chopped
1 small onion, chopped
½ clove garlic, minced
3 cloves, 1 sprig thyme
2 bay leaves
3 tablespoons lemon juice
1 teaspoon salt
½ teaspoon pepper
½ teaspoon cayenne
5 drops Tabasco sauce

Melt fat, add flour and brown slightly. Add remaining ingredients and simmer for 45 minutes. Serves 6.

FISH STOCK

2 pounds white fish or 2 pounds
    head and trimmings
1¼ quarts cold water
2 peppercorns, 1 clove
Sprig parsley, 1 bay leaf
1 tablespoon diced carrot
1 tablespoon diced celery
1 tablespoon diced onion

Cut fish into small pieces, combine with other ingredients and simmer for 1 to 2 hours. Strain through several thicknesses of cheesecloth. Reheat and serve hot, or use as stock in which to boil fish. Makes 1 quart stock.

Use fish stock as all or part of the liquid in fish recipes such as soups, chowders, creamed mixtures and bisques. It enhances the flavor.

FISH PURÉE

1 small onion, minced
1 quart milk
4 tablespoons butter
4 tablespoons flour
2 teaspoons salt
⅛ teaspoon pepper
2 cups cooked fish
Paprika

Scald minced onion in milk. Melt butter, blend in flour, salt and pepper, add milk gradually, stirring constantly. Force fish through a sieve and add to sauce. Serve hot, garnish with paprika. Serves 6.

BACK BAY FISH CHOWDER

¼ pound fat salt pork, sliced
2 cups diced fish
6 small potatoes, sliced
2 onions, chopped fine
3 cups boiling water
2 cups milk
½ teaspoon salt
Dash pepper
3 pilot biscuits

Fry salt pork in a deep kettle. When crisp remove pieces of pork and add fish, potatoes and onions. Cover with boiling water. Simmer for ½ hour, or until potato is tender. Add milk and cook 5 minutes longer. Season with salt and pepper. Before serving, add pilot biscuits. Serves 6.

Back Bay fish chowder is delicious served any place, for any occasion

POTATO AND FISH CHOWDER

1 pound haddock
5 potatoes; 1 onion, sliced
2 cups evaporated milk
2 cups water
3 tablespoons fat
Salt and pepper

Wash haddock; cut into small pieces. Pare potatoes, cut into small pieces and boil 5 minutes. Add sliced onion and fish. Cook until fish is done, about 20 minutes. Add milk, water and fat. Season with salt and pepper. Heat. Serves 5 or 6.

Use 1 cup tomato pulp in place of ½ cup water and ½ cup evaporated milk.

SMOKED FISH CHOWDER

Dice ½ pound salt pork and brown. Add ½ cup diced onion and cook until tender. Add 4 potatoes, diced; 1 bay leaf; ¼ teaspoon pepper and water to cover. Cook until potatoes are almost tender. Add 4 cups milk and 1¼ pounds smoked fillet of haddock, cubed; heat to boiling and simmer 10 minutes. Serves 6.

NEW ENGLAND CLAM CHOWDER

¼ pound salt pork, cubed
2 small onions, minced
1 quart shucked clams
6 to 8 medium potatoes, diced
5 cups water
Salt, if needed
½ teaspoon pepper
3 cups milk
6 to 8 common crackers, split
Cold milk

Brown salt pork in deep kettle. Add onions and cook together 2 to 3 minutes. Remove stomach from clams, chop hard parts and leave soft parts whole or chop them, as preferred. Combine potatoes and hard parts of clams, add to onions, cover with cold water, heat to boiling and simmer until potatoes are tender. Add soft parts of clams, seasonings and milk. Heat to boiling and add crackers which have been soaked in cold milk. Heat thoroughly. Serves 6 to 8.

MANHATTAN—Brown 2 tablespoons chopped green pepper and ½ cup chopped celery with onion. Use tomato juice instead of milk. Season with dash of cayenne and thyme.

SALT CODFISH CHOWDER

2 cups shredded salt codfish
3 cups diced potatoes
2 small onions, sliced
4 tablespoons salt pork fat
1 cup boiling water
2 tablespoons fat
2 tablespoons flour, Dash pepper
Dash cayenne, 4 cups milk
1 cup cream or evaporated milk

Soak codfish in cold water 1 hour, drain. Parboil potatoes 10 minutes, drain. Cook onions in salt pork fat, add potatoes, fish and boiling water, cook until potatoes are tender. Melt fat, blend in flour, pepper and cayenne, add milk gradually, stirring constantly. Combine mixtures, add cream and cook 5 minutes. Serves 6 to 8.

VARIATIONS

Omit milk and cream. Add 4 cups strained cooked tomatoes. Just before serving add ½ cup cracker crumbs. It may be necessary to add more tomatoes if mixture is thick. Or else, soften 8 common crackers in milk and add to chowder before serving.

With or without tomatoes, clam chowder is still New England's gift to the world

FISH MULLIGAN

1 pound any firm lean fish
4 large potatoes, 2 large onions
6 cups hot water
⅓ cup uncooked rice
2 green peppers, diced
⅓ cup diced bacon or salt pork
2 tablespoons minced parsley
Salt and pepper

Cut fish into chunks, slice potatoes and onions ½ inch thick. Place in a kettle, add water and bring to a boil. Add rice, green peppers, bacon or salt pork. Simmer about 30 minutes or until tender. Add parsley and a few slices of dry bread. Leftover vegetables, such as corn or peas may be added. Season to taste. Bring to a boil. Serves 6 to 8

CREOLE BOUILLA-BAISSE

1 pound fresh shrimp
12 cloves
1 tablespoon salt
1½ quarts boiling water
½ pound fresh mushrooms
2 tablespoons butter
2 large onions, chopped
2 cloves garlic
2 cups tomato pulp
2 cups water
3 bay leaves
1½ teaspoons curry powder
1 cup grated cheese
½ cup sherry
2 pounds fish fillets (red snapper and redfish are preferred)
1 pound scallops
2 tablespoons flour
Hot buttered toast

Wash shrimp thoroughly, add 4 cloves, salt and boiling water and

simmer 10 minutes. Remove shrimp from kettle, saving broth to use later. Cool, shell and remove intestinal vein (black line running along the back); and cut shrimp in half lengthwise. Cut mushrooms into thin slices, add to shrimp and allow to stand until needed. Melt butter and fry onions and garlic in it until golden brown; add tomato pulp and 2 cups water, 4 cloves, bay leaves, curry powder, cheese and ½ of the sherry. Simmer for 30 minutes. Season with more salt, if desired. Meanwhile, bring shrimp broth to boiling, add fillets of fish, scallops, 4 cloves and remainder of sherry, lower heat and simmer for 15 minutes. Combine shrimp and mushroom mixture with fish and cook for 5 minutes. Moisten flour with a little cold water and add to the boiling liquid as a slight thickening. Cook another 5 minutes. Remove pieces of fish from sauce, place on buttered slices of toast on large platter, pour sauce over fish and serve. Makes 12 to 15 portions. If desired, omit onion and curry powder. Add 2 leeks sliced and fry the same as the onions.

CRAB CHOWDER

3 slices salt pork
1 tablespoon onion juice
3 tablespoons flour
2 cups chicken stock or bouillon
2 cups cream or evaporated milk
2 cups tomato juice
1 tablespoon sugar
1 cup cooked potato cubes
4 cups crab meat
½ teaspoon salt
⅛ teaspoon pepper
⅛ teaspoon paprika
1 tablespoon fat

Parboil salt pork for 5 minutes, then place in a skillet and fry, add onion juice and flour and stir until smooth. Add stock and cream gradually, stirring constantly. When heated pour into the top of a double boiler and continue cooking over water. Add remaining ingredients and cook until the consistency of thick purée. Serve hot with croutons. Serves 8.

LOBSTER—Omit salt pork, tomato juice, potatoes and crab meat. Combine 5 tablespoons butter with onion juice. Add 2 cups milk, 4 cups cooked lobster meat, 2 tablespoons minced parsley and 1 teaspoon Worcestershire sauce. Follow directions as above.

CLAM BROTH

2 quarts clams, in shells
1¾ cups cold water
1 teaspoon butter

Wash and scrub clams very thoroughly with a stiff brush. Place clams in a kettle with water, cover kettle with a tight-fitting lid and steam clams until they open. Open the clams all the way to secure all the juice, strain the liquor through cheesecloth or very fine sieve and add butter. Reheat but do not let boil. Add salt if needed. Serve hot, plain or with 2 teaspoons of Salted Whipped Cream in each cup. Serves 6.

CLAM CUSTARD—Beat ½ cup cooled clam juice with 3 eggs. Pour into small baking dish, set in pan of hot water and bake in slow oven (325° F.) until custard is set, about 20 minutes. When cold, cut into small cubes, squares, diamonds or any attractive shape Place in soup bowls or cups and pour hot clam broth over them.

CRAB SOUP

1½ tablespoons butter
1½ tablespoons flour
1 teaspoon dry mustard
¼ teaspoon pepper
2 teaspoons salt
1 tablespoon Worcestershire sauce
3 cups hot milk
1 cup boiled and picked crab meat
1 tablespoon sherry

Melt butter and add flour, mustard, pepper, salt and Worcestershire sauce. Cook together for 10 to 15 minutes, stirring constantly until a smooth sauce results. Pour milk over crab meat; add both to seasoned sauce gradually stirring constantly. Before serving add sherry. Serve with additional Worcestershire sauce and Tabasco sauce. Serves 4.

CRAB AND TOMATO BISQUE

2 tablespoons butter
2 tablespoons flour
2 cups milk
½ teaspoon salt
⅛ teaspoon pepper
1 cup flaked crab meat
1 cup tomato juice

Melt butter in the top of a double boiler and add flour and blend. Add milk gradually and cook until thickened. Add seasonings and crab meat. A few minutes before serving heat tomato juice in another pan. When hot, and ready to serve, add tomato juice gradually to first mixture. Serve immediately. Serves 4.

CRAB GUMBO

¼ cup diced ham
½ clove garlic
2 cups sliced fresh okra
2 tablespoons fat
½ bay leaf
⅛ teaspoon thyme
½ teaspoon salt
6 peppercorns
6 diced tomatoes
1 cup hot water
½ pound crab flakes

Fry diced ham, garlic and okra in fat. When well-coated with fat, but not brown, add remaining ingredients, except crab flakes. Cook 20 minutes, add crab flakes and cook 15 minutes longer. Serve on mounds of flaky steamed rice. Serves 6.

MARYLAND CRAB—Blend 2 tablespoons butter and 1 tablespoon flour, add 2 quarts milk and heat to boiling. Add ¼ cup diced onion, 2 tablespoons minced parsley, ½ cup cooked celery, 1 teaspoon salt and ⅛ teaspoon pepper; cook until slightly thickened; add 2 cups flaked crab meat. Top with whipped cream. Serves 8.

BISQUE OF LOBSTER

1 medium-sized lobster
1 cup cold water
4 tablespoons butter
4 tablespoons flour
1 teaspoon salt
Dash pepper, Few grains cayenne
1 quart milk

Remove meat from freshly boiled lobster. Reserve the coral and green fat. Pour cold water into a kettle and add the broken claws, shell and the finely chopped tail meat. Simmer for 20 minutes. Strain. Melt butter, blend in flour, salt, pepper and cayenne, add milk gradually, stirring constantly. Cook 3 minutes; add lobster liquid. Add remainder of lobster meat, cut in dice. Just before serving, add coral mashed to a paste with green fat. Mix thoroughly, reheat and serve with croutons. Serves 6.

Reduce flour to 2 tablespoons. Add ½ cup very fine cracker crumbs to butter with remaining 2 tablespoons flour.

LOBSTER STEW

2 tablespoons butter
4 tablespoons flour
2 cups thin cream
Salt, Pepper
½ teaspoon sugar
2 cups lobster meat
1 egg yolk—if desired

Melt butter, add flour stirring well until smooth. Add cream gradually. Cook for 10 minutes, stirring constantly. Remove from heat. Season. Add lobster meat cut into small pieces. The stew should have the consistency of a fairly thick white sauce. Egg yolk added to the stew just before serving gives a nice color and richer flavor. The stew must not boil after the yolk has been added. Serves 4.

BOSTON OYSTER CHOWDER

1 quart oysters
6 potatoes, sliced thin
1 onion, sliced thin
1 cup water
2 tablespoons butter
1 tablespoon flour
1½ teaspoons salt
⅛ teaspoon pepper
3 cups milk
3 pilot biscuits

Drain oysters and remove any particles of shell. Strain liquor through a fine wire sieve. Boil potatoes and onion in oyster liquor and water until tender but not mushy. Melt butter, blend in flour, salt and pepper, add milk gradually, stirring constantly. Add oysters and cook 2 minutes. Combine with potatoes and onion and liquor in which they have been cooked. Add additional seasoning if necessary. Place pilot biscuits in the hot tureen. Pour chowder over them and serve. Serves 6.

QUAHOG CHOWDER—Use 1 quart shucked quahogs in place of oysters. Use salt pork fat instead of butter.

Two big bowls of oyster bisque with wafers may constitute the entire supper menu

OYSTER STEW

1 quart oysters
1 quart rich milk
2 tablespoons butter
1 tablespoon minced parsley
Dash onion salt or juice
Salt and pepper

Strain oyster liquor into saucepan; heat but do not boil. Heat milk in double boiler; stir in hot oyster liquor. Add butter and seasonings and oysters. When oysters puff and are crinkled at edge, serve at once. Serves 6.

VARIATIONS

Melt butter, blend in 2 tablespoons flour and add hot milk, stirring constantly, continue as above.

Heat oysters in their liquor about 5 minutes or until edges curl. Skim off top. Combine with scalded milk, add butter and seasonings.

Omit milk, parsley and onion. Dilute oyster liquor with water to make 2 cups. Add 2 cups hot cream, increase butter to 4 tablespoons and add 1 teaspoon celery salt. Use celery salt instead of onion salt.

CLAM STEW—Use clams in place of oysters.

BAKED OYSTER SOUP

3 pints rich milk
2 tablespoons butter
1 stalk celery, diced
12 salted crackers, crushed
Salt and pepper
3 dozen oysters

Bring milk to a boil. Add butter, celery and cracker crumbs. Season with salt and pepper. Drop in the oysters, 2 or 3 at a time, and as soon as the milk is almost ready to boil again pour into a large baking dish and put in the oven. Let brown. Stir under, and brown again until the dish has become a golden brown 3 times. Serve immediately. Serves 6.

BISQUE OF OYSTER

2 cups milk
1 cup dry bread crumbs
1 tablespoon butter
1 tablespoon flour
1 teaspoon salt, ⅛ teaspoon pepper
1 pint oysters, 2 cups water
1 slice onion, chopped fine
¼ cup diced celery
1 sprig parsley, chopped fine
1 bay leaf

Scald milk, add bread crumbs and cook in a double boiler for 20 minutes. Rub through a sieve. Melt butter, blend in flour, salt and pepper, add milk-crumb mixture gradually, stirring constantly, and cook 2 minutes. Chop oysters, place in a saucepan with their own liquor, add water, onion, celery, parsley and bay leaf. Simmer for 20 to 30 minutes. Rub through a fine sieve and combine with white sauce mixture. More milk or cream may be added if the bisque is thicker than desired. Serves 6.

Omit bread crumbs and increase oysters to 1 quart.

CLAM—Omit bread crumbs and use clams instead of oysters.

SALMON BISQUE

4 tablespoons butter
1 small onion, minced
4 tablespoons flour
2 teaspoons salt
1/4 teaspoon pepper
4 cups milk, scalded
1 cup canned salmon
1/4 cup cooked peas
Whipped cream

Melt butter, add onion and simmer 5 minutes, do not brown. Blend in flour, salt and pepper, add milk gradually, stirring constantly. Heat to boiling and cook 3 minutes. Remove skin and bone from salmon and rub through a sieve with peas. Add to milk mixture, reheat and serve at once, . garnished with whipped cream. Serves 6.

CREAM OF SALMON SOUP

1 cup salmon
1 quart milk
1 slice onion
2 tablespoons butter
2 tablespoons flour
1/8 teaspoon pepper
1 teaspoon salt

Drain oil from salmon, remove skin and bones and rub through a coarse sieve. Heat milk and onion to scalding, remove onion. Melt butter, blend in flour, pepper, and salt; add milk gradually, stirring constantly. Add salmon, and cook until smooth and slightly thickened. It is best to prepare the soup in a double boiler, but it can be made over direct heat if care is taken not to scorch or boil. Serves 6.
Omit milk, salt and pepper. Use 2 cans condensed tomato soup and 2 1/2 cups water.
Omit milk, butter, flour, pepper and salt. Add 1 can condensed cream of mushroom soup and 1 can water.

SALMON AND PEA CHOWDER

2 strips bacon
1 medium onion, sliced
3 cups potato slices, 1/4 inch thick
3 cups boiling water
2 teaspoons salt
2 cups flaked canned salmon
2 1/2 cups cooked peas
2 cups milk

Dice bacon, add onion and sauté until a golden brown. Add potatoes and boiling water and cook until potatoes are tender. Add remaining ingredients, heat to boiling and serve hot. Serves 8.

SHRIMP CHOWDER

1/2 cup salt pork, cut in cubes
1 onion, chopped
1 quart boiling water
1 cup diced celery
6 medium potatoes, diced
2 teaspoons salt
1/4 teaspoon pepper
2 cups milk
1 pound shrimp, cooked
2 tablespoons fat
2 tablespoons flour

Fry salt pork carefully, taking care not to scorch it. When crisp, strain meat, add onion and cook to a light yellow. Add water and celery and simmer for 15 minutes. Add potatoes and seasonings and cook until potatoes are tender, about 10 minutes. Add milk and shrimp and heat to scalding; add fat and flour which have been blended together, continue heating 3 or 4 minutes, stirring occasionally to keep smooth. Serve hot, for 6.

SHRIMP AND QUAHOG—Use only 1/2 pound shrimp. Add 1/2 pint shucked quahogs with their liquor to the mixture when the shrimp are added. Serve with minced parsley on top.

SHRIMP GUMBO FILÉ

1 bunch green onions
1 tablespoon bacon drippings
1 cup peeled and chopped tomatoes
6 cups soup stock
1 pod red pepper, diced
1 green pepper, diced
1/2 teaspoon thyme
1 bay leaf, Salt
1 pound shrimp, cooked
1 tablespoon filé

Clean green onions, reserving 1 cup of the green tops. Heat bacon drippings in a saucepan. Sauté onions, which have been chopped fine, about 10 minutes. Add tomatoes and cook for 5 minutes. Add stock, peppers, green onion tops cut into strips thyme, bay leaf and salt. Heat to boiling and cook 10 minutes. Add shrimp which have been cut in halves. Cover kettle closely and cook slowly for 1 1/2 hours. Remove from heat and stir in filé. Serve at once with hot boiled rice. Serves 4.

GUMBO CHOU

1 large onion
1 pound fresh okra
1 clove garlic, Flour
2 tablespoons butter
3 cups boiling soup stock or water
2 tomatoes, chopped
Thyme, Parsley
1/2 pound veal, 1/2 pound ham
1 1/2 pounds shrimp, cooked

Chop onion, okra and garlic. Sprinkle lightly with flour and fry in butter until light brown. Add boiling soup stock or water, tomatoes, thyme and parsley to taste. Chop veal and ham fine and fry until brown; add to above mixture. Heat to boiling, add shrimp and cook slowly for 1 1/2 hours, adding hot water as necessary during cooking. Serve over boiled rice. Serves 6 to 8.

BURGOO FOR SMALL PARTIES

2 pounds pork shank
2 pounds veal shank
2 pounds beef shank
2 pounds breast of lamb
¼ pound salt pork
1 4-pound fat hen
8 quarts water
3 large potatoes
3 large onions
3 large carrots
2 green peppers
2 cups chopped cabbage
1 quart cooked tomatoes
2 cups canned corn
2 pods red pepper
1 cup butter (Lima) beans
1 bunch parsley
Salt and cayenne
4 teaspoons Worcestershire sauce

Cook meat in boiling water until tender. Remove from liquor. Cool. Remove meat from bones and dice. Pare and dice potatoes, onions and carrots. Remove seeds from green peppers and dice. Combine meat, vegetables and meat stock. Cook until mixture is thick. Season with salt, cayenne and Worcestershire sauce. Serves 25.

CORN CHOWDER

¼ pound fat salt pork
1 onion, sliced
3 cups diced boiled potatoes
2 cups boiling water
1 cup cooked corn, fresh or canned
4 cups hot milk
½ teaspoon salt
Dash pepper, Parsley

Cut pork into small pieces and try out. Add onion and cook until tender. Add potatoes, boiling water, corn and hot milk. Season with salt and pepper and heat to boiling. Serve garnished with parsley. Serves 6 to 8.

Chowder day once a week will step up the family's nutrition and be easy on the budget

CORN TOMATO CHOWDER

2 ounces salt pork
1 small onion, sliced
2½ cups (1 No. 2 can) corn
2 cups diced potatoes
1½ cups tomatoes
1 teaspoon salt
1 tablespoon sugar, Dash pepper
1 quart boiling water
1 cup evaporated milk

Cut pork into small pieces and fry slowly to a golden brown in a large saucepan. Add onion and cook slowly without browning for 5 minutes. Add corn, potatoes and tomatoes in alternate layers. Sprinkle with salt, sugar and pepper, then add water and cook slowly until potatoes are tender. Remove from heat and stir milk in slowly. Serves 6 to 8.

CORN AND POTATO CHOWDER

Combine 2½ cups cooked corn, 2 cups diced potatoes, 1 tablespoon butter, ¼ cup diced onion, ½ teaspoon salt, ⅛ teaspoon pepper and 1 cup boiling water. Cook until potatoes are tender. Add 2 cups hot milk and thicken with 1 tablespoon flour mixed with 1 tablespoon cold water. Heat to boiling. Serves 4 to 6.

CELERY CHOWDER

4 cups cooked diced celery
1 small onion, minced
1 cup cooked diced carrots
2 tablespoons butter
1 tablespoon flour, 2 teaspoons salt
¼ teaspoon pepper
3 cups milk, scalded
2 egg yolks, well beaten

Rub celery through a sieve. Sauté onion and carrots in butter until delicately browned and combine with celery. Blend in flour, salt and pepper; add milk, gradually, stirring constantly; heat to boiling and cook 3 minutes. Before serving add egg yolks and cook 2 minutes. Serve with Cheese Puffs, for 6.

LIMA BEAN CHOWDER

2 slices bacon
2 small onions, minced
4 potatoes, pared and diced
3 carrots, diced
2 cups cooked Lima beans
1 teaspoon salt
2 cups Medium White Sauce

Dice bacon, cook until crisp, drain. Cook onions in bacon fat until lightly browned. Add bacon, potatoes, carrots, Lima beans and salt and cover with boiling water. Cook until vegetables are tender. Add white sauce, heat and serve. Serves 6.

PARSNIP CHOWDER

1/8 pound salt pork, diced
1 medium onion, diced
1 1/2 cups diced parsnips
2 cups diced potatoes
3 cups boiling water
1 teaspoon salt
1/4 teaspoon pepper
4 cups milk, scalded
3 tablespoons fat

Sauté salt pork and onion together for 5 minutes. Add parsnips, potatoes, boiling water, salt and pepper; heat to boiling and simmer until vegetables are tender, about 30 minutes. Add milk and fat. Serves 6 to 8.

POLISH SOUR MILK SOUP

4 cups sour milk
2 cups sweet cream
1 cup dill pickle or sour beet juice
1 cup cooked beet tops
Few sprigs dill, chopped
2 cucumbers, pared, sliced and salted
3 hard-cooked eggs
1 1/2 cups cooked veal, diced
1/2 teaspoon salt
Dash pepper

Beat sour milk and cream separately until bubbles show on the surface, add juice, chopped beet tops, dill and cucumbers. Mix all together, adding the chopped hard-cooked eggs and veal. Season to taste, place on ice and when serving, place a piece of ice in each plate. Serves 6 to 8.

POTATO CHOWDER

1/3 cup diced salt pork
2 cups diced potatoes
1 cup diced turnips
1 cup diced carrots
1 medium onion, minced
1 stalk celery, cut into small pieces
1 green pepper or pimiento
2 cups Thin White Sauce
Salt and pepper

Fry pork and brown vegetables in the fat. Add boiling water to cover. Cook until tender. Add white sauce and season with salt and pepper to taste. Serves 6.

TOMATO CHOWDER

1/2 cup diced salt pork
1 medium onion, minced
1 cup diced carrots
1 cup diced potatoes
1 cup diced celery
1/2 cup boiling water
2 cups tomatoes, canned or fresh
4 tablespoons fat
4 tablespoons flour
1/2 teaspoon salt
1/4 teaspoon pepper
4 cups milk, scalded

Sauté pork until brown, add onion, carrot, potato and celery, and sauté until brown. Add boiling water, cover and cook until vegetables are tender. Add tomatoes and heat to boiling. (If fresh tomatoes are used cook until tender.) Melt fat, blend in flour, salt and pepper; add milk gradually and cook until smooth. Add vegetable mixture to milk, heat and serve immediately. Serves 6.

VEGETABLE CHOWDER

3 cups diced potatoes
2 cups diced carrots
1/4 pound salt pork, diced
1/2 cup diced onion
1 green pepper, diced
2 tablespoons flour
2 cups milk
2 cups canned tomatoes, hot
1 teaspoon salt
1/8 teaspoon pepper

Cover potatoes and carrots with water or stock and cook until tender. Sauté pork, onion and green pepper about 5 minutes but do not brown; add flour and blend. Add milk and cook 5 minutes, stirring constantly until smooth. Add remaining ingredients; serve at once. Serves 8.

VEGETABLE CHOWDER DE LUXE

2 cups chopped celery
2 cups cooked corn
1 onion, chopped
2 tablespoons diced green pepper
1 cup cooked tomatoes
2 1/2 cups cold water
1 teaspoon salt
1/8 teaspoon pepper
4 tablespoons butter
3 tablespoons flour
2 cups milk, scalded
1/2 cup grated cheese
1/2 cup diced pimiento
1/4 teaspoon paprika

Combine first 8 ingredients, heat to boiling and simmer 1/2 hour. Melt butter, blend in flour; add milk gradually, stirring constantly; heat to boiling and cook 5 minutes. Add to vegetable mixture with cheese, pimiento and paprika. Heat until cheese is melted. Serves 6.

VEGETABLE AND HAMBURGER CHOWDER

1/4 pound salt pork
1 pound hamburger
2 carrots, chopped
1/2 cup diced celery
1 medium onion, chopped
2 cups cooked tomatoes
2 teaspoons salt
1/8 teaspoon pepper
1/4 cup rice or barley
1 1/2 quarts boiling water
2 cups cubed potatoes

Fry salt pork until browned. When crisp remove pieces of pork and brown hamburger in fat; add carrots, celery, onion, tomatoes, salt, pepper, barley, pork and boiling water. Heat to boiling and simmer slowly 1 hour. Add potatoes and cook another hour or until potatoes are tender. Serve as a main dish for luncheon or supper. Serves 6 to 8.

STANDARD CREAM SOUP

2 tablespoons butter or other fat
2 tablespoons flour
1 teaspoon salt
¼ teaspoon pepper
4 cups milk or milk and stock
2 cups vegetable pulp

Melt butter, blend in flour, salt and pepper. Add milk gradually, stirring constantly, and cook until mixture begins to boil. Add hot vegetable pulp and serve immediately. Other seasonings which may be added are celery salt, onion juice or thyme. Serves 6.

CREAM OF ASPARAGUS SOUP

1 pound asparagus
4 cups milk, scalded
2 tablespoons butter
2 tablespoons flour
1 teaspoon salt
⅛ teaspoon pepper

Wash asparagus, cut off tips 1½ inches from top, cover with boiling water and cook uncovered until tender. Remove and set aside, add remainder of asparagus and cook until tender. Drain, rub through a sieve and add to milk. Melt butter, blend in flour, salt and pepper, add asparagus mixture gradually and heat to boiling, stirring constantly; cook 3 minutes. Add asparagus tips and serve hot with toasted crusts. Serves 6.

Use 2 cups chicken stock for 2 cups of milk.
Omit water and milk. Cook asparagus in 6 cups soup stock. Just before serving add ½ cup cream or evaporated milk.

CREAM OF ARTICHOKE SOUP
—Use 2 cups cubed Jerusalem artichokes in place of asparagus, use 3 cups water. Just before serving, pour soup over 1 well-beaten egg.

CREAM OF BEET SOUP

1 medium onion, minced
1 tablespoon fat
1 cup water
1 cup chopped cooked beets
½ cup meat stock
1 teaspoon salt
Dash pepper
1 cup evaporated milk, scalded

Cook onion slowly in fat until a light yellow. Add water, beets and meat stock, simmer until onions are tender. Add salt and pepper and milk, heat to boiling and serve at once. Serves 4.

CREAM OF CARROT SOUP

2 cups chopped carrots
2 cups water
½ cup rice
2 cups milk
2 medium onions, sliced
4 tablespoons butter
2 tablespoons flour
1½ teaspoons salt
⅛ teaspoon pepper
Chopped watercress

Cook carrots in water until tender. Combine rice and milk in the top of a double boiler and cook until tender. Combine carrot mixture with rice mixture. Sauté onions in butter until a light yellow, add flour, salt and pepper. Blend. Add carrot and rice mixture gradually and cook for 3 minutes, stirring constantly. Press through a sieve, reheat and serve very hot, garnished with watercress. Serves 4.

CREAM OF CARROT AND POTATO SOUP

4 medium potatoes
3 large carrots
1 onion
1 tablespoon butter
1 tablespoon flour
2 cups milk
Salt and pepper

Pare and slice potatoes, carrots and onion; boil in salted water to cover until very tender. Rub through a coarse sieve, saving the stock. Prepare a thin white sauce with butter, flour and milk and add to vegetable pulp and stock. Reheat, season and beat with rotary beater. Garnish with a spoonful of whipped cream, if desired Serves 6.

"Who for such dainties would not stoop? Soup of the evening, Beautiful soup"

When you pop corn Sunday evening use some to garnish the creamed corn soup

FRESH CORN SOUP

1 cup fresh corn
2 cups boiling water
2 tablespoons butter
2 tablespoons flour
½ teaspoon salt
⅛ teaspoon pepper
1 teaspoon minced onion
2 cups milk
Finely chopped spinach

Simmer corn and water together for 20 minutes. Press through a coarse sieve. Melt butter, blend in flour, salt, pepper and onion; add milk gradually. Heat to boiling, stirring constantly, and add strained corn. Cook until thickened, about 5 minutes. Serve garnished with spinach. Serves 4.

VARIATIONS

Increase corn to 2 cups and cook in 1 cup water. Increase milk to 3 cups.
Omit water. Use 2 cups canned corn, creamed style.

POPCORN—Reheat and add to cream of corn soup just before serving.

RIPE OLIVE SOUP

3 cups milk
1 tablespoon grated onion
1½ tablespoons butter
1½ tablespoons flour
1 teaspoon salt
¼ teaspoon pepper
⅓ cup cooked diced celery
⅔ cup diced ripe olives

Combine milk and onion and heat to boiling, strain. Melt butter, blend in flour, salt and pepper, add milk gradually, stirring constantly. Heat to boiling and cook slowly for 5 minutes. Add celery and olives. Reheat and serve with Cheese Sticks. Serves 4.

CAULIFLOWER SOUP

1 medium cauliflower
4 cups boiling water
2 cups milk, scalded
4 tablespoons butter
2 slices onion
4 tablespoons flour
2 teaspoons salt, Dash cayenne
1 egg yolk, slightly beaten
2 tablespoons grated cheese

Cook cauliflower in boiling water, uncovered until tender. Strain, rubbing cauliflower through the sieve into liquid and add milk. Melt butter, add onion and sauté until tender, but not brown. Blend in flour, salt and cayenne, add milk mixture gradually, stirring constantly and cook 5 minutes. . Pour gradually over egg yolk and mix well. Serve in bouillon cups, garnished with cheese. Serves 6.

CREAM OF CABBAGE SOUP

1 small head cabbage
2 cups boiling water
2 tablespoons butter
1 tablespoon minced onion
2 tablespoons flour
1 teaspoon salt
⅛ teaspoon pepper, Dash cayenne
2 cups milk, scalded

Cut cabbage very fine, add boiling water and cook until soft, then press through a sieve and return to liquor. Melt butter, add onion and simmer for 3 minutes. Blend in flour, salt, pepper and cayenne. Add milk and cabbage mixture gradually, stirring constantly. Strain. Reheat and serve hot garnished with Cheese Balls or Puffs. Serves 6.

CREAM OF CELERY SOUP

2 cups finely diced celery
1 slice onion
4 cups hot milk
3 tablespoons butter
3 tablespoons flour
1½ teaspoons salt
½ teaspoon pepper

Cook celery and onion with 1 cup milk in the top of a double boiler until tender, about 20 minutes. Remove onion. Melt butter, blend in flour, salt and pepper, add remaining milk gradually, stirring constantly. Heat to boiling and cook 3 minutes. Add celery and milk mixture. Serve hot garnished with chopped parsley. Accompany soup with hot Cheese Sticks. Serves 6.
Use 1 cup of cream or evaporated milk for 1 cup milk, if a richer soup is desired.

CREAM OF CUCUMBER SOUP

4 cucumbers
1 cup chopped celery
2 tablespoons chopped onion
1 tablespoon chopped green pepper
4 cups milk
4 tablespoons butter
2 tablespoons flour
1 teaspoon salt
Dash pepper
1 cup cream or evaporated milk
Pimiento Soup Cream

Wash cucumbers, pare and chop fine. Place in a double boiler, add celery, onion, green pepper and milk, cook for 20 minutes or until cucumber is tender. Combine butter, flour, salt and pepper, add milk mixture gradually and cook for 10 minutes, stirring constantly until thickened. Press through a sieve, add cream or evaporated milk and reheat. Serve garnished with pimiento soup cream. Serves 6.
Use 4 cups chicken stock for the milk.

CHEF'S CREAM OF MUSHROOM SOUP

4 tablespoons fat
1/2 pound fresh mushrooms
2 tablespoons flour
4 cups chicken or veal stock
1 teaspoon salt
1/8 teaspoon pepper
1 cup cream or evaporated milk

Melt fat, add mushrooms which have been washed and chopped and sauté until tender. Blend in flour, add chicken or veal stock, heat to boiling and cook 5 minutes, stirring constantly until thickened. Add seasonings and cream, heat and serve hot. Serves 4 to 6.
Omit stock and cream and use 5 cups milk.

CREAM OF MUSHROOM SOUP

1/4 pound mushrooms
2 1/2 cups water
2 tablespoons butter
2 tablespoons flour
1 teaspoon salt
2 cups milk
Chopped parsley

Wash and skin mushrooms. Simmer skins in 1/2 cup of water. Chop mushroom caps and stems, add remaining 2 cups water and simmer until tender. Melt butter, blend in flour and salt, add milk gradually and cook in a double boiler, stirring constantly until thickened. Add chopped mushrooms with stock and stock drained from skins. Heat and serve garnished with chopped parsley. Serves 6.

One passes to the entrée with regret when the soup has been cream of mushroom

CHESTNUT SOUP

2 cups blanched chestnuts
3 cups water
2 cups milk, scalded
2 tablespoons minced onion
4 tablespoons butter
2 tablespoons flour
1 teaspoon salt
1/4 teaspoon pepper
1/8 teaspoon celery salt
Dash nutmeg
1 cup cream or evaporated milk
Chopped parsley

To shell and blanch chestnuts: wash and discard those that float. Dry and with a sharp knife make a cross on both sides of the nuts. Place in a baking dish with 1 teaspoon shortening, bake in a hot oven (450°F.) about 10 minutes. Cool and remove shell and brown skin with a knife. Cook chestnuts in water until tender, press through a sieve and add milk. Cook onion in butter until tender, but not brown. Blend in flour, salt, pepper, celery salt and nutmeg. Add milk and chestnut mixture, gradually, stirring constantly. Cook 5 minutes, add cream, heat to boiling garnish with parsley and serve, for 6.

CREAM OF ONION SOUP

6 medium onions
3 tablespoons butter
3 tablespoons flour
1 teaspoon salt
1/4 teaspoon pepper
4 cups hot milk
2 tablespoons grated cheese

Cut onions into slices, cover with boiling water, cook until tender and rub through a sieve. Melt butter blend in flour, salt and pepper, add milk and onion purée gradually, stirring constantly. Heat to boiling and cook 3 minutes. Serve hot garnished with cheese. Serves 6.

A rotary egg beater does the trick when making old-fashioned potato soup

OLD-FASHIONED POTATO SOUP

8 potatoes, cubed
1 quart milk
Salt and pepper
1 tablespoon butter
½ cup flour
1 egg, well beaten
¼ cup milk

Boil potatoes until soft. Drain. Add milk and beat thoroughly, season to taste. Work butter into flour and add egg and milk. Drop by teaspoonfuls into hot milk. Cover saucepan and cook about 10 minutes. Serve at once. Serves 4.

POTATO LEEK SOUP

3 tablespoons fat
1 cup sliced leeks
4 cups cold water
1 bay leaf
2 tablespoons chili sauce or catchup
2 medium potatoes, diced
½ small onion, grated
¼ cup chopped celery
2 tablespoons minced parsley
1 teaspoon salt
⅛ teaspoon pepper
1 cup milk

Melt fat, add leeks and cook but do not brown; add water, bay leaf and chili sauce. Cover and simmer for 20 minutes. Add potatoes, onion, celery, parsley, salt and pepper. Cook until potatoes are soft. Add milk and heat to boiling. Serve with croutons. Makes 4 portions.

GRATED POTATO—Cook thin slice garlic; 2 leeks, sliced; 1 onion, minced and 6 uncooked potatoes, grated in 6 cups soup stock until tender. Season, for 8.

SOUR CREAM POTATO SOUP

2 cups diced potatoes
1 cup boiling water
1 teaspoon salt
1 small onion, sliced
½ teaspoon pepper
2 cups sour cream
Minced parsley

Combine first 5 ingredients and cook together for 15 minutes. Add cream and cook until potatoes are tender. Serve hot. Garnish with parsley. Makes 6 portions.

CREAM OF LIMA BEAN SOUP

½ cups canned or cooked
   Lima beans
. quart cold water
: tablespoons fat
. small onion, diced
¼ cup diced carrot
: tablespoons flour
. teaspoon salt
½ teaspoon pepper
½ teaspoon paprika
Dash Tabasco sauce
2 cups milk, scalded
Chopped watercress

Cook beans with their liquor and
water together until beans are
very tender, then rub through a
sieve. Melt fat, add onion and
carrot, cook for 5 minutes. Blend
in flour, salt, pepper, paprika and
Tabasco sauce and add to bean
mixture. Add milk, heat to boiling, stirring constantly, and serve
hot garnished with chopped watercress. Serves 4 to 6.

KIDNEY BEAN SOUP—Substi-
tute canned or cooked kidney
beans for Lima beans.

CREAM OF PEA SOUP

2½ cups canned peas
½ teaspoon onion juice
4 tablespoons butter
4 tablespoons flour
2 teaspoons salt
¼ teaspoon pepper
4 cups milk, scalded
Whipped cream

Combine peas and liquor with
onion juice and cook for 10 minutes. Rub through a sieve. Melt
butter, blend in flour, salt and
pepper, add milk gradually, stirring constantly. Heat to boiling
and add pea purée. Serve very
hot garnished with whipped cream
or popcorn (popped). Serves 6.

FRESH PEA SOUP—Use cooked
fresh peas, which have been
cooked in a small amount of
water, instead of canned peas.

CREAM OF PEANUT BUTTER SOUP

¼ cup butter
1 tablespoon minced onion
1 tablespoon flour
1 cup peanut butter
1 quart chicken stock
Dash pepper
1 teaspoon salt
1 cup cream

Melt butter, add onion and simmer until tender but not brown.
Add flour and peanut butter and
stir to a smooth paste. Add stock
gradually, season and cook for 20
minutes in a double boiler, stirring constantly until thickened.
Strain and add cream. Serves 8.

CREAM OF SPINACH SOUP

1 pound spinach
4 cups veal or chicken stock
2 tablespoons fat
2 tablespoons flour
½ teaspoon salt
¼ teaspoon pepper
2 cups hot milk; Pimiento, diced

Wash spinach thoroughly. Place
in a kettle and cook until tender.
It is not necessary to add any
water. Rub cooked spinach
through a sieve and combine
with spinach water and veal or
chicken stock. Melt fat, blend in
flour, salt and pepper, add milk
gradually and cook 1 minute.
Add spinach mixture and heat to
boiling. Serve hot garnished with
diced pimiento. Serves 6.
Add dash of nutmeg to soup.

LETTUCE SOUP—Use 2 large
heads of lettuce for spinach.

CHICORY SOUP—Use 3 or 4
heads chicory for spinach.

SPINACH PURÉE—Omit stock
and milk. Use 2 cups liquid, milk
and liquid from spinach. Reduce
fat and flour to 1 tablespoon
each. Season with celery salt.

SQUASH SOUP

4 cups milk
2 slices onion
¼ bay leaf
2 cups cooked and strained squash
3 tablespoons butter
3 tablespoons flour
1 teaspoon salt
Dash cayenne
¼ teaspoon celery salt

Scald milk with onion and bay
leaf, strain and add squash. Melt
butter, blend in flour, salt, cayenne and celery salt, add milk
mixture gradually, stirring constantly and cook 5 minutes. Serve
with croutons. Serves 6.
Add 1 bouillon cube to milk.

POTATO AND CABBAGE SOUP

¼ cup chopped onion
2 tablespoons fat
3 cups water
1 teaspoon salt
2 cups diced potatoes
2 cups chopped cabbage
1 tall can evaporated milk

Cook onion slowly in fat until
yellow. Add water, salt, potatoes
and cabbage and cook until tender, about 20 minutes. Add milk
and reheat. Serve with chopped
parsley, a dash of paprika or
toasted bread cubes. Makes 6
portions.

POTATO AND SPINACH SOUP
—Use spinach in place of cabbage.

DUTCH POTATO—Omit cabbage
and fat. Brown 3 slices bacon.
Add remaining ingredients and 2
tablespoons chopped parsley.

HUNGARIAN POTATO—Omit
cabbage. Add ½ cup diced celery and ¼ cup chopped pimiento.

TURNIP SOUP—Use 1 cup
mashed potatoes and 2 cups
mashed turnips instead of cabbage and diced potatoes. Omit
½ of onion.

CREAM OF TOMATO SOUP

2 cups cooked tomatoes
1/2 tablespoon minced onion
1 teaspoon salt
1/4 teaspoon pepper
Dash cayenne
2 teaspoons sugar
2 tablespoons butter or other fat
2 tablespoons flour
1 quart milk, scalded

Cook tomatoes, onion, salt, pepper, cayenne and sugar together for 15 minutes; strain. Melt butter, blend in flour, add milk gradually, stirring constantly. Add tomato mixture gradually to milk mixture, stirring constantly. Serve immediately with Watercress Cream Garnish. Serves 6.

TOMATO CHEESE SOUP—Add 1 cup grated strong American cheese just before serving.

TOMATO OYSTER—Heat 1 pint oysters in 1 tablespoon fat until edges curl. Add to milk.

For luncheon on a cold day nothing surpasses a rich vegetable creamed soup

MOCK TOMATO BISQUE

4 cups milk
3/4 cup dry bread crumbs
2 cups fresh or canned tomatoes
1/2 onion
6 cloves
2 teaspoons sugar
Sprig of parsley
1/4 bay leaf
1/2 teaspoon salt
1/8 teaspoon pepper
1/3 cup butter

Scald milk with bread crumbs. Cook tomatoes with onion, cloves, sugar, parsley, bay leaf, salt, pepper and butter for 15 minutes. Force through a sieve. Add tomatoes to milk and serve at once with croutons or crisp crackers. Serves 6.

Use cracker crumbs instead of bread crumbs.

CREAM OF VEGETABLE SOUP

1/4 cup uncooked rice
1 quart boiling water
2 teaspoons salt
2 cups chopped vegetables (onions, tomatoes, turnips, carrots, greens)
2 cups evaporated milk

Boil rice in water until almost tender. Add salt and vegetables and continue boiling until vegetables are tender. Add milk and cook until heated. Serves 6.

CREAM OF WATERCRESS SOUP

1 cup chopped watercress
2 cups chicken broth or stock
4 tablespoons fat
4 tablespoons flour
1/4 teaspoon salt
Dash pepper
2 cups rich milk
1 teaspoon chopped parsley
1 teaspoon chopped chives

Simmer watercress in chicken broth or stock 5 to 10 minutes. Melt fat, blend in flour, salt, pepper and add watercress gradually, stirring constantly. Cook until thick and smooth. Add remaining ingredients and heat to boiling. Serve at once, for 4.

Use milk for chicken broth, add 1 teaspoon salt and 1 bouillon cube.

Use spinach or lettuce instead of watercress. Serve with hot toast

CHICKEN BOUILLON

3- to 4-pound stewing chicken
10 chicken feet
3 to 4 quarts boiling water
2 stalks celery or ¼ cup diced celery root
1 onion, sliced
1 tablespoon salt
¼ teaspoon pepper
⅛ teaspoon nutmeg

Clean chicken and cut into small pieces. Scald chicken feet; skin and remove nails. Pour boiling water over chicken, feet, celery and onion, cover, heat to boiling and simmer until chicken is tender, about 3 hours. Remove chicken, strain stock and season. Serves 8.

Chicken meat may be creamed, used for croquettes, salad or casserole dishes.

CHICKEN VEGETABLE SOUP— Add 1 diced onion, 1 diced carrot, ½ cup diced celery, ½ cup tomatoes to strained stock and simmer until tender.

CHICKEN BROTH

3-pound stewing chicken
2 quarts cold water
2 tablespoons sago, tapioca, rice or barley (soaked 1 hour)
1 teaspoon salt

Wash chicken and remove skin and fat. Cut into small pieces, crack the bones, place in a kettle with cold water and let stand ½ hour. Add sago or tapioca, heat to boiling and simmer, covered, for 3 hours. Add salt after 2 hours of cooking. When chicken is tender, strain broth, skim off fat and serve. The fat may be more easily removed if the broth is allowed to cool thoroughly before skimming. Makes 1 quart broth. If desired, add ¼ cup diced carrot, ½ cup diced celery, ½ bay leaf and 1 teaspoon minced onion to recipe.

CHICKEN SOUP

3- to 4-pound stewing chicken
½ pound uncooked ham
1 onion
2 to 3 quarts cold water
¼ cup rice
1 tablespoon chopped parsley
½ teaspoon salt, Dash pepper
1 tablespoon flour
1 tablespoon chicken fat, melted
1 cup hot milk

Cut chicken into quarters, place in a kettle with ham and onion and add water. Heat to boiling and simmer until meat is tender, then strain, reserving the meat to be used in any way desired. Remove all possible fat and to 1¼ quarts of soup (the remainder can be used for sauce with the meat) add well washed rice, chopped parsley, salt and pepper. Simmer until rice is tender. Blend flour and chicken fat together, add milk gradually, combine with stock and cook for 5 minutes, until mixture is thick. Season and serve for 6.

NOODLE—Omit ham, rice, flour fat and milk. Add ½ cup diced celery and ¼ cup diced carrots with onion to water. Add 2 cups noodles and cook 15 minutes.

CHICKEN MUSHROOM SOUP

6 cups chicken broth
¼ cup diced celery
½ onion, diced
12 mushrooms, sliced
½ cup cooked chicken white meat
Salt to taste, Dash pepper
2 tablespoons soy sauce
2 eggs, well beaten

Combine broth, celery and onion, cook until tender, then add mushrooms and chicken. Boil about 10 minutes. Add salt, pepper and sauce, add eggs gradually and cook until firm. Serve at once. Serves 6 to 8.

THRIFTY CHICKEN SOUP

Bones of fowl
Leftover gravy
Cold water
¼ cup sliced carrot
¼ cup diced celery
1 small onion, sliced
1 teaspoon salt
⅛ teaspoon pepper
Chicken scraps, diced

Break carcass into pieces, add gravy and water to cover. Heat to boiling and simmer for 2 to 3 hours. Add carrot, celery, onion, salt and pepper and cook ½ hour longer. Strain and add chicken scraps. If a stronger flavored soup is desired add 1 or 2 chicken bouillon cubes. Serves 4, or more, depending on amount of leftover fowl.

Add 1 cup cream or evaporated milk after straining stock.

Duck, turkey or goose may be used in the same way.

CHICKEN CHOWDER

½ stewing chicken
2 pounds stewing beef
3 quarts cold water
½ cup green or wax beans
½ head cabbage, quartered
4 potatoes, diced
4 sweet potatoes, diced
3 carrots, diced
2 leeks, diced
½ squash, diced
4 ears corn (cut from cobs)
2 teaspoons salt
⅛ teaspoon pepper
6 tablespoons rice

Combine chicken, beef and water. Cook for 1 hour. Add vegetables and seasonings and cook 1 hour longer or until tender. Twenty minutes before serving, add rice which has been thoroughly washed and cook until tender. Serve hot. Serves 8 to 10.

Omit beans and add ½ cup shelled peas when rice is added.

CHESTNUT PURÉE

3 cups chestnuts
1 tablespoon cooking oil
4 cups Chicken Broth
½ teaspoon salt
Dash pepper, Few grains cayenne
2 cups cream or evaporated milk

Wash chestnuts and discard those which float. Shell by cutting a ½-inch gash on the flat side of each nut. Place in a heavy skillet, add oil and shake over heat 5 minutes. Roast in a very hot oven (450°F.) about 10 to 15 minutes. Take from oven and remove shells and skins with a sharp knife. Add chestnuts to chicken broth and cook until chestnuts are soft. Rub nuts through a coarse sieve and return to broth. Add salt, pepper, cayenne and cream or evaporated milk, reheat and serve 6 to 8.

CHICKEN GUMBO

1 small stewing chicken
2 tablespoons flour
1 onion, chopped
3 tablespoons fat, melted
4 cups okra, sliced or chopped
2 cups tomato pulp
Few sprigs parsley, chopped
4 cups water
Salt and pepper

Clean chicken and cut into serving portions. Dredge lightly with flour and sauté with onion in fat. When chicken is browned, add okra, tomatoes, parsley and water. Season to taste with salt and pepper. Simmer until chicken is tender and okra well cooked— about 2½ hours. Add water as needed during cooking. Serves 6.

Add 1 cup diced celery, ½ cup cooked corn, 1½ cups diced potatoes and 1 cup cooked rice. Cook rice separately and add to gumbo as it is served.
Add 1 pint oysters or shrimp.

Another of Alice's "Beautiful soups" is chestnut purée

CHICKEN TOMATO BOUILLON

2 cups chicken stock or broth
4 cups tomato juice
¼ cup diced celery
1 teaspoon chopped chives
2 cloves
¼ clove garlic
1 teaspoon minced onion
½ teaspoon salt
1 teaspoon sugar
½ teaspoon Worcestershire sauce
2 tablespoons beet juice
1 tablespoon lemon juice

Combine first 10 ingredients, heat to boiling and simmer 45 minutes. Add beet juice and lemon juice. Stir well and strain. Serves 6 to 8.

CHICKEN NUT SOUP

1 cup chopped celery
4 cups chicken stock
1 egg, beaten
1 tablespoon flour
1 cup milk
Salt, Pepper
⅓ cup ground nut meats
Whipped cream, Minced parsley

Cook celery in stock until tender. Combine egg, flour and milk and beat well. Add to stock gradually and cook for 5 minutes, stirring constantly. Season. Serve in soup bowls; sprinkle nut meats over top and garnish with whipped cream and parsley. Serves 6.

Cook ¼ cup sliced leek and 2 tablespoons minced parsley with celery, strain if desired.

CREAM OF CHICKEN SOUP

3 tablespoons rice
1/2 cup diced celery
3 cups hot chicken stock
2 cups hot milk
Salt and pepper
Chopped parsley

Cook rice and celery in stock until soft, drain and rub through sieve. Combine with milk and season to taste. Sprinkle with chopped parsley and serve hot. Serves 4 to 6.

Use cream or evaporated milk in place of milk listed and add 1 1/2 cups minced, cooked chicken. Omit rice. Combine 3 tablespoons melted fat with 3 tablespoons flour, add stock and milk and cook until thickened, stirring constantly. Pour over 1 slightly beaten egg yolk, cook for 1 minute. Season.

Combine 4 cups Thin White Sauce with 1 1/2 cups diced cooked chicken, heat to boiling.

ALBUQUERQUE—Omit rice. Cut 1 chayote into small cubes, sauté in 2 tablespoons butter. Add to soup with 1 avocado, peeled and cut into small balls, and 1/2 cup chopped ripe olives. Omit rice. Add 1/2 cup cooked barley at serving time.

BELGIUM CHICKEN SOUP

1 4-pound stewing chicken
1/2 lemon
2 onions, 4 cloves
1/2 cup diced celery
3 leeks, minced
1/2 cup diced carrots
1 tablespoon minced parsley
1 sprig thyme, 1 bay leaf
2 teaspoons salt
1/4 teaspoon pepper
2 cups dry white wine

Clean chicken, leaving it whole, rub thoroughly with lemon and place in a large kettle. Add water to half cover chicken and heat to boiling. Peel onions, leaving them whole and insert 2 cloves in each onion; add to chicken with remaining ingredients. Cover kettle and simmer slowly until chicken is tender. When ready to serve, remove chicken from broth and carve it, placing the carved pieces in a soup tureen. Cover with broth and garnish with sprigs of parsley. Serve at once. Serves 6 to 8.

Chicken barley soup will go down in history as "Mother's own" if you but give it the chance

SOUTHERN CHICKEN OYSTER GUMBO

3-pound stewing chicken
1 pound lean beef, cubed
1 cup diced okra
3 pints water
2 dozen oysters
2 teaspoons salt
1/8 teaspoon pepper
1 onion, sliced
1 tablespoon fat
1 1/2 teaspoons filé

Cut up chicken and cook with beef and okra in water. When a strong broth has been obtained and meat is tender, remove chicken and cut meat from bones into small pieces and return to stock. Add oysters with their liquor and season to taste with salt, pepper and onion browned in fat. Cook until the edges of oysters curl. Add filé, mix thoroughly and serve immediately. Serves 8.

CREOLE GUMBO—Instead of beef use 1/2 pound cubed smoked ham. Instead of oysters use 1 pound shelled fresh shrimp. Cook until shrimp turns pink.

TURKEY SOUP

Bones and scraps of turkey
1 quart cold water
1/2 cup chopped celery
1 onion, sliced
1 tablespoon fat
1 tablespoon flour
Dash mace
Salt and pepper to taste
1 cup cream or evaporated milk, scalded

Place turkey scraps in a kettle and cover with cold water, add celery and onion and simmer 2 to 3 hours. Strain. Melt fat, add flour and when smooth add to soup and cook until slightly thickened. Add mace, season with salt and pepper and simmer a few minutes longer. Add cream or evaporated milk and serve immediately. Serves 4 to 6.

BAKED BEAN SOUP

3 slices bacon, diced
2 cups baked or boiled beans
4 cups cold water
1 tablespoon flour
1 tablespoon fat
1 teaspoon salt
Dash pepper
Dash paprika

Sauté bacon in a soup kettle. Add beans and cold water and cook until beans are soft, then rub through a strainer. Return to heat and add a little more water, if needed. Blend flour, fat, salt, pepper and paprika. Add to beans and cook 2 to 3 minutes stirring constantly. Serves 4.

TOMATO BEAN SOUP—Substitute canned tomatoes for half the water.

CHILI SAUCE BEAN SOUP—Add 1 tablespoon chili sauce. Add ¼ cup diced onion and ½ teaspoon celery salt.

SOUTHERN BEAN SOUP

1 cup dried beans
Cold water
6 cups ham broth
1 cup chopped celery
½ onion, minced
3 tablespoons fat
3 tablespoons flour
Salt and pepper
Lemon
Hard-cooked eggs

Cover beans with cold water and let stand overnight, or at least 6 hours. Drain and add beans to ham broth. Add celery and onion and cook slowly until beans become soft. Strain; press beans through a sieve. If necessary, add more water in order to have 5 cups of soup. Blend fat and flour, salt and pepper; stir into hot bean broth slowly and simmer until thickened. Serve hot with slices of lemon and hard-cooked eggs. Serves 4 to 6.

BEAN PORRIDGE

1 pint black beans
2 tablespoons chopped onion
2 stalks celery, chopped
2 teaspoons salt
2 cloves
2 quarts cold water or soup stock
1 hard-cooked egg yolk
⅛ teaspoon pepper
½ teaspoon dry mustard
1 tablespoon flour
1 tablespoon fat

Wash beans and soak overnight in water to cover. Drain and rinse. When ready to cook add onion, celery, salt and cloves, and cover with cold water or soup stock. Boil slowly until beans are soft. Rub through a strainer. Add sufficient stock or water to make the consistency of a thick cream. Mash the egg yolk with pepper and mustard and stir into soup mixture. Cook flour and fat until a golden brown, thin with a little stock and stir into soup. Cook for 5 minutes, thinning with water if necessary. A teaspoon of cooking sherry may be added. Serves 6 to 8.

"Some like it hot, some like it cold"—but we all enjoy it more with croutons

BEAN SOUP

1 pound navy beans
1½ pounds butt end of ham
2 cups diced celery
½ cup chopped onion
2 cups strained tomatoes
2 teaspoons minced parsley
½ cup diced potatoes
Salt and pepper

Soak beans overnight in cold water to cover. Drain, cover with fresh boiling salted water and cook until almost soft. Wash ham, cover with cold water and boil until tender. Remove, skim fat from broth, add beans and other ingredients, and cook until potatoes are tender. Serves 6.

DUTCH BEAN SOUP

1 cup navy beans
3 quarts water
Salt and pepper
1 small onion, grated
1 cup thick sour cream

Wash beans, cover with cold water and soak overnight. Drain and cook in water listed until they have the consistency of thick cream and have cooked down to 3 pints, add salt and pepper to taste and onion. Heat to boiling and add sour cream. Serve with croutons cut into square and diamond shapes. Serves 7.

Just a dash of paprika or cayenne gives cream of navy bean its party touch

NAVY BEAN SOUP

2 cups navy beans
3 quarts water
1 tablespoon minced onion
½ teaspoon celery salt
2 teaspoons salt
⅛ teaspoon pepper
¼ teaspoon mustard
4 tablespoons butter
4 tablespoons flour
1 tablespoon minced parsley

Soak beans in water to cover overnight. Drain. Add water listed, onion and celery salt and cook until beans are very soft. Press beans through a coarse sieve, add salt, pepper and mustard. Melt butter, blend in flour and add to the bean mixture. Heat to boiling, stirring constantly and cook for 5 minutes. Serve garnished with parsley. Serves 8 to 10.

Omit butter and flour. Add 1 pound smoked pork to soaked beans and proceed as above.

LIMA BEAN SOUP—Use dried Lima beans instead of navy beans. Omit celery salt and mustard. Add ½ cup diced celery and a dash cayenne.

CREAM OF NAVY BEAN SOUP

½ pound uncooked ham
¾ cup finely chopped onions
3 quarts boiling water
1 pound navy beans
1½ teaspoons salt
Dash pepper
¼ bay leaf
Dash cayenne
1 tall can evaporated milk

Cut ham into small bits. Cook slowly in soup kettle to try out fat, then add onions and continue cooking 5 minutes. Add boiling water and beans which have been soaked several hours or overnight and drained. Season with salt, pepper, bay leaf and cayenne. Boil gently 3 to 4 hours. Add milk just before serving, 12 to 15.

BLACK SOYBEAN SOUP

2 cups black soybeans
½ cup diced celery
2 quarts cold water
1 small onion
2 tablespoons butter
2 tablespoons flour
1 teaspoon salt
⅛ teaspoon pepper
¼ teaspoon dry mustard
2 hard-cooked eggs, sliced
1 lemon, cut into thin slices

Soak the beans overnight. Drain, add celery and cold water. Cook 4 hours or until tender and rub through a strainer. Cut onion into thin slices and brown slightly in the butter; add flour, seasoning and bean purée. Reheat, strain and pour over eggs and lemon slices. Serves 8 to 10.

BLACK BEAN SOUP

2 cups black beans
12 cups water
¼ pound salt pork
½ pound diced lean beef
1 carrot, diced
3 small onions, minced
3 cloves, ¼ teaspoon mace
Dash cayenne
3 hard-cooked eggs, sliced
1 lemon, sliced
¼ cup sherry

Wash beans, pick over and soak overnight. Drain and add water listed, salt pork, beef, carrot, onions and seasonings. Cover and cook slowly for 3 hours, or until beans have become very soft. Remove meat and rub beans through a sieve. Place in a tureen, add sliced eggs, lemon, cooked meat and sherry. Serves 8 to 10. If desired, omit mace. Add ¾ cup diced celery, ½ cup cooked tomato and ¼ teaspoon dry mustard when carrot is added.

LENTIL SOUP

2 cups lentils
3 quarts cold water
3 pounds brisket of beef or ham
      bone
½ cup diced celery
1 small onion, sliced
2 tablespoons fat
2 tablespoons flour
2 teaspoons salt
¼ teaspoon pepper

Wash lentils and soak overnight in cold water. Drain, add cold water listed and beef or ham bone. Heat to boiling and simmer for 2 hours. Add celery and cook another 2 hours or until meat and lentils are tender. Remove meat and skim fat from stock. Sauté onion in 2 tablespoons of fat. Add flour, salt and pepper, blend, add 1 cup stock gradually, cook until thick and smooth, then add to remainder of stock. Serve hot with Cheese Puffs. Serves 6 to 8. If desired— Add 1 cup strained tomatoes. Use 1 pound smoked sausage or end of a smoked tongue instead of beef or ham bone.

Grandmother's lentil soup with sliced frankfurters is as popular as ever

GREEN KERN SOUP

2 cups green kern
2 cups boiling water
1 teaspoon salt
1 medium onion, minced
1 slice garlic
1 carrot, diced
Pepper, 2 quarts soup stock

Soak kern overnight. Drain, add water and salt and simmer until tender, 8 to 10 hours. Add onion, garlic, carrot and pepper at the end of 2 hours and add soup stock from time to time as the water evaporates. Serves 6.

Green kern is unripe wheat.

SCANDINAVIAN PEA SOUP

2 cups dried yellow peas
3 quarts water
1 pound fresh (or slightly salted)
      pork
2 teaspoons salt
¼ teaspoon ginger

Soak peas overnight, drain and add water listed. Heat to boiling and cook rapidly to loosen skins. Skim off skins as they rise to the surface. After 1 hour of rapid boiling, add pork and simmer for 2 hours or until pork is tender. Add seasonings. Remove pork and serve separately. Serves 6.

PURÉE OF PEAS AND TOMATOES

½ pound yellow split peas
1 quart water
2 cups fresh or canned tomatoes
1 onion, sliced
2 celery tops, 2 teaspoons salt
⅛ teaspoon pepper
1 tablespoon flour
1 tablespoon butter

Soak peas in water overnight. Drain and add tomatoes, water, onion and celery tops. Cook until peas are tender. Force through a sieve. Season with salt and pepper. Blend flour and butter together, add to peas and cook 3 minutes, stirring constantly. Serve garnished with a thin slice of tomato or lemon and a few cooked fresh peas if available. Serve with croutons. Serves 6.

CREAM OF SPLIT PEA SOUP

1 cup dried split peas
2 quarts cold water
Small piece fat salt pork
½ small onion
4 tablespoons butter or other fat
3 tablespoons flour
1¼ teaspoons salt
⅛ teaspoon pepper
2 cups milk or 1 cup evaporated
      milk diluted with 1 cup water

Pick over peas, cover with cold water and soak overnight, drain. Add cold water, pork and onion. Simmer 4 hours, or until tender. Press through a sieve or potato ricer. Melt butter, add flour and stir to a smooth paste. Add pea pulp, salt, pepper and milk. If too thick, add more milk. Garnish with croutons and toasted almond slices. Serves 6 to 8. During the last hour of cooking add 1 cup chopped celery. **LIMA BEAN**—Use dried Lima beans instead of split peas.

JELLIED BOUILLON

1½ tablespoons unflavored gelatin
½ cup cold water
2 cups canned beef bouillon or
   ½ recipe Bouillon
1 cup canned chicken bouillon
1 onion, sliced
1 small bunch parsley
½ teaspoon salt
Dash pepper
1 hard-cooked egg, sliced

Soak gelatin in cold water 5 minutes. Combine remaining ingredients, except hard-cooked egg. Heat to boiling point and simmer 10 minutes, add gelatin and stir until dissolved. Let stand 5 minutes, strain. Pour into bouillon cups and chill until firm. Just before serving draw a fork through the jelly to break it up. Place a slice of egg in each cup. Garnish with lemon wedges, catchup or horse-radish. Serves 6. Sprinkle finely chopped chives over jellied bouillon.

Jellied consommé stored in a glass jar is ready at any time for its garnish of sliced stuffed olives

JELLIED CONSOMMÉ

½ recipe Consommé
3 tablespoons lemon juice
½ teaspoon Worcestershire sauce
Dash cayenne

Heat consommé to boiling. Add lemon juice, Worcestershire sauce and cayenne. Pour into a shallow dish and chill until firm. Cut into small cubes and serve in chilled bouillon cups. Garnish with chopped cold meat. Serves 6. Instead of meat, sprinkle with sieved hard-cooked egg.

JELLIED VEAL CON- SOMMÉ

3 pounds veal knuckle or shin
   bones
Necks and wings of 2 chickens
3 quarts water
1 tablespoon salt
¼ teaspoon peppercorns
3 stalks celery
2 bay leaves
2 sprigs thyme
2 cloves
1 onion
Dash cayenne
6 tablespoons minced pimiento
6 tablespoons minced green pepper

Wash bones and meat in running water. Place in a kettle with remaining ingredients except pimiento and green pepper. Cover and heat to boiling. Skim off any scum that rises. Simmer for 4 hours. Strain through double thickness of cheesecloth. Chill until firm. Break up with a fork and serve in chilled bouillon cups garnished with pimiento in the center of the top of each cup surrounded by a ring of minced green pepper. Makes 2 quarts.

JELLIED MADRILENE CONSOMMÉ

3 pints peeled diced tomatoes
2 teaspoons chopped chives
¼ small onion, chopped
¼ cup chopped celery
1 bay leaf, 2 cloves
1 teaspoon sugar
Shell and white of 1 egg
1 teaspoon salt, ½ clove garlic
1½ pints strong chicken consommé
1 teaspoon tarragon vinegar
½ teaspoon Worcestershire sauce
Dash cayenne
2 tablespoons unflavored gelatin
   softened in ⅓ cup water

Combine first 9 ingredients in a soup kettle and beat well with a wooden spoon rubbed with garlic. Heat to boiling point; reduce heat at once and simmer for ½ hour. Strain through cheesecloth without pressure. Combine this with chicken consommé and heat; add remaining ingredients. A brilliant red color may be obtained by adding a little beet juice (obtained from steamed beets). Chill. Serve in bouillon cups topped with a thin slice of lemon and finely chopped parsley, or garnish with sliced ripe or pimiento stuffed olives. Serves 8.

JELLIED BORSCH

1 tablespoon unflavored gelatin
4 tablespoons beet vinegar
½ clove garlic
¼ cup minced celery leaves
1 teaspoon salt
Few grains cayenne
¼ teaspoon ginger
1 recipe Consommé, boiling
2 cups minced pickled beets
4 tablespoons lemon juice
1 cup sour cream
1 hard-cooked egg white, minced
Paprika

Soften gelatin in vinegar drained from beets, add garlic, celery leaves, salt, cayenne, ginger and boiling consommé and stir until dissolved. Cool for 30 minutes. Strain. Add beets, lemon juice and sour cream and mix well. Chill until firm. Serve in chilled bouillon cups garnished with minced egg white and paprika. Serves 6 to 8.

CHILLED COURT BOUILLON

2 cups Court Bouillon
1 cup shredded cooked fish (pike, bass, trout or salmon)
2 teaspoons grated onion
⅓ teaspoon salt
¼ teaspoon pepper
½ teaspoon Worcestershire sauce
3 drops Tabasco sauce
2 tablespoons lemon juice
Watercress Cream Garnish

Combine all ingredients except the garnish and chill until firm. Break up with a fork and serve in chilled bouillon cups. Garnish with watercress cream garnish. Serves 4.

JELLIED—Soften 2 teaspoons unflavored gelatin in ¼ cup of court bouillon 5 minutes. Heat remaining bouillon to boiling, add gelatin and stir until dissolved. Chill. Use shredded crab, lobster or shrimp instead of fish.

JELLIED CHICKEN BOUILLON

1 tablespoon unflavored gelatin
¼ cup cold water
2 cups hot chicken stock
1 tablespoon chopped parsley

Soften gelatin in cold water for 5 minutes. Add to hot stock and stir until dissolved. Season to taste with salt and add parsley. Chill. When firm cut in cubes or beat slightly with a fork. Serve in cold bouillon cups with lemon wedges. Makes 4 portions.

CONTINENTAL SOUP

1 cup water, ½ cup sugar
Peel of 2 oranges, chopped
Peel of 2 lemons, chopped
1 cup rum, ⅓ cup kirsch
1⅓ cups milk
⅔ cup lemon juice
1½ cups orange juice

Boil water and sugar together until sugar is dissolved. Add orange and lemon peel and let stand 10 minutes. Strain. Add remaining ingredients and allow to stand 3 hours before serving. Strain and serve cold. Serves 8.

ICED ORANGE BOUILLON

2 tablespoons unflavored gelatin
2 tablespoons water
3 cups orange juice
¾ cup sugar
2 tablespoons lime or lemon juice
6 oranges
2 tablespoons sweet cordial

Soak gelatin in water for 5 minutes. Heat 1 cup orange juice, add gelatin and stir until dissolved. Stir in sugar and strain. Add remaining orange juice (2 cups) and lime or lemon juice. Chill. When mixture begins to congeal beat with a rotary beater. Do this several times during the chilling process. Cut oranges in halves and scoop out the pulp, chopping it fine; combine with orange gelatin, and add cordial. When ready to serve, beat thoroughly. Serve in bouillon cups garnished with orange sections and sprigs of mint. Serves 12.

Each cup of jellied consommé may be molded and garnished separately

SOUPS FROM CANS

Since the majority of canned soups on the market are condensed it is wise to read the label and make certain of the correct dilution to make. Water, milk, evaporated milk (diluted or not as desired), cream or stock may be used for diluting.

The use of the can as a measure for diluting is especially convenient and has the advantage of rinsing out any remaining soup in the can. In the following recipes that list 1 or 2 cans of water, milk, etc., the condensed soup can is the measure indicated.

FOUNDATION
1 CAN CLAM CHOWDER

Heat and add any of the following combinations.

BISQUE OF TOMATO AND CLAM—1 can condensed tomato soup. Heat to boiling and add to 2 cans hot milk. Serve immediately.

CLAM CHOWDER BISQUE—1 can condensed chicken gumbo soup and 2 cans milk. Heat just to boiling.

CLAM CHOWDER, DINNER STYLE—1 can condensed consommé and 1 can water. Heat to boiling.

CREOLE MANHATTAN—1 can condensed chicken gumbo soup and 1 can evaporated milk or cream. Heat just to boiling.

FOUNDATION
1 CAN CREAM OF MUSHROOM SOUP

Add any of the following cominations.

CHICKEN AND CREAM OF MUSHROOM—1 can condensed chicken soup and 1 can water Heat to boiling.

CREAM OF CORN AND MUSHROOM—Simmer ½ cup whole kernel corn in 2 tablespoons butter for 5 minutes. Add to soup

with 1 can water, heat to boiling and serve garnished with chopped pimiento.

CREAM OF MUSHROOM AND PEA—1 can condensed pea soup and 2 cans water. Heat to boiling and serve garnished with chopped mint leaves.

LOBSTER SUPREME—1 can condensed asparagus soup, 1 can cream and 1 (7-ounce) can lobster meat. Heat to boiling and add 3 tablespoons sherry.

FOUNDATION
1 CAN CHICKEN SOUP

Add any of the following combinations.

CHICKEN CELERY—1 can condensed celery soup, ½ can each of water and milk. Heat to boiling. Top with minced parsley.

CHICKEN CUCUMBER SUPREME—1 cup puréed cooked cucumber and 1 tablespoon cream. Heat to boiling and pour over 2 beaten egg yolks. Season with salt and pepper, heat to boiling and serve immediately.

FOUNDATION
1 CAN OXTAIL SOUP

Heat and add any of the following combinations.

IN-A-JIFFY OXTAIL—1 can water. Simmer for 15 minutes and add 1 teaspoon Worcestershire sauce and 1 tablespoon lemon juice.

SUNDAY SUPPER—1 can condensed pea soup, 1 can condensed bean-with-bacon soup and 3 cans water. Heat to boiling and simmer 3 to 5 minutes.

FOUNDATION
1 CAN VEGETABLE SOUP

Add any of the following combinations.

CHICKEN VEGETABLE—1 can condensed chicken soup and 1 can water. Heat to boiling.

PEASANT VEGETABLE—1 can condensed pea soup. Heat to boiling and add 1 can water and ¾ cup milk. Heat. Do not boil.

VEGETABLE POTAGE—1 can condensed pea soup and 1 can condensed tomato soup. Heat to boiling, add to 2 cans hot milk and serve immediately.

A fortifying soup, as clam chowder bisque, is no trouble at all made the jiffy way

FOUNDATION
1 CAN PEA SOUP

Heat and add any of the following combinations.

BISQUE OF PEA WITH BEAN—1 can condensed bean-with-bacon soup, 1 can each of water and milk. Heat to boiling and serve with sautéed sliced frankfurters.

HUNTER'S—1 can condensed tomato soup, 1 can condensed Scotch broth and 2 cans water. Heat to boiling and simmer 3 to 5 minutes.

MOCK LOBSTER BISQUE—1 can condensed tomato soup. Heat to boiling and add to 1 can hot cream and ¾ cup shredded lobster meat. Heat just to boiling and serve immediately.

MOCK TURTLE WITH PEA—1 can condensed mock turtle soup and 2 cans water. Heat to boiling, add 1 tablespoon sherry and serve immediately.

PEA SOUP WITH FRANKFURTERS—Cook 1 frankfurter, sliced, and ¼ cup diced onion in 1 tablespoon butter until lightly browned. Add soup and 1 can milk and heat to boiling.

PEPPER POT POTAGE—1 can condensed tomato soup and 1 can condensed pepper pot soup. Heat to boiling, add to 2 cans hot milk and serve immediately.

PHILADELPHIA—1 can condensed pepper pot soup and 2 cans water. Heat to boiling.

PURÉE MONGOL—1 can condensed tomato soup and 2 cans water. Heat to boiling. Add ¼ cup shredded uncooked carrots. Heat 1 minute and serve.

TRIANGLE—1 can condensed tomato soup, 1 can condensed bean-with-bacon soup and 3 cans water. Heat to boiling and simmer 3 to 5 minutes.

FOUNDATION
1 CAN CONSOMMÉ OR BOUILLON

Add to the following:

CREME VICHYSSOISE—Cook ⅛ cup sliced onion and ¾ cup sliced leek in 1 tablespoon butter until soft. Add 1 pint sliced potatoes and 1 can water and cook 20-30 minutes. Add soup and continue cooking 10 minutes. Force through fine sieve. Add 1 cup heated milk and 1 cup cream, 1 teaspoon salt and dash white pepper. Serve **chilled** with chopped chives. Serves 4-6.

ONION SOUP—Cook 2 cups sliced onion in 2 tablespoons butter until brown. Add consommé and 1 can water and heat 20 minutes. Garnish with toasted French bread sprinkled with Parmesan cheese.

FOUNDATION
1 CAN TOMATO SOUP

Heat and add any of the following combinations.

CHICKEN TOMATO—2 cans condensed chicken soup, heat to boiling. Heat 1 can cream or milk and 1 can water and pour soup into milk mixture. Serve immediately.

DESERT CRAB MEAT—1 can condensed pea soup, 1 can condensed bouillon, 2 cans water, 1½ cups shredded crab meat. Heat to boiling, remove from heat and season with sherry.

EASY FISH—1 can water, 1 teaspoon minced onion. Heat to boiling, add ½ cup flaked salmon and 1 tablespoon butter. Reheat and serve.

MADRILENE—1 can condensed chicken broth and 2 cans water. Strain and heat to boiling.

QUICK CREAM OF TOMATO—Pour hot tomato soup into 2 cups hot evaporated milk, stirring constantly. Serve immediately.

SOUTHERN TOMATO—Heat 1 can condensed chicken gumbo soup. Heat 1 can milk and 1 can water together, combine mixtures and serve immediately.

TOMATO CELERY BISQUE—1 can condensed celery soup. Heat to boiling and add to 1 can hot milk. Serve immediately.

TOMATO CONSOMMÉ DE LUXE—1 can condensed consommé and 2 cans water. Heat to boiling. Garnish with whipped cream and chopped parsley.

TOMATO FISH CHOWDER—1 can condensed clam chowder. Heat to boiling. Add 1 can water to 1½ cups flaked cooked fish, heat to boiling, remove from heat and let stand 5 to 10 minutes. Add soup mixture to 1 can hot milk, stirring constantly; add fish mixture and heat 3 to 4 minutes to blend flavors.

TOMATO WITH PEANUT BUTTER—1½ cans water, ½ cup peanut butter, 1 slice onion, ¼ teaspoon salt and dash pepper. Heat in double boiler for 15 minutes, stirring occasionally. Remove onion and beat mixture with an egg beater.

TOMATO PEPPER POTAGE—1 can condensed pepper pot soup. Heat to boiling and add to 2 cans hot milk.

TOMATO AND VEGETABLE BEEF—1 can condensed vegetable beef soup and 2 cans water. Heat to boiling.

TUNA BISQUE—1 can condensed pea soup, 2 cups rich milk or cream and 1 (7-ounce) can tuna, shredded. If desired, add 2 tablespoons sherry just before serving.

SOUP ACCESSORIES

CRACKER BALLS

1 egg, slightly beaten
2 tablespoons butter, melted
1 tablespoon milk
¼ teaspoon salt
½ cup cracker crumbs

Combine egg and butter, add remaining ingredients and mix thoroughly. Shape into tiny balls and let stand to expand. Drop into boiling soup 15 minutes before serving. Makes 12 balls.

CHEESE BALLS

¼ cup butter
½ cup boiling water
¾ cup flour
¼ teaspoon salt
Dash cayenne
Dash paprika
3 eggs
¼ cup grated American cheese

Combine butter and water, cook for 2 minutes, add flour and seasonings and boil until mixture forms a mass in the center of the pan. Cool slightly, add unbeaten eggs 1 at a time, beating well after each addition. Add cheese and drop from a teaspoon into hot fat. Drain and serve immediately. Makes 2½ dozen balls. CHEESE PUFFS—Fold ½ cup grated cheese, 1 tablespoon flour, ¼ teaspoon salt and dash paprika into 2 beaten egg whites, shape, roll in crumbs and fry.

MARROW BALLS

2 tablespoons melted marrow
1 egg, well beaten
¼ teaspoon salt
Dash pepper
Dash paprika
½ cup soft bread crumbs

Strain melted marrow through cheesecloth, beat until creamy and add beaten egg. Season with salt, pepper and paprika, add bread crumbs and form into balls the size of marbles. Poach balls in boiling water and add to soup when serving. Makes 42. LIVER BALLS—Omit marrow. Add ½ cup ground fresh liver, ½ teaspoon minced onion and 1 teaspoon minced parsley. Form into tiny balls, add to hot soup and cook 10 minutes.

RICE BALLS

1 cup cold cooked rice
2 tablespoons flour
1 egg, slightly beaten
¼ teaspoon salt
Dash cayenne
Dash nutmeg
1 teaspoon grated lemon rind
1 teaspoon minced parsley

Rub rice through a sieve, add remaining ingredients, mix thoroughly and form into balls the size of marbles. Cook in boiling salted water until they become firm on the outside. Makes 18.

Cheese toast and stuffed celery are tempters for everyone

PÂTÉ À CHOUX

1 teaspoon butter
2½ teaspoons milk
¼ cup sifted flour
Salt
1 egg

Heat butter and milk together. When at the boiling point, add flour and few grains of salt, stirring constantly. Remove from heat, add unbeaten egg and beat until thoroughly mixed. When cool, drop small pieces from the tip of a teaspoon into hot deep fat (365°F.). When brown and crisp, drain on absorbent paper. Two tablespoons grated Parmesan cheese may be added. Makes about 1 dozen.

SPINACH BALLS

1 cup cooked seasoned spinach
1 cup fine bread crumbs
1 egg white

Chop spinach very fine. Add crumbs and just enough egg white to moisten. Add more seasoning, if necessary. Let stand 15 minutes to stiffen, then shape into balls the size of marbles. Add to soup 5 minutes before ready to serve. Makes about 20.

DUMPLINGS

2 cups sifted flour
1¼ teaspoons baking powder
¾ teaspoon salt
1 tablespoon butter
¾ cup milk (about)

Sift flour, baking powder and salt into a bowl. Add butter and work in with pastry blender or a fork. Add sufficient milk to make a stiff batter. Turn out on floured board and roll about ½ inch thick. Cut into small squares, drop into hot soup, cover closely and cook for 20 to 25 minutes. Cooking utensil must always have a tight-fitting cover or dumplings will be heavy. Makes 2½ dozen.

FLUFFY DUMPLINGS — Increase baking powder to 4 teaspoons, beat 1 egg with milk and increase butter to 3 tablespoons.

NOODLES FOR SOUP

1 egg
½ teaspoon salt
1 cup flour (about)

Beat egg, add salt and as much flour as can be worked into egg to make a very stiff dough. Knead 3 minutes, cover and let stand 30 minutes. Roll paper-thin and spread on cloth to dry. Roll loosely like a jelly roll and cut across into ⅛-inch strips. Unroll and allow to dry thoroughly. Cook in boiling soup until tender, about 15 to 20 minutes. Makes 1¾ cups cut noodles.

NOODLE PUFFS — Roll dough out and let stand until almost dry, fold dough in half, cut through double thickness. using a very small cookie cutter or a floured thimble. Press edges so that they stick together. Fry in hot deep fat (360° to 370°F.) until a golden brown, about 2 minutes.

Cut dough into tiny fancy shapes.

TOMATO CUBES

1 cup tomato purée
1 bay leaf
Dash Tabasco sauce
¼ teaspoon salt
2 egg whites, stiffly beaten

Cook first 4 ingredients together until reduced to ½ cup. Strain, fold in egg whites and pour into shallow pan to a thickness of ½ inch. Place in pan of water and bake in moderate oven (350°F.) until firm, about 10 minutes. Cool and cut into cubes or fancy shapes with vegetable cutters. Add to soup just before serving. Makes about 12 cubes.

PARSLEY OR WATER-CRESS CREAM GARNISH

½ cup heavy cream, whipped
4 tablespoons minced parsley or
    watercress

Whip cream until stiff, fold in minced parsley or watercress. Serve as a garnish for soups.

SALTED WHIPPED CREAM — Add ⅛ teaspoon salt to cream before whipping.
Grated cheese may be folded into whipped cream.

A stack of pretzels in a ring of filled sliced dills accompanies the soup most gallantly

CHICKEN FORCE-MEAT

2 breasts chicken (uncooked)
½ teaspoon salt
¼ teaspoon pepper
1 cup dry bread crumbs
1 cup milk, ⅛ teaspoon mace
3 tablespoons butter or other fat
2 egg whites

Chop chicken, pound and rub through a purée-sieve. There should be a cup of meat. Add salt and pepper. Boil bread crumbs (no crusts), milk and mace together for 10 minutes, or until cooked to a smooth paste. Remove from heat, add butter, seasoned meat and well-beaten egg whites. Stir until all ingredients blend. Shape into small balls and cook in soup. Makes 36.

Use dark meat instead of light and the egg yolks instead of egg whites. Chicken livers also may be used for forcemeat.

FISH FORCEMEAT — Remove skin, fat and bone from any kind of mild-flavored fish. Pound, strain, use 1 cup fish and proceed as for chicken forcemeat.

TOASTED SOUP RINGS

Bread, Melted butter
Salt, Cayenne

Slice bread ¼ inch thick, remove crusts and dip into melted butter. Cut into rings with a doughnut cutter. Cut some slices into long narrow strips. Season with salt and cayenne and brown in a moderate oven (350°F.). Insert 2 or 3 narrow strips through rings and serve hot with soup.

TOAST ANIMALS

Slice bread ½ inch thick. Cut into animal shapes, using various shaped cookie cutters. Toast.

*Cut them and toast them
and serve them with soup
for baby and me*

BREAD STICKS

4 tablespoons shortening
1½ tablespoons sugar
1 cup scalded milk
½ teaspoon salt
1 yeast cake softened in ¼ cup
   lukewarm water
1 egg, separated
3½ cups sifted flour

Add shortening and sugar to milk. Cool to lukewarm, add salt, softened yeast, beaten egg white and flour. Knead and let rise until doubled in bulk. Shape into sticks about the size of a lead pencil. Place 1½ inches apart on a baking sheet, brush with beaten egg yolk and sprinkle with caraway or poppy seeds, if desired. Let rise until doubled in bulk, place in a hot oven (400° F.) and bake 10 minutes. Reduce heat to moderate (350°F.) and continue baking until sticks become dry and crisp. Makes 48.

TOASTED CHEESE STICKS

Cut bread into slices ½ inch thick, cut into strips ½ inch wide and 4 inches long, spread with butter and then with a thick coating of grated cheese. Place in moderate oven (350°F.) or under broiler to brown. Serve hot with soup. Crackers may be used instead of bread strips.

CROUTONS

Cut dry bread into slices about ⅓ inch thick and remove all crust. Spread generously with butter, cut into cubes and bake in moderate oven (350°F.) until delicately browned. If preferred, these cubes of bread may be fried in hot deep fat or sautéed in just enough fat to keep them from burning. Put into soup at time of serving, or serve separately.

MOCK ALMONDS—These are croutons shaped like almonds.

CALF'S LIVER DUMPLINGS

½ pound calf's liver
1 cup bread or cracker crumbs
1 cup milk or water
1 egg, slightly beaten
1 teaspoon salt
½ teaspoon grated onion
⅛ teaspoon pepper
½ teaspoon grated lemon rind

Skin liver and remove tough fiber. Chop fine. Cook crumbs and milk or water together to a paste. Add remaining ingredients, mix well and form into balls the size of marbles. Drop into boiling soup and cook 10 minutes. Serves 4.

EGG BALLS

4 hard-cooked egg yolks
1 teaspoon salt
½ teaspoon pepper
1 egg, well beaten, Flour

Mash yolks to a smooth paste, add salt, pepper and other egg. Shape into tiny balls, roll in flour and sauté until lightly browned. They may be made some time before needed. Add to soup before serving. Makes 20 small balls.
Mash egg yolks to a paste, season and mix with uncooked egg yolk. Form into small balls. Roll them in the uncooked egg white, then in flour and poach in hot water.

CUSTARD ROYALE

2 egg yolks, slightly beaten
1 egg, slightly beaten
½ cup beef stock
⅛ teaspoon salt
Dash pepper
Few grains cayenne

Combine ingredients in the order listed. Pour mixture into a shallow pan or dish so that the custard will be about ½ inch deep. Set in pan of hot water and bake in moderate oven (350°F.) until firm. The custard should set without bubbling and without forming a brown crust on top. When cold cut into fancy shapes with vegetable cutter. Use care in placing these in the soup so that they will not break. When used in consommé, the name "Consommé Royale" is given to the soup.

Follow method above using 1 egg, 2 tablespoons milk, cream or consommé and ⅛ teaspoon salt.

VEGETABLE CUBES—Add ½ cup pea purée and dash each of celery salt and nutmeg.

GARNISHES FOR SOUPS

Bacon and Onions—Add chopped crisp bacon and onions browned in bacon fat to tomato, celery or bean soup.

Cheese—Sprinkle grated cheese over chowders.

Croutons—Sprinkle over any kind of soup.

Frankfurter Slices—Slice frankfurter crosswise into ⅛-inch slices. Brown in fat. Serve on top of soup. Especially delicious with pea, bean, tomato, celery or asparagus soup.

Lemon Slices—Cut lemon very thin and float slices on top of consommé or clam chowder.

Macaroni Rings—Cut cooked macaroni into thin slices, making tiny rings, and sprinkle over soup or chowder.

Olive Rings—Slice stuffed olives very thin and serve as a garnish for jellied consommé.

Popped Corn—Sprinkle buttered popcorn over corn, pea or tomato soup.

Salami Slices—Cut salami slices into thin strips about ⅛-inch wide. Place in the soup about 10 minutes before serving. Adds good flavor to pea, bean, tomato, celery or asparagus soup.

Sautéed Banana Slices—Cut banana into ⅛-inch slices and sauté in butter until tender. Serve 3 or 4 in chicken soup.

Shredded Almonds and Cereal Flakes—Sauté shredded almonds in butter. Add cereal flakes and blend. Add to tomato, celery or chicken soup just before serving.

Toasted Almonds—Sprinkle shredded almonds in cream soups.

Whipped Cream—Serve slightly salted whipped cream in cream soups and sprinkle with paprika or top with a tiny sprig of parsley or a bit of pimiento cut in an attractive shape.

Whipped Avocado—Cut avocado pear into small pieces. Press through a sieve and beat with an egg beater until the consistency of whipped cream. Serve 1 teaspoon in clear consommé.

FARINA FLOATS

1 tablespoon butter
1 cup hot milk
½ cup farina
2 eggs, separated
½ teaspoon salt
Dash pepper

Combine butter and milk in top of double boiler, add farina gradually and stir until thick and smooth. Cool; add egg yolks, salt and pepper; fold in stiffly beaten egg whites. Shape into balls the size of marbles, drop into boiling soup and boil 10 minutes. They will triple in size and float. Makes about 50 balls.

ALMOND FARINA FLOATS—Add ½ cup grated almonds to mixture before forming into balls.

OYSTER FORCEMEAT

12 oysters
2 cups dry bread crumbs
3 tablespoons butter or other fat
1 teaspoon salt, Few grains cayenne
1 teaspoon minced parsley
1 teaspoon lemon juice
3 tablespoons oyster juice
2 egg yolks, 1 egg, slightly beaten
2 tablespoons water, Bread crumbs

Chop oysters fine and add bread crumbs, butter, salt, cayenne, minced parsley, lemon juice, oyster juice, egg yolks and dash of nutmeg. Pound to a smooth paste and rub through a purée sieve. Add more salt if necessary. Form into balls, dip into beaten egg diluted with water, then into bread crumbs and fry in hot deep fat (370°F.) or dip balls in diluted egg only and brown in a moderate oven (350°F.).

QUENELLES—These are made by forcing forcemeat through a pastry bag and tube into boiling water or stock. They are used to garnish entrées as well as soups.

PIMIENTO SOUP CREAM

2 canned pimientos
½ cup heavy cream, whipped
2 tablespoons egg white
Dash salt

Drain pimientos and wipe dry; force through a sieve to make 2 tablespoons purée. Beat cream until stiff, add egg white, beaten stiff, and salt. Fold in purée. Serve a small amount on soup.

Breads, Biscuits and Rolls

200 Breads, Biscuits and Rolls

FLOURS USED IN BREAD

Many flours, besides white wheat flour, are used to make breads and require understanding to be successfully used.

Whole-wheat and graham flour contain most of the wheat bran and, if used alone, make a dough too sticky to knead. For that reason they are usually combined with at least an equal amount of white flour.

Enriched flour is white wheat flour to which a specified amount of the B vitamins and iron have been added.

Rye flour is more nearly like wheat than any other except that it fails to hold the leavening agent and hence the shape of the loaf. Bread made entirely of rye flour is very dark and heavy. To make lighter rye breads, a sponge is made from wheat flour and allowed to rise in order to develop the yeast and mellow the wheat gluten. Rye flour is then added to make a dough. If more than half the flour used is rye, the dough is very sticky and hard to handle.

Buckwheat flour is heavier than other flours, therefore a smaller amount is used in proportion to the liquids.

Corn meal may be either white or yellow. Since it yields no gluten it is rarely used in yeast breads but is combined with white, whole-wheat or rye flours to make breads raised with soda or baking powder.

Hominy is corn treated with lye and coarsely ground and is used in the same way as corn meal. Soy flour is milled from soybeans that are dehulled, specially treated, oil retained or removed as desired, then nutritionally pre-cooked by heating.

Using two tablespoons of soy flour in each cup of wheat flour makes a soya mix that may be used in practically any recipe instead of all wheat flour. Use a little more water and seasoning. The addition of soy proteins results in an important nutritional increase in the baked product.

HOW MUCH FLOUR TO USE

Since different flours vary in the amount of moisture they can absorb it is not usually possible to give the exact amount of flour required. In general, for yeast breads, sufficient flour should be used to make the dough stiff enough to knead.

SPECIAL INGREDIENTS USED

Wheat germ is used with wheat flour to make bread. Since it becomes rancid very quickly it should be fresh when purchased and must be stored in the refrigerator. Soda or baking powder is used as a leavening agent. Mashed potato used in breads helps feed the yeast and tends to produce a loaf more moist and with better keeping qualities. These breads have a characteristically pleasant flavor.

Buttermilk and sour milk may be used interchangeably in recipes.

ABOUT BAKING TEMPERATURES

Baking temperatures for yeast breads vary from moderate (350° F.) to hot (450°F.) The lower temperatures are used for rich doughs, to prevent excessive browning. Rolls are usually baked at 400°F. to 425°F., while bread may be started at 425°F., then the temperature reduced after 15 minutes to 350°F. If it is baked the entire time at 400°

F. to 425°F., a browner crust results.

When bread has finished baking it shrinks slightly from the sides of the pan and sounds hollow when thumped. Remove bread and rolls from pans immediately. Place loaves uncovered on wire cooling racks away from drafts. To prevent drying out of top crusts, brush with melted shortening or cover with a cloth while cooling. Keep bread in closed, dry, ventilated container.

Any yeast dough may be stored in the refrigerator for later use if the yeast is increased by at least one-half or even doubled. It is also important that the dough contain an adequate amount of sugar. Consequently any good roll dough, that is a little richer and sweeter than plain bread dough, is especially well adapted to use as refrigerator rolls. The length of time a dough can be kept in the refrigerator depends somewhat on the quality of the dough but mainly upon the temperature in the refrigerator. At temperatures of 45°F. to 50°F. most dough will keep well for 4 to 5 days. When part of the dough is being used, the amount desired should be removed from the bowl and the remainder returned at once to the refrigerator so that it does not become warm. After removing from refrigerator the dough must become warm before rising can begin. The chilled dough may be allowed to rise until light, then shaped into rolls and again allowed to rise until light before baking. Just as satisfactory results are obtained in shorter time by shaping the chilled dough immediately and allowing it to rise only once before baking.

WHEN YOU KNEAD THE DOUGH

(Turn page for Illustrations)

The object of kneading is to develop elasticity of gluten and to scatter gas pockets that have been formed around yeast. (1) After the first rising, add remaining flour gradually and mix thoroughly. (2) Turn out on lightly floured board. Knead lightly with lower part of hand, using the wrist in the action. (3) When volume has been reduced about ⅓ and dough springs back under hand, return to bowl and allow to rise a second time; (4) until doubled in bulk. (5) Press dough gently with finger. If impression remains, dough has risen sufficiently. Punch down risen dough in bowl, loosen from sides with a spatula and turn out on a lightly floured board. (6) Knead quickly and lightly, (7-9) turning dough ¼ way around after each push. This insures uniformity and an even texture. Time required for second kneading varies with flour, but in general 8 to 10 minutes of kneading are required. Hold hand on dough for 30 seconds. If dough does not stick, feels satiny and looks smooth, it has been kneaded sufficiently. (10) Divide dough into two equal portions. (11) Shape each into a ball, cover and let rest 10 to 15 minutes. This rest period may be omitted but bread will retain its shape better if given this brief period for recovery after kneading. (12-13) With palms of hands flatten each piece into a sheet. (14) Double over and seal edges of dough with the knuckles. (15) Stretch dough slightly into a long sheet. (16) Fold ends of dough to center, letting them overlap. (17) Fold side of dough nearest you over ⅓, and seal. (18) Shape with hands into a long roll and place in greased pan, smooth side up. Cover with a cloth and let rise until doubled in bulk. Bake in a hot oven (400°F.) 40 to 45 minutes.

A third rising and kneading is permissible but this is not necessary for a good loaf. When returning dough to bowl to rise again, turn smooth side up, grease top, cover with a cloth and let rise in a warm place (about 80°F.), not warmer than a warm room, or place bowl in a pan of warm (not hot) water, since it protects dough from sudden changes in temperature. Dough should be allowed to double in bulk but a dough made with rye or whole-wheat flour will rise less; one made with hard-wheat flour should be allowed to increase 2½ to 3 times.

These help you to measure your ingredients correctly

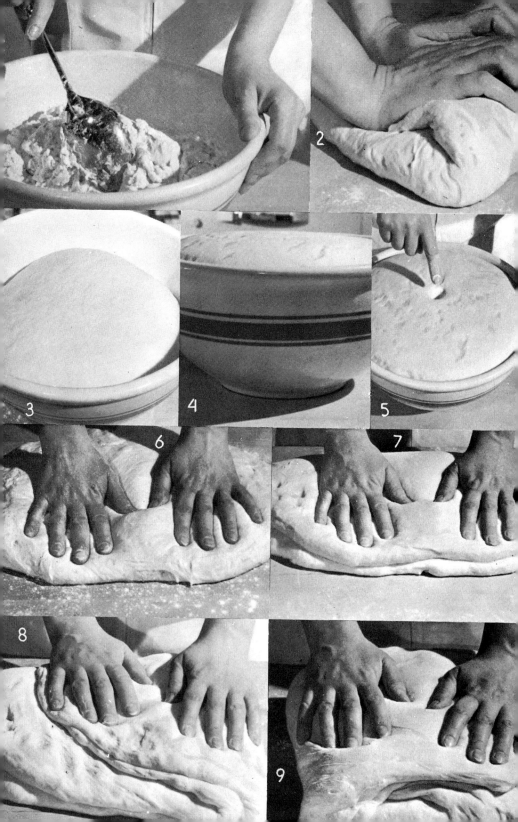

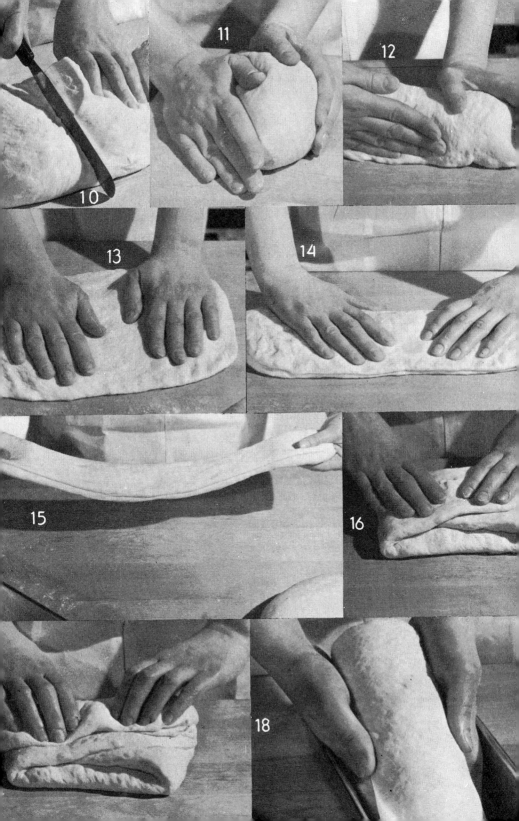

YEAST IN BREAD

Good yeast bread is well raised, well browned, and tender, with a fine even texture, a uniformly creamy white color and good flavor. It is made light by the growth of yeast plants which produce gas (carbon dioxide) which is held in the dough by elastic fibers of gluten. In baking, heat causes the gas to expand, producing the last lift to light fluffy texture, then makes the loaf firm so it remains light and puffy after cooling. Care must be used in making and handling yeast dough to prevent destruction of yeast by heat. Any ingredient mixed with yeast should be lukewarm. Dough should be kept at a warm room temperature (80° F.), covered with a cloth to protect from drafts while rising. Overheating and cold are to be avoided.

COMPRESSED YEAST (moist cake) is grayish-tan in color but may be slightly browned at edges. Keep in refrigerator and use within a week for best results. Soften in lukewarm (80°F) liquid.

ACTIVE DRY YEAST keeps without refrigeration. Soften in warm water (110°F). A package has the leavening power of one cake (3/5 oz.) compressed yeast.

METHODS OF MIXING BREAD

SPONGE METHOD—This is one of the oldest ways of making bread. First a sponge is made by combining the softened yeast with part of the sugar, liquid and flour. Then mixture is set in a warm place until it is bubbly and spongelike. Remaining flour and other ingredients are then added to make a dough which is kneaded.

STRAIGHT DOUGH METHOD—This is the method most commonly used. All ingredients are combined to make a dough which is kneaded to satiny smoothness. It is usually given two risings in a warm place (about 80°F) before shaping. After shaping, dough rises again in pans.

BATTER METHOD—This is the quickest and easiest way to bake bread with yeast. As the name implies, this yeast mixture is a batter rather than a dough and requires no kneading or shaping. The yeast batter is quickly mixed and allowed to rise in the mixing bowl. Batter may be quite thin or fairly thick, depending upon what you are making.

WHITE BREAD STRAIGHT DOUGH METHOD

2 cups milk
1 pkg. active dry or 1 cake
    compressed yeast
¼ cup warm water (110°F.)
    (Use water 80°F. for compressed yeast)
2 tablespoons sugar
1½ tablespoons shortening
2½ teaspoons salt
6 cups flour, about

Scald milk. Soften yeast in warm water; let stand 5 minutes. Pour scalded milk over sugar, shortening and salt in a bowl. When lukewarm blend in 1 cup flour. Stir in yeast and beat well. Add 3 cups flour; continue beating until smooth. Beat in enough remaining flour to make a soft dough. Turn on lightly floured surface; let rest about 5 minutes. Knead until smooth and elastic. Place dough in a greased bowl; turn to bring greased surface to top. Cover; let stand in warm place until dough is doubled, about 1 hour. Punch down, cover and let rise again until almost doubled in bulk. Turn on lightly floured surface. Divide dough in half; let rest 5 to 10 minutes. Shape into loaves. Place in 2 greased loaf pans 9½ x 5¼ x 2¾ inches. Cover and let rise until doubled, about 1 hour. Bake at 400°F. about 50 minutes.

A RICHER BREAD—Use 1 cup milk in place of 1 cup of water; use 2 tablespoons honey, corn sirup or molasses in place of sugar.

CRACKED-WHEAT—Use 4 cups cracked-wheat for 4 cups white.

OATMEAL—Use 4 cups oatmeal for 4 cups white flour.

RAISIN—Add 2 cups raisins or chopped prunes or nuts. Brown sugar may be used instead of white and grated orange or lemon rind added.

WHOLE-WHEAT — Use 6 cups whole-wheat flour· for 6 cups white flour. Use ¼ cup molasses instead of sugar.

CASSEROLE BREAD BATTER METHOD

1 cup milk
3 tablespoons sugar
1 teaspoon salt
1½ tablespoons shortening
1 cup warm (not hot) water
2 packages or cakes yeast,
    active dry or compressed
4½ cups sifted flour

Scald milk, stir in sugar, salt and shortening. Cool to lukewarm Measure the warm water into a bowl. (Use lukewarm water for compressed yeast.) Sprinkle or crumble in the yeast. Stir until softened. Blend in the lukewarm milk mixture. Add flour and stir until well blended, about 2 minutes. Cover; let rise in warm place, free from drafts, about 40 minutes or until doubled in bulk. Stir batter down. Beat vigorously about ½ minute. Turn into greased 1½ quart casserole. A square pan 8 x 8 x 2 inches or an 8-inch tube pan may be used. Bake uncovered at 375°F. about 1 hour. Makes 1 loaf.

FRUIT BREAD

1 pound prunes
1 pound figs
1 pound dates
¼ cup raisins
¼ cup dried currants
1 tablespoon chopped candied
   citron
1 tablespoon chopped candied
   lemon peel
1 tablespoon chopped candied
   orange peel
¼ cup chopped blanched almonds
2 cakes yeast
4½ cups sifted flour
¼ teaspoon cloves
¼ teaspoon cinnamon
¼ teaspoon salt

Soak prunes and figs 1 hour in just enough water to cover. Add dates and cook gently in the same water 20 minutes. Remove fruit, chop and mix with other fruits and nuts. Reduce liquid to ¾ cup. Cool to lukewarm, add yeast and stir until well blended. Add 2 cups flour, beating well. Let rise until light and spongy. Add spices, salt, fruit mixture and remaining flour to make a stiff dough. Knead until smooth. Let rise until doubled in bulk. Shape into oval loaves, brush with slightly sweetened milk and sprinkle with split almonds. Let rise again and bake in hot oven (425° F.) 45 minutes. Makes 3 loaves. If desired, when cool, spread with icing and garnish with candied fruits and nut meats.

LIMPA

2 cups milk, 1 cake yeast
2¼ cups lukewarm water
1 tablespoon sugar
1½ quarts sifted white flour
1 cup dark corn sirup
1½ teaspoons fennel seed
1½ teaspoons aniseed
½ cup molasses
¾ cup shortening
8 cups rye flour, 1 tablespoon salt
Grated rind 2 oranges or ¼ cup
   chopped candied orange peel

Scald milk and cool to lukewarm. Soften yeast in ¼ cup lukewarm water; add sugar, remaining lukewarm water and cooled milk. Add white flour and beat well. Let rise until doubled in bulk. Mix sirup, fennel seed, aniseed and molasses. Heat to boiling and boil 1 minute; strain out seeds. Cool and add shortening. When lukewarm add to sponge with rye flour, sifted with salt. Add grated orange rind and knead well. Let rise until doubled in bulk. Then shape into round loaves. Place in greased pans and let rise again until doubled in bulk. Bake in hot oven (400°F.) 15 minutes; then reduce heat to moderate (350°F.) and bake 45 minutes longer. Makes 4 loaves.

This is well-made bread

SOY BREAD

1 cake yeast, ¼ cup lukewarm
   water
¼ cup brown sugar, 1½ teaspoons salt
2 tablespoons shortening
2 cups milk, scalded
1½ cups soy flour
4½ cups sifted whole-wheat or
   graham flour

Mix and bake as for standard white bread. Makes 2 loaves.

ORANGE BREAD

1 cake yeast
1 tablespoon sugar
1 cup orange juice
1 teaspoon salt, 1 tablespoon butter
1 teaspoon grated orange rind
3 cups sifted flour, ⅓ cup sugar
½ cup shredded candied orange
   peel

Combine yeast and sugar. Let stand a few minutes. Heat orange juice to lukewarm and add to yeast. Add remaining ingredients, except candied orange peel. Beat well. Let rise until doubled in bulk. Knead in orange peel on well-floured board. Shape into loaf and let rise until light. Bake in moderate oven (375°F.) 30 to 40 minutes. Makes 1 loaf.

AMADAMA BREAD

½ cup yellow corn meal
2 cups boiling water
2 tab'espoons shortening
½ cup molasses, 1 teaspoon salt
1 cake yeast
½ cup lukewarm water
5 cups sifted flour (about)

Stir corn meal very slowly into the water just before it boils. Boil 5 minutes. Add shortening, molasses and salt. Cool. When lukewarm, add yeast softened in warm water and enough flour to make a stiff dough. Knead well; let rise until slightly more than doubled in bulk. Shape into loaves, place in greased loaf pans; let rise until light. Bake in hot oven (400°F.) 1 hour. Makes 2 loaves.

WHOLE-WHEAT HONEY BREAD

1 cake yeast
1¼ cups lukewarm water
1 cup milk
3 tablespoons shortening
¼ cup honey
1 tablespoon salt
4 cups sifted flour
4 cups whole-wheat flour

Soften yeast in lukewarm water Scald milk and add shortening, honey and salt. Cool to lukewarm. Add softened yeast and flours. Knead well, cover and let rise in a warm place until dou-

bled in bulk. Punch down and shape into loaves. Place in greased loaf pans. Cover and let rise until doubled in bulk. Bake in moderate oven (375°F.) about 1 hour. Makes 2 loaves.

POTATO BREAD

3 potatoes
1 cake yeast
2 tablespoons shortening
2 tablespoons sugar
1 tablespoon salt
6 to 6½ cups sifted flour

Cook pared potatoes in boiling water until tender; mash in liquid and heat 2 cups to lukewarm. Crumble yeast in ¼ cup of the liquid. To remaining liquid, add shortening, sugar and salt. Add softened yeast and ½ of the flour. Beat; add remaining flour gradually. Knead on floured board until thoroughly elastic. Place in bowl, cover and let rise. When doubled in bulk, divide into 2 parts, shape into loaves and place in greased pans. Let rise again until doubled in bulk. Bake in moderate oven (375°F.) 45 minutes or until bread shrinks from sides of pan. Makes 2 (1-pound) loaves.

If the oven's too slow the crust will be pale, the texture'll be porous; it's sure to fail

ROLLED CINNAMON BREAD

1 cup boiling water
2 tablespoons granulated sugar
2½ teaspoons salt
1 tablespoon melted shortening
1 cup evaporated milk
1 cake yeast
¼ cup lukewarm water
6 cups sifted flour
6 tablespoons brown sugar
1 teaspoon cinnamon

Pour boiling water over sugar, salt and shortening. Add milk and cool to lukewarm. Soften yeast in lukewarm water, add to milk mixture and add flour, ½ cup at a time. Mix until smooth after each addition. Turn out on lightly floured board and knead until dough is smooth and elastic to the touch and bubbles appear under the surface. Place in greased bowl, cover and let rise until doubled in bulk. Turn out on lightly floured board and knead again. Divide dough into 2 portions. Pat and stretch each portion into a sheet about 9 inches square. Sprinkle with mixture of brown sugar and cinnamon. Roll up like jelly roll, and place in greased loaf pans with seam side down. Cover and let rise again' until doubled in bulk. Bake in hot oven (425°F.) 15 minutes, reduce heat to moderate (375°F.) and bake 25 minutes longer. Makes 2 loaves.

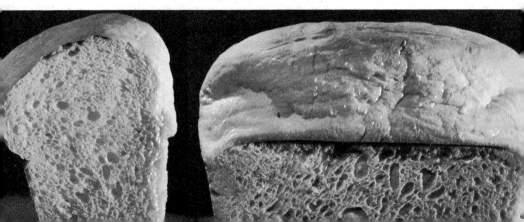

FRENCH BREAD

2 cups scalded (sweet) milk and
  water mixed
1 cake yeast
1 teaspoon sugar
2 teaspoons salt
Enough sifted flour to make a
  smooth dough (about 6 cups)

Scald milk, add water, and cool
to lukewarm. Dissolve yeast,
sugar, and salt in the lukewarm
mixture. Add sufficient flour
gradually to make a stiff dough.
Turn out on lightly floured board
and knead till smooth. Place in
a greased bowl, cover, and let
rise till doubled in bulk; punch
down and let rise again. Knead
well. Divide dough into equal
portions, shape into long loaves
about 2 inches in thickness. Lay
the loaves on a board which has
been lightly sprinkled with flour,
placed so that they do not touch
each other. Let rise till doubled
in bulk. Make diagonal cuts
half way across on each loaf,
about half way through. Place
in hot oven (400° F.) and bake
for 15 minutes. Then lower oven
to 350° F. till the loaves are
crisp. About 10 minutes before
removing from oven, brush loaves
with a mixture of beaten eggs
and water. Makes two loaves.

DARK RYE BREAD

2 cups scalded milk
2 tablespoons sugar
2 tablespoons butter
1 teaspoon salt
1 cake yeast
1/2 cup lukewarm water
6 cups rye flour
1 1/2 cups whole-wheat flour
2 tablespoons caraway seed

Pour scalded milk over sugar, butter, and salt in a large bowl.
Soften yeast in lukewarm water.
When milk mixture is lukewarm,
stir in softened yeast and 3 cups
rye flour. Beat thoroughly, then
beat in remaining rye flour. Cover
and let rise in warm place until
doubled in bulk. Turn onto well-
floured board; knead in whole-
wheat flour and caraway seed.
Knead until dough is smooth and
holds its shape. Divide dough in
half and shape into two round or
oblong loaves. Place round loaves
in greased round pans, oblong
loaves in greased loaf pans. Cover
and let rise in warm place until
doubled. Bake in 350°F oven 15
minutes; reduce heat to 350°F
and bake 35 to 40 minutes longer.
Brush with melted butter the last
5 minutes if a more tender crust
is desired. Makes 2 large loaves.

LIGHT RYE BREAD
WITH RAISINS

1 cup sugar
1/4 cup butter
2 to 3 tablespoons dark
  molasses
1 1/2 tablespoons salt
1 quart hot potato water
2 cakes yeast
1/2 cup lukewarm water
2 cups rye flour
9 to 10 cups white flour
2 cups seedless raisins, scalded
  and drained on absorbent paper
Melted butter or Glaze

Add sugar, butter, molasses, and
salt to potato water. When lukewarm, add yeast softened in lukewarm water. Gradually beat in the
rye flour, then enough white
flour to make a stiff dough. Knead
in the raisins. Turn onto well-
floured board and knead dough
until smooth and elastic. Let stand
in warm place until light; shape
into loaves. Cut tops of loaves
with a few gashes of the knife;
brush with butter or Glaze. Let
rise until light. Bake in 400°F
oven 15 minutes, then reduce heat
to 350°F and bake 30 minutes
longer. (Bread dough may rise
overnight if only one cake yeast
is used.) Makes 4 loaves.

RYE SALT STICKS—Scald 2 cups
milk; pour over 1 tablespoon each
of shortening, salt, sugar, and
caraway seed. Cool to lukewarm
and add 1 cake yeast. Stir in 1
cup sifted rye, and 5 cups sifted
white flour. Let rise until
doubled in bulk. Roll out into
sheets 1/8 inch thick and cut into
pie-shaped pieces. Roll, starting
at large end. Finished roll should
be 1/2 inch in diameter and 5
inches long. Brush with 1 egg
white. Sprinkle with coarse salt
and 1 tablespoon caraway seed.
Bake at 500°F. 20 minutes. Makes
3 dozen sticks.

*In homemade bread, espe-
cially rye, you know there's
more than meets the eye*

NORWEGIAN CHRIST-MAS BREAD

2 cakes yeast, 1 pint milk
¼ cup lukewarm water
1 cup shortening
1 cup sugar, 1 teaspoon salt
2 eggs, well beaten
½ teaspoon ground cardamom
7 cups sifted flour
½ pound seedless raisins
4 ounces citron, sliced
Glaze for Breads

Soften yeast in lukewarm water. Scald and cool milk. Cream shortening, sugar and salt together; add beaten eggs and cardamom. To lukewarm milk add softened yeast and 3 cups of flour; beating until smooth. Add creamed mixture and remaining flour. Mix until smooth, adding more flour, if necessary. Add fruit, sprinkled with flour. Let dough rise until doubled in bulk, stir down and let rise again until about doubled. Turn dough onto floured board, divide into 3 portions and shape into loaves. Place in greased bread pans and let rise until doubled in bulk. Brush tops of loaves with glaze. Bake in moderate oven (350°F.) 50 to 60 minutes. Makes 3 loaves.

TOMATO BREAD

1 tablespoon shortening
1 teaspoon salt
1½ tablespoons sugar
1 cup scalded tomato juice
½ cake yeast
¼ cup lukewarm water
3¾ cups sifted flour

Add shortening, salt and sugar to hot tomato juice. Cool to lukewarm. Soften yeast in lukewarm water. Add to cooled tomato juice mixture. Add half the flour, beat until smooth, add remaining flour and mix well. Knead on floured board about 5 minutes. Let rise in warm place until doubled in bulk, about 2 hours. Shape into loaf, place in greased pan and brush top with melted shortening. Let rise until doubled in bulk and bake in hot oven (400°F.) 15 minutes, then reduce heat to moderate (375°F.) and bake about 45 minutes longer. Makes 1 (9½x4½-inch) loaf.

Try Norwegian Christmas bread, and you're bound to agree; it's just as tasty as tasty can be

SWEDISH COFFEE BREAD

2 cups milk
1 cake yeast
¼ cup lukewarm water
⅞ cup sugar
6½ cups sifted flour
15 cardamom capsules
½ cup shortening
½ teaspoon salt

Scald milk and cool to lukewarm (80°F.). Soften yeast in lukewarm water. Add 2 tablespoons sugar and when dissolved add to milk with 3 cups flour. Beat well. Set aside to rise until doubled in bulk. Remove cardamom seeds from capsules and grind very fine. Cream shortening and remaining sugar (¾ cup). Add ground cardamom seed and mix with sponge. Sift remaining flour with salt; add to sponge and knead into soft dough. Let rise until doubled in bulk. Shape into rolls or loaves. Let rise until doubled in bulk, about ¾ hour. Bake in moderate oven (375°F.) 35 minutes. Makes 2 loaves.

If desired, when cool, spread with a thin sugar glaze, and sprinkle with chopped nuts.

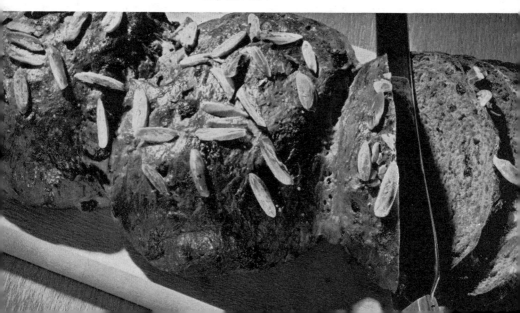

BREADS MADE WITH LEAVENINGS OTHER THAN YEAST

Breads leavened with baking soda or baking powder should not be beaten or kneaded. Because these breads rise only once, any gluten which is developed has no opportunity to stretch and become tender. The usual procedure is to combine the egg, liquid and melted shortening, then to stir in the dry ingredients, mixing only enough to dampen all the flour.

ALMOND BREAD

1¼ cups sifted flour
1½ teaspoons baking powder
⅛ teaspoon salt
4 eggs
⅓ cup sugar
2 tablespoons lemon juice
2 tablespoons softened shortening
½ cup almonds, blanched and halved

Sift flour, baking powder and salt together. Beat eggs until lemon colored; add sugar gradually, beating constantly. Add lemon juice and shortening, continuing to beat until smooth. Add almonds and sifted dry ingredients. Pour into greased (8 x 8-inch) pan and bake in moderate oven (375° F.) 30 to 40 minutes or until well browned. Remove from pan and cut into strips or small squares. Makes 16 (2-inch) squares.

QUICK NUT BREAD

1 cup chopped pecan, walnut or hickory nut meats
2 cups sifted flour
3 teaspoons baking powder
½ teaspoon salt
½ cup brown sugar
1 cup milk
1 egg, beaten
2 tablespoons melted shortening

Place chopped nut meats in boiling water a few minutes and drain. Sift dry ingredients together. Combine milk, egg, shortening and nut meats. Add to dry ingredients, mix, pour into greased loaf pan. Bake in moderate oven (350°F.) about 1 hour or until lightly browned. Makes 1 loaf.

BUTTERMILK NUT BREAD

2 eggs, well beaten
1½ cups brown sugar
3¼ cups sifted flour
2 teaspoons baking soda
½ teaspoon salt
2 cups buttermilk
1 cup chopped nuts

Beat eggs, add sugar and mix well. Sift flour, soda and salt together and add alternately with buttermilk to egg mixture. Add nuts. Pour into 2 greased loaf pans. Bake in slow oven (325° F.) 1 hour. Makes 2 (8x4-inch) loaves.

Your popularity will rapidly spread when you serve specialty fruit-nut bread

BANANA BREAD

½ cup shortening
1 cup sugar
2 eggs
1 cup mashed ripe bananas
1 teaspoon lemon juice
2 cups sifted flour
3 teaspoons baking powder
½ teaspoon salt
1 cup nut meats, chopped

Cream shortening and sugar together. Beat eggs until light and add. Press bananas through sieve and add lemon juice. Blend with creamed mixture. Sift flour, baking powder and salt together and mix quickly into banana mixture. Add nuts. Bake in greased loaf pan in moderate oven (375° F.) about 1¼ hours. Makes 1 (1-pound) loaf.

BANANA-BRAN NUT BREAD— Omit 1 egg, ¼ cup shortening, ½ cup sugar, ½ cup flour, ½ teaspoon baking powder, 1 teaspoon lemon juice, and ½ cup nut meats. Add 1 cup bran, and ½ teaspoon baking soda. Increase mashed banana to 1½ cups. Proceed as for above.

BRAZIL NUT-ORANGE BREAD

3 cups sifted flour
5 level teaspoons baking powder
1 teaspoon salt
1 cup sugar
1 cup sliced Brazil nuts
¾ cup sliced orange peel
2 eggs
1¼ cups milk
2 tablespoons melted butter

Quarter orange and remove peel. Scrape bitter white pulp from inside of yellow peel. Cut peel into thin slices. · Cook until tender in boiling water. Drain and dry. Sift together flour, baking powder and salt. Add sugar, Brazil nuts and cooled orange peel. Mix well. Beat the eggs to lightness and add milk and melted butter. Add to the dry ingredients and mix well. Put into a well-greased loaf pan, and bake in a moderate oven (350°F.) for 1 hour or until well baked.

FRUIT BREAD

2 cups sifted flour
4 teaspoons baking powder
¾ cup sugar
¼ teaspoon salt
½ cup chopped nut meats
2 tablespoons chopped candied
    lemon peel
¼ cup chopped candied citron
¼ cup currants
2 tablespoons chopped candied
    cherries
2 eggs
1 cup milk
3 tablespoons melted shortening

Sift flour, baking powder, sugar and salt together. Add nuts and fruit. Beat eggs, combine with milk and shortening and add to flour mixture. Stir just enough to moisten flour. Pour into greased loaf pan and bake in moderate oven (375° F.) 1 hour. Makes 1 (1-pound) loaf.
If currants are dry soften in warm water 20 minutes, drain and dry.

Brazil nut-orange bread gives that Pan-American touch we all love so much

CORN BREAD

2 eggs, slightly beaten
1¼ cups milk
¼ cup melted shortening
1½ cups yellow corn meal
¾ cup sifted flour
1 teaspoon salt
2 tablespoons sugar
2½ teaspoons baking powder

Beat eggs and add milk and shortening. Sift remaining ingredients together, add to egg mixture and beat well. Pour into greased shallow pan and bake in hot oven (400° F.) until it shrinks from the sides of the pan, about 20 to 25 minutes. Serves 6.

SOUR MILK — Use 1½ cups of sour milk instead of sweet milk, add ¾ teaspoon baking soda and decrease amount of baking powder to 1 teaspoon.

CHOCOLATE ALMOND BREAD

2 eggs
1 cup brown sugar
2 ounces (squares) chocolate,
    melted
½ teaspoon cinnamon
½ teaspoon allspice
½ teaspoon baking powder
⅔ cup sifted flour (about)
2 tablespoons milk
⅓ cup chopped almonds
½ recipe meringue

Beat eggs, add sugar and beat together thoroughly. Add melted chocolate. Sift cinnamon, allspice, baking powder and flour together and add alternately with milk to creamed mixture. Add almonds and stir until mixture is well blended. Spread ½ inch thick in shallow pans and bake in moderate oven (350° F.) ·20 minutes. When baked cut into strips, frost with meringue and brown slightly. Makes 30 strips.

COCOA BREAD

2½ cups sifted flour
3 teaspoons baking powder
½ teaspoon salt
¼ cup cocoa
⅓ cup sugar
1 egg
1⅓ cups milk
¼ cup melted shortening

Sift flour, baking powder, salt, cocoa and sugar together 3 times. Beat egg and add milk and shortening. Stir into dry ingredients, mixing only enough to dampen all flour. Pour into greased loaf pan. Bake in moderate oven (350° F.) 45 minutes. Makes 1 loaf.

DATE NUT BREAD

1 cup cut dates
1 cup boiling water
1 tablespoon shortening
2 cups sifted flour
3 teaspoons baking powder
½ teaspoon salt
¾ cup sugar
1 egg
1 cup chopped nut meats

Combine first 3 ingredients, cover and cool. Sift flour, baking powder and salt together. Beat sugar and egg together and add to dates, alternately with sifted dry ingredients. Add broken nut meats. Pour into greased loaf pan, let stand 20 minutes and bake in slow oven (325° F.) 50 to 60 minutes. Turn onto cake rack to cool. The flavor of loaf improves after standing 24 hours. Makes 1 loaf.

DATE BREAD

2½ cups sifted flour
4 teaspoons baking powder
½ teaspoon salt
½ cup sugar
1¼ cups chopped dates
2 eggs
1¼ cups milk
¼ cup melted shortening

Sift flour with baking powder, salt and sugar. Add dates. Beat eggs, add milk and shortening and add to dry ingredients, stirring only enough to dampen all the flour. Pour into greased loaf pan. Bake in moderate oven (350° F.) 1 hour. Makes 1 (1-pound) loaf. Or use figs instead of dates.

FIG-WALNUT LOAF

2 cups sifted flour
1 teaspoon salt
4 teaspoons baking powder
⅓ cup sugar
1 cup whole-wheat or graham flour
1 cup toasted English walnuts, coarsely chopped
½ cup dried figs, chopped fine
1 egg
1½ cups milk

Sift first 4 ingredients together. Mix in whole-wheat flour, nuts and figs. Beat egg slightly and add milk. Add liquid to dry ingredients, stirring only enough to dampen all the flour. Pour into greased loaf pan and bake in moderate oven (350° F.) 1 hour. Makes 1 (8x4x3-inch) loaf.

Surprise the folks with date nut bread and serve with a variety of mild Cheese spread

FIG BREAD

½ cup raisins
½ cup figs
2 tablespoons shortening
1 cup honey
1 egg
2½ cups sifted flour
½ teaspoon salt
1 teaspoon baking powder
½ teaspoon baking soda
¾ cup milk
¼ cup sour milk
1 cup nut meats

Cut raisins and figs into small pieces. Cream shortening with honey until fluffy. Add beaten egg. Sift dry ingredients together and add alternately with milk. Add nuts and fruit. Bake in moderate oven (325° F.) 1¼ hours. Makes 1 loaf.

HOMINY BREAD

2 cups cold cooked hominy grits
¼ teaspoon salt
1½ tablespoons melted shortening
1½ cups milk
2 eggs, separated

Mix hominy, salt and shortening. Add milk. Beat egg yolks thoroughly and add. Fold in egg whites beaten until stiff but not dry. Bake in greased dish in hot oven (400° F.) about 45 minutes. Serve in baking dish. Serves 6.

GRAPE-NUT BREAD

2 cups milk, scalded
1 cup grape-nuts, 1 teaspoon salt
3 cups sifted flour
4 teaspoons baking powder
½ cup sugar, 1 egg, well beaten
3 tablespoons melted shortening

Pour milk over grape-nuts; cool. Sift flour, baking powder, salt and sugar together. Add egg and shortening to grape-nut mixture and stir well; add flour mixture, stirring only enough to dampen all flour. Turn into greased loaf pan and let stand 20 minutes. Bake in moderate oven (350° F.) 1 hour and 20 minutes. Makes 1 (9x4x3-inch) loaf.

GRAPE-NUT PRUNE BREAD — Increase salt to 1½ teaspoons; add 1 tablespoon grated orange or lemon rind and 1 cup finely chopped prunes.

GRAPE-NUT APRICOT BREAD — Increase salt to 1½ teaspoons; add 1 cup chopped dried apricots.

HONEY-PINEAPPLE BREAD

2 tablespoons shortening
1 cup honey
1 egg
2¼ cups sifted flour
3 teaspoons baking powder
½ teaspoon salt
¾ cup nut meats
1 cup bran
1 cup pineapple juice

Blend shortening and honey. Add egg and beat well. Sift flour, baking powder and salt together and mix ½ cup with nut meats. Add about half the remaining sifted dry ingredients to the egg mixture and mix well. Add bran and pineapple juice and mix, then add remaining flour and nuts. Pour into greased loaf pan and bake in moderate oven (325° F.) 1¼ hours. Makes 1 loaf.

HONEY-DATE NUT BREAD

1 cup dates, 1 cup boiling water
¾ cup honey
2 tablespoons shortening
1 egg, 1 cup nuts
1½ cups sifted flour
¼ teaspoon salt
2 teaspoons baking powder

Cook dates in water until mixture is very thick. Cool. Cream honey and shortening together. Add egg, date mixture and nuts. Sift remaining ingredients together and add to mixture. Pour into greased loaf pan and bake in slow oven (325° F.) 1 hour and 20 minutes. Makes 1 loaf.

HONEY NUT BREAD

2½ cups sifted flour
1 teaspoon salt
1 teaspoon baking soda
2 tablespoons shortening
1 cup honey
1 egg
¾ cup sour milk
1 tablespoon chopped candied
    orange peel
⅔ cup raisins
⅔ cup chopped nuts

Sift flour, salt and soda together Cream shortening and honey thoroughly; add egg and mix well Add sifted dry ingredients alternately with sour milk. Add fruit and nuts and pour into greased loaf pan. Bake in slow oven (300°F.) 1 hour and 40 minutes. Makes 1 loaf.

QUICK ORANGE BREAD

2 cups sifted flour
4 teaspoons baking powder
½ cup sugar
½ teaspoon salt
2 eggs
½ cup orange juice
3 tablespoons melted shortening
1 cup chopped candied orange
    peel

Sift flour, baking powder, sugar and salt together. Beat eggs well and add orange juice, shortening and orange peel. Combine egg mixture with dry ingredients, mixing only enough to dampen all flour. Place in greased loaf pan bake in moderate oven. (350°F.) 1 hour. Makes 1 (1-pound) loaf.

ORANGE-ALMOND BREAD

2 tablespoons shortening, softened
¼ cup sugar, 1 egg
2 cups sifted cake flour
3 teaspoons baking powder
1 teaspoon salt
1 cup orange juice
1 teaspoon grated orange rind
1 cup sliced blanched almonds

Beat shortening, sugar and egg together. Sift flour, baking powder and salt together and add to first mixture alternately with orange juice and rind. Blend thoroughly and add nuts. Pour into greased loaf pan and bake in moderate oven (350° F.) 1 hour. Makes 1 loaf.

ORANGE-HONEY BREAD

2 tablespoons shortening
1 cup honey
1 egg, beaten
1½ tablespoons grated orange
    rind
2⅔ cups sifted flour
2½ teaspoons baking powder
½ teaspoon baking soda
½ teaspoon salt
¾ cup orange juice
¾ cup chopped nut meats

Cream shortening and honey together thoroughly. Add egg and orange rind. Sift flour with baking powder, soda and salt. Add to creamed mixture alternately with orange juice. Add nuts. Bake in greased loaf pan in moderate oven (325° F.) for 70 minutes. Makes 1 loaf.

PEANUT-BUTTER NUT BREAD

TOPPING

2 tablespoons butter
4 tablespoons brown sugar
Peanuts
1 tablespoon water

Spread butter on bottom of loaf pan. Cover evenly with sugar and peanuts. Sprinkle water over mixture. Cover with following:

BATTER

1 egg
1 cup brown sugar
2 tablespoons peanut butter
2 tablespoons melted butter
1 cup sour milk or buttermilk
2 cups sifted, enriched flour
½ teaspoon soda
1 teaspoon baking powder
½ teaspoon salt

Beat egg. Add sugar gradually, beating it in. Stir in peanut butter and melted butter. Add milk. Sift together flour, soda, baking powder and salt. Add egg mixture, stirring until well-blended. Bake in moderate oven (350°F.) 1 hour. Makes one 1-pound loaf.

PRUNE NUT BREAD

1 tablespoon shortening
1 cup sugar
1 egg, beaten
½ cup prune juice
1 cup sour milk
2 cups whole-wheat flour
1 cup sifted white flour
5 teaspoons baking powder
½ teaspoon baking soda
½ teaspoon salt
2 cups chopped pitted, cooked prunes
1 cup chopped walnuts

Cream shortening with sugar. Add egg and blend well. Combine prune juice and sour milk; add alternately with whole-wheat flour to first mixture. Sift white flour, baking powder, baking soda and salt together 3 times. Add with prunes and walnuts to first mixture and beat thoroughly. Pour into greased loaf pans and bake in moderate oven (350° F.) about 1 hour. Makes 2 loaves.

Youngsters sing with all their might. Hooray! It's peanut-butter bread tonite

SOY NUT BREAD

1 cup soy flour
1½ cup white or graham flour
1 teaspoon salt
3 teaspoons baking powder
2 tablespoons sugar
½ teaspoon cinnamon
1 cup chopped nuts
1 cup milk
3 eggs, well beaten
4 tablespoons shortening

Mix and sift first 5 ingredients together; add cinnamon and chopped nuts. Combine milk, beaten egg and shortening and add to dry ingredients, stirring only enough to moisten. Do not beat; batter should not be smooth. Let dough stand in greased bread pan 20 minutes. Bake in a moderate oven (350° F.) for 1 hour.

If desired, ½ cup of chopped dates may be added.

VARIATIONS—¼ soy flour may be substituted for an equal amount of white or whole-wheat flour in any recipe for bread, muffins, biscuits, pastry or plain cakes without any other changes.

BOSTON BROWN BREAD

1 cup yellow corn meal
1 cup rye meal
1 teaspoon baking soda
1 teaspoon salt
1 cup graham flour
¾ cup molasses
1½ cups sour milk or butter-
    milk

Sift first 4 ingredients together, add graham flour and stir in remaining ingredients. Place rounds of greased paper in bottom of 1-pound baking powder cans. Grease sides of cans and fill ⅔ full. Place cans on rack in large kettle. Add hot water to half the height of mold Cover kettle and heat water to boiling. Boil gently 3 hours. More boiling water may have to be added from time to time. Remove from water, uncover· and place in hot oven (400° F.) for a few minutes to dry the top Remove from cans immediately Serve hot with Boston baked beans Makes 3 loaves.

RAISIN BROWN BREAD—Add 1 cup raisins dredged with flour to the above recipe.

STEAMED PEANUT-BUTTER DATE BREAD

¾ cup peanut butter
¼ cup sugar
1 egg, beaten
2 cups sifted cake flour
3 teaspoons baking powder
½ teaspoon salt
1 cup milk
¼ cup chopped dates

Beat peanut butter and sugar together and add egg. Sift flour, baking powder and salt together and add to first mixture alternately with milk. Fold in dates. Fill greased mold ⅔ full, cover tightly and steam 2½ hours. Makes 1 loaf.

Hot, fragrant Boston brown bread is even more tempting and attractive when spread with cream cheese

STEAMED RAISIN NUT BREAD

2 tablespoons shortening
¼ cup brown sugar
1 egg
½ cup chopped raisins
½ cup chopped nut meats
2 cups sifted cake flour
3 teaspoons baking powder
½ teaspoon salt
¼ teaspoon cinnamon
¼ teaspoon allspice
1 cup milk

Cream shortening and sugar and add egg. Beat well. Add raisins and nuts. Sift flour, baking powder, salt, cinnamon and allspice together 3 times. Add to creamed mixture alternately with milk. Fill greased mold ⅔ full, cover and steam 2½ hours. Makes 1 loaf.

PINEAPPLE NUT BREAD

2¼ cups sifted flour
¾ cup sugar
1½ teaspoons salt
3 teaspoons baking powder
½ teaspoon baking soda
1 cup shredded whole bran
¾ cup chopped walnut meats
1½ cups crushed pineapple
    (undrained)
1 egg, well beaten
3 tablespoons shortening, melted

Sift flour, sugar, salt, baking powder and soda together 3 times. Stir in remaining ingredients, mixing only enough to dampen all the flour. Bake in greased loaf pan (9x4x3 inches), in moderate oven (350° F.) 1¼ hours. Makes 1 (2-pound) loaf. This bread keeps moist 7 to 10 days and slices best when a day old. If desired, raisins, or other dried fruit may be used in place of crushed pineapple.

PECAN BREAD

cups sifted flour
teaspoons baking powder
teaspoon salt
¼ cup sugar
cup chopped pecan meats
egg, beaten
½ cups milk
tablespoons melted shortening

Sift flour, baking powder, salt and sugar together. Add nuts. Combine egg, milk and shortening. Add to flour mixture, stirring only enough to dampen all the flour. Place in greased loaf pan. Bake in moderate oven (350° F.) 45 to 60 minutes. Makes 1 loaf.

VERMONT JOHNNYCAKE

2 cups sifted flour
4½ teaspoons baking powder
¾ teaspoon salt
1 cup corn meal
3 eggs, beaten
1 cup milk
½ cup maple sirup
¾ cup melted shortening

Sift first 3 ingredients together, add corn meal and mix thoroughly. Combine remaining ingredients and add to dry ingredients, stirring only enough to dampen all the flour. Pour into greased pan and bake in hot oven (400° F.) 30 minutes. Serves 8.

SOUR-CREAM CORN BREAD

2 cups corn meal
2 tablespoons sugar
1 teaspoon salt
1 teaspoon baking soda
2 teaspoons baking powder
2 eggs
2 cups sour cream

Sift dry ingredients together. Beat eggs and add sour cream. Add to dry ingredients and mix well. Pour into greased pan and bake in hot oven (400° F.) about 30 minutes. Serves 6 to 8.

PRUNE CORN BREAD

1 cup sifted flour
1 tablespoon baking powder
¾ teaspoon salt
1 tablespoon sugar
1 cup yellow corn meal
2 eggs, well beaten
2 tablespoons melted shortening
½ cup pitted cooked prunes, chopped
1 cup milk

Sift flour, baking powder, salt and sugar together. Stir corn meal thoroughly into flour mixture. Combine eggs, shortening, prunes and milk; add to dry ingredients. Mix well, pour into greased pan and bake in moderate oven (375° F.) about 30 minutes. Makes 1 (8x8x2-inch) loaf.

WHOLE-WHEAT FRUIT NUT BREAD

⅔ cup chopped pitted dates
½ cup chopped figs
½ cup chopped nut meats
1½ cups sifted flour
3 teaspoons baking powder
½ teaspoon salt
¼ teaspoon baking soda
1½ cups whole-wheat flour
¼ cup brown sugar
1 egg, beaten
½ cup honey
1⅓ cups milk
3 tablespoons melted shortening
1½ teaspoons grated orange rind

Mix fruits and nuts with 2 tablespoons flour. Sift remaining flour with baking powder, salt and soda; mix in whole-wheat flour thoroughly. Add brown sugar gradually to egg and beat thoroughly; add honey, milk, shortening and orange rind. Add to dry ingredients, mixing only enough to dampen all the flour. Add fruits and nuts. Pour into greased loaf pan and bake in moderate oven (350° F.) 1 to 1¼ hours. Cool thoroughly before slicing. Makes 1 (9x5x3-inch) loaf.

SOUTHERN SPOON BREAD

2 cups white corn meal
2 cups boiling water
1 teaspoon salt
3 tablespoons melted shortening
1½ cups milk
3 eggs, separated

Sift corn meal 3 times and mix with boiling water, stirring until smooth and free from lumps. Add salt, shortening, milk and beaten egg yolks. Beat whites until stiff but not dry and fold in. Pour into greased baking dish and bake in moderate oven (350° F.) 45 minutes. Serve warm in baking dish. Serves 8.

VERMONT GRAHAM BREAD

1 cup sifted flour
1½ teaspoons baking soda
1 teaspoon salt
½ cup maple or brown sugar
2 cups buttermilk or sour milk
2 cups graham flour

Sift flour, soda, salt and sugar together. Add buttermilk and graham flour, mixing only enough to dampen all the flour. Pour into greased pan and bake in moderate oven (350° F.) 1 hour. Makes 1 (9x5x3-inch) loaf.

SWEDISH HARDTACK

1 pint buttermilk
½ cup sugar
½ cup shortening, melted
1 teaspoon salt
⅞ teaspoon baking soda
Coarse rye flour

Mix ingredients to make a thick dough and shape into 24 balls, dipping them in flour. Roll out very thin with a special peg rolling pin (a barbed pin which pricks dough as it rolls). Bake on cookie sheet in hot oven (425°F.) until browned, about 15 minutes. These are very crisp and tender.

YEAST ROLLS

1 cake yeast
½ cup lukewarm water
2 tablespoons shortening
2 tablespoons sugar
2 teaspoons salt
½ cup milk, scalded
1 egg or 2 egg yolks
3½ to 4 cups sifted flour

Soften yeast in lukewarm water. Add shortening, sugar and salt to milk. Cool to lukewarm and add yeast and beaten egg. Stir in flour to make a soft dough. Turn out on floured board and knead until satiny and smooth (8 to 10 minutes). Place in greased bowl, cover and let rise until doubled in bulk. Punch down. Let rise again until doubled in bulk. Punch down and let stand 10 minutes. Shape into rolls. Let rise until doubled in bulk. Bake in hot oven (425° F.) 12 to 15 minutes. Makes 24-36 rolls.

BOWKNOTS—Roll out dough about ¼ inch thick. Cut into strips ½ inch wide and 6 inches long. Tie into knots. Place on greased baking sheet.

BRAIDS—Roll dough out ¼ inch thick and cut into strips 6 inches long and ½ inch wide. Cross 3 strips in the middle and braid from center to each end. Press ends together and fold under. Place on greased baking sheet.

BUTTERLEAF ROLLS—Roll out rectangular sheet very thin. Brush with melted butter. Cut into strips about 1 inch wide. Pile 6 to 7 strips together. Cut into 1½-inch pieces and place on end in greased muffin pans.

CLOVER - LEAF ROLLS—Form dough into small balls. Dip each into melted butter and place 3 balls in each section of a greased muffin pan.

CRESCENTS—Roll part of dough into circular shape about ¼ inch thick. Cut into wedges. Brush with melted butter and roll up, beginning at the wide end. Place point side down on baking sheet. Curve into crescent shape and sprinkle with poppy seed.

SALT ROLLS— Leave straight and sprinkle with salt.

ROSETTES—Follow directions for bowknots. After tying bring one end through center and the other over the side.

WATER ROLLS

1 cake yeast
1 cup lukewarm water
1 tablespoon sugar
1 teaspoon salt
2 tablespoons melted shortening
3 to 4 cups sifted flour
2 egg whites, beaten
Corn meal, 1 egg yolk
1 tablespoon cold water

Soften yeast in ¼ cup lukewarm water. To remaining water add sugar, salt, shortening and 1 cup flour. Beat well. Add egg whites and softened yeast and beat well. Add enough more flour to make a soft dough. Knead thoroughly on a lightly floured board. Place in greased bowl, grease top, cover and let rise until doubled in bulk. Punch down. When again doubled in bulk, punch down and divide into portions. Cover and let rest 10 minutes. Shape into rolls. Place 2½ inches apart on greased baking sheet which has been sprinkled with corn meal, cover and let rise until doubled in bulk. Mix egg yolk with cold water and brush over rolls. Bake in hot oven (450° F.) 20 minutes, with a shallow pan of boiling water on floor of the oven. Makes 24 rolls.

Use some originality in your rolls. Let braids, twists and shamrocks be your goals

REFRIGERATOR ROLLS

2 cakes yeast, 1 cup milk
¼ cup lukewarm water
½ cup corn sirup or ¼ cup honey
   or sugar
1 tablespoon salt, 2 eggs, beaten
6 cups sifted, enriched flour
½ cup shortening, melted

Soften yeast in lukewarm water. Scald milk, add sirup and salt; cool to lukewarm. Add 2 cups flour and beat well. Add yeast, eggs, and shortening; blend well. Add remaining flour to make a soft dough. Knead until smooth and satiny. Place in lightly greased bowl; grease top of dough. Cover well and put into refrigerator. After no less than 12 hours or more than 4 days, remove and punch down. Let stand; mold into any desired shape. Place rolls in greased pans, cover and let rise until doubled in bulk. Bake in hot oven (425° F.) 15 to 20 minutes. Makes 30.

WHOLE-WHEAT ROLLS—Use 3 cups each whole-wheat and white flour.

POTATO REFRIGERATOR ROLLS—Omit 1 cake yeast, 2 teaspoons salt, 1 egg, and ½ cup corn sirup. Add 1 cup hot mashed potatoes, and 5 tablespoons sugar. Increase lukewarm water to ½ cup. Crumble yeast cake into large mixing bowl and add warm water and 1 tablespoon sugar; let stand for 5 minutes. Cream shortening and remaining sugar. Add milk to mashed potatoes and combine with shortening mixture. Cool to lukewarm; add to yeast mixture with egg and salt. Beat in 2 cups of flour; let rise until light. Knead in remaining flour. Continue as for above.

No rolls are simpler to make and easier to eat than clover-leaf

BRIOCHE

1 cup milk, scalded, 1 cup butter
2 teaspoons salt, ½ cup sugar
2 cakes yeast
¼ cup lukewarm water
4 eggs, well beaten
4½ cups sifted flour

Scald milk; add butter, salt and sugar; stir until butter melts. When lukewarm, add yeast softened in lukewarm water; add beaten eggs. Beat flour into mixture. Let rise in warm place 6 hours. Chill until ready to use. Form quickly into small balls ⅓ size of muffin pans. Brush tops with melted butter; let rise until doubled in bulk. Bake in hot oven (400°F.) 20 minutes. Makes 24.

BRAIDS—Dust a breadboard lightly with flour and roll brioche dough gently into a sheet about ½ inch thick. Cut the dough into strips ½ inch wide, leaving one end uncut. Place on greased baking sheet and brush the cut edges with melted butter. Fold the strips over each other to form a braid. Pinch both ends of braid together, flatten and press down on pan to prevent strips separating and losing shape.

BOWKNOTS—Twist strips of brioche dough lightly and tie in a bowknot. Bring the ends down and press to the pan.

CHEESE REFRIGERATOR SQUARES.—Omit ½ cup butter, 1 teaspoon salt, ¼ cup sugar, ¼ cup lukewarm water, and 1 egg. Add 1 cup grated cheese. Increase flour ½ cup. Add cheese with flour. Roll ¼ inch thick. Cut into 3-inch squares. Fold opposite corners of each square to center, pressing together. Bake as for above. Makes 24.

Brioche in any form are always a treat for brunch

*Call them Parker House
or pocketbook;
they're easy to make
for the youngest cook*

PARKER HOUSE ROLLS

2 tablespoons shortening
1 teaspoon salt, ¼ cup sugar
1 cake yeast
1½ cups lukewarm water
3½ cups sifted flour
1 egg, well beaten
Melted butter

Add shortening, salt, sugar and crumbled yeast cake to water; stir until shortening is melted. Stir in sifted flour, cover and set in a warm place, free from drafts, to rise. When doubled in bulk, add egg. Knead lightly and let rise again until doubled in bulk. Roll out ½ inch thick on well-floured board. Cut with biscuit cutter 2 inches in diameter, crease in center with a dull knife, brush with melted butter and fold over, pinching the dough at sides to make a pocketbook. Place on baking sheet and brush tops with melted butter. Let rise and bake in hot oven (400°F.) about 20 minutes. Makes 24.

ORANGE MARMALADE ROLLS
—Omit 1 cup lukewarm water, and 1 egg. Increase shortening to 4 tablespoons, salt to 1½ teaspoons, yeast to 2 cakes, and flour to 5 cups. Add orange marmalade, and 2½ cups milk. Mix as for standard Parker House Rolls. When dough is doubled in bulk, roll out on floured board and cut with a biscuit cutter. Brush with melted butter and place 1 teaspoon of orange marmalade in center. Fold each roll in half and place in greased baking pan. Brush top with butter. Let stand in warm place 30 minutes. Bake in hot oven (425°F.) 20 minutes. Makes 40 rolls.

Grated cheese and nuts in each layer give added zest to butterleaf rolls

ALMOND PUFFS

1 cake yeast, ¼ cup shortening
¼ cup lukewarm water
5 tablespoons sugar, ½ teaspoon
    salt
½ cup scalded milk
2¼ cups sifted flour, 2 eggs
1 cup almonds, blanched and
    chopped

Soften yeast in lukewarm water.
Add shortening, 1 tablespoon
sugar and the salt to scalded milk
and cool to lukewarm. Add flour
and softened yeast, beating thoroughly. Beat in eggs one at a
time. Cover and let rise until
doubled in bulk. Stir in ½ cup
almonds. Fill greased muffin pans
½ full. Sprinkle with remaining
nuts and sugar. Cover and let
rise until doubled in bulk. Bake
in moderate oven (375°F.) 15 to
20 minutes. Makes 24 puffs.

HATCHET-SHAPED
ROLLS

1 recipe Refrigerator Rolls

Divide dough into 2 parts. Roll
out 1 part, cut into strips ½ inch
wide and cut crosswise into
3-inch lengths. Roll out remainder of dough and cut into
strips 1½ inches wide. Cut these
strips into hatchet-head shaped
pieces. Place one hatchet head
at the end of each strip, let rise
until light and bake as directed.

POPPY-SEED CRESCENTS

DOUGH

1 cup scalded milk, 1 cake yeast
½ cup butter
½ cup sugar
½ teaspoon salt
1 teaspoon vanilla
4 eggs, well beaten
4 cups sifted flour

FILLING

2 cups water, 1 cup sugar
1 cup ground poppy seed
½ teaspoon cinnamon
Grated rind of 1 lemon

TOPPING

1 egg yolk
1 tablespoon cold water
Sugar, chopped nuts

Cool milk to lukewarm and soften yeast in ¼ cup of the milk. To remaining milk add butter, sugar, salt and vanilla and stir until the butter has melted. Add beaten eggs and yeast. Sift flour and add gradually, using only enough to make dough stiff enough to be kneaded until smooth and elastic. Cover and let rise until doubled in bulk.

FILLING—Boil water with sugar until sirupy Add the ground poppy seed, cinnamon and lemon rind. Mix well and cool Roll out dough on a floured board until quite thin; cut into triangles, spread with filling and shape into crescents by rolling them from the straight end toward the point. Brush with beaten egg yolk to which cold water has been added and sprinkle with sugar and chopped nuts. Let rise until doubled in bulk and then bake in hot oven (400°F.) 20 minutes or until brown. Makes 36.

Pie-shaped pieces of dough and nimble fingers make crescents straight, curved and flattened

CINNAMON ROLLS

1 cake yeast, 1 cup warm water
½ teaspoon salt, 5 tablespoons
   sugar
Flour (about 6 cups)
1 cup scalded milk
2 eggs, well beaten
½ cup melted butter
FILLING
4 tablespoons sugar
4 tablespoons butter
1½ teaspoons cinnamon
¼ cup broken nut meats

Add yeast to warm water, following directions on package. Pour ½ the scalded milk over salt and 1 tablespoon sugar. Cool to lukewarm and add softened yeast. Sift in about ½ the flour, beating thoroughly until the dough is smooth and falls from spoon in sheets. Place in greased bowl. Lightly grease surface and cover with clean, dry towel. When dough doubles in bulk, punch down. Mix remaining lukewarm milk and sugar with eggs and melted butter before adding to dough. Stir enough of remaining flour in to form ball which does not stick to bowl. Turn out on floured surface and allow to rest 5 to 10 min. Knead dough until smooth and elastic and small blisters are evenly distributed under the surface. Set aside in greased bowl, grease and cover.

Let rise again; roll out on a floured board. To prepare filling: Mix sugar, butter, cinnamon and nuts together with a fork. Spread on dough, roll up like a jelly roll and cut crosswise into 2-inch pieces. Place on greased pan, cut side up, let rise until doubled in bulk and bake in 375°F. oven 20 to 25 minutes. Makes 24 large rolls.

If any time morale is low, just serve cinnamon rolls and watch faces glow

CARAMEL PECAN ROLLS—Roll dough in rectangular sheet to ¼ inch thickness. Spread with filling and roll up as for cinnamon rolls. Melt 6 tablespoons butter in baking pan and add brown sugar to a depth of ¼ inch. Arrange ½ cup pecan halves over sugar. Cut

rolls crosswise into slices 1½ inches in thickness. Place, cu side up, in pan. Cover and le rise until doubled in bulk. Bak at 375°F. 25 to 30 minutes. In vert pan on cooling rack and al low to stand a few seconds befor lifting off pan. Makes about 30

HOT CROSS BUNS

cups sifted flour
¼ cup mixed candied fruits
¼ cup chopped nut meats
2 teaspoon mace
¼ cup seedless raisins
cake yeast
tablespoons lukewarm water
cup milk
¼ cup shortening
1½ teaspoons salt
¼ cup sugar
egg, beaten
2 teaspoon vanilla
¼ teaspoon lemon extract
recipe **Coffee Cake Icing**

Mix flour, candied fruits, nuts
and mace. Wash raisins in hot
water, dry and add to flour. Soften yeast in water. Scald milk
and add shortening, salt and sugar. Add 1 cup flour mixture and
cool to lukewarm. Then add yeast
and beaten egg. Mix thoroughly.
Add flavorings and remaining
flour. Knead well and place in
greased bowl to rise until doubled
in bulk. Knead, form into buns
and place on greased baking
sheet. Cut a cross in top of each
with sharp knife and grease lightly. Let rise until doubled in bulk.
Bake in hot oven (400°F.) about
15 minutes. Dust with confectioners' sugar or make a cross
on each with icing.

CITRON BUNS

1 pint milk, 1 cake yeast
¼ cup sugar
8 cups sifted flour
2 eggs, 1 teaspoon salt
⅓ cup softened butter
1 cup raisins, 4 cardamom capsules
¼ cup chopped citron

Scald milk and cool to lukewarm,
add yeast and let soften. Add
sugar and 4 cups flour to make
a sponge. Beat well. Cover and
let rise in warm place until doubled in bulk, about 1½ hours.
Add unbeaten eggs, salt and butter and mix until thoroughly
blended. Sift remaining flour
over raisins and citron. Remove
cardamom seeds from capsules
and crush fine. Add with flour,
raisins and citron to first mixture. Work to a smooth, elastic
dough. Cover and let rise until
doubled in bulk, about 1½ hours.
Turn onto lightly floured board
and shape into buns. Place on
baking sheet 1 inch apart; let
rise until light, then bake in
moderate oven (375°F.) 20 minutes. Makes 30 buns.

Citron buns add zest to any
meal, and their flavor is as
good as their appeal

BUTTER SEMMELN

½ cake yeast
¼ cup warm water
½ cup mashed potatoes
1 cup granulated sugar
½ cup butter
2 cups milk, scalded
2 eggs, well beaten
½ teaspoon salt
6 cups sifted flour
2 tablespoons butter, melted
¼ cup confectioners' sugar

Make batter in the early evening
and set to rise in a warm place
until morning. Soften yeast in
water and add mashed potatoes
and ½ cup of the sugar. Let
stand in warm place 4 hours.
Add butter to scalded milk and
cool to lukewarm; add eggs, remaining sugar and salt and combine with yeast mixture. Sift
in flour and knead thoroughly.
Cover and let rise in a warm
place until morning. Roll out to
about ¼-inch thickness, brush
with melted butter and cut into
2-inch squares. Turn up corners
toward center. Place about 2
inches apart on greased baking
sheet and let rise until light.
Bake in very hot oven (450°F.)
20 minutes. Remove from oven,
brush with melted butter and
sprinkle with confectioners'
sugar. Makes about 30 rolls.

Biscuits leavened with either baking soda or baking powder or both should have a flaky texture, a smooth brown crust and good flavor. They contain a larger proportion of shortening than most other breads and are mixed in somewhat the same manner as pastry. The cold shortening is cut into the mixture of flour and leavening with knives or a pastry blender, then the cold liquid is added and mixed in quickly and lightly. It is then turned out on a lightly floured board and kneaded very lightly until the dough is smooth (not more than 30 seconds), rolled and cut. If the biscuits are placed close together in the pan, they will have a crust on the top and bottom only; if placed far apart, they will brown all over. Biscuits are baked in a hot oven (450°F.) 10 to 15 minutes, depending on the size of the biscuits.

BAKING POWDER BISCUITS

2 cups sifted flour
3 teaspoons baking powder
½ teaspoon salt
4 tablespoons cold shortening
¾ cup milk

Sift dry ingredients together and cut in shortening. Add milk to make a soft dough. Place on a floured board and knead lightly a few seconds, using as little flour as possible on board. Roll out ½ inch thick and cut with floured biscuit cutter. Place on greased baking sheet and bake in very hot oven (450° F.) about 12 minutes. Makes 14 (2-inch) biscuits.

CHEESE — Add ½ cup grated American cheese to dry ingredients. Continue as above.

DROP — Increase milk to 1 cup and drop from a teaspoon onto a greased baking sheet. Bake as directed.

MAPLE SUGAR—Brush tops of biscuits before baking with butter; .sprinkle generously with grated maple sugar. Or fold ½ cup crushed maple sugar into biscuit dough, then roll and cut.

PEACH — Add 1 cup chopped peaches, drained from juice, 1 teaspoon chopped orange rind and 2 tablespoons sugar.

SOY FLOUR—Use ½ cup soy to 1½ cups white flour. Increase the fat to 5 tablespoons, baking powder to 4 teaspoons, and milk to ⅔ cup.

This is what we like about the South

APPLESAUCE BISCUITS

2 cups sifted flour
3 teaspoons baking powder
¼ teaspoon baking soda
1 teaspoon salt, 1 egg, beaten
3 tablespoons cold shortening
½ cup tart Applesauce
¼ cup thick sour cream
½ cup grated American cheese

Sift flour, baking powder, soda and salt together. Cut in shortening. Combine egg, applesauce and sour cream. Add to sifted dry ingredients, mix quickly, turn out onto a floured board and knead lightly for a few seconds. Roll out to ½-inch thickness. Cut into 2-inch biscuits and place on baking sheet sprinkled with grated cheese. Bake in hot oven (400°F.) 15 minutes. Makes 18

You see the difference in these biscuits, I know. The temperature for the second is too high and the third's too low; the first is the only perfect one in the row

BRAN BISCUITS

¾ cup sifted flour
1 cup bran
2½ teaspoons baking powder
½ teaspoon salt
¼ cup cold shortening
⅓ to ½ cup milk

Combine dry ingredients and mix together thoroughly. Cut in shortening; add enough milk to make a soft dough. Roll out ½ inch thick on lightly floured board, cut into rounds with a floured cutter and place on greased baking sheet. Bake in hot oven (400° F.) 15 minutes. Makes 12.

ORANGE BAKING POWDER BISCUITS

2 cups sifted flour
3 teaspoons baking powder
¾ teaspoon salt
2 tablespoons cold shortening
1 tablespoon grated orange rind
¾ cup milk
Loaf sugar
Juice of 2 oranges
Confectioners' sugar

Sift flour, baking powder and salt together and cut in shortening. Add orange rind and milk. Stir quickly and knead lightly for a few seconds, using as little flour on board as possible. Roll out to ½-inch thickness and cut with floured cutter. Put biscuit rounds together in pairs with a cube of sugar, moistened in orange juice, between. Place on greased baking sheet and spread tops with confectioners' sugar moistened with orange juice. Bake in very hot oven (450° F.) 15 minutes. Makes 18 (2-inch) biscuits.

GRAHAM BISCUITS

2 cups graham flour
1 cup sifted flour
4½ teaspoons baking powder
¾ teaspoon salt
½ cup cold shortening
1 cup milk

Mix dry ingredients. Cut in shortening, add milk, and stir quickly. Knead lightly on floured board. Roll to ½-inch thickness; cut with floured cutter. Bake on greased baking sheet in hot oven (425° F.) 12 to 15 minutes. Makes 25 biscuits.

HONEY CINNAMON BISCUITS

¼ cup butter, ½ cup honey
Cinnamon
1 recipe Baking Powder Biscuit dough

Melt butter and add ¼ cup honey. Spread in greased baking pan and sprinkle with cinnamon. Roll biscuit dough ½ inch thick and spread with remaining honey. Sprinkle with cinnamon. Roll up like jelly roll and cut into ½-inch slices. Place in pan, cut side down and bake in moderate oven (375° F.) 25 to 30 minutes. Makes 12 to 15 biscuits.

SOUR-MILK BISCUITS

2 cups sifted flour, 1 teaspoon salt
½ teaspoon baking soda
1½ teaspoons baking powder
4 tablespoons cold shortening
1 cup thick sour milk
    (less, if milk is not thick)
    or buttermilk

Mix and sift dry ingredients together. Cut in shortening, add milk and mix. Knead lightly, using as little flour as possible on board. Roll to ½-inch thickness, cut with floured cutter, place on greased baking sheet and bake in very hot oven (450° F.) 15 minutes. Makes 12 to 15 biscuits.

FOUR-O-CLOCK-TEA SCONES

cups sifted flour
tablespoon sugar
½ teaspoon salt
teaspoons baking powder
tablespoons cold shortening
½ to ⅔ cup milk
egg, well beaten
Melted butter, Sugar

Sift dry ingredients together and cut in shortening. Add milk to egg, then add to flour mixture gradually, adding more milk if necessary. Knead lightly on a floured board. Roll to ½-inch thickness. Cut into wedges, place on greased baking sheet, brush with melted butter and dredge with sugar. Bake in hot oven (400° F.) 15 minutes. Makes 15 (4-inch) scones.

BEATEN BISCUITS

¾ teaspoon sugar
½ teaspoon salt
3 cups sifted flour
⅓ cup cold shortening
½ cup milk

Sift sugar, salt and flour together; blend in shortening and add just enough milk to make a very stiff dough. Knead on lightly floured board until dough becomes soft and pliable. Run dough through a meat grinder or a biscuit machine, using a coarse knife, or beat steadily with a wooden potato masher 30 minutes, or until dough blisters, keeping edges turned in Roll to ½-inch thickness, cut with biscuit cutter, prick with fork and bake in moderate oven (350° F.) 30 minutes. The biscuits should be a very delicate ivory color. Makes about 1½ dozen.

SWEETPOTATO BISCUITS

1½ cups sifted flour
2 tablespoons baking powder
¾ teaspoon salt
½ cup cold shortening
1 cup milk
1½ cups mashed sweetpotatoes

Sift flour, baking powder and salt together. Cut in shortening. Combine milk and sweetpotatoes. Add to first mixture and stir quickly. Knead lightly, using as little flour as possible on board Roll out to ½-inch thickness; cut with floured cutter. Place on greased baking sheet and bake in hot oven (425° F.) 12 to 15 minutes. Makes 25 biscuits.

It's a beaten biscuit of the Southland, and once you try them you'll understand why the old custom has ne'er been banned

CAMP BISCUITS

2 cups sifted flour
3¾ teaspoons baking powder
1 teaspoon salt
6 tablespoons cold shortening
¾ cup milk

Sift flour, baking powder and salt together. Cut in shortening, stir in milk quickly and knead lightly for a few seconds, using as little flour as possible on board. Roll to ¼-inch thickness and cut with floured 2½-inch cutter. Cook in lightly greased hot skillet over very low heat until biscuits are brown on underside and raised to height of 1 inch. Turn and brown on other side. Makes 18.

LEMON TEA BISCUITS

4 cups sifted flour
¼ cup sugar
1½ teaspoons baking soda
1 teaspoon salt
⅔ cup cold shortening
6 tablespoons lemon juice
1 cup milk

Mix and sift dry ingredients. Cut in shortening with 2 knives .or pastry blender. Stir lemon juice

into milk and add quickly to flour mixture, using only enough to make a soft dough. Knead slightly on lightly floured board. Roll ½ inch thick and cut with floured cutter. Place on ungreased baking sheet and bake in very hot oven (450° F.) 15 minutes. Makes 20 biscuits.

CREAM BISCUITS

3 cups sifted flour
6 teaspoons baking powder
¾ teaspoon salt
1 cup heavy cream

Sift flour, baking powder and salt together. Add cream, stirring just enough to dampen all the flour. Knead lightly for a few seconds, using as little flour as possible on board. Roll to ½-inch thickness and cut with floured cutter. Place on greased baking sheet. Bake in hot oven (425°F.) 12 to 15 minutes. Makes 30 biscuits.

SOUR CREAM—Use 2 additional tablespoons cream. Use only 4½ teaspoons baking powder and add ½ teaspoon baking soda.

RASPBERRY TEA RING

1 recipe Baking Powder Biscuit
   dough
½ cup raspberry jam
Melted butter
1 cup sifted confectioners' sugar
2 tablespoons milk (about)
2 tablespoons raspberry jam

Roll dough into oblong sheet, ⅛ inch thick. Spread evenly with raspberry jam. Roll as for jelly roll; bring ends together to form ring and place on greased baking sheet. With scissors, cut 1-inch slices, almost through ring, turning each slice cut side up and pointing outer edge. Brush with melted butter. Bake in hot oven (400° F.) 30 minutes. Combine sugar, milk and jam. When ring is baked, remove from pan and while hot spread with glaze. Serve warm. For plain glaze, omit jam. Makes 1 ring.

Take along a skillet when you go on vacation. The golden brown camp biscuits will cause a sensation

FOUNDATION SWEET DOUGH

2 cakes yeast
¼ cup lukewarm water
¼ cup shortening, ½ cup sugar
1 teaspoon salt, 2 eggs, beaten
1 cup milk, scalded
1 teaspoon grated lemon rind
5 cups sifted flour (about)

Soften yeast in lukewarm water. Add shortening, sugar and salt to scalded milk; cool to lukewarm. Add softened yeast, eggs, lemon rind and enough flour to make a stiff batter. Beat well. Add enough more flour to make a soft dough. Turn out on lightly floured board and knead until satiny. Place in greased bowl, cover and let rise until doubled in bulk. When light, punch down. Shape into tea rings, rolls or coffee cakes. Let rise until doubled in bulk. Bake in moderate oven (375° F.) 25 to 30 minutes for coffee cakes, 20 to 25 minutes for rolls. Makes 2 (12-inch) tea rings or about 3½ dozen rolls.

Breads and braids
we often eat,
but egg braid with sugar
is quite a treat

ALMOND BUTTER COFFEE CAKE

¼ cup sugar
¼ teaspoon salt
¼ cup shortening
1 cup milk, scalded
½ cake yeast
1 egg
3½ cups sifted flour
⅛ teaspoon—mace
⅛ teaspoon cardamom

Add sugar, salt and shortening to milk and cool to lukewarm. Add crumbled yeast and let stand 5 minutes. Add egg and 1¾ cups flour; beat well. Add remaining flour sifted with spices; then knead well. Let rise until doubled in bulk, about 1½ hours. Knead down and let rise again. Shape into 2 coffee cakes and place in greased pans. Let rise 15 minutes. Spread almond mixture on top and let rise until doubled in bulk. Bake in moderate oven (375° F.) 45 minutes to 1 hour. Makes 2 cakes.

ALMOND MIXTURE

2 tablespoons sugar
1 tablespoon honey or sirup
1 tablespoon butter
1 tablespoon chopped almonds

Cook sugar, sirup and butter until it spins a thread. Add almonds and spread on cake.

EGG BRAID

1 recipe Foundation Sweet Dough
1 egg yolk
2 tablespoons sugar

When dough is light, divide into halves and cut half of dough into 6 pieces. Roll each piece until about 8 inches long. Cross 3 of the rolls in the center, braid to each end and fasten. Place on greased baking sheet. Braid remaining 3 rolls. Place on first braid. Cover and let rise until doubled in bulk. Brush with beaten egg yolk and sprinkle with sugar. Bake in hot oven (400° F.) 30 minutes. Makes 2 braids.

SWEDISH TEA RING

1 recipe Foundation Sweet Dough
Melted butter
Brown sugar
Cinnamon
Coffee Cake Icing
Chopped nuts

When dough is light, shape into 2 rectangular sheets about ¼ inch thick. Brush with melted butter and sprinkle with brown sugar and cinnamon. Roll like jelly roll and shape into rings. Place on greased baking sheet and cut with scissors at 1-inch intervals almost through ring. Turn slices slightly. Cover and let rise until doubled in bulk. Bake in moderate oven (375° F.) 25 to 30 minutes. While warm, spread with icing and sprinkle with chopped nuts. If desired sprinkle 1 cup chopped dried fruit on dough before rolling. Makes 2 rings.

MORAVIAN BREAD — Omit streusel mixture. After dough has risen punch holes in top 1 inch apart. Fill holes with a mixture of 1 cup brown sugar and ½ cup butter. Bake as above.

SPICY APPLE COFFEE CAKE

2 cups sifted flour
1 tablespoon granulated sugar
3 teaspoons baking powder
¾ teaspoon salt
4 tablespoons shortening
½ cup grated nippy cheese
⅔ to ¾ cup milk
2 or 3 apples
⅓ cup brown sugar
½ teaspoon cinnamon
1 tablespoon butter

Sift flour, sugar, baking powder and salt together. Cut in shortening and cheese. Add milk to make a soft dough. Turn out on lightly floured board and knead ½ minute. Pat out dough in ungreased 9-inch layer-cake pan. Pare apples, core and slice thin. Arrange apples in petal design over top. Sprinkle with brown sugar and cinnamon and dot with butter. Bake in hot oven (425° F.) 25 minutes. Makes 1 (9-inch) coffee cake.

COCONUT CURLICUES—Omit cheese. Roll dough into rectangular sheet ¼ inch thick. Brush with melted butter and sprinkle generously with brown sugar and coconut. Roll like jelly roll and cut into 1-inch slices. Spread muffin pans with butter and sprinkle generously with brown sugar and coconut. Place a slice in each pan and bake in hot oven (425° F.) 20 minutes. Makes about 16 (2-inch) rolls.

NAPFKUCHEN

1 cup milk, ¾ cup butter
1 teaspoon salt, ¾ cup sugar
1 cake yeast, 3 eggs
1 teaspoon grated lemon rind
3 cups sifted flour
½ cup chopped almonds
½ cup chopped raisins

Scald milk; add butter, salt and sugar. Cool to lukewarm. Crumble yeast into mixture and mix well. Add remaining ingredients and beat well. Pour into greased tube pan. Let rise until doubled in bulk. Bake in moderate oven (350° F.) 40 minutes. Frost with Coffee Cake Icing and sprinkle a few chopped almonds over the top. Makes 1 (12-inch) kuchen.

Your spicy apple coffee cake can be baked in a square pan with apples marshalled row upon row

DUTCH BREAD

1 cake yeast
¼ cup lukewarm water
½ cup butter
¾ cup sugar
1 cup scalded milk
2 eggs, beaten
2½ cups sifted flour
1¼ cups soft bread crumbs
2 tablespoons melted butter
3 tablespoons brown sugar
¼ teaspoon salt
1 teaspoon cinnamon

Soften yeast in lukewarm water. Add butter and sugar to scalded milk and stir until butter is melted and sugar dissolved. Cool. When lukewarm, stir in softened yeast, eggs and flour (using more flour if necessary to make a stiff batter) Beat thoroughly, cover and let rise until doubled in bulk. When light beat again thoroughly. Grease deep piepans and sprinkle lightly with flour. Spread dough in pans. Combine soft bread crumbs with melted butter, brown sugar, salt and cinnamon and mix well. Sprinkle over cakes, let rise 20 minutes in a warm place and bake in hot oven (400° F.) 20 minutes. Makes 3 loaves.

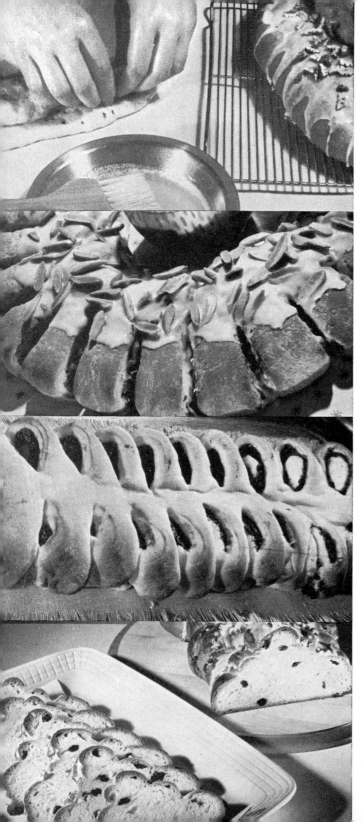

BOHEMIAN CHRISTMAS TWIST

1 cake yeast
¼ cup lukewarm water
1 cup milk
½ cup sugar
¼ cup butter
2 eggs or 4 yolks
Grated rind of 1 lemon
⅛ teaspoon mace
1 teaspoon salt.
4¼ cups sifted flour
½ cup raisins
½ cup chopped blanched almonds
1 recipe Coffee Cake Icing

Soften yeast in lukewarm water. Scald milk and add sugar and butter. Cool to lukewarm. Add softened yeast, beaten eggs, lemon rind, mace, salt and 2 cups flour. Beat well to make a smooth batter. Cover and let rise until light. Add raisins, nuts and remaining flour to make a dough just firm enough to be handled easily. Knead until smooth. Cover and let rise until doubled in bulk. Punch down and divide dough into 3 large portions and 5 smaller ones. Roll each portion into a long roll. Braid the 3 larger rolls loosely and place on greased baking sheet. Then braid 3 of the smaller portions and place on top of the large braid. Twist the last 2 portions together and place on top. Cover and let rise until light. Brush with sweetened milk and bake in hot oven (400°F.) 45 minutes. When cool, spread with icing and sprinkle with chopped nuts. Makes 1 loaf.

Variety is the theme when it comes to making coffee cakes. One recipe of sweet foundation dough, raisins, nuts and such, makes braids, twists, or ladders at your command

CHRISTMAS WREATH RING

¼ cup softened butter
½ cup granulated sugar
2 tablespoons water
¼ cup candied cherries, halved
¼ cup citron, cut into strips
2 cups sifted flour
3 teaspoons baking powder
¾ teaspoon salt
4 tablespoons cold shortening
⅔ to ¾ cup milk
2 tablespoons melted butter
½ cup brown sugar
Cinnamon, ¼ cup currants

Spread softened butter in ring mold and pat granulated sugar over bottom and sides. Sprinkle water in mold. Arrange cherries and citron in bottom to resemble holly. Sift flour, baking powder and salt together. Cut in shortening. Add milk to make a soft dough. Turn out on lightly floured board and knead gently ½ minute. Roll out in rectangle, 6 inches wide and ¼ inch thick. Brush lightly with melted butter, and sprinkle with brown sugar, cinnamon and currants. Roll like jelly roll and cut into 1½-inch slices. Place cut side down in mold. Bake in hot oven (400° F.) 30 minutes. Let stand in pan 1 minute after removing from oven. Serve hot or cold. Makes 1 (9-inch) ring or 12 rolls.

QUICK COFFEE CAKE

1½ cups sifted flour
½ cup sugar
2 teaspoons baking powder
½ teaspoon salt
1 egg, ⅔ cup milk
3 tablespoons melted shortening

Sift flour, sugar, baking powder and salt together. Beat egg and add milk and shortening. Stir liquids into dry ingredients, mixing only enough to dampen all the flour. Pour into greased pan, sprinkle with Crumb Topping and bake in hot oven (425°F.) 25 minutes. Makes 1 (9x9-inch).

PINEAPPLE COFFEE CAKE

2 cups sifted flour
2 teaspoons baking powder
6 tablespoons sugar
¾ teaspoon salt
⅓ cup shortening
1 egg, beaten, ⅓ cup milk
1½ cups drained, diced pineapple
3 tablespoons butter
¼ cup brown sugar
3 tablespoons sifted flour

Sift first 4 ingredients together. Cut in shortening. Combine egg and milk and add all at once to dry ingredients. Blend thoroughly. Spread dough in greased cake pan and arrange diced pineapple on top. Combine remaining ingredients and mix together with a fork until of a crumbly consistency. Sprinkle with diced pineapple. Bake in hot oven (400°F.) about 25 to 30 minutes. Makes 1 (10x6-inch) coffee cake.

Try baking your coffee cake in a ring mold to lend that party air. Ice and sprinkle with chopped nuts and candied fruit

DUTCH CHERRY CAKE

2 cups canned red cherries
1½ cups sifted flour
¼ teaspoon salt
3 teaspoons baking powder
¾ cup sugar
2 eggs, separated
½ cup milk
1 teaspoon vanilla
½ cup shortening, melted

Drain cherries, saving juice. Sift flour, salt, baking powder and ½ cup sugar together. Beat egg yolks and combine with milk, vanilla and melted shortening. Add to flour all at once and beat until smooth. Fold in cherries. Beat egg whites until stiff but not dry, add remaining sugar and fold into mixture. Bake in greased pan in moderate oven (350°F.) 50 minutes. Serve either hot or cold with hot Cherry Sauce. Makes 1 (7x11x1½ inch) cake. Omit cherries and use 1½ cups drained shredded pineapple. Use pineapple juice in sauce.

CRUMB TOPPING

2 tablespoons butter
2 tablespoons sugar
¼ cup sifted flour
¼ cup dry bread crumbs
½ teaspoon cinnamon

Cream butter and sugar together. Add flour, crumbs and cinnamon. Mix to consistency of coarse crumbs and sprinkle over coffee cake batter before baking.

COFFEE-CAKE ICING

1 cup confectioners' sugar
2 tablespoons warm milk
½ teaspoon vanilla

Combine ingredients and mix thoroughly. Frosting for 1 (12-inch) coffee cake.

HONEY TWIST

1 cup milk, scalded
¼ cup shortening
½ cup sugar
1 teaspoon salt
2 cakes yeast
¼ cup lukewarm water
2 eggs, beaten
5 to 6 cups sifted flour

Pour milk over shortening, sugar and salt. Crumble yeast into lukewarm water to soften. Cool milk to lukewarm, add yeast and eggs. Beat in flour to make a soft dough, turn out on a floured board and knead until smooth. Place in a greased bowl, cover and let rise until doubled in bulk. When light, shape into a long roll about 1 inch in diameter. Coil the roll into a greased cake pan beginning at the outside edge and covering the bottom. Brush with Honey Topping. Let rise until doubled in bulk. Bake in moderately hot oven (375°F.) 25 minutes. Makes 1 large twist.

HONEY TOPPING

¼ cup butter
⅔ cup confectioners' sugar
1 egg white
2 tablespoons honey, warmed
Cream ingredients together and brush over twist before baking.

GLAZE FOR BREADS

1 egg yolk
2 tablespoons sugar
3 tablespoons water or milk

Beat egg yolk slightly; add sugar and water or milk. Mix well and brush over breads before baking.

VARIATIONS—In place of water or milk, the juices of various fruits may be used: strawberry, red or black raspberry, blackberry, pineapple, apricot, loganberry, plum or lingonberry. Or melted fruit jelly may be used in place of both milk and sugar.

PRUNE LADDER

1 recipe Honey Twist dough
3 cups sweetened prune pulp
When dough is light, punch down and divide into halves. Roll each piece into a sheet about ½ inch thick. Spread ⅔ with prune pulp. Fold the ⅓ not covered over the center ⅓. Then fold the remaining ⅓ over the top. Clip with a scissors at 1 inch intervals through center. Cover and let rise until doubled in bulk. Bake in moderately hot oven (375°F.) 25 to 30 minutes. While warm, spread with frosting and sprinkle with chopped nuts. Makes 2 ladders.

STREUSEL

½ cup sugar
1 teaspoon cinnamon
¼ cup sifted flour
3 tablespoons soft butter
Few drops vanilla
3 tablespoons chopped nut meats

Mix sugar, cinnamon and flour thoroughly. Rub in butter, working it with fork to form into "crumbs." Add vanilla and chopped nut meats, if desired. Sprinkle over cake before baking. Topping for 2 (1-pound) cakes.

CREAMY COCOA FROSTING

¼ cup butter
1 teaspoon vanilla
3 tablespoons cocoa
3 cups confectioners' sugar, sifted
¼ cup strong coffee (about)

Blend butter and vanilla. Sift cocoa and confectioners' sugar together and add to first mixture alternately with coffee. Use enough coffee to make icing soft enough to spread. Will cover 1 (7½-inch) tube cake.

DOUGHNUTS, FRITTERS AND CRULLERS

The softer the dough, the more delicate the texture of the doughnuts, hence doughnut dough is often mixed a trifle softer than can be handled and then thoroughly chilled until it can be rolled and cut, a small portion at a time. Yeast doughnuts are made stiff enough to handle since they must rise slightly before being fried.

DOUGHNUTS

1 cup sugar
2 tablespoons melted shortening
2 eggs
4 cups sifted flour
4 teaspoons baking powder
¼ teaspoon salt
½ teaspoon cinnamon
½ teaspoon nutmeg
1 cup milk

Beat eggs until light. Add sugar gradually, beating well. Blend in shortening. Sift dry ingredients together and add alternately with milk to sugar mixture. Roll ¼ inch thick on floured board. Cut with doughnut cutter and fry a few at a time in hot deep fat (360°F.), turning once. Drain on absorbent paper and spread with Creamy Cocoa Frosting. Makes 24.

MOLASSES DOUGHNUTS

5 cups sifted flour
½ cup sugar
2 teaspoons baking powder
1 teaspoon salt
1 teaspoon baking soda
½ teaspoon cinnamon
1 teaspoon ginger
1 egg, well beaten, 1 cup molasses
1 cup sour milk or buttermilk
1 tablespoon melted shortening

Sift dry ingredients together 3 times. Beat egg, add molasses, sour milk and shortening and mix well. Add sifted dry ingredients and blend thoroughly. Roll out on a floured board to ¼-inch thickness. Cut with floured doughnut cutter. Fry a few at a time in hot deep fat (370°F.) until brown; turn and brown on other side. Drain on paper. Makes 3 dozen doughnuts. If desired, cover with granulated or confectioners' sugar.

RAISED DOUGHNUTS

1¼ cups milk, scalded
¼ cup shortening
½ teaspoon salt
1 cake yeast
5 cups sifted flour (about)
3 eggs, ¾ cup sugar
1½ teaspoons cinnamon
¼ teaspoon nutmeg, ⅛ teaspoon mace

Combine milk, shortening and salt and cool to lukewarm. Add crumbled yeast; let stand 5 minutes. Add 2½ cups sifted flour. Beat until smooth. Cover and let rise until bubbly. Add eggs and sugar mixed with spices. Mix well. Add enough remaining flour to make a dough that can be kneaded. Knead until smooth. Cover and let rise until doubled in bulk. Roll out ½ inch thick. Cut or mold. Let rise on breadboard until doubled in bulk. Fry a few at a time in hot deep fat (375°F.) 3 minutes or until lightly browned, turning once. Drain on absorbent paper. Makes about 3 dozen doughnuts.

Sinkers! Not these! They'll buoy up any party

Remember the Cala caller in New Orleans' French Quarter; these are his "Belle Cala"

FRENCH RAISED DOUGHNUTS

1 cup boiling water
¼ cup shortening, ½ cup sugar
1 teaspoon salt, 1 cake yeast
1 cup evaporated milk
½ cup lukewarm water
2 eggs, well beaten
7½ cups sifted flour (about)

Pour boiling water over shortening, sugar and salt. Add milk and cool to lukewarm. Soften yeast in water and add to cooled mixture with beaten eggs. Stir in 4 cups flour. Beat hard. Add enough flour to make a soft dough. Place in greased bowl, grease top of dough, cover with waxed paper and a lid or cloth and chill until ready to use. Then roll dough to ¼-inch thickness. Cut with scalloped cookie cutter and fry a few at a time in hot deep fat (360°F. to 370°F.); brown one side, turn and brown on other. Do not let dough rise before frying. Drain on absorbent paper. Cover with a thin frosting. Makes 60 doughnuts.

QUICK CALAS

2 cups cooked rice
3 eggs, beaten, ¼ teaspoon vanilla
½ teaspoon nutmeg
½ cup sugar, ½ teaspoon salt
6 tablespoons flour
3 teaspoons baking powder

Combine rice, eggs, vanilla and nutmeg and mix well. Sift dry ingredients together and stir into rice mixture. When thoroughly mixed drop by spoonfuls into hot deep fat (360°F.) and fry until brown. Drain on absorbent paper, sprinkle with confectioners' sugar and serve very hot. Makes 18 to 20 calas.

CRULLERS

2 tablespoons shortening
1 cup sugar, 2 eggs, well beaten
4 cups sifted flour
3½ teaspoons baking powder
½ teaspoon grated nutmeg
½ teaspoon salt, 1 cup cream

Cream shortening and sugar together until thoroughly mixed. Add eggs and beat well. Sift dry ingredients together and add alternately with cream to creamed mixture. Mix thoroughly. Place dough on floured board and pat and roll to ½-inch thickness, cut into (6x1-inch) strips. Twist dough and press ends together. Fry a few at a time in hot deep fat (360°F.) until brown and drain on absorbent paper. Dust with confectioners' sugar. Makes 2 dozen crullers.

Grandmother's crullers with or without powdered sugar make mighty good eating

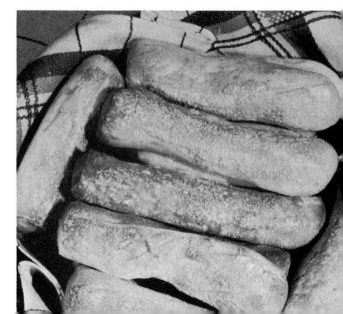

FRUIT FRITTER BATTER

1⅓ cups sifted flour
¼ teaspoon salt
2 teaspoons baking powder
2 tablespoons sugar
1 egg, ⅔ cup milk

Sift dry ingredients and add well-beaten egg and milk. Batter should be just thick enough to coat article. If too thin, add more flour; if too thick, add more liquid. Makes 1½ cups.

APPLE—Pare, core and slice tart apples; dip in fritter batter, covering each slice with batter. Fry in hot deep fat (365°F.) 2 to 3 minutes. Serve with confectioners' sugar, or maple sirup.

BANANA—Omit ⅓ cup milk. Add 2 teaspoons melted shortening. Change flour to 1¼ cups, sugar to ½ cup, and salt to 1¼ teaspoons. Sift 1 cup flour with sugar, salt and baking powder. Mix egg and milk; add to flour mixture gradually, stirring until smooth. Add shortening. Peel bananas, cutting crosswise into halves or quarters. Roll in remaining flour; cover with batter. Fry in hot, deep fat (375°F.) 4 to 6 minutes.

COCONUT—Omit ⅓ cup flour, 1 teaspoon baking powder, ¼ teaspoon salt, and ⅓ cup milk. Add ½ teaspoon grated orange rind, ¼ cup orange juice, and ½ cup shredded coconut. Combine as for Fruit Fritter Batter. Stir in orange rind and juice. Add coconut and mix well. Drop by spoonfuls into hot, deep fat (360°F.) and fry until golden brown. Drain on absorbent paper. Sprinkle with confectioners' sugar. Serves 6.

Don't fret over fritters, just prepare them plain, or fill with fresh fruit for lots of fame

Pancakes and griddlecakes are baked on a griddle either ungreased or very lightly greased, depending upon the material of which the griddle is made. The griddle should be heated until a drop of water will bounce around on it. If the water disappears at once, the griddle is too hot; if it flattens out and sizzles, the griddle is not hot enough.

SOUR-MILK GRIDDLECAKES

1½ cups sifted flour
1 teaspoon baking soda
½ teaspoon salt, 1 tablespoon sugar
2 eggs
1 cup sour milk or buttermilk
1 tablespoon melted shortening

Sift dry ingredients together. Beat eggs, add buttermilk and shortening, then add to dry ingredients gradually, beating until smooth. Drop from a spoon onto a hot greased griddle and cook until top is full of tiny bubbles and underside is brown. Turn and brown on other side. Makes 18 griddlecakes.

BUCKWHEAT OR WHOLE-WHEAT—Use buckwheat or whole-wheat flour instead of half the flour. Increase sugar and shortening to 2½ tablespoons each.

CORN-MEAL PANCAKES—Add 1⅓ cups corn meal. Use ⅔ cup flour instead of flour listed. Increase sour milk to 1½ cups, and melted shortening to 1½ tablespoons. Mix as for above. Pour batter into a pitcher. Heat and grease a griddle or a heavy frying pan. Pour in enough batter to make a cake about 5 inches in diameter. Makes 24.

Just make 'em pancakes in any flavor; you'll hit the spot and stay in favor

BUCKWHEAT CAKES

2 cups milk
2 cups boiling water
1 cake yeast
4 cups buckwheat flour (about)
1/2 teaspoon baking soda
1 cup hot water
1 tablespoon molasses
1 teaspoon salt

Scald milk and add boiling water. Cool to lukewarm and soften yeast in mixture. Sift in enough flour to make a batter thin enough to pour. Let rise overnight. In the morning, dissolve soda in hot water and add to batter with molasses and salt; mix thoroughly. Drop from a spoon onto a hot greased griddle and cook until top is full of tiny bubbles and underside is brown. Turn and brown other side. Makes 3½ dozen cakes. Keep ½ cup of batter in cool place to use in place of yeast for next day's pancakes and proceed as above.

SOUTHERN WAFFLES

2 cups sifted cake flour
2 teaspoons baking powder
1/2 teaspoon baking soda
1/2 teaspoon salt
1 tablespoon sugar
1/3 cup melted shortening
3 eggs, separated
1½ cups buttermilk

Sift dry ingredients together. Combine shortening, beaten egg yolks and buttermilk, then add to dry ingredients, mixing well. Fold in stiffly beaten egg whites and bake in hot waffle iron until brown. Makes 6 waffles.

BUTTERMILK—Omit sugar, use only 2 eggs and increase buttermilk to 2 cups.

RICE—Use 1 cup cold cooked rice instead of 1 cup of the flour. Stir it in last, taking care to avoid mashing.

NEW ENGLAND GRIDDLECAKES

1½ cups sifted flour
1/2 teaspoon salt
1/2 teaspoon baking soda
1 teaspoon sugar
1 egg
1½ cups sour milk
3 tablespoons melted shortening

Sift dry ingredients together. Beat egg, sour milk and melted shortening together. Add liquid mixture gradually to dry mixture, stirring constantly to keep it smooth. Drop the batter by spoonfuls onto a hot greased griddle. Cook slowly until top is full of tiny bubbles and the underside is brown. Turn and brown other side. Serve hot with maple sirup. Makes 2 dozen small cakes.

HUCKLEBERRY OR BLUEBERRY —Fold 1¼ cups washed and drained berries into batter.

RAISED CORN-MEAL GRIDDLECAKES

1/2 cake yeast
1/2 cup lukewarm water
2½ cups scalded milk
2⅔ cups sifted flour
1⅓ cups corn meal
4 teaspoons sugar
1 teaspoon salt
2 eggs, well beaten

Soften yeast in lukewarm water. Cool milk to lukewarm and add softened yeast. Mix dry ingredients together and stir in yeast mixture; cover and let stand overnight in a warm place. Add eggs and let stand 10 to 15 minutes before baking. Drop mixture from tip of spoon onto hot, lightly greased griddle. Cook until top is full of tiny bubbles and underside is browned. Turn and brown on other side. Serve with sirup. Makes 3 dozen cakes.

BRAN GRIDDLE-CAKES

1¾ to 2 cups milk, 1 cup bran
1½ cups sifted flour
3 teaspoons baking powder
1 teaspoon salt, 2 teaspoons sugar
2 eggs, well beaten
1 tablespoon melted shortening

Pour milk over bran. Sift flour, baking powder, salt and sugar together. Add beaten eggs to bran mixture. Add flour and blend; then add shortening, mixing quickly. Bake on hot greased griddle. Serve hot with butter and maple sirup. Makes 2 dozen.

CEREAL FLAKE WAFFLES

1¼ cups sifted flour
2¼ teaspoons baking powder
1/2 teaspoon salt
2 tablespoons sugar
1 cup corn flakes
3 eggs, separated, 1 cup milk
4 tablespoons melted shortening

Sift flour, baking powder, salt and sugar together. Crush corn flakes and add. Combine beaten egg yolks, milk and shortening; add to flour mixture, stirring only until smooth. Fold in stiffly beaten egg whites. Bake in hot waffle iron. Serve with maple sirup. Serves 4.

THIN MAPLE PANCAKES

1 cup sifted flour
1½ teaspoons baking powder
1/2 teaspoon salt
1 tablespoon maple sirup
1 egg, beaten
1 cup milk
3 tablespoons melted shortening

Sift flour, baking powder and salt together. Combine sirup, egg and milk; add gradually to flour, mixing only until smooth. Add shortening. Bake on hot greased griddle. Makes 10 pancakes.

WAFFLES

2 cups sifted flour
3 teaspoons baking powder
½ teaspoon salt
3 eggs, separated, 1½ cups milk
5 tablespoons melted shortening

Mix and sift dry ingredients. Combine beaten egg yolks, milk and shortening; add to dry ingredients, beating until smooth. Fold in stiffly beaten egg whites. Pour a spoonful of batter into each section of a hot waffle iron. Bake until brown. Makes 6.

APPLE—Add 1⅓ cups chopped uncooked apples, ⅛ teaspoon cinnamon and 1 tablespoon sugar to waffle batter before folding in egg whites.

BACON—Sprinkle diced bacon over the batter after it has been poured on the iron.

BANANA—Add 1 tablespoon sugar and 1 cup thinly sliced bananas to batter.

CHEESE—Add 1 cup grated Cheddar cheese to batter.

CHOCOLATE—Add 2 ounces (squares) chocolate, melted, and 1 tablespoon sugar to batter before folding in egg whites.

CHOCOLATE-N U T — Add 2 ounces (squares) chocolate, melted; 1 tablespoon sugar; ½ cup chopped nut meats and ½ teaspoon vanilla to batter before folding in egg whites.

COCONUT—Add 1 cup shredded coconut and 1 tablespoon sugar to waffle batter.

HAM—Add ½ cup finely chopped ham to batter before folding in egg whites.

LEMON OR ORANGE—Add 2 teaspoons of grated lemon or orange rind to batter before folding in egg whites.

NUT—Add ¾ cup broken nut meats to batter before folding in egg whites.

SOY—Add 1½ cups of soy flour, and decrease sifted flour to 1½ cups.

CORN-MEAL WAFFLES

2 cups corn meal
3 cups water
2 teaspoons salt
2 tablespoons shortening
4 eggs
2 cups sifted flour
1 teaspoon baking soda
1 cup sweet milk
Buttermilk or sour milk (about 1¼ cups)

Cook corn meal, water, salt and shortening in double boiler 1C minutes, stirring frequently. Cool. Beat eggs until very light and add to mush. Sift flour with soda and add alternately with sweet milk to mush. Add enough buttermilk to make a thin batter. Bake in hot waffle iron until brown. Makes 12 waffles.

For the hit of the week serve sizzling hot waffles with fruit, nuts or sirup

RICE WAFFLES

1 cup sifted flour
2 teaspoons baking powder
½ teaspoon baking soda
½ teaspoon salt
1 tablespoon sugar
3 eggs, separated
⅓ cup melted shortening
1½ cups buttermilk
1 cup cooked rice

Sift dry ingredients together. Beat egg whites and yolks separately. Combine shortening, beaten egg yolks and buttermilk then add to dry ingredients, mixing well. Fold in rice and stiffly beaten egg whites and bake in hot waffle iron until browned. Makes 8 waffles.

POTATO PANCAKES

3 pounds uncooked potatoes
3 eggs, separated
1¼ cups sifted flour
½ teaspoon salt
1 large sour apple
½ teaspoon grated onion

Peel potatoes, let stand in cold water, grate and drain. Add egg yolks, flour, salt, grated apple and onion. Fold in stiffly beaten egg whites. Pour a small amount onto a hot greased griddle to make thin pancakes. Brown on both sides. Serve for 6.

SOUTHERN GRIDDLECAKES

1½ cups sifted flour
½ teaspoon salt
½ teaspoon baking soda
1 teaspoon sugar
1 egg
1½ cups sour milk
3 tablespoons shortening, melted

Sift dry ingredients together 3 times. Beat egg, sour milk and melted shortening together. Add liquid mixture gradually to dry mixture, stirring constantly to keep it smooth. Drop batter from tablespoon onto a heavy metal griddle, well greased and hot or on a hot ungreased metal griddle. Keep the heat low, so the cakes will not cook too fast. When the top is full of tiny bubbles the under side should be sufficiently brown. Turn and brown the other side. Serve hot with corn sirup. Makes 2 dozen small cakes.

CORN-MEAL — Decrease white flour to 1 cup; decrease sour milk to 1 cup. Add ½ cup corn meal with ½ cup boiling water. Bake as above. Add 2 slices cooked bacon, diced.

Just mention hot waffles for breakfast and watch everyone get to the table on time

SUNDAY WAFFLES

2 cups sifted flour
1 tablespoon sugar
2 teaspoons baking powder
1 teaspoon soda
½ teaspoon salt
3 egg yolks, well beaten
2 cups buttermilk
½ cup melted butter
3 egg whites, stiffly beaten

Sift flour, sugar, baking powder, soda and salt together. Combine beaten egg yolks, milk and melted butter; blend thoroughly. Add liquid mixture all at one time to dry ingredients; mix only until batter is smooth. Fold in beaten egg whites and bake on hot waffle iron. Makes 8 waffles.

SWEET MILK WAFFLES—Omit baking soda and increase baking powder to 3 teaspoons. Substitute milk for buttermilk.

BACON—Add 1 tablespoon crisply fried, chopped bacon to each waffle before closing iron.

BUCKWHEAT—Substitute 1 cup buckwheat for 1 cup white flour; increase baking powder to 4 teaspoons.

SHREDDED COCONUT or CHOPPED NUTS—Add 1 cup of either to batter.

STRAWBERRY — Cover baked waffles with crushed berries; top with sweetened whipped cream.

FLANNEL CAKES

2 cups sifted flour
3 teaspoons baking powder
¾ teaspoon salt
1 tablespoon sugar
2 eggs, separated
1½ cups milk
2 tablespoons melted butter

Sift dry ingredients together; beat egg yolks, add milk and melted butter and add gradually to dry ingredients, beating until smooth. Fold in stiffly beaten egg whites. Drop onto hot griddle and brown on both sides. Makes 24 cakes.

Good muffins are light, fluffy and tender, fine in texture and well browned. The tops are well rounded with a pebbly surface. To achieve good results over-mixing must be avoided unless the recipe calls for an unusually large amount of shortening. Stir the liquid ingredients into dry ingredients just enough to dampen all the flour, leaving the batter rough and lumpy. Twelve to fifteen stirs are usually sufficient. Place batter in the well-greased pans with as little further mixing as possible. If nuts, dates or other extra ingredients are added, mix them with the flour before adding liquids, to avoid necessity for any extra stirring. Knobs and peaks on the tops and long holes or tunnels are caused by over-mixing.

MUFFINS

2 cups sifted, enriched flour
4 teaspoons baking powder
½ teaspoon salt
¼ cup sugar
1 egg, beaten
¼ cup melted shortening
1 cup milk

Sift dry ingredients together. Mix egg, shortening and milk together thoroughly. Combine mixtures, stirring just enough to dampen flour. Fill greased muffin pans ⅔ full. Bake in hot oven (400°F.) 25 minutes. Makes 12 to 15.

BACON OR HAM—Reduce sugar to 2 tablespoons and add ½ cup coarsely chopped, crisp bacon or fine-cut, boiled ham to dry ingredients.

BLUEBERRY—Add 1 cup blueberries to dry ingredients.

CHEESE—Add ½ cup grated cheese and ⅛ teaspoon paprika.

CHERRY—Add ⅔ cup drained, chopped cherries.

CORN-MEAL—Use 1 cup corn meal and 1 cup white flour.

CRANBERRY — Add ⅔ cup chopped cranberries mixed with 2 tablespoons sugar.

DRIED FRUIT—Add to dry ingredients ½ cup of one of the following fruits, chopped, sliced, or whole: apricots, currants, dates, figs, peaches, prunes, or a combination of two or more.

NUT—Add ⅓ cup chopped nuts.

PINEAPPLE—Add 1 cup crushed pineapple to dry ingredients.

RAISIN—Add ⅓ cup raisins.

WHOLE-WHEAT — Use 1 cup each whole-wheat and white flour. Add bacon bits or cracklings, if desired.

Muffins of a fine texture will result if your batter is not over-mixed and your oven is correctly heated

BANANA BRAN MUFFINS

1 cup sifted flour
¾ teaspoon baking soda
½ teaspoon salt
2 tablespoons shortening
¼ cup sugar
1 egg, well beaten
2 tablespoons sour milk
2 cups thinly sliced bananas
1 cup bran

Sift flour, soda and salt together. Cream shortening and sugar together until fluffy; add egg, milk and bananas. Mix and add bran. Let stand until bran softens. Add sifted dry ingredients, stirring only enough to dampen all the flour. Place in greased muffin pans and bake in moderate oven (375° F.) 35 minutes. Makes 6

BUTTERMILK MUFFINS

4 cups sifted flour, 1 teaspoon salt
2 tablespoons corn meal
1 teaspoon baking soda
2 eggs, beaten, 1 tablespoon sugar
2½ cups buttermilk

Sift flour, corn meal, salt and soda together. Beat eggs and add sugar and buttermilk; then add to dry ingredients, stirring only enough to dampen all the flour. Fill greased muffin pans ⅔ full and bake in hot oven (400° F.) 20 minutes. Makes 20 muffins.

CARAMEL CINNAMON MUFFINS

3 tablespoons butter
⅔ cup brown sugar
2 cups sifted flour
3 teaspoons baking powder
½ teaspoon salt
1 teaspoon cinnamon
1 egg
1 cup milk
2 tablespoons melted shortening

Grease muffin pans and place ½ teaspoon butter and 1 teaspoon brown sugar in each cup. Sift flour, baking powder, salt and cinnamon together. Beat egg; add milk, shortening and remaining ¼ cup brown sugar. Add to sifted dry ingredients, stirring only enough to dampen all the flour. Fill prepared muffin pans ¾ full and bake in hot oven (425° F.) 20 minutes. Makes 18. If desired, chopped nuts or raisins may be added to the butter and brown sugar in the bottom of the cup.

If the oven is too hot, all the good mixing has gone to naught. Muffins turn out poorly shaped, full of holes, and are often tough

CEREAL FLAKE-PECAN MUFFINS

1 cup sifted flour, ¼ teaspoon salt
2½ teaspoons baking powder
2 tablespoons sugar
1 cup corn flakes
½ cup finely chopped pecans
1 egg, beaten, ⅔ cup milk
3 tablespoons melted shortening

Sift flour, baking powder, salt and sugar together. Crush corn flakes and add; then add pecans. Combine egg, milk and shortening; add to flour mixture, stirring only enough to dampen all flour. Bake in greased muffin pans in hot oven (425° F.) 25 minutes. Makes 10 muffins.

Too low a temperature and muffins fall flat, with heavy tunnels inside

FAVORITE BRAN MUFFINS

1½ cups sifted flour
1 teaspoon salt
1½ teaspoons baking soda
2½ cups bran
½ cup chopped raisins, dates, prunes or figs
2 eggs
½ cup sugar
¼ cup molasses
1½ cups sour milk or buttermilk
2½ tablespoons melted shortening

Sift flour, salt and soda together; add bran and raisins. Beat eggs; add sugar, molasses, sour milk and shortening. Add to dry ingredients all at once and stir only enough to dampen all the flour. Fill greased muffin pans ⅔ full and bake in hot oven (400° F.) 25 minutes. Makes 1½ dozen.

ORANGE BRAN MUFFINS— Make ⅓ cup of Orange Sugar. Sprinkle 1 teaspoon Orange Sugar on each muffin. Bake as for above.

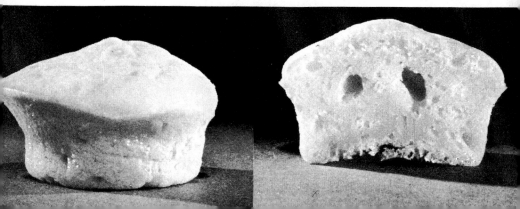

HONEY BRAN MUFFINS

2 cups sifted flour
3 teaspoons baking powder
½ teaspoon salt
½ teaspoon nutmeg
½ cup seedless raisins
2 cups bran, 1 egg
½ cup strained honey
¼ cup sugar, 1¼ cups milk
¼ cup melted shortening

Sift first 4 ingredients together. Stir in bran and raisins. Beat egg well; add honey, sugar, milk and melted shortening. Add to dry ingredients and fruit, stirring only enough to dampen all the flour. Fill greased muffin pans about ⅔ full and bake in hot oven (425° F.) 25 minutes. Makes 16 to 18.

PINEAPPLE BRAN MUFFINS

1½ cups sifted flour
3 teaspoons baking powder
¼ cup sugar, 1½ cups bran
1¼ teaspoons salt, 1 egg, beaten
½ cup evaporated milk
¼ cup pineapple juice
½ cup drained crushed pineapple
¼ cup melted shortening

Sift flour, baking powder, sugar and salt together. Add bran. Combine beaten egg, milk, pineapple juice, pineapple and shortening. Add to dry ingredients and stir just enough to dampen the flour. Fill greased muffin pans ⅔ full and bake in hot oven (400°F.) 25 minutes. Makes 18 medium muffins.

MOLASSES MUFFINS

2 cups sifted flour
1 teaspoon baking powder
½ teaspoon salt
½ teaspoon baking soda
2 tablespoons sugar
1 egg
½ cup sour milk or buttermilk
½ cup molasses
2 tablespoons melted shortening

Sift flour, baking powder, salt, soda and sugar together. Beat egg; add milk, molasses and shortening. Add to dry ingredients, stirring only enough to dampen all the flour. Fill greased muffin pans ⅔ full and bake in hot oven (400° F.) 25 minutes. Makes 18.
GRAHAM MUFFINS — Add 4 tablespoons melted shortening to buttermilk and 1 teaspoon baking powder to flour mixture. Fill greased muffin pans ⅔ full and bake in moderate oven (375° F.) 30 minutes.

SOY MUFFINS

1 cup soy flour
1 cup white or graham flour
1 teaspoon salt
2 teaspoons baking powder
2 tablespoons sugar
¾ cup milk
1 egg, well beaten
1 tablespoon shortening

Sift first 5 ingredients together; combine milk, beaten egg and shortening and add to dry ingredients, stirring only enough to moisten. Do not beat; batter should not be smooth. Fill greased muffin pans ⅔ full and bake in hot oven (425°F.) 15 to 25 minutes, depending upon size. Makes 1 dozen muffins.

Sizzling hot popovers properly baked are delicious as shells for creamed dishes you make

MINCEMEAT BRAN MUFFINS

2½ cups sifted flour
1 teaspoon salt, ½ cup sugar
3 teaspoons baking powder
2 cups bran, 2 eggs
1½ cups milk, 1 cup mincemeat
6 tablespoons melted shortening

Sift first 4 ingredients together and add bran. Beat eggs well; add milk, melted shortening and mincemeat. Add to dry ingredients and stir only enough to dampen all the flour. Fill greased muffin pans about ⅔ full and bake in hot oven (400° F.) about 25 minutes. Makes 18 muffins.

ENGLISH MUFFINS

3 tablespoons butter
1¼ teaspoons salt
2 tablespoons sugar
1 cup milk, scalded
1 cake yeast
¼ cup lukewarm water
1 egg, beaten
4 cups sifted flour

Add butter, salt and sugar to milk and cool to lukewarm. Soften yeast in water. Add yeast, egg and 2 cups of flour to cooled milk. Stir to blend well, then knead in remaining flour until firm and elastic. Let rise until doubled in bulk, about 1 hour. Roll out ¼ inch thick on floured board. Cut into 4-inch circles. Leave on board. Cover and let rise until doubled in bulk, about 1 hour. When light, sprinkle with corn meal, if desired, and bake slowly on hot ungreased, heavy griddle or frying pan about 7 minutes on each side. Brown slowly. Makes 12 muffins.

The English muffin, so light golden brown, is a favorite with many the whole year roun'

A good popover is a crisp hollow shell which is well browned and tender. To achieve this the batter is thoroughly beaten in order to develop the gluten so that the steam formed in baking will be held in a larger pocket and cause the popovers to rise.

POPOVERS

1½ cups sifted flour
½ teaspoon salt
3 eggs, 1½ cups milk

Sift flour and salt. Beat eggs, add milk and stir gradually into flour to make a smooth batter. Beat thoroughly with egg beater. Fill greased custard cups or heavy metal muffin pans ⅔ full. Bake in very hot oven (450°F.) 15 minutes, then reduce temperature to moderate (350°F.) and continue 20 minutes. Makes 12.

WHOLE-WHEAT POPOVERS

⅔ cup sifted flour
¼ teaspoon salt
⅓ cup whole-wheat flour
2 eggs, 1 cup milk
1 tablespoon melted shortening

Sift flour and salt together and stir in whole-wheat flour. Combine unbeaten eggs, milk and melted shortening and add to dry ingredients. Beat well. Fill greased custard cups or heavy metal muffin pans about ⅓ full. Bake in very hot oven (450°F.) 25 minutes, reduce temperature to moderate (350°F.) and bake 10 to 20 minutes longer. Makes 8 to 10 popovers.

It's steam that makes popovers pop, but if the oven's too hot they brown before popping; when it's too cold they start and then flop

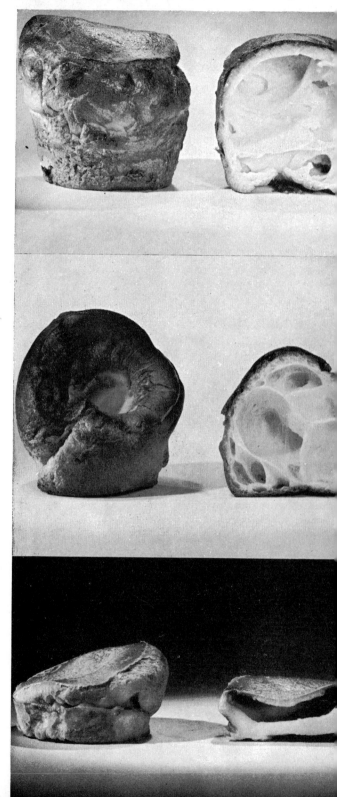

Sandwiches

300 SANDWICHES, FILLINGS AND SPREADS

SANDWICH FILLINGS

Combine all ingredients for filling selected. Use as directed in sections on Party Sandwiches and Closed Sandwiches. Most sandwich fillings may be stored in screw-topped jars in refrigerator for several days. Cream cheese fillings, however, should not be stored more than 1 day since they have a tendency to dry out and turn yellow. Fillings made of chopped uncooked vegetables should be prepared just before using to avoid loss of vegetable juices and crispness.

CHEESE SANDWICH FILLINGS

AMERICAN CHEESE AND BACON

½ cup grated American cheese
¼ cup minced cooked bacon
6 drops onion juice
1 tablespoon minced pickles
3 tablespoons mayonnaise

When the filling forms part of the decoration of the sandwich it should help to carry out the color scheme

AMERICAN CHEESE AND DILL

¾ cup grated American cheese
¼ cup minced dill pickles
2 tablespoons mayonnaise

AMERICAN CHEESE AND EGG

½ cup grated American cheese
2 tablespoons chopped pimiento
1 tablespoon minced onion
2 tablespoons minced sweet pickle
2 hard-cooked eggs, chopped

AMERICAN CHEESE, ONION AND ANCHOVY

1 cup grated American cheese
1 tablespoon minced onion
2 tablespoons anchovy paste
1 teaspoon Worcestershire sauce
2 tablespoons mayonnaise

CHEESE AND SALTED ALMONDS

1 cup grated American cheese
¼ cup chopped salted almonds
2 tablespoons mayonnaise

CHEESE AND PEPPER RELISH

1 cup grated American cheese
¼ cup pepper relish

LIMBURGER CHEESE AND ONION

⅔ cup Limburger cheese
⅓ cup chopped onion

SHARP CHEESE SANDWICH FILLING

2 cups tomato juice
2 tablespoons quick-cooking tapioca
⅛ teaspoon pepper
¼ teaspoon dry mustard
½ pound cheese, grated
¼ pound dried beef, finely ground
½ teaspoon Worcestershire sauce

Heat tomatoes to boiling in top part of double boiler. Add tapioca, pepper and mustard and heat to boiling, stirring constantly. Place over boiling water, and cook 5 minutes, stirring occasionally. Add cheese gradually and stir until melted. Add beef and Worcestershire sauce. Cool. Makes 2½ cups.

CREAM CHEESE AND CHICKEN

¼ cup cream cheese
¾ cup chopped cooked chicken
Salt

CREAM CHEESE AND CHIPPED BEEF

⅓ cup ground chipped beef
⅔ cup cream cheese

CREAM CHEESE AND CHIVES

1 cup cream cheese
2 tablespoons minced chives

CREAM CHEESE AND JAM

½ cup cream cheese
½ cup strawberry jam
Spread each separately.

CREAM CHEESE AND MARMALADE

½ cup cream cheese
½ cup orange marmalade
Spread each separately.

CREAM CHEESE AND NUT

1 cup cream cheese
⅓ cup minced nut meats
   (walnut, pecan or pistachio)

CREAM CHEESE AND PIMIENTO

cup cream cheese
tablespoons minced pimiento

CREAM CHEESE, CUCUMBER, RADISH

1/4 cup cream cheese
1/4 cup chopped cucumber
1/2 cup chopped radishes

CREAM CHEESE, NUT, RAISIN

1/4 cup cream cheese
1/4 cup mayonnaise
1/4 cup ground nut meats
1/4 cup ground raisins

CREAM CHEESE COMBINED WITH:

Chopped candied ginger
Chopped dates
Chopped dill pickle
Chopped green pepper
Peanut butter

CHEESE APRICOT SANDWICH FILLING

1/2 cup dried apricots
1 cup water
2 tablespoons sugar
3 ounces cream cheese
Dash salt

Wash apricots; cut into pieces and add water. Cover and simmer 10 minutes. Add sugar, then cool. Cream the cheese with apricot sauce and add salt. Makes 1 1/2 cups.

COTTAGE CHEESE AND BACON

3/4 cup cottage cheese
1/4 cup chopped cooked bacon

COTTAGE CHEESE AND CELERY

2/3 cup cottage cheese
1/3 cup minced celery
3/4 teaspoon chopped chives
1 tablespoon mayonnaise
1/4 teaspoon salt

COTTAGE CHEESE AND CHIVES

1 cup cottage cheese
2 to 3 tablespoons minced chives
Salt
Paprika

COTTAGE CHEESE AND WATERCRESS

1/2 cup cottage cheese
1/2 cup chopped watercress

COTTAGE CHEESE AND EGG

1/2 cup cottage cheese
2 hard-cooked eggs, chopped
2 tablespoons chopped pickle
2 tablespoons mayonnaise

COTTAGE CHEESE AND GINGER

1/4 cup cottage cheese
2 1/2 tablespoons chopped preserved ginger
1 1/2 teaspoons preserved ginger sirup
3 tablespoons chopped nut meats

COTTAGE CHEESE AND HAM

2/3 cup cottage cheese
1/3 cup chopped cooked ham
1 1/2 tablespoons sweet pickle relish

COTTAGE CHEESE AND JELLY

1/2 cup cottage cheese
1/2 cup grape jelly
Spread each separately.

COTTAGE CHEESE AND OLIVE

3/4 cup cottage cheese
3 tablespoons chopped stuffed olives
3 drops onion juice
1/4 teaspoon salt

COTTAGE CHEESE, CARROT AND NUT

1/2 cup cottage cheese
1/4 cup grated carrots
2 tablespoons chopped nut meats
1/4 teaspoon salt
Dash pepper
1 tablespoon mayonnaise

COTTAGE CHEESE COMBINED WITH:

Chopped dried fruit: raisins, dates, apricots or prunes
Diced tomato
Finely chopped pickles
Preserves, jams, marmalades or honey
Relish

Choose garnishes that enhance the flavor of the filling to make sandwiches that taste as good as they look

CHICKEN SANDWICH FILLINGS

CHICKEN AND MAYONNAISE — Season finely chopped chicken and mix with mayonnaise or salad dressing to moisten.

CHICKEN AND SANDWICH SPREAD—Add enough sandwich spread to finely chopped chicken to moisten.

CHICKEN AND WHITE SAUCE —Moisten chicken with hot white sauce and spread on hot toast.

CHICKEN AND NUT—Moisten chicken with mayonnaise or salad dressing, add chopped nut meats, lemon juice and celery salt.

CHICKEN AND ORANGE MAR-MALADE —Spread slices of bread with orange marmalade; cover with finely chopped chicken, moistened with mayonnaise or salad dressing.

CHICKEN AND MUSHROOM— For a hot sandwich combine sautéed slices of fresh mushrooms and diced cooked chicken. Cover with a cream sauce.

Rolled sandwiches can be hearty as well as dainty, if generously spread with meat or chicken

CHICKEN AND DILL PICKLE— Place thin slices of dill pickle on sliced chicken. Cover with mayonnaise or salad dressing and lettuce leaves.

CHICKEN AND ALMOND SANDWICHES

1 cup cooked chicken meat, ground
½ cup minced celery
¼ cup ground almonds
¼ cup mayonnaise
8 slices toast
4 lettuce leaves

Mix chicken, celery and almonds. Moisten with mayonnaise or salad dressing. Spread on buttered toast, cover with lettuce and a second slice of toast. Cut into triangles or finger shapes. Makes 4 sandwiches.

CHICKEN LIVER SANDWICHES

1 cup mashed cooked chicken livers
2 tablespoons diced crisp bacon
Salt and pepper
4 drops Tabasco sauce
1 tablespoon lemon juice
8 slices bread

Combine first 5 ingredients. Spread between slices of bread. Makes 4 sandwiches.

CHICKEN AND CELERY FILLING

1 cup minced cooked chicken
1 cup minced celery
1 tablespoon minced green pepper
4 tablespoons mayonnaise
¼ teaspoon salt
Dash pepper

Mix all ingredients together thoroughly. Makes about 2 cups.
Omit celery and green pepper, increase chicken to 2 cups and add ½ teaspoon powdered sage.

CHICKEN AND EGG SANDWICHES

1 cup minced cooked chicken
2 hard-cooked egg yolks
1 teaspoon chicken stock
1 teaspoon lemon juice
1 teaspoon butter, melted
Salt and pepper, 8 slices bread

Combine first 7 ingredients. Blend thoroughly. Spread between slices of bread. Makes 4 sandwiches.

CHICKEN HAM SANDWICHES

1 cup diced cooked chicken
½ cup diced cooked ham
½ cup chopped celery
⅓ cup salad dressing or
    mayonnaise
8 slices bread
Lettuce

Combine first 4 ingredients and blend. Spread between slices of bread, topping with lettuce leaf. Makes 4 sandwiches.

Add chopped pickles or olives. Use cucumber instead of celery.

PINEAPPLE—Omit lettuce and mayonnaise. Brown ½ cup drained crushed pineapple in butter and spread over chicken. Serve hot.

EGG SANDWICH FILLINGS

EGG AND CATCHUP

4 hard-cooked eggs, chopped
3 tablespoons tomato catchup

EGG AND PICKLE

4 hard-cooked eggs, chopped
¼ cup chopped sweet pickles
¼ cup mayonnaise

EGG SALAD

2 hard-cooked eggs, minced
1 tablespoon chopped pickles
1 teaspoon chili sauce
6 small stuffed olives
2 tablespoons mayonnaise

CHOPPED HARD-COOKED EGGS COMBINED WITH:

Chopped boned sardines or anchovies, French dressing.
Chopped crisp bacon or boiled ham, mayonnaise.
Chopped olives, cooked salad dressing.
Chopped pickle, mayonnaise.
Diced cooked chicken, meat or fish, chopped pickles, mayonnaise.
Minced celery, pimiento, mayonnaise.
Minced onion, mayonnaise.
Minced pickle, minced cooked tongue, mayonnaise.
Minced pimientos, diced green pepper, chili sauce, mayonnaise.
Salt, pepper, sliced tomato, mayonnaise.

EGG AND ANCHOVY

Lettuce
3 stalks celery hearts, diced
6 hard-cooked eggs
6 to 8 anchovies or sardines
French dressing
Worcestershire sauce

Shred lettuce and add celery. Chop whites and add to lettuce. Put yolks through a sieve, add anchovies or boned sardines and mix into paste. Add French dressing and Worcestershire sauce. Makes about 1½ cups.

preads for canapés must e savory and stimulating to he appetite

NOVEL CHICKEN FILLING

cup cooked white meat of chicken
½ teaspoon salt
ew grains cayenne
teaspoon unflavored gelatin
tablespoons cold water
tablespoons cream

Chop chicken very fine and pound to a paste; season with salt and cayenne. Soften gelatin in cold water for 5 minutes, add cream and dissolve gelatin over boiling water. Add to chicken and blend thoroughly. Spread in thick layer and chill until firm. Divide into squares, cut these squares into very thin slices and arrange on thin buttered slices of bread. Remove crusts and cut into fancy shapes. Makes 1 cup filling.

CHICKEN SALAD FILLINGS

CHICKEN AND ASPARAGUS SALAD—1½ cups diced cooked chicken, 1 cup asparagus tips, 2 tablespoons minced green pepper, ¼ cup shredded cabbage and ¼ cup mayonnaise.

CHICKEN AND BACON SALAD —1 cup diced cooked chicken, ½ cup diced crisp bacon, 1 cup diced tomatoes and ½ cup mayonnaise or salad dressing.

CHICKEN AND CABBAGE SALAD—½ cup diced cooked chicken, 2 cups shredded cabbage, ½ cup diced cooked ham and ¾ cup mayonnaise or salad dressing.

CHICKEN AND CHESTNUT SALAD—1 cup diced cooked chicken; ½ cup chopped boiled chestnuts; 1 cup diced celery; 2 hard-cooked eggs, chopped; ⅓ cup sliced stuffed olives; ½ cup mayonnaise or salad dressing.

CHICKEN AND CUCUMBER SALAD—2 cups diced cooked chicken, ½ cup chopped celery, ½ cup diced cucumbers, 2 tablespoons capers and ¾ cup mayonnaise or salad dressing.

CHICKEN AND TONGUE SALAD —1 cup diced cooked chicken, 1 cup diced cooked tongue, ½ cup chopped celery, ½ cup sliced stuffed olives and ¾ cup mayonnaise or salad dressing.

CHICKEN SALAD WITH PINEAPPLE—Mix 2 cups diced cooked chicken, 1 cup minced celery and 1 green pepper, chopped. Marinate in French dressing. Drain and mix with mayonnaise. Serve on lettuce with pineapple spears.

FISH SANDWICH FILLINGS

SALMON AND CUCUMBER

1 cup flaked cooked salmon
½ cup mayonnaise
¼ cup chopped cucumber

SALMON AND HAM

½ cup flaked cooked salmon
½ cup ground ham
½ cup mayonnaise

SALMON AND NUT

1 cup flaked cooked salmon
3 tablespoons chopped nut meats
3 tablespoons minced celery
½ cup mayonnaise

SALMON AND PICKLE

1 cup flaked cooked salmon
2 tablespoons chopped pickle
3 tablespoons mayonnaise

SHRIMP AND CREAM CHEESE

¾ cup mashed cooked shrimp
¼ cup cream cheese

TUNA SALAD

1 cup flaked tuna
2 tablespoons mayonnaise
1 teaspoon tarragon vinegar
¼ teaspoon paprika
1 tablespoon minced capers

CUCUMBER SHRIMP CRESCENTS

½ cup chopped unpared cucumber
1 teaspoon chopped chives
1 (5¾-ounce) can shrimp,
   cleaned and minced
1 tablespoon French dressing
1 tablespoon mayonnaise

Combine cucumber, chives and shrimp. Add dressing and mayonnaise. Spread on buttered bread cut into crescent shapes. Makes 1½ cups spread.

KIPPERED HERRING SALAD

½ pound kippered herring
2 cups chopped celery
1 green pepper, chopped
1 Spanish onion, chopped
2 hard-cooked eggs, chopped
¼ teaspoon salt
⅛ teaspoon pepper
½ teaspoon paprika
½ cup French dressing

Chop herring and vegetables very fine. Add eggs and seasonings. Toss together with dressing. Makes about 4 cups.

The beauty of mosaic sandwiches depends on the contrast between the fillings and the breads

CRAB-MEAT SALAD FILLING

1½ cups cooked crab meat
¾ cup diced celery
1 tablespoon minced pimiento
1 tablespoon minced green pepper
¼ teaspoon salt
Mayonnaise

Shred crab meat and discard all tough spines. Mix crab meat, celery, pimiento, green pepper and salt and add enough mayonnaise to moisten. Serves 4.

LOBSTER SALAD FILLING

2 cups flaked cooked lobster
¼ cup chopped stuffed olives
2 hard-cooked eggs, chopped
1 teaspoon capers
⅓ cup mayonnaise

Combine all ingredients and chill for 1 hour. Serves 6.
Omit capers and add 1 teaspoon minced chives and ½ cup diced celery.

PICKLED HERRING SALAD

½ cup diced boned pickled herring
¾ cup diced cold cooked potatoes
1½ cups diced pickled beets
3 tablespoons vinegar
2 tablespoons sugar

Combine herring with vegetables and season with vinegar and sugar. Makes about 3 cups.

ANCHOVY SALAD — Use anchovies instead of herring and sliced onions instead of beets.

SALMAGUNDI SALAD — Add ½ cup diced roast meat and 1 apple, diced.

ROE FILLING

1 cup mashed cooked fish roe
2 teaspoons lemon juice
Salt
Blend ingredients thoroughly.

FRUIT, NUT AND NUT BUTTER FILLINGS

DATE AND NUT

⅔ cup ground dates
⅓ cup ground pecan meats
1½ tablespoons mayonnaise
1 tablespoon lemon juice

DATE AND ORANGE

1 cup chopped dates
¼ cup orange juice

PEANUT

¾ cup chopped salted peanuts
¼ cup mayonnaise

PEANUT-BUTTER AND BANANA

½ cup peanut butter
⅓ cup mashed ripe banana
¼ cup mayonnaise

PEANUT-BUTTER AND JAM

½ cup peanut butter
½ cup raspberry jam
Spread each separately.

PEANUT-BUTTER AND PICKLE

½ cup peanut butter
½ cup mayonnaise
3 tablespoons chopped pickle

TOASTED NUT

1 cup minced toasted nut meats
¼ cup mayonnaise

LEMON NUT SANDWICH FILLING

3 tablespoons lemon juice
1 teaspoon grated lemon rind
½ cup sugar
4 egg yolks, slightly beaten
1 tablespoon butter
⅓ cup slivered blanched almonds

Combine lemon juice and rind, sugar, egg yolks and butter. Cook in double boiler, stirring constantly, until thick. Cool and stir in almonds. Makes 1 cup.

For rolled sandwiches, select a filling that will hold the sandwich together

FRUIT NUT SANDWICH FILLING

1 cup dried figs
1½ cups water
⅛ teaspoon salt
3 tablespoons quick-cooking tapioca
½ teaspoon cinnamon
½ cup pitted dates, ground
½ cup nut meats, chopped
1 tablespoon lemon juice

Cook figs in water 5 minutes or until softened. Drain and place 1 cup of the liquid in top of double boiler. Heat to boiling, add salt, tapioca and cinnamon and reheat to boiling, stirring constantly. Place over boiling water and cook 5 minutes, stirring constantly. Put figs through food chopper and add with remaining ingredients to tapioca mixture. Cool. Makes 2½ cups.

COMBINATIONS WITH NUT MEATS:

Chopped almonds with chicken, tuna or crab meat.

English walnut meats and chopped ham.

Chopped nut meats and olives.

Chopped peanuts or pecan meats with chopped carrots, cabbage or apples.

Chopped peanuts or pecan meats and cream cheese.

Pecans or peanuts, honey, butter and chopped whole orange if desired.

Pecans or peanuts with jelly or jam.

Cream cheese, chopped stuffed olives and chopped nuts.

Cream cheese, crushed pineapple and chopped nuts.

Cottage cheese and pickles, olives, nuts or pimientos.

Minced orange peel with cream cheese or mayonnaise mixed with chopped nuts and raisins.

Currant jam with minced walnut meats and creamed butter. Serve with cream cheese. Preserved currants may be used instead of currant jam.

Ground boiled ham and chopped pickles or chopped peanuts.

Chopped stuffed olives and chopped nuts, moistened with salad dressing.

Chopped raisins, figs, dates or prunes, chopped nut meats and mayonnaise or lemon juice.

MEAT FILLINGS

BACON

7 slices crisp bacon, chopped
1 pimiento, chopped
¼ cup mayonnaise

BACON AND PICKLE

8 slices crisp bacon, chopped
4 medium dill pickles, chopped
⅓ cup mayonnaise

BEEF

1½ cups cold roast beef
½ teaspoon salt
½ tablespoon chili sauce
¼ teaspoon Worcestershire sauce
1 tablespoon melted butter

HAM

1 cup ground cooked ham
½ tablespoon minced onion
½ teaspoon dry mustard
2 tablespoons mayonnaise

DEVILED HAM SPREAD

2 (5-ounce) cans deviled ham
½ cup mayonnaise
1 cup cottage cheese

HAM AND CHEESE

½ cup ground boiled ham
½ cup ground American cheese
2 tablespoons ground sweet or dill
   pickle
½ teaspoon ground onion
Mayonnaise to moisten

HAM AND PICKLE

2 (5-ounce) cans deviled ham
⅓ cup mayonnaise
6 small sweet pickles, minced
½ cup chopped lettuce

HAM SALAD

¾ cup chopped cooked ham
1 tablespoon chopped onion
1 hard-cooked egg, chopped
¼ cup chopped green pepper
¼ cup mayonnaise

LAMB

1¼ cups chopped cooked lamb
½ teaspoon salt
¼ teaspoon pepper
½ tablespoon minced onion
1 teaspoon minced mint leaves
1 tablespoon lemon juice

LIVER AND BACON

½ cup chopped cooked bacon
½ cup ground cooked liver
⅛ teaspoon pepper
Dash cayenne
¼ cup cream

LIVER AND RAISIN

¾ cup chopped cooked liver
⅓ cup chopped raisins
⅛ teaspoon salt
2 tablespoons mayonnaise
¼ teaspoon mustard
¼ teaspoon grated onion
⅛ teaspoon pepper
3 tablespoons chili sauce

VEAL AND CARROT

½ cup chopped cooked veal
½ cup grated carrot
Dash salt, Dash pepper
1 teaspoon lemon juice
3 tablespoons mayonnaise

LIVER SAUSAGE

½ cup chopped liver sausage
2 teaspoons minced cooked bacon
2 teaspoons minced pimiento
½ teaspoon lemon juice

TONGUE

1½ cups minced cooked tongue
2 tablespoons prepared horse-radish
½ teaspoon salt
¼ cup mayonnaise
Dash cayenne

VEAL

1¼ cups chopped cooked veal
1 tablespoon lemon juice
¼ teaspoon salt
¼ teaspoon pepper
1 teaspoon prepared mustard

GROUND BEEF SANDWICH

½ pound ground round steak
1 tablespoon minced onion
Salt and pepper

Blend ingredients and use at once, uncooked. Serves 4 to 6.

GROUND BEEF SANDWICH DE LUXE

Cut clove garlic
½ pound ground round steak
2 hard-cooked eggs, chopped
½ teaspoon anchovy paste
1 tablespoon minced onion
Salt

Rub cut side of garlic around mixing bowl. Discard garlic. Blend remaining ingredients in seasoned bowl. Use at once, uncooked. Serves 6.

Savory spreads for canapés may go on crackers instead of toast rounds

SANDWICH BUTTERS

GENERAL METHOD — Cream butter thoroughly. Grind fish, meat or vegetables to a paste and combine with the seasoning and butter. If mixture is not entirely smooth rub through a sieve. Spread on bread or toast cut into dainty attractive shapes and garnish appropriately or use as a base for sandwich fillings.

ANCHOVY BUTTER

1 cup butter
½ cup minced anchovies
2 teaspoons lemon juice
4 drops onion juice
4 hard-cooked egg yolks

Use herring, bloaters, crawfish, lobster, smoked salmon, whitefish, sardines or 4 tablespoons anchovy paste instead of anchovies.

CHEESE BUTTER

½ cup butter
¼ cup grated Parmesan cheese or
    1½ ounces Roquefort or ½
    cup snappy cheese spread

CHILI BUTTER

¼ cup butter
2 tablespoons chili sauce, drained

CHIVE BUTTER

½ cup butter
¼ cup chopped chives
4 drops Worcestershire sauce

EGG BUTTER

½ cup butter
4 hard-cooked egg yolks
Few grains cayenne
6 drops Worcestershire sauce

FILÉ BUTTER

½ cup butter, melted
1 tablespoon filé
1 teaspoon paprika

GARLIC BUTTER, STRONG

1 tablespoon minced garlic
½ cup butter

GARLIC BUTTER, MILD

4 teaspoons minced fried garlic
½ cup sweet butter

HAM BUTTER

½ cup butter
¼ pound cooked ham, ground
2 hard-cooked eggs, chopped
Dash pepper

HORSE-RADISH BUTTER

½ cup butter
¼ cup grated horse-radish

LEMON BUTTER

½ cup butter
Grated rind 1 lemon
1½ tablespoons lemon juice
1 tablespoon minced onion

MUSTARD BUTTER

½ cup butter
¼ cup prepared mustard

OLIVE BUTTER

¼ cup butter
2 tablespoons chopped olives
¼ teaspoon lemon juice

PARSLEY BUTTER

⅔ cup butter
⅓ cup minced parsley

PIMIENTO BUTTER

½ cup butter
¼ cup mashed pimiento
2 teaspoons India relish, drained

POPPY-SEED BUTTER

½ cup butter
½ cup hot poppy seeds, ground

Use caraway seeds or sesame seeds instead of poppy seeds.

SHRIMP BUTTER

1 cup butter
1 cup minced cooked shrimp
¼ teaspoon salt
Dash paprika
1 tablespoon lemon juice

SUGGESTIONS FOR GARNISHES

Red or green peppers, cut into thin strips or circles.
Celery stuffed with a savory cheese mixture, celery curls or hearts of celery.
Radishes cut into thin slices.
Stalks of endive stuffed with Roquefort cheese paste.
Sieved hard-cooked egg yolks.
Finely chopped hard-cooked egg whites or egg wedges.

For the sandwich loaf, fillings must harmonize in flavor and contrast in color and texture

TOASTED SHARP CHEESE SANDWICHES

1 hard-cooked egg
½ pound American cheese, grated
1½ tablespoons chopped pimientos
2 tablespoons minced onion
½ teaspoon salt
Dash cayenne
1 tablespoon butter
1 tablespoon flour
1 tablespoon sugar
2 tablespoons vinegar
½ cup evaporated milk
8 or 16 slices bread

Chop egg, add cheese, pimiento, onion, salt and cayenne. Melt butter, blend in flour and sugar, add vinegar and milk. Cook until smooth, stirring constantly. Add cheese mixture and stir until melted. Spread on slices of bread and brown under broiler. Makes 8 sandwiches.

Spread filling between slices of bread, brush with melted butter and toast in a sandwich grill or under broiler.

Bread cut in attractive shapes makes the unusual hot sandwich

RAREBIT SANDWICHES

1 tablespoon butter
½ pound American cheese
½ teaspoon salt
1 teaspoon prepared mustard
1 teaspoon Worcestershire sauce
¾ cup milk
1 egg, well beaten
2 tomatoes, sliced
6 slices toast
Salt and pepper
6 slices bacon, cooked

Melt butter over low heat, add cheese and stir until melted. Add salt, mustard and Worcestershire sauce. Stir in milk slowly, remove from heat and pour over egg, beating constantly. Place 2 slices tomato on each slice of toast, sprinkle with salt and pepper, cover with rarebit sauce and top with bacon. Serve at once. Serves 6.

BLENDED CHEESE SANDWICHES

½ cup Camembert cheese
½ cup Roquefort cheese
2 tablespoons butter

Melt together in double boiler and spread on hot toast, for 6.

COTTAGE CHEESE DREAMS

1 cup cottage cheese
¼ cup chopped pecans
8 slices bread
1 egg
2 tablespoons water
4 tablespoons butter

Mix cottage cheese and pecans and spread on 4 slices of bread. Cover with remaining slices. Dip sandwiches into beaten egg diluted with water and fry in hot butter. Serves 4.

BAKED TOMATO CHEESE SANDWICHES

8 slices toast, without crust
8 slices crisp bacon, chopped
8 slices tomatoes
½ pound cheese, shredded
2 cups medium white sauce
Buttered bread crumbs

Place toast in buttered baking pan, cover each slice with chopped bacon, then with a slice of tomato and top with cheese. Pour white sauce over all and sprinkle with bread crumbs. Bake in moderate oven (350°F.) 25 minutes. Serves 8.

CHEESE ROLLS

pound aged Cheddar cheese
 spread
green peppers (seeds removed)
medium onion
(7-ounce) can tuna, drained
pint stuffed olives, chopped
2 cup melted butter
(8-ounce) can tomato sauce
8 to 24 hard French rolls

orce cheese, peppers, onion and
 una through food chopper, using
 edium blade. Add olives, butter
 nd tomato sauce and mix. Cut
 ff tops of rolls and remove cen-
 ers. Fill with mixture and wrap
 ach roll in heavy waxed paper.
 wist ends securely, place in
 aper bag and heat in slow oven
 300°F.) 20 minutes. Serve at
 nce. Serves 9 to 12. A covered
 oaster may be used instead of
 aper bag. Place rolls in roaster
 ithout waxed paper, cover and
 eat.

CHEESE SOUFFLÉ SANDWICHES

 slices bread
2 teaspoon salt
 ash pepper
 ash paprika
 eggs, separated
 cup grated sharp cheese

Remove crusts and toast bread on
1 side. Combine salt, pepper,
paprika and egg yolks and beat
until light. Fold yolks and cheese
into stiffly beaten egg whites.
Heap onto untoasted side of bread
and bake in moderate oven (350°
F.) about 15 minutes or until
puffy and brown. Serves 8.

HOT BAKED CHEESE SANDWICHES

2 tablespoons butter
2 tablespoons flour
1 teaspoon salt
1/8 teaspoon pepper
3 cups milk
3 eggs, beaten
12 slices toast
3/4 pound American cheese,
 thinly sliced

Melt butter; blend in flour, salt
and pepper; add milk and cook
until thickened, stirring constantly. Add to beaten eggs. Place
half the toast in a shallow baking pan with half of cheese on
top. Pour on milk and egg mixture and cover with remaining
toast and cheese. Place dish in
pan of hot water and bake in moderate oven (350°F.) until cheese
is melted and egg mixture is firm.
Serves 6.

EGG AND CHEESE TOAST

6 eggs, slightly beate
1/2 teaspoon salt
Pepper
1/2 cup milk
2 tablespoons butter
8 slices hot toast
Tomato catchup
1 cup grated cheese

Combine eggs, salt, pepper and
milk. Melt butter in double boiler, pour in egg mixture and cook
slowly, stirring from sides and
bottom of pan as eggs begin to
thicken. Spread toast with catchup, cover each piece with scrambled eggs and sprinkle with
cheese. Place under broiler to
brown and melt cheese. Serve at
once. Serves 8.

**SCRAMBLED EGG AND FRANK-
FURTER**—Omit cheese. Slice
frankfurters and add to eggs before cooking. Serve in split buns.

SCRAMBLED EGG AND HAM—
Omit cheese. Dice cooked ham
and add to eggs before cooking.
Spread toast with chili sauce.

*With a basket of hot toast
and a hot entrée everybody
makes his own*

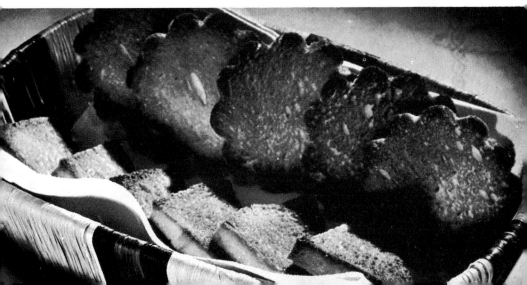

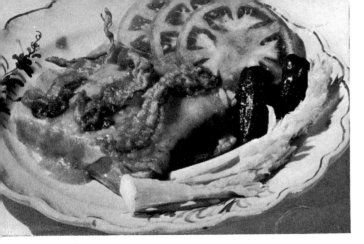

A grilled cheese and bacon sandwich with crisp pickles, celery and tomatoes makes a quick and easy lunch

BROILED HAM SANDWICHES

¼ cup chopped cucumber pickle
1 cup grated American cheese
3 tablespoons mayonnaise
8 (¼-inch slices) cold ham loaf
8 slices bread, buttered

Combine pickle, grated cheese and mayonnaise. Spread on meat, toast under broiler and place on buttered bread. Serve hot. Makes 8 open sandwiches.

Cheese sandwiches, rolled and toasted are suitable for either luncheon or a tea party

OPEN CHEESE SAND-WICHES

¼ pound American cheese, grated
1½ teaspoons Worcestershire
    sauce
8 slices bread
Softened butter
Cayenne

Mix cheese and Worcestershire sauce. Spread bread with softened butter, cover with cheese, sprinkle with cayenne and broil slowly until cheese has softened. Makes 8 sandwiches.

Top each sandwich with crisp bacon.

Mix cheese with 1 or 2 beaten eggs before spreading on bread and broil slowly.

BACON AND CHEESE TOAST

1 egg
3 tablespoons milk
¼ pound cheese, grated
8 slices bread
8 slices bacon

Beat egg, add milk and cheese. Mix well. Spread on bread and place a strip of bacon on top. Toast under broiler. Makes 8 open sandwiches.

TASTY TOASTED SANDWICHES

1 pimiento
1 small onion
¼ pound American cheese
2 hard-cooked eggs
¼ teaspoon salt
Dash pepper
¼ teaspoon paprika
2 tablespoons prepared mustard
16 slices bread
Melted butter

Force pimiento, onion, cheese and eggs through a food chopper. Add salt, pepper, paprika and mustard. Mix thoroughly. Spread between slices of bread, brush bread with melted butter and toast under a preheated broiler or in a sandwich grill. Makes 8 sandwiches.

BACON PEANUT-BUT-TER SANDWICHES

8 slices bread
Peanut butter, Tomato catchup
12 slices bacon cut into halves
Sliced gherkins

Toast slices of bread on 1 side. Spread untoasted side with peanut butter, then with catchup. Slash edges of bacon to prevent curling and place 3 slices on each sandwich. Broil slowly until bacon is slightly browned and crisp. Serve immediately with sliced gherkins. Makes 8 sandwiches.

188

CREAMED EGG AND ASPARAGUS SANDWICHES

4 tablespoons butter
6 tablespoons flour
1 teaspoon salt
½ teaspoon pepper
4 cups milk
6 hard-cooked eggs, diced
16 slices buttered toast
8 slices ham, cooked
48 cooked asparagus tips

Melt butter and blend in flour and seasonings. Add milk gradually, stirring constantly and cook until thickened. Add diced eggs. Cover 8 slices of toast with ham. Cover ham with sauce, place 3 asparagus tips on sauce, cover with another slice of toast, add more sauce and top with 3 asparagus tips. Makes 8 large sandwiches.

PIMIENTO SARDINE SANDWICHES

½ cup mashed sardines
⅓ cup minced pimientos
Mayonnaise
4 slices toast

Mix sardines, pimientos and mayonnaise; broil on toast.

SHRIMP SPECIAL SANDWICHES

¾ cup whole cooked shrimp
1 cup Medium Cream Sauce
6 slices hot toast
3 slices American cheese
Parsley

Clean shrimp and add to hot cream sauce. Pour over 3 slices of fresh buttered toast, cover with remaining toast and top each sandwich with slice of cheese. Toast under low broiler heat until cheese is melted. Garnish with additional shrimp and parsley. Serves 3.

Lobster or flaked tuna, salmon or crab meat may be used instead of shrimp.

189

A creamed egg and asparagus sandwich for the children's lunch will solve many problems

SHRIMP RAREBIT SANDWICHES

1 tablespoon chopped onion
2 tablespoons chopped green pepper
6 tablespoons butter
1 pound cooked shrimp, cleaned
1 tablespoon flour, ½ cup milk
½ teaspoon Worcestershire sauce
⅛ teaspoon dry mustard
Dash salt, Dash pepper
¼ pound sharp Cheddar cheese
5 slices hot toast

Cook onion and green pepper very slowly in 5 tablespoons butter 5 minutes. Add cleaned shrimp, mix carefully with a fork and cook slowly until shrimp are hot. Melt remaining butter, blend in flour, add milk gradually, stirring constantly. Add seasonings and cook until thickened, continuing to stir. Add cheese; stir until melted. Serve shrimp on toast with sauce, for 5.

Hot shrimp rarebit sandwiches are another cold weather lunch solution

The poached egg luncheon sandwich may be bordered with asparagus tips and cheese sauce

FRIED EGG SANDWICHES

1 small onion, minced
1 small green pepper, minced
2 tablespoons butter
1 cup cooked tomatoes
¼ teaspoon salt
Dash pepper
4 slices toast, 4 fried eggs
Grated Swiss cheese

Cook onion and green pepper in butter until tender. Add tomatoes, salt and pepper and cook until reduced one-half. Spread sauce on fresh hot toast, place egg on each slice and cover egg with grated cheese. Melt cheese under broiler. Serve hot with bacon curls. Makes 4 sandwiches.

PEANUT-BUTTER RAREBIT

2 eggs
1½ cups milk
6 tablespoons peanut butter
1 teaspoon salt
4 slices toast

Beat eggs slightly, add milk, peanut butter and salt. Cook in double boiler 12 minutes and pour over hot buttered toast. Serves 4.

CHEESE POACHED EGG—Place hot poached egg on round of buttered toast. Cover with hot Cheese Sauce and sprinkle with paprika. Serve with crisp vegetable salad.

Or pour cheese sauce over the poached egg and serve with a vegetable salad

FRANKFURTER AND CHEESE SANDWICHES

6 frankfurters
6 long thin slices American cheese
Softened butter
6 finger rolls

Steam frankfurters for 10 minutes, then split lengthwise and place a slice of cheese in the opening. Place in buttered split finger rolls and place in moderate oven (350°F.) 10 minutes or until cheese is melted, for 6

TOASTED TOMATO HAM FINGERS

1 cup ground boiled ham
1 cup grated cheese
½ teaspoon horse-radish
½ teaspoon prepared mustard
½ cup condensed tomato soup
5 slices bread

Mix ground ham, cheese, horse-radish, mustard and tomato soup together. Toast bread, trim off crusts and cut each slice into 3 or 4 strips. Spread with mixture, then toast under broiler. Makes about 15 fingers.

BARBECUED BEEF SANDWICHES

½ cup catchup
½ cup water
¼ clove garlic
1 teaspoon chili powder
½ teaspoon Worcestershire sauce
¼ cup sugar
1 teaspoon mustard
Slices roast beef
12 slices bread or 6 buns

Mix first 7 ingredients together and cook slowly for 10 minutes. Add roast beef slices and heat thoroughly. Place on 6 slices of bread, spread remaining slices with barbecue sauce, place on beef and cut each into halves diagonally. Serves 6.

BARBECUED PORK — Use slices roast pork instead of beef.

190

FOUR-LEAF CLOVERS

¼ cup butter
½ cup grated sharp cheese
½ cup dry bread crumbs
12 slices bread

Cream butter and cheese together, then add dry bread crumbs and mix well. Cut bread into four-leaf clover shapes with a small cookie cutter. Spread with cheese mixture and toast under broiler. Makes 24 four-leaf clovers (1¾ inches across).

MUFFIN SANDWICH — Cover toasted English muffins with sliced hard-cooked eggs. Cover with cheese and melt under broiler. Top with crisp bacon.

TOASTED FRANKFURT ROLLS

Remove crusts from a loaf of bread. Cut bread lengthwise into long slices. Spread with butter and a relish cream spread. Cut frankfurters crosswise into halves and place a half on each slice of bread. Roll bread around each frankfurter, secure with a toothpick and toast under broiler heat until rolls are lightly browned.

ASPARAGUS-TOMATO-CHEESE SANDWICH

¼ cup American cheese, grated
1½ teaspoons Worcestershire sauce
2 slices bread
Softened butter, Cayenne
4 cooked green asparagus tips
Strip of pimiento

Mix cheese and Worcestershire sauce. Spread slice of bread with soft butter, cover with cheese, sprinkle with cayenne, broil slowly until cheese has softened. Pile asparagus on other slice toasted and band with pimiento. Serves 1. For variety, place tomato slices under asparagus and cover with Cheese Sauce. Omit pimiento.

191

EGG AND CHEESE TRIANGLES

1 egg, Dash cayenne
⅛ teaspoon salt
½ cup grated aged cheese
3 slices sandwich bread

Beat egg until foamy, add cayenne, salt and cheese and heap on slices of bread. Place under broiler until lightly browned. Cut each diagonally into 4 triangles. Serve on watercress or parsley. Makes 12.

Use ½ cup minced ripe olives instead of cheese. Bake in tiny pre-baked tartlet shells in a 350°F. oven 12 minutes.

A toasted English muffin is the foundation for this egg, cheese and bacon sandwich

SALAMI TIDBITS

3 ounces cream cheese
¼ cup condensed celery soup
1 cup ground salami
Toast or crackers

Mix cheese and celery soup thoroughly. Add salami and mix well. Spread mixture on toast or crackers and brown under broiler. Serves 6 to 8.

Open-faced sandwiches are a complete meal in themselves, deserving their popularity

HAMBURGER CHEESE BUNS

1 pound ground beef
¾ teaspoon salt
⅛ teaspoon pepper
5 round buns
5 slices snappy cheese
India relish (or piccalilli)

Combine beef with salt and pepper and form into 5 round flat cakes. Fry or broil on both sides until browned. Split buns, toast and cover the lower half of each bun with a slice of cheese. Melt cheese under low broiler heat, cover each with a hot hamburger, spread with relish and cover with the top half of bun Serves 5

VARIATIONS — Spread hamburger with mustard, omit cheese. Or omit cheese and relish. Combine 1 cup chopped lettuce, 4 tablespoons mayonnaise and ½ teaspoon prepared mustard. Serve in buns with hamburgers.

Place a grilled onion slice on top of meat.

Omit India relish and add 2 tablespoons toasted poppy seeds or toasted pine nuts.

When the guest list is brief, try waffle sandwiches for the bridge party luncheon

WAFFLE SANDWICHES

½ cup cream cheese
½ cup ground boiled ham
Bread
Butter

Combine cream cheese and ham. Slice bread thin, spread half with softened butter and remaining half with ham mixture. Put sandwiches together. Place 2 at a time in hot waffle iron and bake until browned. Serve at once. Makes 8 sandwiches.

TOMATO DELIGHTS — Split thin baking powder biscuits, butter and top with a slice of tomato and a slice of cheese. Sprinkle with chopped cooked bacon and melt cheese under broiler.

Slice the bread rather thin and remove the crusts before toasting it in the waffle iron

HAM ROLLS

18 finger rolls
Butter
⅓ pound boiled ham, ground
3 hard-cooked eggs, ground
¼ teaspoon salt
1 teaspoon ground onion
2 tablespoons tomato catchup
2 tablespoons tart cooked salad dressing

Split rolls and butter. Combine remaining ingredients. Spread in rolls. Place rolls in paper bag and heat thoroughly. Makes 18 ham rolls.

*Hot biscuits, lavishly but-
tered are ideal to use in
making sandwiches*

HAM SANDWICHES
AU GRATIN

8 slices toast
5 tablespoons butter
1 cup deviled ham
2 tablespoons flour
¼ teaspoon sugar
½ teaspoon salt
Dash pepper
1 cup milk
2 hard-cooked eggs, chopped
3 tablespoons chopped green
     pepper or pimiento
Grated cheese

Spread toast with 3 tablespoons
butter, then with deviled ham
and cover with a second slice of
toast. Melt remaining butter;
blend in flour, sugar, salt and
pepper. Add milk and cook until
thickened, stirring constantly.
Add chopped eggs, green pepper
and cheese, if desired. Pour over
toast. Serves 4.

BROILED HAM AND
CHEESE
SANDWICHES

12 slices white bread, buttered
6 slices boiled ham
6 slices American cheese
2 tablespoons tomato catchup
2 tablespoons prepared mustard
Melted butter

Top half of the buttered bread
with 1 slice each of ham and
cheese. Mix catchup with prepared mustard, spread on remaining slices of bread and place
mustard side down on ham and
cheese. Brush outside with melted butter and toast under broiler
or in sandwich grill. Makes 6
sandwiches.

Omit catchup and mustard.

OPEN-FACED HAM
SURPRISE

8 slices bread
8 slices cooked ham
2 egg whites
¾ cup mayonnaise
2 teaspoons prepared mustard

Cover bread with ham slices.
Beat egg whites until stiff, fold
in mayonnaise and mustard carefully. Cover ham with mixture
and bake sandwiches in very hot
oven (450°F.) about 5 minutes
or until browned. Serve hot.
Makes 8 sandwiches.

ASPARAGUS CROWNS

Cut baking powder biscuit dough
into rounds using biscuit cutter
for half of dough and doughnut
cutter of the same size for remainder. Bake in hot oven
(425°F.) 12 to 15 minutes. Put
together into sandwiches with
creamed chicken or ham, using
doughnut shaped biscuits for
tops. Insert several asparagus tips
in center of each.

*Asparagus tips make these
crowns as gay as a new
spring bonnet*

French fried sandwiches with grilled sausages and fruit make the Sunday morning brunch memorable

FRENCH FRIED SANDWICHES

Sandwiches, filled as desired
2 eggs, slightly beaten
½ cup flour
½ teaspoon salt
Dash pepper
1 cup milk

Prepare sandwiches as usual with cheese, meat or jam fillings. Combine eggs, flour, salt, pepper and milk. Beat until smooth. Dip sandwiches into egg batter and fry in hot deep fat (390°F.) until brown or fry in skillet half filled with hot fat.

Dip sandwiches into beaten egg mixed with ½ teaspoon salt and ¼ cup milk, instead of dipping in above egg batter.

SALMON FRENCH TOAST SANDWICHES

1 (8-ounce) can salmon
3 tablespoons mayonnaise
1 teaspoon grated onion
Salt and pepper
6 slices white bread
1 egg
1 tablespoon milk
Butter

Drain salmon, bone and flake. Mix with mayonnaise, onion and seasonings. Spread on 3 slices of bread and cover with remaining bread. Beat egg, add milk, salmon liquor and salt. Dip sandwiches into this mixture and brown on both sides in butter. Cut diagonally and serve hot. Makes 3 sandwiches.

Cook in hot deep fat (390°F.) until browned.

FRENCH FRIED LIVER SANDWICHES

1 pound liver
1 teaspoon prepared mustard
3 or 4 sweet pickles, diced
¼ cup minced onion
10 slices bacon, fried and diced
3 tablespoons salad oil
20 slices bread
3 eggs, well beaten
¾ cup cream or top milk
½ teaspoon salt
Dash pepper

Simmer liver in salted water with mustard 45 minutes or until tender. Chop and mix with pickles, onion, bacon and salad oil. Spread on bread and cover with second slice of bread. Mix eggs, cream, salt and pepper together. Dip sandwiches in egg mixture and brown on both sides in hot fat. Drain on absorbent paper and serve at once. Makes 10 sandwiches.

Hot toasted cheese points are delicious served with a salad plate

SALMON SAND- WICHES DE LUXE

¾ pound cooked salmon
2 tablespoons horse-radish
1 teaspoon lemon juice
⅓ cup mayonnaise
Salt and pepper
10 slices bread (crust trimmed)
3 tablespoons butter, melted
½ pound American cheese, grated
⅓ cup milk

Flake salmon, remove bones and mix salmon with horse-radish, lemon juice, mayonnaise and seasonings. Spread on slice of bread and cover with another slice, brush outside of each sandwich with melted butter and toast sandwiches under low broiler heat. Melt cheese slowly in top of double boiler and add milk gradually, stirring constantly until sauce is smooth. Pour over sandwiches and garnish with sweet Pickle Fans and parsley. Serves 5.

OYSTER BISCUITS—Break open small hot baking powder biscuits and butter generously. Place a hot baked or fried oyster in each, sprinkle with salt and serve at once.

Bits of bacon and onion mixed with the cheese before grilling gives extra richness and flavor

HOT SARDINE SANDWICHES

2 tablespoons butter
2 tablespoons flour
1 cup milk
½ teaspoon salt
⅛ teaspoon paprika
2 tablespoons tomato catchup
½ cup grated sharp American cheese
2 (3¼-ounce) cans sardines
6 slices toast

Melt butter, blend in flour and add milk gradually, stirring constantly. Add seasonings and cook until thickened, stirring constantly. Stir in cheese. Arrange 3 or 4 sardines on each slice of toast, heat under broiler and pour some of sauce over each sandwich. Makes 6 sandwiches.

Use flakes of kippered herring instead of sardines.

SHRIMP AND LIEDER- KRANZ SANDWICHES

1 cup chopped cleaned cooked shrimp
6 slices hot toast
1 package Liederkranz cheese

Spread shrimp on toast and cover with slices of Liederkranz. Melt cheese under broiler. Makes 6 sandwiches.

CHICKEN CURRY SANDWICHES

1 cup chopped cooked chicken
1 cup chopped cooked ham
¾ cup Thick White Sauce
1 teaspoon or more curry powder
½ teaspoon salt
6 slices bread
1 cup buttered crumbs

Combine chicken, ham, white sauce and seasonings. Toast bread on 1 side and spread untoasted side of bread with filling. Sprinkle with buttered crumbs. Bake in hot oven (425°F.) 15 minutes. Makes 6 sandwiches.

ROYAL CHICKEN SANDWICHES

8 slices buttered toast
8 slices cooked chicken
8 slices tomato
Salt
1 cup grated American cheese
2 teaspoons Worcestershire sauce

Place slices of buttered toast in shallow baking pan. Place chicken on toast and tomato on chicken. Sprinkle with salt. Spread thickly with grated cheese mixed with Worcestershire sauce. Melt cheese under broiler. Serve at once. Serves 8.

OPEN SAVORY CHEESE SANDWICHES

5 slices bacon
½ pound American cheese
2 slices onion
1 tablespoon prepared mustard
6 slices bread

Grind bacon, cheese and onion together. Add mustard and mix thoroughly. Toast bread on 1 side, spread thick layer of cheese mixture on untoasted side and brown under broiler, 4 to 5 minutes. Makes 6 sandwiches.

BROILED SARDINE TOAST

12 large sardines
12 (2-inch) toast strips, Paprika
½ pound pimiento cheese, grated

Place a sardine on each strip of toast and cover with grated cheese. Sprinkle with paprika. Heat slowly under broiler until cheese melts. Serve with lemon wedges. Serves 6.

HAM, EGG AND MUSHROOM SANDWICHES

1 cup ground cooked ham
2 hard-cooked eggs, chopped
½ can condensed cream of mushroom soup
10 or 12 slices bread, buttered

Mix ham, eggs and soup, thoroughly. Spread on slices of buttered bread. Makes 5 or 6.

MUSHROOM-EGG SANDWICHES

8 eggs
1 cup condensed cream of mushroom soup
½ teaspoon salt, Dash pepper
16 slices buttered toast

Beat eggs slightly. Add soup, salt and pepper and mix thoroughly. Pour into top of double boiler and cook over hot water until thick, stirring constantly. Spread between slices of buttered toast. Makes 8 sandwiches.

DRIED BEEF ON TOAST

4 tablespoons butter
4 tablespoons flour
1 cup beef stock
1 cup evaporated milk
⅓ pound dried beef
⅛ teaspoon pepper, Parsley
Hot buttered toast

Melt butter, add flour and stir until flour is browned. Add beef stock and milk gradually, stirring constantly until thickened. Shred beef, add to sauce and simmer 5 minutes. Add pepper and parsley. Garnish with strips of pimiento or sliced pimiento-stuffed olives. Serve hot on toast. Serves 6.

HOT MUSHROOM SANDWICHES

2 tablespoons butter
3 tablespoons flour
1 (No. 2) can ready-to-serve cream of mushroom soup
16 slices bread
Thin slices beef, chicken or veal
Minced parsley
1 hard-cooked egg yolk, sieved

Melt butter, blend in flour, add soup gradually, stirring constantly, and cook until thickened. Toast bread on 1 side and place meat between untoasted sides. Place sandwich on plate and cover with mushroom sauce. Sprinkle with parsley and sieved egg yolk. Serves 8.

GRILLED LIVER SAUSAGE SANDWICHES

1 cup liver sausage
4 teaspoons minced cooked bacon
4 teaspoons minced pimiento
1 teaspoon lemon juice
12 slices rye bread
Butter, softened

Mix liver sausage, cooked bacon, pimiento and lemon juice together. Spread on 6 slices rye bread and top with 6 corresponding slices. Spread butter on top and bottom of sandwiches. Grill. Makes 6 sandwiches.

If desired, omit bacon and add ⅓ cup ground corned beef.

SARDINE FINGERS

Cut thinly sliced bread into long narrow strips, and brown on one side in butter. Roll whole sardines in grated Parmesan cheese and place one on untoasted side of each piece of bread. Sprinkle with salt and brown quickly under broiler. Garnish with tiny sprigs of parsley and serve at once.

ROLLED SANDWICHES

Cut crusts from thin slices of bread, spread with a cheese filling, roll and fasten with toothpicks. Place under broiler and toast lightly on all sides. Remove toothpicks and serve immediately.

CHILI ROLLS—Cream 3 ounces snappy cheese, 2 tablespoons chili sauce and 1 teaspoon minced onion together. Spread on bread and proceed as above. Makes 8 sandwiches.

Rolled cheese sandwiches, hot and crispy from the broiler give pleasant variety to the sandwich tray

In addition to sandwiches described below others may be made using fillings listed in section on Sandwich Fillings. Spread desired filling on a slice of buttered bread, add lettuce, watercress or chicory, if desired, and top with a second slice of buttered bread. Mayonnaise or salad dressing may be used instead of butter for spreading bread. Whole-wheat, graham or rye bread should be used as well as white.

BAKED BEAN SAND-WICHES

1 cup baked beans with pork and tomato sauce
¼ teaspoon salt
2 sweet gherkins, chopped
4 stuffed green olives, chopped
Mayonnaise
16 slices Boston brown or whole-wheat bread

Press beans through sieve or ricer. Add salt, gherkins, olives and mayonnaise to moisten. Spread between buttered slices of bread. Makes 8 sandwiches.

Omit gherkins, olives and mayonnaise and add 2 tablespoons tomato catchup or chili sauce.

The luncheon sandwich plate with fruit and cream cheese is growing in popularity

GARDEN SALAD SANDWICHES

1 green pepper, shredded
6 cooked beets, minced
1 stalk celery, minced
¼ cup mayonnaise
Few drops onion juice
½ cup chili sauce or catchup
16 slices rye bread, buttered
8 lettuce leaves

Combine vegetables, mayonnaise, onion juice and chili sauce. Spread half of bread with filling and put slices together with lettuce between. Makes 8 sandwiches.

MAN'S DELIGHT

8 slices rye bread
Softened butter
4 slices baked ham
4 slices Swiss cheese
Prepared mustard
Lettuce

Spread bread with butter. Place slice of ham, then slice of cheese on 4 slices bread. Spread cheese with mustard; cover with lettuce Top with remaining 4 slices bread. Cut into halves. Serve with dill Pickle Fans. Serves 4.

Use American cheese instead of Swiss cheese.

Use minced mustard pickles instead of mustard.

AMBER SANDWICHES

6 ounces cream cheese
⅓ cup strained honey
12 slices whole-wheat bread
Peanut butter
6 lettuce leaves

Blend cream cheese and honey and spread on half of bread. Spread remaining slices with peanut butter. Put slices together with lettuce leaf between. Makes 6 sandwiches.

DEVILED EGG AND SWISS CHEESE SANDWICHES

3 hard-cooked eggs
1 tablespoon prepared mustard
½ teaspoon salt
1 teaspoon Worcestershire sauce
6 slices whole-wheat bread, buttered
3 wafer-thin slices Swiss cheese
Watercress
Dill pickles

Cut eggs crosswise into halves. Mash yolks and blend with mustard, salt and Worcestershire sauce, mixing well. Fill whites. Cut eggs into thin slices and arrange on 3 slices of bread. Top egg with slice of cheese and second slice of bread. Cut into halves and garnish with watercress and pickles. Makes 3 sandwiches.

CREAM CHEESE AND PEANUT SAND-WICHES

3 ounces cream cheese
½ cup chopped parsley
½ cup chopped salted peanuts
½ teaspoon lemon juice
⅛ teaspoon salt
12 slices white or whole-wheat bread, buttered

Cream the cheese until soft; add parsley, peanuts, lemon juice and salt. Spread between slices of bread. Makes 6 sandwiches.

CHICKEN AND PINE-APPLE SANDWICHES

1 (8-ounce) can crushed pineapple, drained
1 cup chopped cooked chicken
2 cups English walnut meats, chopped
½ cup cooked salad dressing
24 slices white bread, buttered

Combine pineapple, chicken, nut meats and salad dressing. Spread between buttered slices of white bread. Remove crusts and cut each sandwich diagonally into quarters. Makes 4 dozen small sandwiches.

CHICKEN SAND-WICHES DE LUXE

2 cups diced uncooked ham
3 tablespoons butter
2 cups diced cooked chicken
1 cup cream
1 cup Cream Sauce
Salt and pepper
2 egg yolks
12 slices toast
½ pound American cheese, sliced

Cook ham in butter 1 minute Add diced chicken and cream Cook very slowly 3 minutes. Add cream sauce and seasonings and cook slowly 2 minutes. Add to beaten egg yolks and cook, stirring constantly until thickened. Cover 6 slices of toast with the chicken and ham mixture, top with remaining slices of toast and cover each with a slice of cheese. Melt cheese under low broiler heat. Serve immediately, garnished with curly endive, sections of tomato and stuffed olives Serves 6.

VEAL AND CHICKEN—Use 2 cups diced cooked veal instead of ham and add ½ cup sliced stuffed olives to mixture just before serving. Add ¼ cup chili sauce.

SLICED CHICKEN SANDWICHES

8 slices bread
Softened butter
4 slices breast of chicken
Piccalilli, Mayonnaise
Lettuce

Spread bread with butter. Cover 4 slices with chicken, spread with piccalilli and mayonnaise, top with lettuce and cover with remaining slices bread. Serves 4.

To go with luncheon salads cut sandwiches larger, in sticks, circles or triangles

Cut tea sandwiches with small fancy cutters to suit the occasion

JACK HORNER SAND-WICHES

¾ cup condensed cream of mushroom soup
½ cup ground cooked ham
1 cup ground cooked chicken
12 slices bread, buttered

Combine mushroom soup with ham and chicken. Mix well. Spread between slices of buttered bread. Makes 6 sandwiches.

CORNED BEEF SAND-
WICHES

12 slices bread
Softened butter
6 (⅛-inch) slices cooked corned
    beef
Prepared mustard

Spread bread with butter. Cover
6 slices with corned beef, spread
with mustard and top with remaining slices bread. Cut diagonally into halves. Serves 6.

TONGUE
SANDWICHES

1½ cups sliced cooked tongue
½ cup minced sweet pickles
⅓ cup mayonnaise
8 slices white bread
½ cup softened butter
8 slices whole-wheat bread
Watercress

Mix tongue, pickles and mayonnaise together. Spread on white
bread. Butter whole-wheat bread,
put slices together and garnish
with watercress sprays. Makes 8.
Use ham or corned beef instead
of tongue.

*Use dark breads as well as
light and garnish with an
orange curl, carrot and radish roses and watercress*

HAM AND TOMATO
SANDWICHES

1 cut clove garlic
1 cup minced cooked ham
1 teaspoon minced parsley
Dash cayenne
Dash mace
½ teaspoon lemon juice
¼ teaspoon onion juice
½ cup butter, softened
16 slices bread, 8 slices tomato

In mixing bowl rubbed with garlic combine remaining ingredients except bread and tomato.
Spread bread with ham mixture
and place slices together with
slice of tomato between. Makes
8 sandwiches.

ROAST PORK SAND-
WICHES

8 slices bread
Softened butter
Chili sauce
Slices roast pork
Salt, Pepper, Lettuce

Spread bread with butter, then
with chili sauce. Cover 4 slices
with slices of roast pork, sprinkle
with salt and pepper and cover
with lettuce and the remaining
slices bread. Cut into halves, diagonally. Serves 4.

HAM AND PRUNE
SANDWICHES

½ cup cooked prunes
1 can (¼ cup) deviled ham
2 tablespoons tomato catchup
Few drops Tabasco sauce
Dash salt
2 tablespoons chopped sour pickles
2 tablespoons minced parsley
2 tablespoons minced onion
10 slices bread, buttered
Lettuce

Remove pits from prunes and cut
into pieces. Add next 7 ingredients and blend lightly. Spread
between slices of buttered bread
with lettuce between each. Cut
into desired shapes. Makes 5
sandwiches.

SLICED TURKEY
SANDWICHES

8 slices bread
Softened butter
Slices turkey
Salt and pepper
Mayonnaise
Lettuce

Spread bread with butter. Cover
4 slices with turkey, sprinkle
with salt and pepper, spread with
mayonnaise and top with lettuce
and remaining slices bread. Cut
diagonally into quarters. Serves 4.

Filling for ribbon, checkerboard, tile or rolled sandwiches should be of the type which will become firm when chilled in order to hold the pieces of bread together. Savory butters of all kinds and cream cheese mixtures are especially good for this purpose. Cream cheese may be mixed with fish paste, olives, pimientos, parsley, chives, chopped nuts, lemon juice or herbs to give variety in color and flavor. A small amount of vegetable coloring may be used to give delicate tints. Do not attempt to use salad mixtures for this type of sandwich.

CINNAMON SANDWICHES

2 tablespoons butter
6 tablespoons sugar
2 teaspoons cinnamon
4 slices bread, white or brown
Pecans

Cream butter, sugar and cinnamon together until smooth and well blended. Spread on bread and cut into strips, triangles, circles or other fancy shapes. Place a pecan half on center of each. Serve with fruit salad.

Use hot thin toast instead of bread.

Use nut bread instead of white.

Start the filled pinwheel roll with a row of stuffed olives

PINWHEEL SANDWICHES

Cut bottom, side and end crusts from unsliced loaf of white or whole-wheat bread. Spread bottom of loaf with butter and desired filling. Cut as thin and even a slice as possible from bottom of loaf. Start at 1 end of the slice and roll up tightly as a jelly roll. Wrap in a damp cloth and chill. Cut into thin slices across the roll. Serve plain or toast lightly under broiler.

VARIEGATED PINWHEELS — Cut crusts from a loaf of white and a loaf of whole-wheat bread, spread ends of loaves with butter and filling and slice very thin. Roll 1 slice of white bread as for jelly roll, around it roll a whole-wheat slice and then a second white slice. Chill and slice roll.

STUFFED PINWHEELS — Place a row of stuffed olives end to end along one end of a slice of buttered bread. Roll bread as for Pinwheel or Variegated Pinwheel Sandwiches. Chill and slice so each pinwheel has a slice of stuffed olive in the center.

Use small sweet pickles instead of olives.

EGG PINWHEELS — Cut off rounded ends of hard-cooked eggs and use instead of olives in Stuffed Pinwheels.

PARTY PINWHEELS—Spread 1/3 of each slice with mixture of 1 cup cream cheese and 1 cup minced parsley. Spread remainder of slice with deviled ham and sprinkle with paprika. Roll, starting at cheese end. Wrap in damp cloth and chill. Slice thinly. Each roll makes 10 to 15 sandwiches.

MOSAIC SANDWICHES

Cut thin slices of white and whole-wheat bread, and cut into fancy shapes. Spread half of each kind of bread with butter and desired filling. Cut small shapes from centers or corners of unspread slices with tiny cutters and put sandwiches together, using a white and a dark slice for each. If desired the tiny shapes cut from center of dark slices can be inserted into openings of similar shape cut in white slices and the white shapes inserted into the dark slices, rather than having the filling of sandwich showing through the opening. For instance, if a star has been cut from center of a top slice of whole-wheat bread it may be inserted in the star-shaped opening cut in a slice of white bread. The sandwich itself may also be star shaped. See Page 182.

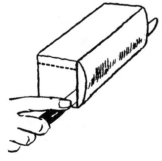  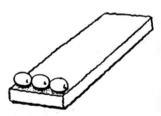

OPEN-FACED SAND-WICH SUGGESTIONS

Remove crusts from loaf of bread and slice thin. Cut into fancy shapes—rounds, stars, squares, diamonds, crescents, horseshoes, triangles, etc., with fancy cookie cutters. Spread with softened butter, cover with desired filling and decorate with edible garnish.

OTHER SUGGESTIONS

Cream cheese with border and center of chopped or sliced candied or maraschino cherries.

Slice of tomato on bread, cut the same size; top with slice of hard-cooked egg and sprinkle with minced pickles or parsley.

Slice of hard-cooked egg in center of round of bread. Garnish with border of caviar.

Garnish buttered circle of bread with border of sieved hard-cooked egg yolk. Fill center with caviar, pâté de foie gras or ground cooked chicken livers. Place a slice of stuffed olive in center.

Slice of smoked salmon. Garnish with spray of dill or thin slice of sweet or dill pickle.

Cut bread into diamond shape. Place a sardine across top and arrange a row of radish slices on each side of sardine.

Cut bread into rectangle and arrange Salmagundi Salad across center. Place strips of pickled beets or circles of hard-cooked egg on each side of the salad.

Slice of cheese on bread with border of Egg Butter forced through a pastry tube or garnish of sliced radishes.

Arrange strips of kippered herring across slice of buttered rye bread. Sprinkle minced onion between strips.

Cut bread into diamond shape, spread half with cream cheese and half with tart jelly. Cover jelly with slices of ripe banana.

Spread white bread with orange marmalade and garnish with halves of seedless grapes.

Slice an apple crosswise, cut out core, place on round of buttered bread and fill center of apple with a grape, a cherry or a spoonful of jelly or peanut butter.

Slice of roast chicken, turkey or cured ham on whole-wheat bread. Garnish with slices of cranberry jelly, cut into fancy shapes.

Cover small squares of buttered bread with chopped or sliced hard-cooked eggs; arrange a row of anchovy or herring fillets diagonally across bread.

Spread diamond of bread with mayonnaise, place slice of hard-cooked egg in center and small slices of cucumber on each end. Use anchovy fillets for cucumber.

Place tomato slice on bread, add asparagus tips and mayonnaise.

Cut meat from cooked lobster claw into halves, place on buttered bread and garnish with mayonnaise and sprigs of dill.

Place row of sliced stuffed olives across center of bread. Decorate on each side with mayonnaise forced through a pastry tube.

Slice of boiled ham cut to fit shape of bread. Garnish with strips of pickled beets.

Mix grated uncooked carrots with enough honey to hold together and spread on whole-wheat bread.

Cut slice of bread into diamond shape and spread 1 end with thick cranberry sauce. On other end place slice of meat loaf cut to fit bread.

Cut slice of bread into rectangle. Spread with mayonnaise, arrange a slice of hard-cooked egg at one end and bits of green pepper to resemble stem and leaves of a flower.

Spread crackers with mayonnaise, cover with thin slice of pared cucumber and garnish with rosette of soft sharp cheese.

Place slice of plum tomato on round of toast the same size. Top with ring of green pepper and garnish with mayonnaise.

Slice the pinwheel roll so that a slice of stuffed olive garnishes the center

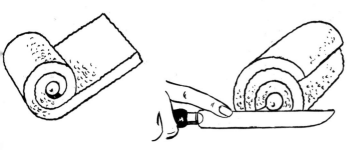

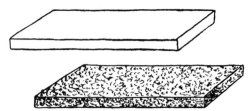

Two long slices of white bread and two of whole-wheat start the ribbon sandwich

PINEAPPLE CHEESE WAFERS

3 ounces cream cheese

3 tablespoons mayonnaise

½ cup chopped pecan meats

½ cup drained crushed pineapple

Crisp crackers

Blend cheese and mayonnaise; add pecan meats and pineapple. Spread on crisp crackers or whole-wheat bread. Makes 24 wafers.

Chill the ribbon sandwich loaf well before cutting it into slices

CINNAMON TOAST

Remove crusts from loaf of bread and cut slices 1¼ inches thick. Cut each slice into 3 strips and toast each on all sides. Dip into melted butter, then roll quickly in mixture of ½ cup confectioners' sugar and 2 teaspoons cinnamon.

APRICOT BANANA TOAST

Toast bread on 1 side and butter the other side. Spread with mashed cooked dried apricots. Cover with slices of banana and sprinkle with brown sugar and a little cinnamon. Arrange on preheated broiler rack and broil slowly until brown sugar is melted. Serve hot.

Use thinly sliced apples instead of apricots.

TILE SANDWICHES

1 unsliced loaf white bread

1 unsliced loaf whole-wheat bread

⅔ cup softened butter, sandwich butter or cream cheese filling

Cut all crusts from white and whole-wheat bread. Cut a 1-inch slice lengthwise from bottom of white loaf. Cut this slice lengthwise into 2 strips, 1x1 inch. Cut 2 similar strips from whole-wheat loaf. Butter 1 side of each strip and press each white strip together with a whole-wheat strip. Spread top of these combined strips with butter and place buttered sides together so that the white sections are opposite whole-wheat sections. Press together and wrap in waxed paper. Chill until butter or filling is firm, about 2 hours. Slice and serve.

DOMINO SANDWICHES

Make closed sandwiches with any desired filling. Cut into oblong shapes and divide crosswise through the center with a strip of pimiento, green pepper or sweet pickle. Cut tiny dots or diamonds from same material and arrange on top to resemble dominoes. Make open sandwiches and use in the same way, selecting material for decorating that will give a good color contrast

Four ribbon sandwiches, two inverted make the checkerboard

RIBBON SANDWICHES

Cut all crusts from unsliced loaf of bread. Spread bottom of loaf thinly with butter and desired filling, then cut a thin slice from bottom of loaf. Spread bottom again with butter and the same or different filling, cut a second slice lengthwise from loaf of same thickness as before and continue until as many slices as desired are prepared. Repeat same procedure with a loaf of whole-wheat bread. Place white and whole-wheat bread slices together in alternate layers with filling and butter between, using 3, 4, or 5 layers depending upon thickness of slices. Use white bread for top and bottom, with an unbuttered slice on top. Press layers together lightly to make a compact loaf. Chill and slice bread down across layers to make thin sandwiches.

CHECKERBOARD SANDWICHES

—Proceed as for ribbon sandwiches, but cut all the slices ½ inch thick and use only 4 layers. To be successful all slices must be as uniform in thickness as possible and the filling must be spread evenly. Cut loaf of ribbon sandwiches into ½-inch slices and spread slices with butter and filling. Pile 4 of these slices one above the other with the strips of bread all running in the same direction and with dark strips above light strips and light strips above dark in checkerboard design. Place the top slice buttered side down. Press stack together firmly. Make similar stacks of remaining slices, chill thoroughly and cut each stack into thin slices.

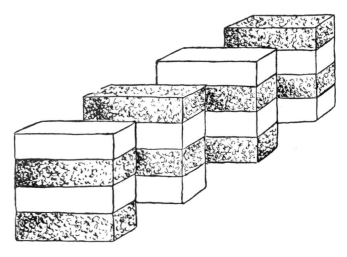

GANGPLANK

Cut all crusts from unsliced loaf of bread. Cut slice lengthwise from bottom of loaf. Butter slice and arrange following fillings, beginning at 1 end in parallel rows to other end. Allow 1 slice to each serving.

Slices of hard-cooked eggs and anchovies

Pickled Herring Salad
Scrambled eggs with sliced frankfurters or chopped bacon
Lobster salad
Sliced roast beef and chopped onions
Roquefort cheese spread

Well pressed together and chilled, the checkerboard will hold together when it is sliced

A bacon cheese roll with a flavorful fruit salad makes an ideal lunch on a hot summer day

SAVORY PINWHEELS

¼ cup butter
½ cup grated sharp cheese
2 tablespoons chopped parsley
1 teaspoon prepared mustard
1 tablespoon tomato catchup
1 teaspoon Worcestershire sauce
Bread

Cream butter and cheese togeth er and remaining ingredients ex- cept bread. Cut 6 slices bread about ⅛ inch thick and spread generously with cheese mixture. Roll like a jelly roll and fasten with toothpicks. Wrap in waxed paper and chill ½ hour or longer. Just before serving, cut into thin slices and toast under broiler. Makes 48 pinwheels.

CORNUCOPIA TEASERS

2 tablespoons meat or fish paste
2 tablespoons sieved hard-cooked
   egg
2 tablespoons softened butter
Few drops lemon juice
Dash cayenne
4 thin slices white bread

Combine meat paste, egg, butter and seasonings. Blend well, spread on bread, trim off crusts and cut each slice into 4 squares. Roll each into a tiny cornucopia and fasten with a toothpick. Place in shallow pan and cover with damp cloth or wet parchment paper. Chill 1 to 2 hours. Remove tooth- picks and garnish as desired. Makes 16 cornucopias.

CORNUCOPIA HORS D'OEU- VRES — Brown cornucopias in moderate oven (350°F.) and re- move toothpicks. Garnish with slice of stuffed olive in tops.

LILY SANDWICHES

Cut thin slices of bread into 2½- inch squares, removing all crusts. Spread with butter and filling. Using 1 corner of bread as stem end and opposite corner as flow- er end of lily, roll 1 of remaining corners to center as a cornucopia. Wrap opposite corner around this roll. Fasten with toothpick and chill until firm. Cut a strip of whole-wheat bread and insert in- to top of lily for stamen.

BACON CHEESE ROLL

Remove crusts from large loaf bread and cut into lengthwise slices, ⅓ inch thick. Spread generously with cheese filling and roll up each slice. Wrap each roll with slice of bacon and toast under broiler, turning frequently.

Lily and cornucopia sand- wiches are glorified versions of rolled sandwiches and just as easy to make

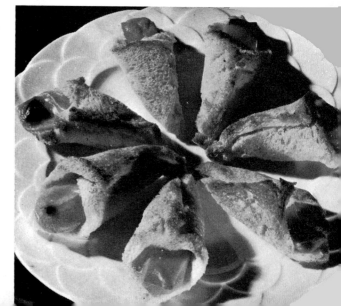

PARTY SANDWICHES

FROSTED PARTY SPECIAL

6 hard-cooked eggs, chopped
1 (4-ounce) can pimientos, chopped
½ teaspoon salt
6 tablespoons mayonnaise
½ pound ground cooked ham
3 medium sweet pickles, chopped
48 thin slices sandwich bread
9 ounces cream cheese
3 tablespoons cream

Combine eggs, pimientos, ¼ teaspoon salt and 3 tablespoons mayonnaise; mix thoroughly. Combine ham, pickles and remaining mayonnaise and mix. Cut bread into rounds, spread 16 of these with egg mixture, top each with second round, spread with ham mixture, top with third round. Press firmly together. Mix cheese, cream and remaining salt and beat until fluffy. Spread over tops and sides of sandwiches and chill 2 to 3 hours. Top each sandwich with a slice of stuffed olive and small sprigs of parsley. Makes 16 sandwiches.

Use watercress for parsley.

Here is the frosted sandwich loaf in all its glory ready to meet all comers

Cut bread into squares, rectangles, triangles, or other fancy shapes instead of circles. After frosting sandwiches, sprinkle generously with hard-cooked egg yolks pressed through a sieve. Use graham or whole-wheat bread for center slice of sandwich. Tint cream cheese frosting any color desired with food coloring.

Individual round sandwich loaves, frosted and garnished look like tea cakes

FROSTED SANDWICH LOAF

1 unsliced loaf sandwich bread
Butter
Mayonnaise
Sliced tomatoes
Ham Filling
Lettuce
9 ounces cream cheese
Milk, Parsley

Remove all crust from a loaf of day-old bread. Cut 4 lengthwise slices about ½ inch thick and spread with butter. Place a slice on a platter, spread with mayonnaise, then cover with sliced peeled tomatoes. Spread another slice with mayonnaise and place it mayonnaise side down on tomatoes. Spread top of this slice with ham filling, cover with third slice of bread. Spread it with mayonnaise and cover with lettuce. Spread fourth slice of bread with mayonnaise and place it mayonnaise side down on lettuce. Press firmly together. Soften cream cheese with milk, beat until fluffy and frost the outside of the loaf. Garnish with parsley. Chill at least 1 hour. Slice crosswise to serve. Serves 8.
Some suggested fillings are:

PARTY SANDWICHES

1.

Sliced tomatoes and cucumbers, mayonnaise
Salmon and Nut Filling
Lettuce and mayonnaise

2.

Cheese and Bacon Filling
Sliced chicken or Chicken and Almond Sandwich Filling
Lettuce or tomato; mayonnaise

3.

Veal and Carrot Filling
Cottage Cheese and Celery Fillin
Egg and Pickle Filling

4.

Cream Cheese and Nut Filling
Orange marmalade
Date and Orange Filling

5.

Egg and Pickle Filling
Chicken and Celery Filling
Cheese Apricot Filling

6.

Anchovy Salad Filling
Bacon Filling
Egg Salad Filling

When cut square or oblong they still look like small individual cakes

PYRAMID SANDWICHES

1 large loaf unsliced sandwich bread
1 cup softened butter
8 slices cold chicken
Russian dressing
½ head lettuce
4 hard-cooked eggs, chopped
¼ cup mayonnaise
¼ teaspoon salt
⅛ teaspoon pepper
2 tomatoes, peeled and sliced
1 cucumber, pared and sliced
3 ounces cream cheese
½ cup chopped olives
8 rolled anchovies
Watercress
Radish Roses

Slice bread thin. For each sandwich cut 5 rounds of bread varying in diameter from 1 to 4 inches. Spread the rounds with softened butter. Cover the largest rounds with sliced chicken, then with Russian dressing. Cover the next smaller rounds with shredded lettuce and a mixture of hard-cooked eggs, mayonnaise, salt and pepper; then place them on the first rounds. Cover the third rounds with a slice of tomato, then with cucumber and place it on top of the egg mixture. Spread next rounds with mixture of cream cheese and chopped olives, add the smallest buttered round, place a rolled anchovy on the top fastened with a frilled toothpick. Place both together on top of the third rounds. Garnish with watercress and radish roses. Makes 8 sandwiches. Omit chicken and use slices of cooked ham, tongue, pork, veal, turkey or smoked salmon. Instead of lettuce use watercress. Omit eggs and add ½ cup chopped pickle to mayonnaise or use 2 eggs and add ¼ cup chopped pickle. Omit cucumber; use sliced radishes. Use cottage cheese for cream cheese.

SKYSCRAPER SANDWICHES

1 large loaf unsliced sandwich bread
1 cup softened butter
3 ounces cream cheese
½ cup orange marmalade
½ cup ground dates
¼ cup ground walnuts
¾ cup drained shredded pineapple
4 slices cooked ham
4 candied cherries
Watercress

Slice bread and spread as described in Pyramid Sandwiches. Mix cheese and marmalade and spread on largest rounds. Cover with next smallest round, spread with date and nut mixture. Cover third round with pineapple and place on date nut filling. . Cover fourth round with ham, place on pineapple. Place smallest round with buttered side down on ham. Garnish with a cherry half and watercress.

TRIANGLE CLUB SANDWICHES

15 slices toast
Chili sauce
5 slices American cheese
Mayonnaise
10 slices cooked tongue
Lettuce
10 stuffed olives
15 sweet pickles

Spread 5 slices of toast with chili sauce. Cover each with a slice of American cheese, then with a second slice of toast. Spread top of toast with mayonnaise, cover each sandwich with 2 slices of tongue and a third slice of toast spread with mayonnaise. Cut off crusts, cut each sandwich into 4 triangles and stand them upright on a plate. Garnish center with crisp lettuce, stuffed olives and sweet pickles. Serves 5.

Everyone loves to demolish these pyramids, since each layer offers a fresh surprise

NIGHT CAP

4 eggs, beaten
2 tablespoons milk or cream
¼ teaspoon salt
Dash pepper
1 tablespoon minced onion
2 tablespoons minced pimientos
½ can Vienna sausages, thinly
    sliced
2 tablespoons butter
8 slices rye or whole-wheat toast,
    buttered

Beat eggs and add milk, salt, pepper, onion, pimientos and sausage. Cook mixture slowly in buttered skillet, stirring slowly. Pour mixture over half of hot buttered toast and top with second slice. Cut diagonally and serve immediately. Makes 4 sandwiches.

TOMATO ROYAL SANDWICHES

¼ cup butter
¼ pound Roquefort cheese
¼ cup Worcestershire sauce
6 slices bread
Sliced tomatoes, Lettuce

Cream butter and cheese thoroughly. Add Worcestershire sauce and beat until smooth.

Spread on unbuttered slices of bread. Top with thin slices of tomato and garnish with lettuce. Cut into quarters and serve as an appetizer or with a Dutch lunch. Makes 6 sandwiches.

PARTY SANDWICH LOAF

1 (1¼-pound) unsliced loaf
    bread
2 cups diced cooked corned beef
6 tablespoons chopped sweet
    pickles
1 cup mayonnaise
½ teaspoon salt
¼ teaspoon pepper

Remove all crusts from bread and cut a long slice ½-inch thick from the top of loaf. Remove center of loaf, leaving a wall ½ inch thick on bottom, sides and ends. Break bread removed from center into crumbs and combine 2½ cups of crumbs with corned beef and pickles. Add mayonnaise and seasonings, mix well and pack into center of loaf. Cover with top slice and chill. Serve in slices. Serves 6 to 8

A very sharp long-bladed knife is an essential for removing top, bottom and center of the loaf to make this treasure chest of sandwiches

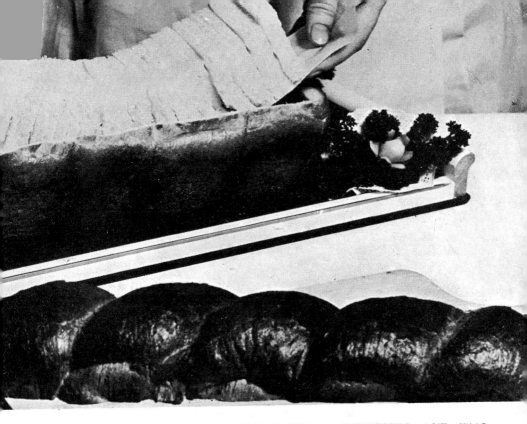

When the filled sandwiches are replaced in the chest, they will stay moist and fresh until used. Arrange nosegays of parsley and radish roses for garnish

TREASURE SAND-WICH CHEST

Cut the rounded top (about ¼ of loaf) from a loaf of bread. Turn loaf upside down on this cut edge and working on the bottom of the loaf with a sharp, pointed knife cut along each edge leaving a ½-inch margin all around. Cut through to the top side so that the entire center may be pushed through the crust-shell in one piece. Cut the bread from center into slices, spread with butter and a sandwich spread or filling and cut off bottom crusts. Place sandwiches on a double fold of waxed paper just the width of the sandwiches, lower all at one time into the "chest" and pull paper out as sandwiches are slipped into place. Use top crust for the cover to the "chest."

PIMIENTO AND WAL-NUT SANDWICHES

½ cup chopped English walnut meats
½ cup chopped pimientos
3 ounces cream cheese
½ cup mayonnaise
⅛ teaspoon salt
Butter
Brown or nut bread

Mix walnut meats with pimientos, cream cheese, mayonnaise and salt. Spread between buttered slices of brown or nut bread. Makes about 12 sandwiches.

POCKETBOOKS

Bread
1 recipe Salmon and Pickle Filling

Cut bread in very thin slices, 5x3 inches. Spread with filling, and fold ends over center to make 3 layers. Makes 12.

DOUBLE-DECKERS AND TRIPLE-DECKERS

CLUB SANDWICHES

24 slices bread
Butter
8 slices cold cooked white meat of chicken
Mayonnaise
16 crisp slices bacon
16 slices tomato

Toast bread and spread with butter. Cover 8 slices with chicken, spread with mayonnaise and cover each with another slice of toast. Spread these with mayonnaise, place 2 slices bacon and 2 slices tomato on top of each and cover with remaining toast. Fasten securely with toothpicks, cut each sandwich diagonally into 4 triangles and stand them upright on a plate. Garnish with pickles, olives, Celery Curls or Radish Roses. Serves 8.

Place a leaf of lettuce on top of tomato; cover with toast.

TUNA—Omit chicken. Drain tuna; slice or flake and arrange on toast in place of chicken.

TURKEY—Use turkey meat instead of chicken.

A rich cheese sauce on the club sandwich gives a new angle to an old favorite

CHICAGO SPECIAL

1 trimmed slice rye bread
1 full slice Swiss cheese
Lettuce
1 slice chicken or turkey breast
Russian dressing
1 thick slice tomato
1 slice hard-cooked egg
Pickle slices, 2 slices crisp bacon

Place bread in center of serving plate. Cover with cheese then large leaf lettuce. Add sliced breast of chicken and another layer of lettuce. Cover generously with dressing. Garnish with tomato topped with egg, pickle and hot bacon. Serves 1.

TOMATO CHEESE CLUB SANDWICHES

12 slices bread, Softened butter
8 slices tomato
8 slices crisp bacon
½ pound Cheddar cheese
⅓ cup milk

Toast bread; spread with butter, cover with tomato slices. Place another slice of toast over tomato; cover with bacon. Top with third slice of toast. Melt cheese in double boiler. Add milk gradually, stirring constantly. Pour sauce over each sandwich. Garnish with Radish Roses. Serves 4.

LIVER SAUSAGE CLUB

12 slices bread
Softened butter
4 thick slices liver sausage
8 thin slices tomato
Salt and pepper
4 leaves lettuce
Mayonnaise

Spread 4 slices bread with butter, cover with liver sausage, place another slice of bread over sausage, spread top with butter, cover with slices tomato, sprinkle with salt and pepper, top with lettuce and mayonnaise and the third slice bread. Stick toothpicks down into center of each side to hold in place and cut diagonally into quarters. Turn cut edges up and serve with dill pickle slices. Serves 4.

Use salami for liver sausage.

MIDNIGHT FEAST

½ teaspoon grated onion
1 (3¼-ounce) can kippered herring, mashed
18 slices bread
6 slices American cheese
2 hard-cooked eggs, mashed
2 tablespoons mayonnaise
½ teaspoon prepared mustard
¼ teaspoon salt
Dash pepper
6 lettuce leaves
6 slices tomato
6 stuffed olives, sliced

Combine onion with mashed kippered herring and spread on 6 of the slices of bread. Cover each with 1 slice of cheese, then with another slice of bread. Combine mashed egg, mayonnaise, mustard, salt and pepper; spread over top of each sandwich. Cover each with lettuce leaf and another slice of bread; on top place tomato slices and cut sandwiches diagonally. Place slices of stuffed olives on corners. Makes 6 sandwiches.

snacks
and
appetizers

300 Snacks,
Appetizers
for Entertaining

THE SMÖRGÅSBORD

TRANSPLANTED to America the Smörgåsbord,—an old Scandinavian custom,—has grown strong deep roots in our national affections until now we feel that it belongs to us. The very sound of the word smörgåsbord implies relaxation—the leisure to enjoy food, friends and conversation of our selection and in the combination and quantity we like. It has become a favorite Sunday night dinner.

It is particularly useful as a means of entertaining sumptuously, larger numbers of guests than can be otherwise entertained in the average home. Perhaps the chief charm of the smörgåsbord is the opportunity our hostess gives us to enjoy our very own choice from the enticing selections she places before us. We help ourselves to the dishes we want, returning to the board again and again.

There are two favored arrangements for the smörgåsbord. If space is limited it is well to push the dining table against the wall, allowing ample space on the three sides for guests to move easily. If there is plenty of space, the table may remain in the center of the room and the guests circulate freely.

The table may be covered with a cloth, or mats and tray cloths. China, silver and napery are carefully arranged at the nearest end or the end of the near side.

Types of food are grouped not only for convenience, but also that the cold and jellied salads may not be warmed by hot dishes. Also if electric heat is used for chafing dishes, casseroles and coffee, the connections usually come from one source. Coffee may be made in the kitchen or brewed at the table. Sweets are usually at the far end of the table and if the preferences of all the guests are known, the coffee may be there too.

The return of the chafing dish is a further indication of the popularity of informal entertaining. Time was when the chafing dish went to college with the daughter of the house and thereby began a long and picturesque social career. The hostess of today will find it a charming and useful addition to her smörgåsbord, for hot entrées and hors d'oeuvres.

Maids may circulate among the guests, frequently seated at small bridge tables. They remove plates, serve desserts and beverages, and replenish plates.

All of these recipes are ready for the smörgåsbord and the clever hostess will make her choice, knowing the preferences of her guests.

DAISY CANAPÉS

8 rounds bread
1/3 cup softened butter
1/2 ounces anchovy paste
8 hard-cooked eggs

Spread untoasted rounds of bread with butter and then with anchovy paste. Cut narrow strips out of hard-cooked egg whites. Arrange in petal fashion on paste and place sieved hard-cooked egg yolk in center. Makes 8 canapés.

HALF AND HALF CANAPÉS

1/2 cup flaked cooked salmon
2 tablespoons mayonnaise
1 1/2 tablespoons lemon juice
1/4 teaspoon salt
Dash pepper
8 toast rounds
3 tablespoons softened butter
1/2 cup mashed avocado
8 strips pimiento

Mix salmon, mayonnaise, 1/2 tablespoon lemon juice, salt, and pepper. Spread toast rounds with softened butter. Spread half of each round with salmon mixture, the other half with avocado mixed with remaining lemon juice. Mark the division with a pimiento strip. Makes 8 canapés.

OLIVE CANAPÉS

8 rectangles bread
3 ounces cream cheese
16 stuffed olives, sliced

Spread bread with cream cheese. Place a row of olive slices down center of bread allowing slices to overlap slightly. Makes 8 canapés.

Use diamond-shaped bread slices and place a slice of stuffed olive in center and a border of finely chopped stuffed olives or thin slices, cut into halves, around edge of each.

OLIVE PINWHEELS

6 tablespoons ground boiled ham
2 tablespoons mayonnaise
1 teaspoon horse-radish
1 loaf sandwich bread
4 tablespoons butter
6 stuffed olives

Combine ham, mayonnaise, and horse-radish. Remove all crusts from bread. Cut bread lengthwise into slices 1/4 inch thick. Spread with softened butter and with ham mixture. Place olives in a line crosswise at 1 end of the bread; roll bread starting at the end of slice. Wrap roll in a damp cloth or in oiled paper and place in refrigerator for several hours. When ready to serve cut crosswise into slices any thickness desired. This makes sufficient filling for 1 full-length slice of bread which will cut 8 thin pinwheels.
TO VARY—Use peanut butter instead of ham; omit horse-radish.
Use any ground poultry, fish or meat instead of ham.
Spread with a mixture of 3 ounces cream cheese and enough chili sauce to make cheese of spread-

The olive, black, green or stuffed will help make attractive canapés

ing consistency.
Arrange chopped olives, pimientos, egg white, parsley or chives, crosswise on slices spread with desired filling.

SHRIMP CANAPÉS

8 cooked jumbo shrimp split from head to tail
1/2 cup French dressing
16 toast rounds
4 tablespoons Lemon Mayonnaise
1 1/2 ounces caviar
Parsley

Marinate shrimp in French dressing for 1 hour. Spread toast rounds with lemon mayonnaise. Place shrimp, flat side down, on toast. Fill curve formed by shrimp with caviar. Garnish with tiny sprig of parsley at the head of shrimp. Serves 8.

IGLOO CANAPÉS

4 hard-cooked eggs
1 recipe Anchovy Filling for Stuffed Eggs (page 221)
8 rounds bread
3 ounces cream cheese

Shell eggs, cut into halves crosswise and remove yolks. Fill whites level-full with anchovy filling. Spread bread with softened cream cheese, turn filled egg white flat side down on bread. Makes 8.

Beautiful canapés begin with the clever cutting of assorted breads

TOMATO AND EGG CANAPÉS

8 rounds bread
2 tablespoons mayonnaise
Sliced tomatoes
Hard-cooked eggs, sliced
Salt
4 stuffed green olives, sliced

Toast rounds of bread on 1 side and spread the untoasted side with mayonnaise. Add thin slices of tomato, then slices of hard-cooked egg. Sprinkle very lightly with salt and garnish with a slice or 2 of stuffed olives. Makes 8 canapés.

CANAPÉ SUGGESTIONS

Place sliced smoked breast **of** goose or turkey on toast rounds, garnish with white grapes and mayonnaise.

Spread toast rounds with Egg Butter. Cover with sliced smoked ham. Garnish with sliced stuffed olives.

Place thin sliced tongue on toast rounds. Spread with tomato purée and garnish with olive slice.

Spread toast rounds with Anchovy Butter, top with slices of roast veal and garnish with capers.

Spread French toast or crackers with Anchovy Butter, garnish with anchovy fillets and minced hard-cooked egg.

Spread toast fingers with prepared mustard and top with whole sardines marinated in lemon juice.

Place rings of hard-cooked egg whites on toast rounds.

CANAPÉ BUTTERS

All these butters are prepared as follows: Cream butter thoroughly. Grind fish, meat, or vegetables to a paste and combine with the seasoning and butter. . If mixture is not entirely smooth rub through a sieve. Spread on toast rounds and garnish appropriately or use as a base for sandwich fillings.

SHRIMP BUTTER

1 cup butter
1 cup minced cooked shrimp
¼ teaspoon salt
Dash paprika
1 tablespoon lemon juice

CHIVE BUTTER

½ cup butter
¼ cup chives
4 drops Worcestershire sauce

ANCHOVY BUTTER

1 cup butter
½ cup minced anchovies or
    4 tablespoons anchovy paste
2 teaspoons lemon juice
4 drops onion juice
Substitute herring, bloaters, crawfish, lobster, smoked salmon, whitefish, or sardines for the anchovies.

HORSE-RADISH BUTTER

½ cup butter
¼ cup grated horse-radish

MUSTARD BUTTER

½ cup butter
¼ cup prepared mustard

HAM BUTTER

½ cup butter
¼ pound cooked ham
2 hard-cooked eggs, chopped
Dash pepper

EGG BUTTER

½ cup butter
4 hard-cooked egg yolks
Few grains cayenne
6 drops Worcestershire sauce

CHEESE BUTTER

½ cup butter
¼ cup grated Parmesan cheese or
    1½ ounces Roquefort or ½
    cup snappy cheese spread

PIMIENTO BUTTER

½ cup butter
¼ cup mashed pimiento
2 teaspoons India relish, drained

FILÉ BUTTER

½ cup butter, melted
1 tablespoon filé
1 teaspoon paprika

OLIVE BUTTER

¼ cup butter
2 tablespoons chopped olives
¼ teaspoon lemon juice

CHILI BUTTER

¼ cup butter
2 tablespoons chili sauce, drained

POPPY SEED BUTTER

½ cup butter
½ cup hot poppy seeds, ground
    Use caraway seeds instead.

CANAPÉ SUGGESTIONS—
Cont.

Fill centers of rings with caviar, anchovy rolls, or sliced stuffed olives. Garnish with sieved hard-cooked egg yolks. Mix 3 ounces caviar with 4 teaspoons minced onion. Spread on toast rounds and garnish with cream cheese or strips of pimiento.

Cook 8 cleaned cooked shrimp in 2 tablespoons butter. Add ¼ teaspoon curry powder, ⅛ teaspoon dry mustard, 1 teaspoon sherry wine. Serve hot on small bread croustades or packaged appetizer shells. Spread rounds of bread with Horse-radish Butter, then with cream cheese. Garnish with flowers made from olives or pimientos.

Spread toast with butter, then with cream cheese. Garnish with strips of pimiento or sprinkle with sieved pimiento.

Spread crackers with mayonnaise cover with thin slices of cucumber and garnish with rosettes of snappy cheese spread and sprig of parsley. Spread bread fingers with cream cheese or with equal parts of Roquefort and cream cheese. Top with walnut meats.

Spread toast triangles with Egg Butter then with pickled beets pressed through ricer. Sprinkle with a few drops French dressing and garnish with sieved egg yolks.

Spread rounds of graham bread with Mustard Butter. Top with slice of tomato and sprinkle with salt. Or spread with Chive Butter and top tomato with slice of cucumber and a dash of paprika.

Make tomato mold, adding minced cucumber to the minced celery. Chill in ½-inch layer and cut into rounds. Serve on crackers.

Spread toast generously with thick mayonnaise. Dip into minced watercress and sprinkle with salt. Garnish with minced hard-cooked egg white.

Spread toast squares with mixture of ¼ cup each of peanut butter and raspberry jam and 2 tablespoons butter.

Spread toast with mixture of strawberry jam and nut meats.

MOSAIC SANDWICHES

16 slices white bread
16 slices brown bread
Any desired Canapé Spread or
Butter

Slice bread ¼ inch thick. Cut into fancy shapes, hearts, diamonds, spades or clubs, and spread half of them with desired filling. With a smaller cutter cut out the center of remaining pieces in the same shape as the original. For example if the original shape was a heart, cut a heart shape out of center. Insert white heart into brown bread and brown heart into white bread. Place each on corresponding shape spread with filling. Makes 8 sandwiches.

Ribbon, rolled and mosaic
sandwiches, dress up the
simplest evening snack

HAM SPREADS

1 cup minced boiled ham, ¼ teaspoon ground cloves, ¼ teaspoon mace, ¼ teaspoon salt, 4 tablespoons cream.

½ cup minced cooked ham, ½ cup chutney.

¾ cup ground cooked ham, ¼ cup minced walnut meats, 1 teaspoon prepared mustard, 3 tablespoons heavy cream, ¼ teaspoon salt, ⅛ teaspoon pepper.

1 cup ground boiled ham, ½ cup pepper relish.

¾ cup deviled ham, 1 chopped hard-cooked egg, 1 tablespoon mayonnaise, 1 tablespoon chili sauce.

1 cup ground ham, vinegar or pickle juice to moisten, 4 teaspoons peanut butter, salt, pepper, celery salt.

½ cup flaked salmon, ½ cup deviled ham, enough mayonnaise to bind mixture.

MISCELLANEOUS

½ cup ground cooked tongue, ¼ cup chopped cooked mushrooms, 1 tablespoon chopped dill pickle, 2 tablespoons Thousand Island dressing.

½ cup mashed cooked goose livers, 2 tablespoons goose fat, 3 chopped hard-cooked eggs, ⅛ teaspoon paprika, ½ teaspoon grated onion, salt, and pepper.

1 cup ground Bologna sausage, 2 teaspoons chopped onion, 2 tablespoons chopped celery, enough mayonnaise to bind mixture.

6 boiled frankfurters, ground; ½ teaspoon prepared mustard; 5 tablespoons mayonnaise.

¾ cup ground dried beef, ¼ cup grated cheese, ¼ cup minced celery, enough mayonnaise to bind mixture.

¼ pound finely chopped salted almonds, ¼ cup chopped stuffed olives, 2 tablespoons mayonnaise, 1 teaspoon French dressing.

½ cup minced ripe olives, ½ cup minced celery, mayonnaise to moisten.

½ cup chopped celery, 4 tablespoons chopped sweet pickle, 4 tablespoons chopped pimiento, 3 tablespoons mayonnaise.

PIE CANAPÉ

1 round loaf rye bread
1 cut clove garlic
⅓ cup softened butter
¼ cup mayonnaise
1½ ounces caviar
Minced parsley
Sieved egg yolk
6 ounces cream cheese
½ cup anchovy paste
⅔ cup Shrimp Spread
1 cup Salmon Spread

Cut a slice horizontally (½ inch thick) from the widest part of a round rye loaf. Trim off crust. Rub a bowl with a cut clove of garlic and mix butter and mayonnaise in it. Spread bread generously with the mixture. Mark the round slice in concentric circles using cutters and bowls of various sizes. Fill center ring with caviar, marking center point with chopped parsley or sieved egg yolk. Fill next ring with cream cheese (tinted if desired) pressed through a pastry tube. Fill the next rings with anchovy paste, then shrimp paste and the largest ring with salmon paste separated by cream cheese. Cut in wedges like pie, with a sharp knife, but do not separate. Serve cold within a few hours. Serves 12 to 16 depending on the size of the loaf.

Cheese spreads, minced ham with mayonnaise, minced stuffed olives and sieved yolks may be used for the various sections instead of fish pastes.

Garnish with pickled onions, stuffed olives, radish roses or vegetable curls. Sliced stuffed olives, small pickles or piccalilli may be used for one of the sections.

The pie canapé will add a new luster to your entertaining—try it and hear the cheers

HOT CRAB-MEAT CANAPÉS

½ cup salad dressing
½ teaspoon prepared mustard
1 teaspoon Worcestershire sauce
2 teaspoons grated horse-radish
1½ cups flaked crab meat
8 shallow Croustades
½ cup grated Parmesan cheese

Mix salad dressing, mustard, Worcestershire sauce and horse-radish with crab meat. Heap crab-meat mixture into croustades, top with cheese and brown in moderate oven (350°F.). For 8.

CURRIED CRAB-MEAT CANAPÉS—Omit cheese. Fill croustades with crab meat as above and cover with Curry Sauce (Page 232), then buttered bread crumbs. Brown crumbs before serving.

HOT CELERY CANAPÉS

3 ounces cream cheese
¼ cup condensed celery soup
1 cup ground salami

Cream cheese and add celery soup. Then add ground salami and mix well. Spread mixture on toast or crackers and heat under broiler until browned. Makes 20 canapés.

TOASTED TOMATO HAM CANAPÉS

1 cup ground boiled ham
½ cup grated cheese
½ teaspoon horse-radish
½ teaspoon prepared mustard
½ cup condensed tomato soup
5 slices bread, toasted

Mix first 5 ingredients together. Toast bread, trim off crusts and cut each slice into 3 or 4 strips. Spread with mixture, then toast under broiler until browned. Makes 15 to 20 canapés.

MUSHROOM AND CRAB-MEAT CANAPÉS

½ pound crab meat
1 cup cooked mushrooms, sliced
4 tablespoons cream
½ teaspoon salt
6 drops Tabasco sauce
Few grains cayenne
18 toast diamonds
1 recipe Anchovy Butter
¼ cup grated Parmesan cheese
¼ cup buttered bread crumbs

Flake crab meat, add mushrooms, cream, salt, Tabasco sauce, and cayenne. Toss together lightly. Spread diamond-shaped pieces of toast with anchovy butter, cover with crab-meat mixture, sprinkle with cheese, then with crumbs. Bake in hot oven (425°F.) 10 minutes or until brown. Serves 8.

BROILED FILLED MUSHROOMS—Use 8 large mushrooms and ½ cup crab meat. Combine crab meat, 2 tablespoons cream and seasonings. Remove stems of mushrooms, wash and peel. Broil rounded-side up 5 minutes. Turn, fill each with crab-meat mixture, cover with cheese and crumbs. Broil again 5 minutes.

FINNAN HADDIE CANAPÉS

½ tablespoon finely chopped onion
2 tablespoons finely chopped mushroom caps
3 tablespoons butter
2 tablespoons flour
⅔ cup thin cream
2 tablespoons grated cheese
2 egg yolks
1 cup finnan haddie, soaked and flaked
Salt and cayenne
12 circles toast
Grated cheese
Buttered bread crumbs

Fry onion and mushrooms in butter for 5 minutes Blend in flour. Add cream gradually and heat to boiling, stirring constantly. Remove from heat and stir in 2 tablespoons cheese, egg yolks, slightly beaten, finnan haddie, salt, and cayenne. Pile mixture on toast circles, sprinkle with cheese and buttered crumbs and brown in hot oven (400°F.). Serve hot for 12.

Few canapés are as luscious as this croustade filled with hot curried crab meat

HOT CANAPÉS

BROILED ROUND STEAK—Place broiled ground round steak patties on toast rounds, season with onion juice, salt, and pepper.

FLOWER CANAPÉS—Spread American or pimiento cheese on thin slices of Bologna (with casing on). Broil until sausage curls.

DOUBLE-DECKED CANAPÉS—Spread crackers with a mixture of deviled ham, a little lemon juice and Worcestershire sauce. Cover with another cracker and snappy cheese spread. Toast under broiler.

SARDINE AND CHEESE CANAPÉS—Mix equal portions of sardines and cream cheese, spread on thin slices of bread and roll. Toast under broiler before serving.

Rolled hot sandwiches will delight your family as well as your friends

BRAZIL-NUT CHEESE CANAPÉS—Mix grated American cheese, paprika, and onion juice. Spread on toast rounds. Place under broiler to melt cheese. Sprinkle with chopped Brazil nuts.

HOT SWISS CHEESE CANAPÉS—Cover toast rounds with a thin slice of onion, then with mayonnaise and a circle of Swiss cheese Melt cheese under broiler.

HOT TONGUE CANAPÉS—Combine 1 cup minced cooked tongue, 2 tablespoons cream, 1 egg yolk, ¼ teaspoon salt, 3 drops Tabasco sauce, few grains cayenne. Spread on hot toast squares and sprinkle with bread crumbs. Cut twice diagonally and brown in hot oven (400°F.) 4 to 5 minutes. Spread 8 slices toast for 32 canapés.

CANAPÉ TURNOVERS—Roll pastry ⅛ inch thick, cut into 2-inch squares, place 1 teaspoon of any of the following mixtures in center of each square. fold into a triangle and press edges together with a fork. Fry in hot deep fat (370°F.) 4 minutes. Serve hot, garnished with chopped parsley. One cup ground liver, 4 tablespoons minced bacon, 2 tablespoons minced parsley, ⅛ teaspoon pepper. One cup ground salami, ½ teaspoon grated horseradish. One cup ground chicken, ¼ teaspoon curry powder, ¼ teaspoon salt, 3 tablespoons minced parsley.

SMOKED SALMON CANAPÉS—Spread toast fingers with Lemon Butter. Place ¼-inch slice smoked salmon on toast. Cover with buttered crumbs and brown under broiler.

SAUSAGE CANAPES—Toast rounds of graham bread on 1 side, butter other side. Broil on 1 side only patties shaped from pork sausage. Place on buttered side of toast rounds and brown under broiler.

ROLLED CANAPES

TOASTED CHEESE ROLLED CANAPÉS—Spread thin slices of bread with butter then with snappy cheese spread. Roll and toast under broiler until browned.

BAKED BEAN CANAPÉS—Season ½ cup baked beans with 1 tablespoon chili sauce. Pile on thin slices of bread. Roll, fasten with toothpicks, wrap in slice of bacon and toast under broiler until bacon is crisp.

EGG CANAPÉS—Scramble eggs, season with salt, pepper and Worcestershire sauce, pile on thin slices of bread, roll, toast under broiler.

HOT FISH CANAPÉS—Spread bread with minced kippered herring, sprinkle with lemon juice, roll tightly, fasten with toothpicks, brush with melted butter and brown lightly under broiler.

CORNED BEEF CANAPÉS—Spread thin slices of bread with butter, then spread ½ cup ground corned beef, seasoned with horseradish and mixed with 4 tablespoons beaten egg. Roll, fasten with toothpicks and toast under broiler.

LIVER CANAPÉS—Force enough cooked liver through food chopper to make 1 cup. Mix with 3 tablespoons cream, ½ teaspoon grated onion, dash salt and pepper. Spread on thin slices of buttered bread, roll, fasten with toothpicks and bake in very hot oven (450°F.) 5 minutes.

ASPIC APPETIZERS

(See page 229)

METHOD—Prepare aspic gelatin, add 1 cup chopped vegetables when mixture begins to thicken. Pour into individual molds, or into layer ½ inch thick and chill. Unmold or cut layer into squares, circles or fancy shapes and serve on crisp crackers, or slices of vegetables such as tomatoes, large carrots, cucumbers, turnips or celery root.

SUGGESTIONS

1. ½ cup uncooked diced celery and ½ cup grated carrots.

2. ¼ cup diced celery, ¼ cup minced onion, ¼ cup diced cooked beets, ¼ cup minced sweet pickle.

3. ½ cup diced uncooked tomatoes, 1 tablespoon grated onion, ½ cup grated carrot.

4. ⅛ teaspoon minced garlic, ¾ cup grated carrot, ¼ cup minced parsley.

JELLIED MÉLANGE

2 tablespoons unflavored gelatin
¼ cup cold water
4 cups hot chicken broth
tablespoons onion juice
1 cup chopped cooked chicken
½ cup chopped cooked ham
½ cup chopped celery
pimiento, minced
Mayonnaise, Parsley

Soften gelatin in cold water for 5 minutes and dissolve in hot broth. Add onion juice. Cool; when mixture begins to thicken, stir in chicken, ham, celery, and pimiento and pour into small molds. Chill. Serve on lettuce garnished with mayonnaise and parsley. Serves 8.

SHRIMP MÉLANGE—Omit ham, use tomato juice instead of chicken broth and chopped, cleaned shrimp instead of chicken.

BEEF MÉLANGE—Omit ham. Use beef broth and chopped beef instead of chicken broth and chopped chicken.

BOLOGNA SAUSAGE CUBES

2 slices Bologna sausage, ¾ inch thick
8 small pickled onions

Cut Bologna into ¾-inch cubes. Spear a Bologna cube, then an onion on an hors d'oeuvre pick. Place onion-up on a server.

Use cervelat, salami, or summer sausage instead of Bologna sausage.

Use cubes of pickled beets instead of onion or use 1 onion and 1 beet cube.

Use slices of small dill pickle instead of onions.

BANANA HORS D'OEUVRES

2 large bananas
1 cup lemon juice
3 ounces cream cheese
⅓ cup chopped nut meats

Peel bananas and cut crosswise into 1-inch pieces. Marinate in lemon juice for 1 hour. Drain, cover with cream cheese and roll in nut meats. Makes 8 hors d'oeuvres.

—Use pineapple, grapefruit or orange juice for the marinade.

CRAB MEAT IN ROLLS

8 finger rolls
1½ cups flaked crab meat
1½ cups diced celery
2 hard-cooked eggs, chopped
½ teaspoon salt
¼ teaspoon pepper
Dash Tabasco sauce
3 tablespoons lemon juice
½ cup salad dressing
Lettuce

Make a lengthwise cut in center of top of each roll, spread apart and remove soft part. Mix crab meat, celery, eggs, salt, pepper, Tabasco sauce, lemon juice, and salad dressing together and fill centers of rolls. Place rolls on crisp lettuce to serve.

A tray of filled nuts and vegetables is a treat

FILLED FRUITS AND VEGETABLES

FILLED BEETS—Marinate small cooked beets overnight in French dressing. Remove centers and fill with paste made of hard-cooked eggs, dry mustard, minced sweet pickles, salt, pepper, and mayonnaise.

Fill beets with mixture of cream cheese, chopped walnuts, French dressing, salt, and pepper.

FILLED CELERY—Mix 1 cup mashed avocado, 2 tablespoons grated horse-radish, ½ teaspoon Tabasco sauce. Fill celery stalks and chill.

CELERY TRUNKS—Fill matching stalks of celery with 1 of the fillings below, press together firmly. Chill. Stand upright to resemble tree trunks.

CUCUMBER CUPS—Scoop out centers of 2-inch lengths of cucumbers and fill with a mixture of 1 cup flaked tuna, ¼ cup minced sweet pickle, 1 tablespoon lemon juice, ½ teaspoon onion juice, salt, and pepper. Chill. Serve garnished with sections of ripe olives.

FILLED DILLS—Remove centers of dill pickles and fill with a mixture of snappy cheese spread and butter. Pack tightly and chill. Cut crosswise into ½-inch slices.

Fill pickles with liver sausage or deviled ham instead of cheese filling.

FILLED MUSHROOMS — Sauté mushrooms in butter. Cool. Fill caps with Pâté de Fois Gras, chill. Place on crisp crackers to serve.

FILLED PRUNES—Fill cooked prunes with a mixture of cream cheese, pineapple juice, and chopped nut meats.

OTHER FILLINGS—Anchovy, shrimp, salmon, tuna, smoked whitefish or sardine paste.

Cream cheese and minced olives.

Cream cheese, chives and Worcestershire sauce.

Roquefort cheese and cream.

Roquefort cheese blended with mayonnaise.

Aged Cheddar cheese blended with cream.

Minced ham, mustard, mayonnaise, minced pickle.

Cottage cheese and chili sauce.

TOMATO SANDWICH HORS D'OEUVRES

8 tablespoons deviled ham
3 tablespoons mayonnaise
½ teaspoon minced onion
4 large tomatoes
Parsley

Combine the ham, mayonnaise, and onion. Wash, dry, core, and cut each tomato into four ¼-inch crosswise slices. Spread deviled ham mixture on half the tomato slices and top each with a second tomato slice to make sandwiches. Garnish with mayonnaise and a sprig of parsley and serve as a first course. Serves 8.

STUFFED CELERY RINGS

1 medium bunch celery
Tangy cheese spread or creamed aged Cheddar cheese

Cut top from celery, wash, and dry each stalk. Fill smallest stalk with cheese, then the next smallest stalk and press firmly into the first one. Continue filling and pressing stalks together until all the celery is formed into a bunch. Tie with string and chill. Slice crosswise into ½-inch slices and serve on lettuce or watercress with French dressing. Serves 8.

Use Roquefort cheese spread or pineapple cheese spread for tangy cheese spread.

Fill with Shrimp, Anchovy or Ham Butter (page 214) instead of cheese.

PECAN AND CHEESE HORS D'OEUVRES

16 pecan or walnut halves
½ cup pineapple cheese spread

Make cheese balls of the spread and press a pecan half on 2 sides. Chill. Makes 8.

Any canapé butter makes delicious filling for celery

HARLEQUIN EGGS

1 cooked carrot
1 cooked beet
½ cup minced green beans
¼ cup mayonnaise
¼ teaspoon salt
⅛ teaspoon pepper
4 hard-cooked eggs
Paprika

Shred carrot and beet, mix with beans and blend with mayonnaise and seasoning. Cut eggs into halves lengthwise, remove yolks and fill with vegetable mixture. Sprinkle with sieved egg yolks. Dust with paprika. Makes 8 harlequin eggs.

STUFFED EASTER EGGS

8 hard-cooked eggs
1 cup flaked cooked crab meat
½ cup minced celery
½ cup chopped walnuts
2 tablespoons minced green pepper
1 teaspoon prepared mustard
¼ teaspoon salt
Mayonnaise
Watercress or chicory

Shell eggs and cut into halves lengthwise. Remove yolks and mash. Add remaining ingredients except watercress, mixing in enough mayonnaise to moisten. Stuff whites with mixture and arrange on bed of cress. Serves 8.

A tiny smörgåsbord—jellied loaf, cheese, sliced tomatoes and stuffed eggs

STUFFED HARD-COOKED EGGS

Cut hard-cooked eggs into halves lengthwise or crosswise. Remove yolk and fill whites with any of the following fillings:

Anchovies, minced parsley and white sauce
Caviar with lemon juice—Chicken livers, sautéed
Chopped celery mixed with mayonnaise or salad dressing
Chopped stuffed or ripe olives and cheese
Chopped onions and mushrooms browned in butter
Chopped nuts and cheese
Cottage cheese, chives, pimiento and Tabasco sauce
Crisp bacon, mashed egg yolk, parsley and mayonnaise
Egg yolk, finely chopped pickle and mayonnaise
Egg yolk, mayonnaise and Worcestershire sauce
Finely ground chicken or meat
Finely ground seasoned fish
Green and red peppers, cheese and egg yolk
Liver sausage — Minced ham — Pâté de foie gras—Sardine paste
Mashed vegetables as asparagus, peas, spinach and beets.
Sieved egg yolk mixed with liver paste and salad dressing
Tartare sauce and egg yolks

To Serve:

Arrange at one end of cold meat and cheese platter.
Top serving of beet or potato salad with egg.
Refill whites, place halves together and mold individually in aspic gelatin.

EGG SHRIMP HORS D'OEUVRES

4 hard-cooked eggs
5 teaspoons French dressing
32 small cooked shrimp
⅓ cup chili sauce
Watercress

Chill, shell and cut eggs into halves. Remove yolks, mince and mix with dressing. (A cut clove of garlic added to the dressing at least ½ hour before using improves its flavor.) Refill whites with yolk mixture. Place a stuffed egg in the center of each plate. Surround each with 4 shrimp and garnish each shrimp with chili sauce. Arrange watercress between shrimp on each plate. Serves 8.

BALLS ON PICKS

Form these mixtures into balls. Chill. Serve on picks.

ANCHOVY BALLS—Mash 4 ounces anchovy paste with 2 hard-cooked eggs, add 5 drops Worcestershire sauce, few grains cayenne and ¼ cup minced parsley.

CELERY BALLS—1 cup minced celery, 3 ounces cream cheese, ¼ teaspoon salt, dash pepper, few grains cayenne. Roll in chopped parsley.

GREEN BALLS—½ cup grated Swiss cheese, ½ cup minced ham, ½ teaspoon prepared mustard, 1 egg yolk, ¼ teaspoon salt, dash pepper. Roll in minced chives or parsley.

BURNING BUSH—3 ounces cream cheese, ½ teaspoon minced onion. Roll in minced dried beef.

LIVER SAUSAGE BALLS—1 cup liver sausage, ¼ cup minced celery, 2 tablespoons minced green pepper. Rub bowl with garlic, mix ingredients, then roll balls in minced dill pickle.

CHEESE CARROTS

3 ounces cream cheese
⅓ cup grated carrot
¼ teaspoon salt
Dash cayenne
4 drops Worcestershire sauce
1 tablespoon chopped chives or onion
Parsley sprigs

Mix cream cheese and carrot, season with salt, cayenne, Worcestershire sauce and chives. Roll into miniature carrot shapes. Chill until firm. Stick a tiny sprig of parsley into each "carrot" to resemble tops. Makes 8 "carrots."

CHEESE SPEARS

8 (¾-inch) cubes American cheese
8 walnut halves
8 tiny sweet pickles

Spear a cheese cube, a walnut half, then a sweet pickle on an hors d'oeuvre pick. Serve on an hors d'oeuvres holder. Makes 8.

PINEAPPLE SPEARS—Spear a cube of fresh pineapple, then a cube of sharp Cheddar cheese and top with a cherry.

Use pecan or walnut halves instead of cheese.

HAM MOLD, NEW ORLEANS STYLE

2 teaspoons unflavored gelatin
2 tablespoons cold water
3 ounces cream cheese
1 can condensed chicken gumbo soup
1 cup ground ham
4 to 5 tablespoons salad dressing

Soften gelatin in water. Heat cream cheese and ⅓ of the can of chicken gumbo soup until cheese and soup are blended. Add remaining soup and heat and dissolve softened gelatin in hot mixture. Cool and add ham and salad dressing. Pour into molds and chill until firm. Makes 6 to 8.

SAILBOATS

8 small dill pickles
8 slices salami
2 tablespoons cream cheese

Cut pickles into halves lengthwise and make a lengthwise slit in each pickle on cut side. Cut salami into shapes of sails and insert into the slit. Flute the edges of sail with cream cheese pressed through a pastry tube. Makes 8 hors d'oeuvres.

CHEESE CUSTARD SNACKS

1 recipe Snack Pastry (page 235)
1 egg
1 cup milk
¼ teaspoon salt
3 tablespoons minced green onions
3 tablespoons grated cheese

Line small muffin pans or tartlet pans with pastry. Beat egg slightly, add remaining ingredients and pour into pans. Bake in slow oven (300°F.) 30 minutes Chill Makes 8 small snacks.

Brazil nuts add the nicest party touch to this snappy cheese custard snack

CORNUCOPIAS

Spread 2½-inch squares cut from thin slices fresh bread with softened butter, spread as desired and roll into cornucopias. Fasten with toothpicks. Chill. Remove toothpicks before serving.

CHEESE—Spread with snappy cheese spread, and place a watercress spray on top.

SALMON—Spread with any Salmon Spread.

LILY CANAPÉS—Spread with any Fish Spread. Partly fill cornucopias with minced egg white. Mix mashed yolks to a paste with butter, form into balls and place a ball on top of each cone. Use strips of green pepper for stems.

TOMATO—Place ¼ slice tomato in the top of each cornucopia.

HERRING ON PICKS

½ pint pickled herring
16 small pickled onions

Cut herring into 1-inch squares. Drain thoroughly. Spear an onion, then a square of herring and another onion on an hors d'oeuvre pick. Serve from an hors d'oeuvres holder. Serves 8.

HAM CORNUCOPIAS

3 ounces cream cheese
3 tablespoons horse-radish
8 (2½-inch) squares cold boiled ham

Mix cheese and horse-radish, spread ham slices with the mixture and roll into a cornucopia. Fasten with a toothpick and chill. Makes 8 servings.

Substitute boiled Canadian bacon or corned beef for the boiled ham. Substitute dried beef for ham and flavor cheese with ¾ teaspoon onion juice and 2 teaspoons Worcestershire sauce. Omit horse-radish.

Fill cornucopia with cottage cheese, seasoned with chives and a few drops Tabasco sauce.

ROLLED HORS D'OEUVRES

DRIED BEEF ROLLS—Spread (⅛ inch thick) slices of dried beef with a mixture of cream cheese and India relish. Roll and chill.

CAVIAR BLINTZES—Season caviar with onion and lemon juice. Place ½ teaspoon on small thin pancakes and roll. Serve with sour cream seasoned with Tabasco sauce and salt.

HAM AND ASPARAGUS ROLLS
—Marinate asparagus tips in French dressing Roll in thin slices of cooked ham. Chill. Slices of ham may be spread with mayonnaise.

HAM STICKS—Spread ham with prepared mustard. Wrap around bread sticks allowing 1 inch of of bread stick to be free as a handle.

LETTUCE ROLLS — Cut (1 x 3 inch) strips from lettuce leaves. Place ½ teaspoon of a mixture of cream cheese, horse-radish, few drops Tabasco sauce and a small amount mayonnaise, on the lettuce and roll. Chill.

SMOKED SALMON AND CELERY ROLLS—Spread very thinly sliced smoked salmon with cream cheese. Roll around crisp (2-inch) stalks of celery.

TONGUE AND CHEESE ROLLS
—Combine cream cheese, catchup, chopped stuffed olives, and chopped pickles. Spread on thin slices cooked tongue and roll.

A simple tray of cold cuts is unusual when some of the meats are filled, rolled and stuck on picks

HARD-COOKED EGGS IN JELLIED BOUILLON

1 tablespoon unflavored gelatin
2 cups bouillon
4 hard-cooked eggs
1/4 teaspoon dry mustard
1/4 teaspoon salt
Dash pepper
1 teaspoon vinegar
1 tablespoon melted butter
8 slices summer sausage

Soften gelatin in 2 tablespoons cold bouillon and dissolve in 1 cup bouillon heated to boiling. Add remaining bouillon. Cool. When beginning to thicken pour a small amount into tiny molds and chill until firm. Cut eggs into halves crosswise; remove yolks and mash with remaining ingredients except sausage. Refill whites, leveling off tops. Place yolk side down on gelatin. Pour remaining gelatin in mold to cover eggs. Chill until firm. Unmold and place on slices of summer sausage. Garnish with lettuce, watercress, parsley, or chicory. Makes 8 servings.

Try serving individual jellied salads on the cold meat tray as well as singly

FROSTED MELON MOLD

1 small melon
1 package lemon gelatin
2 cups boiling water
6 ounces cream cheese
Milk, Chicory
French dressing

Peel a whole melon. Cut a slice from 1 end and remove seeds. Turn upside down to drain. Dissolve gelatin in boiling water and cool. Then pour into melon and chill until gelatin is firm. Soften cream cheese and add just sufficient milk to give a spreading consistency; frost the entire outside of melon. Serve in slices on crisp chicory with French dressing. Serves 4 to 6. Other congealed fillings may be used if in the choice the melon is always kept the predominant flavor.

RHUBARB SALAD RING

1 package raspberry or
    lemon gelatin
1 cup boiling hot rhubarb sauce
1 cup cold water or pineapple juice
1 cup chopped apples
1 cup chopped walnuts or pecans

Dissolve gelatin in hot sauce, add cold water or pineapple juice and let cool. Add apples and nuts and pour into small ring molds. Chill until firm and unmold onto lettuce. Serves 8.

JELLIED APRICOT SALAD

1 package lemon gelatin
2 cups hot water
2 No. 2½ cans whole peeled
    apricots
1/3 cup peanut butter
1/4 cup chopped walnuts
1/2 cup chopped dates
3 tablespoons lemon juice
French dressing

Dissolve gelatin in 2 cups hot water and chill until almost firm. Drain apricots and remove pits. Combine peanut butter, chopped walnuts, and chopped dates with lemon juice and mix well. Fill the cavity of each apricot with a spoonful of this mixture, pressing halves together so that fruit retains its whole appearance. Put 1 filled apricot into each individual mold. Then fill molds with gelatin and chill until firm. Unmold on lettuce and serve with French dressing. Serves 8.

LIVER SAUSAGE HORS D'OEUVRES

¾ cup liver sausage
1 teaspoon minced pickle
1 teaspoon lemon juice
1 teaspoon mayonnaise
Food coloring
1 cup very fine bread crumbs

Mix sausage, pickle, lemon juice and mayonnaise together. Color half the crumbs red and the other half orange. Roll part of the sausage mixture into the shape of strawberries and roll in the red crumbs, place a small piece of parsley in the top for the stem, shape remaining mixture into "kumquats" and roll in orange crumbs. Makes 8 "strawberries" and 8 small "kumquats."

1. Roll the mixture into "radish" and "tomato" shapes and cover with red crumbs.
2. Use cream cheese instead of liver sausage.

SALTED SOYBEANS

Soybeans
Salt
Hot deep fat

Use varieties which are good for cooked dried beans. Wash and soak beans overnight; drain and spread out in a single layer at room temperature to dry, or dry with a clean towel. Fry a few at a time in hot deep fat (350°F.) for 8 to 10 minutes. Drain on absorbent paper and salt while still warm.

CRISP ROLL CUPS

4 long crisp rolls
1 cup minced cooked chicken
6 tablespoons India relish
4 drops Worcestershire sauce
2 tablespoons salad dressing
½ teaspoon grated onion
¼ teaspoon salt
8 stuffed olives, sliced

Cut off ends 2 inches long from rolls. Remove soft center from ends and fill hollow with mixture of all remaining ingredients except olives. Slice a stuffed olive and place in overlapping slices on each cup or garnish with sieved egg yolks. Serve on hors d'oeuvres picks. Makes 8.

Fill roll cups with any of fillings for Stuffed Eggs (pages 307, 308) instead of chicken filling.

COLD SHRIMP HORS D'OEUVRES

8 canned or fresh, cooked cleaned shrimp
8 rounds bread
¼ cup mayonnaise
8 drops Worcestershire sauce
Curry powder, Parsley

Place shrimp on round of bread cut the same size. Top each shrimp with mayonnaise, season with Worcestershire sauce and a dash of curry powder. Garnish with sprig of parsley. Makes 8

SHRIMP BASKETS

8 large cooked shrimp
2 tablespoons mayonnaise
¼ teaspoon lemon juice
Dash pepper
1 tablespoon minced parsley
¼ teaspoon minced onion

Spear both ends of a shrimp on a toothpick, pressing the ends as closely together as possible without breaking shrimp Combine remaining ingredients and fill "basket" (formed by shrimp on pick). Makes 8 servings.

A cheese and wafer tray may be your family's choice for the evening's snack

BACON ROLLS

8 strips bacon
4 tablespoons peanut butter

Spread strips of uncooked bacon with peanut butter. Roll up tightly and fasten with toothpick. Broil until crisp and serve on hors d'oeuvres server. Makes 8 servings.

Broil each of the following until bacon is crisp:

Spread a slice of bacon with 1 teaspoon finely grated cheese and ¼ teaspoon chutney or India relish. Roll as above.

Roll ½-inch cube of aged Cheddar cheese in the bacon.

Roll large pickled onion in ½ slice of bacon.

Wrap rolled anchovies in bacon.

Wrap shrimp in bacon.

Cut stuffed olives into halves, put together with cheese spread, wrap in bacon.

Stuff large cooked prunes with American cheese.

Almost anything you like can be rolled in bacon, oven or pan-broiled and served on picks

GHERKINS IN DRIED BEEF ROLLS

8 sweet gherkins
8 slices dried beef
3 tablespoons butter

Wrap gherkins in dried beef, fasten with toothpicks. Brown in butter. Serve hot. Serves 8.

STUFFED FRANKFURTERS

8 frankfurters
1 cup bread crumbs
1 tablespoon minced onion
1 teaspoon melted butter
¼ teaspoon salt
Dash pepper
Boiling water to moisten
8 slices bacon

Partly split frankfurters lengthwise. Combine bread crumbs, onion, butter, salt, and pepper. Add boiling water to moisten. Fill mixture into opening of sausage, wrap bacon around each frankfurter, and broil until bacon is crisp. Serves 8.

Use strips of cheese, or wedges of dill or sweet pickle instead of bread crumb mixture.

COCKTAIL SAUSAGES IN BLANKETS

2 cups sifted flour
3 teaspoons baking powder
½ teaspoon salt
¼ cup shortening
¾ cup milk (about)
8 cooked cocktail sausages

Sift dry ingredients together 3 times. Cut in shortening with a pastry blender. Add milk, stirring until a soft dough is formed. Knead on floured board for 20 seconds or until dough forms a smooth ball. Roll ¼ inch thick and cut into small oblongs. Place sausages on oblongs of dough, fold over, moisten edges with water and press together to seal. Place on greased baking sheet and bake in hot oven (450°F.) until browned, about 15 minutes. Serve immediately Makes 8 rolls.

SARDINES IN BLANKETS—Use small canned sardines in place of sausages.

ANCHOVIES IN BLANKETS—Use canned anchovy fillets in place of sausages.

Instead of ham use cooked smoked tongue, corned or peppered beef if you like

HAM BANANA ROLL

6 thin slices boiled ham
Prepared mustard
6 firm bananas
Cheese Sauce

Spread slices of ham with mustard. Wrap a banana in each ham slice and place in shallow baking dish. Pour cheese sauce over bananas and bake in moderate oven (350°F.) 30 minutes.

BANANA SCALLOPS

1 egg
1½ teaspoons salt
6 firm bananas
¾ cup fine cereal crumbs, bread or cracker crumbs

Beat egg slightly and add salt. Slice peeled bananas crosswise into 1-inch thick pieces. Dip into egg, roll in crumbs, and fry in hot deep fat (375°F.) 1½ to 2 minutes or until brown and tender. Drain and serve immediately. Serves 6.

Bananas may be prepared for frying several hours in advance.

SAUSAGES BAKED IN BANANAS

8 bananas, unpeeled
8 to 16 link sausages

Slit each banana lengthwise from tip to tip to form a pocket, being careful not to cut through the skin on the under side. Place 1 or 2 link sausages in the opening of each banana. Arrange bananas in baking dish, slit side up and bake in moderate oven (375°F.) about 15 to 20 minutes. Serves 8. To brown sausages, place under broiler 2 or 3 minutes after baking, or fry until light brown before inserting into bananas for baking.

ROQUEFORT PUFFS

1 egg white
2 ounces Roquefort cheese spread
8 crackers or 8 (2-inch) bread rounds
Paprika

Beat egg white until stiff; cream cheese, fold in beaten egg white, and heap on crackers. Bake in slow oven (300°F.) 15 minutes or until brown. Garnish with paprika. Makes 8 puffs.

MIDNIGHT SNACK

½ pound Cheddar cheese
4 slices bacon
8 slices toast

Force cheese and bacon through food chopper and mix together. Spread on slices of hot toast. Place on broiler rack under low heat until brown. Serve at once. Serves 8.

SWEDISH EGGS

8 hard-cooked eggs
1 egg white, slightly beaten
1 pound sausage meat
Sieved dried bread crumbs

Shell eggs. Brush with slightly beaten egg white. Cover with sausage meat. Dip in egg white. Roll in bread crumbs. Fry in hot deep fat (370°F.) until brown. Cut into halves lengthwise. Serve hot. Serves 8.

ROLLS-IN-LOAF

Trim sides and top crusts from a loaf of unsliced white bread. Cut lengthwise down through the center of loaf, just to the lower crust, but not through it. Then make crosswise cuts to the lower crust, spacing cuts so that the "rolls" will be even in size. Brush with melted butter and toast in moderate oven (375°F.) until the edges of loaf are golden brown. Serve hot. Excellent with salads for luncheon, with jam and coffee for breakfast, or with marmalade for afternoon tea.

GARLIC BREAD—Cut loaf into ¼-inch slices instead of into rolls. Press slices together and tie loosely with string. Cream ¼ pound butter with 1 clove garlic, grated. Spread liberally over top of bread (about ¼ inch thick). Place in loaf pan and toast.

CROUSTADES — Cut slices of bread 1 to 2 inches thick. Trim off crust and cut each slice into 4 cubes. Insert the point of a sharp knife ½ inch from edge of sides and cut out the center to within ½ inch of the bottom. Brush with melted butter. Toast in oven or broiler.

CHICKEN LIVERS EN BROCHETTE

8 chicken livers
8 slices bacon
Salt
Pepper

Cut each liver into 4 pieces and each slice of bacon into 5 pieces. Season liver with salt and pepper. Alternate pieces of bacon and liver on skewers. Allow 4 pieces of liver and 5 pieces bacon to each skewer. Bake in hot oven (425°F.) until bacon is crisp and livers are cooked. Serve hot. Serves 8.

CHICKEN LIVER-ANCHOVY TOAST

5 cooked chicken livers
3 tablespoons anchovy paste
3 tablespoons butter
1/8 teaspoon pepper
1 teaspoon salt
4 egg yolks
8 slices hot toast
1 1/3 cups cream or evaporated milk

Make a paste of livers and anchovy paste, add butter, pepper, 1/2 teaspoon salt and 1 egg yolk. Spread on toast and place under preheated broiler for 1 minute. Make a sauce by cooking remaining 3 egg yolks, salt and cream in a double boiler. Serves 8.

SCALLOPS EN BROCHETTE

1 quart scallops
4 tablespoons butter
8 slices bacon
Salt and pepper
Lemon juice

Wash scallops; drain. Melt butter, add scallops and cook over low heat for 5 minutes. Cool. Cut bacon into 1 1/2-inch pieces and spear scallops and bacon alternately on skewers. Sprinkle lightly with salt and pepper. Place under preheated broiler and broil for 15 minutes or until bacon is crisp and scallops brown. Turn during the broiling period Serve with lemon juice. Serves 8. Use thick slices of salami or smoked tongue instead of bacon if desired.

Try dressing up the brochette platter with broiled pineapple, apricots or oranges

HAMBURGER PINWHEELS

1 small onion, minced
2 tablespoons fat
1 pound ground beef
1/4 pound pork sausage
1 teaspoon salt
1/8 teaspoon pepper
1/4 teaspoon Worcestershire sauce
1 recipe baking powder biscuits

Cook onion in fat until tender but not brown. Add meat and cook until browned. Season with salt, pepper, and Worcestershire sauce. Roll out biscuit dough into a rectangle 1/4 inch thick. Spread meat on dough and roll like a jelly roll. Cut into slices about 1 1/2 inches thick. Place cut side up, on greased baking sheet and bake in hot oven (400°F.) about 15 minutes. Serves 8.

HAM ROLLS—Use chopped ham and hard-cooked eggs with sweet pickle and mayonnaise instead of beef mixture. Bake as above.

CORNED BEEF ROLLS—Blend a 12-ounce can corned beef with 3/4 cup evaporated milk. Use instead of beef mixture.

ASPIC ENTRÉES

1 tablespoon unflavored gelatin
¼ cup cold water
1½ cups hot seasoned stock

Soften gelatin in cold water. Dissolve in hot stock. Add any of following mixtures when gelatin begins to thicken. Pour into desired mold and chill until firm. Unmold and garnish with Vegetable Curls or Cups, Radish Roses, endive or parsley.

JELLIED BOUILLON WITH FRANKFURTERS—Use beef stock; place frankfurters upright; hard-cooked eggs, sliced; diced celery.

SLICED VEAL IN ASPIC—Use veal stock, highly seasoned; ½ cup cooked peas; 1 hard-cooked egg; slices of veal.

HAM AND CIDER JELLY LOAF—Use cider instead of stock, add ½ cup raisins, 4 whole cloves, 2 tablespoons brown sugar, 1 cup cubed ham.

LUNCHEON RING—Use beef stock, 1½ cups chopped corned beef, ¼ cup sliced stuffed olives, 1 tablespoon each chopped green pepper and onion. Pour into ring mold and chill.

TONGUE MOUSSE—Use beef stock and 1½ tablespoons unflavored gelatin; 1 cup mayonnaise; 1 teaspoon dry mustard; ½ teaspoon salt; 2 tablespoons each minced onion, green pepper, and parsley; 2 cups ground tongue.

JELLIED CALF'S LIVER—Use liquid from cooking liver; add 1 onion, minced; 3 sprigs parsley; 2 tablespoons vinegar.

JELLIED TUNA—Omit stock. Use ½ cup water. Combine with 2 cups flaked tuna, 1 cup mayonnaise and ¼ cup minced sweet pickles.

TOMATO HAM SALAD LOAF

2 tablespoons unflavored gelatin
½ cup cold water
3 cups tomato juice
1 tablespoon grated onion
½ teaspoon salt
⅛ teaspoon pepper
1 teaspoon sugar
1 cup ground cooked ham
1 teaspoon prepared mustard
6 tablespoons mayonnaise
9 ounces cream cheese
3 tablespoons cream

Soften gelatin in cold water for 5 minutes. Combine tomato juice, onion, salt, pepper, and sugar, heat to boiling, and simmer for 5 minutes. Add gelatin and stir until dissolved. Cool. Combine ham, mustard, and mayonnaise. Thin cream cheese with cream. Pour ⅓ of tomato mixture into loaf pan (8½ x 5 x 3 inches). Chill until firm. Spread ham mixture on top and cover with half of remaining tomato mixture. Chill until firm. Spread with cream cheese and cover with last of tomato mixture. Chill until firm. Unmold on a platter, garnish with greens.

TOMATO ASPIC—Combine gelatin, water, tomato juice, onion, salt, pepper and sugar as described above. Cool, pour into a ring mold and chill. Unmold and serve.

PÂTÉ DE FOIE GRAS IN ASPIC

1 tablespoon unflavored gelatin
¼ cup cold water
2 bouillon cubes
1½ cups hot water
2 ounces Pâté de Fois Gras
8 small rounds from breast of chicken
Watercress
French dressing

Soften gelatin in cold water for 5 minutes. Dissolve bouillon cubes and gelatin in hot water. Pour into small molds and chill until firm. With a hot spoon remove center of molds. Fill centers with pâté de foie gras and chill. Unmold onto rounds of chicken, garnish with watercress and serve with French dressing. Serves 8.

Use aspic gelatin instead of bouillon cubes, gelatin and cold water. Or dissolve aspic gelatin in 1½ cups hot tomato juice and proceed as above.

Fill centers with a fish paste or Filling for Stuffed Eggs.

LIVER SAUSAGE IN ASPIC—Use veal stock. Blend 2 cups mashed liver sausage with aspic while still warm. Garnish with sliced hard-cooked eggs and ripe olives.

Frankfurters take on new glamour in this gleaming aspic

Whole hard-cooked eggs in this jellied tuna loaf add a gay and decorative note

FISH BALLS

1½ cups boned cooked fish
1 cup soft bread crumbs
2 tablespoons minced onion
¼ cup grated carrot
½ teaspoon sugar
1 egg, beaten
¼ teaspoon pepper
½ teaspoon salt
½ cup bread crumbs
1½ quarts fish stock
2 tablespoons flour
¼ cup minced parsley

Mix first 9 ingredients and roll into balls. Heat fish stock to boiling, drop in fish balls and cook for 45 minutes. Remove balls from stock and thicken stock with flour mixed with a little cold water. Add parsley and pour over fish balls. Chill well. Serves 8.

SWEET-SOUR SNACKS

1 cup stock
¼ cup vinegar
¼ cup brown sugar
Salt
Pepper
½ teaspoon minced onion

Cook all ingredients together until smooth and slightly thickened. Pour sauce over cooked fish or meat and added seasonings (below). Marinate at least 3 hours. Drain and serve.

1. 2 pounds boned pike, pickerel or trout, 6 slices lemon, ¼ cup raisins.
2. 2 pounds beef tongue, 2 bay leaves, 4 peppercorns, 4 ginger-snaps.
3. 1 set calf's brains, ½ green pepper, 2 bay leaves, 3 sprigs parsley.
4. 8 small trout, use wine vinegar and 1 tablespoon mixed spices. Omit sugar and onion in sauce.

CRANBERRY CHICKEN MOLD

Red Layer—Jellied Cranberry

1 package lemon gelatin
1 cup hot water
1½ cups cranberry orange relish
1 tablespoon lemon juice

(To make cranberry orange relish: Grind 4 cups cranberries. Pare an orange, remove seeds and white membrane. Then grind pulp and orange rind. Mix with cranberries and add 2 cups sugar.)
Dissolve gelatin in hot water. Then add cranberry orange relish and lemon juice. Pour into mold and chill until firm, then cover with Chicken Mousse.

White Layer—Chicken Mousse

2 teaspoons unflavored gelatin
2 tablespoons cold water
1 can condensed chicken soup
1 cup diced chicken
1 egg, separated
1 tablespoon lemon juice
Salt and pepper
¼ cup heavy cream, whipped

Soften gelatin in cold water.
Strain chicken soup and heat slowly. Force rice, chicken, and celery from the soup and the chicken through food chopper, using fine blade. Beat egg yolk and add hot soup. Then cook slowly until slightly thickened. Pour hot mixture over gelatin and stir until dissolved. Cool and when it begins to thicken, fold in ground chicken and rice, lemon juice, seasonings, beaten egg white and whipped cream. Pour mixture on the firm cranberry layer and chill until firm. Turn out on lettuce, chicory or watercress. Serves 8.

VEAL ROLL

4 to 5 pounds breast of veal, boned
½ pound sausage
3 hard-cooked eggs
1 teaspoon salt
3 peppercorns
Roll up breast of veal with sausage and eggs on the inside. Tie securely in a cloth, cover with boiling water, add salt and peppercorns. Simmer for 3 hours. Remove from liquid. Cool, then chill overnight under heavy weights. Slice thin. Serves 8.

CHEESE SOUFFLE

3 tablespoons butter
5 tablespoons flour
1⅓ cups hot milk
1 teaspoon salt
Dash pepper
⅓ cup grated cheese
4 eggs, separated

Blend butter and flour, add hot milk, salt, pepper, and grated cheese. Cook slowly, stirring constantly until cheese is melted and sauce thickens. Cool, add well-beaten egg yolks, fold in stiffly beaten egg whites, and pour into greased baking dish. Place in pan of hot water and bake in moderate oven (350°F.) 50 to 60 minutes or until firm to the touch. Serve at once. Makes 8 portions.

FISH SOUFFLÉ—Omit cheese and add 1½ cups flaked cooked fish.

MEAT SOUFFLÉ—Omit cheese and add 1 cup ground ham, corned beef or roast lamb to eggs before cooking. Season with horseradish, mustard or Worcestershire sauce. Garnish with parsley.

The chafing dish will be your "steady" for serving any hot entrée at any time

NEUFCHÂTEL FONDUE

2 pounds Swiss cheese, shredded
2 tablespoons flour
2 cups dry white wine
Clove garlic, cut
½ teaspoon salt
¼ teaspoon pepper
½ teaspoon nutmeg
¾ cup kirsch

Mix cheese and flour. Heat dry white wine to simmering in cooking dish that has been rubbed with garlic. Add cheese and stir with a fork until cheese is melted. Add salt, pepper, and nutmeg. Heat to boiling, add kirsch, and serve at once on toast for 8.

NUT VEGETABLE LOAF

1 cup cooked tomatoes
1 cup cooked peas
1 cup diced cooked carrots
½ cup chopped nut meats
1 teaspoon salt
3 tablespoons minced onion
1 cup soft bread crumbs
½ cup milk
2 eggs, beaten
1 tablespoon melted butter
⅛ teaspoon pepper

Combine all ingredients and turn into greased loaf pan. Bake at 350°F 60 minutes. Serves 8.

WELSH RAREBIT

2 pounds American cheese, diced
1 tablespoon butter
½ teaspoon salt
½ teaspoon paprika
1 teaspoon dry mustard
Few grains cayenne
1 cup beer
Toast, bread Croustades, or crackers

Melt cheese and butter in double boiler, add seasonings, then beer, stirring constantly until smooth. Serve on toast, bread croustades, or crackers. Serves 8.

DRIED BEEF RAREBIT—Add ½ pound shredded dried beef.

SARDINE RAREBIT—Arrange cleaned sardines on toast and pour rarebit over them.

OYSTER, SHRIMP, LOBSTER, CRAB MEAT, OR TUNA RAREBIT—Omit 1 pound cheese, add 1 cup fish, ¼ cup chopped green pepper, and 1 tablespoon chopped onion to the rarebit and cook until thoroughly heated.

FINNAN HADDIE RAREBIT—Use 1 cup milk instead of beer, 1 cup grated cheese, and 1 cup flaked, cooked finnan haddie instead of 2 pounds cheese.

MILK RAREBIT—Use 1 cup milk instead of beer.

CHEESE AND TOMATO RAREBIT—Omit paprika, mustard, and beer. Use 1 pound cheese, 1 cup bread crumbs, and 2 cups strained tomatoes.

FLUFFY EGG RAREBIT—Cook 1 minced small onion and 1 minced green pepper in 2 tablespoons butter. Add 2 cups canned tomatoes and 1 cup grated cheese and heat until cheese melts. Add slowly to 2 well-beaten eggs. Cook in double boiler until thickened. Season with salt and cayenne.

LIVER PATTIES

1½ pounds liver
Boiling water
⅓ cup bread crumbs
4 tablespoons bacon fat
⅓ cup tomato purée
1 egg, well beaten
1¼ teaspoons salt
¼ teaspoon pepper
1 teaspoon onion juice
8 slices bacon

Cover liver with boiling water and let stand for 2 minutes, dry, and force through meat grinder. Combine liver with remaining ingredients, except bacon, mix well and shape into patties about 1 inch thick and 2½ inches in diameter. Wrap a slice of bacon around each patty, fasten with toothpick, place in oiled pan, and bake in slow oven (300°F.) 1 hour. Serves 8.

Wrap patties in slices of Canadian bacon, corned beef or in thin slices salt pork.

Omit tomato purée. Pour 2 cups tomato juice over all. Bake at 350°F

Baked liver patties can be a party especially served with the Spring's fresh greens

CHICKEN SNACKS

CHICKEN SHORTCAKE—Combine cooked chicken with medium white sauce, season highly, and serve over 3-inch rounds of baking powder biscuits.

CHICKEN À LA KING—Flavor rich white sauce with chopped pimientos, chopped cooked green pepper, cooked mushrooms and egg yolks. Cook until thickened. Serve in patty shells, bread croustades or on toast. Cooked rabbit may be used in the same way.

CHICKEN CURRY—Make a medium white sauce with chicken stock, add curry powder, paprika, and sherry wine if desired. Serve in patty shells with ground almonds sprinkled over top.

SAUTÉED CHICKEN LIVERS—Season and dredge chicken livers lightly with flour. Fry a little onion in butter, add livers and brown. Add small amount of stock, heat to boiling and serve.

CHICKEN PATTIES—Combine 2 cups seasoned, ground chicken with 1 egg. Brown in butter.

CURRY SAUCE

1 cup Medium White Sauce
1 teaspoon minced onion
1 teaspoon lemon juice
1 teaspoon curry powder

Combine all ingredients and heat to boiling.

BROILED MUSHROOMS

1½ pounds mushrooms
Salt
Pepper
4 tablespoons butter
8 slices toast

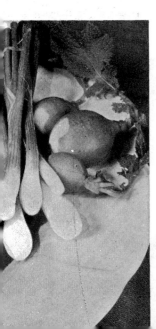

Clean mushrooms by wiping or washing. Skin, if desired. Separate stems from caps. Place stems and caps, gill side down, under the broiler for 2 or 3 minutes, turn, sprinkle with salt and pepper, and dot each cap with butter. Broil 2 or 3 minutes longer or until tender. Serve with their own juice on buttered toast. Serves 8.

PAN-BROILED MUSHROOMS— Cook slowly in butter in a skillet for 5 to 8 minutes. Season as above.

MUSHROOM SAUCE

2 tablespoons butter
½ pound mushrooms, sliced
2 tablespoons flour
1 cup chicken broth
¼ teaspoon salt
⅛ teaspoon pepper

Melt butter, add mushrooms and cook about 5 minutes. Blend in flour. Add chicken broth gradually, cook until thickened, stirring constantly, add seasonings and serve hot. Makes 1¾ cups.
Use rich milk or thin cream instead of chicken broth.

Your friends will certainly enjoy chicken shortcake when served individually

STUFFED PIMIENTOS

1½ cups cooked peas
1 cup cottage cheese
½ teaspoon grated onion
Salt and pepper
8 pimientos
Buttered bread crumbs

Mix peas, cheese, and onion, season with salt and pepper. Stuff pimientos and cover with crumbs. Bake in moderate oven (350°F.) 20 minutes. Serves 8.

PIMIENTOS WITH EGG— Omit peas, cheese, and onion. Break an egg into each pimiento, season, and bake as above. Sprinkle with grated cheese.

PIMIENTOS WITH CORN— Omit peas and cheese. Mix 1½ cups cooked corn, ¼ cup chopped dill pickle and 1 cup thick white sauce.

PIMIENTOS WITH RICE AND BACON— Use 2 cups cooked rice and ½ cup chopped cooked bacon instead of peas and cheese.

DUCHESSES

½ cup butter
⅛ teaspoon salt
1 cup boiling water
1 cup sifted flour
3 eggs, unbeaten

Add butter and salt to boiling water and stir over medium heat until mixture boils. Reduce heat, add flour all at once and beat vigorously until mixture leaves the sides of pan. Remove from heat and add 1 egg at a time, beating thoroughly after each addition. Shape puffs very small, using about 1 teaspoon paste for each one. Bake in very hot oven (450°F.) for about 8 minutes or until points begin to brown, then reduce heat to moderate (350°F.) and continue baking 10 to 12 minutes longer. When cold cut a small slit carefully on 1 side, open and fill with a savory mixture, using the fine tube of a pastry bag. Makes 4 dozen small duchesses.

FILLINGS—

Shrimp Butter
Anchovy Butter
Herring Butter
Bloater Butter
Crawfish Butter
Lobster Butter
Smoked Salmon Butter
Smoked Whitefish Butter

GENERAL METHOD—

1 cup minced cooked fish
1 cup butter
¼ teaspoon salt
Dash paprika
1 tablespoon lemon juice

Force boned fish through food chopper, using fine blade. Cream butter and add fish and remaining ingredients. Use as directed above or as butter for canapés. Instead of using pastry tube, cut tops from duchesses, fill lower half and press top over filling.

CHEESE TOAST

2 eggs, beaten
3 tablespoons cream
3 tablespoons flour
2 cups grated American cheese
½ teaspoon salt
Dash pepper
8 slices of bread

Beat first 6 ingredients together. Spread on slices of bread cut 1½ inches thick. Fry in hot deep fat (375°F.) until browned, placing the cheese side down first; then turn over. Serves 8.

TOASTED CUBES

2 slices bread (1½ inches thick)
1 egg
¼ teaspoon salt
1 tablespoon melted butter
½ cup grated cheese

Cut four 1½-inch cubes from each slice of bread. Dip into mixture of egg, salt, and butter. Roll in grated cheese and place on baking sheet. Bake in moderate oven (350°F.) until cheese is melted and slightly browned. Makes 8 cubes.

Do yourself proud some fine day and add these duchesses to your repertory as hostess

SPICE STICKS

1 cup sifted flour
½ teaspoon salt
⅓ cup shortening
About 3 tablespoons water
2 tablespoons sugar
1 teaspoon cinnamon

Sift flour and salt together, cut in shortening with 2 knives or pastry blender until mixture resembles coarse meal. Add cold water a few drops at a time, until dough is just moist enough to hold together. Chill. Roll into rectangle and sprinkle with mixture of sugar and cinnamon. Fold ends of dough into center, then fold through center to make 4 layers. Roll out to ¼-inch thickness, fold as before and roll again to ⅛-inch thickness. Cut into narrow sticks and bake in very hot oven (450°F.) 8 to 10 minutes. Makes 4 to 5 dozen (4-inch) sticks.

CHEESE STICKS—Use ½ cup grated cheese instead of sugar and cinnamon mixture.

ORANGE STICKS — Use orange juice instead of water and use 1 tablespoon grated orange rind instead of cinnamon.

CHEESE PUFFS

½ loaf bread
Butter
¼ pound sharp cheese, grated
¼ teaspoon baking powder
1 egg, separated

Cut bread into slices ⅓ inch thick. Cut slices into rounds 2 inches in diameter. Toast on 1 side. When cool spread untoasted side with butter. Combine cheese, baking powder, and beaten egg yolk; blend thoroughly. Fold in stiffly beaten egg whites. Spread a thick layer on buttered side of toast, place on baking sheet under the broiler to puff up and brown. Serve hot. Makes 8 puffs.

CHEESE BROCHETTES

½ loaf white bread, sliced
1½ pounds Swiss cheese, sliced ¼ inch thick
1½ cups milk
⅓ cup flour
2 egg yolks
¼ teaspoon salt
1 tablespoon water
Tomato Sauce

Cut bread and cheese into small squares or triangles and spear alternately with a small skewer until skewer is filled. Dip into milk, roll in flour, then dip into a mixture of egg yolks, salt, and water. Fry in hot deep fat (375°F.) until brown. Serve with tomato sauce. Serves 8.

MEAT AND CHEESE TURNOVERS

½ pound butter or other shortening
½ pound cream cheese
2 cups sifted flour

Work butter and cream cheese into flour. Chill thoroughly. Roll pieces of dough very thin, working quickly and cut into circles, 3 inches or more in diameter. Spread with: 4 tablespoons goose liver paste seasoned with 1 teaspoon Worcestershire sauce, or 4 tablespoons ground cooked ham, seasoned with 1 teaspoon hot sauce and 1 teaspoon tomato catchup or chutney. Fold over, press edges together, cover with caraway seeds, if desired, and bake in hot oven (400°F.) until brown. Shape earlier and bake just before serving. Serves 8.

Snack pastries are dramatic when shapes are combined

SNACK PASTRY

½ teaspoon salt
1 cup sifted flour
⅔ cup shortening
6 ounces cream cheese

Sift salt and flour together. Blend in shortening and cheese with 2 knives or pastry blender. Mix thoroughly. Roll out very thin on a floured board, cut into desired shape and bake in moderate oven (375°F.) until very light brown, about 6 minutes. Makes about 50 small snacks.

PEANUT-BUTTER TWISTS — Roll ½ the pastry as thin as possible, spread with peanut butter, and cover with the other half rolled thin. Cut through both layers into strips (¼x3½ inches) then twist 2 strips together. Bake as snack pastry.

CELERY-SEED SNACKS — Make snack pastry, roll out, then sprinkle generously with celery seed and a little salt. Cut and bake as snack pastry.

ANISEED SNACKS—Follow directions using aniseed instead of celery seed.

CARAWAY-SEED SNACKS—Use 1 tablespoon caraway seeds mixed with the pastry before rolling.

WHOLE-WHEAT SNACKS — Use ⅔ cup whole-wheat flour and ⅓ cup sifted flour instead of all white flour.

EGG BREAD

½ loaf of day old bread
⅓ cup butter or other fat
3 eggs, beaten until light
½ cup milk
Salt and pepper

Cut bread into cubes and brown in melted butter. Beat eggs, add milk and salt and pepper to taste. Pour over bread and fry until brown. Serve at once. Serves 8.

CONTINENTAL PLATEAU FOR HORS D'OEUVRES

1 large loaf sandwich bread, unsliced
½ cup melted butter

Remove crust from top, sides and ends of loaf. One and a half inches up from the base at one end of loaf make a horizontal cut 3 inches deep toward the center. Cut down from the top of this 3-inch distance and remove the section. Repeat on the other end of loaf. This makes the first step of the plateau. For the second step, 3 inches toward the center from the vertical cut edge, cut down to within 3 inches of the base of loaf, then cut horizontally from the edge at this point and remove this section. Repeat on the other end of loaf. Brush with melted butter and toast on all sides under broiler. Place in center of tray or platter, cover with hot or cold hors d'oeuvres on picks or canapés. This makes an especially attractive center piece when placed on a mirror.

Nimble fingers have a way with tomatoes that is easy to learn

HORS D'OEUVRES SERVERS

If there is need for extra space on which to serve hors d'oeuvres, attractive vegetables and fruits may be used very successfully. A large eggplant gives a colorful base for hors d'oeuvres on picks and has space for 20 or more depending on size of eggplant. A honeydew melon or cantaloupe is a good base for the more colorful hors d'oeuvres. Melons may also be cut into halves, seeds removed and center filled with ripe or stuffed olives or radish roses and the edge used for the hors d'oeuvres base. A very large orange or red apple serves well for the small party.

VEGETABLE CURLS—Carrot, turnip, or beet curls may be made by piercing the center of the uncooked vegetable, then cutting a thin continous ring from the vegetable holding knife flat against the top surface. Crisp in ice water.

PAPRIKA CELERY CURLS—After celery has curled, drain, dip in melted butter then in paprika. Chill.

SUGAR PLUM TREE

1 large pineapple
½ pound sweet cherries

Cut a 1-inch slice from top of pineapple, keeping all the spiny leaves intact. Wash leaves thoroughly and wipe dry. Press leaves outward, curving them to represent branches of a tree. Set upright on the cut surface and stick cherries on ends of leaves. Use as a center of a large salad plate arrangement or as hors d'oeuvres server.

For the children's party: Use various colored gumdrops or tiny animal crackers instead of cherries.

FOR TOMATO SALADS

PREPARATION—Dip firm ripe tomatoes (1 for each serving) into boiling water and peel carefully. Chill, cut and serve in any of the following ways:

1. Turn tomato stem-end down and cut tomato into 7 petals about ⅔ down toward stem-end. Spread petals out, remove center and fill center with chopped vegetable salad.

2. Turn tomato stem-end down and with the knife slanted toward center cut a circular section from tomato so that the depth at center is 1 inch. Remove section, fill hollow with a cream cheese filling and place section cut-side up on the filling with sprigs of parsley arranged around edge of cover.

3. Turn tomato stem-end down and cut into sections from top to within ½ inch of stem-end, making cuts ½ inch apart Turn tomato ¼ way around and make the same number of cuts in the same way, thus cutting tomato into criss-cross design or cubes.

Leftovers

300 DISHES
FROM
LEFTOVERS

LEFTOVER BREAD, CRACKERS AND CAKE

BAKED APPLE PUDDING

4 medium apples, pared and sliced
½ cup brown sugar
1 cup graham cracker crumbs
¾ cup water
3 tablespoons lemon juice

Combine all ingredients and mix well. Turn into greased baking dish and bake in moderate oven (375°F.) 30 minutes, or until apples are tender. Serve hot with cream. Serves 4.

BLUEBERRY BETTY

3 cups blueberries
¾ cup sugar
⅛ teaspoon salt
½ teaspoon lemon juice
French Toast
Confectioners' sugar
Nutmeg

Cook blueberries, sugar, salt and lemon juice for 10 minutes. Pour into shallow baking dish and arrange slices of French toast on top. Sprinkle with confectioners' sugar and nutmeg and bake in hot oven (425°F.) about 20 minutes. Serve with cream. Serves 6.

BRAZIL-NUT BREAD PUDDING

4 slices buttered bread
⅓ cup sliced Brazil nuts
2 eggs
½ cup sugar
¼ teaspoon salt
1 teaspoon vanilla
2 cups milk

Cut buttered bread into finger-width pieces. Arrange in layers in buttered baking dish, sprinkling each layer with Brazil nuts. Beat eggs slightly, add sugar, salt, vanilla and milk. Mix well and pour over bread. Garnish top with Brazil nuts and bake in slow oven (325°F.) 1 hour. Serves 6.

STEAMED BLUEBERRY PUDDING

1 cup sifted flour
1½ teaspoons baking powder
½ teaspoon salt
½ cup shortening
½ cup dry bread crumbs
½ cup sugar
1 egg, beaten
⅔ cup milk
1½ cups blueberries

Sift flour, baking powder and salt together. Cut in shortening and add bread crumbs and sugar. Add egg and milk, mix thoroughly and carefully fold in blueberries. Pour into greased mold, cover and steam 2 hours. Serve with any sweet pudding sauce. Serves 6.

STEAMED BLACKBERRY PUDDING—Use blackberries instead of blueberries.

STEAMED CRANBERRY PUDDING—Use cranberries which have been cut into halves. Add 4 more tablespoons of sugar.

This delicious Brazil-nut bread pudding is an ace favorite with everybody

SPICE PUDDING

1 cup seeded raisins
1 egg
½ cup sugar
2 cups milk
1½ cups bread crumbs
1 teaspoon cinnamon
½ teaspoon cloves
½ teaspoon allspice
¼ teaspoon nutmeg
1 teaspoon melted butter
⅛ teaspoon salt

Cut raisins into halves. Beat egg until light, add sugar and milk, then pour over crumbs. Add spices, butter, salt and raisins, stir well, pour into baking dish, set in pan of water and bake in slow oven (300°F.) 45 to 50 minutes, or until firm. Serve hot or cold with any sauce. For 8.

BROWN BREAD BREWIS

1½ cups milk
½ cup cream
1½ tablespoons butter
¼ teaspoon salt
2 cups dry brown bread, broken

Scald milk, cream and butter together. Add salt and brown bread, and soak for 5 minutes. Simmer until milk has been absorbed. Serve with cream. Serves 4.

APPLE BETTY

3 cups sliced apples
1½ cups soft bread crumbs
⅓ cup brown sugar
1 teaspoon cinnamon
4 tablespoons butter, melted
¾ cup water, hot or cold

Mix apples, 1 cup bread crumbs, brown sugar and cinnamon. Place in buttered baking dish and pour melted butter and water over top. Mix remaining crumbs with a little extra melted butter and sprinkle over top. Bake in moderate oven (350°F.) 30 to 45 minutes. Serve hot or cold with Hard Sauce. Serves 6.

PECAN BROWNIES

2 egg whites
1 cup brown sugar
½ teaspoon maple flavoring
1 cup pecans, chopped
1 cup fine dry bread crumbs

Beat egg whites until stiff, add sugar and flavoring. Stir well. Combine nuts and crumbs and fold into egg whites. Shape into small balls, place on greased baking pan, bake in slow oven (325°F.) about 20 minutes. Makes 3 dozen balls.

CURRANT FRITTERS

2 cups scalded milk
2 cups fine bread crumbs
1 tablespoon shortening
5 eggs, separated
½ cup sugar
2 tablespoons flour
½ teaspoon cinnamon
¼ teaspoon nutmeg
2 cups fresh currants

Pour hot milk over crumbs and shortening, mix well and let cool. Beat egg yolks well and add. Sift dry ingredients together and beat into first mixture. Add currants, fold in stiffly beaten egg whites and drop by tablespoons into hot deep fat (365°F.). Fry until brown, drain on rack between layers of absorbent paper. Serve hot with a wine sauce for 8.

NEW ENGLAND APRICOT PUDDING

½ pound dried apricots
½ cup sugar
Cinnamon toast

Soak apricots overnight. Stew until tender and add sugar. Arrange squares of cinnamon toast in bottom and around sides of a casserole. Pour in the boiling hot apricots, cover casserole and cool gradually. Serve with cream for 4.

LEFTOVER CAKE

Keep leftover pieces of cake or cookies in a covered metal box. Crumble into pieces or grind into crumbs; combine with cooked leftover fruits (with juice) for steamed fruit puddings. Serve with Lemon Sauce.

1. Cut white, sponge or chocolate cake into rectangles to fit refrigerator tray. Line tray with waxed paper. Put cake together in layers with sweetened whipped cream. Place in freezing compartment and freeze for 8 hours. Lift out, remove paper and frost with whipped cream. Serve whole; cut into slices at table.

2. Arrange squares of spongecake spread with jam or marmalade in pudding dish; top with boiled custard and chill for 3 hours. Sprinkle with chopped toasted almonds before serving.

3. Cut angel food cake into rounds; spread with a paste of chopped figs and preserved ginger sirup. Place a marshmallow in center of each and bake in moderate oven (375°F.) until marshmallows soften.

4. Combine broken up chocolate or angel food cake with whipped cream, marshmallows, chopped nut meats and chopped candied or cooked pineapple. Chill for 3 hours.

CHOCOLATE REFRIGERATOR CAKE—Melt 2 squares (ounces) chocolate over hot water, add 1½ cups evaporated milk and stir until thick. Add ½ cup water. Alternate layers of chocolate mixture with squares of leftover spongecake in narrow bread pan lined with waxed paper. Chill 12 hours; unmold, slice and serve with whipped cream. Serves 4.

LIVER LOAF WITH PAN GRAVY

1½ pounds beef liver
1½ cups boiling water
2 slices salt pork, ¼ inch thick
1 medium onion
¼ cup chopped parsley
2 cups soft bread crumbs
2 eggs, slightly beaten
1 teaspoon salt
¼ teaspoon pepper
2 tablespoons flour
1½ cups cold water

Rinse liver, cover with boiling water and let stand 10 minutes; drain. Grind with salt pork and onion; add parsley, crumbs, eggs, salt and pepper, and mix thoroughly. Press into baking pan (8x4x3 inches) and bake in moderate oven (350°F.) about 1 hour, or until browned. Remove loaf to hot platter. Stir flour into drippings and brown; add water gradually and cook 5 minutes, until thickened; season and pour over loaf. Serves 6.

LIVER PATTIES—Omit water and 1 cup crumbs. Shape into round patties, wrap each in bacon and broil until browned.

If you like, omit gravy and garnish your liver loaf with crisp, brown bacon

CORN BREAD STUFFING

4 cups broken corn bread
4 cups boiling water
1 onion, grated
1 cup diced celery
2 eggs, beaten
½ cup salt pork fat, melted
Salt and pepper

Combine bread and boiling water and squeeze out water while still hot. Add remaining ingredients, mix well and stuff fowl. This amount is sufficient for a duck or a 4-pound chicken.

BREAD LEFTOVERS

Keep on hand in a dry place a large container for dry or leftover bread. When enough bread has been collected, put through food chopper for crumbs Keep the crumbs in a metal box with cover (perforated) or in glass jars with ventilated tops. Use for au gratin dishes, meat and vegetable casseroles, etc.

1. Remove crusts from slices of rye or whole-wheat bread and cut hole in center with small cookie cutter; arrange slices in skillet in browned butter; place 1 egg in center of each and sauté. **2.** Remove crusts from dry bread; sauté in butter and serve with maple sirup.

3. Mix dry bread crumbs with cinnamon and sugar; place 2 tablespoons each in custard cups; fill with custard mixture and bake.

4. Save ends of French bread; rub with cut clove of garlic, brush with melted butter, and toast in oven. Serve with green salad.

5. Remove crusts from dry bread slices. Cream 6 tablespoons butter with ½ clove garlic (grated). Spread each slice of bread, tie slices together and bake in hot oven until slightly toasted.

6. Combine 4 slices bread, diced, with 1⅓ cups scalding milk and 4 tablespoons horse-radish in top of double boiler; heat until thick and serve with meat or fish.

7. Scoop out center of leftover muffins, dot with butter and reheat in oven until butter melts. (A) Fill centers with jam or marmalade and serve hot. (B) Fill centers with creamed fish or eggs; sprinkle with grated cheese and bake in hot oven.

Any sliced leftover meat rolled and filled with corn bread stuffing will make this luscious dinner ➡

BACON AND HOMINY

3 cups cooked hominy
1 small onion, chopped
1 green pepper, chopped
2 tablespoons fat
2 cups cooked tomatoes
1 tablespoon sugar
1 teaspoon salt
½ pound sliced bacon

Place hominy in greased shallow baking dish. Sauté onion and pepper in fat until light brown. Add tomatoes, sugar and salt and simmer 10 minutes. Pour mixture over hominy and cover with sliced bacon. Bake in slow oven (325°F.) about 30 minutes until bacon is brown and crisp. Serves 6 to 8.

BATTER BREAD

½ cup cold cooked hominy
1 egg, beaten
1 teaspoon salt
1 cup white corn meal
2½ to 3 cups boiling water
1 tablespoon butter

Mix cold hominy, egg, salt and corn meal with enough boiling water to make a batter of the consistency of milk. Heat butter in a deep baking pan until it begins to smoke, add batter. Bake in moderate oven (350°F.) 40 minutes. Makes 1 loaf.

FRIED CORN-MEAL MUSH

Pack hot leftover corn-meal mush into a mold and let stand until cold and solid. Cut into ½-inch slices, roll in flour and brown on both sides on a hot greased griddle. Serve with sirup and sausage.

1. Hominy grits may be used in place of corn meal.

2. Slice and fry. Cover each slice with chopped cooked spinach and top with a poached egg.

BAKED HOMINY GRITS

½ cup milk
1 tablespoon butter
1 cup cold boiled grits
1 egg
½ teaspoon salt
Dash of pepper

Heat milk and butter, add grits and mix until smooth. Add beaten egg and seasoning, pour into buttered baking dish and bake in moderate oven (350°F.) until firm and brown, 25 to 30 minutes. Serves 4 to 6.

All good cooks are proud of their batter breads

COOKED CEREALS

BREAKFAST CEREAL—1. Pour hot cereal into custard cups and chill; hollow out centers and fill with Maple Sugar Mousse, fresh fruit or berries. Serve with cream as a dessert.

2. Mold hot cereal in small oblong pan (dipped in cold water) and chill. Slice, dip into bread crumbs and fry. Serve with creamed eggs, meat or fish.

HOMINY (COOKED GRITS) — Cut cold hominy into rings; sauté in butter or bacon fat; top with sautéed apple rings and serve with ham.

MACARONI—Combine cold macaroni with tomato purée, mushroom soup or White Sauce; pour into greased casserole, sprinkle with grated cheese and bake in moderate oven (350°F.) 30 minutes.

1. Spaghetti, noodles or rice may be used instead of macaroni.

RICE—Combine cold rice with whipped cream and sweetened leftover fruit or berries or cooked fruit with juice. Chill and serve with Fruit Sauce.

CREOLE SOUP

1 tablespoon chopped green pepper
1 tablespoon chopped red pepper
1 tablespoon butter, melted
1 tablespoon flour
1½ cups soup stock
1 cup tomato pulp
½ cup canned corn
Salt and pepper

Brown peppers lightly in butter; blend in flour. Add soup stock and tomato pulp slowly, place over heat and stir until soup boils. Reduce heat, cover and simmer 20 minutes. Strain, add corn and season with salt and pepper. Serves 6.

SCALLOPED CHICKEN

¼ cup fat
½ cup flour
1 teaspoon salt
4 cups chicken broth or milk
3 cups diced cooked chicken
2 cups coarse bread crumbs
1 cup cooked macaroni
2 hard-cooked eggs, sliced
Buttered crumbs

Melt fat, blend in flour and salt; add broth and cook until thickened, stirring constantly. Add chicken, bread crumbs and macaroni. Place alternate layers of egg, and chicken and macaroni mixture in greased baking dish. Top with buttered crumbs and bake in moderate oven (350°F.) about 1 hour. Serves 8.

CURRIED RICE

2 cups cooked rice
1 green pepper, diced
1 onion, minced
2 cups canned tomatoes
4 tablespoons fat
1½ teaspoons curry powder

Mix all ingredients. Bake in greased casserole in slow oven (325°F.), about 30 minutes. Serves 6.

HOMINY SALMON LOAF

1 cup cooked hominy grits
1 pound cooked salmon
Corn meal
Fat

Combine hot grits with flaked salmon and pack into a loaf pan. Cool, slice, dredge with corn meal and brown in a small amount of fat. Serves 6.

MACARONI LOAF

1 package aspic gelatin
1 cup boiling water
¾ cup cold water
⅔ cup Russian dressing
1 cup cooked elbow macaroni
⅔ cup chopped white cabbage
2 tablespoons minced pimiento
2 tablespoons minced green pepper

Dissolve gelatin in boiling water; add cold water. Chill until mixture begins to thicken. Beat in dressing. Add remaining ingredients. Mold in loaf pan. Chill until firm. If desired, add few drops Worcestershire sauce or onion juice. Serves 8.

CHICKEN AND MACARONI

¼ cup fat
¾ cup hot milk
2 eggs, beaten
½ cup soft crumbs
1½ cups diced cooked chicken
2 tablespoons grated cheese
1 cup cooked macaroni
2 teaspoons minced parsley
2 teaspoons minced onion
Salt and pepper

Melt fat in milk, then cool. Pour over beaten eggs, add remaining ingredients and season. Pour into greased casserole, place in moderate oven (350°F.) until firm. Serve with Mushroom Sauce. Serves 6.

SPAGHETTI CREOLE

2 slices bacon, diced
¼ pound onions, diced
½ green pepper, diced
½ pound ground beef
1 cup cooked tomatoes
1 cup cooked Lima beans
1¼ cups cooked spaghetti
Salt and pepper

Fry bacon until crisp. Remove bacon and sauté onions and green pepper in bacon fat. Fry beef until well browned and add tomatoes, Lima beans, spaghetti, bacon and sautéed vegetables. Blend thoroughly. When mixture starts to simmer, season well. Cook 10 to 15 minutes. Serves 4.

MACARONI SALAD

2 cups cooked macaroni
1 cup diced celery
¼ cup diced cucumber
¼ cup diced sweet pickle
¼ cup diced American cheese
½ pimiento, cut fine
Mayonnaise to moisten
5 green peppers

Chill ingredients and combine. Chill for several hours. Serve in pepper cups. Serves 5.

The satiny green pepper makes a crisp container for your macaroni salad

RICE WAFFLES

1 cup sifted flour
3 teaspoons baking powder
1/2 teaspoon salt
2 eggs, separated
1 cup milk
4 tablespoons shortening, melted
1 cup cold cooked rice

Sift flour, baking powder and salt together. Combine beaten egg yolks and milk and add to dry ingredients, beating until smooth. Add melted shortening and rice, and stir. Fold in stiffly beaten egg whites and bake in hot waffle iron. Makes 6 waffles.

The rice left from Sunday's chicken dinner makes these delicious waffles for supper

RICE CAKES

4 slices bacon, chopped
3 tablespoons chopped onion
3 tablespoons chopped green pepper
1 teaspoon salt
1/2 teaspoon pepper
3 cups cooked rice
1 cup sifted flour
1 teaspoon baking powder
1 cup tomato pulp

Fry bacon crisp and add to remaining ingredients. Mix thoroughly. Drop by tablespoons into skillet containing bacon drippings and brown on both sides. Makes 16 cakes.

RICE AND PINE-APPLE

2 cups cooked rice
Butter
4 slices pineapple, halved
1/2 cup brown sugar
Pineapple juice

Place 1/2-inch layer of cooked rice in bottom of casserole, dot with butter and arrange a layer of pineapple over the top. Sprinkle with brown sugar. Repeat until all ingredients are used, having top layer of pineapple. Cover with pineapple juice and bake in moderate oven (350°F.) 30 minutes. Serve hot or cold. Serves 4.

RICE GRIDDLECAKES

1 cup cooked rice
2 cups milk
1/2 teaspoon salt
1 tablespoon sugar
1 tablespoon shortening
1 1/2 cups sifted flour
2 teaspoons baking powder
1 egg, beaten

Soak cooked rice in 1 cup of milk overnight. Add salt, sugar, shortening, flour and baking powder. Beat the mixture well, then add egg and remaining cup of milk. Bake on hot greased griddle. Makes about 20 small cakes.

LEMON RICE CROQUETTES

1 cup cooked rice
1/4 cup milk
1 tablespoon sugar
1 teaspoon salt
Grated lemon peel
2 eggs
2 tablespoons water
Crumbs

Combine rice, milk, sugar, salt, lemon peel and 1 egg, beaten. When cold, shape into cylinders or pyramids, roll in remaining egg (diluted with water), then in bread crumbs or rolled crackers and fry in hot deep fat (375°-390°F.) until brown. Serves 3.

RICE MUFFINS

1 cup boiled rice
1 cup milk
2 eggs, beaten
5 tablespoons melted shortening
1 1/2 cups sifted flour
2 teaspoons sugar
1/2 teaspoon salt
3 teaspoons baking powder

Beat rice, milk, eggs and shortening well. Sift flour, sugar, salt and baking powder into batter. Mix only enough to combine. Pour into greased muffin pan and bake in hot oven (400°F.) 25 minutes. Makes 12 muffins.

OATMEAL MUFFINS

2 cups sifted flour
3 teaspoons baking powder
2 tablespoons sugar
1/2 teaspoon salt
1 egg, well beaten
2/3 cup cold cooked oatmeal
1 cup milk
2 tablespoons shortening, melted

Mix and sift dry ingredients. Combine remaining ingredients and add to first mixture. Stir only enough to dampen flour. Fill greased muffin pans 2/3 full and bake in hot oven (425°F.) about 25 minutes. Makes 12 large muffins.

CHEESE FONDUE

1 cup milk
1 cup soft bread crumbs
½ cup grated cheese
2 tablespoons butter
½ teaspoon salt
⅛ teaspoon pepper
3 eggs, separated

Scald milk in double boiler; add crumbs, cheese, butter and seasonings. Stir in unbeaten egg yolks. Beat egg whites stiff and fold into mixture. Pour into greased baking dish, set in pan of hot water and bake in moderately slow oven (325° F.) 30 to 45 minutes, or until firm. Serves 6.

CHEESE PUFFS

12 slices bread (⅓ inch thick)
4 tablespoons butter
¼ pound cheese, grated
¼ teaspoon baking powder
1 egg, separated

Cut 2-inch rounds from bread and toast lightly on one side. Butter untoasted side. Mix cheese, baking powder and beaten egg yolk, then fold in stiffly beaten egg white. Spread thickly over buttered side of bread and place on cookie sheet. Place under preheated broiler until puffed and light brown. Makes 12 puffs.

EGGS AU GRATIN

1½ cups milk
1 teaspoon salt
⅛ teaspoon pepper
4 tablespoons grated Swiss cheese
4 eggs

Add milk, seasoning and cheese to slightly beaten eggs. Turn mixture into greased baking dish, place in pan of hot water and bake in moderately slow oven (325°F.) 40 to 45 minutes or until firm. Remove from oven; let stand 3 minutes and unmold onto platter. Serve with Tomato Sauce. Serves 4.

MASHED POTATOES AU GRATIN

3 tablespoons fat
½ teaspoon salt
½ teaspoon paprika
2 eggs
6 cooked potatoes, riced
¼ cup grated cheese
½ cup buttered crumbs

Add fat, seasonings and eggs to hot riced potatoes. Beat until light and arrange in greased baking dish. Cover with cheese and crumbs. Bake in hot oven (400° F.) 10 minutes, or until crumbs are browned. Serves 6.

SUMMER SQUASH TOMATO CASSEROLE

1½ pounds summer squash
4 tomatoes, sliced
2 medium onions, sliced
1 teaspoon salt
⅛ teaspoon pepper
½ cup dry bread crumbs
½ cup grated cheese
2 tablespoons butter

Cut squash into halves, remove seeds and cover with tomatoes and onions. Sprinkle with next 4 ingredients and top with bits of butter. Cover, bake at 350° F. 45 minutes. Serves 6.

A casserole of au gratin eggs, vegetable or fish makes the budgeteer's best luncheon

SALMON À LA MORNAY

4 cooked potatoes
½ cup grated Swiss cheese
1 egg yolk
1 cup Medium White Sauce
2 cups flaked canned salmon
Buttered crumbs

Mash potatoes and line greased baking dish with them. Add cheese and egg yolk to the white sauce and pour ½ of it over potatoes. Add fish and cover with remaining sauce and buttered bread crumbs. Bake in moderate oven (350° F.) 20 minutes. Serves 6.

CHEESE FRANKFURTERS

6 frankfurters
¼ pound American cheese
6 slices bacon

Cut a lengthwise slit in each frankfurter. Cut strip of American cheese the length of frankfurter and about ¼ inch thick. Fill slit with strip of cheese; wrap slice of bacon around each frankfurter and fasten ends with toothpicks. Broil frankfurters slowly, turning often, until the bacon and frankfurters are cooked through and browned. Serves 3.

CHEESE NAPOLEON

Use any leftover plain pastry or puff paste. Roll out ¼-inch thickness, sprinkle half with grated cheese. Fold over the other half and roll out again. Sprinkle with cheese and proceed as before; repeat 3 times. Cut into narrow strips and bake in very hot oven (500°F.) 10 minutes.

EGG AND SPINACH CREOLE

2 cups chopped cooked spinach
Dash mace
½ teaspoon salt
Dash pepper
2 tablespoons butter
1 tablespoon flour
2 tablespoons pimiento cheese
⅓ cup milk
2 tomatoes, sliced and sautéed
4 eggs

Season spinach with mace, salt and pepper. Keep hot while preparing cheese sauce. Melt butter and add flour, stirring until smooth Combine pimiento cheese and milk and add to butter. Cook until thick, stirring constantly. Place spinach in shallow baking dish and cover with sautéed slices tomato. Poach eggs, place on tomatoes and cover with cheese sauce. Heat thoroughly in moderate oven (350°F.). Serves 4.

MEXICAN BEANS

2 cups mashed pinto beans
2 teaspoons fat
2 cloves garlic, mashed
7 green onions, chopped
1 cup grated American cheese

Use leftover beans. Heat fat, add beans and remaining ingredients, cook until onions are tender and serve hot. Serves 4 to 6.

Lovely to look at, delightful to eat, are these cheese gems

CHEESE GEMS

2 cups sifted flour
3 teaspoons baking powder
½ teaspoon salt
4 tablespoons shortening
¾ cup milk
1 cup grated American cheese

Sift dry ingredients together, cut in shortening with a fork or dough blender. Add milk to make a soft dough. Toss onto a floured board, knead lightly and roll ⅓ inch thick. Cover with the grated cheese. Cut into strips 2 inches wide; place 4 strips one on top of the other. Cut this strip into pieces 1¾ inches wide. Place each of these pieces upright in a greased custard cup with cut edges on top and bottom. Bake in hot oven (425°F.) until lightly browned. Makes 12 gems.

FRIED SPINACH BALLS

2 cups cooked spinach, chopped
2 tablespoons butter, melted
2 eggs
1 cup bread crumbs
2 tablespoons grated onion
2 tablespoons grated cheese
⅛ teaspoon allspice
¼ cup water
Bread crumbs

Combine spinach with butter, 1 beaten egg, crumbs, onion, cheese and allspice and mix thoroughly. Let stand for 10 minutes; shape into balls. Combine remaining egg and the water and beat together until well blended. Roll spinach balls in crumbs, dip into egg and again into crumbs. Fry in hot deep fat (375°F.) until brown. Drain on absorbent paper before serving. Serves 6.

CREAM OF CORN SOUP

5 cups fresh corn
5 cups milk or ½ milk, ½
    white stock
2 tablespoons flour
2 tablespoons butter, melted
Salt and pepper
2 egg yolks

Cook corn in double boiler with 4 cups of milk for 20 minutes. Blend flour and butter, add corn and milk mixture and seasoning. Cook for 5 minutes. Rub through a coarse sieve. Beat egg yolks and add the remaining cup of cold milk. Stir into the soup and cook for 1 or 2 minutes, stirring constantly. Beat and serve at once. Serves 6.

GOLDEN BUCK

3 cups grated Cheddar cheese
1 tablespoon butter
¾ cup beer, ale or milk
1 egg yolk, slightly beaten

Melt cheese and butter in top of double boiler, add half the beer when cheese is partly melted and cook, stirring constantly. Combine remaining beer with egg yolk and add slowly; stirring constantly until smooth and thick. Serve on hot toast. Sprinkle with cayenne. Serves 4.

LEFTOVER EGGS

EGG YOLKS

1. Poach in boiling water until hard; cook and force through a sieve as garnish for salads, canapés, spinach, creamed fish or thick soups.
2. Add to eggs when making omelets or scrambled eggs.
3. Add to white sauce or fish sauces for thickening and a richer flavor and color.
4. Add to eggs for eggnogs.

SCRAMBLED EGGS AND OMELETS

1. Break up with a fork and add to hot soups.
2. Reheat in top of double boiler, break up with fork and combine with chopped bacon or hot minced ham for sandwiches.
3. Cut into tiny cubes for oxtail or other thick soups.

CHEESE APPETIZER

2 egg whites
1 cup grated American cheese
Dash of cayenne
¼ cup grated dry bread crumbs

Beat egg whites stiff, add cheese, cayenne and bread crumbs. Pat into small balls and fry in hot deep fat (375° F.) until light brown. Makes about 16 balls.

POACHED FISH WITH LEMON SAUCE

3 pounds pike
¼ cup sugar
1 lemon, juice and rind
2 egg yolks
1 cup hot fish stock
½ teaspoon salt
1 teaspoon chopped parsley

Poach the fish 30 minutes; skin, bone and arrange on a platter. Mix sugar, grated rind and lemon juice with well beaten egg yolks and add strained fish stock gradually. Cook until thick, stirring constantly. Add salt and parsley and pour over fish. Serve cold. Serves 6.

MASHED POTATO BALLS

2 cups cold mashed potatoes
Salt and pepper
1 egg yolk
Butter

Mix seasoned mashed potatoes with egg yolk and shape mixture into balls. Place in greased pan and make a depression on the top of each. Place a bit of butter in each hollow and brown in hot oven (400°F.). Serves 4.

Crispy, browned cheese ball appetizers are a happy surprise to almost everyone

YOLK RINGS

3 hard-cooked egg yolks
⅓ cup butter
½ cup sugar
1 tablespoon hot water
1 uncooked egg, separated
2 cups sifted cake flour
⅛ teaspoon mace
½ teaspoon salt
Grated rind of ½ lemon

Rub egg yolks through a sieve. Cream butter, sugar and hot water together and add cooked egg yolks and uncooked yolk. Sift flour, mace and salt together and mix with creamed mixture. Add grated lemon rind. Knead sufficiently to blend well. Roll about ⅛ inch thick and cut into rings with doughnut cutter. Brush tops with egg white and sprinkle with colored sugar. Bake in moderate oven (375°F.) 10 to 15 minutes. Makes about 2 dozen rings.

MERINGUED PEARS

6 large pears
6 tablespoons sugar
Grated lemon rind or
    candied ginger
3 egg whites
¼ cup confectioners' sugar

Pare and core pears, place in a baking dish and fill the center of each with one tablespoon sugar and a little grated lemon rind or candied ginger. Add 3 to 4 tablespoons water and bake until tender. Cover with a meringue made with the stiffly beaten egg whites and confectioners' sugar. Brown quickly. Serves 6.
Use fresh peach or apricot halves instead of pears. Dip cooked prunes or figs in meringue, roll in coconut; bake in (350°F.) oven for 20 minutes. Dip currants, cherries, berries or citrus fruit sections in beaten egg white, roll in confectioners' sugar and dry out in a warm place.

PEANUT MOLASSES DIVINITY

2 cups sugar
½ cup water
1 tablespoon molasses
2 egg whites, stiffly beaten
1 teaspoon lemon extract
1 cup roasted peanuts, rolled

Place the sugar, water, and molasses in a saucepan, stirring until the sugar is dissolved. Cook to 240°, or to the soft-ball stage. Pour over the stiffly beaten egg whites, beating constantly. Add the lemon extract. Beat until creamy, then add the peanuts and drop by spoonfuls on waxed paper.

LEMON SHERBET

1 quart water
3 cups sugar
¾ cup lemon juice
2 egg whites

Boil water and sugar together for 5 minutes. Add lemon juice, cool and freeze to a mush. Add stiffly beaten egg whites and continue freezing. Serves 12.
Use other citrus fruit juices or 1 cup crushed berries.

One-egg cake can be chocolate too, when two squares are used for one-half cup flour

TIPSY PUDDING

3 egg yolks
¼ cup sugar
⅛ teaspoon salt
2 cups milk, scalded
1 tablespoon sherry
6 slices of spongecake
Whipped cream

Beat egg yolks and add sugar and salt. Add scalded milk gradually, stirring constantly. Cook in the top of a double boiler until mixture thickens, stirring constantly. Remove from heat and add sherry. Cool. When custard is cold, pour it over slices of spongecake or any plain dry cake and cover with whipped cream. Garnish with chopped nuts, if desired. Serves 6.

GLAZE FOR BREAKFAST BREADS

1 egg yolk
2 tablespoons sugar
3 tablespoons water or milk

Beat egg yolk slightly, add sugar and water or milk. Mix well and brush over breads before baking.

BOILED ICING

2 cups sugar
⅛ teaspoon cream of tartar
½ cup cold water
2 egg whites, beaten
1 teaspoon vanilla

Combine sugar, cream of tartar and water and boil to 238°F. or until a little sirup forms a soft ball when dropped into cold water. Pour hot sirup very slowly into the beaten egg whites, beating constantly. Add vanilla and beat until icing is cool and of proper consistency to spread. Will frost tops and sides of 2 (9-inch) layers.

CHOCOLATE—Fold 4 tablespoons grated chocolate into the warm icing.

MAPLE—Use maple sirup instead of half the sugar.

WALNUT—Use brown sugar in place of granulated. Omit cream of tartar and add ½ cup chopped walnut meats.

VERMONT MAPLE—Use maple sirup in place of sugar and water. Omit cream of tartar and add ½ teaspoon baking powder during last of beating.

TINTED—Lemon juice will whiten icing, grated orange rind will give a yellow color and strawberry, raspberry or cranberry juice will give a pink color.

NEVER-FAIL OR SEVEN-MINUTE ICING

2 egg whites
1½ cups sugar
⅓ cup water
Few grains salt
¼ teaspoon cream of tartar or 1½ teaspoons corn sirup
1 teaspoon vanilla

Combine all ingredients except vanilla in the top of a double boiler. Cook over boiling water, beating constantly with a rotary

Few desserts are so easy to make or so easy on the purse as a glorious baked Alaska

egg beater. Cook for 7 minutes or until mixture holds a point when beater is lifted. Remove from heat, add vanilla and continue beating until cool enough to spread. Will frost tops and sides of 2 (9-inch) layers.

LEMON—Use lemon juice instead of 2 tablespoons of the water, omit cream of tartar and vanilla and add ¼ teaspoon grated lemon rind.

ORANGE—Use only ¼ cup water. Use juice and rind of ½ orange instead of vanilla.

PEPPERMINT—Flavor with a few drops of oil of peppermint instead of vanilla and, when frosting on cake is cold but still soft, make a 1-inch border of chocolate flakes around top of cake. Make flakes by scraping bitter chocolate with a knife.

CARAMEL—Use brown sugar in place of granulated.

CHOCOLATE—Stir 2 squares chocolate, melted, into icing just before spreading on cake.

BAKED ALASKA

½ square spongecake
1 pint ice cream
2 egg whites, beaten stiff
⅓ cup sugar

Cover cake with ice cream. Combine egg whites with sugar and beat well. Spread meringue thickly over ice cream and sides of cake and place on baking board, or on several thicknesses of heavy paper on baking sheet. Bake in hot oven (400°F.) about 6 minutes, or until meringue is lightly browned. Serves 6 to 8.

1. Scoop out center from sponge cupcakes; fill with ice cream, cover ice cream and sides of cakes thickly with meringue and bake as directed.

2. Arrange spongecake layers with filling of ice cream; top with ice cream; cover with meringue and bake as above.

3. Cut leftover plain or frosted layer cake into squares or oblongs at least ½ inch thick, cover with ice cream, frost with meringue and bake as above. If desired, garnish with fresh strawberries, raspberries, or slices of fruit and nut meats.

BEEF MIROTON

4 onions
1 tablespoon fat
1 tablespoon flour
2 tablespoons vinegar
⅔ cup bouillon or
    ⅓ cup water mixed with ⅓
    cup Tomato Sauce
Salt and pepper
1 pound cooked beef
Bread crumbs

Slice onions and brown in fat. Add flour and brown. Then add vinegar, bouillon or water and tomato sauce. Cook together until slightly thickened, stirring constantly. Season with salt and pepper. Simmer slices of beef in sauce a few minutes. Pour into baking dish, sprinkle crumbs over top and bake in hot oven (400°F.) 10 minutes. Serves 4.

BEEF HASH

3 onions
1 tablespoon fat
2 cups diced cooked beef
½ cup cubed cooked potatoes
½ cup meat stock
Salt and pepper

Cut onions into cubes and fry in fat until brown. Add beef, potatoes and stock. Season and cook about 15 minutes. Serves 4.

MEAT AND POTATO CASSEROLE

3 cups mashed potatoes, seasoned
2 cups diced cooked meat
Gravy
½ teaspoon onion juice
1 tablespoon butter

Cover bottom of shallow baking dish with a layer of mashed potatoes; over this spread any kind of leftover meat, leftover gravy and onion juice. Cover with layer of mashed potatoes. Dot with butter and place in hot oven (400°F.) 20 minutes or until heated through and brown on top. Serves 6.

MEAT SOUFFLÉS

3 eggs, separated
2 tablespoons bacon fat, melted
1 cup milk
½ teaspoon salt
1½ cups minced cooked meat
1 tablespoon minced onion

Beat egg yolks well, add bacon fat, milk, salt, meat and onion. Beat thoroughly. Fold in stiffly beaten egg whites. Pour into greased custard cups, place in pan of hot water and bake in moderate oven (350°F.) until firm, 25 to 30 minutes. Serves 6.

A very effective casserole is this one of sausage and corn

PLANKED EGGS WITH HAM

1 cup minced cooked ham
1 cup crumbs
Cream
1 quart mashed potatoes
6 poached eggs
Garnish of tomato slices
Green pepper rings

Mix meat with crumbs and enough cream to make a paste. Spread on heated plank. Make a narrow border of mashed potatoes around edge of plank and inside the border make 6 nests of the potato. Slip a poached egg into each nest and place in oven until potatoes brown. Garnish with alternate slices of tomato and green pepper rings. Serves 6.

SPANISH POTATOES

1 tablespoon minced onion
2 tablespoons chopped green pepper
2 tablespoons chopped pimiento
4 tablespoons fat
2 cups diced boiled potatoes
½ cup chopped cooked ham
1 teaspoon salt
½ teaspoon paprika

Sauté onion, pepper and pimiento in fat until light brown, add potatoes, ham and seasonings and cook until heated through. Serves 4.

CASSEROLE OF SAUSAGE AND CORN

10 Vienna sausages
2 cups cooked whole grain corn
½ green pepper, chopped
Salt and pepper
2 cups Medium White Sauce

Wash sausages. Mix corn, green pepper, salt and pepper. Place in casserole in alternate layers with white sauce. Arrange sausages on top to radiate from center. Bake in moderate oven (350°F.) 20 minutes. Serves 5.

SPINACH AND HAM SALAD

1/2 cups cooked spinach
Juice of 1 lemon
slices cold boiled ham
Lettuce

Drain spinach and add lemon juice. Pack tightly into 8 small molds and chill. Arrange slices of cold boiled ham on lettuce and place 2 molds of spinach on opposite sides of each ham slice. Serve with French dressing or mayonnaise. Serves 4.

PORK SCRAPS

Slice fat salt pork, cut into cubes and place in a single layer in skillet. Place in slow oven or over very low heat, turning often so all sides will brown evenly. When sufficiently crisp, drain and serve sprinkled over the top of codfish baked with milk gravy or as an accompaniment to griddlecakes.

CORNED BEEF HASH

cups chopped cooked corned beef
cups chopped cooked potatoes
Salt and pepper
1/2 cup milk or water
tablespoons fat

Mix beef and potatoes together lightly and season. Heat milk with half the fat and when warm add hash, spreading it evenly and placing the rest of the fat, cut into pieces on top. Cover pan and simmer for 1/2 hour. Do not stir. Fold as an omelet and place on a hot platter. Serves 4.

MEAT AND RICE AU GRATIN

2 cups diced cooked meat
Milk or soup stock
2 cups boiled rice
2 tablespoons fat
1/2 cup grated cheese
1 teaspoon salt
1/8 teaspoon pepper

Cut meat into small pieces and moisten with a little milk or stock. Spread a layer of rice in greased baking dish. Place several small pieces of fat on top and sprinkle with grated cheese. Season with salt and pepper. Then add layer of chopped meat, several pieces of fat and a little grated cheese. Repeat. Bake in moderate oven (350°F.) 15 to 20 minutes. Serves 6.

A different one every time is the score of the clever hostess with her meat pies

MEAT AND VEGETABLE PIE

1 onion, diced
2 tablespoons fat
2 cups cubed cooked meat
1 1/2 tablespoons flour
1 1/4 cups milk or gravy
1 tablespoon Worcestershire sauce
1 cup cooked peas
1 cup sliced cooked carrots
1 cup sautéed mushrooms
Salt and pepper
1/2 recipe pastry

Brown onion in fat and add meat. Brown well. Remove meat and onion from skillet and add flour, milk or gravy and Worcestershire sauce to remaining fat. Blend well. Fill greased baking dish with meat, vegetables and sauce; season and cover with pastry. Make several gashes in pastry to permit steam to escape. Seal around edges by pressing with a fork. Bake in hot oven (425°F.) until crust is brown, about 30 minutes. Serves 6.

EGGPLANT STUFFED WITH HAM

1 large eggplant
Salted water
1 onion, minced
1 green pepper, chopped fine
2 tomatoes, quartered
2 tablespoons butter
½ teaspoon salt
⅛ teaspoon pepper
1 cup diced boiled ham
Bread crumbs

Wash and dry eggplant and cut off a slice from top. Scoop out inside to within ½ inch of skin. Cover shell with salted water and set aside. Chop eggplant pulp and combine with onion, pepper and tomatoes. Cook in a small amount of boiling salted water until tender. Drain and mash. Add butter, salt, pepper and ham. Drain shell well and fill with mixture. Sprinkle top with bread crumbs and bake in moderate oven (350°F.) about 25 minutes. Serves 4 to 6.

LEFTOVER COOKED BACON

Reheat in skillet until very crisp; drain on absorbent paper; chop fine. Use:
For canapé spreads: Combine with chopped chicken livers; liver paste; pâté de foie gras; with chopped onion or chopped pickle. Add to French dressing; or make into hot bacon sauce.
As sandwich spread; with jelly or peanut butter.
Sprinkle over baked vegetables with cheese (such as cauliflower, Brussels sprouts, broccoli, corn, peppers or cabbage).
Sprinkle over broiled or baked fish.
Sprinkle over broiled tomatoes.
In stuffed baked potatoes.
Over candied sweet potatoes.
In bean, baked bean and lentil soups.

Peppers are delicious whether stuffed with leftover meat, fish, vegetables or cereals

FRICADELLONS WITH NOODLES

1 large onion, chopped
2 tablespoons fat
1 cup dry bread softened in 1 cup water
2 cups leftover ground meat
1 egg
2 tablespoons chopped parsley
⅛ teaspoon allspice
¼ teaspoon salt
Dash pepper
3 cups leftover cooked noodles
½ cup warm milk

Brown onion lightly in 1 tablespoon fat. Press water from bread; add onion, meat, egg, parsley, and seasoning. Mix well. Shape into small balls or flat cakes and sauté until crisp in remaining fat. Moisten noodles with warm milk and reheat. Make a ring of noodles, fill center with Succotash and border with the fricadellons. Serves 4.

Combine all ingredients, add 2 additional eggs and pack into a greased ring mold. Bake at 325°F. 1 hour or until firm.

STUFFED PEPPERS

6 green peppers
1¼ cups minced cooked meat (veal, chicken or ham)
1¼ cups moistened bread crumbs
Salt and pepper
1 tablespoon fat
½ onion, grated
1 cup water or stock

Cut a slice from stem end of each pepper. Remove seeds and par boil peppers 10 minutes. Mix minced cooked meat with moistened bread crumbs, add salt, pepper, melted fat and onion. Stuff peppers with mixture and place in baking pan. Add water or stock. Bake in moderate oven (375°F.) 30 minutes, basting frequently. Serves 6.

ROAST BEEF SALAD

1 cup diced cooked beef
2 hard-cooked eggs, sliced
2 tomatoes, quartered
1 small head lettuce
French dressing or mayonnaise

Toss first 2 ingredients together. Serve on lettuce with French dressing or mayonnaise. Serves 6. Use diced cooked ham, tongue or corned beef instead of the beef, if desired.

IRISH STEW WITH DUMPLINGS

2½ cups meat stock or water
1½ pounds cooked lamb, diced
1 teaspoon salt
¼ teaspoon pepper
2 onions, sliced
1 turnip, diced
2 carrots, diced
1 stalk celery, diced
Sprig parsley
2 cups cubed potatoes

Add enough stock to cover meat; season. Add onions, turnip, carrots, celery, parsley and potatoes and cook 35 to 40 minutes. Thicken liquid with flour if necessary and serve stew with dumplings. Serves 6.

DUMPLINGS FOR STEW

2 cups sifted flour
1¼ teaspoons baking powder
¾ teaspoon salt
1 tablespoon butter
Milk (about ⅔ cup)

Sift dry ingredients together. Cut in butter. Add milk to make a soft dough. Turn onto floured board and roll ½ inch thick. Cut into small squares, drop into hot liquid, cover closely and cook 20 minutes. Makes 12.

SHEPHERD'S PIE

1 tablespoon fat
2 cups hot mashed potatoes
2 cups cold lamb, cut into small cubes
1½ cups lamb gravy

Grease a shallow baking dish and spread ½ inch thick with mashed potatoes. Fill with lamb and gravy and garnish top with mashed potatoes in large spoonfuls. Bake in moderate oven (375°F.) about 20 minutes. Serves 4 to 6.

LEFTOVER MEAT AND STOCK

Any small pieces of uncooked meat may be made attractive by broiling on the skewer or preparing as a mixed grill. For any of these there need be only a few pieces of meat with accessories such as a few mushrooms, a few slices of tomato, an onion or two, small cubes of eggplant, turnip or other vegetables, a few slices of bacon or a tiny sausage or two. To cook "en brochette" (arrange them on skewers) dip in melted butter, and broil. Bacon and sausage need no butter.

LEFTOVER MEAT STOCK — Always save bones from cooked meats for soup stock. Smoked meat bones, such as ham, tongue roots and ham hocks can be made into stock for lentil, navy bean or split pea soups.

Bones from broiled steaks, roasts, braised short ribs, veal and lamb chops may also be utilized for soup stock. Place bones in soup kettle in cold water with a cut onion, celery, and carrots; add canned tomatoes, salt, pepper and ¼ teaspoon ginger and heat to boiling. Simmer for 1 hour. Add any leftover gravy to stock.

Use leftover meat stock in sauces, aspics and with vegetables.

LEFTOVER GRAVY — If fat gathers on top, remove before using. Thin the gravy and use instead of meat stock in any of the preceding recipes.

Use instead of milk in scrambled eggs.

Combine with stock in meat sauces.

Combine with leftover cooked meats in meat pies, turnover, or shortcakes.

CRACKLING BREAD

1½ cups white corn meal
¾ cup sifted flour
½ teaspoon baking soda
2 teaspoons baking powder
¼ teaspoon salt
1 cup sour milk
1 cup cracklings, diced

Mix dry ingredients together Add milk and stir in cracklings. Form into oblong cakes and place in greased baking pan. Bake in hot oven (400°F.) 30 minutes. Makes 8 to 10 small cakes.

This gorgeous shepherd's pie is dressed up enough for any occasion

JELLIED CHICKEN BOUILLON

1 tablespoon unflavored gelatin
¼ cup cold water
2 cups hot chicken stock
Salt
1 tablespoon chopped parsley

Soften gelatin in water for 5 minutes and dissolve in hot stock. Season with salt and add parsley. Chill. When firm cut into cubes or beat slightly with a fork. Serve in cold bouillon cups. Serves 4.

If the feet were used in making chicken stock, no gelatin need be added.

CHICKEN HASH

1½ cups chopped cooked chicken
1 cup diced boiled potatoes
2 tablespoons fat
1 tablespoon minced parsley
Salt and pepper
½ cup stock or water

Mix chicken and potatoes together. Melt fat, add first mixture, parsley, seasoning and stock and cook until browned. One-fourth cup chopped green pepper may be added. Serves 4.

Golden brown and crispy chicken croquettes never lose their lure for us

CHICKEN CAKES

2 eggs, slightly beaten
1 tablespoon cream
Salt and pepper
1 cup cooked chopped chicken
Bread crumbs, rolled fine
½ cup minced celery
1 cup Medium White Sauce

Add 1 egg, cream, salt and pepper to chopped chicken. Form into small flat cakes, dip into remaining egg mixed with a little milk and roll in bread crumbs. Fry until well browned. Add celery to white sauce and pour over cakes. Serve on toast and garnish with parsley. Serves 4.

CHICKEN CRO-QUETTES

1¾ cups ground cooked chicken
¼ teaspoon celery salt
1 teaspoon lemon juice
Few drops onion juice
1 teaspoon chopped parsley
Salt and pepper
1 cup Thick White Sauce
Fine crumbs
1 egg, beaten

Add chicken, celery salt, lemon juice, onion juice, parsley, salt and pepper to white sauce. Cool, shape, dip into crumbs, then into egg and again into crumbs. Fry in hot deep fat (375°F.) from 2 to 5 minutes. Serves 4.

CHICKEN CORN CAKE

¼ pound mushrooms
1 tablespoon butter, melted
1 tablespoon flour
1 cup chicken stock
Salt and pepper
2 cups diced cooked chicken
Leftover corn bread

Sauté mushrooms in butter. Remove mushrooms, add flour to remaining butter and mix well; add stock and cook until thickened, stirring constantly. Season. Add chicken and mushrooms to sauce. Cut corn bread into 4-inch squares and split. Cover lower halves with some of the chicken mixture. Place on these the top crusts and cover with more of the chicken mixture. Serves 4.

CHICKEN STOCK

Leftover chicken stock may be used:

1. As a base for clear soups and bouillons.

2. In cream soups to enrich flavor.

3. Combined with white sauce for use with chicken.

4. In chicken gravies and sauces.

5. In aspic for jellied soup or salad.

CREAMED CHICKEN

1 tablespoon parsley
2 cups diced cooked chicken
1 cup Medium White Sauce
1 egg yolk
2 tablespoons milk

Add parsley and chicken to white sauce and heat. Beat egg yolk, adding milk and pour into mixture. Cook for 2 minutes, stirring constantly. Serve in ring or in Croustades. Serves 6.
Mushrooms or chopped cooked eggs, chopped pimientos and olives may be added.

SCALLOPED CHICKEN

2 cups chicken broth
2 tablespoons flour
2 tablespoons chicken fat
Salt and pepper
Bread crumbs
2 cups diced cooked chicken
2 cups sliced cooked potatoes

Thicken broth with a paste made of flour and fat and season with salt and pepper. Fill baking dish with alternate layers of bread crumbs, chicken and potatoes. Cover top with crumbs. Add gravy and a few bits of butter and bake in moderate oven (350° F.) 30 minutes. Serves 5.

BROWNED CHICKEN HASH

1½ cups chopped cooked chicken
1 cup diced boiled potatoes
1 tablespoon chopped parsley
½ teaspoon salt
¼ cup chopped green pepper
½ cup stock or water
2 tablespoons fat

Combine chicken, potatoes, parsley, salt, green pepper and stock. Melt fat in a skillet, spread chicken mixture evenly over the bottom and cook slowly until browned on bottom. Fold over as for omelet, serve on hot platter and garnish with parsley. Serves 4.

CHICKEN MOUSSE

2 cups ground cooked chicken
½ cup mayonnaise
2 tablespoons lemon juice
¾ teaspoon ground celery seed
¾ cup heavy cream, whipped
Salt and pepper
1½ tablespoons unflavored gelatin
½ cup cold chicken stock
Lettuce
Radish Roses

Blend chicken, mayonnaise, lemon juice and celery seed; fold in the whipped cream and season. Soften gelatin in chicken stock for 5 minutes, dissolve over hot water and cool. Fold into chicken mixture. Pour into a ring mold and chill until firm. Unmold, fill center with tiny lettuce cups and garnish with radish roses. Serves 4 to 6.

FROZEN CHICKEN SALAD

1½ cups diced cooked chicken
¾ cup drained crushed pineapple
½ cup chopped pecans
1 cup heavy cream, whipped
1 cup mayonnaise

Toss chicken, pineapple and nuts together. Fold cream into mayonnaise, add to chicken mixture and freeze from 2 to 3 hours, or until firm. Serves 6.

Creamed chicken takes on a new glamour when it appears in a noodle or rice ring

MOCK TERRAPIN STEW

2 tablespoons flour
½ cup melted fat
1 pint scalded milk
Salt and pepper
6 egg yolks
3 cups diced cooked chicken
½ cup sherry

Blend flour with fat and add milk. Cook until slightly thickened, stirring constantly. Season. Cover and keep hot. Just before serving remove from heat, add slowly to beaten egg yolks, stirring constantly. Add diced chicken and wine and serve at once. Serves 6.

HOT CHICKEN SANDWICHES

½ cup stock
¼ cup evaporated milk
1 tablespoon flour
1 tablespoon butter
1 teaspoon onion juice
¼ teaspoon salt
1 cup minced cooked chicken
Thin slices toasted bread

Make a sauce of stock, milk, flour and butter. Add next 3 ingredients and heat thoroughly. Place on slices of toast and serve on a hot platter. Serves 2.

LEFTOVER FOWL

Cut cooked chicken into large pieces and reheat in leftover gravy. Cover split hot baking powder biscuits with the chicken and replace top of biscuits as for shortcake.

Arrange alternate layers of sliced chicken or turkey in buttered casserole with slices of cold stuffing. Pour gravy over this and top with reheated creamy mashed potatoes. Brush with butter and bake in moderate oven (350°F.) about 20 minutes or until potatoes are browned.

Season minced chicken or turkey with curry powder, combine with turkey gravy and fill bread croustades with mixture.

Sauté slices of chicken or turkey in butter; add 1 cup currant jelly and stir until melted. Serve on boiled rice in center of platter.

Reheat slices of roast duck in gravy; add sliced ripe or green olives and arrange on slices of fried corn-meal mush.

Slice cold turkey stuffing and fry; cover the slices with scrambled eggs.

SOUP FROM CHICKEN OR TURKEY BONES

Break the cooked bones and cover with cold water in soup kettle. Add celery, carrots, onion and a little salt; cover, and simmer for 2 hours. Strain and add 1 cup chicken or turkey meat, diced, for every quart of stock.

SOUP FROM CHICKEN FEET

Singe the feet, wash well and drop into scalding water for 10 minutes. Skin; break and cover with cold water in a kettle; season and cook until they fall apart. Strain and use as chicken stock.

Glistening stuffed onions on a favorite chop plate will intrigue your family and guests

BAKED STUFFED ONIONS

6 large onions
¾ cup soft bread crumbs
¾ cup chopped cooked chicken
¾ cup Thin White Sauce
1 egg yolk
Salt and pepper
½ cup buttered cracker crumbs

Remove skins from onions and boil in salted water, uncovered, for 10 minutes. Drain and turn upside down to cool. Remove centers of onions, leaving a shell sufficiently thick to retain shape Chop onion which was removed from center and combine with remaining ingredients except buttered cracker crumbs. Stuff onion shells with mixture, sprinkle with cracker crumbs, and bake in moderate oven (350°F.) until onions are tender — about 40 minutes. Serves 6.

TAMALE PIE

1 cup corn meal
4 cups water
1 teaspoon salt
1 medium onion
1 green or chili pepper
3 tablespoons olive oil
2½ cups cooked tomatoes
2 cups ground cooked fowl
1 teaspoon salt
Dash cayenne or chili powder

Cook corn meal, water and salt in top of double boiler 45 minutes. Chop onion and pepper and fry in hot oil. Add tomatoes, meat, salt and cayenne or chili and cook until thickened. Line a greased baking dish with half the mush, pour in meat mixture, cover with remaining mush and bake in moderately hot oven (375°F.) about 30 minutes or until top is lightly browned. Serves 6 to 8.

The pastry cook of your family will have a good time making these savory salmon rolls

SALMON ROLLS

1 recipe baking powder biscuits
1½ cups flaked salmon
1 small onion, chopped
1 green pepper, chopped
½ teaspoon salt

Roll biscuit dough to ¼-inch thickness on floured board. Combine salmon, onion, green pepper and salt; moisten slightly with salmon liquid, mix well and spread mixture on dough. Roll as for jelly roll and slice 1½ inches thick. Bake in greased pan in hot over (400°F.) ½ hour. Serves 6.

FISH PUFF

1 cup cooked fish
1 cup mashed potatoes
½ cup milk
Salt and pepper
2 eggs

Mix cooked fish with mashed potatoes, milk, salt and pepper. Stir in 1 egg, well beaten. Turn into mold and heat in moderate oven (350°F.). Beat white of remaining egg stiff and fold the beaten yolk seasoned with salt and pepper into it; heap this over the fish and brown. Serves 5.

FISH FRITTERS

1 pound cooked fish
3 eggs, separated
3 tablespoons flour
Salt and pepper
⅛ teaspoon minced garlic
1 tablespoon minced parsley

Mash fish. Beat egg yolks until light and thick, add flour, salt, pepper, garlic, parsley and fish. Add whites of eggs beaten to a froth. Drop by tablespoons into hot deep fat (360°F. to 370°F.) and fry until brown. Serves 4.

FISH CAKES

1 cup flaked cooked fish
1 teaspoon minced onion
1 teaspoon lemon juice
¼ teaspoon salt
Pepper
1 egg, slightly beaten
1 cup cold mashed potatoes
2 tablespoons flour
¼ cup fat

Combine fish, onion, lemon juice, seasoning, egg and potatoes. Form into cakes, coat with flour and sauté in hot fat. Serves 4.

FISH IN RAMEKINS

1 cup leftover fish
8 mussels or clams
½ cup bread crumbs
⅔ cup milk
1 clove garlic
1 teaspoon chopped parsley
1 onion, chopped
Salt and pepper
3 tablespoons fat
Buttered crumbs

Chop fish and mussels or clams. Add crumbs (soaked in 2 tablespoons of milk), garlic, parsley, onion, salt and pepper. Cook in fat several minutes. Stir in remaining milk and fill small ramekins or scallop shells. Cover with buttered crumbs and bake in moderate oven (350°F.) about 15 minutes. Serves 5.

SOUTHERN EGG-PLANT

1 large onion, sliced fine
3 tablespoons fat
1 large eggplant
1 cup uncooked rice
1 cup cooked shrimp
Salt and pepper

Sauté onion in melted fat. Pare eggplant; cut into cubes and combine with remaining ingredients. Steam in top of double boiler 30 to 35 minutes or until rice is tender. Pile on platter and garnish with parsley. Serves 6.

A loaf pan does just as well for the fish mold piquante

FISH MOLD PIQUANTE

½ tablespoon unflavored gelatin
¼ cup cold water
1½ teaspoons salt
1½ teaspoons mustard
Dash cayenne
2 egg yolks, slightly beaten
¾ cup milk
1½ tablespoons melted butter
4 tablespoons lemon juice
1 cup flaked salmon
Lettuce

Soften gelatin in cold water 5 minutes. Combine seasonings, egg yolks and milk in top of double boiler, and cook over hot water 6 to 8 minutes or until thickened, stirring constantly. Add butter, lemon juice and gelatin, stirring until gelatin is dissolved. Fold in salmon. Turn into fish mold; chill until firm. Unmold on bed of crisp lettuce and serve with Cucumber Cream Dressing. Serves 4.

FISH STOCK

The seasoned stock in which any fish or sea food is boiled should be used for Court Bouillon, for fish jelly or molds, and other fish dishes. It may be used instead of milk or water in any recipe calling for the former. Besides the fine flavor, this stock is high in sea minerals and should not be discarded. If fish is fried or baked the heads and bones may be used in Court Bouillon.

COURT BOUILLON

½ cup chopped carrots
1½ cups chopped onion
½ cup chopped celery
3 sprigs parsley
½ clove garlic, crushed
2 tablespoons butter
4 peppercorns
2 whole cloves
1 bay leaf
2 teaspoons salt
¼ cup vinegar
¼ teaspoon ground ginger
3 quarts water
2 pounds fish heads and trimmings

Sauté first 5 ingredients in butter 4 minutes; combine with remaining ingredients in soup kettle, cover and heat to boiling; simmer 5 minutes. Makes 3 quarts.
Use court bouillon as base for fish sauces, in fish soups, bisques or chowders. In cream soup use stock for part of milk.

KEDGEREE

2 cups cooked rice
2 cups flaked cooked fish
4 hard-cooked eggs, chopped
2 tablespoons minced parsley
½ cup cream or evaporated milk
1 teaspoon salt
⅛ teaspoon pepper

Combine all ingredients and re heat in top of a double boiler. Serve at once. Serves 6.

TUNA TURNOVERS

3 tablespoons fat
3 tablespoons flour
1 cup milk
¾ teaspoon salt
1 teaspoon Worcestershire sauce
1 cup flaked tuna
2 hard-cooked eggs, chopped
Pastry

Melt fat, blend in flour, add milk, and cook until thickened, stirring constantly. Add remaining ingredients, except pastry; mix well. Roll out pastry, cut into 3-inch squares, place a teaspoon of filling on each square, fold over to form a triangle. Press edges together, cut a gash in top, and bake in hot oven (400°F.) about 20 minutes. Makes 12.

SHRIMP AND WAX BEAN CURRY

2½ cups cooked wax beans
1 small onion, minced
1 tablespoon fat
1 tablespoon flour
1 teaspoon curry powder
½ teaspoon salt
⅛ teaspoon pepper
1 cup cooked shrimp

Drain beans, reserving liquor. Brown onion in fat, blend in flour, curry powder, salt and pepper. Add bean liquor slowly, cook until slightly thickened, stirring constantly. Add beans and shrimp, mix well and cook 3 minutes. Garnish with hard-cooked eggs if desired. Serves 6.

GREEN BEANS WITH BACON

½ cup lean bacon, diced
2 cups cooked green beans
½ cup sugar
½ cup vinegar
Salt and pepper

Fry bacon until crisp and add remaining ingredients. Cook slowly for about 8 minutes. Serves 6.

TOMATOES STUFFED WITH BEANS

6 tomatoes
2½ cups cooked Mexican beans
3 slices broiled bacon

Scoop out centers of tomatoes. Fill with beans and bake in moderate oven (350°F.) until beans are heated and tomato skins are slightly wrinkled. Top each with half-slice bacon. Serves 6.

CARROT CRO- QUETTES

2 cups puréed cooked carrots
1 tablespoon fat, melted
1 egg yolk, beaten
½ teaspoon salt
Dash nutmeg
Fine bread crumbs
1 bunch parsley

Combine carrot purée with fat, egg yolk, salt and nutmeg. Shape into carrot-shaped pyramids; roll in crumbs and chill for 2 hours. Fry in hot deep fat (375°-380°F.) for 3 to 6 minutes or until brown. Drain on absorbent paper. Arrange croquettes radiating from the center of a round platter, with parsley sprigs at the wide end to resemble carrot tops. Any leftover meat, fish, chicken or vegetables may be made into croquettes and decorated in the same manner. Serves 6.

Served with green beans these carrot croquettes with parsley tops are very nearly real

CARROTS AND PEAS

2 cups cubed cooked carrots
1 cup cooked peas
3 tablespoons butter
Salt
Pepper

Combine carrots and peas, heat and serve with melted butter. Season with salt and pepper. Serves 4.

WITH MINT — Combine carrots and peas as directed above, add ½ cup mint leaves and a little boiling water and boil for 5 minutes. Drain, add salt, pepper and butter and sprinkle with sugar. Serve with a garnish of fresh mint leaves.

GOLDEN MOUNTAIN

2 cups cooked mashed carrots
2 eggs, beaten slightly
¼ cup evaporated milk
1 teaspoon sugar
½ teaspoon salt

Combine ingredients and mix thoroughly. Place mixture in greased mold, set in pan of hot water and bake in moderate oven (350°F.) 45 minutes or until a knife inserted in the center comes out clean. Serves 4 to 6.

CORN CAKES

1 cup cooked corn, crushed
½ cup milk
2 teaspoons sugar
2 eggs, well beaten
¾ cup sifted flour
1 teaspoon baking powder
¼ teaspoon salt

Combine corn, milk, sugar and eggs. Sift flour with baking powder and salt. Combine mixtures. Fill greased muffin pans ⅔ full and bake in moderate oven (350°F.) 15 to 20 minutes or until browned. Makes 8 cakes.

BAKED BEAN CRO- QUETTES

2 cups baked beans
1 minced onion
1 teaspoon salt
¼ teaspoon pepper
1 egg, beaten
2 tablespoons water
Cracker crumbs, sifted

Mash beans with a fork, add onion, salt and pepper and shape into croquettes. Mix egg and water. Roll croquettes in crumbs, then in egg, in crumbs again and fry in deep fat (375°F.) until browned. Drain. Serves 4.

CORN OYSTERS

2 cups corn pulp
2 eggs, separated
2 tablespoons flour
½ teaspoon salt
¼ teaspoon pepper

To corn pulp, add beaten egg yolks, flour and seasoning. Add stiffly beaten egg whites and blend. Drop by teaspoons onto hot greased frying pan and brown. Serves 6.

SUCCOTASH

2 cups cooked corn
2 cups cooked Lima beans, fresh or dried
½ teaspoon salt
Dash pepper
2 tablespoons butter
½ cup milk

Combine corn and beans. Add seasonings, butter and milk and heat slowly. Serves 6. To vary—
1. Omit milk and increase butter to 4 tablespoons.
2. Add 2 tablespoons minced green pepper.
3. Add 4 tablespoons chopped pimiento.

The spinach or Swiss chard ring is luscious, piled high with a creamed filling

BAKED CORN AND TOMATOES

1½ cups cooked corn
1½ cups cooked tomatoes
1 teaspoon salt
Dash pepper
½ teaspoon sugar
¾ cup bread crumbs
2 tablespoons fat

Mix corn and tomatoes with seasonings and pour into greased baking dish. Spread with crumbs, dot with fat and bake in moderate oven (350°F.) ½ hour. Serves 5.

SPANISH LIMAS

1 onion, chopped
1 green pepper, chopped
2 tablespoons fat
2 cups strained cooked tomatoes
2 cups cooked dried Lima beans
½ teaspoon salt
¼ teaspoon pepper
1 teaspoon Worcestershire sauce
1 cup grated American cheese

Sauté onion and pepper in fat. Add tomatoes and simmer 10 minutes. Add beans and seasonings and cook 20 minutes. Place beans and cheese in a greased casserole and bake at 350°F. 20 minutes. Serves 6.

STUFFED ENDIVE

Cottage cheese
Salt and pepper
Chives, chopped
French endive
Stuffed olives
French dressing

Season cottage cheese with salt, pepper and chives. Fill crisp stalks of endive with cottage cheese. Arrange in petal fashion on a round chop plate and fill center with stuffed olives. Serve with French dressing.

MACEDOINE OF VEGETABLES

2 cups mixed cooked vegetables
1 teaspoon beef extract or ½ cup stock
1 teaspoon sugar
½ cup water
Salt and pepper
2 tablespoons butter

Combine ingredients and cook 8 to 10 minutes. Serves 3.

SPINACH OR SWISS CHARD RING

2 tablespoons butter
2 tablespoons flour
½ cup milk
3 eggs, separated
1¾ cups cooked chopped spinach or Swiss chard
½ teaspoon salt
⅛ teaspoon pepper
½ teaspoon grated onion

Melt butter, blend in flour, add milk and cook until thickened, stirring constantly. Add slowly to beaten egg yolks. Add spinach, salt, pepper and onion. Cook for 1 minute, then fold in stiffly beaten egg whites. Pour into greased ring mold, place in pan of hot water and bake in moderate oven (350°F.) until firm, about 30 minutes. Unmold and fill center with creamed fish or vegetables. Serves 6.

PEA-POD SOUP

Pods from 2 quarts peas
1 onion, diced
1 teaspoon salt
1 teaspoon pepper
1 teaspoon sugar
Dash nutmeg
2 cups milk
3 tablespoons butter
3 tablespoons flour

Wash pea pods and cut into pieces; cover with water and boil with onion for 1½ hours. Purée mixture, add seasonings, sugar, nutmeg and hot milk. Heat to boiling and thicken with butter and flour mixture. Serves 4.

POTATO PUFFS

2 cups mashed potatoes (without milk)
Salt and pepper
2 eggs, beaten

Mix seasoned mashed potatoes and eggs. Drop mixture from a spoon into hot deep fat (375°F.), fry until brown, about 2 minutes and drain on brown paper. Serve with a garnish of parsley. Serves 5.

VEGETABLE CROQUETTES

2 cups mashed, cooked vegetables
2¾ cups cracker or bread crumbs
Salt, pepper, nutmeg, chopped parsley
1 egg, beaten
2 tablespoons melted butter

Mix vegetables with 2 cups crumbs, season with salt, pepper, nutmeg and chopped parsley. Add egg and butter (and milk if mixture is dry). Form into cone-shaped croquettes. Roll in remaining cracker crumbs and fry in hot deep fat (375°F.) until browned. Serve hot with Thick White Sauce, garnished with chopped parsley. Serves 4.

SWEETPOTATO PIE

4 tablespoons butter
½ cup sugar
3 tablespoons lemon juice
1 tablespoon grated lemon rind
3 eggs, separated
¼ teaspoon cinnamon
2 cups mashed sweetpotatoes
1 cup top milk
1 unbaked Pastry shell

Cream butter until soft, add sugar gradually and continue to cream until sugar is well blended. Add lemon juice and rind. Add beaten egg yolks, cinnamon, potatoes and milk. Mix thoroughly and fold in stiffly beaten egg whites. Pour into pastry-lined pie plate. Bake in hot oven (425°F.) 10 minutes, then lower temperature to moderate (350°F.) and continue baking for about 40 minutes longer or until a knife inserted in the center comes out clean. Makes 1 (9-inch) pie.

DUTCH LETTUCE

1 pound leaf lettuce
2 cold boiled potatoes, diced
3 thick slices bacon
½ cup vinegar
2 hard-cooked eggs, sliced

Shred lettuce and mix lightly with potatoes. Cut bacon into squares; fry and sprinkle over lettuce. Mix vinegar with bacon fat and pour over salad. Garnish with eggs. Serves 6.

Here's a sweetpotato pie that melts in your mouth

POTATO SOUFFLE

2 cups hot mashed potatoes
2 tablespoons butter
2 eggs, separated
1 cup milk

Combine potatoes, butter, egg yolks beaten until light, and milk. Fold in stiffly beaten egg whites. Mix lightly and pile mixture in greased baking dish. Place in pan of hot water and bake in moderately slow oven (325°F.) 20 to 30 minutes. Serves 4.

SWEETPOTATO CASSEROLE

6 cooked sweetpotatoes, sliced
½ cup brown sugar
5 tablespoons butter
2 medium oranges
½ cup orange juice
¼ cup strained honey
¼ cup fine bread crumbs

Arrange layer of potatoes in greased casserole, sprinkle with 3 tablespoons brown sugar, dot with 2 tablespoons butter and cover with a layer of thinly sliced, unpeeled oranges. Repeat layers. Over all, pour orange juice mixed with honey. Combine crumbs with remaining brown sugar and butter and sprinkle over top. Cover casserole and bake in moderate oven (350°F.) 30 to 40 minutes, removing cover last 15 minutes. Serves 6.

SALAD CONTAIN-ERS AND FILLERS FROM LEFTOVERS

ARTICHOKES — Remove outside leaves from cooked artichokes. Spread center leaves and remove chokes. Cut stems straight so that artichokes will stand upright. Fill centers with mixture of sliced beans, carrots, asparagus tips or peas marinated in French dressing. Serve with mayonnaise between artichoke leaves.

Other Fillings —
Highly seasoned coleslaw.
Chopped hard-cooked egg, minced onion and chopped beet centers.
Chopped peanuts, celery and chopped beet centers.
Chopped dill pickle and beet centers, covered with grated sharp cheese.
Chopped celery, green beans, flavored with horse-radish.

BEET SAUCERS — Cut thick slices from cooked or pickled beets and hollow out to hold a small serving of salad. If slices are small 2 or 3 may be used for each serving.

CUCUMBER CUPS — Peel or score large cucumbers. Cut into 2-inch lengths and remove centers. Place in salted ice water for 1 hour or until needed. Drain; fill with any of the artichoke fillings or with one of the following:

1. Shrimp or crab flakes with lemon juice or mayonnaise or marinated in French dressing.
2. Minced green pepper, celery and uncooked carrots with French dressing.
3. Chicken or meat salad.

CUCUMBER BOATS — Cut a slice from 1 side of small cucumbers, hollow out in boat shape. Marinate in French dressing and chill. Fill with fish or sea food salad, or other suitable mixtures.

Try serving your relishes in small vegetable cups on the platter of cold cuts

VEGETABLE STOCK

The juices from canned or cooked vegetables, with the water in which they are cooked, are rich in vitamins and minerals and should always be saved. Keep in a jar in the refrigerator (any or all combinations are good) and use as a base for vegetable soup, or in combination with meat stock for meat soups. Cook the soupbone in water as usual and add the vegetable stock at the last to preserve the vitamins.

STEAMED CHOCO-LATE PUDDING

2 cups sifted flour
4½ teaspoons baking powder
¼ teaspoon salt
1 cup corn sirup
½ cup water
½ cup hot mashed potatoes
1 egg, beaten
2½ ounces (squares) chocolate
3 tablespoons shortening, melted

Mix and sift flour, baking powder and salt together. Mix sirup with water and add to flour mixture. Stir in potatoes and egg. Add chocolate, melted over hot water, and shortening. Mix well, pour into greased individual molds and steam for 2 hours. Serve with any desired sauce. Serves 5.

SWEETPOTATO WAFFLES

¾ cup sifted flour
2 teaspoons baking powder
¼ teaspoon salt
1 tablespoon sugar
1 teaspoon nutmeg
1 egg, separated
1 cup milk
1 cup mashed sweetpotato
4 tablespoons fat, melted

Sift flour, baking powder, salt, sugar and nutmeg together. Combine with beaten egg yolk and milk and beat until smooth. Add sweetpotato and fat and continue beating. Fold in stiffly beaten egg white. Bake in heated waffle iron until brown. Sprinkle with sugar and cinnamon and serve with roast duck or turkey. Serves 4.

VEGETABLE PUFFS

1 cup leftover mashed potatoes
2 eggs, beaten
3 tablespoons milk
1 teaspoon baking powder
1 cup grated fresh corn or canned whole kernel
½ cup sifted flour
1 tablespoon chopped parsley
1 teaspoon salt

Mix all ingredients together thoroughly. Drop by teaspoons into hot deep fat (350°F.) and cook until brown. Drain on absorbent paper. Makes about 8 puffs.

CHEESE BLINTZES

Filling:

1½ cups cream-style cottage
  cheese, drained
¼ cup thick sour cream
1½ tablespoons sugar
½ teaspoon salt

Pancakes:

1½ cups sifted flour
3 tablespoons sugar
½ teaspoon salt
2 eggs, well beaten
2 tablespoons butter, melted
1¼ cups milk
  Oil or butter
  Thick sour cream

Mix thoroughly the ingredients for filling; place in refrigerator. Sift flour, sugar and salt together. Add melted butter and milk to beaten eggs. Combine egg mixture with dry ingredients. Beat with rotary beater until smooth. Heat a heavy 6-inch skillet; grease lightly. Pour only enough batter to coat skillet thinly; tilt skillet back and forth to spread batter evenly. Cook pancake over medium heat about 2 minutes or until lightly browned on bottom and firm to touch on top. Remove to a plate, brown side up. Stack pancakes. Spoon 1½ tablespoons filling on center of brown side of pancake. Roll, tucking in edges to retain filling. Brown on all sides over medium heat in lightly greased large, heavy skillet. Serve at once with thick sour cream. Serves 4.

SPICED CRUMB PUDDING

1 cup dry bread crumbs
1 cup sour milk
¼ cup shortening
1 cup brown sugar
2 tablespoons molasses
½ cup sifted flour
½ teaspoon cloves
½ teaspoon cinnamon
1 teaspoon baking soda
¾ cup raisins

Soak crumbs in sour milk for ½ hour. Cream shortening and sugar together until fluffy, add molasses and beat well. Sift flour with spices and soda and add to creamed mixture. Add raisins and crumbs and beat thoroughly. Bake in a buttered baking ring in slow oven (300°F.) 45 minutes. Serve hot or cold with any pudding sauce. Serves 8.

A bowl that fits the center of your pudding ring mold is just the thing for sauce

BUTTERMILK SOUP

3 eggs
½ cup sugar
2 tablespoons grated lemon peel
2 quarts (8 cups) buttermilk

Beat eggs until very thick. Gradually add sugar, beating thoroughly after each addition. Beat in grated lemon peel. Pour buttermilk into the egg mixture gradually, stirring until blended. Chill in refrigerator about 2 hours and serve the day it is prepared.
About 2½ quarts soup.

HERRING BITS IN SOUR CREAM

1 16-ounce jar herring fillets
1 cup thick sour cream
3 tablespoons lemon juice
1 large onion, sliced thin
1 tablespoon peppercorns
1 teaspoon salt

Drain jar of herring fillets. Mix together remaining ingredients and pour over herring. Stir carefully with a fork to coat all pieces evenly. Cover; let stand in refrigerator at least 2 hours before serving. Garnish with lemon slices and paprika. Makes about 3 cups.

BEAN SOUP

1 cup navy beans
3 quarts water
Salt and pepper
1 small onion, grated
1 cup thick sour cream

Soak beans overnight in water and boil until they have consistency of thick cream and have cooked down to 3 pints. Add salt, pepper and onion. Heat to boiling and add sour cream. Serves 7.

CORN-MEAL SOUR MILK WAFFLES

2 cups corn meal
3 cups water
2 teaspoons salt
2 tablespoons butter
4 eggs
2 cups sifted flour
1 teaspoon baking soda
1 cup sweet milk
Sour milk (about 1¼ cups)

Cook corn meal, water, salt and butter in top of double boiler for 10 minutes, stirring frequently. Cool. Beat eggs until light and add to mush. Sift flour with soda and add alternately with sweet milk. Add enough sour milk to make a thin batter. Bake in hot waffle iron until brown. Makes 12 waffles.

DATE-FILLED OATMEAL COOKIES

1 pound pitted dates
1 cup white sugar
2 cups hot water
1 cup shortening
1 cup brown sugar
¼ cup sour milk
2 cups oatmeal
½ teaspoon baking soda
1 teaspoon salt
Enough flour to roll

Combine first 3 ingredients and cook together until thick. Cool. Cream shortening, add sugar and remaining ingredients, adding flour last. Roll mixture thin and cut half the cookies with round cutter. Cut remainder with doughnut cutter. Bake in moderate oven (350°F.) 15 minutes. Place together with 1 spoonful of date mixture on the round cookie and top with the cookie with the hole in it. If put together just before serving they will remain crisp. Makes 2 dozen cookies. To vary, use figs or raisins for dates, or combine all 3 with nut meats. Or use jelly, jam or marmalade.

MOLASSES COOKIES

¾ cup melted shortening
1 cup molasses
1 cup brown sugar
1 cup thick sour milk
6 cups sifted flour
½ teaspoon salt
2 teaspoons ginger
4 teaspoons baking soda
1 tablespoon lemon extract

Mix melted shortening, molasses and sugar until smooth. Add sour milk, then flour sifted with salt, ginger and soda. Add lemon extract. Mix to a smooth stiff dough and chill until firm. Roll out on a lightly floured surface to a thickness of ⅓ inch. Cut into crescents or other shapes. Place on greased baking sheet and bake in a moderate oven (350°F.) 8 to 10 minutes. Roll thin for crisp cookies. Makes 150 cookies.

PRUNE NUT BREAD

1 tablespoon shortening
1 cup sugar
1 egg, beaten
½ cup prune juice
1 cup sour milk
2 cups whole-wheat flour
1 cup sifted white flour
4 teaspoons baking powder
½ teaspoon baking soda
½ teaspoon salt
2 cups chopped, pitted, cooked prunes
1 cup chopped walnuts

Cream shortening with sugar. Add egg and blend well. Combine prune juice and sour milk; add alternately with whole-wheat flour to first mixture. Sift white flour, baking powder, soda and salt together 3 times. Add with prunes and walnuts to first mixture and beat thoroughly. Pour into greased loaf pan and bake in moderate oven (350°F.) 1 hour. Makes 2 small loaves.

SOUR CREAM SPICE COOKIES

⅓ cup shortening
2 cups brown sugar
2 eggs, beaten
1 teaspoon vanilla
3 cups sifted cake flour
1 teaspoon baking soda
1 teaspoon cinnamon
½ teaspoon cloves
½ teaspoon nutmeg
½ teaspoon salt
⅔ cup thick sour cream

Cream shortening and sugar until fluffy. Add eggs and vanilla and mix well. Sift dry ingredients together and add alternately with sour cream to creamed mixture. Mix well. Drop from teaspoon onto a greased baking sheet and bake in moderate oven (350°F.) about 12 minutes. Makes about 3½ dozen cookies.

Properly used leftovers keep the cookie jar full

SOUR MILK GRIDDLE-CAKES

1½ cups sifted flour
1 teaspoon baking soda
½ teaspoon salt
1 tablespoon sugar
2 eggs
1 cup sour milk or buttermilk
1 tablespoon melted butter

Sift dry ingredients together. Beat eggs, add sour milk and butter, and add to dry ingredients gradually, beating until smooth. Drop from spoon onto hot greased griddle and brown on both sides. Makes 18 griddlecakes.

FLAPJACKS

2 cups sifted flour
1½ teaspoons baking soda
½ teaspoon salt
1 tablespoon sugar
2 eggs
2 cups sour milk or buttermilk
1½ tablespoons melted butter

Sift flour, soda, salt and sugar together. Beat eggs until light, add milk, then add gradually to flour mixture. Beat until smooth and free from lumps and add melted butter. Pour batter into a pitcher. Heat and grease a griddle. Pour in enough batter to make a cake about 5 inches in diameter. Cook until brown underneath, turn and brown on other side. Makes 24 flapjacks.

CRISP CORN BREAD

2 cups corn meal
1 teaspoon salt
1 teaspoon baking soda
1 tablespoon shortening, melted
2 cups sour milk or buttermilk

Mix corn meal, salt and soda together, add shortening and sour milk and mix well. Pour to a depth of not over ¾ inch in a greased shallow pan. Bake in moderate oven (375°F.) without browning. When it begins to shrink from the sides of pan, remove from oven, brush top with melted butter and return to hot oven (425°F.) to brown. Repeat twice in order to get brown crisp crust. Serves 6.

MAPLE SIRUP GINGERBREAD

1 cup maple sirup
1 cup sour cream
1 egg, beaten
2⅓ cups sifted flour
1¾ teaspoons baking soda
1½ teaspoons ginger
½ teaspoon salt
4 tablespoons melted shortening

Blend maple sirup, cream and egg together. Sift dry ingredients and stir into liquid, beating well. Add shortening and beat thoroughly. Pour into a greased oblong cake pan and bake in moderate oven (350°F.) 30 to 40 minutes. Serves 8 to 10.

RYE PANCAKES

1 cup rye flour
1 cup sifted white flour
1 egg, beaten
6 tablespoons molasses
1 cup sour milk or buttermilk
1 teaspoon baking soda

Mix rye and white flour together, combine egg, molasses and sour milk in which soda has been dissolved. Mix with dry ingredients to form a stiff batter. Drop by teaspoons into hot deep fat (360° F.) and fry until brown. Serve with maple sirup. Makes 24.

TENDER-RICH BUTTERMILK BISCUITS

2 cups sifted flour
2 teaspoons baking powder
1 teaspoon salt
⅓ cup lard, hydrogenated vegetable shortening, or all-purpose shortening
¾ cup buttermilk
Milk

Sift together the flour, baking powder and salt. Cut shortening in with a pastry blender or two knives until mixture resembles coarse cornmeal. Make a well in center of dry ingredients. Add buttermilk all at once. Stir with fork only until dough follows fork. Gently form dough into a ball and put on lightly floured surface. Knead lightly 10 or 15 times. Roll out to ½ inch thickness. Cut with floured cutter or knife. Put biscuits on baking sheet, close together if soft-sided biscuits are desired, or 1 inch apart for crusty sides. Lightly brush tops of biscuits with milk. Bake at 450°F. 10 to 15 minutes or until golden brown. Makes 2 dozen 1½ inch biscuits.

If you like, frost and decorate your gingerbread, then cut into squares

SAUERBRATEN

4 pounds beef chuck or rump
Salt and pepper
1 onion, sliced
3 bay leaves
1 teaspoon peppercorns
Vinegar and water
½ cup sugar
¼ cup raisins
4 to 6 gingersnaps
1 cup thick sour cream

Rub meat with salt and pepper. Place in deep earthen dish with onion, bay leaves and peppercorns. Heat enough water and vinegar to cover (equal parts if vinegar is strong); add ¼ cup sugar. Pour while hot over meat. Cover and keep in a cool place for 3 to 4 days. Remove meat from liquid and brown in hot oven (450°F.) 20 minutes. Add 1 cup spiced liquid, cover and cook in a slow oven (300°F.) 3 hours or until tender. Add more of the vinegar during the cooking if necessary. Remove the meat, slice for serving and keep hot. Strain the liquid; skim off fat. Melt remaining sugar (¼ cup) in skillet, add strained liquid gradually, then raisins and gingersnaps. Cook until thickened and smooth; add sour cream and when hot pour over meat. Serves 10.

SAUERKRAUT VIENNESE

3 cups sauerkraut
3 whole cloves
1 bay leaf
½ teaspoon salt
1 cup sour cream
1 pound link sausage

Place sauerkraut, cloves, bay leaf and salt in a saucepan and cook until the liquid has evaporated. Remove cloves and bay leaf, add sour cream and reheat. Bake sausages in moderate oven (350°F.) until brown. Place sauerkraut on a platter and top with baked sausages. Serves 6.

HASSENPFEFFER

1 rabbit
Vinegar and water
1 large onion, sliced
Salt and pepper
Cloves, bay leaves, fat
1 cup thick sour cream

Cut rabbit into serving portions place in jar and cover with equal parts vinegar and water. Add onion, salt and pepper, cloves and bay leaves. Let meat remain in this solution for 2 days, remove meat and brown in hot fat, turning often. Add some of the sauce in which the meat was pickled. Simmer until meat is tender, about 30 minutes. Just before serving, stir sour cream into sauce. Serves 4 to 6.

CHICKEN AND MUSHROOM SALAD—2 cups diced cooked chicken, ½ cup cold sautéed mushrooms, ½ cup chopped celery, 6 grapefruit segments and ¾ cup mayonnaise or sour cream salad dressing.

CHICKEN AND OLIVE SALAD— 2 cups diced cooked chicken, ½ cup chopped celery, ½ cup sliced stuffed olives and ¾ cup mayonnaise or sour cream salad dressing.

You will enjoy sour cream potato salad served on cold cuts for the evening snack

SOUR CREAM POTATO SALAD

4 cups diced cooked potatoes
½ cup diced cucumber
1 tablespoon minced onion
¾ teaspoon celery seed
1½ teaspoons salt
½ teaspoon pepper
3 hard-cooked eggs
1½ cups sour cream
½ cup mayonnaise
¼ cup vinegar
1 teaspoon prepared mustard

Combine potatoes, cucumber, onion, celery seed, salt and pepper. Toss together lightly. Separate yolks from whites of eggs. Dice whites and add to potato mixture. Mash yolks and combine with sour cream, mayonnaise, vinegar, and mustard. Add to potatoes and toss together lightly. Allow to stand 15 minutes before serving. Garnish with crisp salad greens. Serves 8.

SOUR CREAM SALAD DRESSING

1 teaspoon salt
1 teaspoon sugar
⅛ teaspoon cayenne
1 tablespoon lemon juice
2 tablespoons vinegar
1 cup sour cream

Combine seasonings with lemon juice and vinegar, add cream and beat until smooth and thick. Makes about 1¼ cups dressing.

Scoop out spice puffs and fill with fruit garnished with whipped cream

SPICED PUFFS

⅓ cup shortening
1 cup brown sugar
1 egg, beaten
1 teaspoon vanilla
2 cups sifted flour
1 teaspoon baking soda
1½ teaspoons cinnamon
½ teaspoon cloves
¼ teaspoon nutmeg
⅛ teaspoon salt
1 cup sour milk

Cream shortening, add sugar and cream until fluffy. Add egg and vanilla and beat. Sift flour, soda, spices and salt together 3 times. Add dry ingredients alternately with milk to the creamed mixture, blending after each addition. Half fill greased muffin pans with batter and bake in moderate oven (350°F.) 15 minutes. Makes 16 puffs.

OLD LADY CAKE

¼ cup butter or other shortening
1 cup brown sugar
1 egg, well beaten
2 cups sifted cake flour
1½ teaspoons baking powder
½ teaspoon baking soda
½ teaspoon nutmeg
½ teaspoon allspice
½ teaspoon ground cloves
½ teaspoon cinnamon
¼ teaspoon salt
1 cup sour milk

Cream butter and sugar together. Add egg and beat thoroughly. Sift flour, baking powder, soda, nutmeg, all-spice, cloves, cinnamon, and salt together 3 times. Add dry ingredients and milk alternately to creamed mixture. Bake in a greased tube pan in a moderate oven (350°F.) for 45-60 minutes. Makes 1 (9-inch) cake.

STRAWBERRY JAM CUPCAKES

1 cup sugar
½ cup shortening
2 eggs, beaten
2 cups sifted cake flour
½ teaspoon salt
1 teaspoon cinnamon
1 teaspoon nutmeg
1 teaspoon baking soda
½ cup sour milk
1 cup strawberry jam

Cream sugar with shortening until fluffy, add eggs and blend. Sift flour, salt, spices and soda together and add alternately with milk to creamed mixture. Fold in jam and bake in greased muffin pans in moderate oven (375°F.) 20 to 25 minutes. Remove from pans and frost with any favorite frosting. Makes 20 cupcakes.

SOUR CREAM BISCUITS

2 cups sifted flour
1 teaspoon baking soda
1 teaspoon baking powder
1 teaspoon salt
1 cup thick sour cream

Sift dry ingredients together. Gradually work into the cream, making a soft dough, and roll out ½ inch thick. Cut with a large biscuit cutter, place on a greased pan and bake in hot oven (400° F.) about 12 to 15 minutes. Serve hot with maple sirup, preserves or honey. The same recipe may be used for shortcakes or as a pastry for meat pies. Makes 14 (2-inch) biscuits.

BRAN MUFFINS

2 eggs
½ cup sugar
¼ cup molasses
1½ cups sour milk
2½ tablespoons shortening, melted
1½ cups sifted flour
1 teaspoon salt
1½ teaspoons baking soda
2½ cups bran
½ cup chopped raisins, dates, prunes or figs

Beat eggs, add sugar, molasses, sour milk and shortening. Sift flour with salt and baking soda; add bran and raisins or other fruit, then the liquid mixture, mixing only enough to moisten all the flour. Fill greased muffin pans ⅔ full and bake in hot oven (400°F.) 25 minutes. Makes 1½ dozen muffins.

SOUR CREAM CAKE

2 eggs, separated
1 cup sugar
1 cup sour cream
1½ cups sifted cake flour
1 teaspoon baking soda
1 teaspoon baking powder
¼ teaspoon salt
½ teaspoon nutmeg
½ teaspoon cinnamon
½ cup chopped nut meats
1 cup raisins

Beat egg yolks, add sugar and sour cream and blend. Sift flour, soda, baking powder, salt, nutmeg and cinnamon together. Add with nuts and raisins to first mixture, stirring only enough to moisten all the flour. Fold in stiffly beaten egg whites. Pour into greased loaf pan. Bake in moderate oven (350°F.) 35 to 45 minutes. When cool, cover with any icing. Makes 1 (8x8 inch) cake.

Omit spices, nuts and raisins; bake in loaf pan; sprinkle with confectioners' sugar and nuts, or butter, cinnamon and sugar.

DRIED APRICOT CAKE

1 cup dried apricots
2 cups water
6 tablespoons sugar
½ cup shortening
1 cup sugar
2 egg yolks
1 teaspoon vanilla
1¾ cups sifted cake flour
½ teaspoon salt
½ teaspoon baking soda
1 teaspoon baking powder
¼ cup water

Simmer first 3 ingredients together 30 minutes. Mash and measure ½ cup pulp. Cream shortening and sugar thoroughly, add yolks and vanilla; beat. Sift dry ingredients together and add alternately with water and pulp. Bake in a cake pan (8x8 inches), lined with waxed paper (350°F.) 45 minutes.

MAPLE UPSIDE-DOWN CAKE

3 tablespoons butter
1 cup maple sugar
4 slices pineapple
3 eggs, separated
1 cup sugar
¼ cup water
½ teaspoon vanilla
½ teaspoon lemon extract
1 cup sifted cake flour
1½ teaspoons baking powder

Melt butter in a heavy skillet. Remove from heat, spread maple sugar over bottom of skillet and cover with sliced pineapple. To beaten egg yolks add sugar, water, vanilla and lemon extract; beat until thick and lemon colored. Add dry ingredients, sifted together, and beat for 3 minutes. Fold in beaten egg whites. Pour over pineapple and bake in moderate oven (350°F.) about 45 minutes. Loosen cake from sides and bottom and turn out on a cake rack immediately. Serves 8.

MINT APPLES

1 cup sugar
½ cup water
Green food coloring
2 drops mint flavoring
4 small apples

Boil sugar and water together for 5 minutes. Add a few drops of food coloring and flavoring. Pare apples, keeping them whole. Place in pan with sirup and cover tightly. Simmer slowly until apples are just tender. Serve as a garnish for roast lamb. Serves 4.

APPLESAUCE RELISH

1 package lemon gelatin
1 cup boiling water
1 cup tart Applesauce
½ teaspoon cinnamon
⅛ teaspoon nutmeg

Dissolve gelatin in boiling water, mix applesauce and spices, add to gelatin, sweeten to taste and mold in tiny forms. Red cinnamon candies (dissolved in the boiling water) may be substituted for the cinnamon and nutmeg. Serve with pork. Serves 6.

Brilliant red cranberries add a beautiful luster to the breakfast baked apple

STRAWBERRY PINE-APPLE DELICIOUS

½ cup sliced hulled strawberries
2 slices pineapple, cut into ½-inch pieces
6 marshmallows, cut
¼ cup nut meats
1 cup heavy cream, whipped
8 Ladyfingers, split

Combine first 4 ingredients and let stand for ½ hour. Drain and add whipped cream. Mix well and chill at least 1 hour. Serve in dessert dishes lined with split ladyfingers. Serves 4.

BAKED APPLES WITH CRANBERRIES

4 apples
1½ cups whole Cranberry Sauce
4 tablespoons sugar

Wash apples, core and place in baking dish. Fill centers with cranberry sauce, pouring remaining sauce around apples. Sprinkle sugar over top of apples and bake in moderate oven (350°F.) about 40 minutes or until apples are tender. Baste apples frequently with the cranberry sauce. Serves 5.

CANDIED ORANGE OR GRAPEFRUIT PEEL

3 grapefruit shells or
   6 orange shells
1 teaspoon salt
3 cups sugar
1 cup water

Save fruit shells from breakfast fruits. Cut peel into strips ¼ inch wide from stem to blossom end. Add salt and cover with cold water. Boil 15 minutes, pour off water and add fresh water. Boil 20 minutes. Change water again and boil another 20 minutes. Drain thoroughly and cover with 2½ cups of sugar and water listed. Simmer, stirring continually to prevent scorching, until remaining sirup has boiled away. Spread on waxed paper and roll each piece of candied fruit in remaining sugar.

PRUNE CAKE

⅔ cup shortening
1 cup sugar
3 eggs, separated
1 teaspoon vanilla
2½ cups sifted cake flour
1 teaspoon baking soda
1 teaspoon cinnamon
½ teaspoon salt
½ cup buttermilk or sour milk
¼ cup broken nut meats
1 cup chopped cooked prunes

Cream shortening and all but 3 tablespoons sugar until fluffy Add egg yolks and vanilla and beat thoroughly. Sift flour, soda, cinnamon and salt together 3 times and add to creamed mixture alternately with milk. Add nuts and well drained prunes and mix well. Beat egg whites and remaining sugar until stiff and fold into batter. Pour into greased loaf pan and bake in moderate oven (350°F.) 60 to 70 minutes. Cool thoroughly and spread with orange butter frosting. Makes 1 (8x12 inch) cake.

DAMSON PLUM PUDDING

½ cup shortening
1 cup sugar
3 eggs, beaten
1 cup plum pulp
1 cup sifted flour
½ teaspoon cinnamon
1 teaspoon baking soda
¼ teaspoon nutmeg
3 tablespoons sour milk

SAUCE

1 cup plum juice
½ cup water
2 teaspoons cornstarch
1 cup sugar
2 tablespoons butter

Cream shortening and sugar together until fluffy. Add eggs and plum pulp. Mix well. Sift dry ingredients together and add alternately with milk. Pour into greased shallow pan. Bake in moderate oven (350°F.) 20 to 30 minutes. Cut into squares and serve hot with sauce. Heat plum juice and water. Mix cornstarch with sugar, pour a little hot liquid over it and stir. Pour back into hot juice and cook until thickened, stirring constantly. Add butter. Serves 6 to 8.

Fruit glazes on ham can be enhanced by studding with cranberries or cherries

FRUIT GLAZES

APPLE—Save cores and peelings from 3 pounds tart red apples; cook in 1¼ cups water for 20 minutes, strain, add ¼ cup sugar and cook down to a sirup. Cool and cover hot open apple pie.

APRICOT—Boil down 1 cup apricot juice with 1½ cups sugar until thick. This transparent glaze may be used for the top of strawberry or cherry tarts.

C R A N B E R R Y—Cook 1 cup strained cranberry sauce with ⅜ cup each corn sirup and water. Cook slowly until thick.

FOR MEAT—Use apricot, apple or cranberry or make cherry glaze of cherry juice the same way.

GLAZE FOR CANAPÉS

1 tablespoon unflavored gelatin
4 tablespoons cold water
½ cup boiling water
½ teaspoon salt
1 teaspoon onion juice
4 tablespoons vinegar
Few grains cayenne

Soften gelatin in cold water. Add boiling water and stir until dissolved. Add remaining ingredients, let cool, but not harden, before brushing over prepared canapés. Chill. The glaze will harden, keeping the canapés moist.

OLD-FASHIONED TARTS

1¼ cups cooked prunes or dates
¼ cup walnut meats
¼ cup orange juice
Pastry

Pit prunes or dates and chop fine. Add nut meats and orange juice. Prepare pastry, roll ⅛ inch thick and cut into rounds 3½ inches in diameter. Place 1 teaspoon filling on each. Fold over, moisten edges and press together. Bake on ungreased cookie sheet in hot oven (450°F.) 15 minutes. Makes 18 tarts.

PRUNE WHIP PIE

2 cups stewed prunes
1 cup sugar
1 tablespoon lemon juice
3 egg whites
Baked Pastry shell

Rub prunes through a strainer, add ½ of sugar and heat to boiling, stirring to dissolve sugar. Add lemon juice. Beat egg whites until nearly stiff; add remaining sugar gradually, continuing to beat until stiff enough to hold its shape. Fold in hot prune pulp, pour into pastry shell and bake in slow oven (300°F.) until firm, about 30 minutes. Makes 1 (9-inch) pie.

Half apricot pulp and half prune pulp may be used.

APPLESAUCE PIE

⅓ cup melted butter
15 graham crackers, crushed fine
½ cup sugar
½ teaspoon cinnamon
2 cups thick Applesauce (sweetened)
¼ teaspoon cloves
1 tablespoon confectioners' sugar
½ cup heavy cream, whipped

Add melted butter to graham cracker crumbs and mix well. Stir in sugar and cinnamon. Press crumbs into a piepan and bake in moderate oven (350°F.) 15 minutes. Remove from oven and when cool, place in refrigerator to chill. Just before serving fill with applesauce to which cloves have been added. Add confectioners' sugar to whipped cream and cover top of pie. Serves 6.

FRUIT COCKTAIL

½ cup each of any 4 fruits, diced
1 cup ginger ale
4 sprigs mint
Confectioners' sugar

Combine fruits and chill. Pour iced ginger ale over the top just before serving. Garnish with a sprig of fresh mint sprinkled with confectioners' sugar. Serves 4.

Use leftover prunes for prune whip pie and the apricots left from lunch to garnish the dinner chop plate ➡

FRUIT ROLLS

2 cups sifted flour
4 teaspoons baking powder
1 teaspoon salt
3 tablespoons shortening
¾ cup milk
¼ cup melted butter
Cherries, strawberries or blackberries (sweetened)

Sift flour, baking powder and salt together. Cut in shortening with 2 knives or pastry blender. Add milk (sufficient for a soft dough). Place on floured board and roll into rectangular sheet ½ inch thick. Brush with melted butter and spread with any sweetened fruit. Roll up like jelly roll and cut into pieces about 3 inches long. Bake in hot oven (425°F.) about 15 minutes. Rolls should be turned once or twice so that they will brown evenly. Serves 6.

GRAPEFRUIT PIE

1 cup sugar
⅛ teaspoon salt
4 tablespoons cornstarch
½ cup water
1 cup grapefruit juice
1 tablespoon butter
2 egg yolks, beaten
1 baked pastry shell

GRAPEFRUIT MERINGUE

2 egg whites
6 tablespoons confectioners' sugar
2 tablespoons grapefruit juice

Combine sugar, salt and cornstarch; add water and grapefruit juice and cook slowly, stirring constantly, until thick. Simmer 5 minutes, add butter and egg yolks and remove from heat. Beat well; cool. Turn into pastry shell. Beat egg whites until stiff, add sugar slowly and stir in grapefruit juice. Cover top of pie with meringue and bake in slow oven (300°F.) 10 to 15 minutes or until meringue is browned lightly. Makes 1 (9-inch) pie.

Rhubarb or cranberry ring makes a beautiful container for chicken salad

Marshmallow or orange icing for gingerbread.
Whipped cream garnishes for fruit desserts.
Meringue for lemon or orange pie or tarts.
Creamy rice or tapioca puddings.
Orange or lemon fluffs.

Make into:
Candied orange or grapefruit peel.
Orange baskets.

LEFTOVER COOKED FRUITS

APPLESAUCE — Combine thick unsweetened applesauce with 1 tablespoon honey for each cup sauce; pour into baked tart shells and top with whipped cream.

BAKED STUFFED PEARS — Pare and core large pears and stuff with dates, raisins or chopped nuts and tart marmalade. Place close together in baking dish, cover bottom of pan with water and bake in slow oven (300°F.) until tender.

CANDIED FRUITS — Drain cooked fruit, such as peaches, apricots or pineapple and cook a few minutes in heavy sirup of 1 cup sugar to ⅓ cup water. Coat thickly with sugar, spread out on paper towels in a pan and dry out for several hours on the radiator or in a slow oven.

COOKED PEACH OR PEAR HALVES — Drain fruit; arrange in baking dish with a marshmallow in each center. Combine sirup from fruit with ⅔ cup sugar and 2 tablespoons lemon juice; boil for 5 minutes. Pour over fruit, dot with butter and bake in hot oven, basting with sirup. Serve with meat.

Use leftover halves of cooked fruits for garnishes on meat platters or with mixed grills.

RHUBARB SALAD RING

1 package raspberry or lemon gelatin
1 cup hot Rhubarb Sauce
1 cup cold water
1 cup chopped apples
1 cup chopped walnuts, pecans or almonds

Dissolve gelatin in hot sauce, add water, cool and pour into ring mold. Chill until firm; unmold on lettuce. Make Waldorf salad with apples and nut meats and fill center of mold. Serves 6.
Use strained Cranberry Sauce or crushed berries instead of rhubarb and fill center with chicken salad.

FRUIT JUICES

Always save fruit juices, both fresh and canned. They make excellent:

COLORED ICE CUBES — Freeze fruit juices in refrigerator tray. Use fruit juice in concentrated form for bright colors; dilute with water for pastel shades. Serve with lemonades or other fruit drinks.

FRUIT LEMONADES — Add fruit juices to lemonade for attractive color and flavor.

APPETIZERS — Serve fruit juices in combination for the first course of luncheon or dinner. Suggested combinations:

Pineapple and strawberry juice.
Grape juice, lemon juice and pineapple juice.
Grapefruit juice, pineapple juice and orange juice.
Grape juice, orange and lemon juice.
Stewed rhubarb and pineapple juice.
Loganberry or raspberry juice and pineapple juice.

FROZEN APPETIZERS — Freeze sweetened fruit juices in refrigerator tray for 1 hour, stirring every 20 minutes. Loganberry, pomegranate, raspberry or cherry juice are especially good frozen.

SHERBETS — Use fruit juices for sherbets or ices. Citrus fruits in combination with other fruit juices are best.

CITRUS FRUIT RINDS

Dry out:
Grate and keep in covered jars.
Sprinkle over:
Crumb cake or coffee cake batter, before baking.
Cake frostings or icings.
Orange icing for orange rolls.

LEFTOVER JAMS, JELLIES, PRESERVES

APPLE PRESERVE CAKE

¾ cup shortening
1 cup sugar
¼ cup sour cream
½ cup Apple Preserves
3 eggs
2 cups sifted cake flour
1 teaspoon baking soda
1 teaspoon baking powder
1 teaspoon cinnamon
1 teaspoon nutmeg
1 teaspoon allspice
½ cup chopped walnut meats
½ cup seedless raisins

Cream shortening and sugar together until fluffy. Add sour cream and apple preserves, mixing well. Add eggs, 1 at a time, beating hard after each addition. Sift flour, soda, baking powder and spices together 3 times, add gradually. Fold in nuts and raisins which have been dredged with flour. Pour into greased loaf pan and bake in moderate oven (350° F.) 50 minutes or bake in layers for 25 to 30 minutes. Ice with lemon icing. Makes 1 (8x4 inch) loaf or 2 (9-inch) layers.

APPLE BUTTER PIE

½ cup sugar
3 tablespoons flour
½ cup Apple Butter
2 tablespoons butter, melted
2 eggs
2½ cups milk
½ teaspoon nutmeg
1 unbaked Pastry shell

Combine ingredients and beat thoroughly. Pour into pastry shell. Bake in hot oven (450°F.) 10 minutes, reduce temperature to moderate (350°F.) and bake 40 minutes longer, or until firm. Makes 1 (9-inch) pie.

CRAB APPLE PUFFS

Line muffin pans with pastry; fill with crab apple jelly, cover with pastry and bake in hot oven (450° F.) 10 minutes. Then reduce heat slightly to 425° F. and complete baking. Remove from pans while hot. Serve cold for luncheon.

A few tricks with jelly and a pastry tube dress up the simplest rennet custards

ORANGE MARMA-LADE BREAD PUDDING

1⅓ cups dry bread crumbs
1⅓ cups scalded milk
1⅓ cups sugar
1 tablespoon melted butter
2 eggs, slightly beaten
1 teaspoon vanilla
½ cup Orange Marmalade
½ teaspoon nutmeg

Soak bread crumbs in hot milk; when cool add remaining ingredients. Place in buttered baking dish and set in pan of hot water. Bake in moderate oven (350°F.) 45 to 50 minutes or until a knife inserted in the center comes out clean. Serve hot with pudding sauce or cream. Serves 6.

JELLY CORN MUFFINS

Make a batter for corn-meal muffins. Fill greased muffin pans ¼ full, place a teaspoon of jelly on top of batter in each pan, cover jelly with more batter and bake in hot oven (400°F.) about 20 minutes.

ORANGE MARMALADE ROLLS

2½ cups milk
4 tablespoons butter
4 tablespoons sugar
1½ teaspoons salt
2 yeast cakes
½ cup lukewarm water
5 cups sifted flour
Melted butter
Orange marmalade

Scald milk, add butter or other shortening and stir until melted; stir in sugar and salt. Cool. Soften yeast in lukewarm water and add to the cooled mixture. Stir in 2½ cups of flour and mix well. Cover and keep in a warm place to rise (about 2 hours). Add more flour to make a stiff dough, kneading well. Cover and let rise until double in bulk (about 2 hours). Roll out on floured board and cut with a biscuit cutter. Brush wtih melted butter and place 1 teaspoon of orange marmalade in center. Fold each roll in half and place on a well-greased baking pan. Brush top with butter. Let stand in a warm place about 30 minutes. Bake in a hot oven (425°F.) for 20 minutes. Makes about 40.

JELLY-CENTERED SUGAR COOKIES

½ cup shortening
1 cup sugar
2 eggs, beaten
1 tablespoon milk
1 teaspoon lemon juice
2½ cups sifted flour
2 teaspoons baking powder
Jelly or jam

Cream shortening and sugar and add eggs, milk and lemon juice. Blend. Sift flour and baking powder, and add to first mixture, mixing well. Chill thoroughly. Place dough on a floured board and roll to ⅛-inch thickness. Cut with round cookie cutter and place half of rounds on greased cookie sheet. Place a teaspoon of jelly or jam in center of each. Place a second round of dough over each jelly-filled cookie and with a fork press edges of cookies together. Sprinkle lightly with sugar and bake in moderate oven (350°F.) about 15 minutes. Makes 2 dozen cookies.

Pastry turnovers will often save the day for the busy hostess. Make them small with fruits for dessert or large, with meat for the main dish

JAMS AND JELLIES

MARMALADE STRIPS—Place a thin layer of pastry on an inverted baking sheet. Spread with thick marmalade. Cover with another thin layer of pastry. Cut into strips 4 inches by 1½ inches. Bake in hot oven (425°F.) about 10 minutes. When cool, spread with a thin icing made of confectioners' sugar and water. Sprinkle with chopped nuts.

PASTRY ROLLOVERS — Cut 4 inch circles from pastry. Prick, spread with jelly and sprinkle with chopped nuts. Roll up, place on an inverted pan and bake in hot oven (400°F.) 10 to 15 minutes.

STRAWBERRY OR OTHER FRUIT TURNOVERS—Cut pastry into 3-inch squares. Moisten half the edge of square with cold water and in the center place a teaspoon of thick strawberry preserve. Fold ½ of square over the other. Press edges together and mark with a fork dipped in flour. Brush with beaten egg, prick the top with a fork and chill before placing in the oven. Bake in a very hot oven (450°F.) 15 minutes. Dust with sugar before serving.

Add orange marmalade to apple pie, with a little chopped crystallized ginger.

Cover hot gingerbread with apple butter; add a layer of whipped cream and bits of preserved ginger.

Toast 1 side of bread; spread untoasted side with jelly; top with slices of bacon and roll.

Add a spoonful of any tart jelly to chicken or turkey gravy.

Put a spoonful of quince jelly in apple pie or in hard sauce for holiday puddings.

COFFEE NUT MUFFINS

3 cups sifted cake flour
4 teaspoons baking powder
¾ cup brown sugar
½ teaspoon salt
1 cup pecan meats, broken
1 egg
1¼ cups cold strong coffee
2 tablespoons shortening, melted

Sift dry ingredients together and add nut meats; beat egg, add coffee and shortening and add to dry ingredients. Mix only enough to dampen all the flour. Bake in greased muffin pans in hot oven (400°F.) 20 to 25 minutes. Makes 16 large or 30 small muffins.

COFFEE SPICE LAYER CAKE

½ cup shortening
1 cup sugar
2 eggs, separated
2 cups sifted cake flour
2 teaspoons baking powder
⅛ teaspoon salt
1 teaspoon cinnamon
1 teaspoon nutmeg
½ cup strong coffee

Cream shortening, add sugar gradually. Add egg yolks and beat well. Sift flour, baking powder, salt and spices together. Add alternately with coffee to first mixture. Add stiffly beaten egg whites. Bake in greased layer-cake pans in moderate oven (350°F.) 25 to 30 minutes. Spread with Mocha Icing. Makes 2 (9-inch) layers.

COFFEE SAUCE

2 egg yolks
⅓ cup sugar
⅛ teaspoon salt
1 cup hot clear black coffee

Beat eggs, sugar and salt together. Add coffee gradually, stirring constantly. Cook over water until mixture coats a spoon. Chill. Makes 1 cup sauce.

COFFEE CREAM PIE

⅔ cup sugar
5 tablespoons cornstarch
½ teaspoon salt
1 cup evaporated milk
1 cup strong coffee
1 egg, slightly beaten
1 teaspoon vanilla
1 baked Pastry shell
Whipped cream

Combine sugar, cornstarch and salt. Heat milk and coffee together. Add to cornstarch mixture gradually, stirring constantly. Cook over boiling water until thick and smooth, stirring frequently (about 15 minutes). Pour part of mixture over egg, blending thoroughly. Return to double boiler and cook 2 minutes longer. Cool. Add vanilla. Turn into pastry shell. Cover with whipped cream. Makes 1 (9-inch) pie.

LEFTOVER COCOA

1. Combine with coffee; serve hot or cold. Top with whipped cream.
2. Substitute for liquid in chocolate sauce, candy or icings; adding more cocoa for flavor.

A coffee cream pie is the perfect finish for dinner

MOCHA ICING

½ cup sweet butter
2½ cups confectioners' sugar
2 tablespoons cocoa
2 tablespoons hot coffee
½ teaspoon vanilla

Cream butter until soft and pliable. Add sugar gradually, beating well between additions. As it becomes thick, add cocoa, mixed with hot coffee and vanilla. Continue to beat and add more sugar until light and fluffy and thick enough to spread. Use for filling and to frost top and sides of cold cake. Will frost tops and sides of 2 (9-inch) layers.

BAKED COFFEE CUSTARD

2 eggs
⅓ cup sugar
Few grains salt
1 cup milk
1 cup cold strong coffee

Beat eggs slightly. Add sugar and salt. Add milk and coffee. Pour into greased custard cups. Place in pan with hot water about 1 inch deep. Bake in moderate oven (350°F.) about 1 hour, or until firm. Serves 3.

HOT SANDWICHES

1. Broiled hamburger steaks on round rolls, with chopped pickles, carrots, celery or radishes added to the meat before broiling.
2. Broiled pineapple with sliced hot chicken, turkey or duck on whole-wheat bread.
3. Broiled ham or sliced roast lamb with grilled pineapple on toasted English muffins.
4. Hot roast veal and grilled tomato on rye roll.
5. Grilled tomato with Cheddar cheese on rye toast.
6. Hot smoked tongue with fried apples on toasted English muffins.
7. Scrambled eggs with minced ham, dried beef, liver sausage, pork sausage, sliced frankfurters, salmon, smoked fish, cheese, tomatoes or mixed vegetables.
8. Broiled meat loaf on toast with gravy.
9. Broiled hash on toast with coleslaw.
10. Mashed baked beans with chili sauce and chopped pickle on toasted Boston brown bread.
11. Minced chicken livers and giblets with chopped bacon on toast.

HOT BISCUIT SANDWICH

Break reheated baking powder biscuits apart and butter the halves. On 1 side place slice of tomato, mayonnaise and a layer of minced bacon. Cover with the other half of biscuit and serve hot.

On buttered half of biscuit place thick slice of Bermuda onion and slice of tomato. Broil.

GRILLED TONGUE AND EGG SANDWICHES

1 cup chopped tongue
1 teaspoon onion juice
2 tablespoons mayonnalse
Bread
1 egg
1 cup milk

Mix tongue with onion juice and mayonnaise and spread on thin slices of unbuttered bread. Press slices together and cut into halves diagonally. Beat egg, add milk and dip sandwiches into mixture. Brown in butter, garnish with parsley and serve on a hot platter. Serves 4 to 6.

An excellent place for leftovers is in the making of hot grilled sandwiches

BUTTERS FOR SANDWICHES

ANCHOVY BUTTER

Yolks of 4 hard-cooked eggs
4 boned anchovies
½ cup butter
Paprika

Rub yolks of eggs to smooth paste with anchovies and butter and add paprika to taste.

HAM BUTTER

½ cup cooked ham
¼ cup butter
Yolks of 2 hard-cooked eggs
Pepper

Grind ham and pound smooth with butter and yolks of eggs. Season with pepper.

SHRIMP BUTTER

1 cup cooked shrimp
Salt
⅛ teaspoon cayenne
1 cup butter
About ¼ cup tarragon vinegar or lemon juice

Grind shrimp, add salt, cayenne and butter; moisten with vinegar or lemon juice.

SUGGESTIONS FOR SANDWICH FILLINGS

GENERAL DIRECTIONS — Combine ingredients and spread on bread, toast or buns. Cover with a similar slice and cut into triangles or quarters. Garnish with watercress; celery or carrot curls; pickles or radishes.

BEEF

1½ cups cold roast beef
½ teaspoon salt
½ tablespoon chili sauce
¼ teaspoon Worcestershire sauce
1 tablespoon melted butter

CHICKEN SALAD

1 cup chopped cooked chicken
½ cup minced celery
1 tablespoon minced green pepper
¼ cup mayonnaise

SANDWICH FILLINGS—Cont.

CREAM OR COTTAGE CHEESE

6 ounces cream cheese or
    1 cup cottage cheese
⅓ cup minced stuffed olives
¼ cup chopped nut meats (optional)
1 tablespoon softened butter
¼ teaspoon salt

EGG SALAD

4 hard-cooked eggs
¼ teaspoon mustard
2 teaspoons chili sauce
¼ cup minced celery
2 tablespoons mayonnalse

HAM SALAD

1 cup ground cooked ham
½ tablespoon minced onion
½ teaspoon dry mustard
2 tablespoons mayonnaise

LIVER AND BACON

½ cup chopped cooked bacon
½ cup ground cooked liver
⅛ teaspoon pepper
Dash cayenne
¼ cup cream

LAMB

1¼ cups chopped cooked lamb
½ teaspoon salt
¼ teaspoon pepper
½ tablespoon minced onion
1 teaspoon minced mint leaves
1 tablespoon lemon juice

SALMON OR TUNA SALAD

1 cup fish flakes
½ cup minced celery
1 tablespoon lemon juice
¼ teaspoon salt
⅛ teaspoon pepper
2 tablespoons mayonnaise

TONGUE

1½ cups minced cooked tongue
2 tablespoons prepared horse-radish
½ teaspoon salt
¼ cup mayonnaise
Dash cayenne

VEAL

1¼ cups chopped cooked veal
1 tablespoon lemon juice
¼ teaspoon salt
¼ teaspoon pepper
1 teaspoon prepared mustard

Raisins with cream cheese.

Cream cheese and chopped stuffed olives.

Cream cheese and crushed pineapple.

Cream cheese and chopped nuts.

Cottage cheese and pickles, olives, nuts or pimientos.

Boston brown bread with cream cheese or mayonnaise mixed with chopped nuts and raisins.

Rounds of brown bread spread with chopped olives, minced lettuce and watercress, paprika, parsley and chives mixed with mayonnaise.

Pimientos, cucumbers and onion or chives, minced, mixed with mayonnaise and spread on buttered bread.

Green pepper, pimiento and olives with mayonnaise.

Currant jam with minced walnut meats and creamed butter. Serve with cream cheese. Preserved currants may be used instead of currant jam.

Ground boiled ham and chopped pickles or chopped peanuts.

Chopped stuffed olives and chopped nuts, moistened with salad dressing.

Chopped raisins, figs, dates or prunes, chopped nut meats and mayonnaise or lemon juice.

A beautiful plate of individual aspic, apricot halves with cream cheese, a petal-cut plum, chicory and sandwiches

HOT HORS D'OEUVRES

1. On thin slice of Bologna place 1 teaspoon American or pimiento cheese. Heat in moderate oven (350°F.) until cheese melts and Bologna curls.

2. Remove stones from cooked prunes, fill with cheese, wrap in short strips of bacon, fasten with a toothpick. Broil until bacon is crisp, serve hot on a cocktail pick.

3. Spread strips of uncooked bacon with peanut butter, roll tightly, fasten with toothpick. Broil until crisp and serve on cocktail picks stuck into an eggplant.

4. Cut large stuffed olives crosswise into halves and put together with softened Cheddar cheese. These may be wrapped in bacon slices and placed in the broiler until bacon is crisp.

5. Wrap shrimp in bacon slices and place in the broiler until bacon is crisp. Serve hot.

6. Roll large stuffed olives with anchovy fillets. Place in broiler to brown slightly.

7. Wrap rolled anchovies in ½ slice bacon. Place in broiler until bacon is crisp.

Leftover salads in cups of broiled leftover sausage are an attractive luncheon plate

COLD HORS D'OEUVRES

1. Mash avocado, season with horse-radish and Tabasco sauce and spread on crackers or small rounds of toast.

2. Spread paper-thin slices of smoked salmon with cream cheese, wrap around 2-inch stalks of celery. Chill.

3. Mash avocado, season well with lemon juice, salt and onion juice. Fill crisp celery stalks. Chill.

4. Hollow out crisp radishes, cucumber cup, or hard-cooked egg whites, and fill with caviar.

5. Fill small tomatoes with crab meat, garnish with mayonnaise.

6. Slice peeled bananas crosswise into 1-inch pieces. Dip into grapefruit, pineapple, orange or lemon juice. Spread with cream cheese or salad dressing and roll in finely chopped nut meats.

7. Stuff plum-tomato cups, cut lengthwise, with liver paste; garnish with pearl onions.

8. Fill tiny cooked beet cups with chopped egg pickle spread.

LEFTOVERS WITH PLAIN OMELET

CHEESE—Sprinkle grated cheese over center of omelet while cooking.

FISH — Use any cooked fish. Chop fine, season with salt and pepper and moisten with a little cream. Spread on omelet before folding.

HAM, CHICKEN OR TONGUE — Scatter minced cooked meat over the center of omelet while cooking.

JELLY—Spread any jelly or jam through the middle of the omelet just before folding.

ONION—Mix 1 tablespoon chopped onion and 1 teaspoon chopped parsley. Add to omelet mixture before cooking.

PARSLEY—Sprinkle minced parsley over center of omelet while cooking.

VEGETABLE — Use leftover cooked vegetable. Force vegetable through a sieve, moisten with a little milk, cream or gravy and season with salt and pepper. Spread mixture lightly over omelet before folding.

LEFTOVERS WITH SCRAMBLED EGGS

For every 6 eggs add:
1. 1 cup diced sautéed bread cubes with 1 teaspoon chopped chives.
2. 1 cooked chicken liver, chopped, with slices cooked bacon, chopped.
3. ½ cup minced cooked ham, tongue or dried beef.
4. ½ cup flaked cooked fish (smoked or fresh).
5. ½ cup minced cooked chicken, turkey or duck.
6. ½ cup ground cooked meat.
7. ½ cup flaked lobster, crab meat or shrimp.
8. ¼ cup chopped cooked mushrooms.
9. 3 tablespoons minced parsley and chives.
10. ½ cup cooked corn-meal mush.
11. ⅔ cup grated cheese.
12. ½ cup chopped or cooked tomatoes (omit milk).

SAUCES FROM LEFTOVERS

Use 1 cup Medium White Sauce as the basis for each sauce.
CAPER SAUCE — Add 2 to 4 tablespoons chopped capers.
CELERY SAUCE — Add ½ cup chopped cooked celery.
CHEESE SAUCE — Add 2 to 4 ounces grated cheese. Set over hot water and stir until the cheese is blended with sauce. Season to taste with mustard and paprika.
CREAM GRAVY — Use 2 tablespoons meat drippings for butter in white sauce recipe.
CREAM SAUCE — Use cream instead of milk in white sauce.
EGG SAUCE—Add 1 hard-cooked egg, chopped.
MUSHROOM SAUCE — Add ½ to ⅓ cup chopped or sliced cooked mushrooms to sauce.

Egg Dishes

350 Ways to Serve Eggs

FRIED EGGS

METHOD 1—Have eggs at room temperature if possible. Grease frying pan just enough to keep egg from sticking. Slip egg carefully into heated pan. Add a little water and cover. The steam helps to form a coating over the yolk. Cook very slowly. Egg may be turned if desired.

METHOD 2—Put bacon drippings or other fat in a frying pan and heat. Slip egg carefully into pan. Cook slowly. Dip hot fat over top of egg during cooking. Egg may be turned if desired.

SERVING FRIED EGGS

Bread thick slices of eggplant and sauté in butter. Grill tomato slices. Cover each eggplant slice with a tomato slice and top with fried egg. Season and serve hot.

Serve in a nest of fried white cabbage, buttered celeriac, spinach or chard.

BLACK-BUTTER EGGS

8 fried eggs
5 tablespoons butter
4 teaspoons sherry

Remove eggs from pan to hot platter. Place butter in pan and heat until browned but not burned. Add sherry and pour over eggs. Serves 4.

EGG CHEESE CAKES

6 eggs, beaten
1 onion, chopped
½ cup sifted flour
1 teaspoon baking powder
½ teaspoon salt
½ pound cheese, cubed

Combine all ingredients. Using a large spoon, take up a piece of cheese with as much batter as the spoon will hold and fry in hot fat, browning both sides. Serve with hot Tomato Sauce. Serves 4.

EGGS FRENCH STYLE

2 tablespoons butter
4 tablespoons flour
1 cup milk
½ teaspoon salt
½ teaspoon paprika
⅛ teaspoon pepper
6 hard-cooked eggs
Bread crumbs

Melt butter, blend in flour and add milk and seasonings. Cook until thickened, stirring constantly. Dip eggs into the sauce, cool and roll in bread crumbs. Fry in hot deep fat (375°F.) until brown. Drain on absorbent paper. Serve with Tomato Sauce, for 3.

Cut hard-cooked eggs lengthwise into halves. Fill centers with sieved egg yolks, 2 tablespoons minced green pepper and 2 tablespoons grated sharp cheese. Refill whites and fasten halves together with picks. Prepare as above.

EGGS IN POTATO BLANKETS

3 cups mashed potatoes
4 hard-cooked eggs
1 egg, slightly beaten
Bread crumbs

Divide potatoes into 4 equal parts, shape around hard-cooked eggs. Dip into egg (diluted with 2 tablespoons water) then into bread crumbs. Fry in hot deep fat (375° F.) until brown. Drain, cut into halves and serve hot with Tomato Sauce. Serves 4.

Use sweetpotatoes instead of Irish potatoes.

Used mashed rutabaga or Hubbard squash instead of potatoes.

Pat a layer of liver sausage around the eggs, roll in egg and crumbs and bake in moderate oven for 15 minutes.

Wrap egg in a slice of baked or boiled ham and heat in the oven.

EGG CROQUETTES

3 tablespoons butter
3 tablespoons flour
¾ cup milk, ½ teaspoon salt
Dash paprika
4 hard-cooked eggs, chopped
Cracker crumbs
1 egg, slightly beaten

Melt butter in top of double boiler, add flour and stir until blended. Add milk and seasonings and cook until mixture is thickened. Remove from heat and add hard-cooked eggs. Set aside to cool. When cold, shape into croquettes; roll in cracker crumbs, dip into egg (diluted with 2 tablespoons water) and again in crumbs. Fry in hot deep fat (365° to 380°F.) until brown, 2 to 5 minutes. Serves 6.

Americans share their favorite breakfast with their neighbors to the north →

HAM AND EGG CROQUETTES

1 can mushroom soup
6 hard-cooked eggs, chopped
1 teaspoon salt
½ teaspoon Worcestershire sauce
½ teaspoon prepared mustard
1½ cups soft bread crumbs
1 cup chopped cooked ham
Dry bread crumbs; 1 egg, beaten

Heat mushroom soup. Combine eggs, salt, Worcestershire sauce and mustard. Add eggs, soft crumbs and ham to soup. Heat and cook for 4 to 5 minutes. Chill. Shape into croquettes. Roll in bread crumbs, dip into egg (diluted with 2 tablespoons water) and roll again in crumbs. Fry in hot deep fat (375°F.) 2 to 5 minutes or until brown. Drain on absorbent paper. Serves 6.

PUFFY OMELET

6 eggs, separated
6 tablespoons hot water
¾ teaspoon salt
Dash pepper
1½ tablespoons butter or
   other fat

Beat egg whites until stiff. Beat yolks until thick and lemon colored, beat hot water into them and add salt and pepper. Fold yolks and stiffly beaten whites together. Melt butter in omelet pan, grease bottom and sides of pan. Turn egg mixture into pan, cover and cook over low heat until it is puffy and a light brown underneath, then place in a moderate oven (350°F.) for 10 to 15 minutes or until top is dry. Touch top of the omelet lightly with the finger and if the egg does not stick to the finger the omelet is done. Do not overcook it or it will shrink and be tough. Loosen edges of omelet, cut through the center, slip a spatula or flexible knife under side next to handle of pan, fold ½ over the other and press slightly to make it stay in place, slip onto a hot plate and serve at once. Serves 6.

FRENCH OMELET

6 eggs
¾ teaspoon salt
Dash pepper
2 tablespoons butter

Beat eggs just enough to mix whites and yolks; add salt and pepper. Heat butter in an omelet pan, pour a little of it into the beaten eggs and reheat the remainder. Turn eggs into pan and as mixture cooks on the bottom and sides, prick it with a fork so that the egg on top will penetrate the cooked surface, and run under the sides. While the eggs are still soft, but thickened,

fold over, let stand a few minutes to brown and turn onto a hot dish. Serves 6.

VARIATIONS OF PUFFY OMELET OR FRENCH OMELET— may be made by adding one of the following to the omelet before it is cooked.

ANCHOVY — Omit salt and add 1 teaspoon each of anchovy paste and minced parsley.

ARTICHOKE—Heat 6 artichoke hearts, cooked and chopped; 1 clove garlic, minced; 4 tablespoons minced onion in 2 tablespoons olive oil; add to eggs before cooking.

BEAN SPROUT—Add 1 cup drained bean sprouts and ½ cup chopped cooked bacon or ham to egg yolks.

BREAD—Soften 2 slices dry bread in cream or evaporated milk. Omit water in puffy omelet and add bread, with as much cream as the bread will hold, to the egg yolks and proceed as for puffy omelet.
Sauté bread cubes in butter, add with ½ cup milk to yolks and cook as French omelet.

CHEESE—Sprinkle ⅓ cup grated or ground cheese over the center of omelet while it is cooking.

CLAM—Add 1 cup minced cooked clams to egg yolks. Serve omelet with a highly seasoned tomato sauce.

CORN—Add 2 cups cooked corn to eggs in French omelet.

COTTAGE CHEESE—Add 1 cup cottage cheese and ¼ cup chopped pimiento to egg yolks.

CREOLE—Cook 3 onions, chopped; 4 tomatoes, diced; 3 green peppers, chopped; 1 teaspoon paprika in 2 tablespoons olive oil until vegetables are tender. Serve with French omelet.

DANDELION—Sauté 1½ cups white dandelion tips in 3 tablespoons butter. Mix with eggs before cooking.

FISH—Chop 1 cup any cooked fish, season with salt and pepper and moisten with a little cream Add to egg yolks.

HAM OR OTHER MEAT—Sprinkle 1 cup minced cooked meat over the center of the omelet while it is cooking. The meat may be browned in a smal amount of fat before it is added

JARDINIÈRE—Stir into the beaten eggs a mixture of chopped parsley, onion, chives, shallots and a few leaves each of sorrel and chervil, minced Add 3 tablespoons of the mixture.

LOBSTER—Add 1 cup minced cooked lobster, 2 tablespoons chili sauce and 1 teaspoon minced onion to egg yolks.

MUSHROOM—Add ½ cup sliced sautéed mushrooms to eggs before cooking.

ONION—Mix 1 tablespoon chopped onion and 1 teaspoon chopped parsley. Add to the omelet mixture before cooking.

OYSTER—Chop 12 oysters, combine with 1 cup Thin Cream Sauce, season with cayenne and Worcestershire sauce. Add to eggs in French omelet.

PARSLEY—Scatter 3 tablespoons minced parsley over the center of the omelet while it is cooking.

RUM—Omit pepper, use ⅛ teaspoon salt; add 1½ teaspoons confectioners' sugar and 2¼ tablespoons rum to beaten eggs, cook as directed. Pour 6 tablespoons rum around omelet on platter, ignite rum and serve at once. If desired, sprinkle omelet with sugar.

FILLINGS FOR OMELET

Variations of the plain Puffy Omelet or the plain French Omelet may be made by spreading one of the following on top just before the omelet is folded.

APRICOT AND BRANDY—Spread 1 cup apricot jam to which has been added 1 tablespoon brandy, on omelet.

BACON—(A) Sprinkle chopped crisp bacon over omelet. (B) Fry ½ cup diced bacon until crisp and brown. Remove from pan and fry 1 cup ¼-inch potato cubes in fat until brown, drain and mix with bacon. Fold part in omelet and surround omelet with remainder.

CHEESE—Season grated cheese with Worcestershire sauce and sprinkle over omelet.

CHICKEN OR TONGUE—Pour creamed chicken or tongue over omelet, fold and serve with additional cream chicken or tongue.

CHICKEN LIVERS AND MINCED ONION—Sprinkle cooked livers and onion over omelet.

CRANBERRY—Spread omelet with ¾ cup Cranberry Sauce. Fold. Omit pepper.

CROUTONS—Sauté dry bread cut into ¼-inch cubes in butter. Sprinkle over omelet before folding.

FISH—Use any cooked fish as oysters, shrimp, salmon, tuna, crab meat or lobster. Chop fine, season with salt and pepper and moisten with Cream Sauce. Spread on omelet.

FRUIT — Cover omelet with fresh or canned drained berries or diced fruit before folding.

HASH—Spread corned beef hash over omelet before folding.

JELLY OR MARMALADE—Spread any jelly, jam or marmalade over omelet just before folding. Omit pepper and reduce salt one-half.

KIDNEY—Highly seasoned stewed kidneys may be chopped and added to omelet when baked.

RICE—Add ⅓ cup cooked rice and dash of tomato catchup to egg yolk-milk mixture of puffy omelet.

SAUSAGE—Spread cooked sausage meat over omelet before serving.

SWEETBREADS—Serve boiled, braised, broiled or creamed sweetbreads over omelet.

TOMATO—Spread omelet with Tomato Sauce before folding.

TOMATO AND CHEESE — Cover omelet with thin slices fresh tomatoes, then with grated cheese. Place under broiler until cheese melts.

VEGETABLE—Cooked vegetable as chopped spinach, broccoli, braised chicory, sautéed mushrooms, creamed asparagus or creamed peas are delicious fillings for omelets. Omelets may be served on a bed of buttered and seasoned vegetables.

Speed this fluffy golden omelet to the table on a hot platter accompanied by succulent sautéed mushrooms

EGG FOO YUNG OR CHINESE OMELET

½ cup finely diced cooked bacon
    or ham
½ cup minced onion
¼ cup sliced water chestnuts
1 cup bean sprouts
5 eggs

Combine meat, onion, chestnuts and sprouts and mix well. Beat eggs until thick. Add meat and vegetables. Divide into 6 portions, mold into a soup ladle cup and pour carefully into a shallow pan of hot fat or oil and brown. Serves 3 to 6.

Use 1 No. 2 can mixed Chinese vegetables and ½ cup shredded cooked chicken, instead of first 4 ingredients above.

EGG FOO YUNG WITH CHICKEN—Use finely diced chicken instead of bacon or ham.

EGG FOO YUNG WITH SHRIMP OR LOBSTER—Use shrimp or lobster instead of bacon or ham.

EGG FOO YUNG WITH GREEN PEPPER—Use ½ cup diced celery and 1 large green pepper, chopped, instead of water chestnuts.

SALT MACKEREL OMELET

5 eggs, separated
¾ teaspoon paprika
¼ cup water
1 cup cooked and flaked
    freshened mackerel
2 tablespoons butter

Beat yolks and whites of eggs separately. To yolks add paprika, water and mackerel. Fold in egg whites carefully. Melt butter in a heavy skillet or omelet pan and pour in egg mixture. Cook until omelet is puffy and golden brown. Fold carefully and serve at once no a hot platter. Serves 5.

OMELET WITH FLOUR

1 cup milk
2 tablespoons flour
½ teaspoon salt
4 eggs, separated

Add ¼ cup milk to flour and salt and beat until smooth. Add remainder of milk. Beat yolks until thick and lemon colored. Add milk mixture and fold in stiffly beaten egg whites. Pour into hot buttered skillet or omelet pan and cook as for Puffy Omelet. For 4.

SWEDISH OMELET—Add ½ cup grated sharp cheese to milk.

POTATO OMELET

3 eggs, separated
3 tablespoons cream or milk
1 cup mashed potatoes
1 teaspoon salt
¼ teaspoon pepper
Onion juice
Chopped parsley
Butter

Add egg yolks and cream to potatoes and beat until smooth. Season to taste with salt, pepper, onion juice and chopped parsley. Beat whites until stiff. Fold into potato mixture. Place in buttered skillet and bake in moderate oven (350°F.) until brown. Fold and turn onto a hot platter. Serve at once. Serves 4 to 6.

OMELET WITH BACON

8 slices bacon
8 eggs
½ teaspoon salt

Fry bacon until crisp. Beat eggs with salt. Reduce heat under bacon. Arrange bacon neatly in skillet and pour eggs over it. As egg cooks cut slits in it to allow uncooked egg to run underneath. When eggs are set, loosen from skillet and serve whole on a hot platter. For 6.

SPANISH OMELET

½ green pepper, minced
1 tablespoon minced onion
2 tablespoons fat
6 stuffed olives, sliced
1¾ cups cooked tomatoes
1 tablespoon sliced mushrooms
1 tablespoon capers
¼ teaspoon salt
Few grains cayenne
Puffy Omelet

Sauté pepper and onion in fat until tender but not brown. Add olives and tomato and cook down to a thick sauce. Add remaining ingredients. Place 4 tablespoons sauce on omelet before folding and pour remainder over top. Serves 4.

OMELET WAFFLES

4 eggs, separated
¼ cup flour
6 tablespoons hot water
½ teaspoon salt
⅛ teaspoon pepper
2 tablespoons melted butter
2 tablespoons chopped parsley

Beat egg yolks until lemon colored. Combine flour, hot water, salt, pepper and butter. Beat until smooth, add to egg yolks. Fold in the stiffly beaten egg whites and parsley Bake for 2 minutes on hot waffle iron. Serves 2 to 4.

NOODLE OMELET

1 cup broken noodles
½ cup butter
3 eggs, well beaten
Salt
Pepper

Cook noodles in boiling salted water 10 minutes. Drain well. Heat butter in skillet, add noodles and brown lightly. Season eggs with salt and pepper. Stir into noodles and cook slowly until eggs are firm. Serve with Applesauce. Serves 6.

SHRIMP OMELET

5 eggs
1 tablespoon soy sauce
½ cup chopped onions
2 tablespoons peanut oil or
      butter
½ cup minced cooked shrimp

Beat eggs well, add soy sauce and onions. Heat oil in skillet. Add half the egg mixture. Spread shrimp on top and add remaining egg. Cook over low heat until eggs are set. Serves 4.

STRAWBERRY OMELET

1 pint strawberries
¼ cup sugar
1 French Omelet

Wash and hull berries; cut in halves and cover with sugar. Let stand several hours. Prepare omelet. Spread strawberries on 1 half, fold and serve on hot platter. Garnish with whole berries, if desired. Serves 6.

CANTON OMELET

4 eggs
2 tablespoons chopped cooked
      ham
3 water chestnuts, chopped
2 mushrooms, chopped
2 teaspoons soy sauce
2 tablespoons butter

Beat eggs slightly. Add ham, chestnuts, mushrooms and soy sauce. Heat butter in skillet. Pour in egg mixture and cook over low heat until eggs are set. Serves 4.

CHEESE CUBE OMELET

¼ pound cheese, diced
½ cup cooked diced celery
1 tablespoon minced pimiento
1 cup hot seasoned White Sauce
1 Puffy or French Omelet

Just before serving, combine cheese, celery, pimiento and sauce. Pour over omelet. For 6.

TAPIOCA OMELET

¾ cup milk
2 tablespoons quick-cooking
      tapioca
½ teaspoon salt
⅛ teaspoon pepper
1 tablespoon butter
4 eggs, separated

Scald milk. Add tapioca, salt and pepper. Cook 20 minutes in a double boiler, stirring occasionally. Add butter and beaten egg yolks. Fold in stiffly beaten egg whites. Pour into hot buttered skillet and bake in moderate oven (350°F.) 20 minutes. Serves 4.

If desired, add 1 cup diced cooked chicken or any of the variations of Puffy or French Omelet. The tapioca makes this omelet less likely to fall.

Some like cheese shredded and folded into the omelet; some like it cubed on top

CRÊPES SUZETTE

3 eggs, well beaten
2 tablespoons flour
½ teaspoon salt
1 tablespoon milk
1 tablespoon water
1 teaspoon grated orange rind

SAUCE

3 tablespoons butter
½ cup sugar
⅓ cup orange juice
½ teaspoon grated orange rind
Curacao

Combine ingredients for crêpes and beat well. Bake in thin cakes on hot greased griddle, browning both sides. Make sauce by creaming butter and sugar together, beating orange juice and rind in gradually. Spread on cakes as they are baked and roll up quickly. To serve, pour curaçao over crêpes and ignite; turn crêpes over as blazing continues. Serve as soon as flame goes out. Serve with additional sauce. Serves 4.

If preferred fold crêpes in quarters.

SWEDISH PANCAKES WITH LINGONBERRY

3 eggs
1 cup milk
1½ cups sifted flour
1 tablespoon sugar
½ teaspoon salt
½ cup cream
2 tablespoons melted butter
2 cups Lingonberry Sauce
Confectioners' sugar

Beat eggs until very light. Add half the milk and fold in flour sifted with sugar and salt. Add cream, butter and remaining milk. Bake in large cakes on a hot griddle. Place 2 tablespoons sauce on each and roll up. Sprinkle with confectioners' sugar or stack small cakes with sauce between. Serves 6.

DUTCH PANCAKE

4 eggs
½ cup sifted flour
½ teaspoon salt
½ cup milk
2 tablespoons soft butter
Confectioners' sugar
Jam

Beat eggs. Sift flour and salt together and add to eggs alternately with milk, to make a smooth batter. Spread butter over bottom and sides of cold frying pan. Pour in batter and place in a hot oven (400°F.). Bake 20 to 25 minutes, reducing heat gradually to moderate (350°F.) during baking. Pancake should puff up at the sides and be crisp and brown. Sprinkle with confectioners' sugar and spread with jam. Roll like an omelet. Serve on hot platter. Serves 4.

POLISH PANCAKES

3 eggs
6 tablespoons milk
1 teaspoon flour
¼ teaspoon salt
1 teaspoon sugar
4 teaspoons butter
¾ cup strawberry jam
2 cups sliced peaches
Confectioners' sugar

Beat eggs until foamy, add milk, flour, salt and sugar. Beat well. Melt 1 teaspoon butter in 9-inch skillet, tilting to cover entire bottom. Pour ¼ of egg mixture into hot skillet covering surface evenly. Cook until firm enough to roll. Slip pancake from skillet onto a clean cloth, spread with jam and peaches and roll up. Repeat, making 4 filled pancakes in all. Sprinkle with confectioners' sugar, slice and serve warm. Serves 4.

Other fruit and jam combinations may be used: apricot and raspberry; pear and blackberry.

FILLED PANCAKES

(These pancakes are eaten with soup. The meat in the filling is that cooked in preparing the soup stock.)

1 cup sifted flour
½ teaspoon salt
½ teaspoon baking powder
1 cup milk
5 eggs
1 cup ground meat (from soup)
1 egg yolk
1 cup minced onion
2 tablespoons butter
Bread crumbs

Sift flour, salt and baking powder together. Add milk and 3 eggs, well beaten, and mix to a smooth batter. Bake in thin cakes in a greased skillet. Let cool. Mix meat with egg yolk and 1 egg. Season with salt and pepper to taste. Sauté onion in butter, add meat mixture and cook 2 minutes. Spread on pancakes and roll tightly. Beat remaining egg. Dip rolled pancakes in egg and then in crumbs and fry in hot fat until well browned. Serve with bouillon or other thin soup. Serves 6.

POTATO PANCAKES

2 cups thoroughly drained grated uncooked potatoes
4 eggs, separated
¼ teaspoon baking powder
1 teaspoon salt
1 tablespoon flour

To prepare potatoes, pare and soak in cold water 12 hours. Grate and drain thoroughly. Add egg yolks, baking powder, salt and flour and beat well. Fold in stiffly beaten egg whites. Drop from a tablespoon onto a hot well greased skillet. Brown on both sides. Serve with Applesauce. Serves 4.

SCRAMBLED EGGS

6 eggs
¾ teaspoon salt
⅛ teaspoon pepper
⅓ cup cream or rich milk
2 tablespoons butter

Beat eggs slightly until yolks and whites are broken, but not too well mixed. Add seasonings and cream and mix. Heat butter in skillet until melted and hot enough to sizzle when a drop of egg is added. Add eggs, reduce heat and cook slowly, stirring the eggs from the bottom as they become firm and browned slightly. Serve as soon as eggs are fairly firm (but not dry) throughout. Garnish with slices of crisp bacon. Serves 6.

ANCHOVY—Rub 3 anchovies into a smooth paste, season with lemon juice, paprika and a few drops of onion juice and add when eggs are nearly done. Serve on toast with tart or jellied garnish.

Spread hot toast with anchovy paste just before serving.

BACON AND PEAS—Add ⅓ cup chopped crisp bacon and ¾ cup cooked peas.

CHEESE—(A) Add ½ to ¾ cup grated cheese to the eggs before cooking.

(B) Add ¾ to 1 cup cottage cheese and 1½ teaspoons minced chives to eggs when they begin to pile. Finish cooking.

COOKED VEGETABLE — Add ¾ cup any cooked vegetable desired.

CROUTON — Sauté bread cubes in bacon drippings until brown; add to scrambled eggs.

CURRIED—Add 4 tablespoons curry powder to egg mixture. Serve on toast or biscuits.

FOWL OR MEAT—Add ¾ cup diced cooked fowl, dried beef, fried sausage or other meat to egg mixture.

HAM—Sauté cubes of ham, add egg mixture and cook as described.

HERRING—Add ¾ to 1 cup shredded smoked herring when eggs are nearly finished cooking.

LIVER—Add sautéed chicken or calf's liver.

MUSHROOM — Use mushroom soup instead of milk or cream or add sautéed mushrooms.

ONION AND PARSLEY—The addition of onion juice and chopped parsley improves the flavor of the eggs.

POTATO—Make a depression in stuffed baked potato and fill with scrambled eggs.

SPANISH EGGS—Cook chopped green pepper, pimiento with equal parts chili sauce and grated cheese in butter about 5 minutes. Add to eggs before cooking.

UNUSUAL SCRAMBLED EGGS— Use ½ cup thick sour cream instead of cream or milk. Add ½ teaspoon prepared mustard.

EGG FRIZZLE

¼ pound chipped beef
4 teaspoons butter
4 eggs, beaten
⅛ teaspoon pepper
¼ cup milk

Cook dried beef in butter until slightly crisp. Combine eggs, pepper and milk and mix well. Pour over beef and cook as for Scrambled Eggs. Serve garnished with sprigs of parsley. Serves 4.

EGGS À LA CARACAS—Heat 1 tablespoon grated cheese with beef. Use 1 cup tomatoes instead of milk. Add onion juice and ¼ teaspoon Worcestershire sauce, if desired.

Use 1 cup diced cooked beef or veal instead of chipped beef and tomato catchup instead of milk.

EGGS AND PORK SAUSAGE

½ pound bulk pork sausage
3 cups dry cubed bread
6 eggs, beaten
6 tablespoons milk
½ cup grated cheese

Sauté sausage in skillet until well browned. Pour off most of the fat. Add bread cubes and brown. Combine eggs, milk and cheese and add to sausage mixture. Cook as for Scrambled Eggs. Serve at once with grilled tomatoes. Serves 6.

EGGS IN ONION SAUCE

3 medium onions, sliced
1 sweet pepper, sliced
2 tablespoons fat
6 eggs
Salt and pepper
Parsley

Cook onions and sweet pepper in fat until tender and brown. Beat eggs slightly; add seasoning and pour over the onions. Cook as for Scrambled Eggs. Remove to a hot platter and garnish with parsley. Serves 6.

EGGS WITH SHERRY AND ORANGE

6 eggs
1 tablespoon sherry
3 tablespoons Tomato Sauce
½ teaspoon salt
Dash cayenne
Butter
Grated orange rind

Beat eggs until frothy. Blend in sherry and tomato sauce. Add seasonings. Melt butter in frying pan and pour in the mixture. Cook slowly, stirring until thickened. Sprinkle with grated orange rind and serve immediately. Serves 6.

EGGS WITH SHRIMP

½ cup sautéed mushrooms
½ cup cooked shrimp
3 tablespoons butter
5 eggs, beaten
Salt and pepper

Cook mushrooms and shrimp in butter until lightly browned. Beat eggs, add seasonings and pour over the shrimp mixture. Cook as for Scrambled Eggs. Slip onto hot platter. Serves 4.

METHODS OF SERVING SCRAMBLED EGGS

EGG AND CHEESE TOAST — Spread hot buttered toast with heated tomato catchup, heap scrambled eggs on toast, cover with grated cheese and place under broiler to melt cheese.

EGGS WITH HOMINY AND CHEESE SAUCE—Serve hot buttered hominy covered with Cheese Sauce surrounded with scrambled eggs, garnished with parsley.

EGGS IN SAUSAGE CUPS—Fry summer sausage (with casing left on) in hot butter until edges curl up forming a cup. Remove casing, fill cups with scrambled egg, garnish with paprika and chopped parsley.

EGGS ON SPANISH TOAST — Combine 2 eggs, slightly beaten, ¾ cup tomato juice, 1 teaspoon sugar and ¼ teaspoon salt. Dip 5 or 6 slices of bread into mixture, moistening both sides. Brown on both sides in greased hot frying pan. Place on hot platter and heap with scrambled eggs.

EGGS IN MUFFINS — Hollow out centers of muffins or buns. Toast lightly and fill with eggs.

EGGS WITH RICE AND CHEESE — Pile hot rice on platter. Surround with eggs and top with hot Cheese Sauce.

SCRAMBLED MATZOTH

6 matzoth soaked in water
4 eggs, beaten
½ teaspoon salt

Squeeze any excess water from the matzoth; add beaten eggs and salt. Mix well. Pour into hot greased skillet and cook as for Scrambled Eggs. Serve at once. Serves 4.

CHOW EGGS

6 eggs
½ cup chopped cooked meat
¼ cup chopped mushrooms
½ cup chopped water chestnuts
1 cup chopped bamboo shoots
½ teaspoon salt

Beat eggs and add remaining ingredients. Cook as for Scrambled Eggs. Garnish with parsley and serve with soy sauce. Serves 6.

SCRAMBLED EGGS WITH ASPARAGUS

6 eggs
½ cup cooked asparagus tips
Salt and pepper
1 tablespoon butter

Add unbeaten eggs to asparagus and mix together. Season with salt and pepper. Melt butter in frying pan, add eggs and cook slowly, stirring constantly, until eggs are set. Serve on hot buttered toast. Serves 6.

CAULIFLOWER — Use cooked cauliflowerets instead of asparagus.

CELERY — Use cooked chopped celery instead of asparagus.

KIDNEY — Use chopped cooked kidney instead of asparagus.

SAUSAGE — Use chopped Vienna sausages instead of asparagus.

TOMATO — Use chopped tomato instead of asparagus. Omit asparagus. Serve on bed of buttered spinach.

SCRAMBLED EGGS WITH MUSHROOMS

5 eggs
½ teaspoon salt
⅛ teaspoon pepper
½ cup mushroom soup
½ cup water
1½ tablespoons butter

Combine first 5 ingredients and mix well. Melt butter in frying pan, add eggs and cook slowly, stirring constantly, until eggs are set. Serve on hot buttered toast with bacon. Serves 5.

WITH OYSTERS — Combine 4 eggs, ½ pint oysters, ¾ teaspoon salt, ⅛ teaspoon pepper and 2 tablespoons cream. Cook as above in 2 tablespoons butter. Serves 6.

SCRAMBLED EGGS WITH PRESERVES

6 eggs
2 tablespoons marmalade
1 tablespoon butter

Add unbeaten eggs to marmalade and mix. Melt butter in frying pan, add eggs and cook slowly, stirring constantly until eggs are set. Serve on hot buttered toast. Serves 6.
Use apricot or prune purée instead of marmalade.

OLIVE SCRAMBLED EGGS

4 eggs
¼ cup water
¼ teaspoon salt
⅛ teaspoon pepper
⅛ teaspoon paprika
3 strips bacon
¼ cup minced stuffed olives

Beat eggs slightly with water. Add salt, pepper and paprika. Cut bacon into 1-inch pieces, fry lightly, add olives and eggs and cook slowly, stirring constantly until eggs are as firm as desired. Serves 4.

BAKED EGGS OR SHIRRED EGGS

6 or 12 eggs
Salt and pepper

Melt 1 teaspoon of butter in each custard cup. Break 1 or 2 eggs into each cup. Sprinkle with salt and pepper and dot with butter. Bake in moderate oven (350°F.) until the eggs are firm but not hard, about 15 minutes. Serve in the cups. Serves 6.

CHEESE—Sprinkle grated American cheese over eggs before baking.

CHICKEN LIVERS—Line custard cups with sautéed chicken livers, add egg and 1 tablespoon cider to each and sprinkle with bread crumbs.

PORK SAUSAGE—Line custard cups with thin slices of cooked pork sausage; add egg, salt, pepper and 1 tablespoon Tomato Sauce or catchup to each and

sprinkle with buttered crumbs

ROQUEFORT BAKED EGGS—Place 2 teaspoons Roquefort cheese in bottom of each greased custard cup, melt cheese in oven, add eggs and continue as described above. Serve with Tomato Sauce.

EGGS À LA SUISSE—Cover bottom of buttered custard cups with grated cheese, add eggs, pour in enough thin cream to cover egg and top with layer of grated cheese. Bake as above. Serve Eggs à la Suisse in Patty Shells filled with Curry Sauce.

EGGS IN MUSTARD SAUCE—Add 1 teaspoon prepared mustard and 3 tablespoons grated cheese to 1 cup White Sauce. Break 6 eggs into a buttered baking dish, pour sauce over them and cover with buttered bread crumbs. Bake as above. Serves 6.

Sprinkle chopped parsley in dish before adding eggs.

FLUFFY EGG NESTS

6 eggs
Salt and pepper
6 slices hot buttered toast

Separate eggs, leaving each yolk in the shell until ready to use. Season whites with salt and pepper and beat until stiff enough to form sharp peaks. Heap onto toast and make a hollow in the center of each mound. Slip egg yolks into hollow, season and bake in moderate oven (350°F.) until white is browned and yolks are firm. Garnish with paprika and parsley. Serves 6.

One cup grated or shredded American cheese may be sprinkled over eggs before baking.

Brown 6 slices baked ham in butter and place on toast slices before heaping egg whites on top. Or use rusks instead of toast.

For the ever-popular brunch your gang will like fluffy egg nests with plenty of broiled bacon

EGGS IN TOMATO CASES

6 small tomatoes
2 tablespoons butter
Salt and pepper
6 eggs

Cut tops from ripe tomatoes. In the center of each make a hollow large enough to hold an egg. Add 1 teaspoon butter, season with salt and pepper and break an egg into each. Bake in moderate oven (350°F.) until eggs are firm and tomatoes are cooked. For 6.

EGGS WITH MUSHROOM CAPS

9 Stuffed Hard-Cooked Eggs
18 mushroom caps, sautéed
2 cups mushroom soup

Top each egg half with a mushroom cap. Place in baking dish and add soup. Heat thoroughly in 350°F. oven. Serves 6.

Stuffed eggs have a pixie look when they wear caps of nut-brown broiled mushrooms

EGGS IN BACON RINGS

6 slices bacon
6 eggs
Salt and pepper
Rounds of hot buttered toast
Parsley

Grease bottoms of custard cups, curl a slice of bacon around inside of each cup. Break an egg inside each bacon ring, season with salt and pepper and bake in moderate oven (350°F.) until firm, but not hard. Remove carefully from cup so that the egg and bacon will remain together. Place on rounds of toast. Arrange on platter and garnish with parsley. Serves 6.

If preferred, bacon may be fried or broiled until cooked but not crisp, before placing in custard cups.

Use seasoned mashed potatoes instead of hot buttered toast.

Serve on toasted English muffins or rusks.

EGGS IN PIMIENTO CUPS

6 canned pimientos
6 eggs
Salt and pepper
6 tablespoons cream or evaporated milk
2 tablespoons butter
3 tablespoons flour
1 cup milk
3 tablespoons grated cheese
Buttered toast

Place pimiento cups in custard cups and drop an egg into each. Season with salt and pepper and add 1 tablespoon cream to each one. Bake in moderate oven (350°F.) until eggs are firm. Meanwhile, blend butter and flour, add milk and cook until thick, stirring constantly. Add cheese. Serve pimiento cups on toast covered with sauce, for 6.

EGGS NEW ORLEANS

2½ cups tomatoes
½ green pepper, chopped
1 small onion, chopped
½ cup chopped celery
1 teaspoon sugar
¾ teaspoon salt
⅛ teaspoon pepper
1 bay leaf
¾ cup bread crumbs
4 eggs
½ cup grated American cheese

Cook tomatoes, pepper, onion, celery, sugar and seasonings together for 10 minutes. Remove bay leaf, add bread crumbs and place in casserole. Break eggs on top, sprinkle with salt and pepper and cover with grated cheese. Bake in moderate oven (350°F.) until eggs are firm and cheese has melted, 15 to 20 minutes. Serves 4.

If desired, place mixture in 4 buttered individual baking dishes and break an egg into each. Serve in baking dishes.

EGGS BAKED IN CHEESE SAUCE

¼ cup butter
¼ cup flour
½ teaspoon salt
⅛ teaspoon pepper
2 cups mllk
½ cup grated sharp cheese
4 eggs

Prepare a sauce of the butter, flour, seasonings and milk. Add cheese and stir until melted. Pour cheese sauce into greased baking dish and let cool slightly to thicken. Make 4 hollows in sauce with back of spoon and break 1 egg into each. Season eggs, cover and bake in moderate oven (350°F.) until eggs are firm. Serves 4.

A dish about 7 inches by 1½ inches or small ramekins or custard cups for individual service may be used.

EGGS À LA BENEDICTINE—

Place slice of ham on slice of buttered toast, then a slice of grilled tomato, next the baked egg, cover with the sauce flavored with ¼ cup sherry.

EGGS BAKED IN POTATOES

3 large potatoes
3 tablespoons butter
½ teaspoon salt
⅛ teaspoon pepper
4 tablespoons hot mllk
6 eggs

Scrub and dry potatoes. Bake in hot oven (425° to 450°F.) until tender, about 45 minutes. Cut into halves and scoop out potatoes, being careful not to break skin. Mash potatoes; add butter, salt, pepper and milk. Beat until light and fluffy. Fill potato shells, leaving a hollow in each. Place an egg in each hollow. Season with additional salt and pepper and bake in moderate oven (350°F.) until eggs are firm. Serves 6.

BAKED EGGS WITH HAM—

Break eggs into buttered baking cups, dot with butter and bake in a moderate oven (350°F.) until firm, about 15 minutes. Remove carefully from cups and serve with slices of broiled ham. Garnish with parsley.

Eggs need not be round just because it's customary. Try using square pans, just to be different

EGGS IN MORNAY SAUCE

2 tablespoons butter
2 tablespoons flour
½ teaspoon salt
⅛ teaspoon pepper
½ bay leaf
1 teaspoon minced parsley
1½ teaspoons minced onlon
1 cup milk
2 tablespoons Parmesan or Gruyère cheese
6 eggs

Melt butter, add flour, salt, pepper, bay leaf, parsley and onion. Blend. Add milk and cook until thickened, stirring constantly. Remove bay leaf; add cheese. Place 1 tablespoon sauce in each custard cup, place egg in each and cover with 2 additional tablespoons sauce. Bake in moderate oven (350°F.) until eggs are firm. Serve in the cups. Serves 6.

Or bake in large shallow dish and serve on toast with sauce.

BAKED EGGS, SPANISH STYLE

3 tablespoons chopped onion
3 tablespoons chopped green pepper
¼ cup butter
6 eggs
Salt and pepper
¼ cup bread crumbs
½ cup grated cheese

Brown onion and pepper in butter, then pour into baking dish. Break eggs into dish, being careful not to break the yolks. Season with salt and pepper. Mix crumbs with cheese and sprinkle over eggs. Bake in moderate oven (350°F.) about 15 minutes or until eggs are firm. Serve in baking dish. Serves 3 to 6.

Omit pepper and use grated Parmesan cheese over onion.

Add 1 tablespoon flour and 1 cup tomato purée after browning onion and pepper. Add 2 tablespoons chopped celery, ¼ teaspoon salt and 1 teaspoon chili powder. Simmer until thickened and celery is tender. Break eggs into custard cups and add 2 tablespoons sauce to each.

Use olive oil and pimiento instead of butter and green pepper, add 1 cup tomato pulp instead of crumbs and cheese. Cover each egg with sauce and bake as above.

BAKED EGGS FOR LUNCHEON

1½ cups chopped cooked meat
1½ cups cracker crumbs
Salt and pepper
¾ cup gravy or milk
6 eggs

Combine meat, crumbs, salt, pepper and gravy or milk. Heat. Fill buttered muffin pans ⅔ full with mixture. Break an egg into each pan. Bake in a moderate oven (350°F.) until eggs are set. Serves 6.

EGGS FLORENTINE

3 cups cooked spinach
6 eggs
Salt
½ pound American cheese
1 tall can evaporated milk
2 cups buttered crumbs

Chop spinach very fine and heat; turn into shallow baking dish. Make 6 small wells in the spinach, drop an egg into each and season with salt. Prepare a cheese sauce by heating the cheese and milk over boiling water until cheese is melted. Pour hot sauce over eggs and spinach. Sprinkle with crumbs and bake in moderate oven (350°F.) until brown, about 25 minutes. Serves 6.

Bake in individual baking dishes and garnish with a border of mashed potatoes put through a pastry tube.

Asparagus or Swiss chard may be used instead of spinach.

Add the cheese sauce and your eggs Florentine are ready for the oven

BAKED EGGS ON SPANISH RICE

1 cup uncooked rice
2½ cups cooked tomatoes
½ small onion, sliced
¾ teaspoon salt
1 bay leaf, 2 cloves
2 tablespoons melted butter
2 tablespoons flour
6 eggs
2 tablespoons grated cheese
½ cup buttered crumbs

Cook rice in boiling salted water until tender; drain and rinse with hot water. Simmer tomatoes, onion, salt, bay leaf and cloves together for 10 minutes. Strain. Blend butter with flour in saucepan and add strained tomatoes stirring constantly. Cook until thickened. Arrange layer of rice in greased casserole and make 6 depressions in the rice. Place an egg in each depression. Pour tomato sauce over all and sprinkle with cheese and bread crumbs. Bake in moderate oven (350°F.) until eggs are firm, about 15 minutes. Serves 6.

BAKED TOMATOES AND HARD-COOKED EGGS

2 medium tomatoes, peeled
6 slices bread
6 hard-cooked eggs, sliced
2 cups Cheese Sauce
12 strips cooked bacon
Parsley

Cut each tomato into 3 slices crosswise. Toast bread lightly. Arrange sliced egg on each slice of toast, cover with a slice of tomato and bake in 350°F. oven 15 minutes. Pour hot cheese sauce over tomato and return to oven to heat until sauce begins to bubble. Remove from oven, garnish each service with 2 bacon strips and parsley. Serves 6.

RUFFLED EGGS — Make a border of mashed potatoes around a shallow baking dish; brown in oven. Brown ½ cup each pearl onions and chopped mushrooms in butter. Spread in baking dish. Break 4 eggs on top. Dot with butter and sprinkle with salt and pepper. Bake in moderate oven (350°F.) 15 minutes or until eggs are set. Serves 4.

SHIRRED EGGS AND SAUSAGES

6 link sausages
1 cup catchup
6 eggs

Cut sausages into 1-inch pieces and brown lightly. Place in shallow baking dish and cover with catchup. Break eggs over catchup and bake in moderate oven (350°F.) 15 minutes. For 6.

EGGS WITH CHICKEN LIVERS

6 chicken livers
2 tablespoons butter
6 tablespoons cream
6 eggs
Salt and pepper
Paprika

Cut livers into pieces and fry lightly in butter. Place in 6 buttered ramekins. Add 1 tablespoon cream and 1 egg to each. Season with salt, pepper and paprika. Bake in moderate oven (350°F.) 15 minutes or until eggs are set. Serves 6.

Baked eggs in tomatoes in individual casseroles with a cheese sauce and rusk make a stellar appearance at luncheon

EGGS IN TOMATOES

1 small onion
2 cups cooked tomatoes
1 teaspoon salt
¼ teaspoon pepper
6 eggs
6 slices buttered toast

Cut onion into small pieces and place with tomatoes in shallow baking pan. Bake in moderate oven (350°F.) for 10 minutes. Add salt and pepper. Break eggs and place on tomatoes, being careful not to break yolks. Bake in moderate oven (350°F.) until whites of eggs are thickened, then prick yolks and let them mingle with the tomato and the whites. Serve at once on toast. Serves 6.

EGGS WITH HERBS IN RAMEKINS

4 hard-cooked eggs
2 tablespoons mixed herbs
    (thyme, basil, summer savory,
    sweet marjoram and parsley)
2 tablespoons butter
Salt and pepper
2 eggs, beaten
½ cup cream or evaporated milk

Mince eggs. Sauté herbs in butter for 5 minutes, being careful not to brown butter. Add minced eggs, salt, pepper, eggs and cream; mix thoroughly. Pour into greased ramekins, set in pan of hot water and bake in moderate oven (350°F.) until firm, about 20 minutes. Serves 4.

EGGS WITH MINCED CHICKEN — Moisten 1 cup minced cooked chicken with cream of mushroom soup. Divide among 4 baked pastry shells. Break an egg on top of each and add salt, pepper and 1 tablespoon cream. Bake in a moderate oven (350°F.) 15 minutes or until eggs are set. Serve with crisp bacon for 4.

POACHED EGG

2 cups water
½ teaspoon salt
Pepper
½ tablespoon vinegar
1 egg
Hot buttered toast

Heat water to simmering in a shallow pan; add salt, pepper and vinegar. Break egg into a cup and slip it carefully into water. Make a whirlpool with spoon or fork. Let egg cook below boiling point for about 5 minutes or until white is firm and a film has formed over yolk. Remove egg with skimmer, drain and serve on toast.

NOTE—Water should cover egg. Vary quantity of water according to number of eggs used and size and shape of pan.

TO SERVE POACHED EGGS—
ANCHOVY—Spread toast with anchovy paste, place poached egg on toast.

ASPARAGUS—Spread a buttered piece of toast with purée of asparagus. Cover with poached egg and garnish with cooked asparagus tips. A Cream or Cheese Sauce may be poured over all.

CHEESE—Eggs may be garnished with shredded cheese, American, Swiss, Parmesan or Gruyère.

CHICKEN—Place equal amounts of sautéed mushrooms and chicken or other meat on toast and cover with poached egg.

CORNED BEEF HASH — Place eggs on top corned beef hash patties.

CREAMED—Place poached egg on toast, cover with Cream Sauce and sprinkle with grated cheese.

CROUSTADE — Pour Cheese Sauce into toasted bread Croustades place a poached egg in the center of each one. Garnish with paprika and parsley.

MILK—Eggs may be poached in milk, Tomato Sauce, meat or vegetable stocks.

MUSHROOM—C o v e r poached egg with creamed mushrooms.

PÂTÉ DE FOIE GRAS—Spread toast with pâté de foie gras; place a poached egg on toast; serve with Tomato Sauce.

POTATO—Serve poached eggs on browned potato patties.

SPINACH—Line a greased individual baking dish with seasoned spinach. Place poached egg on top, cover with browned butter, grated cheese, pimiento cheese sauce or Hollandaise Sauce.

TOMATO—Serve poached eggs on broiled tomato slices.

CHEESE EGGS

6 eggs
1 cup cream or evaporated milk
2 tablespoons grated cheese
Salt and pepper

Poach eggs in cream and place on a hot platter. To the cream remaining, add cheese and seasonings. Stir until cheese is melted; pour over eggs. Serves 6.

Back up the luncheon egg by poaching in meat nests like browned corned beef hash

EGG TOAST

6 slices toast
Butter
6 eggs, separated
Salt and pepper

Spread toast with butter, moisten the edges with hot water and poach the egg yolks in salted water until soft-cooked. Place 1 on each slice of toast. Beat the whites until stiff, spread in circles around the yolks, season with salt and pepper and brown in moderate oven (350°F.). Serve hot. Serves 6.

EGGS WITH BROWNED BUTTER

2 eggs
1 tablespoon wine vinegar
1 tablespoon butter
1 teaspoon finely chopped parsley

Poach eggs in water to which a little vinegar has been added. Remove while still soft and place in a dish in the oven. Boil the vinegar until it is ½ its original quantity; then pour it over eggs. Simmer butter for a few minutes in a pan. Add parsley and continue cooking until both butter and parsley are browned. Pour over eggs and serve at once. Serves 1.

EGGS BENEDICT

3 English muffins
6 slices broiled ham
6 poached eggs
Hollandaise Sauce

Split and toast English muffins. Cut ham same size as muffin; place on muffin, slip egg on ham and cover with hollandaise sauce. Serve hot. Serves 6.

Toast may be used in place of English muffins.

Use Cheese Sauce instead of Hollandaise Sauce.

EGGS ROBIN HOOD—Place slices of broiled tomato on ham and muffin and top with poached egg. Serve with Cheese Sauce or Hollandaise Sauce.

EGGS DOREMUS

4 tablespoons butter
3 tablespoons flour
¾ teaspoon salt
1 teaspoon Worcestershire sauce
2 cups milk
6 mushroom caps
6 Tartlet shells
1½ cups minced chicken
6 eggs, poached

Make a white sauce of 3 tablespoons butter, the flour, salt, Worcestershire sauce and milk. Brown mushroom caps in 1 tablespoon butter. Fill shells with hot minced chicken. Place an egg on each, top with mushroom cap and serve with sauce. For 6.

Buttered toast, mashed potatoes, patty shells or rice may be used in place of tartlet shells.

Use ham instead of chicken.

EGGS POACHED IN WHITE WINE

1 tablespoon butter
½ cup dry white wine
4 eggs
Salt and pepper
Few grains cayenne
2 tablespoons grated Roquefort cheese
Hot buttered toast

Melt butter in a skillet, add wine. Slip in eggs one at a time, season with salt, pepper and cayenne, and poach until whites are nearly firm. Sprinkle with cheese and cook until melted. Serve on toast for 4.

Start the day with gold and white poached eggs on toast and crisp brown bacon

EGGS WITH MUSHROOMS

½ pound mushrooms, cut into pieces
4 tablespoons butter
2 tablespoons flour
1 teaspoon salt
¼ teaspoon pepper
¼ teaspoon paprika
1 teaspoon Worcestershire sauce
2 cups milk
6 poached eggs
6 slices hot toast

Sauté mushrooms in butter until tender, about 5 minutes. Add flour and seasonings; blend. Add milk and cook, stirring constantly. Boil for 3 minutes. Place eggs on toast and cover with sauce. Serves 6.

1 cup lobster may be added to the sauce.

Sauté 2 tablespoons chopped green pepper and 2 tablespoons minced pimiento with mushrooms. Garnish with pepper rings.

POACHED EGGS IN RICE NESTS WITH CHEESE AND OLIVE SAUCE

1 cup rice
⅓ cup butter, ⅓ cup flour
1 teaspoon salt
⅛ teaspoon pepper
3 cups milk
1½ cups grated cheese
⅔ cup sliced stuffed olives
8 poached eggs

Cook rice in rapidly boiling salted water until tender. Drain and rinse. Melt butter, blend in flour, salt and pepper. Add milk and cook until thickened, stirring constantly. Remove from heat, add cheese and olives and stir until cheese is melted. Form rice into 8 nests, place egg into each and cover with sauce. Garnish with parsley or watercress. Serves 8.

POACHED EGGS ON POTATO CAKES

4 large potatoes
2 tablespoons butter
2 tablespoons grated cheese
Salt and pepper
Fat for frying
2 onions, sliced
3 tomatoes, sliced
6 poached eggs

Pare and boil potatoes until tender. Mash, add butter, cheese, salt and pepper. Shape into flat cakes and fry in hot fat. Prepare a sauce by browning onions in fat and adding the tomatoes; simmer slowly about 20 minutes. Cover fried potato cakes with sauce and top each with a poached egg. Serves 6.

Use 2 cups leftover mashed potatoes and 2 cups minced cooked ham. Omit tomato sauce and serve with Horse-radish Sauce.

Use corned beef hash for patties, instead of potatoes.

POACHED EGGS WITH CHEESE SAUCE

2 tablespoons butter
1 tablespoon flour
Salt
Pepper
1 pimiento, chopped
2 cups scalded milk
1 cup grated cheese
6 slices toast
6 poached eggs

Melt butter in double boiler. Blend in flour, salt, pepper and pimiento. Add milk and cook until thickened, stirring constantly. Add cheese and stir until melted. Pour sauce over hot toast and place a poached egg on sauce. Garnish with sliced pimiento and a dash of paprika. Serves 6.

Serve on bread Croustades filled with cheese sauce.

A beautiful breakfast service for poached eggs is this bread croustade with a favorite sauce

POACHED SWEET-SOUR EGGS

1 tablespoon butter
1 small onion, minced
1 teaspoon flour
½ cup water
3 or 4 cloves
2 bay leaves
2 tablespoons vinegar
¼ teaspoon salt
1 tablespoon sugar
6 eggs

Melt butter in a saucepan, add onion and cook slowly. Do not brown. Add flour and brown slightly. Add water, cloves and bay leaves and cook until smooth, stirring constantly. Simmer 5 minutes longer. Strain through a coarse sieve. Add vinegar, salt and sugar and heat to boiling, add eggs 1 at a time, breaking each into a saucer and then slipping it into boiling liquid. Cover and cook a few minutes. Eggs may be cooked soft or hard as preferred. Serves 6.

CHINESE POACHED EGGS

1 cup rice
2 tablespoons butter
Salt and pepper
2 tablespoons flour
1 cup milk
1 teaspoon grated onion
1 tablespoon chopped celery
6 eggs, poached

Cook the rice in boiling salted water. Drain and blanch. Prepare a white sauce by melting butter and blending in salt, pepper and flour. Add milk, salt, pepper, grated onion and chopped celery. Cook until thickened, stirring constantly. Arrange hot rice on platter, place eggs on top and cover with sauce. Garnish with paprika and parsley. Serves 6.

Use Tomato Sauce instead of white sauce.

Use Mushroom Sauce instead of white sauce.

PLANKED EGGS

1 cup finely chopped cooked ham
  or corned beef
1 cup crumbs
Cream or evaporated milk
4 cups mashed potatoes
6 poached eggs
Garnish of tomato slices
Green pepper rings

Mix meat with crumbs and enough cream to make a paste. Spread the mixture on a heated plank of suitable size. Around the edge of the plank make a narrow border of mashed potatoes and inside the border make 6 nests of potato. Slip a poached egg into each nest and place in hot oven (425°F.) until potato is browned. Garnish with alternate slices of tomato and green pepper rings. Serves 6.

Omit meat, crumbs and cream.

Every hostess who serves such perfect pinkish poached eggs will use only the freshest and handle with skill

POACHED EGGS IN SHERRIED SHRIMP

½ clove garlic or slice onion
2 tablespoons butter
2 tablespoons flour
½ cup tomato pulp
2 teaspoons chopped parsley
¼ cup cream
¼ cup sherry
1 tablespoon Worcestershire sauce
1 cup cooked shrimp, cleaned
Salt and pepper
Buttered crumbs (about 1 cup)
4 poached eggs

Brown garlic in butter. Remove garlic, add flour, tomato and parsley. Cook about 2 minutes, stirring constantly. Add cream, sherry, Worcestershire sauce and shrimp. Cook about 5 minutes longer. Season. Pour into greased individual casseroles lined with buttered crumbs and bake for 10 minutes in moderate oven (350°F.). Place a hot poached egg in center of each casserole and garnish with pepper and paprika. Serves 3 or 4.

POACHED EGGS ON APPLE RINGS

2 large apples
2 tablespoons fat
6 eggs
Salt and pepper

Wash and core apples; cut crosswise into slices ½ inch thick. Fry apples in fat 2 or 3 minutes to each side. Place an egg on each apple slice. Season. Cover pan closely and continue cooking over low heat until eggs are firm. Transfer to warm platter and garnish with other fried apple slices. Serves 6.

Cut thick crosswise slices from large cooked beets. Heat in butter, being careful not to break the slices. Sprinkle with few drops orange juice and serve a poached egg on each slice.

CREAMED EGGS

(For instructions on hard-cooked eggs, see page 44)

CREAMED EGGS

6 hard-cooked eggs
2 cups White Sauce

Cut eggs into eighths lengthwise or slice. Heat slowly in white sauce. Serve hot on toast, Baking Powder Biscuits or bread Croustades, garnished with chopped parsley. Serve 6.

ANCHOVY—Add 1 teaspoon dry mustard to white sauce and garnish eggs with fillets of anchovies.

CELERY—Add ¾ cup diced celery.

CHEESE—Add ½ cup grated cheese.

DRIED BEEF—Add ¼ pound shredded dried beef.

HAM—Add 1½ cups diced cooked ham.

MUSHROOM—Add ½ cup sautéed mushrooms.

SARDINE—Add ½ cup boned, chopped sardines.

SCALLOPED — Place alternate layers of egg mixture and buttered bread crumbs (1 cup) in greased baking dish; bake in moderate oven (350°F.) until heated and crumbs are browned.

TOMATO CATCHUP—Add 2 tablespoons tomato catchup.

TOMATO SAUCE — Use Tomato Sauce instead of white sauce.

VEGETABLE—Add ½ cup of any cooked vegetables desired.

CREAMED EGGS AND MUSHROOMS

¾ cup evaporated milk
½ pound American cheese, grated
4 hard-cooked eggs
½ cup sautéed mushrooms

Scald milk in top of double boiler. Add cheese, eggs and mushrooms. Serve on toast or in Quick Toast Timbales. Serves 6.
Asparagus, string beans or boiled ham may be used.

DUTCH EGGS

6 hard-cooked eggs
2 tablespoons butter, melted
1 teaspoon minced chervil
1 teaspoon minced parsley
¼ teaspoon dry mustard
Salt and pepper
½ cup chopped cleaned shrimp
1 cup cream' or evaporated milk
Grated cheese, Butter

Chop eggs, add butter, seasonings, shrimp and cream and mix well. Pour mixture into greased baking dish, sprinkle top with grated cheese and dot with bits of butter. Bake in hot oven (400°F.) about 10 minutes or until cheese melts and begins to brown. Serves 6.

CREAMED EGGS AND CARROTS

4 tablespoons butter
4 tablespoons flour
2½ cups milk
1 teaspoon salt
¼ teaspoon pepper
6 hard-cooked eggs, quartered
6 cooked carrots, sliced
6 slices hot toast

Melt butter in top of double boiler. Blend in flour, add milk and stir until thickened. Cook for 3 minutes longer. Add salt, pepper, eggs and carrots and heat thoroughly. Serve on toast and garnish with parsley. Serves 6.

EGGS À LA KING—Omit carrots and add 1 cup sautéed mushrooms, ½ cup peas and 1 pimiento, cut into strips.

FRENCH BREAD CROUSTADE—Slice top off a round loaf of bread; remove soft interior, brush with melted butter and toast. Fill with 1 of the above mixtures.

IN PASTRY SHELLS — Cover bottom of baked Pastry shells with grated cheese. Fill with either of above mixtures.

TOMATO EGGS ON TOAST

4 tablespoons butter
6 tablespoons flour
1 teaspoon salt
3 cups cooked tomatoes
9 hard-cooked eggs, quartered
6 slices buttered toast
Parsley

Melt butter; stir in flour and salt. Add tomatoes gradually and cook until thickened, stirring constantly. Add eggs to sauce and serve on hot toast. Garnish with parsley. Serves 6.
Use 6 eggs instead of 9; add 1 cup cooked mushrooms.
Serve on Melba toast, zwieback or Patty Shells instead of toast.
Add minced chives, if desired

CATALAN EGGS—Heat 1 cup Tomato Sauce in skillet. Add 4 skinned slices Italian sausage and continue heating, turning over and over. Fry 4 eggs in butter or olive oil. Serve an egg on each slice sausage. Pour sauce over.

EGG AND SOUR CREAM CASSEROLE

9 hard-cooked eggs
6 tablespoons softened butter
1 teaspoon grated onion
4 teaspoons minced parsley
1⅔ teaspoons prepared mustard
½ teaspoon salt
⅛ teaspoon pepper
1 cup sour cream
½ cup dry bread crumbs

Cut eggs lengthwise into halves, remove yolks and mash. Add 3 tablespoons butter, onion, parsley, mustard, salt and pepper to yolks. Fill egg whites with mixture. Place, cut side down, in shallow casserole. Cover with sour cream, sprinkle with crumbs, dot with remaining butter and bake in moderate oven (350°F.) 25 minutes. Serves 6.

SCALLOPED EGGS AND ONIONS

10 onions, sliced
¼ cup chopped crisp bacon
6 hard-cooked eggs, sliced
2 cups White Sauce
½ cup buttered bread crumbs

Arrange alternate layers of onions, bacon, eggs and white sauce in greased baking dish. Sprinkle with crumbs. Bake in moderate oven (350°F.) 1¼ hours or until onions are tender. Serves 5.

EGGS FAIRLEE

4 onions, sliced
3 tablespoons butter
8 hard-cooked eggs
½ teaspoon salt
Dash pepper
1 cup White Sauce
Buttered cracker crumbs

Brown onions in butter and place a layer in greased casserole. Slice eggs over top, season and cover with remaining onions. Pour white sauce over all and sprinkle top with buttered crumbs. Bake in hot oven (400°F.) until crumbs are brown. Serves 4.

EGGS AND SHRIMP À LA NEWBURG

4 tablespoons butter
1 quart cream or evaporated milk
Dash mace
1 teaspoon salt
2½ cups cleaned cooked shrimp
Paprika
¼ cup Newburg Sauce
3 uncooked egg yolks
3 hard-cooked eggs
Toast

Melt butter. Add 3 cups cream, mace, salt, shrimp, paprika and Newburg sauce. Add uncooked egg yolks to remaining cup of cream and beat together until well blended. Add to hot shrimp sauce and cook until thickened. Cut each egg into quarters and heat in sauce. Serve on hot toast. Serves 8 to 10.

CURRIED EGGS — Add ¼ teaspoon or more curry powder to 1 cup hot White Sauce. Add 3 hard-cooked eggs, quarered. Serve hot on cooked rice, for 4.

Hard-cooked eggs combine with cooked carrots in the luncheon casserole

EGGS FARCI

6 hot hard-cooked eggs
½ teaspoon salt
¼ teaspoon pepper
1 tablespoon butter
4 tablespoons milk
Few drops onion juice
1½ cups White, Curry or Tomato Sauce

Cut eggs into halves crosswise, then cut an even slice from end of each half, so that it will stand upright. Remove yolks, mash and add salt, pepper, butter, milk and onion juice. Mix thoroughly and heap into whites. Set in shallow pan and bake in slow oven (325°F.) about 5 minutes, then arrange on a hot dish and pour sauce over them. Serves 6.

Add ½ cup chopped boiled ham and 2 tablespoons minced parsley to egg yolk mixture.

EGGS FRICASSEE

3 tablespoons butter
3 tablespoons flour
Salt and pepper
Chopped onion
Minced parsley
3 cups stock
¼ cup cream or evaporated milk
6 hard-cooked eggs, cut into eighths

Mix butter, blend in flour, salt, pepper, onion and parsley. Add stock and cook for an additional 3 minutes, stirring constantly. Add cream, heat and add eggs. Serve hot on toast, rice, potatoes or noodles. Serves 6.

SCALLOPED EGGS AND CARROTS — Cut 6 hard-cooked eggs lengthwise into halves, arrange eggs, ¾ cup sliced cooked carrots, ½ cup crumbs and 1 cup White Sauce in alternate layers in casserole. Cover with buttered crumbs. Bake in 350°F. oven until crumbs brown. Serves 6.

EGGS À LA DUCHESSE

1 onion, sliced
1 tablespoon fat
1 cup milk
6 hard-cooked eggs
2 uncooked egg yolks
2 teaspoons chopped parsley
4 tablespoons grated cheese
Paprika
Salt and pepper
1½ tablespoons lemon juice

Brown onion in fat, add milk and eggs cut into halves. Cook for 3 or 4 minutes, add to beaten egg yolks, parsley, cheese and seasonings. Cook over hot water for about 8 minutes, stirring constantly. Add lemon juice and serve hot. Serves 6.

EGG AND CHEESE SCALLOP

4½ tablespoons butter
1½ tablespoons flour
1 cup milk
¼ teaspoon salt
Dash pepper
Dash paprika
½ teaspoon Worcestershire sauce
1 cup soft bread crumbs
6 hard-cooked eggs, sliced
½ cup grated cheese

Prepare a sauce of 1½ tablespoons butter, flour, milk and seasonings. Melt remaining butter in casserole in oven. Add about ¼ cup of crumbs and set aside for top. Arrange in casserole in layers, the remaining crumbs, eggs, cheese and sauce. Top with buttered crumbs. Bake in moderate oven (350°F.) until the sauce begins to bubble and top is browned. Serve plain or with Tomato Sauce. Serves 4 to 6.
TO VARY—Use tomato juice instead of milk.
Add 1 uncooked egg yolk to sauce before using.
Use 1 cup flaked cooked salmon or tuna instead of cheese.

EGGS AND CRAB MEAT

6 hard-cooked eggs
1 cup cooked crab meat, flaked
1 tablespoon melted butter
3 egg yolks, uncooked
1 teaspoon chopped parsley
½ teaspoon salt
⅛ teaspoon pepper
1 cup sour cream

Cut eggs into halves, remove yolks. Chop crab meat and yolks; add melted butter, 1 of the uncooked egg yolks, parsley, salt, pepper and 2 tablespoons sour cream. Mix thoroughly and heap into egg whites. Place eggs in greased shallow baking dish. Mix remaining uncooked yolks and sour cream and season with salt and pepper. Pour over stuffed eggs. Bake in moderate oven (350°F.) until sauce is firm, 30 to 40 minutes. If desired bake in individual baking dish, using 2 stuffed egg halves in each. Unmold and serve. Serves 6.

Use shrimp instead of crab meat.

Eggs and asparagus are teammates, everybody's choice: en casserole

EGGS À LA DIABLE

6 hard-cooked eggs
6 slices toast, buttered
1 cup tomato catchup
½ cup chili sauce
2 tablespoons Worcestershire sauce
1 tablespoon butter
1 teaspoon mustard
1 teaspoon vinegar
½ teaspoon salt
½ teaspoon pepper

Slice eggs onto buttered toast and cover with a sauce made by heating remaining ingredients to boiling. Serve hot. Serves 6.

EGG AND ASPARAGUS CASSEROLE

8 hard-cooked eggs
½ cup mushrooms
1 tablespoon butter
½ teaspoon salt, Dash pepper
1 cup cut cooked asparagus
1 cup White Sauce

Cut eggs into lengthwise wedges. Brown mushrooms in butter; add seasonings, asparagus, white sauce and 7 of eggs. Turn into baking dish, garnish with remaining egg wedges and bake in 350°F. oven 20 minutes. Serves 6.

EGGS PONCE DE LEON

6 hard-cooked eggs
½ onion, chopped
1 tablespoon butter
1 tablespoon flour
2 cups tomato juice
½ cup chopped celery
¼ cup chopped green pepper
½ cup mushrooms
Salt and pepper
½ teaspoon Worcestershire sauce
½ cup thin White Sauce
Cracker crumbs
Butter

Chop whites of eggs and mash yolks. Brown onion in butter add flour and blend. Add tomato juice, celery and green pepper and heat to boiling, stirring constantly. Simmer until celery and pepper are tender. Add mushrooms, seasonings, Worcestershire sauce, white sauce, egg whites and yolks. Place in greased casserole. Sprinkle with crumbs, dot with butter and brown in hot oven (400°F.) Serves 6.

EGGS WITH CODFISH

1 cup salt codfish
4 tablespoons fat
2 tablespoons flour
Salt and pepper
2 cups milk
2 uncooked eggs
Chopped parsley
3 hard-cooked eggs

Cover fish with cold water and soak overnight. Drain, flake and sauté in fat for a few minutes; sprinkle with flour and seasonings. Add milk and cook until thickened. Stir into the slightly beaten uncooked eggs and cook 3 minutes more. Serve on a platter garnished with chopped parsley and hard-cooked eggs cut into quarters. Two additional tablespoons of flour may be used instead of the uncooked eggs. Serves 4 to 6.

EGGS STUFFED WITH MUSHROOMS

¼ pound fresh or ½ cup canned mushrooms
2 tablespoons butter
2 tablespoons flour
½ teaspoon salt
½ cup boiling water
1 cup evaporated milk
6 hard-cooked eggs
¼ cup almonds, blanched and chopped
2 tablespoons evaporated milk
Salt, Pepper
Buttered bread crumbs

Clean mushrooms. Chop stems but leave caps whole. Sauté in butter. Remove mushrooms. Blend flour and salt with remaining fat in pan. Add boiling water. Cook until sauce begins to thicken, then add cup of milk. Cut eggs into halves. Mash egg yolks and mix with chopped mushroom stems, almonds, 2 tablespoons milk and seasonings. Refill egg whites with mixture. Place in buttered baking dish with mushroom caps and pour sauce over eggs. Top with buttered bread crumbs and brown in moderate oven (350°F.) Serves 6.

EGGS IN HIDING

1 tablespoon butter
1 can (1¼ cups) condensed tomato soup
½ pound American cheese, diced
6 hard-cooked eggs
1 cup cereal flakes, crushed

Heat butter and soup in top of double boiler. Add cheese and cook until melted, stirring constantly. Arrange halves of hard-cooked eggs (cut lengthwise) in buttered baking dish. Pour cheese mixture over eggs. Sprinkle with cereal flakes. Brown under broiler. Serves 6.

SCALLOPED HAM AND EGGS
— Arrange ¾ cup buttered bread crumbs, 1 cup diced cooked ham, 1½ cups White Sauce and 4 hard-cooked eggs, sliced, in alternate layers in greased baking dish, topping with thin layer of crumbs. Bake in moderate oven (375°F.) 20 minutes or until crumbs are browned. Serves 6. Add chopped green pepper.

White and gold hard-cooked eggs crown the green spinach ring while red tomato slices set the stage

Hard-cooked eggs added to macaroni and cheese increase flavor and food value

EGGS WITH HORSE-RADISH SAUCE

6 hard-cooked eggs
¾ teaspoon salt
⅛ teaspoon pepper
2 tablespoons cream
Horse-radish Sauce

Cut eggs crosswise into halves. Rub yolks through a sieve; add salt, pepper and cream. Refill the whites. Place eggs in covered baking dish and cover with the horse-radish sauce. Heat for 10 minutes. Sprinkle chopped parsley over the top. Serves 6.

GOLDENROD EGGS

4 hard-cooked eggs
1½ cups White Sauce
Toast

Chop the whites of eggs and add to the hot white sauce. Put yolks of eggs through a ricer. Pour sauce over hot toast and garnish with the yolks. Serve at once. Serves 4.

One-third cup cooked drained peas, carrots, or spinach may be added to sauce.

Serve in Patty Shells or bread Croustades.

Use cream instead of milk in making White Sauce.

SCALLOPED EGGS DE LUXE

6 tablespoons butter
2 tablespoons flour
½ teaspoon salt
⅛ teaspoon pepper
1½ cups milk, or half milk and half pea stock
4 eggs, beaten
1 cup cooked peas
8 hard-cooked eggs, sliced

Prepare a sauce, using 4 tablespoons butter, the flour, salt, pepper and milk. Cool slightly. Pour over beaten eggs and beat thoroughly. Grease a baking dish with remaining butter and place peas on bottom of dish with sliced hard-cooked eggs on top. Pour sauce over eggs. Bake in slow oven (325°F.) until firm. Let stand for several minutes before unmolding, garnish and serve hot with or without a sauce. A well-seasoned white sauce to which ½ cup chopped, blanched almonds is added may be served. Serves 6 to 8.

EGGS AND MACARONI — Cook ½ pound macaroni in boiling salted water until tender. Arrange in casserole with 8 hard-cooked eggs, sliced, 2 cups White Sauce, 2 pimientos, chopped, and ¼ pound cheese, grated. Bake in moderate oven (350°F.) 20 minutes. Serves 8.

NOODLE OYSTER LOAF WITH CREAMED EGGS

¼ pound noodles
¾ cup milk
¼ teaspoon salt
3 eggs, beaten
½ pint oysters
4 hard-cooked eggs
2 cups White Sauce
Parsley, Paprika

Cook noodles 15 minutes in boiling salted water. Drain. Combine with milk, salt, eggs and oysters and mix thoroughly. Pour into greased pan dusted with flour or sifted crumbs. Set in pan of hot water and bake in moderate oven (350°F.) 45 minutes. Unmold on a platter and slice. On each slice place a hard-cooked egg cut into halves lengthwise, cover with white sauce and garnish with parsley and paprika. Serves 4.

SPAGHETTI WITH EGGS

½ pound spaghetti
¼ pound American cheese cut into small pieces
2 cups White Sauce
8 hard-cooked eggs
Sliced tomatoes
Parsley

Cook spaghetti in boiling salted water until tender. Drain. Heat cheese and white sauce in double boiler until cheese melts. Arrange spaghetti in mound on serving platter, border with hard-cooked eggs cut into halves and garnish with tomatoes and parsley. Serve with hot cheese sauce. Serves 6. For variety, use olive oil as the fat for white sauce and in it sauté chopped onion, ½ cup diced celery and 1 tablespoon chopped green pepper. Proceed as above.

CODDLED EGGS

Cover eggs with cold water, heat to boiling, remove from heat and let stand in hot water 4 to 8 minutes, according to desired consistency.

Place eggs in boiling water, cover, remove from heat; let stand 4 to 8 minutes, according to desired consistency.

EGGS YORKSHIRE

2 eggs, beaten
1 cup milk
1 cup sifted cake flour
1 teaspoon baking powder
½ teaspoon salt
⅓ cup butter, melted
4 hard or soft-cooked eggs

Heat greased casserole in oven. Beat eggs and milk thoroughly; sift flour, baking powder and salt together. Add milk and butter and beat mixture until smooth. Cover bottom of hot casserole with layer of eggs (whole, halved, quartered or sliced). Fill casserole about ⅔ full with batter and place in very hot oven (450°F.) until mixture begins to expand and brown slightly, reduce temperature to (350°F.) and bake 25 minutes longer. Serve at once from baking dish. Serves 4.

SOFT-COOKED EGGS

Have eggs at room temperature. Prick large end with pin to prevent breaking. Cook by any one of the following methods:
Cover eggs with boiling water. Simmer for 3 to 5 minutes, depending on desired consistency.
Cover eggs with cold water and heat to boiling.
Place hot water in both parts of double boiler. When water in lower part is boiling place eggs in upper part. Cook 12 to 15 minutes. (See page 44)

EGGS AND SPINACH

2 quarts spinach
4 tablespoons butter
½ teaspoon pepper
1 teaspoon salt
6 hard-cooked eggs
1 cup Tomato Sauce

Wash spinach, cook, drain and add butter and seasonings. Arrange 2 nests of spinach on a small platter and place 3 eggs in each nest. Serve with tomato sauce. Serves 6.

Use other cooked greens instead of spinach, if desired.

Eggs Yorkshire served with prunes are an unusual treat with or without sliced almonds on top

BOILED EGGS WITH DUMPLINGS AND VEGETABLES

6 soft or medium-cooked eggs
1 head cauliflower
2 cups sifted flour
4 teaspoons baking powder
¾ teaspoon salt
1 egg, beaten
¾ cup milk (about)
Stock or water, Melted butter

Remove shells from soft-or medium-cooked eggs. Break cauliflower into flowerets and cook in boiling salted water until tender. To prepare dumplings sift flour, baking powder and salt into mixing bowl. Add egg and enough milk to make a rather stiff batter. Mix thoroughly. Drop into boiling salted water or stock and cook closely covered for 12 to 15 minutes. Arrange dumplings in center of large platter, reheat eggs in stock, alternate vegetables and egg as a border around dumplings. Serve with melted butter, hot Tomato Sauce or some of the stock. Sprinkle with minced parsley or garnish with parsley or cress. Serves 6.
Onions, asparagus, peas, broccoli or carrots may be used instead of cauliflower.

BATTER BREAD

3 eggs
1 cup buttermilk
1 cup sweet milk
1/3 cup fine white corn meal
2 teaspoons baking powder
1/4 teaspoon baking soda
1/2 teaspoon salt
2 tablespoons melted butter or
    other shortening

Set baking pan in oven to heat. Beat eggs, add buttermilk and sweet milk, beat well and add dry ingredients sifted together, then butter. Grease heated pan, pour in batter and bake in hot oven (400°F.) until set in center, about 1 hour. Serve at once. Serves 6.

CHINESE EGGS—Heat 1/2 pound minced roast pork and 3 cups cold cooked rice in fat. Add 2 tablespoons soy sauce. Add 6 eggs and cook, stirring constantly, until eggs are set. Serves 8.

SUMMER CASSEROLE

6 hard-cooked eggs
3 ripe tomatoes
3 tablespoons butter
3 tablespoons flour
2 teaspoons salt
1 1/2 cups milk
1/2 cup grated cheese
Buttered crumbs

Cut eggs into halves and arrange around edge of a greased casserole or baking dish. Slice peeled tomatoes into the center of dish. Make a white sauce of butter, flour, salt and milk. Add cheese and heat slowly until cheese is melted. Pour over tomatoes and eggs. Cover with crumbs and bake in moderate oven (350°F.) until heated through, about 20 minutes. Scoop out centers of tomatoes and place a whole egg in each, before covering with sauce, if desired. Serves 6 to 8.

TINY EGG BALLS

2 hard-cooked egg yolks
1/4 teaspoon salt
1/8 teaspoon pepper
1 egg white
1 tablespoon flour
2 tablespoons butter

Force egg yolks through a sieve, add salt, pepper and enough egg white to moisten. Shape into small balls, roll in flour and sauté in butter until lightly browned. Add to soup just before serving. Makes 10 small balls.

CARROT CUSTARD

3 eggs
1 1/2 cups grated uncooked carrots
    or mashed cooked carrots
3 cups milk
1 teaspoon salt
3 tablespoons butter

Beat eggs slightly and add remaining ingredients. Pour into greased baking dish, place in pan of hot water and bake in moderate oven (350°F.) about 1 hour or until a knife inserted in center of custard comes out clean. Serve hot. Serves 6.

Turnips may be used instead of carrots.

CHEESE CUSTARD

1 1/2 cups milk
1 teaspoon salt
1/8 teaspoon pepper
1/2 cup grated Swiss cheese
4 eggs

Add milk, seasoning and cheese to slightly beaten eggs. Turn the mixture into greased baking dish, place in a pan of hot water and bake in moderate oven (350°F.) 25 to 30 minutes or until firm. Remove from oven; let stand 3 minutes and unmold on a platter. Serve with Tomato Sauce, for 4. Place slices of tomato, ham or cooked bacon in bottom of baking dish before adding custard.

CHEESE AND OLIVE CUSTARD

5 slices bread
2 tablespoons butter
1 cup grated cheese
1/2 cup stuffed olives, sliced
3 eggs
1/4 teaspoon prepared mustard
1/3 cup olive liquor
2 cups milk, scalded

Remove crusts from bread, spread with 1 tablespoon butter, cut into cubes, and arrange 1/3 in greased casserole. Cover with 1/3 of cheese and 1/2 of olives. Repeat, having cheese on top. Dot with remaining butter. Beat eggs slightly, add mustard, olive liquor and then add milk gradually, stirring constantly. Pour into casserole, set in pan of hot water and bake in slow oven (325°F.) until firm, about 60 minutes. Serves 6.

Use 1/2 cup shredded cooked shrimp instead of cheese.

CORN PUDDING

3 tablespoons corn meal
1 tablespoon salt
1/2 teaspoon paprika
1/2 cup cold milk
2 cups hot milk
1 tablespoon butter
2 cups fresh corn pulp
2 eggs, slightly beaten

Blend corn meal with salt, paprika and cold milk. Add gradually to hot milk, stirring constantly. Cook over boiling water until mixture thickens Remove from heat and stir in remaining ingredients. Turn into buttered casserole. Set in pan of boiling water and bake slowly in moderate oven (350°F.) until center is firm, 45 minutes to 1 hour. Serve hot with meat course. Serves 6.

A tablespoon of chopped green or red pepper may be added.

EGG NOODLES

1 egg
¼ teaspoon salt
⅔ cup flour (about)

Beat egg slightly, add salt and enough flour to make a stiff dough. Knead well, let stand covered ½ hour. Roll out paper-thin spread on cloth to dry. It must not be sticky or brittle. Roll like a jelly roll and slice across roll into fine strips. Spread out to dry thoroughly. When ready to use drop into boiling salted water and cook until done, about 10 minutes. Serves 5.

EGGS WITH NOODLES

Egg Noodles
½ cup butter
3 eggs
½ teaspoon salt

Make noodles, cutting them much broader than for soup. Cook in boiling salted water until tender, about 10 minutes. Drain. Sauté noodles in butter until light brown. Beat eggs with salt and stir into noodles. Continue cooking until eggs are set. Serve at once. Serves 5.

Add ½ cup shredded dried beef, ham or other cooked meat.

EGG MOUNDS IN SAVORY SAUCE

Biscuit dough (using 2 cups flour)
6 soft-cooked eggs, peeled
⅓ cup fat
2 tablespoons flour
1 teaspoon minced onion
3 cups cooked tomatoes
1½ teaspoons salt
1 teaspoon sugar
¼ teaspoon pepper

Roll dough about ¼ inch thick. Divide into 6 parts and wrap around eggs. Prepare tomato sauce of remaining ingredients. Pour hot sauce into a shallow baking dish, place wrapped eggs in sauce and bake in hot oven (400°F.) until biscuit is browned. Serves 6.

Hard-cooked or deviled eggs may be used if preferred.

Any kind of well-seasoned sauce may be used (curry, mushroom, paprika, sour cream, etc.).

Wrap soft-cooked eggs in pastry or hard-cooked eggs with sausage. Brush with egg, roll in bread crumbs and brown in hot deep fat (375°F.).

Soft-cooked, hard-cooked or stuffed eggs may be wrapped in biscuit dough and baked in savory sauce

EGG NOODLE RING

¼ pound noodles
¾ cup cream
3 eggs, slightly beaten
Fine dry bread crumbs

Cook noodles in boiling salted water. Drain; add cream and eggs. Butter a ring mold and dust with crumbs. Pour noodle mixture into mold and set in pan of hot water. Bake in moderate oven (350°F.) for 45 minutes. Unmold on hot platter and fill center with Creamed Eggs, creamed fish or fowl. Serves 6.

MACARONI AND EGG
—Honeycomb Style

2½ ounces long strip macaroni
4 eggs, slightly beaten
2 cups milk
1½ teaspoons salt
¼ teaspoon pepper
Dash cayenne
1 to 2 cups grated sharp cheese

Cook macaroni in boiling salted water until tender. Drain and arrange macaroni strips lengthwise in square or rectangular greased casserole. Combine remaining ingredients except the cheese. Pour all but ¾ cup of milk mixture over macaroni. Place casserole in pan of hot water and bake in moderate oven (350°F.) about 30 minutes. Meanwhile cook remaining mixture (¾ cup) in top of double boiler until slightly thickened. Cool and add cheese. When macaroni mixture is almost firm, cover top with cheese layer. Continue cooking until cheese is melted and surface is browned. To serve cut across the macaroni. Serves 4.

LUNCHEON CUSTARD

6 eggs
1 teaspoon salt
1 tablespoon minced parsley
½ tablespoon onion juice
1½ cups milk

Beat eggs and add remaining ingredients. Pour mixture into 6 greased custard cups and set in pan with hot water. Bake in hot oven (400°F.) until firm, about 20 minutes. Turn out on serving plates and serve with Tomato Sauce. Serves 6.

MUSHROOM CUSTARD

½ pound mushrooms, sautéed
1 tablespoon grated onion
¼ cup grated cheese
Salt and pepper
1 tablespoon chopped parsley
4 eggs, slightly beaten
3 cups milk

Place a layer of mushrooms in greased casserole. Mix remaining ingredients together and pour over mushrooms. Bake in moderate oven (350°F.) until firm, about 40 minutes. Serves 4.

Use sautéed chicken livers instead of mushrooms.

ONION CUSTARD

2 cups sliced onions
2 tablespoons fat
6 eggs, beaten
½ cup milk
¾ teaspoon salt

Cook onions, covered, in the fat until tender but not browned. Place in greased baking dish. Mix eggs, milk and salt and pour over onions. Place casserole in pan of hot water and bake in moderate oven (350°F.) for 45 to 60 minutes or until firm. Garnish with chopped parsley. Serve plain or with a well-seasoned sauce. Serves 4 to 6.

SOUTHERN CORN CUSTARD

3 eggs, 2 cups canned corn
2 tablespoons melted butter
2 cups milk, 1 teaspoon salt
⅛ teaspoon pepper
½ teaspoon sugar
Cracker crumbs, Butter

Beat eggs well. Combine with corn, melted butter and milk. Stir well. Add seasoning and sugar. Pour into buttered casserole, sprinkle with cracker crumbs, dot with butter and bake in moderate oven (350°F.) 40 minutes or until custard is firm. Serves 6.

CHEESE AND MUSHROOM SOUFFLÉ

½ pound aged Cheddar cheese
1 cup cream of mushroom soup
    (ready-to-serve)
4 eggs, separated
Salt, Pepper
¼ cup chopped bacon, cooked
¼ cup sliced blanched almonds

Heat cheese slowly with soup until melted. Add to beaten egg yolks and cook, stirring constantly until thickened. Season. Fold in stiffly beaten egg whites. Pour into casserole, sprinkle with crisp bacon and almonds. Bake in slow oven (315°F.) 1 hour. Serves 6 to 8.

INDIVIDUAL HAM AND EGG SOUFFLES

5 eggs, separated
2 tablespoons butter, melted
1 cup milk
Salt and pepper
1 cup diced cooked ham or pork

Beat egg yolks well, add butter, milk, salt, pepper and ham or pork. Beat thoroughly. Fold in beaten egg whites. Pour into custard cups, place in pan of hot water and bake in moderate oven (350°F.) until firm, 25 to 30 minutes. Serves 6.

EGG TIMBALES

1 tablespoon butter
1 tablespoon flour
⅔ cup scalded milk
3 eggs, separated and beaten
1 tablespoon chopped parsley
½ teaspoon salt
⅛ teaspoon pepper
Dash cayenne
Dash celery salt

Prepare a white sauce of butter, flour and milk and add to egg yolks, beaten until thick and lemon colored. Add seasonings, fold in stiffly beaten egg whites. Fill greased custard cups ⅔ full of mixture. Set dishes in pan of hot water and bake in moderate oven (350°F.) until firm, about 40 minutes. Turn out onto platter and serve with Tomato Sauce. Serves 4.

CHEESE—Add 1 cup grated cheese to egg mixture before baking.

Add 2 tablespoons each chopped green pepper and pimientos.

TOP-OF-THE-RANGE SOUFFLÉ

1½ cups milk
2 tablespoons butter
¾ teaspoon salt
¼ teaspoon pepper
6 eggs, beaten
1 sprig parsley, finely chopped

Heat milk and butter in upper part of double boiler. Add seasonings to eggs and beat very light. Add hot milk to eggs and beat thoroughly. Return to upper part of double boiler and cook over simmering water for 30 minutes. Serve hot. Garnish with chopped parsley. Serves 4 to 6. Serve with well-seasoned Mushroom Sauce or a Thin White Sauce to which a few toasted nuts have been added. The nuts may be toasted in the fat used in making the sauce.

HARD-COOKED EGGS

Cover eggs with boiling water, let simmer for 15 to 20 minutes. Plunge into cold water to keep yolks from discoloring and to remove shells easily.

Place hot water in both parts of double boiler. When water is boiling in lower part place eggs in upper part. Cook for 25 to 30 minutes. (See page 44)

SALAD EGGS

6 hard-cooked eggs
1 tablespoon butter
1 tablespoon cream
½ teaspoon mustard
Dash cayenne, Salt
1 tablespoon anchovy paste

Cut hard-cooked eggs into halves. Remove yolks and mix to a paste with butter, cream, mustard, cayenne, salt and anchovy paste. Fill egg whites and place the eggs in a nest of lettuce or watercress. Garnish with radishes and small onions. Serves 4 to 6. For an extra party touch, force yolks through a pastry tube when filling egg whites.

BACON—Substitute 3 tablespoons chopped crisp bacon for anchovy paste.

OLIVE—Add chopped olives.

OTHER VARIATIONS

1. Combine ¼ to ½ cup chopped peanuts or peanut butter with yolks and omit butter, seasonings and anchovy paste. Garnish with peanut halves and celery curls.
2. Rub bowl used for mixing yolks with a cut clove of garlic.
3. Fill whites only level full and serve flat side down. Garnish tops with pimiento or green pepper strips or small designs, cut with tiny vegetable cutters.
4. Mix egg yolks with ¼ cup mayonnaise, ½ teaspoon minced onion and 1 tablespoon tomato catchup instead of butter, cream, mustard and anchovy paste.

PICKLED EGGS

2 tablespoons sugar
1 teaspoon salt
1 teaspoon mixed spices
2 cups cider vinegar
12 to 16 hard-cooked eggs

Add sugar, salt and spices to vinegar (dilute ⅓ with water if strong) and simmer about 8 minutes. Strain and pour over the peeled eggs arranged in a quart jar. Seal and let stand 2 days before using.

Add sprig of dill, a few caraway seeds, a slice of garlic, a clove or onions to the brine as desired.

CREAMED DEVILED EGGS

4 hard-cooked eggs
1½ teaspoons vinegar
½ teaspoon dry mustard
¼ teaspoon salt
Dash pepper
½ teaspoon sugar
1½ tablespoons melted butter
¼ teaspoon Worcestershire sauce
1 cup White Sauce

Cut eggs lengthwise into halves. Combine egg yolks with next 7 ingredients. Beat together until well blended and smooth. Fill whites with yolk mixture. Place in baking dish and cover with white sauce. Bake in a moderate oven (350°F.) 15 minutes. Serve on hot biscuits or toasted English muffins. Serves 4.

Use ¾ cup condensed mushroom soup thinned with ¼ cup milk instead of white sauce.

Omit white sauce and bake in Tomato Sauce.

EGGS STUFFED WITH CRAB MEAT

6 hard-cooked eggs
1 teaspoon dry mustard
½ teaspoon salt
1 cup flaked crab meat
1 cup chopped celery
2 tablespoons chopped green pepper
¾ cup Mayonnaise
Paprika

Cut eggs into halves crosswise Remove yolks, mash and mix with remaining ingredients. Fill whites, sprinkle with paprika. Makes 12 stuffed eggs.

Put your imagination to work on fillings for eggs; their variety is infinite

Serve savory eggs in halves on toast or in pairs on broiled mushroom caps

DEVILED EGGS IN TOMATO SAUCE

4 hard-cooked eggs
¾ cup chopped mushrooms
1 tablespoon minced parsley
1 tablespoon butter
2 tablespoons chili sauce
Salt and pepper
⅔ cup cooked tomatoes
2 tablespoons grated cheese

Cut eggs into halves. Remove yolks and mash. Sauté mushrooms and parsley in butter until tender and combine with egg yolks, chili sauce, salt and pepper. Refill whites. Place in baking dish, cover with tomatoes and cheese and bake in moderate oven (350°F.) until heated through Serves 4.

SAVORY EGGS

6 hot hard-cooked eggs
Salt and pepper
¼ cup hot cream or evaporated milk
Chopped parsley
Anchovy paste
6 slices hot buttered toast
1 cup hot Thin White Sauce

Cut eggs into halves, lengthwise and remove yolks. Mash yolks, add seasonings, cream, parsley, anchovy or any desired relish and refill the whites. Place on slices of toast and pour white sauce over them. Serves 6.

HERB—Mix yolks with chives, thyme, chervil and sweet marjoram.

THURINGER—Mix yolks with ½ cup minced cooked Thuringer sausage and 1 tablespoon chopped pimiento.

SCALLOPED STUFFED EGGS

6 hard-cooked eggs
3 cups bread crumbs
¾ cup milk
1½ teaspoons salt
Dash pepper
1½ teaspoons minced onion
1½ tablespoons minced green pepper
1 egg, beaten

Cut eggs into halves lengthwise. Remove yolks and mash. Soak bread crumbs in milk until it has been absorbed. Add salt, pepper, onion, green pepper, beaten egg and mashed yolks and mix thoroughly. Fill egg whites with this mixture. Spread the remaining stuffing in a thin layer on the bottom of greased baking dish. Place the stuffed egg halves on top and bake in moderate oven (350°F.) 20 minutes. Garnish with parsley. Serves 4 to 6.

STUFFED EGGS

8 hard-cooked eggs
½ teaspoon salt
1 teaspoon dry mustard
Dash cayenne
2 teaspoons French Dressing
2 tablespoons melted butter

Cut eggs into halves. Remove yolks and mash. Season with salt, mustard, cayenne, dressing and butter. Refill the whites with mixture, press halves together and wrap each egg in a square of oiled paper; twist ends to keep the halves in place.

If desired, add 3 drops onion juice and 1 tablespoon Mayonnaise or Thousand Island Dressing.

CELERY—Add chopped celery to egg yolks.

FRENCH FRIED—Stuff eggs as described, roll each half in beaten egg, then in fine bread crumbs. Fry in hot deep fat (375° F.) until brown. Drain on absorbent paper. Serve hot or cold with or without a cream sauce.

Minced ham may be added to the yolks.

Yolks may be mixed with Mayonnaise to moisten.

Egg yolks may be mixed with a combination of Mayonnaise, drop of Tabasco sauce, horse-radish, lemon juice and minced celery, or mixed with Mayonnaise and chopped sweet pickle.

Mix egg yolks with 1 cup cooked peas, puréed; 2 slices chopped cooked bacon; 1½ tablespoons cream; 1 teaspoon vinegar; 2 teaspoons minced onion; 1 pimiento, minced; salt and Mayonnaise.

Fish
AND
Sea Food

**300 WAYS
TO SERVE
FISH AND
SEA FOOD**

WHAT YOU SHOULD KNOW ABOUT FISH

FISH

FRESH FISH may be identified by its bright bulging eyes, bright red gills, firm elastic flesh which holds no imprint when pressed and its characteristic fresh fishy odor, which should have no trace of foreign odor. The scales should adhere closely to the skin and should be free from slime.

FROZEN FISH, which are cleaned and frozen as quickly as possible after being caught are generally sold as fillets. Such fish can hardly be distinguished from fresh fish if they have been kept properly frozen and are cooked as soon as or before they have thawed. Frozen fish are particularly good buys for those living at considerable distance from sources of supply for fresh fish.

CANNED FISH such as salmon, tuna and sardines are ready to use.

CAVIAR—Is the salted eggs of sturgeon, the best coming from Russia. Eggs of other fish are also used but must be labelled to indicate the source.

SALTED FISH — Are prepared either by "dry-salting" or by pickling in a brine. Firm coarse-fleshed fish such as cod, hake and haddock are dry-salted by packing in dry salt after cleaning. Fat and oily fish are "salted" in brine, then are frequently smoked. Finnan haddie is prepared in this way.

SMOKED FISH, such as salmon, whitefish, herring, oysters and sturgeon are generally eaten without further cooking.

FISH PURCHASED "in the round," that is with skin, bones, head and tail included, requires 1 pound for each serving. If fish is purchased cleaned and scaled, 1 pound will serve 2. A pound of fish fillet or steak will serve 3.

TO FRESHEN DRIED SALT FISH

METHOD 1. Wash fish to remove salt on surface, then soak in cold water 2 to 12 hours with skin side up. If fish is very salty, change water several times. METHOD 2. Shred fish, wash several times to remove salt on surface. Cover with cold water, heat to boiling, drain and repeat 1 or 2 times, depending upon saltiness of fish.

PURCHASING GUIDE

KIND	HOW COOK	SIZE-POUNDS	SEASON	MARKET UNIT	TYPE
Bass, Black ...	Bake, broil, fry	½-5	All year	Whole, fillets	Lean
Sea	Bake, broil, fry	½-4	Summer	Whole	Lean
Striped . .	Bake, broil, fry	2-5	All year	Whole	Fat
Bluefish	Bake, broil, fry	3-6	Winter, Spring, Summer	Whole	Lean
Butterfish	Bake, broil, fry	¼-1	Spring, Summer, Fall	Whole	Fat
				(Fresh or smoked)	
Carp	Bake, boil, fry	2-8	All year	Whole, fillets	Lean
				(Fresh or smoked)	
Catfish	Bake, fry	1-40	All year	Whole, fillets, steak	Lean
Clams	Fry, steam		All year	Dozen or quart	Lean
				(Fresh, canned)	
Cod	Bake, broil, boil, fry	4-75	All year	Whole, fillets, steak	Lean
				(Fresh, salted & smoked, canned, froz	
Crabs, alive ...	Boil (Hard shell)		All year	Dozen	Lean
	Fry, broil (Soft shell)				
Meat				Pound (Fresh, canned)	
Eel	Broil, boil, fry	½-10	All year	(Fresh, smoked, pickled)	Fat
Flounder	Bake, broil, fry	½-6	All year	Whole, fillets	Lean
Grouper	Bake, broil, boil, fry	2-100	All year	Whole, fillets, steak	Lean
Haddock	Bake, broil, boil, fry	2-8	All year	Whole, fillets	Lean
				(Fresh, smoked as finnan haddie, frozen, canned)	
Hake	Broil, boil	3-8	All year	Pound, fillets	Lean
				(Fresh, salted, smoked)	
Halibut	Bake, broil, boil, fry	5-80	All year	Whole, fillets, steak	Fat
				(Fresh, smoked)	

PURCHASING GUIDE—Continued

KIND	HOW COOK	SIZE-POUNDS	SEASON	MARKET UNIT	TYPE
Herring	Bake, broil, boil, fry	½-1	All year	Whole (Fresh, salted, canned, smoked, pickled)	Fat
Lobsters, alive	Boil, broil, bake		All year	Whole	Lean
Meat				Pound (Fresh or canned)	
Mackerel	Bake, broil, boil, fry	¾-10	All year	Whole, fillets, steak (Fresh, pickled, salted, smoked and canned)	Fat
Mullet	Bake, broil, fry	1-5	All year	Whole (Fresh, salted)	Fat
Oysters	Bake, broil, fry		Fall, Winter, Spring	Dozen, quart (Fresh, canned)	Lean
Perch	Bake, broil, fry	½-5	All year	Whole, fillets	Lean
Pickerel	Bake, broil, boil, fry	2-40	All year	Whole, steak	Lean
Pike	Bake, broil, fry	1-40	All year	Whole, fillets	Lean
Pompano	Bake, broil	1-2	Winter	Whole	Fat
Red Snapper ..	Bake, broil, boil, fry	10-20	All year	Pound	Lean
Salmon	Bake, broil, boil, fry	4-25	Summer, Fall	Whole, fillets, steak (Fresh, smoked, salted, canned)	Fat
Scallops	Broil, fry		Spring, Fall, Winter	Pound, quart (Fresh, canned)	Lean
Shad	Bake, broil, boil, fry	1½-6	Fall, Winter, Spring	Whole (Fresh, salted)	Fat
Sheepshead ...	Bake, broil, boil, fry	4-15	Fall, Winter	Whole	Lean
Shrimp	Boil		Spring, Fall	Pound (Fresh, canned)	Lean
Smelt	Bake, broil, fry	4 oz.	Fall, Winter, Spring	Pound	Fat
Sturgeon	Bake, broil, boil	50-500	Spring, Summer, Fall	Pound, fillets, steak (Fresh, smoked)	Fat
Swordfish	Bake, broil, fry	Up to 800	Summer, Fall	Pound, steak	Lean
Trout	Bake, broil, boil, fry	1-20	Spring, Summer, Fall	Whole (Fresh, smoked)	Fat
Tuna	Bake, broil, boil	30 up	Spring, Summer, Fall	Pound, steak (Fresh, canned)	Fat
Weakfish ..... (Sea trout)	Bake, broil, boil, fry	1-6	Fall, Summer	Whole	Lean
Whitefish	Bake, broil, boil, fry	1-30	Spring, Summer, Fall	Whole, steak, fillets (Fresh, salted, smoked)	Fat
Whiting	Bake, broil, boil, fry	½-2	Summer, Fall	Whole (Fresh, salted)	Lean

WHY EAT FISH

Fish and sea foods have always been highly prized as delicious food by those who had access to fresh supplies. Refrigerated shipping facilities now make them available to everyone. Fish are especially valuable for their very high content of mineral salts. For the inlander the most valuable of these is iodine, an absolute essential for maintenance of health in the glandular system and one in which other foods are apt to be deficient.

Iron and copper needed for the health of the blood stream are supplied in considerable quantity. Oysters are especially valuable for copper as well as for iodine because they are so often eaten uncooked and there is no chance for the latter to escape in cooking. Besides this, all fat fish carry some vitamins A and D. Fish livers and many fat fish are indeed, our principal source of these vitamins.

TO PREPARE FISH FOR COOKING

TO CLEAN FISH—To remove scales scrape fish beginning at the tail and working toward head. Use the back of a heavy knife and hold it nearly flat against the fish.

The head and tail are usually left on small fish and on large fish to be served whole. Make a slit down body cavity from gills to vent, remove entrails and wash away any blood. Scrape backbone clean and remove black membrane if present by rubbing with salt. Remove fins, gills and eyes. If head and tail are to be removed, cut off gills with head. When preparing large flat fish such as flounder, the entrails, which are near the head, are easily removed when the head is cut off; or they may be removed after cutting a small opening just under the head. Wash fish thoroughly and wipe dry. If head and tail are removed boil with fins to make stock.

TO SKIN FISH—Remove fins along backbone and cut off a narrow strip of skin down the entire length of backbone. Loosen the skin from bony part of gills on both sides. Draw the skin off toward the tail. If the fish is fresh the skin can be drawn off easily. If flesh is soft, work carefully and loosen skin with knife when necessary to avoid tearing flesh. After removing skin from one side, turn fish over and remove skin from other side. To skin flat fish such as flounder, do not cut off head and tail. Cut the skin across the body just above the tail and loosen. Work the skin loose along one side of the body toward the head and pull gently toward other side of body to strip off skin. Strip the

skin from the other side in the same way.

Fish may also be skinned after boning and cutting into fillets. Fat fish should not be skinned before cooking.

TO BONE FISH—Clean fish and skin if desired. Continue cut beyond vent to tail. Beginning at the tail, insert a sharp knife under flesh close to backbone being careful not to pierce skin on other side of body. Making as clean a cut as possible, follow backbone to head with knife, thus loosening flesh from entire side of fish in one piece. Loosen flesh from other side in same way. Remove backbone in one piece and any small bones. Spread fish open in one piece.

FISH FILLETS—A piece of fish, large or small, freed from skin and bones is called a fillet. Fillets are soft-meated, so must be handled carefully. Before cooking trim off ragged edges and any bits of fin bone. Cut

It's safer for the children and the grown ups like it better when fish is boned

into serving pieces, if desired. Fillets may be sautéed, fried, baked, broiled or boiled. Some of the fish from which fillets may be cut are:

Bass	Halibut	Salmon
Bluefish	Mackerel	Smelt
Cod	Perch	Trout
Eel	Pickerel	Tuna
Flounder	Pike	Weakfish
Haddock	Pompano	Whitefish
Hake	Red Snapper	

SERVING FISH

Remove threads or skewers if fish is stuffed. Garnish with Radish Roses, cucumber, parsley, watercress or lemon cut into attractive shapes. With lean fish, serve a rich sauce; with fat fish or fried fish serve a relish or tart sauce. Lemon cups are colorful containers for tartare sauce.

Tie the fish securely in cheesecloth and lower into boiling court bouillon

➡

BAKED FISH

Clean fish, leaving heads and tails on if desired, season and bake as for Baked Stuffed Fish.

BAKED CARP

1 green pepper, chopped
¼ cup diced celery
1 carrot, diced
1 onion, sliced
2 tomatoes, chopped
½ cup cooking oil
4 pounds carp
Salt and pepper
Flour
Paprika

Combine vegetables and place in baking dish with oil. Use carp, whole or sliced; season with salt and pepper, roll in flour, place on vegetables and sprinkle with paprika. Bake uncovered in moderately hot oven (375°-400° F.) 40 minutes or until browned, basting frequently with liquid in pan. Serves 6 to 8.

A fish is its own excuse for being when baked to flaky perfection

BAKED BUFFALO

Place fish in a shallow baking pan, brush with oil and bake as for Stuffed Fish.

BAKED PICKEREL

Fill fish with any desired stuffing (see page 343), place strips of salt pork over fish and bake as for Baked Stuffed Fish. Garnish with cucumber.

BAKED SHAD

Clean 3-pound shad, split, season, brush with oil and bake in hot oven (400°F.) 30 minutes.

BAKED TROUT

Rub a 3½-pound trout with salt. Place in a baking pan, cover with 2½ cups cooked tomatoes, ¼ cup diced onion and ½ cup diced celery. Bake as for Stuffed Fish. When trout is cooked, place on a hot platter and keep in a warm place while preparing sauce. Strain tomato mixture. Beat 1 egg yolk with ½ cup cream, tomato sauce and ½ teaspoon Worcestershire sauce. Heat to boiling and cook 2 minutes. Pour over fish.

BAKED SALMON NEW ORLEANS

1 teaspoon sugar
2 pounds whole salmon
⅛ teaspoon salt
Dash pepper
1 clove garlic
1 red pepper pod
1 onion
2½ cups cooked tomatoes
1 tablespoon Worcestershire sauce
½ cup olive oil
1 tablespoon vinegar
2 cups uncooked Potato Balls
1 cup mushrooms

Brown sugar in pan. Sprinkle salmon with salt and pepper, place garlic and pepper pod inside. Mince onion fine, place onion and salmon in pan with sugar. Cover with tomatoes; add Worcestershire sauce, olive oil, vinegar and potatoes. Bake in hot oven (400° F.) 15 minutes, add mushrooms and bake 15 minutes longer or until fish and potatoes are tender. Serves 6.

RED SNAPPER—Use red snapper instead of salmon and proceed as above.

COD STEAKS WITH MUSHROOM SAUCE

4 fresh codfish steaks, (¾ inch
   thick)
1 small onion, chopped
¼ pound mushrooms, chopped
6 tablespoons boiling water
3 tablespoons butter
3 tablespoons flour
2 cups milk
Salt and pepper
Paprika

Place steaks in oiled baking dish.
Cook onion and mushrooms 3
minutes in water; add butter, stir
in flour and mix. Add milk, heat
to boiling, stirring constantly; season and pour over cod. Sprinkle
with paprika. Bake in moderate
oven (350°F.) 30 to 35 minutes
or until fish is tender. Serves 4.

BAKED FISH FILLETS

1 pound fish fillets
1 cup milk
1 tablespoon salt
Fine dry bread crumbs
1 tablespoon oil or melted butter

Cut fillets into serving pieces.
Combine milk and salt. Dip fish
into milk, then into crumbs, being sure fish is completely covered with crumbs. Place in
greased baking dish or on oven-
proof platter, sprinkle with oil
and brown quickly in very hot
oven (500°F.) 10 to 20 minutes.
Do not add water. Serve with
Almond Butter Sauce, melted
butter, Maître d'Hôtel Butter or
Lemon Butter. Serves 2.

BAKED FISH CREOLE

1 recipe Creole Sauce
1½ pounds fish fillets or steaks

Pour creole sauce over fish in
baking dish. Bake in hot oven
(400°F.) 20 minutes. Serves 5.
HERRING CREOLE—Use fresh
herring instead of fillets or
steaks.

PLANKED FISH

Select any fish suitable for baking. Large fish may be split,
boned, seasoned and planked flat,
or small fish may be cleaned,
seasoned and planked whole. Oil
plank and preheat thoroughly in
hot oven. Place fish in center
of plank, brush lean fish with
melted butter or French dressing.
Bake in very hot oven (450°F.)
10 to 15 minutes, reduce temperature to moderate (350°F.)
and bake until fish is nearly tender, allowing about 10 minutes
per pound. About 15 minutes
before fish is done, remove plank
from oven, garnish with mashed
potatoes pressed through a pastry
tube and other vegetables as desired. Return to oven to finish
baking fish and to brown potatoes. Garnish.

BAKED TROUT FOR CAMPERS

Reserve the large fish for this
overnight cooking. At night,
clean fish and remove heads.
Season inside and out with salt
and pepper, roll separately in
waxed paper, folding ends in, and
wrap in thick wet newspaper.
Dig a trench for each fish just
deep enough to allow 1 inch of
earth on top. Bury bundles, build
the campfire over the trenches
and leave until breakfast time.

*Planked fish has an elegance
well worth the extra time
and preparation*

FISH FILLETS FLORENTINE

3 pounds spinach, ¼ cup butter
1½ tablespoons flour
½ teaspoon salt
⅛ teaspoon pepper
1½ cups milk
½ cup grated cheese
2 pounds fish fillets

Wash spinach in several waters
and cook without adding water.
When spinach is barely tender,
drain and chop coarsely. Place
in baking dish. Melt butter and
blend in flour and seasonings. Add
milk and cook until thickened,
stirring constantly. Add cheese
and continue heating until cheese
has melted. Pour sauce over
spinach, place fillets on top and
bake in moderate oven (375°F.)
30 minutes. Serves 6 to 8.

BAKED EEL

Have eel skinned, split and backbone removed. Cut into 2- or 3-
inch pieces, wash in salted water
and dry thoroughly. Dredge with
flour, season with salt and pepper,
place in buttered baking pan and
add ½ cup water. Cover. Bake
in hot oven (400°F.) for 20 minutes or until eel is browned.

BAKED STUFFED FISH

Stuffing:

3 cups cracker crumbs
⅔ cup butter
¾ cup chopped celery
¼ cup finely chopped onion
2 tablespoons lemon juice
2 teaspoons minced parsley
¼ teaspoon rosemary
½ teaspoon salt
¼ teaspoon pepper
¼ cup hot water

Fish:

4 to 5 pound fish, with or
        without head and tail removed
1 tablespoon salt
Cooking or Salad oil

Measure crumbs into a bowl. Heat butter in a skillet; add celery and onion. Cook slowly until onion is transparent, stirring occasionally. Add to crumbs with a mixture of lemon juice, parsley, rosemary, salt and pepper. Add hot water and mix thoroughly.

Rinse body cavity of fish with cold water, drain, and pat dry with absorbent paper. Rub cavity with salt. Lightly pile stuffing into fish; skewer or sew opening. Place in shallow baking pan lined with aluminum foil or parchment

Unbroken beauty in baked stuffed fish demands careful handling

paper Brush surface with oil or cover with thin slices of salt pork or bacon. Bake at 350°F. 45 to 50 minutes, or until fish flakes easily. Serves 8.

Fish suitable for baking are: Whitefish, lake trout, pike, carp, pickeral, shad and bass.

SAUCES TO SERVE WITH BAKED FISH: White sauce, White Sauce with Egg, Tomato Sauce, Brown Almond Sauce, Onion Sauce, Almond Butter Sauce, Drawn Butter Sauce, Egg Sauce, Bercy Sauce, Oyster Sauce, Shrimp Sauce, and Horse-radish Sauce.

BAKED STUFFED FILLETS— Place stuffing between two fish fillets, season, brush with oil and bake. Or spread stuffing on fillets and roll up; bake.

FISH BAKED IN MILK

2 tablespoons butter
1½ pounds fish (halibut, haddock,
        whitefish, etc.)
1 teaspoon salt
⅔ cup water
⅔ cup evaporated milk

Melt butter in baking pan. Place fish in pan, sprinkle with salt, add water and milk and bake in moderate oven (350°F.) until fish is tender, about 45 minutes.

FILLETS OF SOLE, MARGUÉRY

8 flounder fillets
Salt and paprika
⅓ cup white wine
2½ cups fish stock
1 boiled lobster
18 littleneck clams or small
        cooked shrimps
3 tablespoons butter, melted
3 tablespoons flour
Pepper
¼ cup grated Parmesan cheese

Place fillets in buttered baking dish, sprinkle with salt and paprika and add wine. Cover with buttered paper and bake in moderate oven (350°F.) 15 minutes. Combine fish stock, shell of lobster and 6 clams. Simmer until liquid is reduced to 1 cup. Blend butter and flour, add strained fish stock and ¼ cup liquid from fillets. Season with salt and pepper. Arrange fillets on serving platter, pour strained sauce on top and garnish with sliced lobster meat and remaining clams. Sprinkle with cheese and bake in moderate oven (350°F.) until cheese is melted and fillets are hot. Serves 8.

Use water and lemon juice instead of wine.

Garnish fish with watercress.

POMPANO EN PAPILLOTES

3 green onions, chopped
3 ounces mushrooms, chopped
1 tablespoon butter
1 tablespoon flour
2 cups stock
Salt and pepper
¼ cup white wine
2 pounds pompano fillets
1 cup crab meat
4 tablespoons butter
1 tablespoon white wine
½ teaspoon salt, 1 egg yolk
1 lemon, sliced

Brown onions and mushrooms lightly in butter, mix in flour, add stock, season and boil 5 minutes. Add wine. Sauté fillets and crab meat separately in butter 5 minutes; add wine, salt and slightly beaten egg yolk to crab meat and cook until thickened, stirring constantly. Place some of crab-meat mixture on half of each fillet, fold other half on top, cover with sauce, fold well in parchment cooking paper, or place in paper bag and bake in hot oven (425°F.) about 10 minutes. Arrange on platter garnished with lemon. Serves 6.

SMOTHERED FISH STEAKS

½ teaspoon salt
¼ teaspoon pepper
¼ cup flour
2 (1-pound) fish steaks
1½ cups milk
2 mild onions, sliced
1 tablespoon fat
2 slices bacon

Combine salt, pepper and flour and sprinkle over fish. Place on bottom of shallow baking dish, add milk and bake in hot oven (425°F.) 10 minutes. Brown onions in fat. Place onions and bacon on fish and bake 10 to 15 minutes longer or until fish is tender. Serves 6.

POTTED CARP

⅓ cup cooking oil
2 pounds sliced carp
2 onions, sliced
2 carrots, sliced
5 gingersnaps
1½ cups warm water
½ teaspoon whole mixed spices
¼ teaspoon salt

Pour half of oil in baking dish, arrange half of fish on top, cover with half of onions and carrots, add remaining fish and vegetables. Soften gingersnaps in water and stir until smooth. Add spices and salt and pour over fish. Add remaining oil and more water, if necessary to cover fish. Cover dish and bake in slow oven (325°F.) about 1 hour. Serves 4.

FISH LOAF

2 cups flaked cooked fish
½ teaspoon salt
2 eggs, separated
1 cup Medium White Sauce

Combine fish, salt, beaten egg yolks, white sauce and beaten egg whites. Pour into greased baking dish and bake in moderate oven (350°F.) 20 to 30 minutes. Serves 4.

Bake in baking shells and top with buttered crumbs.

Skinned and boned fish take naturally to stuffing

SMELT À LA BENEDICTINE

1 pound smelt
5 tablespoons butter
5 tablespoons lemon juice
4 medium sweet potatoes
⅛ teaspoon pepper
½ teaspoon salt
1 cup cream or top milk
Bread crumbs

Boil smelt until bones and skin can be removed easily. Mash fine. Add 1 tablespoon butter and 3 tablespoons lemon juice. Cook sweet potatoes, drain and mash. Add pepper, 2 tablespoons butter, 2 tablespoons lemon juice, salt and cream. Blend with prepared fish. If mixture is too thick and dry add a little milk. Place in baking dish, cover with crumbs and dot with remaining 2 tablespoons butter. Bake in very hot oven (425°F.) for 20 minutes. Serves 4.

Use Irish potatoes instead of sweet potatoes and tomato juice instead of cream. Add 1 tablespoon minced parsley. Use perch or herring for smelt.

POACHED FISH

Lean fish generally give best results for poaching since they do not fall apart as readily as fat fish. Whole fish, slices or fillets may be used. Wrap the fish in cheesecloth or parchment paper, place in wire basket or place fish on plate and wrap both in cheesecloth. Lower into simmering Court Bouillon or water seasoned with ½ teaspoon salt and ½ tablespoon lemon juice or vinegar for each quart. Simmer, allowing 6 to 10 minutes per pound for whole fish, depending upon thickness; allow 10 to 20 minutes for slices or fillets. Some of the fish suitable for poaching are:

Carp	Hake	Sea Bass
Cod	Halibut	Shad
Eel	Mackerel	Sheepshead
Haddock	Salmon	Weakfish
		Whitefish

Serve poached fish with any of sauces suggested for Baked Fish.

COURT BOUILLON — Cook ½ cup each chopped carrots, onions and celery and ½ clove garlic, crushed, in 2 tablespoons butter 4 minutes. Do not brown. Add 4 peppercorns, 2 cloves, 1 bay leaf, 2 teaspoons salt, ¼ cup vinegar, ¼ teaspoon ginger, 3 quarts water. Cook 5 minutes.

Fish slices are placed cut side down on the plate and tied in cheesecloth

POACHED FISH WITH EGG SAUCE

3 pounds pike or other fish
1 tablespoon butter
1 tablespoon flour
1 cup hot fish stock
1 egg yolk

Clean and salt the fish and poach 30 minutes, reserving 1 cup fish stock. Melt butter, add flour and hot fish stock. Remove from heat and pour gradually on the beaten yolk. Pour while hot over fish and garnish with parsley. Serves 6.

FILLED FISH

3-pound fish
2 onions
¼ cup cracker or bread crumbs
1 egg, slightly beaten
1 teaspoon salt
⅛ teaspoon pepper
1 cup water
¼ cup minced celery

Remove skin from fish all in one piece, starting at backbone. Remove bones from fish and grind flesh. Grind onions, combine ⅓ of onions with fish and grind again. Add crumbs to fish with egg, salt, pepper and water. Mix until smooth. Wash fish skin, fill with mixture and sew or skewer together. Place in kettle, add celery and remaining onion. Cover with boiling water and boil for 5 minutes, then simmer about 1 hour, adding water if necessary to prevent fish from burning. Serves 4.

Cut fish into steaks, remove flesh and bones carefully from skin, leaving skin in whole rings. Proceed as above, then stuff skin with mixture.

STEWED EEL

2-pound eel
½ teaspoon salt
1 tablespoon minced parsley
Water
1 tablespoon butter
1 tablespoon flour
⅛ teaspoon pepper

Skin and clean eel; remove all fat carefully from inside. Cut eel into 1½-inch lengths, place in saucepan with salt, parsley and water to cover; cover pan closely and simmer for 1 hour or until tender. Remove eel. Blend remaining ingredients together, add to liquid in pan and cook 3 minutes longer. Pour over eel. Serves 6.

COD CREOLE

¾ cup minced celery and leaves
1 onion, chopped
¼ cup oil
2½ cups cooked tomatoes
1 teaspoon salt
⅛ teaspoon pepper
3 pounds fresh cod
6 potatoes, pared

Cook celery and onion in oil until tender, add tomatoes, salt and pepper and heat to boiling. Add cod and potatoes. Cover and simmer about 30 minutes or until fish is tender, basting fish frequently. Serves 6.
Cook 3 tablespoons chopped green pepper with celery and onions.

FISH IN WINE SAUCE

1½ pounds fish fillets
1 cup white wine
1½ tablespoons lemon juice
12 large mushrooms, sliced
¼ cup butter
2 egg yolks
1 cup heavy cream
1 tablespoon chopped parsley
¾ teaspoon salt
⅛ teaspoon pepper

Poach fish fillets in wine and lemon juice until tender. Sauté mushrooms in 1 tablespoon butter. Remove fish to hot platter and keep warm while making sauce. Heat wine in which the fish was cooked to boiling and continue cooking for 10 minutes. Beat egg yolks and add cream. Pour wine over mixture, stirring constantly. Add remaining butter, mushrooms, parsley, salt and pepper. Pour over hot fish and serve. Serves 6.

PICKLED FISH

4 pounds fish (trout, pike, salmon or carp)
Salt
2 large onions, sliced
1 quart water
1 cup vinegar
2 tablespoons mixed pickling spices
1 tablespoon sugar
½ lemon, sliced

Clean fish without removing skin or bones. Slice and season with salt. Cook onions in water for 20 minutes. Add vinegar, whole spices tied in cheesecloth bag, sugar, lemon and fish. Boil for 1 hour. Remove fish, strain liquid and pour over fish. Store in liquid in stone crock. Serves 8.

SWEET AND SOUR FISH

3½ pounds pike or other fish
1 cup hot fish stock
4 gingersnaps
½ cup brown sugar
¼ cup vinegar
¼ cup seeded raisins
½ teaspoon onion juice
1 lemon, seeded and sliced

Clean, slice and salt fish and let stand for several hours. Boil 20 minutes, drain and bone, reserving 1 cup of the fish stock. Combine remaining ingredients; cook until smooth and thick, and pour over fish. Serve cold. Serves 6.

POACHED FISH WITH GRAPES

3 pounds pike or trout
¼ cup sugar
1 lemon, juice and grated rind
2 egg yolks, beaten
1 cup hot fish stock, Salt
1 teaspoon chopped parsley
1 cup chilled seedless green grapes

Cook fish as for Poached Fish. Remove skin and bones and arrange fish on platter. Combine sugar, grated lemon rind and lemon juice with yolks and add strained fish stock gradually. Cook until thickened, stirring constantly. Add salt and parsley. Pour over fish, sprinkle with grapes and serve immediately. Serves 6.

SMELT À LA STOEHER

2 pounds smelt
½ cup water
4 tablespoons butter
½ teaspoon salt
1 tablespoon flour
1 cup fish bouillon
2 egg yolks, well beaten
Grated cheese

Clean smelt and simmer until tender in water with 2 tablespoons butter and salt. Melt remaining butter, blend in flour smoothly. Combine fish bouillon and egg yolks and add to flour mixture. Cook until slightly thickened. Pour over cooked smelt, cover with grated cheese and brown under preheated broiler. Serves 6.

STEAMED FISH

Select fish as for Poached Fish, season and steam over boiling water or Court Bouillon, allowing same time as for poaching. Serve as for Poached Fish.

Allow ½ pound (as purchased) per person or ⅓ pound boned weight.

BROILED FISH

WHOLE FISH—Remove head and tail if desired, split and clean. Wipe dry, sprinkle with salt and pepper and place on greased broiler, flesh side up. Place 3 inches under moderate broiler heat and broil 10 minutes, or until browned. Turn and broil just long enough to make skin brown and crisp.

SLICES—Brush with oil, season and brown on both sides.

FILLETS—Cook as for slices or sprinkle with flour after oiling and seasoning.

Some of the fish suitable for broiling are:

Bass	Mullet	Shad
Bluefish	Oysters	Smelt
Cod	Perch	Swordfish
Eel	Pike	Trout
Flounder	Pompano	Weakfish
Haddock	Red Snapper	Whitefish
Halibut	Salmon	Whiting
Mackerel	Scallops	

Serve broiled fish with melted butter, Maître d'Hôtel Butter, Almond Butter Sauce, Lemon Butter Sauce or Hollandaise Sauce.

BROILED SHAD ROE

4 pairs shad roe
2 quarts boiling water
1 teaspoon salt
2 tablespoons lemon juice
4 tablespoons butter
8 slices toast
8 slices crisp bacon
Watercress, Lime wedges

Wipe roe carefully with damp cloth. Drop into boiling water, add salt and lemon juice. Boil for 5 minutes. Drain, brush with butter and place under preheated broiler until browned but still soft. Serve on hot toast with slice of bacon. Garnish with watercress and wedges of lime or lemon. Serves 8.

BROILED FINNAN HADDIE

2 pounds finnan haddie
Hot water
2 tablespoons butter
Pepper

Cover finnan haddie with hot water and let stand 10 minutes. Drain. Place on greased broiler rack. Spread with butter, sprinkle lightly with pepper and broil in preheated broiler under moderate heat until brown, turning once. Serves 4.

MACKEREL GRILL

1 (4-pound) mackerel
Salt and pepper
1 tablespoon butter
1 mackerel roe
8 strips bacon
2 tomatoes, cut into halves

Place cleaned split mackerel on greased broiler, skin side up. Season, place 4 inches under moderate broiler heat and broil 5 or 6 minutes. Turn fish, brush with butter, add roe and bacon and continue cooking 5 minutes more; add tomatoes, turn roe and bacon, cook 5 minutes longer or until browned. Serves 4.

SEA-FOOD GRILL

4 small lobsters
8 soft-shelled crabs
24 scallops
1 cup melted butter
¾ cup soft bread crumbs
24 large mushroom caps
24 large oysters
Salt and pepper

Prepare lobsters as for Broiled Lobsters. Kill and clean crabs. Place scallops on 8 skewers. Brush lobsters, crabs and scallops with butter. Mix crumbs with remaining butter. Fill each mushroom cap with an oyster and place on a shallow pan. Cover each with buttered crumbs. Sprinkle lobsters with salt and pepper and broil 10 minutes. Arrange crabs, scallops and pan of oysters on broiler rack and season with salt and pepper. Broil 6 minutes, turning crabs and scallops at the end of 3 minutes. Serve with hot melted butter and lemon wedges. Serves 8.

Bits of butter added before broiling give flavor and richness to lean fish

FRIED FISH

Clean fish, leaving heads and tails on small fish. Cut large fish into 1-inch slices or fillets. Cook plain or dip into milk or egg mixed with 2 tablespoons water; then roll. in salted flour, corn meal or fine dry crumbs. Place in hot frying pan containing ⅛-inch layer of melted fat; brown on one side, then turn and brown on other side, allowing 8 to 12 minutes total cooking time, depending on thickness of slice.

Some of the fish suitable for frying are:

Bass	Mackerel
Butterfish	Perch
Carp	Pickerel
Catfish	Pike
Clams	Salmon
Cod	Shad
Eel (parboil	Smelt
10 minutes)	Trout
Flounder	Weakfish
Haddock	Whiting
Halibut	

Serve fried fish with Maître d'Hôtel Butter, Lemon Butter, Tartare Sauce, Creole Sauce or Hollandaise Sauce.

FRENCH FRIED FISH — Clean and coat fish as directed for Fried Fish. Fry in hot deep fat (365°F) 5 to 7 minutes or until brown and tender. Drain on absorbent paper.

CODFISH BALLS

1 cup flaked cooked fresh cod
1½ cups mashed potatoes
1 egg, beaten
1 tablespoon butter, melted
¼ teaspoon salt
⅛ teaspoon pepper
½ teaspoon onion juice

Mix ingredients and beat until smooth and fluffy. Shape lightly into balls or cakes. Sauté or fry in hot deep fat (375°F.) until browned. Serve hot with Tomato Sauce. Serves 4.

To use salt cod instead of fresh cod, freshen cod and simmer until tender, 30 to 35 minutes per pound. Use as above.

Add 1 teaspoon dry mustard and 2 teaspoons lemon juice.

Salmon, halibut, pike, perch, freshened salt mackerel and other fish may be used instead of cod. Boil uncooked potatoes and fish together until tender, drain thoroughly, dry over low heat and beat until fluffy and smooth. Add remaining ingredients and proceed as above.

Add ¼ cup cheese to the Tomato Sauce.

CODFISH PUFFS — Use 2 eggs instead· of 1. Beat mixture 2 minutes with rotary beater. Drop from spoon into hot fat.

Make your codfish balls light and fluffy to please the New Englander

FISH-FLAKE CROQUETTES

2 cups flaked cooked fish
1 teaspoon onion juice
Salt and pepper
Chopped parsley
1 cup Medium White Sauce
Cracker crumbs
1 egg, beaten

Mix fish flakes with seasonings, add to white sauce and chill thoroughly. Mold into croquettes, roll in cracker crumbs, dip into slightly beaten egg and roll in crumbs again. Fry in hot deep fat (375°F.) about 3 minutes or until brown. Makes 6 medium croquettes.

FISH FRITTERS

1 pound small fish
3 eggs, separated
3 tablespoons flour
½ teaspoon salt
⅛ teaspoon pepper
⅛ teaspoon minced garlic
1 tablespoon minced parsley

Cook fish, remove skin and bones and mash. Beat egg yolks until light and .thick, then add flour, salt, pepper, garlic, parsley and fish. Fold in whites of eggs beaten until stiff. Drop by tablespoons into hot deep fat (360° to 370°F.) and fry until brown. Serves 4.

Add ½ cup diced drained pineapple.

Serve with tomato catchup, Tartare Sauce or Egg Sauce.

FROGS' LEGS

The hind legs of the frog are the only part that is eaten. These have a flavor similar to chicken and are considered a delicacy by many.

To prepare legs for use, cut from body, wash legs in cold water, turn skin down and strip off like a glove. Cover with boiling water, drain quickly, dry and use as desired.

FRIED FROGS' LEGS

Season prepared legs with salt and pepper, dip into fine cracker or bread crumbs, into slightly beaten egg and again into crumbs. Let stand for 15 to 20 minutes. Fry in hot deep fat (375°F.) 3 minutes or until browned. Allow 2 legs per portion.

SAUTÉED FROGS' LEGS—Prepare frogs' legs as above and brown in skillet in a small amount of hot fat. Serve with Tartare Sauce or Maître d'Hôtel Butter.

OUTDOOR FISH FRY

Fish fries, held on the bank of a fishing stream, afford a convivial means of cooking and eating fish freshly caught by members of the party. The fish are cleaned and rolled in corn meal, then fried over an open fire in a large kettle or frying pan of hot fat. After the fish are cooked, Hush Puppies are fried in the fat remaining in the frying pan These are made by mixing 2 cups corn meal, 1 cup milk or water 1 teaspoon salt, 2 teaspoons baking powder and 1 onion, finely chopped. Shape into pones and fry until well browned. Serve the fried fish and hush puppies with coffee or other suitable beverage.

Be sure your fish fillets drain on absorbent paper between kettle and platter

FRIED SEA FOOD

Season clams, oysters, shrimp or scallops; dip into batter of 1 cup flour, 1 cup milk and 1 egg. Fry in hot deep fat (365°F.) until golden brown.

Black-eyed Susans of grilled pineapple and ripe olives garnish the fish fillets

BEET AND FISH HASH

¾ cup flaked cooked fish
¾ cup chopped cooked potatoes
2 cooked medium beets, chopped
1 tablespoon minced onion
1 tablespoon minced parsley
½ teaspoon salt
¼ teaspoon paprika
1 teaspoon Worcestershire sauce
3 tablespoons cream or milk
1½ tablespoons fat

Mix first 8 ingredients and moisten with cream. Cook in fat stirring until hot; then pat lightly into a cake and cook until well browned underneath. Fold like an omelet. Serves 4 to 6.

MAINE BAKED FINNAN HADDIE

1 teaspoon chopped onion
1 tablespoon chopped green pepper
3 tablespoons butter
3 tablespoons flour
¼ teaspoon paprika
2 cups milk
2 cups cooked finnan haddie
1 cup buttered bread crumbs

Cook onion and green pepper in butter until tender. Mix in flour and paprika and add milk gradually. Heat to boiling and pour over fish in greased baking dish. Cover with crumbs and bake in moderate oven (350°F.) 20 minutes or until crumbs are browned. Serves 4.

SCALLOPED FISH WITH NUTS

1 cup flaked cooked fish
2 cups Medium White Sauce
1 cup finely chopped nuts
2 hard-cooked eggs, minced
Cracker crumbs
Butter

Combine fish, white sauce, nuts and eggs. Pour into greased casserole, cover with cracker crumbs and dot with butter. Bake in moderate oven (350°F.) 25 minutes, or until crumbs are brown. Serves 4.

No haddock is plebeian when baked in cream and abundantly seasoned

FISH CHOWDER

¼ pound fat salt pork
2 onions, sliced
3 cups uncooked potatoes cut into ½-inch cubes
4 cups boiling water
3 pounds salt or fresh cod or haddock
1¾ cups evaporated milk
1 teaspoon salt
⅛ teaspoon pepper
1 tablespoon minced parsley
1 tablespoon butter
1 tablespoon flour
Pilot crackers

Cut fat salt pork into small pieces and fry slowly in soup kettle. Add onions and cook 5 minutes. Add potatoes, boiling water and fish cut into small pieces. Simmer until potatoes are soft. Add milk, salt, pepper and parsley. Melt butter, add flour and blend thoroughly. Add gradually to chowder, stirring until slightly thickened. Cook 5 minutes longer. Pour over pilot crackers. Serves 8.

FISH FROMAGE

1 onion, chopped
½ pound American cheese, grated
2½ pounds pike or bass
1½ teaspoons Worcestershire sauce
1 teaspoon mustard
1 teaspoon salt
½ teaspoon pepper
1 cup milk

Spread onion and half the cheese over bottom of baking dish. Place fish on top and cover with remaining cheese. Combine remaining ingredients and pour over fish. Bake in hot oven (425°F.) 25 to 30 minutes. Serves 4.

HERRING ROLLMOPS

6 salt herring
2 tablespoons bread crumbs
2 tablespoons butter
1 tablespoon chopped parsley
1½ tablespoons lemon juice
Pepper
Hot water

Soak herring in cold water overnight, drain and clean. Remove skin and separate each fish into 2 fillets, removing bones. Mix remaining ingredients to a smooth paste. Spread each fillet with paste, roll, fasten with string or toothpicks. Place in baking dish, cover with oiled paper and bake in moderate oven (375°F.) 10 to 15 minutes. Remove string or toothpicks, serve hot. Serves 6.

HADDOCK IN CREAM

1½ pounds fillet of haddock
2 tablespoons lemon juice
1 teaspoon prepared mustard
½ teaspoon Worcestershire sauce
1 teaspoon salt
¼ teaspoon pepper
3 small onions
1 cup cream
Parsley
Paprika

Wipe haddock with damp cloth and place in baking dish. Mix lemon juice, mustard, Worcestershire sauce, salt and pepper together and pour over haddock. Add onions and cream. Bake in hot oven (400°F.) about 30 minutes. Garnish with parsley; sprinkle with paprika. For 6. To vary, add ½ cup chopped celery and 1 tablespoon chopped green pepper. Omit pepper listed.

FISH ROLL

Baking Powder Biscuit dough
  (using 2 cups flour)
1½ cups flaked cooked fish
1 small onion, chopped
1 green pepper, chopped
½ teaspoon salt
Milk

Roll biscuit dough to ¼-inch thickness on floured board. Combine fish, onion, green pepper and salt; moisten slightly with milk, mix well and spread mixture on dough. Roll as for jelly roll and cut into 1½-inch slices. Bake on greased baking sheet in hot oven (400°F.) ½ hour. Serves 6.

SALMON CUSTARD

2 eggs, slightly beaten
1 cup evaporated milk
½ teaspoon salt
Dash pepper
Paprika
1 (1-pound) can salmon, flaked

Combine eggs, milk and seasonings; add salmon. Pour into greased baking dish, set in pan of hot water and bake in moderate oven (350° F.) 25 to 30 minutes or until firm. Serves 4.

SALMON CHOWDER

1 (1-pound) can salmon
1 cup cooked tomatoes
1 small onion, finely sliced
2 cups water
¼ cup flour, 3 cups milk
1½ teaspoons salt
⅛ teaspoon pepper

Flake salmon. Add tomatoes, onion and water. Simmer 20 minutes. Combine flour, milk and seasonings; cook until thickened, stirring constantly. Add salmon mixture and serve at once. Serves 6.

SALMON RAREBIT

¼ pound sharp cheese
1 cup tomato purée
½ teaspoon salt
1 teaspoon prepared mustard
1 tablespoon Worcestershire
    sauce
2 eggs, slightly beaten
1 cup evaporated milk
1 (1-pound) can salmon

Melt cheese over boiling water, blend in tomato purée and seasonings gradually. Add eggs to milk and stir slowly into cheese mixture. Add salmon broken into large pieces and heat 5 minutes. Serve on hot toast, for 6.

SALMON IN RICE NESTS

1 cup rice
1 egg yolk
2 cups Medium White Sauce
2 tablespoons lemon juice
⅛ teaspoon pepper
2 tablespoons cooking sherry
    or sherry seasoning
1 (1-pound) can salmon, flaked
⅓ cup sautéed mushrooms
2 hard-cooked eggs, sliced

Cook rice in boiling salted water until tender and drain. Beat egg yolk slightly; add white sauce slowly. Add lemon juice, pepper, sherry, salmon and mushrooms. Heat thoroughly. Shape rice into mounds on plates; make depression in center of each to form nests. Fill with salmon mixture. Garnish with egg slices. Serves 8.

BAKED SALMON AND RICE — Arrange rice and salmon mixture in layers in a baking dish and bake in a moderate oven (350° F.) 20 minutes. Unmold and garnish with egg slices.

Dinner is ready when you unmold this salmon ring and fill with vegetables

SALMON FONDUE

5 slices bread
1 cup milk
2 tablespoons butter
1 cup flaked cooked salmon
3 eggs, separated
½ teaspoon salt
¼ cup grated American cheese

Trim crusts from bread and cut bread into ½-inch cubes. Heat milk in double boiler. Add bread cubes, butter, liquid from salmon and well-beaten egg yolks; season with salt and cook until thickened, stirring constantly. Remove from heat and stir in cheese. Cool for 10 to 15 minutes. Add salmon. Beat egg whites until stiff and fold into mixture. Pour into greased baking dish. Place dish in shallow pan of hot water and bake in moderate oven (350° F.) 1 hour, or until a knife inserted in center comes out clean. Serves 6.

Chopped shrimp, flaked tuna or minced clams may be used instead of salmon.

SALMON RICE LOAF

1 cup cooked rice
¾ cup toasted buttered bread
    crumbs
2 eggs, beaten
½ teaspoon salt
½ teaspoon celery salt
⅛ teaspoon pepper
1 tablespoon chopped onion
1 tablespoon chopped parsley
1 tablespoon chopped pimiento
4 cups flaked canned salmon

Combine ingredients in order given and place in buttered ring mold. Bake in moderate oven (350°F.) 30 to 40 minutes. Remove from oven and brush with melted butter. Turn onto serving platter, fill center with buttered peas and carrots and garnish with tomato wedges. Serve with Lemon Butter Sauce. Serves 8 to 10.

SALMON SOUFFLÉ

3 tablespoons butter
3 tablespoons flour
1 cup evaporated milk
½ cup water
¼ teaspoon salt
4 eggs, separated
1 (1-pound) can salmon, flaked

Melt butter and blend with flour. Add milk, water and salt; cook until thickened, stirring constantly. Pour slowly over stiffly beaten egg yolks. Add salmon. Fold in stiffly beaten egg whites. Pour into buttered baking dish, place in pan of hot water and bake in moderate oven (350°F.) 45 to 50 minutes. Serves 6.

SAVORY SALMON LOAF

½ cup buttered bread crumbs
2 eggs, slightly beaten
½ cup milk
1 (1-pound) can salmon, flaked
1 teaspoon lemon juice
½ teaspoon salt
Dash pepper
½ teaspoon sage
2 teaspoons finely chopped onion
1 tablespoon chopped parsley
1 tablespoon melted butter

Combine ingredients in order given. Pack firmly into buttered loaf pan and bake in moderate oven (350°F.) 30 to 40 minutes. Turn out onto platter and garnish with sliced hard-cooked eggs and sliced pickles. Serves 6.

DEVILED SALMON IN POTATO NESTS

2 tablespoons minced onion
2 tablespoons minced pepper
3 tablespoons fat
1 cup condensed tomato soup
1 teaspoon prepared mustard
½ teaspoon salt
1 teaspoon lemon juice
1 (1-pound) can salmon, flaked
3 cups mashed potatoes
½ cup bread crumbs
3 tablespoons melted butter

Brown onion and green pepper in fat. Add soup and seasonings. Simmer for few minutes; add salmon. Shape potatoes into 6 nests on buttered baking sheet and fill with salmon mixture. Top with crumbs mixed with melted butter. Bake in hot oven (400° F.) until crumbs are browned, about 15 minutes. Serves 6.

SALMON STUFFED POTATOES

6 medium potatoes
⅓ cup hot milk
1 egg, well beaten
1 teaspoon salt
¼ teaspoon paprika
1 tablespoon lemon juice
1½ cups flaked cooked salmon
⅓ cup minced onions
2 tablespoons butter
Buttered crumbs

Bake potatoes, remove from oven and split lengthwise into halves. Scoop out potatoes, mash and add milk, egg, salt, paprika, and lemon juice; beat until light and fluffy. Fold in salmon and onions which have been sautéed in butter. Refill potato shells, sprinkle with buttered crumbs and bake in moderate oven (350°F.) 20 minutes. Serves 6.

Corral your family before serving this soufflé; it waits for no man

SALMON AND VEGETABLES IN-A-DISH

2 tablespoons diced onion
2 tablespoons butter
2 cups cooked peas
1 (1-pound) can salmon
2 cups diced cooked potatoes
Dash pepper
½ cup sour cream

Cook onion in butter until tender but not browned. Add liquid from peas and salmon and cook until reduced to about ½ cup. Place potatoes in shallow baking dish, add peas and sprinkle with pepper. Break salmon into large pieces and arrange on top of vegetables; combine r e d u c e d liquid mixture with sour cream and pour over vegetables and fish. Bake in moderate oven (350°F.) 40 minutes, or until vegetables have absorbed most of the liquid. Serves 6.

Instead of potatoes, use cooked rice mixed with 2 tablespoons minced pimiento.

Your bridge luncheon guests will be flattered by this tuna baked in shells

SCALLOPED TUNA AND POTATOES

5 cooked potatoes
1 (7-ounce) can tuna
1 tablespoon diced onion
1 can condensed celery soup
Paprika

Slice potatoes and flake tuna. Fill greased casserole with alternate layers of potatoes, tuna, onion and celery soup until all are used. Pour the oil from tuna over mixture and sprinkle with paprika. Bake in hot oven (425° F.) about 30 minutes. Serves 6. Salmon, shrimp, oysters or clams may be used instead of tuna.

TUNA LOAF

1 large can tuna, flaked
1 can ready-to-serve cream of tomato or mushroom soup
2½ cups soft bread crumbs
½ cup milk
¼ cup minced pimiento
3 tablespoons minced parsley
1 teaspoon salt
⅛ teaspoon pepper
2 eggs, beaten

Force tuna through food chopper, using small blade. Combine with soup. Soak crumbs in milk and add tuna mixture, pimiento, parsley, seasonings and eggs. Mix thoroughly. Place in greased loaf pan and bake in moderate oven (350°F.) 30 to 40 minutes. Serve with creamed peas. For 6. To vary, bake in greased muffin pans, unmold and serve as above. Use celery soup for mushroom. Add ¼ teaspoon each basil, and summer savory.

TUNA AND MUSHROOM CASSEROLE

4 tablespoons butter
4 tablespoons flour
¼ teaspoon pepper
2½ cups milk
3⅛-ounce package potato chips, crushed
2 (7-ounce) cans tuna, flaked
¾ cup sliced cooked mushrooms

Melt butter in top of double boiler; blend in flour and pepper; add milk gradually and cook until thickened. Combine ¾ of potato chip crumbs with fish, mushrooms and sauce. Pour into greased casserole; cover with remaining potato chips. Bake in moderate oven (350°F.) 30 minutes. Serves 6.

TUNA BAKED IN SHELLS

1 (7-ounce) can tuna
1 tablespoon butter
1 tablespoon flour
1 cup milk
Salt and pepper
Paprika
Bay leaf
½ cup bread crumbs
2 hard-cooked eggs, minced
3 tablespoons lemon juice
1 teaspoon Worcestershire sauce
4 tablespoons grated cheese

Flake tuna. Melt butter, blend in flour and add milk and seasonings. Cook until thickened, stirring constantly. Remove bay leaf. Add tuna, crumbs, eggs, lemon juice and Worcestershire sauce; fill baking shells and sprinkle with additional crumbs and grated cheese. Bake in moderate oven (350°F.) 30 minutes. Serves 4.

TUNA SUPREME

¾ cup sliced mushrooms
2 tablespoons butter
1 tablespoon flour
1 cup milk
½ cup soft bread crumbs
1 (7-ounce) can tuna, flaked
2 tablespoons chopped parsley
1 teaspoon salt
⅛ teaspoon pepper
2 eggs, beaten

Sauté mushrooms in butter. Blend in flour, add milk and cook until thickened, stirring constantly. Add crumbs, tuna, parsley, seasonings and eggs. Pour into greased shallow baking dish. Place in shallow pan of hot water and bake in moderate oven (350°F.) about 40 minutes. Serves 6.

Salmon, crab meat, lobster or minced clams may be used instead of tuna.

Use 1 cup chicken gravy instead of flour and milk. Add 2 tablespoons pimiento.

CLAMS

There are two general types of clams, the soft clams and the hard or quahog clams. The latter group is divided into 3 classes: The littlenecks, small in size; the cherry stone, medium-sized; and the large chowder clams. The littleneck and cherry stone clams may be used uncooked.

When purchased the shells should be tightly closed or close at a touch as an indication of freshness. They may be opened with a knife or steamed open.

CLAM COCKTAIL

5 clams in shells
Cocktail Sauce

Open clams with a knife. Arrange clams, in deeper half of shells, on a soup plate full of crushed ice. Sink small glass in center and fill with cocktail sauce. Garnish with parsley and lemon. Serve as soon as thoroughly chilled. Serves 1.

STEAMED CLAMS

Wash clams in several waters, scrubbing shells well to remove any sand. Place in large kettle, using ½ cup of water to cover bottom of kettle. Cover kettle tightly, place over low heat and steam until shells open (about 15 minutes). Serve in the shells in soup plates, accompanying each serving with a small dish of melted butter to which a few drops of lemon juice have been added, and a cup of the hot clam liquor.

STEAMED MUSSELS—Wash and cook mussels as above. Trim and discard horny beard. Serve as directed for Steamed Clams.

Clams for cocktails should be very chilly morsels; the sauce hot and spicy

NEW ENGLAND CLAMBAKE

The seashore is the traditional and ideal spot for the clambake, but any flat open space may serve as the locale. The only other essentials are the clams, firewood, a supply of stones, seaweed or hay, a barrel and a piece of tarpaulin.

Besides the clams other foods which may be steamed are included in the bake. Corn with all but the inside husks removed, lobsters, potatoes and chickens wrapped in cheesecloth are among the traditional favorites. The clams should be washed many times in clean sea or fresh water to remove the sand.

When all necessary materials have been assembled, arrange a mound of stones so they will provide adequate draught for the fire. Build a large hot fire on top the stones and when it is blazing well, dump 3 more buckets of stones on the fire, pile on more wood, then more stones and continue in this way, keeping the fire wigwam shaped. Heat the stones 1 hour until they are crackling hot.

In the meantime cover a large barrel with burlap, unless a wooden hooped barrel is used, in which case the burlap may be omitted. Dig a deep hole in the beach and sink the barrel into it to within 3 inches of the top. Cover the bottom of barrel with ½ inch of sea water. If fresh water is used, sprinkle ½ cup salt over the clams. Empty 5 to 6 bucketfuls of hot stones from the fire into the barrel. Put in a layer of seaweed or wet hay, 5 inches deep. Then pour in the clams, add another layer of seaweed, live lobsters, more seaweed, then the corn and potatoes. Pack in more seaweed until barrel is filled. Spread tarpaulin over the top, tie securely and cover the entire barrel with sand. Let it steam for 1½ hours. Open the barrel and serve the flavorful contents with plenty of melted butter. For 20 people 1 bushel of clams, 20 small lobsters or 10 small chickens cut into halves, 20 ears of corn, 20 potatoes and 2 pounds of butter should suffice.

CLAM RAREBIT

½ cup chopped green pepper
½ cup chopped celery
6 tablespoons fat
3 tablespoons flour
3 cups milk
½ pound Cheddar cheese, broken
1 teaspoon salt
1 tablespoon horse-radish mustard
1 teaspoon Worcestershire sauce
½ teaspoon paprika
1 pint clams
Toast

Cook green pepper and celery in fat until tender. Stir in flour, add milk and cook until thickened, stirring constantly. Add cheese and seasonings and cook over hot water, stirring until cheese is melted. Simmer clams in their own liquor until tender, add to cheese mixture and serve at once on hot toast. Serves 10 to 12.

Pour mixture into a casserole and top with small Baking Powder Biscuits. Bake in a hot oven (400°F.) 15 minutes.

Pour into individual casseroles. Top each with large biscuit.

BACON STUFFED CLAMS

24 littleneck clams
3 fresh mushrooms, chopped fine
2 slices cooked bacon, chopped fine
1 teaspoon minced parsley
Salt and pepper
Bread crumbs
Butter

Scrub clams well and place in dripping pan, having bottom covered with rock salt. Place in hot oven (400°F.) until clams begin to open, take from oven, remove from shells, save liquor, chop, and combine with the clam liquor, mushrooms, bacon, parsley, salt and pepper. Add enough bread crumbs to thicken, so that the mixture will hold its shape in shells. Mix thoroughly and fill the clam shells. Sprinkle with bread crumbs and place a small piece of butter on each shell. Bake in moderate oven (350°F.) until brown on top, about 12 minutes. Serves 4.

Clam rarebit takes as kindly to baking powder biscuits as it does to toast

NEW ENGLAND CLAM CHOWDER

¼ pound salt pork, cubed
2 small onions, minced
1 quart shucked clams
6 to 8 medium potatoes
Water
Salt, if needed
½ teaspoon pepper
1 to 2 (14-ounce) cans evaporated milk
6 to 8 common crackers, split
Cold milk

Fry salt pork in deep kettle until golden brown. Add onions and cook 2 to 3 minutes. Remove stomach from clams, chop hard parts and leave soft parts whole or chop them, as preferred. Arrange potatoes and hard parts of clams in layers over onions, cover with cold water, heat to boiling and simmer until potatoes are soft. Add soft part of clams, seasonings and evaporated milk. Heat to boiling and add crackers softened in cold milk. Heat thoroughly. Serves 6 to 8.

MANHATTAN CLAM CHOWDER

¼ pound salt pork
2 large onions, chopped
1 carrot, diced
1 cup chopped celery
1 green pepper, diced
2 cups cooked tomatoes
4 cups water
Thyme
Salt and pepper
2 dozen large clams, shucked and minced
Crackers

Dice salt pork, brown and remove cracklings from fat. Brown onions, carrot, celery and green pepper lightly in the fat. Add tomatoes, water and seasonings. Cook for 10 minutes. Add clams with liquor and simmer until tender. Thicken with crushed crackers. Serves 6.

OYSTER COCKTAIL

3 to 6 oysters
COCKTAIL SAUCE
2 tablespoons tomato catchup
½ tablespoon lemon juice
¼ teaspoon salt
3 to 4 drops Tabasco sauce
1 teaspoon horse-radish
¼ teaspoon Worcestershire
   sauce

Prepare oysters on the half shell and place on bed of ice in soup plates. Combine remaining ingredients, place sauce in small glass in center of plate with lemon wedge. Serves 1.

OYSTERS IN CASSEROLE

2 tablespoons butter
1 tablespoon flour
¾ cup cream
⅔ cup tomato catchup
1 teaspoon Worcestershire
   sauce
Few drops lemon juice
Salt and pepper
1 pint oysters

Melt butter, blend in flour and add cream and catchup gradually. Cook until thickened, stirring constantly. Add Worcestershire sauce, lemon juice, salt and pepper. Cook oysters slowly in their own liquor until edges curl. Drain, place oysters in individual buttered casseroles and cover with the sauce. Bake in moderate oven (375°F.) 15 to 20 minutes. Serves 4.

OYSTER STEW

6 cups milk, 1 quart oysters
¼ cup butter
1½ teaspoons salt
2 teaspoons celery salt
Dash pepper

Scald milk; heat oysters in their own liquor for about 5 minutes or until edges begin to curl. Add butter, seasonings and hot milk. Serve immediately. Serves 6.

CLAM FRITTERS

1 pint clams
2 cups sifted flour
1½ teaspoons baking powder
1 teaspoon salt
1 egg, beaten
1 cup milk (about)

Remove soft part from clams, mince hard parts and combine. Sift flour, baking powder and salt together. Combine egg and clams and add to flour with enough milk to make a thick batter. Drop by teaspoons into hot deep fat (360°F.) or sauté until brown. Serves 6.

CLAM CORN CASSEROLE

1 (7-ounce) can clams, Milk
3 eggs, beaten
1 tablespoon minced onion
2 tablespoons chopped pimientos
½ teaspoon salt, Dash cayenne
1 cup cream style corn
½ cup cracker crumbs
1 tablespoon melted butter

Crisp crackers are a natural complement for oysters in casserole

Drain liquid from clams, add enough milk to make 1·cup liquid and combine with beaten eggs. Add remaining ingredients and pour into greased casserole. Bake in moderate oven (375°F.) until firm, about 45 minutes. Serves 6.

OYSTERS

Oysters in the shell are sold by the dozen; "shucked" oysters by the dozen, pint or quart. If bought in the shell they should be tightly closed as an indication of freshness. Shucked oysters should be plump with no sunken areas or evidence of shrinkage. The liquor should be clear, fresh and sweet smelling.

Wash oyster shells thoroughly and rinse in cold water but do not soak. Insert a strong thin knife between shells near the thick end and run it around back of shell until muscle holding shells is cut. Discard flat shell, save liquid from oysters and remove any small pieces of shell from oysters. Serve oysters on the deep half of shell or use in recipes as desired.

SCALLOPED OYSTERS

1 quart oysters
1 teaspoon salt
1 cup fine cracker or toasted
    bread crumbs
4 tablespoons butter
1 cup milk

Drain liquor from oysters and reserve. Be sure oysters are free from shell and sand. Place 1 layer of oysters in large baking dish, sprinkle with salt and cover with layer of crumbs. Repeat with another layer of oysters, salt and crumbs. Dot with butter. Pour on reserved oyster liquor and add milk just to the top layer of oysters. Bake in moderate oven (350°F.) until edges of oysters curl and top is browned. Serve hot. Serves 6.

If desired, add 2 teaspoons chili powder, sprinkling some over each layer of oysters.

Use 1 pint of oysters and 2 cups cracker crumbs instead of amounts given above. Use 1 can condensed chicken gumbo soup instead of milk. Pour half of soup over each layer of oysters.

FRIED OYSTERS

24 large shucked oysters
2 eggs
½ teaspoon salt
⅛ teaspoon pepper
2 tablespoons cold water
1 cup bread crumbs

Drain oysters. Beat eggs with seasonings, add water and mix. Dip oysters into egg mixture, then into crumbs. Let stand 5 minutes before frying. Fry in hot deep fat (375°-380°F.) until brown. Serve at once. Serves 4.

Scalloped oysters on the menu are a cause for thanksgiving at any time of year

OYSTERS ROCKE-FELLER

4 dozen oysters in half shell
SAUCE
8 slices cooked bacon
2 cups cooked spinach
3 tablespoons minced parsley
6 celery hearts
2 green onion tops
1/2 teaspoon salt
1/4 teaspoon pepper
1/4 teaspoon paprika
1/2 cup butter, melted
6 tablespoons lemon juice
4 tablespoons cracker crumbs

Heat a 1-inch layer of rock salt in pans and arrange oysters in the half shell over the salt. Broil under moderate heat until edges begin to curl. Prepare sauce: Chop first 5 ingredients very fine. Add remaining ingredients and heat to boiling. Pour hot sauce over each oyster, return pan to oven to brown the sauce slightly and serve at once, serving each guest a panful of oysters. The salt is used to keep the oysters hot and to hold them upright. Serves 8.

BAKED OYSTERS AND BACON —Omit all ingredients above except oysters, bacon, parsley, salt and pepper. Season each oyster and cover with minced bacon and parsley. Broil as above.

PANNED OYSTERS

1 pint oysters
4 tablespoons butter
1/2 teaspoon salt
1/8 teaspoon pepper
4 slices hot toast, Parsley

Place oysters in saucepan and cook in their own liquor until edges begin to curl. Add butter, salt and pepper. Serve oysters on toast and garnish with parsley. Serves 4.

Add 2 tablespoons lemon juice and a few drops Worcestershire sauce.

OYSTERS À LA KING

1 pint oysters
2 1/2 cups milk and oyster liquid
1/2 pound mushrooms, sliced
4 tablespoons butter
4 tablespoons flour
1/2 cup chopped green pepper
2 tablespoons minced pimiento
1 1/2 teaspoons salt
1/8 teaspoon pepper
Dash nutmeg
Buttered toast

Simmer oysters in their own liquid for 5 minutes. Drain thoroughly; reserve liquid. To this liquid add enough milk to make 2 1/2 cups. Sauté mushrooms in butter for 5 minutes. Stir in flour, then add remaining ingredients, except oysters and toast. Simmer until thick. Add oysters. Serve on toast. Serves 6.

OYSTER KEBOBS

1 1/2 cups fine bread crumbs
1 cup minced celery
1/2 teaspoon salt
1/8 teaspoon pepper
30 large oysters, shucked
2 eggs, slightly beaten
2 tablespoons melted butter
Toast

Mix crumbs, celery, salt and pepper. Drain oysters, dip into egg and roll in crumb mixture until well coated. Place on skewers, allowing 5 oysters to each. Arrange skewers across top of a pan. Pour a drop of butter on each oyster, place in hot broiler, 4 inches from source of heat and brown quickly. Turn, add remaining butter and brown. Serve at once on toast. Serves 6.

BROWNED OYSTERS

1 quart oysters
Flour
4 tablespoons butter
3 tablespoons lemon juice
Worcestershire sauce
Salt
Pepper

Drain oysters, dredge in flour and brown in 2 tablespoons butter. Arrange in hot serving dish and keep hot. Brown 1 1/2 tablespoons flour in remaining butter, stir in liquid from cooked oysters, add lemon juice and a few drops Worcestershire sauce and season with salt and pepper. Heat to boiling. Pour over oysters and serve. Serves 4 to 6.

Place oysters on toast and pour sauce over them. Garnish with parsley and lemon wedges.

Panned oysters should be plump and juicy. Be careful not to overcook

CRABS

Crabs are generally divided into 2 classes, the hard-shelled crab and the soft-shelled crab; the latter of which is not a different variety, but merely a crab caught after it has shed its shell and before a new one has developed. Crabs when purchased alive should be vigorous and lively. The cooked crab meat may be purchased by the pound or in cans. Soft-shelled crabs are usually fried or broiled, while the hard-shelled crabs are boiled and the meat removed for use in various dishes.

To kill soft-shelled crabs, insert a small sharp knife into the body between the eyes or cut off the face. Lift up the pointed ends of the soft shell and remove the spongy white fibers between the two halves of the body and between the sides of the top shell and the body. Turn crab on its back and remove the apron or ventral placque—the small loose shell running to a point about the middle of the undershell. Wash crabs and cook at once.

BOILED HARD-SHELLED CRABS

Drop live crabs one at a time into boiling salted water to cover. Reheat water to boiling after adding each crab. Cook 20 to 25 minutes, drain and rinse.

Break off claws. Remove the hard top shell, working from tail end. Discard the spongy fiber and apron as above. Crack claws with a nut cracker. Remove meat, discarding all body spines. A 1-pound crab will yield about 1 cup of meat. Crab meat may be used instead of lobster in most recipes for lobster meat.

FRIED SOFT-SHELLED CRABS

Kill and clean crabs, dip into egg and roll in flour or corn meal. Sauté or fry in hot deep fat (365°F.) until brown. Serve on toast with Tartare Sauce. Allow 1 crab per serving.

Dip crabs into batter instead of egg and crumbs.

DEVILED CRABS

1 cup Medium White Sauce
1 egg, beaten
1 cup flaked cooked crab meat
2 tablespoons tomato catchup
1 green pepper, chopped
½ teaspoon salt
1 teaspoon chili powder
2 hard-cooked eggs, chopped
4 crab shells
½ cup buttered crumbs
2 tablespoons chopped parsley

Add white sauce to egg and mix with next 6 ingredients. Heap mixture into crab shells, sprinkle with crumbs and parsley and bake in hot oven (400°F.) until crumbs are browned, about 10 minutes. Serves 4.

CRAB-MEAT CASSEROLE

1 cup cooked crab meat
3 cups Thick White Sauce
2 cups grated cheese
　　(½-pound)
1 teaspoon celery salt
1 green pepper, chopped
1 (4-ounce) can mushrooms,
　　sliced
Buttered cracker crumbs

Remove spines from crab meat. Heat white sauce and cheese in double boiler and stir until smooth. Add celery salt, green pepper, mushrooms and crab meat. Pour into casserole, cover with buttered crumbs and bake in moderate oven (350°F.) about 30 minutes or until browned. Serve hot. Serves 6 to 8.

Bake in individual shells.

Bake in individual casseroles and cover with rich Pastry instead of buttered crumbs.

Use ¼ cup chopped pimiento instead of green pepper.

Crab meat, mushrooms and cheese sauce are hidden under buttered crumbs

CRAB-MEAT RAREBIT

¾ cup cooked crab meat
2 tablespoons fat
2 tablespoons chopped green
    pepper
3 tablespoons flour
¼ teaspoon dry mustard
¾ teaspoon salt
Few grains pepper
¾ cup tomato juice
¾ cup grated American
    cheese
⅓ cup milk

Remove spines from crab meat. Melt fat, add green pepper and cook for 5 minutes. Blend in flour and seasonings. Add tomato juice gradually and cook, stirring constantly until thickened. Add cheese. Pour into milk, stirring constantly. Fold in crab meat and heat to boiling. Serve in bread Croustades, in parboiled halves of green peppers or on toast. Serves 6.

Brown individual croustades in oven to make crisp containers for crab rarebit

AVOCADO CRAB CUTLETS

2 cups cooked crab meat
3 tablespoons butter
4 tablespoons flour
½ teaspoon salt
⅛ teaspoon pepper
1½ cups milk
2 cups diced avocado
Fine bread crumbs
3 eggs, beaten

Remove spines from crab meat. Melt butter, remove from heat and stir in flour until smooth. Add salt, pepper, and milk and cook, stirring constantly, until thick. Cool. Add avocado and crab meat and blend thoroughly. Shape into cutlets, roll in bread crumbs, then in beaten eggs and again in bread crumbs. Fry in hot deep fat (360°F.) until brown, 2 to 5 minutes. Serves 6. To vary, omit eggs. Add ½ cup cream and pour into buttered baking dish. Cover with buttered crumbs and bake in a moderate oven (350°F.) until crumbs are brown.

CRAB CUTLETS

3 tablespoons butter
5 tablespoons flour
1½ cups milk
Salt and pepper
1 egg, beaten
Dash celery salt
1 teaspoon grated onion
2 cups cooked crab meat
Mayonnaise
Dry bread crumbs

Melt butter, blend in flour, add milk and cook, stirring constantly until thick. Add salt, pepper, beaten egg, celery salt and onion and cook until very thick. Remove spines from crab meat and add to first mixture. Chill for several hours. Form into cakes or cut into small steak-shaped pieces, dip into flour, then spread generously on both sides with mayonnaise and roll in crumbs. Brown in hot butter and serve with creamed peas, catchup or Cheese Sauce and wedges of lemon. Serves 6.

Add minced pimiento and parsley to sauce.

CRAB MEAT WITH MUSHROOMS

½ pound mushrooms
5 tablespoons butter
3 tablespoons flour
½ teaspoon salt
⅛ teaspoon pepper
1½ cups milk or vegetable
   stock
1 cup cooked crab meat, flaked
2 cups cooked macaroni
1 tablespoon grated American
   cheese

Clear mushrooms and sauté in 2 tablespoons butter. Melt remaining butter, blend in flour and seasonings, add milk and cook over low heat until thick, stirring constantly. Add crab meat, mushrooms and macaroni. Pile into sea shells. Top with cheese and heat in moderate oven (350° F.) 20 to 25 minutes. Serves 6.

Use avocado cubes instead of cooked macaroni. Add 2 tablespoons minced pimiento. Add ¼ teaspoon each basil, savory and celery salt.

CRAB MEAT IN SHELLS

½ cup butter, ½ cup flour
½ teaspoon salt
⅛ teaspoon pepper
3 cups milk
1 cup cooked crab meat
½ cup minced parsley
4 hard-cooked eggs, chopped
½ cup buttered bread crumbs

Melt butter; blend in flour, salt and pepper; add milk and cook, stirring constantly, until thickened. Flake crab meat and add to sauce with parsley and eggs. Blend thoroughly. Fill greased baking shells, sprinkle crumbs on top and bake in moderate oven (350°F.) for 10 minutes. Serve immediately. Serves 8.

SCALLOPED CRAB MEAT—Omit eggs and add 1 cup dry bread crumbs to the mixture.

CRAB-MEAT AND VEGETABLE CASSEROLE—Use 1½ cups drained cooked peas and 2 tablespoons grated onion instead of eggs and parsley. Bake in casserole at 350°F., 30 minutes.

CRAB LEGS SAUTÉ À LA NEWBURG

½ pound crab legs
¼ cup butter
2 cups cream
¼ teaspoon salt
Dash cayenne
2 egg yolks
1 tablespoon cream
1 tablespoon sherry

Brown crab legs in butter until butter begins to brown, add cream and heat to boiling. Season. Beat egg yolks with tablespoon cream and add. Stir until thickened but do not boil Add sherry and serve on toast. For 4.

CRAB NEWBURG — Use ½ pound crab meat and 1 cup cream. Heat crab meat in butter; add seasonings and sherry. Add combined egg yolks and cream. Heat only to boiling.

Whether you use baking powder or beaten biscuits, crab Newburg is "tops"

Your most honored guest will be delighted with this crab soufflé and its shredded almonds

CRAB SPAGHETTI CASSEROLE

1 (9-ounce) package spaghetti
1¼ cups condensed cream of mushroom soup
3 tablespoons butter
1 cup milk
½ pound sharp **American** cheese, grated
1½ cups flaked crab meat
⅛ teaspoon pepper

Cook spaghetti in boiling salted water until tender. Drain. Heat soup, stirring until smooth; add butter and milk. When hot remove from heat and stir in grated cheese, saving some to sprinkle on top. Combine cheese sauce with spaghetti, crab meat and pepper. Place in greased shallow casserole and sprinkle with remaining cheese. Bake in hot oven (400°F.) about 30 minutes. Serves 8.

Use ½ cup rice instead of spaghetti.

Use White Sauce instead of mushroom soup.

Use only ½ cup cheese, sprinkled over top.

CRAB SOUFFLÉ

3 eggs, separated
1½ cups Medium White Sauce
¼ teaspoon salt
1 teaspoon onion juice
¼ teaspoon paprika
½ cup dry bread crumbs
2 cups flaked cooked crab meat

Thoroughly beat egg yolks; add remaining ingredients, folding in stiffly beaten whites. Pour into buttered dish, place in pan hot water and bake at 350°F. 50 minutes. Carnish with sliced blanched almonds. For 6.

CRAB POLENTA

⅓ cup cubed salt pork
1 clove garlic, 1 bay leaf
2 tablespoons tomato catchup
1 (8-ounce) can crab meat, flaked
Corn-meal Mush

Brown salt pork; add finely chopped garlic and brown. Add bay leaf, catchup and liquid drained from crab meat. Simmer a few minutes. Remove bay leaf; add crab meat. Slice mush, place in bottom of greased shallow casserole and cover with crab mixture. Bake in moderate oven (350°F.) about 20 minutes or until thoroughly heated. Serves 6.

CRAB THERMIDOR

2 pounds cooked crab meat
¼ cup chopped mushrooms
1 green pepper, chopped fine
1 pimiento, chopped fine
4 green onions, minced
2 tomatoes, peeled and chopped
2 tablespoons butter
1 cup cream
1 tablespoon chopped parsley
Salt and pepper
Buttered crumbs

Remove spines from crab meat and combine with mushrooms, green pepper, pimiento, onions and tomatoes; cook in butter for 10 minutes. Add cream and cook for 5 minutes. Add parsley, salt and pepper. Fill washed crab shells with mixture, cover with buttered crumbs and brown in moderate oven (350°F.). Garnish with lemon. Serves 6 to 8.

CURRIED OYSTERS AND CRAB MEAT

3 cups cooked rice
1 medium onion, chopped
1 small clove garlic, crushed
4 tablespoons cooking oil
2 dozen shucked oysters
2 cups milk
2 teaspoons curry powder
¼ teaspoon salt
Dash pepper
4 tablespoons flour
1 cup flaked cooked crab meat

Press hot rice into oiled timbale shells or ring mold. Cook onion and garlic in oil until clear. Cook oysters over low heat until they are plump and the edges begin to curl. Drain, saving liquor. Heat milk. Stir curry powder, salt, pepper and flour into onion mixture. Add hot milk and oyster liquor. Cook until thickened, stirring constantly. Add oysters and crab meat. Heat just to boiling. Serve with rice. For 6.
Use Boiled Shrimp for crab meat.

LOBSTER

LOBSTER

Live lobsters should be heavy for their size, a mottled bluish-green color, should show evidence of life by movement of claws and have all of their claws. Cooked lobster should be a bright red color, heavy for its size, the tail should be firmly curled under the body and should be firm-fleshed and rigid. When the tail is straightened out it should spring back into place. If it does not the lobster was not alive when boiled.

LOBSTER À LA NEWBURG

1½ pounds cooked lobster
3 tablespoons butter
1½ cups Madeira wine or sherry
1½ cups cream
3 egg yolks, beaten
¼ teaspoon salt
Dash cayenne

Cut lobster meat into large pieces and heat slowly in butter about 5 minutes. Add wine and simmer slowly until the wine is almost all reduced. Beat cream into egg yolks, add lobster and season. Cook, stirring constantly until thickened. Serve at once in Timbales or on hot toast, for 8.

LOBSTER MEXICAN

2 cups cooked lobster
6 tablespoons fat
1 large onion, minced
1 green pepper, minced
4 cups cooked tomatoes
¾ teaspoon salt
1 tablespoon sugar
¼ teaspoon cloves
1 bay leaf
1 cup mushrooms, sautéed
Dash Tabasco sauce

Cut lobster meat into pieces the size of a walnut. (Be careful to remove all spines.) Melt 3 tablespoons fat in a saucepan. Add

onion, green pepper, tomatoes, salt, sugar, cloves and bay leaf and simmer 15 minutes. Remove bay leaf. Add mushrooms, remaining fat, Tabasco sauce and lobster meat. Simmer until lobster is heated and serve, for 6.

LOBSTER OMELET

5 eggs, separated
¼ teaspoon salt
¼ teaspoon sugar
1 cup thin cream or milk
1 recipe Lobster Stew (page 106)

Beat egg yolks well with salt and sugar. Add cream, then egg whites, beaten until stiff. Pour into greased omelet pan or baking dish. Bake in a moderate oven (350°F.) until brown, about 20 to 25 minutes. Do not open the oven door for the first 15 minutes. If baked in omelet pan mark omelet through center. Turn onto dish. Pour lobster stew over half, fold over the other half and pour remainder of stew over it. If made in baking dish in which omelet is to be served, pour stew over omelet before serving. Serves 5.

BAKED LOBSTER AND SHRIMP

¼ cup chopped green pepper
¼ cup chopped onion
1 cup chopped celery
1 cup cooked lobster meat, cut into pieces
1 (5¾-ounce) can shrimp, cleaned
½ teaspoon salt
⅛ teaspoon pepper
1 teaspoon Worcestershire sauce
1 cup mayonnaise
1 cup buttered crumbs

Combine all ingredients except crumbs; place in individual baking shells. Sprinkle with buttered crumbs and bake in moderate oven (350°F.) 30 minutes. Serves 8.

LOBSTER CROQUETTES

1 cup Thick White Sauce
1 egg yolk, beaten
2 cups lobster meat, cut
1 teaspoon chopped parsley
1 tablespoon chili sauce
¼ teaspoon salt
¼ teaspoon mustard
2 eggs, well beaten
Bread crumbs

Pour a little of the hot white sauce over the beaten egg yolk. Return to the double boiler and cook 1 minute. Remove from heat, add next 5 ingredients and chill. Form into cone shapes or balls, dip in beaten eggs and roll in bread crumbs. Fry in deep fat (375°F.). Drain on absorbent paper. Serve with Tartare Sauce. Serves 8.

LOBSTER THERMIDOR

1 Boiled Lobster
3 mushrooms, sliced
¼ cup butter
Dash paprika
⅛ teaspoon mustard
1 tablespoon minced parsley
½ cup sherry
1½ cups Cream Sauce
2 tablespoons grated Parmesan cheese

Cut lobster lengthwise into halves, remove meat and break it into small pieces. Cook mushrooms 5 minutes in butter; add paprika, mustard, parsley, sherry and 1 cup cream sauce. Mix well, fill lobster shell with mixture, cover with remaining sauce and sprinkle with cheese. Bake in hot oven (450°F.) about 10 minutes. Serves 2.

The cream sauce may be seasoned more highly if desired. Increase mustard to 1 teaspoon, add 1 teaspoon grated onion and dash celery salt instead of parsley. Increase mushrooms to ¾ cup. Proceed as above.

BOILED LOBSTER

Lobster should be alive when boiled. Heat enough water to cover lobster completely and add 1 tablespoon salt for each quart of water. When water is boiling, grasp lobster firmly by the middle of the back with the claws held away so it cannot nip, straighten tail and plunge lobster head first into water. If a second lobster is to be cooked, reheat water to boiling before adding. Cover kettle and simmer 15 to 20 minutes, depending on size of lobster. Be careful not to overcook since overcooking toughens the meat. Plunge lobster immediately into cold water to stop the cooking.

When cool enough to handle, pull off small claws close to body; pick out the meat with nut picks or skewer leaving claws whole to use as garnish. Crack large claws with nut cracker or hammer and remove meat as whole as possible. Twist and pull off tail, break off tail fins and push the meat out the other end. Break open the meat and remove all traces of the intestinal canal which runs down the center of the tail. The canal may be white, brown or pink, but must be removed. Turn lobster on back and split body lengthwise with a very sharp knife, being careful not to break stomach or "lady"—a small sac just back of the head. Remove body from shell, leaving stomach in shell. Discard spongy tissue or lungs between meat and shell. Remove intestinal canal running length of body near the back. Pick meat from body spines. Save the bright red "coral" if present and the green liver for sauce or garnish.

A 2½-pound lobster will yield about 2 cups flaked meat.

Boil shell and trimmings with celery, a slice of onion and some herbs to make a fish stock for lobster bisque.

Chill lobster after boiling, split and remove stomach, intestinal vein and lungs. Serve lobster in the shell with mayonnaise.

BROILED LOBSTER

Kill lobster by inserting sharp knife into joint where tail and body-shell come together, thus cutting the spinal cord. Place lobster on back, make deep incision at mouth and with a quick cut, split lobster lengthwise to end of tail. Open and remove stomach, intestinal vein running length of body, liver and coral. Save liver and coral for sauce. Crack large claws. Spread lobster as flat as possible, place split side up on greased broiler; brush with melted butter, sprinkle lightly with salt and pepper. Broil slowly for 15 to 20 minutes or until delicately browned. Turn and broil 10 minutes longer on shell side. Serve at once with melted butter. Allow ¾ to 1 pound lobster per portion.

BAKED LOBSTER—Prepare lobster as above, but bake in hot oven (425°F.) 15 to 20 minutes, instead of broiling.

LOBSTER ORLEANS

2 medium onions
2 tablespoons butter
1 cup flaked cooked lobster meat
Flour
1 cup sour cream
Salt and pepper
Toast or Corn Bread

Dice onions and brown in butter. Dredge lobster with flour and add to onions. Cook for about 5 minutes, but do not brown. Pour cream over lobster and simmer for 15 to 20 minutes, season and serve on toast, for 4.

LOBSTER PUFF

3 tablespoons granulated tapioca
1 cup milk
1½ cups Boiled Lobster meat
¼ teaspoon salt
¼ teaspoon paprika
2 teaspoons lemon juice
2 eggs, separated

Cook tapioca with milk in top of double boiler until tapioca is clear and transparent. Chop lobster and add. Add salt, paprika, lemon juice and beaten egg yolks. Fold in stiffly beaten egg whites, pour into greased baking dish and bake in moderate oven (350°F.) 40 minutes or until firm. Serve immediately. Serves 4.

LOBSTER FRITTERS

1⅓ cups sifted flour
2 teaspoons baking powder
¼ teaspoon salt
¼ teaspoon paprika
1 egg, beaten
⅔ cup milk
1½ cups Boiled Lobster meat, ground

Sift dry ingredients together. Combine egg, milk and lobster. Add to dry ingredients and mix. Drop by tablespoons into hot deep fat (375°F.) and fry until brown, 3 to 5 minutes. Serves 4

BOILED CRAWFISH

1 tablespoon salt
1 tablespoon caraway seeds
2 quarts boiling water
2 pounds crawfish

Add salt and caraway seeds to boiling water. Drop live crawfish into the water, boil 5 minutes and let cool in the liquid. Drain chill and serve. Serves 6.

SHRIMP

Fresh uncooked and cooked shrimp are sold by the pound with the heads removed. The uncooked shrimp should be firm-fleshed and grayish-green.

BOILED SHRIMP

Wash shrimp and cover with boiling salted water or boiling Court Bouillon. Simmer 10 to 15 minutes or until shells turn pink. Cool in the cooking water, remove shells and black line down the back. One pound of fresh shrimp yields 2 cups cooked shrimp. Allow ⅓ pound for 1 serving.

SHRIMP COCKTAIL

½ cup Cocktail Sauce
1 cup Boiled Shrimp
¼ cup diced celery

Reduce horse-radish in sauce by ½. Serve shrimp and celery in cocktail glasses with sauce.

Shrimp creole with a rice border is Charleston's delicious gift to the world

BAKED STUFFED AVOCADOS

3 large avocados
3 tablespoons lemon juice
1 teaspoon salt
4 tablespoons butter
6 tablespoons flour
⅛ teaspoon pepper
1½ cups milk
½ cup cooked sliced celery
¼ cup minced pimiento
1 cup Boiled Shrimp
⅔ cup grated American cheese

Cut avocados lengthwise into halves and peel. Sprinkle with lemon juice and ½ teaspoon salt. Melt butter, blend in flour, add remaining salt, pepper and milk; cook until thickened, stirring constantly; add celery, pimiento and shrimp. Fill avocados with shrimp mixture and cover with grated cheese. Place in baking pan, pour in water to depth of ½ inch and bake in moderate oven (350°F.) 15 minutes. For 6. Use crab meat instead of shrimp.

Use only 3 tablespoons flour and add 1 egg yolk slightly beaten just before adding celery and shrimp.

SHRIMP CREOLE

1 cup uncooked rice
3 onions, sliced
1 bunch celery, chopped
4 tablespoons bacon fat
2 tablespoons flour
1 teaspoon salt
⅛ teaspoon pepper
2 teaspoons chili powder
2 cups water
3 cups cooked tomatoes
3 cups drained cooked peas
1½ tablespoons vinegar
2 teaspoons sugar
3 cups cleaned cooked shrimp

Cook rice in boiling salted water until tender; drain. Brown onions and celery slowly in bacon fat. Blend in flour and seasonings and add water slowly, stirring constantly. Simmer 15 minutes, covered. Add remaining ingredients and continue cooking for 10 to 15 minutes until shrimp are thoroughly heated. Pile hot rice in center of platter and surround with shrimp. Serves 6.

CASSEROLE OF SHRIMP

⅔ cup broken uncooked
    thin noodles
1 cup whole kernel corn
1 (5¾-ounce) can shrimp,
    cleaned
½ cup sliced cooked mushrooms
1 cup Cheese Sauce
½ cup grated cheese

Cook noodles in boiling salted water until tender; drain and place in casserole. Arrange corn, shrimp and mushrooms over noodles. Cover with sauce, mix gently and sprinkle with cheese. Bake in moderate oven (350°F.) about 30 minutes. Serves 6.
Use peas instead of corn.

SHRIMP SUPREME

Combine 2 cups cleaned cooked shrimp with ¼ teaspoon salt, ⅛ teaspoon pepper, 2 tablespoons each minced chives and parsley and 1 cup fine bread crumbs. Place in individual baking shells and top each with 2 tablespoons butter. Bake at 350°F. 20 minutes. Serves 4.

Press slices of bread into muffin pans and brown to make these timbales for creamed shrimp

CREAMED SHRIMP

1½ pounds Boiled Shrimp
2 cups Medium White Sauce
½ teaspoon celery salt
1 tablespoon minced pimiento
6 Toast Timbales

Shell and clean shrimp. Add white sauce, celery salt and pimiento. Heat to boiling and serve in toast timbales. Serves 6. Add ¾ cup sautéed mushrooms to shrimp mixture, if desired.

FRENCH FRIED SHRIMP

1½ pounds Boiled Shrimp
1 pint milk
1 egg
Flour
Corn meal or bread crumbs
⅛ teaspoon salt
Dash pepper

Clean shrimp. Mix milk with egg, add shrimp and let stand for 3 minutes. Mix equal parts of flour and corn meal with seasonings. Coat shrimp well with mixture. Cook in hot deep fat (375°F.) until brown. Shrimp will rise to the top of fat when cooked. Drain on absorbent paper. Serves 6.

SHRIMP DE JONGHE

1 pound uncooked shrimp
2 tablespoons white wine
Dash white pepper
2 teaspoons butter
2 slices dried bread or 1 slice bread
    and 1 slice toast, crumbed
1 clove garlic, diced
2 tablespoons diced leek
⅛ teaspoon salt

Clean and rinse uncooked shrimp and arrange in shallow baking dish. Add wine and pepper and dot with butter. Add garlic, leek and salt to crumbs and rub to a smooth paste. Spread on shrimp and bake at 350° 20 minutes. Serve at once in the baking dish, for 2.

SHRIMP GUMBO

2 pounds fresh shrimp
3 onions or 1 bunch green
    onions
½ cup vinegar
2 quarts boiling water
1 tablespoon butter
1 tablespoon flour
4 cups okra, cut fine
1 cup cooked rice
6 large tomatoes, peeled
2 bay leaves
¼ teaspoon salt
⅛ teaspoon pepper

Wash shrimp. Combine 2 onions, vinegar and water; heat to boiling, add shrimp and boil 15 to 20 minutes or until pink. Remove shrimp, shell and clean. Save the stock. Chop remaining onion and brown in butter; blend in flour and add okra. Add strained stock slowly, stirring constantly. Add rice, tomatoes, seasonings and shrimp. Simmer until okra and tomatoes are cooked. Remove bay leaves. Serves 8.

SCALLOPS

Scallops are derived from a variety of shellfish of which the only part considered edible is the eye muscle which opens the shell. This muscle is cut out and the remainder discarded. There are 2 types, the bay or cape scallops which are small and sea scallops which are larger. Scallops should be cream color rather than white and are sold by the pound or quart. Scallops may be used instead of oysters in almost all oysters recipes.

FRIED SCALLOPS

1 cup dry bread crumbs
1 teaspoon salt
½ teaspoon celery salt
1 pound scallops
1 egg
2 tablespoons water

Combine crumbs and seasonings. Dip scallops into crumbs, then into egg diluted with water and dip into crumbs again. Sauté or fry in hot deep fat (365°F.) 4 to 5 minutes. Serve with Tartare Sauce. Serves 4.

BROILED SCALLOPS HAWAIIAN

Bacon, Scallops
Pineapple wedges

Use strips of bacon about 4 inches long. On one end place a small scallop and on other end a drained pineapple wedge. Roll both to the center so each will be wrapped in bacon. Place 2 or 3 of these on a skewer and broil until bacon is crisp and brown and scallops are tender, about 10 minutes. Turn once during broiling.

BROILED SCALLOPS

1 pound scallops
French dressing, Seasoned crumbs

Dip scallops into French dressing and roll in crumbs. Place on greased baking sheet in a preheated broiler (550°F.) and cook for about 15 minutes, or until the scallops are browned. Turn occasionally. Serves 4.

Use a fork when dipping scallops into crumbs to make crust smooth and even

DEVILED SCALLOPS

1 quart scallops
½ cup butter
1½ teaspoons prepared
    mustard
¾ teaspoon salt
Dash cayenne
1 cup hot milk
Buttered crumbs

Chop scallops, heat and place in baking dish. Beat butter until creamy and add mustard, salt and cayenne. Add to scallops and pour on milk. Sprinkle with buttered crumbs and bake in moderate oven (350°F.) 20 minutes. Serves 6.

SAUTÉED SCALLOPS

1 pound scallops
1 small onion, minced
2 tablespoons fat
½ teaspoon salt
⅛ teaspoon pepper

Wash scallops quickly and cook 5 minutes in a small amount of boiling water. Drain and dry. Cook onion in fat until tender. Add scallops and cook until brown. Season and sprinkle with parsley. Serves 4.

FRICASSEE OF SCALLOPS

2 pounds scallops
2 tablespoons butter
1 onion, sliced
1 tablespoon flour
1 cup stock from scallops
1 teaspoon minced parsley
Salt and pepper
1 egg yolk
1 teaspoon lemon juice

Simmer scallops 5 to 6 minutes. Melt butter in top of double boiler, add onion and cook about 3 minutes; stir in flour and when well blended, add stock and cook until sauce thickens, stirring constantly. Add parsley, salt and pepper. Beat egg yolk and pour a little of the hot sauce over it, mixing well. Return to double boiler and cook for 2 minutes. Add scallops and lemon juice and heat thoroughly. Serve at once. Serves 6

Pineapple wedges and scallops rolled in bacon give Hawaiian touch to en brochette (page 341)

SCALLOPS EN BROCHETTE

1 pound scallops
3 tablespoons butter
6 to 8 slices bacon
Salt
Pepper

Cook scallops in butter for 5 minutes. Cut bacon into 2-inch pieces. Arrange bacon and scallops alternately on skewers and sprinkle with salt and pepper. Stand skewers upright by inserting through mesh of cake cooler placed over a pan, or insert skewers into large uncooked potato. Bake in hot oven (475°F.) about 20 minutes or until bacon is crisp and scallops are browned. Serves 4 or 5.

SEA FOOD SOUTHERN

¾ cup small scallops
2 eggs
2 cups boiled rice
¾ cup Boiled Shrimp
2 tablespoons diced onion
2 tablespoons fat
¼ cup tomato catchup
½ teaspoon celery salt
1 teaspoon curry powder

Combine liquid from scallops with slightly beaten eggs; add rice, scallops and shrimp. Brown onion lightly in fat and add catchup, celery salt and curry powder; stir into rice mixture. Place in buttered shallow baking dish; bake in moderate oven (350°F.) about 30 minutes or until firm. Serves 6.

SCALLOP FRITTERS

2 eggs, separated
1½ cups milk
½ teaspoon salt
⅛ teaspoon pepper
2½ cups sifted flour
24 scallops ·

Beat egg yolks until thickened, add milk, seasoning and flour and beat until smooth. Fold in stiffly beaten egg whites. Drain scallops, season and drop one at a time into the batter, take up in a tablespoon with all the batter the spoon will hold and fry in hot deep fat (360°F.) until brown. Serves 4 to 6.

Use only 1½ cups flour and 1 egg, not separated. Coat scallops lightly with batter. Fry.

STUFFINGS AND SAUCES

BREAD STUFFING

2 cups fine soft bread crumbs
1 teaspoon grated onion
½ cup chopped celery
1 tablespoon lemon juice
½ teaspoon salt
3 tablespoons melted butter
2 tablespoons water

Combine ingredients lightly but thoroughly. Stuffing for 3 to 4 pound fish.

MUSHROOM STUFFING—Omit lemon juice Cook ½ to 1 cup sliced mushrooms in the butter before combining with remaining ingredients.

SAVORY STUFFING—Omit lemon juice. Add 2 tablespoons minced parsley, ¼ teaspoon savory seasoning and ¼ teaspoon celery seed.

SPICY STUFFING—Omit celery. Add 2 tablespoons chopped green pepper and ¼ teaspoon mace.

SWEET PICKLE STUFFING— Omit lemon juice. Add ¼ cup chopped sweet pickle. Especially good with pike and other white-fleshed fish.

VEGETABLE STUFFING—Omit lemon juice and water. Increase salt to 1 teaspoon and use ½ cup ground onion instead of 1 teaspoon. Add ¾ cup ground uncooked carrots.

OYSTER OR CLAM STUFFING FOR FISH

½ cup chopped oysters or clams
2 cups fine cracker crumbs
2 tablespoons butter, melted
1 teaspoon salt
2 teaspoons chopped pickle
2 tablespoons lemon juice
½ cup water

Mix ingredients in order given, adding more water if stuffing seems dry. Oyster or clam liquor may be substituted for part of the water. Stuffing for 3 to 4 pound fish.

Simple, effective garnishes of lemon or cucumbers add much to the serving of fish

DILL STUFFING

3 cups soft bread crumbs
½ teaspoon salt
⅛ teaspoon pepper
3 tablespoons minced onion
⅓ cup melted butter
¼ cup chopped dill pickle
2 tablespoons chopped parsley

Mix bread crumbs with seasonings and onion; add butter slowly and toss stuffing with a fork until mixed. Add dill pickle and parsley. Stuffing for 4-pound fish.

SHRIMP STUFFING

2 tablespoons butter
½ tablespoon water
1 teaspoon anchovy paste
1 cup soft bread crumbs
2 teaspoons chopped olives
½ cup minced Boiled Shrimp
¼ teaspoon grated onion
1 tablespoon lemon juice

Heat butter, water and anchovy paste together until butter is melted. Add to bread crumbs with remaining ingredients. Especially good stuffing for trout. Stuffing for 3 to 4 pound fish.

CREOLE SAUCE

2 tablespoons chopped onion
¼ cup minced green pepper
2 tablespoons butter
1½ cups cooked tomatoes
¼ cup sliced mushrooms
¼ cup sliced olives
¼ teaspoon salt
Few grains pepper
2 tablespoons sherry

Cook onion and green pepper in butter until tender. Add tomatoes, mushrooms and olives and cook 2 minutes. Add seasonings and sherry. Makes about 2 cups sauce.

For thicker sauce, blend 1 tablespoon flour with butter and add tomatoes gradually, stirring until thickened.

CUCUMBER SAUCE FOR FISH

1 cup chopped cucumber
⅓ cup water
2 tablespoons butter
2 tablespoons flour
1 cup fish stock
2 teaspoons lemon juice
1 teaspoon grated lemon rind
½ teaspoon grated onion
½ teaspoon salt

Cook cucumber in water until tender. Drain. Prepare sauce of butter, flour and fish stock; when thick add lemon juice, rind, onion and salt. Add cooked cucumber last. Makes 2 cups.

HORSE-RADISH SAUCE

¼ cup prepared horse-radish, drained
¾ teaspoon salt
¼ teaspoon pepper
1 tablespoon vinegar
½ cup heavy cream, whipped

Mix first 4 ingredients thoroughly and fold into whipped cream. Makes 1 cup sauce.

MAÎTRE D'HÔTEL BUTTER

½ cup butter
1 teaspoon salt
⅛ teaspoon pepper
1 tablespoon chopped parsley
1½ tablespoons lemon juice

Cream butter until fluffy, add salt, pepper and parsley and mix well. Work in lemon juice slowly. Makes about ½ cup sauce.

LEMON BUTTER

½ cup butter
3 tablespoons lemon juice

Cream slightly softened butter, adding lemon juice gradually as it becomes pliable. Serve on fish.

ALMOND BUTTER SAUCE — Melt butter, add ¼ cup ground almonds and reduce lemon juice to 1 teaspoon. Serve hot with fish or sea food.

Fillets may be stuffed flat or rolled before baking

DRAWN BUTTER — Melt butter, allow salt to settle; pour off oil into small hot cups.

LEMON BROWNED BUTTER — Brown butter and add ⅓ teaspoon Worcestershire sauce with lemon juice.

PARSLEY BUTTER — Add 1 teaspoon salt, ¼ teaspoon pepper and 1 tablespoon minced parsley. Reduce lemon juice to 2 tablespoons.

QUICK LEMON BUTTER — Reduce butter to 4½ tablespoons and add salt, pepper and 1½ tablespoons minced parsley.

ROAST OYSTER SAUCE — Reduce butter to 2 tablespoons and add 4 drops Tabasco sauce and the juice of ½ onion. Serve hot.

MEATS

500 Ways to Prepare Meats

In most cities it is possible for the homemaker to buy meat which has been graded for quality by the packer and stamped by Federal inspectors. Most packers indicate the grade by various brand names. The Federal stamp guarantees that the meat is wholesome but does not indicate quality.

The woman who does not buy branded meat must rely upon the appearance of the meat to secure her money's worth, since a sirloin steak from low grade beef is apt to be less tender than a rump steak from high grade beef.

HOW MUCH SHALL I BUY— One pound boneless meat serves 4. This includes boned meats, ground meats, flank steak, liver, sausages and most canned meats. One pound meat with a small amount of bone serves 3. This includes round steak, ham slices, etc. One pound meat with larger amount of bone serves 2. This includes such cuts as most steaks, shoulder cuts, chops, etc.

ALL FRESH MEAT should be kept in a refrigerator; handled with clean hands and tools.

GOOD QUALITY VEAL is light grayish pink in color. The meat is very fine-grained, velvety and fairly firm, with little surface fat and no marbling. The fat is clear, firm and white and the bones are porous and red.

GOOD QUALITY BEEF is of fresh red color, has a smooth covering of brittle creamy fat and small streaks of fat distributed through the lean. In other words it is well marbled with fat. The lean is firm, fine-grained and velvety. The bones in young beef are porous and red, in older animals they are white and flinty.

GOOD QUALITY LAMB varies in color from a light to a dark pink, since the color darkens as the animal grows older, and in mutton deepens to red. The fat of young lambs is quite soft and slightly pink in color. As the animal grows older it becomes harder and whiter, so that mutton fat is white and rather brittle.

GOOD QUALITY PORK is grayish pink, changing to a delicate rose in older animals. The flesh is relatively firm, fine-grained, well marbled and covered with firm white fat.

TENDERIZED FRESH MEAT is aged by hanging in a warm humid room under sterile conditions. The high temperature hastens the action of the natural enzymes which soften the muscle fibers, thus reducing the usual time for aging from weeks to a matter of days. High humidity prevents loss of moisture from the meat, while an electric sterilizing lamp prevents its deterioration by bacterial action. Cook as directed by the packer.

FROZEN MEAT

Preservation of meat and other foods by freezing during the winter months has always been a common practice in rural communities. During recent years freezing plants with locker space for rent have made it possible for farmers to slaughter and use frozen fresh meat all year round. Town and city families have been quick to see the economy of buying quarters, halves or the live animals, then freezing and storing the meat in lockers until used. There are an increasing number of these plants.

The length of time meat can be held in lockers depends upon several factors, though in general beef will keep longer than pork. Rapid chilling after slaughtering, proper wrapping to prevent moisture losses, quick freezing and a uniform low temperature in the lockers are all important for good preservation of the meat. Thawing and refreezing are undesirable, since this impairs the quality of the meat and gives an opportunity for increased bacterial action. Meat should be cooked as soon as it has thawed. Meat may be thawed before cooking or the cooking may be started while the meat is still frozen. Soaking the meat in water to hasten thawing impairs the flavor and should be avoided.

TIME REQUIRED TO THAW MEAT

CUT	42°F. (REFRIGERATOR)	ROOM TEMPERATURE
Thick cuts (3 to 5 pounds)	30 to 50 hours	6 to 20 hours
Thin cuts	20 to 24 hours	3 to 5 hours
2-rib standing beef roast		2 hours per pound
3-pound rump pot roast		2-2½ hours per pound
1½-inch porterhouse steak		2 hours per pound
1-inch ground beef patties		2 hours
Pork loin roast	13 to 14 hours	2-2½ hours per pound
Pork chops (¾ inch thick)	24 hours	

TIME TABLE FOR COOKING THAWED AND UNTHAWED CUTS

Frozen meat which has been thawed before cooking may be cooked in exactly the same way and by the same methods as meat which has not been frozen. Meat which is started cooking before thawing may be cooked by the same methods also, but a longer cooking time is required. The following chart lists the cooking time required for various cuts when they are cooked after thawing or while still frozen. In some cases the minutes per pound is given and for some the total cooking time is given.

CUT	MINUTES PER POUND THAWED	UNTHAWED
Standing Rib Roast		
(Roast at 300°F)		
Rare	18	43
Medium	22	47
Well done	30	55
Rolled Rib Roast		
(Roast at 300°F)		
Rare	32	53
Medium	38	57
Well done	48	65
Beef Rump (Braise)	30	50
Porterhouse Steak		
(Broil, rare to medium)		
1 inch	8-10	21-33
1½ inches	10-15	23-38
2 inches	20-30	33-43
Boneless Lamb Shoulder		
(Roast at 300°F.)	40	60
Leg of Lamb		
(Roast at 300°F.)	30-35	45-55
Pork Loin		
(Roast at 350°F.)		
Center cut	35-40	50-55
Rib or loin end	50-55	70-75
Club Steak	Total Time	Total Time
(Broil, rare to medium)	Minutes	Minutes
¾ inch	16-20	24-28
1 inch	20	30
Round Steak (Pan-broil)		
½ inch	7	11
Beef Patties (Pan-broil)		
1 inch	8	10
Lamb Chops (Pan-broil)		
¾ inch	10	15
1½ inches	20	25
Shoulder Lamb Chops (Braise)		
½ inch	15	20
Pork Chops (Braise)		
¾ inch	45	55

DIRECTIONS FOR ROASTING MEAT

Roasting meat at a constant low roasting temperature gives better results than the old method by which the meat was first seared at a high temperature and the roasting finished at a low temperature. The searing does not retain the juices as was once thought and causes excessive shrinkage and loss of weight. Use any shallow pan large enough to hold the meat and place a wire rack in bottom to hold the meat up out of the juices and to allow the heat to penetrate evenly from all sides. A wire cake rack may be placed in the bottom of the pan or hooked securely over the sides.

1. Wipe meat with a damp cloth, but do not wash.

2. Rub with salt in proportion of 1 teaspoon per pound of meat. Use pepper, onion or garlic if desired.

3. Place meat, fat side up, on rack of pan. If meat has little or no fat, place strips of bacon, salt pork or suet over it. This will baste the roast and no other basting is needed.

4. Do not add water and do not cover pan.

5. If meat thermometer is to be used, insert into center of thickest part of cut. Be sure bulb of thermometer does not touch bone or fat.

6. Roast at temperature given on page 8 for the required time or until the thermometer registers the desired internal temperature. If a roast is not cut immediately upon removal from oven, it will continue to cook and the temperature at the center will continue to rise. The cooking may go on from 30 to 45 minutes.

ROAST	WEIGHT POUNDS	OVEN TEMPERATURE CONSTANT	INTERIOR TEMPERATURE WHEN DONE	TIME PER POUND IN MINUTES
BEEF				
Standing ribs (3 ribs)	7-8	300°F	140°F	18-20 Rare
			160	22-25 Med.
(2 ribs)	5-6		170	27-30 Well done
Standing ribs (1 rib)	1.8	350	140	33 Rare
			160	45 Med.
			170	50 Well done
Rolled ribs	6-8	300	140	32 Rare
			160	38 Med.
			170	48 Well done
Chuck ribs	5-8	300	150-170	25-30
Rump	5-7	300	150-170	25-30
Whole tenderloin	4-6	300	140	25 Rare
			160	30-35 Med.
PORK—Fresh (Always cooked well done)				
Loin—Center	3-4	350	185	35-40
Whole	8-15		185	15-20
Ends	3-4		185	50-55
Shoulder—Whole	12-14	350	185	30-35
Boned and rolled	4-6	350	185	40-45
Cushion	4-6	350	185	35-40
Spareribs	1½-1¾	350	185	40-45
Pork Butt	4-6	350	185	45-50
Ham	10-18	350	185	30-35
PORK—Smoked				
Ham—Whole	10-12	300	170	25
Tenderized	10-12	300	145-150	15
Half	6	300	170	30
Tenderized	6	300	145-150	20
Shank end	3	300	170	40
Butt end	3	300	170	45
Cottage Butt	2-4	300	170	35
Picnic	3-10	300	170	35
LAMB				
Leg	6½-7½	300	175-180	30-35
Shoulder-Rolled	3-4	300	175-180	40-45
Shoulder	4½-5½	300	175-180	30-35
Cushion	3-4	300	175-180	30-35
Rack of ribs	2	300	175-180	45-50
(6-7 ribs)				
Crown (12-15 ribs)	4	300	175-180	30-35
VEAL				
Leg roast	7-8	300	170	25
Loin	4½-5	300	170	30-35
Rack (4-6 ribs)	2½-3	300	170	30-35
Shoulder	7	300	170	25
Shoulder-Rolled	5	300	170	40-45

BRAISING

Braising, a method of cooking by moist heat, is used for the less tender cuts of meat which require long slow cooking and presence of moisture to bring out the full flavor and make the meat tender.

To braise meat, brown it in a small amount of hot fat, then cover tightly and cook slowly in juices from the meat or in added liquid such as water, milk, cream, stock, diluted vinegar, fruit or vegetable juices. Add only a small amount of liquid at a time and do not allow to boil, but keep at a simmering temperature. Pot roasts, fricassees, casserole meats, smothered steaks and similar favorites are all cooked by braising. The following table gives the approximate cooking time for braising various cuts after they have been browned in fat.

TIME TABLE FOR BRAISING

CUT	AVERAGE WEIGHT OR THICKNESS	COOKING TIME
BEEF		
Pot roast	3-5 pounds	3-4 hours
Swiss steak	1½-2½ inches	2-3 hours
Fricassee	2-inch cubes	1½ hours
Beef birds	½x2x4 inches	1½ hours
Short ribs	Pieces 2x2x4 inches	1½ hours
Round steak	¾ inch	45-60 minutes
Stuffed steak	½-¾ inch	1½ hours
PORK		
Chops	¾-1½ inches	45-60 minutes
Spareribs	2-3 pounds	1½ hours
Tenderloin		
Whole	¾-1 pound	45-60 minutes
Fillets	½ inch	30 minutes
Shoulder steak	¾ inch	30-45 minutes
LAMB		
Breast—Stuffed	2-3 pounds	1½-2 hours
Breast—Rolled	1½-2 pounds	1½-2 hours
Neck slices	¾ inch	1 hour
Shanks	½ pound each	1-1½ hours
VEAL		
Breast—Stuffed	3-4 pounds	1½-2 hours
Breast—Rolled	2-3 pounds	1½-2 hours
Birds	½x2x4 inches	45-60 minutes
Chops	½-¾ inch	45-60 minutes
Chops—Breaded	½-¾ inch	45-60 minutes
Steaks or cutlets	½-¾ inch	45-60 minutes
Shoulder chops	½-¾ inch	45-60 minutes

The inexpensive cuts of meat make flavorful pot roasts. Brown the meat well in a Dutch oven and add only a little liquid at a time. Long slow cooking does the trick. Add your favorite vegetables when the meat is nearly tender

Rolled veal roast is delicious when larded with salt pork or the fat of smoked beef. Use the larding needle and draw it through carefully or fold frankfurters into meat as you roll

Boned and tightly rolled with the layer of fat on the outside, your roast needs only the thermometer and a trivet to baste itself to juicy perfection

BROILING

Broiling means to cook by direct heat and may be done over hot coals, under a flame or an electric unit. This method may be used for tender cuts of meat with adequate amounts of fat. Veal should not be broiled since it is low in fat; pork is more satisfactorily cooked by other methods. Preheat the broiler with the oven door closed, about 10 minutes. Slash the fat edge of meat in several places to prevent curling. If meat thermometer is used insert at the side and force bulb into center of cut. Place meat on broiler rack with the surface of meat about 4 inches from source of heat. Turn when surface is browned and about half the total cooking time has been used. Sprinkle browned side with salt, turn meat and cook until brown or to same internal temperature as for roast beef and lamb.

A thick juicy steak is a rare treat when carefully broiled, a thermometer at its center and served with broiled tomatoes or radish fans

TIME TABLE FOR BROILING

CUT	WEIGHT	COOKING TIME	
		Rare	Medium
	Pounds	Minutes	Minutes
BEEF			
Filet mignon—1 inch	⅓	5	6-7
1½ inches	½	9-10	12
2 inches	¾	15	18
Club steak—1 inch	1	9-10	12-14
1½ inches	1¼	14-16	18-20
2 inches	1½	18-22	24-30
Sirloin steak—1 inch	3	10-12	14-16
1½ inches	4¼	15-20	20-25
2 inches	5¾	20-25	25-30
Porterhouse steak—1 inch ...	2	9-10	12-15
1½ inches	2½	14-16	18-20
2 inches	3	18-22	25-30
Ground patties (1 x 3 inches)	4 ounces	15	25
LAMB			
Shoulder chops—1 inch	3 ounces	10	12
1½ inches	6 ounces	15	18
2 inches	10 ounces	18	22
Rib chops—1 inch	2 ounces	10	12
1½ inches	4 ounces	15	18
2 inches	5 ounces	18	22
Loin chops—1 inch	3 ounces	10	12
1½ inches	5 ounces	15	18
2 inches	6 ounces	18	22
Ground patties (1 x 3 inches)	4 ounces	15	18
PORK			
Ham slice—½ inch	¾-1 pound	Ham always	20
1 inch	1½-2	cooked well done	25-30
Ham slice—tenderized			
½ inch	¾-1		10-12
1 inch	1½-2		16-20

ROAST BEEF

5- to 6-pound rolled rib roast of beef
Salt and pepper

Wipe meat with damp cloth sprinkle with salt and pepper. Place on rack in pan and roast uncovered in slow oven (300°F.) allowing 35 to 40 minutes per pound. Serves 8. Yorkshire Pudding (p. 354) may be added.

BROILED STEAKS

1 porterhouse or sirloin steak, 1½ inches thick
Salt, Pepper, Butter

Preheat oven to 350°F. about 10 minutes. Place meat on broiler rack 3 inches below moderate broiler heat. Broil 6 to 8 minutes for rare steak or 9 for medium steak. Sprinkle with salt and pepper, turn and broil 6 to 9 minutes longer. Place on hot platter, sprinkle with salt and pepper and spread with soft butter. Serves 4 to 6. **Broil filet mignon, club** and **rib steaks** as above, allowing about 5 to 6 minutes for each side for rare steak and 8 minutes for medium steak.

CHARCOAL BROILED STEAKS

2 club steaks, 1½ inches thick
Salt, Pepper, Butter

Place steaks on rack over glowing charcoal; broil for 9 minutes. Turn, sprinkle with salt and pepper and broil for 9 minutes. Place, hottest side up, on hot platter. Sprinkle with salt and pepper and spread with butter. Serves 4.

Ribs down in the roasting pan with the thermometer at its heart, a standing roast will baste itself and make an attractive dinner dish

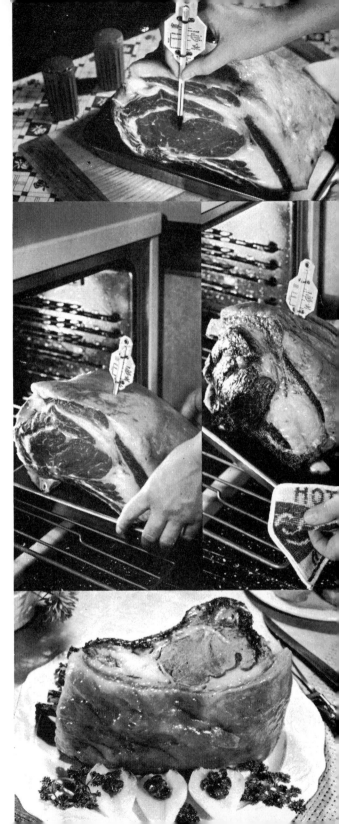

BEEF À LA MODE

5 pounds beef rump roast
¼ pound fat salt pork
Pepper
1 clove garlic, chopped
Salt, Cayenne, Flour
2 onions, sliced
4 tablespoons bacon drippings
1 bay leaf
1 sprig parsley
3 carrots, sliced
1 turnip, sliced
¼ cup boiling water

Cut deep gashes in beef. Slice salt pork very thin, rub with pepper and place in the gashes in meat. Rub meat with garlic, salt and cayenne and dredge with flour. Brown onions in bacon drippings, remove onions, place meat in kettle and place onions, bay leaf and parsley over meat. Cover and cook slowly until well browned on 1 side. Turn and brown on other sides. Add vegetables and brown well. Add boiling water, cover closely and simmer for 3 hours, or longer, adding more water as necessary. Serve with vegetables and gravy Serves 10.

For the budgeteer, flank steak is ideal when stuffed and rolled, tied in tufts to make a turtle or cut in strips for skewered fillets

BEEF POT ROAST

1 tablespoon flour
2 teaspoons salt
¼ teaspoon pepper
3 pounds beef (chuck or rump)
1 onion, chopped
1½ tablespoons fat
2 cloves
2 cups boiling water

Mix flour with salt and pepper and dredge meat with mixture. Brown meat and onion in fat, add cloves and a small amount of boiling water. Cover and simmer

for about 3 hours, or until meat is tender, adding more water as needed. One-half hour before meat is tender, potatoes may be added if desired. Serves 6.

VARIATIONS

Omit onion and cloves. Pour ⅓ cup grated horse-radish over meat after browning. Add water and proceed as above.

Use 1 cup cooked tomatoes instead of 1 cup water. Omit flour and cloves. Add whole or diced vegetables to meat ½ to 1 hour before meat is tender, or just soon enough for vegetables to be tender when meat is cooked. Carrots, potatoes, onions, green beans or peas may be used. Sprinkle meat with 1 teaspoon brown sugar, ½ teaspoon ginger, salt and pepper before browning.

STUFFED FLANK STEAK

1 flank steak
Salt, Pepper, Flour
4 cups bread cubes
2 small onions, chopped
¾ cup chopped celery
1½ teaspoons sage
3 tablespoons butter

Have flank steak scored lightly crosswise. Sprinkle with salt and pepper, dredge with flour and pound well with potato masher. Combine bread cubes, onions, celery, sage and butter. Moisten with water and season with salt and pepper. Spread stuffing over flank steak, roll meat and tie or fasten edge with toothpicks. Brown in fat, add about ½ cup water, cover pan and cook in moderate oven (350°F.) about 1½ hours or until tender. Baste meat occasionally. Serves 6.

FLANK STEAK FILLETS—Roll steak around strips of salt pork, skewer, cut into slices. Brown in hot fat. Braise with tomatoes, onion and green pepper.

YORKSHIRE PUDDING

1 cup sifted flour
¼ teaspoon salt
3 eggs
1 cup milk

Sift flour and salt together. Beat eggs until light and add sifted ingredients, mixing well. Add milk gradually and beat 2 minutes with rotary egg beater. Prepare pudding in time to pour into pan 30 minutes before beef has finished roasting. Place beef to one side of roasting pan. Pour off all fat except ¼ cup and pour in pudding to depth of ½ inch. Return to hot oven (400° F.) to cook 30 minutes. Cut into squares and serve at once. Serves 6.

Yorkshire pudding may be baked separately in oblong pan heated very hot and well greased with beef drippings.

CRANBERRY MEAT LOAF

¼ cup brown sugar
½ cup Cranberry Sauce
1½ pounds ground beef
½ pound ground smoked ham
¾ cup milk, ¾ cup cracker crumbs
2 eggs, 1½ teaspoons salt
⅛ teaspoon pepper
2 tablespoons diced onion
3 bay leaves

Spread sugar over bottom of greased loaf pan. Mash cranberry sauce and spread over sugar. Combine remaining ingredients, except bay leaves. Shape into loaf and place on cranberry sauce. Place bay leaves on top of loaf. Bake in moderate oven (350°F.) about 1 hour. Remove bay leaves before serving. Serves 12.

You never know what's under the blanket crust. This time it's a savory meat loaf

MEAT LOAF IN BLANKET

1 onion, chopped
Bacon drippings
2 cups finely chopped cooked
    potatoes
1½ cups chopped cooked beef
2 eggs, ½ cup milk
Salt and pepper
Baking Powder Biscuit dough
    (made with 2 cups flour)

Brown onion in drippings, add potatoes, mix well and combine with next 5 ingredients. Heat thoroughly. Roll biscuit dough into rectangle ¼ inch thick. Shape hot meat mixture into a loaf and draw dough up over mixture to form a roll. Press edges of dough firmly together. Slash top, place on baking sheet and bake in hot oven (425°F.) 15 to 20 minutes. Serve with Mushroom Sauce for 8. Other cooked meat may be used.

Starring meat loaf, with a supporting cast of onions, tomatoes and duchess potato planked for company dinner

JELLIED MEAT LOAF

1½ tablespoons unflavored gelatin
¼ cup cold water
¾ cup boiling water
¼ cup vinegar
½ teaspoon salt
2 cups diced cooked beef
½ cup diced celery
1 pimiento, chopped
½ green pepper, chopped
½ tablespoon minced onion
2 hard-cooked eggs, sliced

Soften gelatin in cold water, then dissolve in boiling water. Add vinegar and salt. Cool. When mixture begins to thicken add remaining ingredients except eggs. Arrange egg slices on bottom and sides of mold, pour in the meat mixture. Chill. Unmold and serve on lettuce. Serves 6.

BARBECUED HAMBURGERS

1½ pounds ground beef
3 tablespoons chopped onion
½ cup bread crumbs
1½ teaspoons salt
¼ teaspoon pepper
Fat, Barbecue Sauce

Combine beef, onion, crumbs, salt and pepper. Form into patties and brown slowly in fat. Cover with barbecue sauce and cook 15 minutes longer, turning occasionally. Serves 6.
HAMBURGERS—Omit crumbs and sauce. Broil instead of frying.

BEEF BRISKET WITH SAUERKRAUT

4 pounds beef brisket
Hot water
1 tablespoon salt, Pepper
1 quart Sauerkraut
1 cup vinegar
3 tablespoons brown sugar
1 uncooked potato, grated

Cover brisket with water, season and simmer 1 to 1½ hours. Add sauerkraut, vinegar and brown sugar. Cook about 1 hour longer or until meat is tender. Add potato and cook 10 minutes longer. Serves 8.

Sauerkraut is the ideal partner for beef brisket simmered to tenderness

BEEF UPSIDE-DOWN PIE

1½ cups sifted flour
2 teaspoons baking powder
1 teaspoon salt
1 teaspoon paprika
1 teaspoon celery salt
¼ teaspoon white pepper
5 tablespoons shortening
¾ cup milk
¼ cup sliced onion
1 can condensed tomato soup
½ pound ground beef

Sift flour, baking powder, ½ teaspoon salt and other seasonings together. Cut in 3 tablespoons of the shortening with 2 knives or pastry blender until mixture resembles coarse meal. Add milk and mix until blended. Cook onion until soft in remaining shortening. Add remaining salt, soup and meat and heat to boiling. Cover with biscuit mixture, bake in very hot oven (475°F.) about 20 minutes. Turn upside down on plate. For 6.

BREADED OXTAILS

2 oxtails
3 sprigs parsley, chopped
3 sprigs thyme
1 bay leaf
Salt and pepper
Dash cayenne
1 egg, beaten
1 cup sifted dry bread crumbs

Wash oxtails and cut into 4-inch lengths. Cover with boiling water. Add parsley, thyme, bay leaf, salt, pepper and cayenne; simmer until tails are tender, 2 to 3 hours. Let cool in the stock. Drain meat, dip into egg and roll in crumbs. Fry in hot deep fat (370°F.) until brown. Serves 4.

HUNGARIAN BEEF STEW

5 onions, chopped
6 tablespoons fat
2 pounds beef, cut into long strips
½ teaspoon salt, Dash marjoram
¼ teaspoon pepper
1 clove garlic, mashed
¾ cup white wine
½ pound bacon, chopped
2 cups sour cream

Brown onions in fat; add meat, salt, marjoram, pepper, garlic and wine; simmer until meat is nearly tender, about 1 hour. Cook bacon until crisp and add to meat mixture. Stir in sour cream and continue cooking until meat is tender, 15 to 30 minutes longer. Serves 8.

DINNER-IN-A-DISH

5 tablespoons fat
1 medium-sized onion, chopped
2 green peppers, sliced
1 pound hamburger
1½ teaspoons salt
¼ teaspoon pepper
2 eggs, well beaten
2 cups canned corn
4 medium tomatoes, sliced
½ cup dried bread crumbs

Sauté onion and peppers in 4 tablespoons fat 3 minutes. Add meat and seasonings. Remove from heat. Stir in eggs and mix well. Place 1 cup of corn in a baking dish, then half the meat mixture, then a layer of sliced tomatoes. Repeat. Cover with crumbs. Dot with remaining fat. Bake at 350°F. 45 minutes. Serves 4.

POT ROAST WITH PRUNES

4-pound chuck or rump roast
3 tablespoons fat
2 onions, sliced
½ pound uncooked prunes, soaked
4 cloves
Salt and pepper
1 cup water, 1 cup cider

Brown meat on all sides in hot fat. Add onions and when browned, add remaining ingredients. Reduce heat, cover and simmer slowly until tender, 3 to 4 hours. Add more water from time to time if necessary. Serve with Potato Pancakes or buttered Noodles. Serves 6 to 8.

Diluted vinegar may be used instead of cider.

MEXICAN SCRAMBLE

1 cup diced cooked steak
3 tablespoons chopped onion
1 tablespoon green pepper
2 tablespoons fat
1 No. 2 can whole kernel corn
1½ cups tomato juice
½ teaspoon chili powder
1¼ teaspoons salt

Sauté meat, onion and green pepper slowly in fat until lightly browned. Add corn, tomato juice and seasoning, and simmer in covered skillet for 30 minutes. Serve with browned rice for 6.

Prunes and apricots with pot roast add glamour to the meat and flavor to the gravy

SAUERBRATEN

3 pounds beef shoulder
Garlic (if desired)
2 teaspoons salt
Pepper
2 cups vinegar
2 cups water
½ cup sliced onion
2 bay leaves
1 teaspoon peppercorns
¼ cup sugar
Fat, Flour
1 cup sweet or sour cream

Rub meat with a cut surface of garlic, salt and pepper and place in bowl. Heat vinegar, water, onion, bay leaves, peppercorns and sugar together, but do not boil. Pour hot mixture over meat, cover bowl, and let stand in cool place 4 to 8 days, turning meat each day. Drain, saving vinegar mixture. Brown meat in fat, add ½ of strained vinegar, cover pan and simmer until tender, 2 to 3 hours, adding more vinegar as required to keep liquid about ½ inch deep in pan. Strain liquid and thicken with 2 tablespoons flour for each cup liquid. Cook until thickened and add cream. Serves 6.

MEAT CROQUETTES

1 tablespoon fat
4 tablespoons flour
1 cup milk
2 cups finely ground cooked meat
2 teaspoons lemon juice
½ teaspoon salt
⅛ teaspoon pepper
1 teaspoon minced parsley
Fine dry bread crumbs
1 egg

Melt fat, add flour and blend. Add milk and cook until very thick, stirring constantly. Add meat, lemon juice, seasonings and parsley. Chill thoroughly. Form into cylinders, pyramids or patties. Dip into crumbs, then into slightly beaten egg mixed with 2 tablespoons water and into crumbs again. Chill. Fry in hot deep fat (385°F.) until brown. Serves 4.

Omit lemon juice and add 1 tablespoon minced onion.

MEXICAN TAMALE PIE

1 cup corn meal
4 cups water, 1 teaspoon salt
1 medium onion
1 green or chili pepper
3 tablespoons cooking oil
2½ cups cooked tomatoes
2 cups ground cooked meat
1 teaspoon salt
Dash cayenne or chili powder

Cook corn meal, water and salt in top of double boiler for 45 minutes. Chop onion and pepper and fry in hot oil. Add tomatoes, meat, salt and cayenne or chili and cook until thickened. Line greased baking dish with half the mush, pour in meat mixture, cover with remaining mush and bake in hot oven (375°F.) 30 minutes or until top is lightly browned. Serves 6 to 8.

Use 3 cups cooked rice instead of first 3 ingredients.

CORNED BEEF LOAF

4 crackers, crushed
1½ pounds cooked corned beef, ground
1 egg, slightly beaten
¼ cup water
Pepper
½ teaspoon sage
1 onion, minced

Combine crackers with corned beef, add remaining ingredients and mix thoroughly. Pack into greased loaf pan and bake in moderate oven (350°F.) 45 to 60 minutes. Serve hot or cold. Serves 6.

NEW ENGLAND BOILED DINNER

4 pounds corned beef
1 head cabbage
6 carrots, 6 onions
6 white turnips
8 potatoes, 8 beets

Cover meat with cold water; simmer for 3 hours. Prepare vegetables, cutting turnips into quarters and cabbages into eighths. Cook beets in boiling water. Add remaining vegetables to meat and cook until tender. Drain and serve vegetables on platter with meat. Serves 4. Leftovers are made into Red Flannel Hash.

RED FLANNEL HASH

9 cooked beets, chopped
6 cooked potatoes, chopped
1½ cups chopped cooked corned beef
½ cup fat, melted
2 teaspoons salt
⅛ teaspoon pepper
6 tablespoons water

Combine beets, potatoes, corned beef, fat, salt, pepper and water. Place in greased baking dish and bake in moderate oven (350°F.) about ¾ hour. Serves 6.

CORNED BEEF AND CABBAGE

4 pounds corned beef
1 large head cabbage

Cover meat with cold water and simmer 3 hours. Add cabbage, cut into eighths, and cook until tender. Serves 8.

CORNED BEEF DELICIOUS

1½ tablespoons unflavored gelatin
⅓ cup cold water
2 bouillon cubes
2 cups boiling water
¼ teaspoon Worcestershire sauce
½ teaspoon salt
1 cup diced celery
¾ cup drained canned peas
¼ cup sliced radishes
½ cup diced Pickled Beets
¾ cup diced corned beef

Soften gelatin in cold water. Dissolve bouillon cubes in boiling water, pour over gelatin and stir until dissolved. Add Worcestershire sauce and salt. Chill until mixture begins to thicken. Fold in remaining ingredients and chill until firm. Serves 8.

New Englanders like plenty of vegetables with corned beef in their boiled dinner

BAKED CORNED BEEF

4 pounds corned beef
1 cup brown sugar, Whole cloves

Cover corned beef with cold water, heat to boiling and skim. Reduce heat and simmer meat until tender 3 to 4 hours. Remove from water, place on rack in roaster. Rub brown sugar over corned beef. Insert whole cloves into meat in diagonal rows and bake in moderate oven (325°F.) until browned. Serves 10 to 12

BAKED SAUERKRAUT WITH CORNED BEEF HASH

1 No. 2½ can sauerkraut
1 No. 2 can corned beef hash
1 cup tomato juice
2 tablespoons chopped onion
2 teaspoons prepared horse-radish
1 strip bacon

Place sauerkraut in bottom of greased baking dish. Combine hash, tomato juice, onion and horse-radish; spread over sauerkraut. Cut bacon into ½-inch strips and arrange over top of hash. Bake in very hot oven (450°F.) about 20 minutes. Serves 8.

CORNED BEEF HASH

⅓ cup minced onions
1 tablespoon bacon drippings
⅛ teaspoon pepper
3 cups diced cooked potatoes
2½ cups chopped cooked corned
    beef
2 tablespoons fat

Brown onions in drippings in skillet; add pepper, potatoes and beef and mix thoroughly. Shape into patties and sauté in hot fat. Serves 6.
Serve with poached eggs.

Instead of making patties, if desired add ½ cup hot milk to mixture, spread evenly in skillet, cover and simmer ½ hour. Do not stir mixture. To serve, fold like an omelet.

STUFFED VEGETABLE MARROW

1 large vegetable marrow
1½ cups chopped cooked meat
½ cup bread crumbs
1 tablespoon minced onion
2 tablespoons tomato catchup
¼ teaspoon salt, Dash cayenne
1 egg, beaten

Cut marrow crosswise into halves; remove seeds. Combine remaining ingredients and pack into marrow halves. Place halves together and fasten with toothpicks, or place in pan of same length as marrow to hold halves together. Bake in a moderate oven (350°F.) 30 minutes or until tender. Serve in slices. Serves 6.

LIMA BEANS WITH CORNED BEEF

1 cup dried Lima beans
2 cups shredded cooked corned beef
1 medium onion, sliced
2 tablespoons fat, melted
2 tablespoons flour
⅛ teaspoon pepper
½ teaspoon dry mustard
½ teaspoon salt
1 cup milk
¼ cup catchup

Wash beans and soak overnight. Simmer 2 hours; drain. Arrange beans, corned beef and onion slices in alternate layers in greased casserole. Melt fat, add flour, seasonings and milk. Stir until smooth. Cook until thickened. Add catchup, stirring constantly. Pour sauce over beans. Bake in moderate oven (350°F.) 30 minutes. Serves 6.

MEAT DUMPLINGS

1 recipe Baking Powder Biscuit
    dough
½ pound ground cooked meat
2 tablespoons minced onion
¼ teaspoon salt
Dash pepper
¾ cup condensed tomato soup
    or ½ cup cooked tomatoes
1¼ cups cooked green beans

Roll biscuit dough ¼ inch thick and cut into 6-inch squares. Combine remaining ingredients, divide mixture into 6 portions and place 1 portion on each square. Bring edges of dough together on top of meat mixture, rolling back edges in center leaving square opening. Bake in hot oven (450°F.) 10 minutes, reduce heat to 350°F. and bake 20 minutes longer. Serves 6.

Don't be surprised if these meat dumplings create a sensation at your next luncheon

SHORT RIBS OF BEEF

3 pounds beef short ribs
1 clove garlic
1 small onion
2 cups canned tomatoes
1 teaspoon paprika
Salt and pepper

Cut short ribs into serving pieces. Rub with cut clove of garlic. Place in kettle and slice onion over top. Cover with water, cover kettle tightly and cook slowly for 2 hours. Transfer short ribs to greased baking dish, add tomatoes and seasonings, cover and cook in slow oven (300°F.) about 1 hour, or until short ribs are very tender. Remove cover for last 15 minutes of cooking so that short ribs will brown slightly. Serves 6.

BRAISED—Brown 2 pounds short ribs, add 1½ teaspoons salt and water to cover bottom of pan Cover tightly; cook in 300°F. oven 2½ hours. Serves 4.

SMOTHERED MEAT BALLS

2 pounds ground beef
1 cup soft bread crumbs
2 eggs
½ cup milk
Salt and pepper
2 tablespoons fat
1 can onion soup

Combine beef and crumbs. Add eggs, milk and seasonings and mix thoroughly. Shape into balls and brown in fat. Add onion soup and cook slowly for 20 minutes or until meat balls are tender. Serves 8.

Use mushroom soup instead of onion soup.

Flatten balls into patties and wrap each with strip of bacon.

WALNUT—Add 1 cup chopped walnut meats to meat and use tomato soup instead of onion soup. Garnish with watercress.

There's plenty of flavor and nourishment in braised short ribs of beef

STUFFED CUBED STEAKS

4 cubed steaks (1 pound)
¼ teaspoon salt
Pepper
2 tablespoons flour
1 cup soft bread crumbs
¼ teaspoon poultry seasoning
1 teaspoon minced onion
2 tablespoons butter, melted
2 tablespoons water
⅓ cup rice, cooked
2½ cups canned tomatoes
¼ teaspoon salt
2 tablespoons butter

Wipe steaks with a damp cloth; roll in mixture of salt, pepper and flour. Combine crumbs, poultry seasoning, onion, butter and water to make a stuffing. Place steaks with cut side up, and cover each with a fourth of stuffing. Fold steaks over stuffing, fasten with skewers or toothpicks and place in greased shallow baking dish. Place rice around meat rolls, add tomatoes, salt and butter. Cover dish and bake in moderate oven (350°F.) about 1 hour or until steaks are tender. Serves 2 or 4.

Use Sage Stuffing and omit crumbs, poultry seasoning, onion, butter and water.

SPANISH RICE

6 slices bacon, chopped
1 onion, chopped
1½ pounds ground beef
1 teaspoon salt
1 cup uncooked rice
4 cups (about) tomato juice, heated
1 teaspoon paprika

Sauté bacon slowly and pour off part of fat. Brown chopped onion and beef in hot fat. Add salt. Wash rice, drain and add with 1½ cups tomato juice and paprika to meat. Pour into greased casserole and bake in moderate oven (350°F.) until rice is tender, about 30 minutes, adding more tomato juice as it is absorbed. Serves 6.

SWISS STEAK IN SOUR CREAM

3 pounds round steak (2 inches thick)
Flour, Salt, Pepper, Fat
2 onions, sliced
½ cup water
½ cup sour cream
2 tablespoons grated cheese
¾ teaspoon paprika

Dredge steak with flour and season with salt and pepper. Brown on both sides in hot fat. Add remaining ingredients, cover pan closely and simmer until meat is tender, about 2½ hours. Serves 6 to 8.

CHILE CON CARNE WITH KIDNEY BEANS

1 onion, diced; 1 tablespoon fat
2 cups cooked tomatoes
1 pound ground beef
2 cups cooked red kidney beans
½ teaspoon chili powder
1 teaspoon salt

Brown onion in fat, add remaining ingredients, cover and simmer 20 minutes. Add water if mixture becomes too dry. Serves 6.

MEAT AND CHEESE LOAF

2 pounds ground beef
1½ cups diced cheese
2 eggs, beaten
1 large onion, chopped
1 large green pepper, chopped
2 teaspoons salt
1 teaspoon pepper
1 teaspoon celery salt
½ teaspoon paprika
3 cups milk
1 cup dry bread crumbs

Combine ingredients in order given; mix well. Press into 2 greased loaf pans and bake at 350°F about 1½ hours. Serves 10.

APRICOT MEAT ROLL

1½ pounds ground beef
¾ pound ground ham
2 teaspoons salt
¼ teaspoon pepper
1 egg
STUFFING—
½ cup dried apricots
4 cups toasted bread cubes
⅓ cup minced onion
2 tablespoons minced parsley
2 teaspoons salt
⅛ teaspoon pepper
¼ teaspoon sage
⅔ cup water or soup stock

Mix meats, seasonings and egg. Spread out on waxed paper into a square about ½ inch thick. Chop apricots and combine with remaining ingredients. Spread evenly over meat, roll as for jelly roll, place in greased pan and brush with fat. Bake in moderate oven (350°F.) 1½ to 2 hours. Serves 8.

Stuff Spiced Ham Loaf or Sausage Loaf as above.

To vary your apricot meat loaf, spread the meat flat and roll in strips of bread. Garnish with broiled pineapple and sweetpotatoes

SPICY MEAT RING

2 pounds ground beef
1 pound ground pork
¼ cup minced onion
½ cup prepared horse-radish
1 teaspoon prepared mustard
2 eggs, beaten
1 teaspoon salt
⅛ teaspoon pepper
½ cup tomato catchup

Combine first 8 ingredients and mix well. Pour catchup into bottom of greased ring mold. Fill mold with meat mixture and bake in moderate oven (350°F.) 1 hour. Unmold and fill center with creamed mushrooms. For 8.

SAVORY MEAT LOAF

2 pounds ground beef
1 egg, slightly beaten
¼ cup minced onion
1½ teaspoons salt
¼ teaspoon pepper
1¼ cups condensed vegetable soup
2 cups cereal flakes, crushed
½ cup fat

Mix ingredients thoroughly in the order listed except the fat. Shape into loaf and place in greased baking pan. Bake in moderate oven (350°F.) about 1½ hours. Baste meat every 15 minutes with a mixture of ½ cup fat and 1 cup boiling water. Serves 8.

SALISBURY STEAK

4 strips bacon
1½ pounds ground beef (chuck or round)
½ pound ground pork
1 tablespoon chopped onion
1 tablespoon minced green pepper
1 tablespoon chopped parsley
1 teaspoon salt
½ teaspoon pepper

Chop bacon and mix lightly with meat, onion, green pepper, parsley and seasonings. Shape into cakes and place them 3 inches under broiler heat. Broil 12 minutes, turning once. Serves 6.

ITALIAN SPAGHETTI AND MEAT BALLS

1 pound beef
½ pound pork shoulder
2½ cups cracker crumbs
½ cup minced onions
⅓ cup chopped celery tops
2 tablespoons minced green pepper
1 teaspoon salt
1 egg
¼ cup milk
2 tablespoons olive oil
1 recipe Spaghetti Sauce
1 pound spaghetti, cooked
½ cup grated cheese

Grind meat together twice. Combine with next 7 ingredients. Shape into balls. Sauté in olive oil, or other fat in skillet, until browned. Remove from oil; add sauce and simmer 30 minutes. Serve with hot spaghetti and cheese. Serves 6 to 8.

SWEDISH MEAT BALLS

2 cups bread crumbs
2 cups milk
¼ pound pork shoulder, ground
1¾ pounds beef, ground
2 eggs
1 small onion, minced
1 teaspoon salt
¼ teaspoon pepper
¼ teaspoon nutmeg
2 tablespoons fat

Soak crumbs in milk, add next 7 ingredients and mix well. Shape into tiny balls, roll in flour, brown in fat in skillet; cover. Simmer 30 minutes. Serves 8.

DRIED-BEEF CURRY ON RICE

4 ounces dried beef
¼ cup fat, ¼ cup flour
2½ cups milk
¼ teaspoon curry powder
2 cups hot cooked rice

Shred dried beef and brown lightly in fat in skillet. Add flour, stir in milk and cook until thickened. Add curry powder; blend well. Serve over rice. Serves 5.

BEEF PATTIES

1 pound beef chuck, ground
1 cup mashed potatoes
2 tablespoons minced onion
½ teaspoon salt
⅛ teaspoon pepper
2 tablespoons fat

Combine beef, potatoes, onion, salt and pepper. Form into patties. Brown patties slowly in hot fat in shallow skillet. Serves 6.

Bake mixture in muffin pans. Bake mixture in ring mold. Shape into individual loaves. Shape into balls; broil or bake. Wrap each ball in bacon strip. Arrange meat balls around hot spaghetti and mushrooms.

Streamlined design in this variety of patterns for beef patties extended with or without mashed potatoes

BEEF ROLL

1 flank steak
1 egg, beaten
1 cup minced carrots
½ cup minced onion
¼ cup chopped celery
½ cup cooked tomatoes
1 teaspoon salt
1 cup soft bread crumbs
¼ cup flour, ½ teaspoon pepper
3 tablespoons fat
1½ cups hot water
1 cup mushrooms, if desired

Have flank steak deeply scored. Mix egg, vegetables, salt and crumbs together thoroughly. Spread vegetable stuffing on flank steak, roll and tie with string. Roll in flour and pepper; brown in hot fat in roasting pan. Add hot water and mushrooms, cover tightly and cook in moderate oven (325°F.) 1½ to 2 hours. Serves 6.

BEEF AND VEGETABLE PIE

¾ pound beef
¾ pound pork
¼ cup flour
3 tablespoons fat
2 cups water
12 small white onions
    (or 1¼ cups chopped onions)
¾ cup sliced carrots
1 cup tomatoes
2 teaspoons salt
½ teaspoon pepper
2 cups slightly undercooked rice
¼ cup flour
¼ cup water
2 tablespoons Worcestershire sauce
1 recipe Pastry

Cut meat into 1- to 1½-inch cubes. Roll in flour and brown in hot fat in deep kettle. Add water, cover tightly and simmer 40 to 60 minutes or until meat is tender. Add onions, carrots, tomatoes, salt and pepper and cook until carrots are tender. Add water if necessary. Add rice. Combine flour, water and Worcestershire sauce and add to meat. Roll ⅔ of dough ⅛ inch thick. Line casserole with dough. Pour in meat and vegetable mixture. Cover with remaining dough rolled ⅛ inch thick. Cut a large hole in the dough. Bake in a 400°F. oven 40 to 50 minutes. For single crust omit bottom keeping remainder in refrigerator for later use. Serves 8.

When shortening is low, an attractive meat pie is made by filling a casserole with stew and topping with cereal flakes.

EMERGENCY PIES—Prepare filling and line greased refrigerator trays with dough, add filling and cover. Freeze in refrigerator and bake in the refrigerator trays, without thawing.

High-vitamin vegetable stuffing is the clever meat stretcher for savory beef roll

FRUITED MEAT ROLL

1½ pounds beef, ground
½ pound pork, ground
3 teaspoons salt
¼ teaspoon pepper
1 egg
½ cup seedless raisins
4 cups toasted bread cubes
⅓ cup minced onion
2 tablespoons minced parsley
¼ teaspoon sage
⅔ cup water or soup stock

Combine meat, 2 teaspoons salt, pepper and egg; mix thoroughly. Spread on waxed paper into a square ½ inch thick. Wash raisins, dry and combine with remaining ingredients. Spread evenly over meat, roll as for jelly roll, place in greased pan and brush with fat. Bake in moderate oven (350°F.) 1¾ hours. Serves 8.

You can serve 10 people from 1½ pounds of meat in this loaf enriched with whole-wheat walnut stuffing

MEAT LOAF WITH WALNUT STUFFING

1½ pounds beef, ground
½ cup chopped green pepper
¾ cup chopped onion
1 teaspoon salt
1 tablespoon Worcestershire sauce
1 cup white bread crumbs
½ cup milk
2 eggs, ¼ cup fat
2 cups whole-wheat bread crumbs
½ cup chopped celery
½ cup chopped walnuts
¼ teaspoon pepper
¾ cup water or meat stock

Combine beef, green pepper, ½ cup of onion, salt, Worcestershire sauce, white bread crumbs, milk and 1 egg; mix thoroughly. Place ½ mixture in bottom of greased loaf pan. Combine all remaining ingredients, mix thoroughly and place on top of meat mixture. Arrange remaining meat mixture on top of stuffing. Bake at 350°F., 1½ hours. Cool a few minutes before removing pan. Serves 10.

Meat loaf baked in a ring, filled with cauliflower and garnished with spiced pears offers piquant contrast of flavor and texture →

MEAT LOAF RING

2 pounds beef, ground
1 pound pork, ground
¼ cup minced onion
1 teaspoon prepared mustard
2 eggs, beaten
1 cup cracker crumbs
1 teaspoon salt
⅛ teaspoon pepper
¾ cup milk
1 head cauliflower, cooked
Spiced cooked pear halves
Whole cloves

Combine first 9 ingredients and mix well. Press into greased ring mold. Bake in moderate oven (350°F.) 1½ hours. Unmold and fill center with cauliflower. Arrange pears around meat and stud with cloves. Serves 12.

Instead of cauliflower use cooked carrots and peas.

BRAISED LAMB NECK SLICES WITH VEGETABLES

4 double lamb neck slices
2 tablespoons flour
2 tablespoons fat, 1 cup water
4 carrots, 2½ cups green beans
3 potatoes, pared
Salt and pepper

Have double lamb neck slices cut ¾ to 1 inch thick. Dredge with flour and brown in hot fat. Add water, cover, and cook slowly for 1 hour. Cut carrots, green beans and potatoes into small pieces and place in greased casserole. Season. Place lamb neck slices on top. Pour liquid from neck slices into casserole, cover and place in slow oven (300°F.). Cook until vegetables are tender, about 30 minutes. Serves 4.

LAMB CURRY PIE

2 pounds lamb (shoulder or breast)
1 onion, diced; 1 tablespoon fat
3 cups hot water
¼ teaspoon thyme
2½ teaspoons salt
2 tablespoons flour
1 teaspoon curry powder
¼ cup water
3 cups cooked rice

Cut lamb into 1-inch cubes. Brown lamb and onion in fat; add water, thyme and salt; simmer 1½ hours or until meat is tender. Combine flour and curry powder; add cold water and mix to a smooth paste; add to lamb. Line greased baking dish on sides and bottom with rice, pressing rice firmly into place. Fill center with lamb mixture and bake in moderate oven (350°F.) 20 minutes. Serves 6.

Omit rice and cover top of curry with Baking Powder Biscuit dough. Bake in hot oven (425°F.) 15 to 20 minutes.

HASHED MEAT IN CABBAGE LEAVES

1 head cabbage
1 pound lamb, minced
2 onions, chopped
1 cup uncooked rice
Salt and pepper
3 to 4 tomatoes, sliced
½ cup water
Meat stock

Cook cabbage until tender; drain and carefully separate leaves from stem end. Combine lamb, onions, rice, salt and pepper and mix well. On each cabbage leaf place 1 tablespoon of meat mixture, roll leaf over filling and turn ends under so as to secure each roll. Place filled leaves in greased pan, add tomatoes, water and sufficient stock to half cover rolls. Cook in moderate oven (350°F.) about 1 hour or until rice is tender. Serves 6.

ENGLISH HOT POT

6 potatoes, pared and sliced
1½ pounds lamb shoulder or breast
2 lamb kidneys (optional)
1 large onion, sliced
Salt and pepper
1 cup water
2 tablespoons butter, melted

Place half of potatoes in greased casserole, then add meat, cut into cubes. Cover with sliced onion and season with salt and pepper. Add water. Place remaining potatoes on top, covering meat completely. Brush with melted butter. Place in moderate oven (350°F.) and cook for 2 hours. Serves 4 to 6.

LAMB CASSEROLE

2 pounds lamb shoulder
2 teaspoons chopped onion
2 tablespoons bacon fat
2 tablespoons flour
¾ cup meat or mushroom stock
Salt and pepper
1 cup tomatoes, 1 cup mushrooms

Cut meat from shoulder into pieces. Brown meat and onions in fat. Place in casserole, add flour to remaining fat in pan and stir until browned. Add meat stock and cook until thickened. Pour over meat, add seasoning, tomatoes and mushrooms. Cover casserole and bake in moderate oven (350°F.) 1 hour. Sprinkle with chopped parsley. Serves 4.

There are tender morsels of meat on these neck slices. Braise with vegetables

A regal cut of meat, Crown Roast of Lamb is ideal for Easter dinner. Serve it with mint sauce, new potatoes and fresh asparagus Hollandaise

CROWN ROAST OF LAMB

½ cup melted butter or
   margarine
1 cup water
1 8-ounce package bread stuffing
   mix
1 egg, beaten
2 cups finely chopped celery
1 cup chopped onions
½ cup chopped parsley
1 5-pound crown roast of lamb
1 tablespoon cornstarch
½ cup sugar
1⅓ cups water
¼ cup chopped fresh mint
Few drops green food coloring
2 teaspoons lemon juice

Combine butter or margarine, 1 cup water and bread stuffing mix in large mixing bowl. Add egg, celery, onions and parsley; blend thoroughly. Place lamb on a rack in shallow roasting pan. Fill crown roast with stuffing. Place in slow oven (325°F.) about 2½ hours, or until meat thermometer registers 175°-180°F. (depending upon desired degree of doneness). Meanwhile, combine cornstarch and sugar in a saucepan. Slowly stir in the 1⅓ cups water. Add mint and food coloring. Cook over low heat, stirring constantly, until sauce is thickened and clear. Stir in lemon juice. Serve the mint sauce with roast lamb. Serves 6 to 8.

STUFFED BREAST OF LAMB

1 lamb breast
Salt and pepper
2 cups Celery or Prune Stuffing
Fat
½ cup water or stock

Have pocket cut in lamb breast, season inside of pocket and fill with stuffing; sew or skewer edges of pocket and brown in fat. Add water, cover pan closely and cook in moderate oven (350°F.) 2 hours or until tender. Allow ½ to ¾ pound per serving.

STUFFED LAMB ROLL—Have breast boned. Spread stuffing over top of breast, roll and tie. Proceed as above, cooking 30 to 35 minutes per pound.

STUFFED LAMB SHOULDER— Remove bone from shoulder, fill with Apple Stuffing and skewer. Season, place on rack of roaster and cook, uncovered in 300°F. oven 35 minutes per pound.

If a leg of lamb is too large for your family try a stuffed lamb breast

Dress up a rolled roast of lamb with a piquant mustard glaze which imparts an exotic Far-East flavor to the meat

ROAST LEG OF LAMB

1 leg of lamb (about 5 pounds)
1 clove garlic, 1 teaspoon ginger

Wipe meat with a damp cloth. Do not remove fell, the thin paperlike covering over meat. With a sharp knife, make 4 gashes in the roast. Cut garlic into 4 slivers and insert a piece into each gash. Rub meat with the ginger, season with salt and pepper and dredge with flour.

Place in roaster, fat side up and roast, uncovered, in slow oven (300°F.) until tender. Allow 30 to 35 minutes per pound for roasting. When meat thermometer registers 180°F., the lamb will be well done. Remove garlic before serving. Allow ½ to ¾ pound per person.

BARBECUED LAMB—Mix 1 teaspoon mustard with the ginger, salt and pepper and rub over meat. Slice 2 onions over meat, and baste frequently while roasting with mixture of 2 tablespoons chili sauce, 1 tablespoon Worces-

tershire sauce, 1 tablespoon vinegar, 2 tablespoons salad oil and 1 cup boiling water.

GLAZED LAMB ROAST

1 3 to 4 lb. boned shoulder of lamb, rolled and tied
1 jar (8-oz.) brown prepared mustard
½ cup brown sugar
1 bottle (7-oz.) lemon-lime carbonate beverage
2 teaspoons prepared horseradish
1 tablespoon Worcestershire sauce

Place lamb on rack in roasting pan. Roast at 325°F. for 1½ hours. Combine remaining ingredients; blend well. (If desired, reserve ½ cup to use as sauce for rice.) Spoon ⅓ of the mixture over lamb. Roast 1½ hours longer or until meat thermometer registers 170°-180°F. (depending on desired degree of doneness). Spoon remaining mustard sauce over lamb during roasting. Heat reserved sauce and serve over hot rice. Serves 6 to 8.

A garnish of broiled pineapple and fresh mint brings leg of lamb to dinner for the most critical guest

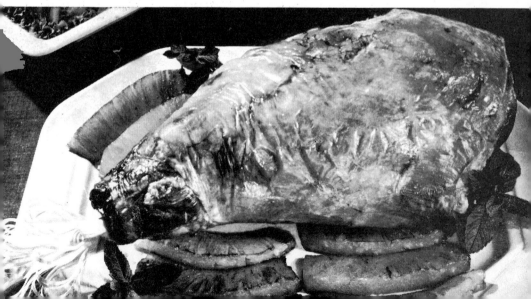

Boned lamb chops rolled and wrapped in bacon slices are held securely with picks

BARBECUED LAMB HASH

3 cups diced cooked lamb
¼ cup grated onion
Fat
2 cups Barbecue Sauce (made without mustard and celery)
4 potatoes, cooked and diced

Brown lamb and onion lightly in fat. Add sauce and simmer for 5 minutes. Add potatoes and heat thoroughly. Serves 6.

Rolled and planked lamb chops in their best bib and tucker are ready for the Easter parade

PLANKED LAMB CHOPS

6 loin lamb chops (1½ inches thick)
Salt and pepper
Brussels sprouts, cooked
Mashed potatoes

Remove bones from meat and roll each chop by wrapping tail of chop around large "eye" of meat. Preheat oven to moderate (350° F.) and place chops 3 inches below broiler heat. Brown chops on both sides and season. Place chops on individual planks, with Brussels sprouts and border with mashed potatoes pressed through a pastry tube. Place under broiler heat until potatoes are browned and serve immediately. Serves 6. Wrap a strip of bacon around each chop before broiling if desired.

BROILED LAMB CHOPS

8 lamb chops, 1½ inches thick
Salt and pepper

Broil chops for 9 minutes in a preheated broiler, 4 inches from heat. Season, turn and broil on the other side for 9 minutes. Season. Serves 4.

LAMB EN BROCHETTE

2 pounds lamb steak (sliced ¾ inch thick)
3 tablespoons cooking oil
6 tablespoons lemon juice
1 onion, minced; 1 teaspoon salt
½ pound mushrooms

Cut lamb into 1-inch squares. Combine oil, lemon juice, onion and salt; pour over lamb and let stand for several hours. Drain lamb and arrange on skewers alternately with mushroom caps. Place 4 inches below moderate broiler heat and broil about 12 to 15 minutes, turning several times. Serves 6.

SPICY LAMB SHANKS

4 lamb shanks
Salt and pepper, Flour
1 cup water
1 cup cooked prunes, pitted
1 cup cooked dried apricots
½ cup sugar
½ teaspoon cinnamon
½ teaspoon allspice
¼ teaspoon cloves
3 tablespoons vinegar
¼ teaspoon salt

Season meat with salt and pepper, dredge with flour and place in greased baking dish. Cover and bake in moderate oven (350°F.) until meat is tender, 1¾ to 2 hours. Combine remaining ingredients, heat to boiling and simmer about 5 minutes. Drain most of fat from cooked shanks, add fruit mixture to meat, cover dish and bake in hot oven (400° F.) about 30 minutes. Serves 4.

LAMB STEW

2 pounds lamb cubes, shank,
   breast, neck or shoulder
2 tablespoons flour
Salt and pepper, Hot water
5 potatoes, 5 carrots
3 onions, 3 white turnips
¾ cup fresh peas, 3 tomatoes
Flour

Dredge lamb with flour and brown well in hot pan. Season with salt and pepper, cover with water and simmer until nearly tender, 1 to 1½ hours. Add vegetables, except tomatoes, whole or cut into cubes and simmer 30 minutes longer or until tender. Add tomatoes and simmer 10 minutes longer. Mix a little flour with water to a smooth paste and add enough to the liquid to thicken slightly Serves 5.

RICE CASSEROLE—Use leftover stew. Line baking dish with hot cooked rice. Fill center with hot stew, cover with additional rice and place in hot oven (425°F.) 15 minutes or until browned.

Cooked lamb combines with celery soup, rice and cheese in a tempting casserole

MEAT-FILLED BISCUIT RING

1 recipe Baking Powder Biscuit
   dough
3 tablespoons melted fat
1 cup ground cooked lamb
1 egg, beaten
½ teaspoon salt
Dash pepper

Roll dough ¼ inch thick and brush with fat. Combine meat, egg and seasoning; spread over dough; roll as for jelly roll and cut crosswise into 1-inch slices. Place cut side down in greased ring mold and bake in moderately hot oven (400°F) 20 minutes Turn out and fill center with creamed vegetables. Serves 6.

SCRAMBLED EGGS HUNTERS' STYLE

2 cups chopped cooked lamb
½ cup chopped onions
2 tablespoons fat
6 eggs, slightly beaten

Cook meat and onions in hot fat in skillet until onions begin to brown. Add eggs. Cook slowly, stirring constantly, until eggs are set. Do not cook eggs until too firm. Serve immediately. Serves 6.

CEREAL-LAMB PIE

½ cup chopped onion
2 tablespoons fat
2 cups cooked tomatoes
2 cups chopped cooked lamb
½ teaspoon salt, if needed
4 cups cooked cereal (corn meal,
   oatmeal or whole wheat)

Brown onion in fat in skillet. Heat tomatoes to boiling; add onion, meat and salt. Place half of cereal in greased pan, add meat mixture and cover with remaining cereal. Bake in moderate oven (350°F.) 30 minutes. Serves 8.

SOUTHERN HASH

2 tablespoons flour
1 cup water
2 cups diced cooked lamb
¼ cup chopped onions
2 cups diced cooked potatoes
1 teaspoon salt
½ teaspoon pepper
½ cup cooked tomatoes
½ pod hot red pepper, if desired

Make smooth paste of flour and water. Combine with remaining ingredients and mix thoroughly. Place in greased casserole and bake in moderate oven (350°F.) 1 hour. Add water if gravy cooks down too much. Serves 4 to 6.

MEAT AND RICE AU GRATIN

2 cups diced cooked lamb
1 can cream of celery soup,
   undiluted
1 can (4-oz.) sliced mushrooms
½ cup milk
½ teaspoon rosemary
Salt and pepper
2 cups cooked rice
¾ cup shredded cheese

Combine all ingredients except cheese and blend thoroughly. Turn into a 2-quart casserole and sprinkle with cheese. Bake at 350°F. about 35 minutes or until thoroughly heated and cheese is melted. Serves 6.

Lamb shoulder cubes, peaches, bananas and dates make a flavor-compatible kebab combination of foods to grill on an open fire

PICNIC MEAT ROLL

2½ pounds forequarter of lamb
6 tablespoons onion
6 tablespoons green pepper
2 teaspoons salt
½ teaspoon pepper
2 eggs
2 cups crumbs
4 hard-cooked eggs

Force lamb, onions, and green pepper through food chopper, add remaining ingredients, excepting hard-cooked eggs, and mix thoroughly. Turn out on a slightly floured board. Place hard-cooked eggs in center of meat, shape into roll, and dredge with flour. Place in roasting pan and bake in moderate oven (350°F.) 45 minutes. Serve sprinkled with chopped parsley. Serves 8.

BRAISED NECK SLICES

4 double lamb neck slices
    (¾ inch thick)
2 tablespoons flour
2 tablespoons fat
1 cup water
4 carrots, diced
2½ cups cooked green beans
3 potatoes, diced
Salt and pepper

Dredge neck slices with flour; brown in hot fat in kettle. Add water, cover and simmer 1 hour. Arrange vegetables in greased baking dish. Season. Place neck slices on top. Add liquid from neck slices, cover and cook in a slow oven (300°F.) 30 minutes, or until vegetables are tender. Serves 4.

Use 2½ cups peas instead of green beans, if desired.

EMINCE OF LAMB

2 cups ground cooked lamb
2 cups cooked rice
1½ cups cooked tomatoes
2 onions, minced
1½ teaspoons salt
1 teaspoon paprika
1 teaspoon Worcestershire sauce
6 large green peppers
1 cup boiling water

Combine first 7 ingredients. Remove tops and seeds of peppers. Fill with meat mixture; place in baking pan and add water. Bake in moderate oven (350°F.) 40 minutes. Serves 6.

STUFFED LAMB SHANKS

6 lamb shanks
2 tablespoons fat
2 cups water, 1 teaspoon salt
¼ teaspoon pepper
¼ pound barley

Brown meat in hot fat in kettle, add water and seasonings, cover and simmer 1½ hours or until tender. Remove meat from broth, cool and remove bones. Cook barley in lamb broth 2 hours, adding water as necessary. Stuff boned shanks with cooked barley; place in baking dish. Add gravy made by thickening remaining broth. Simmer 25 minutes. Serves 6.

MEAT EN BROCHETTE

Insert diced shoulder lamb (1 lb.) on skewers. Drain 1 can (1 lb., 13 oz.) peaches. Cut 4 peeled bananas into 1-in. pieces; brush with peach sirup. Insert peach half, 3 pitted dates, 3 banana pieces and 3 maraschino cherries on each of 8 skewers. Brush with mixture of 2 tablespoons melted butter, 1 tablespoon lemon juice, 1 teaspoon cinnamon and ¼ teaspoon cloves. Cook lamb on grill 7 min. and turn. Place fruit kebabs on grill; cook both 7 min., brushing fruit with sauce often. Season the meat.

LAMB AND LIMAS

¼ pound dried Lima beans
1½ pounds lamb shoulder
2 tablespoons bacon fat
1 small onion or clove of garlic,
    chopped
1½ teaspoons salt
⅛ teaspoon pepper
1 cup boiling water

Wash beans and soak overnight; drain. Cut lamb into 1-inch pieces; brown in fat with onion in skillet. Add salt and pepper and place in casserole. Add beans and water, cover, and cook in slow oven (300°F.) 1 hour, or until tender. Serves 6.

Saucy meat pasties cut in fancy shapes with fluted edges give an air to any luncheon

MEAT PASTIES

½ pound beef or lamb, ground
2 tablespoons fat
2 cups diced potatoes
1½ cups diced carrots
1 cup diced celery and leaves
1 teaspoon salt
¼ teaspoon pepper
2 recipes Baking Powder Biscuit dough

Brown meat in fat in skillet. Remove from heat, add next 5 ingredients and mix thoroughly. Divide into 6 equal portions. Roll dough ¼ inch thick; cut into 8-inch rounds. On half of each round place 1 portion of meat mixture; fold other half of round over filling and seal edge with fork. Bake on ungreased baking sheet in moderate oven (375°F.) 50 to 60 minutes. Makes 6.
OPEN-FACED—Cut hole in upper half of each round.
SQUARES—Roll dough thin and cut into small rectangles.

BRAISED LAMB RIBLETS

2 pounds lamb riblets
1 clove garlic, cut
Salt and pepper
2 tablespoons flour
4 tablespoons fat
1 quart water
5 medium onions, 5 carrots
¾ pound green beans, cooked

Cut riblets into serving portions; rub with garlic, salt, pepper and flour. Heat fat in a heavy kettle, add riblets and brown on all sides. Add water, cover closely and simmer 1 hour. Add onions and carrots and cook 1 hour longer or until meat and vegetables are tender. Arrange meat in center of platter and garnish with vegetables. Serves 5.

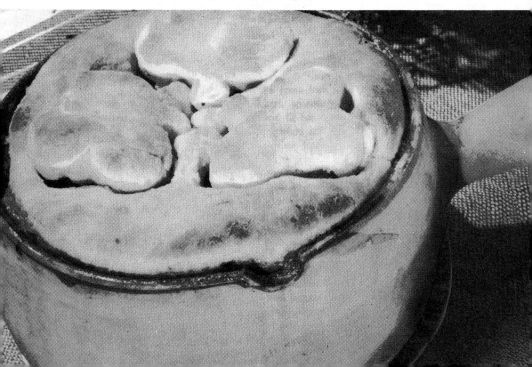

LAMB PIE

1 pound breast of lamb
½ clove garlic, if desired
¼ cup flour
2 tablespoons fat
¾ cup hot water
2 cups cubed potatoes
12 small onions
½ cup sliced carrots
1 cup cooked string beans
½ cup diced ripe olives
1½ cups Brown Gravy

Cut lamb into 1-inch cubes, rub with garlic, roll in flour and brown in hot fat in skillet. Place in a deep casserole, add hot water, cover tightly and cook in a moderate oven (350°F.) 1 hour. Add potatoes, onions and carrots; cover tightly and continue cooking until vegetables are tender, 45 to 60 minutes. Add beans, olives and gravy. Return to oven 15 minutes longer. Serves 6.

Top with biscuit dough last half hour, if desired; brown.

BENGAL LAMB CURRY

3 cups ground cooked lamb
½ cup minced onion
1 green pepper, chopped
3 tablespoons minced parsley
1 cup water, 2 tablespoons flour
1 teaspoon Worcestershire sauce
4 tablespoons catchup
2 teaspoons salt
1 teaspoon paprika
½ teaspoon curry powder
3 cups hot cooked rice
1 hard-cooked egg, minced

Combine first 4 ingredients and ¾ cup of the water in kettle; simmer until onions are tender. Mix remaining ¼ cup water with flour and add with Worcestershire sauce, catchup, salt, paprika, and curry powder. Simmer a few minutes longer. Arrange rice in center of a platter. Surround rice with lamb mixture and garnish with egg. Serves 8.

Feathery crispy biscuit crust enhances the flavor of appetizing lamb en casserole

LAMB HARICOT

2 cups dried Lima beans
½ cup chopped onions
1 pound lamb stew meat
    (neck cuts are satisfactory)
1 cup cooked tomatoes
1 teaspoon salt
¼ teaspoon pepper
2 cups boiling water

Wash Lima beans, soak overnight; drain, place in kettle, cover with water and cook 1 hour or until nearly tender. Place cooked beans in a casserole and add remaining ingredients. Cover tightly and cook in moderate oven (350°F.) 3 hours. Remove cover after 2 hours. Serves 8.

SHEPHERD'S PIE

3 cups hot mashed potatoes
2 cups diced cooked lamb
1½ cups lamb gravy

Arrange half of potatoes in greased baking dish. Add lamb and gravy. Cover with remaining potatoes. Bake in moderate oven (350°F.) 20 minutes. Serves 6.

PORK

CANDLE ROAST OF PORK

Loin of pork
1½ tablespoons salt
Pepper, Cubes of salt pork

Have pork prepared at the market as for crown roast but without rolling. Meat should be in one straight piece. . Rub salt and pepper into meat. Place in pan, cover tip of each bone with salt pork. Roast in a moderate oven (350°F.) allowing 30 minutes per pound. To serve, replace salt pork with paper frills. Four pounds serves 8.

PORK ROAST, PADRE—Place leg or shoulder of pork in crock. Combine 3 bay leaves, 12 peppercorns, 1 chili pepper, 3 teaspoons salt, 1 clove garlic and 1 onion, sliced. Add to meat with vinegar to cover. Let stand 4 days. Remove from vinegar; roast in 350°F. oven 35 to 40 minutes per pound, basting frequently with the vinegar.

The candle roast of pork or lamb is the unrolled crown and just as decorative

TO COOK BACON

BROILED—Place slices of bacon on rack of broiler, 4 inches below medium broiler heat. Broil about 2 minutes, turn and cook 2 minutes longer or to desired crispness.

FRIED—Place bacon in cold frying pan over low heat. Cook slowly to desired crispness, turning frequently. Pour off fat as it accumulates. Drain on absorbent paper.

BAKED—Place strips of bacon on wire rack placed over shallow baking pan. Bake in hot oven (400°F.) 12 minutes or to desired crispness. Do not turn. Use bacon fat as fat in Apple Stuffing, to fry potatoes or for shortening in biscuits.

BRAISED PORK STEAKS WITH GRAPE APPLES

2 pounds pork shoulder steaks
2 tablespoons flour
2 tablespoons fat
Salt and pepper
3 large apples
½ glass grape jelly
¾ cup boiling water

Dredge pork shoulder steaks in flour and brown in hot fat. Season with salt and pepper. Add ¼ cup water, cover tightly, and cook very slowly until tender, about 45 minutes. Pare apples, core and cut into halves. Dissolve grape jelly in boiling water, add apples and cook until tender. Serve around pork steaks for 4.

PORK ROAST WITH SPICY SAUCE

Fresh picnic shoulder
Salt and pepper
2 small onions, minced
1 tablespoon Worcestershire sauce
1 tablespoon sugar
½ teaspoon paprika
½ cup vinegar, ½ cup water
2 tablespoons catchup

Have picnic shoulder boned and rolled at the market. Season with salt and pepper. Place fat side up on rack in open roaster. Roast in moderate oven (350°F.) until meat thermometer registers 185° F., or allow 40 to 45 minutes per pound. Combine other ingredients and cook together for 5 minutes. Serves 6.

CREOLE PORK AND SPAGHETTI

1 cup minced onions
1 pound ground pork shoulder
2 cups cooked spaghetti
¾ cup cooked tomatoes
1 cup grated cheese
½ teaspoon salt
½ cup dry bread crumbs
2 tablespoons fat

Brown onions and meat in skillet; mix with spaghetti, tomatoes, cheese and salt. Place in greased baking dish. Sprinkle crumbs on top, dot with fat and bake in moderate oven (350°F.) 30 minutes. Serves 6.

GLAZED PORK AND SWEETPOTATOES

2 cups diced cooked pork
3 cups diced cooked sweetpotatoes
⅓ cup honey or corn sirup
1 cup orange juice

Place pork in shallow pan or casserole. Add sweetpotatoes and cover with honey and orange juice. Bake in a moderate oven (350°F.) 30 minutes or until browned. Serves 6 to 8.

CORN-MEAL MUSH WITH PORK

1 pound lean pork, including bones
1 cup corn meal
1 teaspoon salt
½ teaspoon powdered sage

Simmer pork in water in kettle until meat falls from bones. Remove meat and bones. Chill broth and remove fat. Bring measure of broth to 1 quart by boiling down or by adding water as necessary. Add corn meal and cook, stirring frequently, until thickened. Chop meat fine, season with salt and sage. Add to mush and pack in bread pans. Chill, slice and sauté. Serves 6.
Beef may be used instead of pork.

BACON CRISPIES

6 rusks
3 ounces cream cheese
3 slices bacon

Spread rusks with cream cheese, top with ½ slice of bacon and toast in broiler until cheese melts and bacon is crisped. Serves 6.

MEAT LOAF WITH OATMEAL

½ pound pork, ground
½ pound beef, ground
1 cup minced onions
2 cups cooked oatmeal
1 teaspoon thyme
1 teaspoon salt
1 teaspoon marjoram, if desired
½ teaspoon pepper
½ cup milk
1 tablespoon melted fat

Mix all ingredients thoroughly. Pack in greased loaf pan. Bake in moderate oven (350°F.) 1½ hours. Let stand several minutes before removing from pan. Serves 6 to 8.

Garnish with hot spiced peaches. To make: Stick cloves into cooked whole peaches; simmer in sirup of 1 cup peach sirup, ½ cup vinegar, 1 stick cinnamon and ½ cup sugar for 3 minutes. Drain peaches and serve hot.

Hot spiced peaches make an effective garnish for a pork and beef loaf made with oatmeal

Boned stuffed lamb or pork shoulder is an idea in good food worth investigating

CUSHION STYLE PORK SHOULDER WITH APPLE AND PRUNE STUFFING

Pork shoulder (picnic)
8 to 10 prunes
3 tart apples
2 tablespoons butter
1 cup bread crumbs
½ lemon rind, grated
½ teaspoon brown sugar
¼ teaspoon cinnamon
Salt and pepper

Have picnic shoulder boned and sew on 3 sides, leaving 1 side open for stuffing. Cook prunes in water until tender, pit and cut into halves. Pare apples and cut into wedges, about ¾ inch thick. Melt butter, add bread crumbs, prunes and apples. Sprinkle with lemon rind, brown sugar and cinnamon. Season pork shoulder with salt and pepper and fill opening with prune and apple stuffing. Place on rack in open roaster. Cook in moderate oven (350°F.), allowing 35 to 40 minutes per pound. Serves 8.

PIG'S KNUCKLES AND SAUERKRAUT

4 pig's knuckles
3 teaspoons salt
2 quarts boiling water
1 quart Sauerkraut

Place whole knuckles in boiling salted water. Cover and simmer until meat is tender about 2½ to 3 hours. Twenty minutes before serving, pour off most of the water and add sauerkraut. Heat thoroughly. Serve the meat on a bed of sauerkraut. Serves 4.

CROWN ROAST OF PORK

Crown roast of pork
Salt and pepper
Stuffing

Have crown roast prepared at market. Season meat with salt and pepper. Place crown roast, rib ends down, on a rack in roasting pan. Roast, uncovered, at 350°F. for 1 hour. Then remove roast from oven and invert so the rib ends are up. Now fill cavity with stuffing. Insert a roast meat thermometer in thickest part of roast, being careful that it does not rest in fat or on a bone. Continue roasting until thermometer registers 185°F. (Allow about 40 minutes per pound.) Use Apple, Raisin, Sage or Corn Bread Stuffing.

MARYLAND STUFFED "HOG MAW"

1 hog stomach
1-pound loaf bread
1 quart diced potatoes
1½ pounds pork sausage meat
2 medium onions, diced
Salt and pepper
2 tablespoons minced parsley

Enlarge opening at lower end of stomach and turn inside out. Scrape out inside lining. Wash in warm water and turn right side out. Sew shut at upper end Dice bread and let dry overnight. Mix thoroughly with remaining ingredients, pack loosely into hog stomach and sew opening shut. Place in roaster, add enough water to cover bottom of pan, cover tightly and cook in moderate oven (350°F.) about 2½ hours. Serves 8 to 10.

Crown roast of pork with a savory stuffing is a rewarding experience ➡

AMERICAN CHOP SUEY

1/8 pound salt pork, diced
1/2 pound round steak, cubed
1/4 pound veal, cubed
1/4 pound pork, cubed
Flour
1 1/2 cups diced celery
1 1/2 cups diced onions
1/2 cup sliced mushrooms
1/2 cup tomato catchup
1/2 cup boiling stock or water
1 tablespoon Worcestershire sauce
1 tablespoon soy sauce
Salt, Pepper

Cook salt pork until crisp, remove from pan. Dredge beef, veal and pork with flour and brown in salt pork drippings. Add remaining ingredients and simmer 45 minutes. Serve with boiled rice or fried noodles. Serves 4.

Omit tomato catchup and use 1 1/2 cups stock.

If desired, use only one kind of meat: beef, pork or veal.

HAWAIIAN BAKED PORK

2 cups crushed pineapple
3 medium sweetpotatoes
2 tablespoons brown sugar
4 shoulder pork steaks, cut into individual servings
Salt and pepper
4 strips bacon

Place pineapple in 1 large baking dish or 4 individual ones. Pare and slice sweetpotatoes, place over pineapple and sprinkle with brown sugar. Season pork steaks with salt and pepper and place on top of sweet potatoes. On top arrange bacon strips. Cover and bake in moderate oven (350° F.) until sweetpotatoes and chops are tender, about 1 hour. Remove cover and increase the temperature to very hot (450°F.) for the last 10 minutes of cooking to brown the steaks and bacon. Serves 4.

PORK CHOPS

Heat heavy frying pan until very hot. Add 1 tablespoon fat, or if the chops have a good covering of fat, place in the pan with fat edge down and cook out enough fat to grease frying pan. Brown chops on both sides. Do not add water. Reduce temperature, cover pan closely and cook slowly until chops are thoroughly done, about 45 minutes. Turn chops occasionally to cook uniformly.

BARBECUED PORK CHOPS

6 pork chops
12 tablespoons Barbecue Sauce

Brown chops on both sides in skillet. Spread 1 tablespoon of sauce on top of each chop. Cover and cook very slowly for 5-8 minutes. Turn chops and put one tablespoon of sauce on other side of each chop. Cover and cook slowly until tender, 30 to 40 minutes. Turn chops several times so that they are thoroughly covered with sauce. Serves 6.

STUFFED PORK CHOPS

6 double pork chops
1 1/2 cups whole kernel corn
1 1/2 cups bread crumbs
3/4 teaspoon salt
1/4 teaspoon pepper
1 1/2 tablespoons minced parsley
3/4 teaspoon sage
1 tablespoon grated onion
1 cup diced apple, 1 egg
3 tablespoons milk, Fat

Cut a pocket on the bone side of each chop. Combine next 10 ingredients and mix well. Stuff each chop with corn mixture. Brown chops in fat, season, add a little water and bake in moderate oven (350°F.) about 1 hour or until tender. Serves 6.

STUFFED PORK CHOPS DE LUXE—Stuff chops with Sage or Onion Stuffing and bake as above. When meat is half done, place a thick slice of apple (cored but not pared) on each chop and sprinkle with brown sugar.

NEW ENGLAND STUFFED PORK CHOPS—Stuff chops with mixture of 1/2 cup chopped celery, 2 tablespoons minced onion, 2 tablespoons chopped parsley, 1 cup soft bread crumbs, 1 teaspoon melted butter, 1 cup Cranberry Sauce and 1 teaspoon salt.

PORK TENDERLOIN PIQUANTE

2 slices bacon
1 pork tenderloin
6 medium onions, chopped
1 tablespoon fat
6 small sweet pickles, minced
1 teaspoon capers (optional)
1 tablespoon minced parsley
2 tablespoons vinegar
1/2 cup Tomato Sauce

Arrange bacon over the top of tenderloin, place on rack of roaster and roast uncovered in moderate oven (350°F.) until tender, allowing about 30 minutes per pound for cooking. Brown the chopped shallots or onions in melted fat. Add sweet pickles, capers and parsley. Season with salt and pepper. Add vinegar and tomato sauce. Cook for 10 minutes and serve with roast tenderloin. Serves 6 to 8.

PORK TENDERLOIN IN SOUR CREAM

1 1/2 pounds pork tenderloin
Fat, Sour cream
1 tablespoon flour

Cut tenderloin into 1-inch slices and brown in fat. Cover with sour cream and simmer about 20 minutes or until tender. Remove meat, add flour to cream and simmer 4 minutes. For 6.

BAKED HAM

1 smoked ham
Glaze, Whole cloves

Have ham warmed to room temperature and bake according to directions given by packer, or as follows: Wipe ham with clean cloth, wrap loosely in one of the papers wrapped around ham or in clean wrapping paper and place fat side up on rack of shallow pan. Do not cover pan or add water. For baking allow 15 minutes per pound for hams, 12 pounds or over; allow 18 minutes per pound for hams, under 12 pounds; allow 22 minutes per pound for half hams; or bake to an internal temperature of 150°F., being sure bulb of thermometer is inserted into center of thickest part of meat and does not touch bone. Bake in slow oven (325°F.) until within 45 minutes of total baking time. Remove paper and rind from ham, make a series of shallow cuts across fat to cut into squares or diamonds, spread with desired glaze and insert 1 clove into each square of fat. Bake uncovered in 325°F. oven for remaining 45 minutes.

GLAZES:

One cup brown sugar, juice and grated rind of 1 orange.

One cup brown or white sugar and ½ cup maraschino cherry juice, cider or sweet pickle juice from pickled fruit.

One cup honey.

One cup brown sugar, 1 tablespoon mustard.

One cup puréed apricots, rhubarb or applesauce.

One glass currant jelly, melted. Use maraschino cherries and mint cherries fastened with pieces of toothpicks instead of cloves.

Three-fourths cup pineapple juice, ¾ cup strained honey and ½ teaspoon mustard cooked until thick.

One-half cup maple sirup, ½ cup cider or apple juice and 2 tablespoons mustard.

One-half cup orange marmalade. Cook ½ pound fresh cranberries with 1 cup maple sirup until skins pop open. Press mixture through sieve and spread over ham.

Decorate baked ham with golden stars of orange peel to give dinner an extra sparkle

HAM AND RICE SCALLOP

1 cup uncooked rice
2 thin slices ham, Salt
3 cups milk

Wash rice and cut ham slices into serving pieces. Arrange rice and ham in alternate layers in greased baking dish, using rice for bottom and top layers. Season, add milk and bake in moderate oven (350°F.) 1 hour. Serves 6.

HAM BAKED IN MILK

1 teaspoon dry mustard
4 tablespoons brown sugar
1 slice ham (2 inches thick)
Milk

Mix mustard and brown sugar together and spread over ham. Place in casserole, add enough milk to barely cover ham. Bake in slow oven (300°F.) 1 hour. Center slice of ham will serve 6.

BAKED HAM WITH PINEAPPLE

—Omit milk, increase sugar to ½ cup; add ½ cup crumbs and ¾ cup pineapple juice. Spread ham with mixture of mustard, sugar and crumbs. Add pineapple juice and bake as above. After 15 minutes add 5 or 6 slices pineapple and cook with ham during remainder of baking period.

HAM CHEESE SAVORY

2 tablespoons fat
2 tablespoons flour
1 cup milk
1 cup grated American cheese
1 cup chopped spiced or boiled ham
Salt, pepper and paprika

Melt fat, blend in flour, add milk and cook until thickened, stirring constantly. Add cheese and stir until melted. Add ham and seasonings. Cook slowly until well heated. Serve on rice, for 4.

HAM SOUFFLÉ

2 tablespoons flour
2 cups milk
¾ cup ground cooked ham
¼ pound cheese, grated
3 eggs, separated
½ teaspoon salt
⅛ teaspoon pepper

Mix flour with milk, heat to boiling and cook for 3 minutes; add to ham, cheese and slightly beaten egg yolks; fold in stiffly beaten egg whites. Season with salt and pepper, pour into baking dish, set in pan of hot water and bake in moderately slow oven (325°F.) until firm, 45 to 60 minutes. Serve with or without a Thin White Sauce. Serves 6.

SWEETPOTATO HAM PUFFS

1 cup ground cooked ham
2 cups mashed sweetpotatoes
1 egg, beaten
¾ cup sifted flour
1 teaspoon baking powder
½ teaspoon salt

Combine ham, sweetpotatoes and egg. Sift flour, baking powder and salt together, and add to ham mixture. Drop by spoonfuls onto a hot greased griddle; brown on each side. Serves 5.

CRANBERRY HAM SLICE

1 slice ham (1 to 2 inches thick)
Whole cloves
1½ cups cranberries
¾ cup strained honey

Trim ham and insert cloves into fat. Wash cranberries, dry and mix with honey. Pour over ham and bake in moderate oven (350° F.) about 1½ hours or until ham is tender. Baste occasionally with liquid in pan. One center slice serves 6.

HEADCHEESE

1 hog's head, 1 hog's tongue
Salt and pepper
Sage or chili powder

Clean and scrape hog's head and wash thoroughly. Wash and trim tongue. Cover head and tongue with slightly salted water and simmer until meat falls from bone. Drain meat, shred and season. Pack tightly in bowl, cover and weight it down. Let stand 3 days in a cold place. Slice. Makes 6 to 8 pounds.

HAM LOAF

2 cups ground cooked ham
1 cup bread or cereal crumbs
1 egg
2 tablespoons chili sauce
1 cup ground carrots
1 cup milk

Combine ingredients. Bake in loaf pan in moderate oven (350°F.) about 45 minutes. Serves 6.

SPICED HAM LOAF—Omit chili sauce and carrots, reduce milk to ½ cup. Add ½ pound ground lean ham, 1 tablespoon brown sugar and ¼ teaspoon cloves. Soften cereal crumbs in milk, then mix and bake as above. Serve with Horse-radish Sauce.

SAVORY HAM LOAF—Omit chili sauce and carrots. Add 1 pound ground fresh ham and 1 tablespoon mustard. Increase crumbs to 1½ cups and milk to 1½ cups. Use 2 eggs. Bake about 1 hour.

HAM WITH GREEN BEANS

Cover 3 pounds smoked ham with water and simmer 2 hours. Clean 1 quart green beans and break into small pieces. Pare and quarter 6 medium potatoes. Add beans and potatoes to ham, cook 10 minutes, add salt and pepper and cook 15 minutes longer or until vegetables are tender. Serves 6.

UPSIDE-DOWN HAM LOAF

1½ tablespoons fat
4 tablespoons brown sugar
3 apples
1 recipe Savory Ham Loaf
1 tablespoon minced onion

Melt fat and sugar in heavy skillet and cover with ½-inch thick slices of pared, cored apples. Brown fruit slightly. Combine ham mixture with onion and spread over apples. Pat down firmly and bake in moderate oven, (350°F.) about 45 minutes. Pour off any excess fat and turn out upside down on serving platter. Serves 4 to 6.

Use pineapple slices instead of apples. Arrange them in an attractive design and place a maraschino cherry in the center.

SUNSHINE HAM

1½ cups dried apricots
½ cup granulated sugar
2 large slices ham, ¾ inch thick
⅓ cup brown sugar
¼ teaspoon cloves

Wash apricots and boil in water to cover 10 minutes, add granulated sugar and cook 5 minutes longer. Drain, saving 1 cup liquid. Place ham in baking dish and arrange apricots over ham slices. Mix brown sugar and cloves; sprinkle over apricots. Pour reserved liquid over all. Cover pan and bake in hot oven (425°F.) 30 minutes, uncover and bake 45 minutes longer, basting often. Serve with liquid from pan over ham. Serves 6.

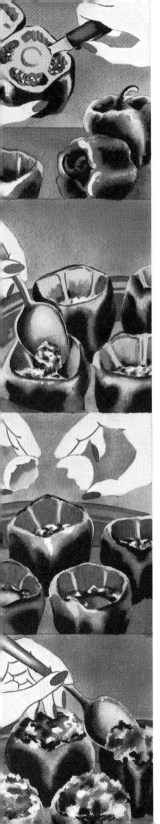

Shirred eggs add nourishment to baked green peppers stuffed with ham and rice

STUFFED PEPPERS

6 green peppers
4 slices bacon or salt pork, chopped
1 cup chopped onions
¾ pound ham, ground
1 teaspoon salt
½ teaspoon paprika
2 cups cooked rice
½ cup water

Cut stem and top from each pepper and remove core and seeds. Sauté bacon in skillet until crisp, add onions and cook until slightly browned. Add ham and brown. Stir in salt, paprika and rice. Fill peppers with mixture. Place peppers in greased pan, add water, cover and bake in moderate oven (350°F.) 40 minutes. Remove cover and bake 10 minutes longer. Top with a bacon slice during the last baking period, if desired. Serve when bacon is browned. Serves 6.

After 40 minutes of baking, top each pepper with an egg, sprinkle with buttered crumbs and bake until eggs are set.

BACON AND HOMINY

3 cups cooked hominy
1 small onion, chopped
1 green pepper, chopped
2 tablespoons fat
2 cups cooked tomatoes
1 tablespoon sugar
1 teaspoon salt
¼ pound sliced bacon

Place hominy in greased shallow baking dish. Sauté onion and pepper in fat in skillet until light brown. Add tomatoes, sugar and salt and simmer 10 minutes. Pour mixture over hominy and cover with sliced bacon. Bake in slow oven (325°F.) about 30 minutes. Serves 6 to 8.

HAM GUMBO IN RICE RING

1 pound ham or smoked shoulder, diced
1 tablespoon bacon fat
1 onion, chopped
1 green pepper, chopped
1 tablespoon minced parsley
2 or 3 stalks celery, chopped
2 cups water
4 cups cooked tomatoes
4 cups sliced okra
1 bay leaf
Salt and pepper
3 cups hot cooked rice

Brown ham in bacon fat in skillet. Add onion, green pepper, parsley and celery; cook 5 minutes. Add water and tomatoes; simmer 40 minutes. Add okra and bay leaf; simmer 20 minutes longer or until stew has thickened. Season. Arrange rice in ring and fill center with ham mixture. Serves 6.

HAM FRITTERS WITH CORN

1½ cups cooked corn
¾ cup ground cooked ham
⅛ teaspoon pepper
½ cup flour
2 teaspoons baking powder
3 eggs, slightly beaten
6 tablespoons fat

Mix corn, ham, pepper, flour, baking powder and eggs together. Heat fat in a skillet; drop in corn mixture by tablespoons. Sauté until golden brown. Serves 6.

BROILED AND FRIED HAM

Place slice of smoked ham on broiler rack, snip edges to prevent curling. Broil at 350°F. Allow 10 minutes for slice ¼ inch thick, 20 minutes for slice ½ to ¾ inch thick and ½ hour for 1-inch thick slice. Turn often.

TO FRY HAM—Rub moderately —hot heavy frying pan with fat and brown on both sides. Cover pan and cook slowly until tender. Turn frequently. Allow same time as for broiling.

Flaky cheese biscuits float atop rich gravy in a savory ham pie fit for a king

SAVORY HAM PIE

3 tablespoons chopped onion
¼ cup chopped green pepper
¼ cup fat
6 tablespoons flour
1 (10½-ounce) can condensed chicken soup
1⅓ cups milk
1½ cups diced cooked ham
1 tablespoon lemon juice
1 recipe Cheese Biscuit dough

Sauté onion and green pepper in fat, stir in flour, add soup and milk and cook until thickened. Add ham and lemon juice, mix and pour into greased baking dish. Roll out biscuit dough on floured board, cut with doughnut cutter and arrange on top of ham mixture. Bake in hot oven (450°F.) 15 minutes, reduce heat to 425°F. and bake 10 minutes longer. Serves 6.

SWEETPOTATO HAM LOAF

1 pound smoked ham, ground
¼ pound beef, ground
¼ pound pork, ground
¼ teaspoon salt
⅛ teaspoon pepper
¼ cup minced onion
1 small green pepper, minced
½ cup chopped celery
⅓ cup quick-cooking cereal
1 egg, beaten
½ cup milk
3½ cups mashed sweetpotatoes

Combine all ingredients, except sweetpotatoes, and mix well. Arrange half of meat mixture in greased loaf pan, cover with sweetpotatoes and top with remaining meat mixture. Bake in moderate oven (350°F.) about 1 hour. Serves 10.

HAM AND APPLES WITH DUMPLINGS

1 quart dried apples
3 pounds ham
2 tablespoons brown sugar
1 recipe Dumplings

Wash apples and soak overnight. Cover ham with cold water in kettle and simmer 2 hours. Add apples and water in which they have been soaked; simmer 1 hour longer; add brown sugar. Drop dumplings by spoonfuls into hot liquid. Cover tightly; cook 18 minutes. Serves 12.

HAM ROLL UPS

2 cups mashed sweetpotatoes
3 tablespoons melted fat
½ cup crushed pineapple
¼ cup chopped pecans
½ cup cracker crumbs
3 tablespoons brown sugar
6 slices, ⅛-inch thick, smoked or boiled ham
¾ cup pineapple juice

Combine potatoes, fat, pineapple, pecans, cracker crumbs and brown sugar; mix well. Spread filling on each slice of ham, roll as for jelly roll, fasten with toothpicks or tie. Place in baking dish, add pineapple juice and bake in moderate oven (350°F.) 1 hour for smoked ham and 20 minutes for boiled ham. Baste frequently. Serves 6.

PORK SHANKS AND SAUERKRAUT

3 pounds pork shanks
1 large onion
6 cups water
1 teaspoon salt
4 cups Sauerkraut

Simmer pork and onion in salted water in kettle 2½ to 3 hours. Place sauerkraut in baking pan and arrange cooked shanks on top. Add 1 cup of pork stock. Bake in moderate oven (350°F.) 30 minutes. Serves 6.

APPLE-STUFFED SPARERIBS

1 onion, chopped
1 tablespoon minced parsley
3 stalks celery, chopped
6 tart apples, chopped
¼ cup sugar
1 cup bread crumbs
2 matching spareribs (about 1½
      pounds each)
Salt, Pepper

Combine onion, parsley, celery, apples, sugar and crumbs. Spread 1 section of ribs with stuffing. Cover with other section and season. Bake uncovered in moderate oven (350°F.) until tender, about 1½ hours. Serves 6.

BOILED SPARERIBS AND POTATOES

2½ pounds spareribs
6 cups water
2 teaspoons salt
1 pod red pepper, if desired
6 medium potatoes

Wipe ribs with a damp cloth. Place in kettle, add water, salt and red pepper; simmer 1½ hours or until almost tender. Add potatoes and simmer until potatoes are tender, about 30 minutes longer. Serves 6.

Instead of spareribs use 4 pounds neckbones.

Add 3 cups sauerkraut to kettle with potatoes, if desired.

SPARERIBS WITH SWEET POTATO STUFFING

2 tablespoons butter, melted
½ cup chopped onion
1 cup chopped apple
2 cups cooked rice
2 cups chopped cooked sweet
      potato
2 tablespoons brown sugar
1 teaspoon salt
¼ teaspoon paprika
4 lbs. spareribs

Cook onion and apple in butter 5 min.; toss with next 5 ingredients. Cut ribs in 2 or 4 pieces; season with salt and pepper, Spread ½ with stuffing; cover with remaining ribs. Tie together. Bake on rack in shallow pan at 450°F. 15 min. Reduce heat to 325°F.; bake until ribs are tender. Brush frequently with glaze. Serves 4.

Apple Sauce Glaze—Blend ½ cup each honey and apple sauce with 2 tablespoons lemon juice. ↓

SLAVIC OVEN STEW

10 medium onions, minced
8 to 10 large tomatoes, sliced
½ cup uncooked rice
6 to 8 potatoes, pared and sliced
5 lamb chops
5 pork chops
1 eggplant
6 green peppers
1 cup diced okra
Salt and pepper
2 tablespoons butter

Cover bottom of roaster with onions; arrange half of tomatoes on onions and then spread rice over tomatoes. Then add potatoes; then chops, alternating pork and lamb. Pare and dice eggplant. Remove seeds from peppers and cut into fine rings. Cover chops with diced eggplant and sliced peppers; add another layer of sliced tomatoes and top with okra. Sprinkle with salt and pepper and dot with butter. Cover roaster and bake in very hot oven (450°F.) 1 hour. Remove cover from pan and continue roasting in moderate oven (350°F.) 30 minutes longer   Serves 5.

Pork, beef or lamb patties are still better for a snug wrapping of bacon

SPARERIBS AND SAUERKRAUT

1 quart Sauerkraut
¼ cup brown sugar
4 pounds spareribs
Salt and pepper
½ cup hot water

Place sauerkraut in greased baking dish and sprinkle with brown sugar. Brown spareribs under broiler heat, season and place on sauerkraut. Add hot water, cover and cook in moderate oven (350° F.) ¾ to 1 hour. Serves 6.

Sprinkle sauerkraut with 1 teaspoon caraway seeds instead of brown sugar.

BARBECUED SPARERIBS

4 pounds spareribs
2 onions, sliced
Salt and pepper
1 recipe Barbecue Sauce

Place spareribs in roaster and add sliced onions. Sprinkle with salt and pepper. Pour the sauce over spareribs. Cover pan and cook in moderate oven (350°F.), 1½ hours. Remove cover and roast 20 minutes longer. Serve with cooked rice for 6.

SPARERIBS AND BREAD STUFFING

1½ cups bread crumbs
¾ teaspoon salt
¾ teaspoon pepper
3 teaspoons minced parsley
⅜ teaspoon sage
3 teaspoons grated onion
¾ cup diced apples
½ cup milk
4 pounds spareribs

Mix first 8 ingredients thoroughly. Break spareribs through the center and remove any surplus fat. Spread bread mixture on bony side of half of ribs, fold in center to cover filling with other half of ribs. Place in baking pan with heavy meat side on top. Season meat and dredge with flour. Cover bottom of pan with boiling water and cook in moderate oven (325°F.) 1½ to 2 hours or until tender. Serves 4.

HAM PATTIES

2 pounds ground smoked ham

Shape into patties ¾ to 1 inch thick. Cook slowly 15 minutes, pouring off fat as it accumulates. Serves 6.

SAUSAGE PATTIES—Use pork sausage instead of ham.

APPLE SAUSAGE ROLL

1 pound sausage
2 cups diced apples
2 cups bread crumbs
1 small onion, diced

Roll out sausage, on waxed paper, into a rectangle ½ inch thick. Combine apples, bread crumbs and onion; spread over meat. Roll like a jelly roll. Place in baking dish; bake in moderate oven (350°F.) 45 minutes. Serves 8.

CASSEROLE OF SAU-SAGE AND CORN

12 Vienna sausages
2½ cups cooked whole-kernel corn
½ green pepper, chopped
Salt and pepper
2 cups Medium White Sauce

Wash sausages. Combine corn, green pepper, salt and pepper. Place in casserole in alternate layers with white sauce. Arrange sausages on top to radiate from center. Bake in moderate oven (350°F.) 20 minutes. Serves 6.

LIVER SAUSAGE BOLOGNA LOAF

⅔ pound Bologna
2 tablespoons chili sauce
4 tablespoons mayonnaise
1 tablespoon lemon juice
⅔ pound liver sausage
3 tablespoons minced dill pickle
4 tablespoons chopped celery
2 teaspoons onion juice
1 tablespoon Worcestershire sauce
1 loaf unsliced bread
3 tablespoons butter
3 slices Bologna
3 slices liver sausage
Tomato wedges, Stuffed olives

Put Bologna through food chopper; add chili sauce, 2 tablespoons mayonnaise and lemon juice; mix to a smooth paste. Mash liver sausage; add pickle, celery, onion juice, Worcestershire sauce and remaining mayonnaise; mix to a smooth paste. Cut crust from bread, slice in 3 lengthwise slices. Place one slice on baking sheet and spread with Bologna paste; top with second slice of bread; spread with liver sausage paste.

Top with remaining slice of bread. Spread entire loaf with butter. Arrange alternate slices of sausage on top. Bake in moderate oven (350°F.) 30 minutes. Garnish with tomatoes and stuffed olives. Serves 6.

SAUSAGE, CABBAGE AND APPLES

1 pound sausage meat
1 medium cabbage, shredded
3 apples, sliced
Salt
1 tablespoon vinegar

Shape sausage into flat cakes and sauté in skillet until crisp. In a greased baking dish arrange layers of cabbage and apples, salting each layer and ending with apples. Place sausage cakes on top. Rinse skillet with vinegar and pour over sausages. Cover and bake in moderate oven (350°F.) about 45 minutes. Serves 6.

Use 4 cooked sliced sweetpotatoes instead of cabbage.

A gorgeous toasted luncheon loaf, with liver sausage and Bologna in the leading rolls

BOLOGNA CUPS WITH PEAS

6 slices Bologna, cut ⅛ inch thick
2 tablespoons fat
2 cups cooked peas
1 tomato, cut into wedges
2 cups hot cooked rice

Spread Bologna with fat and broil. As slices heat they will curl into cups. Fill with hot peas, and arrange cups alternately with tomato wedges around rice heaped in center. Garnish, if desired, with sliced hard-cooked egg and green pepper rings. Serves 6.

BOLOGNA NOODLE CASSEROLE

3 cups cooked Noodles
1 cup chopped Bologna
½ teaspoon salt
⅛ teaspoon pepper
1 cup milk
½ cup cracker or bread crumbs
1 tablespoon fat

Arrange alternate layers of noodles and Bologna in greased baking dish. Add salt, pepper, milk; cover with crumbs. Dot with fat and bake in hot oven (400°F.) 30 minutes. Serves 6. Use macaroni or spaghetti instead of noodles if desired.

À L'ITALIENNE WIENERS

6 ounces spaghetti
1 small onion, chopped
¼ cup fat
⅓ cup flour
1 No. 2 can tomatoes
1 bay leaf
1 pound frankfurters
Salt

Cook spaghetti in boiling salted water. Cook onion in fat but do not brown; add flour and blend. Add tomatoes and bay leaf. Cook until thickened, stirring constantly. Arrange spaghetti and sliced frankfurters in alternate layers in baking dish, strain tomato sauce and add. Season and bake in moderate oven (350°F.) 20 minutes. Serves 4.

PRUNE AND SAUSAGE CANAPÉS—Place pan-fried Sausage Patties on toast rounds, cover with cooked prunes stuffed with minced apple, brush with melted butter, sprinkle with sugar and bake in hot oven (400°F.) 5 minutes.

Broiled Bologna slices will curl into cups; fill with peas and alternate with tomato wedges around rice

FILLED FRANKFURTERS

1½ cups broken macaroni
¾ cup evaporated milk
1¼ teaspoons dry mustard
1¼ teaspoons salt
⅛ teaspoon pepper
2½ cups grated American cheese
1½ pounds frankfurters

Cook macaroni in boiling salted water until tender. Drain. Combine milk, mustard, salt, pepper and 2 cups cheese in double boiler and cook until cheese is melted and sauce is smooth, stirring frequently. Add macaroni and mix well. Split frankfurters lengthwise without separating and fill with macaroni mixture. Sprinkle with remaining cheese, place in baking pan and bake in hot oven (400°F.) 15 minutes. Serve at once. Serves 6.

COVERED FRANKFURTERS—Mix macaroni and cheese as above, then place frankfurters in bottom of buttered baking dish. Cover with macaroni mixture and bake as above.

SAUSAGE VEGETABLE CASSEROLE

½ pound link sausages
1 onion, diced
½ green pepper, diced
2 tablespoons flour
1 teaspoon salt
¼ teaspoon pepper
2½ cups whole-kernel corn
2½ cups cooked tomatoes
1 cup cereal flakes

Brown sausages in skillet and remove from pan. Brown onion and pepper in remaining fat. Add flour and seasonings; blend. Add corn and tomatoes; simmer until juice has partly evaporated. Pour into casserole. Arrange browned sausages on top; sprinkle with cereal flakes. Brown in moderately hot oven (400°F.) about 15 minutes. Serves 8.

TO COOK PORK SAUSAGES

Broiling gives the most satisfactory results. To broil sausages arrange on wire rack and place 4 to 5 inches under broiler heat in unheated broiler. Broil slowly for 10 to 12 minutes. Turn several times while cooking to brown on all sides.

To pan-fry sausages, place in cold pan and cook slowly until browned. Pour off fat as it accumulates. Allow ⅓ pound per person. Serve with Fried Apples.

SAUSAGE BALLS

1 pound pork sausage meat
1 pound fresh pork, ground
½ teaspoon salt
½ cup uncooked rice
1 cup boiling water
3 tablespoons flour, 2 cups milk
⅛ teaspoon cloves, Salt
¼ teaspoon cinnamon

Combine sausage, pork, salt and rice. Shape into balls about 1½ inches in diameter. Brown slowly, cooking 10 to 12 minutes. Add water and simmer 1½ hours or until all water is absorbed. Remove balls, blend flour into fat in pan; add milk, spices and salt and cook until thickened. Pour over meat balls. Serves 8.

A breakfast of sausages and fried apples will drive away even those Monday blues

APPLES STUFFED WITH SAUSAGES

8 baking apples
1 pound pork sausage meat
8 fresh mushrooms

Prepare apples for baking. Core. Stem mushrooms. Slice stems and mix with sausage meat. Arrange apples in baking dish. Fill cores of apples with mixture and cap with mushrooms. Bake at 350°F. 30 minutes. Serves 8.

A crown roast of wieners is an ideal solution for guest problems when the budget is low

BARBECUED FRANKFURTERS

1½ pounds frankfurters
Barbecue Sauce

Prick skins of frankfurters, place in shallow pan, cover with sauce and cook, uncovered, in moderate oven (350°F.) 45 minutes. For 6.

STUFFED CROWN ROAST OF FRANKFURTERS

20 frankfurters
2 cups cooked Sauerkraut

Arrange frankfurters side by side, with curved side up. Using large needle and string, sew through all the frankfurters ½ inch from the bottom and ½ inch from the top. Tie ends of top string together, bringing first and last frankfurter of the row together. Repeat with bottom string. Stand frankfurters on end to form a crown. (Concave side should be out.) Fill center of crown with sauerkraut. Bake filled crown in moderate oven (375°F.) about 20 minutes. Serves 10.

Fill crown with stuffing, creamed cabbage, creamed cauliflower or Potato Balls instead of sauerkraut.

SAUSAGE LOAF

1½ pounds pork sausage meat
1½ cups bread or cracker crumbs
1 tablespoon grated onion
2 tablespoons tomato catchup
2 tablespoons horse-radish
½ teaspoon prepared mustard
1 egg, slightly beaten
½ cup milk

Mix sausage and crumbs. Add onion, catchup, horse-radish, mustard and egg. Moisten with milk. Shape into a loaf and bake in moderate oven (350°F.) about 1 hour. Serves 6.

DOWN EAST SUPPER

1 tablespoon chopped onion
2 tablespoons chopped green pepper
2 tablespoons fat
2 (16-ounce) cans pork and beans
1 tablespoon brown sugar
½ cup chopped celery
2 (4-ounce) cans Vienna sausage

Brown onion and pepper in fat. Add beans, brown sugar and celery and place in 1 large or 5 individual casseroles. Place 3 sausages on each casserole and bake in moderate oven (350°F.) until browned, about 30 minutes. Serves 5.

VEGETABLE SAUSAGE SALAD

1 quart diced cooked potatoes
2 cups cubed salami or Thuringer sausage
2 tablespoons vinegar
2 cups cooked large peas
1 cup chopped celery
1 pimiento, chopped
6 sweet pickles, diced
2 hard-cooked eggs, sliced
Mayonnaise
Salt

Mix all ingredients together, adding enough mayonnaise to moisten, salt to taste and extra vinegar if desired. Heap in large wooden bowl lined with crisp lettuce and garnish with tiny whole pickled beets, and slices of hard-cooked egg. Serves 6.

SAUSAGE ROLLS

12 link sausages
12 thin slices bread

Broil sausages. Remove crusts from bread. Roll each sausage in a slice of bread. Toast under broiler. Serves 4.

Either pork sausages or frankfurters may be tucked into crisp toast blankets

SOUTHERN SAUSAGE CASSEROLE

4 large sweetpotatoes, cooked
1 pound pork sausage meat
4 large apples, unpared
Salt
Water
Brown sugar

Peel potatoes, cut into thin slices and place half in bottom of greased casserole; cover with sausage shaped into 4 cakes and add apples cut into thick slices. Sprinkle with salt, cover with remaining potatoes, brush with water and sprinkle with brown sugar. Bake in moderate oven (350° F) about 1 hour. Serves 4.

BAKED STUFFED FRANKFURTERS

2 cups soft bread crumbs
¼ teaspoon salt
Dash pepper
2 teaspoons sage
1 small onion, minced
¼ cup melted butter
10 frankfurters
5 strips bacon

Combine crumbs with seasoning and onion; add melted butter and blend well. Split frankfurters lengthwise; fill with the stuffing; wrap each with a half strip of bacon and fasten with toothpicks. Bake in moderate oven (350°F.) for ½ hour; or broil 10 minutes. Serves 5.

CHEESE-STUFFED FRANKFURTERS—Place slice of cheese in frankfurters instead of stuffing. Bake or broil long enough to melt cheese and brown bacon.

APPLE-STUFFED FRANKFURTERS—Place finely chopped apple in frankfurters instead of stuffing.

PICCALILLI-STUFFED FRANKFURTERS—Fill frankfurters with piccalilli and proceed as above.

VEAL AND PORK EN BROCHETTE

1 pound veal steak
1 pound pork shoulder
1 egg
1 cup fine crisp cereal crumbs
Fat
1¾ teaspoons salt
½ cup water
½ cup sour or sweet cream

Cut veal and pork into 1½-inch squares. Place 2 squares of pork and 2 of veal alternately on each of several skewers. Dip each into egg, then into crumbs and brown in fat. Season, add water, cover and· simmer until tender, about 1 hour. Remove to hot platter and pour cream into pan. Heat to boiling and serve with meat. Serves 8.

MOCK CHICKEN LEGS—Use only ½ pound veal and ½ pound pork and grind meat instead of cutting into cubes. Combine with 2 teaspoons salt, ¼ teaspoon paprika, 2 tablespoons chopped green pepper and ½ cup drained crushed pineapple. Shape around skewers, coat and cook as above. Omit cream. Garnish ends of skewers with stuffed olives

VEAL FRICASSEE, JARDINIÈRE

2 pounds veal rump
2 tablespoons flour, **Fat**
Salt and pepper
1 teaspoon minced parsley
2 bay leaves, minced
2 carrots, sliced
1 cup water or stock
½ cup sliced celery
2 onions, sliced
1 cup cooked peas or mushrooms

Cut veal into 1-inch cubes, dredge in flour and brown in fat; season and add parsley, bay leaves, carrots, water, celery and onions. Cover tightly and cook in moderate oven (350°F.) 45 to 60 minutes, or until meat is tender. Remove veal. Add peas and thicken liquid with flour mixed with a little cold water. Cook until thickened. Pour over veal. Serves 4 to 6.

Omit peas and carrots. Blend 2 tablespoons flour with ½ cup sour cream and add to liquid after removing veal. Cook slowly until thickened.

Veal and pork brochette garnished with spiced peaches makes a quick, simple and inexpensive luncheon

BRAZIL-NUT JELLIED VEAL LOAF

1 package lemon gelatin
2 cups veal stock
2 hard-cooked eggs, sliced
Whole Brazil-nut meats
1½ cups chopped cooked veal
Salt
1 teaspoon vinegar
2 tablespoons minced parsley
2 teaspoons minced onion
½ cup chopped Brazil-nut meats

Dissolve gelatin in 1 cup hot stock; add remaining stock. Pour ⅓ cup into bottom of loaf pan and chill until firm. Garnish jelly in bottom of loaf pan with sliced eggs and a few whole Brazil nuts. Add veal, salt, vinegar, parsley, onion and Brazil nuts to remaining gelatin. Pour in the veal mixture and chill for several hours, until firm. Unmold and serve with lettuce and mayonnaise. Serves 6.

To vary, use cooked pork for veal.

TWO-TONE MEAT LOAF

PART 1

1 pound ground veal
¼ pound ground fresh **pork fat**
3 crackers, crushed
1 tablespoon milk
2 teaspoons lemon juice
1 teaspoon salt
Dash pepper
1 tablespoon minced onion

PART 2

1 pound ground fresh pork
½ pound ground smoked ham
2 eggs
½ cup bread crumbs
½ cup condensed tomato soup
1 teaspoon salt
Dash pepper

Combine ingredients of part 1 and pack into greased loaf pan. Combine ingredients of part 2 and pack firmly on top of veal mixture. Bake in moderate oven (350°F.) 2 hours. Serves 8 to 10.

The family will need no second call if they know veal cutlets are waiting

BREADED VEAL CUTLETS

6 veal cutlets, ½-inch thick
Salt
Pepper
1 cup fine bread crumbs
2 eggs, slightly beaten
Fat

Season cutlets with salt and pepper. Dip into fine bread crumbs, then into eggs and again into crumbs. Sauté slowly in fat until well browned, allowing 15 minutes for each side. Serve with Tomato Sauce. Serves 6.

SPECIAL BREADED VEAL CUTLETS—Mix 2 teaspoons prepared mustard, 1 teaspoon salt, dash of pepper and 1 tablespoon butter. Rub into steak. Then dip into egg and crumbs and cook as above. Omit tomato sauce.

Dip chops into buttermilk instead of egg.

BRAISED VEAL STEAK WITH MUSHROOMS

2 pounds veal steak
1 egg, slightly beaten
2 tablespoons milk
2 cups crushed cereal flakes
4 tablespoons fat
1 small can mushrooms

Have veal steak cut 1 inch thick. Cut into pieces for serving. Dip into mixture of egg and milk. Roll in finely crushed cereal flakes. Brown in hot fat and cover with mushrooms and mushroom liquid. Cover tightly and cook very slowly until tender, about 45 minutes. Thicken liquid for gravy and serve with veal steaks. Serves 4.

MOCK CHICKEN

1½ pounds veal round
Salt and pepper
Flour
⅓ cup fat
1 green pepper, chopped
½ cup minced celery
½ cup boiling water
½ cup mushrooms, sliced

Cut veal into serving portions. Season, dredge with flour and brown in fat. Add green pepper and celery. Add water, cover pan closely and cook in moderate oven (350°F.) 1½ hours. Add mushrooms and cook about ½ hour or longer. Thicken gravy if necessary before serving. Serves 4.

PAPRIKA CREAM SCHNITZEL

4 slices bacon, cut fine
1½ pounds veal steak
2 tablespoons chopped onion
1 teaspoon paprika
Salt
1 cup sour cream
½ cup Tomato Sauce

Fry bacon until crisp, add veal (cut into serving portions) and brown in hot bacon fat. Add onion and brown. Season with paprika and salt. Stir in sour cream and tomato sauce. Cover pan and cook about 30 minutes. Serve cutlets with the sauce and cover with boiled or fried noodles. Serves 6.

QUICK MEAT STEW

2 cups diced cooked meat (beef, pork or veal)
2 tablespoons fat
2 tablespoons flour
1 (16-ounce) can vegetable soup

Brown meat in fat, add flour and brown. Add soup and cook until thickened. Serve on hot toast, biscuits or cooked rice. Serves 4. Use mushroom or onion soup, if desired.

WIENER SCHNITZEL

6 veal chops or steaks
Salt and pepper
2 eggs, slightly beaten
Flour
3 tablespoons bacon drippings
Juice of 1 lemon
1 tablespoon flour
1 cup thick sour cream

Sprinkle veal with salt and pepper. Dip into eggs, then into flour. Brown on both sides in hot bacon drippings. Cover and cook slowly until chops are tender, about 1 hour. Sprinkle with lemon juice and arrange on hot platter. Blend flour with fat in pan, add sour cream and cook 3 minutes, stirring constantly. Season with salt and pepper and serve with chops. Garnish with lemon slices. Serves 6.
Melt currant jelly in liquid in which chops were cooked, instead of adding flour and cream.

The variations of veal birds are limited only by the ingenuity of the cook

VEAL BIRDS

2 pounds veal steak (cut ¼ inch
    thick)
1 cup Sage or Mushroom Stuffing
Salt
Flour
Fat
1 cup milk or water

Cut veal into 2 x 4 inch pieces.
Place a mound of stuffing on
each piece, fold veal over stuffing and fasten with toothpick.
Season, roll in flour, brown in fat
and add milk. Cover and simmer
or bake in moderate oven (350°
F.) 1 hour. Serves 6.

Wrap veal around sausages or
cooked whole carrots instead of
stuffing.

Use Sage or Onion Stuffing. Pour
mushroom soup over browned
meat instead of milk.

Wrap veal around uncooked meat
balls.

Stuff with chopped pickles and
olives and narrow beet strips.

VEAL RING

1½ pounds veal, knuckle or shin
¼ pound salt pork
2 teaspoons salt
1 teaspoon chopped onion
1 cup cracker crumbs
1 egg, ½ teaspoon sage
1 cup water or stock
2 tablespoons margarine

Grind veal and pork very fine and
add salt, onion, crumbs, egg, sage
and ½ cup water. Mix well. Pack
into greased ring mold and cook
in moderate oven (350°F.) 1½
hours, basting occasionally with
remaining water combined with
margarine. Unmold on plate and
fill with well seasoned cooked
green beans. Serves 5.

ROAST VEAL

3½ pounds veal (leg, loin or rib)
Strips of salt pork or bacon

Wipe meat with a damp cloth. Place strips of salt pork over meat. Roast uncovered in a slow oven (300°F.) allowing 35 minutes per pound. Serves 6.

VEAL STEAK WITH WINE SAUCE

1 pound veal steak, 1 inch thick
1 tablespoon cooking oil
Salt, Pepper
Wine sauce (optional)

Sauté veal steak in oil until browned; cover and cook very slowly 30 minutes or until tender, turning frequently. Place on hot platter, sprinkle with salt and pepper; pour wine sauce over and around steak. Serves 2.

KIDNEY VEAL CHOPS

6 kidney veal chops (¾ to 1 inch thick)
Flour, Fat, Salt and pepper
½ cup hot water

Dredge chops with flour and brown on both sides in hot fat. Season, add water, cover tightly and simmer slowly or bake in moderate over (375°F.) about 45 minutes. Serves 6.

VEAL AND MACARONI SALAD

2 cups cooked elbow macaroni
1 cup chopped celery
6 sweet pickles, chopped
1½ cups diced cooked veal
Mayonnaise

Mix macaroni, celery, pickles and veal. Add mayonnaise to moisten thoroughly. Serves 5.

Kidney veal chops are an English idea which good cooks have quickly adopted

RUMANIAN MEAT AND VEGETABLE CASSEROLE

Beef drippings or other fat
2½- to 3-pound slice veal
Salt and pepper
2 pounds fresh tomatoes, sliced, or
    3½ cups cooked tomatoes
1 clove garlic, chopped
2 cups condensed tomato soup
2 cups water
1 pound green beans
1 onion, sliced
2 tablespoons flour

Melt 3 tablespoons drippings in a baking pan. Season veal with salt and pepper and place in pan. Cover with tomatoes, garlic and 1 cup each of soup and water. Bake in moderate oven (350°F.) about 1 hour or until meat is tender. Cut beans diagonally into thin slices and cook in boiling salted water for 10 minutes. Drain; fry beans and onion in fat for 10 minutes. Push beans and onions to one side of pan and brown flour in fat. Add remaining soup and water and heat to boiling. Pour over meat, return to oven, reduce heat to slow (325°F.) and continue cooking 20 minutes longer. Serves 6.

STUFFED BREAST OF VEAL

1 veal breast
Salt and pepper
2 cups Onion or Raisin Stuffing

Have pocket cut in veal from the large end. Season inside of pocket with salt and pepper, fill with stuffing and skewer or sew edges together. Place on rack of roaster, cover and cook in slow oven (300°F.) about 2 hours. Remove cover during last 30 minutes. Allow ½ pound per serving.

STUFFED VEAL SHOULDER

5-pound veal shoulder
Salt and pepper
Chili or Raisin Stuffing
Melted fat or salt pork

Have bones removed from veal shoulder, season cavity and fill with stuffing. Sew or skewer edges together and place on rack of roaster. Brush with fat or cover with strips of salt pork. Bake uncovered in moderate oven (325°F.) allowing 40 minutes to the pound, or until meat thermometer registers 175°F., for 10.

VEAL STEW WITH DUMPLINGS

1 pound veal breast, cubed
1¼ cups flour
2 tablespoons fat
2 cups hot water
½ cup diced carrots
½ cup diced potatoes
¼ cup chopped onions
¼ cup chopped celery
1 bay leaf
1 teaspoon salt
1 teaspoon Worcestershire sauce
⅛ teaspoon pepper
1½ teaspoons baking powder
½ cup milk
2 tablespoons melted shortening
1 cup tomato paste

Dredge veal with ¼ cup flour; brown in hot fat in kettle; add water, cover and simmer 1 hour or until tender. Add vegetables, bay leaf, ½ teaspoon salt, Worcestershire sauce and pepper. Simmer 20 minutes. Sift baking powder, remaining flour and salt together. Combine milk and shortening, add to dry ingredients. Mix to a soft dough. Add tomato paste to vegetables; bring to a vigorous boil. Add more water if necessary. Drop dumplings from a spoon into hot liquid. Cover tightly and cook, without removing cover, 15 minutes. Serves 6

BRAISED VEAL

¼ cup diced salt pork
1½ pounds veal breast, cubed
2 tablespoons flour
1 teaspoon salt, 2 cups water
1 cup diced celery
1½ cups noodles
2 tablespoons chopped parsley

Brown salt pork until crisp. Roll veal in flour and brown slowly in salt pork fat in kettle. Add salt and water, cover and simmer slowly 1½ hours. Add celery and noodles; continue cooking about 15 minutes or until noodles are tender. Arrange noodles in center of platter, sprinkle with parsley and border with veal. Serves 6.

RICE VEAL CUSTARD

2 cups cooked brown rice
1 cup diced cooked veal
2 pimientos, diced
½ teaspoon salt
Dash cayenne
1 egg, slightly beaten
½ cup milk
½ cup veal stock

Arrange layers of rice, veal and pimientos in greased baking dish. Combine salt, cayenne, egg, milk and stock; add to first mixture. Cover; bake in moderate oven (350°F.) until firm, about 30 minutes. Serves 6.

CITY CHICKEN CUTLETS

¾ pound veal, ground
6 tablespoons fat
2 cups cooked brown rice
1 cup Thick White Sauce
¾ teaspoon salt
½ teaspoon celery salt
1 tablespoon minced parsley
1 egg, beaten
1 cup bread crumbs

Brown veal in 2 tablespoons fat in skillet. Combine with rice, white sauce, seasonings and egg; cool. Shape into cutlets and roll in crumbs; sauté in remaining fat until lightly browned. Cover and cook slowly 10 minutes. Serve with Mushroom or Tomato Sauce. Serves 6.
Ground cooked veal may be used.

HUNGARIAN GOULASH

1 pound beef chuck
1 pound veal or pork
¼ cup flour
½ teaspoon salt
¼ teaspoon pepper
3 tablespoons fat
3 cups boiling water
¾ cup thick sour cream
3 tablespoons grated onion
2 tablespoons minced parsley
Additional salt (if needed)
1 tablespoon paprika
Cooked noodles

Cut meat into 1-inch cubes. Roll in flour, salt and pepper and brown in fat in kettle. Add water and cover tightly. Simmer 1½ hours or until meat is tender. Remove cover and cook to reduce liquid. Add remaining ingredients and heat to boiling; simmer 10 minutes. Serve with cooked noodles. Serves 8.

The delicious flavor of veal and vegetable stew permeates feathery dumplings sprinkled with chives

VEAL À LA KING

½ green pepper, shredded
¼ pound mushrooms
3 tablespoons fat
6 tablespoons flour
4 cups milk or ½ milk and
    ½ veal stock
Salt and pepper
3 cups diced cooked veal
1 pimiento, diced

Cook green pepper and mushrooms in fat in kettle 8 minutes. Remove from fat; blend flour with fat. Add milk and seasonings and cook until thickened, stirring constantly. Add green pepper, mushrooms and remaining ingredients and heat. Serve on toast or in bread Croustades. Serves 8.

VEAL LOAF

2 cups chopped cooked veal
2 cups cracker crumbs
1 pimiento, chopped
1 green pepper, chopped
3 eggs, beaten
Salt and pepper
Meat broth or milk
3 slices bacon

Combine first 5 ingredients and season; add enough liquid to moisten well. Pour into loaf pan lined with bacon. Bake in moderate oven (350°F.) 30 minutes. Serve with Mushroom Sauce.

SHANGHAI SPECIAL

½ pound veal or pork, diced
2 tablespoons fat
3 cups chopped celery
1 cup minced onions
2 cups coarsley chopped salted
    peanuts
½ cup water
⅛ teaspoon pepper
2 tablespoons soy or meat sauce

Brown meat in hot fat in a skillet. Add celery, onions, peanuts, water, pepper and soy or meat sauce. Cover tightly and simmer 30 to 45 minutes. Add salt, if necessary. Serve with hot cooked rice. Serves 6.

Salted peanuts reinforce the meat in this intriguing Shanghai Special

VEAL SCALLOPINE NAPOLI

2 pounds veal round steak,
    ½ to ¾ inch thick
2 teaspoons salt
1 teaspoon pepper
¾ cup flour
3 tablespoons fat
3 tablespoons salad oil
1 pound mushrooms, sliced
1 cup hot water
1 cup dry white wine
Dash nutmeg
½ cup tomato paste
1 teaspoon sugar
½ cup cream

Cut veal into 4-inch squares. Pound salt, pepper and flour into meat. Brown veal on both sides in hot fat and oil, in skillet. Remove meat, add mushrooms, cover and sauté 10 minutes or until tender. Return meat to skillet. Add water, wine and nutmeg. Cover and simmer 20 minutes or until meat is tender. Add tomato paste, sugar and cream; simmer 5 minutes longer. Serves 8.

TO DRESS AND TRUSS RABBITS

Choose rabbits with soft ears and paws—stiffness is a sign of age. Also, be sure that they are fresh and free from any unpleasant odor. Neither hares nor rabbits should be drawn before hanging, as they may become musty.

To skin and dress a rabbit or hare cut off the forefeet at the first joint, cut skin around the first joint of hind leg, loosen it and with a sharp knife slit the skin on under side of the leg at the tail Loosen the skin and turn it back until it is removed from the hind legs. Tie hind legs together and hang the rabbit to a hook by this fastening. Draw the skin over the head, slipping out the forelegs when they are reached. Cut off the head and thus remove the entire skin. Wipe with a damp cloth. Slit down the front and remove entrails, saving heart and liver, and wipe carefully inside Wash inside and out with acidulated water, using 1 tablespoon vinegar to each cup water. Rinse and wipe thoroughly.

If blood has settled in any part, cut with the point of a knife where it is black and soak in warm water; this will draw out the blood. Skewer firmly between the shoulders; draw the legs close to the body and fasten with skewers. Prepare as desired: roast, broil, fry or fricassee. Squirrels are dressed the same.

FRIED RABBIT

2 young rabbits (2½ to 3½
    pounds)
2 egg yolks, beaten
3 cups milk
1¼ cups flour
1 teaspoon salt
½ cup fat
2 teaspoons currant jelly
1 tablespoon minced parsley

Wash dressed rabbits thoroughly under running water. Dry. Cut into serving pieces. Combine egg yolks and 1 cup milk, add 1 cup flour gradually, then salt and beat until smooth. Dip rabbit into batter and fry in fat until brown, about 15 minutes. Reduce heat and continue cooking until tender, 30 to 40 minutes, turning frequently. To make gravy add remaining flour to fat in pan, add remaining milk gradually, stirring constantly, heat to boiling and season to taste with salt and pepper. Pour over rabbit; garnish with jelly and parsley. Serves 6 to 8.

BELGIAN HARE—Season and roll in flour, then fry in fat until brown, cover and cook over low heat about 40 minutes.

ROAST RABBIT

1 rabbit
Salt
Pepper
Sage Stuffing
2 tablespoons fat

Wash dressed rabbit thoroughly under running water. Dry. Sprinkle with salt and pepper on inside. Fill with stuffing, fasten opening securely and spread with fat. Sprinkle with salt and pepper and roast in uncovered pan in moderate oven (325°F.) 1½ to 1¾ hours or until tender. Serves 4 to 6.

HASSENPFEFFER
(Sweet-Sour Rabbit)

1 rabbit, cut in serving pieces
1½ teaspoons salt
¼ cup butter
1 onion, studded with 4 cloves
1½ cups port wine or claret
1 tablespoon lemon juice
12 peppercorns
    Herb bouquet
3 cups hot stock or bouillon
2 tablespoons butter, melted
1 tablespoon flour

Rinse and pat rabbit dry; rub with salt. Brown in ¼ cup butter. Place in casserole; add onion, ¾ cup wine, lemon juice, peppercorns, herbs (parsley, thyme, bay leaf), and stock. Cook, covered in 350° F oven 2½ to 3 hours. One-half hour before serving, blend remaining flour with melted butter and stir into hot mixture. Add remaining wine and cook 30 minutes longer. Remove rabbit to serving dish; strain gravy over pieces. Serve with currant jelly. Serves 4.

ROAST SQUIRRELS

3 small squirrels
¾ cup cooking oil
¼ cup lemon juice
2 cups bread crumbs
½ cup milk or cream
1 cup sliced mushrooms, sautéed
½ teaspoon salt
⅛ teaspoon pepper
½ teaspoon onion juice
4 tablespoons olive oil or bacon fat

Dress and clean squirrels, wash in several waters and dry. Cover with cooking oil mixed with lemon juice and let stand for 1 hour. Combine crumbs, with just enough milk to moisten, mushrooms, salt, pepper and onion juice. Stuff squirrels with this mixture, sew and truss. Place in roaster. Brush with olive oil or bacon fat. Roast uncovered in slow oven (325°F.) until tender, 1½ to 1¾ hours. Baste every 15 minutes with fat. Serve with pan gravy. Serves 6.

STEWED SQUIRRELS—Clean 3 squirrels, cut lengthwise into halves, simmer in boiling salted water with 1 pound carrots until tender. Blend 6 tablespoons each melted fat and flour, add 2¾ cups strained squirrel stock, ¼ teaspoon minced onion, 1 bay leaf and salt. Cook until thickened and serve over squirrel for 6.

ROAST OPOSSUM

The opossum is a very fat animal with a peculiarly flavored meat. It is dressed much as one would dress a suckling pig, removing the entrails, and if desired, the head and tail. After it has been dressed, wash thoroughly inside and out with hot water. Cover with cold water to which has been added 1 cup of salt. Allow to stand overnight; in the morning, drain off the salted water and rinse well with clear, boiling water. Stuff opossum with Opossum Stuffing; sew opening or fasten with skewers. Place in roaster, add 2 tablespoons water and roast in moderate oven (350° F.) until tender and richly browned, about 1½ hours. Baste every 15 minutes with drippings. Remove skewers or stitches, and place opossum on heated platter. Skim fat from gravy remaining in pan. Serves 10.

BRAISED MOOSE

4 pounds ripened moose
4 strips salt pork
Salt and pepper
⅛ teaspoon cinnamon
⅛ teaspoon cloves
⅔ cup claret or weak vinegar
½ cup water, ½ bay leaf
1 onion, sliced
1 cup claret or cranberry juice
1 cup milk

Trim off any musty parts of moose and lard with salt pork. Sprinkle with salt, pepper, cinnamon and cloves. Marinate in claret or vinegar for 2 or 3 days in cold place. Drain, place in baking pan, add water, cover and cook in slow oven (300°F.) about 1 hour. Add bay leaf, onion and claret or cranberry juice, cover and cook until tender, about 1 hour longer. Remove meat and add milk to drippings. Heat to boiling and serve with moose. Serves 6 to 8.

REINDEER

Composition of the meat differs little from beef or veal of the same grade. In general it contains less fat and slightly more protein. The flavor is characteristic and different from beef or veal, gamy but not strong. The texture is fine and most of the meat is tender. Most desirable cut is the round, which may be used for steaks but is most satisfactory for roasting.

Reindeer meat is shipped frozen and must be handled with the same care as any other frozen meat. It should be allowed to thaw slowly at a low temperature.

REINDEER POT ROAST

2 to 3 pounds reindeer meat
½ pound salt pork
Flour
Salt and pepper
1½ cups water
1 teaspoon salt
¼ teaspoon pepper
1 bay leaf
4 carrots, pared
4 turnips, pared
4 potatoes, pared
6 small onions

Wipe meat with damp cloth and lard with ¾ of the salt pork. Rub with flour, salt and pepper. Fry remaining salt pork in kettle and brown meat in this fat. Remove meat and brown 2 tablespoons flour in kettle. Set meat on low rack in kettle, add water and seasonings, cover pan and simmer until meat is nearly tender. Place vegetables around and over meat and continue cooking until vegetables are tender, about 45 minutes. Serve roast surrounded with vegetables. Thicken the gravy if necessary and serve with meat. Serves 4.

Add Dumplings 15 minutes before vegetables are tender.

BRAISED VENISON

3 pounds venison
3 slices salt pork
Salt and pepper, Flour
¼ cup fat
¼ cup hot water
½ tablespoon vinegar
½ cup chopped celery
1 carrot, diced
1 tart apple, chopped
½ tablespoon lemon juice

Use the less tender cuts of venison for this method. Lard venison with salt pork and rub with salt, pepper and flour. Sauté in hot fat until well browned, turning frequently. Add hot water and vinegar. Cover closely and cook until tender, about 2 to 2½ hours, adding more water as it evaporates. One-half hour before meat is done add remaining ingredients. Cook until vegetables are tender. Serve with a tart jelly. Serves 4 or 5.

BROILED VENISON STEAK

2 pounds venison steak, 1 inch thick
1 clove garlic
2 tablespoons fat, melted
4 large mushroom caps
Salt and pepper
Parsley and watercress

Rub steak on both sides with cut surfaces of garlic and brush with fat. Place on greased broiler rack in preheated broiler and broil for 5 minutes; turn and brush with fat and broil on other side. Broil mushroom caps. Season steak with salt and pepper and garnish with mushroom caps, parsley and watercress. Serves 4.

ROAST LEG OF VENISON— Wipe leg, sprinkle with salt and pepper and dredge with flour. Lard with strips of salt pork unless meat is fat. Roast uncovered in slow oven (300°F.) 20 to 22 minutes per pound. Allow ½ pound per serving.

TO PRECOOK BRAINS AND SWEETBREADS

Place brains or sweetbreads in cold water for 30 minutes, then remove membranes. Simmer for 15 minutes in water to which 1 teaspoon salt and 1 teaspoon lemon juice or vinegar has been added for each quart of water. Drain and drop into cold water. Use as desired. Save cooking water to use as stock.

BRAISED BRAINS

1 set calf's brains
Salt and pepper
Flour or cracker crumbs
Fat

Soak brains in cold water for 30 minutes. Remove veins and membrane. Season, roll in flour or crumbs, brown in fat and cover skillet tightly. Cook slowly about 20 minutes. Serves 2.

Cook sweetbreads in the same manner.

BRAIN RISSOLES

2 cups brains or 1 whole brain
¾ teaspoon salt
2 tablespoons chopped green pepper
1 cup Thick White Sauce
Pastry

Precook brains, chop or force through meat grinder; add salt, green pepper and white sauce. Form into small balls. Roll pastry to ⅛-inch thickness. Place the balls on the pastry equal distances apart. Place another sheet of pastry over all. Stamp out around each ball with round cutter or cut them apart and press upper and lower crusts together. Bake in a very hot oven (450°F.) 15 minutes or brown in hot deep fat (375°F.) before serving Serves 4.

Use stock from cooking brains or meat stock in making sauce.

CALF'S BRAIN FRITTERS

1 set calf's brains
1½ cups sifted flour
¼ teaspoon salt
¼ teaspoon paprika
1 egg
1¼ cups milk
Bacon drippings or other fat

Precook brains, dry and break into small pieces. Sift dry ingredients together; combine egg and milk; add to dry ingredients and mix well. Add brains. Drop by tablespoons into hot skillet greased with drippings and sauté, or drop into hot deep fat (360° F.) and fry until brown. Serves 4.

FRIED BRAINS

1 pound brains
2 tablespoons flour
Salt
Pepper
2 tablespoons fat

Precook brains. Roll in flour, season and brown in fat. Serves 4.

BRAISED SWEETBREADS

1 pair sweetbreads
Salt
Paprika
Flour
4 strips bacon
Stock from cooking sweetbreads
Sherry or lemon juice

Precook sweetbreads, break into large pieces, season and roll in flour. Wrap with bacon strips, place in baking dish and add enough stock to cover bottom of dish. Cover dish and cook in moderate oven (350°F.) about 10 minutes. Combine ½ cup stock and 2 teaspoons flour, add to sweetbreads and cook uncovered until bacon is crisp. Add sherry just before serving for 2.

TO VARY—1. Add 1 dozen oysters after cooking 10 minutes. **2.** Cook minced carrots and celery in stock until tender and add vegetables with stock to sweetbreads. **3.** Add sautéed mushrooms with the stock and flour mixture.

BROILED SWEETBREADS—Prepare sweetbreads as above, but dot with butter and broil under moderate heat about 10 minutes, or until bacon is crisp. Baste occasionally with drippings. Flavor drippings with sherry and serve over sweetbreads

SWEETBREADS WITH FRESH MUSHROOMS

1 pound sweetbreads
4 tablespoons butter
1 tablespoon flour
4 green onions, minced
1 sprig parsley, minced
½ pound fresh mushrooms, sliced
1 egg yolk, well beaten
½ cup heavy cream

Precook sweetbreads. Melt 2 tablespoons butter, add flour and brown. Add sweetbreads, onions, parsley and 1 cup of stock from cooking sweetbreads. Simmer until sauce is quite thick. Meanwhile cook cleaned mushrooms about 5 minutes in top of double boiler with remaining 2 tablespoons of butter, then add sweetbread mixture. About 3 minutes before serving, add egg yolk mixed with cream. Stir continually until heated through and serve at once. Makes 4 servings.

CREAMED SWEETBREADS

1 pair sweetbreads
1 cup Medium White Sauce
1 tablespoon sherry

Precook sweetbreads, break into pieces and heat in white sauce. Add sherry and serve immediately. Serves 2.

HEART EN CASSEROLE, ITALIENNE

1½ cups diced cooked heart
4 tablespoons fat, melted
1 No. 2 can spaghetti with tomato sauce
2 tablespoons chopped pimiento
¼ cup grated cheese
1½ cups cooked string beans
1 tablespoon flour
1 cup boiling water
¾ teaspoon salt
⅛ teaspoon pepper
Buttered crumbs

Brown heart in 3 tablespoons fat. Combine spaghetti, pimiento, cheese and string beans; add heart and place in baking dish. Blend flour with remaining fat, add water, salt and pepper, and cook until thickened, stirring constantly. Add to heart mixture, cover with buttered crumbs and bake in moderate oven (350°F.) about 30 minutes. Serves 8.

Mix grated cheese with buttered crumbs and sprinkle on top of mixture, before baking.

A well-browned beef heart surrounded by fresh vegetables is a real treat

HEART GOULASH

1 cup chopped cooked heart
1 cup chopped cooked pork
½ onion, chopped
1 tablespoon fat
1 cup water
1¼ teaspoons salt
½ cup diced carrot
1 cup diced celery
½ cup diced tomatoes
½ cup sour cream
2 tablespoons cold water
2 tablespoons flour
2½ cups cooked rice or noodles

Brown heart, pork and onion in fat. Add water, salt, carrot and celery. Cook until vegetables are tender, about 20 minutes. Add tomatoes and sour cream. Mix water and flour to a smooth paste and add to meat mixture. Cook slowly until thickened. Serve with rice or noodles. Serves 5.

SWEET-SOUR HEARTS

2 veal hearts
2 tablespoons flour
2 tablespoons fat
1 teaspoon salt
6 tablespoons vinegar
2 teaspoons sugar
¼ teaspoon pepper, 3 cups water
1 small onion, chopped

Clean hearts, remove membrane and large veins, and cut hearts into ½-inch cubes. Brown flour in fat and add meat and remaining ingredients. Cover and simmer for 1½ hours or until tender. Serve with noodles. Serves 4.

STUFFED HEART

1 beef or 2 veal hearts
½ recipe Prune Stuffing
2 tablespoons flour
2 tablespoons fat
1½ cups water

Wash heart, trim and fill with stuffing. Tie firmly with string. Dredge with flour, brown in fat and season with salt and pepper. Add water, cover closely and simmer about 2 hours or until tender. Thicken liquid with additional flour. Serves 6.

Other stuffing may be used.

BRAISED HEART—Reduce water to ½ cup. Prepare as above but cook, covered, in moderate oven (350°F.) instead of simmering. Allow 1½ to 2½ hours for lamb, pork or veal hearts; 2½ to 3½ hours for beef hearts.

Use Onion or Sage Stuffing with braised heart. Cook vegetables in pan with heart.

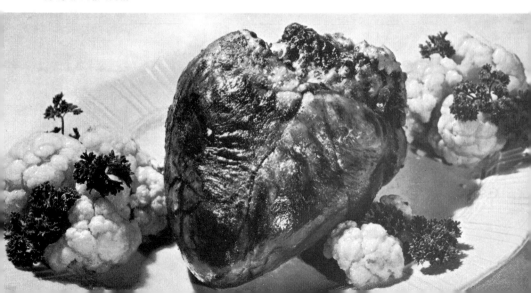

STUFFED HEART

1 beef heart
1 teaspoon salt
½ teaspoon pepper
½ recipe Onion Stuffing
2 tablespoons fat, ½ cup water

Wash heart, remove hard parts, season. Fill with stuffing and sew. Brown in hot fat. Add water. Cover and simmer 3 hours or until tender. Serves 12.

STUFFED LIVER

3 pounds liver
Stuffing
2 teaspoons salt
¼ teaspoon pepper
¼ cup flour
¼ pound sliced salt pork

Buy a chunky piece of liver. Wash and dry. Cut a pocket in thickest part. Fill with stuffing. Season and dredge with flour. Place slices of salt pork over liver. Bake, uncovered, in moderate oven (350°F.) 2 hours. For 12.

STUFFING

⅓ cup melted fat
3 cups fine bread crumbs
⅛ teaspoon pepper
1 teaspoon sage
1 tablespoon minced onion
½ teaspoon salt, Water

Mix ingredients in order given, using enough water to hold crumbs together.

BAKED LIVER ROLLS

1½ cups diced cooked liver
1 small onion
2 tablespoons lemon juice
1 tablespoon chopped parsley
½ teaspoon salt
¼ teaspoon pepper, Milk
1 recipe Baking Powder Biscuit
   dough

Force liver and onion through food chopper. Add lemon juice, parsley, salt, pepper and enough milk to make mixture soft enough to spread. Roll biscuit dough into rectangle, spread with liver mixture and roll as for jelly roll. Cut crosswise into 1½-inch slices, place cut side up in greased baking pan and bake in hot oven (400°F.) 15 to 20 minutes. Serves 8.

Braised beef heart cut into slices reveals delicious flavorful onion stuffing

BRAISED LIVER CASSEROLE

3 slices bacon
1½ pounds beef liver, sliced
2 tablespoons flour
1 small onion, diced
1 cup diced celery
3 small carrots, sliced
½ cup hot beef stock or water
1 teaspoon salt

Cook bacon until crisp and remove from skillet. Dredge liver with flour and brown slowly with onion in hot bacon fat. Place vegetables in casserole, arrange liver over them and top with crisp bacon. Add beef stock and salt, cover and cook in slow oven (300°F.) 45 to 60 minutes. Serves 6.

LIVER BIRDS

1½ pounds liver
2 cups small bread cubes
2 tablespoons minced onion
3 slices cooked bacon, diced
Pepper
½ teaspoon salt
Dash celery salt
½ teaspoon baking powder
Hot water

Have liver sliced as thin as possible and remove membrane from edge of each slice. Combine remaining ingredients, moistening with some of the bacon fat and sufficient water to make stuffing firm but not dry. Place a tablespoon or more of stuffing on each slice of liver, roll up and fasten with toothpicks or skewers. Brown in greased skillet, season with additional salt and pepper and cover bottom of pan with water. Cover pan tightly and simmer about 2 hours, turning rolls occasionally. Remove rolls, make gravy of remaining liquid Serves 6.

Liver braised with vegetables is an ever popular old time favorite

ITALIAN LIVER

1½ pounds liver
2 tablespoons flour
1 onion, chopped
1 green pepper, chopped
¾ cup chopped mushrooms
3 tablespoons fat
3 cups cooked tomatoes
½ clove garlic
1½ teaspoons salt
⅛ teaspoon pepper
3 cups cooked spaghetti
Grated cheese

Dip liver into boiling water; let stand 5 minutes; drain. Cut into cubes and dredge with flour. Brown liver, onion, green pepper and mushrooms in fat. Add tomatoes, garlic and seasonings. Simmer 25 minutes. Serve over spaghetti with grated cheese. Serves 6.

BAKED LIVER

2 pounds beef or pork liver
  (1 thick piece)
4 slices bacon, 1 onion, sliced
2 teaspoons Worcestershire sauce
2 tablespoons catchup
1 tablespoon chopped green pepper
Salt and pepper, Hot water

Place liver in greased baking dish and cover with bacon slices. Add remaining ingredients, using enough hot water to nearly cover liver. Cover and cook in slow oven (300°F.) about 1½ hours. Remove cover for last 15 minutes to brown bacon slices. Serves 6.

LIVER IN SOUR CREAM

1½ pounds liver
⅓ cup butter
2 tablespoons flour
1¼ teaspoons salt
Dash pepper
1½ cups sour cream

Have liver sliced ¾ inch thick. Trim off skin and tough fibers. Brown liver on both sides in butter. Remove liver; add flour, salt and pepper to butter and blend until smooth. Add cream and cook 1 minute, stirring constantly. Return liver to skillet; cover closely, and bake in slow oven (300°F.) about 1 hour, or until liver is tender. Serves 5 or 6.

CREOLE LIVER

4 slices bacon
1 pound lamb liver, sliced
½ green pepper, diced
2 cups chopped tomatoes
⅛ teaspoon cayenne
1½ teaspoons salt
⅛ teaspoon curry powder or
  chili powder

Dice bacon, fry until crisp and remove from fat. Dredge liver with flour and brown in bacon fat. Add remaining ingredients and bacon. Cover and simmer for 45 minutes. Serve with spaghetti. Serves 5.

FRENCH FRIED LIVER

1 pound liver, sliced thin
Flour
Salt
Pepper

Wash liver with cold water and dry thoroughly. Cut into lengths about ⅜ inch wide. Roll in flour, seasoned with salt and pepper. Cook in hot deep fat (375° F.) until brown. Drain on absorbent paper. Serves 4.

LIVER À LA BOURGEOISE

1 carrot, shredded
1 onion, minced
1 turnip, diced
1 bay leaf
2 tablespoons fat
1 tablespoon flour
2½ pounds liver (1 piece)
2 cups water or stock
Salt and pepper

Brown carrot, onion, turnip and bay leaf in fat. Add flour and blend, then add liver and water. Season and simmer for 1¼ to 1½ hours. Serves 6 to 8.

PAN-BROILED LIVER

3 pounds liver
Bacon fat
Water

Cut liver into ¼- to ½-inch slices. Remove outside membrane and any veins or blood clots. Heat skillet, lightly greased with bacon fat and sear liver on both sides, then cook slowly until as well done as desired. A little water or tomato juice may be added during last of cooking. Serves 8.

Pan-fry or broil 16 slices bacon and keep hot to serve with liver.

Baked whole liver with vegetables combines high nutritive value and economy

CORNISH PASTIES

½ pound liver, diced
3 potatoes, diced
1 onion, minced
Salt and pepper
1¾ cups sifted flour
1 teaspoon baking powder
⅛ teaspoon salt
6 tablespoons shortening

Mix liver, potatoes and onion together and season with salt and pepper. Sift flour, baking powder and salt together; cut in shortening and when well blended add sufficient water to make dough. Place dough on a floured board and roll out ¼ inch thick. Cut into squares or circles and place a little of the meat mixture on half of each. Fold dough and press edges together. Bake in a slow oven (325°F.) about 1 hour. Serves 4.

LIVER AND HAM LOAF OR RING

1 pound cooked liver
½ pound cooked ham
½ cup bread crumbs
1 egg, beaten
½ teaspoon salt, Paprika
1 tablespoon grated onion
1 tablespoon minced parsley
Milk

Force liver and ham through food chopper and combine with remaining ingredients, adding enough milk to bind mixture together. Bake in greased loaf pan or ring in 350°F. oven 30 minutes. Unmold and serve for 4.

LIVER DUMPLINGS

¾ pound beef, lamb or pork liver
½ onion
1 strip bacon
3 thick slices dry bread
Water
2 eggs, beaten
2 teaspoons salt
¼ teaspoon pepper
1 teaspoon chopped parsley
¼ cup sifted flour
½ teaspoon baking powder

Slice liver and let stand in hot water for 10 minutes, then grind with onion and bacon. Soften bread in water and squeeze out as much moisture as possible; add eggs, seasoning, parsley and liver. Sift flour and baking powder together and add to liver mixture. Drop by teaspoons into boiling water. Cover tightly and simmer for 10 to 12 minutes. Serve with fried onions or Sauerkraut. Serves 5.

Liver dumplings with sauerkraut was one of grandmother's best ideas

LIVER POT ROAST

¼ cup flour
1½ pounds liver, in one piece
½ cup fat
3 onions, sliced
1 teaspoon salt
¼ teaspoon paprika
1 cup sour cream
½ cup water

Rub flour into liver. Brown in hot fat. Place liver in baking dish. Brown onions in fat and spread over meat. Mix remaining fat with remaining ingredients and pour over meat. Cover, place over low heat or in slow oven (300° F.) and cook gently 1½ hours or until tender. Serves 6.

LIVER SOUFFLÉ

1 cup ground cooked liver
2 eggs, separated
1 cup Medium White Sauce

Stir ground liver and egg yolks into warm sauce. Beat whites until stiff and fold into mixture. Pour into buttered baking dish. Bake in moderate oven (350°F.) Serves 4.

LIVER SAVORY

1 (6-ounce) package noodles
1½ pounds sliced liver
Flour, Salt, Pepper
4 tablespoons fat
¾ cup diced celery
1 cup diced onions
1 green pepper, diced
2½ cups cooked tomatoes
½ pound American cheese, grated

Cook noodles in boiling salted water until tender. Sprinkle liver with flour, salt and pepper. Sauté in fat in skillet until browned. Place in greased baking dish. Combine celery, onions, green pepper and tomatoes; pour over liver. Cover and bake in moderate oven (350°F.) about 1 hour. Place liver on platter. Add cheese to vegetables; stir to melt cheese. Season. Arrange hot drained noodles around liver and border with vegetables. Serves 6.

An appetizing and enticing luncheon—grilled lamb kidneys on broiled fruit slices

STEWED KIDNEYS

3 lamb or pork kidneys
1 sprig parsley, chopped
¼ teaspoon thyme
1 bay leaf, chopped
1½ tablespoons drippings
1 cup sherry wine
1 teaspoon vinegar

Wash kidneys, slice very thin and season with salt and pepper. Cook with herbs in drippings until tender. Add wine and vinegar, heat to boiling and serve at once. Serves 3.

BROILED LAMB KIDNEYS

6 lamb kidneys
1½ cups French dressing
12 slices bacon

Clean kidneys and cut into halves. Marinate in French dressing 12 hours. Drain kidneys and wrap each half in slice of bacon. Place 4 inches below moderate broiler heat and broil 12 to 15 minutes or until bacon is crisp and kidneys are tender. Serve on toast triangles. Serves 6.

Omit bacon. Place each kidney on pineapple or other fruit slice and broil.

SPANISH KIDNEY STEW

4 pork or 6 lamb kidneys
3½ cups water
½ cup chopped onions
2 green peppers, chopped fine
1 cup tomatoes
2 tablespoons cornstarch
1 cup cooked kidney beans
1½ teaspoons salt
¼ teaspoon thyme
½ teaspoon paprika

Wash kidneys and remove tubes and fat. Cut kidneys into ½-inch cubes, place in kettle and cover with 3 cups of water and simmer 1 hour or until tender. Add onions, peppers and tomatoes and cook 20 minutes longer. Mix cornstarch and remaining ½ cup water; add to stew and cook, stirring constantly, until thickened. Add beans, salt and spices and heat to boiling. Serves 6 to 8.

STEAK AND KIDNEY PIE

1½ pounds steak (beef or veal)
½ pound kidney
Flour
Salt and pepper
1 tablespoon chopped onion
1 tablespoon minced parsley
½ pound mushrooms, sliced
Water or stock
Pastry

Cut steak and kidney into ½-inch cubes and dredge with flour. Season with salt and pepper. Arrange meat in greased casserole and add onion, parsley, mushrooms and sufficient water to cover meat. Cover casserole and cook in a moderate oven (350° F.) 1 hour or until meat is almost tender. Remove cover and replace it with pastry, pricking crust to allow steam to escape. Return to a very hot oven (450° F.) and bake for 15 minutes or until crust is browned. Serves 4.

Pastry, rice, mashed potatoes or biscuits in attractive shapes make steak and kidney pies a new experience

SPICED STEAK AND KIDNEY PIE

½ cup flour
½ teaspoon ginger
Dash marjoram
Dash thyme
2 pounds rump or chuck steak
2 lamb kidneys
1 teaspoon salt
1 teaspoon prepared mustard
1 tablespoon Worcestershire sauce
Boiling water
4 onions, sliced
Baking Powder Biscuit dough or Pastry

Mix flour, ginger, marjoram and thyme. Cut meat into cubes and dredge with flour mixture. Place in baking dish, add salt, mustard and Worcestershire sauce. Cover with water and simmer 1 hour. Add onions and simmer until onions and meat are almost tender. Cover with biscuit or pastry crust and bake in very hot oven (450°F.) until crust is brown. Serves 8.

Simmer mixture in saucepan, bake in individual casseroles.

TONGUE

Tongue is sold fresh, pickled or corned, and smoked. Wash tongue thoroughly in warm water and remove blood vessels and clotted blood from fresh tongue. Soak pickled or smoked tongue several hours before cooking.

FRESH TONGUE—Cover with water, add 1 teaspoon salt for each quart of water and simmer until tender. Allow 3 to 4 hours for large beef tongues, 1 to 1½ hours for pork, lamb or veal tongues.

PICKLED TONGUE — Cover tongue with cold water, heat to boiling. Pour off water, cover with fresh water and simmer 4 to 5 hours or until tender.

SMOKED TONGUE — Cover mild-cured tongue with cold water, heat to boiling, reduce heat; simmer 4 hours or until tender.

FOR ADDITIONAL FLAVOR—Add 1 onion sliced, ½ clove garlic sliced, peppercorns and, if desired, thyme or sage.

Cut up the tripe, dip in batter and brown in a skillet if you want something really good and unusual

BOILED BEEF TONGUE

1 fresh beef tongue
2 medium onions
1 carrot
¾ cup diced celery and leaves
6 sprigs parsley
8 peppercorns
1 teaspoon salt
Boiling water

Place ingredients in kettle, using just enough water to cover tongue. Simmer for about 3 hours or until tongue is tender; drain, saving liquid to use for stock. Remove skin and roots from tongue. Serve with Horseradish Sauce. Serves 6 to 8.

BAKED TONGUE AND NOODLES

¾ pound sliced cooked tongue
3½ cups cooked noodles
2 cups cooked tomatoes
¼ cup cracker crumbs
1 tablespoon butter

Arrange layers of tongue and noodles in baking dish. Add tomatoes, cover with crumbs and dot with butter. Bake in moderate oven (350°F.) 30 minutes. Serves 6.

SMOKED TONGUE IN RAISIN SAUCE

1½ cups Raisin Sauce (p. 854)
8 slices cooked smoked tongue

Use stock from cooking tongue in preparing raisin sauce. Heat tongue in sauce. Serves 4.

SPICED TONGUE MOLD

1½ tablespoons unflavored gelatin
¼ cup cold water
2 cups stock from cooking tongue
½ teaspoon salt
⅛ teaspoon pepper
½ teaspoon dry mustard
1 tablespoon lemon juice
1 teaspoon Worcestershire sauce
2 cups chopped cooked tongue
2 hard-cooked eggs, sliced
4 tablespoons chopped sweet pickles
¼ cup mayonnaise

Soften gelatin in cold water and dissolve in boiling stock. Add seasonings, lemon juice and Worcestershire sauce. Chill until mixture begins to thicken, then fold in remaining ingredients. Chill until firm. Serves 6.

SWEET-SOUR TONGUE

2 tablespoons butter
2 tablespoons flour
½ teaspoon salt
¼ teaspoon pepper
1 cup tongue stock
2 tablespoons sugar
2 tablespoons vinegar
8 slices cooked smoked tongue

Blend butter, flour and seasonings. Add stock and cook until thickened. Add remaining ingredients. Heat. Serves 4.

FRIED PICKLED TRIPE

Parboil pickled tripe about 5 minutes. Dry and dip into beaten egg, dredge with flour and brown on both sides in greased skillet.

BOILED TRIPE

Cover fresh uncooked tripe with cold water, heat to boiling, cook 5 minutes and drain. Cover with fresh boiling water, add 1 teaspoon salt for each quart of water, heat to boiling and simmer until tripe is tender, about 4 hours. It tripe is cut into serving pieces before cooking, it should be tender in about 2 hours. Drain tripe, dry thoroughly and use as desired. Marinate overnight in French dressing before using, if desired.

If fresh tripe is purchased already cooked, wash several times in hot water, dry and marinate overnight in French dressing or soak in cold water. Cut into serving pieces, cover with boiling water and simmer 15 minutes. Drain, cover with cold water, heat to boiling and drain.

TRIPE PATTIES

1 pound boiled tripe
1 egg
½ cup bread crumbs
½ teaspoon onion juice
1 teaspoon salt
Dash pepper

Grind tripe and combine with remaining ingredients. Shape into patties and fry in greased skillet until browned. Serves 4.

BAKED TRIPE WITH BACON— Wrap each patty with slice of bacon and bake in hot oven (425°F.) 8 to 10 minutes, or until bacon is crisp.

TRIPE FRITTERS—Sift 1 cup sifted flour with ½ teaspoon salt. Combine 1 cup milk, 1 tablespoon melted shortening and 1 egg, slightly beaten. Add to flour and mix until smooth. Dip tripe patties into the batter and fry in hot deep fat (380°F.) until browned.

Make patties ½ inch thick and brown under low broiler heat.

STUFFINGS FOR MEAT

Many kinds of meat may be roasted and served with stuffing. The stuffing may be baked in a separate pan, arranged in alternate layers with the meat, or filled into a pocket or opening in the meat. The shoulder of lamb, pork or veal may be boned, spread with stuffing and rolled or stuffing put into opening. Stuffing may also be baked in a ring mold and center filled with creamed meats.

BREAD STUFFING

4 cups soft bread crumbs or cubes
¼ to ½ cup melted fat
1 teaspoon salt
¼ teaspoon pepper

Combine ingredients and stuff lightly into meat, allowing room for expansion; or use as desired.

APPLE STUFFING—Use the larger amount of fat in bread stuffing. Add 1 cup chopped sour apples.

CELERY STUFFING—Add 1 cup minced celery to Onion Stuffing.

CHILI STUFFING—Add ½ cup chili sauce or tomato catchup and 1 tablespoon minced onion to bread stuffing. Use ¼ cup fat.

MUSHROOM STUFFING—Add ¾ cup chopped mushrooms to Onion or Celery Stuffing.

ONION STUFFING—Add 2 tablespoons minced onion.

OYSTER STUFFING—Add ½ pint oysters, 1 tablespoon chopped onion, 1 tablespoon chopped pimiento, 1 tablespoon chopped green pepper and ½ cup minced celery to Bread Stuffing.

PRUNE STUFFING—Omit fat; add 2 cups prunes, cooked and chopped; 1 cup diced celery; ¼ cup diced onion and ½ green pepper, chopped. Moisten with meat stock or hot water.

RAISIN STUFFING—Use ½ cup of fat in bread stuffing and add 1 cup seedless raisins.

SAGE STUFFING—Add 2 teaspoons sage, 2 tablespoons chopped onion and 1 tablespoon chopped parsley.

SAUSAGE STUFFING—Omit fat. Brown 1½ cups sausage slightly and add to bread stuffing. Three dozen chopped cooked chestnuts may be added.

CORN BREAD STUFFING

4 cups boiling water
4 cups broken Corn Bread
1 onion, grated
1 cup diced celery
2 eggs, beaten
½ cup melted butter
Salt and pepper

Pour boiling water over bread and squeeze out fairly dry. Add remaining ingredients and mix well. Use for stuffing pork or lamb. Serves 6 to 8.

OPOSSUM STUFFING

1 large onion, chopped fine
1 tablespoon fat
Opossum liver (optional)
1 cup bread crumbs
Chopped red pepper
Dash Worcestershire sauce
1 hard-cooked egg, chopped fine
Salt

Brown onion in fat. Add finely chopped opossum liver and cook until liver is tender. Add crumbs, a little red pepper, Worcestershire sauce, egg, salt and water to moisten.

DUMPLINGS FOR STEW

2 cups sifted flour
4 teaspoons baking powder
½ teaspoon salt
About ¾ cup milk

Sift flour, baking powder and salt together. Add milk all at once and stir to make a soft dough. Drop from tablespoon into simmering stew, cover tightly and cook 12 to 15 minutes without removing cover. Serves 6

Savory stuffing makes a company dish of a boned shoulder of lamb

Poultry

250 Ways

to Prepare

Poultry

CLEANING AND TRUSSING POULTRY

Remove pin feathers from chicken with tweezers or dull edge of knife, singe off hairs quickly and cut off head. About 2 inches above foot insert knife between the leg bone and cartilage to make an opening entirely through leg. Be careful not to sever any of tendons. Pull out tendons one at a time by inserting skewer or pick under each and pulling tendons from drumstick. Make an incision lengthwise of body almost to breastbone. Cut out vent, loosen and remove entrails, giblets, kidneys and lungs, taking care not to break the small green gall bladder and to remove all the lung tissue along the backbone. Slit neck skin down the back, remove crop and windpipe from the neck opening. Cut off neck close to body but leave the neck skin intact. Save neck for soup or stock. Remove thin membrane, arteries, veins and blood around heart. Cut fat and membrane from gizzard and make a long gash along edge through thickest part, cutting in as far as inner greyish lining, but being careful not to pierce it. Pull gizzard open and discard inner lining. Separate gall bladder carefully from liver, removing any of liver that has a greenish tinge. Wash giblets thoroughly and use in stuffing, gravy or as desired. Cut out oil sac above tail, being careful not to break it. Scrub chicken inside and out in warm water to which a little soda has been added but do not soak in water. Dry and rub inside with salt, ⅛ to ¼ teaspoon per pound. Loosen breast skin from meat with handle of spoon and cover meat with a ¼-inch layer of stuffing. This helps to keep breast meat moist. Draw neck skin to back. Turn wing tips up and under back. From this point follow any one of these methods:

METHOD 1—Insert trussing needle through body of chicken below knee joint and pull cord through; continue cord through wings. Tie tightly to hold wings close to body. Stuff neck opening of chicken with stuffing and tuck end of neck skin under

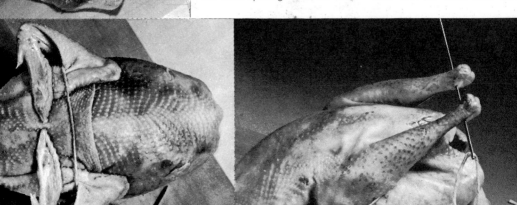

cord. Using another piece of cord, insert needle through legs near joint. Stuff body cavity and truss opening with trussing pins or cord. Draw cord from legs around tail piece and tie legs down close to body.

METHOD 2—Fill neck cavity with stuffing and fasten neck skin flat to back with skewer or cord. Fill body cavity and fasten with steel pins placed across opening at regular intervals. Lace cord around pins to bring edges of skin together. (After roasting remove pins and cord will fall off.) A skewer may be inserted through body under legs as an aid in tying legs close to body. Illustrations, page 441.

METHOD 3—Have incision for drawing cut near one leg instead of down the center. Fill neck cavity with stuffing and fasten neck skin flat to back with skewer or cord. Tie a cord firmly around lower end of drumstick to prevent skin and meat from shrinking away from bone during roasting. Fill body cavity with stuffing, allowing room for expansion. Overlap edges of skin at incision, press leg down firmly to hold edges together and tie both legs with cord to tail piece, holding them firmly against body. Cross cord over back, catch around the wings or skewer, pull wings close to body and tie.

TIME AND TEMPERATURE TABLE FOR ROASTING POULTRY AND GAME

The latest research proves that a constant low temperature produces juicier, more tender meat with less shrinkage than the old method of baking in which the meat was first seared in a very hot oven, then roasted at a reduced temperature for the remainder of the cooking period.

To figure the cooking time for fowl or game multiply the weight of the fowl (after stuffing or before drawing) by the minutes per pound given, using the lower figure for large birds and the higher figure for smaller birds. In the four cases indicated the total cooking time is given instead of the minutes per pound. Time given is based on meat at room temperature which gives the most satisfactory results. If it is chilled add 15 to 30 minutes to the total cooking time.

Birds	Oven Temp.	Time per Pound
Capon	325°F.	22-30 min.
Chicken, Roasting	300°F.	30-45 min.
Duck	325°F.	20-30 min.
Duckling	325°F.	15-20 min.
Goose	325°F.	20-25 min.
Grouse	350°F.	60-75 min. (Total)
Guinea Hen	350°F.	20-22 min.
Partridge	350°F.	30-40 min. (Total)
Pheasant	325°F.	15-20 min.
Quail	350°F.	25-30 min. (Total)
Squab or Pigeon	325°F.	45-60 min. (Total)
Turkey		
8-10 lbs.	300°F.	20-25 min.
10-16 lbs.	300°F.	18-20 min.
18-25 lbs.	300°F.	15-18 min.
Wild Duck or		
Goose (rare)	325°F.	10-12 min.
Well done	325°F.	15-20 min.
Wild Turkey	325°F.	20-25 min.

It is easy enough to truss for roasting. These illustrations show how it is done

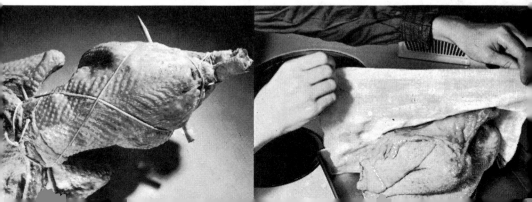

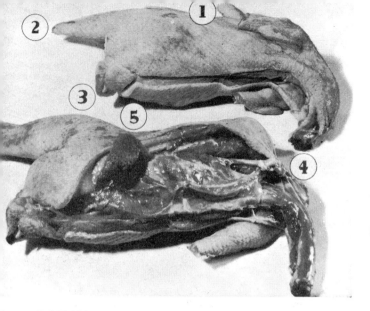

STEP 3. Remove the flesh (with the legs and wings) by pulling away from the carcass. (6) Breast-flesh being pulled away from breastbone. (7) The two parts are pulled away until connected only at the vent and below the tip of the breastbone. Separate here by cutting through the thin layer of flesh and skin.

STEP 4. Remove bones from legs (drumstick and thigh) and wings (1 bone) by cutting and scraping. Work down from inside of body, leaving outside skin intact.

THIGH BONE—Cut through flesh to bone from inside and scrape flesh from bone. Cut through joint between thigh and drumstick. Pull out thigh bone.

DRUMSTICK AND WING BONES—Cut (8) in a circle through skin, flesh and thin tissue at smaller end of drumstick. Hold the bone firmly, small end up at right angles to the table and cut and scrape flesh loose from bone. Pull bone out.
Cut out the wishbone which has remained in the breast.

BONING OF CHICKEN

A frying or roasting chicken may be used for boning. Remove pin feathers, singe and wash but do not draw.

STEP 1. Cut off head, wings up to second joint (1) and legs at knee joint (2). This loosens skin and flesh for easy removal of bone after it has been worked loose from flesh.
Cut along the center back from the neck downward, completing the cut down either side of the tail and around vent (3).

STEP 2. Using a sharp knife, cut the flesh (with skin) away from the back and ribs (4) down to the keel bone. Remove flesh from the keel bone by cutting and by pushing with the fingers. Insert knife tip into each hip joint and turn so as to break this joint. This separates the leg bones from the body. Break wing joints in same way. At eye muscle (5) loosen flesh with skin from the body on both sides, leaving legs and wings attached.

STEP 5. Place the completely boned bird skin side down, sprinkle inside with salt and place stuffing (9) in the center.
The stuffing and meat juices are held in by an envelope fold. Lay one side (10) over the stuffing, overlap with the other side (11) and fold down the neck skin (12)

STEP 6. Tie cords around the body across the breast. Rub unsalted fat thoroughly over skin of bird. Place bird on rack of shallow pan, or place on the center of a sheet of greased paper which extends 2 inches on the sides and 3 inches at the ends beyond the bird. Bring side up to the bird

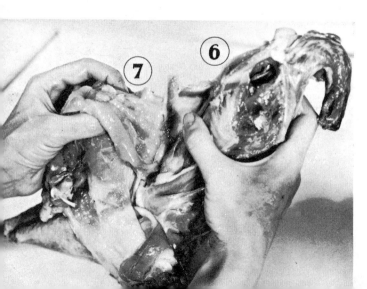

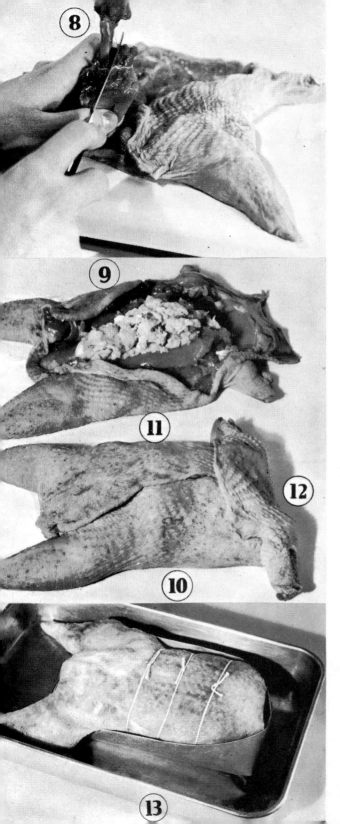

BONING OF CHICKEN—Cont.

folding back enough paper so the sides are not quite as high as the bird—otherwise they would prevent browning. Lap sides over each other at the ends, then slip under the bird. (13) Cook as for Roast Chicken. Clip cords when the bird is half cooked, so that there are no marks over the skin after roasting. Draw carcass; save giblets; use bones for stock.

BAKED CHICKEN WITH HAM STUFFING

5-pound roasting chicken
1 pound cooked ham, chopped
¼ teaspoon salt
Grated rind 1 lemon
8 olives, chopped
1 hard-cooked egg, chopped
Pepper
½ cup seedless raisins
1 potato, finely diced
Chopped cooked giblets

Cover chicken with water and simmer until nearly tender. Drain. Combine remaining ingredients, moistening with stock if necessary. Stuff parboiled chicken and bake in hot oven (425°F.) until tender and browned, basting occasionally with stock. Serves 5.

INDIVIDUAL HALVES OF CHICKENS

3 broiling chickens
3 cups stuffing

Place chickens, split lengthwise into halves, on rack in pan, skin side up. Brown in a hot broiler. Place in baking dish, skin side down; place ½ cup of stuffing in each cavity. Cover tightly and bake in slow oven (325° F.) 45 minutes or until tender Greased brown paper may be placed over the stuffing to prevent drying out. Serves 6.

FROZEN POULTRY

The use of frozen poultry has rapidly increased both because of the high quality of the product prepared by commercial methods and the increasing number of freezing plants in many communities which make it possible for families to prepare and freeze their own poultry for future use. Frozen poultry should be thawed in the refrigerator or at room temperature, though it may be placed in cold water to hasten thawing if necessary. However, some loss of flavor may result. All frozen foods should be cooked as soon as thawed and should never be refrozen.

After poultry has been thawed it may be cooked by any of the methods ordinarily used.

CAPON

Capons are large, plump young roosters weighing 6 to 7 pounds and especially fattened for the table. They are prepared the same as chickens. For stuffing choose a mild flavoring such as oysters, chestnuts, mushrooms, marrons or nuts as the meat is very delicately flavored. Serve with Gravy. Allow ¾ to 1 pound for each serving.

ROAST CHICKEN

4- to 5-pound roasting chicken
Salt (⅛ to ¼ teaspoon per pound)
Stuffing, Melted fat

Singe chicken, clean, wash and dry. Rub inside with salt. Stuff lightly with any desired stuffing and truss. Rub surface with unsalted fat. Place on rack in an uncovered roaster, breast up. Cover with layer of body fat from chicken, then with a clean cloth or with a cloth dipped into melted unsalted fat. Roast uncovered in slow oven (300°F.) until tender, basting occasionally with drippings unless using the layer of body fat, which serves to baste the bird as it melts. Season with additional salt when half done. Remove cloth near the end of roasting period to finish browning. A chicken from 4 to 5 pounds requires 30 to 35 minutes per pound; a smaller chicken, 35 to 45 minutes per pound. Weight should be taken before drawing or after stuffing. Serve on a hot platter with Gravy made from drippings. Cooked giblets may be added to Gravy. Serves 4-5. Use chicken feet for stock.

ROAST CAPON

6-pound capon
Salt
4½ pounds sweetpotatoes
¾ cup fat
2 cups marrons
Chopped leaves 1 bunch celery
1 tablespoon minced onion
½ cup heavy cream

Dress capon, clean and rub inside well with salt. Boil enough sweetpotatoes to make 6 cups mashed. Add salt and ½ cup fat. Mash marrons, reserving 6 for later use, and add to mashed potatoes; mix well. Dice reserved marrons and stir into stuffing. Stuff capon with this mixture and close opening. Rub the capon with unsalted fat. Brown celery leaves and onion in remaining fat in roaster. breast up and cover with cloth Place capon on the sautéed leaves, dipped into melted fat. Bake in slow oven (325°F.) 22 to 30 minutes per pound, basting frequently with melted fat. When capon is nearly tender, remove celery from pan, remove cloth and brush breast with the cream. Continue roasting until tender. Prepare Gravy from the drippings in roaster, strain and serve with capon. Serves 6 to 8.

Use a skewer to pull out the tendons one at a time

BAKED HALF CHICKEN

½ (5- to 6-pound) chicken
1 recipe Giblet Stuffing
Melted fat

Simmer chicken in seasoned water until tender, 2 to 3 hours. Arrange stuffing to keep outline of chicken in bottom of greased shallow pan. Press cooked chicken, cut side down, on stuffing. Brush chicken with melted fat. Bake uncovered in hot oven (400°F.) 30 minutes or until chicken is browned. Serves 4.

BAKED CASSEROLE

4-pound chicken, ¼ cup milk
¼ cup flour
1 teaspoon salt
⅛ teaspoon pepper, ½ cup fat
½ pound mushrooms
1 tablespoon chopped onion
2 cups hot cream or evaporated milk

Cut chicken into serving portions, dip into milk, then into mixture of flour, salt and pepper. Brown chicken in fat and place in deep baking dish. Cook mushrooms for 3 minutes in fat remaining in pan and add with onion to chicken. Cover with the cream. Cook in moderate oven (350°F.) until chicken is tender and the cream cooks to a thick sauce, from 1 to 2 hours. Serves 8.

BAKED CHICKEN IN CREAM —Omit mushrooms and onion.

CHICKEN AND MUSHROOM CASSEROLE—Omit mushrooms, onion and cream. Add ½ cup hot water to chicken before baking. When chicken is tender mix 1 can mushroom soup with ¾ cup milk, heat and pour over chicken. Bake 15 to 20 minutes longer.

The luscious modern way: split or buy the chicken split in half, press down on stuffing and bake

BROILING

Broiling means to cook by direct (radiant) heat from hot coals, a gas flame or an electric element. The small young chicken (1½ to 2½ pounds) customarily chosen for broiling cannot be satisfactorily cooked in less than 45 minutes. The variation in time is allowed for differences in size, equipment and degree of browning desired. When more than 3 broilers are cooked, allow a longer total time.

SNAPPING OUT BREASTBONE

This process makes fried or broiled chicken easier to eat, as well as easier to cook and more attractive in appearance. Cut out backbone by cutting through ribs along both sides of backbone. Remove neck and backbone, open carcass out and slit thin skin covering the breastbone. "Snap out" the breastbone.

Without breast and backbone your broiler should lie flat

DIRECTIONS FOR BROILING

Temperature: moderate (350° F.)
Time: 45 to 60 minutes
(Broiling rack—about 5 inches from heat)
Have chickens at room temperature. Cut into halves, "snap out" the breastbone and, working from inside, break the three or four major joints—hip joint where leg joins body, knee joint between drumstick and thigh and two wing joints. Brush all over with melted or softened fat. Place on heated rack, skin side down, sprinkle each half with ¼ teaspoon salt—slightly less if butter is used for greasing. Replace rack about 5 inches from heat. Adjust heat to moderate so that after cooking about 15 minutes, the surface of the chickens will be only delicately browned. By this time the fleshy portions (sides of breast and thigh which are not in contact with direct heat) may not be browned or well cooked. Place halves supporting each other in a standing position, thus bringing these parts nearer the heat. Turn

again skin side down. Cook about 15 minutes in each position.
Turn skin side up. Brush with fat any parts not satisfactorily browned. Cook about 15 minutes longer, when chicken should be browned and thoroughly cooked. During this last cooking any well browned portions may be covered by parts of other halves, thus bringing a too light portion nearer the heat. Transfer to warm serving platter. Pour pan drippings over chicken. Or, prepare a gravy with the drippings. Giblets previously cooked may be finely chopped and added. Garlic or onion flavor is a delicious addition. Rub broiler rack or service platter lightly with a freshly cut surface of either seasoning. Or simmer a bit of the seasoning in the gravy, then remove it before serving. If chicken won't lie flat, cover with a heavy lid or wire rack. The cooking time can be shortened by placing the bird closer to the heat with fair results, although the appearance of the cooked bird is less attractive. Allow ½ fowl per person.

MARINATED BROILED CHICKEN

2 broiling chickens
½ to ¾ cup olive oil
⅓ cup chopped parsley
1 clove garlic, finely chopped

Split chickens down the back. Combine remaining ingredients to make a marinade. Marinate chickens in this mixture from ½ hour to overnight. The longer they can marinate, the less garlic is necessary. Drain off marinade. Arrange chickens skin side down on preheated broiler, placed about 5 inches from heat; broil about 45 to 50 minutes, basting every 5 to 10 minutes with marinade. Serve at once on preheated or sizzling platter. Serves 4.

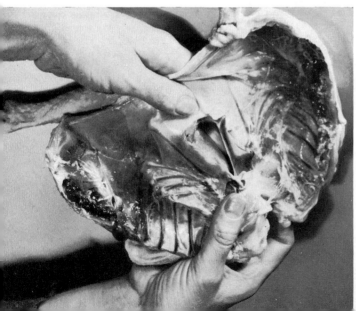

BARBECUED CHICKEN

2 broiling chickens
Melted fat
⅓ cup cider vinegar
1 teaspoon Worcestershire
    sauce
½ teaspoon onion salt
¼ teaspoon garlic salt
½ teaspoon salt
⅛ teaspoon pepper
Dash paprika
1 tablespoon tomato paste
½ cup melted fat

Have chickens split down the back. Clean thoroughly. Brush with melted fat, and place on heated broiling rack, skin side down. Replace rack about 5 inches from heat, broil about 15 minutes, turn, brush with fat and broil on other side, turn again having skin side down. Allow 45 to 60 minutes for broiling chickens. Combine remaining ingredients to make a sauce and baste chicken while broiling. Serves 4.

Combine 5 tablespoons melted fat, 2 tablespoons vinegar, ½ teaspoon dry mustard and ½ teaspoon Worcestershire sauce. Use instead of sauce given above.

CHICKEN À LA TARTARE

1 broiling chicken
½ cup fat, melted
4 sprigs parsley
1 small onion
¼ pound mushrooms
1 clove garlic
½ teaspoon salt
⅛ teaspoon pepper
Bread crumbs

Clean chicken, split into halves and place in skillet with fat. Chop parsley, onion, mushrooms and garlic and add to fat with salt and pepper. Pour over chicken, cover and simmer for 15 minutes, turning occasionally. Dip chicken into bread crumbs and broil until browned. Serves 2.

If you choose, your broiling chicken may be cut completely into halves

BROILED SQUAB CHICKEN WITH SAUTÉED PINEAPPLE

2 (1¼- to 1½-pound)
    broiling chickens
Pineapple juice
Melted fat
Salt
8 slices pineapple
1 tablespoon butter
Toast tips

Split chickens down the back. Cover with pineapple juice for 1 hour, then drain, dry, brush with fat and sprinkle with salt. Place skin side down on greased, preheated broiler rack. Place 4 or 5 inches below heat. Broil for about 15 minutes, then turn birds skin side up. Place rack 6 to 8 inches from heat. Broil birds about 15 minutes longer, turning frequently until brown and tender. Drain and dry pineapple slices, then brown in a small amount of butter. Serve broiled chicken on toast tips with sautéed pineapple topped with jelly. Allow ¾ pound per person.

BROILED CHICKEN WITH TOMATOES

1 broiling chicken
2 tablespoons butter or other
    fat
2 tomatoes
Salt, Pepper
Sugar
4 slices bacon

Clean chicken and steam until tender. Split. Remove ribs and as many small bones as possible without breaking meat. Rub with butter. Broil until crisp on the outside. Cut tomatoes crosswise into halves and season with salt, pepper and sugar. Broil tomatoes. Fry bacon until crisp and shape into curls. Serve chicken on toast and garnish with tomatoes and bacon curls. Serves 2.

Brown 2 chopped onions in 2 tablespoons butter. Add 2 tablespoons each flour and tomato paste, 2 cups boiling water, 2 bouillon cubes, 2 teaspoons Worcestershire sauce, 1 teaspoon each sugar and mustard. Cook 10 minutes and serve over broilers.

TO CUT A CHICKEN FOR STEWING, FRIC-ASSEEING OR FRYING

Clean and draw chicken as for roasting. Using a sharp knife, cut the skin and flesh between the legs and body, bend legs back far enough to snap the hip joints, then cut through the tendons to these joints, taking off the second joint and drumstick from each side in one piece. Separate thigh and leg at the joint. Break the wing joints and cut off the wings. Cut from breastbone following the ribs to the wing joints. Holding the breastbone firmly with one hand and backbone with the other tear them apart. Starting with knife at right angle to upper part of breastbone cut back as far as the wing joint. Split into halves if desired. Cut back into halves.

LESS TENDER POULTRY MEATS

Birds over 1 year old have varying amounts of connective tissue. Moist heat is necessary to soften this tissue and make the meat palatable.

Moist heat methods used are fricasseeing (same as braising or pot roasting in other meats), stewing, simmering and steaming. Dry heat may be used (roasting, frying or broiling) but it must be either preceded or followed by a moist heat method.

FRICASSEEING

Fricasseeing means to brown the meat in a small quantity of fat and then to cook slowly (simmer) in a covered utensil in the meat juices or in added liquid (milk, cream, vegetable juice, wine). Cut the chicken into serving pieces. If desired rub thoroughly with seasoned flour. Brown in a small quantity of fat. Add ½ cup liquid (water, milk, cream, stock, etc.). Add more liquid if necessary during the cooking. Add ¼ teaspoon salt per pound of poultry. Cover tightly and either simmer until tender or transfer to slow oven (300°-350°F.) and bake until tender, 1 to 2 hours. Vegetables may be added during the cooking.

Add the vegetables you like to stewed chicken and drop in dumplings

STEWING

Stewing means to cook by simmering in a large or small amount of water depending upon the dish to be served. The meat of chicken cooked this way is used for creaming, à la king, à la Newburg, pie, frying, for pressed chicken salad, sandwiches, shortcake, soufflés, timbales, stew, etc.

STEAMED CHICKEN

Steaming means to cook in steam with or without pressure. This method is used when it is particularly desirable to retain the shape and preserve maximum of juices within the meat. Steaming requires slightly longer than stewing or simmering. A pressure cooker may be used in which case the cooking time is considerably shortened (⅓ to ½ the time). Poultry cooked by steaming is used in the same manner as stewed chicken.

STEWED CHICKEN AND DROP DUMPLINGS

1 stewing chicken
1 small onion
Salt, Pepper
1 cup sifted flour
2 teaspoons baking powder
½ teaspoon salt
Sprig parsley, minced
½ cup milk

Clean chicken and cut into serving portions; place in kettle and partly cover with water. Add onion, salt and pepper and cook until tender, 2½ to 3 hours. Mix flour, baking powder, salt, minced parsley, and milk to a thick batter and drop from spoon into boiling chicken broth, cover tightly and cook for 20 minutes without raising lid. Place chicken on platter and surround with dumplings. Serves 6.

CHICKEN STEW

4 peppercorns
1 clove
1 small carrot, sliced
1 small onion, sliced
2 ribs of celery with leaves,
    cut up
4-pound chicken, cut into serving
    pieces
1 teaspoon salt

Tie peppercorns, clove and vegetables in cheesecloth and place in kettle with chicken. Add water so the chicken will be covered to depth of ½ inch. Cover and simmer until tender, about 2 hours, adding salt when half done. Remove seasonings and chicken. If a rich flavored gravy is desired, boil stock down to about 2 cups. For each cup of stock use 1 tablespoon flour mixed with a little cold water. Add to hot stock gradually stirring constantly, and cook until thickened. Return chicken to boiling gravy. Add more seasoning if desired. Serve with dumplings, noodles or rice. Serves 8 to 10.

BROWNED CHICKEN WITH MUSHROOM SAUCE—Dredge stewed chicken in mixture of flour, salt and pepper. Brown in fat and serve with Mushroom Sauce.

FRICASSEE OF CHICKEN

4-pound chicken
¼ cup flour
3 tablespoons chicken fat
2 teaspoons salt
Paprika
Boiling water (about 3 to 3½
    cups)

Clean chicken and cut into serving portions; dredge with flour and brown in fat. Add seasonings and enough boiling water to half cover; simmer, closely covered, until tender, about 1½ to 3 hours. Serves 6 to 8.

STEWED CHICKEN À L'ESPAGNOL

5-pound chicken
Salt, Pepper, Flour
¼ cup fat
2 medium onions, sliced
1 cup green olives, chopped
1 green pepper, chopped fine
2 cups chopped tomatoes
1 teaspoon sugar
2 cups peas
1 cup sliced mushrooms
2 teaspoons salt
2 tablespoons flour

Clean chicken and cut into serving portions. Season well with salt and pepper and dredge with flour. Brown chicken in fat, remove, and cook onions, olives, green pepper, tomatoes and sugar in the fat for 10 minutes. Add chicken and sufficient water to cover. Simmer, closely covered, for 1½ hours or until chicken is tender. Add peas, mushrooms and salt. Mix flour until smooth with a little cold water and stir gradually into hot stew. Cover and cook for 20 minutes longer. Serves 8 to 10.

Omit olives, tomatoes, peas, mushrooms and flour. Cook chicken as above, adding 1 cup rice browned in oil and 1 tablespoon saffron after 1 hour.

Mother's old-fashioned boiled chicken dinner is as popular as it ever was

OLD-FASHIONED BOILED CHICKEN DINNER

4-pound chicken (frying, roasting
    or stewing hen)
1 teaspoon salt
3 medium potatoes
6 small onions
1 head cauliflower, or
    ¼ head cabbage
12 small carrots
1 pint Brussels sprouts or
    1 bunch broccoli
Parsley for garnish

Cover chicken with water and simmer until tender, 2 to 3 hours, adding salt when about three-fourths done. Remove chicken from cooking water and cook vegetables in chicken stock until tender. Serve chicken with the vegetables. Garnish with parsley. Serves 6 to 8.

CHINESE CHICKEN STEW — Omit vegetables used above. When chicken is tender add 1 cup chopped bamboo shoots, 1 cup sliced mushrooms and 3 tablespoons soy sauce. Cook 30 minutes longer.

BRUNSWICK STEW

2 onions, sliced
2 tablespoons bacon fat
1 2½-pound frying chicken
Salt and pepper
3 cups water
3 tomatoes, peeled and quartered
½ cup sherry
2 teaspoons Worcestershire sauce
1 pound fresh Lima beans
½ cup okra
3 ears green corn
2 tablespoons butter
½ cup bread crumbs

Brown onions in bacon fat. Cut chicken into serving portions, season and brown in bacon fat. Pour off fat and place chicken and onions in heavy kettle. Add water, tomatoes, sherry and Worcestershire sauce. Cook slowly over low heat for ½ hour, add Lima beans, okra and corn, cut from the cob. Simmer for 1 hour, add butter and bread crumbs and cook ½ hour longer. Serves 6

CHICKEN CURRY

4-pound stewing chicken
5 cups boiling water
1 onion, cut fine
4 tablespoons fat
2 tablespoons curry powder
2 cups chicken stock
1 tablespoon flour
1 egg yolk, beaten

Clean chicken and cut into serving portions; cover with water and simmer until tender, 1½ to 3 hours, then remove from liquor. Cook onion in 3 tablespoons fat, remove and brown chicken in remaining fat. Add curry powder and chicken stock, simmer for a few minutes. Combine remaining 1 tablespoon fat with flour and egg yolk, pour into chicken mixture gradually, stirring constantly and cook until thickened. Serve on platter surrounded with hot boiled rice and a mound of grated fresh coconut. Serves 6.

Deviled chicken will delight your most particular friends

DEVILED CHICKEN

1 broiling or frying chicken
Salt and pepper
½ cup fat, melted
2 tablespoons flour
1 cup hot water or soup stock
1½ teaspoons dry mustard
2 teaspoons Worcestershire sauce
2 teaspoons tomato catchup
Paprika

Cut chicken into serving portions, season with salt and pepper and brown in melted fat; remove from pan. Stir flour into fat; add hot water or soup stock. Cook until mixture thickens, stirring constantly. Add next 4 ingredients to cooked sauce. Place chicken in sauce, cover pan and simmer until chicken is tender, about 1 hour. Allow ¾ pound chicken per person.

CHICKEN AND NOODLES

4-pound stewing chicken
Salt
Pepper
Celery greens
1 chicken heart, cut fine
1 chicken gizzard, cut fine
1 pound egg noodles
⅓ cup chopped green onion
⅓ cup shredded cooked ham

Cut chicken into serving portions, cover with cold water, add salt and pepper, and heat to boiling. Simmer until chicken is tender, then remove and shred meat. Add celery greens, chicken heart and gizzard to stock and simmer until tender. Cook noodles until tender in boiling salted water. Drain and rinse in cold water. Serve noodles in deep bowls, add the hot soup to cover, sprinkle with shredded chicken and a little green onion. Garnish with shredded ham. Serves 6.

CHICKEN WITH RICE

2½- to 3-pound chicken
1 small onion, sliced
2 cloves garlic, mashed
2 bay leaves, Water to cover
½ teaspoon salt
1 cup uncooked rice
3 tablespoons butter
1 small onion, minced
1 clove garlic, mashed
½ cup cooked tomatoes
1 tablespoon minced parsley
1 green pepper, thinly sliced
2 pimientos, mashed
2½ cups hot chicken stock

Cut cleaned chicken into serving portions and cook with next 5 ingredients until tender, about 1 hour. Brown rice in butter and cook with remaining ingredients until tender. Serve with chicken. Serves 5.

CASSEROLE ROASTING CHICKEN

4-pound roasting chicken, split into halves
1 teaspoon salt
⅛ teaspoon pepper
Flour
¼ cup olive or salad oil
¼ cup minced onion
1 clove garlic, minced (optional)
½ cup diced carrots
½ cup diced celery
1½ cups water or stock
1 cup mushrooms, sautéed
12 stuffed olives, sliced (optional)

Sprinkle chicken with salt and pepper and dredge with flour. Brown in olive oil and place in baking dish, skin side down. Cook onion, garlic, carrots and celery in remaining oil until onion is transparent. Pour vegetables and water over the chicken, cover and cook in slow oven (325°F.) until tender, about 1½ hours. Cook mushrooms in fat about 5 minutes and add to chicken with olives about 10 minutes before chicken is done. Serve with gravy made from drippings. If strained gravy is desired, add mushrooms after straining out the vegetables. Serves 6 to 8. Desired stuffing may be placed at one side in roaster to cook during the last hour, or baked in a covered greased baking dish. Serve cold as well as hot.

DEVILED CHICKEN BACKS, LEGS AND WINGS

Back, legs and wings of 2 chickens (1½ pounds)
¼ cup melted fat
1 teaspoon mustard
½ teaspoon paprika
½ teaspoon salt
Few grains cayenne
1 teaspoon vinegar
1 cup buttered soft crumbs

Place chicken in baking dish Pour in melted fat. Mix seasonings and vinegar and spread over chicken. Cover with crumbs and bake, covered, at 350°F. until tender. Serves 4.

Heart, gizzard and neck may be simmered in water until partially tender, then cooked in the same way.

STUFFED CHICKEN LEGS

Select large chicken legs. Remove tendons and bone. Fill cavity with any desired stuffing, keeping legs in shape. Close opening with poultry pins. Place in greased baking dish, cover bottom with ½ inch boiling water and cook in moderate oven (350°F.) until tender, about 1 hour. Allow 1 or 2 legs each.

CHICKEN AU GRATIN

4- to 5-pound chicken
1 teaspoon salt
½ teaspoon pepper
1 tablespoon lemon juice
4 tablespoons olive oil
4 tablespoons fat
3 tablespoons flour, 2 cups stock
1 teaspoon Worcestershire sauce
¼ cup grated cheese
1 cup soft crumbs

Cut chicken into serving portions and marinate overnight in dressing made by mixing together salt, pepper, lemon juice and olive oil. Drain. Cover chicken with hot water and simmer until tender. Drain off stock and save. Place chicken in greased casserole. Melt fat, blend in flour, add stock and Worcestershire sauce and cook until thickened, stirring constantly. Pour over chicken. Cover and cook in moderate oven (350° F.) about 20 minutes. Remove cover, sprinkle with cheese and crumbs and cook, uncovered, until surface is browned and cheese partially melted. Serves 8 to 10.

To vary, omit cheese and use fine crumbs. Roll 1 pint oysters in the crumbs, place in casserole with chicken and sprinkle with remaining crumbs.

A shallow glass casserole is perfect for deviled chicken legs. Dress with paper frills before serving

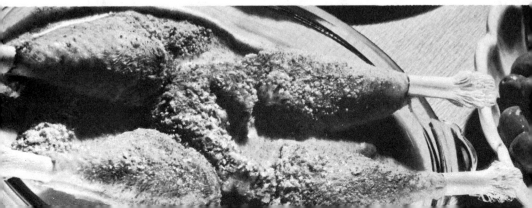

You will enjoy spaghetti more than ever as à la diable

POULTRY SOUFFLÉ

2 tablespoons fat
2 tablespoons flour
1/8 teaspoon pepper
1 teaspoon salt
1/4 teaspoon paprika
1 1/2 cups milk or stock
1/2 cup soft bread crumbs
3 eggs, separated
2 cups chopped cooked turkey,
    chicken, goose or duck
1 teaspoon lemon juice
Chopped parsley, green or red
    pepper or pimiento

Melt fat, blend in flour, pepper, salt and paprika. Add milk and cook until thickened, stirring constantly. Add crumbs, beaten egg yolks, poultry and lemon juice. Cool. Fold in stiffly beaten egg whites and remaining seasonings Pour into greased mold or individual cups. Set in pan of hot water and cook in moderate oven (350° F.) 20 to 35 minutes or until firm Serve with White or Mushroom Sauce. Serves 8.

Chopped mushrooms may be added to mixture before cooking.

JAMBALAYA

1 1/2 cups diced cooked chicken
1 cup cooked rice
1 1/2 cups cooked tomatoes
1 large onion, chopped
1/2 green pepper, chopped
1/2 cup chopped celery
1 teaspoon salt
1/8 teaspoon pepper
Buttered crumbs

Combine chicken, rice and tomatoes and cook for 10 minutes Add onion, green pepper, celery and seasonings. Turn into baking dish and cover with buttered crumbs. Bake in 350°F. oven 1 hour. Serve very hot, for 4.

SPAGHETTI À LA DIABLE

1 (8-ounce) package spaghetti
1 onion, cut fine
1 small clove garlic
2 tablespoons fat
2 1/2 cups cooked tomatoes
Salt and pepper
1 tablespoon sugar
Dash cayenne
1/2 cup diced cooked chicken
1 cup mushrooms, sautéed
Grated cheese

Cook spaghetti in boiling salted water until tender. Drain and place in greased casserole. Sauté onion and garlic in fat until tender but not brown. Add tomatoes, salt, pepper, sugar and cayenne. Heat to boiling, then add chicken and mushrooms and pour over spaghetti. Toss with a fork. Sprinkle with grated cheese and bake in moderate oven (350°F.) until mixture is heated through and cheese is melted. Serves 6 to 8.

The French casserole adds
← *to the beauty of serving*

CHICKEN PILAU

4-pound roasting chicken
1 teaspoon curry powder mixed
    with 1 cup water
2 cups uncooked rice
4 cups chicken drippings and
    water, combined
4 tablespoons fat

Dress chicken as for roasting, omitting the stuffing. Place in uncovered roaster, add curry powder mixed with the water and cook in moderate oven (350°F.), adding more water as needed and basting occasionally. After chicken has cooked about 1/2 hour, drain, replace drippings with 2 cups of water, and continue cooking chicken. Wash rice, add the chicken drippings with enough water to make 4 cups, and cook slowly for about 20 minutes. Set in warm place (where there is no danger of scorching) for another 20 minutes. When chicken is browned, remove from roaster. Combine rice and fat, mix well with gravy and spread over bottom of roaster. Place chicken on top of rice, cover and continue cooking for about 1/2 hour or until chicken is tender and a crust has formed on the bottom of rice. To serve, place chicken on platter and smother with rice, crust side up. Serves 4 to 6.

FRIED CHICKEN

Frying means to cook in fat, either deep fat or a shallow layer ½ to 1 inch deep. Cut chicken into serving pieces: split chicken, 1 to 1½ pounds, lengthwise into halves; split chicken, 2 to 2½ pounds, lengthwise and crosswise to serve 4; 2½ to 5 pounds, cut as for fricassee to serve 6 to 8. Wash pieces and dry to prevent spattering when placed in hot fat. Chicken may be fried without coating or it may be dipped into bread crumbs, eggs and bread crumbs; corn-meal and flour mixture; cracker crumbs or flour. When using corn meal, apply a light coating. Too much will make a dry, hard crust. Heat enough fat in a deep heavy skillet (3 to 4 inches deep) or a chicken fryer to have a ½- to ¾-inch layer. Use 2 skillets if several chickens are to be fried. Any kind of fat may be used. If butter flavor is desired, use ⅓ as much butter as other fat or, after browning, place bits of butter on top of chicken pieces. The melting butter will penetrate and flavor the meat. Brown the chicken lightly in hot fat, then reduce heat and either add a little water or cover the skillet closely and cook slowly until tender, 30 minutes to 1 hour, depending on size of chicken. Simmer gizzard and heart in water until almost tender before frying. Liver requires only a few minutes of cooking. Put thick meaty pieces of chicken in the pan first. Best results are obtained if pieces are not crowded, especially if a thick coating is used.

OVEN METHOD—Fry until thoroughly browned and then transfer to casserole or covered roasting pan. Bake in moderate oven (350°F.) 1 to 1½ hours.

DEEP-FAT FRYING—Chicken coated with egg and crumbs is best fried in deep fat. Cook in hot fat (370° F.) at least 3 inches deep for 10 to 30 minutes, depending on size of pieces. Unless the chicken is very young and the pieces small, results are most satisfactory if the chicken (cut into serving pieces) is steamed or stewed until nearly tender. The deep-fat frying then serves to give a crisp brown covering and to reheat the chicken.

CHICKEN CACCIATORI

2 (2-pound) frying chickens
¼ cup olive or salad oil
2 medium onions, chopped
2 green peppers, chopped
1 red pepper, minced
1 clove garlic, minced
3 tomatoes, peeled and chopped
1½ cups tomato purée
2 tablespoons sour white wine
1½ teaspoons salt
⅛ teaspoon pepper
⅛ teaspoon allspice, if desired

Cut chicken into serving portions and brown in hot olive oil. Add onions, peppers and garlic and brown lightly. Add remaining ingredients and simmer ½ hour or until chicken is tender. Serves 6.

KENTUCKY FRIED CHICKEN

1 young chicken
1½ cups sifted flour
½ teaspoon salt
Dash pepper
1½ teaspoons baking powder
1 egg
½ cup milk

Cut chicken into serving portions; steam or stew until tender. Dry and keep cool until time to fry. This may be done the day before serving if a large quantity is to be cooked. Just before frying mix and sift flour, salt, pepper and baking powder together. Beat egg and add milk. Combine liquids with dry ingredients. Dip each piece of seasoned chicken into batter and fry in hot deep fat (380° F.) until brown. Serve hot. If very young chicken of broiling size (1½ to 2 pounds) is used, it may be cut into halves or quarters and fried without precooking. Serves 2 to 4.

FRENCH FRIED CHICKEN—Instead of using batter dip seasoned cooked chicken into fine crumbs, then into egg diluted with 2 tablespoons milk and roll again in crumbs.

The classic favorite is fried chicken and fritters

*Nothing is ever so welcome
as chicken Maryland*

FRIED CHICKEN
MARYLAND

2 young frying chickens
¾ cup flour
1 teaspoon salt
¼ teaspoon pepper
3 tablespoons fat
1 cup water

Clean and cut chickens into
halves or quarters. Wash carefully and dry, shake in bag with
flour, salt and pepper. Brown
chicken quickly in fat. Reduce
heat, add water and simmer
slowly until tender, about 30
minutes. Remove lid and let
chicken fry slowly. Serve with
Cream Gravy. Garnish with Corn
Oysters or small Corn Fritters and
broiled bacon. Allow ¾ pound
each.

SOUTHERN FRIED CHICKEN —
Prepare chicken as for Fried
Chicken Maryland but cover at
the beginning of the cooking period. Do not add water. Cook
slowly turning only once. Serve
with Cream Gravy in a separate
dish.

CHICKEN HAWAIIAN — Serve
Southern Fried Chicken with hot
cooked rice and sautéed pineapple
slices.

CROQUETTES — Mix 3½ cups
cooked chicken with 2 cups Thick
White Sauce. Shape, roll in egg
and crumbs and brown in hot
deep fat.

ALABAMA FRIED CHICKEN —
Prepare chicken as for Fried
Chicken Maryland but dip portions of chicken into beaten egg
before dredging with seasoning
and flour. Fry quickly in small
amount of fat. Cover as soon as
browned, lower heat and cook
until tender, about 30 minutes.

BABY CHICKEN
BREASTS

2 breasts of chicken
½ teaspoon salt
1½ tablespoons flour
Fat for frying

For Gravy:
2 tablespoons flour
½ cup chicken stock
1 cup cream or rich milk
1 egg yolk, slightly beaten

Remove breast bone from the
meat and split each into 2
fillets. Dip into seasoned flour.
Fry slowly until tender and brown.
Remove to hot serving dish. Remove all fat from skillet except
2 tablespoons, add flour and stir
until well blended. Add stock
and cream, stirring until thickened. Season to taste. Add egg
yolk just before serving and cook
1 or 2 minutes longer. Strain,
if necessary, and pour over the
chicken breasts. Serve on toast or
on fried corn-meal slices. Garnish
with sautéed mushroom caps. Two
tablespoons sherry may be added
to sauce at the last. Serves 2.

SPRING CHICKEN
MARYLAND

3 broiling chickens.
6 tablespoons fat, melted
¼ cup flour
½ teaspoon salt
⅛ teaspoon pepper
2 slices salt pork, cut fine
Dash nutmeg
3 cups cream or evaporated milk
Parsley

Clean chickens and cut into quarters. Brush with fat and dredge
with flour, salt and pepper. Fry
salt pork until brown. Add nutmeg. Place chickens on pork and
baste with melted butter. Cover
the skillet and cook chickens
about 30 minutes. When tender,
pour in 1 cup cream. Remove
cover and let cream cook down.
When it is fairly thick, pour in
another cup of cream, cook and
add the third cup. Cook until
thick. Serve chickens with the
cream gravy. Garnish with parsley. Serves 8 to 10.

CHICKEN SAUTÉ

3-pound frying chicken
¼ cup flour
½ teaspoon salt, Dash pepper
4 tablespoons fat

Steam or stew chicken until tender. Cut into quarters and
remove all bones except upper
wing and drum stick. Dredge
pieces with flour, season with
salt and pepper and sauté in fat
until brown. Skewer the two
halves of the breast so they will
stand upright. Arrange the legs
on either side on the platter
and garnish with sautéed apricots or peaches, filling the hollows of the fruit with currant
jelly. Heap tiny new potatoes,
boiled and rolled in butter and
chopped parsley on the platter.
Serve with Cream Sauce, for 4.

CHICKEN À LA KING

1 tablespoon butter
1 tablespoon flour
Dash white pepper
¼ teaspoon salt
½ teaspoon paprika
1 cup milk or diluted evaporated milk
¼ cup cream
1 cup cooked chicken, cut into pieces
2 olives, chopped
1 pimiento, chopped

Melt butter in top of double boiler, blend in flour, add pepper, salt and paprika. Add milk and cream gradually, stirring constantly until thickened. Beat well. Add chicken, olives and pimiento. Cook for 15 minutes and serve on toast, Baking Powder Biscuits, in Patty Shells or bread Croustades. Serves 2.

Add 1 tablespoon sherry.

Omit olives. Add ½ cup cooked mushrooms and 1 tablespoon chopped green pepper.

CREAMED CHICKEN WITH MACARONI

3 tablespoons butter
1 tablespoon flour
3 ounces cream cheese
1 small pimiento, chopped
1 teaspoon salt
Dash pepper
1 cup milk
1 cup Chicken Broth
2 cups diced cooked chicken
1½ cups cooked macaroni

Melt butter, add flour, cream cheese, pimiento and seasonings. Blend. Combine milk and chicken broth and add gradually to first mixture, stirring constantly. Heat to boiling and cook for 3 minutes. Add chicken and macaroni, pile into greased baking dish and bake in moderate oven (350°F.) 25 to 30 minutes. Serves 8.

CHICKEN AND ASPARAGUS

2 tablespoons fat
1 tablespoon flour
Salt
Pepper
Paprika
2 cups cream or evaporated milk
1 egg, beaten
2 cups diced cooked chicken
2 cups cooked asparagus tips, cut into 2-inch lengths
2 tablespoons chopped pimiento

Melt fat, add flour and seasonings. Add cream and cook until slightly thickened, stirring constantly. Pour over egg and blend. Add chicken, asparagus tips and pimiento and heat thoroughly. Serve on hot toast. Serves 4.

This may be placed in casserole with ½ cup buttered bread crumbs sprinkled over top; brown in the oven.

One cup cooked broccoli cut into 2-inch pieces may be used instead of asparagus.

Serve full length green beans bound with pimiento to set off your chicken in nest

MINCED CHICKEN AND MUSHROOMS

1 tablespoon butter
1 tablespoon flour
½ teaspoon salt
¼ teaspoon pepper
1 cup canned mushrooms, sliced
½ cup milk
2 cups diced cooked chicken

Melt butter, add flour, salt and pepper. Add mushroom liquor and milk and cook until thickened, stirring constantly. Heat to boiling, add mushrooms and chicken and cook 3 minutes. Serve hot on toast points, for 6.

CHICKEN IN NEST

3 tablespoons fat
1½ tablespoons flour
¼ teaspoon salt, Dash pepper
1 cup chicken stock or milk
2 cups diced cooked chicken

Melt fat, blend in flour, salt and pepper. Add chicken stock and cook until thickened, stirring constantly. Add chicken and more seasoning if necessary. Serve in Macaroni ring. Serves 4.

BRAISED CHICKEN WITH SOUR CREAM

4-pound chicken, cut into serving portions
¼ cup lemon juice
½ cup flour
1 teaspoon salt
⅛ teaspoon pepper
¼ cup butter
¼ clove garlic
1 tablespoon minced onion
1 to 2 cups sour cream

Rub chicken with lemon juice and roll in mixture of flour, salt and pepper. Brown chicken in butter, place in baking dish, add remaining ingredients and cover with sour cream. Cook covered in slow oven (325°F.) until tender, 1½ to 2½ hours. Remove garlic clove. Sprinkle with chopped parsley. Serves 4 to 6.

WESTERN PARTY CHICKEN

2 cups chicken stock
1 cup cream
½ cup cooked rice
1½ cups diced cooked chicken
½ cup crushed pineapple, drained
1 cup almonds, blanched
8 Pastry or Cream Puff Shells

Combine first 3 ingredients and heat until mixture starts to thicken. Add chicken, pineapple and nuts, heat again to boiling and cook 5 minutes or until thickened. Be careful when stirring not to mash rice or chicken. Serve hot in pastry or cream puff shells. Serves 8.

CHICKEN AND NOODLE SCALLOP

1 (6-ounce) package noodles
1½ cups diced cooked chicken
2 cups Chicken Gravy
½ cup buttered crumbs

Boil noodles until tender in salted water. Drain. Arrange alternate layers of noodles, chicken and gravy in greased baking dish. Cover with buttered crumbs and bake in moderate oven (350°F.) until liquid starts to bubble through the layer of crumbs on top, about 20 minutes. If dish is prepared in advance of the final baking, more time should be allowed for heating through. Serves 4 to 6.
From ½ to 1 cup of cooked vegetables may be added.

QUICK CHICKEN GRAVY

1½ tablespoons flour
1 cup milk
1 (10½-ounce) can condensed chicken soup

Blend flour and milk and add to chicken soup. Heat slowly to boiling and cook until thickened. Strain. Makes 2⅓ cups.

CHICKEN BREASTS PAPRIKA

Breasts of 2 chickens (broilers or fryers)
¼ cup white wine
¼ clove garlic
1 cup water or chicken stock
1 teaspoon salt
½ tablespoon flour
¼ teaspoon paprika (or more)
1½ cups cream or evaporated milk
1 cup cooked mushrooms

Cut breasts into serving portions and simmer in wine, garlic and stock until tender, about 1 hour. Add salt when almost done. Blend flour and paprika, adding enough cream to make a smooth paste. Add remaining cream to chicken. Stir in flour mixture gradually. Add mushrooms, stir and cook until thickened. Add more seasonings if desired. Remove garlic before serving. Serves 4.

CHICKEN TERRAPIN

2 pairs sweetbreads
1 large chicken, cooked
1 quart cream
1 tablespoon cornstarch
Milk
2 egg yolks, slightly beaten
1 tablespoon butter
Salt and pepper
¼ cup sherry

Cover sweetbreads with boiling water (with 1 teaspoon salt and 1 tablespoon vinegar to each quart of water), cover and simmer for 20 minutes. Drain and cover with cold water until cool. Remove membrane, and cut sweetbreads into small pieces. Cut chicken meat fine and add to sweetbreads. Place cream in double boiler and thicken with cornstarch mixed with a little cold milk. Add egg yolks and stir well. Season with butter, salt and pepper. When thickened, stir in chicken and sweetbreads. Just before serving add sherry. Serve on toast or in Patty Shells. Serves 10 to 12.

CHINESE CHICKEN GRAVY

2½ cups drained crushed pineapple
3 tablespoons butter
¼ cup flour
1 cup chicken stock or boiling water
½ cup diced celery
½ small green pepper, minced
Salt and pepper
1 teaspoon soy sauce
¼ cup almonds, cut into slivers

Sauté pineapple in butter, stir in flour, add chicken stock and cook until thick. Add remaining ingredients except almonds and cook 10 minutes. Use gravy for reheating chicken. Garnish with almonds. Makes 3 cups.

CHICKEN PIE DE LUXE

4-pound stewing chicken
1 small carrot, sliced
1 small onion, sliced
2 stalks celery or few celery tops
1 teaspoon salt
1 whole clove, 3 peppercorns
⅛ teaspoon ginger
3 cups (or more) gravy
1 recipe Baking Powder Biscuits

Cover chicken with boiling water; add carrot, onion, celery, salt, clove, peppercorns and ginger. Simmer until meat begins to fall from bones. Cool meat in the stock. Remove chicken, strain stock and skim fat from the top. Remove meat from bones, cutting the larger pieces across the grain and arrange in casserole, distributing light and dark meat evenly. Add gravy and biscuits rolled about ½ inch thick. Bake in hot oven (400° to 425°F.) for 20 to 25 minutes. Serves 6 to 8.

Omit clove and ginger. Use ¾ cup diced carrot, ½ cup sliced onions and 6 small potatoes.
Omit clove, ginger and carrot. Add 2 tablespoons minced parsley, ½ pound sliced mushrooms and 1 hard-cooked egg, sliced. Use other fowl for chicken.

SWEETPOTATO CRUST

1 cup sifted flour
1 teaspoon baking powder
½ teaspoon salt
1 cup cold mashed sweetpotato
⅓ cup melted fat
1 egg, well beaten

Sift flour with baking powder and salt. Work in mashed potato, fat and egg. Roll ¼ inch thick and cover chicken pie.

For your nicest party nothing equals chicken pie de luxe

CHICKEN HAM PIE

2 cups diced cooked chicken
2 cups diced cooked ham
3 cups Chicken Gravy
½ recipe Pastry, Milk

Place chicken and ham in greased individual ramekins or baking dishes. Cover with the gravy. Roll out pastry ¼ inch thick, cut into strips and place strips crisscross over the top. Brush crust with milk. Place in hot oven (450°F.) and bake until crust is brown and meat is thoroughly heated. Serves 4.

PASTRY

2 cups sifted flour
¾ teaspoon salt
⅔ cup shortening
4 to 6 tablespoons cold water

Sift flour and salt together and cut in shortening with 2 knives or pastry blender, until consistency of coarse meal. Add the water, using only a small portion at a time, until the mixture will hold together. Roll out on a floured board to desired size.

CHICKEN MUSHROOM SHORTCAKE

½ cup milk
1 can condensed mushroom soup
1 egg yolk
1 cup cubed chicken
Baking Powder Biscuits

Combine milk and soup. Mix well and heat. Beat egg yolk and add a little of the hot sauce slowly. Add with chicken to the rest of the mushroom sauce. Heat to boiling, stirring constantly. Split biscuits, butter them and serve chicken mixture between and on top. Serves 4.

CHICKEN OR TURKEY SHORTCAKE

1½ cups diced cooked poultry
2 cups of Gravy or White Sauce
1 recipe Baking Powder Biscuits

Add chicken or turkey to gravy or white sauce and heat in double boiler. Bake biscuits, split, cover ½ with generous serving of hot mixture, top with the other half of biscuit and serve. Serves 6.

DIXIE CHICKEN SHORTCAKE— Use squares of hot Corn Bread instead of baking powder biscuits.

CHICKEN TAMALE PIE

2 to 3 cups Corn-Meal Mush
2 to 3 cups sliced cooked chicken
Salt and pepper
1 can tomato sauce
1 can whole kernel corn
2 tablespoons sugar
2 tablespoons olive oil
½ cup raisins, scalded and chopped
10 ripe olives, sliced
¾ cup grated Parmesan cheese for top

(For 3 cups of corn-meal mush, cook ½ cup dry corn meal in 3 cups boiling water with 1¼ teaspoons salt.)

Spread corn-meal mush in bottom of greased shallow casserole. Arrange chicken over the mush. Sprinkle with salt and pepper. Combine remaining ingredients (except cheese) to make a sauce, adding more salt and pepper if desired. Pour over chicken and sprinkle the cheese over top. Bake in moderate oven (350°F.) about 45 minutes. Serve from casserole. Serves 6 to 8.

CHICKEN HASH

2 tablespoons chicken fat
1½ tablespoons flour
1 cup chicken stock
2 cups chopped cooked chicken

Melt fat, blend in flour, add chicken stock and cook until thickened, stirring constantly. Add chicken; place in greased casserole and bake in moderate oven (350°F.) 20 minutes. Garnish with toast. Serves 4 to 6.

CHICKEN TURNOVERS

1½ cups minced cooked chicken
¾ cup Thick White Sauce
1 tablespoon minced parsley
1 recipe Pastry
1 egg white

Sweetpotato crust has a distinct southern accent

Combine chicken, white sauce and parsley. Roll pastry to ⅛-inch thickness, cut into squares and brush with egg white. Place 2 tablespoons of chicken mixture on each square, fold over and press edges together with a fork. Place on baking sheet. Prick upper crust to allow for escape of steam. Bake in very hot oven (450°F.) until browned. Serve with gravy or seasoned white sauce. Serves 4.

CHICKEN PIE WITH SWEETPOTATO CRUST

3 cups diced cooked chicken
1 cup diced cooked carrots
6 cooked small white onions
1 tablespoon chopped parsley
1 cup evaporated milk
1 cup chicken stock
2 tablespoons flour
1 teaspoon salt
⅛ teaspoon pepper

Arrange chicken, carrots, onions and parsley in layers in casserole. Combine milk and chicken stock Add slowly to flour, blending well. Cook until thickened, stirring constantly. Season and pour over chicken and vegetables in casserole. Cover with sweetpotato crust (p. 426). Bake in moderate oven (350° F.) about 40 minutes. Serves 6 to 8.

CHICKEN YORKSHIRE

2 cups diced cooked chicken
2 eggs
½ cup drippings, melted
1 cup milk
1 cup sifted flour
1 teaspoon baking powder
½ teaspoon salt
Leftover Gravy

Place chicken in bottom of greased casserole and set in oven to heat. Beat eggs, drippings and milk together. Sift dry ingredients together, add to liquid ingredients and beat until free from lumps. Batter will be quite thin. Pour over chicken and bake in moderate oven (350°F.) about 30 minutes. Serve at once from the baking dish with gravy. Serves 6.

COUNTRY CHICKEN LOAF

2 cups diced cooked chicken
½ cup chopped cooked carrots
1 cup cooked peas
½ cup chopped celery
1 tablespoon minced green pepper
1 cup bread crumbs
½ cup milk
2 egg yolks, beaten
1 teaspoon onion juice
1 teaspoon lemon juice
1 teaspoon salt
⅛ teaspoon pepper

Force chicken, carrots and peas through a food chopper. Add remaining ingredients and place in greased loaf pan or ring mold. Bake in moderate oven (350°F.) until firm, about 40 minutes. Serve with Cream or Mushroom Sauce. Makes 1 (8x4 inch) loaf. Serves 6.

CHICKEN AND RICE LOAF — Omit carrots and lemon juice. Use 2 cups whole peas and 1½ cups diced chicken instead of above amounts. Use 2 cups cooked rice instead of bread crumbs.

Use diced pimiento instead of green pepper.

TURKEY-CHICKEN LOAF

1 (10½-ounce) can condensed chicken soup
1 cup diced cooked turkey
1½ cups soft bread crumbs
1 tablespoon chopped pimiento
1 tablespoon chopped parsley
½ teaspoon salt
2 eggs, slightly beaten

Strain rice, celery and chicken from soup. Combine with turkey and grind. Add bread crumbs, chicken broth, pimiento, parsley, salt and eggs. Bake in greased loaf pan in moderate oven (350° F.) 45 to 60 minutes or until firm. Garnish with grilled apricots or grilled apple rings. Serve hot or cold. Serves 4 or 5.

Chicken ring served cold may be filled with fresh combination salad

CHICKEN RING OR LOAF

2 cups hot milk (or stock and cream)
2 eggs or 3 egg yolks, slightly beaten
1 cup soft bread crumbs
½ teaspoon salt
¼ teaspoon paprika
1 teaspoon Worcestershire sauce
3 cups diced cooked chicken
½ cup chopped celery
1 green pepper, chopped
1½ tablespoons lemon juice

Pour hot milk slowly onto eggs, stirring constantly. Add remaining ingredients, mix well and pour into buttered mold. Bake in slow oven (300°F.) until knife inserted in center comes out clean, about 45 to 60 minutes. It will take less time in a ring mold than in a loaf pan. Be careful not to overbake. Let stand 10 minutes before unmolding. Serve Mushroom Sauce in center of ring. Serves 6 to 8.

Omit milk, lemon juice and Worcestershire sauce. Use only 3 tablespoons crumbs. Add 3 tablespoons diced pimiento, 1½ teaspoons minced onion and ¾ cup each tomato juice and cooked rice. Pour into mold packed with ¾-inch layer cooked rice and bake.

HOT CHICKEN LOAF

4- to 5-pound chicken, cut up
1 small carrot
1 small onion
Few celery leaves or 2 stalks
1 clove
3 peppercorns
1 teaspoon salt
2 cups fresh bread crumbs
1 cup cooked rice
1½ tablespoons salt
2 tablespoons chopped pimiento
3 cups Chicken Broth, milk or both mixed
5 eggs, beaten

Place chicken in large kettle. Add carrot, onion, celery, clove, peppercorns and salt. Cover with cold water and simmer until tender, about 2 hours. Strain stock and let chicken cool in stock. When cold drain, saving stock, discard skin of chicken, remove meat from bones and dice meat. Combine diced meat with remaining ingredients. Add more seasoning if necessary. Place in greased baking pan so that mixture is about 2 inches deep. Bake in moderate oven (350°F.) until firm, about 1 hour. Cut into squares or oblongs and serve with Mushroom Sauce. Serves 8 to 10. For variety, use 1½ cups cooked spaghetti in place of rice and add 2 tablespoons finely minced green pepper.

SALADS

CHICKEN AND FRUIT SALAD

1 orange, 15 large grapes
15 salted almonds, 1 banana
1 apple diced
3 cups diced cooked white meat of chicken
1 cup mayonnaise

Remove seeds and membrane from orange segments and cut into halves. Cut grapes into halves, removing seeds. Split almonds, slice banana, mix all ingredients lightly but thoroughly. Chill and serve on lettuce for 8.

MOLDED CHICKEN AND VEGETABLE SALAD

1½ tablespoons unflavored gelatin
3 tablespoons cold water
1 can condensed chicken soup
¾ cup cooked chicken
1 egg, separated
¼ cup heavy cream, whipped
1 tablespoon lemon juice
½ cup diced cooked carrots
½ cup cooked peas
½ cup diced cooked celery

Soften gelatin in cold water for 5 minutes. Strain chicken soup and heat. Grind the ¾ cup chicken with the rice, chicken and celery from the soup. Beat egg yolk and add the hot soup slowly. Cook 3 to 4 minutes, stirring constantly. Pour over softened gelatin and stir until gelatin has dissolved. Cool; when mixture begins to thicken, add chopped chicken mixture, then fold in beaten egg white, whipped cream, lemon juice, carrots, peas and celery. Pour into ring mold and chill. Unmold, fill center with salad dressing or mayonnaise, garnish with spiced peaches and sprigs of watercress. Serves 5 or 6.

Sunday supper will be gayer for this chicken fruit salad

CHICKEN SALAD

1 cup diced cooked chicken
French dressing
½ slice pineapple, or ⅛ cup drained, crushed pineapple
½ cup diced celery
½ teaspoon scraped onion or few drops onion juice
⅛ cup shredded, toasted almonds
Salad dressing

Marinate chicken in French dressing for 1 hour or longer. Drain, if necessary. Add pineapple, celery, onion and almonds with just enough salad dressing to moisten. Season with salt and pepper, if necessary. Chill and serve garnished with a few of the shredded almonds. Serves 4

Add 6 ripe olives, diced.
Heap salad into cucumber boats.

CHICKEN AND SWEETBREAD SALAD

2 cups diced cooked chicken
1 cup diced cooked sweetbreads
1 cup chopped celery
½ teaspoon salt
1 cup mayonnaise or salad dressing
Lettuce cups

Combine first 4 ingredients. Add mayonnaise and toss together lightly. Serve in lettuce, for 5. If desired, garnish with sieved yolks.

CHICKEN SALAD IN MOLDED EGG RING

2 tablespoons unflavored gelatin
½ cup cold water
½ cup boiling water
1½ cups mayonnaise
4 tablespoons lemon juice
½ teaspoon salt
2 drops Tabasco sauce
1 teaspoon grated onion
½ green pepper, chopped
½ cup chopped parsley
12 hard-cooked eggs
1 recipe Chicken Salad

Soften gelatin in cold water 5 minutes and dissolve in boiling water. Cool. Add mayonnaise, lemon juice, salt, Tabasco sauce, onion, green pepper, parsley and 10 eggs chopped. Cover bottom of mold with a 1-inch layer of mixture. Slice remaining eggs, arrange slices around side of mold and chill until firm. Add remaining mixture and chill until firm. Unmold, fill center with chicken salad and garnish with whole almonds and tomato wedges. Serve with mayonnaise or French dressing. Serves 8.

Use a ring of Tomato Aspic, Cranberry Jelly or jellied cucumbers and pineapple instead of the Molded Egg Ring.

Lettuce hearts at the center add to the frosty freshness of chicken almond mousse

CHICKEN AND ALMOND MOUSSE

1½ tablespoons unflavored gelatin
2 cups chicken stock
3 egg yolks
1 teaspoon salt
¼ teaspoon pepper
Dash cayenne
½ cup finely chopped almonds
1 cup diced white meat of cooked chicken
½ cup heavy cream, whipped

Soften gelatin in ½ cup cold stock for 5 minutes. Heat remaining stock and add slowly to beaten egg yolks and seasonings. Cook in double boiler until thickened, stirring constantly. Add gelatin, stir until dissolved and mix in almonds and chicken. Chill until mixture begins to thicken and fold in whipped cream. Pour into mold and chill until firm. Serve on crisp cold lettuce leaves, garnished with additional chopped nuts and Radish Roses. Serves 6. Add ¼ cup each sieved pimientos and minced celery. Remove centers from tomatoes and pour in mixture. Chill. Nuts may be omitted if desired.

LAYERED PRESSED CHICKEN

5-pound cooked chicken
6 hard-cooked eggs
Concentrated chicken stock
½ cup finely chopped parsley
Mayonnaise

Remove the bones and skin from fowl. Separate light and dark meat. Chop light and dark meat, whites and yolks of eggs separately rather fine. Moisten each with stock. Add more seasoning if necessary. Arrange dark meat, egg yolks, parsley, light meat and egg whites in layers in loaf pan or ring mold. Chill overnight, covered and weighted. Unmold, slice and serve on crisp cold lettuce leaves. Garnish with mayonnaise. (Cook the chicken in advance so that stock may be reduced to assure a firm jelly.) Serves 8.

FROZEN CHICKEN AND RICE
— Combine 2 cups cooked rice with ¼ cup mayonnaise. Add 1 cup cooked peas or asparagus tips, 1½ cups diced cooked chicken, 2 sliced hard-cooked eggs, salt and pepper. Freeze until firm, slice and garnish with slices of hard-cooked eggs and mayonnaise.

CHICKEN SALADS
CHICKEN AND ASPARAGUS SALAD—1½ cups diced cooked chicken, 1 cup asparagus tips, 2 tablespoons minced green pepper, ¼ cup shredded cabbage and ¾ cup mayonnaise. Serves 6.

CHICKEN AND BACON SALAD —1 cup diced cooked chicken, ½ cup diced crisp bacon, 1 cup diced tomatoes and ½ cup mayonnaise or salad dressing.

CHICKEN AND CABBAGE SALAD— ½ cup diced cooked chicken, 2 cups shredded cabbage, ½ cup diced cooked ham and ¾ cup mayonnaise or salad dressing.

CHICKEN AND CHESTNUT SALAD—1 cup diced cooked chicken; ½ cup chopped boiled chestnuts; 1 cup diced celery; 2 hard-cooked eggs, chopped; ⅓ cup sliced stuffed olives; ½ cup mayonnaise or salad dressing.

CHICKEN AND CUCUMBER SALAD—2 cups diced cooked chicken, ½ cup chopped celery, ½ cup diced cucumbers, 2 tablespoons capers and ¾ cup mayonnaise or salad dressing.

CHICKEN AND ORANGE SALAD —2 cups diced cooked chicken; 2 oranges, separated into segments; ¼ teaspoon salt, 1 cup chopped celery, ½ cup chopped salted almonds and ¾ cup mayonnaise or salad dressing.

CHICKEN AND TONGUE SALAD —1 cup diced cooked chicken, 1 cup diced cooked tongue, ½ cup chopped celery, ½ cup sliced stuffed olives and ¾ cup mayonnaise or salad dressing.

CHICKEN SALAD WITH PINEAPPLE—Mix 2 cups diced cooked chicken, 1 cup minced celery and 1 green pepper, chopped. Marinate in French dressing. Drain and mix with mayonnaise. Serve on lettuce with pineapple spears.

GIBLET PIE

Giblets (heart, gizzard and liver)
3 cups water
Soup stock or milk
4 tablespoons chicken fat
4 tablespoons flour
½ teaspoon salt
1 cup diced cooked fowl
2 small onions, peeled
1 cup cubed uncooked potatoes
1 recipe Pastry or Baking Powder
    Biscuits

Cut heart and gizzard into cubes, add the water, cover and simmer until tender, about 45 to 60 minutes. Add liver the last 20 minutes of cooking. Add enough soup stock or milk to make 3 cups liquid. Blend melted chicken fat, flour and salt, add to giblets and cook until thickened, stirring constantly. Add fowl, onions, and potatoes. Pour into a casserole and cover with rich pastry or biscuit dough. Place in hot oven (400°F.) until brown, 15 to 20 minutes. This may be baked in individual casseroles. Serves 4.

CHICKEN LIVERS EN BROCHETTE

Chicken livers
Thinly sliced bacon
Salt, Pepper

Cut livers into halves and bacon into squares. Season with salt and pepper. Alternate pieces of bacon and liver on skewers. Allow 4 pieces of liver and 5 pieces of bacon to each skewer. Bake in hot oven (425°F.) until bacon is crisp and livers are cooked.

SAUTÉED CHICKEN LIVERS

3 or 4 uncooked chicken livers
½ teaspoon salt
⅛ teaspoon pepper
2 tablespoons flour
1 onion, diced
1 tablespoon fat
½ cup stock

Cut livers into quarters, sprinkle with salt, pepper and flour. Sauté onion in fat, add livers and brown. Add stock and simmer 3 minutes. Serve on toast, for 2.

CHICKEN LIVERS WITH ANCHOVY

4 cooked chicken livers
2 tablespoons anchovy paste
2 tablespoons butter
⅛ teaspoon pepper
1 teaspoon salt
3 egg yolks
1 cup cream or evaporated milk
5 slices hot toast

Press livers through sieve and mix to a paste with anchovy paste; add butter, pepper, ½ teaspoon salt and 1 egg yolk. Prepare a sauce by combining remaining egg yolks, salt and cream in double boiler and cooking until thickened, stirring constantly. Spread liver mixture on toast and broil for 1 minute. Cover with sauce and serve hot. Serves 5.

CHICKEN LIVER OMELET

½ pound chicken livers
¼ teaspoon salt
Dash pepper
Dash cinnamon
Dash mace
1 teaspoon flour
1 tablespoon butter
1 tablespoon cooking sherry
Omelet made with 4 eggs

Season livers with salt, pepper, cinnamon and mace; dredge with flour and sauté in butter over low heat until brown. Just before removing, stir in sherry until mixture thickens but does not boil. Fold into the cooked omelet and serve at once. Serves 6.

Omit spices and sherry. Combine browned livers with hot Tomato Sauce or condensed cream of mushroom soup before folding into omelet.

If you like, add small whole carrots, green peas, green beans and sautéed mushrooms to your giblet pie. It is ideal for Saturday night

CHICKEN LIVERS WITH CURRY

6 chicken livers, Salt
Pepper, Bread crumbs
1 egg diluted with 2 tablespoons milk
3 tablespoons fat
1 teaspoon minced onion
2 tablespoons flour
½ teaspoon curry powder
1 cup chicken stock

Cut livers into quarters. Season with salt and pepper, roll in crumbs, dip in egg and roll again in crumbs. Sauté livers in fat until tender; remove and sauté onion. Add remaining ingredients and cook until thickened. Pour over livers. Serves 4 to 6.

SPAGHETTI WITH CHICKEN LIVERS

2½ cups cooked tomatoes
1 clove garlic, chopped
1 onion, chopped
2 teaspoons celery salt
½ teaspoon ginger
1 teaspoon salt
⅛ teaspoon pepper
1 teaspoon sugar
Dash cayenne
1 cup beef stock
1 cup uncooked chicken livers
1 cup sliced mushrooms
4 tablespoons fat
2 tablespoons flour
½ cup grated Parmesan cheese
1 (8-ounce) package spaghetti

Combine tomatoes and seasonings and cook together slowly for 30 minutes. Add stock. Sauté chopped livers and sliced mushrooms in fat until tender. Add flour and tomato mixture. Cook slowly for 15 minutes.
Cook spaghetti whole in boiling salted water until tender. Drain. Add sauce to spaghetti; sprinkle with cheese. Serves 6.
One cup diced cooked chicken may be used in place of livers.

Whether pâté de foie gras or other chicken liver filling, rolled sandwiches are the perfect vehicle

MOCK PÂTÉ DE FOIE GRAS

½ pound chicken giblets or chicken livers
1¼ teaspoons salt
½ cup butter
2 teaspoons Worcestershire sauce
1 teaspoon mustard
½ teaspoon nutmeg
¼ teaspoon cloves
⅛ teaspoon cayenne
2 tablespoons onion juice

Simmer giblets in water to cover until tender, about 20 minutes for liver; 1 to 3 hours for gizzard, depending upon the chicken. Add 1 teaspoon salt when almost done. Cool in the stock. Remove cartilage from gizzard, grind giblets to a smooth paste and add softened butter, seasonings and enough of the stock to make a paste. Add more seasonings, if desired. Pack into greased jelly glasses. Cover with paraffin and store in a cool place. This may be kept all winter. Tomato catchup may be used for additional seasoning. Makes 1 cup.

PÂTÉ DE FOIE GRAS

½ cup goose livers
2 tablespoons goose fat
3 hard-cooked eggs
Salt and pepper to taste
⅛ teaspoon paprika
½ teaspoon grated onion

Sauté goose liver in goose fat until tender. Mash into a paste with eggs, add salt, pepper, paprika and onion. If too stiff add additional goose fat. Spread on thin slices of toast. Makes ½ cup paste.

CHICKEN LIVER FILLING

½ cup chopped cooked chicken livers
2 hard-cooked eggs, chopped
¼ teaspoon salt
⅛ teaspoon pepper
1 teaspoon minced onion
Cream

1. Combine ingredients, adding just enough cream to moisten. Spread on toast, crackers or slices of tomato. Makes ⅔ cup spread.
2. Cut stem ends from 6 small ripe tomatoes, scoop out centers to form cups. Turn upside-down to drain. Stuff with above filling and serve on lettuce.

Chilled peeled tomatoes filled with goose livers in jelly and served with tiny sandwiches are for the hostess who seeks new ideas

GOOSE LIVERS IN JELLY

4 pairs goose feet
1 teaspoon salt
1 small onion, minced
½ clove garlic
½ teaspoon salt
⅛ teaspoon pepper
1 cup water
4 goose livers

Clean, scald and strip feet. Cover with water, add salt and cook until bones fall apart, about 2 hours, adding water as it evaporates to keep original amount. Strain and boil liquor down to ½ its volume. Combine onion, garlic, salt, pepper and water and cook 15 minutes. Add livers and simmer 15 to 20 minutes, adding more water to keep livers covered. Grind livers with onion and garlic, using a little of the liver liquor to rinse the grinder and adding it to the ground livers. Half fill small molds with liver mixture and fill with stock made by boiling feet. Chill. Serve as appetizer for 12.

A thin slice of lemon may be floated on top of mold.

A small loaf pan may be half filled with liver and filled with stock and a design of lemon slices and strips of red and green peppers floated on top. The loaf may be cut into squares and served as an appetizer.

Use hollowed tomatoes for molds. Chill 1 cup of the stock until firm, dice or break with a fork and use as garnish for tomatoes.

EGGS STUFFED WITH CHICKEN LIVERS

2 chicken livers
½ teaspoon onion juice
2 tablespoons fat
4 hard-cooked eggs
1 teaspoon chopped parsley
Salt and pepper
Worcestershire sauce to taste
¼ cup grated cheese

Clean livers, chop fine and sprinkle with onion juice; fry in fat. Cut eggs into halves; remove yolks and rub through sieve, add parsley, salt, pepper and Worcestershire sauce to taste, then mix with chicken livers. Refill whites with mixture, sprinkle with grated cheese and bake in hot oven (400°F.) until cheese melts. Serve with toast and Tomato Sauce. Serves 4.

CHICKEN LIVER ROLLS

6 chicken livers
2 tablespoons prepared mustard
2 tablespoons minced olives
6 slices bacon, cut into halves
Bread crumbs

Cut livers into halves, spread with mustard and olives. Wrap bacon around each piece and secure with toothpicks. Roll in crumbs and bake in hot oven (425°F.) 10 to 15 minutes. Serves 6.

CHICKEN LIVERS WITH MUSHROOMS

1 slice bacon, diced
2 tablespoons fat
1 teaspoon chopped onion
6 chicken livers
2 tablespoons flour
½ teaspoon salt
⅛ teaspoon pepper
1 teaspoon lemon juice
¼ cup sliced mushrooms
1 cup chicken stock
1 tablespoon chopped parsley

Sauté bacon until browned. Remove bacon, add fat and onion and when onion is tender but not brown add livers and sauté for 2 minutes. Add flour, salt, pepper, lemon juice and mushrooms. Blend. Add stock gradually and cook until mushrooms are tender. Garnish with chopped parsley. Serves 4 to 6.

LIVER AND EGG SALAD

6 chicken livers
4 hard-cooked eggs
3 small onions, chopped fine
French dressing
Lettuce

Broil or fry livers. Chop eggs and livers, add onion and cool. Mix with French dressing. Serve cold in lettuce cups. Serves 4.

DUCKS

ROAST DUCK

5-pound duck
Salt, Pepper, Clove garlic
3 cups pared quartered apples
1 cup seedless raisins
1 cup orange juice, if desired

Wash, singe and clean duck, season, rub with garlic and fill with apples mixed with raisins; place in pan and roast uncovered in slow oven (325°F.), allowing 20 to 30 minutes per pound. Baste every 10 minutes using 1 cup of orange juice, if the flavor is desired. Serve with Currant or Cranberry Jelly. Serves 5.

DUCK WITH SAUERKRAUT

6-pound duck
Salt, Pepper, Clove garlic
2 quarts Sauerkraut
1 cup water
3 tablespoons sugar

Prepare a young duck for roasting as above. Place in pan, add sauerkraut, water and sugar. Cover and bake in moderate oven (325°F.) until tender and brown, allowing 20 to 25 minutes per pound. Serves 6.

CANETON À LA BIGARDE

2-pound duckling
Rind of ¼ orange
⅔ cup thinly sliced carrots
½ cup thinly sliced onions
Juice 1 orange
¾ cup Currant Jelly
¼ cup kümmel
2 slices toast

Roast duckling in moderate oven (325°F.) 30 to 40 minutes or until tender. Cut orange rind into thin strips and cook in boiling water for a few minutes, until slightly tender. Fry vegetables quickly in fat from duckling. Remove from pan. Add orange juice, jelly and kümmel to remaining fat. Blend thoroughly. Place duckling on toast, surrounded with carrots, onions and orange rind. If desired, garnish duckling with orange segments placed on the breast, a half orange and a lettuce heart on a skewer run through breast of duck. Serves 2.

Roast duck is the perfect ending for an outdoor day

BRAISED DUCK

4-pound duck
3 slices bacon
1 carrot, diced
1 onion stuck with cloves
½ teaspoon powdered thyme
2 tablespoons minced parsley
1 teaspoon salt
⅛ teaspoon pepper
4 cups boiling water
1 small turnip, diced
2 tablespoons melted fat
4 tablespoons flour
¼ cup cold water

Prepare duck as for roasting. Place in a large kettle with bacon, carrot, onion, thyme, parsley, salt and pepper, and cover with water. Simmer until duck is tender, then remove from stock. Sauté turnip in fat until brown, then drain and cook in stock until tender. Strain stock. Blend flour and cold water together until smooth and add gradually to stock, stirring constantly. Pour the gravy over duck. Garnish with pieces of turnip. Serves 6.

WITH MUSHROOMS — Omit bacon and carrot. Use ½ pound mushrooms, sliced, for turnip.

FRICASSEE OF DUCK

5-pound duck
Salt
Pepper
Flour
6 tablespoons fat
2 tablespoons minced onion
½ bay leaf
1 cup chopped mushrooms

Clean duck and cut into serving portions. Dredge with salt, pepper and flour. Brown in 4 tablespoons fat with onion and bay leaf. Cover with water and simmer until tender in covered pan. Sauté mushrooms in remaining fat and add to duck. Simmer 10 minutes longer. Serves 5.

DUCK IN CREAM—Omit mushrooms, bay leaf and onion. After browning duck as above, sprinkle with ½ teaspoon thyme and add 1 cup heavy cream instead of water.

DUCK À LA CREOLE

2 tablespoons fat
1 tablespoon flour
2 tablespoons chopped ham
¾ teaspoon salt
⅛ teaspoon pepper
Paprika
2 tablespoons minced onion
½ cup chopped celery
2 tablespoons chopped sweet pepper
1 tablespoon chopped parsley
1½ cups Consommé or Bouillon
1 whole clove
¼ teaspoon mace
2 cups diced cooked duck

Melt fat, add flour, and stir in ham. Season with salt, pepper, paprika, onion, celery, sweet pepper and parsley. Stir for 2 minutes, add consommé or bouillon, clove and mace. Simmer 1 hour Strain sauce and stir in cooked duck. Heat and serve with fried Hominy or Mush. Serves 4.

DUCKLING WITH SAUCE PIQUANTE

5-pound duckling
Salt, Pepper
1 minced onion
3 tablespoons fat
2 tablespoons peanut butter
1 finely chopped pimiento
½ tablespoon flour
Cayenne
Finely chopped parsley

Cut duckling into serving pieces. Simmer in a small amount of water until almost tender. Season with salt and pepper. Sauté with minced onion in fat until brown. To stock in which duckling was cooked, add peanut butter, pimiento and flour mixed with water. Cook until thickened, stirring constantly. Season with salt, pepper, cayenne and parsley. Serve duckling hot covered with sauce. Serves 5.

PINEAPPLE DUCK

3-pound duck
2 cups boiling water
Salt and pepper
2 tablespoons soy sauce
1 No. 2 can sliced pineapple, diced

Cut duck into serving portions, cover with boiling water and simmer until nearly tender, about 1 hour. Add salt, pepper, soy sauce, pineapple and pineapple sirup. Cook 30 minutes longer. Serves 4.

DUCKLING FRUIT SALAD

2 cups diced cooked duckling
2 cups orange sections
1 cup grapefruit sections
¼ cup French dressing
Lettuce

Mix all ingredients together. Chill. Serve on crisp lettuce leaves. Serves 6.

DUCK SOUP

5-pound duck
1 dried onion sprout
3 to 4 quarts boiling water
4 dried orange peels, ground
3 stalks celery, diced
1 small onion
Salt and pepper
4 tablespoons soy sauce

Cover duck and onion sprout with boiling water. Add orange peel, celery and onion. Cook for 2 to 3 hours or until duck is tender. Remove duck and add remaining ingredients. Serves 10. The duck may be fried or served with soy sauce.

CHESTNUT DUCK

3-pound duck
2 cups boiling water
6 cups chestnuts
2 cups sliced mushrooms
Salt and pepper
4 tablespoons soy sauce

Cut duck into serving portions, cover with boiling water and simmer for 1 hour. Drop chestnuts into cold water and discard those which float. Heat water to boiling and simmer chestnuts for 5 minutes. Drain and peel. Add chestnuts, mushrooms, salt, pepper and soy sauce to duck. Cook 30 minutes longer. Serves 4 to 5

ORANGE DUCK

3-pound duck
2 cups boiling water
12 dried orange peels, ground
2 cups mushrooms, cut into halves
Salt and pepper
3 tablespoons soy sauce

Cut duck into serving portions and cover with boiling water. Add ground orange peels and simmer for 1 hour. Add mushrooms, salt, pepper and soy sauce. Cook 20 minutes longer. Garnish with slices of boiled ham. Serves 3.

GEESE

Geese have very short legs and the breast meat as well as the legs is dark. Since they contain more fat than any other poultry, none is added during the cooking. Very young geese, which are in the market from August to November, may be broiled. Geese for roasting, the most popular method of preparation, are in the market from November to January and weigh 8 to 16 pounds. Older fowls are less tender and so must be prepared in moist heat as fricasseeing or braising. Goose livers are a delicacy which are used for pâté de foie gras.

GOOSE ORANGE SALAD

2 cups diced cooked goose
2 cups diced celery
2 cups orange slices
½ cup French dressing
Lettuce or chicory
¾ cup toasted almonds

Combine first 4 ingredients. Marinate for 1 hour. Drain and arrange in salad bowl lined with lettuce or chicory. Garnish with almonds. Serves 6.

ROAST GOOSE WITH BAKED APPLES

8-pound goose
2 quarts bread crumbs
2 onions, chopped
2 tablespoons fat
1 teaspoon sage
2 teaspoons salt, Dash pepper
6 to 8 apples
¼ cup brown sugar
3 cooked mashed sweetpotatoes

Cook giblets (gizzard, heart and liver) until tender; chop and mix with bread crumbs, onion, fat, sage, salt and pepper. Clean goose; remove fat from body cavity. Remove neck at body, leaving on neck skin. Rinse bird, pat dry. Rub cavities with salt. Spoon stuffing into body and neck; close cavity and fasten neck skin back with skewer. Place, breast side down, on rack in roasting pan. Roast uncovered at 325°F. for 2½ hours. Drain off fat occasionally. Turn goose, breast side up. Place apples in pan; bake 1 hour longer, or until goose tests done. **BAKED APPLES—** Wash and core apples; sprinkle with brown sugar and stuff with seasoned sweet potatoes. Serves 8.

ROAST GOOSE STUFFED WITH SAUERKRAUT—Omit bread stuffing. Drain 2 quarts Sauerkraut and stuff into goose. Roast in slow oven (325°F.) until tender, about 25 minutes to the pound. Apples with sweetpotatoes may be omitted.

STUFFED GOOSE NECKS

Goose meat (uncooked scraps)
Bread Stuffing
Goose neck skins, removed whole
1 onion sliced
1 cup hot water

Grind scraps of goose meat fine and mix with stuffing. Tie one end of the neck skin tight with clean string and stuff with mixture. Tie other end. Place in baking pan, add onion and water and bake in moderate oven (350°F.) until brown and crisp, basting occasionally. Serve hot, sliced. Beef casing, which may be purchased at the market, or chicken, turkey and duck necks may be used instead of the goose neck skins.

If you like, serve goose with stuffed oranges instead of baked apples

TO SKIN A GOOSE

Goose fat has always been highly prized by the housewife, especially if she raised her own birds or lived in a community that raised flocks. Its peculiar flavor, low melting point and easy accessibility make it very popular. The best process of preparing it for rendering was called "shinding" or less colloquially skinning. The best flavored fat is that lying just under the skin. Birds were and still are bred and fed to increase the depth of this layer, not alone to supply more fat but to improve the texture and flavor of the meat beneath. Geese are killed or come to market in the fall and continue until spring.

Singe plucked geese, wash in a solution of baking soda with a cloth or soft brush, enclose in a clean paper bag and chill well or freeze so fat will be firm.

To skin: Use a sharp, small knife and cut the skin down the backbone, around the base of the neck and wings and around the first joint of the legs. Then using a small dull knife, lift the layer of fat off the flesh underneath, holding the skin and fat in the left hand while the knife in the right continues to separate the fat from the meat. In some places the layer of connective tissue makes the process very easy. In other places the fat is all but attached to the muscle and care must be taken not to cut into the meat. As the pieces detached become too large to handle comfortably cut them off and drop into a heavy kettle containing 1 pint of cold water. When completely removed there should be just enough water to cover. Heat to boiling, then reduce heat and simmer until water has completely boiled away, as evidenced by the sputtering. Cool and pour off the fat into clean jars or cans. Store in a cold place. The remaining cracklings may be further reduced until the cracklings are brown. This fat should be stored separately, since it has a slightly "browned" flavor. It is reserved for meat cookery.

After the skin has been removed, break the body at the joint below the ribs, remove the entrails with their envelop of fat, and with great care remove the envelop and the fat that surrounds the giblets. This is then rendered separately, and used in meat cookery when a clear fat is wanted. In all cases, a slice of uncooked potato or fresh bread in the rendering kettle will help to carry off any odor or flavor.

The cracklings, well salted, are sometimes called "grieben" and served as appetizers.

The same method may be used for chicken or other poultry fat.

GOOSE GRIEBEN

(Cracklings)

Fat skin of a goose
Salt, 1 cup cold water

Cut the fat skin of a goose into 1 to 1½ inch squares, sprinkle with salt and let stand 12 hours. Wash well and drain. Add cold water, cover and simmer for 1 hour. Water is added to prevent fat from browning too rapidly and also to permit the steam to carry away any strong flavor the fat might have, giving the cracklings a delicate flavor. Drain and fry slowly to prevent scorching. If soft grieben are desired, remove them as soon as the fat is clear. To make crisp grieben, leave them in the hot fat until well browned and then place in oven a few minutes. Drain well on paper.

ROAST GOOSE AND CABBAGE

8- to 10- pound goose
3 onions, sliced
3 heads cabbage, chopped fine
Salt and pepper

Clean and prepare goose for roasting. Cut into serving portions, place in roasting pan and roast in slow oven (325°F.) until almost tender, about 2½ hours. Pour off most of the fat into a large saucepan; sauté onions in the fat and when brown add cabbage. Cook for several minutes; season. Then place pieces of goose on top of cabbage. Sprinkle with salt and pepper. Cover tightly and simmer for 1 hour or until goose is tender and cabbage is cooked. Serves 8.

SMOKED GOOSE

Meat from neck, wings and back of goose
Neck skin, left whole
Breast and legs
⅔ cup salt
1 tablespoon sugar
1 teaspoon saltpeter
½ clove garlic

Scrape edible meat from neck, wings and back of goose and chop fine. Stuff into neck skin and tie both ends. Rub breast, legs and filled neck with salt. Combine remaining ingredients and rub over goose meat; place in crock, cover with clean cloth, weight down with plate and set in a cool place for 7 days, turning occasionally. Drain, cover each piece with cheesecloth and smoke. Chill and slice thin to serve.

SMOKED DUCK OR TURKEY —
Use duck or turkey meat instead of goose. Sausage casings may be used instead of neck skin.

WILD DUCK WITH PECAN STUFFING

4 cups soft bread crumbs
1 cup finely chopped celery
1 cup finely chopped onion
1 cup seedless raisins
1 cup pecan meats, chopped
½ teaspoon salt
½ cup milk, scalded
2 eggs, beaten
2 (2½-pound) wild ducks
6 slices bacon
1 cup tomato catchup
¼ cup Worcestershire sauce
¼ cup A-1 sauce
½ cup chili sauce

Mix bread crumbs, celery, onions, raisins, nuts and salt together. Add hot milk to the beaten eggs and then add to dry mixture. Dress ducks and fill with stuffing. Close the slits by using poultry pins or by sewing. Place in roaster and cover each duck with 3 strips of bacon. Roast uncovered in moderate oven (350°F.) allowing 15 to 20 minutes per pound. Twenty minutes before serving time, combine the last 4 ingredients and baste the ducks

with the sauce. Garnish with parsley and slices of oranges with a few candied cranberries in center of each slice. Skim the fat from the sauce and serve the sauce with ducks. Salt pork may be used in place of bacon. Serves 4 to 6.

BRAISED MALLARD DUCKS

Dress the mallards; stuff with a bread, apple, nut and egg stuffing; truss and place in a covered roaster. Add water to the depth of 1 inch, a slice of onion and a small amount of thyme. Cover roaster and cook in a slow oven (325°F.) about 1 hour, remove cover so bird will brown and cook another 30 minutes. Use only enough water to prevent burning. Make gravy from the juices and pour over ducks.

In general, the carving of all fowl is much the same. Begin with a firm hold on the end of the drumstick. It comes off easily at the second joint

WILD DUCK

To pluck wild duck remove large feathers dry. Then prepare the following mixture:

⅜ pound paraffin
7 quarts boiling water

Melt paraffin in water. Dip duck in and out of boiling mixture 4 or 5 times or until paraffin has coated feathers. Cool duck to let paraffin harden, then strip off feathers and paraffin at the same time. Singe and remove any remaining pinfeathers.

Cut heads and feet from birds, remove entrails and wash with cold salt water. Dry thoroughly. The duck shot in the fall after a summer in the northern feeding grounds generally has a fine-flavored meat. Any stuffing may be used. Ducks shot in the spring may have a strong-flavored meat which is improved by soaking the cleaned bird 2 to 3 hours in fairly strong salt water to which 1 tablespoon baking soda has been added. The duck should then be rinsed, dried and stuffed with sliced apple or celery. The stuffing helps to absorb the strong flavor and should be removed before serving the duck.

Ducks must not be overcooked or the meat will be dry and crumbly. Roast uncovered in slow oven (325°F.) ¾ to 1½ hours. Brush frequently with fat while roasting.

PAN ROASTED WILD DUCK

Wrap bird in cloth dipped in melted fat. Place in roaster, breast down. Roast uncovered in moderate oven (350°F.) allowing 20 minutes per pound. Turn breast up when about half done. Baste frequently. Remove duck from oven when tender. Unwrap cloth.

GAME PIE

6 quail, pigeons or partridge
1 quart water
Salt and pepper
¼ cup minced parsley
½ onion, chopped
2 whole cloves
¼ pound salt pork, diced
2 tablespoons flour
2 tablespoons fat
2 cups diced cooked potatoes
½ recipe Pastry

Clean birds thoroughly and split into halves. Cover with water and heat to boiling. Skim, add salt, pepper, parsley, onion, cloves and salt pork. Simmer until tender, keeping birds covered with water. When birds are tender, thicken liquid with flour and heat gravy to boiling. Add fat, remove from heat and cool. Place birds in casserole, add potatoes and gravy. Cover with crust, slashed in the center, and bake in hot oven (425°F.) 15 to 20 minutes or until browned. Serves 10.

One cup sherry and 1½ cups sautéed mushrooms may be added when birds go into casserole.

ROAST WILD GOOSE

1 wild goose
Salt and pepper
1 tablespoon vinegar
1 onion
Flour

Clean goose well, season with salt, pepper and vinegar. Place an onion in cavity. Let stand overnight. Remove onion, dredge with flour and place in roasting pan in slow oven (325°F.). Roast uncovered until tender and browned, 20 to 25 minutes per pound, basting with juices in pan. Goose may be filled with stuffing if desired. Allow 1 pound per person.

QUAIL, SNIPE, PLOVER, WOODCOCK

Follow the directions for Broiled Chicken. Broil only 8 to 12 minutes. A strip of bacon, smoked butt, or salt pork may be placed over the top of each bird. Serve on toast with Currant Jelly. Allow 1 bird per person.

Remove wings at the joint nearest the body and cut the leg at the first joint

QUAIL BAKED IN WINE

½ cup fat
2 small onions, minced
2 whole cloves
1 teaspoon peppercorns
2 cloves garlic, cut fine
½ bay leaf
6 quail, cleaned and trussed
2 cups white wine
½ teaspoon salt
⅛ teaspoon pepper
Few grains cayenne
1 teaspoon minced chives
2 cups cream or evaporated milk

Melt fat, add onions, cloves, peppercorns, garlic and bay leaf; cook for several minutes. Add quail and brown on all sides. Add wine, salt, pepper, cayenne and chives and simmer until tender, about 30 minutes. Remove quail to hot serving dish. Strain sauce, add cream and heat to boiling point. Pour over quail. Allow 1 quail for each serving.

Insert fork between the ribs firmly to steady the bird while the breast and back meat is sliced off

ROAST GROUSE

Grouse are very dry birds and need larding to make them palatable. Clean bird and wipe with damp cloth. Cover completely with strips of bacon or salt pork. Roast in moderate oven (350°F.) until tender, about 1 hour. Baste frequently. Just before serving, remove bacon, brush the bird with melted fat, dredge with flour and return to the oven to brown. Gravy is served with grouse. Use the thickened juices from the roasting pan. One bird serves 4.

BROILED GROUSE—Parboil for 30 minutes before broiling. Drain and dry between towels; proceed as for other broiled game.

ROAST GUINEA HEN

1 guinea hen
¼ pound salt pork
Stuffing

Clean hen and lard with salt pork. The market will do this, if requested. Fill with stuffing.

Close opening and truss. **Place** breast side down in an uncovered roaster. Roast in moderate oven (350°F.) until tender, about 2 hours. Roast with breast down half of the time, turn and cook remaining time with breast up. Baste at half-hour intervals. One guinea hen serves 2 or 3.

FRIED PRAIRIE CHICKEN

1 young prairie chicken
Salt
Pepper
Flour
1 tablespoon butter
3 tablespoons other fat

Clean prairie chicken, dress and cut into serving portions. Plunge into cold water; drain thoroughly but do not wipe dry. Season well with salt and pepper and dredge thickly with flour. Fry chicken slowly in hot fat until brown and tender, about 45 minutes. Make Cream Gravy in the skillet and serve with the chicken. Serves 4.

PRAIRIE CHICKEN OR PHEASANT IN CREAM—Prepare prairie chicken or pheasant as for Duck in Cream.

PARTRIDGE

Partridges may be baked in a casserole, whole or cut, roasted, broiled, pan-fried, or braised.

LARDED STUFFED PARTRIDGE

3 partridges
Stuffing
Salt pork for larding
¼ cup water
½ cup sherry

Clean, stuff, lard and truss birds. Place in greased casserole, add water and bake in moderate oven (350°F.) 15 minutes. Add sherry, cover and continue cooking until tender, about 25 minutes. Serve with a grapefruit sauce for 6.

PHEASANT MULLIGAN WITH DUMPLINGS

2 young pheasants
2 cups diced carrots
1 cup diced onions
1 cup finely shredded cabbage
2 cups diced potatoes
2 tablespoons fat
Salt and pepper

DUMPLINGS
2 cups sifted flour
3 teaspoons baking powder
½ teaspoon salt
1 egg, ¾ cup milk

Clean pheasants, cut into serving portions and cover with water. Add carrots, onions and cabbage and cook slowly until nearly tender. Add potatoes, fat, salt and pepper. Cook until meat and vegetables are tender. Make dumplings as follows: sift flour, baking powder and salt together; beat egg, add milk and stir into dry ingredients, adding more milk, if necessary, to form a drop batter. Drop by tablespoons into the hot mulligan and cover kettle tightly. Cook for 15 minutes without lifting the cover. Serves 8.

ROAST TURKEY

Singe turkey while dry and remove pinfeathers with berry clip or dull edge of knife. Remove leg tendons as directed for chicken, or cut through skin around leg of turkey, 2 inches above the foot and insert knife beneath tendons to loosen from bone and muscle, being careful not to cut tendons. Place leg with the cut at edge of board and press downward sharply to snap bone. Pull foot away from body to remove tendons with the foot. If feet have been cut off, remove tendons by inserting a strong metal skewer into ends of tendons. Then pull them out. Make incision for drawing by cutting lengthwise of body. Remove vent, entrails and giblets, gall bladder, kidneys and lungs, being careful not to break gall bladder. Remove windpipe and crop from neck opening. Clean heart, liver and gizzard as for chicken, and use in stuffing or gravy if desired. Cut off neck of turkey close to body but leave neck skin. Save neck for soup or turkey stock. Cut out oil sac at base of tail. Scrub inside and out with warm water in which 1 tablespoon of baking soda has been dissolved. Dry turkey and rub cavity with salt.

Fill neck cavity with stuffing, covering breast with stuffing as directed for chicken, draw neck skin to back of turkey and fasten flat with skewer. Fold wing tips up toward back, tying in place across the back, if necessary. Fill body cavity loosely with stuffing, allowing for expansion. Close incision by inserting 3 skewers across opening and lacing together with cord, then wrap this cord around end of legs and tie securely to tail piece, so legs are close to body. Place breast up, on rack of shallow pan. Brush turkey with melted unsalted fat and cover with cloth dipped into melted unsalted fat, being sure breast, wings and legs are well covered; or cover with layer of body fat, then with clean cloth. Roast, uncovered, in slow oven (300°F.) until tender. Allow 25 minutes per pound for birds under 12 pounds, or 20 minutes per pound for larger birds. Baste several times with melted fat or with drippings in pan. Season when half done. Cloth may be removed during last ½ hour for additional browning. Remove string and skewers before serving. Allow ¾ to 1 pound per serving.

Turkey is trussed for roasting just as other poultry, see illustrations pages 408-12

TURKEY PIE

12-pound turkey
1 onion, 2 whole cloves
4 carrots, sliced
½ white turnip, sliced
1 small clove garlic
3 slices parsnip
½ cup flour, ½ teaspoon pepper
1 teaspoon salt
½ teaspoon nutmeg
3 cups turkey stock
½ teaspoon lemon juice
2 cups cream or evaporated milk
2 recipes Pastry

Cut turkey into pieces, half cover with boiling water. Add onion, cloves, carrots, turnip, garlic and parsnips. Simmer until turkey is tender. Remove turkey and cool. Strain stock, chill and skim off fat. Melt ½ cup turkey fat, add flour, pepper, salt and nutmeg. Blend. Add turkey stock, lemon juice and cream. Cook until thickened, stirring constantly. Cut turkey into ¾-inch cubes and add 6 cups diced turkey to sauce. Cool. Roll pastry and line individual piepans. Fill with creamed turkey, brush the edges of pastry with water, cover with top crust and press edges together. Make a few slits in top crust to allow for escape of steam. Bake in hot oven (400°F.) for 15 minutes, reduce heat to moderate (350°F.) and bake until brown. Serves 10.

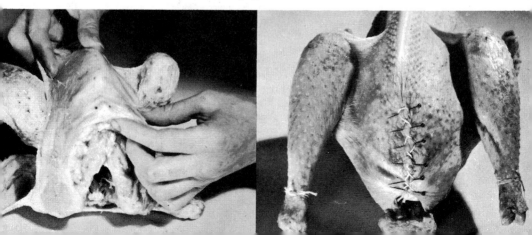

BROILED TURKEY

Use a very young turkey (poult) or older bird steamed 1 hour. Cut bird into serving pieces and use breast, thighs and drumsticks. The other pieces are best cooked in some other way, though they may be broiled if desired. Brush pieces with melted butter, place under slow broiler heat and cook slowly until tender, 30 to 60 minutes, depending upon thickness of piece. Turn pieces as required to brown on all sides. For each cup of drippings blend 2 tablespoons melted fat and 2 tablespoons flour. Add drippings and simmer until thickened, stirring constantly. Add chopped cooked giblets and serve gravy with the turkey.

If additional gravy is desired, combine drippings with water in which giblets were cooked.

BRAISED TURKEY

8-pound turkey
Stuffing
½ pound salt pork, sliced thin
½ cup chopped celery
½ cup chopped carrots
½ cup chopped onion
½ cup chopped turnip
4 cups water or stock

Stuff turkey and truss. Spread slices of salt pork over the breast and legs. Spread remaining salt pork and the chopped vegetables in a double roaster. Place turkey on this mixture with the breast up; cover roaster tightly; cook in moderate oven (350°F.) until tender, about 25 minutes per pound. At the end of 30 minutes add water or stock. During the last ½ hour uncover and remove pork from turkey. Serve with Mushroom Sauce, or with the gravy in the pan, strained and thickened. Serves 10.

TURKEY CURTIS

3 tablespoons fat
4 tablespoons flour
½ teaspoon salt
2 cups turkey stock
⅔ cup diced cooked turkey
½ cup sautéed mushrooms
1 egg yolk, beaten
2 tablespoons chopped pimiento
6 rounds hot buttered toast
⅓ to ½ cup grated cheese
1 tablespoon minced parsley
Paprika

Melt fat, blend in flour and salt. Add stock and cook until thickened, stirring constantly. Add turkey, mushrooms, egg yolk and pimiento. Cook for 1 minute stirring constantly. Place toast in a greased shallow pan, cover with turkey mixture and sprinkle with cheese. Bake for 4 minutes in hot oven (400°F.) or under broiler until cheese melts. Garnish with parsley and sprinkle with paprika. Serves 6.

TURKEY CURRY

1 cup mushrooms
⅓ cup minced onion
1 large apple, pared and diced
3 cups diced cooked turkey
6 tablespoons fat
3 tablespoons flour
½ teaspoon salt
1 to 1½ teaspoons curry powder
1½ cups turkey stock and top milk or cream

Cook mushrooms, onion, apple and turkey in the fat until onion and apple are tender, 10 to 15 minutes. If fresh mushrooms are used, sauté several minutes before adding other ingredients. Remove from heat, blend in flour, salt and curry powder. Add liquid and cook until thickened, stirring constantly. Place over hot water, cover and cook 15 minutes longer. Add more seasoning if desired. Serve with hot rice cooked without salt. Serves 6.

FILLETS OF TURKEY WITH RICE

Breast fillets of turkey
1 egg
2 tablespoons water
Bread crumbs
3 cups turkey or chicken stock
1 cup rice
½ teaspoon onion juice
1 teaspoon salt
2 teaspoons butter
1 tablespoon grated cheese
Pepper
6 tablespoons oil or melted fat

Skin breast of a cooked turkey and separate into fillets about ½ inch thick and as uniform as possible. Beat egg and add water. Dip fillets into egg, then into crumbs, again into egg and into crumbs. Chill. Heat stock with rice, onion juice and ½ teaspoon salt; cover and simmer until liquid is absorbed. When rice is tender add butter and cheese; season with remaining salt and pepper. Cook fillets slowly in oil until brown. Heap rice in center of hot dish and arrange the fillets around it. Serves 6.

ESCALLOPED TURKEY AND CAULIFLOWER

1 head cauliflower
3 tablespoons turkey fat
Salt and pepper
3 tablespoons flour
1½ cups turkey stock or milk
1 to 2 cups diced cooked turkey

Break cauliflower into flowerets and cook in boiling salted water about 6 minutes, or until almost tender. Drain. Melt fat and add salt, pepper and flour. Add stock and cook until thickened, stirring constantly. Arrange cauliflower and turkey in greased casserole, add sauce and bake in moderate oven (350°F.) until heated through, about 20 minutes. Serves 4 to 6.

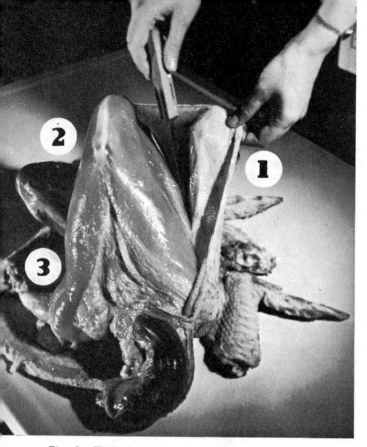

Fig. 1. *With the turkey on a table where you have freedom of action, slit the skin from the neck down the breast bone to the vent*

STEP 3. Loosen muscles at the end of the breast bone and pull meat from breast bones, pulling up toward the neck. Loosen with knife where necessary. Remove remaining meat on carcass by pulling and cutting away with knife.

STEP 4. Spread skin into square or rectangle on flat surface.

STEP 5. Place light and dark meat over the skin to form a fairly even layer. The meat may be mixed or the light and dark meat kept separate and arranged to make distinct layers. Season with salt and pepper.

STEP 6. (**Figure 2**). Roll the turkey muscle and skin tightly together and tie roll firmly. Rub with fat, place on rack of roaster (**Figure 3**) and roast uncovered in slow oven (325°F.) 30 to 35 minutes per pound, or to an internal temperature of 185°F. Baste occasionally with drippings or melted fat. Remove strings and slice hot or cold. (**Figure 4.**) Draw carcass, save giblets and use bones for soup.

SILHOUETTE TURKEY ROLL— Place white meat next to skin, cover with dark meat including cooked or ground giblets. Proceed as above.

TURKEY ROLL

Fig. 2. *Hold the roll firmly with one hand while rolling with the other*

STEP 1. (**Figure 1**). Remove skin all in one piece from turkey. Cut skin around small end of drumstick. Remove wings at the second joint. Slit skin from neck to vent, cutting down the center of breast and along keel bone. Remove skin by pulling from flesh, loosening with knife where necessary. (1) Skin removed from 1 side; (2) Skinned leg; (3) Wing joints.

STEP 2. Remove legs by disjointing at the hip in the usual way.

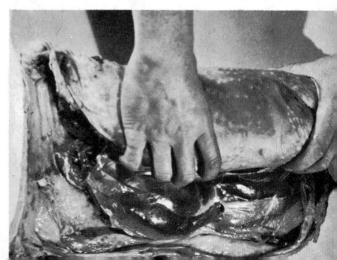

STUFFED TURKEY ROLL—Cut off legs before removing skin. Use only the white meat for the roll. Spread white meat over skin and cover with desired stuffing. Roll and bake as above. Bone legs, stuff and truss into individual rolls.

TURKEY IN CASSEROLE

8-pound turkey
1 quart water
3 tablespoons minced onion
1 cup fat
Salt and pepper
Celery salt
3 stalks celery, chopped
½ pound fresh mushrooms
2 tablespoons flour
1 quart heavy cream or evaporated milk

Cut turkey into serving portions. Simmer drumsticks, neck, back and wings in water to which onion has been added. Simmer until tender, about 2 hours. Fry remaining turkey in hot fat until brown on all sides. Arrange pieces in a casserole; sprinkle with salt, pepper and celery salt and add celery. Pour over them about half the fat remaining in the skillet and 1 cup turkey broth (from neck, etc.). Cover closely and bake in moderate oven (350°F.) until tender, about 2 hours. Clean mushrooms, slice and sauté for 5 minutes in the rest of fat in skillet. About ½ hour before turkey is done add mushrooms. Blend flour with remaining fat, add cream and cook until thickened, stirring constantly. Pour over turkey and continue baking until cream sauce is blended with gravy and turkey is tender Serves 10.

FRENCH FRIED TURKEY—Prepare turkey in the same way as French Fried Chicken.

ROASTED HALF TURKEY

METHOD 1. Prepare the half turkey for roasting the same as a whole turkey. If necessary lace the gash made by drawing. This will make a more bowl-like cavity to hold the stuffing. Tie the leg end to the tail piece. Wrap a double fold of cheesecloth dipped in melted fat around this end to prevent drying out. Fold wing against the breast. Place a spoonful of stuffing in the neck, bringing the neck skin over it and down toward the cavity. Fill the cavity with stuffing and cover with a sheet of parchment paper. With cord hold the parchment to body by tying at both ends. Place rack of roaster over parchment and invert into open roaster. Brush turkey with melted unsalted fat, cover with cloth dipped into melted unsalted fat and bake in slow oven (300°F.) until tender, allowing 18 to 25 minutes per pound. Baste with fat at ½ to 1 hour intervals while roasting. Remove cloth during last ½ hour, if deep brown color is desired. Allow ¾ to 1 pound per person.

METHOD 2—Truss the half as described above, but do not stuff. Bake in open roaster in slow oven (300°F.) skin side up, until browned, about ½ the total cooking time. Remove from oven, invert and place stuffing in cavity. Cover with parchment paper Return to oven and cook the remainder of the time with skin side down. Roast 18 to 25 minutes per pound. Allow ¾ to 1 pound per person.

FRIED TURKEY—Use young birds, or older birds steamed or parboiled. Cut turkey into serving portions, prepare and cook as for Alabama Fried Chicken.

Fig. 3. Tie the roll tightly folding the skin under

TURKEY RING

2 cups diced cooked turkey
1 cup soft bread crumbs
1 tablespoon fat, melted
½ teaspoon salt
⅛ teaspoon pepper
1 cup hot milk
2 eggs, beaten
¼ cup chopped celery
2 tablespoons minced green pepper
2 tablespoons minced pimiento

Combine ingredients in the order listed and mix thoroughly. Pour into greased ring mold or loaf pan. Bake in moderate oven (350°F.) about 35 to 40 minutes. Let stand 5 minutes before unmolding. Fill center with sautéed or creamed mushrooms. Serves 6.

Fig. 4. Stuffed rolled turkey is delicious for any party

TURKEY AND HAM MOUSSE

1 tablespoon unflavored gelatin
¼ cup cold water
2 tablespoons fat
2 tablespoons flour
1¼ teaspoons salt
¼ teaspoon pepper
2 cups milk or equal parts milk and stock
½ cup ground cooked turkey
½ cup ground cooked ham
1 hard-cooked egg, minced
½ cup finely cut celery
¼ cup chopped pimiento
½ cup mayonnaise

Soften gelatin in cold water. Melt fat, blend in flour, salt and pepper; add milk and cook until thickened, stirring constantly. Dissolve gelatin in hot sauce. Add turkey, ham, egg, celery, pimiento and mayonnaise and mix thoroughly. Pour into ring mold and chill until firm. Unmold and garnish with chicory, tomato wedges and sliced pineapple. Serves 8.

TURKEY CLUB SANDWICHES

18 slices hot toast
¼ cup mayonnaise
Cold cooked turkey, sliced thin
6 lettuce leaves
3 small tomatoes, sliced
1 tablespoon chili sauce
12 slices crisp hot bacon
6 stuffed olives
6 sweet pickles

Spread 6 slices of toast with mayonnaise; cover each with turkey and a lettuce leaf. Cover with a second slice of toast, arrange tomatoes on top; spread with chili sauce and place strips of bacon on tomato. Cover with third slice of toast. Cut diagonally and garnish with olives and pickles. If necessary fasten sandwiches together with toothpicks. Makes 6 double-decker sandwiches.

CASSEROLE OF TURKEY AND NOODLES

1 (6-ounce) package noodles
1 green pepper, chopped
3 tablespoons turkey fat
3 tablespoons flour
½ teaspoon salt
⅛ teaspoon white pepper or few grains cayenne
1½ cups milk
1 to 2 cups diced cooked turkey
⅛ to ¼ pound cheese, chopped or grated
1 small can mushrooms, sliced
4 hard-cooked eggs, sliced

Cook noodles in boiling salted water until tender. Drain. Sauté green pepper in fat until tender but not brown. Blend in flour and seasonings. Add milk (part turkey stock may be used) and cook until thickened, stirring constantly. Arrange noodles, sauce and remaining ingredients in alternate layers in greased casserole and bake in moderate oven (350°F.) about 25 minutes. Serves 4.

Omit cheese and eggs. Add ¾ cup chopped pimientos.

TURKEY SCALLOP

2½ cups bread crumbs
1½ cups diced cooked turkey
1 teaspoon salt
Dash pepper
Few drops Tabasco sauce
2 cups turkey gravy
4 tablespoons milk
2 eggs, beaten
2 tablespoons butter

Arrange alternate layers of 1½ cups crumbs and diced turkey in casserole, seasoning each layer of turkey with salt, pepper and Tabasco sauce. Pour gravy over all. Combine remaining crumbs, milk and eggs; spread over the top of casserole and dot with butter. Bake in moderate oven (350°F.) about 30 minutes. Serves 6.

TURKEY À LA KING

¼ cup mushrooms
2 tablespoons fat
1½ tablespoons flour
¼ teaspoon salt
1 teaspoon Worcestershire sauce
1 cup milk
¼ cup chopped green pepper
¼ cup stuffed olives, chopped
1 cup diced cooked turkey
3 slices hot toast

Cook mushrooms in fat for 5 minutes. Add flour, salt and Worcestershire sauce; blend, add milk and cook until thickened, stirring constantly. Add green pepper, olives and turkey. Heat and serve on toast. Serves 3.

TURKEY OR CHICKEN SOUFFLÉ

2 tablespoons fat
2 tablespoons flour
⅛ teaspoon pepper
1 teaspoon salt
¼ teaspoon paprika
1½ cups milk or stock
½ cup soft bread crumbs
3 eggs, separated
2 cups chopped cooked turkey or chicken
1 teaspoon lemon juice
Chopped parsley, green or red pepper or pimiento

Melt fat, blend in flour, pepper, salt and paprika. Add milk and cook until thickened, stirring constantly. Add crumbs; pour over beaten egg yolks, add turkey or chicken and lemon juice. Cool. Fold in stiffly beaten egg whites and remaining seasonings. Pour into greased mold or individual cups. Set in pan of hot water and cook in moderate oven (350° F.) 20 to 35 minutes or until firm. Serve with White or Mushroom sauce for 8.

Chopped mushrooms may be added to the mixture before cooking.

PIGEONS

Tame pigeons are the most desirable to eat. Wild pigeons are likely to be tough. Allow ½ to 1 pigeon per person, depending on size. Method of preparation is the same as for chicken. Suggested methods for preparing pigeons are braising, broiling, stewing and roasting.

Squabs are the nestlings of pigeons, usually marketed at about 4 weeks of age when they weigh around ¾ pound. They are very tender and delicately flavored. Prepare by any of methods suggested for pigeon.

ROAST PIGEONS

4 small pigeons
Salt
Stuffing
Melted fat

Prepare the same as Roast Chicken, cooking in moderate oven (325°F.) from 45 to 60 minutes or until tender. Serve with Currant Jelly. Garnish with parsley. Allow 1 small pigeon to each person. Serves 4.

The delicacy of roast pigeon is always a delight

ROAST PIGEONS WITH RICE PILAU

6 slices bacon
¾ cup chopped celery
1 onion, chopped
2 cups uncooked rice
4 cups chicken stock
4 eggs
Salt and pepper
4 pigeons
Mustard pickle juice

Dice bacon and fry until crisp. Remove bacon and brown celery and onion in drippings. Boil rice in chicken stock until tender, add bacon, celery and onion. Beat eggs and add rice. Season with salt and pepper. Dress pigeons, fill with rice mixture and place on mounds of remaining rice. Bake in slow oven (325°F.) from 45 to 60 minutes, basting frequently with mustard pickle juice. Serves 4.

DEVILED SQUABS—Cut slashes in 4 dressed squabs, rub in mustard and cayenne and broil squabs. Cream ½ cup butter, add 2 teaspoons mustard, 2 teaspoons Worcestershire sauce, ¼ teaspoon pepper, dash cayenne and ¼ teaspoon salt. Spread over broiled squabs just before serving

AUSTRALIAN ROAST SQUABS

1 onion, chopped fine
4 chicken livers
3 slices bacon, diced
4 tablespoons fat
¼ cup raisins
1 cup soft bread crumbs
¼ cup sherry
Salt and pepper
3 squabs

Cook chopped onion, chicken livers and bacon in 2 tablespoons fat. Chop fine and combine with raisins, bread crumbs and wine; season and mix well. Stuff squabs and truss. Place in casserole, brush with remaining fat, cover and roast in moderate oven (350° F.) until squabs are tender, about 45 to 60 minutes, basting frequently with melted fat. Serve on toast. Allow 1 squab per person.

Stuff with a Mushroom Stuffing.

PIGEON PIE

1 recipe Pastry
4 squabs, parboiled
3 tablespoons flour
3 tablespoons fat, melted
2 cups stock in which squabs were boiled
1 cup milk
Salt and pepper
Buttered bread crumbs

Line a deep casserole with pastry. Fry squabs until well browned and place in casserole. Blend flour with fat; add stock and milk slowly. Season with salt and pepper and cook, stirring constantly, until thickened. Pour sauce over squabs; sprinkle buttered bread crumbs on top and bake in very hot oven (450°F.) 10 minutes. Reduce heat to moderate (350° to 375°F.) and continue baking 8 to 10 minutes, until crumbs and edges of crust are browned. Serves 4.

BREAD STUFFING

1½-pound loaf bread, dried
½ to 1 cup fat, melted
1 teaspoon salt
¼ teaspoon white pepper
¼ cup minced onion
2 tablespoons poultry seasoning

Remove crusts from bread and cut bread into 1-inch cubes. Toss all ingredients together lightly. Will fill a 6-pound fowl.

Stuffing does not necessarily need to be baked in the fowl or meat. If the bird is small or if there is some stuffing left over it may be baked or steamed in a greased ring mold, loaf pan or individual molds. Fill center of ring with vegetables. Croquettes of stuffing may be served around bird.

CELERY—Add 2 cups chopped celery, parboiled or uncooked.

CHESTNUT—Add 1 pound chestnuts, cooked and chopped.

GIBLET—Add chopped, cooked giblets.

MUSHROOM—Add ¼ to ½ pound mushrooms, chopped and sautéed in 1 tablespoon butter for 5 minutes.

OLIVE—Add 1 cup or more coarsely chopped olives.

OYSTER—Add 1 pint oysters, chopped, and heated in 2 tablespoons butter.

PINEAPPLE NUT STUFFING

4 cups dry bread, ½-inch cubes
¾ cup finely chopped celery
¾ cup pineapple wedges
½ cup walnut meats, chopped fine
1 canned pimiento, chopped
Dash cayenne
1 teaspoon paprika
1½ teaspoons salt
¼ cup butter
2 eggs

Combine bread, celery, pineapple, walnut meats, pimiento and seasonings. Melt butter, remove from heat, stir in unbeaten eggs and add to bread mixture. Toss lightly. Use as stuffing for turkey, chicken or duck.

Use chopped cooked bacon instead of nuts, reduce salt to ½ teaspoon and add grated onion or use red or green pepper instead of pimiento.

ALMOND STUFFING FOR SQUAB

½ cup soft bread crumbs
¼ cup milk
Salt and pepper
2 tablespoons butter, melted
¼ cup chopped salted almonds

Soak crumbs in milk, add remaining ingredients and blend thoroughly. Will fill 2 squabs.

When the bird is small, make a ring mold or croquettes of additional stuffing

WALNUT POULTRY STUFFING

Giblets from 1 fowl
1 onion, sliced
1 bay leaf
1 cup boiling water
½ pound dry bread
1 tablespoon salt
2 tablespoons poultry seasoning or sage
2 cups chopped walnuts
4 tablespoons fat, melted

Cook giblets, onion and bay leaf in boiling water until tender. Remove bay leaf, drain giblets and chop fine. Remove crusts from bread and break into fine crumbs. Combine all ingredients and toss together lightly. Moisten with giblet stock. Will fill a 12- to 14-pound fowl.

WILD RICE STUFFING

½ cup wild rice
1 quart boiling water
Salt and pepper
½ pound fresh mushrooms, sautéed
½ teaspoon sage
Dash thyme
1 tablespoon melted fat
1 egg yolk, beaten

Cook rice in the boiling water until tender, approximately 25 minutes. Drain and rinse. Add remaining ingredients and blend well. Will fill a 2-pound bird.

FRUIT STUFFING FOR GOOSE

3 cups bread cubes
½ cup fat, melted
1 cup chopped apples
½ cup chopped cooked prunes
¼ to ½ cup chopped nuts
1 teaspoon salt
¼ teaspoon pepper
1 tablespoon lemon juice

Mix all ingredients lightly. Will fill a 4- to 5-pound goose.

Fresh Vegetables and Potatoes

600 Ways to Serve
Potatoes
and Vegetables

Things You Should Know

SELECTION OF VEGETABLES

IN SEASON
Buy vegetables in their season. Many vegetables are in the market the year round, and modern agriculture has greatly extended the season for many others, but some, when out of season, lack flavor and freshness.

IN GOOD CONDITION
Vegetables should be fresh, firm and ripe. Do not buy vegetables that are old, withered, moldy or bruised, underripe or overripe; there is no saving in cost from purchasing such vegetables. Head vegetables should be solid, with few waste leaves. Cauliflower should be white and firm, with no blemishes. Leafy vegetables should be crisp. Peas and beans should have crisp pods. Buy vegetables of medium size and regular shape.

QUANTITIES
Buy only the amount of summer vegetables you can use immediately, because they deteriorate in quality very quickly and are best when cooked soon after gathering.

Winter vegetables may be bought in larger amounts if there is a suitable dry, cool place for storage.

CARE OF VEGETABLES

SUMMER VEGETABLES — If
these are not to be cooked at once, they should be put into the refrigerator immediately. Peas and corn, especially, should be cooked soon after they are gathered, because they lose their sweetness rapidly. Greens and crisp vegetables should be washed and placed in closely covered enamel or porcelain containers.

WINTER VEGETABLES — These
should be in good condition, firm and uninjured and stored in a dry, cool, well ventilated place. Most of them keep better if they are piled up so that the air is excluded. Squash, however, keep better if they are spread out so that they do not touch one another. Squash and sweetpotatoes require a warmer place than other vegetables. Vegetables cannot be kept well in an unpartitioned cellar containing a furnace.

PREPARATION OF VEGETABLES FOR COOKING

Wash all vegetables before cooking, even though they look clean. A vegetable brush is almost a necessity. Dry winter vegetables may be improved by soaking them before cooking for several hours. Vegetables that are soaked after they are pared lose some soluble food materials. Scrape thin-skinned vegetables; pare thick-skinned vegetables or remove the skin after cooking. Make thin parings except in the case of turnips, from which a thick layer of corky material should be removed. Many vegetables, particularly of the bud, head and fruit groups, should be immersed in cold salt water for ½ hour. This freshens the fiber and drives out any insects that have taken refuge in crevices. Leaf vegetables should be washed in several waters or in running water. The leaves should be lifted out of the water rather than the water poured off.

COOKING TO RETAIN THE PROTECTIVE ELEMENTS

BAKING is the best method to preserve vitamins and minerals. Dry baking in their skins generally used for potatoes, sweetpotatoes, squash, turnips, carrots, onions, and parsnips is a simple method whereby they are baked in a hot oven until they are just tender when pierced with a sharp fork. Baking, however, also includes the roasting of whole vegetables with meat, gravy, or fat, especially when potatoes or sweet potatoes are scraped, preserving minerals under the skin.

AU GRATIN AND SCALLOPING are other forms of baking, especially when fresh vegetables are used with cheese or crumbs. Leftover cooked vegetables may be prepared by these methods also, but the vitamin and mineral value will be determined by the first cooking. Only baking in the jacket will insure the preservation of the vitamins.

WATERLESS COOKING of fresh vegetables is any process in which no water is added. The water in the vegetable itself does the cooking. A thick-walled kettle with a tight-fitting lid is the necessary equipment. Very low heat is used, and the vegetable is tender in a very short time because neither heat nor steam escapes. No minerals are lost and the loss of vitamins is almost as low as in baking.

About VEGETABLES

STEAMING is cooking in live steam and valuable for the vegetables that can stand a high temperature for a longer period: carrots, beets, parsnips, sweetpotatoes, wax beans, or those that are cooked in the meat pot so that the extracted minerals and vitamins are used in the gravy.

BOILING does the most damage to vegetables, yet it is used most frequently by the largest number of homemakers. Although there are methods that reduce the losses to a minimum, the modern woman should remember that boiling is to be used least often, and always to be overbalanced by the better methods. Most of the mineral salts occurring in vegetables are easily dissolved in water and the loss of vitamins during boiling takes place in several ways. They may be destroyed by overheating, by prolonged exposure to the air, and by dissolving out in the cooking water. When this is drained off and discarded, the principal food values gained by the intelligent buying of vegetables have been thrown away.

THE AMOUNT OF WATER

In every case only the smallest possible amount of water should be used and it should be boiling rapidly when the vegetables are dropped in. Then the heat reduced when vegetables are at boiling temperature. They should be cooked only until just tender.

TO BOIL VEGETABLES PROPERLY,

methods must be selected according to the color:

1. The green vegetables are best cooked in an uncovered kettle in water that is slightly alkaline to retain the color. A bit of baking soda the size of a pinhead may be used to intensify the color but it is not recommended for continual use (except for that part of the country where the drinking water is always slightly acid) because it reduces the vitamin content and breaks down the texture. Cook only until tender. If overcooked, green vegetables turn brownish because of chemical changes in the coloring matter, the fine flavor is ruined, while food values are lost.

2. White fresh vegetables such as cabbage, cauliflower and onion are strong-flavored, due to their special oils. Hard water changes these oils so that the white color turns to yellow or brown. To prevent this, add 1 teaspoon of lemon juice or white vinegar. Drop the vegetable into enough rapidly boiling water to cover and cook with the kettle uncovered until just tender to the fork. Add the drained water, if any, to your soup.

3. The red color in vegetables is produced by acid and needs to be kept that way. Tomatoes usually have enough acid of their own to keep the color, but beets and red cabbage need a teaspoon of lemon juice or white vinegar. Cook in a small amount of water in a covered kettle.

4 Yellow vegetables are among the most valuable and stable. That rich yellow color is not only beauty but actually the foundation of vitamin A. Not much damage can be done to it although the minerals and other vitamins can still be destroyed if the vegetable is carelessly handled. Cook covered in a minimum amount of water.

Vegetables may be prepared by other methods such as broiling, sautéing, panning, or combinations of methods according to the family's desires. The recipes included in this book use these various methods. The amount of vitamins and minerals retained depend on which method is most prominent.

IMPORTANCE OF VEGETABLES IN THE DIET

The appreciation of vegetables as food has greatly increased in recent years, with an extended understanding of their peculiar values. The modern woman knows that vegetables provide not only starches and sugars for energy, as well as several forms of protein, but what is most important they provide impressive amounts of vitamins A, B, C, E, and G, in addition to mineral salts. These mineral salts are especially calcium, phosphorus, iron, copper, manganese, and sulphur, as well as iodine, in vegetables grown along the seashore. Besides all this she knows that the generous use of many vegetables helps to keep up the body's normal alkaline balance, which contributes so largely to health and vitality.

The following vitamin and mineral tables will help her choose those vegetables which give maximum protection.

VITAMIN CONTENT OF VEGETABLES

Vegetable	A	B	C	B₂
Artichokes, globe	AA	B	C	
Asparagus	A		CC	
Beans, Lima	A	BB		B_2
Beans, string	AA	BB	CC	B_2B_2
Beets	A	B	C	B_2
Beet leaves	AA	BB		$B_2B_2B_2$
Broccoli	AAAA	BB	C	$B_2B_2B_2$
Brussels sprouts	AA	BB		
Cabbage, cooked	A	BB	C	B_2B_2
Carrots	AAA	BB	CC	B_2B_2
Cauliflower	A	BB	C	B_2B_2
Celery	— to A	BB	CC	
Chicory	A		C	
Chinese cabbage	AA	BB	CCC	B_2
Collards	AAA	BB	CC	B_2B_2
Corn, yellow, sweet	AA	BB		B_2
Cucumbers	— to A	B	CC	B_2
Dandelion greens	AAA	BB	C	B_2B_2
Dasheens	A	B	C	
Eggplant	A	B	C	B_2B_2
Endive	AA		C	
Escarole	AAA		C	B_2B_2
Kale	AAA	B	CC	$B_2B_2B_2$
Kohlrabi		B	C	
Lettuce	A to AA	BB	CC	B_2B_2
Mustard greens	AAA	B	CC	B_2B_2
Okra	AA	BB		
Onions, cooked	— to A	B	C	B_2
Parsley	AAA	BB	CCC	
Parsnips	— to A	BB		
Peas, green	AA	BB	CCC	B_2B_2
Peppers, green	AA	BB	CCC	
Pimientos	AAA		CCC	
Potatoes, white	A	BB	CC	B_2
Radishes	— to A	BB	CC	
Romaine	AA	BB		B_2B_2
Rutabaga	— to A	BB	CCC	
Sauerkraut	A	B	C to CC	
Spinach	AAA	B	CC	B_2B_2
Squash, Hubbard	AAA	B		B_2
Squash, summer	A	B		B_2
Soybeans, fresh	AAA	BB		B_2
Sweetpotatoes	AAA	BB	CC	B_2
Swiss chard	AA	B to BB		
Tomatoes	AA	BB	CCC	B_2
Turnips, white	— to A	BB	CC	B_2B_2
Turnip greens	AAA	BB	CCC	B_2B_2
Vegetable marrow	A	B		B_2
Watercress	AAA	BB	CCC	B_2B_2
Zucchini	A	B		B_2

MINERALS IN THE ORDER OF AMOUNTS CONTAINED

CALCIUM
Turnip tops, Collards
Kale, Watercress
Cauliflower, Endive
Lentils, dried
Swiss chard, Kohlrabi
Spinach, Celery
Dandelion greens

COPPER
Navy beans, dried
Lima beans, dried
Peas, dried
Lentils, dried
Turnips, Radishes
Lettuce, Cauliflower
Onions, Watercress
Asparagus, Beet greens

IRON
Lima beans, dried
Lentils, dried
Navy beans, dried
Turnip tops
Beet greens
Swiss chard
Dandelion greens
Watercress
Sweet corn, dried
Spinach, Kale

MANGANESE
Chestnuts
Peas, dried
Lima beans, dried
Navy beans, dried
Turnip tops
Beet greens
Spinach, Beets
Okra, Sweet corn
Artichokes, String beans

PHOSPHORUS
Beans, dried
Peas, dried
Lentils, dried
Sweet corn, dried
Lima beans, dried
Brussels sprouts
Sweet corn, fresh
Broccoli, String beans

COOKED JERUSALEM ARTICHOKES

1½ pounds Jerusalem artichokes
¾ teaspoon salt
Boiling water

Wash artichokes, scrape and place in cold water. Drain; add salt and boiling water to cover. Cover pan and cook about 30 minutes or until tender. To serve, season with butter and pepper. For 6.

Dice artichokes and serve with Browned Onion Butter.

JERUSALEM ARTICHOKES WITH PARSLEY SAUCE

4 cups Cooked Jerusalem Artichokes
1 recipe Parsley Sauce
Paprika

Combine artichokes and parsley sauce and heat thoroughly. Sprinkle with paprika. Serves 6 to 8.

JERUSALEM ARTICHOKE SOUFFLÉ

2 cups hot Riced Jerusalem Artichokes
½ cup hot White Sauce
2 eggs, separated
½ teaspoon salt
⅛ teaspoon pepper
1 tablespoon grated cheese

Combine artichokes and white sauce and beat thoroughly. Add beaten egg yolks, salt and pepper and beat again. Fold in stiffly beaten egg whites, pour into greased baking dish and sprinkle with cheese. Bake in moderate oven (350°F.) about 25 to 30 minutes. Serves 6 to 8.

Add 2 tablespoons sautéed minced onions to mixture.

Artichokes are a delicious and entertaining vegetable with butter or cheese sauce

COOKED GLOBE ARTICHOKES

6 to 8 globe artichokes
Boiling water to cover
1 teaspoon salt

Wash artichokes in salted water and drain, bottoms up. Remove the thick, loose leaves around base and clip off tip of each leaf if sharp. Place artichokes in saucepan, add water and salt and cook 25 to 35 minutes. Drain with bottoms up. Serve with a small cup of melted butter or mayonnaise.

To eat: Pull off a leaf, hold by the tip and dip into butter or mayonnaise. Remove the fleshy part of the base of the leaf with the teeth and discard the remainder of the leaf. When all the leaves are removed, discard the choke—the "hairy" part above the heart. Eat the heart with a fork. Serves 6 to 8.

WITH CHEESE—Open center of Cooked Globe Artichoke and remove choke. Fill center with Cheese Sauce.

SCALLOPED GLOBE ARTICHOKES

6 Cooked Globe Artichokes
1½ tablespoons lemon juice
1 cup dry bread crumbs
½ teaspoon salt
⅛ teaspoon pepper
2 eggs, beaten
1 cup cream or evaporated milk

Scrape edible portion from inside of artichoke leaves, remove choke and cut heart into pieces. Sprinkle with lemon juice. Mix artichokes, bread crumbs, salt and pepper together and place in greased baking dish. Combine eggs and cream and mix well. Pour over artichoke mixture and bake in moderate oven (375°F.) about 25 minutes or until browned. Serves 6 to 8.

RICED JERUSALEM ARTICHOKES

4 cups Cooked Jerusalem
  Artichokes
2 tablespoons butter
2 tablespoons cream

Force artichokes through ricer into serving dish. Indent center of mound with a spoon. Melt butter, add cream and pour into indentation. Serves 6 to 8.

Serve with Browned Onion Butter.

COOKED ASPARAGUS

2 pounds asparagus
Boiling water
1 teaspoon salt

Wash the asparagus thoroughly and tie in 1 bundle or into 6 to 8 individual bundles. Place bundles upright with stems down in just enough boiling water to cover thick part of stalks, add salt and cook 10 minutes or until stalks are tender. Arrange bundles in water so tips are covered and cook 5 minutes longer. To serve, season with pepper and butter. Serves 6 to 8.

WITH HOLLANDAISE — Serve hot Cooked Asparagus with Hollandaise Sauce poured across the bunches and a strip of pimiento over the sauce.

WITH C H E E S E SAUCE — To vary, serve with Cheese Sauce.

ASPARAGUS SOUFFLÉ

3 tablespoons butter, melted
3 tablespoons flour
1 cup milk
4 eggs, separated
2½ cups diced Cooked Asparagus
¾ teaspoon salt

Blend butter and flour, add milk gradually and cook slowly until thickened, stirring constantly. Beat egg yolks until thick and lemon colored, add asparagus and salt and add to sauce. Beat egg whites until stiff and fold into asparagus mixture, pour into greased casserole, set in pan of hot water and bake in slow oven (325°F.) about 45 minutes. For 6.

Green asparagus with Hollandaise and red pimiento brightens any dinner table

ASPARAGUS WITH HOT MAYONNAISE

1 recipe Hot Mayonnaise Sauce
4 cups Cooked Asparagus
Paprika

Pour mayonnaise over hot asparagus and sprinkle with paprika. Serves 6 to 8.

ASPARAGUS CASSEROLE

3 cups Cooked Asparagus
4 tablespoons fat, melted
2 tablespoons flour
2 cups milk
½ cup grated American cheese
¼ teaspoon salt
¾ cup dry bread crumbs
2 tablespoons butter

Cook asparagus just 5 minutes then place asparagus in casserole. Blend fat and flour, add milk gradually and cook slowly until thickened, stirring constantly. Add cheese and salt. Pour sauce over asparagus, sprinkle with crumbs, dot with butter and bake in slow oven (325°F.) 30 minutes. Serves 6 to 8.

CRUMBED ASPARAGUS

1 recipe Cooked Asparagus
1 cup dry bread crumbs
1 egg, beaten
¼ teaspoon salt
⅛ teaspoon pepper
Butter

Arrange asparagus in bundles of 4 stalks. Roll in crumbs, dip into egg mixed with salt and pepper, and roll again in crumbs. Fry in butter until browned. Serves 6 to 8.

COOKED GREEN OR WAX BEANS

1½ pounds green or wax beans
Water to cover
¾ teaspoon salt

Wash beans and remove ends and strings. Cover with boiling water, add salt and cook uncovered, 20 to 35 minutes or until just tender. Drain, saving liquid for soups and gravies. (Makes about 4 cups, cut.) To serve, season with pepper and butter. Serves 6 to 8.

If desired, after removing strings, cut uncooked beans lengthwise into long slender strips or cut diagonally into 1-inch pieces. Allow 5 minutes less time for cooking.

To retain the greater amount of minerals in the beans and to have a stronger flavor, cook beans as for Cooked Carrots. Lift the cover of pan at the end of 15 minutes and let out steam to keep the color. Cook until just tender.

SOUTHERN GREEN BEANS — Break beans into 2-inch pieces, add 2 cups water and ¼ pound salt pork and simmer 2 to 3 hours. Serve beans, pork and liquor.

GREEN BEANS WITH EGG SAUCE

1 recipe Cooked Green Beans
1 recipe Egg Sauce
Paprika

Combine beans and sauce and heat thoroughly, stirring occasionally. Sprinkle with paprika. Serves 6 to 8

Guests from the South will appreciate green beans cooked with salt pork

GREEN BEANS WITH SOUR CREAM

1 cup sliced mushrooms
2 tablespoons fat
4 cups Cooked Green Beans
1 cup sour cream
¼ teaspoon salt
⅛ teaspoon pepper

Brown mushrooms in fat, add beans, cream, salt and pepper and heat thoroughly. Serves 6.

GREEN BEANS WITH CHEESE

4 cups Cooked Green Beans
¼ teaspoon salt
⅛ teaspoon cayenne
¾ cup grated cheese
2 tablespoons butter
⅓ cup cream

Arrange beans in greased baking dish, season with salt and cayenne, add ½ cup cheese, 1 tablespoon butter and cream. Stir until well mixed. Sprinkle with remaining cheese and dot with remaining butter. Bake in hot oven (400°F.) about 20 minutes. Serves 6 to 8.

BEANS IN
ONION SAUCE

½ cup minced onion
3 tablespoons fat
1 recipe White Sauce
4 cups Cooked Green Beans

Cook onion in fat, add to sauce
and combine with beans. Heat
thoroughly. Serves 6 to 8.

CREOLE WAX BEANS

2 tablespoons chopped onion
½ green pepper, chopped
3 tablespoons fat
1½ tablespoons flour
1½ cups tomato juice
¼ teaspoon salt
⅛ teaspoon pepper
3 cups Cooked Wax Beans

Cook onion and green pepper in
fat until onion is yellow. Blend
in flour, add tomato juice gradually and cook for 5 minutes. Add
salt, pepper and beans. Heat
thoroughly. Serves 6 to 8.

CRUMBED
GREEN BEANS

4 cups Cooked Green Beans
6 tablespoons fat
½ cup fine cracker crumbs
½ teaspoon salt
⅛ teaspoon pepper
Pimiento strips

Heat beans with fat, crumbs,
salt and pepper, mixing until
beans are coated with crumbs
and crumbs are browned. Garnish
with pimiento strips. Serves 6.

SPICY GREEN BEANS

1½ tablespoons chopped onion
3 tablespoons fat
⅓ cup chili sauce
¼ teaspoon salt
4 cups Cooked Green Beans

Cook onion in fat until tender;
add chili sauce, salt and beans.
Heat thoroughly, stirring occasionally. Serves 6 to 8.

DEVILED
GREEN BEANS

4 tablespoons butter
1 teaspoon prepared mustard
1 teaspoon Worcestershire sauce
¼ teaspoon salt
⅛ teaspoon pepper, Dash cayenne
4 cups Cooked Green Beans

Cream butter and add next 5
ingredients. Serve on hot green
beans. Serves 6 to 8.

GREEN BEANS WITH
TOMATO SAUCE

1 medium onion, minced
3 tablespoons fat
3½ cups Cooked Green Beans
¾ cup Tomato Sauce
½ tablespoon sugar
1 teaspoon salt
2 teaspoons lemon juice
⅛ teaspoon pepper

Cook onion in fat until tender
(3 to 4 minutes). Add beans,
tomato sauce, sugar, salt, lemon
juice and pepper. Heat thoroughly, stirring occasionally. For 8.

MINTED
GREEN BEANS

4 cups Cooked Green Beans
¼ cup chopped mint
⅓ cup butter, melted
⅛ teaspoon pepper

Combine beans with remaining
ingredients and heat thoroughly.
Serves 6 to 8.

WAX BEANS,
O'BRIEN

6 tablespoons chopped pimiento
6 tablespoons chopped onion
4 tablespoons fat
¼ teaspoon salt
4 cups Cooked Wax Beans
¼ cup water

Cook pimiento and onion in fat
2 to 3 minutes. Add salt and
beans and cook 5 minutes longer,
stirring frequently. Add water
and heat to boiling. Serves 6 to 8.

COOKED FRESH
LIMA BEANS

4 pounds fresh Lima beans
Water to cover, ¾ teaspoon salt

Shell beans. Cover with boiling
water, add salt and cook uncovered, 25 to 35 minutes, or until just tender. Drain; and save
liquid for soups and casserole
dishes. (Makes about 3½ cups.)
To serve, season with pepper and
butter. Serves 6 to 8.

To retain the greater amount of
minerals in the beans and to have
a stronger flavor, cook as for
Cooked Carrots. Lift the cover
of pan at the end of 10 minutes
and let out the steam to keep the
color. Cook until just tender.

LIMA BEAN
CASSEROLE

2 cups Cooked Fresh Lima Beans
½ cup chopped pimientos
1 cup grated cheese
1 recipe White Sauce
2 tablespoons tomato catchup
½ cup dry bread crumbs
2 tablespoons butter

Combine beans, pimientos, cheese,
white sauce and catchup. Pour
into greased casserole, cover with
crumbs, dot with butter and bake
in moderate oven (350°F.) about
30 minutes. Serves 6 to 8.

PARSLEY PAPRIKA
LIMA BEANS

3 tablespoons butter, melted
1½ tablespoons flour
¼ teaspoon salt, Dash pepper
1 teaspoon paprika
1¼ cups water, 2 bouillon cubes
3½ cups Cooked Fresh Lima Beans
2 tablespoons chopped parsley

Blend butter, flour, salt, pepper
and paprika together. Add water
and bouillon cubes and cook for
5 minutes, stirring frequently.
Add Lima beans and parsley and
heat thoroughly. Serves 6 to 8.

LIMA BEANS DE LUXE

3½ cups Cooked Fresh Lima Beans
3 tablespoons butter, melted
1 teaspoon sugar
1 tablespoon minced parsley
1⅓ cups hot top milk
2 egg yolks, well beaten
¼ teaspoon salt
Paprika

Combine beans, butter, sugar and parsley in saucepan and heat slowly to boiling. Heap beans into serving dish. Stir milk into egg yolks, add salt and cook slowly (do not boil) 1 to 2 minutes. Pour sauce over beans and sprinkle with paprika. Serves 6 to 8.

LIMAS WITH BACON

1 quart dried Lima beans
½ pound bacon
3 onions
¼ cup wine vinegar

Soak beans in cold water overnight. Drain, cover with boiling salted water and cook until tender, 2 to 3 hours. Dice bacon and fry until crisp. Drain on absorbent paper. Slice onions thin and fry in bacon fat. Mix bacon, wine vinegar and onions with beans. Serves 10 to 12.

BAKED LIMA BEANS

5 tablespoons butter
3 tablespoons flour; 1¼ cups milk
3½ cups Cooked Fresh Lima Beans
½ teaspoon salt
⅛ teaspoon pepper
2 eggs, well beaten
½ cup dry bread crumbs

Melt 3 tablespoons butter; stir in flour, add milk gradually and cook slowly until thickened, stirring constantly. Press beans through sieve and combine with the sauce; add salt, pepper and eggs. Pour into greased baking dish, cover with bread crumbs,

dot with remaining butter and bake in moderate oven (375°F.) about 20 minutes. Serves 6 to 8.

LIMA BEANS WITH SAUSAGES

2 cups shelled fresh Lima beans
1 can Vienna sausages

Prepare beans as for Cooked Fresh Lima Beans, adding sausages to beans 10 minutes before beans are tender. Serves 6.

BOSTON BAKED BEANS

1 quart pea beans
½ pound fat salt pork
2 teaspoons salt
1½ tablespoons brown sugar
¼ cup molasses
½ teaspoon dry mustard
1 cup boiling water

Wash and pick over beans. Soak beans overnight in cold water. Drain, cover with water and simmer until skins break; turn into bean pot. Score pork and press into beans, leaving ¼ inch above the beans. Mix salt, sugar, molasses, mustard and boiling water together and pour over beans. Cover and bake in slow oven (275° F.) about 8 hours. Add water as needed. Uncover to brown during last half hour of baking. Serves 8.

VARIATION—As a quick method, use same ingredients as in recipe above, but do not soak the beans overnight. Place them over the fire, cover them with cold water, and slowly bring the water to a boil, then set the kettle where the beans will simmer, but will at no time boil vigorously. When they have cooked in this way for fifteen minutes, drain and add fresh boiling water. Add salt pork to the kettle and simmer

until the beans may be pierced with a straw. Turn the beans into a colander to drain; put into beanpot, season and bake as directed above.

COOKED BEETS

2 pounds beets
½ to 1 cup water, ¾ teaspoon salt

METHOD 1. Pare and dice beets. Heat water and salt to boiling, add beets, cover pan tightly to prevent escape of steam and heat again to boiling. Reduce heat at once and simmer 25 to 40 minutes. Drain if necessary. (Makes about 4 cups.) To serve, season with pepper and butter, for 8.

METHOD 2. Pare and dice beets as Method 1, then place in casserole, add water and salt, cover and bake in moderate oven (375° F.) 45 to 50 minutes.

METHOD 3. Leave roots on beets and cut off tops leaving at least 2 inches of stems. Wash thoroughly, cover with boiling water and boil until tender. Allow 30 to 60 minutes for young beets, 1 to 3 hours for large beets. Drain, rub off tops, skins and roots. Slice, dice or serve whole, season as desired.

HARVARD BEETS

¾ cup sugar
2 teaspoons cornstarch
⅓ cup vinegar
⅓ cup water
4 cups Cooked Beets
3 tablespoons butter
¼ teaspoon salt
⅛ teaspoon pepper

Combine sugar and cornstarch; add vinegar and water and boil for 5 minutes. Add beets and simmer ½ hour. Add butter and season with salt and pepper. Slice or dice beets. Serves 6 to 8.

BAKED BEET CASSEROLE

4 tablespoons butter, melted
4 tablespoons cornstarch
1 cup water
4 tablespoons brown sugar
¼ teaspoon salt
3 tablespoons horse-radish
4 cups Cooked Beets
⅓ cup dry bread crumbs
3 tablespoons butter

Blend butter and cornstarch, add water gradually and cook until mixture begins to thicken, stirring constantly. Add sugar, salt, horse-radish and beets. Pour into greased baking dish; cover with crumbs, dot with butter and bake in moderate oven (375°F.) about 20 minutes or until crumbs are browned. Serves 6 to 8.

BEETS IN ORANGE SAUCE

2 tablespoons butter
2 tablespoons cornstarch
¾ cup water
1½ teaspoons grated orange rind
¾ cup orange juice
¼ teaspoon salt
¼ teaspoon pepper
2 teaspoons sugar
3½ cups Cooked Beets, sliced

Melt butter, stir in cornstarch and add water slowly. Add orange rind, orange juice, salt, pepper and sugar. Cook until smooth and thickened, stirring constantly. Add beets and heat. For 8.

BUTTERED BEETS AND CELERY

3 tablespoons minced onion
3 tablespoons fat
2 cups Cooked Beets
2 cups Cooked Celery
½ teaspoon salt
1½ tablespoons vinegar

Sauté onion in fat until tender, add remaining ingredients and heat thoroughly. Serves 6 to 8.

FRIED BEETS

4 cups sliced Cooked Beets
⅛ teaspoon pepper
4 tablespoons butter

Combine ingredients, cover and fry about 20 minutes. Serves 6.

MINTED BEETS

3 tablespoons mint jelly
2 tablespoons butter
1 recipe whole Cooked Beets

Combine jelly, butter and beets. Heat slowly, stirring occasionally until beets are glazed. For 6.

SOUR BEETS

2 tablespoons butter
2 tablespoons cornstarch
½ cup water
¼ cup vinegar, ¼ cup cream
1 teaspoon sugar
½ teaspoon salt
⅛ teaspoon pepper
4 cups Cooked Beets

Melt butter, stir in cornstarch, add water gradually and cook until smooth, stirring constantly. Add remaining ingredients and heat to boiling. Serves 6 to 8.

SPICED BEETS

4 cups Cooked Beets
2 small onions, sliced
1 cup water
¼ teaspoon salt
⅔ cup vinegar
3 tablespoons sugar
10 cloves
1 (3-inch) stick cinnamon

Combine beets and onions. Mix water, salt, vinegar, sugar, cloves and cinnamon together in a sauce-pan. Simmer for 10 minutes; add beets and onions and heat thoroughly. Serves 6 to 8.

SWEET BEETS

¼ cup butter
2 tablespoons sugar
¼ teaspoon salt
4 cups Cooked Beets

Combine butter, sugar, salt and beets and heat thoroughly, stirring occasionally. Serves 6 to 8.

COOKED BEET GREENS—Prepare and cook as directed for Cooked Spinach.

COOKED BROCCOLI

2½ pounds broccoli
Boiling water
1 teaspoon salt

Wash broccoli and split thick heads. Place broccoli in boiling salted water, with ends down and heads out of water. Cook uncovered 10 to 20 minutes. Then place all of broccoli under water and cook 5 minutes longer. Drain. (Makes about 4 cups.) To serve, season with pepper and butter. Serves 6 to 8.

WITH WHITE SAUCE—Combine with 1 cup White Sauce.

WITH HOLLANDAISE SAUCE—Serve cooked broccoli with 1 recipe Hollandaise Sauce.

BROCCOLI WITH CHEESE

1 onion, minced
6 tablespoons butter
4 tablespoons flour
2 cups milk
½ teaspoon salt
⅛ teaspoon pepper
1 egg yolk
1 cup grated Parmesan cheese
1 recipe Cooked Broccoli
½ cup dry bread crumbs

Cook onion in 4 tablespoons butter until tender, stir in flour, add milk gradually and cook slowly until thickened, stirring constantly. Add salt, pepper, egg yolk and cheese. Pour half of sauce into greased baking dish, arrange broccoli on top of sauce, cover with remaining sauce, sprinkle with bread crumbs and dot with remaining butter. Bake in hot oven (400°F.) about 20 minutes. Serves 6 to 8.

BROCCOLI WITH CHEESE SAUCE

1 recipe Cheese Sauce
1 recipe Cooked Broccoli
4 tablespoons butter
⅓ cup dry bread crumbs

Pour cheese sauce over hot broccoli. Melt butter, stir in crumbs and sprinkle over top of sauce. Serves 6 to 8.

COOKED BROCCOLI RABE—
Prepare and cook as directed for Cooked Spinach.

BROCCOLI PARMESAN

2½ pounds broccoli, cooked
Butter
Salt and pepper
¾ cup grated Parmesan cheese

Arrange broccoli on serving plates, season with butter, salt and pepper. Sprinkle generously with cheese. Serves 6 to 8.

BROCCOLI SOUFFLÉ

3 eggs, separated
½ cup hot Thick White Sauce
1 cup chopped Cooked Broccoli
2 tablespoons grated Parmesan cheese

Beat egg yolks and add to white sauce. Add broccoli and cheese. Fold in stiffly beaten egg whites. Pour into buttered baking dish and bake in moderate oven (350° F.) about 50 minutes. Serve with Cheese Sauce, for 4.

BROCCOLI RING—Use 2 eggs and ¾ cup White Sauce. Do not separate eggs, beat slightly and combine with remaining ingredients. Bake in a buttered ring mold. Unmold and fill center with creamed eggs, creamed shrimp, creamed fish or creamed mushrooms.

Fresh green broccoli with Parmesan cheese is a treat you will not soon forget

COOKED BRUSSELS SPROUTS

1½ pounds Brussels sprouts
Boiling water to cover
¾ teaspoon salt

Remove wilted leaves from sprouts, wash and let stand in cold water 15 minutes. Place sprouts in saucepan, add boiling water and salt and cook uncovered 10 to 20 minutes. (Makes about 4 cups.) To serve, season with pepper and butter, for 6.

If desired, season with salt and pepper only and serve with a small pitcher of melted butter.

BREADED BRUSSELS SPROUTS

4 cups Cooked Brussels Sprouts
1 egg, beaten
¾ cup dry bread crumbs
Fat
¼ cup grated cheese

Dip Brussels sprouts into egg, roll in crumbs and fry in hot deep fat (380°F.) until browned. Sprinkle with cheese. Serves 6

FRIED BRUSSELS SPROUTS

1 onion, chopped
3 tablespoons butter
4 cups Cooked Brussels Sprouts

Cook onion in butter until tender, add sprouts and toss gently until thoroughly heated, for 6.

COOKED CABBAGE

2 pounds cabbage
Boiling water to cover
¾ teaspoon salt

Remove outer leaves; cut cabbage into quarters, chop or shred. Place in saucepan, cover with boiling water, add salt and cook uncovered until tender. Allow 8 to 10 minutes for young cabbage and 15 to 20 minutes for older cabbage. (Makes about 5 cups cooked.) To serve, season with pepper and butter. Serves 6.

SCALLOPED CABBAGE

5 cups Cooked Cabbage
1 recipe White Sauce
½ cup dry bread crumbs
3 tablespoons butter

Place cabbage in greased baking dish, add white sauce, cover with crumbs and dot with butter. Bake in hot oven (400°F.) 15 to 20 minutes. Serves 6 to 8.
CABBAGE WITH CHEESE — Sprinkle with ½ cup grated cheese instead of bread crumbs and butter.

CABBAGE AND CELERY CASSEROLE

½ cup chopped celery
5 tablespoons butter
3½ cups chopped cabbage
½ teaspoon salt
⅛ teaspoon pepper
1 cup White Sauce
1 tablespoon chopped pimiento
¼ cup dry bread crumbs

Cook celery in 3 tablespoons butter 10 minutes, stirring frequently. Add cabbage and cook 10 minutes longer. Pour into greased baking dish, add salt, pepper, white sauce and pimiento. Sprinkle bread crumbs over top, dot with remaining butter and bake in moderate oven (350°F.) about 20 minutes. Serves 6 to 8.

Sprouts and other pungent vegetables may be cooked without telling the whole world when tied in vegetable parchment

BRUSSELS SPROUTS AND CELERY

1½ cups chopped celery
4 tablespoons butter
3 tablespoons flour
1½ cups scalded milk
1 recipe Cooked Brussels Sprouts
½ teaspoon salt
⅛ teaspoon pepper
½ cup dry bread crumbs

Cook celery in 3 tablespoons butter for 2 minutes. Blend in flour, add milk gradually and heat to boiling. Add sprouts, salt and pepper. Pour into greased baking dish, cover with bread crumbs, dot with remaining butter and bake in hot oven (400° F.) about 20 minutes. Serves 6 to 8.

BRUSSELS SPROUTS IN PARCHMENT

1½ pounds Brussels sprouts
2 tablespoons butter
½ teaspoon salt
⅛ teaspoon pepper

Clean sprouts. Place in cooking parchment with butter, salt and pepper. Tie. Cook in boiling water 15 minutes. Serves 6.

CABBAGE COOKED IN MILK

2 cups rich milk
5 cups shredded cabbage
¾ teaspoon salt
⅛ teaspoon pepper

Scald milk in top of double boiler, add cabbage and stir thoroughly. Cover tightly and cook over hot water 15 to 20 minutes, stirring occasionally. Season with salt and pepper. Serves 6 to 8.

SWEET AND SOUR CABBAGE

2½ pounds red cabbage
2 tablespoons fat
½ teaspoon salt
⅛ teaspoon pepper
4 cloves
½ teaspoon allspice
½ cup sugar
Boiling water to cover
3 tart apples
½ cup vinegar

Slice cabbage fine and place in kettle. Add fat, salt, pepper, spices, sugar and water to cover. Heat. Pare, core and slice apples, add to cabbage and cook 1 hour. Add vinegar and simmer 1 hour longer. Serves 6 to 8.

CABBAGE WITH TART SAUCE

1 teaspoon salt
1 teaspoon sugar
2 tablespoons lemon juice
5 tablespoons butter, melted
1½ tablespoons horse-radish
1 teaspoon paprika
5 cups Cooked Cabbage

Combine first 6 ingredients and add to hot cabbage. Serves 6.

COOKED CHINESE CABBAGE

2 pounds Chinese cabbage
1 teaspoon salt
Boiling water

Wash Chinese cabbage, cut into small pieces and cook in salted water to cover for 7 minutes, or until tender. Serves 6 to 8.

CHINESE CABBAGE WITH PARSLEY

4 cups Cooked Chinese Cabbage
½ cup cream
6 tablespoons butter
1 teaspoon salt
2 tablespoons minced parsley

Combine ingredients and heat thoroughly. Serves 6 to 8.

BAKED CHINESE CABBAGE

4 cups Cooked Chinese Cabbage
⅛ teaspoon paprika
2 eggs, beaten
2 cups milk
¼ teaspoon salt

Arrange cabbage in greased baking dish and season with paprika. Combine eggs, milk and salt and pour over cabbage. Place dish in pan of hot water. Bake in moderate oven (350°F.) 40 minutes or until firm. Serves 8.

Omit milk. Add 1 cup Stewed Tomatoes and 1 tablespoon minced onion.

COOKED RED CABBAGE

2 pounds red cabbage
¾ teaspoon salt
Boiling water
4 tablespoons lemon juice

Cut cabbage into eighths, place in saucepan, add salt and cover with water. Cook uncovered 15 to 20 minutes. Drain and sprinkle with lemon juice, for 6.

Cabbage should be white and slightly crisp when it comes to the table

CARROT CROQUETTES

4 cups Cooked Carrots
½ teaspoon salt
½ teaspoon nutmeg
1 egg, beaten
2 tablespoons butter, melted
1 cup dry bread crumbs
Fat, Parsley

Mash or press carrots through coarse sieve. Add salt, nutmeg, egg and butter and mix thoroughly. Form into shapes resembling carrots, roll in bread crumbs and chill for several hours. Fry in hot deep fat (380°F.) until browned. Drain on absorbent paper, tuck a sprig of parsley in top and serve at once, for 8.

BROWNED CARROTS

12 medium carrots
½ teaspoon salt
¼ teaspoon pepper

Scrape carrots. Sprinkle with salt and pepper and bake in pan with pot roast or any meat that is cooked covered. Serves 6 to 8.

MASHED CARROTS

4 cups Cooked Carrots
⅛ teaspoon pepper
3 tablespoons butter, melted
4 tablespoons hot cream

Mash carrots; add pepper and butter. Place saucepan over boiling water or low heat and bea until carrots are light and smooth Add cream. Serves 6 to 8.

CARROTS AND PEAS

2 cups Cooked Carrots
2 cups Cooked Peas
½ teaspoon salt
⅛ teaspoon pepper
3 tablespoons butter, melted

Combine freshly cooked carrots and peas. Season with salt and pepper and add butter. Garnish with parsley. Serves 6 to 8.

RED CABBAGE WITH VINEGAR SAUCE

1 cup vinegar
1 tablespoon brown sugar
2 cloves
½ bay leaf
¼ teaspoon salt
Sprig parsley
2 teaspoons grated onion
5 cups Cooked Red Cabbage

Simmer first 6 ingredients for 5 minutes, strain; add onion and pour over hot cabbage, for 8.

SPICED RED CABBAGE

2 tablespoons mixed spices
3 quarts water
1 teaspoon salt
2 pounds red cabbage, shredded
4 tablespoons brown sugar
4 tablespoons vinegar
3 tablespoons butter

Place spices in a bag. Heat water and salt to boiling, add cabbage and spices and cook 30 minutes. Drain. Dissolve sugar in vinegar, add butter and combine with cabbage. Serves 6 to 8.

Instead of plain vinegar, use 4 tablespoons basil vinegar.

Carrot croquettes with parsley for the green tops will please the grown-ups and delight the children

COOKED CARROTS

2 pounds carrots
½ to 1 cup water
¾ teaspoon salt

Scrape carrots and cut as desired. Heat water and salt to boiling, add carrots, cover pan tightly to prevent escape of steam and heat again to boiling. Reduce heat at once and simmer 20 to 30 minutes. Drain, if necessary. (Makes about 4 cups cooked.) To serve, season with pepper and melted butter, for 6.

BAKED CARROTS

18 small carrots
⅓ cup butter, ½ cup sugar
1 teaspoon salt
⅓ teaspoon cinnamon
⅓ cup boiling water

Scrape or pare carrots and place in casserole. Cream butter, sugar, salt and cinnamon together; add water and blend well. Pour over carrots, cover and bake in moderate oven (350°F.) 1½ hours. Serves 6 to 8.

CARROT SOUFFLÉ

3 tablespoons butter
3 tablespoons flour
¼ teaspoon salt
1 cup hot milk
3 eggs, separated
2 cups Cooked Carrots, mashed

Melt butter, add flour and salt. Add milk gradually; cook slowly until thickened, stirring constantly. Beat egg yolks, add white sauce slowly, then stir in carrots. Cool. Beat egg whites until stiff and fold into mixture. Pour into greased casserole or mold, place in pan of hot water and bake in moderate oven (350° F.) 40 to 50 minutes. Serves 6.

CARROT AND CELERY SOUFFLÉ

1 cup dry bread crumbs, Milk
1¼ cups Cooked Carrots, mashed
½ cup chopped celery
2 tablespoons minced onion
2 eggs, separated
½ teaspoon salt
⅛ teaspoon pepper

Soak bread crumbs in enough milk to moisten, add carrots, celery, onion and beaten egg yolks. Beat egg whites until stiff and fold into mixture; season with salt and pepper. Pour into greased baking dish and bake in moderate oven (350°F.) 30 to 40 minutes. Serves 6 to 8.

LYONNAISE CARROTS

2 small onions, minced
¼ cup butter
½ teaspoon salt
¼ teaspoon pepper
4 cups Cooked Carrots
1 tablespoon minced parsley

Brown onions in butter; add salt pepper and carrots. Cover and cook slowly about 15 minutes Sprinkle with parsley. Serves 8

CARROT AND GREEN BEAN CASSEROLE

1 tablespoon chopped onion
3 tablespoons fat
2 tablespoons flour
½ teaspoon salt
⅛ teaspoon pepper
1½ cups milk; 2 eggs, beaten
½ cup grated cheese
1¾ cups Cooked Green Beans
1¾ cups Cooked Carrots, sliced
½ cup bread crumbs
3 tablespoons butter

Cook onion slightly in fat, add flour and seasonings; blend well. Add milk gradually and cook until slightly thickened; add to eggs and cook slowly 1 minute, stirring constantly. Add grated cheese and stir in vegetables. Pour into greased baking dish, cover with crumbs, dot with butter and bake in moderate oven (350°F.) 30 minutes. Serves 8.

PARSLEY CARROTS

4 cups Cooked Carrots
⅛ teaspoon pepper
2 tablespoons butter, melted
4 tablespoons chopped parsley

Season carrots with pepper and butter. Add parsley and toss carrots lightly until well coated with green. Serves 6 to 8.

CARROTS WITH CHEESE

3 tablespoons butter, melted
3 tablespoons flour
1½ cups milk
½ teaspoon salt
Dash cayenne
¾ cup grated cheese
3½ cups Cooked Carrots

Blend butter and flour, add milk slowly and cook until thickened, stirring constantly. Add seasonings and ½ cup cheese. Place carrots in buttered baking dish, cover with sauce and sprinkle top with remaining cheese. Bake in moderate oven (350°F.) 15 minutes. Serves 6 to 8.

CARROT RING

2 cups diced Cooked Carrots
½ teaspoon minced onion
1 teaspoon salt
⅛ teaspoon pepper
3 eggs, well beaten
1 cup milk

Combine ingredients. Pour into a buttered ring mold and bake in a moderate oven (350°F.) 40 minutes. Unmold and fill with seasoned Cooked Peas. Serves 6.

Ring out the old, ring in the new combination of carrots and green peas

CAULIFLOWER FRITTERS

1 cup sifted flour
1 teaspoon baking powder
½ teaspoon salt
Dash mace
1 cup chopped Cooked Cauliflower
1 egg, beaten
½ cup milk
2 tablespoons butter, melted

Sift dry ingredients together and add cauliflower. Combine egg, milk and butter; add to flour mixture and stir until smooth. Drop by tablespoons into hot deep fat (365°F.). Cook 3 to 5 minutes or until browned. Drain on absorbent paper. Serves 6 to 8.

FRENCH FRIED CAULIFLOWER

4½ cups Cooked Cauliflowerets
1 or 2 eggs, slightly beaten
1 cup dry bread crumbs

Dip cauliflower into egg, roll in crumbs and fry in hot deep fat (380°F.) until brown. Drain on absorbent paper. Serves 6 to 8.

CAULIFLOWER WITH BROWNED CRUMBS

¾ cup bread crumbs
6 tablespoons butter
⅛ teaspoon paprika
4½ cups Cooked Cauliflowerets

Brown crumbs in butter, add paprika and sprinkle mixture over hot cauliflower. Serves 6 to 8.

SAUTÉED CAULIFLOWER

5 tablespoons butter
4½ cups Cooked Cauliflowerets
½ teaspoon salt
¼ teaspoon white pepper

Melt butter, add flowerets, salt and pepper. Cover pan and cook slowly, shaking pan occasionally, until thoroughly heated. For 6.

A cauliflower head is the center of interest ringed about by mashed potato cups filled with fresh peas

SWEET-SOUR CARROTS

2 tablespoons butter
2 tablespoons cornstarch
½ teaspoon salt
Pepper
2 tablespoons sugar
2 tablespoons vinegar
1 cup hot water
4 cups Cooked Carrots

Brown butter, blend in cornstarch and continue browning, stirring constantly. Add seasonings. Combine sugar, vinegar and water and add to first mixture gradually; cook slowly until thickened, stirring constantly. Pour over hot carrots. Serves 6 to 8.

COOKED CAULIFLOWER

3 pounds cauliflower
1 teaspoon salt
Boiling water

Let cauliflower stand in salted cold water, head down, about 30 minutes. Rinse in clear water and place in a saucepan. Add salt and water to cover and cook 20 to 30 minutes. Drain. (Makes about 4½ cups cooked.) To serve, season with pepper and butter. Serves 6 to 8.

COOKED CAULIFLOWERETS— Break cauliflower into flowerets and cook 10 to 12 minutes.

Or serve your cauliflower with foaming hot brown butter sauce with brown crumbs

COOKED CELERY

2½ pounds celery
½ to 1 cup water
¾ teaspoon salt

Wash celery and cut into short lengths. Heat water and salt to boiling, add celery, cover pan tightly to prevent escape of steam and heat again to boiling. Reduce heat at once and simmer about 20 minutes. (Makes about 4 cups cooked.) To serve, season with pepper and butter. Serves 6 to 8.

BRAISED CELERY

2 large Spanish onions, sliced
4 cups celery, cut into pieces
4 tablespoons butter, melted
1 tablespoon cornstarch
2 cups water, 2 bouillon cubes

Place onions in baking dish. Brown celery in melted butter. Blend cornstarch with a little water, add remaining water and bouillon cubes. Combine with browned celery and cook for 5 minutes. Pour over onions and bake in slow oven (325°F.) about 1 hour. Serves 6 to 8.

CAULIFLOWER WITH TOMATO AND CHEESE SAUCE

4½ cups Cooked Cauliflowerets
1 clove garlic, peeled
2 tablespoons fat
1 can condensed tomato soup
½ cup grated American cheese

Brown cauliflower and garlic in fat. Remove garlic, add soup and cheese and heat slowly until cheese is melted. Serves 6 to 8.

COOKED CELERIAC

1 pound celeriac
½ to 1 cup boiling water
¾ teaspoon salt

Pare celeriac and cut into cubes. Place in saucepan, add water and salt, cover pan tightly to prevent escape of steam and heat again to boiling. Reduce heat at once and simmer about 20 minutes or until tender. (Makes about 2 cups.) To serve, season with salt, pepper and butter. Serves 4.

Cream sauce on cauliflower is delicious when light and expertly seasoned. Add crumbs if you like

COOKED CHAYOTE

1½ pounds chayotes
½ cup water, ¾ teaspoon salt

Pare chayotes and slice crosswise into ¾-inch slices. Heat water and salt to boiling, add chayotes, cover pan tightly to prevent escape of steam and heat again to boiling. Reduce heat at once and simmer about 25 minutes. Drain. To serve, season with pepper and butter. Serves 6 to 8.

FRIED CHAYOTE

1 recipe Cooked Chayote
1 egg, beaten
1 cup dry bread crumbs, Fat

Dip slices of chayote into egg, roll in bread crumbs and brown in fat. Serves 6 to 8.

COOKED CHICORY

2 pounds chicory
Boiling water, ¾ teaspoon salt

Wash chicory thoroughly, cover with water, add salt and cook uncovered 15 to 25 minutes. Drain thoroughly. To serve, season with butter and pepper. For 8.

CHICORY WITH HOLLANDAISE

1 recipe Cooked Chicory
1 recipe Hollandaise Sauce

Chop freshly cooked chicory while hot, place in hot serving dish, cover with sauce and sprinkle with paprika. Serves 6 to 8.

COOKED COLLARDS

3 pounds collards
Boiling water to cover
1 teaspoon salt

Wash collards and drain. Cook uncovered in boiling salted water 15 minutes or until tender. Drain, chop and serve with butter and pepper. Serves 6.

COLLARDS WITH MASHED PO-TATOES—Cook 1 pound collards and 1 pound potatoes separately. Mash potatoes and mix with minced collards, add butter and beat thoroughly. Fill buttered baking dish and brown in hot oven (400°F.). Egg yolks may be added before baking.

A casserole of fresh or left-over corn with sausages makes a simple and delicious luncheon

SCALLOPED CORN

3 cups cut uncooked corn
2 eggs, well beaten
½ teaspoon salt
¾ cup cracker crumbs
2 tablespoons butter
1 cup milk

Combine corn, eggs and salt. Place alternate layers of corn mixture and crumbs in greased baking dish; dot each layer with butter. Pour in milk and bake in slow oven (325°F.) about 30 minutes. Serves 6 to 8.

CORN AND SAUSAGES— Use 2 cups Cut Cooked Corn instead of uncooked. Brown ½ pound pork sausages and arrange in alternate layers with corn and crumbs, saving some of sausages for the top. Bake as above.

FRIED CORN

4 cups Cut Cooked Corn
½ teaspoon salt
⅛ teaspoon pepper
3 tablespoons minced green pepper
4 tablespoons fat

Combine corn, salt, pepper and green pepper and cook in fat about 20 minutes, stirring occasionally. Serves 6 to 8.

BUTTERED CORN AND PEAS

2 cups Cut Cooked Corn
2 cups Cooked Peas
5 tablespoons butter
⅛ teaspoon pepper

Combine corn, peas, butter and pepper and heat thoroughly. Serves 6 to 8.

BROILED CORN

3 cups Cut Cooked Corn
¼ teaspoon salt
⅛ teaspoon pepper
8 tablespoons cream
½ cup grated cheese
Paprika

Place corn in greased shallow baking dish; sprinkle with salt and pepper; add cream and cover with grated cheese. Place under moderate broiler heat and broil about 20 minutes or until cheese melts and top is browned. Sprinkle with paprika before serving. Serves 6 to 8.

CORN AND PEPPER FRITTERS

2 cups Cut Cooked Corn
2 tablespoons sugar
½ teaspoon salt
½ cup cream or evaporated milk
2 eggs, beaten
¼ cup chopped green pepper
1½ cups sifted flour
1½ teaspoons baking powder

Combine corn, sugar and salt; add cream, eggs and green pepper. Sift flour with baking powder and add to corn mixture; beat well and drop by tablespoons into greased skillet. Cook slowly until puffed and browned. Serve hot with Tomato Sauce. Serves 6.

For a neat appearance at table, cut the ends from corn before husking

CORN FRITTERS

1 cup sifted flour
1 teaspoon baking powder
¾ teaspoon salt
¼ teaspoon paprika
2 ups Cut Cooked Corn
2 eggs, separated

Sift flour, baking powder, salt and paprika together. Add corn and beaten egg yolks; fold in stiffly beaten egg whites. Fry in hot deep fat (365°F.) until browned. Drain on absorbent paper. Serves 6 to 8.

CORN O'BRIEN

¾ cup shredded green pepper
3 tablespoons butter
3½ cups Cut Cooked Corn
3 tablespoons chopped pimiento
½ teaspoon salt
⅛ teaspoon pepper

Cook green pepper in butter 5 minutes. Add corn, pimiento, salt and pepper and cook 10 minutes longer, stirring lightly with fork. Serve at once. Serves 6 to 8.

SOUTHERN CORN PUDDING

3 cups cut uncooked corn
3 eggs, slightly beaten
1 teaspoon salt
⅛ teaspoon pepper
3 tablespoons melted fat
3 tablespoons sugar
1⅛ cups scalded milk

Combine corn and remaining ingredients. Pour into greased baking dish and bake in slow oven (325°F.) 30 to 40 minutes or until firm. Serves 6 to 8.

One-half cup chopped walnuts and 2 teaspoons grated onion may be added.

CORN ON THE COB

8 ears sweet corn
Boiling water

Remove husks and silks from corn, place in kettle and cover with boiling water. Cook 5 to 8 minutes. Drain. Serve on cob with butter and salt. Serves 6 to 8.

CUT COOKED CORN—Cut kernels from cob with a sharp knife, being careful not to cut too deep. Scrape remainder of kernels from cobs. Makes 2 cups.

CREAMED CORN—Combine 3 cups cut uncooked corn with 1 cup cream, ½ teaspoon salt and ⅛ teaspoon pepper. Simmer 10 to 15 minutes. Serves 6. Use milk instead of cream and add 2 tablespoons butter, if desired.

CORN AND CELERY

2 cups Cut Cooked Corn
1½ cups diced Cooked Celery
½ cup minced ripe olives
½ cup minced green pepper
½ teaspoon pepper
¼ teaspoon salt
4 tablespoons butter
½ cup milk
¼ cup dry bread crumbs

Arrange corn, celery, olives and green pepper in alternate layers in greased baking dish; add seasonings, 2 tablespoons butter and milk. Cover with crumbs, dot with remaining butter and bake in moderate oven (350°F.) 45 minutes. Serves 6 to 8.

Cutting corn from the cob is easier if it is held firmly with a skewer

PLANKED EGGPLANT

1 large eggplant
2 tablespoons butter
2 tablespoons flour
1 cup milk
1½ cups grated American cheese
1½ cups soft bread crumbs
1 tablespoon grated onion
1 tablespoon tomato catchup
2 eggs, separated
Salt and pepper
Whole onions, cooked and buttered
Broiled tomato halves
Mashed potatoes

Wash eggplant, cut lengthwise into halves and scrape out centers, leaving ½-inch shells. Cook pulp in small amount of water until tender, mash and drain. Melt butter, blend in flour, add milk gradually and cook, stirring constantly until thickened. Add mashed eggplant, cheese, crumbs, onion, catchup and egg yolks. Season. Fold in beaten egg whites and fill shells. Bake in moderate oven (350°F.) 1¼ hours. Place hot shells on large plank, surround with onions and tomato halves. Force hot mashed potatoes through a pastry tube for a border. Heat in 350°F. oven 10 minutes. Garnish with parsley. Serves 4.

EGGPLANT CASSEROLE

1½ pounds unpared eggplant, diced
3 medium onions, chopped
2 tablespoons butter
2 egg yolks, beaten
½ cup grated Parmesan cheese
1 teaspoon salt
1 cup dry bread crumbs

Cook vegetables in boiling water to cover about 20 minutes. Drain. Add remaining ingredients and pour into greased casserole. Bake in moderate oven (350°F.) 30 minutes or until browned, for 6.

The skilled producer offers planked stuffed eggplant as a double feature

EGGPLANT FRITTERS

2 tablespoons flour
1 egg, beaten
3 cups Cooked Eggplant, mashed
½ teaspoon salt
⅛ teaspoon pepper
Dash cayenne
Fat

Stir flour and egg into eggplant. Beat until very light. Season. Drop by tablespoons into hot deep fat (375°F.) and fry until brown. Serves 6 to 8.

BREADED EGGPLANT

2-pound eggplant
1 teaspoon salt
⅛ teaspoon pepper
1 egg, beaten
1 cup cracker crumbs
3 tablespoons butter

Pare eggplant and cut into ¼-inch slices. Season. Dip into beaten egg and then into cracker crumbs. Place in greased baking pan; dot with butter and bake at 400°F. 40 minutes. Serves 6 to 8.

BRAISED FENNEL

2 pounds fennel
⅓ cup butter
1 teaspoon salt
1 cup meat stock
Dash pepper

Wash and scrape fennel. Cut into 1-inch pieces. Simmer in butter until lightly browned. Add salt, meat stock and pepper and simmer until tender, about 20 minutes. Serves 6.

KALE WITH SOUR CREAM

4 cups Cooked Kale
1 tablespoon butter
1 teaspoon sugar
1 teaspoon salt
⅛ teaspoon pepper
1 teaspoon lemon juice
1 cup sour cream

Place kale in saucepan; add butter, sugar, salt, pepper and lemon juice and heat thoroughly. Reduce heat and stir in sour cream gradually. Serves 6 to 8.

COOKED KALE

4 pounds kale
Boiling water

Wash kale and remove all the heavy stems. Place in saucepan, add water to cover and cook uncovered 25 to 35 minutes or until tender. (Makes about 3½ cups.) Drain. To serve, season with salt, pepper and butter. Serves 6 to 8.

SCALLOPED — Combine 3 cups Cooked Kale with 3 hard-cooked eggs, chopped, and 1 cup White Sauce. Arrange in alternate layers with 1 cup grated cheese and bake at 400°F. 15 minutes. Serves 6.

KALE IN EGG SAUCE

1 recipe Egg Sauce
4 cups Cooked Kale
Paprika

Pour hot sauce over freshly cooked kale. Sprinkle paprika over top. Serves 6 to 8.

COOKED KOHLRABI

2 pounds kohlrabi
Boiling water
½ teaspoon salt

Pare kohlrabi and cut into cubes or slices. Let stand in water with 2 tablespoons vinegar for 1 hour. Rinse, place in saucepan, cover with water and add salt. Cook uncovered 20 to 35 minutes. (Makes about 4 cups diced, cooked.) Drain. To serve, season with salt, pepper and butter. Serves 6 to 8.

Serve Cooked Kohlrabi with hot Hollandaise Sauce.

KOHLRABI IN EGG SAUCE

4 cups Cooked Kohlrabi
1 recipe Egg Sauce

Combine kohlrabi and egg sauce. Heat thoroughly. Serves 6 to 8.

For a Pan-American accent for your dinner party try mushrooms with Brazil nuts (page 470)

Consider mushrooms baked in cheese sauce with spinach for your vegetable entrée

SAUTÉED MUSHROOMS

1 pound mushrooms
3 tablespoons butter
½ teaspoon salt
Dash pepper

Cut off all but ½ inch of mushroom stems. Wash mushrooms thoroughly, leave whole or slice and cook, covered, in butter 10 to 15 minutes. Season with salt and pepper. Serves 6 to 8.

MUSHROOMS STUFFED WITH BRAZIL NUTS

1½ pounds large mushrooms
1 onion, chopped
¼ cup butter
1 cup soft bread crumbs
1 cup ground Brazil nuts
1 teaspoon salt, Pepper
1 tablespoon tomato catchup
1 tablespoon lemon juice
3 strips bacon
½ cup cream

Wash mushrooms and remove stems. Cook chopped stems and onion in butter 5 minutes. Add crumbs and nuts. Cook 2 minutes. Add seasonings. Stuff mushrooms with mixture, place in baking dish, garnish with narrow strips of bacon and pour cream around them. Bake in hot oven (400°F.) 25 minutes. Serves 6.
BAKED MUSHROOMS—Combine 1 cup milk with 1 cup grated cheese, 1 tablespoon grated onion, 1 teaspoon salt and ¼ teaspoon mustard. Line baking dish with Cooked Spinach, fill with 1½ pounds mushrooms and add milk mixture. Bake in moderate oven (350°F.) 30 minutes or until mushrooms are tender. Serves 6.

LEEKS AU GRATIN

2 bunches leeks
Boiling water
1 teaspoon salt
Pepper
½ cup grated cheese

Wash and trim leeks. Cook until tender, about 15 minutes in boiling salted water to cover. Drain. Arrange in buttered baking dish, sprinkle with pepper and cheese. Heat under broiler until cheese is melted. For 8.

WILTED LETTUCE

1 head lettuce, shredded
½ teaspoon salt
3 slices bacon
1 small onion, diced
½ cup vinegar
1 tablespoon sugar
1 hard-cooked egg, sliced

Shred lettuce into 1-inch strips, place in hot serving dish, sprinkle with salt and let stand 10 minutes. Dice bacon, cook until crisp, remove from fat and cook onion in fat until tender. Add vinegar and sugar; when hot, pour over lettuce, mix with fork, sprinkle with bacon and garnish with egg slices. Serve at once. Serves 6 to 8.

BROILED MUSHROOMS

12 large mushrooms
2 tablespoons butter
¼ teaspoon salt
⅛ teaspoon pepper

Scrub mushrooms and remove stems. Place caps on greased broiler rack, cap side down, about 3 inches below source of heat. Broil 3 minutes, then turn over and broil 3 minutes longer. Put a piece of butter in each cap, sprinkle with salt and pepper and broil until butter melts. Serve on buttered toast. Serves 6.

CREAMED MUSHROOMS

1 pound mushrooms
5 tablespoons butter
½ teaspoon salt
⅛ teaspoon pepper
2 tablespoons flour
1½ cups milk

Cut off all but ½ inch of mushroom stems. Wash mushrooms thoroughly, dry and slice. Cook mushrooms in butter until nearly tender; add salt, pepper and flour and mix well. Add milk gradually and simmer 5 to 8 minutes, stirring constantly. Serves 6 to 8.

COOKED MUSTARD GREENS—
Prepare and cook as directed for Cooked Spinach.

COOKED OKRA

2 pounds okra
¾ teaspoon salt
Boiling water

Wash okra and cut off stems. Cut into ½-inch slices and place in saucepan. Add salt, cover with water and cook uncovered 15 to 25 minutes. Drain. To serve, season with pepper, butter and vinegar. Serves 6 to 8.

FRIED OKRA

2 pounds okra
1 egg, beaten
¾ cup corn meal
Fat

Wash okra, cut off stems and cut into ¼-inch slices. Dip into egg, roll in corn meal and fry in hot deep fat (365°F.) until browned. Drain on absorbent paper. Serves 6 to 8.

OKRA CREOLE—Brown ¼ cup sliced onion and 1 green pepper, chopped, in 3 tablespoons bacon fat. Add 18 okra pods, sliced; cook 5 minutes and add 2 chopped tomatoes and 1 cup cut corn. Simmer 15 minutes or until okra is tender and season with salt and paprika. Serves 8.

OKRA IN TOMATO SAUCE

1½ pounds okra
1 small onion, sliced
3 tablespoons butter
1¼ cups Tomato Sauce
½ teaspoon salt
⅛ teaspoon pepper
3 tablespoons chopped parsley

Wash okra and cut off stems. Cut into ½-inch slices. Brown onion in butter, add okra and cook about 5 minutes. Place in greased baking dish, add tomato sauce, season and sprinkle with parsley. Bake in moderate oven (350°F.) about 30 minutes. Serves 6 to 8.

An excellent use for left-over vegetables: stuffed onions with cheese sauce (page 472)

OKRA AND TOMATOES

2 cups Cooked Okra
2 cups Stewed Tomatoes
1 tablespoon butter
½ teaspoon salt
⅛ teaspoon pepper

Simmer okra and tomatoes together about 5 minutes. Add butter, salt and pepper. Serves 6 to 8.

The silver platter reflects credit upon the cook who stuffs onions with mushrooms (page 472)

BAKED STUFFED ONIONS

6 large onions
½ cup grated cheese
½ recipe White Sauce
½ cup fine bread crumbs
1 tablespoon melted butter

Peel onions, place in a large amount of boiling salted water and boil uncovered 15 minutes. Remove and rinse in cold water. Remove centers, leaving a shell of 2 or 3 layers of onion. Chop centers and mix with grated cheese and sauce. Refill onions, top with crumbs and dot with butter. Bake in a moderate oven (350°F.) 20 to 25 minutes. Serves 6.

Mix ½ cup sliced mushrooms, sautéed with filling.

COOKED ONIONS

2 pounds white onions
Boiling water
1 teaspoon salt

Peel onions under cold water and place in saucepan. Cover with water, add salt and cook uncovered, 15 to 30 minutes. Drain. (Makes about 3½ to 4 cups cooked.) To serve, season with pepper and butter. Serves 6.

Try your Spring tonic cooked and served with Hollandaise sauce

CREAMED ONIONS AND STRING BEANS

6 to 8 small Cooked Onions
3½ cups Cooked Green Beans
1 recipe White Sauce
Paprika

Combine vegetables and white sauce and heat thoroughly. Sprinkle with paprika. Serves 6 to 8.

FRIED ONIONS

1½ pounds dry onions
2 to 3 tablespoons fat
½ teaspoon salt
⅛ teaspoon pepper

Peel onions under cold water. Cut into thin slices and brown well in fat, stirring frequently. Add salt and pepper. Serves 6 to 8.

GLAZED ONIONS

4 tablespoons melted butter
3 tablespoons lemon juice
6 tablespoons honey
3½ cups Cooked Onions

Combine first 3 ingredients, add cooked onions and heat slowly 8 minutes or until onions are glazed. Serves 6 to 8.

GREEN ONIONS

4 bunches green onions
1 recipe Hollandaise Sauce

Trim onions and cook in boiling salted water until tender. Serve with Hollandaise sauce, for 4.

FRENCH FRIED ONIONS

1½ pounds Bermuda onions
1 egg white, slightly beaten
⅓ cup milk
½ teaspoon salt
⅛ teaspoon pepper
¾ cup fine dry bread crumbs
Fat

Peel onions under water and cut into slices about ⅓ inch thick, slash each slice to center and pull rings apart. Combine egg white and milk and dip onions into mixture, dust with salt and pepper and roll in bread crumbs. Place in frying basket and plunge into hot deep fat (365°F.) and fry until browned. Drain on absorbent paper. Serves 6 to 8.

ONION RINGS—Slice onions, separate into rings and fry in hot deep fat (365°F.).

ONION CASSEROLE

3½ cups small white onions
⅓ cup strained honey
½ cup tomato catchup
1 tablespoon butter

Parboil onions in boiling salted water about 5 minutes; drain. Place in casserole. Combine honey and catchup and pour over onions. Dot with butter and bake in moderate oven (375°F.) 45 minutes or until onions are tender. Serves 6 to 8.

ONION SOUFFLÉ

½ cup dry bread crumbs
½ recipe White Sauce
1 egg yolk, beaten
1½ cups chopped Cooked Onions
2 egg whites, stiffly beaten

Soak bread crumbs in white sauce. Beat in egg yolk. Add onions and fold in egg whites. Place in greased baking dish and bake in moderate oven (350°F.) about 20 minutes. Serves 6 to 8.

COOKED PARSNIPS

1½ pounds parsnips
½ to 1 cup water
¾ teaspoon salt

Pare parsnips and cut into crosswise or lengthwise slices. Heat water and salt to boiling, add parsnips, cover tightly to prevent escape of steam and heat again to boiling. Reduce heat at once and simmer 30 to 40 minutes. Drain if necessary. (Makes about 4 cups cooked.) Serve with butter and pepper. Serves 6 to 8.

BAKED PARSNIPS

4 cups diced Cooked Parsnips
¼ cup melted butter
½ cup brown sugar
1 teaspoon dry mustard

Place parsnips in greased baking dish. Pour butter over parsnips and sprinkle with a mixture of sugar and mustard. Bake in hot oven (400°F.) about 20 minutes. Serves 6 to 8.

Arrange Cooked Parsnips in a shallow baking dish. Brush with butter and sprinkle with salt, sugar and paprika. Bake in a moderate oven (350°F.) about 15 minutes.

Butter, salt and pepper are all you need add to garden-fresh early green peas (page 474)

FRIED PARSNIPS

1 recipe Cooked Parsnips
Flour, Fat, ¼ teaspoon pepper

Dredge parsnips with flour. Brown in fat and drain on absorbent paper. Season. Serves 6 to 8.

MASHED PARSNIPS

4 cups Cooked Parsnips
2 tablespoons butter
¼ teaspoon pepper

Mash parsnips and add butter and pepper. Place saucepan over low heat and beat parsnips until smooth and fluffy. Serves 6 to 8. Add 1 tablespoon minced parsley, if desired.

PARSNIP FRITTERS

2 eggs
2 cups Mashed Parsnips
½ teaspoon salt
1 tablespoon butter
¾ cup milk
3 tablespoons flour
Fat

Beat eggs until very light, add parsnips and beat well. Stir in salt, butter, milk and flour. Fry in a small amount of fat, turning to brown both sides. Garnish with parsley. Serves 6 to 8.

Increase butter to 3 tablespoons. Pour into hot greased skillet, cover and cook until browned.

Late-season or canned peas are a luncheon treat with cream sauce and hard-cooked eggs (page 474)

COOKED PEAS

4 pounds peas
Water to cover
1 teaspoon salt

Shell and wash peas. Cover with boiling water, add salt and cook uncovered 15 to 20 minutes. Drain, saving liquid for soup, jellied salad or casserole dishes. (Makes about 4 cups cooked.) To serve, season with pepper and butter. Serves 6 to 8.

To retain the greater amount of minerals in the peas and to have a stronger flavor, cook peas as for Cooked Carrots. Lift the cover of pan at the end of 10 minutes and let out the steam to keep color. Cook until tender.

CREAMED — Combine 4 cups Cooked Peas with 1 to 2 cups White Sauce. Heat in oven or over direct heat. Garnish with sieved hard-cooked egg yolks and sliced hard-cooked egg whites. Serves 8.

Use Cream Sauce instead of White Sauce.

Perfectly cooked vegetables attractively served and beautifully garnished are a real masterpiece

CREAMED PEAS AND ONIONS SERVED WITH HAM

1 slice broiled ham
3 cups hot Cooked Peas
12 hot Cooked Onions
1 recipe White Sauce

Surround a slice of broiled ham with peas, arrange onions on peas and pour white sauce over vegetables. Serves 6 to 8.

MINTED PEAS

4 cups Cooked Peas
4 tablespoons butter
3 teaspoons chopped parsley
3 teaspoons chopped mint
⅛ teaspoon pepper

Combine hot peas, butter, parsley, mint and pepper. Heat thoroughly and serve immediately. Serves 6 to 8.

PEAS AND MUSHROOMS

2 cups Cooked Peas
1 cup Sautéed Mushrooms

Combine vegetables and serve hot. Serves 6.

PEA CROQUETTES

4 cups Cooked Peas
2 tablespoons minced onion
2 eggs, slightly beaten
½ cup bread crumbs
½ teaspoon salt
⅛ teaspoon pepper

Force peas through a sieve and add remaining ingredients. Form into balls and fry in hot deep fat (380°F.) about 3 minutes. Serves 6 to 8.

PEAS AND CELERY

2 cups diced celery
3 tablespoons fat
2 cups Cooked Peas
¼ teaspoon salt
⅛ teaspoon pepper
¼ cup milk

Cook celery in fat until tender, about 4 to 6 minutes, stirring occasionally. Add peas, salt and pepper and heat thoroughly. Stir in milk and serve. Serves 6 to 8.

PEAS AND ONIONS

3 cups Cooked Peas
1 cup tiny Cooked Onions
3 tablespoons heavy cream
½ teaspoon sugar

Combine vegetables, add cream and sugar and heat thoroughly. Shake gently until vegetables are well coated with cream. Serves 6 to 8.

MUSHROOM AND PEA CASSEROLE

1 pound mushrooms, sliced
2 tablespoons minced onion
3 tablespoons butter
2 cups hot cooked rice
2½ cups seasoned Cooked Peas

Sauté mushrooms and onion in butter until tender, add rice and mix thoroughly. Place in buttered individual casseroles and top with peas. Heat in 300°F. oven 15 minutes. Serves 4.

PIMIENTO NOODLE RING WITH PEAS

1 cup broken egg noodles
1½ cups hot milk
1 cup soft bread crumbs
¼ cup melted butter
1 pimiento, chopped
2 tablespoons minced green pepper
1½ cups grated American cheese
⅛ teaspoon onion salt
¾ teaspoon salt
⅛ teaspoon pepper
Dash paprika
6 egg yolks, beaten
48 stalks Cooked Asparagus
12 Broiled Mushrooms
2½ cups Cooked Peas
1 cup White Sauce

Cook noodles in boiling salted water until tender. Drain and rinse with hot water. Combine with next 11 ingredients. Pour into buttered 8-inch ring mold. Place in pan of hot water and bake in moderate oven (350°F.) about 60 minutes. Arrange hot asparagus and mushrooms on round plate. Unmold noodle ring on top and fill with hot, seasoned peas. Pour white sauce around ring and garnish, if desired, with strips of pimiento. Serves 6.

PEA TIMBALES

1¾ cups pea purée
2 tablespoons melted butter
3 eggs, well beaten
½ teaspoon salt
⅛ teaspoon pepper

Blend ingredients and pour into individual molds; set molds in pan of hot water and bake in slow oven (325°F.) about 40 minutes or until firm. Serve with White Sauce. Serves 6.

PEAS COOKED IN LETTUCE

2 pounds peas
1 head lettuce
Salt and pepper
Butter, Chopped fresh mint

Shell peas. Wash outside leaves of lettuce and place several layers in bottom of kettle. Place peas on top and cover with more washed lettuce leaves. Cover kettle closely and cook over low heat 20 minutes. Serve peas with salt, pepper, butter and liquid. Serves 4. Garnish with mint.

PEAS WITH CHEESE

4 cups Cooked Peas
¼ teaspoon salt
⅛ teaspoon pepper
1 cup milk
1 cup grated cheese
2 tablespoons minced pimiento

Place peas in greased baking dish. Add salt, pepper and milk. Sprinkle cheese and pimiento over top and bake in hot oven (400°F.) about 20 minutes or until cheese is melted. Serves 8.

PEAS WITH ONION BUTTER

1 medium onion, chopped
5 tablespoons butter
¼ teaspoon pepper
¼ teaspoon salt
3½ cups Cooked Peas
½ teaspoon cuminseed

Cook onion in butter until tender. Add pepper, salt, peas and cuminseed. Cover and cook slowly until peas are heated through. Serves 6 to 8.

Slice the Bologna straight, leave on the rind and broil for perfect cups

BOLOGNA CUPS WITH PEAS

6 (⅛-inch) slices Bologna
2 tablespoons butter
2 cups seasoned Cooked Peas
2 cups cooked rice
1 peeled tomato

Spread Bologna with butter, and place in heated broiler. As the slices heat they will take the shape of cups. Fill with hot peas and arrange around mound of rice. Cut tomato into wedges and place between cups. Garnish, if desired, with sliced hard-cooked egg and green pepper rings. Serves 6.

MUSHROOM FONDUE WITH PEAS

1½ cups sliced mushrooms
¼ cup minced green peppers
¼ cup diced celery
4 tablespoons butter
3 eggs, separated
1 teaspoon salt
Dash pepper
1 tablespoon minced pimiento
2 cups soft bread crumbs
½ cup milk
2½ cups Cooked Peas
1 cup Cheese Sauce

Sauté mushrooms, peppers and celery in butter until tender. Add beaten egg yolks, salt, pepper, pimiento, crumbs and milk. Mix well; fold in stiffly beaten egg whites. Pour into buttered ring mold and bake in moderate oven (350°F.) until slightly browned, 30 to 45 minutes. Unmold and fill center with buttered and seasoned peas. Pour cheese sauce over top. Serves 4.

This symphony in green and gold will bring a breath of Spring to the table at any time of year (page 475)

FRENCH FRIED PEPPER RINGS

4 to 6 green peppers
1 egg, beaten
¾ cup dry bread crumbs
Fat

Slice peppers into thin rings. Remove seeds and membrane. Dip rings into egg, then into crumbs and fry in hot deep fat (370°F.) until browned. Serves 6 to 8.

PEPPERS STUFFED WITH CORN

6 to 8 green peppers
2 cups Cut Cooked Corn
¾ teaspoon salt
⅛ teaspoon pepper
½ cup grated cheese
2 tablespoons butter

Cut off stem end of peppers, remove seeds and parboil 2 minutes. Combine remaining ingredients and fill peppers with mixture. Place in baking dish and bake in moderate oven (350°F.) 10 to 15 minutes. Serves 6 to 8.

Add ¼ cup stuffed olives, chopped, to mixture.

BROILED PEPPERS

6 green peppers
3 tablespoons melted butter
Salt

Cut peppers into quarters and remove seeds. Broil under moderate heat until edges curl. Add butter and sprinkle with salt. Serves 6 to 8.

PEPPERS STUFFED WITH MACARONI

6 green peppers
1 cup cooked elbow macaroni
⅓ pound American cheese, grated
1 cup cooked tomatoes
1 cup soft bread crumbs
¼ teaspoon Worcestershire sauce
¼ teaspoon salt, Dash pepper

Cut a slice from top of each pepper and cook in boiling salted water 5 minutes. Drain. Mix remaining ingredients, saving ⅓ of cheese for top. Fill peppers with mixture, stand upright in pan and sprinkle remaining cheese on top. Bake in moderate oven (350°F.) 30 minutes. Serves 6.

BAKED POTATOES

This is one of the most desirable methods of preparation. When potatoes are scraped and baked or baked in the skins, they retain most of their vitamins and minerals. If a soft skin is desired rub with fat before baking. Always break the skin immediately upon removal from the oven so steam may escape or potatoes will be soggy. Baked stuffed Irish potatoes when combined with poached eggs, chipped beef or sausage form attractive entrées for luncheons. Potatoes baked in the pan with meat absorb the delicious flavor of the meat besides serving as a garnish for the meat platter. Potatoes may be combined with meat or other vegetables and baked en casserole for one dish meals.

TO BAKE POTATOES

Scrub potatoes and dry thoroughly. Rub well with fat if a soft skin is desired. Bake in hot oven (425°F.) about 45 minutes or until potatoes are soft when pressed together with the fingers. Remove from oven and make 2 gashes in the center of the potatoes, in the form of a cross; press potato with the fingers. Insert a large piece of butter, season with salt and pepper and serve piping hot. Allow 1 potato per person.

AU GRATIN STUFFED POTATOES

6 potatoes
½ pound American cheese, grated

Scrub and dry potatoes. With an apple corer remove a cylinder from the center of each potato. Fill each cavity with cheese. Seal ends with tiny pieces of cylinders which have been removed. Bake in moderate oven (350°F.) until tender, about 45 to 50 minutes. Serves 6.

Instead of cheese, use crisp bacon or chopped cooked meat.

IDAHO POTATOES ON THE HALF SHELL

6 medium potatoes
2 teaspoons prepared mustard
1 tablespoon grated onion
Worcestershire sauce
½ teaspoon salt
Buttered crumbs

Scrub potatoes and parboil for 20 to 30 minutes or until nearly cooked through. Split partially cooked potatoes lengthwise into halves. Spread each half with mustard, onion, sprinkle with Worcestershire sauce and salt. Top with buttered bread crumbs and bake in very hot oven (450° F.) 15 to 20 minutes or until potato is completely cooked and crumbs are brown. Serves 6.

If desired, use 3 large potatoes allowing ½ potato for each serving. Instead of buttered crumbs, use chopped bacon.

Slit baked potatoes as soon as they come from the oven, season and serve piping hot

POTATOES JEANETTE COURRANGELLE

6 medium potatoes
2 cups cooked meat
1 clove garlic, 1 small onion
1 teaspoon chopped parsley
½ teaspoon salt

Pare potatoes, bake in hot oven (425°F.) until tender, 30 to 45 minutes, then cut into halves lengthwise. Scoop out the inside. Chop meat, garlic, onion and parsley together, add salt, fill potatoes with the mixture and reheat. The pulp removed from potatoes may be seasoned with salt, pepper and butter and baked in the oven with Tomato Sauce. Serves 6.

VIENNA POTATOES—Prepare as for Oyster Baked Potatoes, using Vienna sausages instead of oysters. Heat in broiler.

Slide your stuffed potatoes under the broiler to broil the sausages and brown the fluffy potato filling

OYSTER BAKED POTATOES

6 medium potatoes
Oil or melted fat
6 tablespoons butter
1½ teaspoons salt
¼ teaspoon pepper
¼ teaspoon paprika
6 tablespoons cream or evaporated milk
6 large uncooked oysters
⅓ cup French dressing
½ cup buttered crumbs

Brush potatoes with oil and bake as for Baked Potatoes. Cut a slice from 1 side, scoop out potato and mash. Beat mashed potato with butter, seasonings and cream. Refill shells, making a hollow in the center of each with the back of a spoon. In each hollow place an oyster which has been marinated for ½ hour in French dressing. Cover with buttered crumbs and bake in moderate oven (350°F.) 20 minutes or until crumbs are brown. Serves 6.

ARMENIAN POTATOES

¼ cup salad oil
4 cups diced uncooked potatoes
¼ cup tomato pulp
½ cup water
1½ teaspoons salt
1 teaspoon paprika or white pepper
1 garlic, separated into cloves and each clove peeled and sliced
1 bunch parsley or 1 tablespoon dried parsley

Mix ingredients in order given, bake in a covered dish in slow oven (325°F.) 40 minutes. For 6. Reduce garlic to 1 or 2 cloves, or omit garlic and parsley and use ¼ cup minced green onions.

BAKED POTATOES WITH CREAMED DRIED BEEF

3 large potatoes
½ pound dried beef
4 tablespoons fat
4 tablespoons flour
⅛ teaspoon pepper
2 cups milk

Wash potatoes and brush surface with oil. Bake in hot oven (425°F.) until tender, about 1 hour. Shred beef and sauté in fat about 5 minutes. Add flour and pepper; blend well. Add milk gradually, stirring constantly and cook until thickened. Cut potatoes lengthwise into halves, scoop out the inside, mash and beat until fluffy. Partially fill potato skins with chipped beef mixture. Pipe mashed potatoes around edge using a pastry bag and tube. Place in hot oven (400°F.) to brown potatoes slightly. Garnish with parsley and pimiento. Serves 3 or 6.

1½ cups canned or freshly cooked peas may be placed on top of chipped beef.

Potatoes may be garnished with sautéed mushroom caps.

BAKED POTATOES

PIGS IN 'TATERS

6 large potatoes
6 tablespoons butter
4½ teaspoons milk
1½ teaspoons salt, Dash paprika
½ pound small sausages

Bake potatoes as for Baked Potatoes. Cut a slice from 1 side of each, then scoop out the inside. Mash with butter, milk, salt and paprika; beat until fluffy. Refill potato shells, make a hollow in the center of each and fill with sausages. Bake in moderate oven (350°F.) until potato is brown and sausages are thoroughly cooked, about 10 to 15 minutes. Serves 6.

PIGS IN BLANKETS

Wash and pare medium potatoes. Make a hole through each with an apple corer and force a link sausage into each cavity. Place potatoes in baking dish and bake in hot oven (425°F.) 45 minutes or until tender, basting with sausage drippings several times during the baking.

A slice of salt pork or bacon may be placed over each potato.

POTATOES À L'ARCHIODOISE

4 cups sliced potatoes
2 cups tomato sauce
2 cloves garlic, minced
1½ teaspoons salt
1 teaspoon paprika

Wash potatoes, pare and slice into baking dish. Add remaining ingredients and bake, covered, in a moderate oven (350°F.) until potatoes are tender, about 1 hour. Remove cover and bake until browned on top. Serves 6.

Season your potatoes from the inside by stuffing them with pork sausages and dressing with bacon

BRABANT POTATOES

Scrape small new potatoes; parboil 10 minutes. Drain. Place in shallow baking dish, brush with melted butter and bake in moderate oven (350°F.) until tender. Baste with melted butter while baking.

A fleet of potato dug-outs slide down the ways with a crew of cocktail sausages

POTATOES ON THE HALF SHELL

6 medium potatoes
2 tablespoons butter
1 teaspoon salt
¼ teaspoon pepper
¼ cup hot milk

Bake potatoes as for Baked Potatoes. Cut lengthwise into halves. Scoop out the inside, being careful not to break the shell. Mash thoroughly, add butter, salt, pepper and hot milk; beat until fluffy. Pile mixture lightly into shells; do not smooth down the top. Return to hot oven (425°F.) and brown lightly on top. Serves 6 or 12.

Small bits of pimiento, stuffed olives or grated cheese may be sprinkled over top or added to potato mixture.

STUFFED POTATOES — Add ½ cup peanut butter and 2 stiffly beaten egg whites to the potato mixture; proceed as above.

Fold 1 cup cooked fresh Lima beans and ½ cup grated cheese into mashed potatoes before refilling shells. Or fill shells with potatoes and cheese, then arrange Lima beans on top.

POTATO AND LIMA BEAN LOAF

1⅓ cups cooked Lima beans (sieved)
⅓ teaspoon sage
4 tablespoons butter, melted
2 teaspoons salt
½ cup milk
2 cups hot riced potatoes

Mix Lima beans with sage, 2 tablespoons butter, 1 teaspoon salt and ¼ cup milk. Place in bottom of a greased dish. Whip hot potatoes with remaining salt and milk and 1 tablespoon butter. Place on top of Lima bean mixture. Brush with remaining butter. Bake in hot oven (425° F.). Serve with Tomato Sauce. Serves 6.

A greased ring mold may be used in place of loaf pan. Fill center with stewed tomatoes, buttered or creamed carrots, spinach, Swiss chard, peas, broccoli, asparagus or Brussels sprouts. If preferred, fill center with meat or chicken gravy.

The second appearance of vegetables is as successful as their debut when served in stuffed potatoes

SUPREME STUFFED POTATOES

4 medium potatoes
½ cup grated American cheese
2 tablespoons butter
1 teaspoon minced parsley
¼ cup minced celery
¼ cup blanched almonds, chopped
1 cup Thick White Sauce
Salt and pepper
Paprika

Bake potatoes in hot oven (425°F.) 45 minutes or until tender. Cut into halves, scoop out the inside and mash. Add remaining ingredients, beat until fluffy and season to taste with salt, pepper and paprika. Pile mixture back into shells and reheat in oven until lightly browned. Serves 4 or 8.

POTATO PUFF OR SOUFFLÉ

2 cups hot mashed potatoes
2 tablespoons butter
2 eggs, separated
1 cup milk
Salt and pepper to taste

To mashed potatoes add butter, egg yolks which have been beaten until very light, milk, salt and pepper. Beat until light and fluffy. Fold in stiffly beaten egg whites. Mix lightly and pile into greased baking dish. Bake in moderate oven (350°F.) 10 minutes. Serve at once, for 4.

POTATO AND CHEESE SOUFFLÉ — Use 4 eggs and only ½ cup milk. Add ½ cup grated cheese with egg yolks. Add 1 tablespoon minced parsley and 1 tablespoon catchup. Prepare as above; bake 15 to 20 minutes.

POTATO AND SALMON SOUFFLÉ — Use 4 eggs. Add 1 cup flaked salmon, 1 tablespoon minced pimiento and 1 teaspoon minced onion. Prepare as above and bake 15 to 20 minutes.

BAKED POTATOES

POTATO, CELERY AND NUT LOAF

¾ cup diced celery
¾ cup chopped nuts
3 cups mashed potatoes
3 tablespoons fat
1 egg, beaten
1 teaspoon salt
⅛ teaspoon paprika
2 teaspoons grated onion

Cook celery until tender in small amount of boiling salted water. Drain off liquid. (This may be used for soup stock.) Add remaining ingredients in order listed. Mix well, pack in greased loaf pan and bake in moderate oven (350°F.) 35 minutes. Serve with Tomato Sauce. Serves 6.

POTATO CHARLOTTE

1 medium onion, chopped
3 tablespoons chicken fat
2 slices white bread
3 cups grated uncooked potatoes
2 eggs, beaten
1 tablespoon salt
1 teaspoon paprika

Fry onion in fat. Soak bread in cold water, squeeze dry; add to potatoes with onion, eggs and seasonings. Heat a heavy skillet and grease, pour in potato mixture and bake in hot oven (400°F.) until well browned on top. Serve with Pot Roast, Gravy and Applesauce. Serves 5.
Add 1 tablespoon minced parsley or red or green pepper.

A well-scrubbed baked potato, liberally seasoned, may be eaten shell and all

The stuffed baked potato is ideal for the de luxe lunch with an artichoke and broiled fish

POTATO AND CORN ROAST

Husk green corn down to the inner light-green covering. Scrub large, uniform potatoes. Build a good wood or coal fire. When it burns down to coals, bury potatoes and corn in the hot coals and roast 1 hour. Rake from coals.

POTATO AND BEAN CUTLETS

1 cup riced potatoes
1 cup riced Lima beans
1 can pimientos, chopped
½ cup bread crumbs
½ teaspoon salt
1 egg diluted with 2 tablespoons milk
Bread crumbs

Mix first 5 ingredients thoroughly and form into cutlets. Dip into beaten egg and sprinkle with bread crumbs; bake in moderate oven (350°F.) until browned; turn carefully and brown on other side. Serve with a Tomato or Cheese Sauce. Serves 4.

Other riced or mashed vegetables may be used instead of Lima beans: carrots, peas or turnips.

POTATO SHALET

3 large potatoes
1 medium onion, minced
3 tablespoons fat
1 teaspoon salt
3 slices white bread
2 eggs, beaten
¼ teaspoon pepper
½ teaspoon allspice

Pare and dice potatoes. Brown onion slightly in 1 tablespoon fat; add potatoes, water to cover and salt. Cook until water boils away, so potatoes must be watched to prevent sticking. Soak bread in cold water and squeeze dry. Add to potatoes with eggs and seasonings; mix well. Heat skillet with remaining 2 tablespoons fat. Spread potato mixture smoothly in skillet and bake in moderate oven (350°F.) 1 hour. Serve with Pot Roast and Gravy. Serves 4.

The deft application of the pastry tube to stuffed potatoes makes a tempting plate (page 480)

The clever homemaker's second thought after she puts the roast in the oven is Franconia potatoes.

FRANCONIA POTATOES

Pare large potatoes (small ones will bake dry and crusty), boil 15 minutes and drain well. Then place in baking pan with roast and cook 45 minutes, turning often and basting with gravy from the roast. Serve with meat. If preferred, potatoes may be placed in baking pan without parboiling, in which case allow 1 to 1¼ hours for cooking.

POTATO CARROT MOLD

3 medium potatoes
3 medium carrots
1 cup warm milk
2 tablespoons butter
½ teaspoon salt
⅛ teaspoon pepper

Pare potatoes and carrots and cook together in boiling salted water until tender; mash. Add milk, butter, salt and pepper; beat until fluffy. Pour into greased casserole and bake in moderate oven (350°F.) 20 minutes, or until browned. Serve with Tomato Sauce. For 4.

BOILED POTATOES

In order to retain the fullest food value, cook potatoes in rapidly boiling water, with skins on or scraped off. Use only enough water to cover. If skins are to be removed, pare very thin and drop at once into boiling salted water. Save the drained water in which pared potatoes have been cooked to make gravies, soups or bread, as it is rich in minerals.

TO BOIL POTATOES

6 potatoes of uniform size
Boiling water to cover
1 teaspoon salt

Scrub potatoes well. They may be pared before or after cooking. Cover with boiling salted water. Cook covered 20 to 30 minutes, or until just tender. Drain, peel if boiled with jackets and set uncovered in a warm place. Shake over low heat to dry and make mealy. Allow 1 medium potato to a serving. When old potatoes are used, soak in cold water for several hours.

MAÎTRE D'HÔTEL POTATOES— Combine ¼ cup melted butter, ¼ teaspoon paprika, ¼ teaspoon salt, dash pepper, ¼ cup minced parsley and 1 tablespoon lemon juice. Add to drained cooked potatoes, turning carefully until potatoes are coated.

FRENCH POTATO BALLS— Pare potatoes and cut into balls using a French vegetable cutter. Let stand in cold water 15 minutes. Drain, cover with boiling salted water and cook until tender, 12 to 15 minutes. Drain. Toss together with 2 tablespoons melted butter and 4 tablespoons minced parsley. Cook remaining potato for salad or for use in creamed or scalloped dishes.

POTATO TRIUMPH— Combine ¼ cup melted butter; 2 tablespoons olive oil; 1½ teaspoons grated lemon rind; 1 tablespoon each chopped parsley and chives; ⅛ teaspoon nutmeg; ½ teaspoon salt; ⅛ teaspoon pepper and 3 tablespoons lemon juice. Pour over potatoes and serve hot.

BOILED NEW POTATOES

1½ pounds small new potatoes
¼ cup butter, melted
Salt and pepper to season

Wash potatoes and cook with jackets on in boiling salted water to cover until tender, 15 to 20 minutes. Peel. Pour butter over potatoes and season with salt and pepper. Juice of ½ lemon may be added to butter. For 6.

CHIVES— Roll boiled potatoes in 2 tablespoons minced chives.

MINT— Roll boiled potatoes in ⅓ cup finely chopped mint leaves.

PAPRIKA— Sprinkle boiled potatoes with paprika.

PARSLEY— Roll boiled potatoes in ⅓ cup chopped parsley.

STEAMED POTATOES

Pare potatoes and cut into halves. Add to pot roast or stew when meat is nearly tender; cover and cook potatoes, turning occasionally, until tender, 30 minutes.

AMERICAN KEDGEREE

1 medium onion
¼ cup fat, melted
2 teaspoons curry powder
1 teaspoon lemon juice or vinegar
2 teaspoons salt
½ teaspoon pepper
2 cups diced cooked potatoes
2 cups cooked kidney beans or soybeans
2 hard-cooked eggs

Chop onion fine, brown in fat, add curry powder, lemon juice, salt and pepper; cook 5 minutes. Add potatoes, beans and chopped whites of the eggs. Heat in saucepan or baking dish. Cover top with sieved egg yolks. Serves 6. If desired, add ½ to 1 cup sweet or sour cream and 1 tablespoon minced pimiento.

Parsley butter sauce is one of the favorites for serving on boiled potatoes

When you are planning meat loaf, consider baking it in a ring and filling it with French potato balls (page 483)

DUTCH STEWED POTATOES

1 onion, sliced
1 tablespoon fat, melted
½ teaspoon salt, Dash pepper
1 teaspoon minced parsley
2 cups diced uncooked potatoes
1½ cups boiling water
2 teaspoons flour

Cook onion in fat 5 minutes. Add salt, pepper, parsley and potatoes; cover with boiling water and cook until tender. Thicken with flour which has been mixed with a little cold water. For 4.

BOILED POTATOES AND ONIONS

6 potatoes
2 medium onions
1 teaspoon salt
2 tablespoons butter

Pare potatoes and cut them into halves. Peel and slice onions and add to potatoes with water to half-cover them. Add salt. Cover and cook until tender. Drain, if necessary, add butter and shake over low heat to dry. Serves 6.

LANCASTER POTATOES AND LIMA BEANS

1 pound fresh Lima beans
4 or 5 potatoes, diced
2 cups milk
2 tablespoons butter
1 teaspoon salt
⅛ teaspoon pepper

Boil beans in water to cover for 15 minutes, add potatoes and continue cooking until both are tender. Drain and add milk and butter. Season to taste with salt and pepper. Serves 8.

POTATOES IN SAUCE (A Sunday Night Dish)

1 tablespoon fat
1 onion, sliced
1 teaspoon chopped green pepper
5 cold boiled potatoes
1 teaspoon parsley
Salt and pepper
1 cup Gravy or thick Broth

Melt fat in a heavy pan and sauté onion and green pepper. Do not brown. Slice potatoes in thick slices and add to onion. Add parsley, seasonings to taste and gravy. Cover pan and simmer until most of the liquid has evaporated. Serves 4.

POTATOES AND GREEN BEANS

4 medium potatoes
1 pound green beans
1 tablespoon butter
Salt and pepper to season
1 tablespoon minced parsley

Pare and slice potatoes. Cook in a small amount of boiling salted water until tender. Evaporate any excess water. Break beans into 1-inch lengths and cook uncovered until nearly tender in just enough rapidly boiling salted water to cover. Combine potatoes, beans, butter, seasonings and parsley. Blend all together lightly, continue simmering until remainder of water is evaporated and beans are tender. Serves 6.

CHEESE POTATOES

8 hot boiled potatoes
¼ cup melted butter
½ cup grated cheese
½ teaspoon salt
⅛ teaspoon pepper

Roll hot potatoes in melted butter and then in cheese mixed with salt and pepper. Place on a baking sheet and bake in a hot oven (400°F.) 15 minutes or until brown. Serves 8.

BROILED POTATOES WITH HAM

4 boiled potatoes
Melted butter
Salt and pepper
1¼-pound slice ham, ¾ inch thick

Cut potatoes into halves and brush with melted butter. Season. Place potatoes and ham in a preheated broiler and broil 8 minutes. Turn and broil 6 minutes on the other side. Serve at once. Serves 4.

If desired, tomato halves spread with mustard and sprinkled with salt, celery salt and pepper may be cooked with potatoes and ham.

CREAMED AND SCALLOPED POTATOES

CREAMED OR SCALLOPED POTATOES

Potatoes may be cooked or un-cooked for this method. Since milk is such an essential food in our daily diet, its combination with potatoes makes an ideal dish for body building. There are many seasonings which may be added to the milk to give a wide variety of flavors, such as: thyme, bay leaf, paprika, parsley, lemon juice, pimientos, green pepper, onion, crisp bacon, ham and cheese. Evaporated milk may be used instead of cream but when it is used in place of fresh milk dilute it with an equal amount of water.

STEWED POTATOES

2 cups potato cubes ·
2 tablespoons butter, melted
2 cups milk
Salt and pepper to season
2 tablespoons flour

Mix together and cook in a double boiler 20 minutes or un-til potatoes are tender. Serves 4. Soup stock or meat gravy may be substituted for milk.

CREAMED POTATOES

2 tablespoons butter
2 tablespoons flour
Dash mace
1¼ teaspoons salt
¼ teaspoon pepper
2 cups milk
Few drops lemon juice
6 cooked potatoes, cubed

Melt butter, blend in flour, mace, salt and pepper. Add milk and cook until thickened, stirring con-stantly. Add lemon juice and potatoes. Cook until potatoes are heated throughout. Serves 6.

CREAMED STEAMED POTATOES

6 potatoes
Oil or melted fat
2 teaspoons salt
1 cup water
1½ cups Medium White Sauce
Parsley

Wash and pare uniform-sized potatoes. Brush with oil, place in baking dish and sprinkle with salt. Add water, cover closely and steam in slow oven (300°F.) 2½ hours. Place in serving dish, cover with hot white sauce and garnish with parsley. Serves 6.

CREAMED NEW POTATOES WITH PARSLEY

8 to 10 small potatoes
½ cup milk
Dash pepper
½ teaspoon salt
2 tablespoons butter
1 tablespoon chopped parsley

Boil potatoes in their jackets un-til tender. Peel. Cover with milk and cook slowly until milk is all absorbed. Add remaining ingredients and cook for a few minutes longer. Serves 4.

Add chopped pimientos, green pepper or chopped broiled crisp bacon.

One cup cooked fresh peas may be added to potatoes.

POTATOES IN CHEESE SAUCE —Prepare 1 cup White Sauce and add ⅓ cup grated cheese. Stir until melted. Cut 4 hot boiled potatoes into ¾-inch cubes and add to sauce. Add 1 tablespoon diced pimiento and mix carefully so as not to break the cubes of potato. Serves 4.

You will not regret taking a few extra minutes to stir up a savory cream sauce for plain boiled potatoes

POTATOES WITH SAVORY SAUCE

4 potatoes
2 small onions, cut into rings
4 tablespoons fat
2 tablespoons flour
1 cup milk
2 teaspoons salt
¼ teaspoon pepper
2 tablespoons pimiento, chopped
Grated cheese

Pare potatoes and cut into long matchlike strips. Cook them in boiling salted water until tender. Drain and place in a warm serving dish. Brown onion rings in fat. Add flour and blend; add milk, salt, pepper and pimiento and cook, stirring constantly until thickened. Pour over hot cooked potatoes and sprinkle with grated cheese. Serves 4.

WITH SALMON—Omit onions. Blend butter and flour, add milk gradually and cook, stirring constantly, until thickened. Add remaining ingredients and 1 cup flaked cooked salmon. Pour over potatoes.

Pork chops are as popular as ham on scalloped potatoes and are prepared in the same manner

DELMONICO POTATOES

2 cups diced cooked potatoes
2 cups Medium White Sauce
Salt and pepper
Buttered crumbs

Mix potatoes, white sauce and seasonings. Pour into greased baking dish, cover with crumbs and bake in hot oven (450°F.) 15 minutes. Two tablespoons chopped pimiento may be added to white sauce. Serves 4.
Add ¼ teaspoon basil.

RUSSIAN STYLE POTATOES

4 medium potatoes
1 small onion, minced
Salt and pepper
Boiling water
2 tablespoons butter
3 tablespoons sour cream

Pare potatoes and cut into cubes. Place in a saucepan. Add onion, salt and pepper. Cover with water and simmer until tender. Drain. Add butter and sour cream and cover. Shake pan gently. Let stand a few minutes before serving. Serves 4.

POTATO AND CLAM PIE

4 cups sliced cooked potatoes
6 young onions, sliced
1 tablespoon butter
¾ teaspoon salt
⅛ teaspoon pepper
½ cup chopped celery
2 cups minced clams
1 cup milk
1 tablespoon quick-cooking tapioca
Baking Powder Biscuit dough

Combine all ingredients except biscuit dough, mix well and pour into a greased baking dish. Cover top with biscuits. Bake in hot oven (400°F.) ½ hour. Serves 6.

SCALLOPED POTATOES

6 medium potatoes
Salt and pepper
2 tablespoons flour
4 tablespoons butter
Milk

Pare potatoes and cut into thin slices. Place in a greased baking dish in 3 layers 1 inch deep, sprinkling each layer with salt, pepper and flour and dotting with butter. Add milk until it can be seen between slices of potato, cover and bake in moderate oven (350°F.) until potatoes are tender when pierced with a fork, 1 to 1¼ hours. Remove cover for the last 15 minutes to brown. Serve from baking dish. Serves 6.

WITH HAM—Prepare Scalloped Potatoes and place a 1-inch slice of ham on top. Do not cover. Bake as above.
Ham may be cut into servings and arranged in layers with the potatoes. Bake covered as above.

FRIED POTATOES

There are two well-known methods of frying potatoes, namely, pan-frying with a small amount of fat, or deep fat frying in a large amount of fat. Bacon or meat drippings; lard; olive, corn, coconut, peanut or cottonseed oils; butter; margarine or any of the vegetable shortenings may be used for pan-frying. The choice is not so wide for deep fat frying. Only fats which are free from moisture can be used, such as olive, corn, coconut, peanut or cottonseed oils, vegetable shortenings or lard.

A thermometer is the accurate gauge of the temperature of deep fat, but there. is a simple test which is very satisfactory. When an inch square of bread browns in 40 seconds the fat is hot enough for all previously cooked foods, such as croquettes. For uncooked foods, such as fritters or potato chips, the bread should brown in 60 seconds.

AMERICAN FRIED POTATOES

6 large potatoes
Garlic
3 tablespoons melted fat
¾ teaspoon salt
¼ teaspoon pepper
½ teaspoon minced onion

Pare potatoes and slice very thin. Rub skillet with the cut edge of a clove of garlic. Add fat and when hot add potatoes, salt, pepper and onion. Sauté slowly, turning occasionally so that potatoes brown evenly on all sides. Cook until tender, about 25 to 30 minutes. Serves 6.

Turn the lyonnaise potatoes lightly with a fork to preserve the cubes intact and brown them on all sides

COTTAGE FRIED POTATOES

Cut cold boiled potatoes into slices or chop. Put into a hot skillet which contains a generous amount of fat. Season with salt, pepper and a little minced onion. Sauté until potatoes are brown. Serve hot. Allow 1 large potato for each serving.

HASHED BROWN POTATOES

2 cups cold boiled potatoes
1 tablespoon flour
Salt and pepper
3 tablespoons fat

Chop potatoes fine, sprinkle with flour and season with salt and pepper. Melt fat in a frying pan. Add potatoes and brown quickly, turning over several times with a fork. When well heated form into an oval-shaped mound about ½ inch thick and brown. Turn with a pancake turner and brown on the other side. Remove carefully to a small platter so potatoes are served with the appearance of an oval-shaped pancake. Serves 4.

Cook in fat from salt pork.

LYONNAISE POTATOES

2 cups diced boiled potatoes
Salt and pepper
1 teaspoon minced onion
2 tablespoons fat
1 tablespoon chopped parsley

The potatoes should be slightly under-done to produce the best results. Season with salt and pepper. Cook the onion in fat until light brown, add the potatoes, and stir with a fork until all sides are brown, being careful not to break the potatoes. Add more fat if necessary. When done, transfer potatoes to a hot dish, sprinkle parsley over top and serve hot. Serves 4.

SOUTHERN FRIED POTATOES

Wash and pare small potatoes, cut into lengthwise strips ¼-inch thick, soak in cold water 1 hour. Dry, dip in slightly beaten egg, then in bread crumbs and place in a frying basket. Immerse in hot deep fat (380°F.) and cook 3 to 5 minutes or until brown. Drain on absorbent paper; sprinkle with salt. Serve hot.

FRENCH FRIED POTATOES

6 medium potatoes
Deep fat for frying
Salt

Wash potatoes, pare and cut into long strips ¼ to ½ inch thick. Soak in cold water for 1 hour. Drain, wipe very dry between towels. Place just enough potatoes in frying basket to cover bottom. Immerse in hot deep fat (380°F.) and cook until lightly browned, about 3 to 5 minutes. Keep shaking potatoes while cooking. Drain and place on absorbent paper. Sprinkle with salt and serve hot. Allow 1 potato for each serving.

BALLS—Cut into balls, using a French vegetable cutter.

BASKETS—Cut as for chips or julienne. Arrange in a potato-basket mold or between 2 strainers, being careful potatoes overlap on sides and bottom.

A few simple cutters plus imagination will produce all the attractive shapes for French fried potatoes

CHAINS—Cut into ¼-inch slices and place in ice water. Cut a ring from each slice with a small cookie cutter. Cut a slit in 1 ring and slip in 2 rings making a chain of links.

CHIPS—Cut into very thin slices.

CUBES—Cut into ¾-inch cubes.

JULIENNE OR SHOESTRING—Cut into matchlike shapes.

LATTICE—Cut with a lattice vegetable cutter.

POTATO TWIRLS—Cut pared medium-sized potatoes crosswise into ¾-inch slices. Starting at the outer edge cut around and around in each slice to form a spiral. Fry as above.

PUFFED—Slice ⅛ inch thick. Dry each slice. Place in heated deep fat (275°F.), cook until browned, about 10 minutes. Drain and cool. Heat fat to 390°F. and immerse potatoes in it. Potatoes should puff up immediately. Drain and sprinkle with salt.

SARATOGA CHIPS—Cut into very thin slices. After potatoes have soaked in cold water, drain and plunge into boiling water. Drain, dry and proceed as above.

POTATOES PRINCESSE

4 large potatoes
1 tablespoon butter or fat
⅛ teaspoon salt
Dash white pepper

Pare firm, white potatoes and slice ¼ inch thick. Grease a large, heavy frying pan and lay slices of potato shingle-wise around pan. Season. Fry at low heat about 20 minutes, until edges are golden brown, place under broiler 8-10 minutes until top is browned. Lift whole onto chop plate and serve 4.

LIVER SAUSAGE POTATO CAKES

6 slices liver sausage
2 cups cold mashed potatoes
½ teaspoon salt
¼ teaspoon pepper
2 eggs
2 tablespoons water
Bread crumbs

Cut liver sausage into ¼-inch slices and remove rind. Mix potatoes thoroughly with seasonings and 1 egg. Make very thin patties of the potato mixture, placing one on either side of each slice of liver sausage. Shape into even, round cakes. Dip in remaining egg, which has been beaten with water, and in bread crumbs and fry slowly in fat until well browned on both sides. Garnish with crisp celery sticks or parsley. Serves 6.

Potato patties may be made ½ inch thick and placed on slices of cooked salami or Thuringer. Place on a baking sheet, dot with butter and bake in a moderate oven (350°F.) to heat through and brown.

LLAPINGACHOS

4 large potatoes
2 tablespoons butter
Salt and pepper
2 tablespoons grated cheese
Fat for frying
2 onions, sliced
3 tomatoes, sliced
6 poached eggs

Pare potatoes and boil until tender. Mash well, add butter; season to taste with salt and pepper, then stir in the cheese. Shape into flat cakes and fry in hot fat. Brown onions in fat and add tomatoes; simmer about 20 minutes. Pour over the fried potato cakes and top each with a poached egg. Serves 6.

PIGS IN POTATOES

¼ teaspoon onion juice
1 tablespoon minced parsley
1 egg yolk
2 cups mashed potatoes
6 to 8 cooked sausages (small links)
Dry bread crumbs
1 egg diluted with 2 tablespoons cold water

Add onion juice, parsley and beaten egg yolk to mashed potatoes. Season if necessary. Beat thoroughly. Coat sausages with potato mixture; shape into croquettes. Roll in bread crumbs, dip in diluted egg, then roll in crumbs again. Fry in hot deep fat (375°F.). Makes 6 to 8 croquettes.

Crispy potato nests for holding creamed foods are easy to make

POTATO NESTS

Pare 3 large potatoes; cut lengthwise into tiny strips. Heat in small amount of hot fat until nearly tender, but not brown. Remove from fat, sprinkle with salt and arrange potatoes against sides and bottom of large deep muffin pans, pressing firmly into place. Bake in hot oven (450° F.) 15 minutes. Serve hot filled with any creamed fish, meat or poultry. Makes 6 nests.

Cut potatoes into thin slices as for chips or with lattice vegetable cutter instead of into strips and use as above.

POTATO CODFISH BALLS WITH TOMATO SAUCE

1 cup salt codfish
2½ cups cubed uncooked potatoes
1½ tablespoons fat
⅛ teaspoon pepper
1 egg, beaten slightly

Soak codfish 12 hours in cold water. Pour off water and shred by placing on cutting board and pulling apart with a fork. Cook potatoes until tender, drain thoroughly and return to kettle in which they were cooked. Shake over heat until thoroughly dry, mash well, add fat and pepper and beat until light; add flaked codfish, beaten egg and continue beating until mixture is light and fluffy. Add more salt if necessary. Form into balls by dropping from a spoon. Fry in hot deep fat (385°F.) for 1 minute, or until brown. Drain on absorbent paper. Serves 4 or 5.

French fried chains of potatoes will enchant all the family (page 488)

TOMATO SAUCE

2½ cups canned tomatoes
1 small onion, sliced
4 cloves, 2 tablespoons fat
2 tablespoons flour
½ teaspoon salt
¼ teaspoon pepper

Cook tomatoes, onion and cloves together for 10 minutes. Melt fat, add flour, salt and pepper and blend. Add tomato mixture and cook 2 minutes longer, stirring constantly. Strain. Makes 1 cup sauce.

SPANISH POTATOES

1 tablespoon minced onion
2 tablespoons chopped green pepper
2 tablespoons chopped pimiento
4 tablespoons fat
2 cups diced cold cooked potatoes
½ cup chopped cooked ham
1 teaspoon salt
½ teaspoon paprika

Fry onion, pepper and pimiento in fat until light brown, add potatoes, ham and seasonings and cook until thoroughly heated. Serves 4.

POTATOES O'BRIEN

6 medium potatoes
Fat for frying
Salt
Chopped pimientos
Onion juice

Wash potatoes, pare and cut into ½-inch cubes. Dry between towels. Fry in a generous amount of fat until a delicate brown. Drain on soft paper, sprinkle with salt; then sauté them in just enough fat to prevent burning, adding finely chopped pimientos and a few drops of onion juice. These should be tossed frequently during cooking and not pressed close to the pan. Serves 6.

TOASTED POTATO BALLS

2 eggs, beaten
½ cup milk
Salt and pepper to taste
3 cups cooked potato balls
1 cup bread crumbs
Fat

(Potato balls are made by cutting fresh Irish potatoes with a French ball cutter. Cook until tender in boiling salted water.)
Combine eggs, milk and seasonings. Roll potato balls in egg mixture and then in bread crumbs. Sauté in generous amount of fat in a heavy frying pan until potatoes are a golden brown. Serves 6.

CREAMED FRENCH FRIED POTATOES

½ tablespoon lemon juice
1 teaspoon minced parsley
1 cup Medium White Sauce
3 cups French Fried Potato Cubes

Add lemon juice and parsley to white sauce. Pour over potato cubes and serve at once. Serves 6.

PIEDMONT POTATO CROQUETTES

2 cups hot riced potatoes
2 tablespoons butter
3 egg yolks, ½ teaspoon salt
Dash of paprika and pepper
1 cup sifted flour
1 whole egg, beaten
½ cup blanched almonds, minced

Mix potatoes, butter, egg yolks, salt, paprika and pepper and beat thoroughly. Shape in balls using 1 tablespoon of the mixture for each ball. Roll in flour, then dip in beaten egg and roll in almonds. Fry in hot deep fat (390°F.) until golden brown. Makes 20

POTATO CROQUETTES

2 cups cold riced potatoes
½ teaspoon salt
⅛ teaspoon pepper
¼ teaspoon celery salt
2 tablespoons butter
1 egg yolk, slightly beaten
1 teaspoon chopped parsley
Few drops onion juice
Bread crumbs; 1 egg, well beaten

Combine first 8 ingredients; beat until light and fluffy. Shape into cylinders. Dip in bread crumbs, in egg, and again in bread crumbs. Fry in hot deep fat (380°F.) until brown. Drain on absorbent paper. Serve hot Makes 6 to 8 croquettes.

POTATO AND SPINACH CROQUETTES

2 cups hot mashed potatoes
1½ tablespoons butter
2 egg yolks, slightly beaten
⅓ cup minced cooked spinach
Salt and pepper
1 egg, slightly beaten
Fine dry crumbs

Combine first 6 ingredients and beat until fluffy. Shape into croquettes, dip into egg and roll in crumbs. Fry in hot deep fat (380°F.) until brown. For 4.

FILLED POTATO CROQUETTES

2 cups hot riced potatoes
3 tablespoons cream
½ teaspoon salt
Dash pepper and cayenne
¼ teaspoon onion juice
1 egg yolk
½ cup chopped cooked meat
3 tablespoons Gravy
1 egg, slightly beaten
Fine dry bread crumbs

Combine first 7 ingredients and beat thoroughly. Combine meat and gravy and heat. Shape potatoes into nests, fill with hot meat mixture and cover with additional potato mixture. Roll lightly until of desired length, flatten ends, dip into egg, then roll in crumbs. Fry in hot deep fat (380°F.) until brown. For 5.

Omit meat and gravy. Fill potatoes with hot creamed salmon.

Omit meat and gravy. Fill potatoes with hot ham à la King.

Omit meat and gravy. Fill potatoes with smoked fish moistened with tartare sauce.

POTATOES DE LUXE

2 medium potatoes
1 small onion
¼ green pepper
Salt, Pepper
1 egg, slightly beaten
3 tablespoons bacon fat

Pare potatoes and force through a food chopper with onion and green pepper. Add salt, pepper and egg and beat well. Heat bacon fat in a skillet, add potato mixture, lower heat and cook until brown on one side. Turn and brown other side. Serves 3 or 4.

SALMON CAKES

6 cooked potatoes, chopped
2 cups flaked salmon
1 green pepper, chopped
1 egg

Combine ingredients and shape into cakes. Brown in greased frying pan. Serve with Tartare Sauce and parsley. Serves 6.

When leftovers are served in potato twirls, they'll seem like a treat instead of an economy. See Page 488

DUMPLINGS

Serve these with soups, stews and with meats having a rich gravy as roast or chicken fricassee. In order that dumplings should be very light, it is a good plan not to add all of the flour at one time. Add ⅔ of the amount specified and then test the mixture by dropping small spoonfuls into the boiling liquid. If it holds together, it is stiff enough and no more flour is needed. However, if the dumpling falls apart more flour will be required. Too much flour makes heavy, soggy dumplings. Be sure there is enough solid matter under the dumplings so that they float and cook in the steam. Cover cooking pan tightly and do not lift until cooking time is completed.

POTATO DUMPLINGS

⅔ cup mashed potatoes
1 cup flour
4 teaspoons baking powder
1 teaspoon salt
2 teaspoons butter or other fat
Milk, about ½ cup

Mix ingredients, roll out to ½-inch thickness. Cut dough with a biscuit cutter. Place dumplings close together in a greased steamer over boiling water, cover closely and steam dumplings for 12 minutes. Makes 12 (2-inch) dumplings.

SOUP WITH POTATO DUMPLINGS

1 cup mashed potatoes
1½ tablespoons fat
1 egg yolk
2 tablespoons grated Parmesan cheese
Dash of nutmeg
Salt
6 cups beef or veal Broth

Combine mashed potatoes with all ingredients except broth. Mix thoroughly; place long strips (about ½ inch in diameter) of potato mixture on floured board. Roll strips carefully in flour, cut into ½-inch pieces, then form into balls. Brown in hot deep fat (365°-380°F.) and serve with very hot beef or veal broth poured over them. Serves 6.

BERKS COUNTY POTATO DUMPLINGS

6 uncooked potatoes
10 slices bread
Salt and pepper to season
1 onion, grated
1 teaspoon minced parsley
2 eggs, well beaten

Pare potatoes and grate. Soak bread in cold water and squeeze out as much of the water as possible. Mix together bread, salt, pepper, grated onion and parsley. Add grated potatoes and eggs; mix well. Form into balls, roll in flour gently; drop into boiling salted water, cover closely and cook for 15 minutes. These dumplings are excellent with sauerkraut, stewed chicken or meat. Serves 6.

WITH HOMINY GRITS—Omit bread. Prepare potatoes as above, place in a cloth and squeeze as dry as possible. Add 2 cups hot cooked hominy grits.

Potato dumplings, light as a feather are an excellent foil for spareribs

DUTCH POTATO DUMPLINGS

9 medium potatoes
1 teaspoon salt
3 eggs, well beaten
1 cup sifted flour
⅔ cup bread crumbs or farina
½ teaspoon nutmeg
1 cup fat
½ cup bread crumbs
2 tablespoons chopped onion

Boil potatoes in their jackets until tender, remove skins and put potatoes through a ricer, into a bowl and add salt, eggs, flour, ⅔ cup bread crumbs and nutmeg. Mix thoroughly. Form mixture into dry balls about the size of walnuts (if mixture is too moist, add more bread crumbs). Drop the balls into boiling salted water. When balls come to the surface, allow to boil uncovered for 3 minutes. Remove one from liquid and cut open; if center is dry, they are sufficiently cooked. Remove balls from liquid to a hot platter and pour over them a dressing made as follows: Brown fat in a skillet, add bread crumbs and onion and cook for several minutes. Two tablespoons mushrooms browned in fat may be used instead of onion. These dumplings may be reheated in a double boiler several times without impairing the flavor. For 12.

IRISH DUMPLINGS

2 tablespoons fat
1 tablespoon onion, chopped
½ cup grated, drained and
    uncooked potatoes
2 pounds boiled potatoes or 5 cups
    riced and cooled
1 tablespoon salt
¾ cup flour
2 eggs, slightly beaten

Heat fat in frying pan, add onion and fry until golden brown. Add grated potatoes. Cook until mixture forms a paste; let cool, add riced potatoes, salt, flour and eggs; stir until smooth and form into balls size of a walnut. Drop into boiling salted water. Cook until dumplings rise to the top and are cooked through center, about 15 minutes. Drain. Serves 5.

POTATO STUFFING

2 tablespoons onion
¼ cup salt pork cubes
2 cups hot mashed potatoes
1 teaspoon poultry seasoning
Salt and pepper
1 cup cooked sausages, chopped

Cook onion and pork until brown; add remaining ingredients and mix well. Use for stuffing chicken, turkey and goose. Makes enough stuffing for 1 3-pound fowl.

CROUTON DUMPLINGS

1 cup bread cubes
Butter
2 large cold cooked potatoes
2 tablespoons flour
1 tablespoon melted bacon fat
2 egg yolks, beaten
Salt and pepper
Bread crumbs, Fat

Brown bread cubes in butter. Rub potatoes through sieve and add remaining ingredients. Shape into balls with a bread cube in each. Cook in boiling water until they float. Drain. Roll in bread crumbs and fry in butter or in deep fat. Serves 6.

BOHEMIAN POTATO STUFFING

5 large potatoes
1 onion, grated
1 teaspoon caraway seeds
1 tablespoon minced parsley
1 tablespoon melted butter

Boil potatoes in their skins until tender. Drain, peel and mash. Add remaining ingredients and mix well. Makes 4 to 5 cups.

IRISH POTATO STUFFING

8 potatoes
4 tablespoons melted goose fat or
    butter
1 cup chopped onions
½ cup chopped celery
1 cup bread crumbs
½ teaspoon sage
½ teaspoon celery salt
½ teaspoon summer savory
1 teaspoon salt
¼ teaspoon pepper
2 eggs, beaten

Pare potatoes and cook until tender. Drain and rice. Add remaining ingredients and mix well. Will fill 10-pound goose. Save potato water for basting goose during roasting.

POTATO AND CELERY STUFFING

2 onions
2 tablespoons melted butter
½ cup pork sausage
¼ cup chopped celery leaves
5 large uncooked potatoes
2 stalks celery
1 teaspoon salt
½ teaspoon paprika

Dice 1 onion and sauté in butter until golden brown. Add sausage and celery leaves and cook 2 minutes. Pare potatoes and put through food chopper with celery stalks and remaining onion. Add to cooked mixture with salt and paprika and mix well. Will fill a 3 to 4-pound fowl.

COUNTRY POTATO STUFFING
—Use 3 cups hot mashed potatoes instead of uncooked potatoes. Use only 1 onion; omit butter. Dice celery and onion and mix all ingredients together without sautéing. Add ½ cup bread crumbs; 1 egg, beaten; ¼ cup cream and ½ teaspoon mustard. Mix together thoroughly and use to stuff poultry or crown roast of lamb or pork.

MASHED POTATOES

There are endless ways in which mashed potatoes may be combined and served. Preparing light and fluffy mashed potatoes, however, is an art. Add hot milk to boiled potatoes and beat hard with a potato masher or a fork, being sure no lumps remain in the potatoes. A very small amount of baking powder may be added to keep the potatoes white and light, but only hard beating will make them creamy. Be sure they are very hot when served. One pound or 3 medium-sized potatoes will make 2 cups mashed potatoes.

RICED POTATOES

Wash potatoes, pare and boil until tender. Drain. Force through a potato ricer or coarse strainer. Pile lightly in hot dish. Garnish with parsley and paprika. Allow 1 medium potato for each serving.

Bake the meat loaf in a ring mold and fill the center with a snowy peak of mashed potatoes

MASHED POTATOES

6 potatoes
3 tablespoons butter
⅓ cup hot milk
1 teaspoon salt
Few grains pepper

Boil potatoes with jackets on, until tender. Peel, force through a ricer, add butter, milk, salt and pepper. Beat until creamy and very light. Serve hot, for 6.

ONION—Add few drops onion juice to potatoes before beating.

BAKING POWDER—To make potatoes very light, add ½ teaspoon baking powder to riced potatoes and proceed as above.

CHANTILLY POTATOES

3 cups mashed potatoes
½ cup heavy cream
⅓ cup grated cheese

Season potatoes well and pile into a greased baking dish. Top with cream, whipped stiff and sprinkle with grated cheese. Bake in hot oven (450°F.) until cheese is melted and the top is slightly brown. Serves 6.

DUCHESS POTATOES

2 cups hot mashed potatoes
2 tablespoons butter
½ teaspoon salt
2 eggs, separated

Combine mashed potatoes, butter and salt with beaten egg yolks and form into balls, hearts or other shapes (a pastry bag may be used). Place in a buttered baking dish and brush with slightly beaten egg whites. Brown in hot oven (450°F.). Serves 6.

COLCANNON

2 onions, minced
⅔ cup milk
4 large potatoes, boiled
2 parsnips, boiled
Salt and pepper
1 cup cooked shredded cabbage
1 tablespoon butter
1 tablespoon minced parsley

Cook onions in milk until tender. Mash potatoes and parsnips together; season with salt and pepper. Add onions and milk slowly, beating well. Combine with cabbage. Serve garnished with bits of butter and minced parsley. Serves 6.

CURATE'S PUDDING

1 cup hot mashed potatoes
½ cup top milk or cream
½ teaspoon salt
1 tablespoon butter, melted
2 eggs, separated
1 tablespoon lemon juice
1 teaspoon grated lemon rind
¼ cup grated cheese

Beat mashed potatoes until smooth. Add cream, salt, butter and egg yolks, slightly beaten. Beat egg whites stiff and fold into potatoes with lemon juice and rind. Place in a greased baking dish and sprinkle with cheese. Bake in moderate oven (375°F.) 20 minutes. Serve with roasts. Serves 4 to 6.

CABBAGE AND POTATOES

8 medium potatoes
1 head cabbage
4 tablespoons butter
Salt, Pepper
½ cup cream

Cook potatoes and cabbage separately in boiling salted water until tender. Drain and mash together with butter, salt and pepper. If mixture is too dry, add cream. Serves 8 to 10.

HUTSPOT

6 onions
6 carrots
8 potatoes
Salt and pepper
½ cup rich milk
2 to 4 tablespoons butter

Dice onions and carrots, cover with boiling salted water and cook until tender. Drain. Pare potatoes, cut in pieces and cook in boiling salted water until tender. Drain and shake over heat to dry thoroughly. Add onions and carrots and mash well. Season with salt and pepper; add milk and butter. Heat thoroughly. Serves 8.

MASHED POTATOES AU GRATIN

3 tablespoons butter
½ teaspoon salt
½ teaspoon paprika
2 eggs, well beaten
6 potatoes, riced
¼ cup grated cheese
½ cup buttered crumbs

Add butter, seasonings and eggs to the hot riced potatoes. Beat until light and pile into baking dish. Cover with cheese and then with buttered crumbs. Bake in moderate oven (350°F.) until crumbs are brown, 15 minutes. Serves 6.

MASHED POTATO RUTABAGA COMBINATION

4 medium potatoes
1 medium rutabaga
Salt and pepper to taste
2 tablespoons butter
¼ cup hot milk

Pare vegetables, slice and cook separately in boiling salted water until tender. Drain. Combine and mash; add remaining ingredients and whip until light and fluffy. Serves 6 to 8.

POTATO-STUFFED FRANKFURTERS

8 frankfurters
Prepared mustard
½ cup grated cheese
2 cups mashed potatoes

Let frankfurters stand in boiling water, off heat, for 7 minutes. Partially split frankfurters lengthwise and spread inside lightly with mustard. Add grated cheese to mashed potatoes, beating until light and fluffy. Fill frankfurters with potato mixture, using a pastry tube or heaping mixture lightly with a fork. Place on broiler rack far enough below heat to brown in 10 minutes. Serves 4.

A vegetable plate will be even more appetizing if mashed potatoes are heaped lightly in the center

MASHED POTATO CANAPÉS

Spread strips of dried beef with prepared mustard, place a spoonful of mashed potatoes at one end, and roll. Fasten with a toothpick and broil. Serve as hot appetizers.

PORK SAUSAGE WITH POTATOES

2 pounds pork sausage links
4 medium potatoes
1½ tablespoons butter
½ cup rich milk
½ teaspoon salt
⅛ teaspoon pepper
1 egg, well beaten

Prick sausages and arrange them in the bottom of a baking dish. Boil potatoes until tender, peel, mash well, and beat thoroughly with butter, milk, salt and pepper. Spread potatoes over sausages and cover evenly with beaten egg. Bake in moderate oven (350°F.) 30 minutes. Serves 6.

Use sausage patties instead of sausage links.

Omit egg; sprinkle with cheese.

POTATO CRAB AU GRATIN

2 cups mashed potatoes
2 tablespoons butter
2 tablespoons flour
1 cup milk, scalded
½ teaspoon salt
⅛ teaspoon pepper
2 cups flaked crab meat
½ cup buttered bread crumbs

Line a greased casserole with mashed potatoes. Melt butter, blend in flour, add milk gradually, stirring constantly, heat to boiling and add salt, pepper and crab meat. Cook 3 minutes. Pour into lined casserole, sprinkle top with bread crumbs and bake in moderate oven (350°F.) 20 to 30 minutes. Serves 4.

Use creamed meat, eggs or other creamed fish instead of creamed crab meat.

Potato cups for holding the other vegetables may be made from mashed potatoes as well as from fried

POTATO CASSEROLE WITH EGGS IN BACON NESTS

4 cups mashed potatoes
Salt and pepper
Milk or cream, Butter
2 eggs, well beaten
12 bacon strips
6 whole eggs

Season potatoes very well with salt, pepper, milk or cream and butter. Add 2 beaten eggs and beat until light and fluffy. Pile lightly into greased casserole and, with the back of a spoon, make in the surface 6 hollows, each large enough to hold 1 egg. Meanwhile partially cook bacon and line each hollow with 2 strips. Place an egg in each. Bake in moderate oven (350°F.) until eggs are set and bacon is browned. Season eggs. Grated cheese may be sprinkled over the top just before eggs are done. Serves 6.

POTATO CASES

Form well-seasoned mashed potatoes into rounds 3 inches in diameter. Hollow out center, leaving a thickness of ½ inch on bottom and building up sides so that they are 1½ inches high. Potatoes may be put through a pastry tube to form cups. Place on a baking sheet, brush with melted butter and bake in moderate oven (350°F.) until heated through and browned. Transfer to platter and fill with well-seasoned vegetables, creamed fowl or meat. Serve piping hot.

POTATOES WITH PEANUT BUTTER—To 3 cups hot mashed potatoes add 3 tablespoons peanut butter, and 1 tablespoon grated onion. Mix thoroughly and place in a buttered baking dish. Blend ½ tablespoon peanut butter with 1 tablespoon butter, brush over potatoes. Brown in moderate oven (350°F.). For 4.

POTATO CRUST PIE

CRUST:
1 cup hot mashed potatoes
½ teaspoon salt
1 teaspoon baking powder
1 egg, beaten
2 tablespoons melted shortening
Flour (enough to make soft dough)

Combine ingredients in the order given. Roll mixture to about ⅛ inch in thickness on a well-floured board.

FILLING:
1 medium onion, chopped
2 tablespoons fat
1 cup cooked meat, cut in cubes
1 cup milk
1 cup chopped cold cooked carrots
1 cup chopped cold cooked potatoes
1 cup cooked peas

Brown onion in fat. Add meat and sear well. Add milk, vegetables, salt and pepper to taste. Pour into a baking dish, cover with potato crust and bake in moderate oven (350°F.) for 30 minutes or until well browned. Serves 6.
Cover with mashed potatoes instead of crust.

POTATO SURPRISE

2 cups cold mashed potatoes
Melted fat
1 egg, slightly beaten

If potatoes are cold and firm, cut into strips 2 inches long, 1 inch wide and ½ inch thick; otherwise shape into flat cakes ½ inch thick. Dip strips or cakes first into melted fat and then into egg. Place on greased pan and brown in hot oven (400°F.). Serves 4.

POTATOES AND WHITE CABBAGE

½ head cabbage
8 medium potatoes
½ pound pork steak, chopped
½ cup barley

Shred cabbage. Pare potatoes, cut in quarters; chop pork steak in pieces; combine and place in pan with barley and cover with water. Cook slowly for 2 hours. When tender, mash and mix thoroughly. Season to taste. Serves 8.

POTATO PUFF BALLS

2 cups warm mashed potatoes
2 eggs, separated
1 tablespoon chopped parsley
½ teaspoon minced onion

Beat potatoes, egg yolks and seasonings together. Beat egg whites until stiff and fold in. Bake in greased muffin pans in moderate oven (350°F.) until browned. Serves 4.
Drop by tablespoons onto greased baking sheet and bake as above. Shape into nests on greased baking sheet and bake as above.

The potato topping on shepherd's pie may conceal or reveal the savory filling as the maker desires

POTATO PASTRY SAUSAGE ROLLS

1 cup flour, ¼ teaspoon salt
¼ cup shortening
¼ cup riced potatoes
Ice water
½ pound sausage meat
1 egg white, unbeaten

Sift flour and salt together 3 times. Cut in shortening with 2 knives or a dough blender until of a crumbly consistency. Cut in potatoes. Add only enough water to hold ingredients together. Roll out on a lightly floured board to a thickness of ⅛ inch. Cut into 3-inch squares. Form sausage into rolls 3 inches long, place on pastry square, roll in jelly roll fashion and brush edge with egg white. Place on a greased baking dish with joining on bottom. Make several gashes in pastry, brush with egg white and bake in moderate oven (350°F.) until brown, 30 to 35 minutes. Makes 4 to 6 rolls.

POTATO CAKES

Form cold mashed potatoes into rounds 3 inches in diameter and ½ inch thick. Place in a hot skillet which contains a generous amount of fat. Brown on one side; turn and brown on other side. Serve hot.

POTATO PATTIES

6 potatoes
2 tablespoons flour
2 tablespoons butter
1 tablespoon grated Swiss cheese
½ teaspoon salt
Tomato Sauce

Boil potatoes in their jackets, peel, mash and add flour, butter, grated cheese and salt. Mix well and shape into thick round patties; make a hole in the middle. Bake in greased shallow baking dish, in hot oven (400°F.) until browned on both sides. Serve with tomato sauce. Serves 4.

PUFFY POTATO OMELET

3 eggs, separated
1 cup mashed potatoes
¼ teaspoon onion juice
½ teaspoon minced parsley
1 teaspoon salt
¼ teaspoon pepper
3 tablespoons cream or milk

Add egg yolks to potatoes and beat until there are no lumps. Add onion juice, parsley, salt, pepper and cream or milk. Beat egg whites until stiff and fold into potato mixture. Transfer to greased frying pan and bake in moderately slow oven (325°F.) until brown. Then turn and fold on hot platter. Serve at once. Serves 4.

When the mashed potatoes left from dinner reappear as browned cakes, they are sure of a warm welcome

Either duchess or plain mashed potatoes piped around each planked chop gives the final touch of elegance

POTATO SALMON CASSEROLE

2 cups mashed potatoes
2 cups salmon, skinned, boned and flaked
½ teaspoon salt
⅛ teaspoon pepper
¼ cup grated American cheese

Mix together potatoes, salmon, salt and pepper. Transfer to a greased casserole, sprinkle cheese over top, and bake in moderate oven (350°F.) 30 minutes or until heated through and brown on top. Serves 6.

MASHED POTATOES AND CHESTNUTS

1 pound chestnuts
1 pound potatoes (3 or 4)
Salt
Pepper
2 tablespoons butter
1 cup cream

Shell, blanch and peel chestnuts. Pare potatoes. Cook chestnuts and potatoes separately in boiling salted water until tender. Drain each thoroughly. Combine and press through ricer. Add salt, pepper, butter and cream. Beat until very light. Reheat over hot water and serve at once. Serves 8.

BAKED SWEET-POTATOES

Potatoes should be baked in their jackets to retain the most nourishment. Select uniform-sized, medium sweetpotatoes. Wash, remove blemishes, and bake in a moderate oven (350°F.) until easily pierced with a fork, 30 to 40 minutes. Remove from oven, slit and insert a large piece of butter or margarine. Serve piping hot.

In place of butter use i tablespoon sour cream or butter that has been whipped with lemon juice.

BAKED SWEET-POTATOES À LA ROXY

Select small, uniform sweetpotatoes, and parboil until the skins slip off easily. Roll in finely chopped pecans and place in a well-greased baking dish. Sprinkle lightly with sugar, dot with butter, cover and bake in moderate oven (350°F.) for 30 minutes.

DUCHESS SWEET-POTATOES

3 cups cooked sweetpotatoes
¼ teaspoon salt
2 teaspoons honey
¼ cup orange juice
2 eggs, separated
3 tablespoons butter

Rice potatoes into a mixing bowl. Add salt, honey, orange juice, egg yolks and butter; whip thoroughly. Fold in stiffly beaten egg whites. Heap individual mounds of this mixture on a well-greased baking sheet, or make individual rosettes using a pastry tube. Bake in a hot oven (425°F.) until brown. Arrange potatoes on serving platter, top with a preserved cherry. Makes 12 rosettes.

GRILLED SWEET-POTATOES

Use baked or boiled sweetpotatoes. Peel and cut in halves lengthwise. Dip in melted butter, sprinkle with salt and sugar. Place on broiler rack 3 inches below heat. Cook 10 to 15 minutes or until brown and heated throughout. Serve with broiled ham, sausage, bacon, or chops. Potatoes may also be browned in a skillet.

NEW ORLEANS POTATOES

6 sweetpotatoes
2 tablespoons butter
1½ cups brown sugar
1½ cups cold water
¼ teaspoon salt

Pare potatoes and cut in slices ½ inch thick. Place in a heavy skillet and add remaining ingredients. Cover and bake in moderate oven (350°F.) for 20 minutes. Uncover and continue baking for 20 minutes or until potatoes are tender. Serves 6.

PALESTINIAN SWEET-POTATO AND PRUNE ZIMES

1 pound prunes, soaked overnight in 3 cups cold water
1 pound brisket of beef
Salt and pepper
5 medium sweetpotatoes, pared and sliced
½ cup sugar
1 tablespoon lemon juice

Place soaked prunes, water and meat in a kettle and season with salt and pepper. Simmer for 1½ hours or until meat is almost tender. Remove meat and prunes from broth and add sliced sweetpotatoes. Place meat and prunes on top of potatoes and sprinkle with sugar and lemon juice. Cover kettle and bake in moderate oven (350°F.) about 40 minutes or until potatoes are tender and meat is brown. Serve hot with gravy. Serves 4 to 6.

It was a talented cook who first served grilled sweetpotatoes and pineapple with meat

SWEETPOTATOES WITH PORK ROAST

Pare sweetpotatoes and cut in halves, lengthwise; parboil 10 minutes; drain and place in the pan with pork roast 1 hour before pork is done. Cook until tender, basting the potatoes when basting the meat.

GLAZED SWEET-POTATOES

6 sweetpotatoes
1 cup brown sugar
¼ cup water
Salt and pepper
Butter

Boil potatoes until tender, drain and skin. Make a thick sirup of sugar and water. Cut each potato in half, dip it in the sirup and place in a baking dish; season each piece with salt, pepper and butter. Bake in a moderate oven (375°F.) until the potatoes are brown, about 15 minutes, basting occasionally with the sirup. Serves 6 to 8.
Add ½ cup sliced Brazil nuts and 6 cloves to the sirup.

STUFFED—Hollow centers from halves before glazing. Fill glazed potatoes with mincemeat or Cranberry Sauce. Heat thoroughly in oven.

MAPLE CANDIED SWEETPOTATOES

6 medium sweetpotatoes
½ cup maple sirup
1 tablespoon butter
1 teaspoon salt
1 cup apple cider
½ cup water

Boil potatoes in jackets until nearly tender. Peel and slice into baking dish. Heat remaining ingredients to boiling, pour over potatoes and bake in slow oven (300°F.) 1 hour. Serves 6.

ORANGE CANDIED SWEETPOTATOES

6 medium sweetpotatoes
1 cup orange juice
½ teaspoon grated orange rind
1 cup water
1 cup sugar
¼ cup butter
½ teaspoon salt

Pare potatoes, slice in ¼-inch slices and arrange in a greased baking dish. Combine remaining ingredients, heat to boiling, and boil until sugar is dissolved; pour over the potatoes. Cover and bake in moderate oven (350°F.) until tender, about 45 to 60 minutes. Baste occasionally. Uncover to brown during the last 10 minutes. If desired, a layer of marshmallows may be added and browned just before removing from the oven. Serves 6.

SWEETPOTATOES WITH APPLESAUCE

3 large sweetpotatoes
¼ cup butter
¼ cup brown sugar
2 cups thick Applesauce

Pare sweetpotatoes and cut into 1-inch cubes. Cook for 15 minutes in rapidly boiling water. Place sweetpotatoes in greased baking dish, dot with butter and brown sugar. Pour applesauce over potatoes. Bake in moderate oven (350° F.) until tender, about 30 minutes. Serves 6.

SWEETPOTATOES EN BROCHETTE

Wash and pare potatoes; cut in 1-inch squares. Arrange 3 or 4 squares on skewers, cook in boiling salted water to cover for 6 to 10 minutes, drain. Brush with melted butter, sprinkle with brown sugar and bake in hot oven (400°F.) until tender and well browned.

STUFFED SWEET-POTATOES

6 sweetpotatoes
½ teaspoon salt
2 tablespoons butter
Thin cream to moisten

Bake potatoes, scoop out centers, mash and add salt, butter and cream. Refill skins and bake in very hot oven (450°F.) about 5 minutes. Serves 6.

WITH PORK SAUSAGE—When potatoes are baked, slit and open far enough to admit 1 peeled sausage for each potato. Place on broiler rack and broil 5 minutes until edges begin to brown.

ORANGE SWEETPOTATOES

6 medium sweetpotatoes
4 slices bacon, diced
½ cup hot water
3 tablespoons Orange Marmalade

Cook sweetpotatoes until tender. Peel and cut into halves lengthwise. Brown bacon lightly. Add hot water to bacon and drippings and add potato halves. Cover skillet and heat slowly until potatoes are thoroughly hot. Remove potatoes to a hot dish. Add marmalade to liquid in skillet, heat to boiling and pour over sweetpotatoes. Serves 6.

SWEETPOTATOES IN HONEY

6 sweetpotatoes
¼ cup honey
Juice 1 orange
Salt

Pare potatoes and cut in ¼-inch slices, lengthwise. Boil for 15 minutes. Drain and place in a greased casserole. Add remaining ingredients and bake in moderate oven (350°F.) until potatoes are tender, about 30 minutes. For 6. Juice of 1 lemon may be used in place of orange.

SUPREME SWEETPOTATOES WITH BANANAS

6 medium sweetpotatoes
3 bananas
15 gingersnaps
1 tablespoon butter
1 cup boiling water

Cook potatoes, peel and slice about ¼ inch thick. Peel and slice bananas. Roll gingersnaps into crumbs. Arrange alternate layers of potatoes, bananas and gingersnaps in a greased casserole. Repeat layers. Dot with butter and add boiling water. Bake, covered, in hot oven (400° F.) 25 minutes. Uncover and brown. Serves 6.

PICKANINNY CREOLE

Cut boiled sweetpotatoes in halves lengthwise and arrange in a shallow pan. Cover with plenty of butter and brown sugar. Add a dash of mace, a sprinkle of salt, and the grated rind of an orange. Bake in a moderate oven (350°F.) until the sugar and butter have formed a thick sirup, 30 to 45 minutes. Serve with grilled bacon, ham or game.

HAM SMOTHERED WITH SWEETPOTATOES

3 sweetpotatoes, 1 slice ham
2 tablespoons sugar
1 cup hot water

Boil potatoes until almost tender, peel and slice. Brown ham slightly on both sides in a skillet and place in a baking dish. Spread sliced sweetpotatoes over ham and sprinkle with sugar. Add hot water to drippings in skillet and pour over ham and sweetpotatoes; cover and bake in moderate oven (350°F.) until ham is tender. Baste occasionally with gravy; when ham is nearly tender remove lid and let top brown. Serves 3 or 4.

Add 2 tart apples, peeled and sliced, to sweetpotatoes.

WITH CRANBERRIES—Use 2 thin slices ham and 6 potatoes. Place 1½ cups cranberries mixed with ¾ cup strained honey between and on top of ham slices and bake as above 45 minutes. Place cooked whole potatoes around ham, sprinkle with sugar and bake 45 minutes longer or until ham is tender. Baste potatoes occasionally with sirup in pan. Serves 6.

SWEETPOTATO CASSEROLE

6 sweetpotatoes, cooked and sliced
½ cup brown sugar
5 tablespoons butter
2 oranges
½ cup orange juice
¼ cup strained honey
¼ cup fine bread crumbs

In greased casserole, arrange a layer of sliced sweetpotatoes, sprinkle with 6 tablespoons brown sugar, dot with 4 tablespoons butter and cover with a layer of thinly sliced, unpeeled oranges. Repeat layers. Over all, pour orange juice with which honey has been mixed. Combine bread crumbs with remaining 2 tablespoons brown sugar and 1 tablespoon butter and sprinkle over top. Cover casserole and bake in moderate oven (350° F.) 30 to 40 minutes, removing cover last 15 minutes. This is most attractive if baked in orange baskets, which are surprisingly easy to make; see Page 508 for directions.

Ham and sweetpotatoes are inseparable; cranberries prove three's not a crowd

LOUISIANA PONE

½ cup sifted flour
½ teaspoon nutmeg
1 teaspoon cinnamon
¾ teaspoon salt
4 cups grated sweetpotatoes
1 egg, well beaten
¾ cup sirup, 1 cup milk
3 tablespoons butter, melted

Sift dry ingredients together. Combine with remaining ingredients. Pour mixture into a greased baking dish and bake in slow oven (325°F.) 2½ hours, stirring occasionally during the first of the cooking. During the last 30 minutes discontinue stirring and allow pone to brown. Serves 10. Serve cold with milk or cream or serve hot as a vegetable.

MARSHMALLOW SWEETPOTATOES

8 medium sweetpotatoes
2 tablespoons butter
½ cup hot milk
½ teaspoon salt
1 teaspoon cinnamon or nutmeg
¼ teaspoon paprika
1 cup chopped walnuts
½ pound marshmallows

Cook sweetpotatoes until tender, remove skins and mash. Add butter, milk, salt, cinnamon or nutmeg and paprika. Beat until free from lumps and light and fluffy. Fold in walnuts. Turn into a greased casserole, cover with marshmallows and bake in a moderate oven (350°F.) until mixture is heated through and marshmallows are brown. For 8.

SWEETPOTATOES AND CHESTNUTS

6 medium sweetpotatoes
1 pound chestnuts
½ cup brown sugar
¼ cup hot water
¼ cup butter
½ cup buttered bread crumbs

Wash, pare and slice potatoes. Boil 5 minutes, drain. Wash chestnuts and discard those which float. Shell and simmer in boiling salted water to cover until tender, 8 to 15 minutes; drain. Place potatoes and chestnuts in alternate layers in a greased casserole. Boil together brown sugar, hot water, and butter; pour over potatoes. Cover with bread crumbs. Bake in a moderate oven (350°F.) until potatoes are tender, about 45 minutes. Serves 6.

SWEETPOTATO CREOLE

8 cooked sweetpotatoes
1 sliced lemon (rind removed)
3 sliced orange sections
1⅓ cups crushed pineapple
2¼ cups pineapple juice
1 cup brown sugar
½ teaspoon salt
5 tablespoons butter

Peel sweetpotatoes and cut into 4 lengthwise strips. Place alternate layers of sweetpotatoes, lemon, orange and pineapple in a greased casserole. Combine remaining ingredients and cook to a thick sirup. Pour sirup over potatoes. Bake in moderate oven (350°F.) 30 to 40 minutes. For 8.

SWEETPOTATO AND BACON CRISP

Sweetpotatoes
Bacon
Parsley

Select sweetpotatoes about 2 inches in diameter. Cook in boiling water until tender, peel and cut into pieces 2 inches long. Around each piece wrap a thin slice of bacon and fasten with a toothpick. Place on a pan and bake in a hot oven until bacon is crisp. Serve with parsley garnish.

PINEAPPLE-FILLED SWEETPOTATOES

3 large sweetpotatoes
1 tablespoon butter
½ teaspoon salt
1 tablespoon cream
½ cup crushed pineapple, drained
6 marshmallows, cut in pieces
2 tablespoons hot pineapple juice

Wash sweetpotatoes, dry thoroughly and bake in hot oven (450°F.) until soft. Remove from oven, split in halves lengthwise and scoop out potatoes, being careful not to break shells. Mash potatoes and add butter, salt, cream and pineapple and mix well. Refill shells and top with bits of marshmallows. Place in a pan and baste with hot pineapple juice. Bake in moderately slow oven (325°F.) about 20 minutes or until well heated and brown. Serves 6.

Or use ½ cup thick hot Applesauce for pineapple and juice.

SWEETPOTATOES AND CRANBERRIES

6 large sweetpotatoes
1½ cups Cranberry Sauce
3 tablespoons butter
⅓ cup brown sugar
1 teaspoon salt
½ cup finely chopped nuts

Boil potatoes in jackets until tender, peel, cut in halves lengthwise; scoop out halves slightly. Place 6 halves in greased baking dish, fill centers with cranberry sauce, and top with remaining halves. Hold potatoes together with toothpicks. Combine remaining ingredients and spread over potatoes. Bake in a moderate oven (350°F.) until lightly browned, about 20 to 25 minutes. Serves 6.

Or fill potatoes with a mixture of 1 cup cranberry sauce and ½ cup orange marmalade.

BOILED AND CREAMED SWEETPOTATOES

BOILED SWEET-POTATOES

Sweetpotatoes
Boiling water
Salt

Sweetpotatoes and yams are usually cooked with skins on. Wash and rinse; cover with boiling salted water and cook until tender, 20 to 30 minutes. Drain, peel and serve piping hot. Allow 1 medium potato to a serving.

SAVORY STEW OF SWEETPOTATOES

¼ pound diced bacon
1 small onion, chopped
6 tablespoons fat
3 pounds sweetpotatoes, cooked
1 cup Stock
1 cup tomato purée, Cheese

Fry bacon and onion in fat. Peel potatoes and cut lengthwise into thick slices; add to bacon and onion and cook 10 minutes, turning potatoes frequently. Add stock and tomato purée, cover and cook 20 minutes. Spread grated cheese over top. Serves 10.

CANDIED SWEET-POTATOES

4 medium yams
Salt
Paprika
⅓ to ½ cup brown sugar
3 tablespoons butter
Cinnamon
½ cup boiling water

Parboil sweetpotatoes or yams, pare and cut in halves, lengthwise. Arrange in casserole, sprinkling each layer with salt, paprika and brown sugar. Dot with bits of butter and add a few dashes of cinnamon. Add water, cover and bake in moderate oven (350°F.) for 30 minutes or until tender. When half baked, turn layers over so that top layers are at the bottom of the dish in sirup. Add more water, if necessary. Serves 4.
Use 1 cup honey and juice of 1 orange for paprika and brown sugar above.
Omit paprika, increase amounts of brown sugar and water to 1½ cups each. Pour over uncooked yam slices (cut ½-inch thick) and bake 50 minutes.

SUGARED YAMS

2 cups water
2 cups sugar
2 tablespoons butter
Dash nutmeg
8 uncooked yams

Heat water and sugar to a boil and add butter and nutmeg. Pare and slice yams, drop into boiling sirup, cover and let simmer until yams are tender and transparent. Serves 8.

CREAMED SWEET-POTATOES, CLUBHOUSE STYLE

4 cold boiled sweetpotatoes
3 tablespoons butter, Salt
2 tablespoons flour
1 cup milk

Peel sweetpotatoes and cut into ½-inch cubes. Heat butter in a skillet, add potatoes, season with salt and sprinkle with flour. Add milk and cook slowly 20 minutes. Serves 4 to 6.

Sugared yams simmered to tender transparency in a rich sirup are a delicacy we owe the South

BREADED SWEET-POTATOES

Cut boiled or baked sweetpo-tatoes into lengthwise slices. Dip the slices in beaten egg, then in crumbs and fry in hot deep fat (375°F.) until brown, about 3 minutes. Drain on absorbent paper. Serve hot.

FRENCH FRIED SWEETPOTATOES

Cut uncooked sweetpotatoes in-to 1-inch strips, soak in cold salt water for a short while, drain and dry between towels. Fry in hot deep fat (365°F.) until browned, 3 to 5 minutes. Drain on absorbent paper and sprinkle with salt.

Uncooked sweetpotatoes may be fried in butter. Pare potatoes, slice ¼ inch thick and soak in cold salted water ½ hour. Drain and dry on paper towels. Fry in butter, turning to brown on both sides. Sprinkle with salt.

GEORGIA FRIED SWEETPOTATOES

Remove skin from boiled sweet-potatoes and cut potatoes in nar-row strips lengthwise. Fry to a golden brown in hot deep fat (390°F.), drain on soft paper, sprinkle with salt and serve with chops or steaks.

HASHED SWEET-POTATOES

3 cups cooked sweetpotatoes
1 cup finely chopped meat or fowl
4 tablespoons fat
½ teaspoon salt

Peel and chop potatoes, add meat or fowl. Melt fat in a skillet, add potato mixture and salt. Cook slowly without stirring until browned on under side; turn and brown on other side. Serves 6.

MALLOW SWEET-POTATO BALLS

3 cups warm mashed sweet-potatoes
Salt and pepper to taste
3 tablespoons melted butter
8 marshmallows
1 egg
1 tablespoon cold water
1 cup almonds, blanched and chopped

Season potatoes and add butter. Mold potato mixture around marshmallows, forming 8 balls with a marshmallow in center of each. Beat egg and add cold water. Dip sweetpotato balls in egg and then in almonds. Fry in hot deep fat (365°F.) until brown. Turn while frying. For 8.

SWEETPOTATO AND PEANUT CROQUETTES

2 cups mashed sweetpotatoes
2 cups finely ground peanuts or pecans
2 eggs, well beaten
1 teaspoon salt
Cayenne
2 tablespoons flour
Bread crumbs
1 egg diluted with 2 tablespoons milk

Combine the first 6 ingredients; shape mixture into croquettes. Roll them in bread crumbs, di-luted egg and again in crumbs. Fry in hot deep fat (380°F.) until a golden brown. Drain on absorbent paper. Serves 10.

GEORGIA SWEETPOTATO CROQUETTES—Omit flour, use only 1½ cups chopped nuts. Add to mixture: 1 cup fine bread crumbs, 1 tablespoon milk and 2 tablespoons peanut butter. If desired, use only 1 egg in mix-ture. Mix and shape as above. Roll in egg and crumbs and fry. Serve with Cream Sauce or Orange Sauce.

SWEETPOTATO BALLS

2 cups hot mashed sweetpotatoes
2 tablespoons melted butter
½ teaspoon salt
1 egg, beaten
Bread crumbs
Deep fat

Combine first 4 ingredients. Beat thoroughly. Shape into balls, roll in sifted bread crumbs or finely crushed corn flakes. Fry in hot deep fat (365°-380°F.) until a golden brown. Drain on unglazed paper. Serves 4 to 6.

One-half cup chopped, blanched almonds may be added to potato mixture before shaping into balls. Add ¼ cup chopped pecans to potato mixture.

Serve with an Orange Sauce.

SPICED SWEETPOTATO BALLS —Add ⅛ teaspoon nutmeg, ⅛ teaspoon allspice, ¼ teaspoon cinnamon and 1 cup broken nut meats. Roll balls in flour instead of in bread crumbs. Fry as above. Pecans and black walnuts are most often used in sweet potato mixtures but other nuts may be used.

SWEETPOTATO CHIPS

Sweetpotatoes
Lemon juice or vinegar

Select well-shaped, medium po-tatoes, wash and pare, slice thin and even into chips just as in making Irish potato chips. Drop slices into water which contains a little lemon juice or vinegar (about a teaspoon of lemon juice to 4 cups of water). This acid will keep the chips from dark-ening and will give them a bet-ter color. Drain and dry between towels. Fry in hot deep fat (365° F.) until browned, 3 to 5 min-utes. Drain on absorbent paper and sprinkle with salt.

SWEETPOTATO CROQUETTES

2 cups mashed sweetpotatoes
2 eggs, beaten
2 tablespoons butter
½ teaspoon paprika
¼ teaspoon salt
½ cup chopped pecans
2 tablespoons milk
Bread crumbs

Combine all ingredients except 1 egg, milk and crumbs. Mix well. Form into croquettes, roll in remaining egg diluted with milk, then in bread crumbs. Fry in hot deep fat (365°-380°F.) until a golden brown. Serve with Orange Sauce for 8.

Omit pecans and add 1 teaspoon minced parsley and ½ teaspoon onion juice.

ORANGE SAUCE—Cook yellow rind of 1 orange, shredded, in 2 cups bouillon 5 minutes. Brown ¼ cup flour in ¼ cup butter. Add bouillon and cook to a smooth sauce. Add 1 cup orange juice, pulp of 2 oranges and 2 tablespoons sherry. For sweetpotato croquettes.

SWEETPOTATOES À LA NORFOLK

¼ to ½ cup cream
3 cups mashed sweetpotatoes
½ cup sugar
½ teaspoon salt
2 eggs
¾ cup grated coconut
Marshmallows
Bread crumbs

Add cream to · potatoes using only enough to moisten; add sugar, salt, 1 beaten egg and coconut. Let stand until cool. Shape into balls with a marshmallow in the center of each. Roll in remaining beaten egg, then in bread crumbs and fry in hot deep fat (365°-380°F.). Drain on brown paper and serve while hot. Serves 8.

SWEETPOTATO SURPRISES

2 cups mashed sweetpotatoes
1 egg, beaten
½ teaspoon salt
⅛ teaspoon pepper
8 marshmallows
½ cup crushed cereal flakes

Combine warm potatoes with egg, salt and pepper. If mixture is too dry, add a little milk. Form into 8 balls with a marshmallow hidden inside of each. Roll in crushed cereal flakes. Fry in hot deep fat (375°-385°F.) until brown; drain on absorbent paper. Serves 4 or 8.

Balls may be rolled in bread crumbs instead of cereal flakes.

Add ¾ cup shredded coconut to potato mixture.

Add 1 teaspoon lemon juice to potato mixture.

ORANGE—Instead of marshmallow use orange segments with membrane removed. Cut into halves; shape potato around 2 halves.

PINEAPPLE—Instead of marshmallow use a cube of canned pineapple in each potato ball.

SOUTH CAROLINA CROQUETTES

3 large sweetpotatoes
1 tablespoon brown sugar
1 teaspoon salt
1 tablespoon butter
1 egg yolk
Flour

Wash sweetpotatoes and bake in a moderate oven (350°F.) until tender. Peel and press through a sieve. Add remaining ingredients except flour. Shape into small cylinders and roll in flour. Fry in hot deep fat (375°F.) until golden brown. Garnish with parsley. Serves 4.

BLAZING SWEETS—Cut 5 boiled sweetpotatoes, peeled, into ½-inch slices. Brown in 2 tablespoons butter. Add ½ cup sugar and 2 tablespoons butter and mix gently until butter is melted and blended with sugar. Add ½ cup rum and ignite. Baste potatoes with sirup and blazing rum. Serves 5 or 6.

Potato chips to go with steak may be made from sweepotatoes as well as from white potatoes (page 504)

MASHED SWEET-POTATOES

6 medium boiled sweetpotatoes
3 tablespoons butter
1/3 cup hot milk

Combine ingredients and beat until light and fluffy. It may be necessary to add more milk if potatoes are dry. Makes 4 cups mashed sweetpotatoes. Serves 6. Add dash of nutmeg.

Form mashed sweetpotatoes into balls with a half or a whole marshmallow in center of each. Roll in shredded coconut and bake in a moderate oven (350° F.) until heated through and a delicate brown.

Form balls of mashed sweetpotatoes and roll in crushed cereal flakes. Brown in the oven.

One or 2 eggs or egg whites, beaten, may be added to mashed sweetpotatoes before shaping into balls and baking.

Sweetpotatoes and maple sirup never combine more delightfully than in this mashed sweetpotato caramel

GEORGIAN SWEET-POTATOES

3 cups mashed sweetpotatoes
2 tablespoons molasses
1 tablespoon butter

Place sweetpotatoes in buttered casserole. Heat molasses and butter together slowly until butter is melted. Pour over sweetpotatoes and bake in moderate oven (350° F.) 30 minutes or until delicately brown. Serves 4 to 6.

SWEETPOTATOES WITH SHERRY

4 sweetpotatoes
2 tablespoons cream
1 tablespoon butter
Salt and pepper
2 tablespoons sugar
3 tablespoons sherry

Boil sweetpotatoes until tender, peel and mash. Add remaining ingredients and beat until fluffy. Place in a buttered baking dish and bake in a moderate oven (350°F.) 15 minutes or until slightly brown. For 4. Add chopped nuts if desired.

GRAPEFRUIT AND SWEETPOTATO CASSEROLE

4 cups mashed sweetpotatoes
1/2 teaspoon salt
1/4 teaspoon nutmeg
4 tablespoons cream
3 tablespoons butter
1 egg, well beaten
8 grapefruit sections
Candied grapefruit peel
3 tablespoons granulated sugar

Combine potatoes, salt, nutmeg, cream, 2 tablespoons butter and egg; beat until light and fluffy. Place in a well-greased casserole. Over top arrange grapefruit sections, free from seeds and white skin, in pinwheel fashion, radiating from the center. Between each two sections arrange a strip of candied grapefruit peel. Dot with remaining butter and sprinkle granulated sugar over top. Bake in moderate oven (350°F.) 25 minutes, or until potato is thoroughly heated and sugar on top is melted. Serves 6.

MASHED SWEET-POTATO CARAMEL

2 cups mashed sweetpotatoes
Milk
Pepper and salt
1/2 cup maple sirup
1/4 cup butter

Mash potatoes with sufficient milk or cream to make smooth and moist. Season with pepper and salt. Place in well-greased casserole or baking dish and pour in thick maple sirup which has been boiled with butter. Bake in a moderate oven (350°F.) until top begins to caramelize, 20 to 30 minutes. Serves 4.

The potatoes may be cut into quarters instead of mashed, and then basted with maple sirup and butter. Continue as above.

PINEAPPLE MARSHMALLOW SWEETPOTATOES

2 cups mashed sweetpotatoes
1 cup milk
½ cup pineapple juice
1 cup diced pineapple
2 tablespoons butter
½ teaspoon cinnamon
Marshmallows

Mix all ingredients except marshmallows and beat until light and fluffy. Use more milk or fruit juice, if needed. Place in well-greased casserole and bake in a moderate oven (350°F.) until heated through, 20 to 30 minutes. Remove from oven and cover top with marshmallows. Return to oven to brown. Serves 6.

SWEETPOTATO PUDDING— Omit pineapple and juice. Increase butter to ¾ cup. Add ½ teaspoon grated lemon rind, ½ teaspoon nutmeg, ¼ teaspoon allspice, 4 eggs, beaten separately, and 2 tablespoons brandy. Rub potatoes through fine sieve, combine ingredients, bake at 350°F. 1 hour.

SWEETPOTATO STUFFING FOR SPARERIBS

2 cups mashed sweetpotatoes
1 tablespoon minced onion
1 cup boiled rice
1½ cups minced celery
2 tablespoons melted butter
Salt and pepper
Spareribs

Mix first 6 ingredients together thoroughly. Remove surplus fat from a strip of spareribs which have been broken through the center. Spread potato mixture on the inner or bony side of the strip, fold on broken line and place in a baking pan with meaty side on top. Dredge with salt, pepper and flour. Cover bottom of pan with boiling water and cook in moderate oven (350°F.) until the meat is tender. Serve with tart Applesauce or Cranberry Jelly. Serves 4 to 6.

STUFFING FOR HAM SLICES— Omit butter and half the celery. Combine ¼ cup diced bacon with ingredients. Roll in ham slices. Skewer and bake as above.

TURKEY IN SWEET-POTATO CUPS

3 cups mashed sweetpotatoes
1 egg, well beaten
3 cups diced cooked turkey
½ cup chopped onion
2 cups turkey broth
4 tablespoons flour
6 tablespoons water

Combine mashed sweetpotatoes with egg and mix well. Line greased custard cups with mixture; fill about half full with turkey and onion. Heat broth. Stir in flour that has been mixed smooth with water. Cook for 5 minutes stirring constantly. Pour over turkey and onion. Bake in a moderate oven (350°F.) for 30 minutes. Serves 8.

Chicken, duck, goose, veal or pork may be used for turkey.

Or line baking dish with part of sweetpotato mixture, fill with turkey and gravy and spread remaining potato on top.

Instead of baking sweetpotatoes with ham, try making sweetpotato stuffing and rolling it up inside

SWEETPOTATOES IN APPLE CUPS

4 medium sweetpotatoes
3 tablespoons butter
½ teaspoon salt
2 tablespoons sugar
4 red-skinned baking apples
4 marshmallows

Boil sweetpotatoes until tender, peel and mash. Add butter, salt and sugar to potatoes and blend thoroughly. Scoop out inside of apples leaving a margin of about ¼ inch all around. Fill apples with mashed sweetpotatoes. Place in a baking dish and bake in a moderate oven (325°F.) until apples are cooked, about 15 minutes. Place marshmallows on top of potato mixture, return to oven and allow marshmallows to brown. Serves 4.

SWEETPOTATOES IN ORANGE CUPS

2 cups mashed sweetpotatoes
2 tablespoons butter
½ teaspoon salt
½ cup orange juice
3 large oranges
6 marshmallows, quartered

Combine sweetpotatoes, butter, salt and orange juice. Mix well. Cut oranges in halves, crosswise, and remove juice and pulp (use part of this juice, when mashing potatoes). Scrub shells well. Fill with the mashed potatoes and decorate with marshmallows. Bake in hot oven (400°F.) about 15 minutes. Serves 6.

SWEETPOTATO PIE—Omit oranges and marshmallows. Increase butter to ⅓ cup, add 1 cup sugar, 4 eggs, beaten, 1 cup milk, 1 teaspoon cinnamon, ½ teaspoon nutmeg and 1 teaspoon grated orange rind. Mix well and bake in 2 pastry lined pans at 350°F. until firm.

SWEETPOTATOES ON PINEAPPLE RINGS

2 cups mashed sweetpotatoes
½ teaspoon salt
½ cup brown sugar
4 tablespoons butter
4 slices canned pineapple
4 marshmallows
4 maraschino cherries

Combine sweetpotatoes, salt, sugar and 3 tablespoons butter in a mixing bowl and beat until light and fluffy. Place slices of pineapple on a baking sheet. Dot with remaining butter. Force sweetpotato mixture through a pastry bag, using the rose tube, onto the slices of pineapple for individual servings. Top each serving with a marshmallow and a cherry. Bake in a hot oven (400°F.) until heated through, about 10 minutes. Serves 4. Potatoes may be formed into round cakes and placed on pineapple if a pastry bag is not available.

SWEETPOTATOES WITH SOUR APPLES

3 large sweetpotatoes
3 large sour apples, cored
¼ cup butter, melted
1¼ teaspoons salt
¼ teaspoon white pepper
1 tablespoon onion juice
1 teaspoon paprika
¼ cup buttered bread crumbs

Bake potatoes and apples until tender, then press through a colander that will retain only the skins. Add remaining ingredients quickly so that the fruit and vegetable will retain their heat. Place into a greased baking dish, sprinkle with buttered crumbs, and bake in moderate oven (350°F.) until brown. Serves 6.

If preferred, 2 cups crushed pineapple may be used instead of apples. Add after pressing potatoes through colander.

SWEETPOTATOES WITH SAUSAGE PATTIES

Mashed sweetpotatoes
Brown sugar
Sausage Patties

Fill a deep buttered pie plate with mashed sweetpotatoes and sprinkle lightly with brown sugar. Cover with sausage patties which have been pan-browned. Add a few teaspoons of the drippings for flavor. Bake in a 350°F. oven 15 to 20 minutes.

SWEETPOTATO PUFF

2 cups mashed sweetpotatoes
2 tablespoons butter
Salt and pepper
¼ cup milk or cream
1 egg, separated

Combine mashed potatoes, melted butter, seasonings and milk. Add beaten egg yolk and beat until light and fluffy. Fold in stiffly beaten egg white. Place in greased casserole and bake in moderate oven (350°F.) 30 minutes or until puffy and browned. If desired, ¼ cup of pecans or black walnuts may be added. Serves 4.

A greased ring mold may be used and center filled with creamed ham, fowl, veal or pork.

YAM PUFF

4 large yams or sweetpotatoes
¼ cup butter
2 well-beaten eggs
⅓ cup sugar
2 teaspoons baking powder
1 teaspoon salt

Pare potatoes and boil until tender. Mash and add remaining ingredients. Beat well and transfer to buttered casserole. Dot with additional butter and bake in moderate oven (350°F.) until brown, 30 to 40 minutes. For 6.

PIMIENTOS FILLED WITH EGGPLANT

4 cups Cooked Eggplant
2 eggs, well beaten
½ cup soft bread crumbs
¼ cup butter
½ teaspoon salt
⅛ teaspoon pepper
Few drops onion juice
4 canned pimientos
¼ cup buttered crumbs

Mash eggplant and mix with eggs, crumbs, butter, salt, pepper and onion juice. Place pimientos in muffin pans and fill with eggplant mixture. Cover with buttered crumbs and bake in moderately hot oven (375°F.) 15 minutes. Remove from pans. Serves 4.

BRAISED RADISHES

3 bunches radishes
3 tablespoons butter
½ teaspoon salt
¼ cup cream

Wash radishes, slice and cook in water to cover for 10 minutes. Drain. Cook in butter for 5 minutes, add salt and cream, cover and simmer 5 minutes longer. Serves 6 to 8.

COOKED RADISHES

3 bunches radishes
Boiling water
½ teaspoon salt

Wash radishes and remove leaves and roots; place in saucepan, cover with water, add salt and cook uncovered 15 to 20 minutes. Drain. To serve, season with pepper and butter. Serves 6 to 8.

FRIED RADISHES

3 bunches radishes
2 tablespoons fat
½ teaspoon salt
⅛ teaspoon pepper

Wash radishes and slice. Fry in fat about 15 minutes, turning frequently. Season. Serves 6 to 8.

COOKED SALSIFY

8 roots salsify or oyster plant
1 tablespoon vinegar
Boiling water
1 teaspoon salt

Wash salsify, scrape clean and slice thin into water to which vinegar has been added. Drain. Cover with boiling water, add salt and cook until tender, 40 to 50 minutes. (Makes about 2½ to 3 cups.) To serve, add butter and pepper. Serves 6.

MOCK OYSTERS — Combine 2 cups mashed Cooked Salsify, 1 egg, ½ teaspoon salt, dash paprika and 1 tablespoon butter. Shape into cakes and brown in fat.

Tangy green peppers lend themselves admirably to a variety of fillings (pages 252 and 381)

SALSIFY IN CREAM SAUCE

4 cups Cooked Salsify
1 recipe Cream Sauce
Paprika

Combine salsify and cream sauce and heat thoroughly. Sprinkle paprika over top. Serves 6 to 8.

Add ⅓ cup grated cheese to hot cream sauce, if desired.

Try stuffing peppers with macaroni and cheese for a new flavor treat (pages 804 and 874)

SALSIFY CASSEROLE

3½ cups Cooked Salsify
¾ cup chopped celery
1 recipe White Sauce
½ cup dry bread crumbs
3 tablespoons butter

Place alternate layers of salsify and celery in greased baking dish. Add white sauce, cover with bread crumbs and dot with butter. Bake in moderate oven (375°F) about 25 minutes. Serves 6 to 8.

SALSIFY PATTIES

4 cups Cooked Salsify
4 tablespoons butter
½ teaspoon salt
⅛ teaspoon pepper
Flour
4 tablespoons fat

Mash salsify, add butter, salt and pepper and mix thoroughly. Shape into small cakes, roll in flour and brown in fat. Serves 6 to 8.

FRIED SALSIFY—Boil whole salsify until tender. Drain, cut lengthwise into halves and roll in seasoned flour. Brown in fat.

Fill the spinach ring with creamed shrimp (page 340) and garnish with hard-cooked egg wedges

SALSIFY WITH CHIVES

4 cups Cooked Salsify
3 tablespoons butter
2 teaspoons chopped parsley
¾ teaspoon chopped chives
½ teaspoon salt
⅛ teaspoon pepper

Combine salsify and butter and heat thoroughly. Add parsley, chives, salt and pepper. For 8.

COOKED SPINACH

2 pounds spinach

Discard wilted leaves and remove the roots of spinach. Wash quickly in warm water (not hot) to release sand, then wash several times in cold water. Place in saucepan, do not add water, cover tightly to prevent escape of steam and cook over low heat 10 to 15 minutes. Drain. (Makes about 3 cups cooked.) To serve, season with salt, pepper and butter.

SPINACH SOUFFLÉ—Combine 2 cups chopped Cooked Spinach, ½ cup White Sauce and 3 egg yolks, well beaten. Fold in 3 stiffly beaten egg whites, pour into greased baking dish and bake in 350°F. oven 25 to 30 minutes. Serves 6.

BAKED SPINACH

2 pounds spinach
6 tablespoons flour
5 tablespoons fat, melted
1 cup milk; ½ teaspoon salt
⅛ teaspoon pepper
4 tablespoons grated cheese
¾ cup bread crumbs

Wash and chop spinach. Arrange in layers in greased baking dish, sprinkling flour between layers. Mix fat, milk, salt and pepper and pour over spinach. Combine grated cheese and bread crumbs and sprinkle over top. Bake in moderate oven (350°F.) about 1 hour. Serves 6 to 8.

CHOPPED SPINACH

3 cups Cooked Spinach
½ teaspoon salt
¼ teaspoon pepper
⅛ teaspoon nutmeg
2 tablespoons butter
1 tablespoon flour; ½ cup milk
2 hard-cooked eggs, sliced

Chop spinach very fine and sprinkle with salt, pepper and nutmeg. Melt butter, stir in flour and cook until smooth. Add spinach and simmer 5 minutes; add milk and cook 3 minutes, stirring constantly. Garnish with egg slices. Serves 6 to 8.

CREAMED SPINACH — Brown 1 tablespoon minced onion and 1 thin slice garlic in butter. Increase milk to 1 cup.

SPINACH RING

3 cups Cooked Spinach
1 cup White Sauce
3 eggs, beaten; ½ teaspoon salt
⅛ teaspoon pepper

Chop spinach fine, combine with white sauce, add eggs, salt and pepper and pour into greased ring mold. Place in pan of hot water and bake in moderate oven (350°F.) 30 to 40 minutes. Serves 6 to 8.

SPINACH DUMPLINGS

4 tablespoons butter
4 teaspoons flour
2 teaspoons cream
1¼ cups Cooked Spinach, chopped
3 eggs
½ teaspoon salt
⅛ teaspoon pepper
Dash mace
½ teaspoon sugar
1 recipe Cream Sauce

Melt butter, add flour and blend; add cream and spinach. Remove from heat, add eggs and seasonings and mix well. Drop from spoon into boiling salted water. Poach for 5 minutes or until firm. Serve in cream sauce. Serves 6 to 8.

SPINACH CASSEROLE

3 cups Cooked Spinach
4 tablespoons minced onion
½ teaspoon salt
¼ teaspoon pepper
2 eggs, slightly beaten
1 cup milk
½ cup dry bread crumbs
2 tablespoons butter

Combine spinach, onion, salt and pepper. Stir eggs into milk and add to spinach mixture. Pour into greased casserole, sprinkle with crumbs, dot with butter and bake in hot oven (450°F.) about 15 minutes or until browned. For 6. Garnish, if desired, with sliced hard-cooked eggs.

SPINACH WITH PEPPERS

3 tablespoons minced green pepper
1 tablespoon minced pimiento
3 tablespoons minced onion
6 tablespoons fat
3 cups Cooked Spinach
1 teaspoon salt
2 tablespoons lemon juice

Cook green pepper, pimiento and onion in fat. Add spinach and salt, heat thoroughly, add lemon juice and serve. Serves 6 to 8.

SWEET-SOUR SPINACH

3 cups Cooked Spinach
½ teaspoon salt
1 teaspoon sugar
1 tablespoon vinegar
2 tablespoons butter

Chop spinach very fine, add salt, sugar and vinegar. Melt butter in saucepan, add spinach mixture and cook slowly until thoroughly heated, stirring constantly. Serves 6 to 8.

LEFTOVER SQUASH

Brown leftover acorn squash in butter and sprinkle with a little sugar before serving. Or else, steam leftover pieces of squash until soft; mash and serve with melted butter, salt and pepper.

Stuffed acorn squash are as luscious as they are beautiful

STUFFED ACORN SQUASH

3 to 4 Baked Acorn Squash
3 tablespoons chopped onion
2 tablespoons fat
½ cup soft bread crumbs
¼ cup water
1 egg
½ teaspoon salt
⅛ teaspoon pepper
½ cup dry bread crumbs
3 tablespoons butter

Remove squash from shells and mash. Brown onion in fat, soak soft crumbs in water, mash and add to onion. Add squash and cook about 15 minutes, stirring occasionally. Stir in egg. Add salt and pepper, place mixture in squash shells, sprinkle with bread crumbs and dot with butter. Bake in moderate oven (375°F.) about 20 minutes or until browned. Serves 6 to 8.

Instead of above stuffing, fill 4 cooked squash with mixture of mashed squash pulp, 1 tablespoon each chopped onion and green pepper, ½ cup melted butter, 2 cups grated cheese, 4 cups soft bread crumbs, salt and pepper. Bake as above. Serves 8.

BAKED ACORN SQUASH

3 to 4 acorn squash
4 tablespoons butter, melted
1 teaspoon salt
Pepper

Wash squash; cut into halves and remove seeds and fibers. Wipe dry; brush with butter; sprinkle with salt and pepper. Place cut side down on cookie sheet and bake in slow oven (325°F.) 1¼ hours. Serves 6 to 8.

SQUASH IN CASSEROLE

3 cups mashed Baked Squash
1 teaspoon salt
¼ teaspoon pepper
1½ cups White Sauce
½ cup butter
¾ cup dry bread crumbs

Combine squash, seasonings and white sauce and stir well. Place alternate layers of squash and dots of butter in greased casserole. Top with crumbs, dot with butter and bake in moderate oven (350°F.) 30 minutes. Serves 6 to 8.

Your family will vote this whole stuffed squash as good to eat as it is to look at

BAKED SQUASH

2 to 3 pounds Hubbard squash
2 teaspoons salt
6 tablespoons butter

Wash squash, remove seeds and cut into pieces for individual servings. Sprinkle each piece with salt and dot with 2 or 3 bits of butter. Place in casserole, cover closely and bake in moderate oven (350°F.) about 1 hour or until squash is tender. To serve, dot each piece with butter and sprinkle with pepper. Serves 6 to 8.

Sprinkle 1 teaspoon brown sugar on each piece before baking.

Spread 1 teaspoon honey on each piece and sprinkle with cinnamon before baking.

GLAZED HUBBARD SQUASH

4 cups pared cubed squash
⅓ cup butter, melted
½ teaspoon salt
1½ tablespoons brown sugar
2 tablespoons lemon juice

Combine squash, butter, salt, brown sugar and lemon juice. Bake in shallow covered pan in hot oven (400°F.) 30 minutes. Remove cover, cook 15 minutes longer or until tender, for 8.

BAKED SUMMER SQUASH WITH TOMATOES

2 pounds summer squash
3 tomatoes, sliced
2 medium onions, sliced
1 teaspoon salt
⅛ teaspoon pepper
2 tablespoons butter

Wash squash, cut into halves, remove seeds and place in greased baking dish. Cover with tomato and onion slices, sprinkle with salt and pepper and dot with butter. Cover and bake in moderate oven (350°F.) about 45 minutes. Serves 6 to 8.

COOKED SUMMER SQUASH

4 pounds summer squash
½ cup water
1 teaspoon salt

Pare squash, remove seeds and cut into cubes. Heat water to boiling, add salt and squash, cover pan tightly to prevent escape of steam and heat again to boiling. Reduce heat at once and cook 15 to 20 minutes. Drain if necessary. (Makes about 4 cups.) To serve, season with pepper and butter. Serves 6 to 8.

STUFFED—Cut off top of squash,. remove seeds and steam 25 minutes. Cook ⅓ cup diced celery, ¼ cup minced green pepper and ½ pound cubed ham in ¼ cup fat until tender. Add 3 tablespoons flour and 1½ cups milk. Cook until thickened. Add ¼ cup sliced stuffed olives, 3 hard-cooked eggs, sliced, salt and pepper. Fill squash and heat in 325°F. oven 15 minutes. Serves 4.

SUMMER SQUASH IN SOUR CREAM

4 pounds summer squash
1 teaspoon salt, 4 tablespoons fat
¼ teaspoon paprika
2 cups sour cream
2 tablespoons flour
2 onions, minced

Pare squash, cut into julienne strips, sprinkle with salt and let stand 1 hour. Drain. Melt fat, add paprika and squash and cook slowly 20 minutes or until tender. Combine sour cream and flour and add to squash mixture. Add onions and simmer about 5 minutes, stirring carefully. Serves 6.

FRIED SUMMER SQUASH

4 pounds summer squash
½ teaspoon salt
⅛ teaspoon pepper
1 cup dry bread crumbs
1 egg, beaten

Wash, pare and cut squash into ½-inch slices. Sprinkle with salt and pepper, cover with crumbs, dip into egg and again into crumbs. Fry in hot deep fat (375°F.) until brown. Drain on absorbent paper. Serves 6 to 8.

COOKED SWISS CHARD—Prepare and cook as directed for Cooked Spinach.

SWISS CHARD WITH CHEESE SAUCE—Cut stems from leaves and cook separately. Serve stems with Cheese Sauce. Chop greens and mix with sauce or serve with pepper, butter and vinegar.

BAKED TOMATOES WITH ONIONS

18 small onions
3½ cups Stewed Tomatoes
1 teaspoon salt
⅛ teaspoon pepper
2 tablespoons brown sugar
¼ cup bread crumbs
2 tablespoons butter

Peel onions and drop into boiling water; parboil 20 minutes. Drain; combine tomatoes, salt, pepper and sugar and turn into casserole. Place onions in center. Sprinkle with bread crumbs and dot with butter. Bake uncovered in slow oven (325°F.) about 20 minutes. Serves 6 to 8.

Wrap strips of bacon around tomatoes and crown with onions before broiling

BROILED TOMATOES

6 tomatoes
Salt and pepper
¼ cup butter, melted

Cut firm, round tomatoes into halves and sprinkle with salt and pepper. Broil under medium heat about 10 minutes or until tender. Pour butter over tomatoes, garnish with parsley and serve at once. Serves 6.

WITH BACON—Omit butter and salt. Wrap each half tomato in 2 strips of bacon placed at right angles to each other, fastening on top with picks. Broil in preheated broiler until bacon is crisp. Top each with a pearl onion before serving.

STEWED TOMATOES AND CELERY

1 pound tomatoes
1 cup cut celery
½ teaspoon salt
⅛ teaspoon pepper
1 tablespoon butter

Peel tomatoes and cook with remaining ingredients, 15 minutes. Serves 4.

Use chopped cabbage instead of celery; add 1 teaspoon grated onion.

BAKED TOMATOES

6 tomatoes
¼ cup chopped green pepper
¾ cup Cooked Corn
1 teaspoon salt
¼ teaspoon pepper
6 tablespoons dry bread crumbs
6 teaspoons butter

Cut tops from tomatoes and remove pulp, leaving a shell ¼-
inch thick. Cover green pepper
with boiling water and let stand
5 minutes. Drain. Mix tomato
pulp, green pepper, corn and
seasonings and fill tomato shells.
Cover each with crumbs, dot
with butter and bake in moderate oven (375°F.) 25 minutes.
Serves 6.

WITH RICE — Omit corn and
bread crumbs. Use 1 cup rice and
1 tablespoon onion with pulp.

BAKED TOMATOES AND CORN

2 cups Stewed Tomatoes
2 cups Cut Cooked Corn
1 green pepper, chopped
1 small onion, sliced
1 tablespoon butter
½ teaspoon salt
⅛ teaspoon pepper
1 cup dry bread crumbs
2 tablespoons grated cheese

Simmer tomatoes about 5 minutes. Add corn, green pepper,
onion, butter, salt and pepper
and cook slowly 15 minutes.
Place alternate layers of vegetable
mixture and bread crumbs in
greased baking dish ending with
layer of crumbs. Sprinkle cheese
over top and bake in hot oven
(400°F.) about 20 minutes or until browned. Serves 6 to 8.

*Plump ripe tomatoes filled
with a hearty stuffing and
baked for luncheon are a
credit to any hostess*

FRIED GREEN TOMATOES

6 to 8 green tomatoes
Flour
Salt and pepper
Fat

Wash tomatoes and cut into
½-inch slices. Roll in mixture
of flour, salt and pepper and fry
slowly in fat until browned.
Serves 6 to 8.

STUFFED TOMATOES

6 firm tomatoes
2 teaspoons minced onion
Fat
½ teaspoon salt
⅛ teaspoon pepper
1½ cups soft bread crumbs
1 egg, slightly beaten
2 tablespoons chopped green pepper
2 tablespoons chopped celery
¼ cup finely chopped cabbage

Wash tomatoes, cut off tops and
scoop out centers. Chop pulp of
tomatoes. Cook onion in fat until tender and combine with remaining ingredients. Fill tomato
shells with mixture, replace tops
and place in greased baking dish.
Bake in moderate oven (375°F.)
about 30 minutes. Serves 6.

SAUTÉED TOMATOES

6 ripe tomatoes
4 tablespoons oil
2 tablespoons flour
1 tablespoon sugar
⅛ teaspoon nutmeg
½ teaspoon salt, Dash pepper
½ cup dry bread crumbs
4 tablespoons fat

Wash tomatoes and cut into ¼-
inch slices. Marinate in oil and
sprinkle lightly on both sides with
mixture of flour, sugar and seasonings. Dip again into oil, then
into bread crumbs and brown in
fat. Serves 6 to 8.

TOMATOES STUFFED WITH SPINACH

6 firm tomatoes
2 cups Cooked Spinach
1 tablespoon melted butter
½ teaspoon salt
½ onion, minced

Wash tomatoes, cut off tops and
scoop out centers. Combine
spinach, butter, salt and onion
and pack into tomato shells.
Place in greased casserole and
bake in moderate oven (375°F.)
about 20 minutes. Serve with Egg
Sauce. Serves 6.

STEWED TOMATOES

2 pounds tomatoes
1 teaspoon salt
⅛ teaspoon pepper
2 teaspoons sugar
1 tablespoon butter

Wash tomatoes, peel and cut into pieces. Place in saucepan, cover tightly to prevent escape of steam and cook slowly about 15 minutes, stirring occasionally. Season with salt, pepper, sugar and butter. (Makes about 4 cups cooked.) To serve, sprinkle with Croutons. Serves 6 to 8.
Add 1 tablespoon minced onion.

SCALLOPED TOMATOES

4 cups Stewed Tomatoes
Few drops onion juice
1 cup dry bread crumbs
2 tablespoons butter

Season tomatoes with onion juice. Place ½ cup crumbs in bottom of baking dish, add tomatoes, cover with remaining crumbs and dot with butter. Bake in hot oven (400°F.) about 20 minutes or until browned. Serves 8.

TOMATO FRITTERS

1 cup sifted flour
2 teaspoons baking powder
¼ teaspoon salt
1 egg, beaten
½ cup milk
1 tablespoon butter, melted
6 firm medium tomatoes, chilled

Sift dry ingredients and add beaten egg. Stir milk in gradually. Add melted butter and beat mixture vigorously. Cut tomatoes into 3-inch thick slices and dip into the batter. Fry in hot deep fat (380°F.) until browned tender. Serves 6 to 8.

BAKED TURNIPS

2 pounds turnips
¼ cup butter
1½ teaspoons salt
1½ teaspoons sugar
⅓ cup water

Pare turnips and cut into cubes. Place in baking dish with remaining ingredients. Cover closely and bake in moderate oven (350°F.) about 1 hour or until tender. Serves 6 to 8.

COOKED TURNIPS OR RUTABAGAS

2½ pounds turnips
½ to 1 cup water
1 teaspoon salt

Pare turnips and cut into cubes. Heat water and salt to boiling, add turnips, cover pan tightly to prevent escape of steam and heat again to boiling. Reduce heat at once and simmer 20 to 35 minutes. Drain if necessary. (Makes about 4 cups, mashed.) To serve, season with pepper and melted butter. Serves 6 to 8.
To prepare milder-flavored vegetable, cook as for Cooked Cabbage, being very careful not to overcook the turnips. Diced young white turnips will cook tender in 15 to 20 minutes.

MASHED TURNIPS

4 cups Cooked Turnips
⅛ teaspoon pepper
3 tablespoons butter

Mash turnips and add pepper and butter. Beat over low heat until smooth and most of liquid has evaporated. Serves 6 to 8.

TURNIPS WITH PEPPER SAUCE

½ cup chopped onion
1 cup chopped green pepper
4 tablespoons fat
1 recipe White Sauce
3 cups Cooked Turnips

Cook onion and green pepper in fat until tender. Add white sauce and turnips and heat thoroughly. Serves 6 to 8.

CHAPEAU VEGETABLE PLATE— Cook vegetables separately and arrange as illustrated.

The celebrated chapeau with a crown of peas and cauliflower and brim of sliced carrots and asparagus tips tied in bundles

VEGETABLE SOUFFLÉ

1 small onion, chopped
1 tablespoon fat
2 cups Cut Cooked Corn
1 pimiento, minced
½ teaspoon salt
¼ teaspoon paprika
½ cup Stewed Tomatoes
1 cup grated cheese
2 eggs, separated

Sauté onion in fat until partially cooked. Add corn, pimiento, salt, paprika, tomatoes, cheese and beaten egg yolks. Fold in stiffly beaten egg whites, pour into greased baking dish and bake in moderate oven (350°F.) 30 to 40 minutes or until firm and browned. Serves 6 to 8.
Use asparagus instead of corn. Use Cream Sauce instead of tomatoes and ½ cup cheese.

A minimum of effort in arrangement can produce a maximum of beauty from the simplest vegetable plate

VEGETABLE CUSTARD — Use eggs whole instead of separated. Increase tomatoes to 1½ cups. Bake in casserole in pan of hot water in moderate oven (350°F.) 40 minutes or until firm.

VEGETABLE CASSEROLE

2 large mild onions
4 large firm tomatoes
2 cups diced potatoes
1 cup chopped celery
1 cup sliced carrots
1 teaspoon salt
¼ teaspoon pepper
1 teaspoon paprika
4 tablespoons fat

Slice onions and tomatoes about ½ inch thick and place in layers in greased casserole with potatoes, celery and carrots. Sprinkle each layer with salt, pepper and paprika; add fat, cover and bake in moderate oven (375°F.) 1 hour or until tender. Serves 6 to 8.

CREAMED VEGETABLE

4 cups cooked vegetable
1 recipe White Sauce

Combine any suggested cooked vegetable with white sauce and heat thoroughly. Serves 6 to 8. Suggested vegetables:
Asparagus, Beet Greens
Broccoli, Broccoli Rabe
Brussels Sprouts, Cabbage
Carrots, Cauliflower
Celery, Chicory
Chinese Cabbage
Cucumbers, Eggplant
Globe Artichokes
Green Beans
Jerusalem Artichokes
Kale, Kohlrabi
Lima Beans
Onions
Parsnips, Peas
Potatoes, Radishes
Salsify, Spinach
Swiss Chard
Turnips
Wax Beans

VEGETABLE MARROW HUNGARIAN STYLE

1½ pounds vegetable marrow
¾ cup boiling water
1½ teaspoons salt
1 tablespoon lemon juice
2 tablespoons flour
1 cup milk, ½ cup cream
1 tablespoon butter
3 tablespoons chopped onion

Pare vegetable marrow. Cut into narrow pieces 2 inches long. Place in saucepan, add boiling water and salt, cover and cook slowly for 15 minutes. Add lemon juice and continue cooking 5 minutes longer. Blend flour and milk and stir into squash. Cover and cook 10 minutes longer. Pour in cream, heat to boiling and add more seasoning if desired. Melt butter in saucepan and brown onion lightly. Serve marrow with browned onion over top. Serves 6 to 8.

VEGETABLE MARROW WITH SOUR CREAM

1½ pounds vegetable marrow
⅓ cup water
1 tablespoon butter
1½ teaspoons salt
Dash pepper
½ teaspoon sugar
2 teaspoons lemon juice
½ cup sour cream
½ tablespoon minced fresh dill

Pare and cut vegetable marrow into ½-inch cubes, discarding centers if seeds are large. Place in saucepan with water, cover and heat slowly for 10 minutes or until cubes are tender but still firm. Drain if necessary. Add butter, seasoning, sugar and lemon juice. Stir together until butter is melted and add sour cream and dill. Heat to boiling. Serves 5 or 6.

STUFFED VEGETABLE MARROW

1 large vegetable marrow
1½ cups chopped cooked meat
½ cup bread crumbs
1 tablespoon minced onion
2 tablespoons tomato catchup
¼ teaspoon salt
Dash cayenne

Cut marrow crosswise into halves. Remove seeds from each half. Mix remaining ingredients together and pack into marrow halves. Place halves together and fasten with picks or place in pan of same length as marrow to hold halves together. Bake in a moderate oven (350°F.) 30 minutes or until tender. Serve in slices, for 6.

Marrows may be baked in Tomato Sauce after they are stuffed.

Another filling may be made by combining 1½ cups cooked rice, 1 cup grated cheese, ½ teaspoon Worcestershire sauce and 1 tablespoon minced green pepper. Bake as above.

COOKED VEGETABLE MARROW

2 pounds vegetable marrow
½ cup water

Pare marrow, remove seeds and cut into cubes or slices. Heat water to boiling, add marrow, cover pan tightly to prevent escape of steam and heat again to boiling. Reduce heat at once and simmer 15 to 20 minutes. Drain if necessary. (Makes about 2 cups.) To serve, season with salt, pepper, and butter, for 6.

SUCCOTASH

½ recipe Cut Cooked Corn
½ recipe Cooked Fresh Lima
  Beans
2 tablespoons butter
1 teaspoon salt
⅛ teaspoon pepper
Parsley

Combine vegetables, add butter and seasonings. Heat thoroughly. Garnish with parsley. Serves 6.

Stuffed vegetable marrow will be a welcome addition to your list of favorites

BAKED VEGETABLES

8 small carrots
8 small potatoes
8 small onions
¾ teaspoon salt
⅛ teaspoon pepper
1 recipe White Sauce
2 tablespoons butter

Pare carrots and potatoes and cut into slices. Peel onions and mince. Combine vegetables in greased baking dish, season with salt and pepper, add white sauce and dot with butter. Bake in moderate oven (350°F.) about 1½ hours or until tender. Serves 6 to 8.

OTHER VEGETABLE COMBINATIONS FOR BAKING

Cauliflower, onion, carrots and peas.
Turnips, carrots and leeks.
Lima beans, onion and corn.
Salsify, carrots, mushrooms and onion.

UPSIDE-DOWN VEGE-TABLE CAKE

2 cups sifted flour
2 teaspoons baking powder
½ teaspoon salt
¼ cup shortening
1 egg, beaten
1 cup milk
4 cups mixed cooked vegetables (peas, carrots, celery, Lima beans)
½ cup vegetable stock
2 tablespoons butter

Mix and sift dry ingredients together and cut in shortening. Combine egg and milk; add to dry ingredients, stirring until mixed. Arrange hot seasoned vegetables in bottom of greased shallow baking pan, add vegetable stock, dot with butter, cover with first mixture and bake in hot oven (425° F.) 20 to 25 minutes. Turn out on hot serving plate with vegetables on top and serve with Tomato or Mushroom Sauce. Serves 6.

Either fresh or cooked vegetables may be combined for this delicious casserole

MIXED VEGETABLES

Chop, combine and sauté in butter until browned. Or reheat with leftover gravy and serve with sliced meat. Or make into vegetable loaf and bake.

Bake the vegetable upside-down cake in a casserole for variety

VEGETABLE PIE

3 medium onions, chopped
3 medium green peppers, chopped
⅓ cup butter
6 medium tomatoes, diced
1½ cups Cut Cooked Corn
1 teaspoon salt
⅛ teaspoon pepper
1 baked Pastry Shell
¼ cup grated cheese

Cook onions and peppers in butter 5 minutes. Add tomatoes and corn and cook 10 minutes longer, but do not brown. Season. Fill pastry shell and sprinkle with cheese. Serves 6 to 8.

VEGETABLE LOAF

½ cup cooked peas
½ cup cooked string beans
½ cup chopped cooked carrots
1½ cups milk
1 egg
1 cup soft bread crumbs
½ teaspoon salt
⅛ teaspoon pepper
½ teaspoon paprika

Press peas through a sieve, cut beans into small pieces and combine all vegetables. Add milk, slightly beaten egg, crumbs and seasoning. Turn into greased baking dish and bake in moderate oven (350°F.) until firm. For 6.

MIXED GRILL

Bake Breaded Eggplant in a shallow pan. Place a slice of peeled tomato on each slice of eggplant. Top each with 2 crossed half-slices bacon. Broil until bacon is crisp. Sprinkle with grated cheese and return to broiler to melt cheese. Garnish with parsley.

LEFTOVER COOKED VEGETABLES

CABBAGE — Purée; reheat with butter and a little cream; serve on toast.

CELERY — Purée and add to cream soups, chowders or meat gravies.

LETTUCE — Cook outside leaves of lettuce with other greens, such as spinach or kale.

ZUCCHINI IN TOMATO SAUCE

5 tomatoes
¼ cup butter
½ teaspoon salt
⅛ teaspoon pepper
1 pound zucchini
2 tablespoons chopped parsley

Peel tomatoes, remove seeds and stew tomatoes in butter until cooked to a thick sauce, stirring constantly. Season with salt and pepper. Wash zucchini, dice very fine, add to tomato sauce and simmer about 15 minutes or until tender. Sprinkle with parsley. Serves 6 to 8.

ZUCCHINI AND TOMATOES AU GRATIN

2 pounds zucchini
3 tablespoons chopped onion
3 tablespoons fat
2 cups Stewed Tomatoes
½ teaspoon salt
⅛ teaspoon pepper
¾ cup grated cheese

Wash zucchini and cut into ¼-inch pieces. Cook onion in fat, add zucchini and cook slowly 5 minutes, stirring frequently. Add tomatoes, salt and pepper. Cover and cook 5 minutes longer. Turn into greased baking dish, sprinkle cheese over top and bake in moderate oven (375°F.) about 20 minutes. Serves 6 to 8.

FRIED ZUCCHINI

2 pounds zucchini
Salt
1 teaspoon chopped onion
¼ cup butter

Wash and cut zucchini into ¼-inch slices. Sprinkle with salt. Add onion and cook slowly in butter about 10 minutes, stirring constantly. Cover and simmer 5 minutes. Serves 6 to 8.

If you've never tried zucchini have it stuffed the first time and you'll want to have it often

STUFFED ZUCCHINI

3 zucchini
2 tablespoons minced onion
3 tablespoons butter
1 cup soft bread crumbs
½ cup cooked tomato
Salt and pepper

Cook zucchini in boiling salted water 10 minutes. Cut in halves and scoop out centers. Mix pulp with remaining ingredients. Fill zucchini. Bake in 350°F. oven 15 minutes. Serve with bacon, for 6.

Green onions provide realistic foliage for the turnip narcissus and jonquil

VEGETABLES AS A GARNISH

VEGETABLE FLOWERS

EASTER LILY — Pare and slice a large white turnip very thin. Roll each slice into a cornucopia and insert a stamen of carrot. Thrust a toothpick through the base to hold parts together. Tint some of the turnip slices yellow with food coloring. When made, dip lillies into warm (not hot) clear gelatin, place on rack in drip pan of refrigerator.

SHASTA DAISY — From pared thin slices of 3-inch white turnips cut V-shaped sections, leaving narrow petal-shaped sections. For the center, cut a partial ball from carrot and fasten into center with a toothpick.

NARCISSUS—Use thin slices of pared turnip about 2 inches in diameter. Cut V-shaped sections from the slice leaving petals about ½ inch across. Use a slightly hollowed-out section of turnip for the center. Tint the upper edge of the turnip with brown food coloring. Dip into warm (not hot) clear gelatin. Place on rack to drain. Chill.

ROSE—Use small turnips or the ends of cucumbers. With a sharp-pointed knife, cut out sections of the vegetable leaving petal forms intact. The skin may be left on the cucumber and triangular sections cut from it leaving green petals as a background for the rose.

JULIENNE VEGETABLES

Cut uncooked carrots and celery or cooked turnips, beets or potatoes into matchlike shreds. Arrange in a row around vegetable platter or in bundles with a strip of pimiento over top.

Remove filling from stuffed olives and fill centers with Julienne carrots or celery.

VEGETABLE BASKETS

EGGPLANT — Make 2 cuts in eggplant ½ inch on each side of stem down about 3 inches. Cut in from each side to meet first cuts and remove sections of eggplant to make handle. Scoop out center and fill with vegetable salad, olives or celery.

PEPPER—Parboil peppers 5 minutes. Cut as for eggplant if a handle is desired, or cut off top portion, remove seeds and membranes; fill with hot creamed mixture.

ARTICHOKE — Cook artichokes until tender. Spread leaves and remove choke. Fill center with creamed sea food, fish or meat.

VEGETABLE CUPS

Make cups from (2-inch) lengths of large cooked carrots, whole turnips or beets or uncooked cucumbers or plum tomatoes.

These delicate blossoms are ingeniously carved from turnips and carrots

Salads

*500
Delicious
Salads*

ANCHOVY APPETIZER SALAD

1 small head lettuce or romaine
2 cans rolled anchovy fillets
8 ripe olives, sliced
½ small can caviar
2 hard-cooked eggs
Horse-radish French Dressing

Arrange lettuce on 4 plates and in center of each place 2 anchovies. Arrange olive slices in circle around anchovies and fill center of each olive slice with caviar. Border with sieved hard-cooked egg yolks and arrange chopped egg whites in outer circle. Serve with dressing. Serves 4.

Use the less expensive salted Italian anchovies instead of fillets. Soak for 4 hours, skin, fillet and roll.

Use chopped pickled herring instead of anchovies.

Use chopped smoked salmon instead of anchovies.

Use slices of stuffed olives instead of ripe olives with caviar.

ARTICHOKE AND CRAB-MEAT SALAD

1 cup diced cooked artichoke
   hearts
1 cup crab meat
½ cup heavy cream, whipped
1 cup Mayonnaise
½ cup tomato catchup
½ teaspoon Worcestershire sauce
Salt and pepper

Mix artichokes and crab meat and chill. Whip cream and combine with mayonnaise, catchup, Worcestershire sauce, salt and pepper. Chill. When ready to serve combine sauce with the artichoke and crab mixture. Serves 6.

Use cooked shrimp or lobster meat instead of crab meat. Add ¼ cup chopped ripe or green olives.

AVOCADO COCKTAIL SALAD

1 avocado
2 tablespoons lemon juice
Salt
Watercress, romaine or lettuce
2 cups avocado balls or cubes
½ cup Appetizer Mayonnaise

Cut avocado crosswise into halves and remove seed. Slice 2 rings from each half and peel. Sprinkle with lemon juice and salt, arrange on watercress, and fill rings with avocado balls. Serve with the mayonnaise. Serves 4.

Use 1 cup avocado balls and any of the following:

1 cup diced asparagus tips.

1 cup diced tomatoes and cucumber.

½ cup diced lobster, shrimp or crab meat and ½ cup chopped celery.

⅓ cup shredded anchovies, ⅓ cup pearl onions, and ⅓ cup chopped celery.

½ cup diced pickled beets and ½ cup pickled onions.

Use Frozen Tomato Mayonnaise instead of the Appetizer Mayonnaise.

GRAPEFRUIT APPETIZER SALAD

Remove seeds from halves of grapefruit. Cut around inside edge as close to shell as possible. Separate grapefruit segments from membrane, cut out remaining membrane and arrange romaine, escarole or chicory around inside of shell. Cut grapefruit segments into pieces and heap up in shell. Serve with French Dressing.

Arrange endive stalks inside grapefruit shell. Heap grapefruit segments at base of stalks and sprinkle with grated Cheddar cheese.

Alternate slices of avocado and segments of grapefruit in grapefruit shell.

Alternate wedges of cantaloupe or honeydew melon with grapefruit segments in shell.

Alternate whole marinated shrimp and segments of grapefruit in shell.

Nothing sharpens the edge of appetites like tart grapefruit and crisp fresh chicory

CELERY CHEESE SALAD

Clean celery and cut stalks into equal lengths. Fill center stalk with pimiento cheese paste, fill next stalk and place it against first stalk and so on until all stalks have been used to form a large compact bunch of celery. Wrap tightly in waxed paper, slip tight rubber bands around stalk at both ends and center and chill. Remove paper, cut into slices, arrange on shredded lettuce and serve with French or Thousand Island Dressing. The slices may be used without dressing as an appetizer. Serves 6 to 8.

SARDINE SALAD APPETIZERS

Chicory
2 cans small sardines, boned and flaked
2 tablespoons chopped onion
2 tablespoons chopped parsley
4 ripe olives
4 Pickled Beets, sliced
4 Pickled Eggs, sliced

Arrange chicory on 4 salad plates and place sardines in center of each. Sprinkle with chopped onion and parsley and top each with a ripe olive. Surround with border of alternate overlapping slices of beets and eggs. Serve with French Dressing.

Marinate sardines in French dressing; serve on shredded lettuce and garnish with chopped eggs and pickled onion rings.

Combine flaked sardines with chopped celery and minced onion. Serve on watercress with Caper French Dressing.

Serve sardines whole on thin slices of dill pickles, placed on slices of lettuce. Garnish with tomato sections, sprinkled with chopped egg, and serve with Chive French Dressing.

SPRING FLOWER SALADS
FLOWERPOTS

2 teaspoons unflavored gelatin
2 tablespoons cold water
3 ounces cream cheese
Milk, Dash salt
2 tablespoons anchovy paste
1/2 teaspoon grated onion

Soften gelatin in cold water. Mash cream cheese and add enough milk to make 1 cup. Blend with salt, anchovy paste and grated onion. Melt gelatin over hot water and stir into cheese mixture. Pour into 2 small custard cups or flared jelly glasses and chill until firm. Unmold and cut each mold into 4 lengthwise slices. Place each slice on colored salad plate to represent flowerpots, and decorate with strips of Tomato Aspic, ripe olives, pimiento or green pepper. Makes 8.

Use 2 tablespoons softened Roquefort cheese instead of anchovy paste and grated onion.

FLOWERS

TULIPS—Cut a slice of pineapple into halves, then spread open about 2 inches at the top. Place a thin wedge of tomato in center and another wedge on each side over pineapple, resembling tulip petals. Make stem from strip of green pepper, celery or romaine, with leaves (1 on each side of stem) of French endive or romaine.

LILIES OF THE VALLEY—Make 3 leaves of French endive or romaine, with 5 long stems of chives arranged in a spray. With pastry bag and small plain tube, pipe softened cream cheese in dots along one side of each stem, to represent lilies. Six ounces cream cheese will be sufficient to make flowers for 8 salads.

HYACINTHS—Make 2 leaves of French endive or romaine. Cut piece from slice of fresh pineapple the shape of a hyacinth cluster and arrange between the leaves. With pastry bag and star tube cover pineapple completely with blossoms of softened cream cheese, either white or delicately tinted pink or yellow.

Serve these salads as first course for a spring luncheon, accompanied by Lemon French Dressing.

TOMATO ANCHOVY APPETIZER SALAD

2 tomatoes
Lettuce or watercress
1 small onion, sliced thin
6 rolled anchovies
1 teaspoon lemon juice
1 hard-cooked egg yolk
French Dressing

Peel tomatoes and cut into thick slices; chill. Arrange lettuce on 6 salad plates; place a tomato slice on each, cover with onion slice and top with anchovy. Sprinkle with lemon juice and garnish with sieved egg yolk. Serve with French dressing. Serves 6.

Use 2 teaspoons chopped chives instead of onion slices.

Use whole sardines instead of anchovies.

Use pickled herring instead of anchovies.

Use chopped cooked chicken liver or Pâté de Foie Gras instead of anchovies.

Use hard-cooked egg slices instead of onion slices and minced chives instead of egg yolk.

The salad platter served like a buffet is new and very attractive

SHRIMP SALAD

8 tender stalks celery with leaves
1½ cups cleaned cooked shrimp
1 large dill pickle
1 orange, cut into wedges
2 carrots, cut into strips
Mayonnaise
Pimiento stars

Divide a chop plate into 4 sections with celery stalks. Place shrimp, dill pickle cut into strips, orange wedges and carrots in each section. Serve mayonnaise in bowl in center topped with pimiento stars. Serves 4 or 5.

SHRIMP AND GRAPEFRUIT SALAD

1 cup shrimp
2 cups grapefruit segments, chilled
3 ounces cream cheese
2 tablespoons mayonnaise
5-6 pieces crisp celery
Lettuce
French dressing

Clean shrimp; cut into small pieces. Drain grapefruit from juice. Mash cheese; add mayonnaise; cream together; add shrimp and mix well. Pack grooves of celery tightly with mixture; cut in ¾ inch slices. Arrange on crisp lettuce leaves with grapefruit segments. Sprinkle with French dressing. Serves 8.

LOBSTER PLATTER

4 cups cooked lobster
½ cup diced celery
½ teaspoon salt
⅛ teaspoon paprika
French dressing to moisten
Lettuce
Mayonnaise
1 hard-cooked egg, sliced
Capers
Stuffed olives

Cut lobster in small pieces and mix well with celery, salt and paprika. Marinate in French dressing and chill thoroughly. Place crisp lettuce leaves on a platter and pile the lobster in the center. Cover with mayonnaise and garnish with slices of hard-cooked egg, capers, and sliced stuffed olives. Serves 8.

LOBSTER GRAPEFRUIT SNACK

4 grapefruit
2 cups flaked lobster
1 cup French dressing
Tartare Sauce

Cut grapefruit into halves, with scissors cut out membrane and alternate sections of grapefruit and fill the space with lobster flakes that have been marinated in French dressing. Garnish center with tartare sauce. Serves 8.

HALIBUT SALAD

3 cups cold cooked halibut
French dressing to moisten
1 cucumber, peeled and cubed
1 tablespoon chopped onion
1 teaspoon salt
¼ teaspoon pepper
Mayonnaise
Lettuce
Capers
1 pimiento

The halibut should have been cooked in very salty water—at least 2 teaspoons of salt to each quart of water. Flake the halibut in rather large pieces. Moisten with French dressing and chill thoroughly. Mix the halibut, cucumber, onion, salt and pepper with sufficient mayonnaise to hold the ingredients together. The mayonnaise may be thinned with a little cream. Serve on crisp lettuce leaves on a large platter. Garnish with capers and pimiento cut into fancy shapes. Serves 8.

OLIVE AND FISH SALAD IN GREEN PEPPER CASES

1 large can tuna
1 cup stuffed olives
10 red radishes
French dressing, or Mayonnaise and chili sauce
8 small green peppers
Lettuce

Flake tuna. Cut olives and radishes into eighths, lengthwise. Mix all ingredients together, chill, moisten with dressing and serve as a salad in green peppers from which seeds have been removed. Place peppers on bed of lettuce for serving. Serves 8.

BEET CUPS—Hollow out large cooked beets. Fill with salad mixture and garnish with wedges of hard-cooked eggs.

TURNIP CUPS—Fill cooked white turnip cups with salad mixture.

APPLE AND NUT SALAD

4 apples, diced
2 tablespoons lemon juice
¾ cup Pineapple Cream Dressing
Lettuce, ¾ cup salted almonds

Combine apples, lemon juice and dressing. Arrange in salad bowl on lettuce. Garnish with almonds. Serves 6.

AUTUMN FRUIT SALAD BOWL

1 head romaine
½ pineapple, pared and sliced
1 grapefruit, peeled and sectioned
½ red apple, sliced
¼ pound red grapes, seeded
1 orange, peeled and sectioned
Whipped Cream Mayonnaise

Line salad bowl with romaine. Divide bowl into 4 divisions with half slices of pineapple. Arrange alternate sections of grapefruit and apple slices in 1 division and place remaining fruits in separate divisions. Fill center with mayonnaise. Serves 4.

Bright red cherries and blush pink cantaloupe with golden pineapple and fresh greens form a colorful salad

AVOCADO SALAD

3 avocados
1 cup pineapple cubes
1 cup grapes, cut into halves
2 oranges, peeled and cut into pieces
French Dressing
Lettuce
Fresh mint

Cut avocados into halves lengthwise and scoop out pulp with a French vegetable cutter. Save shells. Combine with other fruit and marinate in French dressing about 20 minutes. Fill avocado shells and serve on lettuce. Garnish with fresh mint. Serves 6. Add ½ cup grapefruit segments, if desired.

AVOCADO SALAD WITH FROZEN TOMATO MAYONNAISE

2 avocados, Salt
4 tablespoons lemon juice
Frozen Tomato Mayonnaise
Watercress

Pare avocados. Cut into halves lengthwise and remove seeds. Sprinkle with salt and lemon juice. Fill centers with mayonnaise and serve on watercress. Serves 4.

BANANA SALMON SALAD

3 ripe bananas, diced
½ cup diced canned pineapple (about 2 slices)
1½ cups canned salmon
¼ cup diced celery
½ teaspoon salt
1 tablespoon chopped pickle
Mayonnaise to moisten

Mix bananas and pineapple together. Add flaked salmon. Fold in remaining ingredients. Garnish with crisp lettuce or other greens and lemon slices. Serves 8.

CANTALOUPE CHERRY SALAD BOWL

2 ripe cantaloupe, chilled
1 head lettuce
Cottage Cheese Mayonnaise
2 cups fresh red cherries, pitted

Cut cantaloupe into crosswise halves and remove seeds. Cut balls from 1 cantaloupe using a French cutter; pare the other cantaloupe and cut crosswise into thin slices. Cut each slice into halves to form a semicircle. Tear lettuce into large pieces and toss in salad bowl with mayonnaise. Arrange cantaloupe, balls and slices, in bowl alternating with cherries. Serve with additional mayonnaise. Serves 6.

Arrange red cherries and cantaloupe balls in center of bowl and border with overlapping cantaloupe slices.

Use fresh red raspberries for cherries.

Use fresh strawberries for cherries.

Use oxheart cherries for red cherries; stuff with cream cheese and serve with Mint French Dressing.

Use honeydew melon for cantaloupe; and Lime French Dressing for Cottage Cheese Mayonnaise.

FRUIT SALAD COMBINATIONS

Serve on Salad Greens with French Dressing.

Alternate slices of avocado, grapefruit and tomato.

Alternate slices of avocado, Japanese persimmon and grapefruit segments.

Diced avocado and pineapple cubes, garnished with ripe olives.

Sliced oranges and quartered bananas sprinkled with lemon juice and rolled in chopped nuts.

Alternate grapefruit segments and Japanese persimmon wedges on split banana.

Grapefruit segments, cantaloupe or honeydew melon slices with cottage cheese.

Melon balls, white grapes, fresh peach slices and pineapple spears.

Watermelon, cantaloupe and honeydew melon balls, pineapple cubes and Brazil nuts or toasted almonds.

Fresh pineapple, fresh red cherries, orange sections.

Orange slices, diced fresh figs, toasted almonds, red raspberries.

Sliced orange segments, fresh cherries, white grapes, sliced bananas and chopped mint.

Fresh diced pears, sliced bananas and red raspberries.

Diced fresh pear, chopped nut meats and ginger ale cubes.

Sliced fresh pear, cream cheese and chopped preserved ginger.

Cheese-stuffed prunes on orange slices.

Diced apples, sliced bananas and Tokay grapes.

FRUIT SALAD BOWL

1 bunch chicory, washed, dried
1 avocado, sliced lengthwise
3 bananas, cut into eighths
Pineapple juice
3 slices pineapple, cut into halves
6 plums, pitted
12 orange slices
6 wedges cantaloupe
18 watermelon balls
2 cups seedless grapes
Pineapple French Dressing

Have ingredients well chilled. Arrange chicory in salad bowl. Dip avocado and bananas into pineapple juice to prevent discoloration; drain. Arrange fruit attractively on chicory, grouping all of each kind together. Serve with dressing, arranging some of each fruit on individual plates. Serves 6.

FRUIT SALAD IN ICE BOWLS

Serve fruit salads or semifrozen fruit combinations in 1 large, or individual small ice bowls, colored in pastel shades. Serve with any preferred fruit dressing.

ICE BOWLS

Freeze water, colored pale green, in bowl shaped mold. When sufficient ice is formed for wall, break through thin ice layer in center and pour out the water.

Freeze water in enamel bowl, covered and packed in ice and salt. When frozen 1 inch thick press down small bowl until water runs out. When freezing process starts again remove smaller bowl. To unmold dip bowl into hot water.

Repeat process for individual bowls, coloring each in different pastel shade.

GRAPE AND PEAR SALAD

Chicory or 8 grape leaves
8 pear halves
6 ounces cream cheese
1/4 cup cream
2 pounds white seedless grapes
French Dressing

Cover salad plates with chicory or a large grape leaf. Place a pear half on each, flat-side down. Mix cream cheese and cream and spread the pear liberally with the mixture. Cut grapes into halves and place flat-side down on the covered pear, close together to resemble a bunch of grapes. Place a piece of grape stem in large end of pear. Serve with French dressing. Serves 8.

Use seeded purple grapes or seeded Tokay grapes instead of white grapes.

Use Whipped Cream Dressing instead of French dressing.

Cries of delight will greet this frosty bunch of grapes when the layers below are explored

AVOCADO FRUIT SALAD BOWL

2 grapefruit
2 oranges
French Dressing
Romaine
French endive
1 avocado
Cottage Cheese Mayonnaise

Peel grapefruit and oranges, removing segments whole. Marinate in dressing; chill. Line salad bowl with romaine and endive. Pare and halve avocado, removing seed. Cut one half into serving portions, and place in salad bowl. Fill cavity of remaining half with mayonnaise. Arrange orange and grapefruit sections around avocado. Serves 4.

CINNAMON APPLE SALAD

6 apples
1 cup water
1 cup red cinnamon drops
2 cups sugar, Lettuce
Chopped nut meats
Cream cheese
Mayonnaise

Pare and core apples. Heat water, cinnamon drops and sugar in a large saucepan until sugar and cinnamon drops are melted. Add apples and cook slowly, turning apples frequently in the sirup. When apples are tender, lift from sirup carefully, chill and place on lettuce. Fill centers with chopped nuts and softened cream cheese and serve with mayonnaise. Serves 6.
Instead of cheese and nut filling: Fill centers with celery and nuts mixed with mayonnaise.
Fill centers with chopped raisins and nuts moistened with lemon juice.
Fill centers with chopped dates, celery and mayonnaise.

CORONATION SALAD

6 fresh pears
Lemon juice
½ cup cottage cheese
2 tablespoons Mayonnaise
Red Bar-le-Duc
Romaine
Whipped Cream Mayonnaise

Peel pears and sprinkle with lemon juice. Hollow out bottom portion; stuff with cottage cheese mixed with mayonnaise. Scoop out center of top slightly and fill with 2 teaspoons of red Bar-le-Duc. Arrange on romaine and serve with mayonnaise. Serves 6.

COTTAGE CHEESE FRUIT SALAD BOWL

1 grapefruit, in segments
2 oranges, in segments
1 avocado, pared and sliced
Lemon French Dressing
½ head lettuce
½ head French endive
½ bunch watercress
1½ cups cottage cheese

Marinate fruit in dressing and chill. Toss salad greens together in salad bowl with dressing, pile cottage cheese in center and arrange border of orange and grapefruit segments alternating with avocado slices. Serves 6.
Use tomato wedges instead of orange segments.
Use pineapple spears and strawberries instead of grapefruit and avocado.
Use fresh figs and ripe cherries instead of avocado.

FRESH FRUIT SALAD BOWL

2 bananas, cut lengthwise
4 slices avocado
Lemon juice
1 head chicory, shredded
4 long strips cantaloupe
4 half-slices fresh pineapple
8 orange segments
12 black cherries
12 honeydew melon balls
12 watermelon balls
Fruit French Dressing

Dip banana and avocado in lemon juice. Line a salad bowl with chicory and on this arrange banana and cantaloupe. Alternate pineapple, avocado, and oranges in bowl. Make a nest of cherries and garnish with melon balls. Serve with dressing. Serves 4.

Red Bar-le-Duc provides coronation jewels for stuffed fresh pears

AVOCADO CRESCENTS

Halve fruit lengthwise, remove seed, pare, cut each half crosswise and slice to form crescents. Sprinkle with lemon juice and salt. Serve plain with rounded edges overlapping, on salad greens with a section of lemon, or alternate with grapefruit or orange segments, halves of sliced pineapple, melon crescents, apple wedges, pear or peach slices, tomato wedges or halved slices.

FRUIT SALAD SUPREME

1 pineapple
Pineapple Cream Dressing
1 head lettuce
3 oranges, peeled and sliced
2 cups fresh strawberries

Remove top from pineapple; hollow out center and fill with dressing. Arrange lettuce on chop plate or large salad plates. Place tips of pineapple spines, cut from removed portion, in center and around this arrange orange slices and strawberries. Serves 6.

GRAPEFRUIT AND ALMOND SALAD

2½ cups grapefruit segments
1 cup shredded blanched almonds
½ cup chopped dates
1 green pepper, cut into rings
Cream Cheese Ginger Dressing
Lettuce

Toss first 5 ingredients together and serve in lettuce cups. Serves 8. Use equal amounts of orange and grapefruit segments; omit dates.

ORANGE LUNCHEON SALAD

8 oranges
3 Spanish or Italian onions
Cream cheese and nut balls
French Dressing

Peel oranges removing all exterior membrane and skin. Peel onions, and slice onions and oranges thin. Arrange in a circle with slices of orange and onion alternating. Place a ball in center of each plate and serve with French dressing. Serves 8.

PAPAYA SALAD

2½ cups diced papaya
1½ cups diced pineapple
1 cup sliced celery
2 tablespoons finely chopped onion
½ teaspoon salt
¾ cup Mayonnaise, Lettuce

Prepare fruit, combine with remaining ingredients, serve on crisp lettuce leaves. Dress with mayonnaise and a dash of paprika. Serves 8.

PEACH AND BERRY SALAD

12 fresh or canned peach halves
1 head lettuce, separated
3 dozen red raspberries
Raspberry jelly, Watercress

If fresh peaches are used, peel, stone and halve them. If canned peaches are used, drain well. Arrange 2 peach halves on lettuce for each serving. Arrange several raspberries on each, fill centers with jelly, and garnish with watercress. Serve with mayonnaise. Serves 6.

The richness of avocado is best set off by the crisp juiciness of oranges

PEAR SALAD WITH GINGER CHEESE

6 pear halves (fresh or canned)
3 ounces cream cheese
2 tablespoons cream
3 tablespoons chopped crystallized ginger
1 bunch watercress
Orange French Dressing

Drain pear halves, if canned; chill. Soften cream cheese with cream and blend with ginger. Heap 1 tablespoon cheese mixture in hollow of each pear and arrange on watercress. Serve with dressing. Serves 6.

Omit ginger and use Ginger Ale French Dressing instead of orange.

Omit ginger and use Bar-le-Duc Mayonnaise instead of Orange Dressing.

Use Cranberry Sauce instead of ginger.

PEACH—Use peach halves instead of pears. Use chopped dates or nut meats instead of ginger.

APRICOT—Use apricots instead of pears. Use drained crushed pineapple instead of ginger.

ROYAL SALAD

Romaine
1 orange
1 grapefruit
1½ pears
1 green pepper
6 strawberries
Strawberry Cream Mayonnaise

Arrange romaine on individual salad plates. On this arrange 3 segments of orange, 2 of grapefruit, 2 sections of pear, separating the different fruits with a slice of green pepper. Top with strawberry crown. Serve with mayonnaise. Serves 6.

SEMIFROZEN FRUIT COMBINATIONS

Peeled fresh figs, fresh strawberries and fresh pineapple cubes.
Orange and grapefruit segments with peeled and seeded Tokay grapes.
Sliced Japanese persimmon, grapefruit segments and sliced avocado.
Sliced fresh pears, peeled white grapes and red raspberries.
Quartered peaches, pears and plums.
Watermelon, honeydew and cantaloupe balls.
Pears, Peaches, seedless grapes and chopped maraschino cherries.

PINEAPPLE AND BANANA SALAD

1½ cups pineapple cubes
3 ounces cream cheese
2 tablespoons lemon juice
¼ cup pineapple juice
4 bananas
Chicory or lettuce
Lemon French Dressing

Drain pineapple, mash cheese and add lemon and pineapple juice gradually. Beat until creamy. Slice bananas lengthwise, spread with cheese mixture. Arrange fruit on salad greens. Serve with dressing. Serves 4.

Brush bananas with honey and dip into chopped toasted almonds.

PINEAPPLE BASKET SALAD

1 pineapple
2 cups fruit salad
Mayonnaise

Cut pineapple into halves lengthwise and scoop out the pulp in cubes or balls. Mix with fruit salad and pile in pineapple baskets. Serve with mayonnaise.

Nature and art combine to produce these lovely pineapple baskets

STRAWBERRY MELON SALAD BOWL

1 cantaloupe
½ honeydew melon
½ clove garlic
Lettuce
1 pint strawberries or red
    raspberries
Lime French Dressing

All melons should be served very cold. The melon pulp may be shaped into balls with a French vegetable cutter, diced, or scooped out in large spoonfuls. Rub bowl with garlic. Line with lettuce leaves and arrange berries and melon balls on lettuce. Serve with dressing. Serves 6.
Serve with Lemon Mayonnaise instead of French Dressing.

SUN GLOW SALAD

6 large slices pineapple
Chicory
6 large peach halves
Cream Cheese Mayonnaise
6 cocktail cherries

Place a slice of pineapple on chicory, and top with a peach half filled with mayonnaise. Garnish with cherry. Serves 6.

WALDORF SALAD

6 tart red apples
4 celery hearts
2 ounces English walnut meats
Whipped Cream Dressing
Lettuce

Pare apples, cut into long slender strips and dip into lemon water. Cut celery the same way. Shave walnuts into fine pieces. Combine walnuts, apples and celery with enough dressing to moisten. Heap on lettuce on salad plates. Serves 6.
Leave skins on apples and dice. Use black walnuts, toasted almonds or pecans instead of English walnuts.

YOUR SALAD BOWL

Wooden salad bowls develop a fine patina with age, and the flavor of garlic rubbed into the wood is preserved if the bowls are not washed. Drain the bowl each time after use, rub dry with absorbent paper and polish with oiled paper. This method also keeps the bowl from cracking. Keep in an oiled container or cheesecloth bag when not in use. If made of unfinished wood rub inside of bowl thoroughly with olive oil and dry out before using the first time. If possible, keep one bowl for green salads alone. Large pottery, china or glass bowls may be used if preferred, especially for fish, fruit and other salads mixed with mayonnaise. These should be chilled before salad is added and should, of course, be washed each time after using.

SALAD GREENS

Remove wilted leaves from greens and wash well. Drain and chill in ice water for ½ hour or refrigerate until crisp. Dry thoroughly by wrapping in towel or shaking in wire basket.

Never cut salad greens. Tear into large pieces or shred. Rub salad bowl with cut clove of garlic, add greens and toss with French dressing, using salad fork and spoon.

If you prefer to mix your dressing at table, put seasoning in salad spoon and fill with oil, sprinkle over greens and then pour over just enough additional oil to coat greens; toss lightly, sprinkle with lemon juice or vinegar (preferably tarragon) and toss again.

Instead of rubbing the bowl with garlic you may rub a small crust of dry bread with a cut clove of garlic and drop into bowl before adding greens. This may be taken out before serving, or cut into small cubes and mixed with the salad.

COMBINATIONS FOR GREEN SALAD BOWLS

Lettuce, chicory, uncooked spinach, chives.
Watercress, dandelion greens, Spring onions.
Uncooked spinach, chervil, chopped onion, parsley.

Romaine, watercress, parsley.
Lettuce, escarole, chicory, chives.
Romaine, lettuce, watercress, sliced green pepper.
Lettuce, escarole, romaine, pearl onions.
Lettuce, basil, parsley, thyme.
Tomato sections, cucumber slices or chopped hard-cooked eggs may be added.

SPRING SALAD BOWL

2 cups cooked peas
6 cooked cauliflowerets
2 cups cooked green beans
2 tomatoes, peeled and sliced
French or Roquefort Dressing
1 head lettuce
Watercress
Radish Roses

Marinate vegetables separately in French dressing and chill for 1 hour. Line salad bowl with outside leaves of lettuce, and place 4 lettuce cups around center of bowl. Fill each with one of the vegetables, and garnish center of bowl with watercress and radish roses. Serves 6.

Tear greens into manageable pieces and arrange around the salad bowl

EGG AND ONION SALAD BOWL

1 head lettuce
Lemon French Dressing
4 medium onions
8 hard-cooked eggs
⅓ cup grated sharp cheese
1 tablespoon minced parsley

Shred lettuce and toss with dressing. Arrange alternate layers of sliced onions and eggs over lettuce in salad bowl. Moisten with additional dressing, sprinkle with cheese and garnish with parsley. Serves 6.

GREEN BEAN SALAD BOWL

3 cups cooked green beans
1 small onion, minced
⅓ cup French Dressing
1 canned pimiento, cut into fine strips
Lettuce leaves

Combine beans and onion with French dressing. Chill for 1 hour. Drain; add pimiento and toss in salad bowl. Garnish with lettuce. Serves 6.
Use ½ cup sliced radishes instead of pimiento.
Use 1 tablespoon chopped chives instead of onion.

Score unpared cucumbers with a fork to produce green scalloped slices and cut radishes almost through to form fans

CHICORY SALAD BOWL

Lettuce hearts
Small crust French Bread rubbed with garlic
1 head chicory
2 tablespoons chopped chervil
2 tablespoons minced tarragon
Olive or salad oil
½ teaspoon salt
Dash pepper
Tarragon vinegar

Line salad bowl with lettuce and add crust of bread. Break chicory into pieces and add with chervil and tarragon. Toss with just enough oil to coat salad greens; chill for 15 minutes. Add salt and pepper to vinegar using ¼ as much vinegar as oil; pour over salad and toss again. Serves 5.
Use Chicken Liver Dressing instead of oil and vinegar as above.
Use Anchovy French Dressing.
Use Roquefort French Dressing
Sprinkle with grated uncooked cauliflower and carrots.

FRENCH POTATO SALAD BOWL

4 to 6 large new potatoes, boiled in their jackets
1 cup chopped celery
½ cup pearl onions
1 tablespoon chopped pimiento
2 tablespoons chopped parsley
1 teaspoon salt, Dash pepper
Caper French Dressing
Lettuce hearts

Peel potatoes and cut into thin slices; add celery, onions, pimiento, parsley and seasonings. Pour on just enough dressing to coat each potato slice; chill. Toss lettuce hearts in bowl with dressing, and heap potato salad on top of lettuce. Serves 6.

GREEN SALAD BOWL WITH COTTAGE CHEESE

½ head lettuce
½ head chicory
½ bunch watercress
¾ cup thinly sliced carrots
Chiffonade French Dressing
1 cup cottage cheese

Shred lettuce, chicory and watercress and combine with carrots in a salad bowl. Toss together with dressing; heap cottage cheese in center. Serves 6.

GREEN SALAD BOWL WITH CLARET DRESSING

FOR DUCK OR GAME DINNER

1 clove garlic, cut into halves
½ head lettuce
½ head escarole
½ head chicory
½ bunch watercress
¾ teaspoon salt
Dash pepper
½ cup olive or salad oil
2 tablespoons lemon juice
2 tablespoons claret

Rub large salad bowl with garlic. Tear salad greens into pieces. Place in bowl, season with salt and pepper, pour olive oil slowly over greens and toss together until coated but not saturated. Pour lemon juice and claret over salad and toss once more. Serves 8 to 10.

Use 4 tablespoons red wine vinegar instead of claret and lemon juice.

Use 4 tablespoons chopped chives instead of garlic.

PICNIC SALAD BOWL

1 No. 2 can asparagus tips
Mustard French Dressing
3 hard-cooked eggs
⅓ cup deviled ham
Hearts of lettuce
2 strips pimiento
6 wedges Swiss cheese

Marinate asparagus in dressing; chill. Cut eggs lengthwise and remove yolks. Stuff with deviled ham mixed with mashed egg yolks and moisten with dressing. Toss lettuce hearts in salad bowl with dressing. Arrange asparagus tips in center (held together with pimiento strips), surround with cheese and border with stuffed egg halves. Serve with potato chips. Serves 6.

Use cooked green beans instead of asparagus tips

SALAD BOWL COMBINATIONS

Avocado, grapefruit, romaine.
Avocado, orange and watercress.
Avocado, peeled white grapes and chicory.
Avocado, tangerine, pecans and lettuce.
Avocado, tart apple and romaine.
Chicory, escarole and grapefruit.
Chicory, shredded cabbage and lettuce.
Escarole, Chinese cabbage and watercress.
Chinese cabbage, tomato, radish and olives.
Endive, carrot sticks and grapefruit.
Shredded carrot, Chinese cabbage and romaine.
Orange, Bermuda onion and romaine.
Potato diced, celery, cucumber, green pepper and pimiento.
Green peas, mint leaves, lettuce.
Dandelion, escarole, pimiento and onion.
Lettuce, fresh spinach, watercress, radishes, carrot sticks.
Cabbage, carrot sticks, diced apples, shredded green pepper.

Ingredients for the salad bowl should be arranged in order with an eye to color and contrast

MIXED VEGETABLE SALAD BOWL

3 tomatoes, cut into wedges
1 cucumber, cut into thin slices
1 green pepper, cut into rings
6 green onions, sliced
6 radishes, sliced
1 head lettuce, shredded
Garlic French Dressing

Prepare and chill vegetables. Toss together with dressing in salad bowl. Serves 6.

STAR SALAD BOWL

1 cup sliced cooked beets
1 cup sliced cooked zucchini
1 cup sliced cooked green beans
1 cup sliced boiled potatoes
1 large head lettuce, shredded
2 hard-cooked eggs, chopped
1 cup French Dressing
1 cup Mayonnaise
2 cans fillets of anchovy
½ cup capers, chopped
6 ripe olives, chopped
2 hard-cooked eggs, sliced

Combine first 6 ingredients in salad bowl, moisten with the French dressing and a little mayonnaise. Cover top of salad with thin layer of mayonnaise; arrange anchovies on top in shape of 5-pointed star and border with capers. Arrange chopped olives in center and garnish with egg slices. Serves 8 to 10.

SUPPER SALAD BOWL

1 clove garlic, cut into halves
1 head lettuce, shredded
1 bunch chicory, shredded
3 tomatoes, quartered
1 cucumber, sliced
6 scallions, sliced
6 radishes, sliced
3 stalks celery, diced
Fines Herbes French Dressing
3 hard-cooked eggs, sliced
6 slices bacon, fried until crisp

Rub salad bowl with cut surface of garlic. Toss lettuce, chicory, tomatoes, cucumber, scallions, radishes and celery together in salad bowl with dressing; garnish with border of egg slices and sprinkle chopped bacon over all. Serves 6 to 8.

TONGUE SALAD

1½ cups diced cold cooked tongue
1 cup cold cooked green beans
Pearl Onion French Dressing
1 head lettuce
Stuffed olives, chopped
2 tomatoes, diced

Marinate tongue and green beans (separately) in dressing for 1 hour. Toss lettuce in salad bowl with dressing, add remaining ingredients and toss lightly again. Serves 6.

ONION SALAD BOWL

1 bunch watercress
4 Bermuda onions, cut into rings
2 cucumbers, pared and cut into eighths
Lemon French Dressing

Chill watercress. Marinate onion rings and cucumbers in French dressing and chill. Toss cress in salad bowl with dressing, and arrange onion rings and cucumbers on top. Serves 4.

Line bowl with lettuce, place cress in center, tomato wedges and cucumbers around it and top with overlapping onion rings.

SHRIMP SALAD WITH PEAS

2 cups fresh cooked shrimp
Mayonnaise, Cream
1 cup diced celery
4 hard-cooked eggs
1 cup cooked peas, lettuce

Clean shrimp. Thin mayonnaise with cream and mix all ingredients together lightly. Season and serve on crisp lettuce. Serves 8.

Overlapping rings of sweet onion form an interesting arrangement with the watercress center

STUFFED CABBAGE SALAD BOWL

1 small head cabbage
1 onion, minced
4 tablespoons chopped parsley
6 stuffed olives, sliced
3 pickled beets, cut into strips
Sour Cream Dressing

Wash cabbage and remove outside leaves. Hollow out, leaving a shell. Shred cabbage removed from center; combine with onion, parsley, olives and beets and add dressing to moisten. Refill cabbage shell, arrange in its own leaves in a salad bowl and garnish top with slices of olives. Serve with additional dressing. Serves 6. Use thin slices of tart apple instead of onion; 4 tablespoons shredded green pepper instead of parsley; and 3 uncooked carrots, grated, instead of beets. Omit olives. Toss together with French Dressing instead of sour cream dressing.

CABBAGE PINEAPPLE—Mix together 2 cups finely shredded cabbage, 1 cup drained diced pineapple, ½ teaspoon salt, 1 cup shredded coconut and 12 marshmallows, quartered. Whip 1 cup cream stiff and fold in cabbage mixture. Arrange in cabbage bowl and serve at once, for 8.

SALAD BOWL OF VEGETABLES JULIENNE

1 small cucumber, pared
1 cup shredded cooked green beans
1 cup shredded cooked carrots
French Dressing, Lettuce
Olive or salad oil

Cut cucumber into long slender strips, add beans and carrots and marinate in dressing. Shred lettuce into large pieces and toss in salad bowl with olive oil. Drain marinated vegetables and arrange in center of bowl. Serves 6.

TOMATO AVOCADO SALAD BOWL

4 tablespoons olive or salad oil
4 tablespoons lemon juice
4 tomatoes, peeled and cut into eighths
1 avocado
½ teaspoon salt
1 clove garlic, cut into halves
½ head lettuce
½ head chicory
½ bunch watercress
Roquefort French Dressing

Pour olive oil and 2 tablespoons lemon juice over tomatoes; chill. Cut avocado lengthwise into halves, remove stone, pare and cut fruit into crescents. Sprinkle with remaining lemon juice and salt. Rub salad bowl with garlic; shred salad greens and toss together in bowl with tomatoes, avocado and dressing. Serves 6 to 8.
Alternate tomato and avocado crescents in overlapping border around edge of salad bowl.
Cut tomatoes into thin slices and avocado into rings. Arrange tomato slices in border around bowl and top each with avocado ring. Dice avocado and tomatoes instead of cutting as above.
Use 2 teaspoons chopped chives instead of garlic.

VEGETABLE AND SMOKED HERRING SALAD BOWL

⅔ cup diced cooked potatoes
⅔ cup diced cooked beets
⅔ cup diced cooked carrots
2 tablespoons minced onion
⅔ cup shredded smoked herring
½ teaspoon salt
Dash allspice
Lettuce hearts
⅓ cup olive or salad oil
Lemon juice

Combine vegetables, herring, salt and allspice in salad bowl lined with lettuce hearts or endive. Pour oil over mixture gradually and toss together; add enough lemon juice to give tartness and toss again. Serves 4.

VEGETABLE SALAD BOWL

1 clove garlic, cut into halves
1 small head lettuce, shredded
2 cups shredded uncooked spinach
1 bunch chicory, chopped
1 carrot, shredded
3 tomatoes, diced
6 green onions, sliced
6 radishes, sliced
3 stalks celery, chopped
½ cup Cucumber French Dressing

Large wedges of lettuce and tomato form an effective star pattern

Rub salad bowl with garlic. Add greens, vegetables and dressing and toss together until well mixed. Chill 15 minutes before serving. Serves 8.

WINTER SALAD BOWL

4 cooked cauliflowerets
½ cup cooked beets, cut into strips
½ cup cooked green beans, cut into strips
½ cup cooked carrots, cut into strips
½ cup cooked peas
Lemon French Dressing
1 small head lettuce
3 ounces Swiss cheese

Marinate each of the vegetables separately in French dressing; chill for 1 hour. Drain vegetables and save dressing. Shred lettuce into salad bowl and toss with enough dressing to coat the leaves. In center of bowl arrange the cauliflowerets; around these arrange remaining vegetables in groups. Sprinkle with grated Swiss cheese. Serves 6.

ARTICHOKE RING

2 cups artichoke pulp
1 tablespoon unflavored gelatin
¼ cup cold water
1 teaspoon salt
½ cup French Dressing
½ cup chili sauce
½ cup Mayonnaise
½ cup whipped cream
¼ teaspoon paprika
5 hard-cooked eggs, chopped fine
½ cup stuffed olives, cut fine

Prepare artichokes by cooking in boiling salted water until tender, 30 to 40 minutes. When cooked, drain well. Remove leaves and scrape off the tender part of each. Chop the hearts and combine with other pulp. Soften gelatin in cold water for 5 minutes and then dissolve over hot water. Add salt, French dressing, chili sauce, mayonnaise, whipped cream and paprika to gelatin. Stir in artichoke pulp, eggs and olives. Pour into a ring mold and chill until firm. Unmold on crisp, cold salad greens and fill center with Crab Meat, Shrimp, Salmon or Lobster Salad. Serves 8.

The whole leaves make a charming container for cabbage salad

CABBAGE SALAD

1 small head cabbage, shredded
   fine
1 pimiento, chopped
1 green pepper, chopped
½ teaspoon salt
Dash pepper
Cooked Dressing to moisten
Combine ingredients, chill for 2 hours. Serves 6 to 8.

Use 3 small chopped tomatoes instead of pimiento and green pepper; use Mustard French Dressing instead of cooked dressing.

Use 2 chopped tomatoes instead of pimiento; marinate cabbage, tomatoes and green pepper in French Dressing and chill. Drain; mix with Mayonnaise; pack in small molds and chill again. Unmold; serve on romaine or lettuce.

CALIFORNIA COLESLAW

1 pound cabbage
¾ cup French dressing

Shred cabbage fine and mix with dressing. Serves 5.

CELERY CABBAGE SALAD—Use celery cabbage.

COLESLAW—Use cooked dressing instead of French.

CHAYOTE, CARROT AND AVOCADO SALAD

1½ cups diced carrots
1½ cups diced chayote
French Dressing
Lettuce
1½ cups diced avocado

Cook carrots and chayote separately in boiling salted water until tender. Drain, add a little French dressing and chill. Cover salad plate with shredded lettuce; pile chayote in center, surround with a ring of carrots and a ring of avocado. Serve with French dressing or Mayonnaise. Serves 6.

CUCUMBER BOATS

3 large cucumbers
½ cup French Dressing
Watercress

Pare cucumbers and cut lengthwise into halves. Hollow out, sprinkle with dressing and chill ½ hour. Fill center with any of the following; garnish with watercress.
Shrimp, Crab Meat or Lobster Salad.
Fish Salad, Chicken Salad.
Frozen Tomato Mayonnaise.

CUCUMBER COTTAGE CHEESE SALAD

2 cups cottage cheese
½ cup sour cream
¼ cup chopped chives
½ cucumber, diced
1 tablespoon chopped watercress
Salt and pepper
Crisp lettuce

Mix cottage cheese and sour cream lightly with a fork. Add vegetables, season with a few grains of salt and pepper and shape into mounds. Place on lettuce leaves, garnish with watercress and serve cold. Serves 4.

DUTCH SLAW

2 pounds cabbage
Boiling water
1 egg
1 tablespoon sugar
1 teaspoon salt
Dash pepper
¼ cup vinegar

Shred cabbage fine, add water to cover and cook until tender. Beat egg, add sugar, salt, pepper and vinegar and pour over drained cooked cabbage. Heat for 5 minutes. Serves 6.

Add ½ teaspoon caraway seeds and ½ cup diced cooked ham or frankfurters.

CREAMY LETTUCE SALAD

4 slices bacon, diced
1 tablespoon flour
1 cup sour cream
2 tablespoons sugar
1 teaspoon salt
2 tablespoons vinegar
Lettuce

Fry bacon until crisp; stir in flour and blend. Add cream and cook, stirring constantly, until mixture begins to thicken. Add sugar, salt and vinegar. Separate lettuce leaves and wash thoroughly. Dry well, cover with hot sauce and mix. Serves 4.

HOT GREEN BEAN AND BACON SALAD

2 pounds fresh green beans
3 slices uncooked bacon, diced
1 onion, minced
½ cup vinegar
Dash pepper

Wash and string beans; cut into diagonal strips and cook in salted water until tender. Drain and keep hot. Fry bacon until crisp; add onion, stir for a minute and add vinegar, letting it boil up once. Pour over the beans, add pepper and serve hot. Serves 6.

Red tomatoes filled with a mixed vegetable salad appeal to both eye and appetite

HARVEST SALAD

1 cup cooked peas
1 cup cooked green beans
1 cup cooked sliced carrots
1 cup uncooked cauliflowerets
1 cup diced celery
French Dressing
6 large tomatoes
½ teaspoon salt
1 head lettuce
Mayonnaise
Parsley

Combine first 5 vegetables with French dressing; chill. Peel tomatoes, sprinkle with salt, invert and chill. Drain tomatoes and cut each into 5 sections, leaving whole at stem end. Place each on lettuce cup, fill with vegetables, and top each with mayonnaise and parsley. Serves 6.

HOT CABBAGE SALAD

¾ cup vinegar
2 tablespoons butter
½ teaspoon salt
3 cups crisp shredded cabbage

Cook vinegar, butter and salt together for a few minutes. Cool and mix with cabbage. Serves 4 to 6.

Add 1 small onion, minced.

HOT CHICORY BOWL

1 head chicory, torn into pieces
2 tablespoons chopped chives or minced green onion tops
½ teaspoon salt, Pepper
4 slices bacon, diced
¼ cup cider vinegar
3 hard-cooked eggs

Combine chicory, chives, salt and pepper in salad bowl. Fry bacon until crisp; add vinegar, let boil up once and pour over salad immediately. Toss quickly, stirring in chopped or sliced eggs at same time. Serves 4.

Use tarragon vinegar instead of cider vinegar.

Use uncooked spinach or half spinach and half chicory.

GREEN LIMA BEAN SALAD

⅔ cup cooked green Lima beans
1 tablespoon chopped sweet pickles
¼ cup French dressing
2 leaves lettuce
1 tomato, peeled and sliced
1 hard-cooked egg, sliced
4 strips pimiento
Mayonnaise

Mix beans with sweet pickles and French dressing. Place on lettuce leaves and add to each a half-circle of overlapping slices of tomato. Garnish with egg and pimiento and serve with mayonnaise.

LETTUCE SALAD WITH ROQUEFORT DRESSING

1 head lettuce
1 tablespoon chopped chives
1 tablespoon chopped parsley
Roquefort French Dressing

Remove outside leaves and core from lettuce; wash and drain. Cut lengthwise into quarters; arrange each on a salad plate; sprinkle with chives and parsley, and serve with dressing. Serves 4. Instead of Roquefort French Dressing use:
Avocado Dressing.
Cottage Cheese Dressing.
Frozen Tomato Mayonnaise.

MACEDOINE LUNCHEON SALAD

½ cup diced cooked carrots
½ cup diced cooked beets
½ cup cooked peas
Lettuce hearts
½ head cauliflower (uncooked) broken into cauliflowerets
1 cup Roquefort Mayonnaise

Arrange carrots, beets and peas in groups on lettuce on salad plates; arrange cauliflowerets in center of each and serve with mayonnaise. Serves 6.

KIDNEY BEAN SALAD

3 cups canned kidney beans
1 cup chopped sweet pickle
5 hard-cooked eggs, sliced
¾ cup diced celery
1 cup Mayonnaise, Lettuce

Drain beans; add pickle, eggs, and celery and toss together lightly. Add mayonnaise and blend. Chill thoroughly. Serve on shredded lettuce, garnish with egg wedges. Serves 8.

LIMA BEAN SALAD

3 cups cooked Lima beans
½ cup finely chopped sweet pickle
½ cup finely cut celery
½ cup chopped stuffed olives
¾ cup Mayonnaise
½ teaspoon salt

Toss all ingredients together lightly. Chill for at least an hour before serving. Serve on chicory or romaine with additional dressing. Serves 8.
Drain and mix with other ingredients using Horse-radish Cream Dressing for Mayonnaise.

Try a kidney bean salad for a rare combination of flavor, nourishment and economy

MEXICAN SLAW WITH ROQUEFORT CHEESE

1 small head cabbage, shredded
1 green pepper, chopped
1 pimiento, chopped
½ teaspoon salt
Dash cayenne
¾ cup Roquefort French Dressing

Combine all ingredients and chill for ½ hour. Serves 8.

Use 3 small diced tomatoes instead of pimiento and green pepper; increase Roquefort dressing to 1 cup, or use 1 cup French Dressing.

Omit green pepper, pimiento and Roquefort dressing. Mix shredded cabbage with plain French dressing in amounts given above; add 3 tablespoons chili sauce and 2 tablespoons chopped watercress. Chill.

MIXED GREENS AND GRAPEFRUIT SALAD BOWL

2 cups shredded lettuce
2 cups shredded chicory
1½ cups diced grapefruit
½ cup Cottage Cheese French Dressing

Toss all ingredients together in salad bowl with dressing. Serve from bowl. Serves 6.

PEANUT AND CARROT SALAD

2 cups grated carrots
1 cup ground peanuts
1 tablespoon grated onion
½ teaspoon salt
½ cup Mayonnaise
Lettuce or chicory
1 tomato cut into thin wedges

Combine carrots, peanuts, onion, salt and mayonnaise. Mix lightly and serve on crisp lettuce. Garnish with tomato wedges. Serves 6.

POTATO SALADS

Potato salads may be served as the main dish for luncheon or supper. Many of the recipes included in this group are whole meals in themselves. The salads fall into two classes, the warm and the cold type. Be sure to have all the ingredients which make up the salad at the same temperature. Bits of leftover vegetables and meats may be added to potatoes to make a delicious meal. Mix ingredients lightly and add only enough dressing to flavor the salad but not make it "runny." Prepare the salad several hours before serving, so the flavor can penetrate through all the ingredients.

CREAMY MASHED POTATO SALAD

6 potatoes
3 hard-cooked eggs, coarsely
   chopped
½ green pepper, minced
1 teaspoon minced onion
1 teaspoon sugar
1 teaspoon salt
1 teaspoon prepared mustard
2½ tablespoons vinegar
1 egg, well beaten
2 tablespoons cream

Boil potatoes in jackets until soft. Peel and mash. Mix while hot with eggs, pepper and onion. Prepare dressing by cooking together in double boiler, sugar, salt, mustard, vinegar and beaten egg. When thick, add cream and blend thoroughly with the potato and egg mixture. Chill and serve on lettuce leaves. Serves 4 to 6.

Add 2 pimientos, chopped, with pepper and onion.

"Hot dogs" and potato salad are as good for luncheon or supper as for picnics

BUFFET POTATO SALAD

2 cups cubed cold cooked potatoes
4 hard-cooked eggs, diced
1 cup cold cooked peas
2 small onions, diced
1 green pepper, diced
½ teaspoon salt
1 cup Mayonnaise

Combine potatoes, eggs, peas, onions, green pepper and salt. Mix with mayonnaise. Chill thoroughly and serve on lettuce. Garnish with Deviled Egg and tomato. Top with mayonnaise. Serves 4 to 6.

CREOLE POTATO SALAD

3 cups diced cooked potatoes
   (warm)
2 tablespoons grated onion
1 tablespoon minced green pepper
¾ cup finely diced celery
1 hard-cooked egg
1 tablespoon chowchow
5 tablespoons oil
2 tablespoons vinegar
1 teaspoon salt
¼ teaspoon pepper
Lettuce

Combine ingredients in the order given. Chill and serve with a garnish of lettuce. Serves 6.

POTATO SALAD

2 cups diced cooked potatoes
1 large onion, chopped fine
2 hard-cooked eggs, diced
2 tablespoons water
¼ teaspoon salt
Dash pepper
2 tablespoons butter
2 tablespoons vinegar
½ cup minced parsley

Mix potatoes, onion and eggs together lightly. Heat water, salt, pepper and butter until butter is melted; add vinegar. Pour over potato mixture; mix thoroughly, then chill. Sprinkle parsley over the top. Serves 4.

GARDEN POTATO SALAD

3 cups cold cubed cooked potatoes
½ teaspoon salt
¾ cup chopped celery
½ cup cubed cucumbers
½ tablespoon chopped onion
1 tablespoon chopped parsley
12 radishes, sliced
Mayonnaise

Combine ingredients in the order listed using enough mayonnaise to moisten (about 1 cup). Chill. Serve in nests of lettuce leaves. Garnish with Radish Roses, parsley and hard-cooked egg. For 6.

POTATO ASPIC SALAD

2 packages aspic gelatin
4 cups tomato juice
2 cups Potato Salad

Dissolve aspic gelatin in 2 cups boiling tomato juice, add remaining juice. Pour half of gelatin mixture into an oiled mold. When partially set, add a layer of potato salad and pour remaining aspic on top. Chill until firm. Unmold. Serves 8.

Mold aspic in 2 layers. When firm place potato salad between.

POTATO CUPS FOR SALAD

6 medium potatoes
½ cup French dressing

Wash potatoes and boil with jackets on until just tender. Cool and peel. Cut a slice from the bottom so that potato will stand and carefully scoop out inside to make a shell. Pour French dressing over potatoes and let them stand 2 hours. Drain and fill with vegetable, meat or fish salad. Serves 6.

RUSSIAN POTATO SALAD

4 large new potatoes
1 medium onion, grated
½ teaspoon celery seed
1 teaspoon salt
2 teaspoons sugar
¼ teaspoon pepper
½ cup Russian Dressing
½ cup mayonnaise
1 tablespoon vinegar
3 bunches radishes, diced
1½ cups diced celery

Boil potatoes in jackets, peel, cut into cubes; while still warm add seasonings, Russian dressing and mayonnaise mixed with vinegar. Chill. Shortly before serving add diced radishes and celery, toss together, adding more dressing if necessary and serve in a lettuce-lined bowl. Serves 8.

SALAD LOAF

Place a layer of potato salad in a glass dish, cover with layer of meat salad. Alternate until dish is full, pressing into firm layers. Chill and unmold on platter. Decorate with mayonnaise dressing and pimiento and serve in slices on lettuce.

SWEET-SOUR POTATO SALAD

8 potatoes
1 stalk celery, diced
2 hard-cooked eggs, sliced
1 onion, minced
3 sweet-sour pickles, diced
1 tablespoon minced parsley
4 slices bacon, diced
2 eggs, well beaten
1 cup sugar
¼ teaspoon dry mustard
½ teaspoon salt
¼ teaspoon pepper
½ cup vinegar, diluted with ½ cup cold water

Boil potatoes in their jackets. When tender, peel and dice. Add celery, hard-cooked eggs, onion, pickle and parsley. Fry bacon until crisp and brown. Beat eggs, add sugar, spices and diluted vinegar. Mix well. Pour egg mixture into the hot bacon fat and cook, stirring constantly, until thickened (about 10 minutes). Pour over potato mixture and mix lightly. Serves 6.

Red layers of tomato aspic with potato salad between will tempt the most wilted summer appetite

BOLOGNA CUPS WITH HOT POTATO SALAD

6 thin slices large Bologna
2 cups sliced cold cooked potatoes
1 hard-cooked egg
2 sweet pickles
2 tablespoons vinegar
1 tablespoon chopped onion
Mayonnaise to moisten

Leave casing on Bologna, place in frying pan, heat gradually until edges curl up to form a perfect cup. Fill with hot potato salad made by mixing potatoes, sliced egg, pickles, vinegar, onion and mayonnaise and heating slowly in top of a double boiler. Add more salt if desired. Place filled Bologna cups on a platter and garnish with parsley. Serves 6.

Serve in pepper cases instead of in bologna cups.

Use hot potato salad as stuffing for Crown Roast of Lamb, Pork or Frankfurters.

Hot potato salad, attractively served and garnished is equally tempting in summer or winter

DUTCH POTATO SALAD

4 slices bacon; 1 onion, diced
Fat; ¼ cup vinegar
2 tablespoons water
3 tablespoons sugar
1 teaspoon salt
⅛ teaspoon pepper
3 cups diced cooked potatoes
1 tablespoon minced parsley

Cut bacon fine and fry. Brown onion in fat, add vinegar, water, sugar, salt and pepper. Heat to boiling, then add potatoes and parsley. Heat thoroughly and serve. Serves 4.

SOUR CREAM POTATO SALAD

4 cups sliced cooked potatoes
½ cup diced cucumber
1 onion, minced
¾ teaspoon celery seed
1½ teaspoons salt
½ teaspoon pepper
3 hard-cooked eggs
1½ cups sour cream
½ cup mayonnaise
¼ cup vinegar
1 teaspoon prepared mustard

Combine potatoes, cucumber, onion, celery seed, salt and pepper. Blend carefully. Cut egg whites into small pieces and add to potatoes. Mash yolks and combine with sour cream, mayonnaise, vinegar and mustard. Blend. Heat sour cream mixture slightly and pour over potatoes. Serves 8 to 10.

HOT POTATO SALAD

6 medium potatoes
2 hard-cooked eggs, chopped
4 slices bacon, diced
¼ cup minced onion
1 egg, beaten
4 tablespoons vinegar
1¾ teaspoons salt

Cook potatoes with skins on, drain, peel and slice while hot and add chopped eggs. Fry bacon and onion until brown. Strain, reserving bacon fat. Add onion and bacon to potato mixture. Add bacon fat slowly to beaten egg, beating well. Add vinegar and salt and pour over potatoes. Mix well and heat in double boiler. Serve hot, garnished with lettuce or watercress. Serves 6.

STUFFED ARTICHOKE SALAD

6 globe artichokes
2 cups dry bread crumbs
4 tablespoons grated Parmesan
   cheese
1 clove garlic, minced
1 tablespoon minced parsley
⅓ cup olive oil
Lettuce or chicory
Lemon French Dressing

Boil artichokes 15 minutes. Combine next 5 ingredients and fill petals with the paste. Place in uncovered baking pan, add salted water to a depth of 1 inch and bake in a hot oven (425°F.) for ½ hour. Serve hot on shredded lettuce or chicory with dressing in individual cups. Serves 6.

SLICED TOMATO SALADS

Arrange thick slice of peeled ripe tomato on watercress or shredded lettuce. Border with alternate overlapping slices of cucumbers and radishes. Sprinkle tomato with chopped green onion tops or chopped chives. Serve with French Dressing.
Arrange thick slice of peeled tomato on lettuce or chicory. Press an uncooked caulifloweret into center of tomato and border with marinated cooked green beans, cut into narrow strips. Serve with Roquefort French Dressing.
Use cooked green peas instead of beans in above recipe.
Arrange thick slice of peeled ripe tomato on romaine or escarole. Press a floweret of steamed broccoli into center of tomato and border with chopped hard-cooked eggs. Serve with French Dressing.
Arrange thick slice of peeled tomato on watercress. Cut pineapple into fine strips, combine with chopped green and red peppers and sprinkle over tomato. Serve with Pineapple French Dressing.
Arrange thick slice of peeled ripe tomato on lettuce. Sprinkle with mixture of chopped watercress, parsley and tarragon. Serve with Tarragon French Dressing.
Arrange thick slice of peeled ripe tomato on watercress. Moisten with White Wine Dressing and sprinkle with grated Roquefort or Parmesan cheese.

TOMATO ROSE SALAD

8 firm tomatoes
12 ounces cream cheese
2 hard-cooked egg yolks
Watercress
French Dressing

Peel tomatoes and chill. Soften cheese with milk. Form 2 rows of petals on each tomato by pressing level teaspoons of softened cheese against the side of tomato, then drawing the spoon down, with a curving motion. Sprinkle center of each tomato with hard-cooked egg yolk pressed through a sieve. Serve on crisp watercress with French dressing. Serves 8.

A tomato rose with its creamy petals and golden heart is as easy to make as it is to eat

STUFFED TOMATO SALADS

Remove skins from tomatoes, scoop out hollow at stem end of each, add ¼ teaspoon salt, invert and chill. Drain. Serve on lettuce, watercress or other salad greens; stuff with any of the following fillings:

Cottage or cream cheese, chopped cucumbers and chopped chives.
Mexican Slaw.
Cabbage salad.
Chicken salad.
Sea food salad; shrimp, lobster or crab meat.
Mixed vegetable salad.
Cubes of Jellied Ginger Ale Cottage Cheese Mayonnaise.
Baked Bean Salad or Kidney Bean Salad.
Potato salad.
Egg salad.
Fish salad: tuna, salmon, or smoked fish.
Meat aspics, cubed.

VEGETABLE SALAD COMBINATIONS

Cooked Vegetables with French Dressing or Mayonnaise

Sliced beets, chopped hard-cooked eggs, grated horse-radish.
Sliced beets in border around marinated green beans.
Green pepper rings filled with cabbage slaw.
Diced asparagus, chopped tomatoes and pearl onions.
Asparagus tips, cauliflowerets, diced carrots.
Peas, chopped celery and cucumbers.

Uncooked Vegetables with French Dressing

Grated carrots, chopped celery and chopped green pepper.
Grated carrots and chopped raisins.
Grated cabbage and carrots.
Cucumber slices topped with radish slices.
Grated cucumber and cabbage, chopped peanuts.
Tomato sections, cucumber slices, green pepper rings, chopped onions and anchovies.

Arrange salad vegetables in groups sometimes instead of mixing them

WILTED LETTUCE BOWL

1 large head lettuce
½ cup minced green onion
½ teaspoon salt
Dash pepper
4 slices bacon, diced
¼ cup vinegar

Shred lettuce coarsely into salad bowl, add onion, salt and pepper. Fry bacon crisp and drain on absorbent paper. Add vinegar to bacon fat and heat to boiling. Pour over lettuce, tossing salad well. Sprinkle top with crisp bacon. Serves 4.
Use dandelion greens or beet greens instead of lettuce.

APPETIZER SALAD

1½ cups thin slices carrots
1 small cucumber
Watercress
1 hard-cooked egg, sliced
Pearl Onion French Dressing

Place carrot slices in ice water for 1 hour until crisp. Score the pared cucumber lengthwise with a fork, cut into thin slices and chill. Arrange carrot and cucumber slices on watercress, place a ring of egg white in center of each salad and sprinkle with sieved yolk. Serve with dressing. Serves 6.

TOMATO CAULIFLOWER SALAD

3 tomatoes, peeled and chilled
½ head cauliflower, Watercress
Roquefort French Dressing

Cut each tomato crosswise into halves. Soak cauliflower in cold salted water for 45 minutes. Separate into small flowerets. Arrange 1 tomato half on watercress on each plate; top with cauliflowerets and serve with dressing. Serves 6.

VEGETABLE SALAD

½ cup chopped ripe olives
½ cup cubed cooked carrots
1 cup diced celery
1 cup cooked peas
1 small mild onion, grated
French Dressing
Salt and pepper
Mayonnaise

Chill first 5 ingredients and toss together lightly, adding enough French dressing to coat them thoroughly. Chill ½ hour, season to taste with salt and pepper and serve in lettuce cups. Garnish with mayonnaise. Serves 6.

VEGETABLE LUNCHEON SALAD

½ head cauliflower, uncooked
½ cup diced cooked beets
½ cup cooked peas
½ cup diced cooked carrots
French Dressing
1 head lettuce
Cottage Cheese Mayonnaise

Soak cauliflower in cold salted water for 45 minutes. Marinate cooked vegetables separately in French dressing. Drain cauliflower; divide into flowerets and arrange on lettuce in center of each salad plate. Arrange beets, peas and carrots in groups around cauliflower. Serve with mayonnaise. Serves 6.

BLACK CHERRY SALAD

2 cups cherry juice and water
1 package cherry gelatin
2 cups cooked black cherries, drained
1 cup chopped blanched almonds
8 stuffed olives, chopped
Lettuce

Heat cherry juice and water, add gelatin, and stir until dissolved. Chill until it begins to thicken, add remaining ingredients, except lettuce, pour into a mold, and chill until firm. Unmold and serve in lettuce cups with salad dressing. Serves 8.

CHICKEN ORANGE SALAD

3 tablespoons unflavored gelatin
1/2 cup cold orange juice
2 cups hot orange juice
Orange sections
2 tablespoons cold water
3/4 cup boiling chicken stock
1 teaspoon salt
1/2 teaspoon white pepper
1 pimiento, chopped
1/4 teaspoon onion juice
3 cups diced cooked chicken
3/4 cup heavy cream, whipped
Lettuce, Mayonnaise

Soften 1 1/2 tablespoons gelatin in cold orange juice for 5 minutes; dissolve in hot orange juice and strain. Cool. Decorate a large mold, ring mold or individual molds, with orange sections and cover with half of the slightly thickened gelatin. Chill until firm. Soften remaining gelatin in cold water for 5 minutes, dissolve in boiling chicken stock and cool until it begins to thicken. Add salt, pepper, pimiento, onion juice and chicken. Fold in whipped cream and pour over orange gelatin. Chill; when firm, add remaining orange gelatin. Chill. Unmold on lettuce and serve with mayonnaise. Serves 12.

CRANBERRY RING SALAD

2 cups cranberries
1 1/2 cups cold water
1 cup sugar
1 tablespoon unflavored gelatin
1/2 cup chopped nuts
3/4 cup diced celery
Lettuce
Mayonnaise

Wash cranberries, add 1 cup cold water. Cook until tender. Add sugar and cook for 5 minutes. Soften gelatin in 1/2 cup cold water, dissolve in hot cranberries. Chill until mixture begins to thicken. Add nuts and celery. Mix thoroughly. Pour into oiled ring mold. Chill until firm. Unmold and place on large salad plate. Place light lettuce around salad, arrange shrimp in center or serve on a bed of chicory on individual plates and garnish with mayonnaise. Serves 8.

CRANBERRY ORANGE MOLDS

2 cups uncooked cranberries
2 small oranges
1 cup sugar
1 package lemon gelatin
1 cup boiling water
Lettuce
Whipped Cream Mayonnaise

Wash cranberries; dry, and peel oranges. Put cranberries and 1 orange peel through food chopper; dice orange pulp and add with the sugar. Dissolve gelatin in boiling water and cool. Combine with cranberry orange mixture, pour into oiled molds and chill until firm. Unmold on lettuce and serve with mayonnaise. Makes 6 large servings.

The brilliant color of cranberry ring filled with shrimp and garnished with pineapple slices and cream cheese makes a real picture

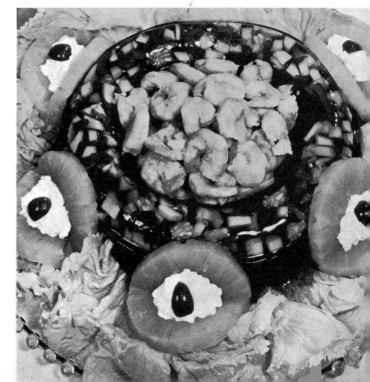

CHICORY CROWN SALAD

3 (3 ounce) packages cream cheese
½ teaspoon salt
2 cups drained grated cucumber
1 cup Mayonnaise
¼ cup minced onion
¼ cup minced parsley
1 cut clove garlic
1 tablespoon unflavored gelatin
¼ cup cold water
1 head chicory
2 hard-cooked egg yolks, sieved

Mix first 6 ingredients in a bowl that has been rubbed with garlic. Soften gelatin in cold water and dissolve over hot water. Cool to lukewarm and combine with cheese mixture. Beat thoroughly and pack into a deep spring-form pan. Select chicory sprays of even height with perfect leaves. Stick whole sprays into the edge of the mixture close enough together to form a complete crown of green. Chill until mixture is firm. Remove from mold onto a bed of chicory and sprinkle sieved egg yolks over top. Garnish with Radish Roses. Serves 8.

This molded chicory crown will add new laurels to your reputation as a hostess

CHICKEN IN ASPIC

5-pound stewing chicken
1 carrot, 1 bay leaf
1 tablespoon salt
4 tablespoons unflavored gelatin
½ cup cold water
6 cups chicken stock
½ tablespoon brandy
2 cups strained canned peas

Clean chicken thoroughly. Cover with boiling water, add carrot, bay leaf and salt. Cook until tender, 2 to 3 hours, depending on the age of chicken. Remove chicken, strain broth, and measure 6 cups. Soften gelatin in cold water 5 minutes, add to hot broth and stir until dissolved. Cool and add brandy. Free chicken from skin and bones and cut into slices. Pour a thin layer of aspic in the bottom of a ring mold or in individual molds. When firm arrange chicken slices and peas in layers on aspic. Fill mold with remaining aspic. Chill until firm. Unmold and fill center with mayonnaise. Serves 12 to 14.

Omit brandy. Chop 4 hard-cooked eggs and use as layer in mold, having a layer of chicken and peas below and above eggs.

CHICKEN AND OLIVE LOAF

2 tablespoons unflavored gelatin
½ cup cold water
3 cups chicken stock
½ teaspoon salt
1 tablespoon lemon juice
⅓ cup sliced stuffed olives
⅓ cup shredded almonds
1 cup diced celery
2 cups diced cooked chicken

Soften gelatin in cold water 5 minutes and dissolve in hot stock. Add salt and lemon juice. Chill until it begins to thicken. Fold in olives, almonds, celery and chicken. Turn into loaf pan and chill until firm. Unmold, for 6.

HAM ASPIC SALAD

1½ tablespoons unflavored gelatin
½ cup cold water
3 cups tomato juice, Dash salt
1 teaspoon sugar, ½ bay leaf
1 tablespoon chopped onion
3 cups minced Baked Ham

Soften gelatin in cold water for 5 minutes. Heat tomato juice, add salt, sugar, bay leaf and onion and simmer 10 minutes. Strain, add gelatin, stir and cool. Add ham, mold and chill. When firm unmold. Serves 6 to 8.

JELLIED SALMON MOLD

1 cucumber
Small bottle stuffed olives
1 package aspic gelatin
1 cup boiling water
⅓ cup lemon juice
½ cup cold water
½ teaspoon salt
¾ cup Mayonnaise
1½ cups cooked red salmon
1 cup diced celery
¼ cup diced green pepper
½ tablespoon minced onion

Pare cucumber, scoop out center, and fill with olives. Dissolve aspic in boiling water. Add lemon juice, cold water and salt. Chill until it begins to thicken. Beat in mayonnaise gradually. Pour layer of aspic mixture into oiled loaf pan or mold. When firm arrange a layer of salmon, celery, green pepper and onion, and place stuffed cucumber in center. Cover with another layer of the aspic mixture, a layer of salmon, celery, green pepper and onion, repeating until cucumber is covered. Chill until firm. Serve on crisp lettuce. Garnish with parsley, lemon sections, cucumber slices and Radish Roses. For 8.

JELLIED SHRIMP SALAD

1 tablespoon unflavored gelatin
¼ cup cold water
1½ cups tomato juice
2 tablespoons vinegar
2 tablespoons lemon juice
Dash salt
1 cup shrimp, halved lengthwise
½ cup diced celery
1 bunch watercress
Cucumber Dressing

Soften gelatin in cold water and dissolve over hot water. Add tomato juice, vinegar, lemon juice and salt and chill; when beginning to thicken add shrimp and celery. Pour into oiled ring mold, chill; unmold and serve on watercress. Fill center with dressing. Serves 8.

Use ½ cup cooked peas instead of diced celery.
Pour mixture into green pepper cups instead of ring mold.
Serve dressing in center of ring mold on lettuce cups.
Dice shrimp and use individual molds.
Mold in Cucumber Boats.
Use cucumber instead of celery and Anchovy Mayonnaise instead of Cucumber Dressing.

SPARKLING FRUIT MOLD

1 package lime gelatin
2 cups boiling water
1 orange
1 cup canned pineapple cubes
1 cup sliced peaches
Chicory or Lettuce
2 small clusters grapes

Dissolve gelatin in boiling water and chill until it begins to set. Pare orange, leaving none of the white-skin. Cube. Add orange and drained pineapple and peaches to gelatin, reserving a few peach slices for garnishing. Pour into a mold and chill until firm. Unmold on bed of chicory and garnish with peach slices and grapes. Serves 8.

Use only 1 cup boiling water, cool mixture and add 1 cup ginger ale. Use lemon or orange gelatin.

Use sliced apricots and seedless grapes instead of orange and peaches.

A shimmering mold of jellied fruit salad will tempt the most languid summer appetite

Mold jellied salads in perky shapes for individual service instead of using large molds. When arranged on a bed of chicory with mayonnaise piled in the center, they'll keep the family coming back for more

A mirror tray is an ideal background to enhance the transparent delicacy of individual molded salads. A garnish of fresh green leaves and ripe whole berries adds the final touch of beauty

MOLDED CUCUMBER SALAD

1 cucumber, pared and diced
½ teaspoon salt
½ sweet pimiento, diced
½ teaspoon lemon juice
2 teaspoons unflavored gelatin
¼ cup cold water
1 cup cream, whipped

Combine cucumber, salt, pimiento and lemon juice. Soak gelatin in cold water 5 minutes; dissolve over hot water and mix thorough-

ly with whipped cream. Add cucumber mixture and pour into molds. Chill. Serves 4.

INDIVIDUAL CHICKEN SALAD IN ASPIC

6 slices tomato (½ inch thick)
Salt, Pepper, Vinegar
1 tablespoon unflavored gelatin
¼ cup cold water
1½ cups seasoned chicken stock
3 tablespoons Mayonnaise
2 tablespoons chopped green
    pepper
½ cup slivered blanched almonds
2 tablespoons diced celery
1⅓ cups chopped cooked chicken

Marinate tomatoes in seasoned vinegar. Chill. Soften gelatin in cold water for 5 minutes. Heat chicken stock to boiling. Add gelatin and stir until dissolved. Cool. When sirupy in consistency add remaining ingredients and place in individual molds. Chill until firm. Unmold each portion onto a slice of tomato and serve with lettuce hearts and mayonnaise. Serves 6.

TOMATO AND CHEESE CROWN

Red Mold

2 tablespoons unflavored gelatin
½ cup cold water
2 cups canned tomatoes
½ teaspoon salt
1/16 teaspoon pepper
1 bay leaf
1 stalk celery, chopped
1 tablespoon vinegar
1 teaspoon onion juice

Soften gelatin in cold water for 5 minutes. Heat tomatoes, add seasonings, bay leaf and celery and cook 10 minutes. Strain and add gelatin, vinegar and onion juice and stir until gelatin is dissolved. Pour into a fluted mold and chill until firm.

White Mold

1½ tablespoons unflavored gelatin
¼ cup cold water
2 cups cottage cheese, sieved
¾ teaspoon salt
⅛ teaspoon paprika
½ cup rich milk

Soften gelatin in cold water for 5 minutes. Combine cheese, salt, paprika and milk. Add gelatin dissolved over hot water; blend thoroughly. Pour into fluted mold the same size as used for tomato and chill until firm. Unmold tomato and cheese and cut each mold in the same number of wedges. Arrange as 1 mold, alternating red and white. Serves 8.
Garnish with mayonnaise.

MOLDED CHEESE SALAD

1 package lemon gelatin
2 cups boiling water
½ cup heavy cream, whipped
1 cup chopped nuts
1 cup grated American cheese
1 cup canned crushed pineapple
½ cup sliced stuffed olives
Cooked Salad Dressing

Dissolve gelatin in boiling water and chill until it begins to thicken. Whip until fluffy and fold in next 5 ingredients. Pour into a ring mold and chill until firm. Fill center with dressing. Serves 8.

TUNA SALAD IN TOMATO ASPIC RING

2 tablespoons unflavored gelatin
¼ cup cold water
¾ cup vegetable stock
1 cup tomato juice
¼ cup vinegar
1 small onion, chopped
⅛ cup sugar
½ teaspoon salt
1 (7-ounce) can tuna
1 cup chopped celery
Mayonnaise, Lettuce hearts

Soften gelatin in cold water. Combine vegetable stock, tomato juice, vinegar, onion and seasoning; heat to boiling and simmer 3 minutes. Strain, pour over gelatin and stir until gelatin is dissolved. Pour into oiled ring mold and chill until firm. Combine tuna, celery and mayonnaise to moisten. Unmold aspic on lettuce, fill center with tuna salad, and garnish with stuffed and ripe olives. Serves 6.

FRUIT AND COTTAGE CHEESE MOLD

2 teaspoons unflavored gelatin
3 tablespoons canned pineapple juice
2½ cups cottage cheese
Lettuce or other greens
Sliced pineapple
Strawberries
Lemon French Dressing

Soften gelatin in pineapple juice and dissolve over hot water. Stir into cottage cheese, pour into 1 large or 6 individual oiled molds and chill until firm. Unmold on lettuce or other greens and garnish with sliced pineapple and halved strawberries. Serve with the French dressing. Serves 6.

Pour cottage cheese into ring mold and fill center with fruit. Garnish with sliced strawberries.

Mold cheese in ring mold and fill center with orange segments and pitted black cherries. Garnish with sliced pineapple and cube of lime jelly.

Vary the fruit with the season so your family can enjoy this cottage cheese ring the year 'round

CHICKEN SALAD LUNCHEON PLATE

Arrange shredded lettuce on luncheon plate. In center place a mound of Chicken Salad. At equal distances place 3 large peeled grapefruit segments. On 1 side of each grapefruit segment place an avocado crescent (dipped in lemon juice) and on other side a wedge of peeled tomato. Place 3 half-slices pineapple between the 3 tomato-grapefruit-avocado groups. Serve with French Dressing.

Use a sea food salad instead of chicken.

SUMMER SALAD PLATE

Chicory
4 slices pineapple
1 cup raspberries
4 bananas

Place a few pieces of chicory in the center of a plate with a slice of pineapple on one side and a mound of raspberries on the other. Arrange rows of sliced bananas on the other two sides. Serves 4.

Use other berries instead of raspberries.

Use a circle of orange segments instead of pineapple.

Always include a bright colored fruit in your salad plate

CRAB LOUIS

¾ head lettuce, shredded
2 cups flaked crab meat
2 hard-cooked eggs, sliced
2 small tomatoes, sliced
1 small cucumber, sliced
Watercress
Appetizer Mayonnaise

Arrange lettuce on 4 salad plates, with mound of crab meat in center of each. Arrange overlapping slices of egg, tomato and cucumber to form a border and garnish with watercress. Serve with mayonnaise. Serves 4.

COMBINATION FRUIT PLATE

1 ripe banana, sliced
4 thin wedges of red apple
   (unpeeled)
4 half-slices peeled orange
Watercress
5 red raspberries
Cottage Cheese Mayonnaise

Arrange 3 rows of fruit, side by side, on a salad plate, using sliced banana for 2 outside rows. For 1 end of center row overlap the apple wedges, with red skin toward outside. Arrange orange slices at other end of row, overlapping, with curved sides toward outside. Garnish center with watercress and berries. Serve with the mayonnaise. Serves 1.

Instead of orange slices, use sections cut from pared orange.

FAN SALAD WITH COLD MEATS

4 slices Baked Ham
4 slices liverwurst
3 cups Potato Salad
Endive
Watercress

Arrange slices of ham and liverwurst in center of platter. On each slice heap mounds of potato salad, arrange endive in upright semicircle around each mound and garnish with watercress. Serves 4.

FRUIT PLATE

Center plate with lettuce cup filled with grapefruit segments and purple grapes. At back on watercress place mound of avocado balls, between 2 finger sandwiches. At front arrange semicircle of orange slices, with groups of orange segments at each end, topped with walnut cheese bonbons (balls of cream cheese placed between walnut halves). Serve with any desired dressing.

HAWAIIAN FRUIT PLATE

Grape leaves
4 oranges
2 cups pineapple cubes
1 cup melon cubes
4 maraschino cherries
Lime French Dressing

On each salad plate arrange 4 grape or geranium leaves or salad greens. Arrange 6 orange slices in groups of 3 separated by a double row of pineapple cubes. Garnish with melon cubes topped with cherry rings and serve with dressing. Serves 4.

Omit oranges and serve the melon balls on whole rings of pineapple.

LOBSTER SALAD

2 cups lobster meat, fresh boiled
  or canned
1 cup French Dressing
1 cup diced celery
½ teaspoon salt
Dash pepper
½ cup Mayonnaise
Salad greens

Break lobster meat into pieces (not too small). Marinate in French dressing for 1 hour, drain and add celery, salt, pepper and mayonnaise. Mix lightly and serve on salad greens. Garnish with lobster claws, wedges of hard-cooked eggs and capers. Serves 6.

Use Coral Mayonnaise instead of mayonnaise and add 1 tablespoon minced pimiento.

SPANISH BEEF SALAD

6 slices cold Roast Beef
Tomato French Dressing
1 head lettuce, shredded
6 thick slices tomato
6 onion slices
6 green pepper rings

Cut roast beef into long narrow strips. Marinate in dressing for 1 hour Toss in salad bowl with lettuce and additional dressing. Border bowl with alternate slices of tomato, onion and green pepper. Serves 6.

Romaine provides a stately background for the giant asparagus tips, shrimp and egg

ROMAINE AND SHRIMP SALAD

12 stalks cooked asparagus
12 slices hard-cooked egg
12 large cooked shrimp
4 long, 4 short leaves romaine
4 green pepper rings
Mayonnaise

Arrange 3 large stalks asparagus, topped with 3 slices of egg and 3 shrimp on each long romaine leaf. Beside it, on the shorter leaf place a pepper ring filled with mayonnaise. Serves 4.

SALAD LUNCHEON PLATES

Potato salad in green pepper cups; slices of ham, tongue or summer sausage; marinated cucumber slices; yellow plum-tomato.

Eggs stuffed with deviled ham; potato chips; marinated green beans; ripe olives.

Half avocado filled with Frozen Tomato Mayonnaise; slices of cold breast of chicken; marinated asparagus.

Slice of cold baked salmon with Cucumber Dressing; marinated mixed vegetables; hard-cooked egg slices; celery curls.

Sardines with lemon slice; tomato slices topped with cottage cheese and chives; toasted crackers.

Tomato stuffed with sea food salad; marinated cold peas; wedges of hard-cooked eggs.

Marinated jumbo shrimp; individual jellied cucumber mold with Mayonnaise; hearts of celery; Melba toast.

Cucumber Boats with Tuna Salad; potato chips; slices hard-cooked egg on tomato slices.

Round slice of frozen Pear and Cream Cheese Salad on tomato slice; border of overlapping cucumber slices; brown bread finger sandwiches.

Alternate grapefruit segments, avocado slices and persimmon sections; fluted banana slices; oxheart cherries stuffed with cream cheese; nut bread.

Fresh pineapple slice; banana half with red raspberries; tangerine flower stuffed with cottage cheese; toasted crackers.

Cottage cheese; alternate slices of avocado and grapefruit segments; peeled fresh figs; strawberries.

Slice of pared honeydew melon; fresh pineapple spears; cream cheese balls rolled in chopped nuts; border of watermelon and honeydew melon balls.

Split banana sprinkled with lemon juice; orange and grapefruit segments; 3 prunes stuffed with cream cheese; peanut butter finger sandwiches.

Sliced smoked sturgeon or whitefish with White Wine French Dressing; pickled beets and potato salad.

SALAD SUGGESTIONS

1. Orange and grapefruit sections with slices of unpared red apple and walnut meats.

2 Canned pineapple with banana and avocado strips and walnut meats.

3. White and red sweet cherries with orange and grapefruit sections and nut meats.

4. Peach halves with cream cheese and walnut meats.

5. Pear halves, a ring of avocado, cream cheese and chopped nut meats.

6 Diced red apples, celery, broken walnut meats and lemon juice.

7. Fresh pineapple wedges, fresh whole strawberries and walnut halves.

8. Halves of canned pears rolled in macaroon crumbs, garnished with cherries and nut meats.

9. Halves of banana split and spread with peanut butter.

10. Diced unpared red apple, dates, lemon juice and nut meats.

11. Alternate slices of cantaloupe and Japanese persimmons.

12. Honeydew melon and nectarine slices with pomegranate seeds.

13. Alternating slices of avocado and Japanese persimmons, garnished with Malaga grapes filled with cream cheese.

WESTERN TREASURE PLATE

Place a lettuce cup filled with fresh pineapple spears at the back of a luncheon plate. Across the front, arrange an apricot half filled with seedless grapes on one side, 3 peach slices in center, and on the other side a half pear filled with cottage cheese and topped with a walnut meat. Serve with Whipped Cream Dressing.

The artichoke is the queen of the luncheon vegetable plate

ARTICHOKE VEGETABLE PLATE

4 artichokes
1 cup cooked peas
French Dressing
Radishes
Mayonnaise

Cook artichokes until tender; chill. Mix peas with French dressing; chill. Serve artichoke on plate with a mound of peas and a few radishes. Serve a small bowl of mayonnaise with each plate. Serves 4.

MOLDED CHICKEN

1 tablespoon unflavored gelatin
3 tablespoons cold water
¾ cup chicken stock, boiling
¾ cup Mayonnaise
1½ cups diced cooked chicken

Soften gelatin in cold water for 5 minutes and dissolve in chicken stock. Cool until sirupy in consistency, then beat until frothy and light. Fold in mayonnaise and chicken. Add more seasonings, if desired. Pour into ring mold or individual molds and chill until firm. Unmold on crisp cold lettuce, garnish with additional mayonnaise, strips of pimiento and tomato wedges. Serves 6.

TOMATO CHEESE SALAD

1½ cups hot condensed tomato soup
½ cup cream cheese
1 tablespoon butter
¼ teaspoon salt
1 tablespoon onion juice
1 tablespoon unflavored gelatin
¼ cup cold water
½ cup heavy cream or evaporated milk
½ cup Mayonnaise
½ cup stuffed olives, chopped

Heat soup, cheese, butter, salt, and onion juice until cheese has softened. Soften gelatin in cold water and dissolve in hot mixture. Cool until mixture starts to thicken; whip cream and add with mayonnaise and stuffed olives. Turn into mold and chill. When firm, unmold on lettuce and garnish with sliced olives. Serve with mayonnaise sprinkled with paprika. Serves 8.

Use 1 cup grated American cheese, 1 green pepper, chopped, 1 cup diced celery, and 3 tablespoons lemon juice instead of the cream cheese, stuffed olives and cream or evaporated milk.

TOMATO MOLDS—Omit cheese, mayonnaise, cream and olives. Use tomato juice instead of soup. Cool. Fold in 1 cup each chopped celery and sweet pickle relish. Season with celery salt and Worcestershire sauce. Chill.

CHICKEN AND HAM SALAD WITH MUSTARD DRESSING

1½ cups diced cooked chicken
1½ cups diced cooked ham
½ teaspoon minced onion
¼ cup French Dressing
6 tomatoes of uniform size
Salt
1 cup Mayonnaise or salad dressing
2 tablespoons prepared mustard
Lettuce

Combine chicken, ham and onion and marinate for 1 hour in French dressing. Drain. Peel tomatoes; salt, invert and chill. Combine mayonnaise with mustard, add to chicken mixture and toss together lightly until thoroughly mixed. Cut each tomato into sixths, cutting to within ½ inch from bottom. Place on lettuce, fill center with chicken salad, garnish with sprig of parsley and dash of paprika. Serves 6.

Instead of cutting tomatoes into petals, leave them whole and scoop out centers.

Serve the salad on thin slices of tomato arranged in a circle with slices overlapping.

Use slices of egg and slices of tomato for the circle.

CAMBRISSON SALAD

1 cup diced cooked beef
2 hard-cooked eggs, sliced
2 tomatoes, quartered
4 anchovies, diced
1 small head lettuce
French Dressing

Combine beef, eggs, tomatoes, and anchovies. Serve on lettuce with dressing. Serves 6.

CELERY STUFFED WITH SHRIMP

1 cup cooked shrimp
2 cups grapefruit segments, chilled
3 ounces cream cheese
2 tablespoons Mayonnaise
¼ teaspoon salt
6 pieces crisp celery, Lettuce
French Dressing

Clean shrimp; cut into small pieces. Drain grapefruit. Mash cheese, add mayonnaise and salt and cream together. Add shrimp and mix well. Pack grooves of celery with mixture; cut into ¾-inch slices. Arrange on lettuce with grapefruit segments. Sprinkle with French dressing, for 6.

Serve crab-flake salad in crisp finger rolls, cucumber boats or pepper cases

AVOCADO FILLED WITH SALMON

2 avocados
Lemon juice, Salt
1 cup diced celery
1 cup flaked salmon
½ cup Appetizer Mayonnaise

Cut avocados lengthwise into halves, remove seeds and sprinkle cut portion with lemon juice and salt. Combine celery and salmon with mayonnaise to moisten. Fill centers of avocados. Serves 4.

Use 1 cup crab meat, lobster, shrimp or oysters instead of salmon.

CALIFORNIA CHICKEN SALAD

3 tablespoons lemon juice
1 cup diced cooked chicken
½ cup finely diced apple
½ cup chopped ripe olives
½ cup diced celery
2 tablespoons Mayonnaise thinned with
2 tablespoons cream, sweet or sour

Sprinkle lemon juice over chicken and apple, mixing lightly. Combine remaining ingredients, using only enough mayonnaise to moisten. Add chicken and apple and toss together lightly. Serve cold with mayonnaise. Serves 4.

CRAB-FLAKE SALAD

2 cups crab flakes, canned or fresh cooked
2 tablespoons lemon juice
2 teaspoons grated onion
1 cup sliced cucumbers
1 cup Mayonnaise
¼ teaspoon salt
Salad greens

Combine all ingredients. Serve in a bowl garnished with salad greens or in lettuce cups as individual servings. Serves 4.

Omit cucumbers and add 2 tablespoons chopped green pepper.

Use celery instead of cucumbers.

SALAD À LA RUSSE

3 cups finely shredded cabbage
1 cup bright colored vegetables,
    cooked peas, beans, uncooked
    carrot, diced tomato
Well-seasoned French Dressing
Thin slices salami or sausage
Anchovies or sardines
Pimiento strips, Salad dressing

Combine vegetables, marinate in French dressing and chill. Serve from salad bowl or use individual service, garnishing with sliced meat, fish, and pimiento strips. Serve salad dressing separately. Serves 8.

STUFFED CABBAGE HEAD

1 head cabbage
Sour Cream Dressing
16 gherkins
16 cocktail frankfurters

Wash cabbage and remove outside leaves. Cut a slice from top and remove center leaving a shell. Shred cabbage from center, mix thoroughly with cream dressing, and chill. When ready to serve fill center with shredded cabbage. Spear gherkins and sausages on hors d'oeuvres picks and stick picks on outside of cabbage head, alternating gherkins and frankfurters.

TOMATO AND SARDINE SALAD

4 tomatoes
1 small can · sardines
Lettuce
2 small onions, sliced
2 teaspoons lemon juice
Mayonnaise
1 hard-cooked egg yolk

Peel tomatoes and cut into slices ¾ inch thick; chill. Drain oil from sardines, remove skin and backbone. Arrange lettuce on a salad plate, place tomato on it, cover with sardine, onion and a few drops of lemon juice. Garnish with mayonnaise and egg yolk which has been rubbed through a sieve. Serves 8.

Another good idea is to serve canapés with the salad

SUNDAY NIGHT COLD MEAT PLATTER

2 cups cottage cheese
12 split celery stalks, curled
6 tomatoes stuffed with Coleslaw
18 thin half-slices cucumber
6 slices cold cooked chicken
12 slices cold spiced tongue
6 Deviled Egg halves
Watercress

Arrange on large glass chop plate as follows:

In center, pile cottage cheese in a mound. Around this stand celery stalks upright in circle, with curled ends on top. Arrange border of stuffed tomatoes alternating with groups of cucumber half-slices. For outer border arrange 6 groups of 3 meat slices alternating with deviled egg halves. Garnish with watercress. Serves 6.

Use cold baked ham and cold roast beef or lamb instead of chicken and tongue.

Use summer and liver sausage instead of chicken and tongue.

Use slices of cold baked salmon instead of cold meats and tomatoes stuffed with Cucumber Dressing instead of coleslaw.

Use coleslaw instead of cottage cheese in center. Stuff tomatoes with cottage cheese instead of coleslaw.

ANCHOVY BEET SALAD

4 medium beets
French Dressing
3 hard-cooked eggs
Lettuce
8 anchovies, rolled
Mayonnaise

Cut the rounded portion from the ends of beets, then cut beets into halves. Marinate in French dressing an hour or longer if possible. Separate yolks and whites of eggs; chop whites fine and rub yolks through sieve. Place sections of beet on lettuce, form a ring around them with egg white, fill center with egg yolk and place an anchovy on top. Garnish with mayonnaise. Serves 8.

SALMON SALAD

1 No. 2 can salmon
3 eggs, hard-cooked
1 teaspoon salt
¼ teaspoon pepper
½ teaspoon prepared mustard
½ cup vinegar, boiling
3 large cucumber pickles

Remove fat and skin from salmon. Cream yolks of eggs, add salt, pepper, and mustard. Heat vinegar to boiling and pour over egg yolk mixture. Chop egg whites and pickles and mix with salmon. Pour dressing over mixture and chill. Serves 8.

PYRAMID SALAD

30 celery sticks
30 Swiss cheese sticks
30 ham sticks
Lettuce, Watercress
Parsley
18 tomato sections
Mustard French Dressing

Arrange sticks on lettuce pyramid fashion. Garnish with watercress, parsley, and tomato sections. Serve with dressing.
Serves 6.

SHRIMP SALAD

1 pound fresh shrimp, cooked
1 egg, hard-cooked
Lettuce
¾ cup diced celery
½ cup Lemon Mayonnaise
Capers

Cook shrimp 10 minutes and cool.
Drain, shell and chill. Chill egg.
Line a bowl with chilled lettuce
leaves, fill with mixture of shrimp
and celery, cover with mayonnaise
and garnish with capers and egg
wedges or slices. Serves 4.

JEAN LAFITTE SALAD

2 cups diced cooked meat
¾ cup diced cooked potatoes
¾ cup diced cooked carrots
¾ cup cooked string beans
1 cup French Dressing
4 sweet pickles, chopped
2 hard-cooked eggs, chopped
1 cup Mayonnaise

Mix meat and vegetables with
French dressing. Let stand for 1
hour; then add pickles, eggs and
mayonnaise. Chill and serve on a
lettuce leaf. Serves 8.

KIPPERED HERRING SALAD

½ pound smoked kippered
herring
2 cups chopped celery
1 green pepper, chopped
1 onion, chopped
¼ teaspoon salt
⅛ teaspoon pepper
½ teaspoon paprika
½ cup French Dressing
1 head lettuce, shredded
2 hard-cooked eggs, sliced

Chop herring and vegetables very
fine. Add seasonings. Toss together with dressing, and serve
on shredded lettuce. Garnish with
hard-cooked eggs. Serves 8.
Use 1 cup chopped tart apple
for 1 of the cups of celery. Omit
green pepper.

*A lettuce cup at the base
and watercress at the top
keep this pyramid in place*

MINTED LAMB SALAD

2 cups thin small slices cold
cooked lamb
2 cups sliced cooked potatoes
¼ teaspoon salt
Mint French Dressing
Lettuce hearts

Combine lamb and potatoes; add
salt and marinate in dressing for
1 hour. Drain. Toss lettuce hearts
with dressing in salad bowl, heap
lamb and potato salad on lettuce,
and garnish with sprigs of mint.
Serves 6.

OYSTER SALAD

1 pint oysters
2 cups chopped celery
French Dressing
Lettuce
8 slices lemon
8 sprigs parsley

Wash and drain oysters. Place in
saucepan with a little water and
simmer until edges begin to curl.
Cool, drain and cut into quarters.
Add celery to oysters and moisten
with French dressing. Place on
lettuce and garnish with lemon
slices and parsley. Serves 8.

DUTCH HERRING SALAD

3 salt herring
2 tart apples, diced
4 cooked potatoes, diced
5 sour gherkins, diced
1 cooked beet, diced
3 scallions in vinegar
¼ teaspoon mustard
Dash pepper
3 hard-cooked eggs, diced
Mayonnaise to moisten

Wash herring and soak 3 hours in
cold water. Tear them lengthwise and cut into narrow strips.
Mix with remaining ingredients,
reserving 2 of the eggs. Combine
reserved eggs with additional
mayonnaise and serve with the
salad. Serves 8.

CHEESE AND VEGETABLE SALAD

Crisp lettuce leaves
2 tomatoes
1½ cups cottage cheese
½ teaspoon grated onion
¼ teaspoon salt
Dash paprika

Line salad bowl with lettuce hearts. Peel tomatoes, cut in wedges and place around edge of bowl. Mix cheese with onion, salt and paprika. Pile in center of bowl. Serves 4.

Add 1 teaspoon chopped parsley. Omit onion and add 1 teaspoon minced chives.

SHRIMP AND PINEAPPLE SALAD

1 cup shrimp
1 cup diced pineapple
¼ teaspoon salt
⅛ teaspoon paprika
4 tablespoons French Dressing
Lettuce or romaine

Combine shrimp, pineapple, salt and paprika and mix well. Chill thoroughly. When ready to serve, mix with French dressing. Arrange on lettuce or romaine. Serves 4.

TONGUE AND CABBAGE SALAD

1 head cabbage
1 cup diced cold cooked tongue
1 cup diced cold cooked ham
1 green pepper, chopped
1 sweet red pepper, chopped
½ onion, chopped
1 cup Mayonnaise

Shred cabbage as for coleslaw. Add next 5 ingredients and blend mayonnaise with cabbage mixture. Sugar and salt may be added if desired. Serves 8.

SCALLOP SALAD

1 pint scallops
1 quart boiling water
1 tablespoon lemon juice
½ tablespoon salt
1 cup Appetizer Mayonnaise
1 cup diced celery
¼ cup chopped sweet pickles
Lettuce or chicory

Cook scallops in water with lemon juice and salt for 10 minutes. Chill and cut into quarters (or more if scallops are large). Add mayonnaise, celery and pickles and mix lightly. Chill for 1 hour. Serve in lettuce cups. Serves 6.

SHRIMP AND ASPARAGUS SALAD

16 cooked shrimp, cleaned
French Dressing
18 cooked asparagus stalks
Lettuce cups, Mayonnaise

Marinate shrimp in French dressing. Chill. Arrange asparagus and shrimp on plate with lettuce cups. Serve with mayonnaise. Serves 4.

Radiating asparagus tips from a shrimp center give a buffet angle to this salad

SMOKED SALMON SALAD BOWL

2 cups shredded smoked salmon
½ cup cooked peas
½ cup chopped celery
½ cup sliced cooked green beans
½ cup diced cooked potatoes
Pearl Onion French Dressing
1 head lettuce or chicory, shredded
2 hard-cooked eggs, separated

Toss all ingredients (except egg yolks) together in salad bowl and chill. Sprinkle with sieved egg yolks and garnish with marinated cucumber slices. Serves 8.

SWISS SALAD BOWL

½ head romaine
½ head chicory
½ bunch watercress
Mustard French Dressing
2 cooked breasts of chicken
¼ pound cold Baked Ham
¼ pound cold tongue
¼ pound Swiss cheese

Shred greens, toss with dressing and arrange in 6 individual salad bowls. Chill. Cut chicken, ham, tongue, and cheese into long narrow strips and marinate in dressing for 15 minutes. Drain; arrange in 4 groups on top of greens in each salad bowl. For 6.

FRUIT SALAD IN ORANGE ICE RINGS

1½ cups orange juice
2 tablespoons lemon juice
Dash salt
⅔ cup sugar
¼ cup water
2 egg whites, stiffly beaten
Segments from grapefruit
4 slices pineapple, diced
Segments from 2 oranges
Fruit Mayonnaise
Lettuce cups
Mint leaves

Combine orange juice, lemon juice and salt and freeze until firm in refrigerator tray. Boil sugar and water together for 3 minutes and pour slowly into stiffly beaten whites, beating constantly. Cool to lukewarm. Scrape up thin layers of frozen mixture with an inverted spoon and fold into egg white mixture; pour into individual ring molds and freeze in refrigerator tray until firm. Combine grapefruit; pineapple and orange with mayonnaise and chill. Unmold orange ice; garnish centers with lettuce cups and fill with fruit salad. Garnish with mint leaves. Serves 4.

Lime, lemon or orange ice may be purchased and frozen in ring molds until firm; then filled with fruit salad and garnished as above.

FROZEN TOMATO APPETIZERS

6 small tomatoes, peeled
1 teaspoon salt
Dash pepper
Watercress or lettuce
Caviar Mayonnaise

Hollow out tomatoes slightly at stem end; sprinkle with salt and pepper; invert and chill. Drain. Frost in refrigerator tray for 1 hour. Serve on watercress and top with mayonnaise. Serves 6.

FROZEN CHICKEN SALAD RINGS

2 teaspoons unflavored gelatin
2 tablespoons cold water
½ cup milk
1 egg yolk
1 cup diced cooked chicken
2 tablespoons sliced cooked mushrooms
4 tablespoons chopped celery
1 teaspoon minced pimiento
1 teaspoon minced green pepper
2 tablespoons chopped parsley
Few drops lemon juice
¼ cup heavy cream, whipped
Lettuce cups
Cucumber Cream Dressing

Soften gelatin in cold water. Combine milk with egg yolk in top of double boiler and cook until thick. Dissolve gelatin in hot milk mixture and cool. When it begins to thicken add next 7 ingredients and fold in whipped cream. Freeze in individual ring molds in refrigerator tray until firm, about 3 hours. Unmold; arrange lettuce cup in center of each ring and fill with dressing. Garnish with tomato sections and watercress. Serves 4.

Use ½ cup diced cooked ham or tongue and ½ cup chicken.

Use 1 cup diced cooked turkey instead of chicken, or use ½ cup turkey and ½ cup ham.

Double the recipe; pour mixture into freezing tray and serve as a loaf, garnished with tomato sections.

STUFFED TOMATOES IN FROZEN DRESSING

6 small ripe tomatoes
1 teaspoon salt
¾ cup grated cucumber
2 tablespoons minced green pepper
2 tablespoons minced chives
1 cup cottage cheese
1 cup Cooked Salad Dressing
1 cup heavy cream, whipped
Lettuce or watercress

Wash tomatoes, remove skins and hollow out centers. Sprinkle with salt, invert and chill. Mix cucumber, green pepper, chives and cheese with 3 tablespoons dressing and pack mixture into tomatoes. Arrange tomatoes upside down in a row in freezing tray. Fold whipped cream into remaining dressing, pour over tomatoes and freeze about 2 hours. Cut frozen mixture into squares between each tomato, and serve on lettuce. Serves 6.

Use 1 cup softened cream cheese instead of cottage cheese and 4 tablespoons chopped olives instead of pepper and chives.

Use 1 cup diced cooked chicken, turkey or game instead of cottage cheese, and mix with 4 tablespoons dressing instead of 3.

Use 1 cup diced cooked ham, tongue, or veal instead of cottage cheese; ¾ cup chopped celery instead of cucumbers, and mix with 4 tablespoons dressing instead of 3.

Use 1 cup flaked crab meat, shrimp or tuna instead of cottage cheese, ¾ cup cold cooked peas instead of cucumbers, and mix with 4 tablespoons dressing instead of 3.

FROZEN OLIVE CHEESE SALAD

3 ounces sharp Cheddar cheese
½ cup cream
10 ripe olives, stoned and chopped
1 teaspoon chopped pimiento
6 tomatoes, hollowed out and chilled
Lettuce or watercress
Mayonnaise

Blend cheese well with cream; add olives and pimiento. Place in 6 small paper cups and freeze 2 to 3 hours in refrigerator tray. Unmold into hollowed-out tomatoes; serve on lettuce with mayonnaise. Serves 6.

FROZEN FRUIT GINGER SALAD

3 ounces cream cheese
3 tablespoons Mayonnaise
¼ cup maraschino cherries, sliced
¼ cup chopped dates
¼ cup preserved kumquats
¼ cup diced pineapple
1 tablespoon chopped candied
   ginger
1 cup heavy cream, whipped
½ cup toasted almonds
Lettuce
Pineapple Cream Dressing

Beat cheese and mayonnaise together until smooth; combine with fruits and fold in whipped cream. Pour into freezing tray of refrigerator, sprinkle with almonds and freeze 2½ to 3 hours, or until firm. Cut into squares and serve on lettuce with dressing. Serves 8.

Use ¼ cup diced oranges instead of chopped dates; and ¼ cup diced bananas instead of kumquats; omit chopped ginger.

Freeze mixture in sealed baking powder cans; slice and serve on slices of tomato; garnish with watercress. Freeze mixture as above; serve on slices of pineapple and garnish with watercress.

FROZEN PEAR AND CHEESE SALAD

3 ounces cream cheese, mashed
1 No. 1 can pears
3 tablespoons French Dressing
Ginger Dressing

To cheese add juice drained from pears and French dressing; beat until smooth. Slice pears and arrange in freezing tray of refrigerator. Pour in cheese mixture and freeze until firm enough to cut into squares. Arrange on lettuce and serve with dressing. Serves 4.

Any fruit from your basket may be combined for frozen fruit salad

FROZEN SPICED APRICOT SALAD

1 pound dried apricots
2 cups water
½ teaspoon cloves
⅓ cup sugar
⅛ teaspoon salt
Grated rind of 1 lemon
2 tablespoons lemon juice
Lettuce
Lemon Mayonnaise

Wash apricots and cook in water with cloves, sugar, salt and rind of lemon until tender. Rub through a coarse sieve, add the lemon juice and freeze for 2 hours. Scrape up into thin layers with an inverted spoon when solidly frozen and serve on lettuce or endive with mayonnaise. Serves 6.

FROZEN SPICED PRUNE—Use prunes and ½ teaspoon cinnamon for apricots and cloves.

FROZEN TOMATO SALAD IN CUCUMBER BOATS

½ cucumber pared and chopped
3 stalks celery, chopped
1 cup cooked asparagus tips
3 cups tomato purée
6 lettuce cups
6. Cucumber Boats
Mayonnaise
3 tablespoons chopped chives

Combine cucumber, celery and asparagus with tomato purée; pour into refrigerator trays and freeze about 1½ hours or until just firm. Arrange lettuce cups on salad plates; place a cucumber boat on each and fill each with frozen tomato mixture. Top with mayonnaise and sprinkle with chopped chives. Serves 6.

Serve frozen tomato mixture in hollowed out chilled peeled tomatoes instead of in cucumber boats.

Slice frozen tomato mixture; serve on lettuce or watercress and garnish with rosettes of cream cheese.

On each round of frozen salad place a ring of avocado and garnish center with Pastel Fruit Mayonnaise.

FROZEN SUMMER FRUIT SALAD

½ cup sliced strawberries
½ cup diced canned pineapple
½ cup diced orange segments
½ cup diced bananas
2 teaspoons lemon juice
1 teaspoon unflavored gelatin
1 tablespoon cold water
4 teaspoons strained honey
⅔ cup heavy cream, whipped
Lettuce

Combine fruits with lemon juice; chill. Soften gelatin in cold water; dissolve over hot water and add to honey and fruit. Fold whipped cream into fruit mixture and freeze in refrigerator tray 3 hours or until firm. Cut into squares and serve on lettuce. Serves 8.

Use ½ cup red raspberries instead of strawberries.

Freeze in sealed baking powder cans, slice, arrange on lettuce. Top each round with pared honeydew or cantaloupe ring; fill center with melon balls and serve with Lime French Dressing.

A sprig of watercress with stuffed olive flowers decorates frozen sea food salad

FROZEN SEA FOOD SALAD

2 teaspoons unflavored gelatin
⅓ cup cold water
2 cups flaked sea food (crab meat, shrimp or lobster)
⅔ cup tomato catchup
2 tablespoons lemon juice
3 tablespoons vinegar
1 teaspoon prepared horse-radish
¼ teaspoon salt
½ cup Mayonnaise
Tomato, Lettuce

Soften gelatin in cold water and dissolve over hot water. Combine with sea food, catchup, lemon juice, vinegar, horse-radish and salt; fold in mayonnaise. Freeze in refrigerator tray until firm, about 2 hours. Cut into cubes and arrange on slices of tomatoes on lettuce. Serves 6.

Serve frozen sea food in hollowed-out whole tomatoes.

Serve frozen sea food in Cucumber Boats.

Serve as a loaf on watercress with border of overlapping cucumber and tomato slices.

Freeze sea food mixture in individual oiled ring molds; unmold, arrange on watercress; fill centers with Cucumber Dressing in lettuce cups.

BUNNY SALADS

1 package lime gelatin
2 cups hot water
6 pear halves
4 tablespoons cottage cheese
Mayonnaise
1 tablespoon chopped blanched
    almonds
Lettuce
24 almonds, blanched
Paprika
Soft pimiento cheese
Parsley

Dissolve gelatin in hot water. Pour into a pan 8 x 8 x 2 inches and chill until firm. For each salad fill pear half with cottage cheese mixed with mayonnaise and chopped almonds. Invert on lettuce leaves on bed of shredded gelatin made by forcing firm lime gelatin through a ricer. Make bunny's ears, mouth and tail of almonds. Make eyes by dipping the pointed end of a knife into paprika. Garnish with small carrot shaped from cheese with a sprig of parsley for top. Serve with mayonnaise. Makes 6.

POINSETTIA SALAD

1 No. 2½ can pears
½ cup red cinnamon drops
3 tablespoons vinegar
1 bunch watercress
4 teaspoons grated sharp
    Cheddar cheese
Lime French Dressing

Combine sirup from pears with cinnamon drops and vinegar and heat to boiling. Cut each pear half into 4 lengthwise slices to represent petals and simmer in sirup for 20 minutes, or until well colored. Chill. Arrange watercress on 4 salad plates. On each arrange 8 petals, clockwise, each curving toward the center to represent a flower. Sprinkle 1 teaspoon grated cheese in center of each flower, and serve with dressing. Serves 4.

FIRECRACKER SALAD

1 package strawberry, raspberry
    or cherry gelatin
1 cup boiling water
¾ cup cold water
16 square marshmallows
Watercress, Mayonnaise
4 marshmallow stars

Dissolve gelatin in boiling water, add cold water and pour to ½-inch thickness in shallow oblong pan. When gelatin is almost set, arrange 4 stacks of 4 marshmallows each, flat sides together, in the gelatin, allowing room between each "firecracker." When firm, pour on remaining cooled gelatin. Chill. Cut between rows of marshmallows and lift out carefully with a spatula. Arrange each plate with watercress, place "firecracker" on it and make a fuse of mayonnaise. Tip each fuse with a star cut from a marshmallow with wet scissors. Serves 4.

Cut pimientos into halves, form a roll of cream cheese the same length as pimiento. Roll cheese in pimiento and chill. Insert a narrow strip of green pepper for fuse. Serve with mayonnaise.

Bunny salads will delight every youngster at the Easter party

CHRISTMAS WREATH SALAD

6 slices pineapple
1 head romaine
Angelica
½ cup red cinnamon drops
Whipped Cream Dressing

Arrange 1 slice pineapple on romaine on each plate. Cut angelica to represent holly leaves and arrange on pineapple. Sprinkle cinnamon drops at intervals between the leaves to represent holly. Fill center of pineapple ring with whipped cream dressing. Serves 6.

DUCK SALAD

1 small head lettuce, shredded
6 large peach halves
1 cup cottage cheese
6 yellow marshmallows
12 currants
⅓ cup toasted almonds
Fruit Mayonnaise

Arrange shredded lettuce on large glass platter or chop plate, fluffing it up with a fork to resemble waves. Stuff each peach half with cottage cheese and invert, rounded side up on lettuce. For each duck's head use a marshmallow, with currants for eyes and a toasted almond, split, for each bill. For each tail use 3 or 4 almonds. Serve with the fruit cream mayonnaise. Serves 6.
Use Whipped Cream Dressing.

EASTER SALAD

2 tablespoons unflavored gelatin
3½ cups chicken broth
Salt, Pepper
Hard-cooked eggs, sliced
1 pimiento, cut into attractive
    shapes
Sliced cooked chicken
Tomato aspic, chopped
Watercress, Mayonnaise
Olives, chopped

Soften gelatin in ½ cup cold chicken broth for 5 minutes. Heat remainder of broth to boiling, add seasoning and gelatin and stir until dissolved. Strain through cheesecloth. When it begins to thicken, glaze a mold with the gelatin mixture. Have the jelly about 1½ inches thick in the bottom. Dip hard-cooked eggs and pimiento in liquid gelatin and place on bottom and sides. Arrange sliced cooked chicken in alternate layers of dark and light meat. Fill with remainder of cooled gelatin. Chill until firm. Unmold and serve on platter, garnished with chopped tomato aspic and cress. Serve with mayonnaise or Tartare Sauce and add chopped olives to either as a relish. Serves 6.

DRUM MAJOR SALAD

⅓ pound cream cheese
Mayonnaise
3 tablespoons chopped walnuts
3 tablespoons chopped olives
¼ teaspoon salt
3 tomatoes, sliced
1 green pepper, cut into strips
Salad greens
12 pitted olives
12 celery sticks, (4 inches)

Beat cheese smooth with mayonnaise, add nuts, olives and salt Spread thickly between 2 tomato slices. Arrange pepper diagonally across filling. Place on nests of greens. Place an olive on end of each celery stick and cross 2 on each salad. Serve with mayonnaise, for 6.

WASHINGTON'S SALAD

Cover a 4-inch straight section of banana with mayonnaise. Roll in chopped nut meats and place on bed of lettuce. Garnish with cherries and a hatchet fastened in a slit in the "log."

Every one will "fall in line" with the drum major salad

INDEPENDENCE DAY SALMON RING

2 tablespoons unflavored gelatin
¼ cup cold water
2 egg yolks
1 teaspoon salt
1 teaspoon dry mustard
¼ teaspoon paprika
2 tablespoons sugar
¾ cup milk
5 tablespoons lemon juice
    (or vinegar)
¾ tablespoon butter
2 cups flaked cooked salmon
1 cup Mayonnaise
2 egg whites (optional)
Cucumber Dressing

Soften gelatin in cold water. Mix egg yolks with salt, mustard, paprika and sugar. Add milk, then add lemon juice very slowly, stirring constantly, and cook over hot water until mixture thickens. Add butter and gelatin and stir until gelatin dissolves. Chill until mixture starts to thicken. Fold in salmon, mayonnaise and stiffly beaten egg whites. Pour into oiled ring mold and chill until firm. Unmold, garnish with watercress, fill center with dressing and place tiny flags at regular spaces around the edge of jellied ring. Serves 6 to 8.

SHAMROCK SALAD

2 green peppers
10 ounces pimiento or cream
    cheese, softened
Lettuce or chicory
French Dressing

Wash, cut off stem end and remove seeds from well-shaped peppers. Stuff with cheese and chill 4 hours. Cut into ¼-inch slices and arrange 3 for each salad on lettuce or chicory. Pipe cream cheese flower in center of each. Serve with French dressing. Serves 6.

ORANGE JACK-O'-LANTERN SALAD

6 small oranges
3 cups Fruit Salad
1 head lettuce, shredded
Mayonnaise

Cut off tops of oranges, remove pulp, and cut eyes, nose, and mouth in the skin. Fill with fruit salad, replace tops, and serve on shredded lettuce with mayonnaise. Serves 6.

ST. PATRICK'S DAY SALAD

1 package lime gelatin
1 cup red sweet cherries, pitted
1 cup white sweet cherries, pitted
1 to 2 cups cottage cheese

Prepare gelatin as directed on package. Arrange dark and light pitted cherries in a mold, pour part of gelatin mixture over them and chill until firm, then add remaining gelatin. Chill. Unmold salad on bed of lettuce and serve with salad dressing and cottage cheese. Serves 8.

Turkey gobbler, sea lion or pussy cat will be the result of your skill and imagination

JACK-O'-LANTERN SALAD

6 large peach halves, canned
2 cups Waldorf Salad
Lettuce, 12 cloves
12 strips pimiento

Stuff peach halves with Waldorf salad and arrange each on lettuce, rounded side up. Use 2 cloves for eyes, and strips of pimiento for nose and mouth. Serves 6.

TURKEY SALAD

6 whole pears
⅔ cup crushed pecans
1 bunch watercress
1 apple, pared and cut into wedges
6 candied cherries
6 strips pimientos
6 half-slices pineapple
Cream Cheese French Dressing

Roll pears in crushed pecans and arrange each on watercress on a salad plate. Stick an apple wedge into stem end of each pear for turkey's neck; top with a cherry for head and attach strip of pimiento underneath for wattles. At other end of pear arrange a half slice of pineapple upright, for tail feathers. Serve with dressing. Serves 6.

VALENTINE SALADS

2 tablespoons unflavored gelatin
½ cup cold water
4 cups tomatoes (fresh or cooked)
1 tablespoon minced onion
Dash celery seed, 2 cloves
½ teaspoon salt
1 teaspoon sugar
1 tablespoon lemon juice
1 head chicory
French Dressing
3 ounces cream cheese
Cucumber Cream Dressing

Soften gelatin in cold water. Cook tomatoes, onion, celery seed, cloves, salt and sugar together 15 minutes. Strain; dissolve softened gelatin in hot liquid. Add lemon juice and cool. Pour into heart-shaped molds and chill until firm. Toss chicory with a little French dressing and arrange on 6 salad plates. Place jellied tomato heart on each, and with pastry bag and tube pipe frilly border of softened cream cheese around each. Serve with dressing. Serves 6.

Tomato jelly mixture may be poured into pans or molds in ¾-inch layers, and cut, when chilled, with heart-shaped cookie cutter.

SALAD GARNISHES

CUCUMBER TULIPS—Cut the ends (2-inch lengths) from unpeeled medium cucumbers. Cut 6 or 7 triangular sections down from cut edge, making petals. Toothpicks may be used as markers so that all the petals will be even. Hollow out remaining seeds, leaving a ¼-inch wall. Place a small rounded bit of carrot, rutabaga or beet on a toothpick and press into the center. Chill in ice water.

CUCUMBER BALLS—Cut large cucumbers into balls with French vegetable cutter and marinate in French Dressing. Sprinkle with paprika and serve as a garnish.

GREEN OR RED PEPPER RINGS—Cut a slice from the top of fresh pepper; remove seeds and partitions. Slice crosswise, making rings as wide as desired. These rings may be used to hold together stalks of asparagus, whole string beans etc., or if cut quite wide they will serve as cups to hold mayonnaise.

JELLIED GINGER ALE CUBES—Sprinkle ½ tablespoon gelatin over 2 tablespoons cold water. Dissolve over boiling water. Cool. Add 1 cup ginger ale and mix thoroughly. Pour into a square pan which has been dipped in cold water. Chill until firm. Cut into small cubes. To make grape juice cubes use ½ cup grape juice and ½ cup ginger ale, instead of the 1 cup ginger ale.

RADISH ROSES—Trim off all but an inch of stem. Cut off root and with a sharp knife cut the outside layer down from the tip toward stem end in 5 or more sections so that the red outside covering stands out like the petals of a flower. Chill radishes in ice water until petals curl. Cut olives, capers, pimientos, slices of hard-cooked egg or beets into fancy shapes.

EGG GARNISHES—To make daisy garnish for green cooked vegetables: cut whites of hard-cooked eggs lengthwise into 5 or more petals, using tip of knife and cutting from larger end to within ½ inch of the smaller end. Open the petals, remove yolks and fill center of white petals with sieved egg yolk.

MELON BASKETS

Locate the center between the ends of a melon. One inch on each side of this point, make a cut downward ⅓ of the distance through the melon, make another cut 1 inch on the other side of the center point, thus making a 2-inch strip through the center down ⅓ way through melon. Cut from each end in toward center to this strip on each side and remove portions of melon. Remove edible portions of melon with French vegetable cutter or a spoon, chill.

WATERMELON BOWL

Cut watermelon lengthwise in a ⅓ to ⅔ proportion. Remove top third. Then cut out melon balls with a French vegetable cutter. Chill. Mark off 2-inch spaces on cut edge of melon and cut out triangular sections between each marker, making a notched edge. Fill bowl with chilled watermelon and cantaloupe balls.

Watermelon bowl or melon baskets for salad service will delight your guests

CREAM CHEESE NOVELTIES

Arrange assorted cheese balls with avocado rings, sliced tomato, sliced beet and artichoke hearts; adding French Dressing.

Make a rainbow garnish as follows:

Line a small deep enameled refrigerator pan or little cake mold with waxed paper. Mix cheese with sufficient cream to mold nicely. Pack in alternate layers with hard-cooked egg yolk mashed with a little mayonnaise, minced green peppers and minced pimientos, or minced fines herbes. Chill or freeze, unmold, remove paper and cut down in slices with knife dipped in ice water. Use striped slices as garnish, or for open-faced sandwiches, or serve alone on lettuce leaves with French Dressing.

SALAD SERVING SUGGESTIONS

Use silver ice tongs to serve salad consisting of large pieces of fruit or vegetables.

Cut a thin slice from stem end of a sweet red or green pepper, remove seeds and use as a container for mayonnaise.

These paddles will make balls of cream cheese, liver, anchovy or fish butters and pastes

SUGGESTIONS FOR SALAD GARNISHES

Red or green peppers, cut into thin strips or circles.

Celery stuffed with a savory cheese mixture, celery curls or hearts of celery.

Radishes cut into thin slices.

Sliced tomatoes, spread with sardine paste, or with horse-radish mixed with whipped cream.

Stalks of endive stuffed with Roquefort cheese paste.

Carrots shredded very fine, or grated.

Paper-thin slices of onions, marinated in French dressing and sprinkled with paprika or chopped parsley.

Asparagus tips, marinated in French dressing and ends dipped in paprika.

Olives—whole, green or ripe and sliced stuffed olives.

Avocado rings, crescents or slices.

Thin slices of a pared, scored cucumber are suitable for fish salads.

Sieved hard-cooked egg yolks.

Finely chopped hard-cooked egg whites or egg wedges.

STUFFED OLIVE GARNISHES

1 (10-ounce) bottle olives
1 package cream cheese
Mayonnaise
½ cup chopped nuts

Cut olives into halves lengthwise, remove pits and chill. Mix cream cheese to a paste with mayonnaise, shape into small balls and roll in chopped nuts. Put the cheese balls between the halves of olives and press together slightly. Serve as garnish for meat or vegetable salads, or aspics.

CELERY CURLS

Cut celery stalks into 2-inch pieces. With a very sharp knife, begin at the outer edge and make 4 to 6 cuts parallel, extending about ⅓ of the way down the stalk. Place in ice water until celery curls. Both ends may be curled.

PICKLE FANS

Cut a small cucumber pickle into 5 or 6 very thin slices from the tip almost down to the stem end but leaving all the slices attached. Press lightly at the stem end to spread the "fan."

STUFFED PICKLES—Fill cored pickles with cream cheese. Chill 3 hours and slice.

Pies and Pastries

300 Superb Pies and Pastries

PASTRY MAKING

Illustrations pages 566-67

Good pastry is flaky, tender, delicate and evenly browned. It is not crumbly, but when broken, shows layers of flat flakes, piled one above the other with air spaces between.

To achieve this result the cook must be quick and "light-handed," since pastry cannot be good if handled roughly or slowly. The flakiness of pastry is caused by many particles of fat which are surrounded and separated by flour. During baking each fat particle melts to form a delicate flake. However, rough, slow handling may cause these particles to melt and blend with the flour to form a solid mass, which is tough and hard after baking.

EVERYTHING MUST BE COLD

Chilled ingredients are important for success and for the beginner even the flour may be chilled. A cold, solid fat and ice water are essentials. Baking powder is sometimes used but with skillful mixing and handling of the dough it is unnecessary.

Sift flour and salt together, then add cold fat and cut in as quickly as possible. A pastry blender is one of the best utensils to use for this purpose, although a quick job can be done with 2 knives. The fingers may be used by those able to work rapidly enough to work in the fat before it starts to melt from the heat of the fingers. Distribute the fat evenly through the flour, being sure not to neglect that at the bottom of the bowl. It has been mixed sufficiently when the largest pieces of fat are the size of small peas. These particles roll out and melt into crisp flakes. The mixture may be placed in a clean jar, covered and kept in the refrigerator.

HOW MUCH WATER

The greatest care is required when adding water No definite amount can be specified since this varies with the dryness of the flour and the amount of shortening used. Usually 2 to 4 tablespoons water are required for 1 cup flour. Sprinkle the water a tablespoon at a time over the flour mixture while tossing it quickly with a fork. Avoid stirring or mixing that would crush fat particles and blend them with the flour. Push moistened portions to one side before adding more water so a dry portion can be sprinkled each time. If allowed to do so, the fat-flour mixture will absorb a great deal more water than should be used, so care must be taken to keep the moisture well distributed. Too much moisture makes the crust hard and brittle. Too little makes a crust which cracks at the edges while being rolled; it may crack open while baking and the finished pie be difficult to serve.

BE SWIFT AND DEFT

When moist enough to hold together under slight pressure, divide into halves, press each into a ball, flatten out with the hands and chill. If too little or too much water has been used, nothing can be done about it, except to profit by experience next time. Sprinkle board and rolling pin lightly with flour and rub into wood. A canvas cloth or coarse linen kitchen towel to cover the board and a "stocking" for the rolling pin are aids to the rolling out process, by preventing sticking without the use of too much flour Excess flour on board and pin make the crust hard. Roll quickly but lightly since heavy pressure makes the pastry stick and breaks the surface. Start each stroke at center of dough and roll to edge, keeping pastry in as circular a shape as possible and keeping edges as thick as the center. Lift and turn pastry occasionally to make sure it is not sticking and rub extra flour over board if necessary. Keep all particles of dough cleaned from uncovered rolling pin since the pastry being rolled will stick to these more readily than to the wood. Roll out to 1/8-inch thickness for lower crust; roll top crust slightly thinner. Place pastry in pans and bake as directed.

Piecrust mixtures, containing all ingredients, except the water can now be purchased. They are especially valuable for the inexperienced cook and small family.

ABOUT THE FILLING

When filling for a two-crust pie is very juicy some precautions are necessary to prevent it from boiling over. The top crust should be well-slashed to allow steam to escape. Some get good results by inserting paper funnels or several 3-inch lengths of uncooked macaroni through the slashes into the filling to act as "chimneys." The edge of the pie may be bound with an inch-wide strip of muslin dipped into water, or with paper pie tape used as directed on the package. A little flour paste will hold the ends together. Remove strip when pie is baked. Another method is to cut the top crust 1/2 inch larger than necessary and turn the excess under the moistened edge of the under crust. Or cut bottom crust 1/2 inch larger and turn it over the top crust. When these are firmly pressed together a tight seal is made. A little flour, cornstarch or tapioca mixed with the sugar helps to thicken the juice. Directions for baking given with each recipe should be carefully followed for best results.

PLAIN PASTRY

2 cups sifted flour
¾ teaspoon salt
⅔ cup shortening
4 to 6 tablespoons cold water

Sift flour and salt together and cut in shortening with 2 knives or pastry blender. Add water, using only a small portion at a time, until mixture will hold together. Divide dough into 2 parts. Roll out on floured board to desired size. Line the piepan with one piece of dough, being careful not to stretch dough. After filling is placed in pastry, dampen edges of lower crust with cold water and cover with remaining dough which has been rolled out and slashed in several places to allow steam to escape while baking. Press edges together with prongs of fork and bake according to recipe for filling selected. Makes 2 (9-inch) shells or one 2-crust (9-inch) pie.

PASTRY SHELL—Roll ½ of the dough ⅛ inch thick, fold in half and lift into piepan. Do not stretch dough. After crust is fitted, trim edges evenly, leaving a 1-inch overhanging border, fold dough under and back to make an upright rim, then flute edges using thumb and index finger of one hand and the index finger of the other hand. Prick crust thoroughly with a fork and use one of the following methods to prevent shrinkage of crust:
Place rolled dough in pan and set aside for 5 minutes, then fit into place with a ball of dough.
Line pastry shell with waxed paper and partially fill with rice or beans, remove paper after first 10 minutes of baking.
Fit a second pan inside on crust, remove pan after first 10 minutes. Bake in a very hot oven (450°F.) about 15 minutes or until delicately browned.

TARTS—Cut pastry into rounds to fit muffin or tart pans and proceed as for pies. Makes 4 (2-crust) or 8 single tarts.

TART SHELLS—Cut pastry into rounds to fit muffin or tart pans and proceed as for Pastry Shell, or shape pastry over the back of muffin or tart pans, trim edge and prick thoroughly with a fork. Makes 8 shells. See page 42.

PASTRY WHEELS—Combine leftover scraps of dough; roll out, sprinkle with cinnamon and sugar and roll up tightly. Slice into tiny circles and bake in hot oven.

HOT WATER PASTRY

2 cups sifted flour
½ teaspoon baking powder
1 teaspoon salt
⅓ cup boiling water
⅔ cup shortening

Sift flour, baking powder and salt together. Pour water over shortening and mix with fork until creamy, add flour mixture and mix into a dough. Chill thoroughly and proceed as for Plain Pastry. Makes 1 (9-inch) double crust pie or 2 (9-inch) single crust pies.

SOUTHERN PASTRY

2 cups sifted flour
½ teaspoon salt
1 cup shortening
6 tablespoons ice water

Mix flour and salt, cut shortening into flour; add water a tablespoon at a time, using only enough to make a workable paste; too little will leave it crumbly. This pastry, being exceedingly rich, must be handled deftly. Roll out pastry and line piepan. Makes 2 (9-inch) pastry shells or pastry for 1 two-crust (9-inch) pie. Thorough chilling before rolling makes pastry easier to handle.

DECORATIONS

Roll out Plain, Southern, Cheese or Hot Water Pastry according to directions and cut out any of the following designs with cookie cutters or cardboard patterns, leave plain or decorate as suggested below. Bake in very hot oven (450°F.) about 10 minutes. Top any open-faced pie or tart.

CAT OR OTHER ANIMALS—After baking, mark to suggest features, using melted chocolate, colored sugar, nut meats, candied or dried fruits.

CHICK—After pastry is baked, mark features using a toothpick and melted chocolate.

CHRISTMAS TREE—Mark to suggest branches and decorate with green sugar.

CRESCENT—Sprinkle with colored sugar.

CROWN—Cut rounds with large scalloped cutter and cut out center with medium cutter.

FLAG—Mark to suggest stars and stripes and decorate with red, white and blue sugar.

HATCHET—Press cutting edge to make it thin and sprinkle red sugar over handle.

HEART—Sprinkle red sugar over all or only on edges. Arrange heart-shaped candies on pastry.

HEARTS, CLUBS, SPADES AND DIAMONDS—Sprinkle colored sugar over top.

PUMPKIN—Mark to suggest ribs and sprinkle stem with green sugar.

SANTA CLAUS—Mark to suggest features and decorate with red sugar.

SHAMROCK—Sprinkle green sugar over all or only on edges.

STAR—Use colored sugar.

TURKEY—Sprinkle with cinnamon and sugar.

WITCH—Mark features.

PUFF PASTE

1 cup butter
2 cups sifted cake flour
½ cup ice water

Wash butter in cold water to remove salt. Allow ⅔ of butter to become soft. Cut remaining butter into flour with 2 knives or a pastry blender; add ice water using only enough to hold ingredients together. Roll out to ¼-inch thickness on a lightly floured board, making a square sheet. Spread ⅔ of dough with ¼ of softened butter; fold unbuttered ⅓ over center ⅓ and fold remaining ⅓ over to cover first ⅓, buttered side down, making 3 layers of dough with butter between each layer. Turn dough ¼ of way around on board and roll to about ¼-inch thickness. Spread with butter. Fold as before and chill thoroughly. Roll, spread with butter, fold and chill 2 more times. Roll, shape and bake as directed in various recipes using Puff Paste. May be baked at once or wrapped in waxed paper and chilled 12 to 24 hours. Makes 15 to 24 fancy pastries.

PATTY SHELLS

Roll puff paste ¼ inch thick, cut into 3-inch rounds with floured cutter. Cut out centers from half of rounds with a small cutter; moisten underside of each ring with cold water and place one on each remaining plain round, pressing down lightly. Bake in very hot oven (450°F.) for 10 minutes, reduce temperature to 400°F. bake for 5 minutes, then reduce temperature to 350°F. and bake 15 minutes longer.

MÜRBE TEIG FOR PIES

1 cup sifted flour
⅛ teaspoon salt
1 tablespoon sugar
¼ cup butter
1 egg yolk, slightly beaten

Combine flour, salt and sugar. Cut in butter with 2 knives or a pastry blender. Add egg yolk and mix thoroughly. Press into a pie plate or spring-form pan to ¼-inch thickness. Fill with a fruit filling. Bake in hot oven (425°) 10 minutes, reduce temperature to 350°F. and bake until fruit is cooked. Makes 1 (9-inch) shell.

VOL-AU-VENT

Roll puff paste 1½ inches thick and cut a circle about 6 inches in diameter, using a cutter or, with a sharp knife, cutting around the edge of a plate placed on the paste. Place circle on a baking sheet and, with a sharp pointed knife or a smaller cutter, cut a circle around the top about 1½ inches from the edge and 1 inch deep. Do not remove the center but bake entire circle in a very hot oven (450°F.) about 8 minutes, reduce temperature to 350°F. and bake 30 minutes longer. When the outer crust is baked, lift out center and remove uncooked paste from below. Place top upside down on a baking sheet and place in oven a few minutes to dry. Fill with any kind of sweetened fresh berries or fruit. Replace top and sprinkle with confectioners' sugar.

Vol-au-vents may be used as containers for creamed fish, fowl or meat.

Another pie plate, some rice or beans will keep the pastry shell in perfect form

Holding the pie plate, press crumbs firmly to form a crust

CRUMB PIE SHELL

1½ cups fine crumbs
¼ cup sugar
½ cup butter, melted

Mix crumbs and sugar together; stir in butter. Line piepan with mixture by pressing it firmly into place. Chill for 20 minutes or bake in moderate oven (350°F.) 10 minutes. Cool. Makes 1 (9-inch) shell.

CINNAMON—Add ½ teaspoon cinnamon to bread or graham cracker crumbs.

Use crumbs of the following:
Chocolate Cookies
Cereal Flakes; Gingersnaps
Graham Crackers; Toasted Bread
Vanilla Wafers; Zwieback

CHEESE PASTRY

½ cup butter
1 cup sifted flour
¼ pound cottage or cream cheese

Cut butter into flour; add cheese and mix to a smooth dough. Chill thoroughly. Roll into desired shapes. Makes 1 (9-inch) single crust pie.

CHEESE STICKS—Use ½ recipe of Plain Pastry. Roll out and sprinkle with ⅓ cup grated sharp cheese. Fold twice, roll out and repeat twice. Cut into strips; bake 12 minutes at 425° F.

BRAZIL-NUT PIE SHELL

1⅔ cups ground Brazil-nut meats
4 tablespoons sugar

Mix nuts with sugar. Line piepan with mixture by pressing it firmly into place. Makes 1 (9-inch) pie shell.

MERINGUE I

2 egg whites
4 tablespoons sugar
½ teaspoon vanilla or
    other flavoring

Beat eggs until frothy. Add sugar gradually and continue beating until stiff. Add flavoring. Pile on pie and bake at 350°F. 10 to 15 minutes. Topping for 1 (8-inch) pie.

II—Use 3 egg whites and 6 tablespoons sugar. Proceed as above. 1 (9-inch) pie.

III—Use 4 egg whites and ½ cup sugar. Proceed as above. 1 (10-inch) pie.

WHIPPED CREAM TOPPING

1 cup heavy cream
¼ cup sugar
1 teaspoon vanilla

1. Whip cream until almost stiff. Add sugar and vanilla and beat until cream holds a peak.

2. Sprinkle ¾ teaspoon unflavored gelatin over 2 tablespoons milk and stir thoroughly. Place over boiling water and stir until dissolved. Add to cream warmed to room temperature. Chill and whip. Top for 1 (9-inch) pie.

MARSHMALLOW MERINGUE

½ pound marshmallows
1 tablespoon milk
2 egg whites
¼ cup sugar
¼ teaspoon salt
½ teaspoon vanilla

Heat marshmallows and milk together, folding over until marshmallows are half melted. Remove from heat and continue folding until mixture is smooth and fluffy. Beat egg whites, add sugar gradually and continue beating until stiff and smooth. Add salt and vanilla. Blend into marshmallow mixture and spread over pie. Bake in very hot oven (450°F.) about 1 minute or until light brown. Meringue for 1 (9-inch) pie.

BROWN SUGAR MERINGUE

2 egg whites
4 tablespoons brown sugar
½ teaspoon vanilla

Beat egg whites until frothy. Add sugar gradually and beat until stiff. Add vanilla and pile on pie. Bake in 350°F. oven for 10 to 15 minutes. Topping for 1 (8-inch) pie.

APPLE PIE

6 apples
1 cup sugar
¼ teaspoon salt
2 tablespoons flour
1 recipe Plain Pastry
1 tablespoon butter

Pare and slice apples. Sift dry ingredients together and mix with apples. Line piepan with pastry, fill with apple mixture, dot with butter and cover with top crust. Bake in very hot oven (450°F.) 15 minutes; reduce temperature to moderate (350°F.) and bake 45 minutes longer. Makes 1 (9-inch) pie.

Add ¼ teaspoon mace to dry ingredients.

Add 1 teaspoon cinnamon to dry ingredients.

Use brown or maple sugar instead of granulated.

APPLESAUCE PIE

¼ teaspoon cloves
2 cups thick applesauce
1 Cinnamon Pie Shell
1 recipe Whipped Cream Topping

Add cloves to applesauce and pour into pie shell. Cover with whipped cream topping and chill. Makes 1 (9-inch) pie.

DAINTY APPLE PIE

3 cups sliced tart apples
2½ cups grapefruit juice
1 Graham Cracker Pie Shell
½ cup sugar
3 tablespoons cornstarch
1 recipe Whipped Cream Topping
8 maraschino cherries, chopped

Cook apples in grapefruit juice until tender. Arrange apples in pie shell. Mix sugar and cornstarch, add to juice and cook until clear and thickened. Pour over apples. Cool. Cover with whipped cream topping and sprinkle cherries over top. Makes 1 (9-inch) pie.

QUINCE APPLE PIE

1 recipe Plain Pastry
5 cups sliced apples
¾ cup quince jelly
1 tablespoon butter

Line piepan with pastry. Arrange half of apples in piepan, dot with half of jelly and butter; add remaining apples and dot with remaining half of jelly and butter. Cover with top crust and bake in very hot oven (450°F.) 10 minutes; reduce temperature to moderate (350°F.) and bake 40 minutes longer or until apples are tender. Makes 1 (9-inch) pie.

APPLE AND RAISIN PIE

4 cups sliced apples
1 cup water
1½ teaspoons flour
½ cup sugar
¼ teaspoon cinnamon
1 cup seedless raisins
1 recipe Plain Pastry
2 tablespoons butter

Cook apples in water (covered) for 5 minutes; cool. Sift flour, sugar and cinnamon into raisins and add to apples. Line piepan with pastry, pour in filling, dot with butter and place strips of pastry over top in lattice design. Bake in very hot oven (450°F.) 10 minutes; reduce temperature to moderate (350°F.) and bake 40 minutes longer or until fruit is tender. Makes 1 (9-inch) pie.

ENGLISH APPLE PIE

5 medium apples
3 tablespoons melted butter
2 egg yolks
1 cup sugar
1 lemon, juice and rind
1 cup heavy cream
½ recipe Plain Pastry
1 recipe Meringue I

Prepare a sauce of apples. When tender, rub through sieve and add butter. Cool, add beaten egg yolks, sugar, lemon juice and rind. Stir in cream. Line piepan with pastry and pour in filling. Bake in hot oven (425°F.) for 10 minutes; reduce temperature to moderate (350°F.) and bake 30 minutes longer. Top with meringue when cold and proceed as directed. Makes 1 (9-inch) pie.

APPLE-BUTTER—Omit apples, cream, lemon and ½ cup sugar. Use ½ cup apple butter, 2½ cups milk and ¼ cup flour.

If you must watch calories sprinkle your apple pie with water and bake without a top crust

APPLE AND RHUBARB PIE

1 recipe Southern Pastry
1 pound rhubarb, cut fine
2 apples, sliced thin
¼ cup brown sugar

Line piepan with pastry. Place rhubarb in bottom, cover with apples and sprinkle sugar over all. Cover with top crust and bake in very hot oven (450°F.) 10 minutes; reduce temperature to moderate (350°F.) and bake 40 minutes longer or until fruit is tender. Makes 1 (9-inch) pie.

APRICOT WHIPPED CREAM PIE

1½ cups dried apricots
1½ cups water
1 tablespoon granulated tapioca
1 cup sugar
1 baked Pastry Shell
1 recipe Whipped Cream Topping
¼ cup coconut, toasted

Wash apricots and cook in water about 20 minutes. Add tapioca and cook until clear, then add sugar and cook until thickened. Remove from heat and chill. Pour into pastry shell, cover with whipped cream topping and sprinkle coconut over top. Makes 1 (9-inch) pie.

JELLIED APRICOT PIE

½ pound dried apricots, cooked and drained
1 cup sugar
1 package orange gelatin
2 cups boiling water and apricot juice
¼ teaspoon salt
1 Cereal Flake Pie Shell
1 recipe Whipped Cream Topping
½ cup shredded coconut

Combine apricots and sugar. Dissolve gelatin in water and juice, add salt and mix with apricots.

Chill. When slightly thickened pour into pie shell and chill until firm. Cover with whipped cream topping and garnish with coconut. Makes 1 (9-inch) pie.

COTTAGE CHEESE APPLE PIE

½ recipe Plain Pastry
1½ cups thinly sliced apples
2 eggs
½ cup cottage cheese
¾ cup sugar
½ cup cream
⅛ teaspoon salt
1 teaspoon grated lemon rind
½ teaspoon cinnamon
¼ teaspoon nutmeg

Line a piepan with pastry and cover with apples. Beat eggs slightly, add cottage cheese, ½ cup sugar, cream, salt and lemon rind. Mix remaining sugar with cinnamon and nutmeg and sprinkle over apples, then cover with egg and cheese mixture. Bake in hot oven (425° F.) 10 minutes, reduce temperature to 350°F. and bake 30 minutes longer. Makes 1 deep (9-inch) pie.

BLUEBERRY PIE

4 cups blueberries
1 cup sugar
4 tablespoons flour
⅛ teaspoon salt
1½ tablespoons lemon juice
1 recipe Plain Pastry

Mix berries with sugar, flour, salt and lemon juice. Line piepan with pastry, pour in filling and cover with top crust. Bake in very hot oven (450°F.) 10 minutes; reduce temperature to 350°F. and bake 20 to 30 minutes longer. Makes 1 (9-inch) pie.

Remove the tape as soon as pie is taken from the oven

One way to protect those precious juices is with muslin or paper tape

SPICY BLUEBERRY PIE

3 cups canned blueberries, drained
1 tablespoon flour
1 cup light brown sugar
1 recipe Hot Water Pastry
1 tablespoon butter
1 teaspoon cloves

Combine first 3 ingredients. Line piepan with pastry, pour in filling, dot with butter, sprinkle cloves over top and cover with top crust. Bake in very hot oven (450°F.) 10 minutes; reduce temperature to moderate (350°F.) and bake 25 minutes longer. Makes 1 (9-inch) pie.

Use fresh or frozen blueberries instead of canned ones.

BLACKBERRY PIE

3 cups fresh blackberries
1 cup sugar
2 tablespoons flour
2 tablespoons lemon juice
⅛ teaspoon salt
1 recipe Plain Pastry
1 tablespoon butter

Combine berries, sugar, flour, lemon juice and salt. Line piepan with pastry, add filling, dot with butter and cover with top crust. Bake in very hot oven (450°F.) 10 minutes; reduce temperature to moderate (350°F.) and bake 25 to 30 minutes longer. Makes 1 (9-inch) pie.

CRANBERRY PIE

4 cups cranberries
1½ cups sugar
2 tablespoons flour
¼ teaspoon salt
3 tablespoons water
1 tablespoon melted butter
1 recipe Plain Pastry

Wash berries, chop and mix with next 5 ingredients. Line piepan with pastry, pour in filling and arrange strips of pastry over top in lattice design. Bake in very hot oven (450°F.) 15 minutes; reduce to moderate (350°F.) and bake about 30 minutes longer. Makes 1 (9-inch) pie.

CRANBERRY MERINGUE PIE

2 cups sugar
1 cup water
4 cups cranberries
2 tablespoons cornstarch
¼ teaspoon salt
3 tablespoons butter, melted
2 egg yolks, beaten
1 baked Pastry Shell
1 recipe Meringue I

Cook sugar and ¾ cup water until sugar is dissolved. Add cranberries and cook until they stop "popping." Combine cornstarch, remaining water, salt, butter and egg yolks and add a small amount of cranberries. Mix thoroughly, add to remaining cranberries and cook until thickened and clear. Pour into pastry shell, cover with meringue and proceed as directed. Makes 1 (9-inch) pie.

MOCK CHERRY PIE

1 recipe Plain Pastry
3 cups cranberries
1 cup seeded raisins
1¼ cups sugar
2 tablespoons flour
¼ teaspoon salt
¾ cup water
½ teaspoon vanilla

Line piepan with pastry. Chop cranberries and combine with remaining ingredients. Pour into pastry shell and cover with top crust. Bake in very hot oven (450° F.) 10 minutes; reduce temperature to moderate (350° F.) and bake about 30 minutes longer. Makes 1 (9-inch) pie.

CRANBERRY AND APPLE PIE

1½ cups cranberries
1½ cups diced cooking apples
½ cup water
1 cup sugar
1 recipe Hot Water Pastry

Cook cranberries and apples in water until tender. Add sugar and cool slightly. Line piepan with pastry and pour in cranberry filling. Cover with ½-inch strips of pastry dough in lattice design. Bake in hot oven (450°F.) 10 minutes; reduce to 350°F. and bake 30 to 40 minutes longer. Makes 1 (9-inch) pie.

HUCKLEBERRY PIE

4 cups fresh huckleberries
2 tablespoons granulated tapioca
1 cup sugar
⅛ teaspoon salt
1 tablespoon lemon juice
1 recipe Plain Pastry
1 tablespoon butter

Stem and wash berries. Mix tapioca, sugar and salt together and sprinkle over berries; add lemon juice. Line piepan with pastry, pour in filling and dot with butter. Cover with top crust. Bake in very hot oven (450°F.) 10 minutes; reduce temperature to moderate (350°F.) and bake 35 minutes longer or until berries are tender. Makes 1 (9-inch) pie.

Let the glistening reds and purples of fruit pies shine through a pinwheel decoration

THREE-IN-ONE PIE

1 cup chopped cranberries
1 cup chopped tart apples
¼ cup crushed canned pineapple
1 cup sugar, ⅛ teaspoon salt
1 recipe Plain Pastry

Combine cranberries, apple, pineapple, sugar and salt and let stand 2 to 3 hours. Line piepan with pastry, add filling and cover with top crust. Bake in very hot oven (450°F.) 10 minutes; reduce temperature to moderate (350°F.) and bake 30 to 40 minutes longer. Makes 1 (9-inch) pie.

RED CHERRY PIE

1 No. 2 can tart red cherries
2½ tablespoons granulated tapioca
⅛ teaspoon salt
1 tablespoon melted butter
½ cup sugar, 1 teaspoon flour
2 drops red food coloring
1 recipe Plain Pastry

Mix cherries and juice with next 6 ingredients and let stand for 15 minutes. Stir well. Line piepan with pastry, pour in filling and cover with top crust. Bake in very hot oven (450°F.) 10 minutes; reduce to moderate (350° F.) and bake about 25 minutes longer. Makes 1 (9-inch) pie.

CURRANT PIE

1 cup fresh ripe currants
2 egg yolks, 1 cup sugar
¼ teaspoon salt, ¼ cup flour
1 tablespoon water
½ recipe Plain Pastry
1 recipe Meringue I

Wash currants and stem. Beat egg yolk, slightly; add sugar, salt, flour, water and currants. Line piepan with pastry and pour in filling. Bake in moderate oven (350°F.) 35 minutes or until filling is firm. Cover with meringue and proceed as directed. Makes 1 (9-inch) pie.

CHERRY PIE

2 cups canned sweetened
    red cherries
2 tablespoons cornstarch
3 tablespoons sugar
⅛ teaspoon salt
1 cup cherry juice
1 tablespoon butter
1 recipe Plain Pastry

Drain cherries, saving juice. Mix cornstarch, sugar and salt; add juice gradually and cook slowly until smooth and thickened. Add butter and cherries. Cool. Line piepan with pastry, pour in filling and cover with top crust. Bake in very hot oven (450°F.) 15 minutes; reduce to moderate (350° F.) and bake about 25 minutes longer. Makes 1 (9-inch) pie.

CHERRY MINCE PIE

1 No. 2 can pitted red cherries
1 cup mincemeat
1 tablespoon granulated tapioca
1 recipe Plain Pastry

Combine cherries, juice, mincemeat and tapioca and let stand 15 minutes. Line piepan with pastry, pour in filling and place strips of pastry over top in lattice design. Bake in very hot oven (450°F.) about 30 minutes. Makes 1 (9-inch) pie.

FRESH CHERRY PIE

1¼ cups sugar
2½ tablespoons flour
¼ teaspoon salt
1 quart tart red cherries, washed
    and pitted
1 recipe Plain Pastry

Mix sugar, flour, salt and cherries together. Line piepan with pastry, add cherry mixture and cover with top crust. Bake in very hot oven (450°F.) 10 minutes; reduce temperature to moderate (350°F.) and bake 25 minutes longer. Makes 1 (9-inch) pie. To vary, decrease flour to 1 tablespoon and add 2 tablespoons quick-cooking tapioca. Dot cherries with 1 tablespoon butter.

CHERRY PIE WITH COTTAGE CHEESE LATTICE—Bake pie without top crust. Cover with cottage cheese forced through pastry tube in lattice pattern.

CHERRY HALO PIE—Omit top crust. Cool slightly. Spread 1 recipe Whipped Cream Topping over pie and pile additional cherries in center or leave cherries in center uncovered.

There need be no guessing the name of this cream pie with luscious red cherries piled in the center

FRUIT SALAD PIE

2 teaspoons unflavored gelatin
3 tablespoons orange juice
½ cup diced fresh apricots
1 cup fresh cherries, pitted
  and cut into halves
½ cup diced oranges
½ cup sugar
1 Vanilla Wafer Pie Shell
1 recipe Whipped Cream Topping

Soften gelatin in orange juice, then dissolve over hot water. Mix with fruits (at room temperature) and add sugar. Pour into pie shell and chill until firm. Cover fruit with whipped cream topping and serve at once. Makes 1 (9-inch) pie.

ELDERBERRY PIE

1 recipe Plain Pastry
2½ cups stemmed elderberries
½ cup sugar
⅛ teaspoon salt
2 tablespoons flour
3 tablespoons lemon juice

Line a piepan with pastry. Fill with elderberries. Mix sugar, salt and flour; sprinkle over berries. Add lemon juice. Cover with top crust. Bake in very hot oven (450°F.) 10 minutes, reduce temperature to moderate (350°F.) and bake 30 minutes longer. Makes 1 (9-inch) pie.

LOGANBERRY PIE

3½ cups cooked loganberries
1 tablespoon butter
⅛ teaspoon salt
1½ tablespoons cornstarch
½ cup loganberry juice
1 baked Pastry Shell
1 recipe Meringue I

Combine berries, butter and salt; heat to boiling. Mix cornstarch and juice together, add to berries and cook slowly until thickened, stirring constantly. Cool. Pour into pastry shell, cover with meringue and proceed as directed. Makes 1 (9-inch) pie.

You will hear plenty of "yum-yums" with the first bite of cherry pie with cottage cheese lattice (page 573)

DATE PIE

1 pound dates
Water
1 cup milk
½ cup sugar
⅛ teaspoon salt
1 tablespoon flour
1 egg, well beaten
1 baked Pastry Shell
1 recipe Whipped Cream Topping

Cut dates into quarters, removing stones. Cover with water and simmer, covered, until tender. Add milk, sugar, salt and flour mixed, then add beaten egg. Cook until thickened. Cool. Pour into pastry shell and when firm cover with whipped cream topping. Makes 1 (9-inch) pie.

GOOSEBERRY DATE PIE

1 quart gooseberries
2¼ cups sugar
1½ cups water
1 cup chopped dates
1 teaspoon cinnamon
¼ teaspoon salt
2 tablespoons cornstarch
1 baked Pastry Shell
1 recipe Whipped Cream Topping

Wash gooseberries. Add 1¾ cups sugar and water, cover and simmer until tender. Drain, reserving juice. Add berries to dates. Mix remaining sugar, cinnamon, salt and cornstarch together. Add 1 cup of gooseberry juice and cook until thick and clear. Add gooseberries and dates. When cool pour into pastry shell and garnish with whipped cream topping. Makes 1 (9-inch) pie.

GOOSEBERRY PIE

3 cups gooseberries
1½ cups sugar, ½ cup water
2 tablespoons flour
¼ teaspoon salt
1 teaspoon cinnamon
½ teaspoon cloves
⅛ teaspoon nutmeg
1 recipe Plain Pastry
1 tablespoon butter

Combine gooseberries, 1 cup sugar and water and cook until berries are tender. Sift remaining sugar, flour, salt and spices together; stir into cooked mixture and cool. Line piepan with pastry, pour in filling and dot with butter. Cover with top crust and bake in very hot oven (450°F.) 10 minutes; reduce temperature to moderate (350°F.) and bake 25 minutes longer. Makes 1 (9-inch) pie.

GRAPE PIE

4 cups Concord grapes, 1 cup sugar
3 tablespoons flour
1 teaspoon lemon juice
1 recipe Plain Pastry
1 tablespoon butter

Remove and save skins from grapes. Bring pulp to a boil; rub through strainer to remove seeds. Mix with skins. Blend in sugar and flour mixed together; add lemon juice. Pour grapes into pie shell; dot with butter. Cover with top crust. Bake at 425°F. 35 to 40 minutes. 1 (9-inch) pie.

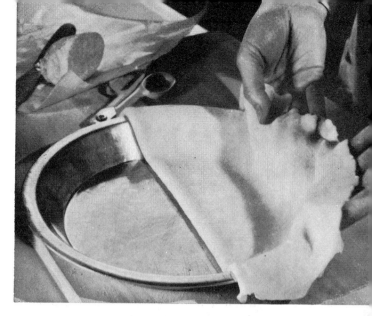

YOUNGBERRY PIE

3 cups youngberries
1 cup sugar
2 tablespoons cornstarch
¼ teaspoon salt
1 recipe Plain Pastry
1 tablespoon butter

Wash and drain berries. Combine with sugar, cornstarch and salt. Line piepan with pastry, fill with fruit mixture and dot with butter. Place strips of pastry over filling in lattice design. Bake in very hot oven (450°F.) 10 minutes, reduce temperature to moderate (350°F.) and bake 20 to 30 minutes longer. Makes 1 (8-inch) pie.

GROUND CHERRY PIE

½ recipe Plain Pastry
1 cup husked ground cherries
2 eggs
⅛ teaspoon salt
⅔ cup sugar
1 tablespoon flour
1 cup milk
1 teaspoon vanilla
1 recipe Whipped Cream Topping

Line piepan with pastry and fill with ground cherries. Beat eggs

To avoid stretching and tearing, handle pastry as you would a delicate flower

with salt and add sugar and flour. Add milk and vanilla and stir well. Pour over cherries and bake in very hot oven (425°F.) 10 minutes, then reduce temperature to moderate (350°F.) and bake 25 to 30 minutes longer or until a knife inserted in center comes out clean. Cover with whipped cream topping. Makes 1 (8-inch) pie.

Be generous with the slits in top crust to keep in the juices

Cut off the surplus pastry before sealing

DOUBLE CRUST GROUND CHERRY PIE

1 recipe Plain Pastry
3 tablespoons flour or granulated tapioca
1 cup sugar
⅛ teaspoon salt
2½ cups husked ground cherries
1 tablespoon butter

Line piepan with pastry. Mix flour with sugar and salt, spread half of mixture in piepan, fill with cherries and sprinkle remaining sugar mixture over top. Dot with butter and cover with top crust. Bake in very hot oven (450°F.) 10 minutes, reduce temperature to moderate (350°F.) and bake 40 minutes longer. Makes 1 (9-inch) pie.

ORANGE AND CRANBERRY PIE

4 cups cranberries, ground
¾ cup orange juice
1 teaspoon grated orange rind
2 cups sugar
½ teaspoon salt
2½ tablespoons granulated tapioca
½ recipe Plain Pastry
1 tablespoon butter
1 recipe Whipped Cream Topping

Combine first 6 ingredients and mix well. Line piepan with pastry, pour in filling and dot with butter. Bake in very hot oven (450°F.) 10 minutes; reduce temperature to moderate (350°F.) and bake 35 minutes longer. Cool; cover with whipped cream topping and garnish with orange segments. Makes 1 (9-inch) pie.

ORANGE PIE

1 cup sugar
⅓ cup flour
¼ teaspoon salt
1½ cups orange juice
2 tablespoons lemon juice
3 egg yolks, beaten
2 tablespoons butter
Grated rind 1 orange
1 Vanilla Wafer Pie Shell
1 recipe Marshmallow Meringue

Sift dry ingredients together, add fruit juices and cook slowly until thickened, stirring constantly. Add slowly to egg yolks, return to heat and cook 2 minutes longer. Add butter and orange rind. Cool. Pour into pie shell, cover with meringue and proceed as directed. Makes 1 (9-inch) pie.

FRENCH—Omit meringue. Whip ¾ cup heavy cream, sweeten and fold ½ into cooled filling. Pour ½ into pie shell, sprinkle with chopped pecan meats, add remaining filling and spread with remaining whipped cream.

ORANGE PINEAPPLE PIE

2 cups canned pineapple juice and water
1 package orange gelatin
2½ cups diced canned pineapple
1 Cereal Flake Pie Shell
1 recipe Whipped Cream Topping

Heat 1 cup liquid to boiling, pour over gelatin and stir until dissolved. Add remaining liquid. Chill until slightly thickened. Arrange pineapple in pie shell, cover with gelatin mixture and chill until firm. Cover with whipped cream topping. Makes 1 (9-inch) pie.

FROSTED ORANGE PIE

1¼ cups sugar
½ cup flour
¼ teaspoon salt
1¼ cups water
2 eggs, separated
½ cup orange juice
2 tablespoons lemon juice
3 tablespoons grated orange rind
½ teaspoon grated lemon rind
1 baked Pastry Shell
⅛ teaspoon salt
2 tablespoons water
1 orange, broken into segments
¾ cup moist shredded coconut

Combine ¾ cup of sugar, flour, salt, water and slightly beaten egg yolks; mix well. Place over boiling water and cook 10 minutes, stirring constantly. Remove from heat and add fruit juice and rind. Cool. Pour into pastry shell. Beat egg whites, remaining ½ cup sugar, salt, and water with rotary beater until thoroughly mixed. Cook over boiling water for 1 minute, remove from heat and beat until mixture will stand in peaks. Pile on pie, arrange orange segments on top and sprinkle with coconut. Makes 1 (9-inch) pie.

SPICED PEAR PIE

½ recipe Hot Water Pastry
1 No. 2½ can pears, drained
   and cut into quarters
¾ cup sugar
⅛ teaspoon salt
1 tablespoon cornstarch
1 teaspoon grated lemon rind
1 tablespoon lemon juice
½ teaspoon cinnamon
½ teaspoon ginger
¼ teaspoon mace
½ cup flour
¼ cup butter, softened

Line piepan with pastry and fill with pears. Mix ¼ cup sugar, salt, cornstarch, lemon rind and juice together and spread over pears. Mix remaining sugar, spices and flour together and add to butter; stir with a fork until of crumb consistency and sprinkle over pears. Bake in very hot oven (450°F.) 15 minutes; reduce temperature to moderate (350° F.) and bake about 30 minutes longer. Makes 1 (9-inch) pie.

PEACH PIE

1 cup sugar
2 tablespoons flour
¼ teaspoon salt
8 peaches, sliced
1 recipe Plain Pastry

Sift dry ingredients together and mix with peaches. Line piepan with pastry, fill with peach mixture and cover with top crust. Bake in very hot oven (450°F.) 15 minutes; réduce to moderate (350°F.) and bake 35 minutes longer. Makes 1 (9-inch) pie.

PERSIMMON MERINGUE PIE

2 cups persimmon pulp
½ cup sugar
½ teaspoon mace
1 teaspoon grated lemon rind
⅛ teaspoon salt
2 teaspoons butter
2 egg yolks
1 baked Pastry Shell
1 recipe Meringue I

The persimmons should be sweet and very ripe. Peel. Press enough through a colander to make 2 cups of pulp. Add sugar, mace, lemon rind and salt and cook slowly for 5 minutes. Add a small amount to butter and beaten egg yolks; return to persimmon mixture and stir until mixture is slightly thickened. Pour into pastry shell, cool and cover with meringue. Proceed as directed. Serve very cold. Makes 1 (9-inch) pie.

AMERICAN PERSIMMON PIE

2 cups persimmon pulp
1 egg, beaten
1 cup milk
½ cup sugar
⅛ teaspoon salt
1 tablespoon cornstarch
½ recipe Plain Pastry

Mix persimmon pulp, egg and milk. Mix sugar, salt and cornstarch and add to first mixture. Line a piepan with pastry and pour in filling. Bake in very hot oven (450°F.) 10 minutes, then reduce temperature to moderate (350°F.) and bake 50 to 60 minutes longer. Makes 1 (9-inch) pie.

PERSIMMON CREAM PIE—Beat 2 eggs with ½ teaspoon cinnamon, ½ cup sugar and ¼ teaspoon salt. Add 2 cups milk or cream, 1 cup persimmon pulp, 2 tablespoons melted butter and 1 teaspoon lemon juice. Pour into unbaked pie shell. Bake in very hot oven (450°F.) 10 minutes, reduce temperature to 350°F. and bake 30 minutes longer.

A pastry wheel cuts perfect lattice strips for a fruit pie

You may like to use pineapple, rhubarb and fresh strawberries in this pie instead of rhubarb alone

RHUBARB PIE

1¾ cups sugar
½ cup sifted flour
¼ teaspoon salt
6 cups fresh rhubarb, cut into small pieces
1 recipe Plain Pastry

Sift together sugar, flour and salt. Line pie pan with pastry and sprinkle 1/3 of the sugar mixture over pie shell. Turn rhubarb into shell heaping slightly at center. Sprinkle remaining sugar mixture over rhubarb. Dot with butter; cover with top crust. (Arrange pastry strips in lattice design over top, if you wish.) Bake at 425°F. 10 minutes, reduce heat to 350° and bake 40 to 50 minutes. Makes 1 (9-inch) pie.

HAWAIIAN PIE

3 tablespoons cornstarch
¼ teaspoon salt
¾ cup sugar
2½ cups unsweetened pineapple juice
2 egg yolks, slightly beaten
2 tablespoons butter
2 tablespoons lemon juice
1 Vanilla Wafer Pie Shell
½ cup crushed pineapple, drained
1 recipe Whipped Cream Topping

Sift cornstarch, salt and sugar together and stir in a little of the pineapple juice. Add remaining juice and cook in top of double boiler until smooth and thickened, stirring constantly. Stir slowly into egg yolks, return to heat and cook 2 minutes longer. Remove from heat and add butter and lemon juice. Cool. Pour filling into pie shell. Fold pineapple into whipped cream topping and spread over filling. Makes 1 (8-inch) pie.

Omit pineapple and juice, lemon juice, ¼ cup sugar and 2 tablespoons cornstarch. Use 1 cup each applesauce and crushed pineapple in filling.

FRESH PINEAPPLE PIE

2 eggs, 1⅓ cups sugar
1 tablespoon lemon juice
2 cups shredded fresh pineapple
1 recipe Plain Pastry
1 tablespoon butter

Beat eggs slightly, add sugar, lemon juice and pineapple. Line piepan with pastry, pour in filling, dot with butter and cover with top crust. Bake in very hot oven (450°F.) 10 minutes; reduce temperature to moderate (350°F.) and bake 35 minutes longer or until pineapple is tender. Makes 1 (8-inch) pie.

FRESH STRAWBERRY PIE

1 cup sugar
2 tablespoons cornstarch
⅛ teaspoon salt
3 cups fresh strawberries
1 recipe Plain Pastry
1 tablespoon butter

Mix sugar, cornstarch and salt together and add to berries. Line piepan with pastry, add filling, dot with butter and cover with top crust. Bake in very hot oven (450°F.) 10 minutes; reduce temperature to moderate (350° F.) and bake 30 minutes longer. Makes 1 (8-inch) pie.

RASPBERRY—Use same quantity raspberries as strawberries.

STRAWBERRY CHEESE PIE

1⅓ cups sweetened condensed milk
⅓ cup lemon juice
2 egg yolks, beaten
3 ounces cream cheese, softened
1 cup sliced strawberries
1 baked Pastry Shell
1 recipe Meringue I

Blend milk and lemon juice and stir until thickened. Add egg yolks, cheese and strawberries. Pour into pastry shell, cover with meringue and proceed as directed. Chill. Makes 1 (8-inch) pie.

STRAWBERRY AND RHUBARB PIE

1¼ cups sugar
¼ cup flour
1 cup fresh strawberries
2 cups diced rhubarb
1 recipe Hot Water Pastry
2 tablespoons butter

Sift sugar and flour together and combine ¾ of it with fruit. Line piepan with pastry, sprinkle remaining dry mixture over bottom and add filling. Dot with butter and arrange pastry strips over top in lattice design. Bake in hot oven (425°F.) 10 minutes; reduce to moderate (350°F.) and bake 30 minutes longer or until fruit is tender. Makes 1 (9-inch) pie.

HONEY RAISIN PIE

1 cup orange juice
3 tablespoons lemon juice
⅔ cup cold water
½ cup honey
¼ teaspoon salt
Grated rind of ½ orange
3 tablespoons cornstarch
1⅔ cups seedless raisins
1 recipe Plain Pastry
1 tablespoon flour
1 tablespoon butter

Combine first 6 ingredients and heat to boiling. Mix cornstarch with a little cold water, add to hot mixture and stir until thickened. Rinse raisins, stir into hot mixture and remove from heat. Line piepan with pastry, sprinkle with flour, pour in filling, dot with butter and cover with top crust. Bake in hot oven (425°F.) 35 to 40 minutes. Serve warm. Makes 1 (9-inch) pie.

PLUM PIE

3 cups pitted fresh plums
1¼ cups sugar
2 tablespoons flour
2 tablespoons lemon juice
⅛ teaspoon salt
1 recipe Plain Pastry
1 tablespoon butter

Combine plums, sugar, flour, lemon juice and salt. Line piepan with pastry, add filling, dot with butter and cover with top crust. Bake in very hot oven (450°F.) 10 minutes; reduce temperature to moderate (350°F.) and bake 35 minutes longer until plums are tender. Makes 1 (9-inch) pie.

Do what you please to the top crust—it's still mince pie

MINCE PIE

1 recipe Plain Pastry
2½ cups mincemeat

Line piepan with pastry, fill with mincemeat and cover with top crust. Bake in hot oven (400° F.) about 35 minutes or until pastry is browned. Makes 1 (9-inch) pie. Serve hot.

MOCK MINCE PIE

2 cups chopped tart apples
1 cup raisins
1 cup brown sugar
⅛ teaspoon cinnamon
⅛ teaspoon nutmeg
⅛ teaspoon salt
1 cup thick sour cream
1 recipe Southern Pastry
1 teaspoon flour

Mix apples, raisins, sugar, spices, salt and sour cream together. Line piepan with pastry, dust with flour, pour in filling and cover with top crust. Bake in very hot oven (450°F.) 10 minutes; reduce temperature to moderate (350°F.) and bake 45 minutes longer or until apples are tender. Serve hot. Makes 1 (9-inch) pie.

Sprinkle grated cheese over baked pie and return to oven until cheese is melted.

DEEP-DISH APPLE PIE

½ recipe Plain Pastry
1 tablespoon flour
1 cup sugar, 5 apples
2 teaspoons butter
¼ teaspoon nutmeg

Line a deep dish with pastry. Sprinkle flour and ¼ cup of the sugar on bottom crust. Pare apples, quarter and place cut side down. Cover with remaining sugar, dot with butter and sprinkle with nutmeg. Bake in 350°F. oven about 35 minutes or until apples are baked and rich sirup has formed. Serves 6.

The deeper the dish, the better the pie

SOUTHERN RAISIN PIE

1½ cups sugar
4 tablespoons flour
1 egg, well beaten
3 tablespoons lemon juice
2 teaspoons grated lemon rind
⅛ teaspoon salt
1 cup seeded raisins
2 cups water
1 recipe Southern Pastry

Mix sugar, flour and egg. Then add lemon juice and rind, salt, raisins and water. Cook over hot water for 15 minutes, stirring occasionally. Cool. Line piepan with pastry, pour in filling and place strips of pastry over filling in lattice design. Bake in very hot oven (450°F.) 10 minutes, reduce temperature to moderate (350°F.) and bake 20 minutes longer. Makes 1 (9-inch) pie.

PRUNE PIE

2 cups stewed prunes, pitted
1 orange, divided into segments
½ cup brown sugar
2 tablespoons butter
¼ teaspoon salt
1 cup prune juice
2 tablespoons cornstarch
1 baked Pastry Shell
1 recipe Meringue I

Cut prunes into quarters. Add orange segments (freed from membrane), sugar, butter, salt and prune juice. Heat to boiling. Mix cornstarch with equal amount of cold water or prune juice, add to hot prune mixture and cook 5 to 10 minutes, stirring occasionally to keep smooth. Cool, pour into pastry, shell, cover with meringue and bake as directed. Makes 1 (9-inch) pie.

DOUBLE FRUIT PIE

2¼ cups chopped cooked prunes
¾ cup chopped cooked apricots
¾ cup sugar
1 recipe Plain Pastry
4 teaspoons flour
1½ teaspoons lemon juice
2 tablespoons prune juice
2 tablespoons apricot juice
1½ tablespoons butter

Combine fruits and sugar. Line piepan with pastry, sprinkle with flour and add filling. Pour combined fruit juices over all, dot with butter and cover with top crust. Bake in hot oven (400°F.) 35 to 40 minutes. Makes 1 (9-inch) pie.

Pies may be made in dishes of any shape and some are made without bottom crust

APPLE NUT CHIFFON PIE

1 tablespoon unflavored gelatin
¼ cup cold water
1¼ cups applesauce
⅛ teaspoon nutmeg
2 egg whites
2 tablespoons sugar
¼ cup chopped nut meats
1 baked Pastry Shell

Soften gelatin in water 5 minutes. Heat applesauce and nutmeg, add gelatin and stir until dissolved. Chill until mixture begins to thicken. Beat egg whites until stiff, add sugar and beat to a stiff meringue. Fold into applesauce mixture and add nuts. Pour into pastry shell and chill until firm. Makes 1 (9-inch) pie.

DREAM PIE

3 egg whites, ¼ cup sugar
1½ cups chopped dates
1 tablespoon lemon juice
1 teaspoon vanilla
1 baked Pastry Shell

Beat egg whites until stiff but not dry. Beat in sugar gradually. Fold in dates, lemon juice and vanilla and pour into pastry shell. Bake in 325°F. oven 25 to 30 minutes. Makes 1 (9-inch) pie.

BANANA CHIFFON PIE

2 teaspoons unflavored gelatin
3 tablespoons cold water
1 cup mashed bananas
1 tablespoon lemon juice
½ teaspoon grated lemon rind
⅛ teaspoon grated orange rind
5 tablespoons sugar
2 eggs, separated
⅛ teaspoon salt
1 Brazil-nut Pie Shell
1 recipe Whipped Cream Topping

Soften gelatin in water 5 minutes. Combine banana, lemon juice and rind, orange rind, 3 tablespoons sugar, slightly beaten egg yolks and salt; cook slowly until consistency of soft custard, stirring constantly. Remove from heat, add gelatin and stir until dissolved. Cool until slightly thickened. Beat egg whites until stiff, beat in remaining sugar and fold into banana mixture. Pour into pie shell and chill until firm. Spread with whipped cream topping. Makes 1 (9-inch) pie.

To make your pie more of a "dream" cover it with marshmallow meringue

CHERRY CHIFFON PIE

1 tablespoon unflavored gelatin
¼ cup cold water
4 eggs, separated; ⅔ cup sugar
½ cup cherry juice
¼ teaspoon salt
1 tablespoon lemon juice
1 cup drained canned
    tart cherries
1 baked Pastry Shell
1 recipe Whipped Cream Topping

Soften gelatin in water 5 minutes. Beat egg yolks and add ½ cup sugar, cherry juice and salt; cook over boiling water until of custard consistency. Remove from heat, add gelatin and stir until dissolved. Add lemon juice and cherries and cool until mixture begins to thicken. Beat egg whites until stiff, beat in remaining sugar and fold into cherry mixture. Pour into pastry shell and chill until firm. Spread with whipped cream. Makes 1 (9-inch) pie.

CIDER NUT CHIFFON PIE

1 tablespoon unflavored gelatin
¼ cup cold water
¼ teaspoon salt, ⅔ cup sugar
1 cup hot cider
½ cup chopped apple
2 tablespoons lemon juice
½ cup chopped nut meats
2 egg whites
1 Graham Cracker Pie Shell
1 recipe Whipped Cream Topping

Soften gelatin in cold water 5 minutes. Add salt and ⅓ cup sugar to cider, add gelatin and stir until dissolved. Chill until thick. Whip. Blend apple with lemon juice and add with nuts to whipped gelatin mixture. Beat egg whites until stiff, beat in remaining sugar and fold into mixture. Pour into pie shell and chill until firm. Spread with whipped cream. Makes 1 (9-inch) pie.

COFFEE PIE

1 tablespoon unflavored gelatin
¼ cup cold water
3 eggs, separated; 1 cup sugar
1 cup cold strong coffee
¼ teaspoon salt
1 teaspoon vanilla
1 Graham Cracker Pie Shell
1 recipe Whipped Cream Topping

Soften gelatin in water 5 minutes. Beat egg yolks until light; beat in ½ cup sugar gradually, add coffee slowly, then salt. Cook over boiling water 5 minutes stirring constantly. Add gelatin and stir until dissolved; chill until mixture begins to thicken. Beat egg whites until stiff, beat in remaining sugar gradually and add vanilla. Fold into gelatin mixture. Pour into pie shell and chill until firm. Cover with whipped cream topping. Makes 1 (9-inch) pie.

CHOCOLATE CHIFFON PIE

1 tablespoon unflavored gelatin
¼ cup cold water
½ cup boiling water
2 ounces (squares) chocolate
4 eggs, separated
1 cup sugar
¼ teaspoon salt
1 teaspoon vanilla
1 Vanilla Wafer Pie Shell
1 recipe Whipped Cream Topping

Soften gelatin in cold water 5 minutes. Mix boiling water and chocolate until smooth. Add gelatin to chocolate mixture and stir until dissolved. Add slightly beaten egg yolks, ½ cup sugar, salt and vanilla; beat thoroughly. Cool until mixture begins to thicken. Beat egg whites until foamy, beat in remaining sugar gradually and fold into gelatin mixture. Pour into pie shell and chill until firm. Spread with whipped cream topping before serving. Makes 1 (9-inch) pie.

Sometimes make your fruity cheese pie with a meringue top and a border of apricots

FRUITY CHEESE PIE

1 tablespoon unflavored gelatin
¼ cup cold water
1 egg, separated
¼ cup sugar
¼ cup milk
¼ teaspoon salt
⅔ cup cottage cheese
½ lemon, juice and grated rind
1 Zwieback Pie Shell
Canned apricot halves
⅔ cup apricot juice
2 teaspoons cornstarch
⅛ teaspoon cinnamon
⅛ teaspoon cloves

Soften gelatin in water 5 minutes. Beat egg yolk, add sugar, milk and salt; cook in top of double boiler until slightly thickened. Add gelatin and stir until dissolved. Add cheese, lemon juice and rind. Beat egg white until stiff, fold into mixture, pour into pie shell and chill until firm. Arrange apricots over top. Combine apricot juice, cornstarch, cinnamon and cloves and cook until thickened. Cool slightly and pour over apricots. Chill. Makes 1 (9-inch) pie.

CHOCOLATE MAL-LOW PIE

½ cup cocoa
¾ cup water
1 teaspoon vanilla
¼ teaspoon salt
¼ cup milk
¾ pound marshmallows
1 baked Pastry Shell
2 bananas, sliced lengthwise
6 marshmallows, cut into halves

Mix cocoa and water to smooth paste and cook over low heat 2 minutes. Cool; add vanilla and salt. Heat milk and add marshmallows; fold over and over until marshmallows are about half melted. Remove from heat and continue folding marshmallows until smooth and fluffy. Chill about 15 minutes, then combine with cocoa mixture and chill about 25 minutes longer, stirring twice. Pour chocolate marshmallow mixture into pastry shell and chill until firm. Arrange slices of banana on top of pie in criss-cross pattern and decorate with halves of marshmallows. Makes 1 (9-inch) pie.

Use strips of pineapple instead of bananas.

PINEAPPLE FLUFF PIE

2½ tablespoons cornstarch
½ cup water
1 cup pineapple juice
¾ cup sugar
1 cup drained crushed pineapple
3 egg whites
¼ teaspoon salt
1 baked Pastry Shell
½ recipe Whipped Cream Topping

Blend cornstarch and water. Add pineapple juice and ½ cup sugar and cook slowly until thickened, stirring constantly. Add pineapple and cook a few minutes longer. Combine egg whites and salt and beat until foamy; add remaining sugar gradually, beating until stiff. Fold into pineapple mixture and pour into pastry shell. Cool. Spread with whipped cream topping. Makes 1 (9-inch) pie.

PINEAPPLE CUSTARD PIE — Mix ¾ cup sugar, 2·tablespoons cornstarch, ⅛ teaspoon salt and 1 cup milk in top of double boiler. Add 3 beaten egg yolks and cook until thickened. Remove from heat, add 1 cup drained, crushed pineapple and 3 stiffly beaten egg whites. Cool. Pour into baked pastry shell.

ORANGE CHIFFON PIE

1 tablespoon unflavored gelatin
¼ cup cold water
4 eggs, separated; 1 cup sugar
½ cup orange juice
1 tablespoon lemon juice
½ teaspoon salt
1 tablespoon grated orange rind
1 baked Pastry Shell
½ recipe Whipped Cream Topping

Soften gelatin in water 5 minutes. Beat egg yolks and add ½ cup sugar, orange juice, lemon juice and salt. Cook over boiling water until of custard consistency. Add grated orange rind and softened gelatin and stir thoroughly. Cool. When mixture begins to thicken fold in stiffly beaten egg whites to which remaining ½ cup of sugar has been added. Fill pastry shell and chill. Spread with whipped cream topping. Makes 1 (9-inch) pie.

LEMON — Use ½ cup lemon juice and 1 teaspoon grated lemon rind instead of orange juice and rind.

The children as well as grownups will enjoy orange segments and coconut instead of whipped cream on the orange chiffon pie

MALLOW PIE

½ pound marshmallows
1 cup strained orange juice
1 tablespoon lemon juice
½ cup heavy cream, whipped
1 Vanilla Wafer Pie Shell
1 orange, sliced
5 marshmallows, toasted

Heat marshmallows in top of double boiler until almost melted. Fold in fruit juice. Cool. Fold in whipped cream and chill until slightly thickened. Pour into pie shell and chill until firm. Garnish with orange slices and marshmallows. Makes 1 (9-inch) pie.

PINEAPPLE CHIFFON PIE

2 tablespoons unflavored gelatin
½ cup cold water
½ cup sugar
Dash salt
2 cups hot crushed pineapple, including juice
1½ tablespoons lemon juice
1 cup heavy cream, whipped
1 baked Cheese Pastry Shell

Soften gelatin in cold water 5 minutes; add sugar and salt, and dissolve in boiling pineapple. Cool slightly and add lemon juice. Continue cooling and when it begins to thicken, beat until light and foamy; fold in whipped cream. Pile into pastry shell and chill until firm. Makes 1 (9-inch) pie.

PINEAPPLE BANANA CHIFFON —Omit whipping cream and use only 1 tablespoon gelatin and 1 cup pineapple. Beat 3 egg yolks and combine with sugar and 1½ cups milk. Cook slowly until mixture coats a spoon. Add softened gelatin, cool and when mixture begins to thicken add pineapple, lemon juice and 2 bananas, sliced. Fold in 3 stiffly beaten egg whites and chill until firm.

PINEAPPLE CHERRY — Prepare as Pineapple Banana using ½ cup maraschino cherries for bananas.

BRAZIL STRAW-BERRY CHIFFON PIE

1 package strawberry gelatin
1 cup hot water
½ cup sugar
1 pint strawberries
½ cup heavy cream, whipped
Brazil-nut Pie Shell
Whole Brazil-nut meats

Dissolve gelatin in hot water. Add sugar to berries; crush and let stand 15 minutes. Drain juice from berries and add juice to gelatin. Chill until mixture begins to thicken. Whip until very fluffy, then fold in berries and whipped cream to which a little salt has been added. Pour mixture into pie shell and chill until firm. Garnish with whole Brazil nuts. Makes 1 (8-inch) pie.

BANANA—Omit heavy cream. Mix 1 cup of the strawberries with sugar and ¼ cup water. Cook slowly 5 minutes to extract as much juice as possible, then strain and add 1 cup of juice to gelatin. Cool until mixture begins to thicken. Slice 2 ripe bananas and remaining strawberries into pie shell. Cover with gelatin mixture and chill until firm. Cover with Whipped Cream Topping. Use baked Pastry Shell instead of Brazil-nut Shell and garnish with whole strawberries.

STRAWBERRY CHIFFON PIE

1 pint strawberries
¾ cup sugar
1 tablespoon unflavored gelatin
¼ cup cold water
½ cup boiling water
1 tablespoon lemon juice
¼ teaspoon salt
½ cup heavy cream, whipped
2 egg whites, stiffly beaten
1 Graham Cracker Pie Shell
½ recipe Whipped Cream Topping

Wash berries. Save ½ cup whole berries for garnishing and crush the remainder; add sugar and let stand ½ hour. Soften gelatin in cold water 5 minutes, then dissolve in boiling water. Combine with crushed berries, lemon juice and salt. Cool and when it begins to thicken fold in whipped cream and egg whites. Pour filling into pie shell and chill until firm. Garnish with whipped cream, whole berries. Makes 1 (9-inch) pie.

RED RASPBERRY—Use red raspberries instead of strawberries.

Change about now and then and use most of the berries on the top of your pie

If you like to use a pastry tube, pile whipped cream on the Brazil strawberry chiffon pie

RHUBARB WHIPPED CREAM PIE

2 tablespoons unflavored gelatin
½ cup cold water
2½ cups stewed rhubarb
1 cup sugar
1 cup heavy cream, whipped
1 Cereal Flake Pie Shell

Soften gelatin in water. Heat rhubarb and sugar to boiling, add gelatin and stir until dissolved. Cool; when mixture begins to thicken fold in whipped cream. Pour into pie shell and chill. Makes 1 (9-inch) pie.

PRUNE CHIFFON PIE

1 tablespoon unflavored gelatin
¼ cup cold water
1 cup chopped cooked prunes
¾ cup prune juice
½ cup sugar, ¼ teaspoon salt
2 tablespoons lemon juice
1 teaspoon grated lemon rind
2 egg whites, stiffly beaten
1 baked Pastry Shell

Soften gelatin in water 5 minutes. Combine prunes, juice, sugar, salt, lemon juice and rind, and heat to boiling. Remove from heat, add gelatin and stir until dissolved. Cool. When slightly thickened, fold in egg whites. Pour into pastry shell and chill. Makes 1 (9-inch) pie.

RUM CHIFFON PIE

1 tablespoon unflavored gelatin
¼ cup cold water
3 eggs, separated; 1½ cups milk
¾ cup sugar, ⅛ teaspoon salt
1 tablespoon rum
1 Graham Cracker Pie Shell
1 recipe Whipped Cream Topping
Sweet chocolate, shredded

Soften gelatin in water 5 minutes. Beat egg yolks, add milk, sugar and salt and cook over low heat, stirring constantly. When mixture coats a spoon stir in gelatin and cool until mixture begins to thicken. Beat egg whites until stiff and fold into custard with rum. Turn into pie shell, cover with whipped cream, sprinkle with chocolate Chill. Serves 6.

STRAWBERRY RE-FRIGERATOR PIE

2 cups sliced strawberries
⅔ cup sugar
1 tablespoon lemon juice
⅛ teaspoon salt
2 teaspoons unflavored gelatin
½ cup water
1 cup heavy cream, whipped
1 teaspoon vanilla
1 Cereal Flake Pie Shell

Combine strawberries, sugar, lemon juice and salt. Chill. Soften gelatin in water 5 minutes, then dissolve over hot water. Fold gelatin, whipped cream and vanilla into strawberry mixture. Pour into pie shell and chill until firm. Garnish with whole strawberries. Makes 1 (9-inch) pie.

PUMPKIN CHIFFON PIE

2 teaspoons unflavored gelatin
¼ cup cold water
3 eggs, separated; 1 cup sugar
1¼ cups mashed cooked pumpkin
½ teaspoon salt
½ teaspoon cinnamon
¼ teaspoon nutmeg
½ teaspoon ginger, ½ cup milk
1 Gingersnap Pie Shell
1 recipe Whipped Cream Topping

Soften gelatin in water 5 minutes. Beat egg yolks and add ½ cup sugar, pumpkin, salt, spices and milk. Cook over low heat, stirring constantly until mixture begins to thicken. Add gelatin to hot pumpkin and stir until dissolved. Cool. When mixture begins to thicken, beat egg whites until almost stiff and beat in remaining sugar, 1 tablespoon at a time. Fold into pumpkin mixture, pour into pie shell and chill until firm. Cover with whipped cream topping. Makes 1 (9-inch) pie.

Thrifty cream pie filling (page 587) may be used as a foundation for the strawberry refrigerator pie in any shell of your choice

TOFFEE CHIFFON PIE

1 tablespoon unflavored gelatin
¼ cup cold water
2 cups hot milk
⅛ teaspoon salt, ⅓ cup sugar
2 eggs, separated
½ teaspoon vanilla
¾ cup crushed pecan toffee
1 baked Pastry Shell
Pecan toffee shavings

Soften gelatin in water 5 minutes. Combine milk, salt and 4 tablespoons sugar; stir until dissolved. Add to slightly beaten egg yolks and cook over boiling water until thickened, stirring constantly. Add gelatin and stir until dissolved. Cool. Add vanilla and toffee when custard begins to thicken. Beat egg whites until stiff, add remaining sugar and fold into custard. Pour into pastry shell and chill until firm. Sprinkle with toffee shavings. Makes 1 (9-inch) pie.

SHERRY—Use almond extract instead of vanilla; add 2 tablespoons sherry, and use ¼ cup chopped almonds instead of toffee and toffee shavings.

ORANGE PUMPKIN PIE

2 tablespoons unflavored gelatin
¼ cup cold water
2½ cups mashed cooked pumpkin
1¼ cups brown sugar
½ teaspoon salt
1½ teaspoons pumpkin pie spice
⅓ cup orange juice, 2 cups milk
2 egg yolks, slightly beaten
2 tablespoons butter
1 baked Pastry Shell

Soften gelatin in water 5 minutes. Combine next 8 ingredients in order listed and cook in top of double boiler until slightly thickened. Add gelatin and stir until dissolved. Cool. Pour into pastry shell and chill until firm. Makes 1 (10-inch) pie.

When you don't want to use the oven make a vanilla or chocolate wafer crust for the two-tone pie

SHARKEY CUSTARD PIE

½ recipe Southern Pastry
¾ cup butter, ½ cup sugar
6 eggs, separated
1 cup wild goose plum preserves
Few grains salt
2 tablespoons whisky
½ cup cream
1 recipe Whipped Cream Topping

Line pie plate with pastry. Cream butter and sugar; beat egg yolks and add to creamed mixture. Add plum preserves, salt, whisky and cream. Beat egg whites until stiff and fold into mixture. Bake piecrust in hot oven (400° F.) 15 minutes. Remove from oven and fill with custard mixture. Reduce oven temperature to moderate (375° F.) and continue baking 40 minutes or until knife comes out clean when inserted in center. Spread with whipped cream before serving. Makes 1 (9-inch) pie.

JELLY PIE—Omit plum preserves and whisky and use only 4 eggs. Add ½ cup strawberry jelly, increase sugar to 1½ cups and add 1 teaspoon lemon juice. If a less rich pie is desired, omit cream and ¼ cup of butter.

TWO-TONE PIE

1 tablespoon unflavored gelatin
4 tablespoons cold water
1 cup sugar
1¼ tablespoons cornstarch
4 eggs, separated
2 cups milk, scalded
2 ounces (squares) chocolate
2 teaspoons vanilla
1 baked Pastry Shell
¼ teaspoon cream of tartar
1 recipe Whipped Cream Topping

Soften gelatin in water. Mix ½ cup sugar and the cornstarch together; add beaten egg yolks and stir in milk. Cook slowly until thickened, stirring constantly. Remove from heat and reserve 1 cup of mixture. Add gelatin to remaining mixture and stir until dissolved. Melt 1½ ounces chocolate and add to the reserved cup of mixture; add 1 teaspoon vanilla and beat with rotary beater. Cool. Pour into pastry shell and chill. Beat egg whites until frothy, add cream of tartar and beat until stiff; beat in remaining sugar. When gelatin mixture is slightly thickened, fold in egg whites and remaining vanilla. Pour in pastry shell, covering the chocolate layer. Chill thoroughly. Cover with whipped cream topping; grate remaining chocolate and sprinkle over top. Makes 1 (9-inch) pie.

CREAM PIE

⅓ cup sugar
⅛ teaspoon salt
3 tablespoons cornstarch
½ cup cold milk
1½ cups scalding milk
3 egg yolks
1½ teaspoons vanilla
1 baked Pastry Shell
1 recipe Meringue III

Mix sugar, salt and cornstarch together; add cold milk and blend. Add scalding milk gradually and cook in top of double boiler, stirring constantly until mixture thickens. Beat yolks until light and pour a small amount of the hot mixture over them, stirring rapidly. Return to remaining mixture in top of double boiler and cook 4 minutes longer. Add vanilla and cool. Pour into pastry shell, cover with meringue, sealing in custard, and bake. Makes 1 (9-inch) pie. Use any variations listed under Thrifty Cream Pie.

APRICOT—Cover filling with 1 cup cooked apricot pulp and spread with Whipped Cream Topping.

PEACH—Cover filling with sliced sweetened peaches and spread with Whipped Cream Topping.

PINEAPPLE—Stir 1½ cups drained crushed pineapple into filling.

THRIFTY CREAM PIE

1½ cups milk
¼ cup sugar
¼ teaspoon salt
3 tablespoons flour
1 egg yolk
1 tablespoon butter
½ teaspoon vanilla
1 baked Pastry Shell
1 recipe Whipped Cream Topping

Scald 1 cup milk over boiling water. Mix sugar, salt, flour and remaining milk together. Stir into hot milk and cook slowly until thickened, stirring constantly. Cover and cook over boiling water for 5 minutes. Add mixture slowly to egg yolk and cook 1 minute longer. Add butter and vanilla. Cool. Pour into pastry shell and spread with whipped cream topping. Makes 1 (9-inch) pie.

BANANA—Use 4 ripe bananas. Fill pastry shell with alternate layers of sliced bananas and cooled filling.

COCONUT—Stir 1½ cups moist shredded coconut into filling.

FRUIT—Stir 1½ cups drained canned fruit salad and a few slices of banana into filling.

Deft handling of meringue, a moderate oven and a short time, gives just a tinge of golden brown

RASPBERRY — Add 1 cup raspberries to cooled filling.

STRAWBERRY—Cover filling with sliced, sweetened strawberries and spread with Whipped Cream Topping.

Any Crumb Pie Shell may be used instead of baked pastry shell.

OLD-FASHIONED CREAM PIE

1 pint heavy cream
4 tablespoons sugar
2 tablespoons flour
⅛ teaspoon salt
2 egg whites, slightly beaten
1 baked Pastry Shell
1 recipe Whipped Cream Topping

Heat cream in top of double boiler. Mix sugar, flour and salt. Pour hot cream over mixture, stirring well. Return to double boiler and cook until thickened, stirring constantly. Remove from heat, add egg whites, pour into pastry shell and bake in hot oven (400° F.) 15 minutes. Chill and cover with whipped cream topping. Makes 1 (9-inch) pie.

SOUR CREAM PIE

½ cup flour
¾ cup sugar
½ teaspoon salt
2 cups sour cream
3 egg yolks
¼ teaspoon almond extract
1 baked Pastry Shell
1 recipe Meringue II

Mix flour, sugar and salt together; stir in cream and cook in top of double boiler until thickened, stirring constantly. Pour hot mixture slowly over egg yolks, stirring constantly. Return to heat and cook 3 minutes longer. Add flavoring and cool. Pour into pastry shell, top with meringue and proceed as directed. Makes 1 (9-inch) pie.

TRANSPARENT CUSTARD PIE

½ recipe Plain Pastry
2 cups sugar
4 tablespoons butter, melted
3 tablespoons cream
4 egg yolks, beaten
½ teaspoon salt
1 tablespoon flour
1 teaspoon vanilla
1 recipe Brown Sugar Meringue

Line a piepan with pastry. Mix sugar, butter and cream. Add egg yolks, salt, flour and vanilla. Pour into pastry. Bake in very hot oven (450° F.) 10 minutes; reduce temperature to moderate (350° F.) and bake 25 to 30 minutes longer or until a knife inserted in center comes out clean. Cover with meringue and bake as directed. Makes 1 (9-inch) pie.

APPLE CUSTARD PIE

½ recipe Plain Pastry
4 tablespoons flour
1 cup sugar
5 apples, pared and cut into halves
1 egg, beaten
1½ cups evaporated milk
¼ teaspoon nutmeg
½ teaspoon cinnamon

Line piepan with pastry, sprinkle 2 tablespoons flour and ¼ cup sugar over bottom. Arrange apples cut side up in pastry shell. Combine egg and milk and pour over apples. Combine remaining flour and sugar with spices and sprinkle over top. Bake in very hot oven (450° F.) 10 minutes; reduce temperature to slow (325° F.) and bake 30 minutes longer, until apples are tender and custard firm. Makes 1 (9-inch) pie.

SOUR CREAM APPLE—Omit egg, milk, cinnamon and ½ of flour. Combine remaining ingredients as above, bake as above, adding 1 cup sour cream after 25 minutes.

Lustrous blackberry cream pie will tempt the most jaded appetite

BLACKBERRY CREAM PIE

1⅓ cups sweetened condensed milk
¼ cup lemon juice
1⅓ cups fresh blackberries
1 baked Pastry Shell
1 recipe Whipped Cream Topping

Combine milk and lemon juice and stir until thickened. Fold in 1 cup of fruit and pour into pastry shell. Cover with whipped cream topping and garnish with remaining berries. Chill. Makes 1 (9-inch) pie.

Any one of the following fruits may be used instead of blackberries: raspberries, sliced apricots, bananas, peaches or strawberries; or 1½ cups drained crushed pineapple.

BLACKBERRY MERINGUE—Use only ½ of lemon juice and add 2 egg yolks. Top with meringue and proceed as directed, omitting berry garnish.

Use any of fruits suggested above.

APPLE CREAM PIE

3 cups chopped tart apples
½ cup sugar
1 tablespoon flour
¼ teaspoon mace
½ recipe Southern Pastry
2 tablespoons butter
1 recipe Thrifty Cream Pie filling
1 recipe Meringue I

Combine apples, sugar, flour and mace. Line a piepan with pastry, add apple mixture and dot with butter. Bake in very hot oven (450° F.) 10 minutes; reduce temperature to moderate (350° F.) and bake 35 minutes longer or until apples are tender. Cool. Cover with cream filling, top with meringue and proceed as directed. Makes 1 (9-inch) pie.

TWIN PIE—Pit 2 cups cooked prunes. Cut into quarters and add 1 cup prune juice, ½ cup orange juice, ½ teaspoon grated orange rind, ½ cup sugar, ¼ teaspoon salt and 3 tablespoons granulated tapioca. Cook slowly until tapioca is clear. Cool. Pour into baked Pastry Shell. Cover with cream filling and meringue as above.

On occasion top the date cream pie with meringue or whipped cream

DATE CREAM PIE

½ recipe Plain Pastry
1 egg
1 cup sugar
½ teaspoon salt
1 cup evaporated milk
2 tablespoons lemon juice
1 cup chopped dates

Line piepan with pastry. Combine remaining ingredients and pour into pastry shell. Bake in very hot oven (425° F.) 10 minutes; reduce temperature to slow (300° F.) and bake 15 minutes longer until firm. Makes 1 (9-inch) pie.

BUTTERSCOTCH PIE

¾ cup brown sugar
¼ cup granulated sugar
⅓ cup flour
2 cups scalded milk
⅛ teaspoon salt
3 egg yolks, beaten
1½ tablespoons butter
1 teaspoon vanilla
1 baked Pastry Shell
1 recipe Meringue II

Combine sugars with flour, add hot milk gradually, stirring constantly to make a smooth mixture. Add salt and cook in top of double boiler for 15 minutes, stirring occasionally, until thickened. Pour part of the hot mixture slowly onto egg yolks, stirring constantly. Pour back into double boiler, mix well, and cook not more than 3 minutes, stirring almost constantly. Add butter, stir until melted. Cool. Add vanilla, pour into pastry shell, cover with meringue and proceed as directed. Makes 1 (9-inch) pie.

BLACK WALNUT PIE—Use all granulated sugar and only 2 teaspoons butter. Add 1 cup black walnut meats, chopped, to cooled filling. Proceed as above.

BARBARA FRIETCHIE PIE

½ recipe Southern Pastry
¾ cup granulated sugar
¾ cup brown sugar
½ cup heavy cream or
    evaporated milk
2 egg yolks, beaten
2 tablespoons butter
½ teaspoon vanilla
⅛ teaspoon salt
2 egg whites, beaten
Nutmeg

Line piepan with pastry. Cook next 5 ingredients in top of double boiler until thickened, stirring constantly. Remove from heat, add vanilla, salt and egg whites. Pour into pastry shell, sprinkle with nutmeg. Bake in hot oven (425° F.) 10 minutes, reduce temperature to slow (300°F.) and bake about 45 minutes longer or until knife inserted in center comes out clean. Serve very cold. Makes 1 (9-inch) pie.

BUTTERMILK PIE

1 tablespoon butter
2 tablespoons flour
2 egg yolks
½ cup sugar
1 cup buttermilk
1 teaspoon lemon extract
½ recipe Plain Pastry
1 recipe Meringue I

Blend butter and flour, add egg yolks and sugar beaten together, buttermilk and extract. Line piepan with pastry, pour in filling and bake in hot oven (425° F.) 10 minutes, reduce temperature to moderate (350° F.) and continue baking 20 to 25 minutes or until firm. Remove from oven, cover with meringue and bake as directed. Makes 1 (9-inch) pie.

RAISIN BUTTER-SCOTCH PIE

3 tablespoons butter
¾ cup brown sugar
2¼ cups milk
1 tablespoon cornstarch
1 cup raisins, ground
⅛ teaspoon salt
2 egg yolks
2 teaspoons vanilla
1 baked Pastry Shell
1 recipe Brown Sugar Meringue

Heat butter and sugar until melted. Add 2 cups milk and scald over boiling water, stirring to dissolve sugar. Combine cornstarch, remaining milk, raisins, salt and egg yolks and beat well. Add to milk mixture and cook until thickened, stirring constantly. Add vanilla. Pour into pastry shell, top with meringue and bake as directed. Makes 1 (9-inch) pie.

SPICED CREAM PIE

2 eggs, 1 cup sour cream
1 cup seedless raisins
1 cup sugar, 1 tablespoon flour
½ teaspoon cinnamon
½ teaspoon nutmeg
⅛ teaspoon salt
½ recipe Hot Water Pastry

Beat eggs until light; add sour cream and raisins. Blend sugar, flour, cinnamon, nutmeg and salt and add to first mixture. Line piepan with pastry and pour in filling. Place thin strips of pastry across top of filling. Bake in hot oven (425° F.) 15 minutes, then reduce temperature to moderate (350°F.) and continue baking until filling is firm, about 30 minutes. Serve hot. Makes 1 (9-inch) pie.

SOUR CREAM RAISIN PIE

2 eggs
1 cup sugar
1 cup thick sour cream
1 cup raisins, chopped
¼ teaspoon nutmeg
⅛ teaspoon salt
1 tablespoon lemon juice
1 unbaked Pastry Shell

Beat eggs, add sugar and beat until light. Whip sour cream and fold into egg mixture. Add raisins, nutmeg, salt and lemon juice and mix. Pour mixture into pastry shell and bake in very hot oven (450°F.) 10 minutes. Reduce temperature to moderate (350° F.) and bake 20 minutes longer. Makes 1 (9-inch) pie.

SIRUP CUSTARD PIE

1 cup corn sirup
½ cup sugar
4 tablespoons butter
3 eggs, 1 teaspoon vanilla
1 recipe Southern Pastry

Cook sirup, sugar and butter together until thickened. Beat eggs until light, pour sirup over them, add vanilla and blend. Line a piepan with pastry and pour in filling. Bake in hot oven (425° F.) 10 minutes; reduce temperature to slow (325° F.) and bake 20 minutes longer or until filling is firm. Makes 1 (8-inch) pie. Sprinkle ½ cup pecan meats over top before baking.

For the "company touch" decorate the cream pie with fruit

CUSTARD PIE

4 eggs, slightly beaten
¼ teaspoon salt
½ cup sugar
3 cups milk, scalded
½ teaspoon vanilla
½ recipe Plain Pastry
Nutmeg

Combine eggs, salt and sugar; add milk and vanilla slowly. Line pie-pan with pastry, pour in filling and sprinkle with nutmeg. Bake in very hot oven (450° F.) 10 minutes. Reduce temperature to slow (325° F.) and bake 30 to 40 minutes longer, or until a knife inserted in center comes out clean. Makes 1 (9-inch) pie.

CARAMEL—Caramelize sugar and add to scalded milk before combining milk with egg mixture.

CARROT — Add 1 cup grated carrot, ½ teaspoon lemon extract and 3 additional tablespoons of sugar to custard before baking.

COCONUT — Add 1 cup shredded coconut to custard before baking.

MODERN CUSTARD PIE—Use 1 baked Pastry Shell in place of pastry. Pour custard into well-greased piepan of same size as used for pastry shell. Bake in slow oven (325°F.) 45 to 55 minutes, or until knife inserted in center comes out clean. Chill thoroughly. Place waxed paper on top of custard, a cookie sheet on paper and turn upside down, leaving custard on sheet. Remove piepan and place pastry shell in its place. Turn right-side up. This method keeps crust from becoming soggy.

STRAWBERRY—Spread 1 cup sliced unsweetened strawberries over cooled pie; top with whipped cream.

PEANUT-BUTTER PIE — Combine 1 cup light corn sirup 1 cup sugar, 3 eggs, ½ teaspoon vanilla and ⅓ cup peanut butter. Pour into unbaked shell; bake as above.

CHOCOLATE BUT-TERSCOTCH PIE

1 cup brown sugar
½ cup flour
2 cups milk, scalded
2 ounces chocolate, melted
1 tablespoon water
⅛ teaspoon salt
2 egg yolks, slightly beaten
1 tablespoon butter
½ teaspoon vanilla
1 baked Pastry Shell
1 recipe Brown Sugar Meringue

Blend sugar and flour and add enough milk to make a thin mixture. Combine with remaining milk, add chocolate and stir until thickened. Cook in top of double boiler, covered, for 5 minutes. Stir water and salt into egg yolks, add a little of the cooked mixture, return to remaining mixture, add butter and cook 1 minute longer. Cool. Add vanilla, pour into pastry shell, top with meringue and proceed as directed. Makes 1 (9-inch) pie.

CHOCOLATE CUSTARD PIE

3 eggs, slightly beaten
½ teaspoon salt
¾ cup sugar
2¾ cups milk
1 teaspoon vanilla
½ recipe Plain Pastry
1½ ounces (squares) chocolate

Combine eggs, salt, ½ cup sugar, 2½ cups milk and vanilla. Line a piepan with pastry and pour in filling. Bake in very hot oven (450° F.) 20 minutes; reduce temperature to slow (325° F.) and bake 15 minutes longer. While pie is baking, melt chocolate over boiling water, blend in remaining sugar and milk and cook until smooth and well blended. Spread over top and bake 15 minutes longer until firm. Makes 1 (9-inch) pie.

CHOCOLATE MERINGUE PIE

¾ cup sugar
3 tablespoons cornstarch
3 tablespoons flour
½ teaspoon salt
2½ cups hot milk
2 ounces (squares) chocolate
2 egg yolks, well beaten
1 teaspoon vanilla
1 baked Pastry Shell
1 recipe Marshmallow Meringue

Blend sugar, cornstarch, flour and salt. Stir into hot milk and cook over boiling water until thickened. Add chocolate broken into small pieces; stir until smooth. Add a small amount of the mixture to egg yolks, blending thoroughly; return to remaining mixture and cook 2 minutes longer. Cool and add vanilla. Pour into pastry shell. Top with meringue and proceed as directed. Makes 1 (9-inch) pie.

CHOCOLATE FRUIT—Use brown sugar instead of granulated. Combine ¼ cup each of finely chopped figs, dates and raisins and spread over filling in pastry shell. Cover with Whipped Cream Topping instead of meringue.

CHOCOLATE NUT—Mix ¾ cup chopped nut meats with filling.

GRAPEFRUIT PIE

⅓ cup cornstarch
1¼ cups sugar
¼ teaspoon salt
1¾ cups boiling water
3 egg yolks, slightly beaten
1 tablespoon butter
½ cup fresh grapefruit juice
1 teaspoon grated grapefruit rind
1 baked Pastry Shell
Grapefruit segments
1 recipe Meringue II

Mix cornstarch, sugar and salt. Add water slowly, stirring until well blended. Cook over boiling water for 15 minutes, stirring until thick and smooth. Pour into egg yolks slowly, return to heat and cook 2 minutes longer. Remove from heat and add butter, grapefruit juice and rind. Cool. Pour into pastry shell, arrange grapefruit segments around edge of pie, pile meringue in center and proceed as directed. Makes 1 (9-inch) pie.

RASPBERRY JUICE PIE—Use 2½ tablespoons cornstarch, ¾ cup sugar, ½ cup water, 1 egg and 1½ cups fresh raspberry juice. Combine and cook as above. Top with whipped cream.

Beauty is only one of the attributes of this grapefruit pie

BANANA BUTTER-SCOTCH PIE

¾ cup brown sugar
5 tablespoons flour
½ teaspoon salt, 2 cups milk
2 egg yolks, slightly beaten
2 tablespoons butter
1 teaspoon vanilla
3 ripe bananas, sliced
1 baked Pastry Shell
1 recipe Whipped Cream Topping

Combine sugar, flour and salt and stir in milk slowly. Cook over boiling water until thickened, stirring constantly. Cover and cook 10 minutes longer, stirring occasionally. Add mixture to egg yolks, stirring vigorously; cook 1 minute longer. Add butter and vanilla and cool. Place alternate layers of filling and bananas in pastry shell and cover with whipped cream. Makes 1 (9-inch) pie.

Pile meringue thick and high on your banana butter-scotch pie

COFFEE CREAM PIE

¼ cup flour
⅛ teaspoon salt
⅔ cup sugar
1 cup strong coffee
1 cup milk
2 egg yolks
2 tablespoons butter
1 baked Pastry Shell
1 recipe Meringue I

Mix flour, salt and sugar thoroughly; add coffee and milk and cook until thickened, stirring constantly. Stir slowly into beaten egg yolks and cook 1 minute longer. Add butter. Cool. Pour into pastry shell, top with meringue and proceed as directed. Makes 1 (9-inch) pie.

CARAMEL PIE

3 tablespoons butter
4 tablespoons flour
1 cup brown sugar, 1 egg
1 cup milk, 1 teaspoon vanilla
1 baked Pastry Shell
1 recipe Whipped Cream Topping

Cream butter, flour and sugar together. Beat egg, add milk and add to creamed mixture. Cook in top of double boiler until thickened, stirring constantly. Cool and add vanilla. Pour into pastry shell and chill. Spread with whipped cream topping. Makes 1 (9-inch) pie.

Hidden under the fluffy sweet meringue is that irresistible flavor of a coffee cream filling

A circle and center of whipped cream decorates the mocha pie

MOCHA PIE

¼ cup ground coffee
2 cups milk, scalded
¾ cup sugar, ⅓ cup flour
¼ teaspoon salt
1 ounce (square) chocolate
2 eggs
1 egg yolk
1 tablespoon butter
1 teaspoon vanilla
1 baked Pastry Shell
1 recipe Whipped Cream Topping

Add coffee to milk as it scalds. Strain. Mix sugar, flour and salt together. Stir in milk and cook over boiling water until thickened, stirring constantly. Add chocolate and continue cooking 10 minutes longer, stirring occasionally. Beat eggs and egg yolk slightly. Add part of hot mixture to eggs, stir and return to double boiler. Cook stirring constantly 2 minutes longer. Remove from heat, add butter and vanilla; cool. Pour into pastry shell, chill and serve with whipped cream. Makes 1 (9-inch) pie.

LEMON MERINGUE PIE

1 cup sugar
¼ cup cornstarch
¼ teaspoon salt
1½ cups boiling water
2 egg yolks
⅓ cup lemon juice
1 tablespoon grated lemon rind
1 tablespoon butter
1 baked Pastry Shell
1 recipe Meringue I

Combine sugar, cornstarch and salt; add water gradually and cook over boiling water until smooth and thickened, stirring constantly. Cover and cook 15 minutes. Beat egg yolks and pour hot mixture over them gradually, stirring constantly. Cook 5 minutes longer. Just before removing from heat add lemon juice, rind and butter. Mix well and cool. Pour into pastry shell, top with meringue and proceed as directed. Makes 1 (9-inch) pie. Use milk instead of water and increase egg yolks to 3.

JIFFY CHOCOLATE PIE

1⅓ cups sweetened condensed milk, ¼ teaspoon salt
2 squares (2 oz.) chocolate
½ cup hot water
½ teaspoon vanilla
1 baked pastry shell
½ cup heavy cream, whipped

Cook milk, salt, chocolate over boiling water until thickened; stir constantly. Add water gradually; cook about 3 minutes longer until mixture thickens again. Add vanilla; pour into pie shell. Cool ½ hour; place in refrigerator and cool at least 3 hours. Spread on whipped cream. Makes 1 (8-inch) pie.

CHERRY CREAM PIE

1 tablespoon unflavored gelatin
¼ cup cold water
2 cups drained canned tart cherries
½ cup sugar
¾ cup cherry juice
⅛ teaspoon salt
1 tablespoon lemon juice
½ cup heavy cream, whipped
1 Graham Cracker Pie Shell

Soften gelatin in cold water 5 minutes. Heat cherries with sugar and juice. Add salt and gelatin. Mix well to dissolve gelatin. Add lemon juice and chill. When mixture begins to thicken, fold in whipped cream. Pour into pie shell. Chill until filling is firm. Makes 1 (8-inch) pie.

FLORIDA PIE

½ cup sugar
4 tablespoons flour
½ teaspoon salt
1 cup orange juice
1 tablespoon lemon juice
3 egg yolks, beaten
1 teaspoon butter
½ cup drained crushed pineapple
1 Graham Cracker Pie Shell
1 recipe Marshmallow Meringue
½ cup moist shredded coconut

Mix sugar, flour and salt together in top of double boiler. Add fruit juices and cook for 10 minutes, stirring occasionally. Add slowly to egg yolks, return to heat and cook 3 minutes, stirring constantly. Remove from heat; add butter and pineapple. Cool and pour into pie shell. Cover with meringue, sprinkle with coconut and bake. Makes 1 (8-inch) pie.

CRANBERRY CUSTARD PIE

2 cups fresh cranberries
1 cup water
1 can (1⅓ cups) sweetened condensed milk
¼ cup lemon juice
2 egg yolks, well beaten
1 baked Pastry Shell
½ cup heavy cream, whipped

Cook cranberries in water until all the skins pop open; force through a sieve. Combine with condensed milk, lemon juice and egg yolks and mix well. Pour into pastry shell. Chill thoroughly. Spread on whipped cream topping. Makes 1 (9-inch) pie.

SOUTHERN LEMON PIE

1½ cups sugar, ⅓ cup flour
1¼ cups boiling water
1 tablespoon butter
⅛ teaspoon salt, 3 egg yolks
1 lemon, juice and rind
1 baked Pastry Shell
1 recipe Meringue II

Mix sugar and flour in top of double boiler. Add water gradually, stirring constantly. Add butter and salt. Beat egg yolks, add first mixture slowly and cook over water until thickened. Remove from heat and cool. Add lemon juice and rind. Pour into shell, top with meringue and bake as directed. Makes 1 (8-inch) pie.

LEMON COCONUT PIE

1⅓ cups sweetened condensed milk
½ cup lemon juice
Grated rind of 1 lemon
2 egg yolks
1 cup shredded coconut
1 Vanilla Wafer Pie Shell
1 recipe Meringue I

Mix first 4 ingredients together, mix well, add ¾ cup coconut and pour into pie shell. Cover with meringue, sprinkle remaining coconut over top and proceed as directed. Makes 1 (8-inch) pie.

HONEY PIE

3 tablespoons flour
⅛ teaspoon salt
⅓ cup honey
2 egg yolks, slightly beaten
2 cups milk
1 Graham Cracker Pie Shell
1 recipe Meringue I

Mix flour, salt, honey and eggs together. Add milk and cook slowly until thickened. Pour mixture into pie shell, cover with meringue and proceed as directed. Chill. Makes 1 (8-inch) pie.

HONEY CHEESE PIE

9 ounces cream cheese
½ cup strained honey
3 eggs, slightly beaten
Juice and grated rind ½ lemon
¼ teaspoon salt
1½ cups milk
½ recipe Plain Pastry

Cream cheese thoroughly. Combine next 5 ingredients and add to cheese gradually. Line piepan with pastry, pour in filling and sprinkle nutmeg over top. Bake in very hot oven (450° F.) 10 minutes; reduce temperature to slow (325° F.) and bake 30 minutes longer or until knife inserted in center comes out clean. Makes 1 (8-inch) pie.

MINCE CUSTARD PIE

½ recipe Plain Pastry
1 pound mincemeat
⅔ cup sugar
1½ cups milk
1 teaspoon vanilla
3 eggs, slightly beaten

Line a piepan with pastry and spread mincemeat over bottom. Add remaining ingredients to eggs and stir until sugar is dissolved. Pour custard gently over mincemeat. Bake in hot oven (400° F.) 5 minutes; reduce temperature to moderate (350° F.) and bake 45 minutes longer or until filling is firm. Makes 1 (9-inch) pie.

PUMPKIN PIE

⅛ teaspoon salt
⅔ cup sugar
2 teaspoons pumpkin pie spice
2 eggs, slightly beaten
1⅔ cups milk
1½ cups mashed cooked
   pumpkin
½ recipe Plain Pastry

Sift dry ingredients together and stir into eggs. Add milk and pumpkin. Line piepan with pastry and pour in filling. Bake in very hot oven (450° F.) 10 minutes; reduce temperature to slow (325° F.) and bake 35 minutes longer or until knife inserted in center comes out clean. Cool. Makes 1 (9-inch) pie.

PUMPKIN NUT—Add ⅓ cup chopped nut meats to custard before baking.

Use 1 teaspoon cinnamon, ¼ teaspoon nutmeg and ½ teaspoon ginger instead of pumpkin pie spice.

PUMPKIN CREAM—Mix ¾ cup sugar, 2 tablespoons cornstarch and 2 teaspoons pumpkin pie spice. Add 1 egg yolk, 1 cup pumpkin and 2 cups milk. Cook until thickened, stirring constantly. Pour into baked Pastry Shell, cover with Meringue and bake.

Sugar crumbs and diagonal lattice are "tops" for many pies

SURPRISE PIE

2 ounces (squares) chocolate
1 baked Pastry Shell
¼ cup chopped nut meats
1 recipe Thrifty Cream Pie filling
1 recipe Whipped Cream Topping

Melt chocolate over hot water and pour into pastry shell; sprinkle nuts over top. Chill until firm. Cover with cream filling. Chill. Spread with whipped cream topping. Makes 1 (8-inch) pie.

PEACH MERINGUE PIE

1⅓ cups sweetened condensed milk
¼ cup lemon juice
2 egg yolks
1 cup sliced peaches
1 Chocolate Cookie Pie Shell
1 recipe Meringue I

Combine milk, lemon juice and egg yolks and mix well. Fold in peaches and pour into pie shell. Cover with meringue and proceed as directed. Makes 1 (8-inch) pie.

Use baked Pastry Shell or other crumb shell instead of above.

If you start the meringue at the rim, you may want to leave the center of this rhubarb pie uncovered

PINE-COT CREAM PIE

½ cup sifted flour
⅔ cup sugar
¼ teaspoon salt
1 cup milk
½ cup pineapple juice
2 egg yolks
1 tablespoon butter
1 cup crushed pineapple
½ cup diced canned apricots
1 baked Pastry Shell
1 recipe Meringue I

Combine flour, sugar and salt in top of double boiler. Add milk gradually and mix thoroughly. Add pineapple juice and cook over boiling water until thickened. Add to slightly beaten egg yolks. Return to heat, add butter and cook 1 minute longer, stirring constantly. Cool, add pineapple and apricots. Pour into pastry shell, cover with meringue and bake. Makes 1 (9-inch) pie.

CARAMEL—Caramelize sugar and add to scalded milk before combining milk with mixture.

VINEGAR PIE

2 tablespoons butter
½ cup sugar
3 tablespoons flour
1 teaspoon cinnamon
¼ teaspoon cloves
¼ teaspoon allspice
⅛ teaspoon salt, 1 egg
2 tablespoons vinegar
1 cup water
½ recipe Plain Pastry

Cream butter and sugar. Add dry ingredients, egg, vinegar and water. Cook in top of double boiler until thickened, stirring constantly. Line piepan with pastry, bake in moderate oven (350°F.) 3 minutes, then pour in filling and continue baking until crust is brown. Makes 1 (8-inch) pie.

RHUBARB CREAM PIE

1 cup sugar
3 tablespoons flour
2½ cups stewed rhubarb
2 egg yolks, slightly beaten
⅓ cup orange juice
Grated rind of 1 orange
1 tablespoon butter
1 baked Pastry Shell
1 recipe Meringue I

Sift sugar and flour together; add to rhubarb and cook slowly until thickened, stirring constantly. Stir into egg yolks, return to heat and cook 1 minute longer. Remove from heat, add orange juice, rind and butter. Cool. Pour into pastry shell, cover with meringue and bake. Makes 1 (9-inch) pie.

SHARTLESVILLE PUMPKIN PIE

½ recipe Plain Pastry
2 cups mashed cooked pumpkin
¼ teaspoon salt
1 cup sugar
4 eggs, separated
½ teaspoon cinnamon
⅓ cup cream
1 cup whisky
¼ cup butter, melted
1 tablespoon cornstarch

Line piepan with pastry. Combine pumpkin, salt, sugar, egg yolks and cinnamon and beat for 5 minutes. Add cream, whisky and butter and mix well. Sprinkle cornstarch over stiffly beaten egg whites and fold into first mixture. Pour into pastry shell. Bake in very hot oven (450° F.) 10 minutes; reduce temperature to moderate (350° F.) and bake about 30 minutes longer or until a knife inserted in center comes out clean. Cool. Makes 1 (9-inch) pie.

PEACH ICE CREAM PIE

16 marshmallows
2 tablespoons crushed peach
2 eggs whites, ¼ cup sugar
¼ teasoon salt
⅔ quart vanilla ice cream
1 baked Pastry Shell
1 cup fresh peaches, sliced
3 tablespoons lemon juice

Heat marshmallows with crushed peach slowly, folding over and over until marshmallows are half melted. Remove from heat and continue folding until mixture is smooth and fluffy. Cool. Beat egg whites until they hold a peak; add sugar slowly, beating constantly. Add salt. Blend lightly with marshmallow mixture. Place ice cream in pastry shell, cover with sliced peaches mixed with lemon juice and top with marshmallow meringue, swirled attractively. Brown quickly in broiler or very hot oven (450° F.) ½ minute or until tips of the meringue swirls are browned. Remove pie from oven, tuck peach slices into the swirls and serve immediately. Makes 1 (9-inch) pie.

PERSIMMON — Use sliced persimmons instead of peaches. Heat marshmallows with 2 tablespoons hot water instead of with crushed peaches.

RASPBERRY — Use fresh raspberries.

CHOCOLATE — Use chocolate ice cream and omit the berries.

FROZEN PUMPKIN PIE

1 cup confectioners' sugar
1 teaspoon cinnamon
1 teaspoon ginger
⅛ teaspoon salt
3 eggs, separated
1½ cups mashed cooked pumpkin
⅔ cup heavy cream, whipped
1 Cereal Flake Pie Shell

Add sugar, spices, salt and slightly beaten egg yolks to pumpkin and cook over boiling water until thickened. Fold in stiffly beaten egg whites, then cream. Pour into refrigerator tray and partially freeze. Pack into pie shell. Serve at once. Makes 1 (9-inch) pie.

Ice cream pie is so simple to make and serve, treat your family often to its cool luxury

PECAN PIE

¼ cup butter
⅔ cup brown sugar, firmly packed
¼ teaspoon salt
¾ cup dark corn sirup
3 eggs, beaten
1 teaspoon vanilla
½ recipe Plain Pastry
1 cup pecan halves

Cream butter and sugar together until fluffy; add next 4 ingredients. Line piepan with pastry and sprinkle with pecans; pour the filling over pecans. Bake in very hot oven (450°F.) 10 minutes; reduce temperature to moderate (350°F.) and bake 35 minutes longer or until knife inserted in center comes out clean. Makes 1 (8-inch) pie.

ICE CREAM PIE

1 Cereal Flake Pie Shell
1 quart ice cream, any flavor
½ ounce (square) chocolate

Fill pie shell with ice cream, grate chocolate over top and serve at once. Makes 1 (9-inch) pie.

Omit chocolate and use sweetened berries, chopped fruit or an ice cream sauce.

TARTS, FANCY PASTRIES, CREAM PUFFS

TARTLETS

Roll out any pastry or Puff Paste to ¼-inch thickness and cut out rounds. Cut centers from half of rounds with a small, scalloped cookie cutter. Brush plain rounds with water and press other round on top. Bake in very hot oven (450°F.) about 10 minutes. Fill centers with jam, jelly, marmalade or any cream pie filling.

Cut pastry into 2½-inch squares, moisten corners, fold toward center and press gently to make them stick. Bake and press centers in slightly. Fill as above.

PASTRY BOATS

Line boat shaped pans with Puff Paste or Plain Pastry. Prick, line with waxed paper and half fill with rice to keep pastry in shape. Bake in very hot oven (450°F.) 15 to 20 minutes or until browned. Discard paper and rice. Remove from pans, fill and garnish as desired.

Fit pastry over inverted muffin pans to make tart shells quickly and easily

GLAZED STRAW-
BERRY TARTS

1 quart strawberries
½ cup confectioners' sugar
1 cup water
½ to ¾ cup granulated sugar
1 tablespoon cornstarch
8 baked Tart Shells
1 recipe Whipped Cream Topping

Wash and stem berries, mix 3 cups of them with confectioners' sugar and let stand at least 1 hour. Cook remaining cup of berries with water until tender and rub through a sieve. Mix granulated sugar and cornstarch, add to strained strawberry juice and cook until clear. If not red enough, add food coloring. Arrange whole berries in tart shells and pour hot glaze over top. Cool. Garnish with whipped cream topping. Makes 8 tarts.

Use 1 quart cherries, ground cherries or gooseberries instead of strawberries. Omit coloring.

Huckleberries, blackberries or red raspberries may be used with 1 tablespoon lemon juice added for each quart of berries.

STRAWBERRY
CHEESE TARTS

¼ pound cream cheese
⅓ cup heavy cream
Baked Tart Shells
½ cup sugar
2 cups sliced strawberries
½ recipe Whipped Cream Topping

Beat cheese and cream together until stiff and smooth. Line tart shells with mixture. Add sugar to berries and pour into shells. Garnish with whipped cream topping. Makes 8 to 10 tarts.

APPLE-BUTTER
TARTS

1 recipe Cheese Pastry
1 cup Apple Butter
3 ounces cream cheese
1 teaspoon lemon juice

Roll out pastry, cut into rounds or squares and bake in very hot oven (450°F.) about 10 minutes. Cool. Put 3 circles or squares together with apple butter between each. Soften cheese with lemon juice and spread over top. Makes 4 to 6 tarts.

APRICOT TARTS

⅓ cup sugar
2 tablespoons cornstarch
1⅛ cups apricot juice
2 tablespoons butter
12 canned apricot halves
6 ounces cream cheese
1 teaspoon rum flavoring
12 baked Tart Shells
½ recipe Whipped Cream Topping

Sift sugar and cornstarch together, stir in apricot juice and butter and cook slowly until thickened, stirring constantly. Add apricots and chill. Beat cheese with a fork and add flavoring. Place 2 tablespoons of cheese in each tart shell, fill with fruit mixture and cover with whipped cream topping. Makes 12 tarts.

BANBURY TARTS

¼ cup chopped raisins
¼ cup chopped dates
¼ cup chopped figs
¼ cup chopped nuts
1 cup brown sugar
1 tablespoon flour
1 egg, slightly beaten
3 tablespoons lemon juice
1 tablespoon grated lemon rind
1 recipe Plain Pastry

Combine first 7 ingredients and cook slowly for 10 minutes, stirring constantly. Remove from heat and stir in lemon juice and rind. Cool. Roll pastry to ⅛-inch thickness and cut into 3-inch squares. Place 2 teaspoons of filling on each square, moisten edges and fold over, making 3-cornered tart. Pinch edges together, make 3 short slits in top. Bake in hot oven (425°F.) about 20 minutes. Makes 12 tarts.

BRAZIL-NUT TARTS

8 baked Tart Shells
1 recipe Cream Pie filling
1 recipe Whipped Cream Topping
8 Brazil-nut meats, sliced

Fill tart shells with cream filling, cover with whipped cream topping and sprinkle nuts over top. Makes 8 tarts.

CHOCOLATE TARTS—Use Chocolate Meringue Pie filling instead of cream filling and proceed as above.

COCONUT TARTS — Add ½ cup shredded coconut to filling and proceed as above. Sprinkle with coconut instead of Brazil nuts.

BUTTER PECAN TARTLETS

½ cup butter
1 cup brown sugar
½ teaspoon salt
1 egg, beaten
½ cup pecan nut meats
1 recipe Plain Pastry

Cream butter and sugar, add salt and beat until fluffy. Add egg and mix thoroughly. Fold in nut meats, broken into coarse pieces. Roll pastry thin and cut into 3-inch squares. Place the squares into small muffin pans, fitting them in so that the points are up like the petals of a flower. Drop a tablespoon of the nut mixture into each case and bake in slow oven (325°F.) 20 to 25 minutes. Makes 15 tartlets.

Crown cherry tarts lend a regal touch to the most informal service

CROWNED CHERRY TARTS

2 tablespoons cornstarch
3 tablespoons sugar
1 cup cherry juice
1 tablespoon butter
2 cups canned sweet cherries
8 baked Tart Shells
8 Pastry Crowns

Mix cornstarch and sugar together, add juice gradually and cook slowly until smooth and thickened; add butter and cook for a few minutes longer. Cool. Add cherries and pour into tart shells. Place crowns on top. Makes 8 tarts.

DATE TARTS

2 cups pitted dates
1 cup cold water
2 tablespoons orange juice
8 baked Tart Shells
1 recipe Whipped Cream Topping

Combine dates and water and cook to a thick paste. Remove from heat, add orange juice, cool. Fill tart shells with date mixture and cover with whipped cream topping. Makes 8 tarts.

GRANDMOTHER'S OLD-FASHIONED TARTS

1¼ cups steamed sweetened
    prunes or dates
¼ cup English walnut meats
¼ cup orange juice
1 recipe Plain Pastry

Pit prunes or dates and chop fine. Add nut meats and orange juice. Roll pastry ⅛ inch thick and cut into rounds 3½ inches in diameter. Place 1 teaspoon filling on each. Fold over, moisten edges and press together. Prick top to allow for escape of steam. Bake on ungreased cookie sheet in very hot oven (450°F.) 15 minutes. Makes 15 tarts.

PINEAPPLE TARTS

2 cups canned crushed pineapple,
    drained
¼ cup maraschino cherries,
    quartered
2 tablespoons pineapple juice
½ cup sugar
¼ teaspoon grated lemon rind
⅛ teaspoon salt
1 recipe Plain Pastry
2 tablespoons butter

Combine first 6 ingredients. Cut pastry into 8 (5-inch) squares. Arrange pastry squares in muffin pans and place 3 heaping tablespoons pineapple mixture into each. Dot with butter. Draw corners of pastry over filling. Bake in hot oven (425°F.) 20 to 25 minutes. Makes 8 tarts.

You can let your imagination run wild when you make tarts

APPLE DUMPLINGS

8 medium apples
1¼ cups brown sugar
⅓ cup butter, ½ teaspoon salt
1 teaspoon cinnamon
1 teaspoon grated lemon rind
1 recipe Plain Pastry

Pare and core apples. Combine next 5 ingredients and fill each apple cavity with part of mixture. Roll pastry to ⅛-inch thickness, cut into squares large enough to cover apple. Place apple on each square and bring corners together at top; moisten edges and pinch together to hold apple in place. Place on baking sheet and bake in moderate oven (350°F.) 30 minutes or until apples are tender. Makes 8 dumplings.

CHESS PIES

1 recipe Southern Pastry
½ cup butter, 1 cup sugar
3 egg yolks, 1 egg white
1 cup chopped raisins
1 cup chopped nut meats
1 teaspoon vanilla
1 recipe Whipped Cream Topping

Line individual pie plates with pastry. Cream butter and sugar, add beaten egg yolks and stiffly beaten egg white. Mix well. Add fruit, nuts and vanilla, pour into pastry shells and bake in hot oven (400°F.) until fillings set, reduce temperature to moderate (350°F.) and bake until browned. Cover with whipped cream topping. Makes 6 individual pies.

FRIED CREAM PIES

FILLING

1 cup milk
¼ cup sugar
¼ teaspoon salt
1 teaspoon butter
4 teaspoons cornstarch
4 teaspoons cold water
2 egg yolks, beaten
1 teaspoon vanilla

Combine milk, sugar, salt and butter; heat to boiling. Mix cornstarch and water together until smooth and add to mixture. Cook slowly until thickened, stirring constantly. Stir slowly into egg yolks. Add vanilla. Cook 5 minutes longer. Cool.

CRUST

2 tablespoons butter
1 cup sifted flour
1 egg yolk
3 tablespoons hot milk
⅛ teaspoon salt

Cut butter into flour. Combine egg, milk and salt and add. Knead well to make a smooth dough. Roll ⅛ inch thick and cut into rounds 4 inches in diameter. Place 1 tablespoon cream filling on half of round, cover filling with other half and pinch edges together. Fry in hot deep fat (360°F.) until brown. Makes 6 pies.

FRIED FRUIT PIES — Place 1½ tablespoons cooked and sweetened mashed fruit, such as prunes, or dried apricots or peaches on each pastry round and proceed as for Fried Cream Pies, or sauté, then bake at 425°F. for 5 minutes.

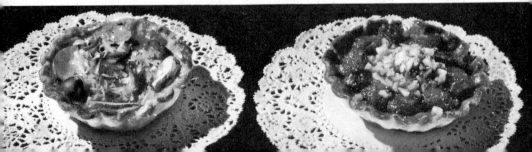

DANISH PASTRY

⅓ cup sugar
2 cakes yeast
1 pint lukewarm milk
8 cups sifted flour
1 teaspoon salt
2 cups butter
3 eggs, well beaten

Dissolve sugar and yeast in luke-warm milk. Sift flour and salt together, rub in 6 tablespoons butter and add eggs and yeast mixture. Knead 5 minutes and roll into rectangle twice as long as wide. Cut remaining butter into pea-sized pieces and spread about ⅓ over ⅔ of dough. Fold unbuttered third of dough over half of butter-covered portion; then fold remaining third on top, to make 3 thicknesses of dough with butter between. Press edges together and roll out fair-ly thin. Repeat twice to incor-porate remaining butter. Cover, set aside at room temperature for ½ hour, roll out and shape as desired. Let rise until light but not quite doubled in bulk. Bake in hot oven (400°F.) 15 to 25 minutes, depending on size of rolls.

TIMBALE CASES

Combine 1 cup milk and 2 eggs, slightly beaten. Sift 1 cup flour, ½ teaspoon salt and 1 tablespoon sugar together; add milk mixture slowly, stirring constantly. Pour small amount of batter into small deep mixing bowl and dip timbale iron into this. Heat iron in hot deep fat (365°F.). Drain iron, wipe off excess fat and dip iron into batter. Place in hot fat, un-til case browns. Drain on ab-sorbent paper and repeat. Fill case with crushed, sweetened fruit. Makes 18 cases.

CREAM PUFFS

½ cup shortening
⅛ teaspoon salt
1 cup boiling water
1 cup sifted flour
3 eggs, unbeaten

Add shortening and salt to boil-ing water and stir over medium heat until mixture boils. Lower heat, add flour all at once and stir vigorously until mixture leaves the sides of pan. Remove from heat and add 1 egg at a time, beating thoroughly after each ad-dition. Shape on an ungreased cookie sheet using 1 teaspoon or 1 tablespoon of paste for one puff (depending upon size de-sired). A pastry bag may be used. Bake in hot oven (450°F.) 20 minutes; reduce temperature to moderate (350°F.) and bake about 20 minutes longer. Re-move from oven and place on rack to cool. When cold, make slit on one side of each puff with sharp knife and fill with Whipped Cream Topping, ice cream or Cream Pie filling. Makes 12 large or 48 small puffs.

FRENCH PUFFS—Make tiny cream puffs, fill with cream fill-ing, and cover with chocolate, coffee, caramel or vanilla frost-ing. Decorate with pastry tube.

LEMON CHEESE STICKS

3 cups sifted flour
1 teaspoon salt
1 cup shortening
1 egg, slightly beaten
3 tablespoons lemon juice
Ice water
1½ cups grated American cheese

Sift flour and salt together. Cut in shortening with 2 knives or a pastry blender. Add egg com-bined with lemon juice, then just enough ice water to bind dough together. Roll dough ¼ inch thick, sprinkle half with grated cheese. Fold and pat edges to-gether, fold again and roll to ¼-inch thickness. Repeat process twice, 4 times in all; cut into strips ¼ or ½ inch wide. Bake in hot oven (450°F.) until lightly browned, about 10 minutes. Ex-cellent with cocktails and salads. Makes 54 sticks (6¼x¼ inches).

PASTRY ROLLS

"Scraps" of pastry
Jelly
Chopped nut meats

Roll pastry ⅛ inch thick and cut into pieces 5x3 inches. Spread with beaten jelly, sprinkle with nuts and roll like jelly roll. Place on cookie sheet, rolled edge down, and bake in very hot oven (450° F.) 15 minutes or until browned. Sprinkle with cinnamon and sugar instead of jelly and nuts.

Tarts, tarts and more tarts —each an expression of the maker's ingenuity

The clever hostess will tuck fruit into her cream puff fillings

PINEAPPLE PUFFS

1 recipe Puff Paste
1 recipe Cream Pie filling
8 slices canned pineapple, drained
Maraschino cherries

Roll puff paste to ⅛-inch thickness. Cut into rounds the size of pineapple slices, place on cookie sheet and chill thoroughly. Bake in very hot oven (450°F.) 10 to 15 minutes. Cool. Put 2 rounds together with cream pie filling, place pineapple slice on top and garnish with cherry. Serves 8.

Garnish with Whipped Cream Topping.

Fill with any cream pie filling and garnish with Whipped Cream Topping.

Fill with orange marmalade and spread with icing.

FRESH STRAWBERRY PUFFS —
Cut cream puffs and fill with fresh strawberries and cream filling or sweetened crushed berries and whipped cream.

CREAM HORNS

1 recipe Puff Paste
1 recipe Whipped Cream Topping

Roll paste to ⅛-inch thickness and cut into strips 1 inch wide. Roll around funnel forms into cornucopia shapes. Bake in very hot oven (450°F.) 12 to 15 minutes or until brown. Remove from forms and fill with whipped cream topping.
Add crushed sweetened berries or fruit to whipped cream.
Add chipped sweet chocolate and nut meats to whipped cream.

NAPOLEONS

1 recipe Puff Paste
1 recipe Cream Pie filling
1 recipe icing

Divide puff paste into 3 portions and roll each portion into as thin a sheet as possible without breaking. Prick thoroughly and chill. Bake until a delicate brown in very hot oven (450°F.), cool and spread 2 sheets with cream filling. Place one upon the other, top with third sheet. Spread with icing. To serve, cut into blocks 2x4 inches. Makes 12.

JAM MERINGUE

1 recipe Puff Paste
1 cup strawberry jam
1 recipe Meringue II
¼ cup shredded blanched almonds
2 tablespoons confectioners' sugar

Roll puff paste to ⅛-inch thickness. Trim edges to make a sheet 10x7 inches. Place on cookie sheet and make a ½-inch rim around the edge. Prick with fork and chill thoroughly. Bake in very hot oven (450°F.) about 10 minutes or until lightly browned. Cool. Spread jam over all, cover with meringue, sprinkle almonds over top, then sugar. Proceed as directed for meringue. Serves 8.
Use any jam desired instead of strawberry jam.

PUFF FLUFFS

1 recipe Puff Paste
2 egg whites
1 cup confectioners' sugar
⅔ cup finely chopped blanched almonds

Roll puff paste to ⅛-inch thickness. Cut into strips about 4 inches long and 1½ inches wide. Beat egg whites until stiff; add ¾ cup sugar gradually, beating constantly; then stir in almonds. Spread mixture over puff strips and sprinkle with remaining sugar. Place on cookie sheet. Bake in moderate oven (350°F.) about 15 minutes. Makes about 25.

LOVERS' KNOTS

Puff Paste
1 egg, slightly beaten
Chopped almonds

Cut wide strips of puff paste, roll thin and tie into knots. Brush with egg and sprinkle nuts over top. Place on cookie sheet and bake in hot oven (400°F.) 10 to 15 minutes.

Cream puff swans on a shimmering mirror lake will carry your summer party to a new high

CREAM PUFF SWANS

1 recipe Cream Puffs
1 recipe Whipped Cream Topping
    or vanilla ice cream

Form 8 large cream puffs on baking sheet and bake as directed. Place remaining cream puff mixture in pastry tube and force S-shaped pieces through large plain tip onto greased baking sheet to form swan necks. Force out small, pointed pieces for tails. Bake in hot oven (450°F.) until double in size, then reduce temperature to slow (300°F) and bake about 20 minutes longer. Cool. Cut off ⅓ of top of cream puff and fill with cream. Cut top into halves and press into filling on each side to represent wings. Insert neck and tail into filling. Makes 8 swans.

TEA PASTRIES

1 recipe Puff Paste
½ cup chopped blanched almonds
¼ cup sugar

Roll puff paste to ⅓-inch thickness. Mix nuts and sugar together and spread over paste. Pat and roll to ⅛-inch thickness. Cut into rounds with small cookie cutter, place on cookie sheet and chill thoroughly. Bake in very hot oven (450°F.) 8 to 10 minutes. Makes 50.

MINSTRELS

1 recipe Cream Puffs
1 quart Chocolate Ice Cream
Candied cherries and fruits

Cut tops from baked cool puffs, fill with scoops of ice cream and make a face with cherry crescent for mouth, citron for eyes.

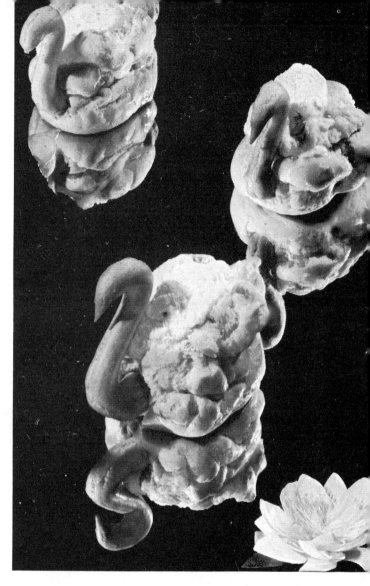

LEMON STICKS

1 recipe Puff Paste
1 recipe Lemon Meringue Pie
    filling

Roll puff paste out to ⅛-inch thickness. Cut into sticks about 4 inches long and 1½ inches wide. Place on cookie sheet and chill thoroughly. Bake in very hot oven (450°F.) about 10 minutes or until browned. Put 2 sticks together with filling. Makes 15.

ORANGE STICKS — Use Orange Pie filling instead of lemon filling

ECLAIRS

1 recipe Cream Puffs
1 recipe Whipped Cream Topping

Shape paste into strips 1 inch wide and 4 inches long on baking sheet and bake as for cream puffs. When cool, split one side, fill with whipped cream topping and frost with chocolate frosting. Makes about 12 éclairs.

Use Cream Pie filling in place of whipped cream topping.

Pastry cats on mincemeat tarts served in the candlelight carry out the gaiety of the Halloween spirit

Break mincemeat into pieces; add water and sugar. Place over heat and stir until lumps are broken up. Cook for about 1 minute. Cool. Line tart pans with pastry, pour in filling and bake in hot oven (400°F.) about 35 minutes. Cut cats from remaining pastry using a cat cookie cutter and bake as pastry shell. Place a cat on each baked tart. Makes 6 to 8 tarts.

FIG TURNOVERS

1 cup sugar
1 tablespoon flour
½ cup water and fig juice
1 tablespoon butter
1 egg, beaten
⅓ cup lemon juice
2 tablespoons grated lemon rind
1 cup canned figs, chopped
1 recipe Plain Pastry

Combine first 8 ingredients and cook slowly until thickened. Cool. Roll pastry ⅛ inch thick and cut into 4-inch circles. Place a tablespoon of fig mixture on half of each circle, moisten edges and fold other half over filling; pinch edges together and prick top. Place on baking sheet and bake in very hot oven (450°F.) about 15 minutes. Makes 8 to 10.

APPLESAUCE TURNOVERS — Combine 2 cups Applesauce, ¼ teaspoon each of nutmeg and cinnamon. Place on pastry as above and sprinkle each with grated American cheese. Continue as above.

MINCEMEAT TURNOVERS — Cut rolled pastry into squares and place a tablespoon of mincemeat on each. Moisten edges, fold to form triangles and seal firmly. Prick with fork and bake.
Use Cheese Pastry instead of plain pastry.

BERRY TURNOVERS — Use strawberry or raspberry preserves as a filling for turnovers.

HALLOWEEN TARTS

1 9-ounce package condensed
    mincemeat
1½ cups cold water
3 tablespoons sugar
1 recipe Plain Pastry

DESSERTS

250
Delectable
Desserts

APPLE CHARLOTTE

Slices of dry bread, ¼ inch thick
Melted butter
Stewed tart apples, mashed and seasoned with sugar and nutmeg
Chopped almonds

Line a greased mold with bread slices brushed with melted butter. Fill center with stewed apples and add almonds. Cover top with slices of bread, buttered, and bake at 400°F. 30 minutes.

BANANA AND APPLE BROWN BETTY

¾ cup sugar
¼ teaspoon salt
½ teaspoon cinnamon
2 apples, pared and sliced
3 bananas, peeled and sliced
3 cups small bread cubes
3 tablespoons butter

Mix sugar, salt and cinnamon together. Combine with sliced apples and bananas. Brown bread cubes in butter. Fill buttered baking dish with alternate layers of bread cubes and fruit, using bread for top and bottom layers. Cover dish and bake in moderate oven (375°F.) 30 minutes. Remove cover and bake 15 minutes longer, or until apples are tender. Serves 6.

PEACH BETTY

4 cups bread crumbs
¼ cup melted butter
3 cups sliced fresh peaches
½ cup water
3 tablespoons lemon juice
1 teaspoon lemon rind
¾ cup sugar, or more if desired

Moisten crumbs with butter. Place alternate layers of crumbs and peaches in buttered baking dish, using crumbs for first and last layers. Sprinkle each layer of peaches with combined water, lemon juice, rind and sugar. Cover and bake in slow oven (325°F.) about 1 hour. Serve with Vanilla Sauce. Serves 12.

TOASTY PRUNE BETTY

4 cups toasted bread cubes
1½ cups cooked prunes, sliced
1½ cups chopped cooking apples
1 cup prune liquid
¾ cup water, ¾ cup sugar
½ teaspoon salt
½ teaspoon cinnamon
2 tablespoons butter

Place half of toasted bread cubes in buttered casserole or pan (about 1½ quart size), add prunes in a layer, apples, then remaining bread cubes. Combine liquids, sugar, salt, cinnamon and butter and boil for 2 to 3 minutes. Pour over bread cubes. Bake covered in moderate oven (375°F.) about 1 hour. Serves 6.

CRACKER PUDDING

⅔ cup cracker crumbs
¾ cup sugar
½ teaspoon salt
4 cups milk, scalded
¼ cup melted shortening
2 eggs, separated
1 teaspoon vanilla
¼ cup confectioners' sugar
1 tablespoon lemon juice

Combine cracker crumbs, sugar, salt and milk. Stir in melted shortening and beaten egg yolks. Add vanilla. Pour mixture into greased baking dish and bake in moderately slow oven (325°F.) 1 hour. Remove from oven and cover with meringue prepared by beating the whites of eggs until stiff, adding confectioners' sugar gradually and lemon juice. Bake in slow oven (300°F.) until meringue is brown, about 20 to 25 minutes. Serves 6.

"Bread 'n butter, applesauce 'n sugar" appears as apple charlotte

INDIAN PUDDING

½ cup yellow corn meal
1 quart milk, scalded
⅔ cup molasses
1 teaspoon salt
2 cups cold milk

Add corn meal slowly to hot milk stirring constantly over boiling water until thick. Add molasses and salt. Pour into greased baking dish and add cold milk. Bake in slow oven (275°F.) 3 hours. Serve hot with hard sauce, ice cream or plain cream. Serves 6.

SPICY—Use ½ teaspoon each of cinnamon and ginger

APPLE—Pare and slice 2 apples and place in alternate layers with the pudding mixture before baking. Use spice or not as desired. Serve with whipped cream

APPLE SLUMP

Baking Powder Biscuit dough
    (using 2 cups flour)
3 pints pared, cored and quartered apples
1 cup sugar
½ cup water
2 teaspoons cinnamon

Cut biscuit dough into 2-inch rounds. Combine apples, sugar, water and cinnamon in saucepan, cover tightly and heat slowly to boiling. When boiling, cover with unbaked biscuits, place tightly fitting cover on pan and continue to cook over low heat about 25 minutes. Remove biscuits; pour cooked applesauce over them. Serve with cream. Serves 8 to 10.

"GRUNTS"—Use 2 cups berries, cherries or peaches instead of apples

APPLE PANDOWDY

4 tart apples
½ cup sugar
½ teaspoon cinnamon
2 tablespoons butter
Baking Powder Biscuit dough
    (using 2 cups flour)

Pare, core and slice apples; arrange in well-greased shallow baking dish. Sprinkle with sugar and cinnamon and dot with butter. Cover with biscuit dough, rolled to ½-inch thickness. Prick dough with fork to allow steam to escape. Bake in moderate oven (350°F.) about 30 minutes. Serve hot with pudding sauce or nutmeg-flavored sweetened cream. Serves 6.

When the cosy old cookstove was used to heat the kitchen an apple Indian pudding was likely to be in the oven

BLACK WALNUT SWEETPOTATO PUDDING

1 pound uncooked sweetpotatoes, grated
½ cup honey or sirup
3 eggs, well beaten
2 tablespoons butter, melted
2 cups sweet milk
1 teaspoon cinnamon
½ teaspoon salt
½ teaspoon nutmeg
½ teaspoon ginger or allspice
½ cup raisins
½ cup black walnut meats

Mix all ingredients together and pour into buttered baking dish. Bake in slow oven (325°F.) 1 hour, stirring occasionally, for 6.

GRATED SWEET-POTATO PUDDING

4 eggs, 2 cups milk
3 cups grated uncooked sweet-potatoes
4 tablespoons butter, melted
2 cups brown sugar
½ teaspoon cinnamon
¼ teaspoon cloves, allspice
¼ teaspoon salt

Beat eggs slightly, add remaining ingredients, mix well and pour into a buttered baking dish. Bake in slow oven (325°F.) 30 minutes, or until well browned, stirring occasionally. Serves 8.

POTATO CUSTARD TARTS

2 cups riced cooked potatoes
4 eggs, slightly beaten
1 cup sugar, ¾ cup milk
⅓ cup butter, melted
3 teaspoons grated lemon rind
3 tablespoons lemon juice
8 unbaked Tart Shells

Combine ingredients (except pastry) in order listed. Beat hard for 5 minutes. Pour into tart pans lined with unbaked pastry. Bake in hot oven (450°F.) 10 minutes, reduce temperature to moderate (350°F.) and bake until custard is firm and knife inserted in center comes out clean. Makes 8 tarts.

SWEETPOTATO PONE

1 cup sugar, ½ cup butter
2 cups grated uncooked sweet-potatoes
½ cup milk, ¼ teaspoon salt
1 teaspoon ginger
⅛ teaspoon cinnamon, nutmeg
Grated rind of 1 orange

Blend sugar and butter, add grated sweetpotatoes and milk. Beat well. Add salt, spices and orange rind. Place in shallow buttered baking pan and bake in slow oven (325°F.) 1 hour. Serves 8.

DATE DESSERT LOAF

1 cup boiling water
1 cup chopped dates
½ cup sifted flour
1 teaspoon baking soda
¼ teaspoon salt
1 cup chopped walnut meats
1 egg
1 cup sugar
1 tablespoon melted butter
½ teaspoon vanilla

Pour water over dates. Sift flour, soda and salt together and add walnut meats. Beat egg and beat in sugar. Add butter and vanilla. Stir into date mixture and add flour and nuts. Turn into buttered loaf pan and bake in slow oven (250°F.) 1¼ hours. Serve hot or cold with Fluffy Brandy Sauce. Serves 6 to 8.

QUICK MAPLE PUDDING

1 cup maple sirup
1 tablespoon shortening
3 tablespoons sugar
1 egg
1 cup sifted cake flour
2 teaspoons baking powder
¼ teaspoon salt
½ cup milk

Heat maple sirup to boiling and pour into greased baking dish. Cream shortening, add sugar and cream together until fluffy. Add beaten egg and mix well. Sift flour, baking powder and salt together and add alternately with milk, in small amounts, beating well after each addition. Pour into hot sirup and bake in hot oven (400°F.) about 25 minutes. Turn out onto serving plate and garnish with chopped nuts. Serve with cream or with Marshmallow Sauce. Serves 4

Black walnuts in the sweet-potato pudding call for more on the top

CRANBERRY NUT COBBLER

2 cups sugar
1 cup water
4 cups (1 pound) cranberries
½ cup chopped walnuts
Grated rind of 1 orange
2 tablespoons butter
1 recipe Shortcake Biscuits

Heat sugar and water to boiling; add cranberries, walnuts, orange rind and butter and let stand while mixing biscuit dough. Roll dough to ¼-inch thickness. Fill individual baking dishes with cranberries and cover each with biscuit dough. Cut slits in top of dough to allow steam to escape. Bake in very hot oven (450°F.) 10 minutes, reduce heat to moderate (350°F.) and bake 20 minutes longer. Makes 6 cobblers.

RAISIN HONEY BREAD PUDDING

¾ cup raisins
½ cup honey
4 cups white bread cubes
1 quart milk
5 eggs
¼ cup sugar
¼ teaspoon salt
2 teaspoons vanilla
Few grains nutmeg

Rinse raisins and drain. Combine honey and bread cubes; cook over low heat and stir until bread absorbs honey (2 to 3 minutes). Blend milk, slightly beaten eggs, sugar, salt and vanilla together; add with raisins to bread cubes; mix well. Pour into buttered baking dish. Sprinkle with nutmeg. Place dish in pan of hot water and bake in moderate oven (350°F.) 1 hour or until knife inserted in center comes out clean. Serve with plain or whipped cream. Serves 6 to 8.

CHOCOLATE BREAD PUDDING

2 ounces (squares) chocolate
3 cups milk
¼ teaspoon salt
½ cup brown sugar
2 eggs, separated
1½ teaspoons vanilla
6 slices dry bread, cut into ½-inch cubes
4 tablespoons granulated sugar

Heat chocolate and milk in double boiler until chocolate is melted. Add salt. Combine brown sugar and egg yolks; add chocolate mixture gradually, stirring vigorously. Add vanilla. Combine bread and chocolate mixture; let stand 10 to 15 minutes, stirring occasionally. Turn into buttered baking dish, place in pan of hot water and bake in moderate oven (350°F.) 30 minutes, or until almost firm. Beat egg whites until foamy; add half of sugar, beating until blended; add remaining sugar and continue beating until mixture will stand in peaks. Pile meringue lightly into mounds in border around edge of pudding. Sprinkle meringue with shaved chocolate and continue baking 8 minutes longer, or until meringue is delicately browned. Serves 6.

PEACH AND RICE CUSTARD LOAF

1 No. 2½ can sliced peaches
¾ cup sugar
4 tablespoons flour
¼ teaspoon salt
1½ cups milk
2 egg yolks
1 teaspoon almond extract
2 cups cooked rice
1 cup sifted dry bread crumbs

Drain peaches. Combine sugar, flour and salt in top of double boiler. Add ½ cup milk and egg yolks; beat well. Add remaining 1 cup milk. Cook in double boiler about 20 minutes or until thick, stirring occasionally. Remove from heat; add flavoring and fold in rice. Cover bottom of buttered loaf pan with half of bread crumbs; pour in a third of rice custard, then cover with half of peaches. Repeat layer of custard, remaining peaches and remaining custard. Sprinkle with remaining bread crumbs. Bake in moderate oven (350°F.) about 40 minutes. Let cool 10 to 15 minutes before unmolding. Slice and serve with Peach Sauce. Serves 8.

Fold the meringue into the chocolate pudding before baking, or spread on top

Brazil-nut pudding with dates and grated apples is something new in the world

HOLIDAY DELIGHT

½ cup butter
¾ cup sugar
2 eggs, unbeaten
2 cups sifted cake flour
¼ teaspoon salt
4 teaspoons baking powder
1½ cups raspberry jam
½ cup blanched almonds, chopped
½ pint heavy cream, whipped

Cream butter and sugar together until fluffy. Add eggs. Sift flour, salt and baking powder together and add to first mixture. Form into balls. Place in buttered muffin pans and press around edges of pans. Fill center with mixture of jam and nuts and bake in hot oven (450°F.) about 10 minutes. Cool and serve with whipped cream. Serves 8.

BRAZIL-NUT BREAD PUDDING

4 slices buttered bread
½ cup sliced Brazil nuts
2 eggs, ½ cup sugar
¼ teaspoon salt
1 teaspoon vanilla
2 cups milk

Cut buttered bread into half-inch wide strips. Arrange in layers in buttered baking dish. Sprinkle each layer with Brazil nuts. Beat eggs slightly, add sugar, salt, vanilla and milk. Mix well and pour over bread. Garnish top with Brazil nuts and bake in slow oven (325°F.) about 1 hour. Serves 4 to 6.

BRAZIL-NUT PUDDING

¼ cup butter
½ cup sugar
1 egg yolk
½ cup grated apple
¼ cup pitted dates, cut fine
½ cup chopped Brazil-nut meats
¾ cup sifted flour
1 teaspoon baking powder
¼ teaspoon salt
½ cup strong coffee
1 egg white

Cream butter and sugar together until fluffy. Add egg yolk, apples, dates and Brazil nuts. Mix and sift flour, baking powder and salt. Add alternately with coffee to first mixture. Fold in stiffly beaten egg white. Turn into buttered loaf pan, small ring mold, or 8-inch square pan. Bake in moderate oven (350°F.) 45 to 50 minutes. Serve with Hard Sauce. Serves 6.

CHERRY COTTAGE PUDDING

1 No. 2 can pitted red cherries
¼ cup shortening
⅔ cup sugar, 1 egg
¼ teaspoon almond extract
1¾ cups sifted flour
1 teaspoon baking powder
½ teaspoon salt
½ teaspoon baking soda
1 cup sour milk

Drain cherries and save juice for sauce. Cream shortening and sugar together until fluffy. Add egg and flavoring and beat well. Sift flour, baking powder, salt and soda together. Add alternately with milk in small amounts, mixing well after each addition. Add cherries. Pour into buttered cake pan and bake in moderate oven (350°F.) about 45 minutes. Cut into squares and serve with hot Cherry Sauce. Makes 1 (9x9 inch) cake.

DEVIL'S FOOD PUDDING

2 cups sifted flour
1 teaspoon baking soda
½ teaspoon salt
3 ounces (squares) chocolate
1½ cups sugar
1½ cups milk
½ cup shortening
2 eggs, beaten
1 teaspoon vanilla

Sift flour, soda and salt together. Melt chocolate in double boiler; add ½ cup sugar and ½ cup milk; cook until thickened, stirring constantly. Cool. Cream shortening with remaining 1 cup sugar until fluffy. Add eggs and beat. Stir in chocolate mixture. Add flour alternately with remaining 1 cup milk and vanilla. Pour into greased paper-lined (9½-inch) tube pan and bake in moderate oven (350°F.) 1 hour and 10 minutes. Serve with desired sauce. Serves 10.

RHUBARB CRISP

½ cup butter
1¼ cups sugar
2 eggs
½ teaspoon nutmeg
½ teaspoon vanilla
2 cups toast cubes
4 cups cereal flakes
4 cups diced fresh rhubarb

Blend butter and ½ cup sugar together thoroughly. Add eggs and beat well. Stir in nutmeg, flavoring, toast cubes and cereal flakes. Spread half of mixture in buttered baking pans; arrange rhubarb evenly over the top; sprinkle with remaining sugar and cover with remaining mixture. Bake in moderate oven (375°F.) about 40 minutes, or until rhubarb is tender. Serve warm with whipped cream. Serves 10.

RHUBARB AND BANANA PUDDING — Omit cereal flakes. Arrange 2 bananas, sliced, over rhubarb. Use brown sugar instead of white. Mix 1 tablespoon each lemon and orange juice with 2 tablespoons water and sprinkle over top before baking.

RHUBARB BROWN BETTY

1 (9-ounce) package condensed
   mincemeat
½ cup cold water
3 cups diced fresh rhubarb
½ cup sugar
¼ teaspoon salt
2 cups soft bread crumbs
¼ cup water
1 tablespoon butter

Break mincemeat into pieces and add water. Heat slowly, stirring until all lumps are thoroughly broken up. Heat to boiling; continue boiling for 3 minutes or until mixture is practically dry. Combine mincemeat, rhubarb, sugar and salt. Place alternate layers of bread crumbs and rhubarb mixture into buttered baking dish with layer of crumbs on top. Add water and dot top with butter. Bake in moderate oven (350°F.) 45 minutes, or until rhubarb is tender. Serve with Hard Sauce. Serves 6.

Other fruits may be used instead of rhubarb: tart apples, peaches or apricots.

RICE TARTS

¾ cup rice
1½ pints milk
½ teaspoon salt
4 egg yolks
1 cup sugar
½ teaspoon vanilla
¼ cup rum
1 cup heavy cream, whipped
8 individual baked Pastry Shells
Cinnamon

Wash rice in cold water. Heat milk, add salt and rice and cook slowly until rice is tender, stirring occasionally. Beat egg yolks, add sugar and combine with rice. Cook 1 minute longer. Cool. Fold in vanilla, rum and whipped cream. Fill baked pastry shells, sprinkle with cinnamon and brown under broiler. Garnish with whipped cream. Serves 8.

Omit rum and vanilla, if desired, and flavor with a mixture of 3 tablespoons orange juice and 1 tablespoon lemon juice.

A Spring tonic for the whole family appears in this baked rhubarb crisp

Fruit hidden in meringue and baked or meringue cups filled with fresh fruit are ready for anybody's party

MERINGUES

6 egg whites
¼ teaspoon cream of tartar
1½ cups sugar
1½ teaspoons vanilla

Beat egg whites until foamy, add cream of tartar and beat until stiff but not dry. Add sugar 2 tablespoons at a time, beating after each addition; then add vanilla. Cover bottoms of medium muffin pans with rounds of heavy brown paper. Do not grease. Pack with meringue, cutting with knife to remove air pockets. Bake in very slow oven (250°F.) 1 hour and 15 minutes. Let stand for a few minutes before removing from pans. Makes 10.

APPLE MERINGUES—Cover baked apples, stuffed or plain, with meringue and bake in a moderate oven (350°F.) 20 minutes.

FRENCH MERINGUES

2 cups sugar
¾ cup water
5 egg whites
1 teaspoon vanilla

Heat sugar and water, stirring until sugar is dissolved. Continue cooking without stirring until the temperature reaches 238°F. or until sirup will form a soft ball when tested in cold water. Remove from heat and pour slowly into stiffly beaten egg whites, beating constantly. Continue beating until mixture is cool. Add flavoring. Shape the meringues into a ring with spoon or pastry tube on a dampened board covered with heavy brown paper. Bake in slow oven (270° F.) for 1 hour or longer, depending on the size. Makes 10 to 12.

STRAWBERRY — Fill meringues with fresh strawberries; top with whipped cream, if desired.

FROZEN BANANA MERINGUE

3 egg whites
¾ cup sugar
½ teaspoon vanilla
¼ teaspoon vinegar
1 cup mashed ripe bananas
¼ teaspoon salt
1½ tablespoons lemon juice
¼ cup confectioners' sugar
1 cup heavy cream, whipped

Beat egg whites to thick foam; beat in sugar 2 tablespoons at a time. Add vanilla and vinegar and beat until well blended. Divide meringue into 2 equal parts and place each part, shaped to fit refrigerator tray, on greased baking sheets. Bake in slow oven (275°F.) 40 to 50 minutes, or until lightly browned. Cool. Combine banana, salt and lemon juice. Fold confectioners' sugar and banana mixture into whipped cream. Place one baked meringue in bottom of refrigerator tray, cover with filling and second baked meringue. Freeze until center is firm. Cut into slices to serve. Serves 6 to 8.

PINEAPPLE—Use ½ cup shredded pineapple and ½ cup nut meats instead of banana.

RUSSIAN MERINGUES

2 cups heavy cream, whipped
¼ cup confectioners' sugar
1 teaspoon vanilla
½ teaspoon almond extract
1 recipe Meringues
¾ cup pecans, chopped
½ cup maraschino cherries,
    quartered
1¼ cups shredded coconut

Combine whipped cream with sugar, vanilla and almond extract. Frost meringues with whipped cream, sprinkle with nuts, cherries and coconut. Serves 10. Bake meringue in 1 large round and slice into pie-shaped servings.

HINTS ON USE OF A FREEZER may be found on page 39.

AMERICAN ICE CREAM

1 tablespoon flour
¾ cup sugar
2 cups scalded milk
1 egg or 2 egg yolks, slightly beaten
2 cups heavy cream
¼ teaspoon salt
1 tablespoon vanilla

Mix flour and sugar thoroughly, add milk slowly and cook over hot water 8 minutes, stirring frequently. Add to egg, cook 2 minutes and cool. Add cream, salt and vanilla. Pour into freezer can and freeze, using 8 parts ice to 1 part salt. Makes about 1¼ quarts.

CHOCOLATE ICE CREAM

3 ounces (squares) chocolate
2 cups milk
1⅛ cups sugar
4 tablespoons flour
⅛ teaspoon salt
2 eggs, slightly beaten
4 cups cream
2 tablespoons vanilla

Heat chocolate and milk over boiling water until chocolate is melted. Beat with rotary beater until blended. Combine sugar, flour and salt; mix thoroughly. Add to chocolate mixture gradually and cook until thickened, stirring constantly. Continue cooking 5 minutes, stirring occasionally. Add to eggs, stirring vigorously; return to double boiler and cook 2 minutes longer, stirring constantly. Cool; add cream and vanilla. Pour into freezer can and freeze, using 8 parts ice to 1 part salt. Makes 2 quarts.

CARAMEL ICE CREAM

⅔ cup sugar
⅓ cup boiling water
2½ cups milk
1 egg, well beaten
⅛ teaspoon salt
1 teaspoon vanilla

Melt sugar slowly in heavy skillet, stirring constantly. When sugar is melted and browned, add water, heat and stir vigorously until sugar is dissolved. Add 1 cup milk and pour mixture into egg and salt. Cook slowly 5 minutes, stirring frequently. Cool. Stir in remaining milk and vanilla. Pour into freezer can and freeze, using 8 parts ice to 1 part salt. Makes 1 quart.
Burnt Almond—Add 1 cup blanched almonds, chopped and toasted.

FRENCH VANILLA ICE CREAM

½ cup sugar
⅛ teaspoon salt
4 to 6 egg yolks, slightly beaten
2 cups scalded milk
2 cups heavy cream
1 tablespoon vanilla

Mix sugar, salt and egg yolks thoroughly. Add milk slowly and cook in top of double boiler until mixture coats a spoon. Cool, strain and add cream and vanilla. Pour into freezer can and freeze using 8 parts ice to 1 part salt. Makes about 1½ quarts.

Nut Custard—Increase sugar to 1 cup, salt to ½ teaspoon and milk to 3 cups. Add ⅓ cup each chopped pistachio, filbert, English walnut and blanched almonds and 1 teaspoon almond extract. Fold in 5 stiffly beaten egg whites before pouring into freezer.

PINEAPPLE ICE CREAM

1 egg
½ cup sugar
3 cups milk
¼ teaspoon salt
1½ cups crushed pineapple (pulp and juice)
1 teaspoon vanilla
2 tablespoons maraschino cherry juice (optional)

Beat egg, add remaining ingredients and mix well. Pour into freezer can and freeze, using 8 parts ice to 1 part salt. Makes about 1½ quarts.

PHILADELPHIA ICE CREAM

1 quart cream
¾ cup sugar
1½ tablespoons vanilla
⅛ teaspoon salt

Scald cream, add sugar and cool. Add vanilla and salt. Pour into freezer can and freeze, using 8 parts ice to 1 part salt. Makes about 1¼ quarts.

LEMON CUSTARD ICE CREAM

1 tablespoon flour
1 cup sugar
⅛ teaspoon salt
1 cup boiling water
2 eggs, slightly beaten
3 cups milk
½ cup lemon juice
2 tablespoons grated lemon rind

Blend flour, sugar and salt in top of double boiler. Add boiling water and heat to boiling over direct heat, stirring frequently. Pour slowly over eggs, return to double boiler and cook 3 minutes, stirring occasionally. Remove from heat. Cool. Add milk, lemon juice and rind. Pour into freezer can and freeze, using 8 parts ice to 1 part salt. Makes 1¾ quarts.

BAVARIAN CREAM

1½ tablespoons unflavored gelatin
1¼ cups water
1 cup evaporated milk
2 eggs, separated
¾ cup sugar
2 teaspoons vanilla
½ cup heavy cream, whipped

Soften gelatin in ¼ cup water. Heat remaining water with evaporated milk to scalding in double boiler. Beat egg yolks and sugar together and add gradually to hot mixture. Cook over boiling water 3 minutes, or until mixture coats spoon. Remove from heat, add gelatin and stir until dissolved, then place in pan of ice water. When mixture begins to thicken, add vanilla. Fold in stiffly beaten egg whites and whipped cream. Pour into mold and chill until firm. Serve with fruit. Serves 8.

MAPLE FLUFF

2 tablespoons unflavored gelatin
¼ cup cold water
1 pint cream
2 eggs, separated
1 cup maple sirup
½ cup shredded coconut
¼ teaspoon salt
½ teaspoon almond extract

Soften gelatin in cold water. Heat cream over hot water, then pour slowly over slightly beaten egg yolks. Return mixture to double boiler and cook 5 minutes, or until it begins to thicken, stirring constantly. Remove from heat and stir in softened gelatin. Add maple sirup and cool. When mixture begins to thicken, add coconut, salt and almond flavoring. Beat egg whites until stiff but not dry and fold into mixture. Pour into individual molds and chill until firm. Serve plain or topped with sweetened whipped cream sprinkled with toasted coconut. Serves 8.

BANANA LIME DESSERT

1 package lime gelatin
2 cups boiling water
Sliced ripe bananas
Strawberries
Sweetened whipped cream

Dissolve gelatin in boiling water. Cool. Place a slice of banana in center of each individual mold. Add a tablespoon of gelatin and chill. When firm fill molds with gelatin and chill. When it begins to thicken add other slices of bananas. Chill until firm. Unmold and garnish with slices of bananas and berries. Serve with sweetened whipped cream. Serves 5.

FIG NUT WHIP

1 cup dried figs
1¾ cups hot water
1 package lemon gelatin
½ cup heavy cream, whipped
½ cup chopped nut meats

Rinse figs; boil in water to cover for 30 minutes. Drain, clip stems and cut into small pieces. Pour hot water over gelatin and stir until dissolved; cool. When gelatin begins to thicken, add whipped cream, figs and nuts and mix thoroughly. Pour into serving dishes, chill until firm and garnish with whipped cream and pecans or fruit. Serves 6.

Use dates instead of figs.

CHERRY RICE

1 No. 2 can pitted tart cherries
¾ cup heavy cream, whipped
½ cup sugar
½ teaspoon vanilla
1½ cups cooked rice

Drain cherries. Whip cream until stiff; beat in sugar; add vanilla. Fold in rice and chill. Fold cherries into chilled cream mixture and serve in sherbet glasses with Cherry Sauce. Serves 6 to 8.

FLUFFY SQUARES

1 tablespoon unflavored gelatin
4 tablespoons cold water
1 cup boiling water
⅔ cup sugar
3 egg whites
¼ teaspoon salt
1 teaspoon vanilla
20 vanilla wafers, rolled fine

Soften gelatin in cold water, dissolve in boiling water and stir in sugar. Cool until mixture begins to thicken then beat until fluffy, fold in beaten egg whites, salt and vanilla. Turn into pan and chill. To serve, cut pudding into small squares and roll in vanilla wafer crumbs. Arrange in dessert glasses and top with Lemon Cream Sauce. Serves 8 to 10.

CARAMEL BAVARIAN CREAM

1 tablespoon unflavored gelatin
¼ cup cold water
¾ cup sugar
½ cup boiling water
1 egg
½ cup milk
1 teaspoon vanilla
¾ cup heavy cream, whipped

Soften gelatin in water 5 minutes. Heat ½ cup sugar slowly in heavy skillet until browned, stirring constantly. Add boiling water and heat until the browned sugar dissolves, stirring constantly. Add gelatin and stir until dissolved. Beat egg, combine with remaining sugar, milk and vanilla and add browned sugar mixture. Cook over boiling water stirring constantly until mixture coats a spoon. Chill. When mixture begins to thicken, fold in whipped cream. Turn into a mold and chill until firm. Unmold and serve plain or with Caramel Sauce. Serves 6.

BUTTERSCOTCH RICE MOLD

⅓ cup rice
¼ teaspoon salt
3 cups milk, scalded
1 cup brown sugar
2 tablespoons butter
1 tablespoon unflavored gelatin
¼ cup cold water

Wash rice; add salt and 2 cups of milk. Cook in double boiler until nearly tender. Cook brown sugar and butter together slowly in a shallow pan until very dark brown. Add to rice and cook until rice is tender and sugar melted. Soften gelatin in water, add remaining 1 cup hot milk and stir until dissolved. Add gelatin to hot rice mixture, pour into mold and chill until firm. Unmold and serve plain or with whipped cream. Serves 6.

CHERRY CREAM

1½ tablespoons unflavored gelatin
½ cup cold water
2 cups heavy cream
¾ cup sifted confectioners' sugar
¾ cup oxheart cherries, cut into small pieces
1 teaspoon vanilla
¼ teaspoon almond extract

Soften gelatin in water 5 minutes, then dissolve over boiling water. Chill until it begins to thicken. Whip cream and fold in sugar, cherries, flavorings and gelatin. Pour into mold and chill until firm. Decorate with additional cherries and leaves. Serves 8.

COCONUT DELIGHT

1 layer fresh white cake
3 cups heavy cream
2 cans moist coconut
½ cup blanched almonds
8 maraschino cherries

Crumble cake very fine. Whip 2 cups cream. Arrange alternate layers of cake crumbs, whipped cream and all but ⅓ can of coconut in a bowl. Cover and chill 12 hours. Unmold, frost with remaining cream, whipped; sprinkle with remaining coconut and garnish with almonds and cherries. Serves 8.

CHILLED ANGEL FOOD

1 Angel Food Cake
1 can moist coconut
1 cup drained crushed canned raspberries
½ teaspoon vanilla
2 tablespoons sugar
2 cups heavy cream, whipped

Cut a slice about 1 inch thick from top of cake and remove center, leaving walls and bottom about 1 inch thick. Crumble cake which has been removed and mix with ½ cup coconut, raspberries, vanilla, sugar and enough whipped cream to hold ingredients together (about ½ cup). Fill cake with fruit mixture and replace top. Chill several hours. Before serving, cover with remaining whipped cream, sweetened, and sprinkle with remaining coconut. Serves 10 to 12.

BERRY FLUFF

1 cup raspberries
1 egg white
⅛ teaspoon salt
⅓ cup sugar
Few whole berries

Clean berries, crush and chill. Beat egg white with salt until stiff. Beat in sugar and add crushed berries. Serve in parfait glasses. Decorate with whole berries. Serves 4.

Red or black raspberries or strawberries may be used. Additional sugar may be used with strawberries.

Use whipped cream instead of egg. Top with grated coconut.

ORANGE BAVARIAN CREAM

1⅓ tablespoons unflavored gelatin
⅓ cup cold water
⅓ cup boiling water
1⅛ cups sugar
¼ cup lemon juice
1 teaspoon grated orange rind
1 cup orange juice and pulp
3 egg whites
1 cup heavy cream, whipped

Soften gelatin in cold water, dissolve in boiling water and add sugar, lemon juice, orange rind and juice. Chill. When thick and sirupy, add egg whites beaten until stiff but not dry and fold in whipped cream. Pour into serving dishes; chill until firm. For 8.

ORANGE CHARLOTTE RUSSE— Line mold with split Ladyfingers before filling with orange mixture.

BAVARIAN CREAM IN ORANGE CUPS—Pour dessert into orange cups and when chilled garnish with whipped cream, candied orange peel or cherry.

PEACH BAVARIAN CREAM

1½ cups chopped fresh peaches
2 tablespoons lemon juice
¼ teaspoon salt
⅔ cup sugar
1½ tablespoons unflavored gelatin
½ cup water
1 cup heavy cream, whipped
1 teaspoon vanilla
½ teaspoon almond extract

Combine peaches, lemon juice, salt and sugar; let stand 1 hour. Soften gelatin in cold water, then dissolve over low heat. Combine with peach mixture and chill. When mixture begins to thicken, fold in whipped cream, vanilla and almond extract. Place in individual molds and chill until firm. Garnish with peach slices or whipped cream. Serves 8.

FIVE-CUP DESSERT

1 cup cold cooked rice
1 cup drained canned crushed
    pineapple
1 cup quartered marshmallows
1 cup chopped walnut meats
1 cup heavy cream, whipped

Combine ingredients in the order listed, chill thoroughly and serve in sherbet glasses. Garnish with additional whipped cream, for 10.

GRAPE JUICE FLUFF

1 tablespoon unflavored gelatin
1½ cups grape juice
¼ cup sugar, ¼ teaspoon salt
1 tablespoon lemon juice
2 egg whites
¼ cup heavy cream, whipped

Soften gelatin in ½ cup grape juice 5 minutes. Heat remaining grape juice, add sugar, salt and gelatin and stir until dissolved. Add lemon juice. Cool and when mixture begins to thicken fold in stiffly beaten egg whites. Half fill individual parfait glasses with ⅔ of this mixture. To remaining grape mixture add whipped cream and fill glasses. Chill until firm. Garnish with whipped cream, sweetened and flavored, or with ripe grapes. Serves 6.

Use your melon mold for pineapple soufflé and garnish generously with fresh peaches

RASPBERRY BAVARIAN CAKE

1½ tablespoons unflavored
    gelatin
¼ cup cold water
2 cups milk
2 eggs, separated
¾ cup sugar
1 teaspoon lemon juice
1 cup raspberries
½ cup heavy cream, whipped

Soften gelatin in water 5 minutes. Scald milk, add gelatin and stir until dissolved. Mix egg yolks with sugar and add hot milk gradually. Cook over boiling water 3 minutes until mixture coats a spoon. Remove from heat and chill. When mixture begins to thicken add lemon juice and raspberries. Fold in stiffly beaten egg whites and whipped cream. Pour into spring-form pan and chill until firm. Unmold and serve in slices like cake. Serves 8.

APRICOT — Use 1 cup cooked dried apricot purée instead of raspberries.

PINEAPPLE SOUFFLE

1 tablespoon unflavored gelatin
¼ cup cold water
3 eggs, separated
1 teaspoon grated lemon rind
2 tablespoons lemon juice
½ cup sugar
¼ teaspoon salt
⅔ cup crushed canned pine-
    apple
½ cup heavy cream, whipped

Soften gelatin in water 5 minutes. Beat egg yolks slightly and add grated rind, lemon juice, sugar and salt. Cook in double boiler, stirring constantly until mixture thickens. Add gelatin and stir until dissolved. Add pineapple and cool. When mixture begins to stiffen, fold in whipped cream and stiffly beaten egg whites. Turn into mold and chill. When firm, remove from mold and garnish with cherries and quarter slices of pineapple. Serves 8.

BANANA—Omit crushed pineapple and use ¼ cup pineapple juice mixed with 1 cup mashed bananas. Line mold with Ladyfingers or thin slices of Spongecake.

CHERRY — Increase sugar to ⅔ cup and use canned drained cherries instead of pineapple.

ORANGE CREAM

1 tablespoon unflavored gelatin
3 tablespoons cold water
½ cup strained orange juice
1 tablespoon lemon juice
1½ cups buttermilk
Dash salt
⅓ cup sugar

Soften gelatin in water 5 minutes. Combine orange and lemon juices, buttermilk, salt and sugar. Melt gelatin over hot water, add to buttermilk mixture and mix well Pour into mold and chill until firm; unmold and garnish with orange sections and whipped cream. Serves 4.

PINEAPPLE DUCHESS

1 No. 2 can sliced pineapple
9 maraschino cherries
1 package lemon gelatin
1 cup hot water
1 cup cold water
½ tablespoon unflavored gelatin
2 tablespoons cold water
2 tablespoons sugar
¾ cup pineapple juice, hot
¾ cup heavy cream, whipped

Drain pineapple, save juice and place 1 slice in bottom of medium-sized (1¼-quart) bowl. Line sides of bowl with 5 slices of pineapple and place 6 halves of maraschino cherries in center of slices. Place a smaller (about 2½-cup) bowl in center of larger bowl and weigh it down with something heavy. Dissolve lemon gelatin in hot water, add 1 cup cold water and pour between the 2 bowls. Chill until firm and remove smaller bowl by filling with lukewarm water and lifting out in ½ minute or less. Soften unflavored gelatin in 2 tablespoons cold water 5 minutes, add sugar and hot pineapple juice and stir until gelatin is dissolved. Add remaining pineapple, diced, and remaining maraschino cherries, sliced. Chill. When mixture begins to thicken fold in whipped cream. Pour into center of mold. Chill. When firm unmold on serving plate. Serves 6.

MOCHA FLUFF

20 marshmallows, cut fine
1 cup hot black coffee
½ cup evaporated milk, chilled

Heat marshmallows and coffee until marshmallows are half melted, folding over and over. Remove from heat and continue folding until marshmallows are melted. Place bowl in larger bowl of cracked ice, stir until mixture begins to thicken, then beat until frothy. Beat milk very stiff and fold in. Place into 1 large mold or 6 individual molds and chill until firm. Serves 6.

MACAROON CREAM

1 tablespoon unflavored gelatin
¼ cup cold water
1 cup milk, scalded
12 marshmallows
½ dozen macaroons
12 candied cherries
2 cups evaporated milk, chilled
½ cup chopped pecan meats
⅛ teaspoon salt
⅓ cup sugar

Soften gelatin in water 5 minutes, then dissolve in hot milk. Cool. Cut marshmallows, macaroons and cherries into small pieces. When gelatin thickens, beat until fluffy, whip milk until very thick and fold in with other ingredients. Chill until firm and serve with whipped cream and additional candied cherries. Serves 10.
Use chocolate or vanilla cookies instead of macaroons.
Use ½ cup drained crushed pineapple instead of macaroons.
Use heavy cream instead of evaporated milk.

ROYAL PINEAPPLE CREAM

1 tablespoon unflavored gelatin
¼ cup cold water
¾ cup milk
½ cup sugar
½ cup drained canned crushed pineapple
½ cup sliced strawberries
1 cup chopped walnut meats
1 cup heavy cream, whipped
1 egg white, stiffly beaten

Soften gelatin in water 5 minutes and dissolve over hot water. Add milk and sugar; chill until mixture begins to thicken; then beat slightly. Fold in remaining ingredients in the order listed and chill until firm. Serve with additional chopped walnut meats. Serves 6.

STRAWBERRY FLUFF PIE

1 pint strawberries
⅔ cup sugar
⅛ teaspoon salt
1 tablespoon lemon juice
1 tablespoon unflavored gelatin
½ cup cold water
1 cup evaporated milk, chilled
1 teaspoon vanilla
1 Graham Cracker Piecrust

Wash berries, hull and cut into small pieces. Add sugar, salt and lemon juice. Chill 1 hour or more. Soften gelatin in water 5 minutes, dissolve over boiling water and add to chilled strawberry mixture. Whip milk very stiff and fold in. Add vanilla, turn into crust and chill until firm. Garnish with berries. For 6. Other berries may be used instead of strawberries.
Use baked Pastry Shell instead of graham cracker pie shell.
Partially fill shell with filling, cover with sliced ripe bananas, then with remaining filling. Top with whipped cream if desired.

PRUNE BAVARIAN

2 tablespoons sugar
1 cup prune pulp
1 tablespoon unflavored gelatin
¼ cup cold water
1 cup evaporated milk, chilled
1 tablespoon lemon juice

Add sugar to prune pulp and stir until dissolved. Soften gelatin in water 5 minutes, dissolve over boiling water and cool slightly. Add to prune mixture. Whip milk stiff, add lemon juice and fold in prune mixture. Pour into a mold or individual molds and chill until firm. Serves 8.

REFRIGERATOR CHEESE PIES

2 tablespoons unflavored gelatin
¼ cup cold water
2 eggs, separated
1 teaspoon salt
½ cup milk
1 cup sugar
1 tablespoon grated lemon rind
3 cups cottage cheese (dry)
⅓ cup lemon juice
2 teaspoons vanilla
1 cup heavy cream, whipped
1 recipe Cereal Crumb Piecrust

Soften gelatin in water 5 minutes. Cook slightly beaten egg yolks, salt, milk and sugar in double boiler until thickened, stirring occasionally. Add lemon rind and gelatin and stir until gelatin is dissolved. Chill. When gelatin begins to thicken, beat in cottage cheese, lemon juice and vanilla with rotary beater. Fold in stiffly beaten egg whites and whipped cream. Butter bottom and sides of 2 (9-inch) piepans. Line pans on bottom with crumb crust saving ¼ cup for top. Pour in cheese mixture and sprinkle remaining crumbs on tops. Chill 4 to 5 hours or overnight before serving. Serves 12.

CHANTILLY SPONGE

1 large Sunshine Cake
1 cup cubed pineapple, drained
12 marshmallows, quartered
1 cup cut strawberries
½ teaspoon vanilla
2 cups heavy cream, whipped
20 large whole berries, cleaned

Cut cool sunshine cake into halves, crosswise. Fold next 4 ingredients into whipped cream. Spread the bottom half of cake liberally with the mixed filling. Cover with the top half and spread remaining mixture over top and sides of cake. Chill for 2 to 3 hours before serving. Garnish with whole berries. Serves 12.

POLKA DOT PUDDING

1 package vanilla pudding
6 ounces (squares) semi-sweet chocolate, chipped

Prepare vanilla pudding as directed on package. Chill. Fold in chocolate. Serves 5.

CHOCOLATE FILLED ANGEL FOOD

1 large Angel Food Cake
6 tablespoons cocoa
6 tablespoons sugar
⅛ teaspoon salt
3 cups heavy cream
1 cup sliced, blanched and toasted almonds

Cut a slice about 1 inch thick from top of cake. Remove center from cake leaving walls and bottom about 1 inch thick. Mix cocoa, sugar and salt with cream and chill thoroughly 1 hour. Then whip cream mixture stiff and add ½ of almonds. Fill cake with ⅓ of cocoa mixture. Place top on cake and frost with remaining cocoa mixture. Sprinkle remaining almonds over cake. Chill 2 to 3 hours before serving. Serves 12.

Omit chocolate mixture and use Cherry Cream. Fill chilled cake with thickened mixture. Chill; frost cake with whipped cream.

You'll be one up on the rest of the crowd if you serve them this luscious chantilly sponge

Apricot rice mold may be made with half peaches or plums as well as apricots

MARASCHINO DELIGHT

1 tablespoon unflavored gelatin
½ cup cold water
½ cup boiling water
¼ cup sugar
Few grains salt
1 tablespoon lemon juice
¼ cup juice from maraschino cherries
½ cup warm water
¾ cup finely chopped moist canned coconut
10 maraschino cherries, chopped

Soften gelatin in cold water 5 minutes and dissolve in boiling water. Add sugar and salt. Cool and add lemon and cherry juice. Pour warm water over coconut and cherries. Let stand a few minutes, drain and add liquid to gelatin mixture. Chill until thickened. Set bowl in chopped ice, beat mixture until light and fluffy, then fold in coconut and cherries. Pile into sherbet cups, garnish each with a whole cherry and chill. Serves 6.

PLUM FLUFF

1 No. 2½ can plums
1 tablespoon lemon juice
2 egg whites
4 tablespoons confectioners' sugar
1 cup heavy cream, whipped

Drain plums, remove pits and mash plums with fork; add lemon juice. Beat egg whites until stiff; beat sugar in gradually. Fold whipped cream and plums into meringue. Chill about 1 hour. Serves 6 to 8.

Sliced fruit adapts itself to garnishing the fluted mold of cool bavarian cream (pages 614 and 615)

APRICOT RICE MOLD

1 No. 2½ can apricot halves
1¼ teaspoons unflavored gelatin
2 cups cold cooked rice
Few grains salt
½ cup heavy cream, whipped

Drain apricots and place a half in each custard cup. Press remaining halves through a sieve. Soften gelatin in 3 tablespoons apricot juice and dissolve over hot water. Combine dissolved gelatin, puréed apricots, rice and salt and mix well. Fold in whipped cream and pour into custard cups. Chill. When firm unmold and garnish with whipped cream. Serves 6.

BAKED CUSTARD

3 eggs, slightly beaten
¼ teaspoon salt
⅓ cup sugar
3 cups scalded milk
½ teaspoon vanilla
Nutmeg

Combine eggs, salt and sugar. Add milk slowly, stirring constantly. Add vanilla. Pour into custard cups. Sprinkle with nutmeg, place in pan of hot water and bake in moderate oven (350° F.) 30 to 35 minutes or until a knife inserted in center of custard comes out clean. Serves 4.

Pour into large mold and bake as above 45 to 50 minutes.

CARAMEL—Add 3 tablespoons caramelized sugar sirup to milk.

CHOCOLATE—Add 1½ ounces (squares) chocolate to milk; heat until melted.

COCONUT—Add ½ cup shredded coconut to mixture.

COFFEE—Scald 2 tablespoons ground coffee with milk, strain. Proceed as for baked custard.

DATE—Add ½ cup chopped dates to custard before baking.

GINGER—Add a little finely chopped candied ginger.

HONEY—Use ½ cup honey instead of sugar.

RICE—Save whites for meringue. Add 1 cup cooked rice and ½ teaspoon grated lemon rind. Bake. Top with meringue and bake until brown.

RUM—Omit vanilla and add 2 tablespoons rum.

SNOWY—Combine 1¼ cups scalded milk, ¼ cup sugar and dash salt. Beat 3 egg whites slightly but not until light. Add milk and ½ teaspoon vanilla. Bake as above. Serve with crushed fruit for 2.

ORANGE CAKE CUSTARD

1 (9-inch) layer Spongecake
1 cup orange juice
2 cups milk
3 eggs, separated
¼ cup sugar
⅛ teaspoon salt
6 tablespoons confectioners' sugar

Cut spongecake into 1-inch cubes and place in greased casserole. Pour orange juice over cake and let stand while preparing custard. Scald milk in top of double boiler. Beat egg yolks with sugar and salt, stir in hot milk slowly and cook over hot water, stirring constantly, until mixture coats a spoon. Pour over cake in casserole. Make a meringue by beating the egg whites with confectioners' sugar until stiff. Pile over dessert and brown in slow oven (300°F.) 12 to 15 minutes. Serve hot or cold. Serves 8. Garnish with orange segments.

Baked custard wears a lovely wreath of berries, whipped cream roses and pineapple

LEMON CUSTARD IN MERINGUE CUPS

½ recipe Meringues
1 cup sugar
⅛ teaspoon salt
3 tablespoons cornstarch
1½ cups boiling water
3 egg yolks, beaten
Juice of 2 lemons
2 tablespoons grated lemon rind

Shape meringue into cups on heavy ungreased paper and bake in slow oven (300°F.) 45 minutes. Remove from paper and cool. Mix sugar, salt and cornstarch; add water slowly and cook until thick, stirring constantly. Add small amount hot mixture to egg yolks, lemon juice and rind; stir into remaining hot mixture. Cook in double boiler until thick, about 10 minutes. Cool, fill meringues with custard and chill. Makes 6 (3½-inch) cups.

Use hollowed out sponge cupcakes instead of meringues.

BANANA TAPIOCA CREAM

2 tablespoons quick-cooking tapioca
¼ teaspoon salt
⅓ cup sugar
2 cups scalded milk
1 egg, separated
1 teaspoon grated orange rind
1 cup sliced or diced ripe bananas
    (1 to 2 bananas)

Mix tapioca, salt and half the sugar together. Add milk and cook over boiling water about 5 minutes, or until tapioca is clear, stirring frequently. Combine egg yolk and remaining sugar. Add a small amount of the tapioca mixture, stirring constantly. Then pour back into remaining hot mixture, beating vigorously. Continue cooking about 5 minutes, stirring constantly. Fold in beaten egg white. Cool. Add orange rind and bananas. Chill. Garnish with sliced ripe bananas. Serves 6.

FLOATING ISLAND PUDDING

5 eggs
½ cup sugar
¼ teaspoon salt
1 quart milk, scalded
1 teaspoon vanilla

Beat 3 egg yolks and 2 whole eggs slightly. Add sugar and salt, mix well and add hot milk gradually, stirring constantly. Cook in top of double boiler until it coats the spoon, stirring constantly. Add vanilla. Pour into large pan. Beat remaining egg whites until foamy; beat in additional 6 tablespoons sugar gradually. Add ¾ teaspoon vanilla. Drop meringue, using large spoon, onto hot custard, cover pan closely until mixture is cool; then chill. Serves 8.

CHOCOLATE—Melt 2 ounces (squares) chocolate in milk.

HOT PEACH PUDDING

1 pound dried peaches
3 cups water

CUSTARD
⅔ cup sugar
Dash salt
3 tablespoons flour
2 eggs
3 cups hot milk

Wash peaches, cover with water and cook until tender; cool and cut into pieces. Sift sugar, salt and flour together. Add to well-beaten eggs, mix well and stir in hot milk slowly. Cook in double boiler and stir until thickened. Remove from heat and add peach juice and peaches. Serve hot. Serves 6.

A touch of sophistication in the garnish makes boiled custard a party dessert

BOILED CUSTARD
(Custard Sauce)

2 eggs, slightly beaten
⅛ teaspoon salt
¼ cup sugar
2 cups milk, scalded
½ teaspoon vanilla

Combine eggs, salt and sugar; add milk slowly and cook in top of double boiler until mixture coats a spoon. Add vanilla, turn into individual serving dishes and chill. Serves 4.

ALMOND—Use almond extract instead of vanilla and when ready to serve garnish with shaved toasted almonds.

CARAMEL—Use brown sugar instead of granulated.

CHOCOLATE—Add 1 ounce (square) chocolate to milk. Heat until melted.

COFFEE—Use 1 cup strong hot coffee instead of 1 cup milk.

FRUIT—Pour custard over fresh or canned fruit. Chill.

PUMPKIN—Fold ⅔ cup sweetened canned pumpkin into custard. Pour into individual serving dishes and decorate tops with Christmas tree design made with fine cookie crumbs.

GLAZED CARAMEL CUSTARD

¾ cup sugar
3 eggs, slightly beaten
⅛ teaspoon salt
1 teaspoon vanilla
1½ cups milk, ¼ cup cream

Caramelize ½ cup sugar in heavy skillet and glaze bottom and sides of custard cups with it. Combine remaining ¼ cup sugar with other ingredients and pour into cups. Place cups in pan of hot water and bake in moderate oven (350°F.) until firm, 30 to 35 minutes, or until a knife inserted in center of custard comes out clean. Cool. Serves 6.

GRAPE-NUT RENNET-CUSTARD

2 cups milk
1 package vanilla rennet powder
⅔ cup grape-nuts

Heat milk slowly, stirring constantly. When warm (120°F.), not hot, remove at once from heat. Stir rennet powder into milk until dissolved. Add grape-nuts and pour at once into dessert glasses. Do not move until firm (about 10 minutes), then chill. Serve with Cherry Sauce and garnish with whipped cream and candied citron. Serves 4 or 5.

NUT SOUFFLÉ

6 eggs, separated
1 cup sugar
1 cup ground nut meats

Beat egg yolks until light, add sugar and beat until thick and lemon colored. Add nuts. Fold in stiffly beaten egg whites. Pour into greased baking dish, set in pan of hot water and bake in slow oven (325°F.) until firm, about 60 minutes. Serves 8 to 10. Garnish with candied orange peel.

A perky garnish gives wings to such simple desserts as grape-nut rennet-custard

RENNET-CUSTARD

2 cups milk (or 1 cup milk and 1 cup cream)
1 package vanilla rennet powder
1 egg white, ¼ cup sugar
¼ cup grenadine sirup

Heat milk slowly, stirring constantly. When lukewarm (120° F.), not hot, remove at once from heat. Stir powder into milk until dissolved. Pour at once (while still liquid) into individual dessert glasses. Do not move until firm, about 10 minutes. Chill. Just before serving, beat egg white until fluffy; add sugar and sirup alternately in small amounts and continue beating until mixture is very stiff. Heap or pipe with a pastry tube onto chilled dessert. Serves 5.

JELLY SOUFFLÉ

1 glass tart jelly
3 egg whites
⅓ cup chopped nut meats

Melt jelly and while very hot add gradually to stiffly beaten egg whites. Fold nuts in carefully. Turn into greased baking dish. Set in pan of hot water and bake in moderate oven (350° F.) 25 to 30 minutes. Serve hot or cold with Boiled Custard or whipped cream. Serves 6.

SWEET SOUFFLÉS

3 tablespoons butter, melted
4 tablespoons flour
¼ teaspoon salt
1 cup milk
4 eggs, separated
4 tablespoons sugar
1 teaspoon vanilla

Blend butter, flour, and salt. Add milk, heat to boiling, stirring constantly; pour over mixture of egg yolks and sugar beaten until thick and lemon colored. Cool. Add vanilla. Fold in stiffly beaten egg whites. Pour into greased baking dish set in pan of hot water and bake in moderate oven (350°F.) until firm, 50 to 60 minutes. Serve at once for 6.

CHOCOLATE—Use only 3 tablespoons flour and 2 eggs. Add 1 ounce (square) melted chocolate to milk mixture.

FRUIT—Place 2 cups drained canned fruit (pineapple, peaches, apricots cut into pieces) on bottom of baking dish. Pour soufflé over fruit and bake as described above.

MACAROON—Omit butter, flour and sugar. Use only 3 eggs. Break 1 dozen macaroons into milk, add salt and proceed as above.

MOCHA—Use ¾ cup strong hot coffee and ¼ cup cream instead of milk.

RICE—Omit flour and increase sugar to ½ cup and milk to 2 cups. Add 1 cup cooked rice to egg yolk and milk mixture. Add ½ cup raisins and ½ teaspoon cinnamon.

SPANISH—Brown ½ cup dry bread crumbs in butter. Omit flour and prepare as above.

Rennet-custard for the children's Christmas party wears sugarplum trees and place cards of meringue or spritz cookies ➡

COFFEE RENNET-CUSTARD

1½ cups milk
4 tablespoons coffee
1 rennet tablet
1 tablespoon cold water
1 cup cream
6 tablespoons sugar

Heat milk and coffee to lukewarm and let stand 20 minutes. Strain through several thicknesses of cheesecloth and return to saucepan. Crush rennet tablet and dissolve in cold water. Reheat coffee infusion slowly with cream and the sugar, stirring constantly until lukewarm (120°F.), not hot. When warm remove immediately from heat. Add dissolved rennet tablet and stir quickly for a few seconds only. Pour at once into dessert glasses. Do not move until firm (about 10 minutes), then chill. Serves 5 or 6.

SPICED RENNET-CUSTARD

½ teaspoon cinnamon
½ teaspoon ginger
⅛ teaspoon cloves
1½ tablespoons boiling water
2 cups milk
1 package vanilla rennet powder
⅓ cup red apple jelly
1½ ounces cream cheese

Combine spices and blend with boiling water. Stir milk while heating to lukewarm (120°F.), not hot. Remove from heat and stir in dissolved spices and rennet powder. Pour at once into 5 sherbet glasses or custard cups. Do not move until firm (about 10 minutes), then chill. Just before serving, garnish with jelly and cream cheese chilled and cut into narrow strips. Serves 5.

Try a "shortcake" effect with creamy pudding sauce and black raspberries

BAKED ORANGE FLUFF

4 eggs, separated
1 cup sugar
½ cup orange juice
1 tablespoon grated orange rind

Beat egg yolks until light; add sugar slowly, beating constantly. Add orange juice and rind. When well mixed fold in stiffly beaten egg whites. Pour into greased baking dish, place in pan of hot water and bake in moderate oven (350°F.) about 35 minutes, or until firm. Serve immediately with whipped cream. Serves 6.

LEMON — Use 3 tablespoons lemon juice and 1 teaspoon grated lemon rind instead of orange.

COCONUT SOUFFLÉ

2 cups milk
⅓ cup quick-cooking tapioca
¼ teaspoon salt, ⅓ cup sugar
3 eggs, separated
2 tablespoons melted butter
1 teaspoon vanilla
½ cup shredded coconut

Scald milk in top of double boiler, add tapioca and salt. Cook until tapioca is clear, stirring frequently. Add sugar and cool. Beat egg yolks until light, combine with first mixture, then add butter, vanilla and coconut. Fold in stiffly beaten egg whites and turn mixture into buttered baking dish. Place in pan of hot water and bake in slow oven (325°F.) 1 to 1¼ hours. Serves 8.

You might like to do a flower of peach slices in the center of your sweetpotato soufflé

RIBBON RENNET-CUSTARD

4 cups milk

2 tablespoons banana purée

1 package vanilla rennet powder

2 tablespoons chopped pistachio nuts

1 to 2 drops green coloring

½ teaspoon pistachio flavoring

½ package maple rennet powder

½ package raspberry rennet powder

SWEETPOTATO SOUFFLÉ

1 cup milk, ½ cup sugar
½ teaspoon salt
3 tablespoons butter
1 teaspoon nutmeg
2 cups mashed sweetpotatoes
2 eggs, separated; ½ cup raisins
½ cup chopped pecans
Marshmallows

Scald milk and add sugar, salt, butter, nutmeg and potatoes; beat until fluffy. Beat egg yolks and add to potatoes. Add raisins and pecans. Beat egg whites stiff, fold into potatoes and pour into greased baking dish. Bake in moderate oven (350°F.) 50 to 60 minutes or until firm. Top with marshmallows, brown, for 8.

Combine 1 cup milk and banana purée and heat slowly, stirring constantly. When lukewarm (120°F.), not hot, remove at once from heat. Pour ½ package vanilla rennet powder into milk and stir until dissolved. Pour at once into 8 parfait glasses. Do not move until firm (about 10 minutes). To another 1 cup milk add pistachios, green coloring and flavoring and warm slowly, stirring constantly. When lukewarm (120°F.), not hot, remove at once from heat. Stir in remaining vanilla powder and pour gently into glasses on top of banana layer. Do not move until firm (about 10 minutes). Warm another cup of milk to lukewarm, stir in maple rennet powder and pour into glasses. When this layer has thickened, warm remainder of milk, stir in raspberry powder and pour into glasses. Do not move until firm (about 10 minutes). Chill. To make slanting stripes, tilt glasses sideways while rennet custards thicken.

Parfait glasses heighten the dramatic effect of ribbon rennet-custard

BRAZIL-NUT MARSHMALLOW CREAM

½ pound marshmallows
½ cup diced canned pineapple
12 candied cherries, sliced
¾ cup sliced Brazil-nut meats
1 cup heavy cream, whipped
6 candied cherries
6 whole Brazil-nut meats

Cut marshmallows into eighths with a wet knife and combine with pineapple, cherries and sliced nuts. Fold whipped cream into marshmallow mixture, chill several hours, pile into sherbet glasses and garnish with cherries and whole nuts. Serves 6.

For Easter Sunday supper these tiny eggs in the nest will excite your most blasé and travelled guest

CREAM PUDDING

1 pint very thick slightly soured cream
½ cup water (to rinse cream jar)
½ cup sifted flour
½ teaspoon salt, 1 pint hot milk
Sugar and cinnamon

Simmer cream and water, 45 minutes to 1 hour, stirring occasionally. Combine flour and salt, sift into hot cream, beat until smooth and cook until thick and butter fat rises to top. Remove fat and save. Stir in hot milk and beat well. Pudding should be very smooth and creamy. Pour into a bowl and make depressions on top for butter fat. Serve hot in dessert dishes with sugar and cinnamon sprinkled on top. The pudding is not a success unless the butter fat rises to top after flour is added. Serves 6 to 8.

CHOCOLATE PUDDING

1 ounce (square) chocolate
1 pint milk
½ cup sugar
3 tablespoons cornstarch
¼ teaspoon salt
1 teaspoon vanilla
1 teaspoon butter
6 tablespoons moist coconut
15 jelly bean "eggs"

Melt chocolate in ½ cup milk, stir until well blended. Heat remaining milk and add chocolate mixture. Sift sugar, cornstarch and salt together and add to hot milk gradually. Cook, stirring constantly, until thickened. Add vanilla and butter. Pour into serving dishes and chill. Serves 5.

For the children's party: Form a nest on the top with a tablespoon of coconut and fill with 3 jelly bean "eggs."

VANILLA PUDDING — Omit chocolate. Prepare as above.

CARAMEL TAPIOCA CREAM

2 tablespoons butter
1 cup brown sugar
2 tablespoons quick-cooking tapioca
2 cups milk
2 eggs, separated
¼ teaspoon salt
1 teaspoon vanilla

Heat butter and ¾ cup sugar slowly. Stir until it boils, cook about 1 minute or until sugar is slightly caramelized. Add tapioca and milk. Cook until tapioca is clear, then pour slowly onto 2 egg yolks mixed with salt. Cook in double boiler and stir occasionally until thickened. Remove from heat and pour mixture over egg whites beaten until stiff with remaining brown sugar. Stir and add vanilla when slightly cool. Serves 8.

Clever designs on simple custards are easy to do with the pastry tube

RICE PUDDING

½ cup rice
1 quart milk
½ teaspoon cinnamon or nutmeg
½ cup sugar (white or brown)
½ teaspoon salt

Wash rice, add remaining ingredients and pour into greased baking dish. Bake in 275°F. oven 3 hours. Stir frequently during first hour. Serves 6. Add ½ cup raisins or 2 eggs during last ½ hour.

MAPLE NUT PUDDING — Mix ⅓ cup cornstarch with ¼ cup cold water. Add 1½ cups brown sugar and 2 cups boiling water. Cook until thickened, then cook over boiling water 20 minutes. Add 3 stiffly beaten egg whites and ½ cup chopped nut meats. Pour into molds. Chill. Serves 6.

PINEAPPLE TAPIOCA CREAM

⅔ cup sweetened condensed milk
2 cups hot water
3 tablespoons quick-cooking tapioca
¼ teaspoon salt
2 eggs, separated
1½ cups crushed pineapple, drained
1 tablespoon lemon juice

Blend milk with hot water and heat in top of double boiler. Add tapioca and salt. Cook 15 minutes. Stir small amount into slightly beaten egg yolks. Then combine with remaining tapioca mixture. Add pineapple and lemon juice. Cook for 2 minutes longer. Remove from heat. Fold in stiffly beaten egg whites; chill. Garnish with whipped cream and diced pineapple, if desired. Serves 6.

POMPADOUR PUDDING

½ cup sugar
2 tablespoons flour
¼ teaspoon salt
3 eggs
2 cups milk, scalded
1 teaspoon vanilla
1 ounce (square) chocolate
½ cup confectioners' sugar

Combine sugar, flour, ⅛ teaspoon salt, 2 egg yolks and 1 whole egg. Add small amount of milk; blend. Stir into remaining milk. Cook in double boiler, stirring constantly. Cool; add ½ teaspoon vanilla. Chill; pour into sherbet glasses. Melt chocolate over hot water. Beat confectioners' sugar into stiffly beaten egg whites. Add chocolate slowly; fold in remaining vanilla and salt. Chill and press through pastry tube in flower design on top of each pudding. Serves 6.

BUTTERSCOTCH PUDDING

1 tablespoon butter
1 cup brown sugar
1¾ cups scalded milk
3 tablespoons cornstarch
¼ teaspoon salt
¼ cup cold milk
1 teaspoon vanilla
2 egg whites, stiffly beaten

Melt butter, add brown sugar, cook, stirring frequently until sugar melts. Add hot milk slowly and heat until smooth, stirring constantly. Mix cornstarch and salt, dilute with cold milk and add to hot mixture, stirring constantly until mixture thickens. Cook 5 minutes longer. Cool slightly, fold in flavoring and egg whites, turn into individual serving dishes, chill and garnish with whipped cream and red raspberries. Serves 6.

DESSERT CAKES

(For general instructions on cake baking see pages 684-687)

APPLE CAKE

1 cup sifted cake flour
1½ teaspoons baking powder
¼ teaspoon salt
6 tablespoons sugar
2 tablespoons shortening
2 egg yolks
½ cup milk
4 apples, pared and sliced thin
½ teaspoon cinnamon
1 teaspoon grated lemon rind
Butter

Sift flour, baking powder, salt and 2 tablespoons sugar together. Cut in shortening and mix well. Beat egg yolks, combine with milk, and stir into first mixture. Beat well. Pour into greased shallow pan and cover with apple slices. Sprinkle with remaining sugar, cinnamon and lemon rind and dot with butter. Bake in hot oven (400°F.) about 35 minutes. Serve with Lemon Sauce, for 8.

STRAWBERRY COFFEE CAKE

2 cups sifted flour
2 teaspoons baking powder
6 tablespoons sugar
¾ teaspoon salt
⅓ cup shortening
1 egg, beaten
⅓ cup milk
1½ cups strawberries, cleaned
3 tablespoons butter
¼ cup sugar
3 tablespoons sifted flour

Sift first 4 ingredients together. Cut in shortening with 2 knives or pastry blender. Combine egg and milk and add all at once to dry ingredients. Blend thoroughly. Spread dough in greased cake pan and arrange strawberries on top. Combine remaining ingredients and mix together with a fork until a crumbly consistency. Sprinkle over strawberries. Bake in hot oven (400°F.) about 25 to 30 minutes. Makes 1 (10x6 inch) coffee cake.

CREAM CHEESE CAKE

1½ cups zwieback crumbs
⅝ cup sugar
2 tablespoons butter, melted
2 tablespoons flour
¼ teaspoon salt
1 pound cream cheese
1 teaspoon vanilla
4 eggs, separated
1 cup cream

Combine zwieback crumbs with 2 tablespoons sugar and butter; blend thoroughly. Line bottom of spring-form pan. Mix remaining ½ cup sugar with flour and salt and blend thoroughly with cream cheese. Add vanilla and beaten egg yolks and beat. Add cream and beat again. Fold in beaten egg whites. Pour mixture on top of crumbs and bake in moderate oven (325° to 350°F.) about 1 hour, or until mixture is firm. Turn off heat, but do not remove from oven for 1 hour or until cool. Makes 1 (9-inch) cake.

HOT FROSTED GINGERBREAD

½ cup shortening
½ cup strong hot coffee
2 eggs
½ cup sugar
½ cup molasses
1½ cups sifted flour
2 teaspoons baking powder
1 teaspoon ginger
1 cup confectioners' sugar
4 tablespoons cream
½ teaspoon vanilla

Melt shortening in hot coffee. Beat eggs and stir in sugar and molasses. Add shortening and coffee. Sift flour with baking powder and ginger and add. Mix well and spread ½ inch deep in greased pan. Bake 25 minutes in moderate oven (350°F.). Mix remaining ingredients and spread on hot gingerbread. Makes 1 (8-inch) cake.

GLAZED APPLE RING

1 cup butter
1 cup brown sugar
4 apples, pared and sliced
1 cup sugar
1 teaspoon vanilla, 2 eggs
1½ cups sifted flour
1½ teaspoons baking powder
½ teaspoon salt
½ cup milk

Melt half the butter in a skillet; add brown sugar and apple slices; simmer 10 to 15 minutes, or until tender. Turn frequently to prevent burning. Cream remaining butter with granulated sugar; add vanilla, then add eggs one at a time, beating thoroughly until fluffy. Add sifted dry ingredients alternately with milk in small amounts. Pour candied apples and sirup into greased ring mold (10-inch), or tube pan. Add cake batter. Bake in moderate oven (375°F.) about 40 minutes. Turn out onto large round plate; serve hot with Butterscotch Sauce. Serves 8.

HAYSTACKS

4 egg whites
¼ teaspoon salt
½ cup sugar
1 teaspoon lemon juice
6 cups dry shredded coconut
1 cup walnuts, chopped
2 cups pitted dates, cut into pieces

Beat egg whites stiff, beat in salt and sugar gradually, then add lemon juice, coconut, walnuts and dates. Moisten hands and mold mixture into small balls. Place on greased cookie sheet and bake in moderate oven (350°F.) 10 minutes or until browned. Makes about 20 haystacks.

Gentle mixing, careful baking and "don't touch" cooling are all important for perfect cheese cake ➡

Use white or chocolate cake batters instead of gingerbread sometimes for apricot upside-down cake

APRICOT UPSIDE-DOWN GINGERBREAD

3 tablespoons butter
1½ cups brown sugar
1 to 1½ cups drained canned apricots
½ cup shortening
2 eggs, beaten
1 cup molasses
2½ cups sifted cake flour
2 teaspoons baking soda
2 teaspoons ginger
½ teaspoon salt
1 cup sour milk

Melt butter in skillet, add 1 cup sugar gradually and stir until melted. Arrange apricots, cut side up, to cover bottom of pan. Cream shortening, add ½ cup sugar gradually and cream until fluffy. Add beaten eggs and molasses and beat thoroughly. Sift flour, soda, ginger and salt together. Add alternately with sour milk in small amounts, mixing thoroughly after each addition. Pour batter over apricots and bake in moderate oven (325° to 350°F.) 35 to 50 minutes. Serve with whipped cream, for 16.

ORANGE CRANBERRY UPSIDE-DOWN CAKE

½ pound cranberries
2 oranges
2 tablespoons butter
1 cup brown sugar
1⅓ cups sifted cake flour
2 teaspoons baking powder
¼ teaspoon salt
¼ cup shortening
1 teaspoon grated orange rind
¾ cup sugar
1 egg
¼ cup evaporated milk
¼ cup orange juice

Wash cranberries and cut into halves. Peel oranges, divide into sections and remove membrane. Melt butter and stir in brown sugar. Mix well and spread evenly over bottom of pan. Cover with cranberries, then with orange sections. Sift flour, baking powder and salt together. Cream shortening with orange rind, add sugar gradually and beat until fluffy. Add egg and beat thoroughly. Mix milk and orange juice and add alternately with dry ingredients in small amounts. Pour batter over fruit and bake in moderate oven (350°F.) 40 to 45 minutes. Makes 1 (10x10 inch) cake.

Here's a symphony in color and flavor that is a real masterpiece

DESSERT CAKES

Add Brazil nuts to the short-cake dough for a delightful new flavor and add more with the apples for the top

APPLE BRAZIL-NUT SHORTCAKE

2 cups sifted flour
3 teaspoons baking powder
4 tablespoons sugar
½ teaspoon salt
6 tablespoons shortening
½ cup sliced Brazil-nut meats
¼ cup milk
1 egg, slightly beaten
Butter
3 cups sweetened stewed apples

Sift flour, baking powder, sugar and salt together. Cut in shortening with 2 knives or pastry blender; add nut meats and milk mixed with egg. Mix lightly. Divide dough into halves, turn out onto floured board and shape each half into a large round cake about ⅓ inch thick. Butter top of 1 cake. Cover with second cake. Place in pan and bake in hot oven (425°F.) about 20 minutes. Separate hot cakes, spread each with butter. Arrange stewed apples between layers and over top. Serve with plain or whipped cream. Serves 6.

ORANGE SHORTCAKE

½ recipe shortcake as for
    Strawberry Shortcake
1 cup orange juice
1 cup sugar
2 tablespoons shredded orange
    peel
6 oranges

Bake shortcake in 2 (8-inch) layer cake pans. Combine orange juice, sugar and orange peel and heat to boiling. Pare oranges and cut sections from 5. Slice remaining orange. Arrange on shortcake layers. Pour sauce over. Serves 6.

SPRING FRUITS SHORTCAKE

2 cups diced, unpeeled young
    rhubarb
1⅓ cups sugar
¼ cup water
2 cups strawberries, cleaned
Shortcake Biscuits

Combine rhubarb, 1 cup sugar and water in shallow pan and simmer until rhubarb is tender, about 20 minutes. Combine strawberries and remaining sugar, add to hot rhubarb sauce and chill. Split and butter hot shortcake biscuits and put together with cold fruit sauce. Top with whipped cream and serve, for 6.

Extend the brief shortcake season through the year by using oranges and other winter fruits

DATE NUT TORTE

¼ cup sifted flour
½ teaspoon baking powder
¼ teaspoon salt
1½ cups chopped pitted dates
1½ cups chopped nut meats
2 eggs, separated
¾ cup sugar
½ teaspoon vanilla

Sift flour, baking powder and salt together; combine with dates and nut meats. Beat egg yolks until very thick. Add sugar gradually while continuing to beat until very thick and fluffy. Fold in flour mixture and vanilla. Fold in whites beaten until stiff but not dry. Turn into greased baking pan and bake in slow oven (275°F.) about 50 minutes. Serve with whipped cream, for 8.

APPLESAUCE TORTE

24 graham crackers, crushed
¼ pound butter, melted
3 pounds apples
6 eggs, separated
1 cup sweetened condensed milk
3 tablespoons lemon juice
1 tablespoon grated lemon rind

Mix crumbs and butter. Line greased torte pan with half of mixture. Pare apples, slice and cook with a little water to a thick sauce. Mash. Add beaten egg yolks, milk, lemon juice and rind and mix well. Fold in stiffly beaten egg whites. Pour into crumb-lined pan, cover with remaining crumbs and bake in moderate oven (350°F.) until firm and lightly browned, 45 to 60 minutes. Cool. Serve with whipped cream. Serves 10 to 12. Use 3 cups prune and apricot pulp instead of applesauce.

Whether the biscuit or cake type, strawberry shortcake is America's great treat

SHORTCAKE BISCUITS

2 cups sifted flour
3 teaspoons baking powder
2 tablespoons sugar
½ teaspoon salt
4 tablespoons shortening
¾ cup milk

Sift dry ingredients together, cut in shortening with 2 knives or pastry blender. Add milk, mix well and place on floured board. Knead lightly, pat out to ½-inch thickness and cut with round cutter. Place on greased baking sheet and chill until ready to bake. Bake in hot oven (425°F.) 20 minutes. Makes 14.

CARROT TORTE

8 eggs, separated; 2 cups sugar
1 tablespoon orange juice
Grated rind 1 orange
1 pound carrots, cooked and grated
1 pound almonds, blanched and
    chopped fine

Beat egg yolks until thick, beat in sugar gradually, then add juice and rind of orange. Add carrots and nuts. Fold in stiffly beaten egg whites. Bake in greased torte pan at 350°F. 50 minutes. Chill; serve with whipped cream, for 12.

STRAWBERRY SHORTCAKE

4 cups sifted flour
6 teaspoons baking powder
½ teaspoon salt
2 tablespoons sugar
1 cup shortening
1¼ cups milk; 2 eggs, beaten
2 teaspoons confectioners' sugar
1 cup heavy cream, whipped
1 teaspoon vanilla
1 quart strawberries, cleaned
½ cup granulated sugar

Sift first 4 ingredients. Cut in shortening with 2 knives or pastry blender, add milk and eggs, mix, knead lightly and divide into halves. Place on lightly floured board and pat into shape to fit pan. Place first layer in pan, brush top with melted butter and place second layer over it. Bake in hot oven (425°F.) about 20 minutes. Fold confectioners' sugar into whipped cream and add vanilla. Reserve about 15 choice strawberries. Crush remaining berries and combine with granulated sugar. Separate shortcake layers. spread with whipped cream and top with crushed strawberries. Replace top layer and spread with whipped cream. Arrange whole berries over top. Serves 8.

MOCHA CAKE

⅓ cup butter
1 cup brown sugar, 3 egg yolks
¾ cup cold strong coffee
¼ teaspoon vanilla
12 Ladyfingers

Cream butter and add sugar gradually, then add egg yolks. Add coffee and vanilla slowly. Place alternate layers of ladyfingers and coffee mixture in oblong pan, using ladyfingers for top and bottom layers. Chill at least 12 hours. Slice, for 6.

PARTY ROLL

¼ pound graham crackers
½ cup chopped pitted dates
8 marshmallows, cut fine
½ cup nut meats, broken
3 tablespoons cream
1 teaspoon vanilla

Crumble crackers fine and reserve 3 tablespoons for coating roll. Combine remaining crumbs with dates, marshmallows and nut meats. Blend with cream, add vanilla and shape into a roll. Coat with cracker crumbs and chill 3 to 4 hours. Serve in slices with whipped cream. Serves 6.

APPLE BUTTER REFRIGERATOR ROLL

⅓ cup Apple Butter
1 cup heavy cream, whipped
15 vanilla wafers
½ cup chopped nut meats

Fold apple butter gradually into whipped cream. Spread wafers with mixture, arrange in piles or form into roll and cover top and sides with remaining filling. Sprinkle with chopped nuts and chill about 3 hours. Cut roll into diagonal slices and serve on individual plates. Serves 4.

FROZEN ROLL—Place roll in refrigerator tray and freeze for 3 hours. Slice as above.

Use apricot or raspberry jam instead of apple butter.

Add chopped maraschino cherries. Use chocolate wafers instead of vanilla wafers.

Use graham crackers, cutting diagonally to serve.

Nothing could be simpler for family or party dessert than one of these rolled cookie refrigerator cakes

CRANBERRY REFRIGERATOR CAKE

1 pound (4 cups) cranberries
1½ cups water
3 eggs, separated
1½ cups sugar
5 tablespoons flour
½ teaspoon salt
Juice and rind of ½ orange
1 tablespoon butter
1 dozen Ladyfingers
Chopped nut meats

Cook cranberries in water until skins pop. Rub through sieve. Combine beaten egg yolks, sugar, flour, salt, orange juice and rind and add to cranberry purée. Cook over hot water until thick. Add butter. Cool; fold in stiffly beaten egg whites. Arrange halved ladyfingers around bottom and sides of a spring-form pan lined with waxed paper; add half the cranberry mixture. Cover with ladyfingers; add remaining mixture. Chill for about 8 hours. Unmold and garnish with nuts. Makes 1 (10x10 inch) cake.

FIG REFRIGERATOR CAKE

1 cup cooked dried figs
1½ teaspoons unflavored gelatin
1 tablespoon cold water
1¼ cups milk
4 tablespoons sugar
2 eggs, separated, Salt
1 teaspoon vanilla
½ cup heavy cream, whipped
Graham crackers
12 marshmallows, quartered

Clip stems from figs and cut figs into pieces. Soften gelatin in cold water. Scald 1 cup milk over hot water. Caramelize 2 tablespoons sugar and dissolve in hot milk. Combine egg yolks, ¼ cup cold milk, remaining sugar and salt and stir into hot milk. Continue cooking until custard coats the spoon. Add figs and gelatin and cool; add flavoring, stiffly beaten egg whites and whipped cream. Line loaf pan with waxed paper. Line sides and bottom of pan with graham crackers. Pour in a 1-inch layer of custard, add some of marshmallows, a layer of crackers, more custard, marshmallows, and so on, until all are used, using crackers for top. Chill overnight. Unmold, slice and serve with whipped cream. Serves 6 to 8.

JIFFY CRANBERRY REFRIGERATOR CAKE

1 egg white
2 cups Cranberry Sauce
1 Spongecake
1 cup heavy cream, whipped

Fold stiffly beaten egg white into cranberry sauce. Arrange alternate layers of sliced spongecake and sauce in pan, finishing with cake. Place a weight on top. Chill. Unmold and garnish with whipped cream. Serves 6.

REFRIGERATOR CHEESE CAKE

½ cup melted butter
¾ cup sugar
2 cups fine zwieback crumbs
2 teaspoons cinnamon
2 tablespoons unflavored gelatin
1 cup cold water
3 eggs, separated
2 cups cream cheese
3 tablespoons lemon juice
1 tablespoon grated lemon rind
¼ teaspoon salt
½ cup heavy cream, whipped

Blend butter, ¼ cup sugar, crumbs and cinnamon. Line spring-form pan with ¾ of mixture. Soften gelatin in ½ cup water. Cook egg yolks, remaining sugar and water in a double boiler until thickened. Add gelatin. Beat into cheese with lemon juice, rind and salt. Chill; beat well. Fold in cream with stiffly beaten egg whites. Pour onto crumbs. Sprinkle with remaining crumbs. Chill until firm. Serves 12.

A dainty wreath of whipped cream and cherries sets off refrigerator cheese cake

REFRIGERATOR CHRISTMAS CAKE

2 tablespoons unflavored gelatin
1 quart milk
2 eggs, separated
¾ cup sugar
¼ teaspoon salt
¾ cup chopped maraschino cherries
⅓ cup maraschino juice
1 teaspoon vanilla
1½ cups heavy cream
2 dozen vanilla wafers

Soften gelatin in ½ cup milk. Scald remaining milk and pour onto beaten egg yolks. Add sugar, salt and softened gelatin; return to double boiler; cook until mixture coats a spoon. Cool. Add cherries, juice and vanilla. Chill until mixture begins to thicken. Fold in beaten egg whites and half the cream, whipped. Butter a cake pan and arrange vanilla wafers around it. Pour in filling and cover top with remaining vanilla wafers. Chill overnight. Unmold and frost sides and top of cake with remaining cream, whipped. Serves 12.

CHOCOLATE REFRIGERATOR CAKE

1 small Spongecake
4 ounces (squares) chocolate
½ cup milk
½ cup sugar
4 eggs, separated
1 teaspoon vanilla
¼ teaspoon salt
1 cup heavy cream, whipped
¼ cup confectioners' sugar

Line small loaf pan with waxed paper Cover bottom and sides with thin slices of spongecake. Melt chocolate over hot water. Add milk and continue cooking over hot water until smooth and blended, stirring constantly. Add sugar to slightly beaten yolks and add chocolate mixture slowly, stirring constantly. Cook until thick and smooth. Remove from heat and while still hot, fold in stiffly beaten egg whites. Add ½ teaspoon vanilla and salt. Pour half of chocolate mixture into cakelined pan. Cover with a layer of spongecake, add remaining chocolate mixture and cover with final layer of cake slices. Chill for 12 hours. Turn out onto plate; cover with whipped cream flavored with confectioners' sugar and remaining vanilla. Serves 12.

REGAL CHOCOLATE — Omit cake, milk, and confectioners' sugar. Soften 1 teaspoon unflavored gelatin in 1 tablespoon cold water. To chocolate add sugar, salt and ¼ cup hot water; blend. Add gelatin; blend. Add to beaten yolks; cook 2 minutes. Add vanilla; cool. Fold in stiffly beaten whites; chill. Use ½ cup cream, whip and fold in. Use 36 Ladyfingers; separate and line bottom and sides of mold. Cover bottom with thin layer chocolate mixture; then alternate ladyfingers and chocolate. Chill 12 hours. Unmold. Serves 12.

ORANGE REFRIGERATOR PUDDING

½ cup sugar
2 teaspoons flour
2 eggs, separated
½ cup scalded milk
1 tablespoon butter
Few grains salt
Grated rind ½ orange
Juice of 1 orange
Ladyfingers
Whipped cream

Mix sugar and flour with beaten egg yolks, then add scalded milk slowly. Add butter and salt and cook over hot water until thick. Add orange rind and juice. Cool slightly and fold in stiffly beaten egg whites. Split ladyfingers and place a layer in pan lined with waxed paper; spread with orange mixture; cover with another layer of ladyfingers and continue until mixture is used. Chill 24 hours. Serve with whipped cream. Serves 6.

Instead of ladyfingers, use Spongecake cut into strips. Garnish with sections cut from pared orange.

Sprinkle 2 tablespoons grated chocolate over cake.

Graham crackers and apple butter stage an exciting return engagement (page 633)

REFRIGERATOR RASPBERRY PIE

¼ cup butter
1 cup graham cracker crumbs
1 pint raspberries
⅔ cup sugar
⅛ teaspoon salt
1 tablespoon lemon juice
2 teaspoons unflavored gelatin
½ cup cold water
1 cup heavy cream, whipped
1 teaspoon vanilla

Melt butter, combine with crumbs and mix thoroughly. Pat buttered crumbs evenly over sides and bottom of pie plate and chill. Hull and wash berries and cut into small pieces. Mix with sugar, salt and lemon juice. Soften gelatin in cold water for 5 minutes, dissolve over low heat and combine with raspberry mixture. Fold in whipped cream, add vanilla and turn into crust. Chill for 1½ hours or until firm. Two or three large berries and a small amount of whipped cream may be reserved for garnishing. Serves 6. Use blackberries, if desired.

BUTTERSCOTCH CHARLOTTE RUSSE

1 tablespoon unflavored gelatin
¼ cup cold water
2½ tablespoons butter
⅔ cup brown sugar
1½ cups milk; 2 eggs, separated
¼ teaspoon salt
1 cup evaporated milk, chilled
½ teaspoon vanilla
1 dozen Ladyfingers

Soften gelatin in water 5 minutes. Melt butter, add sugar and cook together until well blended. Add milk, heat and pour over well-beaten egg yolks, stirring constantly. Add salt and cook over hot water until mixture coats a spoon, stirring constantly. Remove from heat and add softened gelatin. Stir until dissolved, then chill until mixture begins to thicken. Fold in stiffly beaten egg whites, whipped evaporated milk and vanilla. Pour into a mold lined with separated ladyfingers. Chill until firm; unmold. Serves 6.

Spongecake or vanilla cookies may be used for ladyfingers.

CHOCOLATE CHARLOTTE RUSSE

2 teaspoons unflavored gelatin
2 tablespoons cold water
1 ounce (square) chocolate
¼ cup boiling water
6 tablespoons sugar
Dash salt
1¾ cups evaporated milk
½ teaspoon vanilla
10 Ladyfingers

Soften gelatin in water 5 minutes. Melt chocolate over hot water; add boiling water and cook slowly over direct heat to a smooth thickened paste, stirring constantly. Add sugar, salt and ¾ cup evaporated milk and cook 2 to 3 minutes longer. Remove from heat and add gelatin, stirring until dissolved. Cool. Chill remaining milk thoroughly. When chocolate mixture begins to thicken whip chilled milk until stiff and fold into chocolate mixture. Add vanilla and pour into a mold lined with separated ladyfingers. Chill until firm; unmold. Serves 5.

FRUIT REFRIGERATOR LOAF

½ pound marshmallows, quartered
1 cup cream or evaporated milk
1 cup graham cracker crumbs
1 cup chopped candied cherries
1 cup chopped candied pineapple
1 cup chopped dates
1 cup chopped salted pecan meats
2 teaspoons grated orange rind
2 teaspoons sherry or lemon juice

Heat marshmallows and cream over low heat, folding over and over until marshmallows are half melted. Remove from heat and continue folding until mixture is smooth and fluffy. Cool. Sprinkle buttered loaf pan with ¼ cup graham cracker crumbs. Add remaining crumbs, fruit, nut meats, orange rind and sherry to marshmallows, then pour over crumbs. Chill thoroughly. Slice and serve plain or with whipped cream. Serves 12.

If desired add all crumbs to fruit mixture.

When you unmold and garnish this fruit refrigerator loaf your family will vote you especially high honors

MOSAIC CHOCOLATE REFRIGERATOR CAKE

1 teaspoon unflavored gelatin
1 tablespoon cold water
4 ounces (squares) chocolate
½ cup sugar
Dash salt
¼ cup hot water
4 eggs, separated
1 teaspoon vanilla
½ cup heavy cream, whipped
3 dozen Ladyfingers

Soften gelatin in water 5 minutes. Melt chocolate over hot water. Add sugar, salt and hot water, stirring until sugar is dissolved and mixture blended. Add gelatin, stir until dissolved and remove from boiling water. Add egg yolks, one at a time, beating thoroughly after each is added. Place over boiling water and cook 2 minutes, stirring constantly. Add vanilla; cool. Fold into stiffly beaten egg whites. Chill until mixture begins to thicken. Fold in whipped cream. Line bottom and sides of mold with waxed paper, then with separated ladyfingers. Cover bottom with thin layer of chocolate mixture, then arrange ladyfingers and chocolate mixture in alternate layers, topping with chocolate mixture. Cut off ends of ladyfingers around sides of mold and place on chocolate mixture. Chill 12 to 24 hours. Unmold. Serves 12.

Add ½ cup chopped walnut meats to chocolate mixture before turning into mold.

LEMON — Combine 1 teaspoon cornstarch and ½ cup sugar. Add 1 cup milk, 1 tablespoon butter and 3 egg yolks. Cook over hot water until thickened. Chill. Add juice 1 lemon, ½ teaspoon grated lemon rind and 3 stiffly beaten egg whites. Line mold with ladyfingers, fill with mixture and chill. Serves 8.

PINWHEEL REFRIGERATOR CAKE

8 slices Jelly Roll
1 tablespoon unflavored gelatin
¾ cup cold water
1 package orange gelatin
1 cup orange juice
½ cup sugar
⅛ teaspoon salt
1 tablespoon grated orange rind
2 cups heavy cream, whipped
½ cup blanched and chopped almonds (lightly toasted)

Line tube pan with slices of jelly roll made with Orange Marmalade. Soften unflavored gelatin in ¼ cup water 5 minutes. Dissolve orange gelatin in 1 cup hot orange juice, add softened gelatin and stir until dissolved. Add remaining ½ cup water, sugar, salt and grated orange rind. Chill. When mixture begins to thicken, whip until fluffy, fold in whipped cream and ½ of almonds. Pour into tube pan. Sprinkle remaining almonds over top. Chill until firm; unmold. Serves 8.

MAPLE NUT REFRIGERATOR CAKE

1 tablespoon unflavored gelatin
½ cup cold water
2 eggs, separated
¾ cup maple sirup
¼ teaspoon salt
1 cup heavy cream, whipped
10 macaroons, dried and rolled
¾ cup chopped nut meats
2 dozen Ladyfingers

Soften gelatin in water 5 minutes. Beat egg yolks slightly, add maple sirup and salt and cook over boiling water until slightly thickened. Add gelatin and stir until dissolved. Cool and add whipped cream, macaroons and nut meats. Fold in stiffly beaten egg whites. Line a mold with separated ladyfingers and fill with maple mixture. Chill. When firm, unmold and garnish top with whipped cream and whole nut meats. Serves 8.

First aid to the harried hostess is mosaic refrigerator cake prepared ahead of time

The peach marshmallow mixture is equally good molded with layers of chocolate wafers

PEACH MARSHMALLOW REFRIGERATOR CAKE

1 tablespoon unflavored gelatin
¼ cup cold water
⅓ cup butter (softened)
1 cup confectioners' sugar
2 eggs, separated
½ pound marshmallows, cut into small pieces
4 cups sliced peaches
2 cups vanilla wafer crumbs

Soften gelatin in water 5 minutes. Cream butter, add sugar and blend in egg yolks. Cook over low heat, stirring constantly until thickened. Remove from heat, add gelatin and stir until dissolved. Cool slightly, add marshmallows, blend lightly and chill until mixture begins to thicken. Fold in sliced peaches and beaten egg whites. Arrange alternate layers of cookie crumbs and peach filling in a mold, beginning and ending with cookie crumbs. Chill until firm, unmold and serve with or without whipped cream. Serves 8.
Use sweetened cooked apricots instead of peaches.

FRESH RHUBARB REFRIGERATOR CAKE

1⅓ cups (1 can) sweetened condensed milk
¼ cup lemon juice
1 cup unsweetened stewed fresh rhubarb
24 vanilla wafers

Blend milk and lemon juice together. Add rhubarb. Line narrow oblong pan or spring-form pan with waxed paper and fill with alternate layers of fruit mixture and wafers, finishing with layer of wafers. Chill 6 hours or longer. To serve, turn out onto small platter, remove waxed paper and cut into slices. Serves 8.

HAWAIIAN REFRIGERATOR CAKE

1⅓ cups (1 can) sweetened condensed milk
¼ cup lemon juice
10 marshmallows, quartered
½ cup crushed pineapple
10 maraschino cherries, quartered
½ cup heavy cream, whipped
Ladyfingers

Combine condensed milk and lemon juice and stir until thickened. Add marshmallows, pineapple, maraschino cherries and whipped cream. Line 9-inch tube pan with separated ladyfingers, standing halves around inner and outer edge of pan. Pour in filling. Cover with ladyfingers, if desired. Chill in refrigerator 6 hours or longer. To serve, turn out onto small platter. Garnish with whipped cream. Serves 10.

HOLIDAY REFRIGERATOR CAKE

½ pound marshmallows, quartered
1 cup cream
1 cup graham cracker crumbs
1 cup chopped candied cherries
1 cup chopped candied pineapple
1 cup chopped dates
1 cup chopped salted pecan meats
2 teaspoons grated orange rind
2 teaspoons sherry or lemon juice

Heat marshmallows and cream over low heat, folding over and over until marshmallows are half melted. Remove from heat and continue folding until mixture is smooth and fluffy. Cool. Sprinkle buttered loaf pan with ¼ cup graham cracker crumbs. Add remaining crumbs, fruit, nut meats, orange rind and sherry to marshmallows, then pour over crumbs. Chill thoroughly. Slice and serve plain or with whipped cream. Serves 12.

DEEP-DISH APPLE PUDDING

1 cup minced suet
1 cup sifted flour
⅛ teaspoon salt
1 teaspoon baking powder
2 medium apples, sliced
¼ cup sugar

Mix suet with flour, salt and baking powder. Add enough cold water to make a soft dough. Roll out into 2 rounds of ¼-inch thickness and line small greased pan with 1 round of dough. Fill with sliced apples and sprinkle with sugar. Cover with second round and steam for 2 hours. Serves 4.

BURNT SUGAR DUMPLINGS

SAUCE
1½ cups sugar
2 tablespoons butter
⅛ teaspoon salt
2 cups hot water
DUMPLINGS
1½ cups sifted flour
2½ teaspoons baking powder
3 tablespoons sugar
¼ teaspoon salt
3 tablespoons butter
½ cup chopped walnut meats
¾ cup milk

Heat ½ cup sugar in skillet until it melts to a golden brown sirup. Add butter, salt and remaining sugar. Add hot water gradually, stirring constantly. Heat to boiling and cook until sugar is dissolved, about 10 minutes, stirring frequently. Sift flour, baking powder, sugar and salt together. Cut in butter with pastry blender. Add walnuts; stir in milk all at once, mixing only enough to moisten flour. Drop by tablespoons into gently boiling caramel sauce. Cover tightly and simmer gently 12 to 15 minutes without removing cover. Serve at once with sauce, for 6.

ENGLISH SUET PUDDING

3 cups sifted flour
1 teaspoon baking soda
1 teaspoon cinnamon
1 teaspoon cloves
½ teaspoon grated nutmeg
1 teaspoon salt
1 cup suet
1 cup sour milk
1 cup molasses
1 cup raisins

Mix and sift dry ingredients, keeping ½ cup of flour to sift over raisins. Chop suet fine and add to milk and molasses. Combine the 2 mixtures and add the raisins, dredged with flour. Grease pudding molds or baking powder cans and fill ⅔ full. Cover and steam 3 hours. Serve with Hard Sauce or any pudding sauce. Serves 8 to 10.

Use buttermilk instead of sour milk.

Add ¼ cup each diced citron and candied orange peel.

Use currants instead of raisins.

For the holidays serve English suet pudding with flaming brandy or tiny lighted tapers

CANDIED FRUIT PUDDING

½ cup shortening, ½ cup sugar
3 eggs, separated
2 cups candied fruit
1½ cups sifted cake flour
¼ teaspoon salt

Cream shortening and sugar until fluffy. Beat egg yolks until thick and combine with creamed mixture. Chop candied fruits, mix with flour and salt and add gradually to first mixture, blending thoroughly. Fold in egg whites beaten until stiff but not dry. Pour into greased melon mold and steam 1½ hours. Serve hot with Fluffy Brandy Sauce, for 8.

CHERRY ROLY-POLY

1 recipe Shortcake Biscuits
2 cups canned cherries, drained

Roll dough lightly on floured board into an oblong ½ inch thick. Spread with cherries and roll, sealing edges well. Place in buttered pan, cover tightly and steam for 1¼ to 1½ hours. Serve with Cherry Sauce made from juice. Serves 8.
Bake at 400°F. 25 to 30 minutes, instead of steaming.

This lordly plum pudding bears a diadem of hard sauce pinwheels

ENGLISH PLUM PUDDING

¾ cup sifted cake flour
1 teaspoon salt
¾ teaspoon baking soda
1 teaspoon cinnamon
¼ teaspoon nutmeg
½ teaspoon mace
½ pound raisins, chopped
½ pound dried currants, chopped
¼ pound citron, chopped
⅛ pound lemon peel, chopped
⅛ pound orange peel, chopped
⅛ pound blanched almonds, chopped
½ cup fine bread crumbs
¾ cup hot milk
½ pound brown sugar
5 eggs, separated
½ pound suet, chopped
¼ cup fruit juice (any kind)
½ glass currant jelly

Sift flour, salt, soda and spices together; stir in fruit and almonds. Soften crumbs in milk 10 minutes. Beat sugar into beaten egg yolks; add suet and crumbs; stir into flour-fruit mixture. Add fruit juice and jelly and mix well; fold in stiffly beaten egg whites. Pour into greased mold, cover tightly and steam for 3½ hours. Serves 12.

CRANBERRY PUDDING

1 cup sifted flour
1½ teaspoons baking powder
½ teaspoon salt
⅓ cup brown sugar
½ cup bread crumbs
⅔ cup finely chopped suet
1 cup chopped cranberries
1 egg, ⅓ cup milk or water

Mix ingredients in the order given. Turn into greased mold, cover with waxed paper and steam 2 hours. Serve with Foamy Cranberry Sauce. Serves 6.

CRANBERRY ROLY-POLY

1 recipe Shortcake Biscuits
2 tablespoons melted butter
2 cups Cranberry Sauce, drained

Roll biscuit dough on slightly floured board to ¼-inch thickness. Brush with melted butter and cover with cranberry sauce. Roll up like jelly roll. Place seam side down in buttered pan, cover tightly and steam for 1¼ to 1½ hours. Serve with Hard Sauce. Serves 8.

MOLASSES FRUIT PUDDING

¼ cup shortening
½ cup molasses
½ cup milk
1 egg
1 cup sifted cake flour
½ cup bran
½ teaspoon baking soda
1 teaspoon salt
½ cup raisins

Melt shortening, add molasses, milk and beaten egg. Mix dry ingredients together, add raisins and stir into first mixture. Turn into greased mold, cover and steam for 1½ hours. Serves 6.

Use chopped dates for raisins.

DATE PUDDING

2 cups coarse dry bread crumbs
½ teaspoon baking powder
½ teaspoon salt
1½ cups chopped dates
½ cup chopped nuts, 2 eggs
½ cup brown sugar
½ cup water

Combine first 5 ingredients. Beat eggs, add sugar and water. Add to crumb mixture. Pour into a greased mold, cover and steam 45 minutes. Serves 6.

SAILOR'S DUFF

2 tablespoons butter
2 tablespoons brown sugar
1 egg, ½ cup molasses
1½ cups sifted flour
½ teaspoon baking soda
⅛ teaspoon salt
1 teaspoon baking powder
½ cup boiling water

Cream butter and sugar together until fluffy. Add beaten egg and molasses. Sift flour, soda, salt and baking powder together and add alternately with boiling water in small amounts. Mix thoroughly. Turn into greased mold and steam 1½ to 2 hours. Serves 6.

FIG MAPLE PUDDING

¼ pound figs
¾ cup maple sirup
½ cup boiling water
¾ cup sifted flour
1½ teaspoons baking powder
¼ teaspoon salt
1½ tablespoons sugar
3 tablespoons shortening
¼ to ⅓ cup milk

Soften figs in cold water, cut into halves and place in greased baking dish. Mix maple sirup with boiling water and pour over figs. Cover dish and steam for ½ hour. Sift flour, baking powder, salt and sugar together. Cut in shortening with 2 knives or pastry blender, add milk and mix lightly. Remove baking dish from steamer and pour batter over figs. Cover dish, return to steamer and steam 1 hour. This pudding provides its own sauce. Serves 5.

INDIVIDUAL STEAMED FIG PUDDINGS

Figs
¾ cup shortening
1 cup sugar
2 eggs
2 cups sifted flour
½ teaspoon salt
1 teaspoon baking soda
1 teaspoon mace
1 teaspoon cinnamon
½ cup sour milk
1 teaspoon vanilla

Rinse figs, dry on a towel, clip stems and force enough through food chopper to measure ¾ cup. Cream shortening and sugar together until fluffy. Add beaten eggs and mix; then add figs, blending well. Sift flour, salt, soda and spices together; add alternately with milk in small amounts, mixing well after each addition. Stir in flavoring and pour into greased custard cups,

filling slightly over ½ full. Cover and steam for 45 minutes. Serve hot with Lemon, Vanilla or Marshmallow Sauce. These may be reheated. Serves 10.

REGAL PUDDING

1½ ounces (squares) chocolate
1½ tablespoons butter
⅓ cup confectioners' sugar
½ tablespoon flour
2 egg yolks, beaten
¼ teaspoon vanilla, Dash salt
2 egg whites, stiffly beaten

Melt chocolate and add remaining ingredients, folding in egg whites. Pour into greased mold, cover tightly and steam 30 minutes. Serves 6.
Serve with desired sauce.

STEAMED BROWN BREAD PUDDING

2 cups bread crumbs
1 cup cold water
½ cup molasses
1 egg, beaten
1 teaspoon baking soda
1 teaspoon cinnamon
½ teaspoon cloves
½ teaspoon salt
1 cup raisins

Combine ingredients in order given and place in greased mold. Cover tightly. Place in pan of boiling water and steam 3 hours. Serve with a sauce. For 6.

Candied fruit and nuts give a gay touch to the simplest pudding

LAYER PUDDING WITH CRYSTALLIZED GRAPES

Pecan meats
Candied cherries
3¾ cups sifted flour
6 teaspoons baking powder
1 teaspoon salt
⅔ cup shortening
¾ cup sugar
2 eggs
1½ cups milk
¾ teaspoon almond extract
1½ teaspoons vanilla
Green food coloring
1½ ounces (squares) chocolate, melted
¼ teaspoon lemon extract
2 teaspoons grated orange rind

Grease a 2- to 2½-quart mold and decorate with halves of pecans and candied cherries. Sift flour, baking powder and salt together. Cream shortening and sugar until fluffy. Add eggs and beat well. Add milk alternately with dry ingredients, in small amounts, mixing thoroughly after each addition. Remove 1½ cups batter to smaller bowl, add almond extract, ¾ teaspoon vanilla and a few drops green coloring to tint delicate green; mix well to distribute color evenly. Drop green batter by spoonfuls into mold being careful not to disturb the decoration. Remove a second 1½ cups batter to small bowl and add melted chocolate and ¾ teaspoon vanilla; blend well, place on top of green layer in mold. To remaining batter add lemon extract and orange rind; blend well, place on top of chocolate layer in mold. Cover tightly and steam 1¾ hours. Unmold on large platter and garnish with huckleberry leaves and bunches of Crystallized Grapes. Serve hot with Brandy Hard Sauce. Serves 8 to 10.

Grandmother steamed her puddings in baking powder cans; we use a fluted mold

SPICE PUDDING

3 tablespoons butter
¼ cup sugar
1 egg, beaten
1 cup sifted flour
1½ teaspoons baking powder
⅛ teaspoon salt
½ teaspoon cloves
½ teaspoon allspice
½ teaspoon cinnamon
½ cup milk

Cream butter and sugar together until fluffy. Add beaten egg. Sift remaining dry ingredients together; add alternately with milk in small amounts, mixing well after each addition. Beat thoroughly and pour into greased pan. Steam about 45 minutes and serve hot with desired sauce. Serves 6.

OLD-FASHIONED STEAMED PUDDING

1 cup bread crumbs
½ cup sour milk
¼ cup shortening, ½ cup sugar
½ teaspoon vanilla, 1 egg
½ cup sifted flour
¼ teaspoon salt
½ teaspoon baking soda
⅟₁₆ teaspoon nutmeg
½ teaspoon cinnamon
½ cup raisins
½ cup chopped nuts

Soften bread crumbs in sour milk. Cream shortening and sugar until fluffy; add vanilla and blend thoroughly. Beat egg and combine with milk and crumbs, then add to sugar and shortening mixture. Mix thoroughly. Sift flour, salt, soda and spices together; add raisins and nuts. Combine with first mixture. Steam for 1 hour in greased mold. Serves 6.

CHERRY PURÉE

Juice from 1 quart tart cherries,
    freshly stewed or canned
2 teaspoons arrowroot
Grated rind 1 lemon

Heat the juice from the cherries.
Add arrowroot moistened with
cold water, stirring the mixture
rapidly to prevent the forming of
lumps. Flavor with the grated
lemon rind. Serve very cold, with
a whole cherry on each portion.

ORANGE PURÉE

2 cups orange juice
1 teaspoon cornstarch
2 tablespoons cold water
½ cup sugar
1 teaspoon grated orange rind

Place orange juice in saucepan
and when it is thoroughly heated
add the cornstarch mixed with
the cold water. Cook slowly until clear. Add sugar and grated
orange rind. Serve cold in sherbet cups. Serves 4.

RASPBERRY PURÉE

¼ cup quick-cooking tapioca
3 cups water
½ cup currant juice
2 cups raspberries, Sugar

Boil tapioca in water and currant
juice. When tapioca is transparent, add raspberries and sugar
to taste. Serve cold in sherbet
glasses. Serves 8.

SCALLOPED APPLES

6 large tart apples
¼ teaspoon salt
4 tablespoons lemon juice
¾ pound peanut brittle, crushed
    fine

Pare and slice apples, add salt,
lemon juice and peanut brittle
Place in buttered casserole and
bake in slow oven (325°F.) 1
hour. Serves 8.

APPLES STUFFED WITH MINCEMEAT

6 baking apples
¾ cup mincemeat
1 cup sugar, 2 cups water

Wash apples, core and place in
baking pan. Place 2 tablespoons
mincemeat in cavity of each
apple. Mix sugar and water, pour
into pan. Bake in slow oven
(300°F.) 1 hour, or until soft.
Serve with juice in pan. For 6.

APPLES WITH BRAZIL NUTS
— Fill apples with chopped Brazil nuts and sirup mixture.

APPLE MERINGUE PUDDING

Toasted bread, Hot milk
1 dozen apples
Sugar, Nutmeg
3 eggs, separated

Cover the bottom and sides of
a baking pan with toasted bread,
moistened with hot milk. Core
apples and cook them whole;
sweeten with sugar and flavor
with nutmeg. Beat the yolks of
eggs together with a little sugar
and pour over the apples. Place
apples on toast, then cover with
the stiffly beaten egg whites.
Bake at 325°F. 15 minutes.

CRYSTALLIZED GRAPES

Wash 1 pound red or purple
grapes and dry; cut into small
clusters. Boil ½ cup water and
1 cup sugar together for 5 minutes. Dip each bunch of grapes
into sirup, allow excess sirup to
drain off, sprinkle grapes immediately with coarse granulated
sugar. Place on platter and allow sirup to harden. Grapes
crystallize rapidly if chilled.

BAKED PEACHES HAWAIIAN

8 firm medium peaches
½ cup sugar
½ cup canned unsweetened
    pineapple juice

Pour boiling water over peaches.
rub off skins and place peaches
close together in baking dish.
Sprinkle with sugar, add pineapple juice, cover and bake in
moderate oven (350°F.) about 20
minutes. Remove cover and brown
fruit slightly. Serve hot or cold.
Serves 8.

*Brazil-nut filling for baked
apples is only one of endless possibilities (page 644)*

BAKED ORANGES

8 large oranges
½ cup sugar
8 teaspoons butter

Wash oranges and grate the skins slightly. Cover with water and boil for 30 minutes. Drain and cool. Cut off a small slice at blossom end and remove core. Place 1 tablespoon sugar and 1 teaspoon butter in center of each orange. Place in a buttered baking dish, fill ⅔ full of water, cover and bake in moderate oven (350°F.) 2 hours. Serves 8.

STUFFED ORANGES

4 large oranges, 8 dates
4 teaspoons chopped walnuts
4 teaspoons raisins
4 tablespoons sugar
1 egg white, stiffly beaten
4 teaspoons grated coconut

Cut a thin slice from stem end of oranges. Cut triangles evenly

Oranges as well as apples may be stuffed and topped with meringue and served hot or cold for lunch or dinner dessert

from top. Remove centers, dice pulp and combine with dates, walnuts, raisins and 2 tablespoons sugar. Fill orange shells and bake in a casserole with ½ inch water, in 300°F. oven 45 minutes. Fold beaten egg white and remaining sugar together. Remove oranges from oven, top with egg mixture, sprinkle with coconut and return to oven for 15 minutes. Serves 4.

BAKED APPLES

6 apples
⅔ cup sugar
¼ teaspoon nutmeg
¼ teaspoon cloves

Select sound apples; core and place in a baking dish. Sprinkle with sugar, nutmeg and cloves. Add water to cover bottom of dish and bake in moderate oven (350°F.) about 1 hour, or until tender. Serves 6.
Baked apples may be varied by filling the centers with brown sugar and raisins, sections of bananas, red cinnamon candies, marshmallow, marmalade or jelly,

honey or corn sirup and lemon juice, nuts, candied orange peel, candied pineapple, preserved ginger, canned or fresh berries, peaches and other fruits or leftover fruit juice. Meringues, Custard Sauce, whipped cream or Marshmallow Sauce may be used as a garnish for apples.

APPLESAUCE

8 large apples
½ cup water
¾ cup sugar

Wash, pare, quarter and core sour, juicy apples. Place them in a saucepan with water; cover tightly and simmer until tender. Add sugar and cook a few minutes longer. Serve hot or cold. For 6. A few whole cloves or a dash of cinnamon or nutmeg or a little lemon juice or a few seedless raisins may be cooked with the apples. Brown or maple sugar may be used instead of white.

APRICOTS—Wash apricots. Place in enough cold water to cover and boil 40 minutes, or until tender. Add sugar and lemon juice to taste.

PEACHES—Prepare as apricots.

PRUNES—Prepare as apricots.

RHUBARB SAUCE

2 pounds rhubarb
1 cup sugar

Wash rhubarb and cut into ½-inch cubes. Place in a pan containing 1 inch of water. Cover tightly and simmer about 45 minutes. Remove cover and cook until most of water is evaporated. Sweeten with sugar and serve alone as a fruit sauce or with roast lamb or veal or poured over plain cake. Other fruits or fruit juices may be added, if desired. Makes about 3 cups.

HAWAIIAN WEDGES

1 pineapple
Confectioners' sugar
12 orange sections, Mint

Cut unpeeled pineapple from top to bottom into 6 wedges. Remove center core from each piece. Loosen fruit from skin but leave fruit in skin. Cut fruit lengthwise through center and crosswise several times making wedges. Sprinkle with confectioners' sugar. Place two orange sections and sprig of mint in the center cut of each serving. Serves 6.

GLAZED PEACHES

½ cup dried peaches
1 cup sugar
¼ cup white corn sirup
½ teaspoon mace
½ lemon, juice and grated rind

Wash peaches; cover with boiling water; let stand overnight. Drain, reserving ½ cup water. Heat sugar, sirup and water to boiling; add mace, lemon juice and rind. Pour over peaches; cover; bake at 300°F., 2½ hours. For 6.

FRUIT WHIP

1 cup fruit pulp
⅛ teaspoon salt
½ cup sugar
2 egg whites, beaten
1 tablespoon lemon juice

1. Heat fruit pulp, salt and sugar together until sugar is dissolved. Pour hot sirup slowly over stiffly beaten egg whites, beating constantly. Add lemon juice. Pile into parfait glasses and serve immediately. Serves 4.

2. Place mixture in greased baking dish, place in pan of hot water and bake in slow oven (300°F.) about 1 hour. Serve hot or cold.

PINEAPPLE PEACH PYRAMID

1 No. 2½ can sliced pineapple
1 No. 2½ can peach halves
8 marshmallows

Drain fruit separately, reserving peach juice for this recipe and pineapple juice for breakfast juice. Place peach half with hollow side up in center of each slice of pineapple; arrange in shallow baking dish. Place marshmallow in center of each peach. Pour peach juice into baking dish. Bake in moderate oven (375°F.) 20 to 30 minutes, basting occasionally. Serve hot. Serves 8.

PEACHES IN MERINGUES

6 large cooked peach halves
6 teaspoons tart jelly
½ recipe Meringue

Fill peach halves with jelly. Place on baking sheet, cover with meringue and bake in slow oven (275°F.) about 1 hour. Serve hot or cold. Serves 6.

Cover meringue with chopped nut meats or coconut.

Use peanut butter, chopped nut meats or coconut instead of jelly. Use cooked pear, apple or apricot halves.

Quick and easy evening desserts are made of fruits covered with meringue and nuts, then baked

APPLE DUMPLINGS

8 medium apples
1¼ cups brown sugar
⅓ cup butter
½ teaspoon salt
1 teaspoon cinnamon
1 teaspoon grated lemon rind
Baking Powder Biscuit dough

Pare and core apples. Mix brown sugar, butter, salt, cinnamon and lemon rind together and fill each apple cavity with part of mixture Roll baking powder biscuit dough to ⅛-inch thickness; cut into squares large enough to cover apple. Place apple on each square and bring corners together at top; moisten edges and pinch together to hold apple in place. Place on baking sheet and bake in moderate oven (350°F.) 30 minutes or until apples are tender. Serve with a plain Lemon Sauce. Makes 8 dumplings.

They'll come without calling when they know there are apple dumplings for supper

BAKED BANANAS

6 firm bananas
2 tablespoons melted butter
Salt

Peel bananas, place in buttered baking dish, brush with butter and sprinkle with salt. Bake in moderate oven (375°F.) 15 to 18 minutes. Serve with Orange Sauce. Serves 6.

MAPLE BANANAS

6 firm bananas
2 tablespoons lemon juice
¾ cup maple sirup
¼ cup chopped nuts

Peel bananas, brush with lemon juice and place in greased baking dish. Pour maple sirup over bananas. Bake in moderate oven (375°F.) 15 to 18 minutes. Sprinkle with nuts. Serves 6.

COCONUT—Omit sirup and nuts. Roll bananas in coconut. Bake as above. Serve with Orange Sauce.

BROILED GRAPEFRUIT

Cut grapefruit into halves, sprinkle with white or light brown sugar, dot lightly with butter and place under moderate broiler. Heat until butter is melted and sugar is browned slightly.

APRICOT OR PRUNE WHIP

1½ cups sweetened apricot or prune pulp
1½ tablespoons lemon juice
⅛ teaspoon salt
⅓ cup sugar
3 egg whites, stiffly beaten
Chopped nuts

Mix pulp, lemon juice and salt together. Beat sugar into egg whites, fold in fruit mixture and serve garnished with chopped nuts. If desired this mixture may be piled lightly into greased baking dish and baked in slow oven (275°F.) 30 to 45 minutes.

BERRY—Use mashed berries instead of apricot pulp.

FRIED APPLES

1 apple
1 egg, beaten
¼ teaspoon cinnamon
¼ teaspoon sugar
1½ tablespoons fat

Core apple and cut into ¼-inch slices. Dip in egg; sprinkle with cinnamon and sugar. Fry slowly in fat until brown and tender.

BAKED PEARS

4 pears
1 cup brown sugar
1 cup granulated sugar
2 tablespoons butter
¾ cup water
3 ounces cream cheese
Milk

Place pears in baking dish and add sugars, butter and water. Bake in 350° F. oven about 35 minutes. Soften cheese with milk, whip until fluffy and serve on pears for 4.

Refrigerator Desserts

250 Luscious Refrigerator Desserts

Introduction

FREEZING DESSERTS IN THE REFRIGERATOR

The directions supplied by the manufacturer of the refrigerator should be followed to secure the best results. However, a few general suggestions may be given. The larger the proportion of sugar or other sweetening the slower the mixture freezes. In fact, it may not freeze at all if too much sweetening is used, so ingredients should be measured carefully.

Beat the cream only to a soft peak, not to a stiff peak as for toppings of pies and puddings. If cream is whipped too stiff the dessert will not have as good volume and may have a "buttery" flavor.

Do not fold whipped cream or whipped evaporated milk into a warm mixture. It should be either well chilled or partially frozen as directed in the recipe.

If freezing temperature can be adjusted, use lowest possible temperature, since rapid freezing improves the texture.

Do not attempt to freeze ice cubes and a dessert at the same time.

Freezing will be more rapid if the doors are not opened frequently and if the freezing unit is not heavily frosted.

When the mixture contains bits of fruit, do not freeze so hard that the fruit freezes to icy particles. Puréed fruit is best to use, since the flavor is more evenly distributed and there is less possibility of a crystalline texture. If bits of fruit are included they will be less icy after freezing if they are heated with sugar until wilted, then cooled and used in the mixture.

Turn temperature regulator back to normal setting after the dessert is frozen.

To be worthy of its place as America's favorite dessert, ice cream must be smooth and velvety as well as rich and well-flavored. Ice cream made in a freezer achieves this fine texture through the air beaten in by the dasher while the cream freezes. When frozen desserts are made in the automatic refrigerator, other methods have to be used to incorporate air and prevent the mixture from freezing into a solid block of coarse icy crystals.

Whipped cream or evaporated milk, melted marshmallows, beaten eggs, gelatin, rennet tablets and other ingredients are all added to help prevent the formation of large ice crystals as well as to improve or vary flavor. There are a number of products now on the market which are designed to achieve the same result. Stirring or beating while freezing and very rapid freezing are also aids to good texture.

TO WHIP EVAPORATED MILK

Chill milk very thoroughly by placing unopened can in freezing compartment of automatic refrigerator or by pouring milk into freezing tray and freezing until ice crystals begin to form around the edges. Pour milk into thoroughly chilled bowl and whip with cold beater. Beat milk as rapidly as possible and use it at once. Add lemon juice while beating or soften a little unflavored gelatin in cold milk 5 minutes and dissolve in scalded milk before chilling to help milk hold its stiffness longer. If the whipped milk is to be folded into another mixture, the mixture should also be thoroughly chilled.

If milk fails to whip it was not cold enough and may be rechilled and beaten again, since it will not become "buttery" no matter how many times it is whipped.

Evaporated milk triples in volume when whipped and heavy cream doubles in volume, consequently if one is substituted for the other the amounts being beaten may have to be adjusted in some recipes. If a recipe calls for 1 cup evaporated milk, whipped, 1½ cups of heavy cream, whipped, would give the same volume. One cup of heavy cream, whipped, gives the same volume as ⅔ cup evaporated milk, whipped.

BANANA PECAN ICE CREAM

1 cup mashed ripe bananas
2 teaspoons lemon juice
¼ teaspoon salt
⅓ cup milk
2 eggs, separated
¼ cup sugar
1 cup heavy cream
1 teaspoon vanilla
½ cup chopped pecan meats

Mix bananas, lemon juice, salt and milk together, stirring until mixed. Beat egg whites, add sugar and beat until stiff. Beat egg yolks until thick. Whip cream until thick enough to hold a soft peak. Combine banana mixture, egg yolks, egg whites, cream, vanilla and pecan meats. Pour into tray of refrigerator and freeze until firm. Serves 8.
Sprinkle additional nuts on top.

HONEY ICE CREAM

2 eggs, separated
½ cup honey
2 cups cream
1 teaspoon vanilla

Beat egg yolks until thick, adding honey gradually. Blend in cream and vanilla. Freeze until firm. Place in chilled bowl, add egg whites and beat until smooth. Return to freezing tray and freeze until firm. Serves 6.

BUTTER PECAN ICE CREAM

½ cup sugar
½ teaspoon salt
1⅓ cups milk
1 cup broken pecan meats
2 tablespoons butter
2 eggs, separated
1 cup heavy cream
1 teaspoon vanilla

Dissolve sugar and salt in milk. Brown pecans in butter, cool. Beat egg whites until stiff but not dry. Beat egg yolks until thick and lemon colored. Whip cream until thick enough to hold a soft peak; add vanilla and fold in egg yolks, egg whites, milk and pecans. Pour into freezing tray of refrigerator and freeze, stirring every 30 minutes until the mixture will hold its shape, then freeze until firm. Serves 6.

BUTTER CRISP — Instead of pecans, use a mixture of 1 tablespoon melted butter, 2 tablespoons brown sugar, ¼ cup chopped nuts and ¼ cup crushed cereal flakes Bake mixture in 375°F. oven 10 minutes, stirring frequently. Cool and fold into ice cream when half frozen. Freeze until firm.

Line the refrigerator tray with waxed paper and lift out the finished dessert by the folded edges

CHOCOLATE ICE CREAM

1 ounce (square) chocolate
⅔ cup sweetened condensed milk
⅔ cup water
½ teaspoon vanilla
½ cup heavy cream, whipped

Melt chocolate over boiling water, add milk and stir 5 minutes or until mixture thickens. Add water and mix well. Pour into freezing tray of refrigerator and freeze until ice crystals form around sides of pan. Add vanilla. Whip cream until thick enough to hold a soft peak, fold into chilled mixture and freeze. When mixture is half frozen scrape from sides and bottom of tray, beat until smooth but not melted and freeze until firm. Serves 6.

CHOCOLATE COCONUT — Add ½ cup finely chopped shredded coconut just before folding in whipped cream.

CHOCOLATE SHERRY — Add 3 tablespoons sherry or sherry extract, ¼ cup chopped candied cherries and ¼ cup chopped candied pineapple just before folding in whipped cream.

MOCHA — Decrease vanilla to ¼ teaspoon and use 1 cup strong cold coffee instead of water.

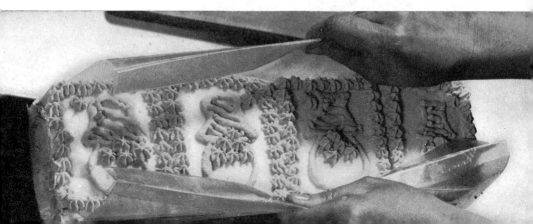

CARAMEL ICE CREAM

½ cup sugar
1 cup milk
⅛ teaspoon salt
2 egg yolks, beaten
1 cup heavy cream
1 teaspoon vanilla

Heat ⅓ cup of sugar slowly in heavy skillet until melted and slightly brown, stirring constantly. Scald milk and add to melted sugar. Cook until sugar is completely dissolved. Add remaining sugar and salt to beaten egg yolks and add hot sugar mixture gradually. Cook slowly until thickened. Chill. Whip cream until thick enough to hold a soft peak, add vanilla and fold into chilled mixture. Pour into freezing tray of refrigerator and freeze until firm. Serves 6.
Line tray with broken nuts.

Make the shamrock of green gumdrops and the face of candied cherries

FRUITY ICE CREAM

½ (9-ounce) package condensed
    mincemeat
⅓ cup cold water
⅔ cup sweetened condensed
    milk
½ cup water
1½ teaspoons vanilla or rum
    flavoring
1 cup heavy cream

Break mincemeat into pieces. Add cold water and cook slowly, stirring constantly until lumps are thoroughly broken up. Heat to boiling and cook 1 minute or until mixture is practically dry. Cool. Blend milk, water and flavoring thoroughly. Add mincemeat and chill. Whip cream until thick enough to hold a soft peak and fold into chilled mixture. Pour into freezing tray of refrigerator and freeze. When mixture is about half frozen, scrape from sides and bottom of tray, beat until smooth but not melted and freeze until firm. Serves 5.

CHOCOLATE CHIP ICE CREAM

⅔ cup evaporated milk
1 egg
¼ cup sugar
Few grains salt
2 ounces (squares) sweet chocolate, shaved or grated
¼ teaspoon vanilla

Chill milk thoroughly, then whip until stiff. Beat egg; add sugar, salt, chocolate and vanilla. Fold into whipped milk. Pour at once into freezing tray of refrigerator and freeze until firm. Serves 3.

COFFEE MALTED ICE CREAM

⅔ cup sweetened condensed
    milk
3 to 4 tablespoons malted milk
½ cup strong cold coffee
½ teaspoon vanilla
1 cup heavy cream, whipped

Mix condensed milk with malted milk. Add coffee and vanilla, blending well. Pour into freezing tray of refrigerator and freeze until crystals form around sides, then scrape from sides and bottom of tray, beat until smooth but not melted, fold in whipped cream and freeze until firm. Serves 6.

CHOCOLATE — Use chocolate malted milk instead of plain and water instead of coffee.

MOCHA — Use chocolate malted milk instead of plain.

If desired, line tray with fine graham cracker or cookie crumbs or with coarsely broken nut meats.

Fold in ½ cup broken nut meats with whipped cream.

Add candied cherries, sliced.

Instead of coffee use fruit juices: prune, apricot, raspberry or grape juice.

HONEY NUT CUSTARD ICE CREAM

1⅔ cups evaporated milk
⅛ teaspoon salt
4 egg yolks, well beaten
2 cups boiling water
1 cup honey
½ cup chopped nut meats

Pour milk into freezing tray of refrigerator and freeze until ice crystals form around edges of tray. Add salt to beaten egg yolks and add boiling water slowly, stirring constantly. Cook over hot water 2 minutes. Cool and add honey. Whip chilled milk until stiff. Fold into cold custard, add nuts and freeze until firm. Serves 8.

Pour warmed honey over servings of ice cream. Sprinkle with crisp cereals or chopped nuts.

ORANGE PEKOE TEA ICE CREAM

1 cup evaporated milk
1 cup hot water
3 tablespoons orange pekoe tea
6 cloves
3 eggs, separated
1½ cups sugar
¼ teaspoon salt
1 tablespoon lemon juice
1½ teaspoons grated lemon
   rind
1 cup heavy cream

Scald milk and water. Add tea and cloves and steep 3 minutes. Strain. Beat egg yolks, 1 cup sugar and salt together, add milk mixture and cook over boiling water until thickened, stirring constantly. Cool. Add lemon juice and rind. Beat egg whites until stiff and beat in remaining sugar. Whip cream until thick enough to hold a soft peak, fold egg whites and whipped cream into chilled mixture, pour into freezing tray of refrigerator and freeze until firm. Serves 8.

PRUNE ICE CREAM

1 teaspoon unflavored gelatin
1 tablespoon cold water
2 cups prunes
1 cup milk
½ cup sugar
4 eggs, beaten
1 tablespoon vanilla
¼ teaspoon salt
1 cup heavy cream

Soften gelatin in cold water 5 minutes. Wash prunes in hot water, cut from pits and force through food chopper using fine blade. Combine milk and sugar and heat to boiling. Add gelatin and stir until dissolved. Pour hot mixture over eggs, stirring constantly; add vanilla, prunes and salt. Chill. Beat thoroughly with rotary beater until fluffy. Whip cream until stiff enough to hold a soft peak. Fold into whipped prune mixture, pour into freezing tray of refrigerator and freeze until firm. Serves 6.

PEACH ICE CREAM

1 No. 2½ can peaches
½ tablespoon unflavored gelatin
½ cup sugar
½ teaspoon vanilla
½ teaspoon almond extract
⅛ teaspoon salt
1 drop red food coloring
1 cup heavy cream

Drain peaches, saving juice to be used at another time. Press peaches through coarse sieve. To ¼ cup peach purée, add gelatin and let soften 5 minutes. To remaining purée, add sugar and heat to boiling. Add gelatin mixture and stir until dissolved. Cool, pour into freezing tray of refrigerator and freeze. When half frozen add flavoring, salt and coloring. Whip cream until thick enough to hold a soft peak and fold in. Freeze. Serves 4.

A circus parade of animal crackers prowls around the party dish of ice cream

NEW YORK ICE CREAM

2 cups milk
1 tablespoon cornstarch
2 tablespoons cold milk
2 eggs, separated
½ cup sugar
½ cup corn sirup
¼ teaspoon salt
1 tablespoon vanilla
1¼ cups heavy cream

Scald milk in top of double boiler. Make a paste of cornstarch and 2 tablespoons milk, add to scalded milk and cook until thickened, stirring constantly. Beat egg yolks; add sugar, corn sirup and salt. Mix well. Add hot milk gradually to egg mixture, then return to top of double boiler and cook 2 minutes. Add vanilla. Chill mixture in freezing tray of refrigerator until ice crystals form around sides of pan, then beat until light. Fold stiffly beaten egg whites into custard. Whip cream until stiff enough to hold a soft peak, fold into mixture, return to freezing tray and freeze, stirring twice. Serves 6 to 8.

ANGEL — Add ⅓ cup maraschino cherry juice with vanilla. Add ⅓ cup chopped candied fruits, ½ cup chopped blanched almonds and 1 cup angel food cake crumbs to chilled custard before folding in egg whites.

BANANA — Add 1 cup mashed ripe bananas to chilled mixture before folding in egg whites.

CHOCOLATE — Melt 2 ounces (squares) chocolate in hot custard mixture.

TUTTI FRUTTI — Add ⅓ cup chopped nut meats, ⅓ cup chopped candied pineapple and ⅓ cup chopped maraschino cherries to chilled custard mixture before folding in egg whites.

Whole red berries add their color and melting sweetness to raspberry ice cream

RAISIN ICE CREAM

½ teaspoon unflavored gelatin
1 tablespoon cold water
1 cup evaporated milk, scalded
1 cup seedless raisins
¾ cup sugar
1 tablespoon cornstarch
1 cup milk
1 egg, separated
2 teaspoons grated orange rind
¾ cup orange juice
2 tablespoons lemon juice

Soften gelatin in cold water 5 minutes and dissolve in hot evaporated milk. Chill thoroughly. Cook raisins in water 5 minutes, drain and cool. Blend sugar and cornstarch thoroughly, add milk and beaten egg yolk. Cook until thick, stirring constantly. Add orange rind, cool and add orange and lemon juices. Whip evaporated milk until stiff, fold in cold orange mixture, raisins and stiffly beaten egg white. Mix together thoroughly, pour into freezing tray of refrigerator and freeze until firm, stirring occasionally. Serves 8.

RASPBERRY ICE CREAM

1 cup sweetened condensed milk
¼ cup water
2 cups fresh raspberries, crushed
2 tablespoons lemon juice
½ cup heavy cream

Mix condensed milk and water Add raspberries and lemon juice Chill. Whip cream until thick enough to hold a soft peak. Fold into chilled mixture, pour into freezing tray of refrigerator and freeze. When half frozen scrape from sides and bottom of tray, beat until smooth but not melted and freeze until firm. Serves 6.

EGGNOG ICE CREAM

2 eggs, separated
½ cup sugar
2 tablespoons brandy
2 tablespoons rum
1 cup scalded milk
1 cup heavy cream, whipped

Beat egg yolks until thick, adding sugar gradually. Beat in brandy, rum and hot milk. Chill. Fold in stiffly beaten egg whites and whipped cream. Pour into freezing tray and freeze until firm. Serves 6.

BASKETS FOR ICE CREAM

APPLE—Remove a slice from blossom end of firm red apples. Leave skin on. Scoop out center of apples and fill with any ice, sherbet or ice cream.

CANTALOUPE—Cut melon crosswise into halves, scoop out seeds and fill with ice cream. Serves 2.

HONEYDEW MELON—Cut melon lengthwise into halves, scoop out pulp and cut a slice off the bottom so that basket will stand upright. Fill with ice cream. Serve from basket or cut each into halves. Serves 4.

ORANGE AND GRAPEFRUIT — Mark off with toothpicks ½-inch strips around centers of large oranges or small grapefruit. Cut out peel in 2 quarter sections, leaving uncut strips ½ inch wide for handles to baskets. Remove pulp, leaving shells intact; flute or scallop edge of shells. Fill with Orange Sherbet or ice cream.

PEAR—Wash large pears. Do not remove stem and blossom ends; cut lengthwise into halves and remove core and seeds. Scoop out pear halves to form baskets. Fill with Ginger Ale Sherbet.

PINEAPPLE—Cut large, well-shaped pineapples into halves lengthwise; scoop out centers leaving a ¼-inch wall. Chop pineapple and sweeten. Fill with ice cream and serve topped with chopped fresh pineapple.

WATERMELON — Scoop out red portion of fruit from end slice of watermelon; hollow out white rim, leaving shell intact; scallop edges with sharp knife; and cut a slice off the bottom so that basket will stand firm. Fill with ice cream or sherbet. Serve from basket.

RENNET ICE CREAM

1 rennet tablet
1 tablespoon cold water
1 cup milk, ½ cup sugar
1¼ teaspoons vanilla
1 cup heavy cream

Dissolve rennet tablet in cold water. Heat milk, sugar and vanilla to lukewarm, not hot, stirring constantly. Remove from heat, add dissolved tablet and stir a few seconds. Pour at once into freezing tray of refrigerator. Let stand at room temperature until firm, about 10 minutes, then cool in refrigerator ½ hour. Whip cream until stiff enough to hold a soft peak, fold into rennet-custard and freeze. When partly frozen, scrape from sides and bottom of tray and beat until smooth but not melted. Continue freezing until firm. Serves 6 to 8.

VANILLA MERINGUE ICE CREAM

2 egg whites
⅛ teaspoon salt
¼ cup sugar
1 cup heavy cream, whipped
½ teaspoon vanilla

Beat egg whites with salt until nearly stiff, then beat in sugar gradually to make a stiff meringue. Whip cream until thick enough to hold a soft peak, add vanilla and fold into meringue. Pour into freezing tray of refrigerator and freeze without stirring until firm. Serves 6.

Shred 2 ounces candied or preserved marrons and add just before freezing.

Fill a chilled cantaloupe with ice cream and garnish the top with fresh fruit and berries in season

MAPLE NUT — Use 2 teaspoons maple flavoring instead of vanilla. After mixture has been partially frozen and beaten fold in ¼ cup chopped walnut meats.

ORANGE — Use orange juice instead of water and ½ teaspoon grated orange rind for vanilla.

PEACH — Omit vanilla. Crush 1 cup fresh sliced peaches, sweeten with about ¼ cup confectioners' sugar and add to blended milk and water. Chill and proceed as above.

PEPPERMINT STICK — Omit vanilla and fold in 1 cup crushed peppermint stick candy after beating half-frozen mixture.

PISTACHIO — Use 1 teaspoon almond extract instead of vanilla. Fold in ¼ cup finely chopped pistachio nut meats, 1 stiffly beaten egg white and a few drops green food coloring with whipped cream.

STRAWBERRY — Omit vanilla. Crush 1 cup strawberries, sweeten with about ¼ cup confectioners' sugar and add to blended milk and water. Chill and proceed as above.

Save the reddest, most perfect berries to serve over scoops of strawberry ice cream

VANILLA ICE CREAM

⅔ cup sweetened condensed
    milk
½ cup water
1½ teaspoons vanilla
1 cup heavy cream

Blend milk, water and vanilla thoroughly, pour into freezing tray of refrigerator and freeze until ice crystals form around sides of pan. Whip cream until stiff enough to hold a soft peak, fold into milk mixture and freeze.

When half frozen scrape mixture from sides and bottom of tray, beat until smooth but not melted and freeze until firm. Serves 6.

APRICOT — Use ½ cup crushed fresh apricots and ½ cup apricot juice instead of water. Reduce vanilla to ½ teaspoon.

CHERRY — Use 1 cup cherry juice and ½ cup minced cherries instead of water. Use 1 teaspoon lemon juice instead of vanilla.

COFFEE — Use strong black coffee instead of water. Reduce vanilla to ½ teaspoon.

COFFEE RUM — Use strong black coffee instead of water and use 2 tablespoons rum for vanilla.

Or mold the ice cream in a lined refrigerator tray and garnish with berries and whipped cream

BAKED ALASKA SANDWICH

1 layer of cake (square or
    oblong)
1 quart ice cream
4 egg whites
½ cup sugar
1 teaspoon vanilla

Cut cake into halves and trim to fit deep refrigerator tray. Line tray with heavy waxed paper so that paper extends 2 inches beyond each side. Pack ice cream into tray and freeze until hard. Lift ice cream from tray with ends of waxed paper and place one of the halves of cake in tray. Place ice cream on top, then the second half of cake. Chill thoroughly. Beat egg whites until nearly stiff, beat in sugar gradually, add vanilla and beat until stiff. Place a board at least 1½ inches thick between 2 pieces of corrugated paper, cover top with waxed paper and place cake and ice cream on top. Cover top and sides of cake with the meringue, making sure it is at least 1 inch thick. Bake in very hot oven (450°F.) until meringue is delicately browned. Serve immediately. Serves 10.

If refrigerator tray is not available spread firm ice cream between chilled layers of cake, cover with meringue and bake as above.

Use any flavor of ice cream desired. Any kind of cake except angel food may be used.

BAKED ALASKA—Prepare meringue as above. Place round of spongecake on board, heap ice cream quickly on top, leaving a 1-inch margin of cake all around; cover thickly with meringue. Brown quickly in very hot oven (450°F.). Serve at once with Chocolate, Caramel or fruit sauce, if desired.

BAKED ALASKA WITH BRAZIL NUTS

1 Spongecake
1 pint ice cream
¾ cup sliced Brazil nuts
3 egg whites
Salt
3 tablespoons sugar
1 teaspoon vanilla

Remove center from top of cake, leaving a shell at least ¾ inch thick. Fill with ice cream and sprinkle ½ cup sliced nuts over ice cream. Beat egg whites until stiff but not dry; beat in salt, sugar and vanilla gradually. Spread on top of cake and sprinkle with remaining Brazil nuts. Bake in very hot oven (450°F.) until light brown, about 5 minutes. Serve at once. Serves 6.

MOCHA BAKED ALASKA

1 layer Spongecake
3 egg whites
6 tablespoons confectioners' sugar
1 teaspoon vanilla
1½ pints Mocha Ice Cream
    frozen in a mold

Place a layer of spongecake which is cut a little larger than the mold of ice cream, on a board covered with heavy brown paper. Beat egg whites until stiff, add sugar gradually and continue beating. Add vanilla. Unmold Mocha Ice Cream onto the cake. Cover thickly with meringue. Place on baking sheet and brown under broiler heat. Serve at once. Serves 6.

Baked Alaska is a gorgeous dessert which deserves to be made more often

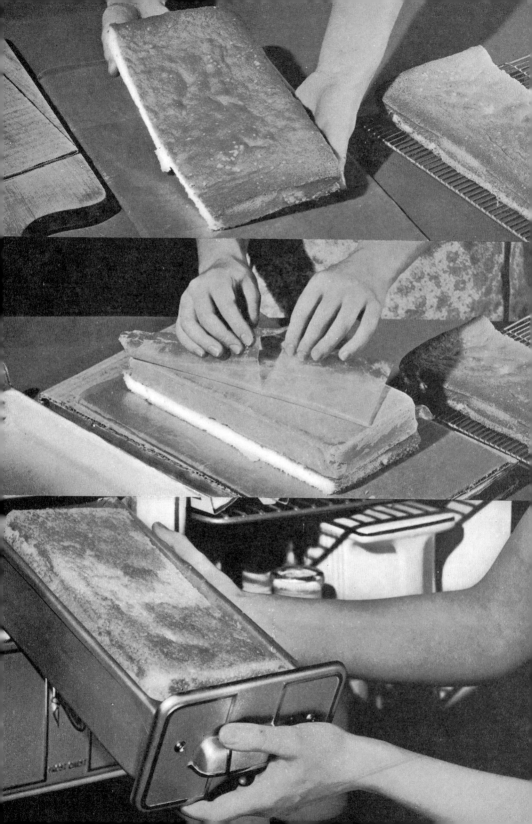

CARAMEL CRUNCH SUNDAE

½ cup brown sugar
2 tablespoons butter
2 cups crisp cereal flakes or
   puffed rice cereal
Chocolate or Vanilla Ice Cream

Place sugar and butter in heavy saucepan and cook over low heat about 5 minutes, stirring occasionally. Add cereal and toss lightly until coated with sirup. Spread out on platter and cool. Sprinkle over ice cream. Serves 6 to 8.

CHOCOLATE SUNDAES

CARAMEL CHOCOLATE—Serve Caramel Ice Cream with Hot Chocolate Fudge Sauce. Top with whipped cream if desired.

CHOCOLATE MINT—Serve Chocolate Ice Cream with Quick Chocolate Mint Sauce.

COCONUT SNOWBALL—Cover bottom of shallow sherbet glass with Chocolate Fudge Sauce. Shape Vanilla Ice Cream into a ball; roll in moist coconut and place in sherbert glass. Toast coconut if desired.

Use chopped walnut, pecan or blanched almond meats instead of coconut.

HOT FUDGE—Serve Chocolate Ice Cream or Vanilla Ice Cream with Hot Chocolate Fudge Sauce. Top with chopped nut meats or plain or toasted coconut.

MARSHMALLOW MINT — Add 2 or 3 drops peppermint flavoring to Marshmallow Sauce and serve over Chocolate Ice Cream, garnish with puffed cereal.

MOCHA PECAN—Serve Coffee Ice Cream with Chocolate Fudge Sauce and garnish with pecan meats.

CHOCOLATE CARAMEL SANDWICH

⅔ cup Caramel Sauce
¼ cup cream
1 layer of white cake
1 pint Chocolate Ice Cream

Combine sauce and cream. Cut cake into squares and slice each through the middle, sandwich fashion. Place ice cream between slices and pour caramel sauce over cake. Serves 4 to 6
Other combinations may be used instead of above. Omit cream.
1. Chocolate Cake, Peppermint Stick Parfait, Chocolate Fudge Sauce, chopped nut meats.
2. Angel Food Cake, Strawberry Ice Cream, sweetened crushed strawberries.
3. Angel Food Cake, Chocolate Ice Cream, Marshmallow or Caramel Sauce.
4. Chocolate Spongecake, Butter Pecan Ice Cream, Chocolate Fudge Sauce.
Spongecake, Vanilla Ice Cream, Maple Sauce.

ORANGE MERINGUE RING

Orange food coloring
5 egg whites, 1½ cups sugar
¾ teaspoon vinegar
⅛ teaspoon salt
¾ teaspoon grated orange rind
¼ teaspoon vanilla
Chocolate Ice Cream

Mix a small amount of orange coloring with egg whites and beat until nearly stiff. Add sugar gradually, beating thoroughly after each addition. Add vinegar, salt, orange rind and vanilla. Shape into a ring on a cookie sheet covered with heavy paper. Bake in very slow oven (250°F.) about 1¼ hours or until dry on surface. Remove from paper and cool. Place on a round platter and fill center with ice cream. Serves 8.

CHOCOLATE WAFFLES WITH ICE CREAM

1 cup sifted cake flour
¼ teaspoon salt
3 tablespoons sugar
1½ teaspoons baking powder
1 egg, beaten
½ cup milk
½ teaspoon vanilla
1 ounce (square) chocolate,
   melted
3 tablespoons melted butter
Chocolate or Peppermint Stick
   Ice Cream
Chocolate Fudge Sauce

Sift flour, salt, sugar and baking powder together. Combine egg, milk, vanilla, chocolate and butter. Add to sifted dry ingredients and mix well. Bake in hot waffle iron. Cut into halves and serve with ice cream and chocolate sauce or cut into quarters, using one quarter below and one above ice cream. Serves 6 to 8.

MINT MERINGUES WITH CHOCOLATE ICE CREAM

2 egg whites
⅔ cup confectioners' sugar
Few grains salt
Few drops green coloring
1 or 2 drops peppermint extract
Chocolate Ice Cream
Whipped cream, Peppermints

Beat egg whites until nearly stiff and add sugar gradually, beating until stiff. Add salt, coloring and flavoring and mix in lightly. Drop by tablespoons onto cookie sheet covered with heavy paper. Bake in slow oven (275°F.) 30 to 35 minutes or until dry on surface. Remove from paper and cool. Pile ice cream in center of plates, place a meringue on each side of plate, garnish ice cream with whipped cream and place peppermints on top. Serves 6.

ÉCLAIR GLACÉ

1½ cups corn sirup
1½ ounces (squares) chocolate
9 marshmallows, cut into pieces
3 tablespoons cream
6 Éclair Shells
1 pint Vanilla Ice Cream

Heat corn sirup, add chocolate and cook slowly, stirring constantly until chocolate is melted. Add marshmallows and stir until melted. Add cream. Split éclair shells, cover each half with ice cream and pour hot sauce over ice cream. If the sauce is to be used cold add more cream, as it thickens when cool. Serves 6.

PEACH BANANA SUNDAE

3 to 4 tablespoons sugar
1 cup sliced peaches
1 ripe banana, diced
2 teaspoons lemon juice
Peach or Vanilla Ice Cream

Combine sugar, peaches, banana and lemon juice and mix lightly until sugar is dissolved. Serve over ice cream. Serves 6.

BOMBES

Do not have frozen mixtures too hard. Scald mold, chill and line sides with ice cream, ice or sherbet, making layer ¾ inch or more in thickness, depending on size of mold. Spread evenly with a spoon, fill center with any desired ice cream, ice, sherbet, mousse or parfait to within ¾ inch of top and cover with first mixture until filled to overflowing. Cover and freeze in freezing unit of refrigerator or in ice and salt. If using ice and salt, (4 parts ice to 1 part salt) seal cover with a strip of cloth dipped into melted shortening. To serve, wrap mold in hot cloth a few seconds, turn onto a platter and slice.

SUGGESTED COMBINATIONS:

Chocolate Ice Cream with:
  Peanut Mousse
  Peppermint Stick Parfait
  Honey Nut Custard Ice Cream
  Banana Ice Cream
Orange Sherbet with:
  Raisin Ice Cream
  Frozen Rice and Pineapple Pudding

Chocolate Chip Ice Cream with:
  Butter Pecan Mousse
Vanilla Ice Cream with:
  Chocolate Coconut Ice Cream
  Maple Nut Ice Cream
  Caramel Ice Cream
  Cranberry Mousse
Plum Sherbet with:
  Honey Nut Custard Ice Cream
  Banana Ice Cream
Mocha Ice Cream with:
  Black Walnut Parfait
Coffee Rum Ice Cream with:
  Fresh Cherry Sherbet
Pineapple Sherbet with:
  Butterscotch Parfait
Fresh Strawberry Ice Cream with:
  Rhubarb Ice
Rennet Ice Cream with:
  Butterscotch Parfait
Cider Mallobet with:
  Cinnamon Parfait

BRICK ICE CREAM

Line refrigerator tray with heavy waxed paper. Separate layers of various colored and flavored ice cream or mousse with dry bread crumbs. Slice when frozen.

A bombe is a luxurious way of serving two ice creams of different colors and textures

Try a delicate meringue shell for your chocolate ice cream pie

CARAMEL CRUNCH RING WITH ICE CREAM

¼ cup water
½ cup butter
1 cup brown sugar
3 cups cereal flakes
½ cup finely cut pecans
Caramel Ice Cream

Heat water and butter slowly. Add sugar and heat until well mixed. Add to cereal flakes and pecans; mix thoroughly. Pack into buttered ring mold and chill 2 hours. Unmold by placing mold in hot water ½ minute. Fill center of ring with caramel ice cream. Serves 8.

COOKIE CRUMB — Use crushed vanilla wafers or gingersnaps instead of cereal flakes.

FRESH RASPBERRY TARTS

1 pint fresh raspberries
⅓ cup sugar
4 to 6 baked Tart Shells
1 pint Vanilla Ice Cream

Crush raspberries, add sugar and chill about 1 hour. Fill tart shells ⅓ full with the raspberries and place scoop of vanilla ice cream in each. Garnish with remaining raspberries. Serves 4 to 6.

ICE CREAM MERINGUE TARTS

¼ cup Currant Jelly
6 baked Tart Shells
3 egg whites, Few grains salt
4½ tablespoons sugar
Butter Pecan Ice Cream

Break jelly slightly with fork and spread in bottom of chilled tart shells. Beat egg whites and salt until nearly stiff and beat in sugar gradually. Fill tart shells with firmly frozen ice cream and cover with meringue making sure ice cream is completely covered with a thick layer. Bake in very hot oven (450°F.) until lightly browned. Serve immediately. Serves 6

STRAWBERRY BASKETS

4 individual Spongecakes
½ tablespoon sugar
¼ teaspoon vanilla
⅓ cup heavy cream, whipped
1 pint Strawberry Ice Cream
2 dozen small strawberries

Hollow out the centers of spongecakes. Add sugar and vanilla to whipped cream. Fill the cake baskets with ice cream, top with whipped cream and garnish with strawberries. Serves 4.

STRAWBERRY PINEAPPLE TARTS

1½ cups diced strawberries
¼ cup sugar
3 tablespoons cornstarch
¾ cup pineapple juice
1 cup diced pineapple
⅛ teaspoon salt
1 teaspoon butter
6 baked Tart Shells
Vanilla Ice Cream

Mix strawberries and sugar. Make a smooth paste of cornstarch and a little pineapple juice. Add remaining pineapple juice, diced pineapple and salt. Cook, stirring constantly until thickened. Add butter, strawberries and more sugar if desired. Pour into tart shells and serve topped with vanilla ice cream. Serves 6.

Use Chocolate Ice Cream or orange ice instead of Vanilla Ice Cream.

STRAWBERRY ICE CREAM PIE

¼ pound (16) marshmallows
2 tablespoons crushed strawberries
Few drops red food coloring
2 egg whites
¼ cup sugar
¼ teaspoon salt
⅔ quart Vanilla Ice Cream
1 baked Pastry Shell
1 cup fresh strawberries, sliced

Heat marshmallows and crushed strawberries slowly, folding over and over until marshmallows are half melted. Remove from heat and continue folding until mixture is smooth and spongy. Add coloring and cool. Beat egg whites until nearly stiff and beat in sugar slowly. Add salt. Fold into cooled marshmallow mixture. Place ice cream in pastry shell. Cover with strawberries and top with marshmallow meringue. Brown quickly under broiler heat ½ minute. Serve immediately. Serves 6.

CHOCOLATE PEPPERMINT ROLL

¼ cup sifted flour
½ teaspoon salt
3 tablespoons cocoa
1 cup confectioners' sugar
5 eggs, separated
1 teaspoon vanilla
1 pint Peppermint Stick Ice Cream

Sift dry ingredients together 3 times. Beat yolks until thick, fold in dry ingredients. Beat whites stiff, add vanilla and fold into mixture. Spread in shallow (11x16 inch) pan lined with waxed paper. Bake at (400°F.) 15 to 20 minutes. Turn out on a damp towel. Remove paper, cut off edges and roll up as jelly roll. When cold unroll, spread with ice cream; reroll. Chill. Slice and serve with Chocolate Fudge Sauce. Serves 8.

ORANGE SURPRISE

2 oranges
1 recipe Orange Sauce
Plain cake batter
1 pint Vanilla Ice Cream

Peel oranges, separate into segments, cover bottom of greased layer-cake pan with orange segments and orange sauce. Cover with plain cake batter. Bake in moderate oven (350°F.) about 35 minutes. Cut into individual servings and top with ice cream. Cake may be used hot or cold. Serves 4 to 6.
Add 2 tablespoons brandy to sauce.
Any upside-down cake may be served in the same manner.

MELBAS

The combination of cake, cooked fruit and ice cream is called a Melba. Originally it was sponge-cake, a peach half and vanilla ice cream. The modern Melba is made of any plain cake, cooked or fresh fruit and ice cream, often with whipped cream garnish. Use your choice of fruits and cake with the following:

PRALINE ICE CREAM

1½ cups broken Praline Kisses
3 cups scalding milk
4 egg yolks, well beaten
¾ cup sugar
Few grains salt
1 teaspoon vanilla
1½ cups heavy cream or chilled evaporated milk

Pound pralines and force through a coarse sieve. Stir milk gradually into egg yolks. Add sugar and salt and cook in top of double boiler until mixture coats the spoon. Chill thoroughly. Add pralines, vanilla and c r e a m (whipped until not quite stiff enough to hold its shape). Freeze. If frozen in a mechanical refrigerator, stir twice during the freezing. Makes 2 quarts ice cream.

KUMQUAT ICE CREAM

1 quart heavy cream
2 cups sugar
4 eggs, separated
1 cup minced kumquats in sirup
1 tablespoon Curaçao

Heat cream to scalding. Mix sugar and beaten egg yolks. Add cream slowly and cook, stirring constantly, until slightly thickened. Remove from heat and cool, then stir in finely minced kumquats and Curaçao. Fold in stiffly beaten egg whites. Freeze in refrigerator tray until firm. Makes 1½ quarts.

BANANA CARAMEL ICE CREAM

1 cup mashed ripe bananas (2 to 3 bananas)
2 teaspoons lemon juice
¼ cup brown sugar
¼ teaspoon salt
⅓ cup milk
2 eggs, separated
1 cup heavy cream
1 teaspoon vanilla

Mix bananas and lemon juice together. Add sugar, salt and milk, stirring until mixed. Beat egg whites until stiff. Whip cream until thickened but not stiff. Beat egg yolks until thick. Combine banana mixture, egg whites, egg yolks, cream and vanilla. Turn into refrigerator tray and freeze, stirring every 30 minutes until mixture holds its shape. Freeze until firm. Serves 8.

ENGLISH TOFFEE ICE CREAM

1 pound marshmallows
3 cups milk
1 cup heavy cream, whipped
1 cup crushed English toffee

Heat marshmallows in 2 tablespoons of milk in saucepan, folding over and over until marshmallows are half melted. Remove from heat and continue folding until mixture is smooth and fluffy. Cool. Then add remaining milk gradually and blend. Pour into refrigerator tray and chill. When mixture just begins to freeze, stir thoroughly and fold in whipped cream. Freeze, stirring several times during freezing period. Just before ice cream becomes firmly frozen, fold in English toffee. Leave the ice cream in freezing tray for several hours. Serves 6 to 8. Garnish with almonds.

Use peanut brittle in place of English toffee.

MOUSSES, MALLOBETS AND MARLOWS

Mousses are very rich mixtures, frozen without stirring. They may be frozen in refrigerator trays, in individual molds or paper soufflé cups packed into the tray, or in a larger mold which will fit into the freezing compartment of the refrigerator.

APRICOT AND BANANA MOUSSE

1 tablespoon unflavored gelatin
¼ cup cold milk
½ cup apricot juice, hot
2 ripe bananas, mashed
1 cup sweetened stewed apricots, puréed
2 cups heavy cream
1 cup confectioners' sugar

Soften gelatin in milk 5 minutes, dissolve in hot apricot juice and cool. Add bananas and apricots. Whip cream until thick enough to hold a soft peak and beat in sugar. Fold in fruit mixture and freeze until firm. Serves 8 to 10. Omit first 4 ingredients. Fold sugar and apricots into cream.

Any frozen dessert which does not need stirring may be frozen in paper cups

APPLE MOUSSE

1 cup evaporated milk, chilled
2 tablespoons lemon juice
2 cups sweetened Applesauce, chilled
Dash nutmeg, Few grains salt

Whip milk very stiff. Fold in lemon juice, applesauce, nutmeg and salt. Freeze until firm. Makes 1 quart.

CHOCOLATE MOUSSE

1 ounce (square) chocolate
1¼ cups evaporated milk
¼ cup water
7 tablespoons sugar
2 egg yolks, beaten
⅛ teaspoon salt
1 teaspoon vanilla

Melt chocolate over hot water. Scald ¼ cup milk, water and sugar over boiling water. Pour over egg yolks, stirring vigorously; add salt, return to double boiler and cook 5 minutes, stirring constantly. Add gradually to melted chocolate, beating until thoroughly blended. Cool. Chill remaining milk and whip very stiff. Fold chocolate mixture into milk, add vanilla and freeze until firm. Serves 6.

CHOCOLATE MINT LAYER

1 cup heavy cream
⅓ cup sugar
¼ teaspoon mint extract
2 ounces (squares) chocolate
1 quart Vanilla Ice Cream
1 dozen toasted almonds

Whip cream until stiff, add sugar and mint extract. Melt chocolate over boiling water, cool slightly and add gradually to whipped cream. Place ice cream in waxed-paper lined freezing tray of refrigerator and spread chocolate whipped cream over ice cream. Decorate top with toasted almonds and place in freezing compartment to freeze whipped cream. Slice. Serves 6.

CRANBERRY MOUSSE

1½ cups Cranberry Sauce
¼ cup orange juice
1 cup evaporated milk, chilled
2 tablespoons lemon juice
Few grains salt

Mash cranberry sauce and add orange juice. Whip milk very stiff. Fold in lemon juice, salt and cranberry mixture. Freeze until firm. Makes 1 quart.

MAPLE MOUSSE

¾ cup maple sirup
4 egg yolks, beaten
⅛ teaspoon salt
1 teaspoon vanilla
1¾ cups evaporated milk, chilled

Combine maple sirup, egg yolks and salt. Cook over boiling water until thickened, beat until cool, add vanilla and chill. Whip milk very stiff, fold in maple custard and freeze until firm. Serves 6 to 8.

MAPLE SUGAR—Melt ⅔ cup maple sugar and use as maple sirup.

MAPLE SURPRISE — Melt 2 tablespoons butter and add 3 tablespoons brown sugar, ½ cup crisp cereal crumbs and ½ cup chopped walnut meats. Heat in slow oven (325°F.) 15 minutes, then cool. Add to cooled custard before folding into whipped milk.

PEANUT MOUSSE

1 cup sugar
1¼ cups boiling water
1 cup evaporated milk
3 eggs, beaten
1 cup heavy cream
1 teaspoon vanilla
½ cup salted peanuts, chopped

Heat sugar in heavy skillet until melted and slightly browned, stirring constantly. Add ¼ cup water and cook, stirring constantly, until sirup is thick. Add remaining water and evaporated milk. Heat slowly until sugar has all dissolved and pour over eggs, stirring constantly. Cook over boiling water until mixture coats a spoon. Chill. Whip cream until thick enough to hold a soft peak and fold in chilled custard, vanilla and chopped peanuts. Freeze until firm. Serve with Chocolate Fudge Sauce or Honey Sauce. Serves 8 to 10.

PEACH MOUSSE

4 to 5 medium peaches
½ cup sugar
1⅔ cups evaporated milk, chilled
2 tablespoons lemon juice
⅛ teaspoon salt

Peel peaches, stone and mash enough to make 1½ cups pulp. Add sugar and stir occasionally until sugar is dissolved. Whip milk very stiff. Fold in lemon juice, salt and peach mixture. Freeze until firm. Makes 1½ quarts.

BANANA — Use mashed bananas instead of peaches. Increase lemon juice to 3 tablespoons and add 1 teaspoon grated lemon rind.

PINEAPPLE — Use canned crushed pineapple instead of peach pulp.

PRUNE MOUSSE

1 cup cooked prunes
2 eggs
½ cup confectioners' sugar
⅛ teaspoon salt
2 teaspoons vanilla
¼ cup lemon juice
1 cup heavy cream

Pit prunes and chop. Beat eggs until thick and light. Add sugar, salt and vanilla. Beat thoroughly and add prunes and lemon juice. Whip cream until thick enough to hold a soft peak and fold into prune mixture. Freeze until firm. Serves 6.

SANTA CLARA—Omit eggs and use only 2 tablespoons lemon juice. Add ¼ teaspoon cinnamon and ⅛ teaspoon cloves.

Children and grownups all agree that cake and ice cream make a party

VANILLA MOUSSE

⅔ cup evaporated milk, chilled
1 egg
¼ cup sugar
Few grains salt
1 teaspoon vanilla

Chill milk thoroughly, then whip until stiff. Beat in egg, sugar, salt and vanilla. Freeze until firm. Makes 1 pint.
Use 1 cup heavy cream for milk.

For a new flavor in frozen desserts try Brazil-nut mousse

PEANUT BRITTLE MOUSSE

1 tablespoon unflavored gelatin
¼ cup cold water
1 cup milk
⅓ cup sugar
¾ cup ground peanut brittle
1 cup heavy cream, whipped

Soften gelatin in water 5 minutes. Scald milk, add gelatin and sugar. Stir until dissolved. Chill. When mixture begins to thicken fold in candy and whipped cream. Pour into freezing tray of refrigerator and freeze until firm. Serves 6.

STRAWBERRY MOUSSE

1 quart strawberries
1 egg white
1 cup sugar
1⅔ cups evaporated milk
2 tablespoons lemon juice
2 teaspoons vanilla
⅛ teaspoon salt

Wash berries and hull. There should be at least 3 cups. Mash strawberries and beat with egg white and sugar until very stiff (about 5 minutes with an electric beater and about 15 minutes with hand beater). Chill milk thoroughly, whip until stiff, add lemon juice gradually, fold into berry mixture and add vanilla and salt. Freeze until firm. Makes 20 servings.

PEPPERMINT MOUSSE

2 cups heavy cream
16 marshmallows
Green coloring
6 drops oil of peppermint

Add ⅓ cup of the cream to marshmallows and heat until softened, fluffy and smooth. Color a light green and stir in oil of peppermint. Cool until thick. Whip cream and fold into marshmallow mixture. Freeze in refrigerator tray without stirring. Serves 6 to 8.
FRANGO—Serve with half portion of one with contrasting color.

BRAZIL-NUT MOUSSE

½ cup chopped Brazil nuts
1 pint Vanilla Mousse mixture
4 whole Brazil nuts
8 candied cherries

Add chopped nuts to mousse mixture; freeze. Serve in sherbet glasses garnished with whole nuts and cherries. For 4.

BUTTER PECAN MOUSSE

1 teaspoon unflavored gelatin
4 teaspoons cold water
1½ cups evaporated milk
½ cup finely chopped pecan
    meats
1 tablespoon butter
6 tablespoons sugar
1 tablespoon vanilla

Soften gelatin in water 5 minutes. Scald milk over boiling water, add softened gelatin and stir until dissolved. Chill. Brown pecan meats in butter and cool. Beat milk very stiff. Fold in nut meats, sugar and vanilla. Freeze until firm. Serves 6.

MOCHA MARLOW

1 ounce (square) chocolate,
    melted
16 marshmallows, quartered
1 cup strong coffee
⅛ teaspoon salt
1 cup heavy cream, whipped
⅓ cup chopped nut meats

Melt chocolate over boiling water. Add marshmallows, coffee and salt. Heat over boiling water, folding over and over until marshmallows are half melted. Remove from heat and continue folding until mixture is smooth and spongy. Cool. Add whipped cream and nuts. Pour into freezing tray of refrigerator and freeze until firm, stirring once when half frozen. Serves 6.

CHOCOLATE — Omit nuts and use milk instead of coffee. Increase chocolate to 2 ounces (squares) and marshmallows to 20. Add 1 teaspoon vanilla. Combine as above.

CHOCOLATE MINT — Add 2 or 3 drops peppermint extract to Chocolate Marlow.

COFFEE — Omit chocolate.

PINEAPPLE MARLOW

24 marshmallows
1 No. 2 can crushed pineapple
1⅔ cups evaporated milk,
    chilled
¼ cup lemon juice

Heat marshmallows and juice from pineapple in top of double boiler, folding over and over until marshmallows are half melted. Remove from heat, add pineapple and continue folding until mixture is smooth and spongy. Whip milk until stiff, add lemon juice slowly and whip until very stiff. Fold pineapple mixture into milk. Turn into freezing tray of refrigerator and freeze until firm. Serves 6 to 8.

ENGLISH TOFFEE MARLOW

½ pound marshmallows
3⅛ cups milk
1 cup heavy cream, whipped
1 cup crushed English toffee

Heat marshmallows with 2 tablespoons milk in double boiler, folding over and over until marshmallows are half melted. Remove from heat and continue folding until smooth and fluffy. Cool. Blend in remaining 3 cups milk gradually and chill in freezing tray until it just begins to freeze. Stir thoroughly and fold in whipped cream. Freeze until firm, stirring several times and adding candy when nearly firm. Let ripen in freezing tray several hours to blend flavors. Serves 12.

RASPBERRY MARLOW — Crush 1½ cups raspberries and heat with 16 marshmallows in double boiler until marshmallows are melted. Add ⅓ cup thinly sliced dates and chill. Fold in 1 cup heavy cream, whipped, and freeze until firm.

LEMON MALLOBET

32 (½ pound) marshmallows
¾ cup water, ¼ teaspoon salt
½ teaspoon grated lemon rind
½ cup lemon juice
2 egg whites, stiffly beaten

Heat marshmallows, water and salt over low heat, folding over and over until marshmallows are half melted. Remove from heat, add lemon rind and juice and continue to fold until mixture is smooth and spongy. Chill, stir, then fold in egg whites. Pour into freezing tray of refrigerator and freeze until firm. Serves 10.

Butter pecan mousse is a grand dessert to serve for evening guests

APRICOT MALLOBET

¼ pound dried apricots
2 cups water
¼ cup orange juice
18 marshmallows
2 egg whites
⅛ teaspoon salt
2 tablespoons sugar

Wash apricots and soak in water overnight. Simmer until tender in same water drain and press through a strainer. (There should be ¾ cup pulp and 1 cup juice.) Mix apricot juice and orange juice, add marshmallows and heat over hot water until marshmallows are half melted, folding over and over. Remove from heat and continue folding until mixture is smooth and spongy. Add apricot purée. Beat egg whites and salt until stiff but not dry and beat in sugar. Fold into apricot mixture, pour into freezing tray of refrigerator and freeze. Stir when half frozen and freeze until firm. Serves 6 to 8.

A generous serving of straw-berry mallobet has two layers with berries between, around and on top

CIDER MALLOBET

24 marshmallows
1½ cups sweet cider
2 tablespoons lemon juice
2 tablespoons sugar
2 egg whites
⅛ teaspoon salt

Heat marshmallows with ¾ cup cider over hot water, folding over and over until marshmallows are half melted. Remove from heat, add remaining cider, lemon juice and 1 tablespoon sugar. Continue folding until mixture is thick and spongy. Cool. Beat egg whites and salt until nearly stiff, add remaining sugar and beat until stiff. Fold egg whites into marsh-mallow mixture, pour into freezing tray of refrigerator and freeze until firm. Serves 6.

PINEAPPLE — Use 1½ cups pineapple juice instead of cider. If sweetened pineapple juice is used, omit sugar.

VANILLA — Use 1½ cups milk instead of cider and add ½ tea-spoon vanilla.

It may be necessary to stir these mixtures once during the freez-ing.

GRAPE MALLOBET

20 marshmallows
1 cup grape juice
¼ cup orange juice
2 tablespoons lemon juice
½ teaspoon grated lemon rind
½ teaspoon grated orange rind
2 egg whites
⅛ teaspoon salt
1 tablespoon sugar

Heat marshmallows and ½ cup grape juice in top of double boiler, folding over and over until marshmallows are half melted. Remove from heat, add remaining grape juice, fruit juices and grated rinds. Fold over and over until mixture is smooth and spongy. Cool. Beat egg whites until nearly stiff, then beat in salt and sugar. Fold into fruit mixture, pour into freezing tray of refrigerator and freeze, stir-ring once when half frozen. Serves 6.

STRAWBERRY MILK MALLOBET

32 marshmallows (½ pound)
2 cups milk, chilled
1½ cups crushed, fresh straw-berries
2 tablespoons lemon juice

Heat marshmallows and 2 table-spoons of milk slowly, folding over and over until marshmallows are about half melted. Remove from heat and continue folding until mixture is smooth and spongy. Cool to lukewarm, then blend in remaining milk, crushed strawberries and lemon juice. Pour into freezing tray of re-frigerator and freeze, stirring several times while freezing. Serves 5 or 6.

LOGANBERRY — Use only 1½ cups milk and 1½ cups logan-berry purée.

RASPBERRY — Use crushed rasp-berries instead of strawberries.

BISCUIT TORTONI

1 teaspoon unflavored gelatin
1 tablespoon cold water
1 cup sugar
½ cup water
¼ teaspoon salt
6 egg yolks
¾ cup crushed macaroons
½ cup chopped nut meats
¾ cup chopped blanched
   almonds
1 teaspoon vanilla
2 cups heavy cream, whipped

Soften gelatin in water 5 minutes. Boil sugar, water and salt to 230°F. or until sirup spins a thread. Pour slowly over beaten egg yolks, stirring constantly. Add softened gelatin and stir until completely dissolved. Cool. Fold in macaroons, nut meats, vanilla and whipped cream. Pour into paper soufflé cups, place in tray of refrigerator and freeze. Serves 15 to 18.

Use 1 cup corn sirup instead of sugar.

If desired, freeze in refrigerator tray instead of paper cups.

FROZEN APRICOT SHORTCAKE

1 cup dried apricots
2½ cups water
⅔ cup sugar
⅛ teaspoon salt
1 teaspoon unflavored gelatin
1 tablespoon cold water
1 teaspoon vanilla
1 egg, beaten
1 cup heavy cream, whipped
Spongecake

Cook apricots in water until very tender, about 25 minutes; add ⅓ cup sugar and salt; heat to boiling, remove from heat and beat to a mush. Soften gelatin in water 5 minutes and dissolve in hot apricots; cool. Add remaining ⅓ cup sugar and vanilla to beaten egg and beat until thick. Fold in whipped cream. Arrange a layer of spongecake cut about ¼ inch thick, in bottom of refrigerator tray, spread with apricots and cover with whipped mixture. Freeze. Cut into squares and serve cream side up. Serves 6.

Sprinkle toasted almonds on top.

FIG BANANA BRICK

2 tablespoons quick-cooking
   tapioca
1½ cups milk
2 tablespoons sugar
⅛ teaspoon salt
1 cup dried figs
1 cup heavy cream
1 cup mashed bananas
½ teaspoon grated lemon rind
2 teaspoons vanilla

Cook tapioca and milk over hot water about 10 minutes; strain but do not rub tapioca through the sieve. Add sugar and salt to strained milk mixture. Chill. Boil figs 10 minutes in water to cover, drain, cool, clip stems and chop. Whip cream until stiff. Combine with figs, cold milk mixture, bananas, lemon rind and vanilla; mix thoroughly. Pour into freezing tray of refrigerator and freeze, stirring 2 or 3 times. Unmold and slice. Serves 8.

Add ½ cup chopped marrons.

Precious things come in small packages as these beautifully decorated biscuit Tortoni prove

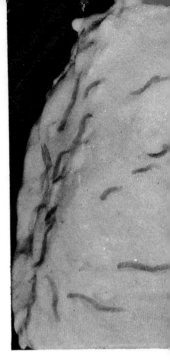

FROZEN RICE

1½ cups evaporated milk
2 tablespoons unflavored gelatin
2 cups cooked rice
1 cup crushed pineapple
    drained
½ cup sugar
⅛ teaspoon salt

Chill 1 cup evaporated milk. Soften gelatin in remaining ½ cup milk 5 minutes and dissolve over hot water. Add dissolved gelatin to rice. Add pineapple, sugar and salt. Whip chilled milk until very stiff, fold into rice mixture and freeze until firm. Serve with whipped cream. Serves 10.

FROZEN CHOCOLATE — Cook ½ cup each sugar and water 5 minutes. Add ¼ pound sweet chocolate, grated. Pour slowly over 6 beaten egg yolks, add 6 stiffly beaten egg whites, chill and fold in 2 cups heavy cream, whipped. Freeze until firm.

Carry out the valentine idea by freezing rice pudding in a heart-shaped mold

FROZEN RICE AND APRICOT PUDDING

½ cup rice, ⅛ teaspoon salt
1 quart milk
1 cup sugar
4 eggs, separated
1 tablespoon lemon juice
½ cup minced cooked apricots

Cook rice 5 minutes in salted boiling water. Drain, add milk and ½ cup sugar, cover and cook over boiling water 50 minutes. Add a small quantity to beaten egg yolks, combine with remaining rice and cook 5 minutes longer. Chill. Beat egg whites until nearly stiff, add remaining sugar gradually and beat until stiff. Fold in lemon juice, apricots and rice. Freeze. Serves 8.

FLUFFY CREAM — Beat 5 egg yolks; add 1 cup each sugar and cream. Cook until thickened. Soften 2 tablespoons unflavored gelatin in ¼ cup milk and add. Cool. Add 2 tablespoons rum, 5 stiffly beaten egg whites and 2 cups cream, whipped. Freeze.

FROZEN RICE AND PINEAPPLE PUDDING

2 cups milk, ⅛ teaspoon salt
2 egg yolks
¼ cup sugar
1 cup cooked rice
1 cup crushed pineapple
½ cup heavy cream, whipped

Scald milk in upper part of double boiler. Add salt. Beat egg yolks with sugar until light and thick. Add milk slowly, stirring constantly. Return to double boiler and cook over hot water until mixture coats a spoon. Add rice and pineapple and cool. When cold, fold in whipped cream and freeze until firm. Serve plain or with crushed or sliced pineapple. Serves 8.

GRAPE JUICE AND RAISIN — Use Concord grape juice instead of milk and seedless raisins instead of pineapple. Cook raisins in grape juice 5 minutes. Proceed as above. Use 1 cup heavy cream, whipped, instead of ½ cup. Serve with Marshmallow Sauce.

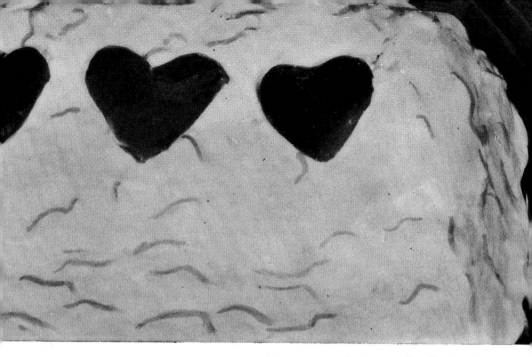

FROZEN FRUIT PUDDING

3 ounces cream cheese
¾ cup heavy cream
2 tablespoons lemon juice
1 tablespoon sugar
⅔ cup shredded pineapple
1 cup small thin slices avocado
¼ cup chopped dates
1 cup thinly sliced cooked
    peaches, Dash salt
12 maraschino cherries, halved

Cream the cheese; add ¼ cup cream gradually, stirring until smooth. Add lemon juice and sugar. Whip remaining ½ cup cream thick but not stiff and fold into cheese mixture. Combine carefully with prepared fruits. Pour into freezing tray of refrigerator and freeze until firm. Serves 8 to 10.

FROZEN FIG — Soak ½ pound chopped figs overnight in ¼ cup orange juice. Whip 2 cups heavy cream; add ½ cup powdered sugar. Line mold with ladyfingers, cover with ½ of cream, then with figs, remaining cream and additional ladyfingers. Freeze.

LEMON CREAM

2 eggs, Dash salt
½ cup sugar
½ cup light corn sirup
2 cups milk
¼ cup lemon juice
1 teaspoon grated lemon rind

Beat salted eggs thoroughly, then beat in sugar gradually until mixture is very thick. Combine with remaining ingredients. Pour into freezing tray of refrigerator and freeze. When half frozen whip until light and creamy and continue freezing until firm. Makes 1 quart.

LEMON FROZEN SANDWICH

Combine 1½ cups graham cracker crumbs, ½ cup melted butter and ½ cup sugar; mix thoroughly. Line tray of refrigerator with waxed paper. Spread bottom with half of cracker mixture, cover with frozen Lemon Cream and top with remaining crumb mixture. Freeze again until firm. Serves 6 to 8.
Use vanilla wafer or cereal crumbs instead of graham cracker crumbs.

Or freeze the dessert in a loaf and cut hearts from cranberry jelly to decorate the top

FROZEN MARSH-MALLOW SPONGE

1¾ cups evaporated milk
1 tablespoon unflavored gelatin
2 tablespoons cold water
½ pound marshmallows
2 tablespoons milk, Dash salt
1 cup canned crushed pineapple

Scald evaporated milk but do not boil. Soften gelatin in water 5 minutes and dissolve in hot milk. Chill thoroughly. Heat marshmallows in 2 tablespoons milk with salt, folding over and over until half melted. Remove from heat and continue folding until mixture is smooth and fluffy. Cool and add crushed pineapple. Whip chilled milk mixture until thick. Fold in marshmallow pineapple mixture and freeze until firm. Serves 8. If desired, cut 2 ripe bananas into thin slices and add to pineapple before combining with marshmallow mixture.

APRICOT ANGEL CREAM

1 cup cooked sieved dried apricots
⅔ cup sugar
Grated rind of ½ lemon
1 teaspoon unflavored gelatin
¼ cup water
1 cup heavy cream, whipped

Combine apricots, sugar and lemon rind. Soften gelatin in water and dissolve over hot water. Add to apricot mixture and blend. Pour into refrigerator tray and chill until slightly thickened. Remove, beat until light and fold in whipped cream. Continue freezing until firm. Serves 6.

FROSTED FRUIT

¼ cup sliced maraschino cherries
¼ cup diced canned pineapple
¼ cup diced orange segments
¼ cup diced banana
1 teaspoon lemon juice
½ teaspoon unflavored gelatin
½ tablespoon cold water
2 teaspoons strained honey
⅓ cup heavy cream, whipped

Combine fruits with lemon juice; chill. Soften gelatin in cold water; dissolve over hot water and add to honey and fruit. Fold whipped cream into fruit mixture and freeze in refrigerator tray 3 hours or until firm.

HEAVENLY HASH

¼ pound (16) marshmallows
1 cup milk
1 cup almonds, blanched and
    chopped
1 cup walnuts, chopped
1 cup maraschino or candied
    cherries
1 cup heavy cream, whipped

Dissolve marshmallows in milk over hot water. Cool. Add nuts and cherries. Fold in whipped cream. Freeze to a mush in refrigerator tray. Beat well and freeze until firm. Serves 8.

TUTTI-FRUTTI TRIFLE

½ grapefruit
1 orange
1 cup fresh pineapple
6 marshmallows
6 maraschino cherries
½ cup moist shredded coconut
2 tablespoons maraschino juice
3 egg whites
6 tablespoons confectioners' sugar

Remove segments from membrane of grapefruit and orange, slice pineapple and cut marshmallows and cherries into eighths. Soak marshmallows and coconut in combined juices. Beat egg whites until stiff and fold in sugar. Combine with fruits and coconut marshmallow mixture. Freeze in refrigerator tray until firm. Serves 8.

Add ½ cup seedless raisins.

Add 1 tablespoon brandy.

Canned cubed or crushed pineapple may be used instead of fresh pineapple.

FROZEN GINGER CREAM

1 teaspoon unflavored gelatin
1 tablespoon cold water
1 cup milk
¼ cup finely chopped preserved
    ginger
2 tablespoons ginger sirup
⅓ cup sugar
⅛ teaspoon salt
2 teaspoons vanilla
1 cup heavy cream, whipped

Soften gelatin in cold water. Dissolve over hot water and add milk slowly. Add preserved ginger and remaining ingredients except whipped cream. Mix and chill. Beat thoroughly and fold in whipped cream. Freeze in refrigerator tray. Serves 6 to 8.

PINEAPPLE CREAM—Omit ginger and ginger sirup. Add ½ cup cooked drained pineapple and 1 tablespoon lemon juice.

ORANGE CREAM—Omit ginger and ginger sirup. Add ½ cup chopped candied orange peel.

PEACH DELIGHT

2 egg whites
4 tablespoons confectioners' sugar
2 teaspoons lemon juice
Few grains salt
⅔ cup peach pulp
½ teaspoon almond extract
½ teaspoon vanilla

Beat egg whites until stiff; add sugar, lemon juice, salt, peach pulp and extracts. Fold together lightly and freeze in refrigerator tray until firm. Serves 6.

FROZEN CHRISTMAS PUDDINGS

1½ cups macaroon or vanilla
    wafer crumbs
½ cup chopped nuts
½ cup chopped dates
½ cup chopped candied fruit peel
Grated rind ½ lemon
¼ teaspoon cinnamon
¼ teaspoon nutmeg
8 marshmallows, quartered
¼ cup hot orange juice
¼ cup sugar
1 cup heavy cream, whipped

Combine crumbs, nuts, fruit, rind and spices. Dissolve marshmallows in orange juice, add sugar and combine with first mixture. Fold in whipped cream. Fill individual paper soufflé cups with mixture, place in refrigerator tray and freeze until firm. Remove paper cups and garnish puddings with holly sprays made of red cinnamon candies and bits of green gum drops. Makes 10 puddings.

SEA-FOAM DESSERT

Spongecake
1 cup heavy cream
¼ cup sugar
¼ cup pistachio nut meats, chopped
½ teaspoon almond extract
1 teaspoon vanilla
Green food coloring
Dash salt
1 egg white

Line bottom and sides of mold with slices of spongecake. Whip cream only until it holds its shape. Fold in sugar, nut meats, flavorings and just enough green coloring to give a tint. Add salt to egg white, beat until stiff and fold into cream mixture. Pour into mold. Cover top with slices of cake. Freeze until firm. Unmold. Serves 6.

GRAHAM CRACKER PUDDING

2 cups graham cracker crumbs
1 cup quartered marshmallows
1 cup chopped walnuts
½ cup confectioners' sugar
1 cup coconut
1 teaspoon vanilla
½ cup cream
½ cup heavy cream, whipped

Mix cracker crumbs, marshmallows, nuts, sugar, coconut, vanilla and cream together thoroughly. Line refrigerator tray with heavy waxed paper and pack mixture into tray. Freeze until firm. Slice with warm knife for serving and top with whipped cream. Serves 10.

COOKIE CRUMB—Use vanilla wafers, chocolate cookies or macaroons instead of graham crackers.

PINEAPPLE—Use ½ cup grated pineapple and ½ cup pineapple juice instead of cream. Omit coconut, if desired.

PRUNE—Use 1 cup cooked prune purée instead of cream.

FROZEN CUSTARD

1 tablespoon cornstarch
⅓ cup sugar
1½ cups milk, scalded
2 eggs, separated
⅛ teaspoon salt
1 cup heavy cream, whipped
2 teaspoons vanilla

Mix cornstarch and sugar thoroughly. Stir in hot milk and cook in double boiler, 15 minutes, stirring occasionally. Beat egg yolks and add hot mixture gradually. stirring constantly. Chill. Fold into stiffly beaten egg whites. Add salt, fold in whipped cream and vanilla. Pour into refrigerator tray and freeze until firm. Serve with or without sauce.

CHOCOLATE—Combine 4 tablespoons cocoa with sugar and cornstarch, before adding milk and prepare as above.

GRAPE-NUT — Add 1 cup grapenuts to chilled mixture, when adding egg whites.

The more the merrier when it's layers of ice cream and devil's food cake

CHESTNUT LAYER

4 egg yolks
¼ cup sugar
½ cup cream
2 tablespoons rum
1 cup heavy cream, whipped
1 cup ground chestnuts
  (or other nuts)
1 cup graham cracker crumbs

Beat egg yolks, add sugar and cream and cook over hot water 5 minutes, stirring constantly until thickened. Chill. Add rum and fold into whipped cream. Pour a ½-inch layer of cream mixture in the bottom of freezing tray, sprinkle with a layer of ground chestnuts and a layer of cracker crumbs. Repeat until all ingredients are used. Freeze until firm. Serves 6 to 8.

Omit rum and cracker crumbs and use 2 tablespoons brandy and 1 cup vanilla wafer crumbs.

COCONUT BISQUE

3 tablespoons quick-cooking
   tapioca
2 cups milk
½ cup sugar
2 eggs, separated
¼ teaspoon salt
1 cup heavy cream, whipped
1 tablespoon lemon juice
1½ teaspoons vanilla
1 cup moist coconut

Add tapioca to milk, cook in double boiler 15 minutes or until tapioca is clear. Stir frequently and add ¼ cup sugar during last few minutes of cooking. Press hot mixture through sieve and add to beaten egg yolks. Chill. Beat egg whites until nearly stiff, add salt and remaining ¼ cup sugar, beat until stiff and fold into cold tapioca mixture. Fold in whipped cream, lemon juice, vanilla and coconut. Freeze until firm. For variety toast coconut in hot oven until browned. Makes about 1½ quarts.

FROZEN GINGER PUDDING — Omit lemon juice, vanilla and coconut. Add ¼ cup sirup from preserved ginger to milk. Fold in ¼ cup minced preserved ginger and ¼ cup chopped pecan meats with whipped cream.

Here is the ice cream sandwich which has two chocolate ice cream layers with fruity cake between

NESSELRODE PUDDING

8 cooked chestnuts, broken into
   small pieces
Maraschino sirup
3 cups milk
½ teaspoon salt
1½ cups sugar
5 egg yolks, beaten
2 cups heavy cream, whipped
¼ cup pineapple juice
1½ cups cooked chestnuts,
   pressed through a sieve
½ cup chopped candied fruit
¼ cup seedless raisins

Soak broken chestnut pieces overnight in maraschino sirup. Scald milk in top of double boiler. Beat salt, sugar and egg yolks together and add milk gradually, stirring constantly. Return to double boiler and cook until thickened, stirring constantly. Strain, cool and add whipped cream, pineapple juice and chestnut purée. Turn half of mixture in mold or freezing tray of refrigerator. To the remaining half, add candied fruit, raisins and broken chestnut pieces. Fill mold or tray with this mixture and freeze. When firm, unmold and serve with whipped cream flavored with maraschino sirup and small pieces of cooked chestnuts. Serves 8.

The maraschino sirup, pineapple juice and seedless raisins may be omitted.

FROZEN PUDDING

½ cup sugar
½ cup water
2 egg whites, stiffly beaten
1⅓ cups heavy cream, whipped
1 teaspoon vanilla
¼ cup seeded raisins, finely cut
½ cup strawberry preserves
½ cup chopped walnut meats

Boil sugar and water together to 230°F. or until mixture spins a thread. Pour hot sirup slowly over egg whites while beating constantly and beat until cool. Fold in remaining ingredients. Pour into freezing tray of refrigerator and freeze until firm. Serves 6.

FRUITY ICE CREAM SANDWICH

1½ cups sifted flour
¾ teaspoon baking soda
¼ teaspoon salt
1 cup seedless raisins
¾ cup water
¼ cup shortening, ¾ cup sugar
1 egg, well beaten
½ cup buttermilk
Orange Ice Cream

Sift flour, soda and salt together 3 times. Cook raisins in water 5 minutes. Drain, reserving liquid for sauce and cool. Cream shortening and sugar together until fluffy and add egg. Add sifted dry ingredients alternately with buttermilk in small amounts, beating well after each addition. Add drained raisins and pour into buttered square pan. Bake in moderate oven (350°F.) 30 to 40 minutes. Cut into squares and slice through the middle, sandwich fashion. Place ice cream between slices, freeze and serve with Raisin Sauce. Serves 8.

CHOCOLATE — Or freeze 1 layer Chocolate Ice Cream, add layer of cake and top with ice cream. Freeze until top layer is firm.

Ices are frozen mixtures made from sweetened fruit juices with the addition of water and are stirred while freezing. Sherbets are frozen mixtures made from sweetened fruit juices and milk to which gelatin, egg whites or marshmallows are added. The egg white is usually beaten into the mixture after it is half frozen.

AVOCADO CRAN-BERRY SHERBET

½ tablespoon unflavored gelatin
1 cup cold water
1 cup sieved cranberries or juice
1 cup sugar
⅛ teaspoon salt
2 tablespoons lemon juice
1½ cups diced avocado

Soften gelatin in ¼ cup water 5 minutes. Combine cranberries, remaining water, sugar and salt and heat to boiling. Add lemon juice and gelatin and stir until dissolved. Pour into freezing tray of refrigerator and freeze until firm. Stir twice while freezing and add avocado before mixture becomes firm. Serves 6 to 8.
Use pineapple juice; orange or lemon juice with grated orange or lemon rind; or apple cider instead of cranberries.

BERRY SHERBET

1½ cups strawberries, washed and hulled
⅓ cup sugar
Few grains salt
⅔ cup sweetened condensed milk
2 tablespoons lemon juice
2 egg whites, stiffly beaten

Combine strawberries, sugar and salt and let stand about 15 minutes. Crush berries and force through sieve. Blend milk, lemon juice and strawberries. Chill. Fold in egg whites. Pour into freezing tray of refrigerator and freeze. When about half frozen scrape mixture from sides and bottom of pan, beat until smooth but not melted and freeze until firm. Serves 6.

RASPBERRY — Use raspberries instead of strawberries.

BUTTER PECAN SHERBET

⅔ cup sweetened condensed milk
2 tablespoons melted butter
½ cup water
½ teaspoon vanilla
⅛ teaspoon salt
2 egg whites, stiffly beaten
½ cup pecan meats, chopped

Blend milk and melted butter thoroughly. Add water, vanilla and salt. Chill. Fold egg whites into chilled mixture. Pour into freezing tray of refrigerator and freeze. When about half frozen scrape mixture from sides and bottom of tray, beat until smooth but not melted, add pecans and freeze until firm. Serves 6.

PINEAPPLE — Omit pecans. Use pineapple juice instead of water and 2 tablespoons lemon juice instead of vanilla. Add 1 cup crushed pineapple before chilling.

COLA MARSH SHERBET

24 marshmallows
2 cups cola beverage
⅛ teaspoon salt
2 tablespoons lemon juice

Place marshmallows and 2 tablespoons cola beverage in saucepan. Heat slowly, folding over and over until marshmallows are about half melted. Remove from heat and continue folding until mixture is smooth and fluffy. Cool slightly, then add remaining cola beverage, salt and lemon juice. Blend thoroughly. Pour into freezing tray of refrigerator and freeze until firm, stirring 2 or 3 times while freezing. Serves 4 or 5.

Serve scoops of sherbet on your favorite devil's food cake

Revive your drooping spirits on a hot day with a frosty glass of sherbet

CRANBERRY SHERBET

1 tablespoon unflavored gelatin
1¼ cups water
½ cup sugar
2½ cups Cranberry Sauce
1 egg white, stiffly beaten

Soften gelatin in ¼ cup cold water. Boil sugar and remaining water together 3 minutes. Add cranberries and boil 5 minutes longer. Press through a sieve, pour over softened gelatin and stir until gelatin is dissolved. Cool and fold in egg white. Pour into freezing tray of refrigerator and freeze until firm, stirring occasionally. Serves 6.

GRAPEFRUIT GINGER SHERBET

1 cup grapefruit juice
1 tablespoon chopped candied
   ginger
16 marshmallows
2 tablespoons lemon juice
2 egg whites
3 tablespoons sugar

Heat grapefruit juice, ginger and marshmallows in top of double boiler, folding over and over until marshmallows are half melted. Remove from heat, add lemon juice and continue folding until smooth and spongy. Beat egg whites until nearly stiff, beat in sugar and fold into marshmallow mixture. Pour into freezing tray of refrigerator and freeze until firm, stirring occasionally. For 6.

If desired, omit ginger. Use ¾ cup grapefruit juice and ½ cup orange juice instead of all grapefruit juice.

Use ¾ cup grapefruit juice and ¼ cup pineapple juice.

PLUM SHERBET

¾ cup sugar
½ cup water
12 fresh plums, blue or red
2 egg whites

Combine ½ cup sugar with water and plums. Boil until plums are tender and press through a sieve. Cool. Beat egg whites nearly stiff, beat in remaining sugar and fold in plum purée. Pour into freezing tray of refrigerator and freeze until firm, stirring once or twice while freezing. Serves 4 to 6.

CHERRY — Use 1 quart cherries instead of plums and reduce water to ¼ cup. Pit cherries, put through food chopper, cook as above and cool without puréeing.

CURRANT — Use 1 quart currants instead of plums. Increase sugar to 1¼ cups if red currants are used and add 1 tablespoon lemon juice if black currants are used.

FRESH PEACH SHERBET

⅔ cup sweetened condensed milk
2 tablespoons lemon juice
2 tablespoons melted butter
½ cup water
1 cup crushed fresh peaches
2 egg whites

Blend condensed milk, lemon juice, melted butter and water. Add peaches and chill. Beat egg whites until stiff and fold into chilled mixture. Pour into freezing tray of refrigerator and freeze. When mixture is about half frozen scrape from sides and bottom of tray, beat until smooth but not melted and freeze until firm. Serves 6.

CIDER SHERBET

1⅛ cups sugar, ½ cup water
3-inch stick cinnamon or 1
    teaspoon ground cinnamon
½ teaspoon cloves
Few grains salt
2 teaspoons grated orange rind
2 cups cider, 2 egg whites

Boil 1 cup sugar, water, spices, salt and grated orange rind together 5 minutes. Chill. Strain through cheesecloth and add cider. Beat egg whites until stiff, beat in remaining 2 tablespoons sugar and blend with spiced cider. Pour into freezing tray of refrigerator and freeze. When half frozen, beat until smooth but not melted and freeze until firm. Serves 8.

GREEN GAGE CREAM SHERBET

12 canned green gage plums
¼ cup confectioners' sugar
½ cup plum juice
½ cup light corn sirup
⅛ teaspoon salt
1 cup heavy cream

Drain plums and reserve ½ cup of the juice. Rub stoned plums through coarse strainer. Add sugar and stir until dissolved. Combine plum juice, corn sirup and salt. Blend well, add to plum mixture and let stand a few minutes. Add cream in thin stream,

Select a rich ice cream and a colorful sherbet to fill your best parfait glasses

while stirring constantly. Pour into freezing tray of refrigerator and freeze, stirring twice during freezing period. Serves 6.

GINGER ALE SHERBET

1 quart ginger ale, chilled
½ cup orange juice
½ cup lemon juice
½ cup water
1¼ cups sugar
4 egg whites
⅛ teaspoon salt

Mix ginger ale and fruit juices and pour into freezing tray of refrigerator. Let freeze until mushy. Boil water and 1 cup sugar to 234°F. or until sirup spins a long thread. Beat egg whites until stiff but not dry, then beat in salt and remaining sugar. Pour hot sirup slowly over whites, beating constantly. Remove the mushy juice and ginger ale mixture from the freezing tray. Place in a chilled bowl and beat until fairly smooth but not melted. Then carefully fold in the egg white mixture. Return to refrigerator trays and freeze. When half frozen, or mushy, place in a chilled bowl and beat until mixture is smooth and well blended. Return to trays and freeze until firm. Serves 10 to 12.

THREE-IN-ONE SHERBET

1 ripe banana, mashed
½ cup orange juice
¼ cup lemon juice
¾ cup sugar
⅛ teaspoon salt
1 cup evaporated milk, chilled

Combine banana, orange juice, 2 tablespoons lemon juice, sugar and salt. Pour into freezing tray of refrigerator and chill thoroughly. Whip chilled milk until fluffy, add remaining lemon juice and continue beating until stiff. Fold into fruit mixture and freeze without stirring until firm, for 6.

APPLE FRAPPÉ

3 cups diced uncooked apples
¼ cup red cinnamon candy drops
⅓ to ⅔ cup sugar
Enough water to nearly cover fruit
⅛ teaspoon salt

Cook apples with cinnamon candies, sugar, water and salt until apples are tender. Press through sieve and cool. Freeze in refrigerator tray until firm. Scrape up thin layers of the frappé with an inverted spoon and beat back and forth in tray until texture is smooth. Serve at once, garnished with a bit of fresh mint. Serves 6.

BANANA SHERBET

2 cups mashed bananas
7 tablespoons lemon juice
½ cup sugar
¼ cup white corn sirup
⅛ teaspoon salt
1 egg white
2 cups milk or 1 cup evaporated
    milk and 1 cup water

Press bananas through a coarse sieve; measure; add lemon juice, sugar, corn sirup and salt. Fold stiffly beaten egg white into banana mixture. Stir slowly into milk. Freeze in refrigerator tray. Beat thoroughly when freezing begins and again just before mixture becomes firm. Serves 6.

FRESH CHERRY SHERBET

1 quart tart red cherries
1¼ cups sugar
½ teaspoon almond extract
6 cups milk

Wash cherries, pit and force through food chopper. There should be 2½ cups juice and pulp. Add sugar and chill, stirring occasionally until sugar is dissolved. Add almond extract and milk. Pour into freezer can and freeze, using 6 parts ice to 1 part salt. Serve with Marshmallow Sauce. Makes 3 quarts.

GREEN GAGE FRAPPÉ

12 plums
1½ cups water
1 cup sugar
¼ teaspoon salt
2 teaspoons lemon juice

Cook plums with water and sugar until tender. Rub through a coarse sieve; add salt and lemon juice. Freeze in refrigerator tray until firm. Scrape up thin layers of the mixture with an inverted spoon, then beat back and forth in the tray until texture is smooth. Serve at once. Serves 8.
Use canned plums; omit sugar.

MINT GRAPEFRUIT ICE

1 teaspoon unflavored gelatin
2¼ cups unsweetened grapefruit
    juice
½ cup water, ⅔ cup sugar
Few drops oil of peppermint
Green food coloring

Soften gelatin in ¼ cup of the grapefruit juice. Heat water and sugar together, stirring until sugar is dissolved. Add gelatin and stir until dissolved. Combine with grapefruit juice and oil of peppermint. Add a few drops of green food coloring to tint a delicate green. Freeze in refrigerator tray until firm, stirring occasionally. Serves 4.

LEMON CREAM SHERBET

1½ cups sugar
¾ cup lemon juice
⅛ teaspoon salt
3 cups milk
1 cup cream

Mix sugar, lemon juice and salt; add slowly to milk and cream. Pour into freezer can and freeze, using 8 parts ice to 1 part salt. Makes 1½ quarts.

RHUBARB ICE

4 cups cut rhubarb
1½ cups sugar
¼ teaspoon salt
1 cup water
Rind of 1 lemon
4 tablespoons lemon juice

Wash rhubarb and cut into small pieces. Add sugar, salt, water and lemon rind; cook until rhubarb is tender; press through a sieve, add lemon juice and freeze in refrigerator tray until firm. Scrape up thin layers of the ice with an inverted spoon and beat back and forth in tray until texture is smooth. Serve at once. Serves 6.

RHUBARB AND STRAWBERRY SHERBET

1 pint strawberries
2 cups cooked rhubarb
2 tablespoons lemon juice
⅛ teaspoon salt
1½ cups sugar
¾ cup heavy cream

Wash berries, hull and mash. Press rhubarb and berries through sieve, add remaining ingredients, pour into freezing tray of refrigerator and freeze without stirring until firm. When ready to serve, scrape up thin layers of the mixture with an inverted spoon, beat back and forth in tray until smooth and serve immediately. Serves 6.

BLACK RASPBERRY SHERBET

1 cup water, ⅛ teaspoon salt
½ cup water
1 No. 2 can black raspberries
2⅓ cups milk

Boil sugar, salt and water 3 minutes. Press berries through a sieve, add sirup to purée and chill. Pour milk into freezer can, add berry mixture and freeze, using 8 parts ice to 1 part salt. Makes 1½ quarts.

ORANGE SHERBET

1½ cups sugar
1 cup water
Few grains salt
2 egg whites, stiffly beaten
2 cups orange juice
3 tablespoons lemon juice

Boil sugar, water and salt together 5 minutes. Pour in thin stream over beaten egg whites, while beating constantly. Add fruit juice, pour into freezing tray of refrigerator and freeze. When half frozen beat until smooth but not melted and freeze until firm. Serves 6.

GRAPEFRUIT — Use grapefruit juice instead of orange juice.

GRAPEFRUIT AND ORANGE — Use 1¼ cups grapefruit juice and ¾ cup orange juice instead of 2 cups orange juice.

LEMON — Omit orange juice, increase sugar to 2 cups, lemon juice to 1 cup and water to 2 cups. Proceed as above.

RHUBARB SHERBET

2½ cups sliced rhubarb (about ¾ pound)
1 No. 1 can crushed pineapple (1⅓ cups)
⅛ teaspoon salt
½ cup sugar
1⅔ cups evaporated milk, chilled
⅛ teaspoon mace or nutmeg, if desired

Wash rhubarb. Remove blemishes but do not peel. Cut into small pieces and combine with pineapple, salt and sugar. Simmer until tender or bake in moderate oven (350°F.) in covered baking dish. Press through a coarse sieve. There should be 2 cups of pulp and sirup. Chill. Whip milk until very stiff, fold in rhubarb mixture and pour into freezing tray of refrigerator. Freeze until firm. Serves 10.

Use 1 pint strawberries instead of pineapple. Do not cook them.

RHUBARB CREAM SHERBET

2 cups cut rhubarb
1 cup water
1 cup sugar
4 teaspoons lemon juice
1 egg white
1 cup heavy cream, whipped
Red food coloring

Simmer rhubarb, water and ¾ cup sugar until rhubarb is tender. Cool. Add lemon juice. Pour into refrigerator tray and freeze until firm. Beat egg white with remaining sugar until stiff. Scrape up thin layers of frozen mixture with an inverted spoon and fold into egg white carefully. Fold in whipped cream and add a few drops coloring, if desired. Return to tray and freeze until firm. Serves 6 to 8.

The Queen of the Snows never looked more fragile and frosty than this cream sherbet on spun sugar

GRAPE SHERBET

1 pint grape juice
2 tablespoons lemon juice
Few grains salt
1/2 cup sugar
1/4 cup water
2 egg whites, beaten

Pour grape juice, lemon juice and salt into refrigerator tray and freeze until firm. Boil sugar and water together for 3 minutes and pour slowly into the stiffly beaten egg whites, beating constantly. Cool to lukewarm. Scrape up thin layers of the frozen grape juice with an inverted spoon and fold into egg white mixture. Replace in the tray and freeze. Serves 6 to 8.

CRANBERRY PINEAPPLE SHERBET

2 cups cranberries
1 cup water
1/4 pound marshmallows
1 cup unsweetened pineapple juice
2 tablespoons lemon juice
1/2 cup sugar
2 egg whites
1/8 teaspoon salt

Cook cranberries in water until skins pop; rub through sieve. Heat marshmallows in pineapple juice until melted; combine with sieved cranberries, lemon juice and 6 tablespoons of the sugar. Freeze in refrigerator tray to a mush. Beat egg whites until stiff with remaining sugar and salt. Fold into partly frozen cranberry mixture and return to tray. Freeze until firm. Makes 1 quart.

CRANBERRY SHERBET

1 pound (4 cups) cranberries
2 1/2 cups water
2 cups sugar
1 tablespoon unflavored gelatin
1/2 cup cold water
1/3 cup lemon juice

Cook cranberries and water until skins pop. Rub through sieve, add sugar and heat to boiling. Soften gelatin in cold water, add to hot cranberry mixture and stir until dissolved. Cool and add lemon juice. Freeze in refrigerator tray until firm. Serves 8 to 10.

CRANBERRY AND APPLE SHERBET — Use 2 cups diced apples and 2 cups cranberries instead of 4 cups cranberries.

PINEAPPLE CREAM SHERBET

1 cup sugar
2 cups water
2 cups crushed pineapple
1/8 teaspoon salt
2 cups heavy cream

Boil sugar and water 5 minutes; cool, add pineapple, salt and cream. Pour into freezer can and freeze, using 8 parts ice to 1 part salt. Makes about 2 quarts.

Provide jam and strawberry ice and let the high school crowd make their own sundaes

STRAWBERRY ICE

1 quart fresh strawberries
3/4 cup sugar
1/4 teaspoon salt
1/3 cup water
2 tablespoons lemon juice

Cook strawberries with sugar, salt and water until tender. Press through sieve, add lemon juice and freeze in refrigerator tray until firm. Scrape up thin layers of the mixture with an inverted spoon and beat back and forth in tray until texture is smooth. Serve at once. Serves 6.

After smoothing mixture, cover with layer of whipped cream, sweetened with 6 tablespoons of berry sugar. Return to refrigerator until cream is frozen.

Omit strawberries and use any of the following: raspberries, loganberries or youngberries.

Frozen parfaits are made of a foundation of beaten egg whites or yolks, cooked with a hot sirup and combined with whipped cream and flavorings. They are frozen without stirring so they. may be frozen in refrigerator tray, in individual molds or paper soufflé cups packed into the tray or in a large mold.

A second type of parfait is a rich sundae made of layers of ice cream, fruit or other flavored sauce and whipped cream.

APRICOT PARFAIT

½ pound dried apricots
⅓ cup sugar
2 egg whites, stiffly beaten
⅔ cup heavy cream

Cook apricots in water to cover until tender. Drain off juice, add to sugar and boil to 230°F. or until sirup spins a thread. Pour sirup slowly over egg whites while beating constantly. Continue beating until cool. Press apricots through sieve and chill. Whip cream until stiff enough to hold a soft peak, fold in apricot pulp and egg white mixture. Freeze until firm. Makes about 1 quart.

BLACK WALNUT PARFAIT

1 cup sugar
⅛ teaspoon salt
½ cup water
3 egg whites, stiffly beaten
1 cup chopped black walnut
  meats
1 teaspoon vanilla
2 cups heavy cream, whipped

Cook sugar, salt and water to 230°F. or until sirup spins a thread. Pour slowly over egg whites while beating constantly. Continue beating until cool. Fold in nut meats, vanilla and whipped cream. Freeze until firm. Makes 1½ quarts.

BUTTERSCOTCH PARFAIT

1¼ cups brown sugar
½ cup water
2 tablespoons butter
3 eggs, separated
1 teaspoon vanilla
½ cup chopped nut meats
1½ cups heavy cream, whipped

Boil sugar and water 5 minutes. Remove from heat, add butter and stir until melted. Pour slowly over beaten egg yolks and beat until cool. Fold in stiffly beaten egg whites, vanilla, nut meats and whipped cream. Freeze until firm. Makes about 1½ quarts.

CHERRY NUT PARFAIT

¾ cup corn sirup
3 egg whites, stiffly beaten
Dash salt
2 cups heavy cream, whipped
1 cup crushed walnut meats
12 maraschino cherries, quartered
1 teaspoon almond extract
3 tablespoons maraschino juice

Heat corn sirup to 230°F. or until it spins a thread. Pour slowly over egg whites, while beating constantly and beat until cool. Add salt. Fold in whipped cream, add nut meats, cherries, flavoring and cherry juice. Place in individual molds and freeze without stirring. Serves 8.

DATE PARFAIT

½ cup chopped pitted dates
1½ cups water
¼ cup sugar
¼ teaspoon salt
4 egg yolks, well beaten
½ cup orange juice
½ cup heavy cream, whipped

Cook dates in water 20 minutes, add sugar and salt and cook 10 minutes longer. Pour slowly over egg yolks. Cook over boiling water until thickened, stirring constantly. Chill and add orange juice and whipped cream. Freeze until firm. Makes 1 quart.

DIVINITY PARFAIT

1 cup sugar
½ cup water
3 egg whites, stiffly beaten
¼ pound marshmallows, cut
  into eighths
½ cup chopped nut meats
1 teaspoon vanilla
1 cup heavy cream

Cook sugar and water to 230°F. or until sirup spins a long thread. Pour slowly over egg whites, beating constantly. Beat until light and fluffy, add marshmallows and beat until cool. Fold in nuts and vanilla; chill. Whip cream until thick enough to hold a soft peak, fold into chilled mixture and freeze. Serves 10 to 12.

PISTACHIO PARFAIT

1 cup sugar
¼ cup water
⅛ teaspoon salt
2 egg whites, beaten stiff
Green food coloring
½ cup chopped pistachio nut
  meats
1 teaspoon almond extract
2 cups heavy cream

Cook sugar, water and salt to 238°F. or until a small amount of sirup forms a soft ball when tested in cold water. Pour sirup slowly over stiffly beaten egg whites, while beating constantly. Continue to beat until cool. Tint delicate green and add nut meats and almond extract. Whip cream and fold into mixture. Pour into molds or parfait glasses and freeze until firm. Serves 6.

For parfait service, place a spoon of pistachio ice cream in glass, top with Marshmallow Sauce and chopped nuts.

BURNT ALMOND PARFAIT

¼ cup heavy cream
⅔ cup Caramel Sauce
1 pint Vanilla or Chocolate Ice
    Cream
½ cup toasted almonds, chopped

Whip cream and add ⅓ cup of caramel sauce slowly, beating constantly. Place about a teaspoon of plain caramel sauce and a teaspoon of cream mixture in bottom of parfait glasses and add ice cream. Sprinkle with nut meats. Repeat until glasses are full. Top with cream mixture. Serves 6.
Use Butterscotch Sauce instead of caramel sauce.

BUTTER PECAN PARFAIT

1 pint Butter Pecan Ice Cream
¾ cup Butterscotch Sauce
⅓ cup chopped pecan meats
¼ cup heavy cream, whipped

Fill parfait glasses ⅓ full with ice cream. Add butterscotch sauce and sprinkle with nut meats. Repeat until glasses are almost full. Top with whipped cream. Serves 6.

STRAWBERRY PARFAIT

1 pint strawberries
½ cup crushed pineapple and
    juice
2 tablespoons sugar
1 pint Strawberry Ice Cream

Hull berries and crush. Cook pineapple with sugar until sugar is dissolved, cool slightly and pour over berries. Place some of mixture in bottom of parfait glasses, add small ball of ice cream, cover with strawberry mixture and add another ball of ice cream. Top with whipped cream. Serves 6.

FIG PARFAIT

½ cup chopped dried figs
¼ cup light brown sugar
½ cup water
¼ cup chopped walnut meats
1 pint Vanilla Ice Cream
Whipped Cream

Cook chopped figs, sugar and water until slightly thickened. Add nut meats and chill. Arrange alternate layers of ice cream and chilled fig sauce in parfait glasses. Top with whipped cream. Serves 6.

MAPLE PARFAIT

½ cup maple sirup
1 egg yolk, well beaten
⅓ cup heavy cream, whipped
¼ cup chopped pecan meats
1 pint Vanilla Ice Cream
Candied pineapple

Cook maple sirup with egg yolk in top of double boiler until slightly thickened. Remove, chill and add to whipped cream. Stir in nut meats. Fill parfait glasses with alternate layers of maple mixture and ice cream. Top with pieces of pineapple. Serves 6.

PINEAPPLE PARFAIT

½ cup sugar
1 cup crushed pineapple and
    juice
1 pint Vanilla Ice Cream
Diced pineapple, Mint leaves

Boil sugar, crushed pineapple and juice together for a few minutes. Chill. Fill parfait glasses with alternate layers of ice cream and pineapple sauce. Garnish with diced pineapple and mint leaves. Serves 6.

Parfaits are luscious served in a bowl with ladyfingers and fresh fruit or berries

CHOCOLATE PARFAIT

¾ cup sugar
¾ cup water
3 egg whites, stiffly beaten
⅛ teaspoon salt
3 ounces (squares) chocolate, melted
2 cups heavy cream
2 teaspoons vanilla

Heat sugar and water slowly to boiling and cook to 238°F. or until a small amount of sirup forms a soft ball when dropped into cold water. Pour sirup in fine stream over egg whites, while beating constantly. Add salt and continue beating until mixture is cool. Add chocolate and blend; whip cream until stiff enough to hold a soft peak; fold in whipped cream and vanilla Freeze. Makes 1¼ quarts.

COFFEE CARAMEL PARFAIT

1½ cups milk
2 tablespoons ground coffee
1 cup sugar
2 egg yolks, well beaten
⅛ teaspoon salt
1½ cups heavy cream
1 teaspoon vanilla

Combine milk with coffee and scald in top of double boiler; strain immediately. Heat ½ cup sugar slowly in heavy skillet until melted and slightly brown, stirring constantly. Add hot coffee mixture and heat until sugar is dissolved. Beat egg yolks with remaining ½ cup sugar and salt and stir in hot mixture slowly. Cook until slightly thickened, stirring constantly. Chill. Whip cream until thick enough to hold a soft peak. Fold whipped cream and vanilla into chilled mixture and freeze. Makes 1½ quarts.

CINNAMON PARFAIT

¾ cup sugar
½ cup water
⅛ teaspoon salt
4 tablespoons cinnamon candies
3 egg whites, stiffly beaten
2 cups heavy cream, whipped
1 teaspoon vanilla

Boil sugar, water, salt and 2 tablespoons candies together to 230°F. or until sirup spins a thread. Pour slowly over egg whites, while beating constantly. Beat until cool. Crush remaining candies and add to egg white mixture. Fold in whipped cream and vanilla. Freeze until firm. Makes 1¾ quarts.

Use 3 drops red food coloring and ¼ teaspoon cinnamon instead of candies, if desired.

COFFEE PARFAIT

½ cup sugar
½ cup strong clear coffee
⅛ teaspoon salt
2 egg whites
1⅔ cups evaporated milk, chilled
1 teaspoon vanilla

Cook sugar and coffee together to 230°F. or until sirup spins a thread. Add salt to egg whites and beat until stiff but not dry. Pour sirup slowly into egg whites, beating constantly. Chill. Whip milk until very stiff. Fold in egg whites and vanilla. Freeze until firm. Makes 1½ quarts.

Make your own parfaits and serve them in layers with whipped cream

Pour maple sirup slowly over slightly beaten egg yolks, add salt, cook until thickened and chill. Whip cream until thick enough to hold a soft peak and fold into chilled mixture. Fold in stiffly beaten egg whites and freeze until firm. Makes about 1½ quarts.

GINGER PARFAIT

¼ cup sugar
Few grains salt
¼ cup water
1 tablespoon ginger sirup
2 egg whites, stiffly beaten
3 tablespoons preserved ginger, chopped fine
1 cup heavy cream

Cook sugar, salt, water and sirup from perserved ginger to 230°F. or until sirup spins a thread. Pour slowly over egg whites, while beating constantly. Beat until cool, add ginger and chill thoroughly. Whip cream until stiff enough to hold a soft peak and fold in. Freeze until firm. Makes 1 quart.

PEPPERMINT STICK PARFAIT

½ cup sugar
½ cup water
⅛ teaspoon salt
2 egg whites
1⅔ cups evaporated milk, chilled
½ cup finely chopped peppermint stick candy (2 ounces)

Cook sugar and water together to 230°F. or until sirup spins a thread. Add salt to egg whites and beat until stiff but not dry. Pour hot sirup slowly into egg whites, beating constantly. Chill. Whip milk very stiff. Fold in egg whites and candy. Freeze until firm. Makes 1½ quarts.

Before freezing add ¼ cup grated sweet chocolate over top in any design desired.

Serve maple parfait
On any hot day
And smuggle within
A banana sliced thin
Top off, to be merry,
With sauce and a cherry
Now shout aloud and spread
the news that here's a cure
for front-porch blues

MAPLE CUSTARD PARFAIT

1 cup hot maple sirup
4 eggs, separated
⅛ teaspoon salt
1 pint heavy cream, whipped

CAKES

*250 Delicious
Cakes*

For many years the art of cake-making remained unchanged. Cakes were classified in two groups—"butter" cakes and egg-. leavened cakes (angel food and sponge). Recently several distinctly new types of cakes have been introduced with quite revolutionary methods of mixing. They are included in the following classification:

"BUTTER" CAKES—Made with butter, margarine, or hydrogenated fats by the conventional "creaming" method. This method is most familiar to homemakers and mixing is done by hand or with a mixer. The method is to cream the fat with sugar and flavoring. (Or flavoring may be blended with liquid). Beaten eggs are then beaten into mixture and dry and liquid ingredients added alternately. When using a mixer, the unbeaten eggs are added, one at a time, to creamed mixture, beating well after each addition. Sifted dry ingredients and liquids are added alternately · in thirds and batter is beaten only until smooth. Overbeating must be avoided as this reduces volume. Nuts, raisins, etc. are usually added last and beaten egg whites are folded in by hand.

"ONE-BOWL" CAKES — Made with only hydrogenated fats. The method is to add softened shortening to sifted dry ingredients. Then add about two-thirds of the liquid to which flavoring has been added. (With all-purpose flour add liquid all at once.) Beat at medium speed 2 minutes, scraping down bowl. Or beat by hand 2 minutes, 150 strokes per minute. Add remaining liquid and unbeaten eggs (or egg yolks or whites) and beat 2 minutes more, scraping down bowl.

CAKES WITHOUT BUTTER—Group includes angel food, sponge cake, etc. Eggs are used for the leavening agent; cakes usually contain no fat or baking powder but occasionally they contain a little of each. The old method of baking these cakes was to place them in a cold oven and bake them at 300°F. an hour or longer. Opinions vary today on the use of a preheated 325 to 350° oven for a shorter period, or a higher temperature of 375 to 400° for even a shorter time.

CHIFFON CAKES—Similar to angel food and sponge cakes in texture, but they contain both fat (oil) and baking powder.

CAKE-MIX CAKES—Formula and mixing methods are almost foolproof. There are many varieties available most of which are of good texture and flavor.

TECHNIQUES FOR SUCCESSFUL CAKES

MEASURING EQUIPMENT—Use only standard measuring cups and spoons.

TO MEASURE FLOUR—Sift flour once before measuring. Then spoon lightly into cup and level off with a spatula.

TO MEASURE SUGAR—Fill cup with granulated sugar and level off with spatula. Pack brown sugar firmly into cup.

TO MEASURE BAKING POWDER, SODA, SALT, SPICES, ETC.—Fill spoon heaping full, level off with spatula and divide as desired. Use fractional spoons when possible.

TO MEASURE SHORTENING—Pack firmly into cup or spoon; level off with spatula. Use fractional measuring cups for amounts less than a cup. When recipe requires hydrogenated fat do not substitute another type.

TO MEASURE LIQUIDS—Use glass measuring cup with extra space above the cup marking.

EGGS—Medium-sized eggs were used for cake recipes. Keep eggs at room temp. several hours before using so that they will beat up

SUCCESSFUL CAKES

to their greatest volume. In separating it is important that none of the yolk gets into the white. If this occurs the white will not whip to a stiff foam.

FLOUR—Two types of flour are used in cakemaking. Cake flour is made from soft winter wheats and all-purpose flour made from spring or winter wheats. Cake flour has been used in most of the following recipes as it produces a lighter, more tender cake. If all-purpose flour is used instead of cake flour reduce the amount of flour by 2 tablespoons per cup and avoid over-beating the batter.

BAKING POWDER—In the following recipes a compromise amount of baking powder has been used, insuring satisfactory results with any brand.

LIQUID—Milk, sweet or sour, is most commonly used; however, cream, buttermilk, water, fruit juices and coffee may be used.

MIXING OF CAKE—Follow directions carefully for each recipe. For cakes with shortening, sift dry ingredients together as directed, cream shortening and add sugar gradually,

creaming until light and fluffy. Always add a small quantity of dry ingredients to creamed mixture first, then add liquids and dry ingredients alternately.

PANS—Prepare pans before mixing cake; grease pans for cakes made with shortening. Do not grease pans for cakes made without shortening as the batter needs to cling to the sides of pan in order to reach top volume. Fill pan ½ to ⅔.

BAKING—Start heating oven before mixing cake. Place cake as near center of oven as possible, do not place one cake pan directly over another. Refrain from unnecessarily opening over door.

TESTING CAKE—Baking time for cake is usually divided into quarters. During first quarter cake rises, second quarter it continues to rise and browns slightly, third quarter rising stops and fourth quarter cake finishes baking. A cake is done when it shrinks slightly from the sides of the pan, springs back when pressed lightly or when a cake tester or toothpick comes out clean from center of cake.

REMOVING CAKE FROM PANS—Place cake made with shortening on rack and let cool in pan 5 minutes. Then turn out. For sponge type, turn pan upside down on rack and let hang until cold.

CAKE BAKING ADVICE

A cake may have—	BUTTER-TYPE CAKES Because of—	SPONGE-TYPE CAKES
A hard top crust	Temperature too high Overbaking	Temperature too high Overbaking
A sticky top crust	Too much sugar Insufficient baking	Too much sugar Insufficient baking
A humped or cracked top	Too much flour or too little liquid Overmixing Batter not spread evenly in pan Temperature too high	Too much flour or sugar Temperature too high
One side higher	Batter not spread evenly Uneven pan Pan too close to side of oven Oven rack or range not level Uneven oven heat	Uneven pan Oven rack or range not level
A soggy layer at bottom	Too much liquid Underbeaten eggs Shortening too soft Undermixing Insufficient baking	Too many eggs or egg yolks Underbeaten egg yolks Undermixing
Fallen	Too much sugar, liquid, leavening, or shortening Too little flour Temperature too low Insufficient baking	Too much sugar Overbeaten egg whites Underbeaten egg yolks Use of greased pans Insufficient baking

Coarse grain	Use of all-purpose flour
	    instead of cake flour
	Too much leavening
	Shortening too soft
	Insufficient creaming
	Undermixing
	Temperature too low
		Use of all-purpose flour
		    instead of cake flour
		Omitting cream of tartar
		  (angel food)
		Undermixing

Tough Crumb	Too much flour Too many eggs Too little sugar or shortening Overmixing Temperature too high	Too little sugar Overbeaten egg whites Underbeaten egg yolks Omitting cream of tartar (angel food) Overmixing Temperature too high Overbaking
A heavy, compact quality	Too much liquid or shortening Too many eggs Too little leavening or flour Overmixing Temperature too high	Overbeaten egg whites Underbeaten egg yolks Overmixing
Crumbled or fallen apart	Too much sugar, leavening or shortening. Undermixing Improper pan treatment Improper cooling	
Fallen out of pan before completely cooled		Too much sugar Use of greased pans Insufficient baking

TWO-EGG CAKE

(Creaming Method Using Mixer)

5/8 cup soft shortening
1 7/8 cups sugar
1 1/2 teaspoons vanilla
2 eggs (1/2 cup)
3 cups sifted cake flour
   or 2 3/4 cups sifted all-
   purpose flour
2 1/2 teaspoons baking powder
1 teaspoon salt
1 1/4 cups milk

Cream shortening, sugar, and vanilla together. Add eggs, one at a time, and beat on medium speed after each addition until mass is light and fluffy. Sift flour, baking powder, and salt together. Turn beater to low speed and add sifted dry ingredients to creamed mixture alternately with the milk in thirds. Beat only until batter is smooth. (Do not over-beat when using mixer as this reduces volume of cake.) Turn batter into prepared pans and bake at 350°F. 30 to 35 minutes. Makes 2 (9-inch) layers.

TWO-EGG CAKE

(One-Bowl Method)

2 1/4 cups sifted cake flour
1 1/2 cups sugar
3 teaspoons baking power
1 teaspoon salt
1/2 cup soft shortening
1 cup milk
1 1/2 teaspoons flavoring
2 eggs (1/3 to 1/2 cup)

Sift flour, sugar, baking powder, and salt together. Add shortening and a little over half of milk mixed with flavoring; beat vigorously with spoon 2 minutes (or 2 minutes with mixer at medium speed). Add remaining milk and unbeaten eggs. Beat 2 minutes with spoon (150 strokes per minute) or 2 minutes with mixer at medium speed. Turn batter into prepared pans; bake at 350° F. for 25 to 30 minutes. Makes 2 (9-inch) layers.

DEVIL'S FOOD CAKE

(One-Bowl Method)

2 1/4 cups sifted cake flour
   or 2 cups sifted all-
   purpose flour
1 3/4 cups sugar
1/3 teaspoon baking powder
1 3/4 teaspoon soda
1 teaspoon salt
2/3 cup cocoa
2/3 cup soft shortening
1 cup water
1 teaspoon vanilla
3 eggs (1/2 to 2/3 cup)

Sift flour, sugar, baking powder, soda, salt and cocoa together. Add shortening, a little over half the water, and vanilla. Beat vigorously with a spoon for 2 minutes (or with mixer at medium speed). Add remaining water and eggs; beat vigorously with spoon 2 minutes (or mixer at medium speed). Turn into prepared pans; bake at 350°F. 30 to 40 minutes. Makes 2 (9-inch) layers.

SILVER CAKE

(One-Bowl Method)

2 7/8 cups sifted cake flour
   or 2 2/3 cups sifted
   all-purpose flour
1 7/8 cups sugar
4 1/2 teaspoons baking powder
1 teaspoon salt
2/3 cup soft shortening
1 1/4 cups milk
2 teaspoons flavoring
5 egg whites (2/3 cup)

Sift flour, sugar, baking powder and salt together. Add soft shortening. Pour in a little over half of milk blended with flavoring. Beat vigorously with spoon 2 minutes (or mixer at medium speed). Add remaining milk and unbeaten egg whites; beat 2 more minutes. Turn batter into prepared pans; bake at 350°F. 40 to 45 minutes. **Makes 1 (13x9-inch) cake.**

LEMON CHIFFON CAKE

2 1/4 cups sifted cake flour
   or 2 cups sifted all-
   purpose flour
1 1/2 cups sugar
3 teaspoons baking powder
1 teaspoon salt
1/2 cup cooking (salad) oil
*5 egg yolks, unbeaten
3/4 cup cold water
2 teaspoons vanilla
2 teaspoons grated lemon rind
7 egg whites (about 1 cup)
1/2 teaspoon cream of tartar
(*Use 7 egg yolks when using all-purpose flour.)

Sift into mixing bowl the flour, sugar, baking powder, and salt. Make a well in center of dry ingredients; add oil, egg yolks, water, vanilla and lemon rind in the order listed. Beat with a spoon until smooth. Put egg whites and cream of tartar into large mixing bowl. Whip until whites form very stiff peaks. Gently fold yolk mixture into beaten whites, using a rubber spatula. Fold only until blended. Pour into ungreased tube pan. Bake at 325°F. for 55 minutes, then at 350° for 10 to 15 minutes. When cake tests done invert and let hang until cool. Makes 1 (10x4-inch) cake.

PINEAPPLE CHIFFON CAKE

Follow recipe for Lemon Chiffon Cake but substitute pineapple juice or sirup for water. Add to the "well" made in center of dry ingredients 1/2 cup of well-drained, finely crushed pineapple.

SPICE CHIFFON CAKE

Follow recipe for Lemon Chiffon Cake but omit vanilla and lemon rind. Add to dry ingredients— 1 teaspoon cinnamon, 1/2 teaspoon each of nutmeg, allspice and cloves.

FLORIDA ORANGE "FLOWER CAKE"

1½ cups sifted cake flour
1½ teaspoons baking powder
¼ teaspoon salt
1 teaspoon grated orange rind
½ cup shortening
1 cup sugar
2 eggs, unbeaten
½ cup orange juice

Sift flour, baking powder and salt together. Add orange rind to shortening and cream thoroughly. Add sugar gradually and cream until fluffy. Add eggs, one at a time, beating thoroughly after each addition. Add sifted dry ingredients and orange juice alternately in small amounts, beating thoroughly after each addition. Pour into greased pans and bake in moderate oven (350°F.) 30 minutes. Makes 2 (8-inch) layers. Place orange segments over 1 layer of cake and cover with sweetened whipped cream. Place second layer of cake on first and spread with whipped cream. Then arrange orange segments in flower design on whipped cream for garnish.

Your "flower cake" may be grapefruit or peach

PEANUT-BUTTER CUPCAKES

2 cups sifted cake flour
2½ teaspoons baking powder
½ teaspoon salt
⅓ cup shortening
1½ cups brown sugar
1 teaspoon vanilla
½ cup peanut butter
2 eggs, well beaten
¾ cup milk

Sift flour, baking powder and salt together. Cream shortening with 1 cup brown sugar and vanilla until fluffy. Add peanut butter and mix thoroughly. Beat eggs until light and beat in remaining sugar. Add to creamed mixture and blend well. Add sifted dry ingredients and milk alternately in small amounts, beating thoroughly after each addition. Pour into greased cupcake pans and bake in moderate oven (350°F.) 25 to 30 minutes. Makes 18.

ORANGE TEA CAKE

2 cups sifted flour
3 teaspoons baking powder
¼ teaspoon salt
¼ teaspoon nutmeg
½ cup shortening
1 cup sugar, 2 eggs, beaten
Grated rind 1 medium orange
¾ cup orange juice

Sift flour, baking powder, salt and nutmeg together. Cream shortening with sugar until fluffy. Add eggs and orange rind; beat thoroughly. Add sifted dry ingredients and orange juice alternately in small amounts, beating well after each addition. Pour into greased pan and bake in moderate oven (350°F.) 50 minutes. Makes 1 (9x9 inch) cake.

LAZY DAISY CAKE

CAKE

⅓ cup milk
1 tablespoon butter
1 cup sifted cake flour
½ teaspoon salt
1¼ teaspoons baking powder
2 eggs
1 cup sugar
1 teaspoon vanilla

FROSTING

3 tablespoons butter
⅓ cup brown sugar
2 tablespoons cream
½ teaspoon vanilla
½ to ¾ cup coconut

Scald milk, add butter and cool to lukewarm. Sift flour, salt and baking powder together. Beat eggs slightly and add sugar gradually, beating constantly until thick and lemon colored. Add vanilla. Add sifted dry ingredients and milk alternately in small amounts, mixing lightly but thoroughly. Pour into greased pan and bake in moderate oven (350°F.) 30 minutes. Combine ingredients for frosting in the order listed. Remove cake from oven, cool for 5 minutes. Spread frosting evenly over cake, using 2 forks. Place under broiler heat until coconut is delicately browned. Makes 1 (8-inch) cake.

LAZY DAISY SPICECAKE — Add ¼ teaspoon each cinnamon and nutmeg and ⅛ teaspoon cloves to flour.

Sometime you want to cut gingerbread after spreading

GINGERBREAD SUPREME

½ cup sugar
1½ cups sifted flour
½ teaspoon baking soda
½ teaspoon baking powder
½ teaspoon salt
½ teaspoon ginger
¼ teaspoon allspice
1 teaspoon cinnamon
¼ cup shortening, melted
¼ cup maple sirup
½ cup sour milk
1 egg, well beaten
1 cup black walnut meats, broken (optional)

Sift first 8 ingredients together. Combine shortening, maple sirup, sour milk and egg. Add liquid mixture to dry ingredients, beat well and pour into greased pan. Sprinkle walnuts and additional cinnamon over top and bake in moderate oven (350°F.) 30 to 40 minutes. Cut into squares, top with whipped cream and garnish with a dash of nutmeg. Makes 1 (8x8 inch) cake.

ANGEL GINGER CAKE

2 cups sifted flour
1 teaspoon baking soda
1 teaspoon ginger
¼ teaspoon salt
6 tablespoons butter
½ cup sugar
½ cup molasses
2 eggs, well beaten
½ cup sour milk or buttermilk

Sift flour, soda, ginger and salt together 3 times. Cream butter with sugar until fluffy. Add molasses, eggs and milk and beat well. Fold in sifted dry ingredients, beat thoroughly and pour into greased pan. Bake in moderate oven (350°F.) 35 to 40 minutes. Makes 1 (6x10 inch) cake.

MISS ROSA'S GINGERBREAD

3 cups sifted flour
1 teaspoon cinnamon
1 teaspoon ginger
1 teaspoon cloves
1 teaspoon baking soda
1 cup brown sugar
½ cup melted shortening
1 cup molasses
2 eggs
1 cup boiling water

Sift flour, spices and soda together. Stir brown sugar into melted shortening, add molasses and unbeaten eggs. Beat well. Add sifted dry ingredients and hot water alternately in small amounts beating thoroughly after each addition. Pour into greased pan and bake in moderate oven (350°F.) 40 to 50 minutes. Makes 1 (10x10 inch) cake.

ORANGE MARMALADE GINGERBREAD

1¾ cups sifted cake flour
¾ teaspoon baking powder
½ teaspoon baking soda
1 teaspoon cinnamon
1 teaspoon ginger
½ teaspoon salt
3 tablespoons shortening
1 egg, well beaten
½ cup molasses
1 cup orange marmalade
4 tablespoons boiling water

Sift flour, baking powder, soda, cinnamon, ginger and salt together. Cream shortening, add egg and mix well. Add molasses and marmalade and beat thoroughly. Add sifted dry ingredients and hot water alternately in small amounts, beating well after each addition. Pour into greased pan and bake in moderate oven (350°F.) 35 to 45 minutes. Makes 1 (8x8 inch) cake.

RICH HONEY GINGERBREAD

1½ cups sifted flour
¼ cup sugar
2 teaspoons baking powder
¼ teaspoon baking soda
½ teaspoon salt
½ teaspoon ginger
½ teaspoon cinnamon
½ teaspoon cloves
1 egg, well beaten
½ cup honey
½ cup milk or water
4 tablespoons melted shortening

Sift dry ingredients together 3 times. Mix egg, honey, milk and shortening. Combine liquid and dry ingredients and beat thoroughly. Pour into greased pan and bake in moderate oven (350°F.) 30 to 35 minutes. Makes 1 (8x8-inch) cake.

The one-egg cake may be very festive with nuts over caramel frosting

HONEY ONE-EGG CAKE

2 cups sifted cake flour
2 teaspoons baking powder
¼ teaspoon salt
⅓ cup shortening
½ cup sugar, ½ cup honey
1 egg, unbeaten, ½ cup milk
1 teaspoon vanilla

Sift dry ingredients together. Cream fat and sugar until fluffy. Add honey gradually, beating after each addition. Add ½ cup dry ingredients; beat well. Add egg; beat well. Add remaining dry ingredients alternately with milk. Stir only enough to blend. Add vanilla. Bake in greased pan in moderate oven (375°F.) for 30 to 35 minutes. Makes 1 (8-inch) cake.

LAYER CAKE

2 cups sifted cake flour
¼ teaspoon salt
2½ teaspoons baking powder
½ cup shortening
1 cup sugar
2 eggs, separated
⅔ cup milk
1 teaspoon vanilla

Sift flour, salt and baking powder together. Cream shortening with sugar until fluffy. Add beaten egg yolks and beat thoroughly. Add sifted dry ingredients alternately with milk and vanilla in small amounts, beating well after each addition. Fold in stiffly beaten egg whites. Pour into greased pans and bake in moderate oven (350°F.) 25 minutes. Cool, fill and frost as desired. Makes 2 (8-inch) layers.

DATE DELIGHT CAKE—Use lemon extract for vanilla. Spread Date Filling between layers and frost with Peanut-butter Frosting.

ONE-EGG CAKE

2 cups sifted cake flour
2½ teaspoons baking powder
¼ teaspoon salt
¼ cup shortening
1 cup sugar
1 egg
1 teaspoon vanilla
¾ cup milk

Sift flour, baking powder and salt together. Cream shortening with sugar until fluffy. Add egg and vanilla and beat thoroughly. Add sifted dry ingredients and milk alternately in small amounts, blending well after each addition. Pour into greased pans and bake in moderate oven (350°F.) 30 to 35 minutes. Makes 2 (9-inch) layers.

CANDIED FRUIT CUPCAKES—Pour batter into greased muffin pans, filling ⅔ full. Sprinkle candied grapefruit or orange peel over top of batter. Bake as above. Makes 24 cupcakes.

ORANGE LOAF

2 cups sifted cake flour
½ teaspoon baking soda
¼ teaspoon salt
⅓ cup shortening
1 cup sugar
2 eggs
Grated rind of 1 orange
¾ cup strained orange juice

Sift flour, baking soda and salt together. Cream shortening with sugar until fluffy. Beat eggs until thick, add to creamed mixture with orange rind and beat thoroughly Add sifted dry ingredients and orange juice alternately in small amounts, beating thoroughly after each addition. Pour into greased loaf pan and bake in moderate oven (350°F.) 50 minutes. Makes 1 (6x10 inch) cake.

SWEETPOTATO CAKE

1½ cups sifted flour
2½ teaspoons baking powder
⅓ cup shortening
2 eggs, well beaten
1 cup hot mashed sweetpotatoes
¾ cup sugar
¼ teaspoon salt
1 teaspoon nutmeg or cinnamon
½ cup milk
2 tablespoons lemon juice

Sift flour and baking powder together. Add shortening and beaten eggs to potatoes while still hot; add sugar, salt and nutmeg. Beat thoroughly. Add flour and milk alternately in small amounts, beating well after each addition. Add lemon juice. Pour into greased loaf pan and bake in slow oven (325°F.) 60 to 65 minutes. Makes 1 (8x4 inch) cake.

CHOCOLATE CAKES

QUICK CHOCOLATE CAKE

2 ounces (squares) chocolate, grated
1 cup boiling water
½ cup shortening
2 cups sugar
½ teaspoon salt
2 cups sifted flour
1½ teaspoons baking soda
½ cup sour milk
2 eggs, beaten

Heat chocolate, water and shortening in top of double boiler until chocolate is melted and the mixture is glossy when beaten slightly. Remove from heat and place in mixing bowl. Add remaining ingredients in the order listed. Beat vigorously for 2 minutes. (This batter is very thin. Do not add more flour.) Pour batter into greased pans and bake in moderate oven (350°F.) 30 to 35 minutes. Makes 2 (8-inch) layers. Fill and frost with Caramel Icing, sprinkle with chopped nut meats.

SPANISH COCOA CAKE

2 cups sifted cake flour
4 tablespoons cocoa
½ teaspoon salt
2 teaspoons baking soda
⅓ cup shortening
1 cup sugar
2 egg yolks, beaten
1 teaspoon vanilla
1⅓ cups thick sour milk

Sift flour, cocoa, salt and baking soda together 3 times. Cream shortening with sugar until fluffy. Add egg yolks and vanilla and beat thoroughly. Add dry ingredients and milk alternately in small amounts, blending after each addition. Pour into greased pan and bake in moderate oven (350°F.) 40-50 minutes. Makes 1 (8x8-inch) cake.

HONEY CHOCOLATE CAKE

2½ cups sifted flour
1 teaspoon baking powder
1 teaspoon baking soda
½ teaspoon salt
½ cup shortening
½ cup sugar
¾ cup honey
1 egg, separated
2 ounces (squares) chocolate, melted
¼ cup water
½ cup sour milk
1 teaspoon vanilla

Sift flour, baking powder, soda and salt together. Cream shortening with sugar and honey until fluffy. Add ½ cup dry ingredients and blend. Add beaten yolk and chocolate; beat thoroughly. Add dry ingredients and liquids alternately in small amounts, blending after each addition. Fold in stiffly beaten egg white. Bake in greased pan in moderate oven (350°F.) 40 to 50 minutes. Makes 1 (8x8 inch) cake.

HONEY DEVIL'S FOOD—Increase baking powder to 2 teaspoons and reduce soda to ½ teaspoon. Use 2 to 4 ounces chocolate and ¾ cup sweet milk. Omit water. Mix and bake as above.

DEVIL'S FOOD CAKE

¾ cup boiling water
3 ounces (squares) chocolate
2¼ cups sifted flour
1½ teaspoons baking soda
¾ teaspoon baking powder
¾ teaspoon salt
¾ cup shortening
1⅞ cups brown sugar
3 eggs, well beaten
1½ teaspoons vanilla
¾ cup sour milk

Pour boiling water over chocolate; stir over low heat until smooth and thick; cool. Sift flour, soda, baking powder and salt together. Cream shortening with sugar until fluffy. Add eggs and beat thoroughly. Blend in chocolate and vanilla. Add sifted dry ingredients and milk alternately in small amounts, blending well after each addition. Pour into greased pans and bake in (350°F.) oven 25 to 30 minutes. Makes 3 (8-inch) layers.

CHOCOLATE MINT CAKE—Prepare chocolate cake using above recipe. Spread Mint Divinity Icing between layers and over top and sides of cake.

A fluffy coconut frosting is the final touch of glory for devil's food

Cut into squares, fudge cake seems even more toothsome than usual

CHOCOLATE FUDGE CAKE

2¼ cups sifted cake flour
1 teaspoon baking soda
½ teaspoon salt
4 ounces (squares) chocolate
1¼ cups milk
¾ cup brown sugar
1 teaspoon vanilla
⅔ cup shortening
1 cup granulated sugar
3 eggs

Sift flour, soda and salt together. Heat chocolate and milk in top of double boiler until chocolate melts. Add brown sugar and beat until smooth. Cool and add vanilla. Cream shortening with granulated sugar until fluffy. Add eggs one at a time, beating thoroughly after each is added. Add sifted dry ingredients and cooled chocolate mixture alternately in small amounts, beating well after each addition. Pour into greased pan and bake in moderate oven (350°F.) 30 to 35 minutes. Makes 2 (9-inch) layers. Spread with Chocolate Frosting flavored with mint extract.

CHOCOLATE NUT CAKE

1¾ cups sifted cake flour
2 teaspoons baking powder
⅛ teaspoon salt
½ teaspoon cloves
½ teaspoon cinnamon
½ teaspoon allspice
¾ cup shortening
1½ cups sugar
4 eggs, separated
4 ounces (squares) chocolate, melted
1 cup milk
1 cup walnut meats, chopped
1 teaspoon vanilla

Sift flour, baking powder, salt and spices together 3 times. Cream shortening with sugar until fluffy. Add unbeaten egg yolks and chocolate and beat vigorously. Add sifted dry ingredients and milk alternately in small amounts, beating well after each addition. Stir in nuts and vanilla. Fold in stiffly beaten egg whites. Pour into greased pan and bake in slow oven (325°F.) about 50 minutes. Makes 1 (9x9-inch) cake. When cool, spread top and sides with ½ recipe Marshmallow Icing or Chocolate Icing. Cut into attractive shapes for the very special party.

SPICED DEVIL'S FOOD CAKE

3 cups sifted cake flour
1½ tablespoons cinnamon
1 teaspoon allspice
1 teaspoon cloves
1 teaspoon baking soda
⅛ teaspoon salt
1 cup shortening
2 cups brown sugar
1 teaspoon vanilla
2 eggs, beaten
4 ounces (squares) chocolate, melted
1 cup buttermilk
½ cup boiling water

Sift flour, spices, soda and salt together 3 times. Cream shortening with sugar and vanilla until fluffy. Add beaten eggs and chocolate and beat thoroughly. Add sifted dry ingredients and buttermilk alternately in small amounts, beating well after each addition. Add boiling water and blend. Pour into greased pans and bake in moderate oven (350°F.) 30 to 35 minutes. Makes 3 (9-inch) layers.

Make cupcakes by baking batter in greased muffin pans instead of in cake pans. When cold and ready to serve, scoop out centers and fill with pecan toffee ice cream.

CHOCOLATE MARBLE CAKE

PART 1

2⅓ cups sifted cake flour
2¼ teaspoons baking powder
¼ teaspoon salt
½ cup shortening
1 cup sugar
1 egg, well beaten
2 egg yolks
1 teaspoon vanilla
¾ cup milk

PART 2

2½ ounces (squares) chocolate, melted
½ teaspoon baking soda
3 tablespoons sugar
2 tablespoons shortening
¼ teaspoon salt
¼ cup hot water

Sift flour, baking powder and salt together. Cream shortening with sugar until fluffy. Combine egg and egg yolks, beat well, add to creamed mixture with vanilla and beat thoroughly. Add sifted dry ingredients and milk alternately in small amounts, beating well after each addition. Combine ingredients of part 2 in order given. Blend thoroughly. Divide batter as follows: Leave ⅓ of the batter white and to the other ⅔ add chocolate mixture (part 2). Blend well. Drop batter by tablespoons into greased pan, alternating white and chocolate batters. Bake in moderate oven (350°F.) about 1 hour. Makes 1 (8-inch) cake.

FUDGE CAKE

2 cups sifted cake flour
¼ teaspoon salt
1 teaspoon baking soda
1 cup shortening
1⅓ cups brown sugar
3 eggs, well beaten
4 ounces (squares) chocolate, melted
1 teaspoon vanilla
⅔ cup milk

Sift flour, salt and soda together. Cream shortening and sugar, beat in eggs. Blend in chocolate and vanilla. Add dry ingredients and milk alternately. Bake in greased pans at 350°F., 30 minutes. Makes 2 (9-inch) layers.

MODERN MARBLE CAKE

1¾ cups sifted cake flour
2 teaspoons baking powder
½ teaspoon salt
½ cup shortening
1 cup sugar
2 eggs, beaten
½ cup milk
1 teaspoon vanilla
1 ounce (square) chocolate
2 tablespoons milk

Sift flour, baking powder and salt together. Cream shortening with sugar until fluffy. Beat eggs thoroughly and add. Add sifted dry ingredients and milk alternately in small amounts, beating well after each addition. Add vanilla. Divide batter into halves. Melt chocolate and add with 2 tablespoons milk to one half; blend well. Drop batter by tablespoons into greased pan, alternating white and chocolate. Bake in moderate oven (350°F.) 50 to 60 minutes. Makes 1 (8x8 inch) cake.

CHOCOLATE PEPPER-MINT CAKE

2 cups sifted cake flour
1 teaspoon baking soda
½ teaspoon salt
⅓ cup shortening
1¼ cups sugar
1 egg, unbeaten
3 ounces (squares) chocolate, melted
1 teaspoon vanilla
½ cup thick sour cream
¾ cup sweet milk

Sift flour, soda and salt together. Cream shortening with sugar until fluffy. Add egg and beat thoroughly; then add chocolate and vanilla and blend. Add about ¼ of the flour and beat well; then add sour cream and beat thoroughly. Add remaining flour and milk alternately in small amounts, beating well after each addition. Pour into greased pans and bake in moderate oven (350°F.) 30 minutes. Spread Peppermint Frosting between layers and over cake. Decorate with a border of chocolate flakes. Makes 2 (9-inch) layers.

The fun of baking a marble cake is to see what designs come through

Combine 1 cup brown sugar, cocoa and 1 cup grapefruit juice. Cook until thickened, stirring constantly. Cool. Sift flour, baking powder and soda together. Cream shortening with remaining cup of sugar until fluffy. Add beaten egg yolks and beat thoroughly. Add sifted dry ingredients and remaining grapefruit juice alternately in small amounts, beating well after each addition. Fold in cooled chocolate sirup and mix thoroughly. Fold in stiffly beaten egg whites. Pour into greased pans and bake in moderate oven (350°F.) 30 minutes. Makes 2 (8-inch) layers.

Fudge icing and pecan meats complete the sour milk chocolate cake

SOUR CREAM CHOCOLATE CAKE

2 cups sifted cake flour
2 teaspoons baking powder
¾ teaspoon baking soda
¼ teaspoon salt
⅓ cup shortening
1 cup sugar
2 eggs, well beaten
2 ounces (squares) chocolate, melted
½ cup milk
½ cup sour cream
1 teaspoon vanilla

Sift flour, baking powder, soda and salt together. Cream shortening with sugar until fluffy. Add eggs and chocolate and beat thoroughly. Add sifted dry ingredients and liquids alternately in small amounts, beating well after each addition. Pour into greased tube pan and bake in moderate oven (350°F.) 45 to 50 minutes. Makes 1 (8-inch) cake. When cake is cold cut slices ½ inch thick, spread with a thick layer of ice cream and cover with another slice of cake.

SOUR MILK CHOCOLATE CAKE

2 cups sifted cake flour
1 teaspoon baking soda
½ teaspoon salt
½ cup shortening
1½ cups sugar
1 teaspoon vanilla
3 eggs, separated
2 ounces chocolate, melted
1 cup sour milk

Sift flour, soda and salt together. Cream shortening with sugar until fluffy; add vanilla and beaten egg yolks and beat thoroughly. Stir in chocolate. Add sifted dry ingredients and milk alternately in small amounts, beating well after each addition. Fold in stiffly beaten egg whites. Pour into greased pans and bake in 350°F. oven, 30 to 35 minutes. Makes 2 (9-inch) layers.

CITRUS DEVIL'S FOOD CAKE

2 cups brown sugar
1 cup cocoa
1½ cups grapefruit juice
2 cups sifted cake flour
½ cup baking powder
1 teaspoon baking soda
¼ cup shortening
2 eggs, separated

YEAST CHOCOLATE CAKE

3 cups sifted flour
½ teaspoon salt
1 teaspoon baking soda
1 cup shortening
2 cups sugar
3 eggs
1 cake yeast
¼ cup lukewarm water
1 cup milk
2 ounces chocolate, melted
½ cup chopped nut meats

Sift flour, salt and soda together. Cream shortening with sugar until fluffy. Add unbeaten eggs, one at a time, beating well after each is added. Soften yeast in water, then beat into first mixture. Add milk, melted chocolate, sifted dry ingredients and chopped nuts. Beat 5 minutes. Pour into greased pans, cover with waxed paper and chill for 6 hours or overnight. Remove from refrigerator and bake at once in moderate oven (350°F.) 45 minutes. Spread Orange Filling between layers. Cover top and sides with Orange Butter Frosting. Makes 2 (9-inch) layers.

COCOA 'LASSES CAKE

2 cups sifted cake flour
½ teaspoon salt
1 teaspoon baking soda
⅔ cup shortening
1 teaspoon vanilla
5 tablespoons cocoa
½ cup brown sugar
2 eggs
½ cup light molasses
1 cup thick sour milk

Sift flour, salt and soda together. Blend shortening, vanilla and cocoa, add sugar and cream until fluffy. Beat in eggs and molasses. Add dry ingredients and milk alternately, beating well after each addition. Pour into greased pan and bake at 350°F., 50 to 60 minutes. Makes 1 (10x10 inch) cake.

MOCHA HALO CAKES

1½ cups sifted cake flour
½ cup cocoa
½ teaspoon baking soda
2 teaspoons baking powder
¼ teaspoon salt
½ cup shortening
1 cup sugar
1 egg
2 egg yolks
½ cup cold strong coffee
½ cup buttermilk

Sift flour, cocoa, soda, baking powder and salt together 3 times. Cream shortening with sugar until fluffy. Combine whole egg and egg yolks, beat well and add to creamed mixture. Combine coffee and buttermilk. Add sifted dry ingredients and liquids alternately in small amounts, beating well after each addition. Pour into greased cupcake pans and bake in moderate oven (350° F.) 20 minutes. Makes 18 medium or 12 large cupcakes. Frost with Fluffy White Icing. Melt 1 ounce (square) chocolate with 1 teaspoon butter and put a band around each cake with teaspoon or pastry brush.

MINT CHOCOLATE CHIP CAKE

1½ cups sifted cake flour
2 teaspoons baking powder
⅛ teaspoon salt
½ cup shortening
1 cup sugar
2 eggs, separated
½ cup milk
1 teaspoon vanilla
2½ ounces (squares) sweet chocolate, cut into pieces

Sift flour, baking powder and salt together. Cream shortening with ⅓ cup sugar until fluffy. Beat egg yolks until thick, add ⅓ cup sugar gradually and continue beating until very thick. Add to shortening mixture. Add sifted dry ingredients and milk alternately in small amounts, beating thoroughly after each addition. Beat egg whites until foamy, beat in remaining ⅓ cup sugar gradually and continue beating until stiff enough to hold a peak. Fold egg whites, vanilla and chocolate into batter, pour into greased pans and bake in moderate oven (350° F.) 25 to 30 minutes. Makes 2 (8-inch) layers. Frost tops and sides with Peppermint Frosting.

BANANA CHOCOLATE CAKE

2¼ cups sifted cake flour
1 teaspoon baking powder
¾ teaspoon baking soda
1 teaspoon salt
⅔ cup shortening
1½ cups sugar
2 eggs
2 ounces (squares) chocolate, melted
1 teaspoon vanilla
1 cup mashed ripe bananas (2 to 3)
½ cup sour milk or buttermilk

Sift flour, baking powder, soda and salt together. Cream shortening with sugar until fluffy. Add eggs, one at a time, beating thoroughly after each is added. Add chocolate and mix thoroughly. Stir in vanilla. Add sifted dry ingredients alternately with bananas and milk in small amounts, beating well after each addition. Turn into greased pans and bake in moderate oven (350°F.) 30 to 35 minutes. Makes 2 (9-inch) layers.

Mocha halo cakes are ideal for the children's party

DELICIOUS FRUITCAKE

4 cups sifted cake flour
1 teaspoon mace
¼ teaspoon nutmeg
2 teaspoons cinnamon
½ teaspoon baking soda
3 pounds currants
2 pounds seeded raisins
1 pound citron, sliced
2 cups blanched almonds, sliced
1 pound shortening
2 cups light brown sugar
9 eggs, separated
1 cup strong cold coffee

Sift flour, spices and soda together 3 times. Mix with fruit and nuts. Cream shortening and sugar together until fluffy. Beat yolks until thick and whites until stiff; add to creamed mixture. Add flour-fruit mixture alternately with coffee. Pour into greased pans lined with greased paper. Bake in very slow oven (275°F.) 3 to 4 hours. Rich fruitcake is sometimes steamed 1 hour, then baked for remaining time. Test with toothpick or cake tester before removing from oven. Makes 9 pounds fruitcake.

OLD-FASHIONED FRUITCAKE —
Omit 1½ pounds of the currants, the mace, nutmeg, citron and coffee. Add 1 tablespoon milk, 3 tablespoons lemon juice, ½ pound chopped orange peel, 1 pound chopped pitted dates, ¼ pound halved candied cherries and ½ pound sliced candied pineapple.

TO RIPEN FRUITCAKES—Place fruitcakes in airtight containers 2 to 4 weeks before using to develop their delicious mellowness to the full.

A flower motive of candied fruit and blanched nuts adds to the glory of the dark Christmas fruitcake

CHRISTMAS FRUITCAKE

2 cups seeded raisins
4 cups seedless raisins
2 cups uncooked prunes
2 cups halved candied cherries
4 cups sliced citron
1 cup sliced candied pineapple
½ cup ground candied lemon peel
1 cup ground candied orange peel
3 cups broken walnut meats
1 tablespoon grated orange rind
½ cup fruit juice
5 cups sifted flour
1½ teaspoons salt
3 teaspoons baking powder
1 pound shortening
2 cups white sugar
1 cup brown sugar
3 teaspoons cinnamon
2 teaspoons cloves
1 teaspoon allspice
2 teaspoons mace
10 eggs, well beaten
1 tablespoon vanilla

Rinse raisins, drain, dry on a towel and slice seeded raisins. Pour boiling water over prunes, cover and let stand 10 minutes; drain, dry and cut from pits into very small pieces. Rinse, drain and dry cherries and citron before slicing. Combine fruit, nuts and orange rind. Pour fruit juice over combined fruits. Sift flour, salt and baking powder together Cream shortening, sugars and spices until fluffy. Add beaten eggs and mix thoroughly. Add flour, prepared fruit mixture and flavoring and stir until fruits are well distributed. Pour into 1 (10-inch) tube pan and 1 loaf pan (about 10x5x3 inches) lined with 2 thicknesses of greased brown paper. Smooth tops and decorate if desired. Bake in very slow oven (275° to 285°F.). Cake in tube pan will require from 3¾ to 4 hours baking time; in loaf pan, about 3 to 3¼ hours. Test with toothpick or cake tester before removing from oven. Baked weight approximately 10 pounds. May be served as soon as cool but improves if ripened a few days longer.

Omit vanilla, 1 cup of seedless raisins, candied fruit peel, prunes, 1 cup of walnut meats, allspice, 1 teaspoon of cloves and 1 teaspoon of mace. Add grated rind and juice of 1 lemon, 3 cups currants, 1 pound chopped dates, 2 teaspoons nutmeg, 1 glass tart jelly and ¼ pound almonds, blanched and sliced.

DARK FRUITCAKE

2 pounds seeded raisins, chopped
1¾ pounds sultana raisins,
    chopped
¾ pound citron, chopped
1 pound currants
½ pound candied pineapple
¼ cup chopped candied lemon
    peel
½ pound candied cherries, halved
¼ cup chopped candied orange
    peel
1 cup grape juice
2 cups chopped nut meats
1 pound cake flour
2 cups shortening
1 pound brown sugar
12 eggs
1 cup molasses
4 teaspoons cinnamon
4 teaspoons allspice
1½ teaspoons mace
½ teaspoon nutmeg
½ teaspoon baking soda
½ teaspoon salt
4 ounces (squares) chocolate,
    melted
2 tablespoons hot water

Combine fruit. Pour grape juice over fruit and let stand overnight. Dredge fruit and nuts with half of the flour. Cream shortening and sugar until fluffy. Add eggs, 1 at a time, to the creamed mixture and continue creaming. Add molasses. Combine remaining flour with other dry ingredients and sift 3 times. Add alternately with grape juice and fruit mixture to creamed sugar and egg mixture. Add chocolate and hot water. Blend thoroughly. Pour into greased loaf pans lined with brown paper. Steam for 2 hours and bake in slow oven (300°F.) for an additional 1½ hours. Makes 8 (10x2x3 inch) loaves. Cakes may be decorated with pieces of fruit before placing in oven.

Peel paper from cakes while warm.

ROSE GARNISH—Cut gelatin candies shaped like lemon or orange segments into thin lengthwise slices. Roll a slice tightly to form center of rose and press other slices around it to form petals. Moisten slices slightly if necessary to make them stick together. Place on fruitcake with artificial rose leaves.

This transparent rose is a beautiful decoration

HARRISON CAKE

1 (9-ounce) package condensed
    mincemeat
½ cup cold water
1 cup shortening
1 cup sugar
2 eggs, slightly beaten
¼ cup molasses
2½ cups sifted cake flour
½ teaspoon baking soda
¼ teaspoon salt
½ cup water
¼ pound citron, chopped

Break mincemeat into pieces. Add cold water. Place over heat and stir until all lumps are thoroughly broken up. Heat to boiling; continue boiling for 3 minutes or until mixture is practically dry. Cool. Cream shortening and sugar until fluffy. Add eggs, beating vigorously until smooth and creamy. Add molasses. Sift flour with soda and salt. Add alternately with water in small amounts, beating thoroughly after each addition. Fold in citron and cooled mincemeat. Pour into paper-lined pan. Bake in moderate oven (350°F.) about 1¼ hours. Test with toothpick or cake tester before removing from oven. Makes 1 (9x9 inch) cake.

Simple fruits and nuts decorate the light fruitcake

LIGHT FRUITCAKE

5 cups white raisins
2 cups chopped dried white figs
5 cups sliced citron
2 cups halved candied cherries
½ cup fruit juice
2 teaspoons cardamom seeds
3 teaspoons nutmeg
4 teaspoons mace
1 teaspoon cinnamon
1½ cups thick Orange Marmalade
4½ cups sifted flour
3 teaspoons baking powder
1½ teaspoons salt
2 cups shortening
2½ cups sugar, 8 eggs
1 teaspoon vanilla
2 teaspoons lemon extract
1½ cups chopped Brazil nuts
2 cups broken walnut meats

Rinse fruits, drain and dry on towel. (If figs are very dry, let stand in hot water about 5 minutes.) Cut figs into thin strips. Combine fruit juice and spices; mix and pour over combined fruit. Add marmalade and mix well. Cover and let stand overnight.

Sift flour, baking powder and salt together. Cream shortening and sugar until fluffy. Add beaten eggs and mix. Add flour, fruit mixture, flavoring and nuts and stir until fruit is well distributed. Pour into 2 (9-inch) tube-cake pans which have been lined with 2 thicknesses of greased brown paper. Smooth tops and decorate if desired. Bake in very slow oven (275°F.) 3¾ to 4 hours. Test with toothpick or cake tester before removing from oven. May be used as soon as cool or ripened. Baked weight is approximately 9¾ pounds.

DRIED APRICOT CAKE

1 cup dried apricots
2 cups water
6 tablespoons sugar
1¾ cups sifted cake flour
½ teaspoon salt
½ teaspoon baking soda
1 teaspoon baking powder
½ cup shortening
1 cup sugar, 2 egg yolks
1 teaspoon vanilla
¼ cup water

Simmer first 3 ingredients together 30 minutes. Mash and measure ½ cup pulp. Sift flour, salt, soda and baking powder together 3 times. Cream shortening and sugar until fluffy. Add yolks and vanilla; beat thoroughly. Add dry ingredients alternately with water and pulp in small amounts. Bake in greased cake pan in 350°F. oven 45 minutes Makes 1 (8x8 inch) cake.

ENGLISH FRUITCAKE

5½ cups sifted cake flour
2½ teaspoons baking powder
¼ teaspoon mace
1 cup shortening
1⅞ cups brown sugar
3 eggs, well beaten
1 teaspoon lemon extract
3¼ cups sultana raisins
¼ cup sliced candied orange peel
¼ cup sliced candied lemon peel
¼ cup sliced citron
¼ cup sliced candied pineapple or cherries
1 cup chopped walnut meats
1 cup fruit juice

Sift flour, baking powder and mace together 3 times. Cream shortening and sugar together until fluffy. Add eggs and beat well. Add lemon extract, fruit and nuts and mix well. Add dry ingredients and fruit juice alternately in small amounts, beating thoroughly after each addition. Pour into tube pan lined with greased brown paper. Bake in slow oven (300°F.) 2 to 2½ hours. Test with toothpick or cake tester before removing from oven. Makes 1 (10-inch) cake.

RAISIN FRUITCAKE—Use 2 cups white sugar instead of brown sugar. Use 3 cups stewed raisins instead of sultana raisins, candied peels, candied pineapple and nuts Use 1 cup raisin juice instead of fruit juice. Omit mace and lemon extract. Add 2 teaspoons cinnamon and 1 teaspoon nutmeg.

WEDDING CAKE

4½ cups (1 pound) sifted cake
    flour
1 teaspoon baking powder
½ teaspoon cloves
½ teaspoon cinnamon
½ teaspoon mace
1 pound shortening
1 pound brown sugar
10 eggs, well beaten
½ pound candied cherries, cut into
    halves
½ pound candied pineapple, diced
1 pound dates, seeded and sliced
1 pound raisins
1 pound currants
½ pound citron, thinly sliced
½ pound candied orange and
.   lemon peel, sliced
½ pound nut meats, chopped
1 cup honey
1 cup molasses
½ cup cider

Sift flour, baking powder and
spices together 3 times. Cream
shortening and sugar until fluffy.
Add eggs, fruit, nuts, honey, molasses and cider. Add flour in
small amounts, mixing well after
each addition. Turn into cake
pans which have been greased,
lined with heavy paper and again
greased. Bake in very slow oven
(250°F.). For large loaves, bake
in 8x4x3 inch pans about 4 hours.
For small loaves, bake in 6x3x2½
inch pans about 2½ to 3 hours.
For 8½ inch tube pan, bake 4
to 5 hours. Test with toothpick
or cake tester before removing
from oven. Makes 10 pounds
fruitcake. Spread Ornamental
Icing on top and sides of cake
and decorate with simple borders,
festoons and rosettes of Ornamental Icing.

*For a terraced cake, bake in
pans of several sizes and use
a pastry tube to decorate*

WHITE FRUITCAKE

1 cup shredded coconut
1 cup sliced citron
1 cup sultana raisins
1 cup chopped candied pineapple
1 cup candied cherries, sliced
2 cups blanched almonds, chopped
3 cups sifted flour
1 teaspoon baking powder
1 cup shortening
2 cups sugar
1 tablespoon vanilla
½ cup fruit sirup
8 egg whites

Combine first 6 ingredients with
1 cup of the flour. Sift remaining flour with baking powder.
Cream shortening with sugar and
flavoring until fluffy. Add sifted
dry ingredients and fruit sirup alternately in small amounts, beating well after each addition. Add
fruit mixture. Beat egg whites
until stiff but not dry and fold
into batter. Pour into greased
pans lined with heavy greased
paper and bake in very slow oven
(275°F.) about 4 hours. Makes
5 pounds fruitcake.

GOLDEN FRUITCAKE

2 cups chopped dried apricots
2 cups seeded raisins, chopped
⅔ cup chopped candied cherries
⅔ cup chopped candied orange
    peel
⅔ cup chopped citron
½ cup blanched almonds, shaved
1 teaspoon grated lemon rind
4 cups sifted cake flour
1½ cups shortening
1½ cups sugar, 8 eggs
1 teaspoon salt
1 teaspoon baking powder

Combine fruits, nuts and rind
with half of flour. Cream shortening and sugar until fluffy. Beat
in eggs, one at a time. Combine
remaining flour, salt and baking
powder and sift together 3 times.
Add to creamed mixture. Add
fruit and nut mixture and blend
well Pour into greased loaf pans
lined with greased brown paper.
Bake in slow oven (300°F.) 1½
hours. Makes 4 (7x3x2½ inch)
loaves.

FRESH APPLE CAKE

2 cups sifted cake flour
¼ teaspoon salt
1 teaspoon baking soda
1 teaspoon baking powder
½ cup shortening
1 cup sugar
2 eggs, well beaten
1½ tablespoons sour milk
1 cup ground, unpeeled apples
¼ cup broken nut meats
1 teaspoon vanilla

Sift flour, salt, soda and baking powder together. Cream shortening with sugar until fluffy. Add eggs and beat thoroughly. Add sifted dry ingredients, milk and apples alternately in s m a l l amounts, beating well after each addition. Add remaining in-gredients, mixing lightly. Pour into greased pan and bake in moderate oven (350°F.) about 1 hour. Makes 1 (8x4 inch) loaf. Frost entire cake with ½ recipe Caramel Icing. When icing is firm, store in a cool, dry place several days to develop flavor.

The blueberry torte is all the more welcome because its season is so short

APPLE PRESERVE CAKE

2 cups sifted cake flour
1 teaspoon baking soda
1 teaspoon baking powder
⅛ teaspoon salt
1 teaspoon cinnamon
1 teaspoon nutmeg
1 teaspoon allspice
¾ cup shortening
1 cup sugar
¼ cup sour cream
½ cup Apple Preserves
3 eggs
½ cup chopped walnut meats
½ cup seedless raisins

Sift flour, soda, baking powder, salt and spices together 3 times. Cream shortening with sugar un-til fluffy. Add sour cream and apple preserves, mixing well. Add eggs, one at a time, beating hard after each is added. Add sifted dry ingredients gradually, beating well. Fold in nuts and raisins. Pour into greased loaf pan and bake in moderate oven (350°F.) 50 minutes or bake in layers 25 to 30 minutes. Makes 1 (8x4 inch) loaf or 2 (9-inch) layers.

BLUEBERRY TORTE

1⅓ cups sifted cake flour
2 teaspoons baking powder
¼ teaspoon salt
⅓ cup shortening
⅔ cup sugar
4 eggs, separated
1 teaspoon vanilla
⅓ cup milk
½ cup sugar
1½ cups blueberries
1 tablespoon sugar

Sift flour, baking powder and salt together. Cream shortening with ⅔ cup sugar until fluffy. Add egg yolks and beat thoroughly. Add vanilla. Add sifted dry in-gredients and milk alternately in small amounts, beating well after each addition. Pour into 2 greased (8- or 9-inch) cake pans and bake in moderate oven (350°F.) 15 minutes. Beat egg whites un-til fluffy, add ½ cup sugar gradu-ally and beat until stiff. Spread over hot cakes and bake in slow oven (300°F.) 20 minutes longer, or until meringue is lightly browned. Cool. Remove from pans. Clean blueberries and mash about 1 tablespoon of them; add remaining sugar and mix together. Sprinkle with a few drops lemon juice, spread over one layer of cake and cover with other layer. Chill. For 8.

FIG CAKE

Sift 3 cups cake flour, 3 tea-spoons baking powder, ¼ tea-spoon salt, 1 teaspoon each cin-namon and nutmeg, and ½ tea-spoon cloves together 3 times. Cream 1 cup shortening and 2 cups brown sugar. Mix in 4 beaten eggs. Add 2 cups chopped raisins and ½ pound figs, finely chopped. Add dry ingredients and 1 cup water alternately, beat-ing well. Pour into greased loaf pan; bake at 300°F., about 2 hours.

BANANA LAYER CAKE

2¼ cups sifted cake flour
2½ teaspoons baking powder
½ teaspoon baking soda
½ teaspoon salt
½ cup shortening
1 cup sugar
2 eggs
1 teaspoon vanilla
1 cup mashed ripe bananas
¼ cup sour milk or buttermilk

Sift flour, baking powder, soda and salt together. Cream shortening with sugar until fluffy. Add eggs, one at a time, beating thoroughly after each is added. Stir in vanilla. Combine bananas and milk. Add sifted dry ingredients and milk mixture alternately in small amounts, beating thoroughly after each addition. Pour into greased pans and bake in moderate oven (375°F.) 25 to 30 minutes. Spread Seven-minute Icing between layers and on top and sides of cake. Makes 2 (9-inch) layers.

Omit icing. Put layers together with whipped cream and sliced bananas. Spread whipped cream over top of cake and garnish with sliced bananas.

ECONOMY CAKE

1 cup brown sugar
⅓ cup shortening
½ teaspoon cloves
1 teaspoon cinnamon
¼ teaspoon nutmeg
¼ teaspoon salt
2 cups seeded raisins
1 cup water
2 cups sifted flour
½ teaspoon baking powder
1 teaspoon baking soda

Heat first 8 ingredients to boiling, boil for 3 minutes and cool. Sift flour, baking powder and soda together, add to cooled mixture and beat 3 minutes. Pour into greased loaf pan and bake in 350°F. oven about 45 minutes. Makes 1 (8x8 inch) cake.

MARIGOLD CAKE

2¼ cups sifted cake flour
¼ teaspoon salt
2½ teaspoons baking powder
½ cup shortening
1¼ cups sugar
3 eggs
1 teaspoon vanilla
⅔ cup milk
Bananas

Sift flour, salt and baking powder together. Cream shortening with sugar until fluffy; add unbeaten eggs, one at a time, beating well after each is added. Add vanilla and mix thoroughly. Add sifted dry ingredients and milk alternately in small amounts, beating well after each addition. Pour into 3 greased cake pans and bake in moderate oven (350°F.) 25 to 30 minutes. When cold, prepare a double recipe of Lemon Filling, spread between layers, add a layer of sliced bananas and cover with more lemon filling to prevent discoloration. Cover top and sides of cake with Divinity Icing and decorate with sliced bananas. Serves 12 to 16.

GOLD NUGGET CAKE

2 cups sifted flour
½ teaspoon baking powder
¾ teaspoon baking soda
½ teaspoon salt
¼ cup sour milk or buttermilk
1 cup mashed bananas (2 to 3)
½ cup shortening
1½ cups sugar
2 eggs, well beaten
1 teaspoon vanilla
3 bananas, sliced

Sift flour, baking powder, soda and salt together. Add milk to mashed bananas. Cream shortening with sugar until fluffy. Add eggs and beat well. Add sifted dry ingredients and milk mixture alternately in small amounts, beating well after each addition. Stir in flavoring. Pour into greased pans and bake in moderate oven (375°F.) 30 minutes. Cool. Put layers together with Banana Frosting and sliced bananas. Spread frosting over top and sides of cake and garnish with sliced bananas. Makes 2 (8-inch) layers.

Gold nugget cake is a "find" for any clever hostess

GOLDEN CROWN CAKE

1⅔ cups cubed pineapple
2½ cups sifted cake flour
1 teaspoon baking powder
½ teaspoon baking soda
½ teaspoon salt
¾ cup shortening
1¼ cups sugar
2 egg yolks
2 eggs
⅔ cup pineapple sirup plus water
½ teaspoon vanilla

Drain pineapple. Sift flour, baking powder, soda and salt together. Cream shortening with sugar until fluffy. Add egg yolks and eggs, one at a time, beating thoroughly after each is added. Add sifted dry ingredients, sirup and vanilla alternately in small amounts, beating well after each addition. Pour into greased ring mold or muffin pans. Fill mold half full. Bake in moderate oven (350°F.) 50 to 60 minutes for ring mold or 20 to 25 minutes for cupcakes. Cool and spread with Cream Cheese Frosting, using a double recipe. Decorate with pineapple. Makes 1 (10-inch) ring cake and 6 cupcakes or about 25 medium cupcakes.

Add this golden crown to your laurels as a hostess

PRUNE CAKE

1 cup drained, pitted cooked prunes
2½ cups sifted cake flour
1 teaspoon baking soda
1 teaspoon cinnamon
½ teaspoon salt
⅔ cup shortening
1 cup sugar
3 eggs, separated
1 teaspoon vanilla
½ cup buttermilk or sour milk
¼ cup nut meats, broken

Chop prunes fine. Sift flour, soda, cinnamon and salt together 3 times. Cream shortening with all but 3 tablespoons of the sugar until fluffy. Add egg yolks and vanilla, then beat thoroughly. Add sifted dry ingredients and buttermilk alternately in small amounts, beating well after each addition. Add chopped prunes and nuts; mix well. Beat egg whites until almost stiff, add remaining sugar and beat until stiff. Fold into batter. Pour into greased loaf pan and bake in moderate oven (350°F.) 60 to 70 minutes. Spread with Orange Butter Frosting. If baked in layers use a hotter oven (375°F.) 25 to 30 minutes. Makes 1 (8x12 inch) cake.
Bake in greased muffin pans at 375°F., 25 minutes. When cold scoop out centers, fill with Cream Filling and top with sweetened whipped cream.

MAPLE FIG CAKE

1 cup dried figs
2¾ cups sifted flour
1 teaspoon salt
3 teaspoons baking powder
¾ cup shortening
1 cup sugar
2 eggs, well beaten
⅔ cup milk
½ teaspoon maple flavoring

Pour boiling water over figs, cover and let stand for 5 minutes. Drain, dry on a towel, clip stems and slice fine. Sift flour, salt and baking powder together. Cream shortening with sugar until fluffy. Add eggs and beat thoroughly. Add sifted dry ingredients and milk alternately in small amounts, beating well after each addition. Add flavoring and figs and mix lightly but thoroughly. Pour into greased pan and bake in moderate oven (350°F.) 1 hour and 20 minutes. Makes 1 (10x5 inch) cake.

GRAPEFRUIT CAKE

3¾ cups sifted cake flour
½ teaspoon salt
½ teaspoon baking soda
3 teaspoons baking powder
1 cup shortening
3 tablespoons grated grapefruit rind
2½ cups sugar
4 eggs
1 egg yolk
¾ cup grapefruit juice

Sift flour, salt, soda and baking powder together. Cream shortening with grapefruit rind and sugar until fluffy. Add whole eggs and yolk, one at a time, beating thoroughly after each is added. Add sifted dry ingredients and juice alternately in small amounts, beating well after each addition. Pour into greased pans and bake in moderate oven (350°F.) 30 to 35 minutes. Makes 3 (9-inch) layers.

HONEY APPLESAUCE CAKE

2¼ cups sifted flour
1 teaspoon baking soda
½ teaspoon salt
1 teaspoon cinnamon
½ teaspoon cloves
1 cup raisins
1 cup broken nut meats
½ cup shortening
1 cup honey
1 egg, well beaten
1 cup thick Applesauce

Sift 2 cups flour with soda, salt and spices. Mix remaining flour with raisins and nuts. Cream shortening with honey until fluffy. Add egg and beat thoroughly. Add floured raisins and nuts. Add sifted dry ingredients and applesauce alternately in small amounts, beating well after each addition. Pour into greased pan and bake in moderate oven (350° F.) 50 to 60 minutes. Makes 1 (8x8 inch) cake.

SOUR CREAM CHOCOLATE CAKE

¾ cup shortening
1¾ cups dark corn sirup
4½ ounces chocolate, melted
3 eggs
2½ cups sifted cake flour
1 cup thick sour cream
1¼ teaspoons vanilla
¾ teaspoon baking powder
1 teaspoon baking soda
¾ teaspoon salt

Cream shortening, mix corn sirup and melted chocolate; add to shortening gradually, creaming continually. Beat in one egg at a time. Add 1½ cups flour and ⅔ cup sour cream; beat thoroughly; add remaining cream and vanilla; fold in remaining cup flour sifted with baking powder, soda and salt. Bake in greased layer pans in a moderate oven (350°F.) 30 to 35 minutes. Makes 3 (9-inch) layers.

CORN SIRUP SPICECAKE

½ cup shortening
1 cup dark corn sirup
3 egg yolks
½ cup milk
2 cups sifted cake flour
2 teaspoons baking powder
½ teaspoon cinnamon
½ teaspoon mace
¼ teaspoon cloves
¼ teaspoon allspice
½ teaspoon salt

Cream shortening, add sirup gradually, creaming continually Add well-beaten egg yolks. Beat in half of milk and 1 cup flour. Add remaining milk and fold in remaining flour sifted 3 times with baking powder, spices and salt. Turn into greased deep 8-inch square pan and bake in moderate oven (350°F.) 45 minutes.

What, no frosting for the spicecake? Top it with canned pears and whipped cream!

SOFT HONEY CAKE

2 cups sifted cake flour
¼ teaspoon salt
1 teaspoon baking soda
½ teaspoon ginger
½ teaspoon cinnamon
½ cup shortening
1 cup honey
1 egg
½ cup sour milk or buttermilk

Sift flour, salt, soda and spices together. Cream shortening and honey until fluffy. Beat egg until light and thick; add to honey mixture. Add sour milk and fold in sifted dry ingredients. Turn into 2 greased (8-inch) layer pans and bake in moderate oven (375°F.) 25 to 30 minutes. Spread with desired icing.

WHITE CAKES

WHITE CAKE

3 cups sifted cake flour
3 teaspoons baking powder
½ teaspoon salt
½ cup shortening
1½ cups sugar
¾ teaspoon vanilla
¼ teaspoon almond extract
1 cup milk
½ cup (about 4) egg whites

Sift flour, baking powder and salt together. Cream shortening with sugar and flavorings until fluffy. Add sifted dry ingredients and milk alternately in small amounts, beating well after each addition. Beat egg whites until stiff but not dry and fold into batter. Pour into greased pans and bake in moderate oven (350° F.) 30 to 35 minutes. Cool layers. Spread Fig Filling between layers, ice with Caramel Icing and decorate sides of cake with shaved almonds. Makes 2 (9-inch) layers.

WHITE MOUNTAIN CAKE — Omit almond extract and increase vanilla to 1 teaspoon. Use only 2½ cups flour. Follow method above. Bake in greased tube pan in moderate oven (350°F.) 45 to 60 minutes. When cake is cold frost with Divinity Icing.

FRENCH PASTRY

4 cups sifted cake flour
4 teaspoons baking powder
½ teaspoon salt
1 cup shortening
2½ cups sugar
1 cup milk
10 egg whites
1 teaspoon almond extract
½ teaspoon vanilla

Sift flour, baking powder and salt together. Cream shortening with sugar until fluffy. Add sifted dry ingredients and milk alternately in small amounts, beating well after each addition. Beat egg whites until stiff but not dry. Fold in egg whites and flavorings, pour into greased large shallow pan and bake in moderate oven (350°F.) 25 to 30 minutes. Cool.

Cut cake into oblongs, squares, circles, diamonds, crescents or any desired shape. Spread top and sides with Butter Frosting. Color some of the frosting and decorate cakes using different tips of the pastry tube. Fill hollows with jam. Press chopped nuts, grated or shaved chocolate or toasted coconut into sides of frosted cakes. Often rounds are cut with centers cut from half of rounds so that a hollowed round may be placed on top of a whole round and the hole filled. The entire pastry is then frosted and decorated. Makes about 50.

LADY BALTIMORE CAKE

3 cups sifted cake flour
3 teaspoons baking powder
½ teaspoon salt
¾ cup shortening
2 cups sugar
½ cup milk
½ cup water
1 teaspoon vanilla
6 egg whites

Sift flour, baking powder and salt together. Cream shortening with sugar until fluffy. Combine milk, water and vanilla. Add sifted dry ingredients and liquids alternately in small amounts, beating well after each addition. Beat egg whites until stiff but not dry and fold into batter. Pour into greased cake pans and bake in moderate oven (350°F.) 25 minutes. Cool. Spread Lady Baltimore Filling between layers and cover top and sides with Divinity Icing. Makes 3 (9-inch) layers.

Beautiful French pastry is the joy of the women with pastry-tube skill

PETITS FOURS

Bake White or True Spongecake in shallow pans. When cool cut into tiny squares, diamonds, circles or other fancy shapes. Use plain or split, hollow centers, fill with whipped cream or Custard Filling and put halves together again. Remove any loose crumbs. Place on cake rack with waxed paper under rack. Allow plenty of space between cakes. Pour Fondant Frosting slowly over cakes allowing surplus to run onto paper beneath. Lift cake rack gently, move to a second sheet of paper, decorate as desired and let stand until frosting is firm. Remove cakes with spatula and trim bottom edges with sharp knife. Scrape frosting from papers, reheat and use for other cakes.

TO DECORATE CAKES — Make flowers, borders or other designs with colored Ornamental Icing using pastry bag or tube; sprinkle with chocolate s h o t, silver dragées, colored candies, shaved nuts or colored coconut; or decorate with candied fruit or flowers.

Silver cake with coconut frosting, on a silver tray is a glittering success

SILVER CAKE

3 cups sifted cake flour
3 teaspoons baking powder
1/2 teaspoon salt
2/3 cup shortening
2 cups sugar
1 teaspoon vanilla
1 cup milk
5 egg whites

Sift flour, baking powder and salt together. Cream shortening with sugar and vanilla until fluffy. Add sifted dry ingredients and milk alternately in small amounts, beating well after each addition. Beat egg whites until stiff but not dry and fold into batter. Pour into greased pans and bake in moderate oven (350°F.) 30 minutes. Makes 3 (9-inch) layers.

CAKE BASKETS — Bake batter in greased (14x9 inch) pan, 45 minutes. When cold cut into oblongs, 3x4 inches. Scoop out centers, frost with Seven-minute Icing. When ready to serve fill with ice cream.

WHIPPED CREAM CAKE

2 cups sifted cake flour
1/2 teaspoon salt
3 teaspoons baking powder
3 egg whites
1/2 pint heavy cream
1 1/2 cups sugar
1/2 cup cold water
1 teaspoon vanilla
1 teaspoon almond extract

METHOD 1. Sift flour, salt and baking powder together 3 times. Beat egg whites until stiff but not dry. Whip cream until stiff and fold into egg whites. Add sugar gradually and mix well. Add dry ingredients alternately with water in small amounts. Add flavoring and blend thoroughly. Pour into pans lined with paper. Bake in moderate oven (350°F.) 25 to 30 minutes. Makes 2 (8-inch) layers.

METHOD 2. Sift flour, salt, baking powder and sugar together 3 times. Whip cream until stiff, fold in stiffly beaten egg whites and flavorings. Add water, then fold in dry ingredients carefully. Proceed as above.

METHOD 3. Use 2 1/4 cups flour. Sift flour with salt and baking powder. Whip cream, add sugar, then flour and water alternately. Fold in stiffly beaten egg whites and flavoring. Bake as above.

METHOD 4. Use 4 egg whites. Sift flour, 1 cup sugar, baking powder and salt together 3 times. Whip cream until stiff, then slowly stir in water. Beat egg whites until foamy, add remaining sugar gradually, beating constantly until mixture holds a peak. Add vanilla. Combine whipped cream and egg mixture, beating with a wire whip. Fold in dry ingredients. Proceed as above.

OLD-FASHIONED POUNDCAKE

1 pound butter (2 cups)
1 pound sifted cake flour (4¼ cups)
10 eggs, separated
1 pound sugar (2 cups)
1 teaspoon vanilla

METHOD 1. Cream butter, work in flour until mixture is mealy. Beat egg yolks, sugar and vanilla until thick and fluffy. Add first mixture gradually, beating thoroughly. Fold in stiffly beaten egg whites. Beat vigorously 15 minutes. Pour into 2 greased loaf pans and bake in slow oven (325° F.) 1¼ hours. Makes 2 (8 x 4 inch) loaves.

METHOD 2. Cream butter with vanilla and sugar until fluffy. Beat egg yolks until thick and add to creamed mixture. Fold in stiffly beaten egg whites, mixing thoroughly. Fold in flour and beat vigorously 15 minutes or longer.

RAISIN POUNDCAKE—Sift half the flour with 1 teaspoon cinnamon and 2 teaspoons mace 3 times; add to 1½ cups raisins. Use method 2. Add flour and raisin mixture first, then remaining flour.

RAISIN HONEY POUNDCAKE

1 cup raisins
3 cups sifted flour
3 teaspoons baking powder
½ teaspoon salt
1 cup (½ pound) butter
1 cup honey
4 eggs, well beaten
1 teaspoon vanilla
1 teaspoon lemon extract
¾ cup chopped walnut meats

Rinse raisins, drain, dry on a towel and slice or chop fine. Sift flour, baking powder and salt together. Cream butter with honey until fluffy. Add eggs and beat thoroughly. Add sifted dry ingredients and beat well. Add flavoring, raisins and nuts and mix well. Pour into greased loaf pan and bake in slow oven (300° F.) about 2 hours. Makes 1 (5½x10x3 inch) cake.

Poundcake has always been one of the family's standbys

THRIFTY POUNDCAKE

3 cups sifted cake flour
1½ teaspoons baking powder
¼ teaspoon mace
⅛ teaspoon salt
1 cup butter
1½ cups sugar
1 teaspoon vanilla
3 eggs, beaten
½ cup milk

Sift flour, baking powder, mace and salt together 3 times. Cream butter with sugar and vanilla until fluffy. Add eggs and beat thoroughly. Add sifted dry ingredients and milk alternately in small amounts, beating well after each addition. Pour into greased tube pan and bake in moderate oven (350°F.) about 60 minutes. Makes 1 (10-inch) cake.

BURNT SUGAR CAKE

2 cups sugar
1 cup boiling water
3 cups sifted cake flour
3 teaspoons baking powder
½ teaspoon salt
1 cup shortening
4 eggs, separated
1 teaspoon vanilla

Place 1 cup of the sugar in a skillet and heat, stirring constantly until sugar melts and becomes brown; remove from heat, add boiling water and stir until sugar is entirely dissolved. Cool. Sift flour, baking powder and salt together. Cream shortening with remaining sugar until fluffy. Add unbeaten egg yolks, one at a time, beating thoroughly after each is added. Add vanilla. Add sifted dry ingredients and caramel sirup alternately in small amounts, beating thoroughly after each addition. Fold in stiffly beaten egg whites. Pour into greased pans and bake in moderate oven (350° F.) 30 to 35 minutes. Makes 3 (9-inch) layers.

Square pans give a new slant to orange marmalade cake

BUTTERSCOTCH CAKE

1¾ cups brown sugar
¼ cup butter
1½ cups milk
3 cups sifted cake flour
3 teaspoons baking powder
½ teaspoon salt
½ cup shortening
1 teaspoon vanilla
3 eggs, well beaten

Combine 1 cup brown sugar, butter and ¼ cup milk and heat, stirring constantly. Cook to 250° F. or until a small amount of sirup forms a hard ball when tested in cold water. Remove from heat. Heat remaining milk and stir into sirup gradually. Cool. Sift flour, baking powder and salt together. Cream shortening with remaining sugar and vanilla until fluffy. Beat eggs until light and add to creamed mixture gradually, beating thoroughly. Add sifted dry ingredients and butterscotch mixture alternately in small amounts, beating thoroughly after each addition. Pour batter into greased pan and bake in moderate oven (350°F.) 50 to 60 minutes. Makes 1 (10x10 inch) cake. Frost with Butterscotch Icing.

IN-A-JIFFY CAKE

1½ cups sifted cake flour
¾ cup sugar
¼ teaspoon salt
2 teaspoons baking powder
¾ cup milk
1 teaspoon vanilla
¼ cup melted shortening
1 egg, beaten

Sift dry ingredients together 3 times. Combine remaining ingredients and add gradually to dry ingredients. Beat mixture 2 minutes. Pour into greased pan and bake in moderate oven (350° F.) 30 minutes. Makes 1 (8x8 inch) cake.

ORANGE MARMALADE CAKE

3 cups sifted cake flour
4 teaspoons baking powder
½ teaspoon salt
¾ cup shortening
1¾ cups sugar
3 eggs, well beaten
½ cup orange juice
1 tablespoon lemon juice
Grated rind 1 orange
½ cup water

Sift flour, baking powder and salt together. Cream shortening with sugar until fluffy. Add eggs and beat thoroughly. Mix fruit juices, orange rind and water together. Add sifted dry ingredients and liquid alternately in small amounts, beating well after each addition. Pour into greased pans and bake in moderate oven (350°F.) 30 minutes. Makes 3 (8-inch) layers. Cool. Spread Orange Marmalade Filling between layers, frost top and sides with Seven-minute Icing.

CRUMB CAKE

PART 1

2 cups sifted cake flour
2 cups brown sugar
½ cup shortening

PART 2

1 egg, beaten
½ cup sifted cake flour
2 teaspoons baking powder
1 teaspoon cinnamon
¾ cup milk

Rub flour, sugar and shortening (part 1) together until crumbly. Reserve ½ cup of crumbs to sprinkle over top of cake. To remainder add ingredients in part 2. Mix thoroughly. Spread in greased cake pan, sprinkle crumbs over the top and bake in moderate oven (350°F.) 30 to 40 minutes. Serves 10 to 12.

BOSTON GINGERBREAD

1 cup molasses
1 cup sour milk
2¼ cups sifted flour
1¾ teaspoons baking soda
2 teaspoons ginger
½ teaspoon salt
1 egg, well beaten
½ cup melted shortening

Mix molasses and milk. Sift dry ingredients together and add. Add egg and shortening and beat until the mixture is smooth and creamy. Pour into greased pan and bake in moderate oven (350° F.) about 30 minutes. Makes 1 (9x9 inch) cake.

LINZER TORTE

2 cups sifted flour
3 teaspoons baking powder
1 cup shortening
1 cup sugar, 3 eggs
1 teaspoon grated lemon rind
3 tablespoons lemon juice
½ pound blanched almonds, grated
1 glass (1 cup) tart red jelly
½ cup heavy cream, whipped

Sift flour and baking powder together 5 or 6 times. Cream shortening until smooth and fluffy. Add sugar, eggs, lemon rind and juice and beat for 5 minutes. Add almonds, fold in flour mixture and pour into greased spring-form pan. Bake in moderate oven (350°F.) about 35 minutes. Garnish top with jelly and whipped cream. Makes 1 (9-inch) torte.

Omit jelly; reduce baking powder to 1 teaspoon and add 1 tablespoon brandy. Separate eggs and fold in stiffly beaten whites last. Roll out ⅔ of the dough and line a spring-form pan, having dough for bottom thicker than for sides. Fill with 2 cups jam or preserves. Roll remaining dough, cut into strips and place crisscross on top. Bake as above, increasing time to 45 minutes. Before serving fill in hollows with additional jam.

GRAHAM CRACKER CREAM CAKE

1 cup sifted cake flour
2 teaspoons baking powder
¼ teaspoon salt
1 cup graham cracker crumbs
½ cup shortening
1 cup sugar, 2 eggs, beaten
1 cup milk
1 teaspoon almond extract

Sift first 3 ingredients together; mix with crumbs. Cream shortening and sugar, beat in eggs. Add dry ingredients and liquids alternately. Bake in greased pan at 350°F. 30 minutes. Makes 2 (8-inch) layers. Fill with Cream Filling.

A party could not possibly fail with this linzer torte

With candles alight, the blitz torte will celebrate any birthday or anniversary

BLITZ TORTE

1 cup sifted cake flour
1 teaspoon baking powder
⅛ teaspoon salt
½ cup shortening
1¼ cups sugar
4 eggs, separated
1 teaspoon vanilla
3 tablespoons milk
½ cup sliced blanched almonds
1 tablespoon sugar
½ teaspoon cinnamon

Sift flour, baking powder and salt together. Cream shortening with ½ cup sugar until fluffy. Add well-beaten egg yolks, vanilla, milk and sifted dry ingredients. Spread mixture in 2 greased pans. Beat egg whites until stiff but not dry, add remaining sugar gradually and beat until eggs hold a sharp peak. Spread over unbaked mixture in both pans. Sprinkle with almonds, 1 tablespoon sugar and cinnamon and bake in moderate oven (350°F.) about 30 minutes. Cool and spread Custard Filling between layers. Makes 2 (9-inch) layers.

CAKES

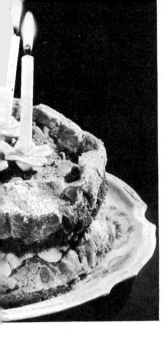

STAR CAKE

2¼ cups sifted cake flour
3 teaspoons baking powder
¼ teaspoon salt
½ cup shortening
1½ cups sugar
2 eggs, separated
1 cup milk
¾ teaspoon lemon extract
1¼ cups tart red jelly
1 cup heavy cream, whipped

Sift flour, baking powder and salt together. Cream shortening with 1¼ cups of the sugar until fluffy. Add egg yolks and beat vigorously. Add sifted dry ingredients and milk alternately in small amounts, beating well after each addition. Beat egg whites until nearly stiff, add remaining sugar and beat until stiff; then fold into cake with flavoring. Turn into 2 greased (8-inch) pans and bake in moderate oven (350°F.) 30 minutes. When cooled, melt jelly over warm water and spread between layers and over top and sides of cake. Chill until set. Just before serving, pipe whipped cream in star shape on top and serve with more whipped cream. Serves 10.

HEAVENLY TORTE

1½ cups butter
¼ cup sugar
¼ teaspoon salt
4 egg yolks
1 teaspoon grated lemon rind
4 cups sifted flour
1 egg white, unbeaten
¼ cup sugar
1 teaspoon cinnamon
½ cup chopped pecan meats

Cream butter with sugar until fluffy, add salt and egg yolks, one at a time, beating thoroughly after each is added. Add lemon rind and flour and mix well. Pat dough into 3 oblong pans, spread the top of each with mixture of unbeaten egg white, sugar, cinnamon and pecan meats. Bake in very hot oven (450°F.) 10 minutes, then reduce heat to 350°F. and bake 20 minutes longer. When torte is cold spread raspberry jam and Heavenly Torte Filling on 2 layers and cover with remaining filling. Makes 3 (7x11 inch) layers.

PRIZE CHOCOLATE CAKE

3 ounces (squares) chocolate
½ cup milk
1 cup sifted cake flour
¼ teaspoon salt
2 teaspoons baking powder
4 eggs, separated
1⅔ cups sugar
1 teaspoon vanilla

Melt chocolate over double boiler. Add milk, stirring constantly until slightly thickened. Cool. Sift flour, salt and baking powder together. Beat egg yolks, add sugar and vanilla and beat until fluffy. Add sifted dry ingredients and chocolate mixture alternately in small amounts, beating well after each addition. Fold in stiffly beaten egg whites. Pour into greased and flour-dusted pan and bake in slow oven (325°F.) 45 minutes. Frost if desired. Makes 1 (9x9 inch) cake.

A star in its own right is this luscious party cake

LORD BALTIMORE CAKE

2½ cups sifted cake flour
½ teaspoon salt
3 teaspoons baking powder
¾ cup butter
1¼ cups sugar
8 egg yolks
¾ cup milk
½ teaspoon lemon extract

Sift flour, salt and baking powder together. Cream butter thoroughly, add sugar gradually and cream together until very fluffy. Beat egg yolks with rotary beater until very thick and light colored, add to creamed mixture and beat for 5 to 10 minutes. Add flour alternately with milk in small amounts, beating very thoroughly after each addition. Add lemon extract and beat vigorously. Pour into greased pans and bake in moderate oven (375°F.) about 20 minutes. Spread with Lord Baltimore Filling and cover top and sides with Divinity Icing. Makes 3 (9-inch) layers.

MALLOW WHITE CAKE

2 cups sifted cake flour
2 teaspoons baking powder
½ teaspoon salt
½ cup shortening
1½ cups sugar
1 teaspoon vanilla
¾ cup water
4 egg whites

Sift flour, baking powder and salt together. Cream shortening with sugar and vanilla until fluffy. Add sifted dry ingredients and water alternately in thirds, beating well after each addition. Beat egg whites until stiff but not dry and fold into batter. Pour into greased pans and bake in moderate oven (350°F.) 30 to 35 minutes. Makes 2 (8-inch) layers.

RIBBON CAKE

3½ cups sifted cake flour
4 teaspoons baking powder
¼ teaspoon salt
½ cup shortening
2 cups sugar
4 eggs, separated
1 cup water
Red food coloring
1 tablespoon molasses
¼ teaspoon mace
¼ teaspoon cloves
½ teaspoon cinnamon
½ cup chopped dates or raisins
⅓ cup chopped figs or nuts

Sift flour, baking powder and salt together. Cream shortening with sugar until fluffy. Add unbeaten yolks, one at a time, beating thoroughly after each addition. Add sifted dry ingredients and water alternately in small amounts, beating well after each addition. Fold in egg whites, beaten until stiff but not dry. Divide batter into 3 equal portions, leave 1 portion uncolored, tint second portion pink with food coloring and add remaining ingredients to third portion. Pour each portion into greased pan and bake in moderate oven (350°F.) 30 to 35 minutes. When cool put layers together with jelly or icing, with dark layer on bottom, uncolored in center and pink on top. Makes 3 (9-inch) layers.

Omit molasses, spices, fruits and nuts and add 1 ounce (square) chocolate, melted, to third layer.

NUT LOAF CAKE

1½ cups sifted cake flour
2 teaspoons baking powder
¼ teaspoon salt
½ cup shortening
1 cup sugar
2 eggs, separated
1 teaspoon vanilla
½ cup milk
1 cup chopped nut meats

Sift flour, baking powder and salt together. Cream shortening with sugar until fluffy. Add egg yolks and vanilla and beat thoroughly. Add sifted dry ingredients and milk alternately in small amounts, beating well after each addition. Add nuts and fold in stiffly beaten egg whites. Pour into greased pan and bake in moderate oven (350°F.) 50 minutes. Makes 1 (8x4x3 inch) loaf.

SEVEN LAYER CAKE

7 eggs, separated
1 cup confectioners' sugar
1 cup sifted cake flour
¼ teaspoon salt
½ pound sweet chocolate
3 tablespoons cold water
3 eggs
1½ cups sugar
½ pound butter
1 teaspoon vanilla

Beat egg yolks until thick and lemon colored. Add sugar gradually, beating constantly. Sift flour and salt together and fold into yolk mixture. Beat egg whites until stiff enough to hold a peak and fold in lightly. Line 7 layer cake pans with paper and grease the paper. Divide batter evenly among pans and bake in moderate oven (350°F.) for 12 minutes. Remove from pans at once. Heat chocolate and water in top of double boiler. Mix eggs and sugar thoroughly, combine with melted chocolate and cook until thick, stirring constantly. Remove from heat; add butter and beat until well blended. Add vanilla and continue beating until filling is stiff enough to spread. Cover each layer and top and sides of cake with filling. It may be necessary to place several toothpicks through top layers to hold them in place until filling sets. Serve after 24 hours. Serves 14 to 16.

CHOCOLATE CHIP LAYER CAKE

8 ounces (squares) semi-sweet
   chocolate
2¼ cups sifted cake flour
2¼ teaspoons baking powder
½ teaspoon salt
½ cup shortening
1 cup sugar
3 egg whites, ¾ cup milk
1½ teaspoons vanilla

Cut each small square of chocolate into 4 to 6 pieces. Sift flour, baking powder and salt together. Cream shortening with sugar until fluffy. Add unbeaten egg whites, one at a time, beating thoroughly after each is added. Add dry ingredients and milk alternately in small amounts, beating well after each addition. Add vanilla. Line cake pans with paper and grease the paper. Pour about 1/6 of batter into each pan. Sprinkle 1/6 of chopped chocolate over each. Repeat, ending with chocolate. Bake in 350°F. oven 30 minutes. Makes 2 (9-inch) cakes.

CUPCAKES—Add cut chocolate to cake batter with vanilla. Bake in cupcake pans as above.

1-2-3-4 CAKF

3 cups sifted cake flour
3 teaspoons baking powder
¼ teaspoon salt
1 cup shortening
2 cups sugar
1 teaspoon vanilla
4 eggs, separated
1 cup milk

Sift flour, baking powder and salt together. Cream shortening with sugar and vanilla until fluffy. Add beaten egg yolks and beat thoroughly. Add sifted dry ingredients and milk alternately in small amounts, beating well after each addition. Beat egg whites until stiff but not dry and fold into batter. Pour into greased pans and bake in moderate oven (375°F.) about 30 minutes. Makes 3 (9-inch) layers.

COCONUT CAKE—Spread Lemon or Orange Filling between layers. Cover top and sides of cake with Seven-minute Icing and sprinkle generously with coconut.

Pile shredded coconut on thick and watch the eyes of your family light up

CIRCUS BIRTHDAY CAKE—Spread Orange Marmalade Filling between layers. Cover top and sides of cake with Marshmallow Seven-minute Icing. Arrange a circle of animal crackers upright on top of cake and another circle around bottom of cake. Place tiny candles on top of cake.

MARYLAND BLACK WALNUT CAKE

2 cups sifted flour
2¾ teaspoons baking powder
¼ teaspoon salt
⅔ cup shortening
1½ cups sugar
1 teaspoon vanilla
3 eggs, separated
¾ cup milk
1½ cups ground black walnuts

Sift flour, baking powder and salt together. Cream shortening with sugar and vanilla until fluffy. Add beaten egg yolks and beat thoroughly. Add sifted dry ingredients and milk alternately in small amounts, beating well after each addition. Add nuts and fold in stiffly beaten egg whites. Pour into greased pans and bake in moderate oven (350°F.) 30 minutes. Makes 2 (9-inch) layers.

SPICE CAKES

BAKED MERINGUE SPICE CAKE

2 cups sifted cake flour
3 teaspoons baking powder
¼ teaspoon salt
1 teaspoon cinnamon
½ teaspoon cloves
½ cup shortening
1 cup brown sugar
1 egg, 2 egg yolks
¾ cup milk

Sift flour, baking powder, salt and spices together 3 times. Cream shortening with sugar until fluffy. Add beaten egg and egg yolks and beat thoroughly. Add sifted dry ingredients alternately with milk in small amounts, beating well after each addition. Pour into greased cake pan, spread with meringue and bake.

MERINGUE

2 egg whites
1 cup brown sugar
½ cup broken nut meats

Beat egg whites until stiff but not dry. Beat in brown sugar gradually until mixture stands in peaks. Spread over cake, sprinkle with nuts and bake at (350°F.) 45 to 50 minutes, or until cake tests done. One (7x11-inch) cake.

SPICE CAKE

2 cups sifted flour
¼ teaspoon salt
1 teaspoon baking soda
2 teaspoons cinnamon
1 teaspoon cloves
½ teaspoon nutmeg
½ cup shortening
2 cups brown sugar
3 eggs, separated
1 cup thick sour cream

Sift flour, salt, soda and spices together 3 times. Cream shortening with sugar until fluffy. Add beaten egg yolks and beat thoroughly. Add sifted dry ingredients and cream alternately in small amounts beating well after each addition. Beat egg whites until stiff but not dry and fold into batter. Pour into greased pan and bake in moderate oven (350°F.) 40 to 50 minutes. Makes 1 (9x9 inch) cake.

Bake batter in 2 (8-inch) layers at 350°F., 30 minutes. When cold, spread with ½ recipe Fig Filling and frost with Seven-minute Icing.

For a party on short notice nothing equals the baked meringue spice cake

APPLESAUCE CAKE

1¾ cups sifted flour
1 teaspoon baking soda
½ teaspoon salt
1½ teaspoons cinnamon
1 teaspoon allspice
1 teaspoon nutmeg
¼ teaspoon cloves
½ cup shortening
1 cup sugar
1 egg, beaten
1 cup unsweetened Applesauce

Sift flour, soda, salt and spices together 3 times. Cream shortening with sugar until fluffy. Add egg and beat thoroughly. Add sifted dry ingredients and applesauce alternately in small amounts, beating well after each addition. Pour into greased pan and bake in moderate oven (350° F.) 45 to 50 minutes. Makes 1 (8x8 inch) cake. Frost with Caramel Fudge Icing.

Omit cinnamon and cloves, reduce allspice and nutmeg to ½ teaspoon each. Add 1 cup seedless raisins.

Omit allspice and cloves, reduce cinnamon to 1 teaspoon and nutmeg to ½ teaspoon. Add 1 cup chopped raisins and ½ cup chopped nut meats.

*Old favorites in any family
are these ginger cupcakes*

TREASURE CHEST CAKE

1 cup seedless raisins
1 orange rind and pulp
1 cup chopped walnut meats
2 cups sifted flour
1 teaspoon baking powder
1 teaspoon baking soda
1 teaspoon salt
1 teaspoon mixture of cloves,
    allspice and cinnamon
½ cup shortening
1 cup sugar
1 egg, well beaten
1 teaspoon vanilla
1 cup sour milk or buttermilk
Confectioners' sugar

Grind raisins, orange and walnuts together. Sift flour, baking powder, soda, salt and spices together 3 times. Cream shortening with sugar until fluffy. Add egg and vanilla and beat thoroughly. Add dry ingredients and milk alternately in small amounts, beating well after each addition. Add ½ of the fruit mixture. Blend thoroughly. Pour into greased pan and bake in moderate oven (350°F.) 45 to 60 minutes. Combine remainder of fruit with enough confectioners' sugar to make mixture thick enough to spread. Spread on cooled cake. Makes 1 (9½x5½-inch) loaf.

BANANA SPICE CAKE

2¾ cups sifted flour
2 teaspoons baking powder
1 teaspoon baking soda
1 teaspoon salt
¼ teaspoon cloves
1½ teaspoons cinnamon
¾ teaspoon nutmeg
⅔ cup shortening
1⅓ cups sugar
2 eggs, well beaten
1⅔ cups mashed bananas
    (4 to 5 bananas)
2 teaspoons vanilla

Sift flour, baking powder, soda, salt and spices together 3 times. Cream shortening with sugar until fluffy. Add eggs and beat thoroughly. Add sifted dry ingredients and bananas alternately in small amounts, beating well after each addition. Stir in vanilla. Pour into greased pans and bake in moderate oven (350°F.) 35 to 40 minutes. Makes 2 (9-inch) layers.

GINGER CUPCAKES

⅔ cup molasses
½ cup sugar
½ cup shortening
1 teaspoon ginger
1 teaspoon cinnamon
1 teaspoon baking soda
2 cups sifted flour
1 cup sour milk
2 eggs, beaten

Heat first 5 ingredients to boiling, stirring constantly. Cool to lukewarm. Sift soda and flour together and add alternately with milk and eggs, beating thoroughly after each addition. Pour into greased muffin pans and bake in moderate oven (350°F.) 15 minutes. Makes 16 cupcakes.

GINGER COCONUT — Frost cakes with Seven-minute Icing and cover with shredded coconut.

SPICED PRUNE LOAF CAKE

1 cup cooked prunes
2 cups sifted flour
2 teaspoons baking powder
½ teaspoon baking soda
½ teaspoon salt
1 teaspoon cinnamon
1 teaspoon nutmeg
½ teaspoon cloves
½ cup shortening
1 cup sugar
2 eggs, well beaten
½ cup cold strong coffee
½ cup coarsely chopped walnuts

Pit prunes and cut into very small pieces. Sift flour, baking powder, soda, salt and spices together 3 times. Cream shortening with sugar until fluffy. Add eggs and beat thoroughly. Add sifted dry ingredients and coffee alternately in small amounts, beating well after each addition. Fold in prunes and nuts. Pour into greased cake pan and bake in moderate oven (350°F.) 35 to 40 minutes. Frost with Mocha Butter Frosting. Makes 1 (7x11-inch) cake.

Omit baking powder, coffee and nut meats. Use 1 cup sour milk and increase soda to ¾ teaspoon.

Spice marble cake cut into squares shows the pattern

SPICE MARBLE CAKE

2 cups sifted cake flour
2 teaspoons baking powder
¼ teaspoon salt
½ cup shortening
1 cup sugar
2 eggs, well beaten
⅔ cup milk
1 teaspoon cinnamon
½ teaspoon cloves
½ teaspoon nutmeg
2 tablespoons molasses

Sift flour with baking powder and salt. Cream shortening and sugar until fluffy. Add eggs and beat thoroughly. Add sifted dry ingredients and milk alternately in small amounts, beating well after each addition. Divide batter into 2 parts. To one part, add spices and molasses. Drop by table-spoons into greased pan, alternating light and dark mixtures. Bake in moderate oven (350°F.) 40 to 50 minutes or until cake tests done. Spread Butter Frosting on top and sides of cake. Makes 1 (8x8-inch) cake.

Pour batter into fluted paper baking cups and bake 25 minutes. Cool and frost.

COFFEE SPICE CAKE

2½ cups sifted cake flour
3 teaspoons baking powder
¼ teaspoon baking soda
¼ teaspoon salt
¼ teaspoon ginger
1½ teaspoons cinnamon
¼ teaspoon cloves
¼ teaspoon nutmeg
¾ cup shortening
1½ cups brown sugar
¼ cup molasses
3 eggs, well beaten
¾ cup cold strong coffee

Sift flour, baking powder, soda, salt and spices together 3 times. Cream shortening with sugar until fluffy. Add molasses and eggs and beat thoroughly. Add dry ingredients and coffee alternately in small amounts, beating well after each addition. Pour into greased pans and bake at (350° F.) 35 to 40 minutes. Frost with Mocha Butter Frosting and place candles on top of frosting. Makes 2 (9-inch) layers.

Bake in cupcake pans 20 to 25 minutes. Cool and frost with Caramel Icing. Sprinkle with coconut or chopped nuts.

GUMDROP CAKE

3 cups sifted cake flour
1 teaspoon baking soda
1 teaspoon salt
1 teaspoon cinnamon
1 cup shortening
1 cup brown sugar
2 eggs, well beaten
1 cup sweetened Applesauce
2 cups seedless raisins
1 pound gumdrops (assorted, but no black ones), cut into pieces with scissors

Sift flour, soda, salt and cinnamon together 3 times. Cream shortening with sugar until fluffy. Add eggs and beat thoroughly. Add 1 cup dry ingredients and blend; add applesauce, raisins and remaining dry ingredients; mix thoroughly. Mix in gumdrops. Turn into tube pan lined with greased paper. Bake in slow oven (300° F.) 2 hours. Makes 1 (9-inch) cake.

TOMATO SOUP CAKE

2 cups sifted flour
1 teaspoon baking soda
2 teaspoons baking powder
1 teaspoon cinnamon
½ teaspoon cloves
1 teaspoon nutmeg
½ cup shortening
1 cup sugar
1 cup condensed tomato soup
1 cup chopped walnut meats
1 cup raisins

Sift flour, soda, baking powder and spices together 3 times. Cream shortening with sugar until fluffy. Add sifted dry ingredients and tomato soup alternately in small amounts, beating thoroughly after each addition. Stir in nuts and raisins. Pour into 8-inch greased tube pan or loaf pan and bake in moderate oven (350°F.) 50 to 60 minutes. Let stand 24 hours before cutting. Cover with Cream Cheese Frosting. Makes 1 (9x9-inch) cake.

ANGEL FOOD CAKE

1 cup sifted cake flour
1¼ cups sugar
1 cup egg whites (8 to 10 eggs)
1 teaspoon cream of tartar
½ teaspoon salt
¾ teaspoon vanilla
¼ teaspoon almond extract

Sift flour and ¼ cup sugar together 4 times. Beat egg whites, cream of tartar and salt until frothy throughout. Add remaining sugar in small amounts and beat after each addition, preferably with a rotary beater. Egg whites should have fine, even texture and be stiff enough to hold a peak but not dry. Add flavorings. Sift ¼ of flour at a time over mixture and fold in lightly. Pour into large ungreased tube pan; cut through batter with spatula to remove large air bubbles. Bake in moderate oven (350°F.) 45 to 60 minutes. Invert pan and let cake hang until cool. Makes 1 (9-inch) cake.

DREAM CAKE

10 eggs, separated
½ teaspoon cream of tartar
Dash salt
1 tablespoon water or lemon
  juice
1 cup sugar
¾ cup sifted cake flour

Beat egg whites until frothy, then add cream of tartar and beat until stiff. Beat egg yolks and salt until very thick and lemon colored, add water, beat in and add sugar gradually, beating until thick enough to hold a soft peak. Fold egg whites and flour into egg yolk mixture. Pour into ungreased tube pan and bake in moderate oven (350°F.) about 40 minutes. Invert pan and let cake hang in pan until cool. Makes 1 (9-inch) cake.

CHOCOLATE ANGEL FOOD CAKE

¾ cup sifted cake flour
4 tablespoons cocoa
1¼ cups egg whites
¼ teaspoon salt
1 teaspoon cream of tartar
1¼ cups sifted sugar
1 teaspoon vanilla

METHOD 1. Sift flour and cocoa together 4 times. Beat egg whites and salt until foamy throughout, add cream of tartar and continue beating until stiff enough to hold a peak but not dry. Fold in sugar lightly, 2 tablespoons at a time, until all is used. Fold in vanilla. Sift small amounts of flour over mixture and fold in quickly but lightly; continue until all is used. Pour batter into ungreased tube pan and cut through batter with spatula to remove large air bubbles. Bake in 350°F. oven 50 to 70 minutes. Invert pan and let cake hang in pan until cool. Makes 1 (10-inch) cake.

METHOD 2. Sift flour, cocoa and sugar together 6 times. Beat egg whites until foamy throughout, add salt and cream of tartar and continue beating until eggs are stiff enough to hold a peak but not dry. Fold in vanilla. Sift 2 to 3 tablespoons dry ingredients at a time over egg whites and fold in lightly until all is used. Bake as above.

MERINGUE ANGEL FOOD CAKE

1½ cups sugar
½ cup water
1¼ cups egg whites
1 teaspoon cream of tartar
¼ teaspoon salt
1 teaspoon vanilla
¼ teaspoon almond extract
1 cup sifted cake flour

Cook sugar and water to 242°F. or until sirup spins a long thread. Beat egg whites until frothy throughout. Add cream of tartar with salt and continue beating until egg whites hold a peak. Pour sirup slowly over beaten egg whites and continue beating until mixture is cold. Add flavoring. Fold in flour. Cut through batter with spatula to remove large air bubbles. Bake in ungreased tube pan in moderate oven (350°F.) 45 minutes. Invert pan and let cake hang in pan until cool. Makes 1 (10-inch) cake.

The snowy white angel food needs no frosting to proclaim its glory

Grandmother's spongecake is a perennial favorite

YOLK SPONGECAKE

3 cups sifted flour
3 teaspoons baking powder
1 teaspoon salt
2 teaspoons lemon extract
12 egg yolks (about 1 cup)
2 cups sugar
1 cup hot water

Sift flour and baking powder together 4 times. Add salt and flavoring to yolks and beat with rotary beater until very thick. Add sugar and hot water alternately in 4 portions, beating until very thick after each addition. Fold in about ¼ of flour mixture at a time. Pour into ungreased tube pan and bake in moderate oven (350°F.) 1 hour. Invert pan and let cake hang in pan until cool. Makes 1 (10-inch) cake.

BANANA YOLK — Reduce lemon extract to 1 teaspoon and use 1½ cups mashed bananas instead of water.

MERINGUE SPONGECAKE

½ cup water
1¼ cups sugar
6 eggs, separated
1 teaspoon cream of tartar
1 tablespoon lemon juice
1⅛ cups sifted cake flour
¼ teaspoon salt

Boil water and sugar together to 238°F. or until a small amount of the sirup forms a soft ball when dropped into cold water. Beat egg whites until stiff but not dry, pour sirup slowly over whites, add cream of tartar and beat until cool. Add juice. Fold stiffly beaten egg yolks into sirup mixture. Fold in flour sifted with salt. Bake in ungreased pan in moderate oven (350°F.) 45 minutes. Invert pan and let cake hang in pan until cool. Makes 1 (9-inch) cake.

Split cake crosswise into halves. Fill with Bavarian cream, replace top and spread entire cake with whipped cream. Serve cold.

ORANGE SPONGECAKE

2 cups sifted cake flour
2 teaspoons baking powder
¼ teaspoon salt
5 egg yolks
1⅞ cups sugar
½ cup water
1 tablespoon grated orange rind
½ cup orange juice
4 egg whites

Sift flour, baking powder and salt together 4 times. Beat egg yolks, add sugar gradually and beat until thick enough to hold a soft peak. Add water gradually and beat very thoroughly. Combine orange rind and juice. Fold in sifted dry ingredients and orange juice alternately in small amounts. Beat egg whites until stiff but not dry and fold in. Pour into ungreased tube pan, cut through batter with spatula to remove large air bubbles and bake in moderate oven (350°F.) 50 to 60 minutes. Invert pan and let cake hang in pan until cool. Makes 1 (10-inch) cake. Frost with Orange Butter Frosting.

TRUE SPONGECAKE

1 cup sifted cake flour
¼ teaspoon salt
Grated rind ½ lemon
1½ tablespoons lemon juice
5 eggs, separated
1 cup sugar

Sift flour and salt together 4 times. Add lemon rind and juice to beaten yolks and beat until very thick. Beat egg whites until stiff but not dry and fold in sugar in small amounts. Fold in egg yolks. Sift about ¼ of flour at a time over surface and fold in. Bake in ungreased tube pan in moderate oven (350°F.) 1 hour. Invert pan and let cake hang in pan until cool. Makes 1 (9-inch) cake.

HOT WATER SPONGECAKE

1 cup sifted cake flour
1½ teaspoons baking powder
¼ teaspoon salt
2 eggs
1 cup sugar
½ tablespoon lemon juice
6 tablespoons hot water

Sift flour, baking powder and salt together. Beat eggs until very thick and light, about 10 minutes. Add sugar gradually, beating constantly until thick enough to hold a soft peak. Beat in lemon juice. Add hot water, 2 tablespoons at a time, and beat until very thick after each addition. Fold in flour in small amounts. Bake in ungreased tube pan in moderate oven (350°F.) 45 minutes. Invert pan and let cake hang in pan until cool.

Pour batter into lightly greased pans and bake in moderate oven (350°F.) 25 to 30 minutes. Makes 2 (8-inch) layers.

MOCHA CAKE

1½ cups eggs (whole)
1¼ cups sugar
½ teaspoon vanilla
¼ teaspoon almond extract
2 cups sifted cake flour
¼ cup butter, melted

Heat eggs and sugar over hot water, beating constantly with a rotary beater until very light and fluffy, about 10 minutes. Keep water hot, but never allow it to boil. Remove from heat, beat until cold; add vanilla and almond extract and fold in flour gradually. Add melted butter, mix well. Pour cake into greased pans and bake in slow oven (325°F.) about 30 minutes. Cool thoroughly and spread Mocha Butter Frosting between layers, on top and sides. Makes 3 (9-inch) layers.

SUNSHINE CAKE

1 cup sifted cake flour
1 cup sifted sugar
¼ teaspoon salt
6 egg whites
½ teaspoon cream of tartar
4 egg yolks
½ teaspoon lemon extract

Sift flour and ½ cup of sugar together 4 times. Add salt to egg whites and beat until foamy. Add cream of tartar and continue beating until foamy throughout. Add remaining sugar, 1 tablespoon at a time and beat well after each addition. Continue beating until air bubbles are very fine and even and egg whites are stiff enough to hold up in peaks but not dry. Beat egg yolks until stiff enough to hold a soft peak and fold into egg whites. Add lemon extract. Sift small amounts of flour over mixture and fold in carefully; continue until all is used. Pour into ungreased tube pan, cut through batter with spatula to remove large air bubbles and bake in moderate oven (350° F.) 45 to 60 minutes. Invert pan and let cake hang in pan until cool. Makes 1 (9-inch) cake.

MOSS ROSE CAKE

2 cups sifted cake flour
½ teaspoon salt
2 teaspoons baking powder
4 eggs
2 cups sugar
½ teaspoon almond extract
1 cup hot milk

Sift flour, salt and baking powder together 3 times. Beat eggs, add sugar gradually and beat until thick enough to hold a soft peak. Add flavoring. Fold in flour mixture in small amounts and add hot milk gradually, mixing quickly until batter is smooth. Turn into lightly greased cake pans. Bake in moderate oven (350°F.) 30 minutes. Makes 3 (8-inch) layers.

BOSTON CREAM PIE

Use recipe for One-Egg Cake or Hot Water Spongecake and bake in 2 layers, spread Cream Filling between layers, sift confectioners' sugar over top and cut into wedges.

Boston's cream pie has conquered the rest of us

PINEAPPLE FEATHER CAKE

1½ cups sifted cake flour
1 teaspoon baking powder
6 eggs, separated
¼ teaspoon salt
1½ cups sugar
½ cup pineapple juice
1 tablespoon lemon juice

Sift flour and baking powder together 4 times. Beat egg whites and salt until stiff but not dry. Add ¾ cup sugar, about 2 tablespoons at a time, beating well after each addition. Beat egg yolks, add remaining sugar and fruit juices and beat until thick enough to hold a soft peak. Fold flour, about ¼ of it at a time, into yolk mixture, folding just enough to moisten flour. Fold in egg white mixture. Pour into ungreased tube pan. Cut through batter with spatula to remove large air bubbles. Bake in slow over (325°F.) 50 to 60 minutes. Invert pan and let cake hang in pan until cool. Makes 1 (9-inch) cake.

FEATHER WHIPPED CREAM CAKE

1½ cups sifted cake flour
1 cup sugar
3 teaspoons baking powder
½ teaspoon salt
½ cup (about 4) egg whites
1 cup heavy cream
1 teaspoon vanilla

Sift dry ingredients together 3 times. Beat egg whites until stiff but not dry. Beat cream until stiff and fold into whites with vanilla. Fold sifted dry ingredients gradually into whipped cream mixture. Do not beat or stir. The batter will be smooth if dry ingredients are folded in gradually. Pour into greased tube pan lined with greased paper and bake in moderate oven (350°F.) 45 to 55 minutes. Makes 1 (9-inch) cake.

The chocolate roll is a delicious party cake

CHOCOLATE SPONGECAKE

¾ cup sifted cake flour
¼ teaspoon salt
4 tablespoons cocoa
1 tablespoon lemon juice
5 eggs, separated
1 cup sifted sugar

Sift flour, salt and cocoa together 4 times. Add lemon juice to beaten egg yolks and beat with rotary egg beater until thick enough to hold a soft peak. Beat egg whites until stiff but not dry. Fold in sugar in small amounts, then fold in egg yolks. Fold in flour mixture in small amounts. Pour into ungreased tube pan, cut through batter with spatula to remove large air bubbles and bake in moderate oven (350°F.) 45 to 60 minutes. Invert pan and let cake hang in pan until cool. Makes 1 (9-inch) cake.

CHOCOLATE CREAM ROLL—Pour batter into large shallow pan lined with paper and bake 15 minutes. Turn out onto towel, cut off crusts, roll and cool. Unroll and spread with sweetened whipped cream, Seven-minute Icing or ice cream. Reroll, chill and slice.

ICE CREAM ROLL—Proceed as for Chocolate Cream Roll; chill thoroughly. Spread with any flavored ice cream (softened enough to spread), roll, slice and place slices in refrigerator tray until served.

DAFFODIL CAKE

¾ cup sifted cake flour
¾ cup egg whites
¼ teaspoon salt
¾ teaspoon cream of tartar
1 cup sifted sugar
¼ teaspoon vanilla
¼ teaspoon grated orange rind
3 egg yolks, well beaten
1½ tablespoons sugar

Sift flour 4 times. Beat egg whites and salt until foamy, add cream of tartar; continue beating until stiff but not dry. Fold in 1 cup sugar carefully, 2 tablespoons at a time. Sift flour over mixture in small amounts, folding carefully. Divide into 2 parts and add vanilla to one. Into other, fold orange rind and egg yolks beaten until very thick with additional 1½ tablespoons sugar. Drop by tablespoons into ungreased tube pan, alternating mixtures. Fill pan only ½ full. Bake in moderate oven (350°F.) 45 to 60 minutes. Invert pan and let cake hang in pan until cool. Makes 1 (9-inch) cake.

ROLLED CAKE

5 eggs
⅔ cup sugar
¼ teaspoon salt
½ cup sifted cake flour
3 tablespoons melted butter
1 teaspoon vanilla
1 cup jelly or jam, slightly beaten

Combine eggs and sugar and beat only until blended. Place over hot water and heat until mixture is slightly hot (140°F.). Remove from heat and beat until mixture holds a soft peak. Combine salt and flour and fold into egg mixture. Fold in butter, a tablespoon at a time. Blend in vanilla. Pour into large (10x15 inch) pan lined with paper. Bake in moderate oven (350°F.) 15 to 20 minutes. Turn quickly onto towel sprinkled with confectioners' sugar, remove paper and trim off crusts. Spread quickly with jelly, roll and cool; or roll cake while hot and when cold unroll, spread with jelly and roll. Just before serving sprinkle cake with confectioners' sugar. Makes 1 roll.

Rolled cake may be served almost any way one chooses

JELLY ROLL

5 eggs, separated
1 cup sugar
1 tablespoon grated lemon rind
2 tablespoons lemon juice
1 cup sifted cake flour
¼ teaspoon salt
Confectioners' sugar
1 cup jelly or jam

Beat egg whites until stiff but not dry. Add ½ the sugar slowly, beating constantly. Beat egg yolks until thick and lemon colored; add remaining sugar gradually, continuing to beat until stiff enough to hold a soft peak; add grated lemon rind and juice. Fold gently into egg whites. Combine flour and salt and fold quickly but lightly into egg mixture. Line large shallow (11x16 inch) pan with paper, pour in batter and bake in moderate oven (350°F.) 15 minutes, being careful not to overbake it. Turn onto a clean towel well sprinkled with confectioners' sugar. Remove paper and trim off crusts. Roll, lifting end of towel nearest you. Wrap in towel and cool. Unroll, spread with whipped jelly and roll again. Serves 8.

LEMON ROLL — Spread roll with Lemon Filling instead of jelly.

MARSHMALLOW CHOCOLATE
ROLL — Spread roll with Marshmallow Seven-minute Icing instead of jelly and roll. Coat with mixture of 1 teaspoon melted butter and 1 ounce (square) chocolate, melted.

FIG ROLL

2 cups sifted flour
1½ teaspoons baking powder
¾ teaspoon salt
6 eggs, separated
1 cup sugar
4 tablespoons cold water
1 teaspoon vanilla

Sift flour, baking powder and salt together 4 times. Beat egg yolks very thoroughly, add sugar and beat until thick enough to hold a soft peak. Add water and flavoring and fold in sifted dry ingredients in small amounts. Beat egg whites until stiff but not dry and fold into batter. Pour into shallow (16½x13½ inch) pan lined with paper and bake in moderate oven (350°F.) 12 to 15 minutes. Turn out onto towel, cut off crusts, roll and cool. Unroll, spread with Fig Filling and roll. Top may be spread with Vanilla Cream Frosting.

CHOCOLATE HONEY LOAF CAKE

2¾ cups sifted cake flour
2½ teaspoons baking powder
½ teaspoon baking soda
½ teaspoon salt
2 tablespoons shortening
1 cup honey
1 egg, beaten
1 tablespoon grated orange rind
¾ cup orange juice
¾ cup chopped nuts
1 (7-ounce) package semi-sweet chocolate, pieces

Sift flour, baking powder, soda and salt together. Blend shortening and honey until fluffy. Add egg and orange rind. Mix well. Add dry ingredients alternately with orange juice. Fold in nuts and ½ of chocolate. Pour into greased paper-lined loaf pan. Sprinkle remaining chocolate over top of batter. Bake in slow oven (325°F.) 70 minutes.

JAM ROLL

1 cup sifted cake flour
¼ teaspoon salt
5 eggs, 1 cup honey
1 tablespoon lemon juice
1 cup jam

Sift flour and salt together. Beat egg whites until stiff but not dry. Beat yolks until thick, add honey gradually and beat until well blended. Add lemon juice. Add flour gradually to yolk mixture. Beat 5 minutes. Fold in stiffly beaten whites. Pour about ½-inch deep in 1 or 2 small shallow oblong baking pans which have been greased on bottom only. Bake in slow over (325°F.) 20 to 30 minutes. Turn onto towel which has been sprinkled with confectioners' sugar and trim off crisp edges. Spread with jelly or jam. Roll. Wrap in oiled paper or towel until cool.

MAPLE SIRUP CUPCAKES

½ cup shortening
¼ cup maple-flavored corn sirup
¼ cup light corn sirup
2 eggs
2 cups sifted cake flour
½ cup water
4 teaspoons baking powder
½ teaspoon salt

Cream shortening; add maple and light sirups gradually, beating constantly. Beat in 1 egg at a time. Add 1 cup flour and ¼ cup water; beat well. Add remaining water and remaining flour sifted with baking powder and salt. Mix well. Turn into greased cupcake pans and bake in moderate oven (375°F.) 15 to 20 minutes. Makes 12 to 18.

Cherry preserves from your well-stocked shelves make this jelly roll another "sugar saver" (page 719)

APPLE UPSIDE-DOWN CAKE

¼ cup butter
1 cup brown sugar
2 large baking apples
½ cup seedless raisins
1½ cups sifted cake flour
½ teaspoon salt
3 teaspoons baking powder
⅓ cup shortening
⅓ cup granulated sugar
2 eggs, well beaten
½ teaspoon vanilla
⅔ cup water

Melt butter in skillet or baking pan. Add sugar and stir until melted. Cool. Peel, core and slice apples; place on sugar. Sprinkle with raisins. Sift flour, salt and baking powder together. Cream shortening with sugar until fluffy. Add eggs and vanilla and beat thoroughly. Add sifted dry ingredients and water alternately in small amounts, beating well after each addition. Pour over apples and bake in moderate oven (350°F.) 40 to 50 minutes. Turn onto plate immediately and serve with whipped cream. Makes 1 (9-inch) cake.

APPLE GINGERBREAD UPSIDE-DOWN CAKE

3 tablespoons butter
4 large tart apples
¾ cup light brown sugar
1 teaspoon cinnamon
1 cup sifted flour
½ teaspoon baking powder
½ teaspoon baking soda
¼ teaspoon salt
½ teaspoon cinnamon
½ teaspoon ginger
¼ cup shortening
¼ cup sugar, white or brown
1 egg, well beaten
½ cup molasses
½ cup sour milk

Spread softened butter over bottom of heavy (8 x 8 inch) baking pan. Pare apples and slice thin. Arrange half of apples over bottom of pan, sprinkle with half of brown sugar and cinnamon mixed together, add remaining apples and sprinkle with remaining sugar and cinnamon. Cook over low heat while preparing batter. Sift flour, baking powder, soda salt and spices together 3 times. Cream shortening with sugar until fluffy. Add egg and beat thoroughly. Add sifted dry ingredients alternately with molasses and milk, beating well after each addition. Pour gingerbread batter over apples and bake in moderate oven (350°F.) about 45 minutes. Turn out upside down. Serves 6.

PEAR — Increase butter to 4 tablespoons, use ½ cup granulated sugar instead of brown, omit cinnamon and use cooked pear halves for apples. Melt butter in pan, add sugar and stir until melted. On this arrange pears, cut side down. Pour gingerbread batter over pears and bake as above. If pears are very large it may be necessary to slice them.

Apple is the beginning but far from the end of many luscious upside-down cakes

MAPLE APPLE UPSIDE-DOWN CAKE

3 tablespoons butter
½ cup maple sirup
2 medium red apples
1½ cups sifted flour
2 teaspoons baking powder
¼ teaspoon salt
¼ cup shortening
¾ cup sugar
2 eggs, separated
½ cup milk
½ cup grated apple

Melt butter in cake pan, add maple sirup and remove from heat. Cut cored unpeeled apples into ½-inch slices and arrange in sirup mixture. Sift flour, baking powder and salt together. Cream shortening with ½ cup sugar and unbeaten egg yolks until fluffy. Add sifted dry ingredients and milk alternately in small amounts, beating well after each addition. Add apple. Beat egg whites until stiff but not dry, beat in remaining sugar and fold into batter. Spread batter over the apple and sirup mixture and bake in moderate oven (350°F.) 40 to 50 minutes. Serve warm with plain or whipped cream. Makes 1 (8x8 inch) cake.

CHERRY PECAN UPSIDE-DOWN CAKE

1 cup butter
2 cups sugar
1 cup pecan meats, chopped
2 cups pitted tart cherries, well drained
2½ cups sifted cake flour
3 teaspoons baking powder
¼ teaspoon salt
2 eggs, well beaten
⅔ cup milk
1 teaspoon vanilla
Whipped cream
Fresh cherries

Melt ⅓ cup butter in heavy skillet, add ½ cup sugar and stir until dissolved. Add nuts and cherries. Sift flour, baking powder and salt together. Cream remaining butter with remaining sugar until fluffy. Add eggs and beat thoroughly. Add sifted dry ingredients and milk alternately in small amounts, beating well after each addition. Add vanilla and pour batter over mixture in skillet. Bake in moderate oven (350°F.) 1 hour. Remove from oven and turn onto large platter. When cool, cover with whipped cream and garnish with fresh cherries. Serves 12.

Fruit leftovers take a new lease on life in this fruit mélange upside-down cake

CRANBERRY UPSIDE-DOWN CAKE

3 tablespoons butter
1½ cups sugar
2 cups cranberries
1½ cups sifted cake flour
1½ teaspoons baking powder
¼ teaspoon salt
¼ cup shortening
1 egg, beaten
½ cup milk
1 teaspoon vanilla

Melt butter and 1 cup sugar in baking pan; add cranberries. Sift flour, baking powder and salt together. Cream shortening with remaining sugar until fluffy; add egg and beat thoroughly. Add sifted dry ingredients and milk alternately in small amounts, beating well after each addition. Add vanilla. Pour batter over cranberries and bake in moderate oven (350°F.) 40 to 50 minutes. Turn upside down. If desired serve with whipped cream. Makes 1 (8x8 inch) cake.

CRANBERRY GLAZE CAKE — Omit butter and use 2½ cups cranberries. Mix 1 cup of the sugar with 1 tablespoon cornstarch, add ½ cup boiling water and cook until slightly thickened. Add cranberries, spread over bottom of pan and proceed as above.

FRUIT MÉLANGE UPSIDE-DOWN CAKE

1 cup cooked prunes or dried figs
1 cup sweetened cooked dried pears, peaches, apricots, apple rings or nectarines
½ cup raisins
½ cup fruit liquid
½ cup sugar
3 tablespoons butter, melted
3 teaspoons ginger
½ cup broken nut meats
2½ cups sifted flour
¾ teaspoon salt
1 teaspoon baking soda
2 teaspoons cinnamon
¾ cup shortening
1 cup sugar
½ cup molasses
2 eggs, well beaten
½ cup boiling water

Remove pits from prunes, or if figs are used, clip stems. Slice all cooked fruits as desired Rinse and drain raisins. Combine fruit liquid, sugar, butter and 1 teaspoon ginger in greased baking pan and blend. Cover with fruits and nuts. Sift flour, salt, soda, cinnamon and remaining ginger together 3 times. Cream shortening with sugar until fluffy. Stir in molasses, add beaten eggs and beat thoroughly. Add sifted dry ingredients and water alternately in small amounts, beating well after each addition. Pour batter evenly over fruit and bake in slow oven (300°F.) about 1½ hours. Loosen sides and turn onto platter. Serve warm with cream. Makes 1 (7x11½ inch) cake.

INDIVIDUAL CAKES — Prepare fruit and sirup as above and distribute mixture evenly into 24 greased muffin pans. Pour batter over fruit mixture and bake in moderate oven (350°F.) 25 to 30 minutes. Remove from pans immediately and serve cold. These are delicious served with or without whipped cream.

RHUBARB UPSIDE-DOWN CAKE

4 cups cut rhubarb
1 cup sugar
1 cup quartered marshmallows
1¾ cups sifted flour
2 teaspoons baking powder
⅛ teaspoon salt
½ cup shortening
1 cup sugar
2 eggs, separated
⅓ teaspoon almond extract
⅓ teaspoon vanilla
½ cup milk

Cook rhubarb over low heat until juice begins to run, add sugar and marshmallow and mix well. Simmer about 10 minutes and pour into greased cake pan. Sift flour, baking powder and salt together. Cream shortening with sugar until fluffy. Add egg yolks and flavorings and beat thoroughly. Add sifted dry ingredients and milk alternately in small amounts beating well after each addition. Beat egg whites until stiff but not dry and fold into batter. Pour over rhubarb mixture and bake in moderate oven (350°F.) 40 to 50 minutes. Loosen cake from sides and bottom with a spatula and turn out onto cake plate. If marshmallows are very fresh, do not add to rhubarb until just before cake batter is poured on. Serves 8.

HUCKLEBERRY—Heat 2 cups cooked huckleberries with 1 tablespoon butter and ½ cup brown sugar 10 minutes. Sift 1 cup flour, ¼ teaspoon salt and 1 teaspoon baking powder together. Cream ¼ cup shortening with ½ cup sugar. Add 1 beaten egg and mix thoroughly. Add sifted dry ingredients alternately with ¼ cup milk with 2 drops almond extract. Turn huckleberries into greased pan (8x8 inch) and cover with batter. Bake at 350°F., 45 minutes.

CHOCOLATE UPSIDE-DOWN CAKE

2 ounces (squares) chocolate
1⅓ cups (1 can) sweetened condensed milk
1½ cups sifted cake flour
¼ teaspoon salt
2 teaspoons baking powder
6 tablespoons shortening
1 cup sugar
2 eggs, well beaten
1 teaspoon vanilla
½ cup milk

Melt chocolate, add condensed milk and mix well. Line greased pans with paper and grease paper. Pour chocolate mixture into pans and cool. Sift flour, salt and baking powder together. Cream shortening with sugar until fluffy. Add eggs and vanilla and beat thoroughly. Add sifted dry ingredients and milk alternately in small amounts, beating thoroughly after each addition. Pour carefully over chocolate mixture and bake in moderate oven (350°F.) 35 minutes. Makes 2 (8-inch) layers.

Add ½ cup chopped nut meats to chocolate mixture. Or sprinkle ½ cup shredded coconut on top of chocolate mixture.

Pineapple slices and walnuts make a very beautiful cake

PINEAPPLE UPSIDE-DOWN CAKE

½ cup butter
1 cup brown sugar
1 No. 2 can sliced pineapple
2 tablespoons large whole pecans
1 cup sifted cake flour
1 teaspoon baking powder
⅛ teaspoon salt
3 eggs, separated
1 cup granulated sugar
5 tablespoons pineapple juice

Melt butter in large baking pan. Spread brown sugar evenly in pan and arrange pineapple slices on sugar, filling in spaces with pecans. Sift flour, baking powder and salt together. Beat egg yolks until light, adding sugar gradually; add pineapple juice and sifted flour; fold in stiffly beaten egg whites. Pour batter over pineapple. Bake in moderate oven (375°F.) 30 to 35 minutes. Turn upside down on cake plate. Serve with whipped cream if desired. Makes 1 (9 x 9 inch) cake. Serves 8.

APRICOT UPSIDE-DOWN CAKE
—Use apricots (stewed, canned or fresh) or apricots and prunes instead of pineapple.

Use canned, fresh or stewed dried peaches instead of pineapple.

Use sliced pears instead of apricots.

FILLINGS and FROSTINGS

APRICOT FILLING

2 cups dried apricots
Cold water
⅔ cup sugar
1 tablespoon lemon juice
½ teaspoon grated lemon rind

Soak apricots and cook in just enough water to cover until tender and practically dry. Beat apricots until smooth. Add sugar, lemon juice and grated lemon rind and cook until sugar has entirely dissolved. Cool. Use for 3 layers.

PRUNE — Use prunes instead of apricots. Cook prunes in the same way, pit prunes and beat pulp until smooth. Continue as above.

HEAVENLY TORTE FILLING

¼ cup sugar
1 tablespoon cornstarch
2 egg yolks, beaten
2 cups thick sour cream
1 teaspoon lemon or orange extract
½ teaspoon vanilla

Mix sugar and cornstarch together thoroughly and add to egg yolks. Stir in cream and cook over boiling water until mixture coats a spoon. Add flavoring and cool. Filling for 3 layers.

CREAM FILLING

⅓ cup sugar
3 tablespoons cornstarch
¼ teaspoon salt
2 egg yolks
2 cups milk, scalded
2 tablespoons butter
1 teaspoon vanilla

Combine sugar, cornstarch and salt very thoroughly. Add egg yolks and beat well. Add a little of the milk slowly, mix and return mixture to remaining hot milk. Cook over boiling water, stirring constantly until mixture thickens. Add butter, cool and add vanilla. If desired add ½ cup chopped nut meats. Filling for 3 layers.

DATE DELIGHT FILLING

1½ cups chopped dates
¼ cup sugar
½ cup water
1 tablespoon lemon juice

Cook dates, sugar and water together until thick. Cool and add lemon juice. Filling for 2 layers.

When the cake is cool, remove crumbs and swish filling onto the first layer

CUSTARD FILLING

3 tablespoons flour
⅓ cup sugar
⅛ teaspoon salt
1 cup milk
1 egg, beaten
½ teaspoon vanilla
1 teaspoon butter

Combine dry ingredients very thoroughly. Add milk and egg. Cook over boiling water, stirring constantly, until thickened. Add vanilla and butter. Cool. Filling for 2 layers.

BANANA — Increase sugar to ½ cup and vanilla to 1 teaspoon. Fold 2 bananas, sliced, into cooled filling.

FIG FILLING

2 cups dried figs
1 cup crushed pineapple
3 cups water
¼ teaspoon salt
2 cups sugar

Rinse figs in hot water and drain. Clip off stems and cut figs into thin strips. Combine with pineapple and water and cook about 10 minutes. Add salt and sugar and cook, stirring occasionally, until figs are tender and mixture is very thick, about 10 to 15 minutes. Cool. Filling for 3 (9-inch) layers.

LEMON FILLING

¾ cup sugar
2 tablespoons cornstarch
⅛ teaspoon salt
1 tablespoon grated lemon rind
⅓ cup lemon juice
½ cup water
1 egg, beaten
1 tablespoon butter

Mix sugar, cornstarch and salt very thoroughly. Add remaining ingredients and blend. Cook over boiling water, stirring constantly until thickened. Cool. Filling for 2 layers.

ORANGE—Reduce sugar to ½ cup. Use orange rind and juice instead of lemon and add 1 teaspoon lemon juice.

LEMON BUTTER FILLING

4 egg yolks
1 cup sugar
1 teaspoon cornstarch
2 tablespoons butter
1 teaspoon grated lemon rind
¼ cup lemon juice

Beat egg yolks. Mix sugar and cornstarch very thoroughly and add to egg yolks. Add butter, lemon rind and juice and cook over hot water, stirring frequently, until thickened, about 20 minutes. Filling for 2 layers.

ORANGE FILLING

2 tablespoons butter
¼ cup sugar
2 eggs, beaten
1 tablespoon grated orange rind
1 tablespoon lemon juice
½ cup orange juice

Combine all ingredients and mix well. Cook over very low heat, stirring constantly until well thickened, about 10 minutes. Chill well before spreading on cake. Filling for 2 layers.

ORANGE COCONUT—Add ½ cup moist coconut.

ORANGE MARMALADE FILLING

1¼ cups Orange Marmalade
1 cup chopped walnut meats

Combine and spread between layers of cake. Fills 3 layers.

SOUR CREAM FILLING

½ cup sugar
2 tablespoons flour
2 eggs, beaten
½ cup sour cream
2 tablespoons butter
½ cup nut meats, chopped

Mix sugar and flour, add eggs, cream and butter. Cook until thickened. Cool and fold in nuts. Filling for 2 layers.

MARSHMALLOW ICING

2½ cups sugar
½ cup light corn sirup
¼ teaspoon salt
½ cup water
2 egg whites
1 teaspoon vanilla
8 (¼ pound) marshmallows

Cook sugar, corn sirup, salt and water together (without stirring) to 250°F. or until a small amount dropped into cold water will form a firm ball. Pour the hot sirup slowly over stiffly beaten egg whites, beating constantly. Add vanilla and continue beating until frosting is cool and thick enough to spread. Add marshmallows, cut into eighths. Will cover tops and sides of 3 (9-inch) layers.

SWIRL ICING

Frost cooled cake with Seven-minute Icing. Dip tines of fork into 1 ounce (square) chocolate, melted; let chocolate drop from tines onto icing. With a toothpick swirl through chocolate dots.

Fit the second layer on carefully and use a clean spatula to swish the frosting on the top and sides

CARAMEL FUDGE ICING

2 cups brown sugar
1 cup granulated sugar
1 cup sour cream or sour milk
1 tablespoon butter
1 teaspoon vanilla

Combine sugars and sour cream. Cook (stirring constantly) to 238°F. or until a small amount forms a soft ball when dropped into cold water. Add butter and vanilla and cool to lukewarm without stirring. Beat until thick enough to spread. If frosting becomes too thick while spreading, beat in a few drops of hot water. Will frost 2 (9-inch) layers.

FRESH COCONUT CREAM FROSTING

1 cup heavy cream
½ teaspoon vanilla
3 tablespoons confectioners' sugar, sifted
1 cup grated fresh coconut

Whip cream until stiff. Add vanilla and fold in sugar. Spread between layers and over top of cake. Sprinkle with coconut. Will frost 2 (8-inch) layers.

BANANA FROSTING

½ cup mashed banana (1 large banana)
½ teaspoon lemon juice
¼ cup butter
1 pound (3½ cups) confectioners' sugar, sifted

Mix banana and lemon juice together. Cream butter with 1 cup sugar, then add banana and enough of remaining sugar to make mixture thick enough to spread. Will cover tops and sides of 2 (8-inch) layers.

BROWN BUTTER FROSTING

6 tablespoons butter
1½ cups confectioners' sugar, sifted
1 teaspoon vanilla
4 tablespoons cream

Heat butter until golden brown, add sugar and vanilla. Add enough cream to make frosting soft enough to spread. Will cover top and sides of 1 (9x9 inch) cake.

Let the white frosting cool before running on this luscious chocolate drip. Waxed paper under the cake catches the run-over

BUTTER FROSTING

½ cup butter
3 cups confectioners' sugar, sifted
4 tablespoons cream or evaporated milk
1 teaspoon vanilla

Cream butter. Add remaining ingredients and continue creaming until mixture is well blended and fluffy. Will cover tops and sides of 2 (8-inch) layers.

LEMON — Add ½ teaspoon grated lemon rind and use lemon juice instead of vanilla and ½ of the cream.

MOCHA — Add 3 tablespoons cocoa and use cold strong coffee instead of cream.

ORANGE — Add 1 tablespoon grated orange rind and use orange juice instead of cream.

PINEAPPLE — Use ⅓ cup crushed pineapple with juice instead of cream.

FUDGE ICING

2 cups sugar
2 tablespoons corn sirup
3 ounces (squares) chocolate
½ cup milk
1 teaspoon vanilla
2 tablespoons butter

Cook sugar, corn sirup, chocolate and milk (stirring constantly) to 232°F. or until a small amount of the sirup forms a very soft ball when dropped into cold water. Remove from heat, add vanilla and butter. Cool to lukewarm without stirring. Beat until creamy and thick enough to spread. Will cover tops and sides of 2 (8-inch) layers.

CREAMY PEANUT-BUTTER FROSTING

Cook 1 can sweetened condensed milk and 2 tablespoons peanut butter over boiling water 5 minutes or until thick, stirring until blended. Cool. Will cover top and sides of 1 (8x8 inch) cake.

Prepared fudge mix makes a quick and easy frosting

UNCOOKED CHOCO-LATE FROSTING

½ cup butter
3 ounces (squares) chocolate
¼ teaspoon salt
3 cups confectioners' sugar, sifted
5 tablespoons cream or evaporated milk
1 egg white, beaten
1 teaspoon vanilla

Heat butter and chocolate over hot water until chocolate is melted. Stir until smooth; then add salt, sugar and cream, beating until smooth and blended. Stir in beaten egg white and flavoring and beat until cool and thick enough to spread. Will frost 2 (9-inch) layers.

CHOCOLATE CREAM FROSTING

3 ounces cream cheese
¼ cup milk
3 cups sifted confectioners' sugar
⅛ teaspoon salt
1 teaspoon vanilla
3 ounces (squares) chocolate, melted

Blend cream cheese with milk. Add confectioners' sugar, salt and vanilla; beat in chocolate. Will frost 2 (8-inch) layers.

COCOA ALMOND FROSTING

6 tablespoons butter
3½ cups confectioners' sugar, sifted
½ cup cocoa
⅓ cup cream
½ teaspoon almond extract

Cream butter; sift sugar with cocoa and add alternately with cream. Beat until fluffy and thick enough to spread. Add flavoring. Will cover tops and sides of 2 (9-inch) layers.

CREAM CHEESE FROSTING

3 ounces cream cheese
1½ cups confectioners' sugar, sifted
1 teaspoon vanilla

Cream all ingredients together until fluffy. Will frost 1 (8x4 inch) cake.

CARAMEL ICING

2 cups brown sugar
1 cup granulated sugar
⅛ teaspoon baking soda
¾ cup cream
1 egg white

Combine sugars, soda and cream. Cook, stirring constantly to 238° F. or until a small amount forms a soft ball when dropped into cold water. Cool to lukewarm without stirring. Beat until creamy, add unbeaten egg white and beat until thick enough to spread. Will frost 3 (8-inch) layers.

Fluffy white icing on a white cake is beauty of the first order

FIVE-MINUTE CHOCO-LATE FROSTING

2 ounces (squares) chocolate
1⅓ cups (1 can) sweetened condensed milk

Melt chocolate over boiling water, add condensed milk and stir 5 minutes or until thickened. Thin with a few drops water if too thick. Will cover top and sides of 1 (9x9 inch) cake.

FLUFFY WHITE ICING

¾ cup sugar
¼ cup water
⅛ teaspoon cream of tartar
1 teaspoon corn sirup
2 egg whites, stiffly beaten
1 teaspoon vanilla

Heat· first 4 ingredients slowly to boiling and cook (without stirring) to 242°F. or until a small amount dropped from tip of spoon spins a long thread. Pour sirup slowly onto stiffly beaten egg whites, beating constantly. Beat until cool and thick enough to spread. Add vanilla. Will frost 1 (9x9 inch) cake.

FONDANT FROSTING

2 cups sugar
⅔ cup water
⅛ teaspoon cream of tartar

Heat ingredients slowly and stir until sugar is dissolved. Cover pan and cook without stirring to 240°F. or until a small amount forms a soft ball when dropped into cold water. Pour onto a lightly greased platter or marble slab and cool until firm enough to retain a dent when pressed lightly. Fold mixture over and over with a spatula until cool enough to handle, then knead until smooth and creamy, about 15 minutes. Form into a ball, wrap in waxed paper and place in covered jar for 24 hours to ripen. Melt fondant in small amounts over hot (not boiling) water, flavor and color very delicately.

CHOCOLATE—Add 2 ounces (squares) chocolate, melted, to fondant when kneading.

COFFEE—Use strong coffee instead of water.

PEPPERMINT FROSTING

¼ cup crushed peppermint stick candy
½ cup milk
1 pound confectioners' sugar, sifted

Heat candy and milk over hot water until candy is melted. Add enough confectioners' sugar to make frosting thick enough to spread. Will cover tops and sides of 2 (8-inch) layers.

ORNAMENTAL ICING

2 cups sugar
1 cup water
3 egg whites
¼ teaspoon cream of tartar
½ teaspoon vanilla

Boil sugar and water (without stirring) to 242°F. or until a small amount dropped from tip of spoon spins a thread. Beat egg whites until stiff but not dry and pour on hot sirup in a thin stream, while beating constantly. Add cream of tartar and vanilla and beat until thick enough to spread. Cover cake smoothly with part of icing and beat remaining icing until cool and stiff enough to hold shape when forced through pastry tube. When coating on cake has hardened decorate as desired with remaining icing forced through pastry tube. If icing becomes too thick to spread smoothly, add a few drops of hot water.

QUICK ICING — Beat 3 egg whites until foamy, add confectioners' sugar gradually and beat until thickened. Add ¼ teaspoon cream tartar and 1 teaspoon vanilla. When thick enough to spread, cover top and sides of cake. To remainder, add more sugar until thick enough to hold shape when forced through pastry tube.

COFFEE-SCOTCH ICING

1 cup granulated sugar
½ cup brown sugar
⅔ cup double-strength coffee
1 tablespoon light corn sirup
2 egg whites

Cook sugars, coffee and corn sirup (without stirring) to 240°F. or until a small amount dropped from tip of spoon spins a long thread. Beat egg whites until stiff but not dry, pour sirup slowly into egg whites, beating constantly. Continue beating until thick enough to spread. Will frost 2 (9-inch) layers.

PEANUT-BUTTER FROSTING

2 tablespoons butter
¼ cup peanut butter
3½ cups confectioners' sugar, sifted
About 6 tablespoons milk

Blend butter and peanut butter together. Sift in confectioners' sugar and add enough milk to make frosting soft enough to spread. Will cover tops and sides of 2 (8-inch) layers. Decorate top with pitted dates.

Cake sticks are fun for any party or picnic

PARTY CAKE STICKS

Bake Sponge or Angel Cake in a tube pan according to directions. When cake is cold, cut into wedges, force a wooden skewer into broad end and cover entire piece with Divinity Icing.

BUTTERSCOTCH ICING

1 cup brown sugar
2 tablespoons butter
¼ cup milk
1 tablespoon light corn sirup
¼ cup shortening
¼ teaspoon salt
2 cups sifted confectioners' sugar
3 tablespoons hot milk

Cook first 4 ingredients to 250°F. or until a small amount of the sirup forms a hard ball when dropped into cold water. Stir constantly after mixture begins to boil. Remove from heat. Combine shortening and salt and add sugar gradually, creaming well. Add hot milk, then add hot butterscotch mixture gradually and beat until smooth and thick enough to spread. Will frost 1 (10x10 inch) cake or 2 (8-inch) layers.

DIVINITY ICING

1½ cups sugar
6 tablespoons water
⅛ teaspoon cream of tartar
2 egg whites, stiffly beaten
1 teaspoon vanilla

Combine sugar, water and cream of tartar. Cook sirup (without stirring) to 238°F. or until a small amount forms a soft ball when dropped into cold water. Pour ⅓ of the sirup in a fine stream over stiffly beaten egg whites while beating constantly. Cook remainder of sirup to 248° F. or until a small amount forms a firm ball when dropped into cold water. Remove from heat and pour ½ of the remaining sirup in a fine stream into the mixture while beating constantly Cook remaining sirup to 268° F or the hard-ball stage. Remove from heat and pour the last of the sirup in a fine stream into the icing, beating thoroughly. Add flavoring and beat mixture until thick enough to spread. Will cover tops and sides of 2 (9-inch) layers.

LADY BALTIMORE FILLING—
Double the recipe. Divide the icing into halves. To ½ add: 1 cup chopped seeded raisins, 1½ cups chopped nut meats, 1 cup chopped figs and ½ teaspoon lemon extract. Mix carefully and spread between layers of Lady Baltimore Cake. Spread remaining icing over top and sides of cake. Sprinkle top with additional chopped figs, nuts and raisins if desired. Will cover 3 (9-inch) layers

LORD BALTIMORE FILLING—
Double the recipe and divide icing into halves. To half add ½ cup dry macaroon crumbs, ¼ cup chopped pecan meats, ¼ teaspoon orange extract, ¼ cup chopped blanched almonds, 12 candied cherries (cut into quarters) and 2 teaspoons lemon juice. Mix carefully and spread between layers of Lord Baltimore Cake. Spread remaining icing over top and sides of cake.

These funny little figures will be welcome at any party

SEVEN-MINUTE ICING

1½ cups sugar
⅓ cup water
2 egg whites
¼ teaspoon cream of tartar
¼ teaspoon salt
1 teaspoon vanilla

Combine all ingredients, except vanilla, in top of double boiler. Beat with a rotary beater until thoroughly mixed. Place over rapidly boiling water and beat constantly for 7 to 10 minutes or until icing will hold a peak. Remove from heat and add vanilla. Beat until cool and thick enough to spread. Will cover tops and sides of 2 (9-inch) layers.
Omit cream of tartar and use 1½ teaspoons corn sirup.
MARSHMALLOW—Add 16 (½ pound) marshmallows, cut into quarters, to hot cooked icing; beating until smooth.
ORANGE MARSHMALLOW — Use grated orange rind instead of vanilla in Marshmallow Seven-minute Icing.
MINT—While hot add ½ cup crushed after-dinner mints and enough green vegetable coloring to tint icing a very delicate green.

VANILLA CREAM FROSTING

3 tablespoons butter
1 teaspoon vanilla
¼ teaspoon salt
3 cups sifted confectioners' sugar
5 tablespoons scalded cream (about)

Blend butter, vanilla and salt; add ½ cup confectioners' sugar. Add hot cream and remaining sugar alternately in small amounts beating well after each addition. Add only enough cream to make frosting soft enough to spread. Will cover top and sides of 1 (10x10 inch) cake.

Cookies

300 Recipes
for
Delightful
Cookies

IT'S FUN TO MAKE COOKIES

Grandmother's cookie jar has come back to stay but now it is apt to be filled with many delectable dainties which would probably have amazed that estimable lady.

THE PERFECT COOKIE—Should have good flavor, tender crumb unless the variety is a hard cookie, soft or crisp texture depending upon variety of cookie, uniform color and shape depending upon type of cookie.

TYPES—Cookies are classified in many ways—by the texture of the baked cookie (soft or crisp), the consistency of batter or dough (soft or stiff), the richness of cookies (plain or rich), or by the method used in shaping cookie.

BAR—Dough is baked in a four-sided pan and cut into bars or squares after baking.

REFRIGERATOR — Dough is pressed into a cookie mold or shaped into a thick roll or bar, chilled in refrigerator until ready to cut into thin slices with a sharp knife, then baked.

DROP—Dough is dropped from a teaspoon onto lightly greased cookie sheet.

MOLDED—Dough is shaped by hand.

PRESSED—Dough is soft enough to hold a shape.

ROLLED—Dough is rolled to desired thickness on a lightly floured surface and cut into shapes with a cookie cutter.

COOKIE WISDOM

Select pans of proper kind and size. Cookie sheets or pans should be bright and shiny. Use pans which allow at least an inch of heat circulation between pan and oven walls. (Too large a pan causes cookies to burn on bottom.) To prevent cookies from browning too much on bottom, use two pans of same size placed one on top of the other. If pans with sides are used, turn upside-down and bake cookies on bottom.

Spatulas are helpful in lifting unbaked cutout cookies onto pans, and for removing hot cookies onto cooling racks. A pastry cloth and rolling-pin stocking are helpful aids in making rolled cookies. A mixture of one part granulated sugar and two parts flour may be used to dust pastry cloth when dough proves difficult to roll out. An alarm clock or range timer is useful in cookie baking. Preheat oven and after cookies are placed in it avoid peeking as it often prevents proper browning. It is advisable to check accurately the timing of the first batch and peeking will not be necessary for subsequent batches.

A variety of cookie cutters adds interest to your cookies baking. Store cooled cookies in a covered cookie jar or canaster. Crisp cookies should not be stored with other types. If they have softened during storage, place them in a 300°F oven for a few minutes to restore their crispness.

WHAT TO USE

FLOUR—Two kinds of flour are available for home use, cake flour and all-purpose flour. Cake flour is made of soft wheat and contains less glutin than all-purpose flour which is made from a blend of hard and soft wheat flours. For these cookie recipes one flour may be used for the other. To substitute all-purpose flour for cake flour, sift it 3 times and take out 2 tablespoons for each cup used in recipe.

SUGAR—A fine granulated sugar will cream much more easily than a coarse sugar and give cookies of a finer texture. All sugar in these recipes is white granulated unless otherwise specified. Brown sugar may be substituted for white in many recipes. As it takes 1¾ cups of confectioners' sugar to be as sweet as 1 cup of granulated sugar, it is difficult to substitute one for the other in most instances. It is also difficult to substitute honey or molasses for sugar because they increase the amount of liquid in a recipe.

SHORTENING—Butter and margarine are the best shortenings for cookie making from the standpoint of flavor and texture, however, it is possible to substitute hydrogenated oils, lard, chicken or goose fat. Remember, though, that solid shortenings make a better textured cookie than the melted or liquid shortenings. When substituting margarine or hydrogenated oil for butter, use the same amount as originally called for in the recipe. If lard or other more concentrated fats are used, the amount of shortening needed is about 1/5 less.

LIQUIDS—One may use milk or water in making cookies. Milk makes a richer cookie, but cookies made with water are more moist and keep better. If cream is used in place of milk, the amount of fat in the recipe should be reduced. When evaporated milk is used in place of whole milk, add an equal amount of water.

EGGS—All of the recipes in this book were tested with eggs weighing 23 to 24 ounces a dozen. If the eggs are small and the recipe requires several, it will be necessary to increase the number used in order to get the desired volume.

CHOCOLATE AND COCOA—To substitute cocoa for chocolate in a recipe use 4 tablespoons cocoa for 1 square chocolate.

DRIED FRUITS—Dried fruits, if purchased in bulk, should be thoroughly washed and then dried before using. Packaged fruit need not be washed. If it has become too dry, plump up by steaming over hot water.

NUTS—Nuts are better chopped than ground in the food chopper.
To Blanche—Almonds, raw peanuts, chestnuts and the like have a skin that is easily removed by blanching, i.e., drop into boiling water for 1 minute. Chill in cold water and drain. Pop the nuts out of their skins and dry on a clean towel.

To Toast—Spread in pan and place in a hot oven for 3-5 minutes.

FLAVORING EXTRACTS—Good quality flavoring extracts are cheaper in the long run. A smaller quantity can be used to give the desired flavor and better retention during baking. Flavoring extracts in oil require only 2 to 3 drops to equal 1 teaspoon of the alcoholic extracts.

SIRUPS—Many types of **molasses** are now available and may be used interchangeably in a recipe. Many varieties of **corn sirup** can be purchased ranging in color from dark brown to clear. One kind may be used in place of another unless it is desirable to retain a particular shade in the finished product. **Honey** comes from many sources and each has its own flavor. They can be used interchangeably so choose the honey with the flavor you prefer. **Sorghum** comes in varying strengths and color and it depends on flavor preference as to which variety is used.

BAKING POWDERS—are classified as double-acting baking powders, phosphate baking powders, and tartrate baking powders. Recipes in this book give amounts which will give satisfactory results regardless of the type used.

SODA—is used in recipes calling for sour milk, (sweet milk soured by adding vinegar or lemon juice), fruit, brown sugar, and molasses. Buttermilk may be substituted for sour milk with satisfactory results.

ACCURATE MEASUREMENTS—Use only standard measuring equipment and all measurements should be level.

STEPS IN MAKING COOKIES

1. Heat the oven.

2. Arrange all needed equipment conveniently.

3. Assemble all ingredients.

4. If chocolate is to be used, put to melt over hot water.

5. Prepare the cookie sheets. If the cookies contain considerable shortening or if you are planning to use the cookie press, do not grease the cookie sheets. For all other cookies grease the cookie sheets with a bland fat that contains no salt; preferably a hydrogenated one. If cookie bars are to be made, grease the cookie sheet, line with waxed paper, and grease again. Macaroons are baked on heavy plain paper.

6. Sift the flour and measure immediately. Pile flour lightly into measuring cup, level with straight edge of knife, and refrain from shaking or tapping the cup. Since flour particles pack readily, it is easy to get an excessive amount of flour in the dough when these directions are not followed.

7. Measure other dry ingredients, add to flour and sift again. Use pieces of waxed paper to hold dry ingredients while measuring and sifting.

8. Prepare fruit and nuts, if to be used, and measure.

9. Measure shortening and liquid ingredients. Liquids should be poured into a level, graduated measuring cup and filled to the mark desired. Fractions of a cup of hard shortening may be measured by displacing cold water. For instance, to get ¼ cup shortening fill measuring cup ¾ full of cold water and add shortening until water is at 1 cup level. Be careful to drain all of water off before using the shortening. Pound bricks of shortening are easily measured. One pound contains 2 cups—cut in half for 1 cup or into quarters for ½ cup. Soft shortening may be measured by packing it into the proper measure and leveling off with a knife.

10. Cream shortening in a bowl. This is done by whipping until it becomes very soft and fluffy. Never melt the shortening as this injures the texture and flavor of the cookie. Shortening creams best between 70° and 80°F.

11. Add sugar gradually and beat well with each addition. The mixture should have a fluffy appearance when thoroughly creamed. Measure granulated sugar the same as flour except that it does not need to be sifted first. Brown sugar should be rolled or sifted to remove lumps and then packed firmly into the desired measure. Powdered sugar should be sifted to remove lumps and measured the same as flour.

12. Flavoring extracts are better distributed if added to the liquids.

13. Eggs are added to the sugar and butter mixture unless otherwise stated in the recipe.

14. Nuts and fruits are added last.

DROP COOKIES

FOUNDATION DROP COOKIES

⅓ cup shortening
¾ cup brown or white sugar
1 egg, beaten
2 cups cake flour
¼ teaspoon salt
1 teaspoon baking powder
⅓ cup milk
1 teaspoon vanilla

Cream shortening, add sugar slowly and cream thoroughly. Add beaten egg. Sift the dry ingredients together and add to the creamed mixture alternately with the milk and vanilla. Drop by teaspoons onto a greased cookie sheet and bake in a moderate oven (375°F.) 10 to 15 minutes. Makes 50 cookies 1½ inches in diameter.

This same dough can be used as a foundation for any of the following variations:

FRUIT—Add 1 cup chopped dates, raisins, or currants.

NUT—Add 1 cup chopped nuts to the mixture.

SPICE—Add 1 teaspoon cinnamon and ½ teaspoon cloves.

COCOA DROPS

1 cup shortening
1⅓ cups brown sugar
2 eggs
1 cup milk
2½ teaspoons vanilla
4 cups cake flour
1 teaspoon salt
3 teaspoons baking powder
¾ cup cocoa
1 cup chopped nuts

Mix shortening and sifted brown sugar together. Add eggs and beat well. Alternate milk and vanilla mixture with sifted dry ingredients. Add chopped nuts. Drop by teaspoons onto a greased cookie sheet and bake at 350°F. 15 minutes. Makes 120 drops 1½ inches in diameter. Keeps only 3 days.

CHOCOLATE MOUNTAINS

1 cup shortening
2 cups brown sugar
2 eggs, well beaten
2½ teaspoons vanilla
3½ cups flour
1 teaspoon salt
2 teaspoons baking powder
1 cup milk
4 ounces chocolate
2 tablespoons additional fat
2 cups chopped nuts

Cream shortening and sifted sugar together. Add eggs and vanilla. Sift flour, salt and baking powder together and add alternately with the milk to the creamed mixture. Add melted chocolate and additional melted fat. Add chopped nuts last. Drop from a teaspoon onto a greased cookie sheet. Top with candied cherries and bake in a moderate oven (350°F.) 15 minutes. Makes 126 cookies 2½-inch diameter.

Drop cookie dough should not be too stiff, neither should it sprawl over the pan during the baking

APPLESAUCE-SPICE COOKIES

½ cup shortening
1 cup sugar
1 egg, beaten
2 cups cake flour
½ teaspoon cinnamon
¼ teaspoon cloves
½ teaspoon salt
½ teaspoon soda
1 teaspoon baking powder
1 cup thick unsweetened Apple-sauce

Cream shortening and sugar together. Beat egg, add to creamed mixture and blend well. Sift all dry ingredients together and add alternately with the applesauce to the creamed mixture. Be sure to add flour first and last. Drop on well-greased cookie sheet. Bake 15 minutes in a moderate oven (375°F.) Makes 2½ dozen large cookies.

VARIATIONS—Add 1 cup chopped nuts, dates or raisins to the batter. Before baking, top each cookie with a red or green maraschino cherry and brush tops with Cream Cheese Spread.

Some like them frosted, some like them plain, but everybody likes them with fruits and nuts

NUGGETS

⅔ cup peanut butter
⅔ cup shortening
1 cup sugar
3 eggs, beaten
⅓ cup milk
2 cups cake flour
½ teaspoon salt
½ teaspoon soda
2 cups rolled oats
1 cup raisins
1 cup chopped dates
1 cup chopped nuts

Cream peanut butter and shortening together until well blended and soft (not melted). Add sugar a little at a time and cream well with each addition. Add beaten eggs to milk. Sift flour, salt and soda together. Add alternately with the milk and egg mixture, to the creamed mixture, blending well after each addition. Add the rolled oats, fruit and nuts. Drop from a teaspoon on a greased cookie sheet and bake in a moderately hot oven (375° F.) until brown, about 15 minutes. Makes 6 dozen small cookies about 2 inches in diameter.

VARIATION—2 cups of one kind of fruit may be used instead of both dates and raisins. Omit chopped nuts and use as garnish after baking.

MINCEMEAT GOODIES

1 cup shortening
2 cups sugar
3 eggs, well beaten
About 4 cups cake flour
1 cup mincemeat
1 teaspoon soda
⅛ teaspoon ginger
1 teaspoon cloves
1 teaspoon nutmeg
½ teaspoon salt
½ cup chopped nuts

Cream shortening and sugar thoroughly. Add the well beaten eggs to the creamed mixture and enough of the flour to keep it from curdling. Mix well and add the mincemeat. Sift the remaining flour with the other dry ingredients and add. The exact amount of flour needed varies with the amount of liquid in the mincemeat; however, the dough should be the consistency of a rolled dough. Add the chopped nuts and drop from a teaspoon onto a greased cookie sheet. Allow 2 inches between each cookie for spreading. Bake at 375°F. 12 minutes. Makes 96 3-inch cookies. These keep fairly well.
Push a plump maraschino cherry into each unbaked cookie.

HERMITS

1 cup shortening
2 cups brown sugar
1 cup milk
2 eggs, beaten
4½ cups cake flour
1 teaspoon baking powder
1 teaspoon salt
1 teaspoon soda
1 teaspoon cinnamon
½ teaspoon allspice
1 cup chopped nuts
1 cup raisins

Cream shortening and sifted sugar together. Add milk to beaten eggs. Sift all dry ingredients together and add to the shortening mixture alternately with liquid ingredients. Add nuts and raisins. Mix well and drop by teaspoons onto a greased cookie sheet. Bake at 350°F. 15 minutes. Makes 116 cookies 1½-inch diameter. They keep about 48 hours.

SPICED OAT DROPS

1 cup shortening
1½ cups brown sugar
2 eggs, beaten
2 cups cake flour
½ teaspoon salt
½ teaspoon soda
2 teaspoons baking powder
1 teaspoon cinnamon
½ teaspoon cloves
⅔ cup sour milk
1½ cups rolled oats
1 cup raisins or chopped dates
1 cup chopped nuts

Cream shortening and sifted sugar together. Add beaten eggs and mix well. Sift dry ingredients together and add alternately with sour milk to the creamed mixture. Add rolled oats, fruit and nuts. Drop by teaspoons onto a greased cookie sheet and bake in a moderate oven (350°F.) 15 minutes. Makes 64 2-inch cookies. Will keep well in a closed jar. Sweet milk may be used instead of sour milk and the soda omitted.

A tall cool glass of chocolate milk topped with whipped cream is an ideal accompaniment for cookies

COCOA FRUIT DROPS

1 cup butter
1⅓ cups brown sugar
4 eggs beaten
2 tablespoons milk
3 cups cake flour
½ cup cocoa
4 teaspoons baking powder
1 teaspoon soda
1 teaspoon salt
2 teaspoons cinnamon
1 cup chopped nuts
1 cup chopped dates

Cream butter with sifted sugar Beat eggs well, add milk. Sift flour, cocoa and other dry ingredients together. Add alternately with the liquid ingredients to creamed shortening. Add chopped nuts and fruit. Drop from a teaspoon onto greased cookie sheet. Bake at 350°F. 20 minutes. Makes 6 dozen cookies.

HONEY CHOCOLATE OATMEAL COOKIES

2½ cups cake flour
1 teaspoon baking powder
¼ teaspoon soda
½ teaspoon salt
1 teaspoon cinnamon
1 cup shortening
1¼ cups honey
2 eggs, beaten
2 ounces chocolate, melted
1½ cups rolled oats
1 cup nuts or coconut

Sift flour, baking powder, soda, salt and cinnamon together. Cream shortening and honey. Add beaten eggs, melted chocolate and rolled oats. Mix thoroughly. Add sifted dry ingredients and nuts or coconut. Drop from a teaspoon onto a greased cookie sheet. Bake in a slow oven (325°F.) 20 minutes. Makes 5½ dozen cookies.

CHOCOLATE CHIP KISSES

2 egg whites
1/8 teaspoon salt
1/8 teaspoon cream of tartar
3/4 cup sugar
4 ounces semisweet chocolate
   (bar or pieces)
1/2 cup chopped walnut meats
1/2 teaspoon vanilla

Beat egg whites until foamy, then add salt and cream of tartar and continue beating until eggs are stiff but not dry. Add sugar, 2 tablespoons at a time, beating thoroughly after each addition. Cut chocolate into pieces if bar is used. Fold in chocolate, nuts and vanilla. Drop from teaspoon onto ungreased heavy paper. Bake in slow oven (300°F.) 25 minutes. Remove from paper while slightly warm. Makes 18 kisses.

CHOCOLATE COCONUT—Add 3/4 cup shredded coconut when folding in chocolate.

CAKE CRUMB COOKIES

2 eggs
1 cup milk
4 cups dry cake or cookie crumbs
2/3 cup molasses
1/2 cup fat, melted
3 cups flour (about)
1/2 teaspoon soda
1 teaspoon baking powder
1/2 teaspoon salt
1 teaspoon cinnamon
1 cup steamed raisins

Beat the eggs, add the milk and the crumbs and let stand fifteen minutes. Add the molasses, melted fat and the dry ingredients which have been sifted together. Add the raisins and drop by teaspoons on a greased cookie sheet about two inches apart. Bake in a moderate oven (350-degrees F.). The amount of flour will vary with the degree of dryness of the cake or cookie crumbs. The batter should be a stiff drop batter which will hold its shape on the cookie sheet but will spread in the oven.

HONEY CHOCOLATE CHIP COOKIES

1 cup flour
1 teaspoon baking powder
1/4 teaspoon salt
1/2 cup shortening
1/2 cup honey
1 egg
1/2 teaspoon vanilla
1/4 cup chopped nuts
1/2 cup semi-sweet chocolate
   pieces

Sift flour, baking powder and salt together. Cream shortening and honey; beat in egg; add vanilla and sifted dry ingredients. Fold in nuts and chocolate pieces. Drop from teaspoon onto greased cookie sheet. Bake in moderate oven (375°F.) 10 to 12 minutes. Makes about 3 dozen cookies.

CHOCOLATE CHIP COOKIES

1 1/8 cups flour
1/4 teaspoon soda
1/2 teaspoon salt
1/2 cup shortening
1/4 cup brown sugar
1/2 cup sugar
1 egg, beaten
1 teaspoon vanilla
1/2 cup chopped walnuts
1/2 pound semi-sweet chocolate

Sift flour, soda and salt together. Cream shortening and brown and granulated sugars together. Add egg and vanilla. Beat thoroughly. Add sifted dry ingredients. Fold in nuts and chocolate cut into small pieces. Drop from teaspoon onto greased cookie sheet. Bake in moderate oven (350°F.) about 10 minutes. Makes 50 cookies.

COCONUT ORANGE JUMBLES

3/4 cup shortening
1 1/4 cups sugar
2 egg yolks, well beaten
1 cup shredded coconut
2 1/2 cups flour
1/4 teaspoon salt
1/2 teaspoon soda
1/3 cup strained orange juice
Coconut and grated orange peel

Cream shortening and sugar together. Add egg yolk and coconut and beat well. Sift together flour, salt and soda and add to the creamed mixture alternately with orange juice. After each addition beat until smooth. Drop from teaspoon onto ungreased cookie sheet. Sprinkle with additional coconut and grated orange peel. Bake in moderate oven (375° F.) 10 to 12 minutes. Makes 50.

FROSTED JUMBLES—Use the above recipe. When cookies are cool, dip them into a thin Confectioners' Icing. Roll immediately in shredded coconut.

HONEY HERMITS

2 1/4 cups flour
1 teaspoon soda
1/4 teaspoon salt
1/2 teaspoon allspice
1/2 teaspoon cinnamon
1/2 cup shortening
1/2 cup honey
1/2 cup brown sugar
2 eggs, well beaten
3 tablespoons milk
1 cup seedless raisins
1 cup dried currants
1 cup chopped dates
1/2 cup chopped nuts

Sift flour, soda, salt and spices together 3 times. Cream shortening with honey and sugar. Add eggs. Add milk, dry ingredients, fruit and nuts and mix thoroughly. Drop from teaspoon onto greased cookie sheet and bake at 400°F. 10 to 12 minutes. Makes 48.

APPLE-RAISIN CHEWS

2¾ cups cake flour
1 teaspoon salt
2 teaspoons baking powder
1 cup shortening
2 cups brown sugar
1½ teaspoons vanilla
1 egg
½ cup evaporated milk
¼ cup orange juice
2 large apples, pared and cored
1 cup seeded raisins
1 tablespoon grated orange rind

Sift flour with salt and baking powder. Cream shortening with sifted sugar, add vanilla and egg and beat well. Add dry ingredients to the creamed mixture alternately with the combined evaporated milk and orange juice. Mix thoroughly. Put apples and raisins through food chopper, add grated orange rind and fold into mixture. Drop from ½ teaspoon onto a well-greased cookie sheet. Bake 12 to 15 minutes in a moderate oven (375°F.). Makes 10 to 12 dozen small cookies. These keep well.

BRAZIL NUT MELTS

½ cup shortening
⅓ cup sugar
2 egg yolks
6 tablespoons ground Brazil nuts
½ teaspoon grated lemon rind
⅛ teaspoon salt
1 cup cake flour
3 tablespoons orange juice
½ cup thinly sliced Brazil nuts
Confectioners' sugar

Cream shortening, add sugar and egg yolks and cream thoroughly. Mix the ground nuts, lemon rind, salt and flour together and add to the creamed mixture alternately with the orange juice. Fold in sliced nuts, drop by teaspoons onto a greased cookie sheet and bake 10 to 12 minutes at 400°F. While hot roll in confectioners' sugar Makes 40 small cookies.

CORN MEAL COOKIES

1 cup shortening
1½ cups sugar
2 eggs
1 teaspoon lemon extract
½ cup raisins, chopped
3 cups cake flour
1 teaspoon baking powder
1 teaspoon nutmeg
½ teaspoon salt
1 cup yellow corn meal

Cream shortening, add sugar, eggs and lemon extract. Beat well. Dredge raisins with ½ cup of flour and add. Sift remaining flour with other dry ingredients and add, mixing thoroughly. Drop by teaspoons onto a greased cookie sheet and flatten out with a fork. Bake 10 to 12 minutes at 400°F. Makes 60 2-inch cookies. They keep very well.

VARIATIONS—Increase raisins to 1 cup and add ½ cup finely chopped nuts.
Omit raisins and add 1 cup chopped dried apricots.

PUMPKIN COOKIES

½ cup shortening
1¼ cups brown sugar
2 eggs
1½ cups cooked, mashed pumpkin
½ teaspoon salt
¼ teaspoon ginger
½ teaspoon nutmeg
½ teaspoon cinnamon
2½ cups cake flour
4 teaspoons baking powder
1 cup raisins
1 cup chopped nuts
1 teaspoon lemon extract

Cream shortening and sifted sugar thoroughly. Add eggs, pumpkin and seasonings. Blend well.° Sift flour and baking powder together, stir in raisins and nuts. Add flour mixture to the creamed mixture and beat. Blend in lemon extract. Drop from teaspoon onto greased cookie sheet. Bake 15 minutes at 400°F. Makes 36.

NUT BUTTER DAINTIES

½ cup peanut butter
¾ cup confectioners' sugar
½ cup ground dates
⅛ teaspoon salt
1 teaspoon vanilla
2 egg whites, unbeaten
2 cups cereal flakes, crushed
½ cup whole cereal flakes

Cream peanut butter with sifted sugar, dates, salt and vanilla. Add egg whites and crushed cereal flakes, mix thoroughly. Drop by ½ teaspoons into whole cereal flakes, turning until well coated. Place on greased cookie sheet and bake 15 minutes at 350°F. Makes about 100 tiny balls.

SPICED PRUNE COOKIES

½ cup shortening
¾ cup brown sugar
1 egg
½ cup molasses
2½ cups cake flour
2 teaspoons baking powder
¾ teaspoon soda
1 teaspoon salt
1½ teaspoons ginger
1½ teaspoons cinnamon
2 cups chopped cooked prunes

Cream shortening and sifted sugar until fluffy. Add egg and molasses, beat well. Sift together flour, baking powder, soda, salt, ginger and cinnamon. Add flour mixture to creamed mixture and mix thoroughly. Add prunes. Drop by teaspoons on ungreased cookie sheet and bake in a hot oven (400°F.) 10 minutes. Makes 10 dozen 1½-inch cookies.

VARIATIONS—Omit prunes, add 2 cups chopped cooked apricots. Omit ginger, add 1 teaspoon cloves. Add ½ cup chopped nuts with either the prunes or apricots.

BUTTER-NUT DROPS

½ cup butter
¼ cup sugar
1 egg, separated
½ teaspoon vanilla
¼ teaspoon salt
1 cup cake flour
1 tablespoon lemon juice
2 tablespoons grated orange rind
1 tablespoon grated lemon rind
½ cup Brazil nuts, ground fine
Candied cherries

Cream butter and sugar well. Add egg yolk and flavoring. Beat well. Sift dry ingredients together and add with lemon juice and rinds. Mix thoroughly and place in covered bowl. Chill. Roll into tiny balls (½ teaspoon of dough per ball). Dip balls into slightly beaten egg white. Roll in ground nuts. Place on greased cookie sheet 1 inch apart. Press ½ candied cherry on top of each and bake at 350°F. 25 minutes. Makes 40.

NUT CRISPS

⅓ cup shortening
1⅓ cups brown sugar
2 eggs, beaten
1⅓ cups cake flour
½ teaspoon salt
1 teaspoon baking powder
1 cup almonds, chopped

Cream shortening and ⅓ cup of sifted sugar. Beat eggs until thick and lemon colored, add remaining sifted sugar and continue beating. Combine the two mixtures and blend until smooth. Sift dry ingredients together and add. Mix in chopped nuts last. Chill. Drop from teaspoon onto greased cookie sheet and bake in a moderate oven (350° F.) 8 to 10 minutes. Makes 100 cookies.

We're called little butter-nut
Dear little butter-nut drops

SOUR CREAM SUGAR COOKIES

4½ cups cake flour
½ teaspoon salt
1 teaspoon soda
3 teaspoons baking powder
½ teaspoon nutmeg
½ teaspoon allspice
1 cup shortening
2 eggs, beaten well
2 cups thick sour cream
1⅓ cups brown sugar
1 cup chopped nuts
1 cup chopped dates or raisins

Mix and sift the dry ingredients. Cut in shortening very fine as for pastry. Beat eggs and add to the cream. Add sifted brown sugar to cream and combine with the dry ingredients. Add nuts and fruit. Drop by teaspoons onto a greased cookie sheet and bake in a moderate oven (350°F.) 16 minutes. Makes 7 dozen 2½-inch cookies.

THRIFT COOKIES

2 cups dry cookie or cake crumbs
1 egg, beaten
½ cup milk
¼ cup shortening
⅓ cup peanut butter
½ cup brown sugar
1 cup cake flour
½ teaspoon salt
1 teaspoon baking powder
⅛ teaspoon soda
½ cup raisins

Grind cookie or cake crumbs and sift. Beat egg, add to milk and pour over crumbs. Cream shortening, peanut butter and sifted sugar, blend well with crumb mixture. Sift dry ingredients together and add with raisins. Drop by teaspoons onto a greased cookie sheet. Bake at 350°F. 15 minutes. Makes 54 2-inch cookies.
Instead of raisins use ½ cup chopped candied lemon or grapefruit peel.

HONEY NUTLETS

1 cup shortening
1 cup honey
1 cup brown sugar
1 egg, beaten
4 cups cake flour
½ teaspoon soda
1 teaspoon salt
1 teaspoon cinnamon
2 cups broken nut meats

Melt shortening, add honey and sifted sugar. Beat thoroughly. Add egg, sifted dry ingredients and mix well. Stir in nuts and drop by teaspoons onto greased cookie sheet. Bake at 350°F. 15 minutes. Makes 48 cookies. Store in airtight jar 10 days to ripen.

BANANA NUT COOKIES

2¼ cups flour
2 teaspoons baking powder
½ teaspoon salt
¼ teaspoon soda
⅓ cup shortening
1 cup sugar
2 eggs, beaten
½ teaspoon vanilla
¼ teaspoon lemon extract
1 cup mashed bananas
½ cup chopped nuts

Sift together dry ingredients.

Cream shortening and sugar thoroughly, add eggs, flavorings and beat well. Add banana alternately with dry ingredients. Stir in chopped nuts. Drop by teaspoons onto greased cookie sheet and bake at 350°F. 15 minutes. Makes about 60 cookies.

SPONGE DROPS

½ cup cake flour
⅛ teaspoon salt
⅔ cup powdered sugar
3 eggs, separated
½ teaspoon vanilla extract

Sift together flour and salt. Beat egg whites until stiff but moist. Add vanilla. Add sugar gradually and continue beating. Fold in egg yolks, beaten until thick and lemon colored. Carefully fold in the flour mixture. Drop from tip of spoon onto ungreased paper-lined pan. Bake in moderate oven (350°F.) for 10 to 12 minutes. Makes about 48 drops. When cool top with Apricot Filling, whipped cream and slice of candied cherry. Serve at once.

Birds, flowers, stars, balls, drops and pinwheels will delight any guest

RAISIN ROCKS

1 cup shortening
2 cups brown sugar
2 eggs, beaten
3 cups flour
½ teaspoon salt
2 teaspoons soda
½ teaspoon cloves
½ teaspoon cinnamon
1 cup sour milk
1 cup chopped nuts
1 cup chopped raisins

Cream shortening. Sift brown sugar and add gradually. Cream thoroughly and add beaten eggs. Sift flour, salt, soda, cloves and cinnamon together. Add to the creamed mixture alternately with the sour milk until all are well blended. Add the chopped nuts and raisins. Drop by teaspoons about 2 inches apart onto a greased cookie sheet and bake in a moderate oven (350°F.) 9 minutes. Makes about 100 2-inch cookies. These cookies will keep in a closed tin for several weeks.

PEANUT BUTTER DROP COOKIES

1 cup chunk-style peanut butter
½ cup butter
2 teaspoons vanilla
½ cup sugar
1 cup honey
2 eggs
2½ cups sifted all-purpose flour
1 teaspoon baking soda

Cream together the peanut butter, butter and vanilla, using rotary beater on medium speed. Gradually add sugar and honey; continue beating. Add eggs, one at a time, and beat well after each addition. Beat until light and fluffy. Add flour and soda, sifted together, and beat on low speed only until blended. Drop by teaspoonfuls onto cookie sheets. Bake at (375°F.) 10 to 12 minutes. Remove to cooling rack. Makes about 8 dozen cookies.

VANILLA WAFERS

⅓ cup shortening
1 cup sugar
1 egg, beaten
¼ cup milk
3 teaspoons vanilla
2 cups flour
2 teaspoons baking powder
½ teaspoon salt

Cream shortening and sugar thoroughly. Beat the egg and add milk and vanilla. Sift all dry ingredients together. Add wet and dry ingredients alternately to the creamed mixture. Drop from a teaspoon onto a greased cookie sheet and bake at 300°F. 20 minutes. Makes 82 2-inch cookies.

LACE COOKIES

½ cup shortening
¾ cup sugar
1 egg, well beaten
½ cup cake flour
½ teaspoon soda
1 teaspoon cinnamon
1 cup finely chopped pecans
½ cup finely ground raisins

Cream shortening and sugar together and add egg and beat. Sift together all dry ingredients and add to the first mixture. Add pecans and raisins. Drop 3 inches apart by ¼ teaspoons onto cookie sheets and bake at 350°F. 10 minutes. Makes 4 dozen cookies 1-inch diameter.

SCOTTISH FANCIES

3 eggs, beaten
1½ cups sugar
¾ teaspoon salt
3 tablespoons melted shortening
1 tablespoon vanilla
3 cups rolled oats

Beat eggs, add sugar gradually and beat well with each addition. Add salt, melted shortening, vanilla and then the rolled oats. Drop from teaspoon onto a greased cookie sheet. Bake at 325°F. 20 minutes. Remove while still warm. Makes 108 cookies.

COCONUT OAT DROPS

1 egg, beaten
½ cup sugar
1 teaspoon melted shortening
½ teaspoon vanilla
½ cup rolled oats
½ cup chopped nuts
½ cup coconut
¼ teaspoon salt
1 tablespoon honey

Beat egg, add sugar gradually, then melted shortening and vanilla. Combine with remaining ingredients. Drop by teaspoons onto greased cookie sheet and flatten with a fork. Bake in a moderate oven (375°F.) 10 to 12 minutes. Makes 60 cookies 1-inch diameter.

SOFT MOLASSES COOKIES

½ cup shortening
½ cup brown sugar
½ cup hot water or sour milk
1 tablespoon vinegar
½ cup molasses
1 egg, beaten
2½ cups flour
½ teaspoon salt
¼ teaspoon soda
1 teaspoon baking powder
½ teaspoon ginger
½ teaspoon cloves
1 teaspoon cinnamon
½ cup raisins

Cream shortening with sifted sugar. Add hot water or sour milk and vinegar to the molasses. Combine with shortening and sugar. Add beaten egg. Sift dry ingredients and add. If desired, chop or grind raisins fine and add. Drop dough from teaspoon onto a greased cookie sheet. Bake in a moderate oven (350°F.) 15 minutes. Makes 7 to 8 dozen.

If desired, brush with Confectioners' Icing and design funny faces with raisins and orange slices.

COOKIE BARS

TWO LAYER WALNUT SQUARES

⅓ cup shortening
⅓ cup confectioners' sugar
1 teaspoon vanilla
1 egg yolk
1⅓ cups cake flour

SECOND LAYER

2 eggs
1 cup brown sugar
2 tablespoons cake flour
¼ teaspoon baking powder
½ teaspoon salt
1 teaspoon vanilla
½ cup coconut
1 cup chopped nuts

Cream shortening and confectioners' sugar together. Add vanilla and egg yolk. Beat. Add flour and mix well. Press dough into a 7x11-inch pan which has been lined with waxed paper. Bake 12 to 15 minutes at 425°F.

To prepare second layer: Beat eggs and sifted sugar together and fold in sifted dry ingredients. Add remaining ingredients and spread over the baked crust. Bake 25 to 30 minutes at 350°F. Cut into 24 1½-inch squares.

VARIATION—Frost with ½ cup confectioners' sugar, 3 tablespoons milk, ¼ teaspoon vanilla and sprinkle with chopped walnuts.

GUMDROP BARS

2 cups cake flour
¼ teaspoon salt
1 teaspoon cinnamon
3 eggs
2 cups brown sugar
¼ cup evaporated milk
1 cup soft gumdrops, cut into small pieces (omit licorice)
½ cup chopped nut meats

Sift flour, salt and cinnamon together. Beat eggs until light and beat in sifted sugar and milk gradually. Add flour mixture in thirds, beating until smooth after each addition. Add gumdrops and nuts. Spread in greased pan and bake in 325°F. oven 35 minutes. Cut into bars, 4x1 inch. Spread tops with frosting and decorate with sliced gumdrops. Makes 40.

The bits of gumdrops decorating the top, hint of the treasures hidden within these gumdrop bars

COCONUT NUT BARS

⅓ cup shortening
1 cup cake flour

Mix ingredients together well, press into a cake pan about 8x8 inches in size and bake until light brown. Cover with the following:

2 eggs
1½ cups brown sugar
1 teaspoon vanilla
2 tablespoons flour
¼ teaspoon baking powder
½ teaspoon salt
½ cup coconut, chopped
1 cup nuts, chopped

Beat eggs, add sifted sugar gradually and blend thoroughly. Add vanilla and flour, baking powder and salt which have been sifted together. Add chopped coconut and nuts. Spread over the above baked mixture and bake in a 325°F. oven 20 minutes. Makes 32 1x2-inch bars. Sprinkle top with tinted coconut.

FUDGE FOUR O'CLOCKS

2 ounces chocolate
¼ cup shortening
3 eggs, beaten
1 cup sugar
1 cup cake flour
½ teaspoon salt
1 teaspoon baking powder
½ cup milk
1 cup toasted nuts

Melt chocolate and pour over shortening. Mix well. Beat eggs until thick and lemon colored. Add sugar gradually, beating well with each addition. Combine mixtures and add a little of the flour. Sift rest of flour, salt and baking powder together and add, alternately with the milk. Add chopped nuts. Spread in 2 8x8-inch pans which have been greased and lined with waxed paper. Bake in a slow oven (325°F.) 20 minutes. Cut into 32 bars 1x4-inches.

CHOCOLATE INDIANS

2 eggs, beaten
1 cup sugar
1 teaspoon vanilla
¼ cup milk
2 ounces chocolate, melted
¼ teaspoon salt
1 cup cake flour
½ cup nuts, coarsely chopped

Beat eggs until thick. Add sugar gradually, vanilla and milk, beating until the sugar is partly dissolved. Add the melted chocolate, salt, flour and nuts. Spread in greased paper-lined 7x11-inch pan. Bake at 350°F. 30 minutes. Remove from pan and cut into 77 1x1-inch bars.

WASHINGTON NUT BARS

1 cup cake flour
2 tablespoons brown sugar
½ cup shortening
2 eggs, beaten
⅓ cup sugar
⅔ cup dark corn sirup
3 tablespoons butter, melted
1 teaspoon vanilla
⅔ cup chopped walnuts

Rub together well, flour, sifted brown sugar and ½ cup shortening. Pat into 8x8-inch pan and bake in moderate oven 350°F. 15 minutes. Remove from oven and cover with following mixture: Beat eggs, add ⅓ cup sugar, corn sirup, melted butter, flavoring and nuts. Bake at 350°F. 25 minutes. Makes 32 1x2-inch bars.

Fudge four o'clocks spread with fluffy frosting and crowned with nuts

BROWNIES

2 ounces chocolate, melted
⅓ cup shortening
1 cup cake flour
¼ teaspoon salt
½ teaspoon baking powder
2 eggs, beaten
1 cup sugar
½ teaspoon vanilla
1 cup nuts, chopped

Combine melted chocolate with shortening and blend well. Sift flour, salt and baking powder together. Beat eggs and add sugar gradually, beating until very light. Add vanilla and the chocolate mixture. Add dry ingredients and nuts. Spread about ½ inch deep in greased paper-lined shallow pan. Bake at 350°F. 30 minutes. Remove from pan and cut into 16 4x1-inch bars.

CHOCOLATE CHIP NUT SQUARES

6 1-ounce squares semi-sweet chocolate
½ cup cake flour
½ teaspoon baking powder
¼ teaspoon salt
1 egg, well beaten
½ cup sugar
1 teaspoon melted butter
2 teaspoons hot water
⅔ cup broken walnuts

Cut each small square of chocolate into 6 pieces. Sift flour, baking powder and salt together. Beat egg, add sugar slowly and continue beating. Combine butter, water, nuts and chocolate with egg mixture. Mix thoroughly. Fold in flour mixture and blend well. Pour batter into an 8x8-inch pan which has been lined with waxed paper and greased. Bake in a slow oven (325°F.) 25 to 30 minutes. Cool, remove from pan and cut in squares. Makes 20 2-inch or 80 1-inch squares.

ROYAL BARS

½ cup shortening
½ cup sugar
2 egg yolks, beaten
¼ teaspoon almond extract
1¼ cups cake flour
½ teaspoon salt
1 teaspoon baking powder
2 tablespoons water

TOPPING
½ cup (⅛ pound) almond paste
¼ cup sugar
2 egg whites

Cream the shortening and sugar together, add the egg yolks which have been beaten until stiff and lemon colored, and the almond extract. Sift the flour, salt and the baking powder together and add alternately with the water to the creamed mixture. Spread in a 7 x 11-inch pan and bake in a moderate oven (350°F.) about 35 minutes.

Cover with the topping made by working the almond paste and sugar together and combining with the stiffly-beaten whites of the eggs. Bake until the topping is firm and lightly colored. Remove from oven and let cool slightly. Cut in bars and place on a rack to cool. Makes 30 bars.

NUT—Omit topping. Beat 1 egg white until stiff. Fold in 1 cup brown sugar, sifted. Spread over unbaked cookie dough and sprinkle with 1 cup chopped nut meats. Bake at 325°F. for 30 minutes.

CHOCOLATE CHEW BARS

½ teaspoon salt
¼ teaspoon baking powder
¾ cup cake flour
½ cup brown sugar
½ cup sugar
½ cup grated semi-sweet chocolate
1 cup finely chopped dates
½ cup chopped walnuts
2 eggs, well beaten

Sift salt, baking powder and flour into mixing bowl. Add sifted brown sugar, granulated sugar, chocolate, dates and walnuts. Mix thoroughly. Whip in well-beaten eggs. Line an 8 x 8-inch pan with waxed paper, grease well and spread mixture in it. Bake 30 to 40 minutes at 375°F., cut into bars while hot and when cool remove from pan. Store in an airtight box. Makes 32 1 x 2-inch bars.

VARIATIONS—Omit nuts and add ½ cup finely-chopped coconut. Omit dates and nuts, add 1½ cups chopped cooked apricots and spread mixture in pan. Cover with shredded coconut and bits of semi-sweet chocolate. Bake.

You can bake cookies and frosting all at one time when you make these nut royal bars

CHINESE CHEWS

2 eggs, well beaten
1 cup sugar
¾ cup cake flour
1 teaspoon baking powder
¼ teaspoon salt
1 cup finely chopped dates
1 cup finely chopped pecans

Beat eggs and add to sugar. Sift all dry ingredients together and mix in dates and nuts. Add flour mixture to sugar mixture. Beat well. Line a 6 x 11-inch pan with waxed paper and spread dough in it to depth of ½ inch. Bake 40 minutes at 350°F. Makes 22 1 x 3-inch bars.

DATE HONEYS

Sprinkle additional nuts over the pecan sticks before baking, for a decorative touch

3 eggs, beaten
1 cup strained honey
1½ cups cake flour
1 teaspoon baking powder
1 teaspoon salt
2 cups ground dates
1 cup chopped nuts

Beat eggs until thick and combine with honey. Sift the flour, baking powder and salt together and add to eggs and honey. Add dates and nuts. Combine all ingredients and pour only to ¼-inch depth, into 2 7x11-inch pans which have been greased and lined with waxed paper. Bake in a moderate oven (350° F.) 40 minutes. Remove from pan and cool. Cut into 22 bars 1 inch wide or wrap the whole cake in waxed paper and store until ready to cut. Honey cookies can be kept 2 or 3 weeks and the flavor will improve.

The bars may be rolled in confectioners' sugar or frosted.

PECAN STICKS

1 cup shortening
1 cup sugar
1 egg yolk
1 teaspoon vanilla
1 teaspoon cinnamon
2 cups sifted flour
1 egg white
1 cup chopped pecans

Cream shortening and 1 cup sugar together, add egg yolk, vanilla, cinnamon and flour. Mix thoroughly. Spread ¼ inch thick in a well-greased 15½x10½x1-inch pan. Beat egg white slightly and brush over top of dough. Cover with thick layer of pecans or add the cup of pecans to dough and sprinkle additional nuts on top. Bake 30 minutes at 350° F. Cut while warm and remove when cool. Makes 75 1x2-inch sticks.

APRICOT BARS

½ recipe Apricot Filling
1 tablespoon lemon juice
1 cup cake flour
1 cup brown sugar
½ teaspoon salt
½ cup shortening
1½ cups rolled oats
3 tablespoons milk
1 tablespoon grated lemon peel

Prepare ½ recipe of Apricot Filling and add lemon juice just before filling is removed from heat. Cool. Sift flour with sifted sugar and salt. Cut in shortening until mixture resembles meal. Add rolled oats and mix well. Add milk, grated lemon peel and blend. Pack ½ of dough into 8 x 8-inch greased pan. Spread Apricot Filling on top and cover with remaining dough. Bake 40 minutes at 350°F. Cool. Cut in bars 1 x 2 inches. Makes about 32 cookies.

VARIATION—Sprinkle cinnamon and sugar mixture over dough before baking.

BUTTERSCOTCH BARS

4 eggs, beaten
2 cups brown sugar

Beat eggs and add the sifted sugar. Cook in a double boiler 20 minutes stirring frequently. Cool and add the following, first sifting the baking powder and salt with the flour:

2 teaspoons baking powder
¼ teaspoon salt
1½ cups cake flour
1 cup chopped nuts

Spread about ¼ inch thick in a well-greased 7x11-inch pan, lined with waxed paper. Bake in a moderate oven (350°F.) 12 to 15 minutes. Cut, cool and roll in confectioners' sugar. Makes about 60 bars 1 x 1½ inches.

FROSTED GINGER CREAMS

1 cup shortening
½ cup sugar
1 teaspoon ginger
1 teaspoon cinnamon
1 egg or 2 yolks, beaten
1 cup molasses
½ cup milk
3½ cups cake flour
2 teaspoons soda
½ teaspoon salt
1 cup raisins

Cream shortening with sugar and spices. Add egg and beat well. Add molasses and milk and blend. Stir in flour sifted with soda and salt. Add raisins. Spread ¼ inch deep in 2 well-greased 10x15-inch pans. Bake 12 minutes at 350°F. Cool in pans and spread with Confectioners' Icing. Cut in squares or diamonds. Makes 140 1½x2-inch cookies.

Top with candied peel.

DATE BARS

¾ cup shortening
1½ cups sugar
1 egg
3 cups cake flour
1 teaspoon salt
1 teaspoon baking powder
½ teaspoon soda
1 cup sour milk
1 cup chopped nut meats
1 cup cut dates
Confectioners' sugar

Cream shortening and sugar until fluffy. Add egg and beat thoroughly. Sift flour, salt, baking powder, and soda together. Add alternately with sour milk to creamed mixture. Fold in nuts and dates. Pour into 2 greased shallow pans. Bake in a moderate oven (350°F.) 20 to 25 minutes. Cut into bars, 1 x 4 inches, when still warm and roll in confectioners' sugar. Store in a tightly covered container. Makes 48 bars.

FUDGIES

1½ cups sugar
1 cup cake flour
¾ teaspoon baking powder
½ teaspoon salt
½ cup evaporated milk
¼ cup water
3 squares chocolate
3 eggs, beaten
¾ cup chopped nuts
½ teaspoon vanilla

Sift sugar, flour, baking powder and salt together. Heat milk, water and chocolate together in double boiler. When chocolate is melted beat mixture until thick and smooth. Cool. Beat eggs until light and lemon colored. Add eggs, dry ingredients, nuts and vanilla to chocolate. Mix thoroughly. Spread in greased 8-inch square pan. Bake in moderate oven (350°F.) 35 minutes. Remove from pan, cut into 1-inch squares and dredge with confectioners' sugar. Makes 64 Fudgies.

GOODIES

1 cup cake flour
1 cup sugar
2½ cups quick oatmeal
1 cup shortening
½ recipe Cinnamon-Prune Filling

Mix together flour, sugar and oatmeal. Cut in shortening until all ingredients have been blended into a crumbly mass. Spread half of crumbs into a greased 6x10-inch baking pan. Spread with Cinnamon-Prune Filling and sprinkle remaining crumbs over top. Bake in a moderate oven (350°F.) 45 minutes. After baking allow cookies to remain in pan 5 minutes before removing. When cold cut in 2-inch squares. Makes 24.

VARIATION — Omit Cinnamon-Prune Filling and spread with mincemeat, thick jam, marmalade or any desired Fillings.

FRUIT SQUARES

2 eggs, beaten
1 cup brown sugar
2 teaspoons vanilla
1 cup cake flour
1 teaspoon baking powder
½ teaspoon salt
⅔ cup chopped nuts
1 cup candied fruits, chopped
1 cup dried fruits (dates, citron, raisins, figs) chopped

Beat eggs until they start to stiffen, beat in sugar gradually and add vanilla. Sift flour with baking powder, salt and add. Fold in chopped nuts and the candied and dried fruits which have been cut into small bits. Bake in a 7x7-inch pan, lined with waxed paper, in a moderate oven (350°F.) 30 to 40 minutes. Remove from pan while warm, cool and cut into 49 1-inch squares.

VARIATION—Frost with Cream Cheese Spread and roll in shavings of semi-sweet chocolate or colored candy beads.

HONEY RAISIN BARS

¼ cup shortening
½ cup sugar
½ cup honey
1 egg
1½ cups cereal flakes
1½ cups cake flour
1½ teaspoons baking powder
¼ teaspoon soda
¼ teaspoon salt
½ cup milk
1 cup seedless raisins

Blend shortening, sugar and honey thoroughly. Add egg and beat well. Crush cereal flakes into fine crumbs, mix with sifted dry ingredients and add to shortening mixture alternately with milk. Stir in raisins. Spread batter ½ inch thick in well-greased 10 x 15-inch pan. Bake 15 to 20 minutes at 350°F. Cool and cut into 35 2-inch squares.

CHOCOLATE-ALMOND SQUARES

2 cups cake flour
2 teaspoons baking powder
¼ teaspoon cinnamon
½ teaspoon salt
½ cup shortening
1 cup brown sugar
2 eggs, beaten
1 square chocolate, grated
1 teaspoon vanilla extract
1 cup chopped almonds

Sift together flour, baking powder, cinnamon and salt. Cream shortening and sifted sugar. Add eggs to creamed mixture, beating well. Add chocolate, vanilla extract and almonds and mix well. Add flour mixture and blend thoroughly. Pat into a well-greased rectangular pan, 9x14 inches. Bake at 375°F. 15 to 20 minutes. While still warm, cut into 1½-inch squares. Makes about 54 cookies.

If desired, frost with a chocolate fudge frosting or melted chocolate candy bar and top with almonds.

NUT TOASTIES

4 slices bread (1 inch thick)
1 egg, beaten
¼ cup milk
½ teaspoon salt
1 teaspoon sugar
1 cup finely chopped nut meats

Remove crusts from bread and cut each slice into strips 1 inch wide. Beat egg, add milk, salt, and sugar and dip bread in batter. Roll in nut meats and fry in hot deep fat (385°F.) until brown or bake in a hot oven (450°F.) 15 minutes. Serve with afternoon tea. Makes 1 dozen.

Use shredded coconut instead of nut meats.

Cut cube horizontally and fill with jam before dipping in egg.

It's a clever cook who can turn bread into cookies but it is simple enough when you know how

CHOCOLATE PECAN SQUARES

⅔ cup cake flour
½ teaspoon salt
½ teaspoon baking powder
⅓ cup shortening
2 squares chocolate
½ cup sugar
2 eggs, well beaten
½ cup honey
½ cup broken pecans
1 teaspoon vanilla extract
64 pecan halves

Sift flour, salt and baking powder together. Melt shortening and chocolate together over boiling water. Add sugar to eggs and beat well. Add honey gradually to egg mixture and beat thoroughly. Add chocolate mixture and continue beating. Stir in flour mixture, nuts and vanilla. Blend well. Pour batter into 8x8-inch pan which has been lined with waxed paper and greased. Arrange pecan halves on batter before baking. Bake about 40 minutes at 350°F. Cut into 64 1-inch squares so that each square has a pecan half in its center. Top with Peppermint Spread.

CURLED WAFERS

Curled wafers are very thin cookies which are limp when hot and can be curled into any shape desired. They become crisp when cool and make a very dainty afternoon-tea cookie. They keep best in a tightly covered jar; however, most of them will not stay crisp for more than 2 days. The batter for curled wafers should be quite thin. This is important as a thick batter cannot be spread thin enough to curl. The secret of removing wafers from cookie sheet is to grease the sheet heavily with a bland fat that contains no salt and after baking, cool them a minute before trying to remove. Then speed is essential. Lift them quickly off the sheet and curl by hand around a wooden-spoon handle. If they become crisp before all have been curled, return to the oven for a few minutes. Curled wafers may be served plain or filled with sweetened whipped cream, thinned cream cheese, cream cheese and crushed pineapple, fruit whips, custard-pie filling or chiffon-pie filling. Serve at once.

MOLASSES WAFERS

¼ cup hot water
¾ cup molasses
¼ cup shortening
1 cup minus 2 tablespoons cake flour
6 tablespoons powdered arrowroot
½ teaspoon soda
½ teaspoon baking powder
½ teaspoon ginger
¼ teaspoon cloves

Add hot water to molasses and combine with shortening. The flour should be sifted and meas-

ured first and 2 tablespoons removed from the cup before the other ingredients are added. Mix and sift all dry ingredients and add to the first mixture. When dough has been thoroughly mixed, drop by half teaspoons and spread each extremely thin over a 2x3-inch area on a heavily-greased cookie sheet. Bake at 325°F. 8 to 9 minutes. Cool 1 minute, lift wafer from sheet and curl around finger or wooden handle. Makes 100 wafers. This wafer should be used within 36 hours. Serve plain or filled.

CURLED PECAN WAFERS

¼ cup shortening
½ cup brown sugar
1 egg
2 tablespoons cake flour
¼ teaspoon salt
¼ teaspoon cloves
½ cup finely chopped pecans

Cream shortening, add sifted sugar gradually and then the unbeaten egg. Beat well. Add sifted dry ingredients and pecans. Drop very small amounts of dough onto a heavily-greased cookie sheet. Spread very thin into a 2-inch square. Bake in a slow oven (300°F.) 10 minutes. Remove, cool 1 minute and curl around

finger or wooden handle. If they become too brittle return to oven for 1 minute. Makes 68 wafers. Serve plain or fill with fillings.

CALLA LILLY—Curl into cornucopia, fill with cream cheese, insert candied orange peel and top with grated lemon rind.

CURLED HONEY AND CINNAMON WAFERS

½ cup cake flour
½ teaspoon cinnamon
¼ cup shredded almonds
¼ cup shortening
¼ cup sugar
½ cup honey
1 egg

Sift flour and spice, add nuts. Cream shortening, add sugar and beat well. Add honey and egg and continue beating. Fold in flour mixture. Drop from ¼ teaspoon onto a heavily-greased inverted cookie sheet. Spread out thin into a 2-inch square. Allow at least 1 inch between cookies. Bake in slow oven (300°F.) about 10 minutes. Cool just 1 minute, remove from pan and curl into cone shape. Makes 60 cones. Serve plain or fill with fillings.

Curling your wafers is simple to do Serve them at tea for something new

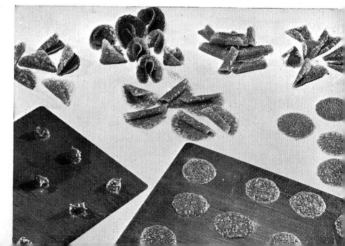

FILLED COOKIES

There are three types of filled cookies. The first and most usual type uses a sugar-cookie dough as a base. The cookie is rolled out about ⅛ inch in thickness, cut in rounds and placed on the cookie sheet. In the center, a teaspoonful of a fruit filling is placed, another cookie is placed on top and the edges are sealed with the fingers or a fork.

To make the second type, roll the dough out in two large pieces about ⅛ inch in thickness and about the same size and shape. Place one sheet of the cookie dough on a greased cookie sheet, spread it with the cookie filling to the depth of about ¼ inch and cover with the second sheet of cookie dough. Bake, cool slightly and cut in bars. This type may also be cut before baking if preferred, baking each bar as a separate cookie.

The third type of cookie might be called the sandwich type. Here thin crisp cookies are first baked and then filled with a fruit filling as one wishes to use them. They will not keep well after filling as the moist filling destroys the crispness of the cookie.

In nearly every recipe, a different filling may be used from among those listed. Fillings should have body, be moist, but should not absorb readily into the cookie as it bakes. A thick jam or preserve will make an excellent filling.

SUGAR GLAZE—Dilute confectioners' sugar with enough milk, cream or water to the consistency of thin cream. Use a pastry brush to cover tops of cookies.

Press the edges together with a fork to keep the filling within and make a pretty fluted edge

FOUNDATION FILLED COOKIES

¾ cup shortening
1 cup sugar
2 eggs, well beaten
3½ cups cake flour
3 teaspoons baking powder
½ teaspoon salt
⅓ cup milk
½ teaspoon vanilla

Cream shortening and sugar together. Add eggs. Sift dry ingredients together and add alternately with milk and vanilla. Mix well after each addition. Roll out dough ⅛ inch thick on a floured pastry cloth. Cut with 2½-inch round cutter. Place on greased cookie sheet, add teaspoon of desired filling and cover with another round. Pinch together with tines of fork or fingers. Brush tops with egg white and bake in hot oven (400°F.) 15 minutes. Makes 78 filled cookies.

FILLINGS

If dried fruit is to be used, soak it until soft enough to chop finely. Use water from the fruit for liquid in the recipe. If fresh or canned fruit is used, drain liquid as much as possible and add only the amount called for in the recipe. Combine all ingredients in the order given. Cook over low heat, stirring frequently, until the consistency of marmalade. Add citrus fruit juices after you have removed filling from stove and cool thoroughly before using.

APRICOT FILLING

2½ cups sugar
1½ cups water
6 tablespoons flour
¼ teaspoon salt
4½ cups chopped dried apricots

APRICOT-ORANGE FILLING

¾ cup water
1½ cups sugar
3 tablespoons flour
1½ teaspoons grated orange rind
¼ teaspoon salt
4½ cups chopped dried apricots
¾ cup orange juice

DATE FILLING

1⅓ cups sugar
1⅓ cups water
2 tablespoons butter
¼ teaspoon salt
2⅔ cups stoned dates
3 tablespoons lemon juice

Cut out centers from some filled cookies; allow the filling to show through attractively

CINNAMON-PRUNE FILLING

1 medium orange, peeled
    and diced
½ cup prune juice
½ cup sugar
1½ teaspoons cinnamon
¼ teaspoon salt
2 tablespoons melted butter
¾ cup chopped walnuts
2 cups chopped prunes

PEACH FILLING

2 cups water
3 cups sugar
¼ teaspoon salt
5 cups chopped dried peaches

TUTTI-FRUTTI FILLING

1 cup sugar
2 tablespoons flour
1 cup water
2½ cups chopped dried fruits
2 tablespoons lemon juice

SPREADS

Blend sugar and paste ingredients with only enough liquid so that the mixture just spreads. Add flavoring.

PEPPERMINT SPREAD

1 cup confectioners' sugar
Small amount milk
¼ teaspoon peppermint flavoring

CREAM CHEESE SPREAD

2 cups confectioners' sugar
3 ounces cream cheese
1 teaspoon orange juice
½ teaspoon grated orange rind

CONFECTIONERS' ICING

2 cups confectioners' sugar
1 tablespoon melted butter
3 to 4 tablespoons cream
1 teaspoon vanilla

DATE-CHERRY FILLING

1 tablespoon flour
1 cup sugar
1 cup water
1 cup raisins
1 cup stoned dates
15 candied cherries

FIG FILLING

1 cup sugar
2 tablespoons butter
1⅓ cups hot water
¼ teaspoon salt
4 cups chopped figs

FIG-LEMON FILLING

1½ cups water
1 cup sugar
4 tablespoons flour
¼ teaspoon salt
2 cups chopped figs
Juice of 2 lemons

FIG-ORANGE FILLING

1 cup water
1 cup sugar
¼ teaspoon salt
1 cup chopped nuts
3 cups chopped figs
½ cup orange juice
4 teaspoons grated orange rind

WALNUT-FIG FILLING

1¼ cups water
1 cup corn syrup
½ cup sugar
4 tablespoons flour
¼ teaspoon salt
¾ cup chopped walnuts
2 cups chopped figs
2 tablespoons lemon juice
2 teaspoons grated lemon rind

PRUNE FILLING

2 tablespoons flour
1 cup sugar
1 cup chopped nuts
¼ teaspoon salt
2 cups chopped prunes
1¼ cups orange juice

RAISIN FILLING

1⅓ cups sugar
1 cup hot water
2 tablespoons butter
1 tablespoon flour
¼ teaspoon salt
4 cups raisins

LEMON-RAISIN FILLING

1 cup sugar
4 teaspoons lemon rind
1 cup hot water
4 cups raisins
¼ cup lemon juice

BUTTERSCOTCH FRUIT BARS

¾ cup butter
2 cups brown sugar
3 eggs, well beaten
1 teaspoon vanilla
4 cups cake flour
½ teaspoon salt
1 teaspoon soda
Tutti-frutti Filling

Cream butter and sugar together. Add beaten eggs, vanilla and ½ cup flour. Blend well. Add remaining dry ingredients which have been sifted together. Chill. Divide dough into 2 parts and roll each part into sheets ⅛ inch thick of approximate size and shape. Spread one sheet with the Tutti-frutti Filling and cover with the second. Press together lightly. Cut bars 2 inches long and 1 inch wide and bake at 350°F. 20 minutes. Makes 40 bars. These bars will not keep longer than 2 days. However, the dough makes an attractive rolled cookie which will keep several weeks.

BUTTERSCOTCH BALLS—Add 1 cup finely chopped pecans to the dough, shape into balls the size of a marble, arrange on cookie sheet and bake 8 minutes. While still warm roll in confectioners' sugar. If desired, imbed a nut half or piece of candied fruit in center of each.

PEPPERMINT FILLED CHOCOLATE COOKIES

2½ cups cake flour
2 teaspoons baking powder
½ teaspoon salt
½ cup shortening
1 cup sugar
1 egg
2 ounces chocolate, melted
¼ cup evaporated milk
Peppermint Spread

Sift dry ingredients together. Cream shortening, add sugar and beat well. Add egg, melted chocolate and continue beating. Then add the evaporated milk and flour mixture slowly. Blend well. Form into a roll 2 inches in diameter, chill overnight and cut in thin slices. Place on greased cookie sheet and bake at 400°F. 10 to 15 minutes. When cookies are cool put together with 1 recipe of Peppermint Spread.

VARIATIONS—Add ½ cup of finely chopped almonds to the Peppermint Spread before spreading on cookie.

Add ½ cup freshly ground coconut to the Peppermint Spread and reduce the liquid.

Any thin crisp cookies may be put together with filling after they are baked

FILLED OAT CRISPS

1 cup shortening
1 cup brown sugar
2½ cups cake flour
½ teaspoon baking soda
½ teaspoon salt
2½ cups rolled oats, ground fine
½ cup water

Cream shortening and sugar thoroughly. Sift flour with baking soda and salt and add rolled oats which have been put through a food chopper. Add dry ingredients alternately with water to the mixture. Chill for at least 15 minutes. Roll out small portion of dough at a time and keep remainder in the refrigerator. Roll as thin as possible (about $\frac{1}{16}$ inch thick) on a slightly-floured pastry cloth. Cut in rounds about 2 inches in diameter. Lift onto a greased cookie sheet and bake in a moderate oven (350°F.) 10 minutes. Makes 13 dozen single cookies. Cool and store. When ready to use spread Date Filling on one cookie and top with another. Cookie does not keep well after being filled, so fill as needed.

For variety add ½ teaspoon cinnamon and ¼ teaspoon cloves to whole recipe and blend well.

Before baking, sprinkle cookies with ground walnuts. When cool spread with Apricot Filling.

ROLLED COOKIES

CHOCOLATE CIRCLES

½ cup shortening
1 cup sugar
1 egg, beaten
¼ cup milk
2½ ounces chocolate, melted
2½ cups cake flour
½ teaspoon salt
2 teaspoons baking powder

Soften shortening, cream well with sugar. Add beaten egg, milk and chocolate. Mix well, sift dry ingredients and add. Chill thoroughly. Remove small amount of dough at a time from refrigerator and roll ⅛ inch thick on pastry cloth. Cut in circles, bake on greased cookie sheet 10 minutes at 350°F. Makes 11 dozen 2-inch cookies. This is a crisp cookie that keeps well.

BREAD CRUMB COOKIES

⅔ cup shortening
1 cup brown sugar
2 eggs, well beaten
½ cup molasses
2½ cups fine bread crumbs
1 cup cake flour
½ teaspoon soda
¼ teaspoon cloves
½ teaspoon cinnamon
1 teaspoon baking powder
Flour, Milk

Cream shortening and sifted sugar thoroughly. Add beaten eggs and molasses. Sift together dry ingredients and add slowly to the liquid mixture. Mix thoroughly. Add enough additional flour to make a stiff dough. Chill and roll thin. Use a simple cookie cutter. Glaze by brushing tops with milk. Bake at 350°F. 6 to 8 minutes. Makes 156 cookies of 2-inch diameter.

Suit the cutter to the occasion; these cookies provide refreshments for the bridge party

CARAMEL SOUR CREAM COOKIES

½ cup shortening
⅔ cup brown sugar
1 egg, beaten
½ cup sour cream
2¼ cups cake flour
½ teaspoon salt
1½ teaspoons baking powder
¼ teaspoon soda
½ teaspoon nutmeg
Brown sugar

Cream shortening, add sifted sugar and cream well. Add beaten egg to sour cream. Sift flour, salt, baking powder, soda and nutmeg together. Add alternately with egg mixture to the creamed shortening and sugar. Chill thoroughly. Use a rolling-pin stocking and pastry cloth and roll only a small portion at a time to ¼ inch thickness. Sprinkle with brown sugar and bake on a greased cookie sheet 15 minutes at 350°F. Makes 4 dozen cookies 2-inch diameter. Will keep well.

This dough may be molded in a cookie press without chilling.

LEMON SNAPS

1/3 cup shortening
1 cup sugar
5 egg yolks or 2 whole eggs
3 tablespoons milk
1½ teaspoons lemon extract
3⅔ cups cake flour
2½ teaspoons baking powder
¼ teaspoon soda
½ teaspoon salt
Egg for glaze, Milk

Cream shortening and sugar. Beat eggs well and add with the milk and lemon extract. Mix and sif dry ingredients and add. Chill. Roll ⅛ inch thick. Cut and brush tops with egg diluted with milk. Bake in moderate oven (375°F.) 10 minutes. Makes 150 cookies 2½-inch diameter.

If desired top each cookie with ½ almond before brushing with diluted egg. Decorate with narrow strips of candied ginger, pineapple, citron or lemon peel.

Round cookies with fluted edges lend themselves to decorating with colored or white sugar

SHREWSBURY CAKES

½ cup shortening
½ cup sugar
½ teaspoon vanilla
1 egg, well beaten
2½ cups cake flour
Egg, Poppy seed,
Colored sugar, Cinnamon

Cream shortening and sugar. Add vanilla and egg, blend. Add flour. Chill. Roll dough out ⅛ inch thick and cut into fancy shapes. Different effects can be obtained by brushing surface with beaten egg or sprinkling cookies with poppy seed or sugar (plain, colored or cinnamon). Bake at 350° F. 15 minutes. Makes 7 dozen 2½-inch cookies. This cookie is like sweet, tender pastry and keeps indefinitely.

QUEENIES

1 cup shortening
¾ cup confectioners' sugar
2 cups cake flour
1 cup chopped nuts
½ cup flour
2 tablespoons confectioners' sugar

Cream shortening and sugar thoroughly. Add flour and nuts. Blend together. Roll ¼ inch thick on a pastry cloth which has been dusted with a mixture of ½ cup flour and 2 tablespoons sugar. Cut into small fancy shapes with cookie cutters. Arrange on a greased cookie sheet and bake in a hot oven (400°F.) 10 minutes. Sprinkle top of cookies with confectioners' sugar as soon as they are removed from the oven. Makes 100 cookies.

VARIATION—Add ¼ teaspoon cinnamon to dough, blend well. Roll, cut and decorate with tiny red cinnamon candies.

MAPLE SUGAR COOKIES

1 cup shortening
2 cups maple sugar, sifted
4 eggs, beaten
1 teaspoon lemon extract
2 tablespoons milk
5 cups cake flour
2 teaspoons salt
5 teaspoons baking powder
Maple sugar

Cream shortening and add the sugar which has been rolled for sifting and cream together well. Add eggs, lemon extract, milk, then part of the flour which has been sifted with salt and baking powder. Beat well and add remaining dry ingredients. Drop by teaspoons onto a greased cookie sheet. Flatten with a fork or glass. Sprinkle with maple sugar. Bake at 350°F. 12 minutes. Makes 96 2-inch cookies.

If maple sugar is not available use brown sugar and add ½ teaspoon of maple flavoring.

PASTEL COOKIES

1 cup shortening
1 cup sugar
2 egg yolks
3¼ cups cake flour
1 teaspoon baking powder
¼ teaspoon salt
6 tablespoons milk
Food colorings

Cream shortening and sugar thoroughly. Add egg yolks and beat well. Sift all dry ingredients together and add alternately with milk to the creamed mixture. This foundation makes the following:

CHECKERBOARD—Use ½ of recipe and divide into 2 portions, one portion slightly larger than the other. To the smaller quantity add 1 square of melted chocolate. Divide the white dough into 5 balls of equal size and the chocolate dough into 4 balls of equal size. Shape each ball into a roll 8 inches long, then flatten sides to form rectangle ½ inch thick. Stack on waxed paper: a white roll, a dark roll and then a white roll. The stacked rolls will be 3 squares wide and 3 squares high and the colors will be alternated to make a checkerboard. When stacking the rolls moisten each side before placing the next roll in position. Wrap the resulting cube in waxed paper and chill for at least 3 hours. Slice ⅓ inch thick and arrange on a well greased cookie sheet. Bake at 375°F. 9 minutes. Makes 80.

PINWHEELS—Use ¼ of the recipe and divide this into 2 portions. Color as desired. Any 2 colors can be used; however it is preferable to have one dark and one light, such as the chocolate and white combination for checkerboards. Roll out the dark layer first making it almost ½ inch thick. Moisten the surface of the

dark dough, place the light dough on top of the dark and press together lightly. Moisten the top of the light layer and with the aid of a sheet of waxed paper roll tightly into a long roll. Chill thoroughly for at least 3 hours and slice about ⅛ inch thick. Arrange on a well greased cookie sheet and bake at 375° F. 9 minutes. Makes 50 cookies.

RIBBON COOKIES—Use last ¼ of recipe and divide into 3 portions. Color each differently. Roll out the doughs about ⅓ inch thick, cut in 2-inch strips and stack 2 inches high alternating colors. Trim sides, press together slightly, wrap in waxed paper and chill. Slice ⅛ inch thick, arrange on a greased cookie sheet and bake at 375°F. 9 minutes. Makes about 50 cookies.

When rolling pastel pinwheels, you will find a sheet of waxed paper a valuable assistant

SUGGESTED COLORS AND FLAVORS—For ½ the recipe: **Green**—Add ½ teaspoon of almond extract and color pale green by adding food coloring a drop at a time.
Pink—Add 2 to 3 drops of cinnamon oil and color pink.
Orange—Add 1 teaspoon of orange flavor and color orange.
White—Add 1 teaspoon vanilla extract, no coloring.

SPECIAL DESIGNS—This recipe makes very attractive rolled cookies. For Halloween color the dough orange and cut out small pumpkins. Decorate with a little green icing for the stem and melted chocolate for the eyes, mouth and nose. Clever hatchet-shaped cookies can be fashioned, adding red icing along the edge of the blade and blue icing on the handle. Card-party cookies can be clubs, hearts, spades and diamonds sprinkled with colored sugar. Bake at 375°F. 7 minutes. Makes about 200 2-inch cookies.

The foundation sugar cookie adapts itself to many variations in shape and flavoring

CARAMEL SUGAR COOKIES

1 cup shortening
1 cup sugar
½ cup brown sugar
3 eggs, beaten
2 teaspoons vanilla
3¾ cups cake flour
1 teaspoon salt
½ teaspoon soda
Brown sugar

Cream shortening. Add sugar and brown sugar a little at a time and cream well. Add beaten eggs and vanilla. Mix. Sift flour, salt and soda together and combine with the mixture. Chill. Roll out ¼ inch thick. Sprinkle with brown sugar. Bake in a moderate oven (350°F.) 15 minutes. Makes 96 cookies 3 inches square.

OLD-FASHIONED SUGAR COOKIES

1 cup shortening
1 cup sugar
2 eggs, beaten
2 teaspoons vanilla
1 cup sour cream
5 cups cake flour
2 teaspoons baking powder
1¼ teaspoons salt
1 teaspoon soda

Cream shortening and sugar. Add eggs and vanilla to sour cream. Sift together the flour, baking powder, salt and soda and add alternately with the liquid to shortening and sugar mixture. Chill thoroughly. Roll out on pastry cloth ¼ inch thick. Cut with large cutter, sprinkle with sugar and press in lightly. Bake in moderate oven (375°F.) 15 minutes. Makes 100 2½-inch cookies.

FOUNDATION SUGAR COOKIES

1 cup shortening
2 cups sugar
6 tablespoons milk
2 teaspoons vanilla
3 eggs, beaten
5½ cups cake flour
1 teaspoon salt
3 teaspoons baking powder

Cream shortening, add sugar gradually and cream well. Add milk and vanilla to beaten eggs. Sift all dry ingredients together and add alternately with liquid ingredients to creamed mixture. Chill. Roll out small portions of dough at a time to ¼ inch thickness on a floured pastry cloth. Keep remaining dough in the refrigerator and save all scraps after cutting for the final rolling so that the dough does not become overworked. Bake in a moderate oven (375°F.) 15 minutes. Makes 168 cookies 2-inch diameter.

CINNAMON—Sprinkle cinnamon and sugar over the top of the unbaked cutouts.

CARAWAY—Sprinkle tops of the unbaked cutouts with caraway seed and sugar.

COCONUT—Add 1 cup shredded coconut to the foundation dough.

JELLY—Place teaspoon of tart jelly on top of unbaked cutouts. For a fancier cookie, roll the dough very thin and cut with a round cutter. Place jelly on top of 1 cookie and cover with a second cookie from which a tiny round center has been cut.

LEMON—Add to dough 2 teaspoons lemon extract, omit vanilla. Decorate unbaked cutouts with bits of candied cherry and lemon peel.

SPICE—Add to dough 1 teaspoon cinnamon, ½ teaspoon nutmeg and ¼ teaspoon cloves. Sprinkle with sugar before baking.

Either gingersnaps or molasses cookies are doubly enchanting when cut with fancy cookie cutters

HONEY ORANGE CRISPS

¾ cup shortening
½ cup sugar
1 egg, beaten
½ cup honey
1½ teaspoons ginger
2 tablespoons orange juice
½ teaspoon orange extract
3 cups cake flour

Cream shortening and sugar together. Add egg, honey and ginger, mixing until smooth. Mix in orange juice and extract. Sift flour and add slowly, beating well between each addition. Chill thoroughly. Roll out very thin on a lightly-floured pastry cloth and cut with various shaped cookie cutters. Bake on ungreased cookie sheet in moderate oven (350°F.) 8 to 10 minutes. Makes about 10 dozen 2-inch cookies.

Sprinkle ground fresh coconut over the top of the unbaked cutout to give attractive flavor, or frost with Cream Cheese Spread, top with candied peel.

WALNUT STRIPS

½ cup shortening
½ cup brown sugar
¼ cup boiling water
½ cup molasses
3 cups cake flour
1 teaspoon salt
1 teaspoon soda
1 teaspoon ginger
¼ teaspoon nutmeg
⅛ teaspoon cloves
1½ cups finely chopped walnuts

Cream shortening and brown sugar. Add boiling water to molasses. Sift dry ingredients and add alternately with molasses and water to creamed mixture. Chill and roll. Cut into strips 1 inch wide and 3 inches long. Sprinkle with walnuts. Bake at 350° F. 12 minutes. Makes 78 strips. These keep very well.

STONE JAR GINGER COOKIES

¾ cup shortening
1½ cups molasses
5 tablespoons boiling water
4 cups cake flour
2 teaspoons soda
¼ teaspoon salt
1½ teaspoons ginger
½ teaspoon cinnamon

Cream shortening, add molasses and water and blend. Sift the dry ingredients and add to mixture. The resulting dough is very soft and must be chilled overnight. Roll out ⅛ inch thick on a well-floured pastry cloth. Use any shape cutter. Bake at 375°F. 12 minutes. Makes 144 cookies 2-inch diameter.

GINGERSNAPS

1 cup shortening
1 cup sugar
⅔ cup hot coffee
⅔ cup molasses
5 cups cake flour
1 teaspoon salt
1 teaspoon soda
2 teaspoons ginger
1 teaspoon cloves
1 teaspoon cinnamon

Cream shortening and sugar thoroughly. Add hot coffee to molasses and add to creamed mixture. Sift dry ingredients together. Add gradually to liquid mixture. Chill thoroughly. Roll out on a pastry cloth ⅛ inch thick, cut out and bake in a moderate oven (350°F.) 17 minutes. Makes 14 dozen 2-inch cookies.

RICHES

1½ cups shortening
2 cups sugar
1 egg and 1 extra yolk
¼ teaspoon almond extract
½ teaspoon salt
4 cups cake flour

TOPPING

4 egg whites
8 tablespoons sugar
2 teaspoons cinnamon
¾ cup almonds, shredded fine

Cream shortening and sugar. Add egg and extra yolk, almond extract, salt and flour. Chill until firm. Roll out on a pastry cloth ⅛ inch thick. Cut into 2-inch circles and in the center of each cookie place a teaspoon of topping made by beating egg whites until stiff and adding sugar and cinnamon. Sprinkle topping with almonds. Bake at 400°F. 12 minutes. Makes 108 cookies.

SCOTCH SHORTBREAD

1 cup shortening
⅔ cup brown sugar
2⅔ cups cake flour
Egg, Milk

Cream shortening and sifted sugar together and work into the flour. Chill. Roll out ⅓ inch thick on a pastry cloth. Cut with small

fancy cutters and brush tops with a mixture of egg and milk for a glaze. This method makes 60 small cookies.

If desired, roll out in a large sheet ⅓ to ½ inch thick and cut lengthwise in strips 1½ inches wide, then diagonally 1½ inches apart to form diamond shapes. Bake in a slow oven (325°F.) 30 minutes or until slightly browned. Store in cool place.

SUGAR CRISPS

½ cup shortening
¾ cup sugar
1 egg, beaten
⅔ cup molasses
½ teaspoon vanilla
2½ cups cake flour
1 teaspoon baking powder
2 teaspoons cinnamon
½ teaspoon soda
½ teaspoon salt

Cream shortening with sugar. Add egg, molasses and vanilla. Sift dry ingredients together and add. Mix thoroughly. Drop dough from a ¼ teaspoon onto a well-greased cookie sheet. Space cookies about 2 inches apart. If desired, cookies may be flattened with a glass covered by a damp cloth. Bake in moderate oven (350°F.) 12 minutes. Makes 75 to 80 cookies 1½-inch diameter.

SAND TARTS

½ cup shortening
1 cup sugar
1 egg, beaten
2 cups cake flour
2 teaspoons baking powder
¼ teaspoon salt
½ cup almonds, blanched
1 egg white
1 tablespoon sugar
¼ teaspoon cinnamon

Cream shortening and sugar thoroughly. Add beaten egg and dry ingredients which have been sifted together. Chill dough until stiff. Roll out ⅛ inch thick and cut with various shaped cutters. Press ½ almond in the center of each, brush tops of cookies with egg white and sprinkle with cinnamon and sugar mixture. Bake in moderate oven (375°F.) 10 minutes. This makes 76 cookies 2½-inch diameter. A crisp cookie which keeps well.

VARIATION—Roll thin, cut with tiny bridge-set cutters, bake 5 minutes, remove from oven and cool. Frost with Peppermint Spread and while moist outline each with candy beads.

For outdoor meals, fill a basket tray with Scotch shortbread, drop cookies and refrigerator cookies

REFRIGERATOR COOKIES

FOUNDATION REFRIGERATOR COOKIES

1 cup shortening
2 cups sugar
2 eggs, beaten
2 teaspoons lemon extract
3½ cups cake flour
½ teaspoon salt
2 teaspoons baking powder

Cream shortening and sugar. Add eggs and flavoring alternately with the sifted dry ingredients. Form in long rolls about 2 inches in diameter, wrap in waxed paper and place in refrigerator until firm. Slice cookies $\frac{1}{16}$ inch thick and bake in moderate oven (375°F.) 10 minutes. Cookies may be sliced and baked as needed. Makes 156 cookies.

For variety, 1 cup of finely chopped nuts may be added.

With a few rolls of dough in the refrigerator, you can provide fresh cookies at the drop of a hat

5 IN 1 COOKIES

1½ cups shortening
3 cups brown sugar
2 eggs, well beaten
2 teaspoons vanilla
½ teaspoon salt
4 teaspoons baking powder
6 cups cake flour

Cream shortening and sifted sugar until light and fluffy. Add eggs and flavoring. Combine and sift dry ingredients. Add to the creamed mixture. Knead in the last of the flour. Divide dough into 5 equal parts and vary each as follows. Shape each portion into a roll, wrap in waxed paper and chill thoroughly. When firm slice very thin and bake at 375°F. Makes about 300 thin, 1½ x 2-inch cookies.

CHOCOLATE—Add 2 squares of melted chocolate. Blend well. Baking time—10 minutes.

SPICE—Add ½ teaspoon cinnamon and ¼ teaspoon nutmeg. Blend well. Bake 9 minutes.

FRUIT—Add ½ cup finely-chopped dried or candied fruits (dates, raisins, figs, currants, apricots, prunes, cherries, peel). Baking time—14 minutes.

NUT — Add ⅓ cup finely-chopped nuts (almond, pecans, Brazil, filberts or walnuts). Baking time—12 minutes.

COCONUT—Add ⅓ cup shredded coconut. Baking time—10 minutes.

ALMOND ROLL

¾ cup shortening
1 cup sugar
1 egg, beaten
½ teaspoon almond extract
2 cups cake flour
¼ teaspoon salt
½ teaspoon soda
1 cup almonds, blanched and chopped very fine

Cream shortening and sugar thoroughly. Add egg and almond extract. Mix well. Sift dry ingredients together and add to the creamed mixture. Form in a roll 2 inches in diameter and roll this in the chopped nuts. Wrap in waxed paper and chill thoroughly. Slice ⅛ inch thick and bake in a moderate oven (350°F.) 12 minutes. Makes 88 cookies. These keep very well.

A white cookie may be made by using 2 egg whites instead of 1 whole egg.

REFRIGERATOR COOKIES
CHOCOLATE WALNUT REFRIGERATOR COOKIES

4 cups sifted cake flour
4 teaspoons baking powder
½ teaspoon salt
1¼ cups softened shortening
1½ cups sugar
2 eggs, unbeaten
4 ounces (squares) chocolate, melted
1 teaspoon vanilla
2 cups broken walnut meats

Sift flour, baking powder and salt together. Cream shortening and sugar until fluffy. Add eggs, chocolate and vanilla, beating until blended; then add nut meats. Add sifted dry ingredients gradually, mixing well. Shape into 2 rolls, 1½ inches in diameter, wrap in waxed paper and chill thoroughly. Cut into ⅛-inch slices and bake on ungreased baking sheet in moderate oven (350° F.) 10 minutes. Makes 13 dozen.

FIG COOKIES

2¼ cups sifted cake flour
½ teaspoon cinnamon
1 teaspoon soda
½ cup shortening
1 cup brown sugar; 2 eggs, beaten
2 tablespoons sour cream
1 cup chopped figs

Sift flour, cinnamon and soda together. Cream shortening with sugar until fluffy; add eggs, cream and figs. Add sifted dry ingredients with more flour if necessary. Chill thoroughly. Roll out on lightly floured board to ⅛-inch thickness, cut with cookie cutter and bake on greased cookie sheet in moderate oven (350°F.) 10 to 12 minutes or until browned. Makes 5 dozen.

It is well to keep a roll of refrigerator cookies on hand to cut and bake as needed

REFRIGERATOR CARAMEL COOKIES

1 cup shortening
2 cups brown sugar
2 eggs, beaten
2 teaspoons vanilla
3½ cups cake flour
2 teaspoons baking powder
½ teaspoon salt

Cream shortening and sifted sugar together. Add beaten eggs and vanilla and beat smooth. Add sifted dry ingredients. Mix well. Form into roll 2 inches in diameter. Roll in waxed paper and chill overnight or until ready to use. Slice ⅛ inch thick and bake in a moderate oven (350°F.) 10 minutes. Makes 100 cookies which are thin, crisp and keep well.
SPICE—Add ½ teaspoon cloves to dough. Bake, glaze with Sugar Glaze to which has been added crushed clove candy.

REFRIGERATOR OATMEAL COOKIES

1 cup cake flour
½ teaspoon soda
¼ teaspoon salt
2 cups rolled oats, finely ground
1 cup chopped coconut
½ cup shortening
1 cup sugar
1 egg
¼ cup evaporated milk
1 teaspoon vanilla

Sift dry ingredients together, grind oats and add with coconut. Cream shortening and sugar, add egg and beat well. Mix milk and vanilla. Add dry ingredients to creamed mixture alternately with milk and vanilla. Mix thoroughly. Form into rolls, wrap in waxed paper and chill overnight in refrigerator. Slice ⅛ inch thick, place on greased cookie sheet and bake at 400°F. 12 minutes. Makes 80 2-inch cookies.

REFRIGERATOR RAISIN COOKIES

1 cup seedless raisins
1½ cups brown sugar
¾ cup shortening
2 eggs
3 cups cake flour
½ teaspoon salt
½ teaspoon baking powder
½ teaspoon nutmeg
½ teaspoon soda

Wash raisins and cut in small pieces with scissors. Cream sifted sugar and shortening, add eggs and raisins and beat well. Sift flour, salt, baking powder, nutmeg and soda together. Add to creamed mixture and mix thoroughly. Chill in refrigerator until stiff enough to handle. Form into rolls 2 inches in diameter, wrap in waxed paper and store in refrigerator. Slice ¼ inch thick, place on greased cookie sheet and bake 10 minutes at 400°F. Makes about 60 cookies.

CHOCOLATE REFRIGERATOR COOKIES

1 cup shortening
1 cup sugar
1 egg, beaten
2 tablespoons milk
2 teaspoons vanilla
3½ cups cake flour
3 teaspoons baking powder
½ teaspoon salt
3 ounces chocolate, melted

Cream shortening and sugar together. Beat egg and combine with milk and vanilla. Sift dry ingredients together. Add melted chocolate to creamed mixture and then add alternately, the dry and liquid ingredients. Work until a smooth dough is formed. Mold into a roll 2 inches in diameter and roll in waxed paper. Chill until firm. Slice ⅛ inch thick and bake at 350°F. for 12 minutes. Makes 150 cookies.

DUTCH SOUR-CREAM COOKIES

½ cup butter
1 cup sugar
1 egg
¼ teaspoon soda
¼ cup sour cream
½ teaspoon lemon extract
½ teaspoon vanilla extract
3 cups cake flour

Cream butter and sugar. Add egg and beat thoroughly. Dissolve soda in cream and add. Stir in flavorings. Sift flour and add. The mixture should be a soft-dough consistency. Shape into a roll, wrap in waxed paper and chill overnight. When firm slice thin and bake in moderate oven (375°F.) 10 minutes. Makes 50 small cookies.

REFRIGERATOR DATE COOKIES

1 cup shortening
2 cups brown sugar
2 eggs
1 cup nuts, ground
1 cup dates, ground
3½ cups cake flour
1 teaspoon salt
1 teaspoon soda

Cream shortening and sifted sugar thoroughly, add eggs 1 at a time and beat well after each addition. Add nuts and dates which have been put through food chopper. Sift dry ingredients together, add to creamed mixture and mix well. Shape in rolls 2 inches in diameter, wrap in waxed paper and store in refrigerator until firm. Slice thin and bake 8 minutes at 400°F. Makes 11 to 12 dozen cookies.

Whether rolled in waxed paper or shaped in a mold, refrigerator cookies need a thin sharp knife ➡

PINWHEELS

⅓ cup shortening
½ cup sugar
1 egg yolk
½ teaspoon vanilla
3 tablespoons milk
1½ cups cake flour
½ teaspoon salt
½ teaspoon baking powder
1 cup ground nuts
1 ounce chocolate, melted

Cream shortening and sugar together. Add egg yolk and beat. Add vanilla and milk. Sift flour, salt and baking powder together and add with the nuts. Divide dough into 2 parts and to 1 part add the melted chocolate. Chill at least an hour. Roll out both parts quickly about ⅛ inch thick and place chocolate dough on top of white. Press together with a rolling pin. Roll up as for jelly roll, wrap in waxed paper and place in refrigerator until very firm. Slice the cookies ⅛ inch thick. Bake in a moderate oven (375°F.) 10 to 15 minutes. Makes 3½ dozen cookies.

PINWHEEL COMBINATIONS—

Prepare ½ recipe Raisin Refrigerator Cookies and 1 recipe Refrigerator Oatmeal Cookies. Roll and chill as for Pinwheels. Slice and bake at 400°F.

Prepare 1 recipe Dutch Sour-Cream Cookies and 1 recipe Date Refrigerator Cookies. Roll and chill as for Pinwheels. Slice and bake at 375°F.

Prepare 1 recipe Lemon-Caraway Cookies and omit the caraway seeds. Roll dough out ¼ inch thick and spread with Date-Cherry Filling. Roll and chill as for Pinwheels. Slice and bake on well-greased cookie sheet 10 to 12 minutes at 400°F.

LEMON-CARAWAY COOKIES

1 egg
1 cup sugar
2 tablespoons lemon juice
½ cup shortening, softened
2 teaspoons caraway seed
3 cups cake flour
½ teaspoon soda
½ teaspoon salt

Beat egg, add sugar gradually and continue beating. Add lemon juice, shortening and caraway seed. Sift the dry ingredients and add. Make into a roll and wrap in waxed paper. Chill until firm enough to slice thin. Bake in a hot oven (400°F.) 10 minutes. Makes 60 thin 2½-inch cookies.

Grandmother's cookie jar would have a hard time competing with this tray of pinwheel cookies

MACAROONS, MERINGUES and KISSES

Macaroons and meringues are among the earliest types of sweet cookies made and were common before baking powder, soda and similar types of leavening agents were known. Most of them depend on the amount of air which can be beaten into the egg whites to make them light.

Care must be taken not to overbeat the egg whites as overbeating makes dry, coarse cookies. Egg whites should be beaten stiff but not dry. When the egg beater is withdrawn from the mass, peaks should form but the beaten egg whites should be smooth and shiny. The whites will flow very slowly when the bowl is tipped and will cling to the side of the bowl if they are beaten just the right amount of time. Egg whites beat better when at room temperature.

When meringues and macaroons are baked on unglazed paper, the paper may be removed by moistening it on the underside with a cloth wrung out of cold water and letting them stand for a few minutes.

SURPRISE KISSES

½ pound semi-sweet chocolate
4 egg whites, beaten
¼ teaspoon salt
¼ teaspoon cream of tartar
1½ cups sugar
1 cup broken walnuts
1 teaspoon vanilla

Cut each small square of chocolate into 6 to 8 pieces. Beat egg whites until foamy, then add salt and cream of tartar and continue beating until eggs are stiff enough to hold peaks, but not dry. Add sugar 2 tablespoons at a time, beating thoroughly after each addition. Fold in chocolate, nuts and vanilla. Drop from teaspoon onto ungreased heavy paper. Bake at 300°F. 25 minutes. Remove from paper while slightly warm. Makes 72 kisses.

VARIATION—Add ¾ cup shredded coconut and fold into egg white mixture with the chocolate pieces.

Omit chocolate and add 1 cup maple sugar pieces. Brown sugar lumps can also be used.

ALMOND MACAROONS

1¼ cups almonds
⅛ teaspoon cinnamon
2 tablespoons grated lemon peel
2 egg whites, beaten
⅝ cup sugar
2 tablespoons lemon juice

Grind almonds, coarsely. Combine cinnamon and lemon and add. Beat egg whites very stiff, fold in sugar and continue beating. Fold in lemon juice with almond mixture and blend. Drop from a teaspoon onto ungreased heavy paper. Bake 30 minutes at 250°F. Remove from paper while still slightly warm. Makes 30 macaroons.

The egg white for macaroons or meringues should be stiff enough to hold its shape on the cookie sheet

COCONUT-ALMOND MACAROONS

⅝ cup sugar
⅝ cup confectioners' sugar
2 tablespoons cake flour
4 egg whites, beaten
⅔ cup ground, blanched almonds
½ teaspoon vanilla
2 cups shredded coconut

Sift together both sugars and flour. Beat egg whites until foamy throughout then add sugar 2 tablespoons at a time. Beat well after each addition. Fold in almonds, vanilla and coconut. Drop from teaspoon onto ungreased heavy paper. Bake 20 to 25 minutes at 325°F. Makes 36 macaroons.

MOON BEAM KISSES

2 egg whites, beaten
1 cup sugar
¾ cup blanched almonds
1½ cups chopped dates
1 teaspoon vanilla

Each guest will want to sample several kinds so be sure to provide plenty of cookies when you entertain

Beat egg whites until stiff, add sugar gradually and beat hard. Shred almonds, chop dates and fold into egg white mixture. Add vanilla and blend carefully. Drop by teaspoons onto ungreased heavy paper and bake 18 to 20 minutes at 250°F. Makes about 36 kisses.

CHOCOLATE MACAROONS

¼ cup cold water
4 egg whites, beaten
⅔ cup sugar
2 teaspoons vanilla
½ teaspoon salt
1 tablespoon cake flour
2 ounces chocolate, melted
3 cups coconut

Add cold water to egg whites and beat until stiff but not dry. Add sugar and vanilla and continue beating. Sprinkle salt and flour over egg whites and blend carefully. Fold in melted chocolate and coconut. Drop by teaspoons onto smooth brown-paper covered cookie sheet. Bake in slow oven (325°F.) 30 minutes. Makes 42 cookies.

Sugar 'n spice 'n everything nice, that's what big and little cookies are made of →

COCOROONS

3 egg whites, beaten
½ teaspoon salt
1 cup sugar
2 teaspoons light corn sirup
¼ teaspoon almond extract
2 cups cereal flakes
1½ cups coconut

Beat egg whites with salt until foamy throughout. Add sugar, 2 tablespoons at a time, beating after each addition until all the sugar has been blended with the egg whites. Beat in corn sirup and almond extract. Fold in cereal flakes and coconut. Drop from teaspoon onto ungreased heavy paper. Bake 20 minutes at 325°F. Makes 3 dozen cocoroons.

VARIATION—Add ½ cup broken pecans with the coconut.

CEREAL FLAKE MACAROONS

2 egg whites, beaten
½ cup sugar
⅓ teaspoon salt
2 cups cereal flakes
½ cup coconut

Beat egg whites until stiff, beating in sugar and salt gradually. Fold in cereal flakes and coconut. Drop mixture from tip of spoon onto ungreased heavy paper and bake in a moderate oven (350°F.) 15 to 20 minutes. Makes 36.

FLAKOROONS

3 egg whites
½ teaspoon salt
1 cup sugar
¼ teaspoon almond extract
2 cups rice flakes
2¼ cups coconut

Combine as in Cereal Flake Macaroons. Bake at 275°F. 18 to 20 minutes. Makes 36.

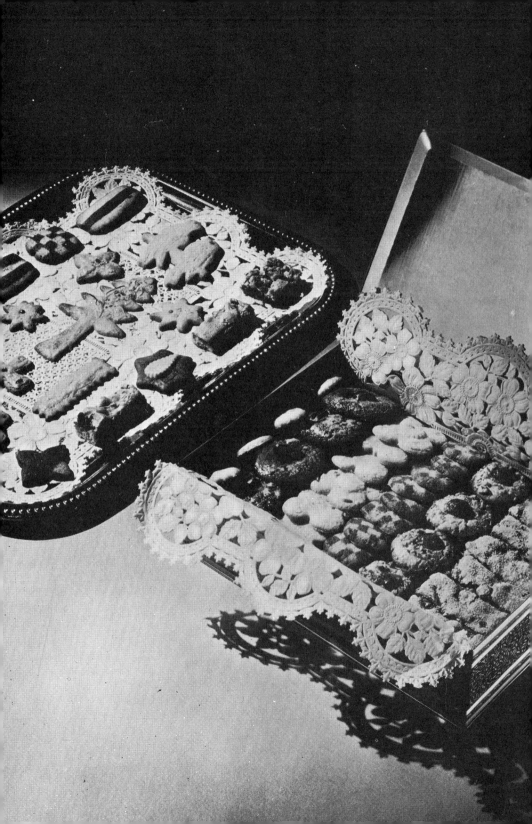

FRENCH MERINGUE

2 cups sugar
1 cup water
6 egg whites, beaten
¼ teaspoon salt
¼ teaspoon cream of tartar
1 teaspoon vanilla

Boil sugar and water to a heavy-thread stage 238°F. Beat egg whites very stiff, add salt and cream of tartar. Pour the sirup gradually over egg whites, beating continuously. Add flavoring and beat until cold. Shape with a pastry bag or drop, from a teaspoon onto letter paper or onto a cookie sheet which has been greased and dredged with cornstarch. Bake at 250°F. 45 minutes. Makes 48 meringues. To remove the center: Bake on a wet board covered with letter paper, remove the center and return to dry out. Fill with ice cream or whipped cream.

VARIATION—Chopped nuts may be added to the meringue mixture or the meringues may be sprinkled with the chopped nuts.

NUT KISSES

½ cup nuts, chopped
2 egg whites, beaten
½ cup sugar
½ teaspoon vanilla
⅛ teaspoon salt

Chop the nuts very fine. Peanuts or pecans are especially good. Beat the egg whites until stiff but not dry. Beat in the sugar, a little at a time. Fold in the vanilla, salt and nuts. Drop by teaspoons on ungreased letter paper. Bake in a slow oven 275°F. 40 to 60 minutes. Makes about 2 dozen kisses. If well dried out in the baking and stored in a tight can, they will keep for a long time.

VARIATION—Instead of the chopped nuts, 1 cup of shredded coconut may be used.

MERINGUE CASES

4 egg whites, beaten
1 cup sugar
⅛ teaspoon salt
1 teaspoon vanilla
1 teaspoon vinegar

Beat egg whites until stiff but not dry. Beat in ⅔ of the sugar gradually and continue beating until it will hold its shape. Fold in the remaining sugar, salt, vanilla and vinegar. Shape in form of cups with a pastry tube or drop from tablespoon onto heavy paper. Bake in a slow oven (275°F.) 1 hour or until thoroughly dry but not browned. Yields 20 cases made by dropping from tablespoon. To fill: Crush or cut off the top.

These cases may be tinted (when mixing) with food coloring, if desired.

PEANUT BRITTLE MERINGUE DROPS

3 egg whites, beaten
1 cup sugar
½ teaspoon vanilla
½ teaspoon vinegar
½ cup crushed peanut brittle

Beat egg whites until stiff and dry. Add sugar slowly and continue beating until all sugar is

Shred blanched almonds and stick them into the kisses before baking to add to their interest

added. Add vanilla and vinegar and blend carefully. Fold in peanut brittle. Drop from teaspoon onto ungreased heavy paper and bake about 1 hour at 275°F. Remove from paper as soon as they come out of the oven. Makes 50 small drops.

FRENCH NUT STICKS

3 egg whites, beaten
1½ cups sugar
¼ teaspoon salt
1½ cups walnuts, chopped
1½ cups pecans, chopped

Beat egg whites stiff, but not dry. Add sugar and salt gradually, beating until thoroughly blended. Add the nut meats chopped fine. Place mixture in the top of a double boiler and stir over hot water until mixture thickens slightly and does not run, 8 minutes. Shape into finger length rolls as slender as they can be rolled or force through a pastry tube or cookie press onto heavy paper. Bake in a moderate oven (350°F.) 12 minutes.

Makes 4 dozen sticks, 1 inch wide and 3 inches long.

MARGUERITES

1¾ cups sugar
½ cup water
2 egg whites, beaten
1 teaspoon vanilla
1 cup nuts, chopped
⅛ teaspoon salt
1 tablespoon butter
40 soda crackers

Boil the sugar and water to the soft ball stage (238°F.), then pour over the beaten egg whites and beat until stiff. Add vanilla, nuts, salt and butter. Drop by spoonfuls on the crackers and bake in a moderate oven (350° F.) until light brown. Makes 40.

VARIATIONS — Add chopped fruit in place of part of the nuts.

Sprinkle the marguerites with shredded coconut before baking.

Sprinkle marguerites with chocolate shot before baking.

Add finely chopped maraschino cherries to the meringue mixture.

Spread round thin crackers with a mixture of cream cheese and currant jelly before spreading with the meringue.

Spread the wafers with a chocolate paste made by mixing cocoa, powdered sugar and cream. Top with meringue and bake.

GRAHAM CRACKER MARGUERITES

1½ cups sugar
½ cup water
5 marshmallows
2 egg whites, well beaten
¼ teaspoon vanilla
2 tablespoons shredded coconut
⅛ teaspoon salt
1 cup pecans, chopped
16 graham crackers

Boil sugar and water together to the soft-ball stage (236°-238° F.). Add the marshmallows which have been cut into pieces and stir until dissolved. Pour over the well-beaten egg whites and beat until stiff enough to hold its shape. Add the vanilla, coconut, salt and pecans. Spread on graham crackers and bake in a moderate oven (350°F.) for about 15 minutes or until light brown.

Use ginger cookies and add chopped raisins, citron and orange peel to the meringue.

Use sifted brown sugar instead of granulated sugar. Top with maraschino cherry.

When the children want to cook let them start with these easy but delicious condensed milk kisses

CONDENSED MILK KISSES

1⅓ cups (1 can) sweetened condensed milk
3 cups (¾ pound) shredded coconut
½ teaspoon vanilla
⅛ teaspoon salt

Combine ingredients and drop by teaspoons onto a greased cookie sheet. Bake at 375°F. for 15 minutes. Remove from the pan while hot. Makes about 30 cookies.

VARIATIONS—FRUIT KISSES— Use 2 cups chopped dried fruits such as raisins, dates or figs.

NUT KISSES—Use 1 cup nut meats such as peanuts, walnuts or pecans.

PEANUT-BUTTER KISSES—Use ½ cup peanut butter. The peanut butter may be combined with the coconut or cereal flakes.

A mixture of fruit and nuts, cereal and nuts, or cereal and fruit may be used, taking care that there is sufficient condensed milk to bind ingredients together.

PRALINE KISSES

1 egg white, beaten
½ teaspoon salt
1 cup brown sugar
1 cup chopped pecans

Beat egg white until stiff, add salt and continue beating. Add sifted sugar gradually beating between each addition. Fold in pecans. Drop from teaspoon onto ungreased heavy paper and bake 60 minutes at 250°F. Cool slightly and remove from paper. Makes about 30 kisses.

MAPLE KISSES—Omit the brown sugar and add 1 cup of maple sugar which has been crushed and sifted to remove lumps.

Molded cookies are usually made by using a cookie press or a pastry bag and tube.

Most molded cookies might be used as rolled cookies by first chilling the dough to the point where it can be rolled satisfactorily. Some rich molded cookie doughs may be rolled and chilled in the refrigerator and used as a sliced cookie.

To mold well, the dough should be only moderately stiff, usually at room temperature, and of a consistency that the dough will retain the imprint of the mold when baked.

Fruit and nut cookie doughs will not usually go through the molding plates of the cookie press but the plainer doughs can be shaped with the press much more quickly and easily than by rolling them out and cutting. The press is also an aid in securing a dainty and uniform cookie. An infinite variety may be made with same dough by using different molds.

In using a cookie press, the following rules should be observed:

1. Do not grease the cookie sheet.

2. The cookie sheet should be cold or the fat in the cookies will melt and the cookies pull away from the sheet when the press is lifted.

3. Observe carefully the directions coming with the press as to how it should be put together, particularly the way the molding plates are placed.

4. Hold the press upright and force out the dough until it appears at the edge of the mold and then lift the press away.

HONEY COOKIES

⅔ cup shortening
½ cup sugar
1 cup strained honey
1 egg, beaten
½ cup sour cream
5 cups cake flour
1 teaspoon soda
1 teaspoon cinnamon
1 teaspoon nutmeg
1 teaspoon cloves
1 teaspoon salt

Cream shortening with sugar. Add honey and blend. Combine egg and sour cream and add to shortening mixture. Sift dry ingredients and add to liquid. Form with cookie mold or drop from teaspoon and flatten with a knife. Bake 15 minutes at 350°F. Makes 130 2-inch cookies.

BUTTER STICKS

⅔ cup butter
½ cup sugar
2 eggs, well beaten
1 teaspoon almond extract
3 cups cake flour
½ teaspoon soda
½ teaspoon salt

Cream butter and sugar thoroughly. Mix eggs and flavoring. Sift all dry ingredients together and add alternately with the liquid to the creamed mixture. Force through a pastry tube or cookie press onto a cold ungreased cookie sheet. Bake in a hot oven (400°F.) 12 minutes. Makes 40 sticks 3½ inches long and ½ inch wide. If desired, dust with confectioners' sugar.

For variety eliminate the almond extract and flavor as follows:

CINNAMON—Add 1 teaspoon of cinnamon and sprinkle with granulated sugar before baking.

CHOCOLATE—Add 1½ ounces of melted bitter chocolate.

Drop cookies can be as well-shaped as cut ones if the pastry tube is used

*Those who make many cook-
ies will find a cookie press
a time-saving piece of equipment*

RICH CINNAMON COOKIES

½ cup shortening
1 cup sugar
1 teaspoon vanilla
2 eggs or 4 yolks
2 cups cake flour
½ teaspoon salt
2 teaspoons baking powder
2 teaspoons cinnamon

Cream shortening and sugar, add
vanilla. Beat eggs well. Sift dry
ingredients together and add to
the creamed mixture alternately
with beaten eggs. Chill for 1 hour.
Mold with cookie press or drop
from teaspoon and flatten with
damp-towel covered glass. Bake
at 425°F. 7 minutes. Makes 60
cookies 2½ inches in diameter.

VARIATION—Shape into balls,
press nut half into each and bake.
Roll in cinnamon-sugar.

TEA DAINTIES

1 cup shortening
⅔ cup sugar
1 egg, beaten
2½ cups cake flour
¾ teaspoon baking powder
¼ teaspoon salt
Flavors, Food colors

Cream shortening. Add sugar
slowly and cream thoroughly, add
egg. Sift dry ingredients together
and add to the first mixture. Divide dough into as many parts as
colors desired. Vanilla is best in
an uncolored dough. Use all alco-
hol-based flavoring in the proportion of 1 teaspoon for entire
recipe. Oil extracts require only
a few drops. To color the dough
add food coloring a drop at a time
until the desired shade has been
attained. Suggested flavors and

color combinations are:
  almond extract and green
  lemon extract and yellow
  cinnamon oil and pink.

Mold the various doughs with a
cookie press or drop from a teaspoon and flatten into tiny circles.
Rolling is also possible if the
dough is thoroughly chilled. Much
variety is possible when all three
methods are used and further interest is created by small frosting
designs and toppings of fruit or
nuts. Bake uncolored cookies at
400°F. and colored ones at 325°F.
15 minutes. Makes 90 1-inch
cookies.

Store in a closed jar. These keep
only 2 days but can be made crisp
again by returning to the oven for
a few moments.

RICH CHOCOLATE TEAS

½ cup shortening
1 cup sugar
1 egg, beaten
½ teaspoon vanilla
½ teaspoon salt
2 tablespoons milk
2 cups cake flour
2 ounces chocolate, melted

Cream shortening, add sugar gradually, cream well. Add beaten
egg, vanilla, salt, milk. Blend and
add half of sifted flour. When
well mixed add melted chocolate
then rest of flour. Mold with
cookie press on cold, ungreased
cookie sheet. Bake in moderate
oven (350°F.) 23 minutes. Makes
6 dozen 2-inch cookies

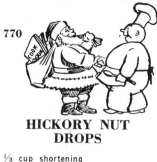

HOLIDAY COOKIES

HICKORY NUT DROPS

⅓ cup shortening
1 cup brown sugar, 2 eggs
2 cups cake flour
2 teaspoons baking powder
½ cup milk
1 teaspoon vanilla
1 cup hickory nuts, chopped

Cream shortening and sugar together until fluffy. Add eggs one at a time beating thoroughly after each addition. Sift flour and baking powder together and add alternately with the milk to the creamed mixture. Fold in vanilla and nuts. Drop from teaspoon onto a greased cookie sheet and bake 15 minutes at 375°F. Makes 60.

The fun of holiday preparations is shaping and decorating an assortment of cookies

SUGAR PLUM DROPS

1 cup shortening
1 cup sugar
1 cup brown sugar
2 eggs, beaten
1 teaspoon vanilla
1 teaspoon soda
1 tablespoon cold water
2 cups cake flour
1 teaspoon baking powder
1 teaspoon salt
2 cups rolled oats
1 cup coconut
1 cup colored gumdrops, chopped

Cream shortening and sugars together. Beat eggs, add vanilla and soda dissolved in the water. Combine egg mixture with the shortening and sugars. Sift flour with baking powder and salt and stir into creamed mixture. Add remaining ingredients. Shape into small balls, place on well-greased cookie sheet and bake 12 minutes at 375°F. Dredge with confectioners' sugar. Makes 120.

CHOCOLATE MOLDS

½ cup shortening
1 cup sugar
1 egg, well beaten
½ teaspoon vanilla
2 ounces chocolate, melted
2½ cups cake flour
½ teaspoon soda
½ teaspoon salt
¼ cup milk

Cream shortening and sugar until fluffy. Add well-beaten egg, vanilla and melted chocolate. Sift flour, soda and salt together and add alternately with the milk to the creamed mixture. Shape with a cookie press or with a pastry tube on an ungreased, cold cookie sheet and bake 12 to 15 minutes at 375°F. Makes 80 2½-inch cookies.

This mixture may be dropped from the tip of a teaspoon. Decorate with halves of nuts or cherries or with shredded colored coconut.

BLITZ KUCHEN

1 cup butter
1 cup sugar
4 egg yolks, beaten
½ teaspoon salt
3 cups cake flour
2 egg whites, beaten

TOPPING

2 egg whites, beaten
¼ cup sugar
¾ teaspoon cinnamon
½ cup almonds, blanched

Cream the butter and sugar together until light. Add the egg yolks which have been beaten until thick and lemon colored. Add salt and flour. Fold in the beaten egg whites. Spread thin on a greased cookie sheet. To make topping: Beat egg whites until stiff but not dry and add half of the sugar and cinnamon mixture. Spread on the batter. Shred the almonds and sprinkle over the topping. Dredge the remaining sugar and cinnamon over all. Bake in a moderate oven (350°F.) 30 minutes. Cool slightly, cut in bars and remove to a cooling rack.

PINEAPPLE-NUT COOKIES

½ cup shortening
½ cup brown sugar
½ cup sugar
1 egg, beaten
2 cups cake flour
2 teaspoons baking powder
¼ teaspoon soda
¼ teaspoon salt
½ cup crushed pineapple
⅔ cup chopped nuts
1 tablespoon lemon juice

Cream shortening and sugars together, add egg and beat well. Sift dry ingredients together and add with well-drained pineapple, nuts and lemon juice. Drop from a teaspoon or shape with a cookie press onto a well-greased cookie sheet. Bake 15 to 20 minutes at 375°F. Makes 48 2½-inch cookies.

FRUIT DREAMS IN COOKIE TARTS

1¾ cups cake flour
½ teaspoon salt
½ cup shortening
½ cup sugar
1 egg
½ teaspoon vanilla extract
1 quart sweetened strawberries
½ pint whipping cream

Sift together flour and salt. Cream shortening and sugar until light and fluffy. Add egg and vanilla extract and mix thoroughly. Add flour mixture to creamed mixture, stirring only enough to combine ingredients. Chill overnight. Roll out ⅛ inch thick and cut with a 2-inch cookie cutter. Line ungreased 3-inch muffin cups with 4 cut outs, overlapping about ½ inch. Place scrap of dough in bottom to cover open place. Moisten overlapping edges slightly and press together so that cookies will maintain their shape after baking. Bake at 375°F. 10 to 15 minutes. When cool fill with sweetened strawberries, top with sweetened whipped cream and serve. Makes 8 to 10 cookie tarts.

Somebody shook the dreamland tree and down came all these luscious cookies

VARIATION—Put 1 heaping tablespoon jam in baked cookie tarts and top with meringue made with 3 egg whites and 6 tablespoons of sugar. Bake at 350°F. about 10 minutes until meringue is a golden brown.

NORWEGIAN KRINGLE

1 cup sugar
1 cup rich sour cream
3 cups cake flour
1 teaspoon salt
1 teaspoon cinnamon
¾ teaspoon soda
1 ounce chocolate (optional)

Dissolve sugar in sour cream. Sift flour, salt, cinnamon and soda together. Combine with the cream and sugar. If chocolate is used melt and add last. Drop by ½ teaspoons on a greased cookie sheet and bake in a moderate oven (350°F.) 20 minutes. Makes 72 1-1½-inch cookies.

CURRANT TREASURES

¾ cup shortening
2½ cups cake flour
½ teaspoon salt
½ teaspoon cinnamon
¾ cup sugar
1 teaspoon baking powder
1 teaspoon grated lemon rind
1 cup nuts, chopped
1 cup currants, washed, dried
2 eggs, well beaten
6 tablespoons milk

Cream shortening. Sift flour, salt, cinnamon, sugar and baking powder together. Cut into shortening with dough blender until the consistency of coarse corn meal. Add remaining ingredients and blend thoroughly. Drop from a teaspoon onto a well-greased cookie sheet. Bake in a moderate oven (350° F.) about 15 minutes. Makes 7 dozen cookies

VARIATIONS—Omit 1 cup currants and add 1 cup washed and dried cranberries and increase sugar to 1 cup.

Omit nuts and add 1 cup chopped, shredded coconut to either the currants or cranberries.

Turn about is fair play; a hungry child can gobble up the big bad wolf

CHRISTMAS CUT OUTS

½ cup shortening
1 cup sugar
1 egg
2 teaspoons baking powder
2½ cups cake flour
½ teaspoon salt
½ cup milk
1 teaspoon vanilla

Cream shortening well. Add sugar and egg and blend together. Sift baking powder, flour and salt together and add to creamed mixture alternately with the milk. Stir in vanilla. Chill. Roll out $\frac{1}{16}$ inch thick on pastry cloth, cut in Christmas designs, brush with egg white, decorate and bake at 350°F. 10 to 12 minutes. Makes 100 2-inch cookies.

DECORATION—Cut cookies in the shape of Santa Claus, frost with red Confectioners' Icing. Using pastry tube, trim with white frosting making a white beard, fur collar and cuffs on pants, hat and jacket. Use raisins for eyes, nose and mouth.

Buy cutters for fairy-tale cookies or cut around a cardboard pattern

PFEFFERNÜSSE

5 eggs, beaten
2 cups sugar
Grated rind 1 lemon
3 tablespoons lemon juice
½ cup citron or other candied
    fruit or fruit peel, chopped
6 cups cake flour
2 teaspoons baking powder
½ teaspoon salt
½ teaspoon cloves
½ teaspoon nutmeg
½ teaspoon mace
1 tablespoon cinnamon
½ cup chopped nuts

Beat eggs well. Add sugar about two tablespoons at a time and beat thoroughly with each addition. Add lemon rind and juice, finely chopped citron, the dry ingredients which have been mixed and sifted together, and the finely chopped nuts. Chill at least an hour, roll ½ inch thick and cut out with a pfeffernüsse cutter, a round cutter about ⅞ of an inch in diameter. Place pfeffernüsse on a cookie sheet and let stand overnight in a cool place to dry. The next morning before baking,

invert each cookie and put a drop of fruit juice or brandy on the moist spot on the bottom of the cookie and bake upside down. This tends to make the pfeffernüsse "pop." Bake in a slow oven (300°F.) 8 minutes. Makes 180-200 cookies. Let ripen and soften before using.

If a pfeffernüsse cutter is not available, a narrow bottle top or round tin bouillon cube box will do very nicely.

BRAUNES LEBKUCHEN

1 cup sugar
⅔ cup honey
⅓ cup shortening
1 egg, beaten
⅓ cup water
4 cups cake flour
1 teaspoon soda
½ teaspoon salt
1 teaspoon cinnamon
1 teaspoon cloves
⅔ cup nuts, chopped
⅓ cup citron, chopped

Boil sugar, honey and shortening together for 5 minutes. Cool. Beat egg and add to water Mix and sift the flour, soda, salt and spices. Add the sifted dry ingredients alternately with the liquid ingredients to the honey mixture. Add nuts and citron last. Chill. If the dough is allowed to ripen for several days before rolling out, the flavor and texture are somewhat improved. Roll out about ¼ inch thick and cut the size of a playing card. Bake in a moderate oven (350° F.) 15 to 20 minutes. Frost with colored icing or with a sugar glaze.

FOR EASTER BASKETS—Place coconut on top of unbaked cutouts in the form of a nest. Arrange 3 colored jelly beans in the center. Bake as above.

Christmas cookies from across the sea include a basket of pfeffernüsse like grandmother used to make

FATTIGMAN

12 egg yolks
3 egg whites
½ teaspoon salt
1⅛ cups sugar
1⅛ cups heavy cream
1 teaspoon ground cardamom
½ cup melted butter
1 teaspoon lemon extract
2 tablespoons brandy
7 cups flour
Confectioners' sugar

Beat egg yolks, whites, salt and sugar together for ½ hour. Add cream and cardamom and stir well together. Add butter, extract and brandy and blend well. Mix in flour thoroughly. Dough should be stiff enough to roll out very thin. Place in refrigerator and chill overnight. Remove small amounts of dough at a time and roll out very thin, cut into diamond shapes and cut a slit in the center of each diamond through which one corner of the diamond should be pulled. Fry in deep hot fat (365° F.) until a delicate brown. Serve cold dredged with confectioners' sugar. Makes about 200 cookies.

They may be decorated by rolling them in colored sugar, after brushing the tops with egg white.

WEISER LEBKUCHEN

5 eggs, beaten
2 cups sugar
1 cup finely shredded citron
¼ cup finely chopped candied
   cherries
¾ cup almonds, finely chopped
4½ cups cake flour
½ teaspoon cinnamon
½ teaspoon cloves
½ teaspoon nutmeg
½ teaspoon salt

Beat eggs till thick. Add sugar gradually and beat well. Add citron, cherries, almonds and the flour which has been sifted with the spices and the salt. Roll and cut in squares. Let stand overnight and bake in a moderate oven (350°F.) 15 to 20 minutes until a very light brown. Makes about 96 squares. To make the following designs, omit citron, cherries and almonds and bake as above.

CHRISTMAS TREES—Cut trees with a knife and cut away the edges of the tree with a corrugated cutter. Sprinkle liberally with green sugar. Ornament with colored candies and bake.

CHRISTMAS WREATHS — Cut with doughnut cutter. Sprinkle liberally with green sugar. Dot with tiny red candies and bake.

SPRINGERLI

4 eggs, beaten
2 cups sugar
4 drops anise oil
4½ cups cake flour
Anise seed for pan

Beat whole eggs till thick. Add sugar gradually, beating well between each addition until all is combined and then beat well for about 15 minutes. This makes the finished cookies fine grained and light. Add the anise oil and blend. Fold in the flour lightly. Roll out the dough about ½ inch thick. Flour the springerli mold carefully and press firmly into the dough. Remove mold and cut the cookies along the line of the imprint. Place on greased cookie sheets. Flour the mold each time it is used. Sprinkle anise seed, if desired, on the greased cookie sheets before placing the cookies on them.

Let cookies stand overnight in a cool place to dry. In the morning, place first in a moderate oven (375° F.) to set the shape but reduce the heat immediately (to about 300°F.). In 15 minutes the cookies should be light in color with the appearance of having been iced. Makes 72.

Keep cookies in a tight can for two or three weeks before using to have the best flavor. To soften them, put a cut apple in the can a day or two before using. The apple also adds a delightful aroma to the cookies.

VARIATION — Spiced springerli are preferred by many. Add to the above recipe 2 teaspoons cinnamon and 1 teaspoon cloves, in place of the anise oil and seeds

Bake a good supply of holiday cookies and serve them early and often

S COOKIES

cup shortening
cup sugar
egg yolks
egg whites
teaspoon almond extract
cups cake flour

LAZE

egg white, beaten
tablespoon water
teaspoon cinnamon
tablespoons sugar
cup blanched almonds

Cream shortening, sugar and eggs together until smooth. Add almond extract and the flour. The dough should be smooth and not stick to the fingers. Make a ball about the size of a hickory nut and roll out to the thickness of a lead pencil. Shape in the form of an S on a cookie sheet. Let stand overnight.

To glaze: Beat egg white slightly with water, brush over tops of cookies with pastry brush, dip in cinnamon and sugar mixture and sprinkle with finely chopped almonds. Bake at 400°F. 8 minutes. Makes 72. If coloring is desired, roll in gaily colored sugars.

CINNAMON STARS

6 egg whites
2 teaspoons cinnamon
2¾ cups confectioners' sugar
1 pound almonds, not blanched
Confectioners' sugar

Mix egg whites, cinnamon and sugar until well blended. Set aside ¼ cup for frosting. Add finely ground almonds. Roll out mixture on sugar-flour dusted board to ⅛ inch thick. Cut with star cutter, frost with egg mixture stiffened with additional confectioners' sugar. Bake 20 minutes at 300°F. Makes 60 cookies.

Your party guests will be delighted to find their names spelled out in spritz cookies

SPRITZ COOKIES

1 cup shortening
¾ cup sugar
1 egg or 3 yolks, beaten
1 teaspoon almond extract
2¾ cups cake flour
¼ teaspoon salt
½ teaspoon baking powder

Work shortening until soft and cream with the sugar until light. Add beaten egg and almond flavoring. Beat until smooth. Add the flour sifted with the other dry ingredients. Mold with a cookie press into any desired shape. Bake in a moderately hot oven (375°F.) 12 to 15 minutes. Makes 45 cookies 2 inches in diameter.

VARIATIONS—Omit the almond extract and add 3 teaspoons melted red peppermint candies or ¼ teaspoon mint extra and color green. Spell out into names with a cookie press.

Use a pastry tube or cookie press to shape these spritz cookies and twist the ends into a knot

A gay box of Christmas cookies makes a charming gift for the hard-to-please

ALMOND PRETZELS

1 cup shortening
2½ cups cake flour
2 eggs, 2 egg yolks, beaten
2 tablespoons cream
1 teaspoon vanilla
1 cup sugar
½ teaspoon salt
1 egg white for icing
1 tablespoon milk
½ cup chopped almonds

Work shortening into the flour as for pie crust. Combine beaten eggs, cream, vanilla, sugar and salt. Add to flour and butter mixture and chill. Roll into rolls about 8 inches long and as thick as a lead pencil. Shape like a pretzel, brush with egg white which has been slightly beaten and to which has been added 1 tablespoon milk. Sprinkle with finely chopped almonds and bake in a moderate oven (350°F.) 12 to 15 minutes. Makes 5 dozen.

SPECULACI

1 cup shortening
2 cups confectioners' sugar
4 eggs, beaten
1 teaspoon lemon extract
1 teaspoon grated lemon rind
1 teaspoon salt
2¼ cups cake flour
1 cup almonds, chopped fine

Cream shortening and sugar until light. Beat eggs well, add to the creamed mixture and mix well. Reserve ½ cup of the creamed mixture for a glaze later on. To the remainder, add the lemon extract, lemon rind, the salt and the flour. Spread about the thickness of a knife blade on a greased cookie sheet and cover with the mixture which was reserved. Sprinkle with the chopped almonds and bake in a moderate oven (350°F.) 20 minutes. When firm and light brown in color, cut in strips 2½ x 1½ inches in size and remove to cooling rack. Makes 50 bars.

SWISS CHRISTMAS COOKIES

1¼ cups strained honey
¾ cup shortening
2 cups sugar
¼ cup fruit juice
Grated rind of 1 orange
Grated rind of 1 lemon
2 cups unblanched almonds, chopped
10 cups cake flour
1 teaspoon salt
1 teaspoon cinnamon
2 teaspoons nutmeg
1 teaspoon cloves
4 teaspoons baking powder

Melt honey and shortening together over hot water. Add sugar and fruit juice and stir until dissolved. Add grated rinds of orange and lemon, chopped almonds, and the dry ingredients which have been sifted together. Chill in refrigerator. The dough may be kept several days to ripen or used at once. Roll about ⅛ of an inch thick and cut in strips about 2 by 2½ inches in size. Bake in a slow oven (300°F.) 20 minutes. Makes 180 cookies. While still warm, frost with Confectioners' Icing.

NORWEGIAN CROWNS

6 hard-cooked egg yolks
6 egg yolks, uncooked
¼ teaspoon salt
¾ cup sugar
1½ cups butter
3 cups cake flour
1 egg white, slightly beaten
Coarse granulated sugar

Force cooked egg yolks through a sieve. Cream with uncooked egg yolks, salt and sugar. Add butter and flour alternately, a little at a time. Cover and chill until stiff. Roll into pencil shape ¼ inch in diameter and 5 inches long. Shape into rings, crossing the ends. Dip in egg whites and in sugar and bake in a hot oven (400°F.) 8 to 10 minutes. Makes about 72.

Candies

**75 WAYS
TO MAKE
CANDY**

CANDY BARS
CARAMEL CUTTER
COPPER KETTLE (Heavy, Deep)
CRYSTALLIZING TRAY AND
   WIRE RACKS
DIPPING FORKS AND RINGS
EGG BEATER
FOOD CHOPPER
FUNNEL
HOOK FOR PULLING CANDY
KNIVES
MARBLE SLAB

MARZIPAN MOLDS
MEASURING CUP
MEASURING SPOONS
METAL BARS
NOUGAT FRAME
PADDLES
PANS
PASTRY BRUSH
PASTRY TUBES AND BAGS
PLATTERS AND BOWLS
ROLLING PIN
RUBBER MATS

SACCHAROMETER
SAUCEPANS AND DOUBLE
   BOILERS
SCALES
SCISSORS
SIEVE (Fine Mesh)
SPATULAS
SPOONS, LARGE
SUGAR SCRAPER
THERMOMETER
WAXED PAPER AND
WAFER PAPER

Candy bars are made of steel and are used to form various sized spaces on the marble slab, into which are poured caramel and taffy mixtures. They can be arranged to hold any quantity of candy.

A candy hook is very useful, labor-saving and inexpensive. Candy is improved by being pulled on a hook, as the pulling makes it lighter in color and fluffier.

A caramel cutter consists of a metal framework filled in with transverse and longitudinal metal bars, which, when pressed on the surface of caramel or taffy, mark it into a number of small squares. The squares are then cut out with a knife.

Crystallizing trays are shallow pans fitted with wire racks to hold candies and prevent their rising during crystallizing. A crystallizing tray is usually fourteen inches long and ten inches wide.

Dipping forks are made of wire with two or three prongs or a loop at the end, and used for lifting the dipped candies out of the coating mixtures. They are very inexpensive.

A marble slab is not absolutely necessary, but it is convenient and useful. When candy is poured out on a piece of marble, it cools quickly. A large platter or an enameled tray may be used

The **saccharometer** is often used for ascertaining the specific gravity of liquids. It is made of glass containing quicksilver, the same as the thermometer, and is divided into degrees or scales. The scale on the saccharometer registers from 0° to 50°, and reads from the top downward. The advantages of the saccharometer are immense, not only as a matter of economy, but as a guide to he candymaker, who cannot work with certainty without knowing the degrees of boiling. For example: The thread, large or small, marks 25°; the pearl, 30°; the blow, 34°; the feather, 36°; the ball, 50°. After this last degree the sugar has become so thick that the saccharometer can no longer be used. The remaining degrees, the crack and caramel, must be determined by other tests. In order to use the saccharometer to test sirup you must have a narrow glass vase, or a glass test tube, or a tall bottle about an inch and a half in diameter. Pour some of the sirup into the tube, wet the saccharometer and drop it into the boiling sugar and it will indicate the density of the sugar.

A good candy thermometer will save its purchase price in many successful batches of candy

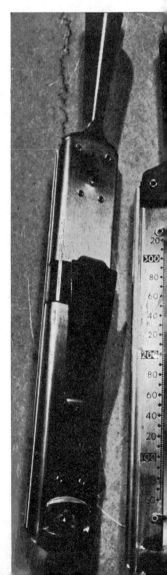

Nougat frames are made of wood, and used for molding nougat and other candies of like consistency. **Rubber mats** are used for the molding of fondants. They come in innumerable designs, and the candies cast in them are perfectly shaped and delicately molded. **Saucepans** may be made of copper, iron, granite, enamel, or aluminum. They must be kept clean inside and outside. Two small lipped pans, holding about one pint each, are convenient for melting fondant and for other minor operations.

A sheet of brightly polished tin, which may be procured at the cost of a few cents, will be found useful for dropped chocolates. **Spatulas** are flat, pear-shaped paddles made of metal or hardwood, and are used for stirring and beating mixtures or for scraping out pans. They are useful little utensils, and often used in place of spoons.

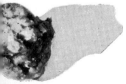

A starch tray is used when molding fondants, liqueurs, fruit jellies, or other candies in starch. Any large flat box or biscuit pan will do for this. Three inches by twenty inches is a convenient size. Fill the box with clean, dry, sifted cornstarch. Smooth the starch with a flat stick; then make the required impressions on it with small plaster molds glued to a piece of wood. They may be made with a cork, a piece of sealing-wax, a thimble, a marble, a glass stopper, or the tip of the finger. The piece of wood should be longer than the box or pan. Pour or pipe in the candy mixture, filling each mold level with the top of the starch. When set, pick up the candies and dust off the starch. Keep the starch dry and clean in tin boxes. It should always be dried and sieved before use.

A sugar scraper is made of a strip of strong metal or tin rolled at one end to form a handle. It is used to scrape up the sugar on the slab or platter. A broad-bladed spatula may take its place.

A confectioner's **thermometer** is required for candymaking, so that the sirup may be removed from the heat at exactly the correct temperature. Such thermometers are made of wood, nickel, brass or copper, and the degrees on them should mark not less than 320°F. A thermometer should always be lowered gently into the boiling sugar.

When not in use, it should be kept hanging up on a nail or hook.

WEIGHTS AND MEASURES

All Measures Are Level

1 tablespoon	3 teaspoons
1 cup	16 tablespoons
½ cup	8 tablespoons
¼ cup	4 tablespoons
½ ounce butter	1 tablespoon
½ pound butter or sugar	1 cup
1 pound butter or sugar	2 cups
1 pound molasses	1½ cups
1 pound corn sirup	1⅓ cups
1 pound chocolate	16 squares
1 pound peanuts	2⅔ cups
3¾ ounces English walnuts	1 cup
1 pound coconut	8 cups
6 ounces brown sugar	1 cup
5½ ounces confectioners' sugar	1 cup
4½ ounces cocoa	1 cup
4 ounces almonds	1 cup

Everyone at one time or another has made a batch of candy. It's fun to do and best of all, when you're through making the candy, you still have the pleasure of eating it. The wise candymaker will find it valuable to learn certain fundamental techniques that will develop added skill and improvement in the finished product.

It is just as easy to be a versatile candymaker as a monotonous one. Simple little tricks such as adding gay food colorings to a mixture; decorating with nuts, shredded coconut, glacé sirup; making fascinating designs with pulled sugar or gossamer nests of spun sugar, lift a candymaker from the mediocre class.

Practice will develop deftness and skill in handling your candymaking materials to get the best possible results. A most important factor in the production of good candy is not to trust to guesswork, but to follow recipes carefully and to use a thermometer.

CANDYMAKING INGREDIENTS

ANGELICA
BUTTER
BAKING SODA
BROWN SUGAR
CORN SIRUP
CHOCOLATE
CREAM OF TARTAR
CHERRIES
CREAM
CORNSTARCH
COCONUT
DATES
EXTRACTS
EGGS
FOOD COLORS
FIGS
FRUITS, Fresh and Candied
GINGER, Preserved and Candied
GOLDEN SIRUP
GELATIN
GLUCOSE
GUM ARABIC
HONEY
JELLY
LEMONS

MAPLE SIRUP
MAPLE SUGAR
MOLASSES
MILK: Fresh, Evaporated, Condensed
MARSHMALLOWS
NUTS
PRUNES
PRESERVES
POPCORN
RAISINS
SUGAR
SPICES
VINEGAR

HOW TO PREPARE CHESTNUTS

With a sharp knife make a slit in each chestnut. Place in boiling water and boil for 4 minutes; then remove and dry thoroughly Melt 3 tablespoons of butter in a saucepan, add the chestnuts and heat, stirring thoroughly until very hot.

With a sharp-pointed knife, both skins can then be removed together, leaving the nut whole.

HOW TO BLANCH PISTACHIO NUTS

Cover the nuts with cold water, then bring to boiling point and boil for 5 minutes. Plunge into cold water, drain and rub off the skins.

SALTED ALMONDS

½ pound shelled Jordan almonds
2 tablespoons olive oil or melted butter
Salt

Blanch the almonds and dry them on a clean cloth. Place the oil or butter in a small frying pan, and when hot add the almonds. Sauté until evenly and delicately browned. Drain on paper and sprinkle with salt. Cool before serving.

Pecan nut meats, blanched pistachio nuts and peanuts may be salted in the above manner

HOW TO COLOR ALMONDS

Blanch 2 cups of almonds; cool and wipe dry. Then place them in a bowl, and add 5 tablespoons of olive oil. Let stand for 1 hour, stirring occasionally. Then place in a baking pan in a hot oven (450°) until evenly browned. Turn out on waxed paper to dry. To color, chop blanched and dried almonds and spread on white paper. Add a few drops of whatever food coloring is desired, rubbing almonds together until color is evenly distributed. Dry carefully and keep for use.

HOW TO COLOR COCONUT

Sprinkle some shredded coconut on waxed paper; add a little food coloring and rub evenly throughout. Dry and store in jars.

HOW TO COLOR SUGAR

Place some granulated sugar on a piece of stiff white paper; sprinkle over it a few drops of the desired food coloring and rub with a wooden spoon or between the hands until evenly distributed. Dry in a moderate oven (350°), occasionally separating the grains by rubbing them between the fingers. Store in an airtight container.

VANILLA OR CLOVE SUGAR

1 ounce vanilla beans, or 2 ounces cloves
1 pound loaf sugar

Chop the vanilla beans (or cloves) and pound them in a mortar or a bowl with the sugar, rubbing all through a fine sieve. Store in airtight containers.

STOCK SIRUP

Place 2 cups of granulated sugar in a saucepan; add 2 cups of water and bring slowly to the boiling point. Remove the scum from the surface. Cover and boil for 4 minutes to allow the condensing steam to clear any crystals of sugar from the sides of the pan. Boil gently for 25 minutes. Then remove from heat, allow to cool, and store in a jar for use in making bonbons.

HOW TO CLARIFY STOCK SIRUP

After making the sirup in the above manner pour it in a steady stream over stiffly beaten egg whites, allowing 2 egg whites to 1 pound of sugar.

Return to pan and simmer until the whites coagulate and rise to the surface; strain.

HOW TO STUFF DATES

Remove the stones from dates and stuff them with any nut meats. Close the dates, then brush over with a little beaten egg white; roll in colored sugar, colored coconut, or chopped pistachio nuts, or spangle with brilliantine.

Dates may be stuffed with flavored and colored fondant, then closed and soaked in a little sherry wine for about 10 minutes. To finish, drain and roll them in fine sugar.

They may also be stuffed with such delicacies as seedless raisins, marshmallows, walnuts chopped to a paste, preserved ginger and cherries chopped together, and finely chopped shredded coconut. Stuffed dates are delicious dipped in melted fondant or chocolate, or glacéed.

TO PREPARE FIGS AND PRUNES FOR STUFFING

Steam figs or prunes 15 minutes or until plump and soft. Remove pits from prunes. Cut slit in sides of figs.

CRYSTALLIZED MINT LEAVES

2 pounds mint leaves
5 cups sugar
2 cups water
Pinch cream of tartar

Remove the mint leaves from the stalks and wash in cold water; spread on white paper to dry.

Place 4 cups of the sugar together with the water in a saucepan and dissolve thoroughly, stirring with the thermometer. When dissolved, add the cream of tartar and cook until it forms a soft ball when tested in cold water, or to 240°.

Remove from heat and add the mint leaves, pressing them down under the sirup. Return to heat and allow to boil up once, then pour gently into a cold bowl. The following day drain on a wire rack. To the sirup add the remaining cup of sugar, and cook without stirring to the soft-ball stage, or to 240°. Drop in the mint and set aside overnight; then drain again, heat to the boiling point and add the mint. Remove from heat and stir gently until the sirup begins to grain; then pour onto sheets of paper; shake and separate the leaves; when dry, pick them from the sugar. Use for decorating candies.

CRYSTALLIZING

8 cups sugar
4 cups water

Put the sugar and water in a saucepan and heat, stirring until the sugar is dissolved. Cook to 225°. Remove the thermometer and gently lift the pan to a table. On the hot sirup lay a piece of paper with a small hole cut in the center and set to cool before using. (The paper should be dipped in cold water and should fit closely around the sides of the pan.)

Place the candies to be crystallized on racks in the pans of a crystallizing tray. Remove any crystals which may have formed on the sirup and lift off the paper covering. Pour enough of the sirup over the candies on each rack to completely cover them. Cover the candies with a piece of damp muslin and leave undisturbed for 10 to 12 hours. When an especially thick coating of crystals is desired, it is necessary to leave the candies in the sirup longer.

Lift off the muslin and drain away the sirup; remove the candies, place on wire racks and leave in a warm place overnight to become dry. The surfaces of the candies should then be covered with fine sugar crystals.

Many candies are improved in appearance and keeping qualities by being crystallized, and some look better if crystallized twice.

TO SEND CANDY BY MAIL

Line buttered tin boxes with waxed paper, pour the candy in while hot, mark in squares when cool enough. Cover and wrap. Wrap hard candies separately.

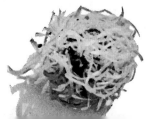

CANDY TEMPERATURE CHART

from
"Terminology Used in Food Preparation"
Published by American Home Economics Association

Product	Stage of concentration desired	Temperature of sirup at sea level (indicating concentration desired)		Behavior at stage desired
		Degrees F.	*Degrees C.*	
Sirup	Thread	230 to 234	110 to 112	The sirup spins a two-inch thread when dropped from fork or spoon.
Fondant Fudge Panocha	Soft ball	234 to 240	112 to 115	The sirup when dropped into very cold water forms a soft ball which flattens on removal.
Caramels	Firm ball	244 to 248	118 to 120	The sirup when dropped into very cold water forms a firm ball which does not flatten on removal.
Divinity Marshmallows Nougat Popcorn balls Salt-water taffy	Hard ball	250 to 265	121 to 130	The sirup when dropped into very cold water forms a ball which is hard enough to hold its shape, yet plastic.
Butterscotch Taffies	Soft crack	270 to 290	132 to 143	The sirup when dropped into very cold water separates into threads which are hard but not brittle.
Brittle Glacé	Hard crack	300 to 310	149 to 154	The sirup when dropped into very cold water separates into threads which are hard and brittle.
Barley Sugar	Clear liquid	320	160	The sugar liquefies.
Caramel	Brown liquid	338	170	The liquid becomes brown.

PULLED SUGAR

4 cups sugar
1 cup water
1 tablespoon glucose
¼ teaspoon cream of tartar

Put the sugar and water in a saucepan and set in a warm place to dissolve. When thoroughly dissolved place on range and add the glucose and cream of tartar. Cook as quickly as possible to 312°, or to the hard-crack stage; remove at once from the heat. Dip the pan in cold water to stop the boiling. Then pour the sirup on a lightly oiled slab, and as the edges cool lift them toward the center of the mass, using a knife.

When the sugar is cool enough to handle, roll into a ball and pull with the fingers from the two sides, turning the ends over from side to side and into the center; pull all parts evenly.

The sugar will soon take on a white sheen and become whiter and whiter. Care should be taken that it does not become too cold. While shaping the pulled sugar into fancy forms, it should be pulled near the heat of an oven or in front of a batch-warmer, but not overheated.

To make a pulled-sugar rose, pull a piece of sugar with the thumb and forefinger of the right hand and break this portion off short. Shape the piece into a round with a thin edge; press in at the center and fold over to bring the thin edges almost together to represent the center of a rose just beginning to open. Pull some petals and arrange three or four of them slightly higher than the bud, adding more if necessary.

Use a real flower as a pattern. Make leaves and stem of green pulled sugar

Try your hand at making spun sugar. It's lots of fun and the results are a joy forever

HOW TO SPIN SUGAR

4 cups sugar, 2 cups water
Pinch cream of tartar
1 teaspoon glucose

Spinning sugar simply consists of drawing the hot sugar, which has been boiled to a hard crack, into fine strands which will harden immediately and retain their form.

Dissolve the sugar in the water while heating and stirring. Cook to 280°, or to the soft-crack stage. Then add the cream of tartar and glucose and continue cooking to 310°, or to the hard-crack stage. Remove quickly from heat and to prevent the sugar from changing its color, set the pan in cold water. Then remove and place in warm water.

Oil a rolling pin or the blade of a large knife and hold it out straight with the left hand; then with the right hand dip a warm spoon into the sirup and shake it backward and forward over the rolling pin. The sugar will fall across the pin in long threads. Continue the operation until enough spun sugar is obtained; then cut off the ends and press as desired into molds, or shape. Another method of spinning the sugar is to oil the handles of two wooden spoons and fasten them in drawers or under weights with the ends projecting over the edge of a table. Cover the floor underneath with clean paper or several large baking pans. Then take a large fork, two forks, an egg beater, or a bunch of wires, and dip into the sirup. Move quickly backward and forward over the oiled spoon handles. Continue until there is a mass of sugar threads resembling silk. The threads may be made either fine or coarse by moving the forks or spinners slowly or quickly.

SUGARS AND ICINGS

If in the course of spinning the sirup becomes too firm to use, warm the pan over a low heat and continue the spinning process.

The sirup may be colored, if desired.

Spun sugar is used for decorating candies and cakes and for garnishing desserts.

It must be made and kept in a very dry atmosphere and used as soon as possible.

HOW TO MAKE BRILLIANTINE

Put 2 ounces of gum arabic and ½ cup of water in a double boiler and stir occasionally while heating over hot water.

When melted, strain through a piece of fine muslin. Dip a stiff brush into the gum and brush it lightly over pieces of clean, polished glass. Dry in a warm room. When dry and set, scrape or brush the brilliantine off. It may then be rolled with a rolling pin or left in tiny flakes, to be used for spangling candies. Color may be added, if desired.

ROYAL ICING FOR DECORATING CANDIES

2 cups confectioners' sugar
2 egg whites
2 teaspoons lemon juice

Sift the sugar into a bowl. Add the egg whites and lemon juice. Stir until well mixed, then beat with a wooden spoon for about 15 minutes. The icing should be creamy but too stiff to drop from the spoon. If too thick, add more egg white; if too thin, add a little more sugar. Tint if desired. Use a small bag and tube for applying icing decorations to candies. Allow to become thoroughly dry before serving.

ORANGE SUGAR

12 oranges
½ pound loaf sugar

Wash and dry the oranges; cut off the thin yellow rinds, rejecting all the white peel. Dry thoroughly. Then place the rinds together with the sugar in a mortar or a bowl, and pound. Rub through a fine sieve and store in an airtight tin.

Tangerine and lemon sugars may be made in the same way.

Flavoring sugars are very useful and economical, and in many instances may be substituted for extracts.

Flavored sugars may be crushed with a rolling pin and used for coating stuffed fruits.

The ethereal delicacy of this centerpiece is due to the spun sugar border and pulled sugar flowers

Spun sugar is a particularly lovely garnish for molded ice cream or other frozen desserts

Fondant is a creamy, smooth confection made of sugar, water and some substance such as glucose, cream of tartar, corn sirup or lemon juice.

Because there are certain important rules involved in fondant making, all simple when they are pointed out, the following standard recipe is given in much detail, with a list of hints and explanations.

DO'S AND DONT'S OF FONDANT MAKING

1. Every particle of sugar should be melted before the sirup is allowed to boil. If this precaution is not taken and the sugar, being partly dissolved, is allowed to boil, these crystals will not dissolve readily and will cause the sirup to grain.

2. The glucose or cream of tartar is used to prevent too rapid crystallization of the sugar and should be added after the sugar is dissolved.

3. Do not stir or move the pan after the mixture boils, or the sirup will become sugar.

4. Allow the sirup to "settle" before creaming the mass.

5. Add the desired coloring and flavoring to the lukewarm fondant at the beginning of the beating period, if desiring one flavor and color for the entire batch; otherwise, add the coloring and flavoring extract to the fondant as it is used in various candies.

6. Allow the fondant to ripen for one hour before using it to make candies.

TO SHAPE BONBONS

Take any quantity of fondant. Add any desired flavor and color and knead thoroughly until well blended. Break off small pieces of the fondant and shape or cut into balls, cubes, strips, patties, diamonds, or odd shapes. Let stand for several hours to dry.

BASIC FONDANT

6 cups sugar
2 cups water
1 tablespoon glucose, or
    Pinch cream of tartar

Place the sugar and water in a large saucepan and heat, stirring until the sugar is completely dissolved; then stop stirring. Wash down the inside of the pan to the sirup's edge with a small brush dipped in water, or with a fork wrapped in a damp cloth. When the sirup begins to boil, add the glucose or the cream of tartar.

Continue the boiling, without stirring, until the thermometer registers 240° or until a few drops form a soft ball when tested in cold water. Remove from heat at once, allow to stand 4 minutes, or until the air bubbles disappear; then pour into a large wet platter or onto a marble slab between candy bars. (The sirup should not be deeper than 1½ inches.) Set in a cool place and when lukewarm (110°) beat with a wooden spoon or a hardwood paddle.

Turn the sugar backward and forward, leaving no part untouched, until the whole mass becomes white and opaque.

Knead until smooth and free from lumps. Wet and wring a small towel, place it over the fondant and allow it to remain there for at least 1 hour. (This is called the curing process.) Remove the cloth and knead just as you would bread dough, until creamy and smooth. Store in an airtight jar. (If left exposed to the air the fondant will get hard and dry.)

TO PREPARE FONDANT FOR DIPPING

Place 1 cup of fondant in top of a double boiler, or in a dish placed in a pan of water. Heat, keeping water just below the boiling point. Stir only enough to blend, adding a very small quantity of stock sirup or boiling water if mixture is too stiff. When melted, add the coloring and flavoring desired; stir as little as possible to prevent crystallization. Remove from heat and lower the centers, one at a time, into the mixture on a dipping fork.

Note: Work quickly so the fondant will not become too thick to manipulate; in that case, however, add a few drops of boiling water to bring mixture back to correct consistency.

BUTTER FONDANT

3 cups sugar
1 cup milk
2 tablespoons butter
1 teaspoon glucose

Place the sugar, milk and butter in a saucepan; when dissolved, add the glucose and cook to 240° or to the soft-ball stage.

Remove from heat and pour into a platter which has been rinsed with cold water. When cool, beat until creamy; then knead until smooth. Keep in an airtight jar. When wanted for use, make into balls for centers.

MAPLE FONDANT

4 cups brown sugar
2 cups maple sirup
2 cups hot water
1 tablespoon glucose

This fondant is cooked and tested in the same way as the Basic Fondant, but usually requires longer beating to make it creamy. It makes delicious centers, which must be allowed to dry before they are crystallized, dipped in melted fondant or chocolate.

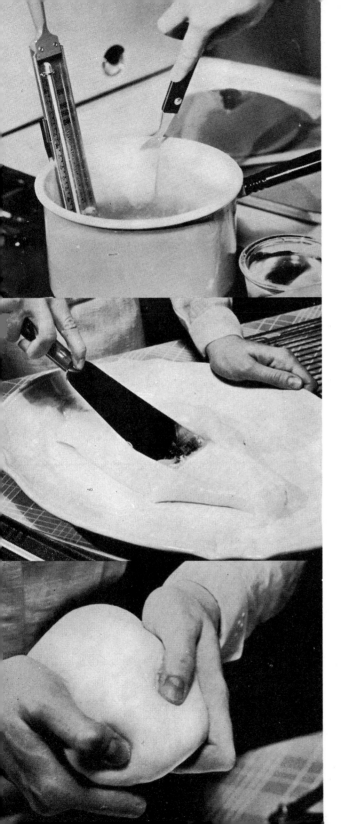

CANDIES WITH BASIC FONDANT

AFTER-DINNER MINTS

Melt the fondant as for dipping, using such flavor and color combinations as:

COLOR	FLAVOR
White	Peppermint, vanilla
Pink	Wintergreen
Green	Spearmint, almond, lime
Red	Cinnamon, clove

The melted fondant may be either dropped from the tip of a spoon or poured through a funnel onto waxed paper or a greased, flat surface. When firm, loosen and lift on a clean, soft cloth.

BURNT ALMOND BONBONS

1 cup blanched almonds
1 cup ground almonds
2 cups flavored Fondant

Brown and chop the blanched almonds. Melt the fondant and add both the browned almonds and the ground almonds. Stir well and pour onto a buttered slab. Roll small portions in strips, then cut the strips into small cushions. Put on waxed paper to dry. Coat with melted fondant, melted chocolate, or glacé sirup.

COCONUT BALLS

Work into 1 cup of vanilla fondant as much chopped, shredded coconut as possible without its becoming too stiff to mold. Roll in balls, allow to dry and dip in melted fondant. Roll in chopped coconut before fondant coating becomes firm.

To insure success in making fondant, use a candy thermometer and remove crystals from sides of pan

CREAMED GRAPES

Cut Malaga or Tokay grapes from the bunches, leaving the stems as long as possible. Wash and dry thoroughly. Holding them by the stems, dip them, one at a time, into some melted flavored fondant; then place on waxed paper to dry. Whole nut meats, pieces of candied fruits, small stemmed fruits and bits of marzipan may also be coated with melted fondant, using a fork to lift them into and out of the fondant.

FRUIT FONDANT

Into 1 pound of unflavored fondant knead the following: chopped raisins, chopped dates, chopped figs, and the desired chopped candied fruits. Press into a flat cake about an inch thick and cut into bars. When dry, dip in melted chocolate or melted fondant, or both.

When dipped in melted fondant, decorate with chopped nuts, silver dragées, tiny candies, or small pieces of candied fruit.

JAM SANDWICHES

Cut fondant into small squares, putting two squares together with a little strawberry or raspberry jam. Dip in melted chocolate.

NUT CREAMS

Tinted and flavored fondant is very delicious combined with chopped nuts and shaped into balls. Whole nut meats may be pressed into the tops, or the balls may be dipped in chocolate. These balls are good when merely rolled in cocoa or cinnamon.

Add flavoring and coloring a drop at a time. Mold and cut slices for dipping into melted fondant or chocolate

CHOCOLATE CANDIES

CHOCOLATE DIPPING

Chocolate dipping is a difficult process. Proper equipment and ingredients must be available. For success follow directions.

1. Temperature is important. Keep room between 60° and 70° F. Never dip on a warm or humid day and avoid all drafts.

2. Arrange all equipment conveniently. Have centers ready and at room temperature. Cover wire racks with waxed paper. Place these to right of dipping pan. Have ready a good, tested candy thermometer, a 1½ quart double boiler and a dipping fork.

3. Use special dipping chocolate and grate fine. Melt grated chocolate over hot water in top of double boiler. Melt slowly, stir constantly but never let water boil. Do not melt less than 1 pound or more than 2 pounds of chocolate at one time. When completely melted, immerse bulb of thermometer in chocolate. Continue stirring until chocolate has reached 130°F.

4. Cool quickly by emptying hot water from bottom of double boiler and refilling with cold water. Stir constantly and rapidly, using circular motion, until chocolate has cooled to 83°F.

5. To keep chocolate at this temperature add hot water to bottom of boiler until water is 85°F. Quickly replace chocolate.

6. Chocolate is now ready for dipping but must always be stirred between each dip. Drop center in chocolate and cover well. Lift out with fork, tap on rim of saucer to remove excess chocolate and draw fork carefully across rim. Invert piece on waxed paper, remove fork and form string across top with chocolate that is still on fork. Work fast. If necessary repeat steps, 3, 4, 5.

CHOCOLATE ALMOND AND RAISIN BALLS

2 cups almonds, blanched and chopped
4 cups seeded raisins
1 teaspoon almond extract
Melted coating chocolate

Mix the nuts, raisins and almond extract and put through the food chopper. Roll the mixture into small balls and allow them to dry. Dip in melted chocolate and drop on a baking sheet.

CHOCOLATE ALMONDS

Almonds, Coating Chocolate

Blanch the almonds and put them on a baking pan in the oven until slightly browned. When cold, dip them into melted coating chocolate and drop onto a pan to harden.

Note: The almonds are very good if they are dipped first into glacé sirup and then into the melted chocolate.

CHOCOLATE NOUGAT

2 cups sugar
1 teaspoon glucose
½ cup water, ¼ cup butter
1 teaspoon almond extract
½ cup grated chocolate, melted
¾ cup preserved cherries, chopped
¾ cup blanched almonds, chopped

Place the sugar in a saucepan, add the glucose, water, and butter. Dissolve and stir slowly over the heat; then cook, without stir-

ring, to 240°, or to the soft-ball stage. Remove from heat and pour at once into a bowl, rinsed in cold water. When nearly cold, stir in the extract and add the melted chocolate. Beat until a firm mass is formed. Cover with waxed paper and a clean cloth and leave in a cool place for about ½ hour. Then knead until smooth and place in a double boiler, heating until warm enough to pour.

Mix in the cherries and the almonds and pour into a nougat frame lined with wafer paper. Cover with wafer paper and set a board and a heavy weight on the top. Leave for about 5 hours, then turn out and cut into strips.

CHOCOLATE BONBONS

4 squares grated chocolate
½ pound vanilla fondant

Knead the chocolate into the fondant on a slab. Form into small balls and allow to dry on waxed paper. Dip in melted fondant or in melted coating chocolate.

DIPPED COCONUT FUDGE

3 cups brown sugar
8 tablespoons golden sirup
2 tablespoons butter
Pinch of salt
3 cups shredded coconut, chopped
1 teaspoon vanilla extract
½ teaspoon almond extract
Melted coating chocolate

Cook the sugar, sirup and butter to 240°, or to the soft-ball stage. Add the salt and remove from heat. Add the coconut and extracts. Spread in a pan lined with waxed paper. Cut into small pieces. When cold, dip in melted coating chocolate.

CHOCOLATE CANDIES

CHOCOLATE DATES

1 pound dates
4 squares chocolate
½ cup confectioner's sugar
2 tablespoons boiling water
½ teaspoon vanilla extract

Wipe the dates and extract the pits through a small lengthwise slit.

Grate the chocolate into a small saucepan; add the sugar, boiling water and vanilla extract, and heat without boiling until smooth; keep mixture fluid by setting saucepan in a pan of boiling water.

Fill dates with the chocolate mixture, gently pressing the edges together. Let stand to harden.

CHOCOLATE MARSHMALLOWS

4 ounces gum arabic
1 cup water
1 cup sugar
1 teaspoon almond extract
3 egg whites
Melted coating chocolate
Confectioners' sugar
Cornstarch

Soak the gum arabic in the water overnight; then strain into a double boiler, add the sugar, and cook until mixture thickens. Remove from heat and add the almond extract with the stiffly beaten egg whites. Beat the mixture until stiff, then pour into a pan which has been dusted with equal quantities of confectioners' sugar and cornstarch. Dust top with the cornstarch mixture. Let stand overnight, then cut in rounds and dip in chocolate.

Dipping centers in melted chocolate is always fun

BROWN SUGAR CARAMELS

2 cups granulated sugar
½ cup boiling water
1 cup cream
1 tablespoon glucose
1 cup light brown sugar
1 cup nut meats, chopped
1 teaspoon vanilla extract

Place 1 cup of the granulated sugar in a saucepan and heat, stirring constantly, until melted. Slowly add the boiling water and stir until blended. Add the cream and glucose and stir for about 5 minutes. Then add the brown sugar and the remaining granulated sugar and cook to 245°, or to the firm-ball stage.

Remove from heat, add the nuts and the extract, and beat until creamy. Pour into a pan lined with waxed paper. Spread out smoothly and mark into squares while warm. Cut when cool.

Use evaporated milk for cream.

BRAZIL CREAM CARAMELS

2 cups sugar
2 cups cream
2 tablespoons glucose
¼ cup butter
1 teaspoon lemon extract
1 cup Brazil-nut meats, chopped

Dissolve the sugar in 1 cup of cream, heating slowly. Add the glucose, and cook, stirring frequently, to 240°, or to the soft-ball stage. Add the remaining cream and the butter. Cook to 252°, or to the hard-ball stage. Remove from heat, add the lemon extract and nut meats, stirring as little as possible. Pour into buttered pan. Cut when cool.
Use English walnuts or black walnuts instead of Brazil nuts and use vanilla instead of lemon extract.

Caramels decorated with whole Brazil nuts or animal crackers will delight grown-ups as well as children

CHOCOLATE MOLASSES CARAMELS

3 cups sugar
1 cup butter
1 cup milk
1 tablespoon glucose
1 cup molasses
4 squares chocolate, chipped
1 teaspoon vanilla extract
½ teaspoon lemon extract

Place the sugar, butter, milk, glucose, molasses, and chocolate in a saucepan and cook, stirring constantly, to 252°; or to the hard-ball stage. Add the extracts and pour into buttered pans. When cool, cut into pieces with buttered scissors.

INEXPENSIVE MILK CARAMELS

2 cups sugar
1 cup light corn sirup
3 cups milk
¼ cup butter
½ teaspoon salt
1 teaspoon vanilla extract

Heat sugar and sirup in 1 cup of milk, stirring until dissolved. Then cook, stirring frequently, to 246°-248°, or to the firm-ball stage. Slowly add the second cup of milk, and repeat the cooking process. Add the final cup of milk, the butter and salt, and cook to 246°-248°, or until a ball tested in cold water is of the firmness desired in the finished caramel.

Remove from heat, add vanilla extract and pour at once into a buttered pan, marking in squares when cool.

Add ½ cup chopped pecans, black walnuts, or coconut. Shape into roll 1½ inches in diameter, roll in chopped nuts and cut in ½-inch slices.

BARLEY SUGAR

3 cups sugar, 2 cups water
1 lemon
Pinch cream of tartar

Dissolve the sugar in the water; then add the thin rind of the lemon and the cream of tartar. Cook to 240°, or to the soft-ball stage, then remove the lemon rind. Add the strained juice of the lemon and cook to 310°, or to the hard-crack stage, taking care that the sirup does not burn. (Sirup should be a delicate straw color.)

Pour onto a well-buttered platter or slab and when candy begins to set, cut in strips. When cool enough to handle, twist each strip. Keep in an airtight container.

BRITTLED ALMONDS

2 cups sugar, ½ cup water
Pinch cream of tartar
1 teaspoon lemon extract
2 cups almonds, blanched and split in halves

Dissolve the sugar in the water, add the cream of tartar and cook to 315°, or to the hard-crack stage. Add the extract.

Sprinkle the almonds in a buttered pan and pour the boiling sirup over them. When cool mark into squares with a sharp knife. Break into pieces when cold.

HOREHOUND CANDY

1 ounce dried horehound
1½ cups water
1¾ pounds brown sugar
¼ cup corn sirup

Cook horehound slowly in water 30 minutes. Remove horehound. To liquid, add sugar and sirup. Cook to 300° or to hard-crack stage. Pour into greased pan and mark into squares.

TROPICAL NUGGETS

¼ cup Brazil nuts, sliced ⅛-inch thick
¼ cup seeded raisins
¼ cup figs, chopped
¼ cup shredded coconut
2 cups sugar
2 tablespoons butter
¼ cup vinegar
¼ cup water
1 teaspoon lemon extract

Place the nuts, raisins, figs and coconut in a buttered pan. Place the sugar, butter, vinegar, and water in a saucepan and cook to 290°, or to the soft-crack stage. Add the lemon extract and pour mixture over the fruit and nuts. Break into pieces when cold.

GINGER BARS

¾ cup molasses
2 tablespoons ground ginger
½ cup butter
1 cup brown sugar

Place the molasses, ginger, butter, and sugar in a large saucepan and cook to 300°, or to the hard-crack stage. Pour in buttered pans and cut into small bars. Wrap in waxed paper.

CINNAMON BARS are made in the same way, substituting ground cinnamon for the ginger.

STICK-JAW

3 cups granulated sugar
3 cups brown sugar
6 tablespoons glucose
4 cups water
1 teaspoon almond extract
1 teaspoon vanilla extract
4 cups shredded coconut

Place the sugars, glucose and water in a large saucepan and cook to 312°, or to the hard-crack stage. Add the extracts and coconut. Pour into an oiled platter and when cold, cut into squares.

BUTTERSCOTCHES

6 cups light brown sugar
2 cups water
Pinch cream of tartar
1½ cups butter, melted
2 teaspoons lemon extract

Place the sugar and water in a large saucepan and heat, stirring occasionally, until the boiling point is reached; add the cream of tartar Cover and allow to boil for 10 minutes. Remove the cover, then cook to 310°, or to the hard-crack stage. Add the melted butter and lemon extract and remove from heat when blended with the sirup. Pour between buttered candy bars, or into buttered pan.

When cold, cut with buttered scissors into small pieces and wrap in waxed paper.

ALMOND BUTTER CRUNCH

1 cup butter
1 cup sugar
½ cup finely chopped blanched almonds, lightly toasted
4 ounces (squares) dipping chocolate

Combine butter and sugar and heat slowly, stirring constantly until sugar is dissolved. Cook to hard-crack stage (310°), stirring occasionally to prevent burning. Add ¼ cup nuts and pour into buttered (8x8 inch) pan. When cold, heat chocolate over boiling water until partly melted. Remove from heat and stir rapidly until completely melted. Spread ½ the chocolate over cooled candy and sprinkle with 2 tablespoons nuts. When firm, invert crunch and cover with remaining chocolate. Sprinkle remaining nuts over top. When firm, break into small irregular pieces. Makes 1¼ pounds.

DIVINITIES

STANDARD DIVINITY

2 cups sugar
½ cup light corn sirup
¼ teaspoon salt
½ cup hot water
2 egg whites
1 teaspoon vanilla extract

Dissolve sugar, sirup, and salt in the hot water. Cook, without stirring, to 248°, or to the firm-ball stage, wash down with a damp cloth any crystals that may form on the sides of the pan during cooking. Remove from heat and pour gradually over the stiffly beaten egg whites, beating constantly with a wire whisk. Add extract and continue beating until mixture will hold its shape when dropped from a spoon. Drop by teaspoonfuls on waxed paper or spread into a buttered pan and mark in squares.

Note: Should the divinity become too stiff to manipulate, add a few drops of hot water to bring it back to spreading consistency. If for some reason the divinity does not harden, cook it over hot water until mixture will hold its shape. Chopped nuts, shredded coconut, or dried or candied fruits add interest to divinity and should be added during the beating process.

CHOCOLATE DIVINITY

From 1 to 2 squares of melted chocolate may be added to the beaten divinity mixture while it is still warm. As the chocolate tends to make the finished candy harder, it will be necessary to add a few drops of hot water to the mixture before turning it out of the bowl.

HONEY NUT DIVINITY

1 cup sugar
2 tablespoons strained honey
½ cup boiling water
2 teaspoons butter
1 egg white
½ teaspoon almond extract
Almonds or pecan nut meats

Place the sugar, honey, boiling water, and butter in a saucepan, stirring until dissolved. Cook slowly, to 240°, or to the soft-ball stage.
Pour the sirup over the stiffly beaten egg white, beating constantly. Add the almond extract and beat until creamy. Drop on waxed paper and decorate with nut meats.

Fluffy nuggets of divinity make lovely candies for the bridge table

CARAMEL DIVINITY

2 cups brown sugar
2 cups boiling water
1 egg white, stiffly beaten
1 teaspoon vanilla extract

Heat sugar in a heavy saucepan over low heat about 5 minutes, stirring constantly. Stir in boiling water slowly and continue cooking to 240°, or to the soft-ball stage. Then pour sirup slowly into beaten egg white, beating constantly until stiff peaks are formed and candy is no longer glossy. Add extract last few minutes of beating. Drop in teaspoonfuls on waxed paper.

SEA FOAM

3 cups light brown sugar
¼ teaspoon salt
¾ cup water
2 egg whites
1 teaspoon vanilla extract

Dissolve the sugar and salt in the water. Cook, without stirring, to 255°, or to the hard-ball stage. Remove from heat and pour gradually over beaten egg whites, beating constantly. Add vanilla extract. Continue beating until candy cools and will hold its shape. Then drop by spoonfuls on waxed paper, or spread into buttered pan and mark in squares.

FUDGES

CHOCOLATE FUDGE

2 cups sugar
2 squares chocolate, chipped
⅔ cup cream, milk or water
2 tablespoons light corn sirup
2 tablespoons butter
Few grains salt
1 teaspoon vanilla extract

Place sugar, chocolate, liquid, corn sirup, butter, and salt in a saucepan and heat slowly, stirring until the sugar is dissolved. Cover until boiling point is reached. Cook without stirring until the temperature 240° is reached, or until a soft ball is formed when a few drops are placed in cold water. Add vanilla extract, then coo', without stirring, to lukewarm (110°). Beat until creamy and mixture loses its shine. Pour into a buttered square pan and mark into squares.
Note: If mixture becomes too stiff to spread, the candy may be kneaded, or a few drops of cream may be added to bring the mixture back to spreading consistency.

BAKED FRUIT FUDGE

2 tablespoons butter
1 cup sugar
2 eggs, separated
2 squares chocolate, melted
1 teaspoon lemon extract
1 teaspoon orange extract
½ teaspoon vanilla extract
½ cup flour
½ cup dates, raisins, figs, candied
    pineapple or cherries, chopped

Cream the butter and sugar together, then add the beaten egg yolks, melted chocolate, and extracts; beat well. Thoroughly blend in the flour and fold in the stiffly beaten egg whites.
Pour over the fruit arranged in a buttered baking pan and bake for about 30 minutes in a slow oven (300°). When cool, cut in squares.

WHITE FUDGE

Make as for Chocolate Fudge, omitting chocolate and corn sirup.

RIBBON FUDGE—Make 1 recipe chocolate fudge, add ½ cup chopped nuts and pour into deep square pan. Pour 1 recipe white fudge on top. Tint a second recipe white fudge a delicate pink, add ½ cup cut candied cherries and spread over top.

FUDGE PINWHEELS—Make 1 recipe chocolate fudge, beat until stiff, place on board dusted with confectioners' sugar and roll out into a rectangle ⅛ inch thick with rolling pin dusted with confectioners' sugar. Make ⅓ recipe Basic Fondant, roll out to rectangle of same size and thickness, place on chocolate fudge and roll crosswise like jelly roll. Chill. Slice.

PANOCHA

2 cups light brown sugar
⅔ cup milk
1 tablespoon butter
1 teaspoon vanilla extract

Place sugar, milk and butter in saucepan, and cook, stirring constantly, to 240°, or to the softball stage. Remove from heat, add vanilla extract and cool, without stirring, to lukewarm (110°). Beat until thick and creamy. Pour into buttered pans and mark into squares.

COFFEE PANOCHA

Substitute ⅔ cup of strong coffee infusion for the ⅔ cup of milk called for in the Panocha recipe, following the same directions for cooking and beating. Add ½ cup nuts, if desired.

ALMOND FUDGE

4 cups sugar
2 tablespoons golden sirup
1 cup milk, 1 teaspoon salt
¾ cup almonds, chopped
1 tablespoon vanilla extract

Place the sugar, sirup, milk and salt in a deep saucepan. Stir until mixture boils up well, then continue boiling without stirring for about 15 minutes, or until it reaches 240°, the soft-ball stage. Remove from heat, add the almonds and vanilla extract. Beat until creamy and pour into a buttered pan.

CHOCOLATE-MAPLE FUDGE

1 cup maple sugar
1 cup brown sugar
2 tablespoons butter
¾ cup golden sirup
2 squares chocolate, chipped
¾ cup cream
½ cup shredded coconut
½ cup nut meats, chopped

Place the sugars, butter, sirup, chocolate and cream in a saucepan; cook, stirring constantly, to 240°, or to the soft-ball stage. Remove from heat, add the coconut and beat until creamy. Pour into buttered pans, sprinkle nuts over the top and mark into squares when cool.

SOUR-CREAM CANDY

3 cups brown sugar
1 cup sour cream
Salt, ¼ cup butter
1 teaspoon vanilla extract
1 cup chopped English walnuts

Combine the sugar and cream and cook to 240°, or to the soft-ball stage. Remove from heat, add a pinch of salt and the butter. Beat until mixture begins to grain. Stir in the vanilla extract and the nut meats and pour into a buttered pan.

MAPLE CREAMS

1 cup maple sugar
1 cup light brown sugar
¼ cup water
½ teaspoon almond extract
Walnut meats

Cook the sugars and water to 240°, or to the soft-ball stage; add the almond extract. Cool to lukewarm, then beat until creamy, yet firm. Knead until smooth, form into small balls, and press a walnut meat into each ball.

MAPLE BRITTLE

3 cups maple sugar
1 cup cold water
1 cup molasses
1 tablespoon maple sirup
Pinch cream of tartar
½ cup butter
2 teaspoons soda
1 tablespoon boiling water
1 teaspoon lemon extract
1 cup Brazil-nut meats, chopped

Cook the sugar, water, molasses, sirup and cream of tartar to 300°, or to the hard-crack stage. Add the butter, boil for 4 minutes, then remove from heat Add the soda dissolved in the boiling water, and the lemon extract. As soon as mixture begins to foam pour out in buttered platters, spreading very thin. Sprinkle with the chopped nuts.

14-MINUTE MAPLE CANDY

4 cups maple sirup
1 cup cream, ¼ cup butter
1 cup nut meats, chopped
1 teaspoon lemon extract

Cook the maple sirup, cream, and butter for 9 minutes after the boiling point is reached. Remove from heat, add the nut meats and extract and stir for 5 minutes. Pour into buttered pans and when cool, cut into squares.

MAPLE-MOLASSES GEMS

4 cups molasses
1 cup brown sugar
1 cup maple sugar
Pinch cream of tartar
½ cup butter
½ teaspoon vinegar
Pinch of salt
1 teaspoon vanilla extract
½ teaspoon almond extract
2 cups pecan nut meats, chopped

Cook the molasses, sugars, and cream of tartar to 256°, or to the hard-ball stage. Add the butter, vinegar, salt, extracts, and the chopped nut meats. Stir lightly to blend and pour into buttered pans, marking off while soft into sticks, squares, cushions, or other desired shapes. Walnuts or butternuts may be used.

Maple candy is just another debt we owe New England

BROWN SUGAR MOLASSES KISSES

1 cup butter
1¼ cups brown sugar
5 tablespoons warm water
1 tablespoon glucose
¾ cup Sugar

Place the butter, sugar, water, glucose, and molasses in a large saucepan and heat slowly until dissolved. Then cook, stirring constantly, to 254°, or to the hard-ball stage. Pour into a buttered pan.

Turn the corners and sides into the middle of the batch with a buttered knife, to cool the candy equally and keep it soft. Pull lightly for about 10 minutes, then pull out in strips and cut. Wrap in waxed paper.

Sprinkle nuts over hot sirup in pan and mix thoroughly through candy when it is pulled.

OLD-FASHIONED MOLASSES TAFFY

1¼ cups sorghum or dark
   molasses
¾ cup sugar
1 tablespoon vinegar
1 tablespoon butter
⅛ teaspoon soda
⅛ teaspoon salt

Combine sorghum, sugar and vinegar and cook to 270°, or to the soft-crack stage; stir occasionally to prevent burning. Remove from heat, add butter, soda, and salt, and stir just enough to blend. Pour into buttered pans. When cool enough to handle, gather into a ball and pull between ungreased finger tips until firm and light in color. Cut into pieces and wrap in waxed paper. Add a few drops of oil of peppermint or of peppermint extract to the above recipe before pulling.

TAFFY APPLES

2 cups sugar
½ cup water
Pinch cream of tartar
½ cup butter
1 teaspoon vinegar
½ cup cream
6 or 8 apples

Place the sugar and water in a saucepan and heat until dissolved. Add the cream of tartar, butter, vinegar and cream. Cook, stirring constantly, to 290°, or to the soft-crack stage. Remove from heat. Dip each apple, held by a skewer, into the boiled sirup and carefully place on a buttered plate to harden.

CHOCOLATE TAFFY

1 cup brown sugar
⅓ cup corn sirup
⅔ cup water
1 cup molasses
¼ teaspoon salt
2 tablespoons butter
4 ounces (squares) chocolate,
   melted
1 tablespoon vanilla

Combine first 6 ingredients. Cook slowly, stirring constantly until mixture boils. Cook to 290° or to soft-crack stage. Pour into buttered pan, pour chocolate over candy and as edges cool fold in toward center. Add vanilla and continue folding until cool enough to pull. Pull until cold and cut into pieces.

WHITE TAFFY

1½ cups sugar, ½ cup water
½ tablespoon vinegar
¼ teaspoon cream of tartar
1 teaspoon lemon extract

Place the sugar, water, vinegar, and cream of tartar in a saucepan. Cook to 290°, or to the soft-crack stage. Add the extract and pour out on a buttered platter. When cool enough to handle, pull until white and glossy. Cut into sticks or cushions.

WINTERGREEN KISSES

1 cup golden sirup
1 cup water
2 cups brown sugar
Pinch cream of tartar
½ teaspoon wintergreen extract
Few drops red food coloring

Place the sirup, water, and sugar in a saucepan and stir until the sugar is dissolved. Add the cream of tartar and cook to 250°, or to the hard-ball stage. Remove from heat and add the wintergreen extract and coloring. Pour into a buttered platter. Pull when cool enough to handle. Roll out, cut, and wrap in waxed paper.

SALT-WATER TAFFY

2 cups sugar
5 tablespoons water
1 tablespoon butter
1 teaspoon vanilla extract
Pinch cream of tartar

Dissolve the sugar in the water. Add the butter and cook, without stirring, to 290°, or to the soft-crack stage. Add the extract and cream of tartar and pour into a buttered pan. When cool enough to handle, pull until white. Stretch out in front of a batchwarmer or in front of the range. Cut and wrap in waxed paper.

Dairy Dishes

50
Health-Building
Dairy Dishes

ENTRÉES

Beat egg yolks and add remaining ingredients. Pour into individual buttered ramekins and bake in slow oven (300°F.) about 15 minutes or until set. Serves 6.

CHEESE PUDDING

5 slices bread
2 tablespoons butter
1 cup grated cheese
½ cup sliced stuffed olives
3 eggs, slightly beaten
⅛ teaspoon dry mustard
⅓ cup olive liquid
2 cups scalded milk

Cut crusts from bread and spread with 1 tablespoon butter. Cut bread into cubes and arrange bread, cheese and olives in alternate layers in buttered baking dish with bread cubes on top. Dot with remaining butter. Combine remaining ingredients, pour over mixture in dish and bake in slow oven (300°F.) 1 hour or until firm. Garnish with parsley or watercress. Serves 5.

SOUR CREAM NOODLE BAKE

8-oz. package medium noodles
1 pound ground beef
2 tablespoons butter
1 teaspoon salt
⅛ teaspoon pepper
¼ teaspoon garlic salt
1 8-oz. can tomato sauce
1 cup creamed cottage cheese
1 cup dairy sour cream
6 green onions, chopped
¾ cup shredded sharp Cheddar cheese

Cook noodles in boiling salted water according to package directions. Rinse and drain. Brown meat in butter. Add salt, pepper, and garlic salt, then tomato sauce. Simmer for 5 minutes. Combine cottage cheese, sour cream, onions and noodles. In a 2 quart casserole alternate layers of noodle mixture and meat mixture, beginning with noodles and ending with meat. Top with shredded Cheddar cheese. Bake at (350° about 25 minutes, or se is melted and Serves 6 to 8.

Sour cream and cottage cheese change everyday beef and noodles into a tasty dish for the pot-luck crowd.

FROMAGE

2 egg yolks
1 cup milk
Paprika
¼ teaspoon salt
4½ cups grated cheese

The bread for cheese strata can be cut into cubes or left in whole slices, if preferred

ASPARAGUS WITH CHEESE SAUCE

2 pounds asparagus tips
1 recipe Cheese Sauce (using 1 cup cheese)

Cook asparagus upright in boiling salted water until stems are nearly tender. Continue cooking with tips in water until tender. Drain. Serve with cheese sauce. For 6.

BAKED NOODLES AND CHEESE

1 tablespoon butter
2 tablespoons flour
1/2 teaspoon salt, Dash pepper
2 cups milk
3 1/2 cups cooked noodles (9-ounce package)
1/2 cup diced cooked ham
1 1/2 cups grated cheese
1 cup soft bread crumbs, buttered
2 tablespoons chopped parsley

Melt butter, add flour, salt and pepper and mix thoroughly. Add milk and cook over hot water until thickened, stirring constantly. Arrange alternate layers of noodles, sauce, ham and cheese in buttered casserole and cover top with buttered crumbs and parsley. Bake in moderate oven (350°F.) about 25 minutes or until crumbs are browned. Serve immediately. Serves 6 to 8.

Cheese sauce enhances many a vegetable, notably asparagus, green beans, cabbage and broccoli

ASPARAGUS LOAF AU GRATIN

1 (1-pound) can asparagus tips
Pimiento strips
2 tablespoons butter
4 tablespoons flour
1 cup milk
1/2 teaspoon salt
1/8 teaspoon pepper
2 cups grated American cheese
1 3/4 cups fine soft bread crumbs
2 eggs, slightly beaten

Drain asparagus and reserve liquid. Line bottom of buttered loaf pan with about half the asparagus tips. Place strips of pimiento between tips. Melt butter, remove from heat, add flour and mix well. Add milk and 1/4 cup asparagus liquid and cook until thickened, stirring constantly. Add salt, pepper and cheese and stir until cheese is melted; stir in crumbs. Add mixture gradually to eggs and fold in remaining asparagus tips cut into 1-inch pieces. Pour into loaf pan and place in pan of hot water. Bake in moderate oven (325°F.) 1 hour or until firm. Serve on platter and surround with watercress. Serves 6.

BAKED NOODLES AND SPINACH

1 recipe Medium White Sauce
3/4 cup grated cheese
1/2 teaspoon salt
1/8 teaspoon pepper
1/8 teaspoon paprika
3 cups cooked noodles
3 cups cooked spinach, chopped
1/2 cup buttered crumbs

Combine white sauce, cheese and seasonings. Arrange noodles, spinach and white sauce in alternate layers in buttered casserole. Sprinkle top with crumbs. Bake in moderate oven (350°F.) about 30 minutes or until browned. Serves 6 to 8.

BEETS A LA RUSSE

12 small beets (cooked)
2 tablespoons sugar
2 tablespoons vinegar
2 tablespoons butter, melted
Salt and pepper
1 tablespoon flour
1/2 cup sour cream

Grate or shred beets and sprinkle with sugar, vinegar, 1 tablespoon butter, salt and pepper. Blend remaining butter with flour. Stir into beet mixture and cook until thickened. Add sour cream. Reheat and serve. Serves 6 to 8.

Cheese blends well with most cereals; with corn-meal mush it makes golden glow casserole

COTTAGE CHEESE CROQUETTES

2 cups cottage cheese
2 cups bread crumbs
½ cup nut meats, chopped
¼ teaspoon paprika
2 tablespoons chopped onion
2 tablespoons chopped green pepper
1 teaspoon salt
1½ cups milk
1 egg
2 tablespoons milk
½ cup crumbs

Combine cottage cheese, crumbs, nut meats and seasonings. Add milk and mix well. Form into croquettes and dip into mixture of egg and 2 tablespoons milk. Then dip into crumbs. Fry in hot deep fat (370°F.). Serve with Cream Sauce. Makes 6 to 8 croquettes.

COTTAGE CHEESE PATTIES — Form mixture into patties instead of croquettes; dip into egg mixture and crumbs and brown in butter.

BAKED RICE AND CHEESE

3 eggs
1½ cups cooked rice
3 canned pimientos, chopped
1½ cups grated American cheese
3 cups milk
½ teaspoon salt
⅛ teaspoon pepper
⅛ teaspoon paprika
⅓ cup dry bread crumbs
2 tablespoons butter

Beat eggs and add next 7 ingredients. Pour into buttered baking dish, cover with crumbs, dot with butter and bake in slow oven (300°F.) 45 minutes or until firm. Serves 6.

CORN WITH CHEESE

1 tablespoon minced onion
2 tablespoons minced green pepper
2 tablespoons butter
1 recipe Medium White Sauce
2 cups cooked corn
2 cups grated American cheese
½ teaspoon salt
⅛ teaspoon pepper
2 eggs, separated

Cook onion and green pepper in butter 3 minutes. Add white sauce, corn, 1½ cups cheese, salt, pepper and beaten egg yolks. Fold in stiffly beaten egg whites. Pour into buttered baking dish, sprinkle with remaining cheese and bake in moderate oven (350°F.) 40 minutes or until firm. Serves 6.

CHEESE PINEAPPLE FRITTERS

1 cup sifted flour
2 teaspoons baking powder
¾ teaspoon salt
1 cup cottage cheese
¾ cup drained canned crushed pineapple
1 egg, separated

Sift flour, baking powder and salt together. Combine mashed cottage cheese, pineapple and slightly beaten egg yolk and mix well. Stir into dry ingredients, mixing just enough to moisten. Fold in stiffly beaten egg white and drop by teaspoons into hot deep fat (360°F.). Fry until brown. Serves 6.

GOLDEN GLOW CASSEROLE

¾ cup corn meal
½ teaspoon salt
3¾ cup boiling water
¾ pound Cheddar cheese
¾ cup milk
Paprika

Add corn meal gradually to boiling salted water, stirring constantly; cook over boiling water 30 to 45 minutes. Pour into shallow pan. When cold, cut into 1-inch squares. Melt cheese in top of double boiler and add milk gradually, stirring constantly. Arrange alternate layers of mush and cheese in casserole and bake in moderate oven (350°F.) 20 minutes. Sprinkle with paprika and serve hot. Serves 6.

CUCUMBERS IN SOUR CREAM

1 large cucumber
1 cup thick sour cream
1 tablespoon chopped onion
3 tablespoons vinegar
¼ teaspoon salt
⅛ teaspoon white pepper

Pare cucumber. Run tines of fork lengthwise of the cucumber and cut crosswise into thin slices. Combine remaining ingredients and pour over sliced cucumber. Marinate 30 minutes. Serves 4.

Golden cheese sauce is a fine foil for snowy white cauliflower

CAULIFLOWER WITH CHEESE SAUCE

1 head cauliflower
1 recipe Cheese Sauce (using 1 cup cheese)

Cook whole cauliflower in boiling salted water to cover 15 minutes or until tender. Drain, place in serving dish and cover with cheese sauce. Serves 6 to 8.

CORNED BEEF HASH WITH CORN AU GRATIN

1 tablespoon minced onion
3 tablespoons butter
1 cup chopped cooked corned beef
1 cup chopped cooked potatoes
1¼ cups evaporated milk
1 teaspoon salt
¼ teaspoon pepper
3 tablespoons flour
½ cup stock drained from corn
2 cups canned whole-kernel corn
6 tablespoons grated cheese

Cook onion in half the butter 3 minutes. Mix with corned beef, potatoes, ½ cup milk and half the salt and pepper. Press into buttered baking dish to form a nest. Melt remaining butter and blend in flour and remaining salt and pepper. Add corn stock and remaining milk. Cook until thickened, stirring constantly. Add corn and pour into hash-lined dish. Sprinkle cheese over corn mixture. Bake in moderate oven (350°F.) 30 minutes. Serves 6.

CHICKEN HASH WITH CORN AU GRATIN—Omit corned beef and potatoes and use 1 cup minced roast chicken and 1 cup chopped leftover stuffing.

FARMERS' CHOP SUEY

1 cup shredded lettuce
½ cup sliced radishes
½ cup diced cucumbers
¼ cup diced green pepper
½ cup shredded carrots
2 recipes Sour Cream Dressing

Have all ingredients cold. Combine and toss together in a salad bowl. Serves 6 to 8.

Corn au gratin in hash-lined casserole is a new slant on a family favorite

PIMIENTO NOODLE RING

1 cup broken egg noodles
1½ cups hot milk
1 cup soft bread crumbs
¼ cup butter, melted
6 egg yolks, beaten
1 pimiento, chopped
2 tablespoons chopped green pepper
1½ cups grated sharp American cheese
⅛ teaspoon onion salt
¾ teaspoon salt
⅛ teaspoon pepper
Dash paprika

Cook noodles in boiling salted water until tender. Drain and rinse. Combine noodles with milk, bread crumbs and butter and add to remaining ingredients. Mix thoroughly. Pour into greased 8-inch ring mold. Place in pan of hot water and bake in moderate oven (350°F.) until firm, about 45 to 60 minutes. Unmold and fill center with cooked peas or asparagus tips. Serves 6.

HAM NOODLE RING—Omit pimiento and green pepper and add 1 cup minced cooked ham and 1 teaspoon dry mustard to mixture before baking.

RINKTUM DITTY

1 tablespoon butter
1 small onion, minced
2 cups cooked tomatoes
1 teaspoon salt
¼ teaspoon pepper
2 teaspoons sugar
½ pound American cheese, grated
1 egg, beaten

Melt butter and cook onion until tender, but not brown. Add tomatoes, salt, pepper and sugar and heat thoroughly. Add cheese and cook until melted, stirring constantly. Add egg slowly, stirring constantly and cook 1 minute longer. Serve on buttered toast. Serves 4.

SCOTCH WOODCOCK

Add 2 to 3 tablespoons anchovy paste and a dash of cayenne to Rinktum Ditty. Chop 4 hard-cooked eggs and place them on toast. Pour sauce over all.

With the return of the chafing dish, Welsh rarebit comes into its own

TANGY RAREBIT

2 cups milk
1 tablespoon cornstarch
½ cup grated or chopped aged Cheddar cheese
4 green onions, minced
⅛ teaspoon paprika
⅛ teaspoon curry powder

Mix ¼ cup cold milk with cornstarch. Scald remaining milk in top of double boiler and add cornstarch mixture. Stir until thickened; add cheese, onions, paprika and curry powder. Heat thoroughly, pour over hot buttered toast and serve. Serves 4.

WELSH RAREBIT

2 tablespoons butter
1 teaspoon Worcestershire sauce
½ teaspoon salt
½ teaspoon paprika
¼ teaspoon prepared mustard
½ pound American cheese, grated
½ cup ginger ale, 1 egg

Melt butter; add seasonings and grated cheese. Stir until cheese is soft, heating over low heat. Add ginger ale, then the slightly beaten egg. Stir until thick. Serve on toast or crackers. For 4.

CHEESE RAVIOLI

3 eggs
2½ teaspoons salt
2 cups sifted flour
3 cups cottage cheese
2 tablespoons cream
⅛ teaspoon pepper
2 quarts boiling water

Beat eggs slightly, add 1 tea-spoon salt and flour. Knead well, cover and let stand ½ hour. Roll dough paper-thin and let stand 1 hour to dry. Cut into strips 3 inches wide. Combine cheese, cream, ½ teaspoon salt and pepper. Place teaspoon of filling 1 inch apart along lower edge of each strip of dough, cover with upper half, cut into squares with filling in center of each square and press edges together. Place on cloth to dry for several hours. Drop a few at a time into boiling water to which remaining salt has been added and cook 20 minutes. Serve with brown sauce. Serves 6.

Use grated aged Cheddar cheese instead of cottage cheese, adding more cream to make the cheese into a paste.

BEEF PATTIES WITH CHEESE

1½ pounds ground beef
1 cup evaporated milk
3 tablespoons minced onion
6 tablespoons quick-cooking rolled oats
2 tablespoons minced parsley
2 teaspoons salt
¼ teaspoon pepper
2 tablespoons butter
3 thin slices American cheese

Mix first 7 ingredients and shape into 6 patties. Place in buttered baking pan and dot with butter. Bake in moderate oven (350°F.) 45 minutes, basting twice with drippings in pan. Cut cheese slices into halves, place a strip on each patty and bake 10 minutes longer. Serves 6.

Spread beef mixture in pie plate. Cover with 6 thin onion slices.

Top with cheese, cut into wedge-shaped pieces. When melted, serve the meat in wedges.

The dinner gong will not be needed when luscious patties with cheese are on the menu

CREAMED MUSHROOMS WITH SHRIMP

1 pound fresh mushrooms
¼ cup butter
¼ cup flour
2 cups milk
¾ teaspoon salt
¼ teaspoon pepper
1 cup shrimp, cleaned
6 patty shells

Wash mushrooms, dry and slice Melt butter in a skillet. Add mushrooms and cook until tender. Sprinkle flour over mushrooms. Mix well and add milk gradually, stirring constantly during the addition. Season with salt and pepper. Cook mixture slowly, stirring constantly, until thickened. Add shrimp and heat thoroughly. Serve hot in heated patty shells. Serves 6. Other foods which may be creamed with mushrooms and served in patty shells: cooked chicken, lamb or veal, sweetbreads, chicken livers, hard-cooked eggs, oysters, lobster, crab meat. Garnish with mushroom caps placed on tomato slices, seasoned and broiled.

Macaroni and cheese for the growing youngsters and the discriminating grown-ups

CORN RING WITH CREAMED DRIED BEEF

1 cup Thick White Sauce
1 teaspoon grated onion
1½ cups fine soft bread crumbs
3 cups cooked or canned
    whole kernel corn
1 egg
Creamed Dried Beef

Combine white sauce, onion, bread crumbs, drained corn and slightly beaten egg. Mix well and pack in ring mold lined with waxed paper. Bake in moderate oven (375°F.) about 50 minutes or until firm. Unmold on serving dish, remove paper and fill the center with creamed dried beef. Serves 6.

Use creamed fish, chicken or sausage instead of dried beef.

MACARONI AND CHEESE

2 cups broken macaroni
8 cups boiling water
2 teaspoons salt
2 cups grated aged cheese
1 teaspoon mustard
¼ teaspoon salt
Dash pepper
1¼ cups scalded milk

Cook macaroni in boiling salted water 15 minutes. Drain and rinse in hot water. Place in layers in buttered baking dish sprinkling each layer with cheese, mustard, salt and pepper. Pour milk around edge and cook in a moderate oven (350° F.) 30 minutes. Serves 6.

Buttered crumbs may be sprinkled over top.

NOODLE RING WITH MEAT BALLS

½ pound ground beef
½ pound ground pork
1½ cups evaporated milk
½ cup bread crumbs
2 tablespoons minced onion
1 teaspoon salt
⅛ teaspoon pepper
1½ tablespoons flour
2 tablespoons fat
1 can condensed vegetable soup
¾ cup water
1 (8-ounce) package noodles

Mix beef, pork, ¾ cup milk and crumbs, onion, salt and pepper and shape mixture into 12 small balls. Roll balls in flour and brown in hot fat. Add soup and water and continue cooking over low heat 30 minutes. Cook noodles in boiling, salted water 20 minutes or until tender. Drain and shape into ring on a hot platter. Arrange meat balls around edge. Add remaining milk to sauce in pan and heat to boiling. Serve in center of noodles. Garnish with parsley. Serves 6.

With discreet anonymity milk adds nourishment to both meat balls and sauce

EGGS A LA SUISSE

1 cup grated Swiss cheese
6 eggs
Salt and pepper
Cream

Cover bottoms of 6 buttered custard cups with grated cheese. Slide an egg carefully into each cup, sprinkle lightly with salt and pepper and cover with cream. Top with a layer of grated cheese. Bake in moderate over (375°F.) about 15 minutes or until eggs are firm but not hard. Serves 6.
Serve in Patty Shells filled with Curry Sauce.

GREEN BEANS WITH SOUR CREAM

2 cups cooked green beans
2 tablespoons chopped onion
2 tablespoons butter
2 tablespoons flour
Dash salt and pepper
1 tablespoon vinegar
1 tablespoon sugar
½ cup sour cream
2 tablespoons chopped parsley

Drain beans and save liquid. Brown onion in butter. Blend in flour, add liquid from beans and cook until thick, stirring constantly. Add salt, pepper, vinegar, sugar and sour cream. Add beans and heat thoroughly. Serve immediately, garnished with chopped parsley. Serves 4.

FRIED CORN WITH SOUR CREAM SAUCE

3 cups canned or cooked
    whole kernel corn
4 tablespoons butter
⅓ cup chopped red and green
    peppers
1 teaspoon chopped onion
4 teaspoons flour
1 cup thick sour cream
¾ teaspoon salt
⅛ teaspoon pepper

Fry corn in 2 tablespoons butter. Melt remaining butter, add peppers and onion and cook over low heat stirring frequently until tender. Add flour and mix well. Add sour cream and cook over low heat, stirring constantly until thickened. Season with salt and pepper and serve with corn. Serves 6.

GOLDENROD BEANS

1½ pounds whole green beans
1½ tablespoons butter
2 tablespoons flour
½ teaspoon salt
⅛ teaspoon pepper
¾ cup evaporated milk
3 hard-cooked eggs, separated
¾ cup mayonnaise

Cook beans in boiling salted water until tender. Save ½ cup of the liquid. Melt butter, blend in flour, salt and pepper. Add bean stock and cook until thickened, stirring constantly. Add milk and chopped egg whites; heat thoroughly. Remove from heat and add mayonnaise. Drain beans, cover with sauce and sprinkle with egg yolks pressed through a sieve. Serves 6.

Cauliflower, asparagus or broccoli may be used instead of green beans.

Flavor sauce with ½ cup grated cheese and ¼ teaspoon Worcestershire sauce.

Goldenrod beans will be a favorite luncheon dish in your family

OYSTER PIE

2 cups Medium White Sauce
1/2 teaspoon celery salt
1 teaspoon onion juice
1 pint oysters
Pastry (made with 1 cup flour)

Combine first 4 ingredients. Pour into greased casserole. Cover with pastry, cut several gashes in it to allow for escape of steam. Bake in very hot oven (450°F.) 20 minutes or until crust is brown. Serves 4.

Instead of pastry use Sourmilk Biscuits.

FISH CROQUETTES

1½ cups Thick White Sauce
1½ cups flaked cooked fish
1 cup cracker crumbs
1 egg, slightly beaten

Combine white sauce and fish, chill. Shape into croquettes; roll in crumbs, then in egg and again in crumbs. Fry in hot deep fat (380°F.). Serves 6.

Oyster pie is a delicious supper dish with either pastry or biscuit top

OYSTER SOUFFLÉ

3 tablespoons butter
6 tablespoons flour
1 teaspoon salt
1/3 cup oyster liquor or milk
1⅔ cups milk
1 tablespoon lemon juice
Few gratings onion
Dash cayenne
1 pint oysters, chopped
6 eggs, separated
1/2 teaspoon cream of tartar

Melt butter, add flour and salt and mix thoroughly. Add oyster liquor and milk, stirring constantly. Cook over boiling water until very thick, stirring constantly. Add seasonings and oysters. Beat in egg yolks, one at a time. Beat egg whites until foamy, add cream of tartar and continue beating until egg whites are stiff but not dry. Fold into oyster mixture and pour into baking dish greased only on bottom. Place in pan of hot water and bake in slow oven (325°F.) until brown and firm, about 1 hour. Serve at once. Serves 6 to 8.

SCALLOPED CORN AND OYSTERS

1 (No. 2) can corn
1 pint oysters
3 tablespoons butter
2 tablespoons flour
1 teaspoon salt
Dash pepper
1½ cups milk
1 cup buttered crumbs

Heat corn. Drain oysters and add enough water to liquid to make 3/4 cup. Melt butter, add flour, salt and pepper and mix well. Add milk and oyster liquor and cook until thickened, stirring constantly. Arrange corn, oysters, white sauce and crumbs in alternate layers in buttered baking dish. Bake in hot oven (400°F.) 12 to 20 minutes. Serves 5 or 6.

SUPPER SPECIALS

2 tablespoons butter
1/4 cup flour
3/4 teaspoon salt
1/8 teaspoon pepper
3/4 cup evaporated milk
1/2 cup stock drained from peas
2 cups flaked cooked salmon
2¼ cups cooked peas
1 cup crushed potato chips

Melt butter and blend in flour, salt and pepper. Add milk and pea stock. Cook until thickened, stirring constantly. Flake salmon and add to half the sauce. Place in buttered custard cups. Add peas to remaining sauce and fill custard cups with mixture. Cover with potato chips. Bake in moderate oven (350°F.) 45 minutes. Unmold if desired. Serves 6.

Mixture may be baked in a large casserole.

Instead of potato chips, 1/2 cup crushed corn flakes and 1/4 teaspoon salt may be used. Dot with 2 tablespoons butter.

Flaked tuna or other fish may be used.

Canning, Freezing and Preserving

250 Ways to Preserve Food

HOME CANNING

To preserve foods by canning two things must be done. First, sufficient heat must be provided to destroy all microscopic life that will cause spoilage in food; and, second, a perfect seal must be made which will prevent the re-entrance of microorganisms. These problems of preventing spoilage have been practically solved by the improved methods of canning which are explained below.

Only the freshest of fruits and vegetables should be canned. Canning does not improve the product; it only preserves it for future use

METHODS OF CANNING

OPEN KETTLE—This method involves cooking the product completely and pouring it into sterilized jars, using sterilized equipment throughout. The jars are then sealed and stored. The open kettle method is recommended only for preserves, pickles, and foods canned in a thick sirup. For other foods use the following methods.

COLD PACK—Cold, raw foods are put into jars and covered with boiling-hot sirup, juice or water.

(Tomatoes are pressed down in jar so they are covered with their own juice.) Jars are partially or completely sealed, following manufacturer's directions. Jars are then processed in boiling water or in steam to simultaneously cook the food and sterilize the jars.

HOT PACK—Fruits and vegetables are preheated before packing causing shrinkage before food goes into jars. This is the preferred method as preheating the food before packing prevents "floating", (especially w i t h fruits) and assures a full pack. Processing time is also lessened when food is hot-packed.

EQUIPMENT

GLASS JARS—Glass jars are sold with various types of closures.

1. Porcelain-lined zinc cap with separate rubber ring — Ring is placed on jar before filling, jar is filled, then cap screwed down firmly and turned back ¼ inch. After canning cap is tightly screwed down to complete the seal.

2. Wire-bale type jar with glass lid and rubber ring. Place ring on jar, fill jar and push long wire over top of glass lid. Leave short

wire up. After canning, push short wire down to complete the seal.

3. Glass lid and top-seal rubber ring with metal screw band — After filling jar, put rubber ring on lid and lid on jar. Screw metal band on until almost tight. Turn back ¼ turn. After processing screw band on tight.

4. Flat metal lid with sealing compound and a metal screw band — Put lid on with sealing compound next to glass. Screw metal band on tight. This is a self-sealing lid and is not tightened further after canning.

WATER BATH CANNER—Fruits, tomatoes and pickled vegetables may be processed in a boiling-water-bath canner. Any metal container will do if it is deep enough to hold water to at least an inch over tops of jars, if it has a cover, and a rack to keep jars from touching the bottom.

PRESSURE CANNER—All common vegetables (except tomatoes) and meat should be processed in a pressure canner. These are low-acid foods and require a higher temperature than that of boiling water to destroy spore-forming bacteria which could cause spoilage. Check canner carefully before using and follow manufacturer's directions.

PROCEDURE

Inspect and test all equipment before preparing food to be canned. Wash jars in hot soapy water; rinse well. For the open kettle method, place jars, lids, knife, spoon, and funnel in boiling water; boil for 15 minutes. (Some metal lids with sealing compound need boiling; others need only a dip in hot water; follow manufacturer's directions.) For cold or hot pack canning, leave jars in hot water until ready to fill.

Choose vegetables that are young and that have made a quick growth.

Do not use very dirty vegetables as more microorganisms are present on these than on clean vegetables.

Do not attempt to handle too large a quantity of vegetables at once, especially in hot weather. The various steps in the canning process must be followed in rapid succession to prevent loss of flavor caused by what is known as flat sour, and large quantities can not be handled rapidly.

Can vegetables as soon as possible after they have been picked. This is particularly necessary with asparagus, peas, beans and corn.

Clean the vegetables thoroughly and prepare them as for cooking. Select firm, well-grown, but not overripe fruit.

If possible, can fruit on the day it is picked.

Wash, pare, and prepare the fruit, removing all bruised or decayed parts.

If there is much variation in size, sort the fruit or vegetables so that the contents of each jar will be as nearly uniform as possible. Precook low-acid vegetables in order to heat them thoroughly. Use the water in which they are cooked to fill jars. Pour boiling water over such foods as tomatoes or peaches to loosen the skins.

Cook berries and fruits in sirup a few minutes before packing, to insure a full pack. Bring tomatoes to a boil before packing.

Fill only as many jars at a time as the cooker will hold. Work rapidly once the food has been heated and avoid letting it stand before processing, since objectionable bacteria develop most rapidly between 105° and 150°F. Add 1 teaspoon salt to each quart of vegetables and ½ teaspoon to each pint. Fill jars to within ½ inch of top, using boiling water for vegetables and boiling sirup for fruits. Air bubbles will rise as the liquid is added. Assist them to rise and break by running a spatula down the side of the jar.

Partially seal or completely seal the jars before processing.

When processing time is complete, let hand on gauge fall to zero then wait about 2 minutes before removing the canner cover.

Top picture

Run knife between tomatoes and jar to remove air bubbles. But be careful not to scrape the side of the jar. Metal objects scratch glass; scratches cause breakage.

Lower picture

Have canner half full of water when jars are put into it for processing. Then add more water to cover tops of jars at least 1 inch.

PROCESSING IN HOT WATER BATH

Place hot filled jars on rack in canner and add boiling water to cover them to the depth of 1 inch. Heat quickly to boiling and count time as soon as bubbles break freely over the jars. .Be sure the water covers the jars during the entire processing time. Add more boiling water if necessary. As soon as processing is completed remove canner from heat.

PROCESSING IN PRESSURE COOKER

Have enough boiling water in the cooker to come up to the bottom of the rack. Place filled jars on rack, adjust cover of cooker and clamp down securely. Make sure that the petcock is open. Place over heat and watch for steam to escape from the petcock. Allow steam to escape for 7 minutes and then close petcock and allow pressure to reach the desired point. Count time from this point. Adjust heat to keep pressure steady. Fluctuations in pressure usually result in loss of liquid from the jars, particularly if the pressure goes high enough to release the safety valve and cause a sudden drop in pressure. Remove cooker from heat as soon as processing time is completed. Allow to cool until pressure reaches zero. Then open petcock slowly. **Do not open cooker until pressure is entirely released.**

The bail type of jar may be completely sealed before processing in the pressure cooker. When this is done, be sure that the pressure is reduced slowly at the end of the processing time. Allow fully 15 minutes for the pressure to drop from 10 pounds to zero Do not tighten seal. Jars need not be inverted.

COOLING JARS

Remove jars from the canner; complete the seal if jars are only partially sealed. Place jars on folded towels away from drafts. Cool jars, top side up, allowing enough room to let air get to all sides. Leakage or bubbles rising in the jar mean that the contents must be used or recanned. When jars are cold wash, label, and store in a cool, dry place.

ALWAYS boil home-canned meats, beans, peas or corn for 10 minutes before using, even if they are to be served cold. These foods may be infected with botulinus from the soil in which they were grown. Death has resulted from a single taste of food thus infected. Boiling destroys botulinous toxins. Never use food showing signs of spoilage.

TO MAKE SIRUPS

Boil sugar and water together 5 minutes using the following proportions:

THIN SIRUP—3 cups water and 1 cup sugar.

MEDIUM SIRUP—2 cups water and 1 cup sugar.

THICK SIRUP—1 cup water and 1 cup sugar.

Honey or corn sirup may be used instead of sugar in making sirup.

Use honey for an equal amount of sugar; use 1½ cups corn sirup for 1 cup sugar. Boiling water or fruit juice may be used instead of sirup to save sugar.

RECIPES FOR CANNING BY HOT WATER BATH

APPLES—Wash apples, pare and cut into slices, quarters or halves. Bake or stew, adding sugar to taste or heat to boiling in thin sirup and cook ½ minute. Pack hot into jars, seal and process.

BERRIES—Wash and sort berries carefully. Can only perfect berries; use imperfect ones in making sirup. Pack berries into jars and fill with boiling thin sirup or cook in sirup ½ minute before packing. Seal and process at once.

CHERRIES (Sweet)—Wash cherries; remove stems and pits. Cover with thin sirup, heat to boiling and cook ½ minute. Pack hot into jars. Seal and process at once.

CHERRIES (Tart)—Proceed as above, using thick sirup.

PEACHES—Immerse peaches in boiling water until skins will slip, plunge into cold water and drain. Peel, cut into halves and remove stones. Pack cut side down into jars and cover with medium sirup or cook 5 minutes in sirup and pack hot into jars. Seal and process at once.

PEARS—Wash and pare fruit. Cut into halves and core. Cover with thin sirup, heat to boiling and cook 4 to 8 minutes, depending upon hardness of fruit. Pack hot into jars. Seal and process at once.

When canning without sugar use boiling fruit juice or boiling water to cover fruit

PLUMS--Wash fruit and prick several times with a needle to prevent bursting. Pack into jars. Fill with boiling thin sirup. Partially seal jars and process

RHUBARB—Wash rhubarb and cut into ½-inch pieces. Pack into glass jars and cover with thick sirup. Partially seal and process at once. If preferred, measure cut rhubarb and add ¼ as much sugar. Bake in a covered baking dish until tender, pack hot into jars and seal. Process.

TOMATOES—Select firm ripe tomatoes of uniform size for canning. Remove spots from any imperfect tomatoes. cut into pieces and cook until soft. Press through sieve and use as liquid for filling jars of whole tomatoes. Scald perfect tomatoes, plunge into cold water, drain and peel. Pack closely into jars. Add salt and tomato juice. Partially seal jars. Process at once.

TOMATO JUICE—Prepare tomato juice as above. Heat to simmering and fill jars. Add salt, seal and process.

CANNING IN PRESSURE CANNER

ASPARAGUS—Wash asparagus carefully and cut into lengths to fit container. Place in pan with boiling water over tough portions only. Cover closely and cook 3 to 4 minutes. Pack hot into jars stem end down, add salt and fill with cooking liquid. Partially seal jars. Process at once.

BEANS (Snap) — Wash beans, remove ends and cut into even lengths. Cover with boiling water and cook 3 to 4 minutes. Pack hot into jars, add salt and boiling cooking water. Partially seal jars. Process at once.

BEANS (Lima)—Use only the small green beans for canning; the large white ones should be dried. Wash the beans thoroughly, shell; cook in water 5 minutes. Pour into jars; add salt; partially seal jars. Process at once.

BEETS—Use only very small beets for canning. Wash thoroughly and cut off tops, leaving about 1 inch of stem. Cook in boiling water about 15 minutes,

remove skins and pack into jars. Add salt, fill with boiling water and partially seal. Process.

CARROTS—Wash carrots and either scrape skins off or cook in boiling water until skins will slip off. Pack into jars. Add salt and fill with boiling water. Partially seal. Process at once.

CORN (Whole kernel)—Simmer ears of corn in water 4 to 5 minutes. Cut from cob but do not scrape cob. Weigh corn and add ½ the weight of water. Add 1 teaspoon salt and 2 teaspoons sugar for each quart. Mix well and heat to boiling. Pack at once into jars; partially seal. Process immediately.

CORN (Cream style)—Remove corn, uncooked, from cob by cutting through grains and pressing out with the back of a knife. Add water, salt and sugar and proceed as above.

GREENS—Remove stems and any imperfect leaves. Wash thoroughly. Add water and simmer until leaves are wilted. Drain, saving liquid. Pack into jars; loosen in center with a knife. Add salt and boiling cooking water; partially seal. Process.

Can the surplus vegetables at the peak of the season when they are at their luscious best

PEAS—Use only very tender young peas for canning. Shell, discarding any imperfect peas. Wash and cook in boiling water 1 minute. Pack into jars. Add salt and boiling cooking water; partially seal. Process at once

TIME TABLE FOR HOT WATER BATH
(Hot Pack)

Product	No. Minutes to Process in Boiling Water Glass Jars	
	Qts.	Pts.
Apples	20	15
Berries	15	10
Cherries	15	10
Peaches	25	20
Pears	25	20
Plums	25	20
Rhubarb	10	10
Tomatoes	10	10
Tomato Juice	10	10

TIME TABLE FOR PRESSURE CANNER
(Hot Pack)

Product	No. Minutes to Process in Pressure Canner at 10 Pounds Pressure	
	Qts.	Pts
Asparagus	30	25
Beans (Snap)	25	20
Beans (Lima)	50	40
Beets	35	30
Carrots	30	25
Corn (Cream Style)		85
Corn (Whole-Kernel)	85	55
Greens	90	70
Peas	40	40

MINCEMEAT

4 pounds beef, diced
2 pounds beef suet
2 pounds sugar
2 pounds seedless raisins, chopped
2 pounds currants
4 pounds apples, chopped fine
½ pound citron, minced
½ pound candied lemon peel, minced
Grated rind 2 oranges
Grated rind 1 lemon
1 nutmeg, grated
1 tablespoon cloves
1 tablespoon cinnamon
1 teaspoon salt
½ cup orange juice
½ cup lemon juice
4 cups hard cider, 2 cups brandy

Boil meat and suet together until tender; drain and cool. Force through food chopper. Combine all ingredients except brandy and cook 1½ hours. Add liquor, pour into sterile jars and seal. Makes about 12 quarts.
Or omit sugar and use 4 cups honey; reduce cider to 3 cups.

BREAKFAST FIGS

6 quarts fresh figs
1 cup baking soda
1 gallon boiling water
6 cups honey, 6 cups water

Select figs of uniform size and ripeness. Add soda to boiling water and pour over unpeeled figs. Let stand 5 to 10 minutes, depending on thickness of skins. When skins become slightly transparent, remove to a bath of cold water and rinse thoroughly. Combine honey and water and heat to boiling. Add figs and simmer until figs can be pierced with a straw and the skins look clear and translucent. Pack in sterile jars; fill with hot sirup. One slice lemon and 1 slice orange may be added to each jar. Adjust rings and covers. Process 25 minutes in hot water bath. Makes 6 quarts figs.

CANNING FRUIT JUICES

Fruit juices are a valuable addition to any pantry when canned. They are used as beverages and for making frozen or molded desserts or molded salads. Unsweetened juices are also used for making jelly later in the season when other fruits are available to combine with them. To can properly they are pasteurized in a water bath at about 180°F. This temperature is high enough to insure the keeping qualities of the fruit juices without appreciably impairing their flavor, color or vitamin content.

EXTRACTING—Very juicy berries, such as blackberries are crushed and strained through a cheesecloth, then heated before pouring into jars. Less juicy fruits and berries are crushed to start the flow of juice, then heated to 180°F. and kept at that temperature until juice flows freely. They are then strained and the juice allowed to stand until the dregs have settled before pouring into jars. Fruits such as apples and quinces are prepared in the same way except that enough water to prevent scorching must be added to the crushed or cut-up fruit before cooking.

PROCESSING—After the dregs have settled, pour or siphon the juice carefully into STERILE jars; then seal. Place jars on a rack in kettle filled with hot water which comes about 2 inches below tops of jars. Process at 180° F. for 20 minutes. Remove jars and invert to cool.

Home canned fruit juices will refresh the family and friends all year around

SPECIAL RECIPES

APPLE JUICE OR CIDER—Put uncooked apples through a cider press and strain the juice. Heat to 180°F., pour into sterile jars, seal and process at 180°F. 20 minutes.

CRANBERRY—Cook cranberries in an equal amount of water until skins burst, about 5 minutes. Strain through cheesecloth but do not squeeze. Add ⅔ cup sugar for each quart of berries used and heat to 180°F. Pour into sterile jars, seal and process at 180°F. 20 minutes.

GRAPE—Use firm ripe grapes. Wash and crush thoroughly. Add ½ cup water for each quart of grapes. Heat slowly to 180°F. and strain through cheesecloth. Pour into glass or enamel container and let stand 24 hours in a cool place. Siphon off clear juice from sediment, strain through heavy jelly bag; heat again to 180°F., adding ½ cup sugar for each quart of juice, if desired. Pour into sterile jars, seal and process at 180°F. 20 minutes.

QUICK GRAPE JUICE—Wash 1 cup grapes and place in sterile quart jar with ½ cup sugar. Fill jar with boiling water, seal and process at 180°F. 30 minutes.

RASPBERRY VINEGAR—Fill jars with raspberries, press lightly and fill with vinegar. Let stand 1 month, then strain and bottle juice. Use as vinegar in salad dressings or sweeten, and add 3 parts water to one of raspberry vinegar for beverage.

STRAWBERRY RHUBARB—Grind strawberry rhubarb and strain juice through jelly bag into glass or enamel container. Let stand 3 hours, then siphon off clear juice and pour into sterile jars. Add ¼ cup sugar to each pint. Seal and process at 180°F. 30 minutes.

NUTRITIVE VALUE

Freezing has very little effect on the vitamin content of foods. During the scalding of vegetables some vitamin B is dissolved in the water. If the vegetables are not sufficiently scalded, oxidizing enzymes will destroy vitamin C. Rapid handling of fruits and vegetables between harvesting and freezing will ensure a minimum loss of vitamin C. Once the foods have begun to thaw, after being frozen, the loss of vitamin C is very rapid. Therefore, fruits are best used before they are completely thawed and vegetables are dropped into a small amount of boiling water while they are still frozen. Vegetables packed in brine are allowed to thaw until there is enough liquid to start the cooking. Cover closely and cook only until tender. Frozen vegetables will cook in slightly less time than fresh.

Frozen meat, fish or poultry may be started cooking while still frozen or they may be thawed first. If started while frozen, allow more time for cooking.

PREPARING FOOD FOR FREEZER STORAGE

Most meats and many fruits and vegetables may be successfully frozen and stored in a home freezer or in lockers available throughout the country. Cleanliness and speed are two important factors in handling foods for freezing. Unlike canning, freezing does not sterilize the product; bacteria, yeasts and molds are not all destroyed. Food must be thoroughly washed and all bruised or injured parts which might harbor bacteria must be discarded. Food must be handled rapidly in order to give bacteria as little time as possible to multiply and to reduce enzyme action which destroys the fresh flavor and texture of fruits and vegetables. As in all other types of storage, use only the best products at the peak of perfection. End-of-season surpluses are not of good enough quality to justify the cost of freezer storage.

PREPARING FRUITS

Select fruits which are fully ripe and firm. Discard bad fruit or cut out bad spots. Sugar or sirup is used with fruit to inhibit enzymatic action which could cause changes in fruit tissues during freezing. A general rule to follow is to use sirup (made by dissolving sugar in boiling water) on fruit with little juice, and sugar on fruit which has plenty of juice to form a natural sirup with added sugar. Exceptions to this rule are fruits such as cranberries, blueberries and sliced apples which may be packed dry with no sirup or sugar. (Apples are steam or water-blanched, or are treated with a sulfide solution before packing.) Never use dry sugar on fruits such as peaches, plums and apricots. These fruits must be covered with sirup to prevent discoloration during freezing. It is often advisable to further treat them with ascorbic acid (vitamin C) purchased at a drug store in powdered form. (Before pouring cold sirup over fruit add ascorbic acid—1 teaspoon to 4 cups prepared sirup.) For people who are on a sugarless diet, saccharine may be used in place of sugar in a ratio of 27 grains of saccharine for each pound of sugar used.

Many combinations of fruits may be successfully frozen. Prepare each fruit individually, then mix together and pack with a 40 or 50% sugar sirup.

Such fruits as apples, grapes, bananas, and melons do not combine well with other fruits. Freeze them separately and add at time of serving. Orange and grapefruit sections combine well with other fruits.

A well-stocked freezer saves many time-consuming trips to the market

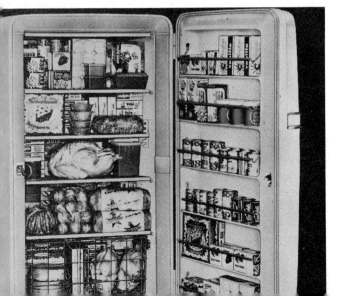

PREPARING SIRUP — Dissolve sugar in boiling water; cool to 70°F before using. Clear white corn sirup mixed with warm water and cooled, may be substituted for sugar solution.

Concentration Desired	Sugar per pint of Hot Water
30%	1 cup
40%	1⅔ cups
50%	2½ cups
60%	3½ cups
65%	4½ cups
70%	5½ cups

Water needed per 5 pound jar corn sirup	
50%	2 pints, 1 cup
60%	1 pint
65%	1 cup
70%	½ cup

Always allow at least ¾-inch headroom when filling containers.

APPLES—Peel and slice. Submerge slices for 5 minutes in a solution of 1½ teaspoons sodium bisulphite and 1 gallon of 70°F. water. Prepare only a few apples at a time. Pack dry.

APRICOTS—Wash, peel, cut into halves and pit. Cover with 60% sirup (ascorbic acid added.)

BLACKBERRIES, DEWBERRIES, BLUEBERRIES—Pick over, wash. Mix 1 pound sugar with 4 to 5 pounds fruit, or use 50% sugar sirup. Blueberries may be packed dry.

BOYSENBERRIES, LOGENBERRIES — Pick over, wash. Cover with 50% sirup.

CANTALOUPE, WATERMELON —Use firm, ripe fruit. Scoop out balls or cut into cubes. Mix with 40 to 50% sirup, or cover with orange or lime juice mixture (⅓ cup each of juice and sugar and 2 cups water).

CHERRIES (Tart) — Wash, chill, pit. Add 1 pound sugar to 4 to 5 pounds fruit. Stir gently to partly dissolve sugar in juice.

CHERRIES (Sweet)—Stem, wash, pit. Cover with 40 to 50% sirup (ascorbic acid added).

CRANBERRIES—Pick over, stem, wash. Pack dry. Or cook as for sauce or puree, adding sugar to taste.

CURRANTS, GOOSEBERRIES— Stem, wash, crush slightly. Mix 1 pound sugar with 3 pounds fruit.

PEACHES — Immerse in boiling water, then in cold. Rub off skins, remove pits and slice into cartons. Cover with 50 to 60% sirup (ascorbic acid added).

PINEAPPLES—Peel, core, slice or dice. Cover with 50 to 60% sirup.

PLUMS, PRUNES — Wash, pit, and quarter. Cover with 50 to 60% sirup.

RASPBERRIES, BLACK, RED — Sort, wash. Add 1 pound sugar to 4 to 5 pounds berries; stir gently. Or cover with 50 to 60% sirup. Or pack dry.

RHUBARB—Wash, trim, cut into 1-inch pieces. Add 1 pound sugar to 4 to 5 pounds fruit. Or cover with 40% sirup.

STRAWBERRIES (sliced) — Pick over; wash in water containing ice; hull. Cut into ⅜-inch slices. Add 1 pound sugar to 4 to 5 pounds berries; mix gently. Cover whole berries with 50 to 60% sirup or add sugar as for sliced berries.

PREPARING FISH AND GAME BIRDS

FISH—Clean, scale, behead, remove entrails; wash thoroughly. Cut fins from small fish with scissors. Cut large fish into steaks and fillets.

Dip lean fish such as haddock and cod into a salt solution for ½ minutes. (1⅓ cups salt per gallon of water). Fatty fish such as salmon and mackerel do not need this dip.

Wrap individual fish fillets or steaks in moisture-proof paper and pack in flat, rectangular folding waxed cartons. Overwrap with cellophane or freezer paper and heat-seal. Or wrap fish in foil or heavy freezer paper and label.

SHELLFISH (Oysters, clams, scallops)—Wash shells in running water; shuck. Dip meat in salt solution (1 tablespoon salt to 2 quarts cold water). Drain. Package in containers and freeze at once.

Crabs and lobsters should be steamed or boiled in water 15 to 20 minutes, then cooled and the meat removed from shells

Package in freezer cartons; freeze at once.

Cooked shrimps toughen slightly during freezing so it is best to remove the heads, then package meat uncooked and unshelled.

GAME BIRDS

Pluck and dress birds as you would poultry for roasting. Game birds are plucked most easily by the wax method. (After scalding and rough-picking, dip or roll birds in melted paraffin wax. Let wax harden, then peel off wax coating which takes off pin feathers and down).

Scald only a pound of vegetables at one time

PREPARING POULTRY

PREPARING VEGETABLES

Use only high quality birds. They should be properly killed and bled, then dry-picked or scalded and picked. Singe off pin feathers and refrigerate birds overnight. Draw and rinse thoroughly. Poultry may be frozen whole but require less space if cut into halves or serving pieces. Wrap giblets and neck in cellophane and insert in cavity of roaster, or between halves of broilers and fryers. Wrap birds in foil or moisture-proof paper. Put cut-up pieces in rectangular-shaped c a r t o n s. Freeze fowl without the dressing; stuff bird before roasting it. Remove meat from bones of cooked fowl when freezing it. Remove stuffing and freeze separately.

Vegetables for freezing should be neither immature or overgrown but at the best stage for immediate table use. To inhibit enzymatic action, scald vegetables a recommended time before freezing. This is done by the boiling-water method or by steaming. To scald in water, put vegetables in a wire basket or cheesecloth and immerse in boiling water. Start timing when water returns to full boil. To scald in steam, pour about two inches of water into a large kettle with a rack or trivet in bottom. When water boils place vegeatbles in a wire basket on trivet, cover the kettle, bring water to boil, and start timing. Immedi-

ately after scalding, immerse vegetables in cold running water or water containing ice. For most vegetables this takes twice as long as scalding. After cooling, drain vegetables and pack in containers. Freeze at once.

ASPARAGUS — Wash, cut off tough ends. Cut stalks to fit cartons or into 2-inch pieces. Steam-blanch small stalks 3½ minutes, large stalks 4½ minutes. Cool; pack.

BEANS, GREEN, WAX—Water-blanch the washed, cut beans 2 minutes, whole beans 2½ minutes. Steam-blanch cut beans 3 minutes, whole beans 3½ minutes. Cool; pack.

BEANS, LIMA — Do not wash after shelling. Water-blanch small beans 1 minute, medium beans 1½ minutes, large beans 2 minutes. Cool; pack.

BROCCOLI—Wash in cold, running water; eliminate c o a r s e leaves. Cut head into pieces not thicker than 1 inch and not longer than 6 inches. Water-blanch small pieces 3 minutes, medium pieces 4 minutes, large pieces 5 minutes. Cool; pack.

BRUSSELS SPROUTS — C u t sprouts from main stem, wash, trim off coarse leaves. Water-blanch 4 minutes. Cool; pack.

CARROTS — Wash, s c r a p e. Water-blanch ¼-inch slices 3 minutes, small whole carrots 4½ minutes. Cool; pack.

CAULIFLOWER—Prepare as for table use; cut into pieces not thicker than 1 inch. Water-blanch small pieces 3 minutes, medium pieces 5 minutes. Cool; pack.

To freeze ears of corn in foil blanch 1 minute longer than the usual time and chill 1½ times longer than the blanching time.

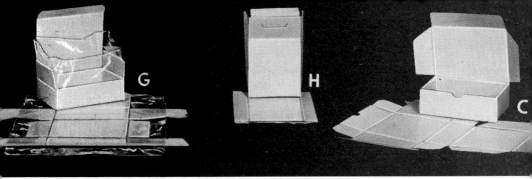

CORN, SWEET—Freeze as soon as possible after harvesting. Husk; illiminate starchy ears. After scalding and cooling, cut off kernels with sharp knife; pick out silk and bits of cob. Steam-blanch small ears 6½ minutes, medium ears 8½ minutes, large ears 10½ minutes. Water-blanch small ears 6 minutes, medium ears 8 minutes, large ears 10 minutes. Chill; cut kernels from cob, pack and freeze. To freeze corn on cob, wrap each chilled ear in moisture-proof cellophane, then pack in cartons.

EGG PLANT—Peel, slice in ⅓-inch slices, or dice in ⅓-inch cubes. Water-blanch 4 minutes. Then dip in 2% citric acid solution (dissolve 1 tablespoon citric acid or ½ cup lemon juice in 5 cups cold water), then dip in cold water. Pack; freeze.

MUSHROOMS—Freeze same day as picked. Wash, cut off base of stem. Steam-blanch small mushrooms 3½ minutes, large 4½ to 6 minutes. Cool first in 2% citric acid solution, then in cold water. Drain well and pack.

OKRA — Wash young, tender pods; cut off stems. Separate into small and large pods. Steam-blanch small pods 3 minutes, large pods 4 minutes. Water-blanch small pods 2 minutes, large pods 2 minutes. Cool; pack.

PEAS—Shell, discard tough peas. Do not wash after shelling. Water-blanch small peas 45 seconds, large peas 1 minute. Chill; pack.

PEAS, BLACKEYED — Do not wash after peas are shelled. Discard hard peas. Water-blanch 2 minutes. Steam-blanch 3 minutes. Chill; pack.

PEPPERS—Wash, trim out stem and seeds. Halve, slice, or dice. Water-blanch pieces 2 minutes, halves 3 minutes. Steam-blanch peices 3 minutes, halves 4 minutes. Cool; pack. (Peppers lose crispness in freezing but are excellent in cooked dishes).

PIMIENTOS — Select dark red and slightly shriveled product. Peel by roasting in 400°F. oven for 3 to 5 minutes. Remove skin under cool, running water. Cut out stem end, remove seeds. Slice or dice; pack dry.

SPINACH—Cut out thick stems; wash thoroughly. Water-blanch 2½ minutes. Use 2 gallons of boiling water per pound of spinach. Cool; pack.

SQUASH, SUMMER—Wash; cut into ½-inch slices. Water-blanch 3½ minutes. Steam-blanch 4½ minutes. Cool; pack.

SQUASH, WINTER — Peel, cut into 1-inch cubes. Cook or steam until tender. Mash and package.

SWISS CHARD — Wash, discard main stems. Water-blanch 2 minutes. Cool; pack.

TURNIPS—Select young, tender product. Cut off tops, peel, dice in ½-inch cubes. Steam-blanch 70 seconds. Water-blanch 60 seconds. Cool; pack.

TURNIP GREENS—Wash; illiminate coarse large leaves. Water-blanch 60 seconds. Cool; pack.

Collapsible boxes: H is easier to fold into shape than G and C

PREPARING MEAT AND LARGE GAME

Freeze only high quality meat and at a temperature of zero degrees or lower. Slaughtering may be done at home if a chilling room is available, or at a locker plant. (Write to your state university extension service for information on selection of meat animals, slaughtering, aging, and cutting up of carcass into suitable cuts for size of family. Or use facilities of a locker plant for this service). It is advisable to remove some bone and fat from large cuts of meat. Make soup stock from bones and freeze for future use.

Fatty meat loses flavor faster than lean meat, therefore freezing sliced ham and bacon is not advised. Whole hams and bacon slabs may be frozen for several months, especially during warm weather when the fat of cured and smoked meats may become rancid. Wrap smoked meat carefully to prevent odors from penetrating to other foods.

Omit salt from sausage to be frozen as it increases rancidity of the fat. Do not let freezer temperature fluctuate much above zero. The lower the storage temperature is kept the longer it is possible to store the product. Variety meats such as heart, liver, etc., may be frozen but stored no longer than 2 to 4 months. Prepare large game as for meat.

PACKAGING FOODS FOR FREEZING

PACKAGING MATERIALS FOR FROZEN FOODS

A home freezer is a very dry storage place and to avoid the drying out of foods placed in storage it is necessary to use wrapping materials specifically recommended for the purpose. For irregularly shaped foods such as meat, fowl, fish, cakes and pies, use heavy aluminum foil, freezer-type cellophane, pliofilm, or polyethylene. Use the "drugstore" wrap when packaging these foods. (Place food in center of wrapping material and draw the two opposite sides of material up together. Then fold over and over until the wrapping is tight around the food).

Overwrap foods packaged in cellophane or other light-weight plastic materials with stockinette, a knitted tubular material. It is advisable to heat-seal the plastic wrapping materials, using a warm hand iron or a special heat-sealing device. Freezer tapes are also available for sealing packages.

CONTAINERS

Pliofilm and polyethylene bags are available in many sizes to use for irregularly shaped foods. Do not use these bags for liquid foods. Some cartons are also lined with this type of bag.

For either liquid or dry-packed foods, many varieties of containers are available. They include— Glass freezer and canning jars, molded plastic containers, and heavily waxed tub-shaped cartons. For fruits and vegetables you may use heavy aluminum-foil cartons or waxed folding cartons which have a moisture-proof liner in them. Tin cans may be used the same as other cartons. Empty coffee and vegetable fat cans may be saved for freezing.

OTHER SUPPLIES

To label packages for the freezer use a labeling pen or pencil which has no odor. Give the name of food, weight or number of servings, percentage of sirup or sugar used with fruits, and date of freezing.

Use sealing tape to fasten freezer wrapping material which is not self-sealing. It is also useful to fasten tops of coffee cans and vegetable fat cans used for freezing. Use various colors of tape for different foods as it is an aid in locating them later.

PLACING FOODS IN FREEZER

Place against side walls or bottom of freezer leaving space between packages for fast freezing. Leave food in contact with walls overnight. Stack packages in orderly fashion the next day.

MONOSODIUM GLUTAMATE

Research on the processing of frozen foods indicates that the addition of monosodium glutamate to many foods prior to packaging improves their flavor and storing qualities.

EGGS AND DAIRY PRODUCTS

EGGS—Select fresh eggs. They may be frozen whole (never in shell) or separated into yolks and whites. Eggs once frozen and thawed should be used at once, never refrozen. Therefore freeze eggs in specific amounts for certain purposes such as for cakes, custards, mayonnaise, etc. To freeze whole eggs add either salt, sugar or corn sirup to prevent from becoming gummy during freezing. Add 1 teaspoon salt or 1 tablespoon sugar or sirup to each cup of liquid eggs. Mix with fork only to break yolks, not to whip air into eggs. Use eggs containing salt for mayonnaise,

salad dressing, etc., and eggs with sugar added for cakes, etc.

To freeze yolks, add 2 tablespoons sugar or corn sirup or 1 teaspoon salt to each cup of yolks. To freeze whites of eggs nothing need be added and use them for any purpose.

To freeze eggs for poaching or frying line muffin pans with paper muffin cups. Carefully drop an egg into each cup, taking care not to break yolk. Freeze, remove paper cups from pans and wrap individually in moisture-proof paper; heat-seal. Put into pliofilm bags and return to freezer.

MILK AND CREAM — Pasteurized, homogenized milk may be frozen not longer than 2 weeks. Allow 2 inches of headroom in carton or bottle for expansion during freezing. Heavy, pasteurized cream containing no less than 40% butter fat may be frozen. For best results add 6½ tablespoons sugar to 1 quart of cream. Hold not longer than 3 months.

CHEESE—Most hard chesses such as Cheddar and brick cheese freeze satisfactorily. Wrap well in foil. After long storage cheese becomes crumbly but flavor is not impaired. Soft cheeses such as Camembert and Bleu may be frozen to prevent further ripening.

CREAM CHEESE—Wrap in foil and hold no longer than 2 months.

COTTAGE CHEESE—Pack solidly in cartons and store for several weeks.

BUTTER, MARGARINE, LARD— Pack in cartons or wrap in foil. Do not freeze butter made from unpasteurized cream as it tends to become rancid during storage.

ICE CREAM — Store in liquid-tight cartons. It keeps about 1 month but spoils if carton is opened frequently.

FREEZING SALADS

Gelatin salads, especially those to which cottage cheese, whipped cream, sour cream, or mayonnaise has been added, freeze satisfactorily. Mayonnaise alone separates during freezing but in combination freezes well. Fresh vegetable salads are unsuited for freezing as vegetables lose crispness during freezing. Salads containing nuts and whites of hard-cooked eggs do not freeze well. Fruit salads which are frozen in refrigerator trays for several hours may usually be kept in the freezer compartment of refrigerator for a longer period, providing the freezer maintains at least a zero degree temperature and food is properly wrapped.

STRAWBERRY SALAD

1 16-ounce package sliced frozen strawberries, partially thawed
1 cup dairy sour cream
1 cup dry cottage cheese
1 tablespoon lemon juice

Beat sour cream with rotary beater until slightly thicker. Fold in remaining ingredients and spoon

FROZEN FRUIT SALADS

BLUEBERRY CREAM CHEESE SALAD

1½ cups mayonnaise
12 ounces cream cheese
2 teaspoons grated lemon rind
¼ cup confectioners' sugar
1 cup well-drained fruit cocktail
1 cup sliced banana
2 cups frozen blueberries, thawed
2 cups heavy cream, whipped

Blend mayonnaise with cream cheese. Beat in grated lemon rind and sugar. Fold in fruit cocktail, banana, blueberries and whipped cream. Pour into three 1½ pint freezer cartons and place in freezer. To serve, unmold and cut into slices. Serve on bed of chickory, watercress, or other greens. Each carton yields 6 slices.

---

into two 1-pint cartons. Place in freezer. To thaw, place carton in refrigerator about 1 hour before serving time. Or thaw at room temperature a few minutes. Each carton yields 6 slices.

FROZEN FRUIT SALAD

1 9-oz. can sliced pineapple, drained (reserve sirup)
½ cup butter
2 tablespoons flour
2 tablespoons sugar
Few grains salt
1 egg, slightly beaten
2 tablespoons lemon juice
¾ cup orange sections, cut into ½-inch pieces
½ cup maraschino cherries, drained, cut into quarters
¼ cup chopped pecans
12 marshmallows, cut in eights
2 cups heavy cream, whipped

Measure pineapple juice into measuring cup; add water to make 1 cup liquid. Melt butter over very low heat; blend in mixture of flour, sugar and salt. Add pineapple liquid gradually, stirring constantly until mixture is thickened and smooth. Remove from heat and stir several tablespoons of hot mixture into beaten egg. Add to thickened sauce; cook over simmering water 3 or 4 minutes, stirring constantly. Stir in lemon juice. Chill. Toss together in a bowl the pineapple, cut into small cubes, orange pieces, maraschino cherries, nuts and marshmallow pieces. Blend together the pineapple juice mixture and whipped cream; fold into fruit until well blended. Spoon into two 1½ pint freezer cartons; freeze until firm.

To serve, place carton in refrigerator until salad is slightly softened, (about 2 hours). Remove from carton or cut carton away from mold. Cut into slices and serve as a salad on a bed of salad greens, or serve plain as a dessert. Each carton yields about 8 slices.

Blueberry Cream Cheese Salad may be prepared with frozen or fresh blueberries. Freeze in square or round cartons.

PIES AND PASTRY—Fresh fruit pies are favorites for freezing although cream-filled pies (fillings thickened w i t h gelatin, cornstarch, or tapioca) may be frozen also. Custard-type fillings tend to separate and crust becomes soggy. Meringue toppings on pies toughen slightly in freezing.

Pies and pie shells may be frozen before or after baking. If a fruit pie is to be frozen unbaked do not pierce top of crust. A solid top prevents drying out of fruit. (Do not thaw a frozen pie for baking.) For easier wrapping, pies may be frozen before packaging, but wrap immediately after they are frozen. Cool baked pies thoroughly at room temperature before wrapping and leave in pie pan. (Or you may prefer using a paper pie plate with a metal rim, or an aluminum foil pie pan.) Baked pies may be thawed at room temperature or set in a 400° F. oven for 10 to 15 minutes. Cool baked pie shells at room temperature and freeze in pie pan. Thaw, unwrapped, at room temperature, about 30 minutes. Then unwrap and pour in filling. Thaw unbaked pie shell (do not let it become warm) and bake in usual manner. If a baked filling is used, pour it into unthawed shell and bake.

CREAM PUFFS, ECLAIRS—Cool thoroughly after baking; wrap and freeze.

YEAST BREAD AND ROLLS—May be frozen baked or unbaked, but the quality of products frozen after baking is superior. Unbaked doughs can be stored for several weeks, while baked bread and rolls keep fresh up to three months. To freeze unbaked, allow dough to rise until doubled in bulk. Shape into rolls or loaves and freeze before dough rises a second time. Freeze in pans or transfer to cartons after freezing. Grease the tops of rolls and put cellophane between layers when packaging.

To freeze baked rolls and bread, cool thoroughly before wrapping, then freeze immediately.

To bake unbaked rolls and loaves of bread, remove freezer wrap and place in greased muffin pans or loaf pans; cover to prevent surface drying and let rise in warm place until doubled in bulk. Bake in the usual manner.

To thaw and serve frozen rolls heat them, unwrapped, in a 400° F. oven for about 10 minutes. (Do not put pliofilm bags in oven.) To thaw bread, leave inside wrap at room temperature about an hour.

Brown-and-serve rolls may be prepared by baking pan rolls until they are slightly browned (about 40 minutes) at 275°F. Then cool them in pans for 20 minutes and turn out to cool thoroughly. Wrap in freezer material and store no longer than 3 months. To serve, place thawed rolls on baking sheet and brown in 450°F. oven about 7 minutes.

FREEZER YEAST ROLLS

1/4 cup sugar
3 teaspoons salt
6 tablespoons shortening
1 cup milk, scalded
3/4 cup water
1 egg, well beaten
2 cakes or packages yeast
1/4 cup lukewarm water (or warm water for active dry yeast)
6 cups sifted flour, about

Combine sugar, salt, shortening and milk in a large bowl. Add water and cool to lukewarm. Add egg and yeast which has been dissolved in lukewarm water. Add flour, beating after each addition. Mix to a soft dough. Knead until dough is smooth and satiny. Put into greased bowl, grease surface, and then let rise until doubled in bulk. Shape dough into rolls and place in greased pan or muffin pans. Grease tops of rolls. (If prepared for freezing, wrap and put into freezer at once.) Let rise until doubled in bulk. Bake in 425°F. oven 10 to 12 minutes. (If frozen, cool before packaging.) Makes about 3 dozen rolls.

Cool rolls thoroughly before wrapping for freezing.

Freezing your favorite biscuits, cakes or cookies to find them still perfect in texture and flavor weeks later is exciting fun.

QUICK BREADS AND BISCUITS
—Are prepared for freezing the same as yeast breads and rolls. They may be frozen baked or unbaked. When freezing batters leave them in the baking pans and thaw, before baking, in the wrapper. Bake in the usual manner.

Thaw baked quick breads, unwrapped, at room temperature. If served warm, heat in 250°F. oven about 20 minutes.

To freeze waffles, bake in the usual manner, cool at room temperature, wrap in moisture-proof paper and freeze. Reheat in electric toaster. Leftover waffle and pancake batter may be frozen in containers, then thawed and baked when served.

CAKES AND FROSTINGS —
Angel food, sponge, butter, and fruit cakes all freeze satisfactorily.

Cake batters may be frozen but the storage time is shorter and finished cake may not be as acceptable. (Batter loses some of its leavening power during storage.)

Cakes which have been kept in freezer storage dry out more quickly when thawed than cakes freshly baked. Consider this factor when you plan the size of cakes to freeze.

For best results, frost a cake after freezing. Frosted cakes may be stored not longer than two months while unfrosted cakes keep up to three or four months.

Fruit cakes keep up to a year. Fillings tend to make a cake soggy and should be added after removing from freezer and thawed. Butter frostings and the cooked candy-type freeze better than those containing egg whites.

To freeze a frosted cake, place on a piece of cardboard, put in freezer until frosting is firm, then wrap in cellophane or pliofilm. For extra protection, place wrapped cake in bakery carton. Thaw cake in wrappings after taking from carton. For a large cake this takes about two hours at room temperature.

Thaw cake batters at room temperature inside container, then pour into greased pans and bake in usual way. If batter is frozen in cake pans, thaw at room temperature and bake as usual.

Cheese cake, as a rule, does not freeze well as the crumb crust tends to become soggy in storage. If you do freeze them you will find that those made with cream cheese freeze better than those made with cottage cheese.

Most cookies, except the meringue-type, freeze satisfactorily.

Cookies may be frozen before or after baking. Cool baked cookies thoroughly before packaging. Put cellophane or pliofilm between layers. To thaw, leave unwrapped at room temperature about one-half hour.

To freeze refrigerator-type cookie dough, shape the rolls and wrap in moisture-proof cellophane; put in freezer cartons and freeze. To bake, slice dough with a sharp knife and proceed as usual. If dough is too hard to slice, soften it in the refrigerator about an hour.

To freeze drop cookie dough, drop by teaspoonfuls on baking pan; freeze until firm. Then remove cookies from pan and pack in containers with cellophane between layers. To bake, return to cookie pan, thaw until dough is just soft; bake in usual manner. (Or dough may be frozen in a carton, then thawed until soft enough to drop by teaspoonfuls on cookie pan.)

FREEZING SANDWICHES AND
CANAPES—Use day-old bread and leave on crusts. Spread a thin layer of softened butter on both slices. Then spread on the filling. Wrap each sandwich separately in moisture-proof material.

Lettuce and tomatoes do not freeze so add them to sandwiches before they are served.

Sandwich fillings which contain mayonnaise, salad dressing and jelly tend to soak into bread so avoid their use.

Sandwich fillings suitable for freezing—Cheddar or cream cheese, sliced or ground meat and poultry, tuna fish or salmon, cooked egg yolks (not whites), luncheon meats, leftover sliced roast beef, roast pork, and baked ham, cheese spreads and peanut butter. (Add honey or marmalade to peanut butter for easier spreading.)

Cut bread in desired shapes for canapes. Coat with softened butter, then with filling or topping. Place canapes on baking sheet and freeze. Remove from freezer and pack in rectangular freezer boxes, putting cellophane between layers. Overwrap container, heat-seal, and return to freezer. Thaw canapes inside container in the refrigerator about an hour before served.

MAIN DISHES—Freezer owners, anticipating future needs, save time and even money by preparing their favorite dishes in double or triple quantities and freezing amounts not served when they are prepared. These dishes are a wonderful convenience to serve on a busy day or when . unexpected guests arrive. Dishes which must be reheated before serving should be only partially cooked before freezing. Meat and vegetables, for example should be under-cooked. When preparing your favorite stew, add the vegetables when meat is almost tender and omit the potatoes. They do not freeze well and can be added when stew is served.

Dishes which are only thawed before serving must be entirely cooked before freezing. Foods containing pepper, garlic, onion, cloves, curry powder and synthetic vanilla flavoring undergo flavor changes during freezing.

For this reason it is best to season foods very lightly before freezing. Cooked foods to be frozen must be cooled rapidly, packaged, and put into the freezer as soon as possible after cooking.

Dishes which contain a large quantity of milk may curdle or separate during thawing but they generally recombine when heated.

Dishes containing macaroni, rice and spaghetti taste warmed-over after freezing and reheating. It is advisable to freeze other parts of these dishes and add the cereal nearer to the time of serving.

SOUPS—Most soups freeze well but if freezer space is limited it is not always advisable to use it for soup storage. However, concentrated broth and meat stock take little space and may be diluted when they are used. Vegetables and cereals may be added at the time soup is made.

Cool soup stock immediately after cooking and pour into liquid-proof containers. Or pour soup into divided refrigerator ice trays and freeze in small blocks. When frozen, wrap each block separately in cellophane, place in polyethylene bags or containers and freeze.

Preparing thick soups such as bean, split pea and lentil soup in large quaintities is a great time-saver and their flavor is unimpaired by freezing. When freezing ingredients for bisques and chowders freeze only the vegetables and sea foods and add them to the liquid base before they are served.

FREEZING COMPLETE MEALS—When precooking and freezing entire meals select foods with a variety of shapes, colors, flavors, and textures to give the meal taste and eye appeal. Include foods in the menu which have the same reheating time so they will be ready to serve at the same time.

Use the same precaution as you do for freezing any food; freeze it soon after cooking and reheat promptly when taking from freezer.

Store foods for picnic menus in your freezer and be ready for an outing at a moment's notice. Hamburger patties and corn ears, ready for cooking, frozen buns, cupcakes, brownies, and cherry pie, ready for eating, all are appetite-appealing picnic favorites

A plan of quantity cooking has been formulated which we call "basic freezer cookery": This plan calls for the preparation of a basic mixture in quantity and subsequent use of the mixture for a number of dishes.

For instance: A basic ground beef recipe is prepared which includes only those ingredients common to all dishes to be made from the mixture. It is then packaged in recipe-sized quantities and frozen. When ready to use, one portion is thawed, additional ingredients are added and the dish may become spaghetti with hamburger, beef hamburger pie, chili con carne, pizza, quick meat loaf, or some other concoction.

Here is the basic ground beef mixture and several dishes which can be made from it.

BASIC GROUND BEEF MIXTURE

4 pounds ground beef
½ cup chopped onion
1 tablespoon shortening
4 10-ounce cans condensed
    tomato soup
2 tablespoons Worcestershire sauce
4 teaspoons salt

Saute ground beef and onion in melted fat. Add tomato soup, Worcestershire sauce and salt. Simmer about 30 minutes, stirring occasionally, until mixture thickens slightly. Divide into 5 equal portions and freeze.

SPAGHETTI WITH HAMBURG-ER—Thaw 1 portion basic mixture over low heat. Meanwhile, saute ½ cup chopped onion and ½ cup chopped green pepper in a small amount of fat until tender. Add onion, pepper, 1 10-ounce can condensed tomato soup, 1 can tomato paste, ½ pound grated Cheddar cheese, 3 tablespoons

sliced olives, ¼ teaspoon oregano, and ¼ teaspoon salt to ground beef mixture. Bring to a boil and simmer 10 minutes. Yields enough sauce for 2 packages of spaghetti.

BEEFBURGER PIE WITH CHEESE PUFF—Thaw 1 portion basic ground beef mixture. Add 1 cup canned tomatoes, 1¼ cups diced carrots, 1¼ cups cooked green beans, and ¼ teaspoon salt. Cook a few minutes. Pour into greased 1½ quart casserole. Sift 1¼ cups sifted all-purpose flour, 2 teaspoons baking powder, ¾ teaspoons dry mustard, and ½ teaspoon salt together; cut in 2½ tablespoons shortening; add ⅓ cup grated sharp cheese, ⅔ cup milk; blend to a soft dough. Drop by spoonfuls over top of meat mixture. Bake 12 to 15 minutes at 400°F. Serves 6.

CHILI CON CARNE—Thaw 1 portion basic ground beef mixture. Saute 3 tablespoons chopped green pepper in melted shortening until tender. Add ½ cup canned tomatoes, 1 No. 303 can undrained kidney beans, 1 teaspoon or more chili powder, dash cayenne pepper, and the green pepper to basic mixture. Bring to a boil and simmer 10 minutes. Serves 4.

AMERICAN PIZZA—Prepare 1 package hot roll mix according to package directions. Roll out dough and line 3 greased 9-inch pie pans with it. Brush with melted butter or margarine. Thaw 1 portion of basic ground beef mixture, add 1 6-ounce can mushrooms, ¼ teaspoon oregano, and ¼ teaspoon salt. Spread mixture on dough. Sprinkle with ¼ pound crumbled Mozzarella or other mild cheese. Bake at 425°F. 15 to 18 minutes.

QUICK BEEF LOAF—Saute ½ cup chopped celery and 2 table-

spoons chopped onion in small amount of fat until tender. Thaw 1 portion basic ground beef mixture. Add vegetables, 3 slices stale bread soaked in water and wrung out, 2 slightly beaten eggs, and ¼ teaspoon salt to mixture. Spoon into a greased 8-inch square pan. Bake at 325°F. for 30 minutes. Serves 4.

Here is a basic beef stew mixture and several recipes made from it.

BASIC BEEF STEW MIXTURE

1 cup flour
1 tablespoon salt
½ teaspoon pepper
5 pounds stew beef, cubed
1 quart (4 cups) water

Combine flour, salt, and pepper. Coat meat in flour mixture and brown on all sides in small amount of hot fat. Add water and simmer 1¼ hours or until tender. Divide into 5 equal parts and freeze.

FAVORITE BROWN STEW—Defrost 1 portion of basic beef stew mixture. Dissolve 2 bouillon cubes in 1½ cups boiling water and add 4 small whole onions, 3 stalks sliced celery, ½ bunch sliced young carrots; cook until vegetables are tender. Combine the mixtures; add 1 tablespoon flour mixed with a little water, ½ clove garlic and 1 bay leaf (wrapped in cloth bag), ½ teaspoon each of sugar and paprika, dash cloves, and ½ teaspoon lemon juice or gravy seasoning sauce.. Simmer 10 minutes. Remove seasoning bag. Serves 4.

BEEF STROGANOFF—Thaw 1 portion basic stew mixture. Blend in 1 tablespoon prepared mustard, 1 teaspoon Worcestershire sauce, ¾ cup sour cream, and salt and pepper to taste. Bring to boil, simmer 5 minutes, and serve over cooked rice. Serves 4.

Here is a basic chicken mixture and several recipes to be made from it.

BASIC CHICKEN MIXTURE

1½ cups butter or margarine
1½ cups flour
6 cups milk
12 cups diced, cooked chicken
    Salt and pepper to taste

Melt fat and stir in flour. Add milk and cook over low heat, stirring constantly, until mixture is thickened and smooth. Add chicken and seasoning. Divide into 8 equal portions and freeze.

CHICKEN VEGETABLE CASSE-ROLE—Defrost 1 portion basic chicken mixture over low heat. Combine with ¼ cup chopped stuffed olives, ½ package frozen or 1 cup cooked peas, ½ cup diced cooked celery, ¾ teaspoon salt, dash cayenne and 1 cup milk. Place 3 cups cooked rice in greased 1½ quart casserole. Pour chicken and vegetable mixture over rice. Combine 1 tablespoon melted butter and ¼ cup bread crumbs; sprinkle over mixture. Bake at 350°F. 25 minutes. Serves 6 to 8.

CHICKEN à la QUEEN—Defrost 1 portion basic chicken mixture over low heat. Saute ¼ slivered, blanched almonds in 1 tablespoon butter or margarine until light golden; set aside. Pour ½ cup milk over 1 beaten egg yolk; add yolk mixture to hot chicken mixture, stirring. Add ¼ teaspoon salt and cook 2 minutes. Add 1 cup drained pineapple tidbits. Pour over canned chow-mein noodles, toast, or rice. Top with

almonds. Serves 6.

CHICKEN SOUFFLE—Thaw 1 portion basic chicken mixture over low heat. Combine with ½ cup soft bread crumbs, ¼ cup milk, ¼ teaspoon paprika, ⅛ teaspoon salt, 1 teaspoon lemon juice, and 3 egg yolks, beaten until light. Fold in 3 stiffly beaten egg whites. Pour into greased ring mold or custard cups. Set in pan of hot water and bake in 350°F. oven 35 minutes. Bake 15-20 minutes when using custard cups. Serve with mushroom sauce. Serves 4 to 6.

CHICKEN FILLING FOR HOT BISCUITS—Bake your favorite recipe for baking powder biscuits. Thaw 1 portion basic chicken mixture over low heat. Add 2 hard-cooked, finely chopped eggs, ¼ teaspoon salt, 2 teaspoons grated onion, 4 tablespoons sliced ripe olives, and ½ cup milk. Cover and simmer 5-10 minutes. Split hot biscuits and spoon filling between and on top of each biscuit. Serves 6.

Here is a basic cookie dough and recipes to make from it.

BASIC COOKIE DOUGH

8 cups sifted flour
1 teaspoon salt
4 teaspoons baking powder
2 cups butter or margarine
2 cups sugar
2 eggs
2 teaspoons vanilla
¼ cup milk

Sift together flour, salt, and baking powder. Cream butter and sugar with rotary beater until light and fluffy. Add eggs, one at a time, and beat well after each addition. Add vanilla. Stir in

sifted dry ingredients and beat only until blended. Divide dough into 4 equal portions. If cookies are to be baked before freezing, proceed with directions for any of the variations which follow. Or wrap dough in freezer material and freeze for baking of cookies at a later date. To bake cookies, defrost dough in refrigerator several hours before using, or 45-60 minutes at room temperature.

FILLED COOKIES—Roll 1 portion of basic cookie dough ⅛-inch thick and cut with round cutter. Remove center from half of cookies. Put 1 teaspoon jam or other filling on plain rounds and top with "doughnut" rounds. Crimp edges with fork or pastry wheel. Bake at 375°F. on greased cookie pans for 12-15 minutes. About 2 dozen filled cookies.

TOFFEE TREATS—Roll half of 1 portion of basic cookie dough between 2 sheets of waxed paper into a ½-inch thick rectangle. Transfer to greased cookie sheet. Repeat with second half of dough. Bake at 375°F. for 10-12 minutes. While still warm, spread with 1 package (6-ounces) semi-sweet chocolate, melted. Sprinkle with ½ cup chopped nut meats. Cut into diamonds or squares.

DATE BARS—In saucepan, combine 1 package (6-ounces) chopped dates, ½ cup sugar, 1 tablespoon lemon juice and ½ cup hot water. Cook 5 minutes. Cool. Spread half of 1 portion of basic cookie dough in greased 9-inch square cake pan. Spread with date mixture. Crumble remaining cookie dough over dates. Bake for about 35 minutes at 350°F. Cut into bars while still warm. Roll in confectioners' sugar. About 2 dozen bars.

JELLY MAKING

Good jelly is clear and sparkling and has a fresh flavor of the fruit from which it is made. It is tender enough to quiver when moved, but holds angles when cut.

EXTRACTING JUICE—Pectin is best extracted from the fruit by heat, therefore cook the fruit until soft before straining to obtain the juice. Since pectin is most abundant in cores and near skins of apples and similar fruits, cook without paring and coring. Cook juicy fruits such as berries or grapes with no water. Heat slowly until juice starts to flow, then cook more rapidly until soft. Cook firmer, less juicy fruits such as apples or quinces with just enough water to prevent burning. Pour cooked fruit into a jelly bag which has been wrung out of cold water. Hang up and let drain. When dripping has ceased the bag may be squeezed to remove remaining juice, but this may cause cloudy jelly.

TEST FOR PECTIN—The amount of pectin in juice may be estimated by testing a little of the juice with Epsom salts. Add ½ tablespoon sugar and ¾ teaspoon Epsom salts to 1 tablespoon extracted fruit juice. Stir until sugar and salts are dissolved and let stand without stirring 5 minutes. If the mixture sets into a jellylike mass in 5 minutes, the juice contains enough pectin to make good jelly and 1 cup sugar to 1 cup juice may safely be used. If the mass is soft, only ½ to ⅔ cup sugar to 1 cup juice should be used. If mixture fails to set, add commercial pectin or a juice rich in pectin such as apple or currant.

COOKING JUICE—Long cooking of the juice reduces the fruit flavor, darkens the color and may even break down the pectin. To make the cooking period as short as possible cook only 4 to 6 cups of juice at a time and use a kettle with large diameter to provide a large surface for evaporation. Always boil the juice as rapidly as possible.

AMOUNT OF SUGAR—The best amount of sugar varies with the amount of pectin and acid present. Too much sugar will make the jelly weak and sirupy; too little makes a tough jelly. In case of doubt it is always better to use too little rather than too much. Add sugar gradually to boiling juice, while stirring constantly.

TESTING FOR JELLY—Take a little cooked juice in a spoon, cool slightly and pour slowly back into kettle from the edge of the spoon. If the jelly is not cooked sufficiently the juice will fall in 2 parallel drops. When the jelly is cooked sufficiently the drops run together and fall from the spoon in a flake or sheet leaving the edge of the spoon clean. Remove from heat and skim. Pour immediately into glasses or jars. Pour carefully to avoid splashes or drops on the rim, since these cause a poor seal with the paraffin.

PREPARING CONTAINERS—Jars, glasses and lids for jellies must be clean and sterile when used. They should be washed in soapy water, rinsed with hot water, then covered with fresh water and boiled 15 minutes. Leave in the water until needed, drain quickly and fill while hot.

SEALING—Cover jelly with paraffin while hot or after cooling as preferred. If jelly is cooled until set, the paraffin should be very hot when poured to sterilize the top of the jelly. Cover jelly with ⅛-inch layer of paraffin. Dip knife blade into very hot paraffin and insert between jelly and glass to a depth of ¼ inch. Pass knife completely around glass to leave a space into which paraffin may flow. When paraffin is firm cover jars with lids. Store in cool dry place.

CORN SIRUP MAY REPLACE:

⅓ of the sugar when no pectin is added

No more than 2 cups sugar in any recipe using liquid pectin

½ of the sugar in recipes using powdered pectin

SELECTION OF FRUIT—A good jelly-making fruit must contain both acid and pectin. Many fruits contain sufficient amounts of both, while others are lacking in one or the other, or both. When such fruits are used, the missing acid or pectin must be supplied by the use of lemon juice, commercial pectin or apple juice. As fruit ripens the quantity of acid and pectin decreases, consequently some underripe fruit to supply acid and pectin is usually combined with ripe fruit.

USING FRUIT PULP—The pulp remaining from fruits rich in pectin and acid may be combined with water and recooked to give a second extraction of juice. Such fruits are currants, crab apples and wild grapes. The pulp from other fruits may be used for making fruit butters.

Pour hot jelly immediately after skimming into sterile glasses; melt paraffin in teapot and seal glasses when cool

CRANBERRY JELLY

4 cups cranberries
1½ cups water
2 cups sugar

Wash cranberries and pick over. Cook with ¾ cup of the water until very soft. Press through a sieve. Combine sugar and remaining ¾ cup of water and cook 10 minutes. Add strained cranberries and cook 10 minutes longer. Strain again and pour into a moistened mold. Chill. When firm, unmold and serve.

APPLE JELLY

4 pounds tart apples
4 cups water
Sugar

Wash and quarter apples without paring or removing the cores. Place in kettle, add water, cover and cook slowly until fruit is tender, 20 to 25 minutes. Pour into jelly bag and let drip. Use pulp for apple butter or add water again and extract juice a second time. Combine this second extraction with the first or use separately. For each cup of juice use ¾ cup sugar. Cook only 3 to 4 cups of juice at a time. Heat juice to boiling, add sugar gradually and boil rapidly until mixture gives test for jelly. Skim and pour into sterile glasses. Seal with paraffin. Makes 4 (6-ounce) glasses.

CRAB APPLE—Make as above with crab apples, using 1 cup sugar to 1 cup juice. If a second extraction of juice is made and cooked separately, use only ¾ cup of sugar to 1 cup juice. If first and second extractions are combined for cooking, use 1 cup sugar to 1 cup juice.

MINT—Wash and mince 2 cups mint leaves. Add ½ cup water and ½ cup sugar. Let stand several hours. Heat to boiling and strain. Color 4 cups of apple juice prepared as for apple jelly with green food coloring, cook and when nearly to jellying point add 1 to 2 tablespoons of mint juice. Finish cooking, skim, pour into sterile glasses and seal.

ROSE GERANIUM—Add 1 rose geranium leaf to juice for every cup of sugar used in apple jelly. Add leaf when juice is nearly at jellying point. Remove leaves when jelly is cooked.

LEMON VERBENA—Use lemon verbena leaves in the same way as rose geranium.

BLACKBERRY JELLY

Blackberries
Water
Sugar

Select blackberries, about half of which are underripe and half fully ripe. Wash, place in kettle and add 1 cup of water for each 3 quarts of berries. Heat slowly to boiling and boil about 5 minutes. Strain through jelly bag Add ¾ cup sugar for each cup juice, cooking only 3 to 4 cups of juice at a time. Boil juice 3 minutes, add sugar and boil rapidly until juice gives test for jelly. Pour into sterile glasses. Cover with paraffin and store in cool place.

DEWBERRY — Use dewberries instead of blackberries.

LOGANBERRY — Use loganberries instead of blackberries.

RASPBERRY — Use raspberries instead of blackberries. Omit water.

CURRANT JELLY

5 pounds currants
Sugar

Wash currants, pick over and crush. Heat slowly to boiling and boil 5 to 10 minutes, or until currants look white. Strain through jelly bag Add 1½ to 2 cups sugar for every pint of juice and boil until it gives test for jelly, about 20 minutes. Skim, pour into sterile glasses and seal with paraffin. Makes about 9 (6-ounce) glasses.

GOOSEBERRY—Use slightly underripe gooseberries instead of currants.

YOUNGBERRY—Use slightly underripe youngberries instead of currants.

As soon as the jelly test is obtained, remove from heat and skim at once

GRAPE JELLY

4 pounds Concord grapes
⅔ cup water
Sugar

Select slightly underripe grapes, remove from stems and wash. Place in large kettle and add water. Heat to boiling and cook slowly about 3 minutes. Drain through a jelly bag and measure juice. Use ¾ to 1 cup sugar for each cup of juice and cook only 3 to 4 cups juice at a time. Place juice in kettle and boil rapidly 3 minutes. Add sugar and boil rapidly until it gives test for

jelly. Strain and pour into sterile glasses. Seal with paraffin and store in cool, dry place. Makes about 8 (6-ounce) glasses.

S P I C E D—Omit water. Cook grapes with ⅔ cup vinegar, 2 teaspoons cloves and 3 (1-inch) pieces stick cinnamon. Strain juice and proceed as above.

HONEY JELLY

3 cups (2¼ pounds) strained
   honey
1 cup water
½ cup (½ bottle) pectin

Mix honey and water, heat to

boiling quickly and add pectin at once, stirring constantly. Then heat to a full rolling boil and immediately remove from heat. Skim; pour quickly into sterile jelly glasses and seal with paraffin at once. Makes about 5 (6-ounce) glasses.

MINT AND HONEY JELLY

¾ cup boiling water
2 tablespoons dried mint leaves
2½ cups strained honey
Green food coloring
½ cup (½ bottle) pectin

Pour boiling water over mint, cover and let stand 15 minutes. Strain and add enough water to make ¾ cup. Add honey and heat to boiling, adding coloring to tint a light green. Add pectin, stirring constantly. Heat to full rolling boil. Remove from heat at once, skim and pour into sterile glasses. Seal with paraffin. Serve with meat. Makes 5 (6-ounce) glasses.

QUINCE HONEY

1½ pounds quinces
2½ cups water
2 tablespoons lemon juice
3 cups sugar

Wash, pare and core quinces. Add water to parings and cook 30 minutes. Grate or grind quinces or slice very thin. Weigh pulp and use 1 pound. Add lemon juice and strained liquid from parings. Cook until tender, add sugar and cook until sirup gives test for jelly. Pour into sterile glasses and seal with paraffin. Makes 6 (6-ounce) glasses.

Strain juice without squeezing for clearest jelly; then measure juice and sugar accurately

BUTTERS

Fruit butters are generally made from larger fruits, such as apples, plums, peaches or grapes. Cook the fruit until softened and run through a sieve to give a smooth consistency. After sieving, cook the pulp rapidly about 5 minutes or until slightly thick. Add sugar and cook as rapidly as possible with constant stirring. As mixture becomes thicker the heat must be reduced to avoid spattering and scorching. Cook until no rim of liquid separates around the edge of the butter when a small amount is dropped onto a cold plate. The finished product should mound up when dropped from a spoon, but should not cut like jelly. Neither should there be any free liquid.

Fruit pulp left after extraction of juice for jelly may be used for butters. Remove pulp from the jelly bag and if it is quite dry add ½ cup water for each 2 cups pulp. Cook 10 minutes and rub through sieve.

CIDER APPLE BUTTER

Apples
2 quarts cider
1½ pounds sugar
1 teaspoon cinnamon
1 teaspoon allspice
1 teaspoon cloves

Wash apples, slice into small bits and use 4 quarts. Cover with cider and cook until soft. Press through a sieve to remove skins and seeds. Add sugar and spices to apple pulp and cook until thick, stirring constantly. Fill sterile jars and seal. Makes about 3 quarts.

The food mill is the simple and easy way to make apple or other fruit butters

JAMS

Jams are usually made from pulp and juice of one fruit, rather than of a combination of several fruits. Berries and other small fruits are most frequently used, though larger fruits such as apricots, peaches or plums cut into small pieces or crushed are also used for jams.

Good jam has a soft even consistency without distinct pieces of fruit, a bright color, a good fruit flavor and a semijellied texture that is easy to spread but has no free liquid.

To make jam from berries, some partially ripe fruit should be used to provide pectin. Wash berries well, remove stems or caps and weigh or measure berries. In general use ½ to ¾ pound sugar to each pound of fruit, or ½ to 1 cup sugar to 1 cup fruit, the amount varying with the ripeness of the fruit and the flavor desired. Crush berries and cook rapidly without adding water until thick. Stir constantly to prevent burning. Add sugar and cook rapidly until mixture gives the sheeting test for jelly. It may also be tested by drawing the spoon across the center of the pan. If the mark does not fill in quickly the jam is thick enough. Pour into sterile glasses and seal as for jelly.

When using larger fruits, pare, remove seeds or stones and cut into small pieces. Add a small amount of water and proceed as above, mashing cooked fruit well before adding sugar.

Corn sirup may be used instead of sugar, about ¾ cup for each cup of fruit.

Mash soft fruits with a potato masher; chop or grind the firmer ones

BLACKBERRY JAM

2½ pounds blackberries
1½ pounds sugar

Wash berries thoroughly, remove caps and crush berries. Heat slowly to boiling, stirring constantly. Add sugar and continue cooking rapidly until mixture gives test for jelly. Pour into sterile jars and seal. If seedless jam is desired rub cooked berries through sieve before adding sugar. Makes 2 pints.

CHERRY AND RASPBERRY JAM

2 cups pitted cherries
2 cups raspberries
4 cups sugar

Crush cherries slightly and cook until skins are tender. Add raspberries and cook until mixture begins to thicken. Add sugar and cook rapidly until thick. Cool slightly, pour into sterile glasses and seal with paraffin. Makes 5 (6-ounce) glasses.

GOOSEBERRY JAM

1 pound gooseberries
1 pound sugar

Clean berries, remove stems and crush slightly to start juice. Cook until soft, add sugar, heat slowly until sugar is dissolved, then boil rapidly until juice gives test for jelly. Pour into sterile glasses and seal. Makes about 2 (6-ounce) glasses.
If ripe gooseberries are used, use only ¾ pound sugar to 1 pound berries.

PEACH JAM

Peaches
¾ to 1 pound sugar

Wash peaches, dip in boiling water for about ½ minute and plunge into cold water. Slip off skins, cut fruit into halves and discard stones. Use 1 pound prepared fruit. Crush fruit and arrange in layers with sugar. Let stand 3 to 4 hours, then heat slowly until sugar is dissolved, stirring constantly. Heat to boiling and cook rapidly, stirring constantly, until fruit is clear and jam is thick. Pour into sterile glasses and seal. Makes 3 (6-ounce) glasses.

APRICOT—Make as above using ¾ pound sugar to each pound of prepared fruit. Add 2 tablespoons lemon juice.

PEAR AND APPLE JAM

1 pint diced pears
1 pint diced apples
Grated rind 1 lemon
Juice 1 lemon
3½ cups sugar

Combine ingredients and heat, stirring thoroughly until sugar is dissolved. Boil rapidly until mixture is thick and clear. Cool slightly, pour into sterile jars and seal. Makes about 1½ pints.

PLUM JAM

1 pound plums
1 cup water
¾ pound sugar

Clean plums, cook in water until skins are tender, 10 to 15 minutes. Cool and remove stones. Add sugar, heat slowly until sugar is dissolved, then cook rapidly until thick. Partially cool, stirring, occasionally, pour into sterile jars and seal. Makes about ½ pint.

RHUBARB JAM

2½ pounds rhubarb
1½ pounds sugar
½ cup water
2 oranges (rind and juice)

Wash rhubarb and cut into small pieces; add sugar and water. Grate rind of oranges and add to rhubarb. Add orange juice and cook 30 minutes, stirring occasionally. Fill sterile glasses and seal. Makes about 6 (6-ounce) glasses.

STRAWBERRY JAM

3 cups large firm berries
3 cups sugar

Wash strawberries carefully, hull and measure. Crush berries in large kettle. Heat slowly to boiling, stirring constantly. Add sugar and continue cooking rapidly until mixture gives sheeting test for jelly or spoon leaves a mark across the center of pan. Pour into sterile glasses and seal. Makes about 3 (6-ounce) glasses.

TOMATO AND APPLE JAM

1 lemon, chopped
1 pint tomatoes, fresh or canned
2 cups diced apples
3 cups sugar

Cook lemon until tender in a small amount of water. Add remaining ingredients and boil mixture until thick and clear. Cool slightly, pour into sterile jars and seal. Makes about 2 pints.

TUTTI-FRUTTI JAM

1 quart currants
1 quart gooseberries
1 quart cherries
1 quart red raspberries
6 pounds (12 cups) sugar

Wash and drain fruits. Stem currants. Stem gooseberries and remove blossom ends. Add 6 cups sugar to currants and gooseberries and let stand 1 hour. Simmer 30 minutes. Pit cherries and add raspberries and remaining sugar. Let stand 1 hour. Add to cooked currants and gooseberries, and continue cooking 20 minutes longer. Pour into hot sterile jars and seal. Makes 9 (8-ounce) jars.

MARMALADES

Marmalades are usually made from fruits which have jelly-making properties. They have a clear jelly in which thin slices or small pieces of the fruit are suspended. Cool the product partly before pouring into glasses and seal with paraffin or cellophane.

CARROT, APPLE AND PEACH MARMALADE

1 pint diced carrots
1 pint diced tart apples
1 cup diced peaches
Juice 1 lemon
3 cups sugar

Combine ingredients and boil rapidly until mixture is clear. Pour into sterile jars and seal. Makes about 2½ pints.

ORANGE MARMALADE

6 large oranges
Water
Sugar
2 tablespoons lemon juice

Wash oranges and cut into halves. Remove seeds and stem end. Slice very thin. Add 2 cups water for each cup fruit and let stand overnight. Simmer until tender, add 1 cup sugar for each cup cooked mixture, add lemon juice and cook 20 minutes or until thick. Remove from heat, cool 5 minutes, stirring frequently to prevent large pieces floating on surface. Pour into sterile glasses and seal. Makes about 8 (6-ounce) glasses.

SEVILLE ORANGE MARMA-LADE—Use 1 pound wild oranges, ½ pound sweet oranges and ½ pound lemons. Follow method above. Seeds of fruit may be heated with 1 cup water, then liquid added as part of the water. Makes 48 ounces.

ORANGE AND GRAPE-FRUIT MARMALADE

2 oranges
1 grapefruit
1 lemon
Honey
Sugar
Salt

Remove peel from fruit and slice very thin. Add 1 quart water to peel, heat to boiling and cook 5 minutes. Drain and repeat twice. Cut pulp into thin slices, removing seeds and membrane. Add to drained peel. To each cup of mixture, add 3 cups water and boil rapidly 40 minutes. Measure and add ⅔ cup honey and ⅓ cup sugar for each cup fruit; add a few grains salt. Boil rapidly 25 minutes or until mixture gives test for jelly. Pour into sterile glasses and seal. Makes about 4 (6-ounce) glasses.

GREEN GAGE MARMALADE

1 quart green gage plums
1 cup cold water
3 cups sugar

Wash plums; cut into small pieces, removing stones but not skins. Add water and cook until plums are tender. Add sugar and cook until mixture is thick and clear. Pour into sterile glasses and seal. Makes about 5 (6-ounce) glasses.

PEAR MARMALADE

8 pounds ripe pears
3 oranges
2 lemons
6 pounds granulated sugar
   (12 cups)

Wash pears, core and grind. Wash oranges and lemons and remove seeds and ends. Grind whole fruit, skin and all. Place all the fruit in a preserving kettle, add sugar and stir well. Bring to a boil and cook until clear. Pour into sterilized glasses and seal. Makes 8 pints.

APRICOT MARMALADE

2 pounds dried apricots
1 dozen oranges
1 grapefruit
¾ cup lemon juice
1¾ cups crushed pineapple
Sugar

Soak apricots overnight. Peel oranges and grapefruit and remove white rind. Cut in pieces and add lemon juice and soaked apricots, cut in pieces. Add pineapple. Measure fruit and add an equal volume of sugar (less if desired). Cook until thick, stirring carefully. Fill sterilized glasses and seal. Makes 12 to 14 (6-ounce) glasses. Chopped piñion nuts may be added.

RHUBARB MARMALADE

4 pounds rhubarb
5 pounds sugar
1 pound seeded raisins
Rind of 1 lemon, cut in shreds
Juice of 2 oranges
½ teaspoon cloves
1 teaspoon cinnamon

Wash rhubarb and cut into 1-inch pieces. Cover with sugar and let stand overnight. Add remaining ingredients. Heat to the boiling point. Reduce heat and simmer about 40 minutes or until thick. Stir frequently to prevent burning. Pour into sterilized glasses, cool and seal. Makes 4 pints.

CONSERVES

Conserves are jam-like products which contain a mixture of fruits, frequently including citrus fruits, raisins or nuts. The consistency should be tender and slightly jellied with little or no sirup. Nuts if used should be dipped into boiling water and skins removed, then chopped or ground Combine prepared fruit with sugar and water it required and cook until thickened. Use same test as for jam. Add nuts, cool slightly and pour into sterile containers. Seal

PLUM CONSERVE

2 oranges
3 pounds plums
3 pounds sugar
1 pound seedless raisins
½ pound broken walnuts

Wash and grind oranges. Remove stones from plums and cut into quarters. Combine oranges, plums, sugar and raisins. Simmer 1½ hours, stirring to prevent scorching. Add walnuts and cook ¾ hour more or until thick. Pour into sterile glasses and seal. Makes 12 (6-ounce) glasses.

RASPBERRY AND CHERRY CONSERVE

1 cup pitted cherries
1 cup raspberries (red or black)
1 pound sugar

Clean and stem fruit. Crush cherries slightly and cook until skins are tender. Add berries and cook until mixture begins to thicken. Add sugar and cook rapidly until thickened Partially cool, stirring occasionally, pour into sterile jars and seal. Makes about 1 pint.

Weigh fruit and sugar accurately; add nuts when conserve is nearly finished and label every glass or jar

PRESERVES

Preserves are whole fruits or pieces of fruit cooked in a heavy sugar sirup. A special effort is made to keep the fruit as whole and well shaped as possible. Good preserves are plump and tender, with natural color and flavor.

PEACH PRESERVES

2 pounds peaches
3 cups sugar
2 cups water

Remove skins from peaches, cut into halves and remove stones Boil sugar and water together until sirup coats a spoon. Add peaches and boil until sirup is thick. Place peaches in clean hot jars, fill jars with boiling sirup and seal. Makes about 3 half-pint jars

STRAWBERRY PRE-SERVES

3 cups strawberries
2 cups sugar

Select berries slightly underripe for eating. Clean, wash and drain carefully to avoid crushing. Use berries whole or cut as desired To 1 cup of berries, add 1 cup of sugar. Heat gradually to boiling and boil 6 to 7 minutes. Add 1 more cup of strawberries and 1 cup sugar. Boil 6 to 7 minutes. Add 1 more cup berries and boil 6 to 7 minutes. Pour into sterile jars and seal. Makes 1½ pints.

GOLDEN TOMATO PRESERVES

2 pounds yellow pear-tomatoes
Boiling water
3 cups sugar
Juice 2 oranges
Grated rind 1 orange
Grated rind 1 lemon
2 lemons. thinly sliced

Select fully ripe tomatoes, cover with boiling water, let stand a few seconds, then drain and dip into cold water. Peel carefully and place in layers in bowl, sprinkling sugar over each layer. Cover and let stand overnight. Drain off juice and sugar and heat to boiling with orange juice, orange rind and lemon rind. Boil until sirup spins a thread. Add tomatoes and sliced lemons. Cook rapidly until sirup is thick. Pour into sterile jelly glasses and seal with paraffin or pour into sterile glass jars and seal. Makes about 2 pints.

RED TOMATO—Use 5 pounds sliced ripe tomatoes and 4 pounds sugar. Omit orange juice and rind and lemon rind. Proceed as above.

APPLE PRESERVES

5 pounds apples
5 pounds brown sugar
Grated rind ½ lemon
1 piece whole ginger root
3⅓ cups water

Pare apples, core and cut into quarters. Combine sugar, lemon rind, ginger root and water. Heat to boiling and add apple quarters. Cook until fruit is clear and tender. Remove apples from sirup and pack into sterile jars. Heat sirup to boiling, pour over apples to fill jars and seal. Makes 5 pints.

FIG PRESERVES

4 pounds fresh figs
1 lemon
4 cups sugar
1 cup water

Wash and peel the figs. Slice the lemon. Boil the sugar and water together for five minutes, then add the figs and lemon. Cook rapidly until the fruit is clear. Seal in clean hot jars.

PLUM PRESERVES

3 pounds fruit
4½ cups sugar
½ cup water

Select small purple plums and be sure they are sound and not overripe. Remove the stems, wash the fruit, and pierce each plum with a fork. Place the plums in an earthen bowl or jar. Cover them with the sugar and add the water. Cover the bowl and set in a cool place over night. Drain the plums and boil the juice for five minutes. Add the plums and cook until clear. This will take only a few minutes, and care should be taken not to overcook, as the sirup thickens or jellies after standing. Pour into hot, clean jars and seal. Makes 3 pints.

GRAPE PRESERVES

4 pounds Concord grapes
1½ cups water
3 cups sugar

Wash the grapes and press pulp from skins. (They are best if seeded.) Boil the sugar and water 5 minutes. Add the fruit and cook until grapes are clear and sirup is thick. Pour into hot, clean jars and seal at once. Makes 2 pints preserves.

CHERRY PRESERVES

2 pounds stemmed tart cherries
2 pounds sugar
2 cups water

Wash cherries, but do not stone. Heat 1 cup of sugar with water, boil 5 minutes, add fruit and cook until tender. Add remaining sugar and cook rapidly until thick. Skim and pour into sterile jars. Seal. Makes about 1½ pints.

PICKLED FRUITS

PICKLED SPICED BLUEBERRIES

5 pounds blueberries
1 cup vinegar
1 cup water
6 cups sugar
1 tablespoon whole allspice
1 tablespoon broken stick
    cinnamon
1 tablespoon whole cloves

Wash berries and drain. Mix vinegar, water and sugar. Tie spices loosely in cheesecloth bag and boil in vinegar mixture 5 minutes. Add well-drained berries and simmer 5 to 10 minutes. If cooked too long, berries will have a shriveled appearance. Remove spices. Pour into sterile jars and seal. Makes about 8 pints.

SPICED CRANBERRIES

2 quarts cranberries
1⅓ cups vinegar
⅔ cup water
6 cups sugar
2 tablespoons ground cinnamon
1 tablespoon ground cloves
1 tablespoon ground allspice

Pick over cranberries and wash. Place in large kettle and add remaining ingredients. Cook slowly over low heat 45 minutes. Pour into sterile jars and seal. Makes 3 pints.

SPICED CHERRIES

2 cups vinegar
8 cups sugar
5 pounds tart cherries, pitted
3 tablespoons cinnamon
1½ tablespoons cloves

Mix vinegar and sugar and boil 1 minute. Skim. Add fruit and simmer 1½ hours. Add spices and mix well. Pour into sterile jars and seal. Makes about 8 pints.

PRESERVED CITRON

4 pounds citron
Salt
4 pounds sugar
4 cups water
1 small piece ginger root
Juice and rind of 4 lemons

Wash citron carefully. Cut into halves and remove seeds; then cut into eighths. Sprinkle generously with salt, cover with cold water and let stand overnight. Drain off water, cover with fresh cold water and let stand overnight. Drain and pare citron. Combine sugar, water, ginger root, lemon juice and rind and heat to boiling. Add citron and cook slowly until citron is tender. Pack in sterile jars, fill jars with boiling hot sirup and seal at once. Makes 4 half-pint jars.

PICKLED CRAB APPLES

1 peck (8 quarts) crab apples
6 sticks cinnamon
¼ cup whole cloves
1 quart vinegar
2½ pounds sugar

Select apples of uniform size, wash and remove blossom ends, but do not pare. Tie spices loosely in cheesecloth bag. Mix vinegar and sugar, add spices and heat to boiling. Add apples and reheat mixture slowly to avoid bursting skins. Simmer until apples are tender. Pack apples in sterile jars, cover with boiling vinegar sirup and seal. Makes 10 pints.

SPICED CURRANTS

2½ pounds ripe currants
2 pounds sugar
1 cup vinegar
1 tablespoon cinnamon
1½ teaspoons allspice
1½ teaspoons cloves

Wash currants, stem and cook with sugar and vinegar over low heat 1 hour. Add spices and continue cooking 30 minutes. Pour into sterile jars and seal. Makes 2½ pints.

Seedless grapes may be used in place of currants. Use same amount of whole spices instead.

Cranberries and oranges make a relish requiring no cooking

SPICED ELDERBERRIES

1 stick cinnamon
1 tablespoon whole cloves
1 tablespoon whole allspice
3 pounds sugar
1 pint diluted vinegar
5 pounds elderberries

Tie spices in cheesecloth bag. Heat sugar, vinegar and spices to boiling and cool. Add cleaned berries, heat slowly to simmering and simmer until berries are tender. Cool quickly and let stand several hours or overnight. Remove spice bag. Pack berries in sterile jars, heat sirup to boiling and pour over berries. Seal. Makes about 5 pints.

SPICED HUCKLEBERRIES—Use huckleberries instead of elderberries.

CRANBERRY ORANGE RELISH

2 large oranges
4 cups cranberries
2 cups sugar or 1½ cups honey

Cut oranges into eighths and remove seeds. Force cleaned cranberries and orange (rind and pulp) through a food chopper. Mix well. Add sugar and stir until thoroughly mixed. Make several hours before using. Pack in sterile glasses and seal. Makes about 1 quart relish.

SPICED GOOSEBERRIES

5 pounds ripe gooseberries
4 pounds brown sugar
2 cups vinegar
2 tablespoons cloves
3 teaspoons cinnamon
3 teaspoons allspice

Wash and pick over gooseberries. Combine with remaining ingredients. Cook slowly until mixture becomes rather thick. Pour into sterile glasses and seal. Makes about 5 pints.

A pointed orange cup forms an attractive serving dish for cranberry orange relish

FIG PICKLES

1 tablespoon baking soda
1 gallon water
7 pounds fresh figs
3 pounds sugar
1 pint vinegar
1 tablespoon cinnamon
½ tablespoon cloves
3 lemons, sliced thin

Dissolve soda in water, heat to boiling and pour over figs. Let stand a few minutes, drain and rinse thoroughly in cold water. Dissolve sugar in vinegar, add cinnamon, cloves and lemons and heat to boiling. Add figs and cook until clear. Lift out figs and pack in jars. Boil down vinegar sirup until thick and pour over figs. Makes about 7 pints.

GINGER PEARS

5 pounds hard pears
3 cups water
5 pounds sugar
1/3 cup chopped preserved ginger
Juice and grated rind 3 lemons

Pare pears, core and dice or cut into slices. Add water and cook until tender. Add remaining ingredients and simmer mixture until thick. Pour into sterile jars and seal. Makes 5 pints.

PICKLED PLUMS

4 quarts plums
2 cups vinegar
6 cups sugar
1 teaspoon whole allspice
1 stick cinnamon
1 tablespoon whole cloves

Wash plums, dry and place in a stone jar. Mix vinegar, sugar and spices and boil 5 minutes. Pour boiling sirup over plums, cover jar and let stand overnight. Drain plums, saving liquid and heat liquid to boiling. Add plums and simmer mixture until plums are clear. Do not cook so long that skins break. Pack fruit in sterile jars, cover with boiling vinegar sirup and seal. Makes about 8 pints.

SPICED PICKLED PUMPKIN

5 pounds pumpkin, pared and cut
   into 1-inch cubes
1 teaspoon whole cloves
1 tablespoon broken stick
   cinnamon
1 quart vinegar
4 pounds sugar

Place pumpkin in a kettle. Tie spices in cheesecloth. Add to vinegar with sugar, heat to boiling and boil 5 minutes; pour over pumpkin. Cook pumpkin in sirup until tender. Place in sterile jars, cover with vinegar sirup and seal at once. Makes 4 quarts.

BRANDIED PEACHES

9 pounds peaches, 9 pounds sugar
1 quart water, 2 sticks cinnamon
2 tablespoons whole cloves,
   heads removed
3 pints brandy

Select large clingstone peaches. Peel and weigh fruit. Boil sugar and water with spices tied in a bag until clear; drop in peaches, a few at a time, and cook until tender, but not soft. They must remain whole. Repeat until all peaches have been cooked. Place fruit on platter to drain. Boil sirup until thick, cool, add brandy and stir well. Place peaches in sterile jars and cover with sirup. Seal. Makes about 4 quarts.

PICKLED PEACHES

3 cups honey, 3 cups vinegar
2 cups water, 1 teaspoon salt
5 quarts peaches
1 tablespoon whole cloves
2 sticks cinnamon

Heat first 4 ingredients to boiling Scald peaches, remove skins and insert 3 or 4 whole cloves into each. Place a few at a time in boiling sirup, add cinnamon and cook until peaches are tender and slightly transparent. Pack in sterile jars, cover with boiling sirup and seal. Makes about 8 pints.

SPICED RASPBERRIES

3 quarts ripe red raspberries
1/2 cup vinegar, 4 cups sugar
2 sticks cinnamon
12 whole cloves

Wash berries, drain and mix with vinegar and sugar Tie spices in cheesecloth bag, add to first mixture and simmer until mixture is thick. Remove spices Pour into sterile jars. Seal. Makes 5 pints.

WATERMELON PRE-SERVES

1 pound prepared watermelon rind
1 tablespoon lime or salt
2 quarts water
2 cups sugar
1/2 lemon, sliced thin
2 tablespoons sliced preserved
   ginger

Pare the rind and remove the pink edge. Cut into 1-inch cubes and let stand overnight in solution of lime or salt and 1 quart water. Drain and rinse with cold water. Cover with boiling water and cook 15 minutes. Drain. Combine sugar and remaining 1 quart water and boil 5 minutes. Add rind, lemon and ginger. Cook rapidly until rind is clear. Let stand in sirup overnight. Reheat to boiling, pour into sterile jars and seal. Makes 1 1/2 pints.
Citron and unripe cantaloupe may be preserved in the same way.

PICKLED WATER-MELON RIND

Watermelon rind
1/2 cup salt
2 1/2 quarts water
2 cups vinegar
1 lemon, sliced thin
4 cups sugar
1 teaspoon whole allspice
1 stick cinnamon
1 tablespoon whole cloves

Pare outside green skin from rind and remove any pink portions. Use 2 pounds prepared rind. Cut rind into small pieces (2x1x1/2 inch), soak overnight in mixture of salt and 2 quarts water. Drain rind, wash with fresh water and drain. Boil rind in fresh water until tender. Combine remaining 2 cups water with remaining ingredients; boil 5 minutes, add rind and boil rapidly until rind is clear. Pack in sterile jars, cover with boiling vinegar sirup and seal. Makes about 4 pints.

PICKLES AND RELISHES

Pickles and relishes add zest, flavor and color to any meal, but have little food value. Both fruits and vegetables may be pickled whole, in halves, quarters or slices. Cucumbers, beets, carrots, onions tomatoes, cauliflower and cabbage are the vegetables most frequently preserved by pickling. Crab apples, peaches, cherries and pears are the most popular fruits.

There are two general processes for making pickles, the quick process and the long fermentation process. The quick process pickles are made from vegetables salted down overnight and combined with vinegar and spices the next day with or without cooking. The fermented pickles are put through a curing process lasting 2 weeks to 2 months. Dill pickles belong to this group. Scrub vegetables carefully in plenty of clear water. Soak for several hours or overnight in a salt solution using ⅛ to ¼ cup salt to 1 quart water. Some vegetables are parboiled before they are placed in a pickling solution. The salt draws the water from the tissues of the vegetable and makes them crisp and

firm and better prepared to absorb the pickling solution. Fruits do not need to be treated in a salt and water solution. Pickles are packed in clean jars, filled to overflowing with specified liquid as described in each recipe and sealed.

Catchups are poured into jars or bottles and sealed. Relishes and chutneys are poured into clean hot jars and sealed at once. Store pickles and relishes in a cool, dry place away from strong light.

CHILI SAUCE

1½ teaspoons ground allspice
1 to 2 tablespoons cinnamon
1½ teaspoons cloves
1 gallon chopped peeled tomatoes
1 cup chopped onions
1½ cups chopped green peppers
1½ cups chopped sweet red peppers
½ to 2 cups vinegar
1 cup sugar
3 tablespoons salt

Tie spices loosely in cheesecloth bag and boil with vegetables until mixture is reduced to half of its original volume. Stir well while cooking to prevent scorching. Add vinegar, sugar and salt. Boil rapidly 5 minutes, stirring constantly. Pour immediately into sterile jars and seal jars immediately. Makes 2¼ quarts.

MUSHROOM CATCHUP

1 peck (8 quarts) mushrooms
1 cup water, 2 cups vinegar
2 tablespoons salt
1 tablespoon cinnamon
½ teaspoon cloves
½ teaspoon mace
2 tablespoons mustard
¼ teaspoon cayenne

Pick over mushrooms, clean, peel and slice. Discard any tough portions of stems. Cook mushrooms in the water until tender, stirring frequently. Press through a sieve and add vinegar, salt and spices. Boil 30 minutes, pour into sterile jars and seal. Makes 12 (½-pint) jars.

CRANBERRY CATCHUP

1 quart cranberries
1½ cups water
1½ cups vinegar
4 whole allspice
8 whole cloves
1 stick cinnamon
2 cups brown sugar

Cook cranberries, water, vinegar and spices (tied in a bag) until fruit is tender. Remove spices and rub cranberries through a sieve. Add sugar, boil 10 minutes and seal in sterile jars. Makes 1 quart.

APPLE CHUTNEY

3 red peppers, 3 green peppers
12 tart apples
12 ripe medium tomatoes
6 medium onions
1 cup diced celery
2 ounces crystallized ginger
1 pound seedless raisins
2 quarts cider vinegar
3 cups sugar, 2 teaspoons salt

Cut peppers into halves and remove seeds. Pare apples and remove core. Force vegetables, apples, ginger and raisins through a food chopper. Combine all ingredients and cook until thick and clear, about 1 hour. Fill sterile jars and seal. Makes about 4 quarts.

PEACH CHUTNEY

1 pound peaches
½ pound tart apples
¼ pound celery
1 sweet red pepper, chopped
1½ cups vinegar
2 cups sugar, 1 teaspoon salt
1 cup seedless raisins

Peel peaches, remove stones and chop. Pare apples, remove cores and chop. Chop celery, cook in small amount of water until almost tender, then drain Combine all ingredients except raisins and boil rapidly until clear and slightly thick. Steam raisins 20 minutes and add. Pour into sterile jars and seal. Makes 2 pints.

LEMON CATCHUP

12 large lemons, grated rind and
   juice
4 tablespoons white mustard seed
1 tablespoon turmeric
1 tablespoon white pepper
1 teaspoon cloves, 1 teaspoon mace
2 tablespoons sugar
2 tablespoons fresh grated
   horse-radish
1 shallot, minced fine
2 tablespoons salt, Dash cayenne

Mix ingredients together and let stand in a cool place 3 hours. Heat to boiling and cook 30 minutes. Pour into a crock, cover closely and let stand 2 weeks stirring well every day. Strain, fill sterile bottles and seal. Makes about 4 pints.

GRAPE AND APPLE CATCHUP

1 pound tart apples
4 pounds grapes
2 teaspoons whole allspice
2 tablespoons stick cinnamon
2 teaspoons whole cloves
1½ cups vinegar
4 cups sugar
½ teaspoon salt

Pare apples, core and dice. Wash grapes, remove from stems, place in pan without water and steam until soft. Cook apples in covered pan in small amount of boiling water until they are just tender. Press fruit through sieve. Tie spices loosely in cheesecloth bag and simmer them with fruit, vinegar, sugar and salt 20 minutes. Remove spices. Pour into sterile bottles and seal. Makes 5 pints.

TOMATO CATCHUP

1 peck ripe tomatoes
5 onions, sliced
1 small clove garlic
2 red peppers, seeded
1½ bay leaves
1 tablespoon salt
1 tablespoon whole allspice
1 tablespoon celery seed
1 teaspoon cayenne
2 inches stick cinnamon
½ cup sugar
2 cups vinegar

Boil first 6 ingredients until soft. Strain through sieve. Add spices (tied in a cloth bag) and sugar to tomato mixture and boil rapidly, stirring occasionally until thick

or quantity is reduced one half. Remove spices, add vinegar and boil 10 minutes longer. Pour into sterile bottles and seal. Makes about 6 quarts.

SAUERKRAUT MADE IN STONE CROCK

10 pounds cabbage
½ cup salt

Wash and scald crock. Remove outer leaves from cabbage but do not wash heads. Wild yeast plants on unwashed cabbage are a factor in fermentation process. Shred cabbage directly into crock, using preferably, a kraut shredder to avoid handling cabbage. The shreds should be long and about the thickness of a nickel. Sprinkle layer of salt over each 1-inch layer of cabbage. Pack each layer down well, using potato masher. When all cabbage and salt are in jar, cover with clean white cloth; place inverted plate on cloth and top with as large a piece of limestone as possible. The weight of stone holds cabbage under brine that soon forms and the small amount of lime that is dissolved by the brine aids in lactic acid fermentation, giving sauerkraut its flavor.

Allow to ferment 4 to 6 weeks in a cool place, preferably at temperature of 60°F. A higher temperature speeds fermentation but kraut is likely to spoil. Skim off any film that may have formed during fermentation period. Sauerkraut may be left in crock for several months if care is taken that brine always covers kraut and that film is removed each time crock is opened. Use clean cut cloth each time crock is covered.

If space is lacking, sauerkraut may be drained, packed tightly into sterilized jars and sealed. Makes 6 to 7 quarts.

CORN RELISH

9 medium ears corn
1 quart vinegar
1 cup sugar
1 tablespoon salt
1½ tablespoons dry mustard
1 teaspoon turmeric
1 small cabbage, chopped
2 medium white onions, chopped
3 red peppers, seeded and
    chopped
2 green peppers, seeded and
    chopped

Cook corn in boiling water 2 minutes. Remove, dip into cold water and cut grains from cob. Mix vinegar, sugar, salt and spices. Heat to boiling and add vegetables. Boil until vegetables are tender, 20 to 30 minutes, stirring constantly. Pour into sterile jars and seal. Makes about 8 pints.

MEXICAN RELISH

1 pint vinegar
2 tablespoons chili powder
1 tablespoon dry mustard
¼ teaspoon salt
4 green tomatoes
2 green peppers
1 onion
½ teaspoon horse-radish

Heat vinegar, add chili powder, and boil 10 minutes. Add mustard and salt. Chop tomatoes, peppers and onion fine; add horse-radish and place in jar. Add boiling vinegar to cover. Serve with meat. Makes 1 quart relish.

PICKLED BEETS

Beets, 3 pounds
1 stick cinnamon
1 teaspoon whole allspice
6 whole cloves
1 pint vinegar
½ cup water
½ cup sugar

Cook beets in boiling water until tender and remove skins, roots and tops. Tie spices in cheesecloth bag. Heat vinegar, water, sugar and spices to boiling. Add beets, whole or sliced, and boil 5 minutes. Remove spice bag, pack beets in sterile jars and fill jars with hot liquid Seal. Makes about 3 pints.

BEET RELISH

3 pounds beets
1 medium white onion, chopped
2 red peppers, seeded and chopped
½ cup grated horse-radish
2 cups vinegar
¾ cup sugar
2 teaspoons salt

Cut all but 1 inch of tops from beets and boil until tender. Remove skins, tops and roots. Chop, measure 1 quart and combine with remaining ingredients. Boil until thick. Pour into sterile jars and seal. Makes about 1 quart.

Colorful corn relish is as delicious as it is easy to prepare

PEPPER RELISH

16 sweet red peppers
16 sweet green peppers
10 small onions
Boiling water
1 quart vinegar
1½ cups sugar
2½ teaspoons salt

Cut peppers into halves and remove seeds. Chop first 3 ingredients fine, pour boiling water over them and let stand 5 minutes. Drain off the water, again cover with boiling water and let stand 10 minutes. Pour into a muslin bag and drain overnight. Add vinegar, sugar and salt and boil 20 minutes. While hot, pour into sterile jars and seal. Makes about 3 pints.

SHORT PROCESS—Grind vegetables, scald and drain. Heat to boiling in vinegar to cover, with salt and 1 tablespoon each pepper corns and celery seed. Add sugar, boil 20 minutes.

INDIA RELISH

4 green peppers
2 sweet red peppers
1 horse-radish root
2 pecks green tomatoes
2 heads cabbage
12 large onions
2 cups salt
Vinegar
1 tablespoon cinnamon
1 tablespoon nutmeg
1 tablespoon allspice
1 teaspoon celery seed
1 teaspoon mustard seed
3 pounds brown sugar

Cut peppers into halves and remove seeds. Grate horse-radish root. Chop vegetables, mix with salt and let stand overnight. Squeeze out moisture. Cover vegetables with cold vinegar and heat to boiling. Drain and add fresh vinegar, spices and sugar. Heat to boiling, cook 5 minutes and pour into sterile jars. Seal. Makes about 12 quarts.

PHILADELPHIA PEPPER RELISH

1 cup minced green pepper
½ cup minced red pepper
3 cups minced cabbage
1 cup minced celery
2 tablespoons salt
2 tablespoons mustard seed
2 tablespoons brown sugar
1½ cups vinegar

Combine minced vegetables and salt and let stand overnight. Drain thoroughly. Add mustard seed and brown sugar to vinegar and heat to boiling. Pour over drained vegetables in earthen jar. Cool. Serve within 3 days. Makes 1½ quarts.

UNCOOKED TOMATO RELISH

2 quarts ripe tomatoes
3 large onions, chopped fine
1 cup sugar
4 tablespoons salt
1 green pepper, chopped fine
1 cup diced celery
1 ounce mustard seed
1 pint white vinegar

Peel tomatoes and chop fine; drain, using only the pulp. Add remaining ingredients. Do not cook. Pour into sterile jars and seal. Let stand at least 5 days before using. Makes 3 quarts.

PICCALILLI

⅔ cup salt
4 pecks green tomatoes, chopped
1 cup grated horse-radish
2 tablespoons ground cloves
2 tablespoons cinnamon
2 tablespoons allspice
2 tablespoons mustard
4 tablespoons pepper
2 cups brown sugar, Vinegar

Sprinkle salt over chopped tomatoes and let stand overnight. Drain in colander. Add horse-radish, spices, sugar and enough vinegar to cover tomatoes; heat to boiling and cook 20 minutes. Fill sterile jars and seal. Makes about 20 quarts.

CUCUMBER OIL PICKLES

12 cucumbers, 4 to 5 inches long
6 small white onions, thinly sliced
⅓ cup salt
2 cups vinegar
2 tablespoons sugar
1 teaspoon celery seed
¼ cup white mustard seed
½ cup salad oil

Slice cucumbers thin, add onions and salt and let stand overnight. Drain, wash vegetables in 2 cups cold water and drain again. Mix vinegar, sugar, spices and oil with vegetables; pack in sterile jars, seal and store in cool place. Makes 4 pints.

SWEET SLICED CUCUMBER PICKLES

3 quarts cucumbers, sliced
3 onions, chopped
2 green peppers, seeded and chopped
½ cup salt
1 quart vinegar
4 cups sugar
1 teaspoon whole cloves
1 tablespoon white mustard seed
6 small sticks horse-radish root

Mix vegetables with salt, let stand 3 hours and drain. Mix vinegar, sugar and spices and boil 5 minutes. Pack pickles in sterile hot jars with a stick of horse-radish in the center of each and cover with boiling vinegar sirup. Seal. Makes 3 quarts.

SENFGURKEN (Ripe Cucumber Pickles)

12 large ripe cucumbers
½ cup salt
4½ cups water
6 cups sugar
1 quart vinegar
2 tablespoons mustard seed
1 tablespoon whole cloves
1 stick cinnamon

Wash cucumbers. Pare, quarter and remove seeds. Cut into strips, 1x2½ inches. Combine salt and water and stir until salt is dissolved. Add cucumber strips and let stand 12 hours or overnight. Drain cucumbers. Combine sugar, vinegar and spices (tied in a cheesecloth bag), heat to boiling and add cucumbers Boil until cucumbers begin to look transparent but are still crisp. Pack in sterile jars and fill to the top with vinegar sirup. Seal. Makes 3 quarts.

If a rich, dark pickle is desired increase vinegar to 1½ quarts, mustard seed to 3 tablespoons, cloves to 1 tablespoon and cinnamon to 1½ sticks. Cover jars but do not seal. Each morning for the following 3 days drain off sirup, boil 5 minutes and pour over pickles. Seal jars on the third morning.

CABBAGE-FILLED PEPPERS

6 sweet red or green peppers
½ head cabbage
½ teaspoon salt
1 tablespoon mustard seed
2 cups vinegar

Wash peppers, remove stems, cut off the tops and remove seeds without breaking shells. Cut cabbage fine as for slaw, add salt and mustard seed. Mix thoroughly and place in peppers, pressing it in tightly If desired place tops on pepper cases and fasten them down with toothpicks Arrange them upright in stone jar and cover with cold vinegar Place cover over jar and store in cool place. They may be kept for several months. Serves 6.

GREEN TOMATOES—Use same filling for tomatoes, pack in crock and pour in scalding vinegar. Drain off vinegar 3 successive days and heat to boiling.

CURING AND PRESERVING MEAT AND POULTRY

CORNED BEEF

Fresh-killed beef
1½ pounds fine salt
½ pound brown sugar
½ ounce saltpeter

Scrub a good oak barrel thoroughly. Put as much fresh-killed beef as desired in barrel and cover with cold water. Have water 2 inches above meat. Let stand 48 hours. Drain off water and measure before discarding. Measure same amount of cold water (spring water if possible) and to every gallon of water formerly used, add same proportions of salt, sugar and saltpeter. Boil 15 minutes and skim. When cold, pour over beef. Place heavy weight on meat to keep it under brine. Store in cool cellar. The corned beef will be ready for use after 10 days.

DRIED BEEF

200 pounds good fresh-killed beef
   (the rounds)
1 pint fine salt
1 teaspoon saltpeter
¼ pound brown sugar

Mix last 3 ingredients well, rub bing out all lumps. Divide mixture into 3 equal portions. Place meat in large crocks and rub

thoroughly with one portion of above mixture. Let stand 1 day. Follow same procedure on second and third days. Turn meat several times a day. Allow meat to remain in crocks 7 more days, then hang in warm place until meat stops dripping. When dripping has stopped, hang in cool shed about 6 weeks to dry thoroughly. Wrap meat in clean muslin bags and keep in cool place. If in 6 months meat becomes too hard, soak it in cold water 24 hours and wipe dry. Wrap again in muslin bags and hang in cool place.

CURED BACON

100 pounds sides of bacon (from
   fresh-killed hogs)
8 pounds fine salt
3 pounds brown sugar
3 ounces saltpeter
4 gallons water

Place sides of bacon on a board and rub with salt Let stand 48 hours. Mix next 3 ingredients and dissolve in water. Heat to boiling and cook 15 minutes. Skim and cool. Place bacon in clean oak barrel and pour liquid over meat. Place heavy weight on bacon to keep it under brine. Bacon prepared like this will

keep about one year. After bacon has been in brine 5 weeks, it may all be hung up to dry and when thoroughly dried, smoked at smokehouse as needed.

CURED HAMS

100 pounds ham
3 ounces saltpeter
½ pound brown sugar
5 pints fine salt
⅛ pound black pepper

Use only corn-fed hogs. Mix saltpeter, sugar and 1 pint salt thoroughly, rub over hams (being sure to get plenty in the hock) and let stand 24 hours Then rub meat with pepper and 2 pints salt. Let stand 5 days, then rub meat again with remaining salt Set aside 30 days, then hang meat and brush off salt. Have hams smoked 10 days with hickory or apple wood. Rub hams with red pepper, wrap in brown paper, then in muslin bags and hang up, hock down. Give the cloth a coating of shellac or suspend hams in a loose bag surrounded by finely chopped straw to the thickness of two or three inches. Hams prepared in this manner will keep indefinitely, and flavor and quality improve with time.

SAUSAGE

20 pounds dressed pork
10 pounds clear fat pork
2 teaspoons sugar
1 teaspoon ginger
½ pound fine salt
2 tablespoons pepper
1 tablespoon sage (optional)

Cut meat into small pieces and add sugar and seasonings. Put through a sausage cutter, grinding twice. Pack into sterilized jars, cover with ½-inch layer of lard and keep in cold place. Makes 30 pounds.

SMOKED SAUSAGE—Omit sugar and ginger. Chop ½ ounce red pepper pods with meat and add 1½ ounces saltpeter. Sage may be increased to 2 cups. Stuff cleaned casings with sausage meat, tie ends securely and smoke with green hickory or apple wood for 3 to 4 days. Hang in dry place.

CHAURICE
(Creole Pork Sausage)

2 pounds fat fresh pork
4 pounds lean fresh pork
3 teaspoons salt
2 teaspoons black pepper
½ teaspoon cayenne
½ teaspoon chili pepper
1 teaspoon paprika
2 large onions
1 clove garlic
1 sprig thyme
Sprig parsley, minced
2 bay leaves
½ teaspoon allspice
Casings (sheep)

Grind pork as fine as possible, mixing fat and lean. Add seasonings and mix thoroughly. Mince onions, garlic and herbs very fine and add with allspice. Scald casings, which have been thoroughly cleaned by butcher, wash again, dry and fill with sausage mixture. Tie in lengths to make 6 to a pound. Makes about 6 pounds or 36 sausages.

PICKLED TONGUE

¼ teaspoon saltpeter
2 quarts water
1 cup salt
2 tablespoons sugar
2 cloves garlic
½ teaspoon paprika
½ tablespoon mixed spices
1 beef tongue

Dissolve saltpeter in ½ cup warm water. Add remaining water, salt, sugar, garlic (sliced), paprika and spices. Place tongue in crock and cover with liquid. Cover with plate and weight down so that tongue remains covered. Let stand 3 weeks, turning occasionally.

HEADCHEESE

4 pounds pork from head or
   shoulder
8 pounds side pork
Salt
Pepper
Ground cloves

Boil pork until extremely tender, the fat and lean in separate kettles (some veal may be used). A layer of fat will come to the surface, which should be skimmed off. While meat is still hot, prepare headcheese. First spread a large piece of muslin in a shallow pan. Then use the cooked rind of the pork to hold the headcheese by placing the rind side next to the muslin, fitting pieces together to cover the bottom. On this place alternating pieces of fat pork and lean pork, seasoning each layer with salt, pepper and ground cloves. Cover top and sides with cooked rind, tie up tightly in muslin. Reheat in liquid, then remove the "cheese" and press in a flat dish under a weight. Chill at once, keeping weighted until cold. A thickness of 2 inches when pressed is convenient for slicing. Keep in a light brine in a cool place until needed. The meat must not freeze. Change brine occasionally. Serves about 30.

MEAT PRESERVED IN FAT

Meat may be preserved by cooking and then packing in a sterile crock and covering with hot fat. Store in a dry place having constant low temperature. To sterilize the crock, wash it and place upside down in a pan half full of boiling water. Boil 15 minutes; remove crock; do not dry.

ROASTS

Wipe meat with damp cloth, place in roasting pan and rub with salt. Place in moderate oven (350°F.) and cook 45 to 50 minutes for rib or shoulder ends, 30 to 35 minutes for center cuts. Pack in crock and cover at once with hot fat.

CHOPS OR STEAKS

Season chops and sear on both sides. Add 2 tablespoons water, cover and continue cooking over low heat. Cook single chops 20 minutes, double chops 40 minutes. Pack closely in crock and cover at once with hot fat.

TO USE—

To use meat which has been packed in fat, scrape off as much fat as possible and heat thoroughly.

GOOSE—Use meat from Skinned Goose, Page 437. Cover with boiling water, simmer 2 hours and drain. Place in crock, cover with clear melted fat. Keep in cool dry place. To use: drain off fat and simmer again in boiling water 1 hour.

SMOKED TONGUE—Boil as on Page 404 for 1½ hours. Drain and cover with melted fat. To serve drain off fat and cook 1½ hours.

SMOKE-FLAVORED TURKEY

There are on the market several smoke-flavored curing mixtures which may be used either dry or in solution to prepare smoke-flavored turkey. Some produce a light smoked flavor; others, notably those intended for fish, produce a more pronounced smoke flavor. Smoke-flavored turkey will keep up to 4 weeks if wrapped carefully and kept in the refrigerator. Prepare turkey as for smoked turkey and place in crock when cooled to 40°F. Prepare brine, following the directions on the package. Usually about 4 pounds of the mixture are dissolved in 2 gallons boiling water. Cool to 40°F. and pour over turkey. Cover and weight down. Let stand 7 to 10 days, depending on size of turkey. The curing may be done in less time if 10 cc. (about 2 teaspoons) of the brine is injected into the thick parts of the turkey and around the thigh and wing joints before the bird is placed in the crock. A glass syringe, costing less than $1.00, fitted with a No. 12 needle is suitable for this process. After curing wash well and hang to drain and dry 12 to 24 hours in a cool place. Wrap in cellophane or heavy paper and keep in a cool place. To use, soak in cold water 2 to 4 hours and bake in a covered roaster to prevent drying. Smoked or smoke-flavored turkeys may be hard frozen and kept almost indefinitely. Do not allow to thaw and refreeze.

THE SMOKEHOUSE

Build a sturdy smokehouse 3 feet square and 6 feet high, hinging one side to form a door. Have the bottom open to the ground but make a false bottom 12 inches from the ground level and bore holes in it at 2-inch intervals. Nail cleats inside the box to hold the trays or smoke sticks, placing the first set 12 inches below the top of the house. Bore a few holes near the top for ventilation. Set the house over a pit 2 feet square and 18 inches deep. Dig a second pit a few feet from the smokehouse, 3 feet square and 18 inches deep. This is the fire pit and should be connected with the smokehouse by a trench 1 foot deep. Cover fire pit and trench with sheets of galvanized iron. (See page 846)

SMOKED TURKEY

PREPARING TURKEY—Use the best quality turkeys, well fattened, for smoking. Thin birds become tough and stringy. The birds should be killed and bled in the usual way, then dry-picked. Hard-scalding spoils the appearance and keeping qualities of the birds. Take particular care not to tear the skin. Draw and remove feet and neck, leaving neck skin. Remove all the viscera so that bird is open at both ends and water may be run through it freely for washing. Wash, including giblets and neck which are placed inside the bird and smoked with it. Cool to 40°F.

CURING—Salt, sugar and saltpeter are used in the curing process. The salt preserves the meat but also tends to harden the fibers and absorb water from them. Sugar helps to counteract the hardening and to keep the muscles tender. Also it improves the flavor of the meat and helps to preserve it. Saltpeter is used to help preserve the meat and to hold its natural color.

4½ gallons water
6 pounds salt
3 pounds sugar
2 ounces saltpeter
Heat water to boiling and boil 10 minutes Add remaining ingredients and stir until dissolved. Cool slightly, then strain and cool to 40°F This should test 70° with a salinometer at 40°F. and will cover 2 turkeys weighing about 12 pounds each, dressed. Pack chilled turkeys close together in a 12-gallon crock. Pour the cold brine over them and weight down with a cover to keep turkeys under the brine Cure about 1½ days for each pound weight of individual turkey. Twelve-pound turkeys require about 18 days. At the end of each week remove turkeys from brine and repack them to make sure that all parts come into contact with the brine The temperature **must** be kept low, not over 40°F. at any time. At the end of the curing period remove turkeys from brine and wash well in warm water. Hang up to drain and dry at 40°F. for 3 days.

SMOKING—Apple, hickory or maple chips or ground corn cobs are used to produce a dense aromatic smoke. The temperature may be kept as high as 140°F., which partially cooks the bird, but a temperature of 110°F. will cause less drying and loss of weight and is generally preferred. Avoid drafts which cause excessive drying. When the turkeys are thoroughly drained, fold the neck skin back and fasten with the wing tips. This will prevent a considerable loss of fat during the smoking. Hang by the legs and smoke as long as desired up to 40 hours. A short smoking time of about 20 hours will give a light smoke which does not hide the flavor of the turkey. The longer smoking will produce a flavor more closely resembling ham and a product which will keep longer. The meat requires further cooking before it is eaten.

Age 1 week at 68°F. to develop the flavor and allow the meat to become more tender. Wrap in cellophane or heavy paper and store in a cool place.

QUICK PROCESS—Prepare turkey as above but do not cut off the neck.

3 pounds salt
12 ounces sugar
8 ounces saltpeter
2 gallons water

Mix salt, sugar and saltpeter and rub 1 pound of the mixture over outside and inside of turkey. Place in crock. Store for 24 hours at 35° to 40°F. Heat water to boiling and add remaining mixture. Stir until dissolved, strain and cool to 40°F. At the end of dry-curing period pour brine over turkey, cover and weight down so that turkey does not float. Let stand 1 week. Remove from brine and soak in warm water 15 minutes. Hang up to drain and dry 3 days at 40°F. Split through the back. Tie a cord tight around neck and a second cord tight around legs. Suspend from both cords to smoke. Smoke at 90° to 100°F. for 48 to 60 hours. Age for 1 week. Wrap in cellophane or heavy paper and store in a cool place.

DRY PROCESS—Prepare turkey as above but do not remove neck.

1 clove garlic, cut
¼ pound salt
2 tablespoons sugar
2 teaspoons saltpeter
1 teaspoon black pepper

Combine ingredients and rub over outside and inside of turkey. Wrap in paper and store for 1 week. Smoke at 110°F. for 24 to 36 hours. Wrap in cellophane or heavy paper and keep in a cool place.

SMOKED GOOSE

Meat from 8-pound goose
⅔ cup salt
1 tablespoon sugar
1 teaspoon saltpeter
½ clove garlic, minced

Scrape edible meat from neck, wings and back of goose and chop very fine. Stuff into neck skin and tie both ends shut. Combine salt, sugar, saltpeter and garlic and rub over breast, legs and filled neck; place in crock, cover with clean cloth, weight down with plate and set in cool place for 7 days, turning occasionally. Drain, cover each piece individually with cheese-cloth and smoke. Chill and slice thin to serve. Serves 10 to 12.

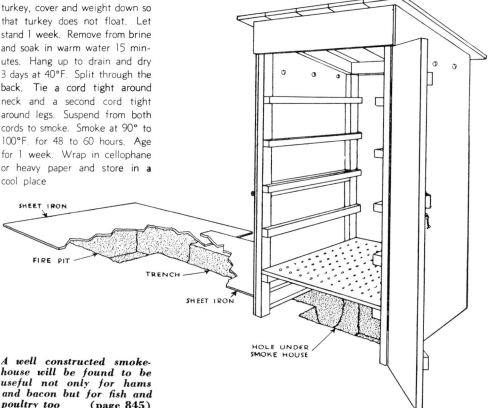

A well constructed smokehouse will be found to be useful not only for hams and bacon but for fish and poultry too **(page 845)**

PRESERVING FISH

PRESERVATION OF FISH

Fish for drying, pickling or smoking must be thoroughly cleaned and none of the steps of the process may be omitted. There are many variables, however, with which one must experiment depending upon the type of product desired, the amount of fat, the size and thickness of the fish and the weather conditions. Some of these variables are the length of time for brining, the time required for drying, the kind of wood used for smoking and the time for smoking.

DRIED SALT FISH

Fish for drying must be absolutely fresh. To prevent spoilage, bleed and clean the fish thoroughly as soon as possible after they are caught. Direct sunshine and rough handling cause fish to spoil more readily; cover with a tarpaulin (which should not rest directly on the fish) and handle gently.

Split fish down the back, close to the backbone, taking care not to cut all the way through at the tail end. The backbone is removed from Spanish mackerel and other fat fish but left in lean fish to help keep their shape. Remove all traces of blood from under the backbone using a wire brush. Wipe out all the dark membrane with a piece of coarse cloth. Clean fish thoroughly and carefully; rinse in clear water. Score with a knife under the backbone and longitudinally through the flesh on the other side. Drop into light brine (2 pounds salt to 5 gallons water). Never use sea water from close to shore, it is invariably contaminated. Let stand 30 minutes. Remove from brine and drain 15 minutes.

Use fine ground-mined salt. Sea salt is likely to be contaminated with a bacteria which thrives on salt and which causes reddening of the fish. Dredge the fish one at a time in a shallow box of salt, working salt well into the gashes. Pick up the fish with as much salt as possible adhering to it and pack skin side down in a box or tub having a thin layer of salt in the bottom. Place each layer at right angles to the one below and scatter a little salt on each layer. Use about 1 pound of salt to 3 pounds of fish. Place the top layer of fish skin side up and weight down to keep the fish under the brine which forms. Leave in a light, cool, airy shed for 36 to 48 hours, depending on the size of the fish.

When the fish are sufficiently salted remove them and scrub them in brine of the same strength as that used in cleaning until there is no salt visible on the surface. Drain 15 to 20 minutes. Spread on chicken wire racks, 3 or 4 feet from the ground; cover with a roof to give protection from the sun. The racks should be over dry ground, preferably gravel, and in a breezy location where there will be a good current of air over the fish. Turn the fish 3 or 4 times during the first day. The time for drying depends upon weather conditions and the size of the fish. Four to 5 days is usually sufficient. The fish must be brought indoors at night or the dampness will cause them to sour and mold. Dry the fish until the surface is dry and hard and the thick part cannot be dented with the thumb. Store in boxes lined with waxed paper, scattering a little salt between layers . . . about 1 pound of salt for 10 pounds of fish. If signs of rust or mold appear, scrub fish in brine and dry in the air for a day or two.

String the fish on two poles for smoking

SMOKED FISH

There are 2 types of smoked fish; cold smoked, which will keep for some time; hot smoked, which are cooked by the heat of smoking and will keep not longer than 1-2 weeks. In any case a smokehouse must be built.

COLD SMOKING—Clean fish, soak in brine and pack in salt as for dried salt fish, except that they should not be scored with a knife or weighted down after packing in salt. If the heads are removed, leave on the hard bony plate just back of the gills. Leave fish in salt from 1 to 3 hours, then rinse in brine, removing all visible traces of salt. Dry on wire racks for 3 hours or until a thin film forms on the surface. Place fish in smokehouse on wire racks or string on rods. The rods are put through the fish just below the bony plate, one in each side. A pair of rods 3 feet long will hold 12 to 14 fish. Be sure the fish are not close enough to touch or the smoke will not penetrate properly.

Start the fire in the fire pit about 2 hours before the fish are hung in the smokehouse. Two sticks of wood 2 feet long and 4 inches thick are sufficient. Use any hard wood which is not resinous. Suggested fuels are alder, beech, birch, oak, hickory, sweet bay, river mangrove, palmetto roots, buttonwood, orange wood, cypress. The fire should be low and smoldering and should not

give off a great deal of smoke during the first 8 to 12 hours. Dense smoke is necessary for the remainder of the smoking period. The fire must never be allowed to blaze up; the air in the smokehouse should not feel warm to the hand. The fire must be tended at night; it must not die out nor can it be built large enough in the evening to last all night.

Smoke the fish for 4 or 5 days if they are to be kept for a long time; 24 hours' smoking will keep fish for 2 weeks. Remove fish from the smokehouse and dry in the air for 1 to 2 hours, then sprinkle lightly with salt and wrap in waxed paper Pack in boxes and keep in a cool dry place. If they begin to mold rinse them in vinegar and smoke again for 3 to 6 hours.

Cold smoked fish must be freshened in cold water and cooked to serve.

HOT SMOKING—Clean fish and soak in brine as for dried salt fish but do not score with a knife. Prepare a spiced brine.

2 pounds salt, 1 pound sugar
½ ounce saltpeter
1 ounce peppercorns, crushed
1 ounce cardamom seeds, crushed

Mix ingredients and add water to test 90° with salinometer.

Remove fish from light brine, making sure they are thoroughly cleaned, drain 15 minutes and drop into spiced brine. Let stand 2 to 4 hours. Rinse in fresh water and dry on wire racks for 3 hours. Then hang on rods and place in the smokehouse. Provide dense cool smoke for the first 8 hours, then increase the fire until the temperature in the smokehouse is 130° to 150° F. and continue smoking at this temperature 2 to 3 hours or until the fish have a glossy brown surface. Remove from the smokehouse, wipe off any moisture and cool thoroughly, about 2 hours. Wrap in waxed paper and store in a cool dry place, not on ice.

The drying rack for fish should have circulation of air over and under it, and protection from the sun

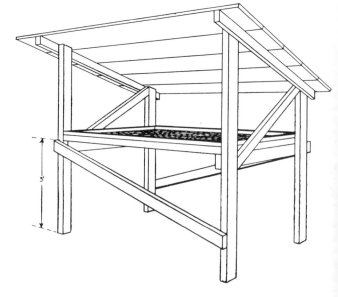

Sauces, Gravies and Dressings

200 Sauces, Dressings and Gravies

AVOCADO COCKTAIL SAUCE

1 cup sieved avocado
1 tablespoon lemon juice
⅓ cup mayonnaise
Few grains salt
¼ cup chili sauce or tomato catchup
½ teaspoon Worcestershire sauce

Combine ingredients and mix well. Makes 1⅔ cups.

COCKTAIL SAUCE FOR AVOCADOS

½ cup heavy cream
½ cup chili sauce
½ cup mayonnaise
1 teaspoon Worcestershire sauce
3 tablespoons lemon juice

Whip cream and fold in remaining ingredients. Serve with avocados. Makes 2 cups.

*Chilled grapefruit
and a minted sauce
Make a cocktail
fit for "the boss"*

SAUCE FOR GRAPEFRUIT CUP

½ cup heavy cream, whipped
1 cup Tomato Sauce
1 tablespoon lemon juice

Fold whipped cream into tomato sauce, add lemon juice and beat well. Serve on grapefruit sections. Makes 1½ cups.

CUCUMBER SAUCE

1 cucumber, grated
½ cup chili sauce
1 teaspoon onion juice
2 tablespoons lemon juice
Few grains pepper
2 drops Tabasco sauce

Combine ingredients and serve on sea food. Makes 1½ cups.

FRUIT SAUCE

1 cup Currant Jelly
½ cup boiling water
1 tablespoon chopped orange peel

Combine ingredients and beat. Serve hot. Makes 1¼ cups.

GRAPEFRUIT MINT COCKTAIL

1 cup Mint Jelly
1½ cups water
1¼ cups sugar

Melt mint jelly in double boiler and beat with egg beater. Boil water and sugar together 10 minutes and add to mint jelly. Chill and pour over grapefruit sections. Makes 2½ cups.

HONEY SAUCE

¼ cup pineapple sirup
¼ cup lemon juice
¼ cup honey
Combine ingredients, chill and pour over fruit. Makes ¾ cup.

HONEYDEW MELON COCKTAIL SAUCE

1 cup sugar
¾ cup boiling water
⅓ cup orange juice
⅓ cup lime juice
2 tablespoons lemon juice

Boil sugar and water together 5 minutes, cool and add fruit juices. Pour over honeydew melon balls. Makes 1¾ cups.

MAYONNAISE SAUCE

½ cup chili sauce
½ cup mayonnaise
2 drops Tabasco sauce
½ teaspoon A-1 sauce
¼ teaspoon salt
1 teaspoon lemon juice

Mix ingredients and chill thoroughly. Serve on fish cocktails. Makes 1 cup.

PINEAPPLE GRAPEFRUIT SAUCE

⅔ cup canned pineapple sirup
⅓ cup grenadine sirup
⅓ cup grapefruit juice

Combine sirups with fruit juice, chill and pour over fruit cocktail. Makes 1⅓ cups.

Manhattan sauce
for oyster cocktail
Promises a dinner
where graces prevail

BALTIMORE SAUCE

1 tablespoon prepared horse-radish
½ cup tomato catchup or chili sauce
3 tablespoons lemon juice
1 teaspoon Worcestershire sauce
½ teaspoon celery salt

Combine ingredients and mix thoroughly. Chill and serve over sea food. Makes ¾ cup.

Use ½ cup minced celery instead of celery salt if desired.

CHILI COCKTAIL SAUCE

⅓ cup chili sauce
⅔ cup mayonnaise
2 tablespoons pineapple sirup
2 tablespoons lemon juice

Combine ingredients, chill and serve. Makes 1¼ cups.

COCKTAIL SAUCE

¼ cup mayonnaise
2 tablespoons French dressing
2 tablespoons chili sauce
1 tablespoon chopped pimiento
2 teaspoons chopped olives
Salt and pepper

Combine ingredients, chill and serve with avocado cocktail. Makes ½ cup.

HORSE-RADISH COCKTAIL SAUCE

1 cup tomato catchup
¼ cup chili sauce
1 tablespoon lemon juice
Few drops Tabasco sauce
1 tablespoon prepared horse-radish
¼ teaspoon salt, Dash pepper

Combine ingredients and mix well. Makes 1⅓ cups.

Rosy and chill
served without scrimp
Mobile sauce for
Mobile's shrimp

MANHATTAN SAUCE

2 teaspoons prepared horse-radish
3 tablespoons tomato catchup
2 tablespoons vinegar
¼ cup lemon juice
¼ teaspoon Tabasco sauce
1 teaspoon salt

Combine horse-radish, catchup, vinegar, lemon juice, Tabasco sauce and salt. Makes ⅔ cup.

MOBILE SAUCE

¼ cup mayonnaise
¼ cup tomato catchup
2 tablespoons fresh tomato
2 tablespoons minced green pepper
2 tablespoons chili sauce

Combine ingredients, chill and serve. Makes ¾ cup.

PIQUANT SAUCE

1 cup tomato catchup
3 teaspoons onion juice
1 teaspoon Tabasco sauce
½ teaspoon salt
¼ teaspoon cayenne

Combine ingredients, chill and serve with sea food. Makes 1 cup.

SEA FOOD SAUCE

1 cup mayonnaise
2 tablespoons anchovy paste
2 tablespoons chili sauce
2 tablespoons tarragon vinegar
¼ cup tomato catchup
Lemon juice and pepper if needed

Combine ingredients, chill and serve. Makes 1⅔ cups.

SAUCES FOR MEAT, FISH, GAME, POULTRY

WHITE SAUCE

MEDIUM—For gravies, sauces, creamed and scalloped dishes.

2 tablespoons butter
2 tablespoons flour
1 cup milk
¼ teaspoon salt
⅛ teaspoon pepper

METHOD 1—Melt butter and blend in flour. Add milk gradually, stirring constantly. Reduce heat and cook 3 minutes longer; add seasonings.

METHOD 2—Blend butter and flour together and add to hot milk, stirring constantly until mixture thickens. Cook 3 minutes longer; add seasonings.

BERCY—Cook 1 tablespoon chopped shallots in the butter before adding flour. Use fish stock instead of milk.

BROWNED ALMOND—Brown ¼ pound sliced blanched almonds in butter before adding remaining ingredients. Thin with additional milk.

CREAM—Use cream for milk.

EGG—Add 1 hard-cooked egg, chopped.

HOT MAYONNAISE—Add 1 cup mayonnaise.

LOBSTER—Add 1 cup diced cooked lobster.

ONION—Chop 2 slices onion and cook in the butter before adding remaining ingredients. Strain sauce before serving.

OYSTER—Cook 1 cup oysters in their liquor until plump, drain and use liquid for part of the milk. Add oysters to sauce just before serving.

PARSLEY—Add 2 tablespoons minced parsley.

SHRIMP—Add ⅓ cup chopped cooked shrimp and 1 slightly beaten egg.

THICK—Use 3 tablespoons butter and 3 tablespoons flour.

THIN—Use 1 tablespoon butter and 1 tablespoon flour.

Try bread sauce for a treat

WHITE ROUX

¼ cup butter
¼ cup flour

Melt butter, add flour and stir until well blended and bubbling throughout. Makes roux for 1 pint sauce.

BLONDE—Cook roux 15 minutes longer.

BROWN ROUX

¼ cup butter
5 tablespoons flour

Melt butter, add flour and cook over very low heat, stirring constantly, until mixture is color of light mahogany. Makes roux for 1 pint sauce.

To make roux to thicken 2 quarts stock use 1 cup butter and 1¼ cups flour.

ALBUQUERQUE SAUCE

2 tablespoons minced onion
¼ cup minced green pepper
3 tablespoons olive oil
¼ cup sliced mushrooms
¼ cup sliced stuffed olives
½ cup cooked tomatoes
1 cup Brown Gravy
Salt and pepper

Cook onion and pepper in olive oil 5 minutes; add mushrooms and cook 3 minutes. Add remaining ingredients and heat to boiling. Makes 2 cups.

BREAD SAUCE

4 cloves
1 small onion
⅓ cup soft bread crumbs
1 cup milk, scalded
½ teaspoon salt
Pepper
1½ tablespoons butter or other fat

Stick cloves in onion and cook with bread crumbs and scalded milk in a double boiler for 20 minutes. Remove onion, add salt, pepper and butter and stir until melted. Makes about 1 cup sauce.

BROWN SAUCE

1½ tablespoons butter
3 tablespoons flour
1 cup Meat Stock
½ teaspoon salt
Dash pepper

Melt butter and add flour. Stir over low heat until flour is brown. Add stock gradually and cook until thickened, stirring constantly. Season. Makes 1 cup.

CHESTNUT—Add 1 cup mashed cooked chestnuts.

CURRANT JELLY—Add ¼ cup currant jelly and 2 teaspoons lemon juice.

OLIVE—Add 6 stuffed olives, sliced.

BÉCHAMEL NORMANDE

Fish skin and bones
Liquor from boiled fish
1 small onion
1 bay leaf
2 cups water
3 tablespoons butter
5 tablespoons sifted flour
⅔ cup heavy cream
4 well-beaten egg yolks
½ teaspoon salt
Few grains white pepper
2 teaspoons lemon juice

Cook skin and bones in liquor in which fish was boiled. Add onion, bay leaf and water, cook ½ hour and strain. Measure 2 cups of the fish stock. Melt butter; add flour, fish stock and cream, and heat to boiling. Add small amount to egg yolks, stir and pour back into sauce. Cook over low heat 3 to 4 minutes, stirring constantly; add salt, pepper and lemon juice. Makes 1 pint.

MORNAY—Add 2 ounces each grated Gruyère and Parmesan cheese, cook over low heat until cheese is melted. Remove from heat and beat in ¼ cup softened butter.

BECHAMEL SAUCE

2 tablespoons chopped onion
¼ cup diced celery
1 small carrot, chopped
2 sprigs parsley
1 sprig thyme
Small piece bay leaf
2 cups Chicken or Veal Stock
2 tablespoons butter
2 tablespoons flour
½ cup cream
Salt and pepper

Add vegetables and herbs to stock and cook 20 minutes. Strain. Melt butter and blend in flour. Add strained stock gradually and cook 10 minutes, stirring constantly until thickened. Add cream, salt and pepper and heat. Makes 2 cups.

YELLOW—Combine a small amount of hot sauce with 2 egg yolks, add to remaining sauce and cook 2 minutes longer. Serve at once.

*A meat ring with
an array of sauces
Makes us soon forget
our losses*

SPANISH CREOLE SAUCE

2 onions, chopped
2 green peppers, chopped
2 tablespoons olive oil
4 fresh or 1 cup cooked tomatoes
¼ teaspoon salt
½ teaspoon paprika

Sauté onions and peppers in olive oil. Add tomatoes, season with salt and paprika and cook slowly until vegetables are tender. Serve with omelets or hot rice. Makes 1½ cups.

RED CHILI—Use chili peppers instead of green peppers. Use only 1 onion. Add 2 cloves garlic, crushed, 1 tablespoon chopped parsley, a sprig of thyme and a leaf of sage. Remove thyme and sage before serving.

CELERY—Cut onions and peppers in thin slices instead of chopping them. Add 1 cup sliced celery, cook in 3 tablespoons oil until transparent and add tomatoes and seasonings.

SAUCE ALLEMANDE

2 tablespoons butter
3 tablespoons flour
1 cup hot seasoned Veal or
    Chicken Stock
Few grains white pepper
⅓ cup cream
1 egg yolk, beaten
1 teaspoon lemon juice
Few grains nutmeg

Combine butter and flour, add stock gradually, heat to boiling and add pepper. Add cream, pour over egg yolk and return to double boiler to thicken. Add lemon juice and nutmeg. Makes 1½ cups.

VELOUTÉ SAUCE

2 tablespoons butter
2 tablespoons flour
1 cup Chicken or Veal Stock
¼ teaspoon salt
Few grains white pepper

Combine butter and flour, stir in stock gradually and heat to boiling. Cook until thickened, stirring occasionally. Add salt and pepper. Makes 1 cup.

MUSHROOM — Add ⅓ cup cream and 5 cooked mushroom caps, sliced, just before serving.

BÉARNAISE SAUCE

4 egg yolks
1 cup butter
1 tablespoon lemon juice
1 tablespoon tarragon vinegar
¼ teaspoon salt
1 teaspoon chopped parsley
1 teaspoon onion juice
Dash cayenne

Place egg yolks with ⅓ of butter in top of double boiler. Keep water in bottom of boiler hot but not boiling. Add remaining butter as sauce thickens, stirring constantly. Remove from heat and add remaining ingredients. Serve with broiled meat. Makes 1 cup.

RAISIN SAUCE

¾ cup brown sugar
3 tablespoons cornstarch
1½ cups broth from ham or tongue
¼ cup vinegar, ½ cup raisins
1 lemon, sliced thin; 1 tablespoon fat
Mix sugar and cornstarch in top of double boiler and add broth gradually, stirring constantly. Add remaining ingredients and cook until raisins are plump and mixture is thickened, stirring occasionally. Serve hot with ham or tongue. Makes about 1½ cups.

TART BARBECUE SAUCE

1 onion, chopped
2 tablespoons oil
2 tablespoons vinegar
2 tablespoons brown sugar
¼ cup lemon juice
1 cup tomato catchup
3 tablespoons Worcestershire sauce
½ teaspoon prepared mustard
½ cup water
½ cup chopped celery
Salt and cayenne

Brown onion in fat and add remaining ingredients. Simmer 30 minutes. Makes 2 cups.

When the wind blows chill
Hot barbecue sauce
Should be on the bill

BARBECUE SAUCE

2 medium onions, sliced
1 cup condensed tomato soup
¾ cup water
3 tablespoons vinegar
2 tablespoons Worcestershire sauce
1 teaspoon salt
¼ teaspoon cinnamon
1 teaspoon paprika
¼ teaspoon black pepper
1 teaspoon chili powder
⅛ teaspoon cloves

Combine all ingredients; heat and use to baste meats or fish. Makes 2 cups.

ROUND-UP BARBECUE SAUCE —Use ¾ cup catchup instead of tomato soup; omit cinnamon and cloves.

CALIFORNIA SAUCE

1½ cups chopped onions
1 clove garlic
⅓ cup salad oil
1 cup seedless raisins
3 cups tomatoes
⅓ cup chopped green chili pepper
½ cup sliced stuffed olives
1½ teaspoons salt

Sauté onions and garlic in oil, add raisins and cook 5 minutes longer, stirring frequently. Add tomatoes, chili pepper, olives and salt and heat to boiling. Cook 5 minutes. Use for braising fresh beef tongue. Makes 6 cups.

CREAM CURRY

4 tablespoons butter
2 tablespoons chives, minced
1 tablespoon parsley, minced
1 teaspoon curry powder
Salt, 1 egg yolk
¾ cup rich cream

Melt butter, add chives and parsley. Blend well, simmer, and add curry powder. Add salt. Just before removing from fire, add egg yolk, mixed with cream. Serve with lobster or crabmeat. Makes 1¼ cups.

BLACK OLIVE—Add ¼ cup sliced black olives with the salt.

DRAWN BUTTER

½ cup butter

Melt butter and allow salt and curd to settle. Pour off clear oil into small hot cups. Serve with globe artichokes, fish or sea food. Makes about ⅜ cup.

ALMOND—Add 1 teaspoon lemon juice and ¼ cup ground almonds. Serve with fish.

DRAWN BUTTER SAUCE

2 tablespoons butter
2 tablespoons flour
½ teaspoon salt
Few grains pepper
1 cup hot water

Melt butter; blend in flour and seasonings. Add water and cook slowly until thickened, stirring constantly. Makes 1 cup.

If desired, fish stock may be used instead of water.

ANCHOVY—Blend a little of sauce with ½ teaspoon anchovy paste. Combine with remaining sauce.

CAPER—Add ¼ cup drained capers. Heat.

MINT—Add ⅛ cup chopped fresh mint leaves.

PARSLEY—A d d 1 tablespoon lemon juice and 1 tablespoon chopped parsley.

Drawn butter, fish soufflé: Friday's fish on a holiday

ESPAGNOLE SAUCE

2 tablespoons minced onion
2 tablespoons minced celery
2 tablespoons minced carrot
2 tablespoons minced parsley
1 shallot
1 teaspoon chervil
2 tablespoons butter
2 tablespoons flour
1 bay leaf, 1 clove
½ teaspoon peppercorns
2½ cups jellied seasoned beef stock
5 tablespoons Brown Roux

Sauté onion, celery, carrot, parsley, shallot and chervil in butter and thicken with flour. Add bay leaf, clove and peppercorns and continue browning. Heat beef stock and add vegetable mixture. Simmer 10 to 15 minutes, strain through fine sieve and thicken with brown roux. Makes 1 pint.

MUSHROOM—Add ½ cup chopped mushrooms. This may be served with sautéed liver.

STUFFED OLIVE—¼ cup sliced stuffed olives may be added. Serve with lamb chops.

NEWBURG SAUCE

¼ cup sherry
⅔ cup cream
½ blade mace
2 egg yolks, beaten slightly
¼ teaspoon salt
Few grains white pepper
1 tablespoon butter

Pour sherry over sautéed lobster, other shellfish or fowl; cook over low heat until sherry is reduced. Heat cream in double boiler with mace until cream is slightly reduced; remove mace. Stir a little of the scalded cream into egg yolks, blend well and add egg yolks gradually to remaining cream, blending with wire whisk. Stir in lobster and heat just long enough for sauce to thicken slightly, until it coats a wooden spoon, stirring constantly. Remove from heat, add salt, pepper and butter and serve at once. Makes sauce for 2 cups cooked lobster or chicken.

RAVIGOTE SAUCE

½ cup white wine
¼ cup vinegar
5 tablespoons butter
4 tablespoons flour
2 cups seasoned Veal or Chicken
    Broth
1 shallot, minced
1 teaspoon minced chervil
1 teaspoon minced tarragon
1 teaspoon chopped chives
Salt, pepper

Combine wine and vinegar and simmer down to ½. Melt 3 tablespoons butter and blend in flour. Add broth and cook until thickened, stirring constantly. Add to wine and simmer 5 minutes. Add herbs and remaining ingredients. Serve with poultry or eggs. Makes 2½ cups.

If fishes had wishes,
Their sauce would be wine

SEA FOOD SAUCE

20 green shrimp
1 cup thick White Sauce
½ cup cream
½ cup fish stock
¼ cup pimientos, chopped
1 (4-ounce) can mushrooms
2 egg yolks, well beaten
⅓ cup sherry
2 tablespoons lemon juice
1 teaspoon Tabasco sauce
Salt and pepper to taste

Peel and thoroughly clean the raw shrimp. Add to white sauce the cream, fish stock and the shrimp. Cook for 10 minutes and then add the pimientos and mushrooms. Cook 10 minutes longer; add the egg yolks, lemon juice, sherry and seasonings. Serve at once with boiled fish. Serves 8.

SANTOS FISH SAUCE

2 tablespoons butter
½ clove garlic, minced
1 clove
Dash powdered thyme
Small piece bay leaf
⅛ teaspoon chopped tarragon
½ teaspoon minced parsley
Salt and pepper
1 cup white wine

Heat butter and add remaining ingredients. Simmer fish in mixture. Remove fish carefully to hot platter. Strain sauce and serve with fish. Sufficient for cooking 1½ pounds fish.

Add 1 teaspoon of chopped capers.

Add 1 tablespoon of chopped pimiento or green pepper.

Omit the white wine. Use 1 cup of red wine and serve with meat.

Swiss steak, sauce of wine
Help to make a meal divine

SAUCE FOR FISH MARGUÉRY

2½ cups Fish Stock
3 tablespoons butter
3 tablespoons flour
18 small shrimp, or ½ cup lobster or littleneck clams
⅓ cup white wine
¼ teaspoon salt, Paprika
⅛ teaspoon pepper
1 tablespoon chopped oysters
1 (4-ounce) can mushrooms
3 hard-cooked eggs, chopped
¼ cup grated cheese

Simmer fish stock until it is reduced to 1¼ cups. Melt butter and blend in flour. Add the liquid gradually, stirring constantly until mixture thickens. Cook 3 minutes longer; cut all but 4 of the shrimp into the sauce. Add the wine, seasonings, oysters, mushrooms and 2 of the eggs. Pour the sauce over Baked Fish, topping with the remaining shrimp, egg and grated cheese. Bake in 350° F. oven until cheese melts. Serves 8.

MATELOTTE — Omit eggs and cheese. Use only 1 cup fish stock. Add 1 cup white wine, 1 small onion, minced, and 3 tablespoons burned brandy. Serve over 2 pounds poached fish or broiled steak.

SHERRY MUSHROOM SAUCE

1 (4-ounce) can sliced mushrooms
3 tablespoons flour
¼ cup butter
¾ cup Meat Stock
1 tablespoon chopped onion
2½ tablespoons chopped green pepper
3 olives, chopped
Salt, pepper
1 tablespoon sherry

Drain mushrooms and measure ¼ cup liquid. Brown flour in 2 tablespoons butter, add meat stock and measured mushroom liquid and cook until thickened, stirring constantly. Sauté onion and green pepper in remaining butter and add to sauce. Add olives. Season with salt and pepper. Simmer 10 minutes, remove from heat and add sherry. Serve with broiled steak or fillet of beef. Makes 1½ cups.

SOUTH AMERICAN ORANGE SAUCE

1 tablespoon bacon, chopped
1 tablespoon onion, chopped
1 cup orange juice
½ cup port wine
2 cups Gravy

Fry bacon and onion until brown. Add other ingredients and heat to boiling. Serve with poultry. Makes 3½ cups.

WINE SAUCE FOR QUAIL

2 small onions, minced
½ cup butter
2 cloves
1 teaspoon peppercorns
2 cloves garlic, minced
½ bay leaf
2 cups white wine
½ teaspoon salt
Dash pepper and cayenne
1 teaspoon minced chives
2 cups cream

Sauté onions in butter with cloves, peppercorns, garlic and bay leaf. Brown quail in mixture, add wine, salt, pepper, cayenne and chives and simmer 30 minutes. Remove quail to hot serving dish. Strain sauce, add cream and heat to boiling. Makes sauce for 6 quail.

WINE SAUCE FOR SWISS STEAK

3 medium onions, sliced
1 green pepper, diced
1 cup celery, diced
1½ cups red wine
1 cup tomato juice

Add the vegetables and half the wine to 3 pounds of steak which has been dredged in seasoned flour and browned in hot fat. Cover and bake in a hot oven (400° F.) for ½ hour. Add remaining wine and tomato juice and bake 1 hour longer. Serves 8.

WINE SAUCE FOR GAME OR TONGUE

1 tablespoon butter
½ glass Currant Jelly
Juice of ½ lemon
Dash cayenne
½ cup water
3 cloves
1 teaspoon salt
½ cup port wine

Simmer all ingredients except wine together 5 minutes. Strain and add wine; add 3 tablespoons meat gravy if desired. Serve hot. Makes about 1¼ cups sauce.

CHAUD-FROID SAUCES AND MEAT GLAZES

CHAUD-FROIDS

This jellied sauce is made up hot but the finished product is served cold. The sauce, which may be white, yellow, brown or other colors, is used to give a smooth, glossy surface to choice cooked meat, fish, fowl, game or molded mixtures, well seasoned and chilled. A decoration is usual, also a final coating of glaze.

WHITE CHAUD-FROID

¼ cup sweet butter
¼ cup sifted flour
1 pint milk
⅛ teaspoon salt
Few grains white pepper
2 tablespoons unflavored gelatin
6 tablespoons cold water
¼ cup mayonnaise

Make white sauce of butter, flour, milk, salt and pepper. Soften gelatin in water, pour hot white sauce over it and stir in mayonnaise. Strain at once through closely woven cloth into a bowl surrounded with cracked ice and stir constantly until the consistency of soft custard. Pour over chilled food to be coated, in smooth layer. If sauce becomes too stiff, reheat slightly in double boiler. Makes about 2½ cups.

BROWN—Use browned butter and flour and brown stock instead of milk.

CORAL—Use lobster coral butter instead of sweet; fish stock instead of milk, and coral mayonnaise, Page 862.

GREEN—Use Green Butter instead of sweet, white stock instead of milk, and Green Mayonnaise.

RED—Use beet juice instead of milk. And use Red Mayonnaise.

YELLOW—Add beaten yolks of 2 eggs just before removing white sauce from heat; omit mayonnaise.

CHICKEN CHAUD-FROID SAUCE

¼ cup rendered chicken fat
¼ cup sifted flour
2 cups concentrated seasoned Chicken Stock
2 teaspoons unflavored gelatin
2 tablespoons cold water
¼ cup cream

Combine chicken fat and flour; add chicken stock gradually and heat to boiling. Soften gelatin in cold water, stir into hot sauce and cool. Add cream and chill until the consistency of soft custard, stirring constantly. Makes about 2½ cups.

VEAL—Use concentrated veal stock instead of chicken.

TOMATO CHAUD-FROID SAUCE

6 tablespoons butter
6 tablespoons sifted flour
3 cups tomato juice
2 teaspoons salt
Few grains pepper
2½ tablespoons unflavored gelatin
6 tablespoons cold water

Combine butter and flour, tomato juice and seasonings as for white sauce. Soften gelatin in water, stir into hot sauce, cool and chill until the consistency of soft custard, stirring constantly. Makes about 3½ cups.

FISH CHAUD-FROID SAUCE

¼ cup sweet butter
¼ cup sifted flour
1 pint Fish Stock
⅛ teaspoon salt
Few grains white pepper
2 tablespoons unflavored gelatin
¼ cup cold water
2 tablespoons lemon juice

Combine butter and flour; add fish stock gradually, heat to boiling and add salt and pepper. Soften gelatin in cold water and stir into hot sauce. Cool, add lemon juice and chill until the consistency of soft custard, stirring constantly. Makes 2½ cups. Use strained court bouillon, Page 318, instead of fish stock. For shrimp or lobster use 2 tablespoons beet juice as part of water.

GLAZES FOR MEAT

Boil 1 quart consommé until it is reduced to 1 cup. For half-glaze, reduce it to 1 pint.

Simmer a small amount of jellied stock with burnt sugar until it becomes sirup.

To cup brown stock, add ½ tablespoon gelatin softened in ¼ cup water. The glaze should be melted over hot water and applied to meat, fish, game or poultry.

HAM GLAZES

Use 1 of the following to glaze ham. Forty-five minutes before ham is done, spread glaze over ham, then finish baking.

BROWN SUGAR—One cup brown sugar, juice and grated rind of 1 orange.

CIDER—One-half cup maple sirup, ½ cup cider or apple juice and 2 tablespoons prepared mustard.

CRANBERRY—Cook ½ pound fresh cranberries with 1 cup maple sirup until skins pop open. Press mixture through sieve and spread over ham.

CURRANT—One glass Currant Jelly, melted.

FRUIT—One cup puréed apricots, rhubarb or applesauce.

HONEY—One cup honey.

MUSTARD—One cup brown sugar, 1 tablespoon prepared mustard.

ORANGE—One-half cup Orange Marmalade.

PINEAPPLE HONEY—Three-fourths cup pineapple juice, ¾ cup strained honey and ½ teaspoon mustard; cook until thick.
SWEET—One cup brown or white sugar and ½ cup maraschino cherry juice, cider or juice from pickled fruit.

LAMB GLAZES

APRICOT—Rub 2 cups cooked apricots and juice through a sieve. Add ¾ cup sugar and cook slowly until thickened. Baste lamb frequently.

GRAPE—Rub meat with ½ cup minced mint leaves. Baste meat frequently during the last hour of roasting with ½ cup Grape Jelly melted in ½ cup hot water.
MINT—Baste lamb while cooking with vinegar flavored with minced mint leaves.
PINEAPPLE—Cover meat with pineapple slices 1 hour before meat is done.
TOMATO—Baste lamb while cooking with mixture of ½ cup tomato catchup and 2 tablespoons Worcestershire sauce.

TRANSPARENT GLAZE

2 tablespoons unflavored gelatin
¼ cup cold water
2¼ cups boiling water
1 tablespoon lemon juice
¼ teaspoon salt
Few grains white pepper

Soften gelatin in water, dissolve in boiling water and add lemon juice, salt and pepper. Cool until mixture begins to thicken. Makes about 2¼ cups.

PINK—Use cranberry juice instead of water.

GRAVIES

The distinction between sauces and gravies is well known but not often defined. Gravies are here considered to be those sauces which depend for their richness and flavor upon stock and drippings left in the pan after meat or poultry has been cooked. This pan stock is usually the fat and browned juices obtained from roasting or frying meat, sometimes called drippings. There is usually an excess of fat which should be removed before making the gravy. In some recipes pan stock referred to is the result of braising meat, in which case the ingredients in which the meat is braised are indicated. Occasionally the meat is braised in the gravy. Pan stock is then obtained by browning the meat in a little fat before placing it in a casserole.

GIBLET GRAVY

Chicken liver, heart and gizzard
¾ teaspoon salt
⅛ teaspoon pepper
4 tablespoons flour
4 tablespoons chicken fat or
  drippings from frying chicken
3 cups giblet stock

Wash liver, heart and cleaned gizzard. Cover gizzard and heart with cold water, add salt and pepper and simmer 20 minutes. Add liver and cook about 20 minutes longer or until tender. Drain, saving stock, and chop giblets fine; brown flour in fat, stirring constantly. Add giblet stock, stirring constantly and cook about 5 minutes. Add chopped giblets. Cream or milk may be used for part of the stock. Makes 3 cups gravy.

PAPRIKA CHICKEN GRAVY

Pan stock from roasted, fried or
  broiled chicken
1 tablespoon chopped onion
1 tablespoon paprika
1½ tablespoons flour
1 (10½-ounce) can chicken soup
Salt and pepper

Leave 1½ tablespoons pan stock in pan, add onion and paprika and cook until tender. Add flour and stir until well blended. Add chicken soup gradually. Cook slowly about 10 minutes. Season and strain. Makes 1¼ cups.

BROWN GRAVY

Pan stock from roast meat
¼ cup flour
2 cups meat stock or milk
Salt and pepper

Leave ¼ cup pan stock in pan, add flour and brown carefully. Add meat stock gradually, stirring until thickened. Cook 5 minutes. Season. Makes 2 cups.

MADEIRA HAM GRAVY

¾ cup pineapple juice
½ cup orange juice
3 tablespoons lemon juice
¾ cup Madeira wine
1½ tablespoons flour
¼ cup water
Salt and pepper

Combine fruit juices with Madeira wine and baste ham with mixture during baking. Remove ham when done, make a paste of flour and water, add to pan stock and cook until thickened, stirring constantly. Add seasoning and a little more wine to gravy just before serving if desired. Makes 2¼ cups.

Use also for baked smoked tongue or for smoked goose and turkey.

ARABIAN SAUCE

½ tablespoon minced onion
1 tablespoon minced celery
½ clove garlic, minced
¼ green pepper, chopped
1 tablespoon butter, melted
1 cup tomato soup
⅛ teaspoon salt, Dash pepper

Sauté onion, celery, garlic and green pepper in melted butter. Add tomato soup and seasonings and heat. Serve with cooked cabbage. Makes 1¼ cups.

ASPARAGUS CHEESE SAUCE

1 (10½-ounce) can asparagus soup
¾ cup milk
2 tablespoons sharp cheese
2 strips crisp bacon, chopped fine

Combine soup with milk. Heat and add cheese, stirring constantly until cheese is melted. Add bacon. Serve over waffles. Makes 2 cups.

NEAPOLITAN SPA-GHETTI SAUCE

2 onions, sliced thin
2 cloves garlic, mashed
½ cup olive oil
1½ pounds finely ground beef
2½ cups tomato juice
1½ cups tomato purée
1 can Italian tomato paste
4 hot chili peppers
1 teaspoon salt
¼ teaspoon pepper
1 teaspoon sugar
12 stuffed green olives, sliced

Brown onions and garlic in oil. Add meat and brown slowly. Heat tomato juice, purée and paste in a deep kettle; add meat mixture, chili peppers, salt, pepper and sugar. Simmer 2½ to 3 hours, until thick. Remove chili peppers and add olives. Simmer 10 minutes longer. Serve with spaghetti, topped with grated Parmesan cheese. Makes sauce for 1 pound spaghetti.

VARIATIONS

Add ½ teaspoon mace and ½ bay leaf with the tomato juice.
Add 1 cup sautéed mushrooms.
Add 1 green pepper, chopped.

BACON SAUCE

6 slices bacon, cut fine
¼ cup flour
2½ cups milk
¼ teaspoon salt

Fry bacon crisp. Add flour, stirring to blend well. Add milk and salt and cook until thick, stirring constantly. Makes 2½ cups. Add 2 teaspoons of onion juice if desired.

BROWNED BUTTER

½ cup butter
Heat butter until slightly browned.
LEMON—Add 3 tablespoons lemon juice and ⅓ teaspoon Worcestershire sauce.
ONION—Add 1½ tablespoons minced onion.

CELERY CHEESE SAUCE

6 tablespoons milk
1 (10½-ounce) can celery soup
2 ounces pimiento cheese

Combine milk with soup and add pimiento cheese. Heat until cheese is melted. Serve on vegetables such as cauliflower and cabbage. Makes about 2 cups.

TOMATO CHEESE SAUCE

2 tablespoons butter
2 tablespoons flour
½ teaspoon minced basil
2 cups tomato juice
¾ teaspoon salt
¼ teaspoon pepper
1 cup grated American cheese

Melt butter, blend in flour and basil, add tomato juice gradually and cook, stirring constantly, until thick and smooth. Add salt, pepper and cheese. Remove from heat and stir until cheese melts.

CHEESE SAUCE

2 tablespoons butter, melted
1 tablespoon flour
1 cup milk
Dash salt and pepper
¾ cup American cheese, grated

Blend butter and flour together, add milk and boil until thickened. Add seasonings and cheese and continue to heat, stirring constantly until cheese is melted. Makes 1¾ cups.

CHESTNUT SAUCE

1 pint chestnuts
Few celery leaves
1½ pints Brown Stock
2 tablespoons Browned Butter
2 tablespoons flour
Salt and pepper

Make small slit on flat side of each chestnut, boil 5 minutes and remove skins and shells with knife. Cook with celery leaves in 1 pint brown stock until tender and stock is entirely reduced. Make a brown sauce of butter, flour and remaining stock and add seasonings and chestnuts. Serve with Brussels sprouts, molded spinach or cauliflower. Makes 1½ pints.

VEGETARIAN SAUCE

¼ cup finely chopped celery
2 tablespoons finely chopped onions
1 teaspoon butter
1 (10½-ounce) can pea soup
¾ cup milk
¼ teaspoon salt

Sauté celery and onions in melted butter. Add soup, milk and salt and heat. Makes 2 cups.

ROQUEFORT SAUCE

2 ounces Roquefort cheese
¼ cup cream
Few drops Worcestershire sauce

Blend cheese with cream and Worcestershire sauce. Serve on asparagus. Makes ½ cup.

GOLDEN EGG SAUCE

6 hard-cooked eggs, diced
1 cup cream
1 tablespoon butter
Salt
Paprika
¼ cup minced parsley

Place eggs, cream, butter, salt and paprika in double boiler and cook until heated through. Add parsley. Serve with vegetables. Makes 2½ cups.

Add ¼ cup chopped pimiento.

HAM AND TOMATO SAUCE

1 clove garlic, minced
1 medium onion, chopped
2 tablespoons cooking oil
¾ cup shredded boiled ham
1 can tomato soup
1 teaspoon sugar

Sauté garlic and onion in oil. Add ham, tomato soup and sugar, cover and cook slowly 10 minutes longer. Makes 2⅓ cups.

When hearts are gay
And time not fleeting
Make Hollandaise sauce
For that special meeting

MOUSSELINE SAUCE

½ cup butter
4 egg yolks
¼ cup cream
¼ teaspoon salt
Few grains cayenne
2 tablespoons lemon juice

Cream half the butter and beat in egg yolks 1 at a time; add cream, salt and cayenne. Cook in double boiler until thickened, stirring constantly; add lemon juice, remove from heat and add remaining butter, cut into bits. Serve with asparagus, broccoli or cauliflower. Makes 1 cup.

GREEN—Press ¼ cup chopped fresh spinach or watercress through fine sieve and add to sauce. Serve with fish.

ROSY—Add ¼ cup pickled beet purée.

HOLLANDAISE SAUCE

½ cup butter
2 egg yolks, well beaten
¼ teaspoon salt
Dash cayenne
1 tablespoon lemon juice

METHOD 1—Divide butter into 3 portions. Place egg yolks with ⅓ of the butter in top of double boiler over hot (not boiling) water. Beat constantly with wire whisk; when butter melts add another portion and as mixture thickens add remaining butter, beating constantly. As soon as mixture is thickened, remove from heat and add seasonings and lemon juice. Should sauce separate, beat in 2 tablespoons boiling water, drop by drop. Makes ¾ cup.

METHOD 2—Melt butter in top of double boiler. Add to egg yolks gradually, stirring constantly. Return to double boiler and cook over hot water until thickened, stirring constantly. Remove from heat and stir in salt, cayenne and lemon juice. Sauce may be prepared 30 to 45 minutes before serving and kept hot by covering and placing pan in hot (not boiling) water.

WITH WATER—Cream butter, add egg yolks 1 at a time, blending each one in thoroughly. Add remaining ingredients and beat. Just before serving add ½ cup boiling water gradually, beating constantly. Cook over hot water, stirring constantly, until thickened. Serve at once.

MUSHROOM PIMIENTO SAUCE

½ cup milk
1 can mushroom soup
2 ounces pimiento cheese

Stir milk into soup and add cheese. Heat in a double boiler until cheese melts. Makes 2¼ cups.

MAYONNAISE

2 teaspoons salt
1 teaspoon dry mustard
Dash cayenne
2 egg yolks
1 pint olive or salad oil
¼ cup cider and tarragon
    vinegar, in equal parts

Combine dry ingredients with un-beaten yolks in a mixing bowl and beat together until stiff. Add part of the oil, beating it into the mixture drop by drop at first, then proceeding more rapidly always keeping the mixture stiff. When it begins to thicken add a little of the vinegar; alternate the oil and vinegar until blended. Makes 2½ cups.

Use 1 cup Mayonnaise:

ANCHOVY—Add 2 tablespoons anchovy paste or mashed an-chovies.

APPETIZER—Add 1 cup chili

You can make perfect may-onnaise in just a jiffy

sauce; 1 teaspoon Worcester-shire sauce; 1 teaspoon pre-pared horse-radish; 2 pickles, minced; 1 stalk celery, minced; 1 tablespoon minced chives and 2 tablespoons chopped parsley.

ASPIC—Beat ½ cup aspic gela-tin (as it begins to thicken) into mayonnaise and chill. Use through pastry bag or tube for garnishing.

BAR-LE-DUC—Add 3 table-spoons Bar-le-Duc and 1 table-spoon lemon juice.

CAVIAR—Add 4 tablespoons caviar and 2 tablespoons pearl onions or prepared horse-radish.

CHEESE—Add 3 ounces cream cheese and 2½ tablespoons Cam-embert cheese.

CHIFFONADE—Add 2 table-spoons each chopped green and red pepper, 1 tablespoon each chopped olives and sweet pickle and 1 teaspoon prepared horse-radish.

COLORED—RED: for vegetable salads add beet juice or cooked beet purée.

GREEN: for vegetable salads add cooked spinach purée, minced parsley or concentrated liquor from boiled artichokes.

CORAL—Add mashed coral from cooked lobster.

COTTAGE CHEESE—Add ⅓ cup cottage cheese and mix well.

CRANBERRY—Add 1 cup minced cranberries.

CRANBERRY CREAM—Add 1 cup Cranberry Jelly and ¾ cup whipped cream.

CREAM CHEESE—Add 3 ounces cream cheese, 1 tablespoon lemon juice, ⅔ cup chopped toasted almonds; fold in 1 cup whipped cream.

CUCUMBER—Add ¼ cup chopped celery and ⅔ cup chopped cucumber.

CURRY—Add 1 teaspoon curry powder and ½ clove garlic, minced.

FRUIT—Add 3 tablespoons fruit juice, ½ cup confectioners' sugar and 1 cup heavy cream, whipped.

GARLIC—Add 1 cup Garlic French Dressing. Beat well.

HERB—Add 1 teaspoon each minced parsley, tarragon, water-cress, chervil, chives and basil. Beat very well.

FLUFFY HORSE-RADISH—Add ¾ cup whipped cream, 4 table-spoons freshly ground horse-radish, and 4 drops Tabasco sauce.

JELLY CREAM—Add 1 cup strained Currant Jelly and 1 cup whipped cream.

LEMON CREAM—Add ½ cup confectioners' sugar, ¼ cup lemon juice, dash salt and 1 cup heavy cream, whipped.

OLIVE—Add ⅓ cup chopped ripe or stuffed olives

SALAD DRESSINGS

PASTEL FRUIT—For fruit salads, add red raspberry juice or cooked red raspberry purée.

PIMIENTO CHEESE—Add 1 ounce pimiento cream cheese, 2 tablespoons chili sauce and ½ teaspoon Worcestershire sauce.

ROQUEFORT—Add 2 tablespoons Roquefort cheese, mashed and 1 teaspoon lemon juice.

SEA FOOD—Add 1 cup chili sauce; 3 hard-cooked eggs, chopped; 2 sweet pickles, minced; ½ cup chopped ripe olives; ¼ pound shredded crab meat, shrimp or lobster.

SHERRY—Add 1 tablespoon sherry or grenadine.

STRAWBERRY CREAM—Add 1 cup mashed fresh strawberries (or red raspberries), ⅓ tablespoon confectioners' sugar, 3 tablespoons lemon juice; fold in 1 cup whipped cream.

THOUSAND ISLAND DRESSING—Add ⅓ cup chili sauce, 2 tablespoons chopped stuffed olives, 1 teaspoon chopped capers, 1 teaspoon chopped chives.

TOMATO—Add 1 cup chopped fresh tomatoes, dash of salt and 1 teaspoon chopped chives. Three tablespoons diced cucumbers may be added.

WHIPPED CREAM—Fold mayonnaise into 1 cup whipped cream.

WHITE WINE—Add ¼ cup fresh strawberries or raspberries; ¼ cup chopped pecans, toasted almonds or pistachios; 2 tablespoons each fruit juice and white wine.

FROZEN LIME MAYONNAISE

1 cup Mayonnaise
⅓ cup heavy cream, whipped
2 tablespoons lime juice
2 tablespoons sugar

Combine mayonnaise with whipped cream; add fruit juice and sugar. Freeze either in refrigerator tray or in small molds. Serve with fruit salads. Serves 6.

EGGLESS MAYONNAISE

½ teaspoon salt
½ teaspoon confectioners' sugar
¼ teaspoon dry mustard
¼ teaspoon paprika
Dash cayenne
1 tablespoon vinegar
1 tablespoon lemon juice
¼ cup chilled evaporated milk
1 cup chilled olive or salad oil

Beat first 8 ingredients with rotary egg beater until well blended. Add ⅓ cup oil and beat well. Add another ⅓ cup oil and beat. Add the remaining oil and beat again. Serve the dressing shortly after making. Makes about 1½ cups.

LEMON MAYONNAISE

1 egg yolk, ¼ cup lemon juice
⅔ cup sweetened condensed milk
¼ cup olive or salad oil
½ teaspoon salt
1 teaspoon dry mustard

Combine ingredients. Beat well until mixture thickens. Add ¼ cup more lemon juice for a more tart flavor. Makes 1¼ cups.

Place the dressing bowl at the side to emphasize the salad arrangement

TARTARE SAUCE

1 teaspoon minced onion
2 teaspoons chopped sweet pickle
1 teaspoon chopped green olives
½ tablespoon minced capers
1 tablespoon minced parsley
¾ cup mayonnaise
1 tablespoon tarragon vinegar

Drain first 5 ingredients thoroughly and fold into mayonnaise. Add vinegar. Makes about ¾ cup sauce.

SHRIMP RÉMOULADE—¾ cup mayonnaise, 1 teaspoon salt, 2 teaspoons dry mustard, 6 green onions minced, 2 stalks celery minced, 1 teaspoon paprika, 2 drops Tabasco sauce, 3 sprigs parsley minced. Combine and pour over shrimp; let stand 4 hours. Serve.

FROZEN TOMATO MAYONNAISE

4 tomatoes, peeled and chopped
1 teaspoon minced onion
1 cup Mayonnaise
⅛ teaspoon salt, Dash cayenne

Combine all ingredients; pour mixture into freezing tray of refrigerator and freeze without stirring. Serve in the hollow of a peeled half avocado garnished with salad greens. Serves 6.

FRENCH DRESSING

1 cup olive or salad oil
¼ cup vinegar
½ teaspoon salt
Few grains cayenne
¼ teaspoon white pepper
2 tablespoons chopped parsley

Combine and beat or shake thoroughly before using. Makes 1¼ cups.

Variations using 1 cup French Dressing as a foundation:

ANCHOVY—Add 2 tablespoons anchovy paste or mashed anchovies and 1 tablespoon pearl onions.

CAPER—Add ⅓ cup minced capers.

CHIFFONADE—Add 1 tablespoon each chopped beets, chopped chives and chopped hard-cooked eggs.

CHIVE—Add 1 tablespoon chopped chives, minced shallot or onion.

COTTAGE CHEESE—Add 3 tablespoons cottage cheese and 1 tablespoon chopped chives.

CUCUMBER—Add 3 tablespoons grated cucumber and 1 tablespoon chopped chives.

FINES HERBES—Add 1 tablespoon each minced parsley, watercress, chervil and basil.

GARLIC—Rub bowl with crushed clove garlic.

GINGER ALE—Use 2 tablespoons each vinegar and ginger ale.

HORSE-RADISH—Add 1 teaspoon prepared horse-radish.

INDIA—Add 2 tablespoons chutney, 2 chopped hard-cooked eggs and ½ teaspoon curry powder.

MUSTARD—Add 2 teaspoons prepared mustard to Garlic French Dressing.

PEARL ONION—Add 2 tablespoons pearl onions.

ROQUEFORT—Add ⅓ cup soft Roquefort cheese, crumbled first and creamed with 2 tablespoons French dressing.

TARRAGON—Use ¼ cup tarragon vinegar.

TOMATO—Add 1 cup tomato juice; ½ clove garlic, minced; and 1 tablespoon confectioners' sugar.

VINAIGRETTE—Add 1 tablespoon chopped chives, 1 tablespoon chopped sweet pickles and 1 teaspoon chopped capers.

WHITE WINE—Use ¼ cup white wine vinegar.

Shake French dressing well and serve it in a bowl which matches your salad plates

LEMON FRENCH DRESSING

½ cup olive or salad oil
½ cup lemon juice
½ teaspoon salt
Few grains cayenne
2 tablespoons sugar or honey

Combine all ingredients and shake well before using. Makes 1 cup.

VARIATIONS WITH 1 CUP LEMON FRENCH DRESSING

CREAM CHEESE GINGER—Beat in 2 tablespoons each cream cheese and chopped ginger.

CRYSTALLIZED—Fold into French dressing 2 cups fruit gelatin just as it begins to thicken; chill. Whip well.

FRUIT—Use 2 tablespoons each lemon, lime, pineapple and orange juice instead of ½ cup lemon juice.

GRAPEFRUIT—Use ¼ cup grapefruit juice instead of ¼ cup lemon juice and reduce sugar to 1 teaspoon.

LIME—Use ¼ cup lime juice instead of ¼ cup lemon juice.

MARASCHINO—Add 1 tablespoon chopped toasted almonds and 1 tablespoon minced maraschino cherries.

MINT—Add 2 tablespoons chopped mint.

ORANGE—Use ¼ cup orange juice for ¼ cup lemon juice and reduce sugar to 1 teaspoon.

PINEAPPLE—Use ¼ cup pineapple juice instead of ¼ cup lemon juice and reduce sugar to 1 teaspoon.

RUBY—Add 2 tablespoons grenadine or maraschino cherry juice and reduce sugar to 1 teaspoon.

RUSSIAN DRESSING

1 cup salad oil
½ cup catchup
1/3 cup vinegar
2 tablespoons sugar
1 teaspoon salt
½ teaspoon grated onion

Combine all ingredients in the order listed and beat until thoroughly blended. Makes 1¾ cups.

WHIPPED CREAM DRESSING

⅔ cup sugar
2 tablespoons flour
2 eggs, beaten
2 tablespoons salad oil
3 tablespoons lemon juice
4 tablespoons orange juice
1 cup pineapple juice
½ cup heavy cream, whipped

Combine sugar and flour in top of double boiler; add remaining ingredients except cream and cook until thickened, stirring constantly. When cool fold in whipped cream. Makes 2 cups.
GINGER—Add 3 teaspoons chopped crystallized ginger.

SOUR CREAM DRESSING

2 hard-cooked egg yolks
1 cup sour cream
1 teaspoon lemon juice
½ teaspoon sugar
Dash each salt and pepper

Press yolks through a sieve and beat into sour cream. Beat in lemon juice, sugar and seasonings. Makes 1¼ cups.

SUGGESTIONS

Add ⅛ teaspoon of ground cardamom seed.
Beaten egg whites may be added.

COTTAGE CHEESE DRESSING

½ cup cottage cheese
½ cup evaporated milk
½ cup lemon juice
1 tablespoon honey or sugar
½ teaspoon salt
Dash paprika
1 tablespoon chopped chives

Beat all ingredients together until smooth. Makes 1⅓ cups.

VARIATIONS

Use 1 tablespoon chopped capers.
Use fresh milk instead of evaporated milk.

CUCUMBER CREAM DRESSING

2 tablespoons lemon juice
1 cup heavy cream, whipped
Dash cayenne
¼ teaspoon salt
Dash white pepper
¾ cup grated cucumber, drained

Stir lemon juice gradually into whipped cream; add seasonings and cucumber. Serve with fish or aspic. Serves 12.
CUCUMBER DRESSING—Use ½ cup mayonnaise with ½ cup whipped cream.

HORSE-RADISH CREAM DRESSING

1 cup heavy cream
1 tablespoon lemon juice
1 tablespoon tarragon vinegar
1 tablespoon red wine vinegar
3 tablespoons grated horse-radish
Dash salt
Dash sugar
¼ teaspoon prepared mustard

Whip cream; add lemon juice and vinegar gradually, and stir in seasonings. Serve with tomato jelly, mixed greens, or cold meats. Makes 2 cups.

Add 2 tablespoons grated cucumber.

PINEAPPLE CREAM DRESSING

3 egg yolks
½ cup sugar
5 tablespoons lemon juice
½ cup pineapple juice
Dash salt
½ cup heavy cream, whipped

Beat egg yolks and sugar together, add fruit juices and salt and cook in top of double boiler until mixture thickens. Cool and fold in whipped cream. Makes 1½ cups.
ORANGE CREAM—Use orange juice in place of pineapple.

COOKED SALAD DRESSING

1 tablespoon sugar
2 teaspoons dry mustard
1 teaspoon salt
⅛ teaspoon cayenne
¾ cup salad oil, 1 egg
¼ cup vinegar
3 tablespoons cornstarch
1 cup cold water

Combine first 7 ingredients in a bowl, but do not beat. Combine cornstarch and cold water and stir until thoroughly mixed. Cook over low heat stirring constantly, until mixture boils and becomes clear. Remove from heat and continue stirring for about 3 minutes. Pour hot mixture into ingredients in bowl and beat vigorously with a rotary beater until smooth. Chill. Makes 2 cups.

CHICKEN LIVER DRESSING

4 cooked chicken livers
4 hard-cooked egg yolks
3 teaspoons prepared mustard
¼ teaspoon salt
Dash pepper
¼ cup olive or salad oil
2 teaspoons red wine vinegar
2 tablespoons red wine

Rub livers and cooked egg yolks through a sieve, add seasonings and mix to a paste. Add oil, drop by drop, blending well, then vinegar and wine. Toss with greens in salad bowl. Makes 1 cup.

SOUR CREAM COOKED DRESSING

3 tablespoons tarragon vinegar
1 cup cider vinegar
1 tablespoon lemon juice
3 eggs
3 tablespoons sugar
1 tablespoon dry mustard
1 teaspoon salt
1 tablespoon celery salt
Dash cayenne
3 tablespoons melted butter
½ cup sour cream

Scald vinegars and lemon juice. Beat eggs with sugar, mustard, salt, celery salt, · and cayenne. Add hot vinegar and simmer until thickened, stirring constantly. Remove from heat, add melted butter and beat until smooth. Add sour cream and beat again. Makes about 2 cups.

Make your own salad and dress it from the center of the bowl

COOKED DRESSING FOR FRUIT SALAD

½ cup sugar
½ teaspoon dry mustard
½ teaspoon salt
½ cup vinegar
6 egg yolks or 3 whole eggs
2 tablespoons butter

Combine sugar, mustard, salt and vinegar, and heat to boiling. Pour over well beaten yolks, stirring constantly. Cook until thickened, beating with rotary egg beater. Add butter. Just before serving add ½ cup heavy cream, whipped, or thin with cream or milk. Do not dilute the vinegar. Makes 1½ cups.

AVOCADO DRESSING

2 tablespoons lemon juice
4 tablespoons evaporated milk
½ teaspoon salt
1 teaspoon prepared mustard
6 drops Tabasco sauce
1 cup sieved avocado

Beat lemon juice and milk together thoroughly; add seasonings and blend. Beat in avocado until thick and creamy. Serve with tomato or vegetable salads. Makes about 1⅓ cups dressing.

DESSERT GARNISHES

The art of garnishing is based upon a knowledge of flavors and how they may be combined to add to the attractiveness as well as the palatability of a dish. Demonstrate the value of garnishing by experimenting with simple desserts. Garnish just before serving.

FLUFFY BRANDY SAUCE

1 egg, separated
¾ cup confectioners' sugar
⅛ teaspoon salt
½ cup heavy cream, whipped
3 tablespoons brandy

Beat egg white; add sugar gradually, beating until stiff. Beat in salt and egg yolk, then fold in whipped cream and brandy. Chill. Makes 1¾ cups.

MADEIRA SAUCE

5 egg yolks, beaten
3 tablespoons sugar
3 tablespoons lemon juice
1 tablespoon grated lemon rind
⅔ cup Madeira wine

Combine ingredients and cook in double boiler, beating constantly, until thickened. Do not boil. Serve at once. Makes 1¼ cups.

VANILLA SAUCE

½ cup sugar
1 tablespoon cornstarch
1 cup boiling water
2 tablespoons butter
1 teaspoon vanilla
Few grains salt

Mix sugar and cornstarch; add water gradually, stirring constantly. Boil for 5 minutes, remove from heat, add butter, vanilla and salt. Stir until butter is melted and serve hot. Makes about 1 cup sauce.

CLARET SAUCE

⅓ cup butter
1¼ cups confectioners' sugar
3 egg whites
⅔ cup boiling water
⅔ cup claret
1 teaspoon grated lemon rind
½ teaspoon cinnamon

Cream butter and sugar until smooth, beat in egg whites and continue beating until light. Just before serving add boiling water, claret, lemon rind and cinnamon. Heat in double boiler and beat until foamy. Makes 3 cups. One-fourth teaspoon of nutmeg may be added.

MARSHMALLOW SAUCE

1 cup sugar
½ cup water
16 marshmallows
2 egg whites

Boil sugar and water together for 5 minutes. Cut marshmallows into small pieces and add to hot sirup. Stir until dissolved and pour mixture gradually over stiffly beaten egg whites. Beat until smooth and well blended. Makes 2½ cups sauce.

This sauce may be flavored with peppermint.

Add 4 marshmallows, cut into eighths, just before serving.

HOT WINE PUDDING SAUCE

1 cup sugar
1 tablespoon flour
2 cups boiling water
⅓ cup butter
¼ cup sherry

Combine sugar and flour, add water gradually, stirring constantly, and cook until mixture thickens. Add butter and sherry. Makes 2½ cups.

HOT RUM SAUCE

½ cup butter
1 cup sugar
¼ cup rum
Dash cinnamon

Combine butter and sugar, heat to boiling and boil for 2 minutes. Remove from heat and add remaining ingredients. Makes about 1 cup.

RUM SAUCE

1 cup sugar
1 tablespoon grated lemon rind
1½ cups boiling water
1 tablespoon butter
1 tablespoon cornstarch
3 tablespoons lemon juice
½ cup rum
Dash salt

Combine sugar and lemon rind with water, add butter and heat to boiling. Mix cornstarch with lemon juice and add. Cook 8 minutes, remove from heat, strain, add rum and salt. Makes 2 cups. Serve hot with puddings.

BRANDY SAUCE

4 egg yolks, beaten
3 tablespoons confectioners' sugar
⅔ cup cream
5 tablespoons brandy

Combine egg yolks and sugar and beat. Add cream, heat to boiling and boil 5 minutes, beating constantly. Remove from heat and add brandy. Makes 1⅓ cups.

BRANDY HARD SAUCE

⅓ cup butter
¾ cup confectioners' sugar
2 tablespoons brandy

Cream butter and sugar, add brandy gradually and continue beating until smooth. Chill. Makes ¾ cup.

SHERRY—Use 2 tablespoons sherry instead of brandy.

BUTTERSCOTCH SAUCE

¼ cup butter
1 cup brown sugar
2 eggs, separated
½ cup cream, Dash salt

Cream butter and sugar. Beat yolks until thick, add cream; beat into butter and sugar mixture. Cook in top of double boiler until thickened. Pour slowly over salted egg whites, beaten until stiff but not dry. Serve hot. Makes 2½ cups sauce.

CARAMEL SAUCE

1 cup sugar
½ cup boiling water
2 tablespoons cream

Place sugar in heavy pan and heat slowly until melted and browned, stirring constantly. Add boiling water slowly, stirring vigorously. Cook until sirupy and all of browned sugar has melted. Remove from heat and add cream. Serve hot or cold. If too thick when cold, add a little more cream. Makes about 1 cup.

RICH CHERRY SAUCE

¼ cup sugar
2 tablespoons flour
1 cup hot red cherry juice
¼ cup butter
2 tablespoons lemon juice
2 drops almond extract

Combine sugar and flour, stir in cherry juice gradually, heat to boiling and cook until thickened, stirring constantly. Add butter, lemon juice and almond extract. Serve hot or cold. Makes 1¼ cups.

HARD SAUCE

⅓ cup butter
1 cup confectioners' sugar
¾ teaspoon vanilla
1 tablespoon cream

Cream butter, beat in sugar gradually and continue creaming until fluffy. Add flavoring and cream. Chill. Makes ¾ cup sauce.

PINWHEEL HARD SAUCE—To ⅓ of recipe add 3 tablespoons finely grated chocolate. Spread white layer on cold damp cloth and spread chocolate mixture on top. Roll as a jelly roll. Chill. Slice and use as a garnish.

HOT FUDGE SAUCE

1 tablespoon butter
1 ounce (square) chocolate
⅓ cup boiling water, 1 cup sugar
2 tablespoons corn sirup
½ teaspoon vanilla
⅛ teaspoon salt

Melt butter in saucepan. Add chocolate and stir over low heat until chocolate is melted. Add boiling water gradually, stirring constantly; heat to boiling. Add sugar and sirup, stirring until dissolved. Simmer 5 minutes, add vanilla and salt. Serves 6.

LEMON SAUCE

1 tablespoon cornstarch
½ cup sugar
¼ teaspoon salt
1 cup water
2 tablespoons lemon juice
1 teaspoon grated lemon rind
1 egg yolk
1 tablespoon butter

Mix constarch, sugar and salt thoroughly. Add water, heat to boiling and cook until clear and thickened, stirring constantly. Add lemon juice and rind and pour slowly over beaten egg yolk. Cook another minute and add butter. Makes 1¼ cups.

CRANBERRY SAUCE

Boil 1½ cups sugar and 2 cups water together 5 minutes. Add 1 pound (4 cups) cranberries and boil without stirring until all skins pop open; about 5 minutes. Re-

move from heat and cool. Makes 4 cups sauce.

LEMON CREAM SAUCE

2 egg yolks, ⅓ cup sugar
⅓ cup melted butter
1 tablespoon grated lemon rind
2 tablespoons lemon juice
⅓ cup heavy cream, whipped

Beat egg yolks until thick, then beat in sugar gradually. Add butter, lemon rind and juice. Fold in whipped cream; chill. Serves 8.

CHOCOLATE MINT SAUCE

2 ounces (squares) chocolate
2 cups sugar
1 cup cold water, Dash salt
2 tablespoons butter
Few drops oil of peppermint

Melt chocolate over hot water. Add sugar, water and salt. Cook over low heat, stirring constantly, until sugar and chocolate dissolve and mixture thickens slightly. Boil about 3 minutes longer (to 230°F.), or until a small amount forms a very soft ball in cold water; remove from heat, add butter and peppermint. If sauce is to be stored, omit butter, seal in a jar and chill. Just before using, reheat and add butter. Makes 2 cups sauce.
Use vanilla instead of peppermint for plain chocolate sauce.

MAPLE SAUCE

½ cup sugar, ¼ cup corn sirup
¾ cup cream
3 tablespoons butter
½ cup maple sirup

Combine sugar, corn sirup and cream and heat to boiling, stirring constantly. Cook to 234°F. or until drop forms very soft ball in cold water. Remove from heat add butter and maple sirup. Use hot or cold. Makes 1½ cups.

Dishes for Children

75
Special Menus and Recipes for Children

MENUS

FOR THE PRESCHOOL CHILD

BREAKFASTS

Sliced Ripe Banana
Oatmeal with Raisins, 872   Milk
Toasted Roll
Orange Nog, 914

Baked Pears
Whole-grain Cereal, 872
Milk
Zwieback
Chocolate Milk

Orange Juice
Farina, 872   Milk
Toast Sticks
Crisp Bacon
Milk

Pineapple Juice
Corn-meal Mush, 872   Milk
Melba Toast
Milk

Orange Sections
Scrambled Egg, 287, 288
Toast   Milk

Strawberries
Rolled Oats and Rice, 872   Milk
Zwieback
Milk

Prune Juice
French Toast, 873
Milk

DINNERS

Monday
Cream of Salmon Soup
Baked Stuffed Onions, 256, 472
Sandwich of
Watercress and Lemon Butter
Stewed Apricots   Milk

Tuesday
Liver and Potato Pie, 874
Peas Cooked in Lettuce
Minced Uncooked Cabbage
with Lemon Juice
Baked Custard   Milk

Wednesday
Boned Halibut Baked in Milk, 316
Baked Potato
Parsley Carrots
Shredded Lettuce Sandwich
Banana Mousse   Milk

Thursday
Creamed Egg and Asparagus
Sandwich, 298
Carrot and Raisin Salad
Sliced Peaches
Old-fashioned Sugar Cookie
Milk

Friday
Back Bay Fish Chowder, 103
Sliced Ripe Tomatoes
Fresh Escarole Sandwich
Brown Rice Pudding
Apricot Shake

Saturday
Broiled Beef Patties, 362
Cabbage Cooked in Milk
Carrot Sticks
Bread and Butter
Prune Whip   Milk

Sunday
Roast Chicken, 412
Mashed Potato
Chopped Spinach
Whole-wheat Bread   Butter
Jellied Fruit Salad
Orange Sherbet   Milk

SUPPERS

Goldenrod Eggs on Toast, 873
Toast and Butter
Jellied Tomato Juice
Baked Apple
Milk

Cream of Tomato Soup
Egg and Uncooked Spinach, 883
Sandwich on Whole-wheat Bread
Sliced Orange and
Ripe Banana

Soft-cooked Egg on Toast, 303
Buttered Spinach
Bread and Butter
Fruit Gelatin
Milk

Potato Soufflé, 261
Bread and Butter
Prune and Cottage Cheese Salad
Apricot Angel Cream
Custard Sauce
Milk

Spaghetti with Chicken Livers, 432
Buttered Kale
Apple Salad
Figs Stuffed with Prunes,
Raisins and Nuts   Milk

Cream of Potato Soup, 114
Buttered Beets
Shredded Lettuce and Parsley
Sandwich
Sponge Drops   Eggnog

Macaroni and Cheese, 874
Shredded Uncooked Cabbage
Sandwich on Whole-wheat Bread
Baked Banana
Grape Juice Shake

FOR THE SCHOOL CHILD

BREAKFASTS	LUNCHES	DINNERS

BREAKFASTS

Orange Juice
Poached Egg, 873
Toast   Crisp Bacon
Hot Chocolate

Stewed Apricots
Buckwheat Grits, 872
Toast
Banana Milk Shake

Half Grapefruit
Whole-wheat Muffins, 172
Jam
Crisp Bacon   Milk

Tomato Juice
Scrambled Egg, 287-288
Toast   Milk

Baked Apple, Milk
Corn-meal Mush, 872   Molasses
Milk

Prune Juice
Poached Egg, 873   Toast
Chocolate Milk

Sliced Orange
Waffles, 170   Brown Sugar
Milk

LUNCHES

Monday
Liver Vegetable Soup, 100
Pineapple and Banana Salad
Toast Animals
Butterscotch Pudding

Tuesday
Peppers Stuffed with
Macaroni, 476
Creamed Onions and String Beans
Bread and Butter
Baked Apple   Milk

Wednesday
Vegetable Ring
Bread and Butter
Watercress and Egg Salad
Old-fashioned Tarts, 270
Milk

Thursday
Lima Bean Chowder, 109
Nut Bread Sandwiches
Bananas with Custard Sauce
Milk

Friday
Eggs in Tomato Cases, 290, 873
Cottage Cheese and Watercress
Sandwiches
Peaches and Cream
Milk

Saturday
Spring Salad Bowl, 530
Bran Muffins
Floating Island Pudding
Fig Cookies   Milk

Sunday
Chicken Broth
Treasure Sandwich Chest, 209
Jack O'Lantern Salad
Milk

DINNERS

Mock Duck, 874
Potatoes on the Half Shell
Waxed Beans, O'Brien
Shredded Lettuce Salad
Strawberries. Cream   Milk

Pot Roast of Beef with
Vegetables, 353
Mashed Sweetpotatoes
Cabbage Salad
Fruit Soufflé   Milk

Bouillon
Broiled Lamb Kidneys, 911
Creamed Potatoes
Buttered Beets and Celery
Honey Cookies
Frosted Apricot Milk

Baked Liver, 401
Carrot Ring
Mixed Vegetable Salad Bowl
Toasty Prune Betty   Milk

Hominy Salmon Loaf, 243
Buttered Broccoli
Cranberry Orange Mold
Peanut-butter Cupcakes   Milk

Panned Liver, 874
Baked Potatoes
Stuffed Zucchini
Sliced Tomatoes
Nutmeg Almond Float

Grapefruit Juice
Chicken and Brown Rice
Tomatoes Stuffed with
Spinach, 514
Green Salad Bowl
New York Ice Cream

PREPARATION OF HOT CEREALS

In general, proportions of water for 1 cup cereal are: for granular cereals such as farina, cornmeal and brown granular wheat, 4 to 5 cups; for flaked cereals such as rolled oats and rolled or flaked wheat, 2 to 3 cups; and for whole grain or cracked cereals such as rice, barley, and wheat, 3 to 4 cups.

To keep granular texture, cereals should be stirred as little as possible using a slotted spoon or fork.

Hot cereals, whether whole grain, flaked or granular, may be quick-cooking or the longer-cooking variety. Follow directions on package. Or —

TO COOK GRANULAR CERE-ALS (such as corn meal, farina and brown granular wheat)—Put ½ cup cereal into a saucepan; stir in 2 to 2½ cups cold water and ½ teaspoon salt. Heat gradually to boiling over direct heat, stirring enough to prevent settling. Tightly cover saucepan and cook over low heat, or place double boiler top over simmering water about 5 to 10 minutes for quick-cooking, or 15 to 30 minutes for longer-cooking variety. Makes 4 servings.

TO COOK FLAKED CEREALS (such as rolled oats and rolled or flaked wheat)—Bring 3 to 4½ cups water and 1 teaspoon salt to a rapid boil over direct heat in top of double boiler. Gradually sprinkle in 1½ cups cereal and boil gently 3 to 5 minutes, stirring occasionally. Cover and place over simmering water in lower part of double boiler. Cook about 5 to 10 minutes for quick-cooking, or 15 to 30 minutes for longer-cooking variety. Makes 4 servings.

TO COOK WHOLE GRAIN OR CRACKED CEREALS (such as rice, barley, and wheat)—Follow method for cooking flaked cereals, using 4½ to 6 cups water. Cook 35 to 45 minutes for rice. Brown and wild rice take a little longer time. Follow directions on package for precooked rice. Other grains require 3 to 4 hours. Makes 8 servings.

Quick Method for Cooking Flaky Rice—Put 1 cup rice, 2 cups cold water and 1 teaspoon salt into 2 quart saucepan with a tight-fitting cover. Set over high heat until rice boils vigorously. Stir with a fork, cover and reduce heat to very low; cook about 15 minutes longer without lifting cover. Rice grains should be separate and fluffy. Remove cover when tender to allow steam to escape.

HOMINY—Hominy is a corn product and is found in these forms: samp (whole kernels), grits (granulated or ground), and hulled corn (cooked product, canned or in bulk). Grits are cooked like a cracked cereal. To cook samp: Wash 1 cup samp; soak 4 hours in 2 cups cold water. Drain. Slowly stir samp into 4 cups rapidly boiling water. Cover and cook over direct heat for 1 hour. Add small amounts of water if necessary but avoid mushy consistency. Drain and rinse with boiling water. Add 2 tablespoons butter and 1 teaspoon salt. Place over hot water and let stand about 30 minutes to "mellow". Makes 4 servings.

CEREALS COOKED IN MILK—Use part or all milk instead of water. Add dried fruits such as raisins, dates and figs.

Soft-eyed bunny dishes will tempt the most finicky child

PUFFED OMELET

6 eggs, separated
6 tablespoons hot water
¾ teaspoon salt
Dash pepper
1½ tablespoons butter or other fat

Beat egg whites until stiff. Beat yolks until thick and lemon colored, beat hot water into them and add salt and pepper. Fold yolks and stiffly beaten whites together. Melt butter in omelet pan, grease bottom and sides of pan. Turn egg mixture into pan, cover and cook over low heat until puffy and light brown underneath, then place in moderate oven (350°F.) 10 to 15 minutes or until top is dry. Touch top of omelet lightly with finger and if egg does not stick to finger omelet is done. Do not overcook it or it will shrink and be tough. Loosen edges of omelet, cut through center, slip a spatula or flexible knife under side next to handle of pan, fold ½ over other and press slightly to make it stay in place; slip onto hot plate and serve at once. Serve 6.

Serve cooked vegetable in center.

EGGS IN TOMATO CASES

6 small tomatoes
2 tablespoons butter
Salt, 6 eggs

Cut tops from ripe tomatoes. In center of each make a hollow large enough to hold an egg. Add 1 teaspoon butter, season with salt and break an egg into each. Bake in moderate oven (350°F.) until eggs are firm. Serves 6.

GOLDENROD EGGS

4 hard-cooked eggs
1½ cups Medium White Sauce
Toast

Separate whites and yolks of eggs. Chop whites and add to hot white sauce. Press egg yolks through a ricer. Pour sauce over hot toast and garnish with yolks. Serve at once. Serves 4.

FRENCH TOAST

3 eggs
2 cups milk
½ teaspoon salt
12 slices bread ½ inch thick

Beat the eggs, add the milk and salt. Dip slices of bread into the mixture and sauté in a little hot fat until a delicate brown on both sides. Serve hot. Sprinkle with confectioners' sugar or serve maple sirup with the toast.

POACHED EGG

2 cups water, ½ teaspoon salt
½ tablespoon vinegar
1 egg, Hot buttered toast

Heat water to simmering in a shallow pan; add salt and vinegar. Break egg into a cup and slip it carefully into water. Make a whirlpool around egg with spoon or fork. Let egg cook below boiling water about 5 minutes or until white is firm and a film has formed over yolk. Remove egg with skimmer, drain and serve on toast or rusk.

NOTE—Water should cover egg. Vary quantity of water according to number of eggs used and size of pan.

**TO SERVE POACHED EGGS—
ASPARAGUS**—Spread a buttered piece of toast with purée of asparagus. Cover with poached egg and garnish with cooked asparagus tips. A cream or cheese sauce may be poured over all.

CHEESE — Garnish eggs with shredded cheese.

CROUSTADE—Pour cheese sauce into toasted bread Croustades and place a poached egg in center of each one. Garnish with parsley.

Eggs are consumed with enthusiasm when you cultivate the art of making perfect omelets

MOCK DUCK

1 shoulder lamb
4 slices salt pork or bacon
Salt and pepper

Have the butcher prepare a mock duck from the shoulder of lamb. Wrap the duck's head in salt pork or bacon. Sprinkle with salt and pepper and place on rack in open roasting pan. Roast in slow oven (300°F.) about 45 minutes per pound or until a meat thermometer registers 180°F.

PANNED LIVER

1 pound liver, (beef, calf or pork)
Bacon fat, Water

Cut liver into ¼- to ½-inch slices. Remove outside membrane and any veins or bloodclots. Heat skillet, lightly greased with bacon fat and sear liver on both sides, then cook slowly until tender. A little water may be added during the last of cooking. Serves 3. Pan-fry or broil 3 slices bacon and keep hot to serve with liver.

LIVER AND TOMATO PIE

2 potatoes, cooked and mashed
1 egg
3 tablespoons fat
½ pound beef liver
½ tablespoon salt
Dash pepper
1 small onion
½ cup liver water or soup stock
1 tablespoon butter

Mix potatoes with egg and fat. Cook liver in boiling salted water about 20 minutes. Drain, saving water. Chop liver with seasonings and onion. Place in greased casserole; add liquid. Cover lightly with potato mixture, dot with butter and bake in moderate oven (350°F.) 40 to 50 minutes or until top is browned. Serves 2.

For a really hilarious dinner nothing equals this schoolmate of Donald Duck

BAKED HAM AND RICE

1 slice ham, 1½ inches thick
  (about 2¼ pounds)
2½ cups rice, 1 quart milk

Trim off part of ham fat, cut ham into 6 pieces and brown lightly in a hot frying pan. Place ½ of rice in baking dish, cover with ham and sprinkle remaining rice over top. Pour a little of the milk into pan in which ham was browned. Stir well and pour into baking dish. Add remaining milk. Bake in (350°F.) oven 1 hour. Serves 6.

MACARONI AND CHEESE

2 cups broken whole-wheat
  macaroni
8 cups boiling water
2 teaspoons salt
2 cups grated aged cheese
¼ teaspoon salt, Dash pepper
1¼ cups scalded milk

Cook macaroni in boiling salted water 15 minutes. Drain and rinse in hot water. Place in layers in buttered baking dish sprinkling each layer with cheese, salt and pepper. Pour milk around edge and cook in a moderate oven (350°F.) 30 minutes. Serves 6.

The older children will enjoy a pastry crust on chicken and vegetable casserole.

CASSEROLE OF CHICKEN AND VEGETABLES

4- to 5-pound stewing chicken
Salt and pepper
Flour
Fat for frying
3 carrots, diced
1 cup diced celery
1 medium onion, diced
1 green pepper, diced
1 cup hot water
2 tablespoons fat
1½ tablespoons flour
½ teaspoon salt
1 cup milk

Cut chicken into serving portions. Season with salt and pepper, dredge with flour and brown in fat. Place in casserole. Add vegetables and hot water. Cover and cook in slow oven (275°F.) until tender, about 3 hours. Add more water if necessary. Melt fat, blend in flour and salt, add milk and cook until thickened, stirring constantly. Add vegetables to sauce and serve with chicken. Serves 8 to 10.

CHICKEN AND BROWN RICE

3½-pound chicken
Salt
1 cup diced celery
3 quarts boiling water
1 cup uncooked brown rice

Clean chicken and cut into serving portions. Season with salt and let stand several hours. Place chicken and celery in kettle, add boiling water and cook slowly 1½ hours or until almost tender. Add rice and cook 30 minutes longer, until tender. Serves 6.

FISH-POTATO CASSEROLE

2 cups mashed potatoes
2 cups salmon, skinned, boned and flaked
½ teaspoon salt
¼ cup grated American cheese

Mix potatoes, salmon and salt together. Transfer to greased casserole, sprinkle cheese over top and bake in moderate oven (350°F.) 30 minutes or until heated through and browned. Serves 6. Use flaked cooked perch, whitefish or other fish instead of salmon. Add minced parsley.

HUNGARIAN CHICKEN

6 onions, sliced
2 tablespoons fat
1 tablespoon paprika
4- to 5-pound chicken, cut into serving portions
Salt
3 tomatoes
3 green peppers, sliced

Brown onions in fat, add paprika and chicken. Season, add a small amount of water and simmer about 1 hour. Add tomatoes and sliced peppers, cover and cook until chicken is tender, about 1 more hour. Serves 4.

STUFFED DRIED FRUITS

16 dates
16 nuts
Brown sugar, coconut or nuts

Remove stones from moist, plump dates. Then place 1 nut in each date. Roll in sugar, coconut or chopped nuts. Makes 16.

Stuff dates or steamed figs, prunes, dried peaches, pears or apricots with nuts, peanut butter or cheese.

Mix enough confectioners' sugar with ¼ cup peanut butter to make a stiff paste. Use as stuffing for dates or stoned prunes.

Chop ½ cup raisins, ½ cup figs and ½ cup nuts and mix thoroughly. Stuff dates or prunes.

Chop ½ cup prunes, ½ cup raisins and ½ cup nuts; mix thoroughly and use as stuffing for steamed figs or apricots.

LOLLYPOPS

1 cup sugar
⅓ cup light corn sirup
⅔ cup water
6-8 drops peppermint oil
Vegetable coloring

Mix sugar, corn sirup and water, cook over low heat, stirring until sugar is dissolved and mixture boils. Continue boiling without stirring, until a small amount is very brittle when dropped into cold water (310°). Wash away crystals from sides of pan with a damp cloth. Cook slowly at end so sirup will not discolor. Remove from heat, add flavor and color and stir only to mix. Drop sirup quickly from tip of spoon onto flat greased surface, press one end of wooden skewer into edge of each lollypop. When firm but still warm, loosen from surface to prevent cracking.

COCONUT BALLS

¼ cup sweetened condensed milk
2 teaspoons orange juice
2 teaspoons grated orange rind
2½ cups sifted confectioners' sugar
1 cup shredded coconut

Mix milk, orange juice and orange rind. Add confectioners' sugar gradually, mixing well. Drop from teaspoon into shredded coconut and roll into small balls. Chill several hours. Makes 24.

FRUIT SLICES

1 cup prunes
1 cup dried figs
1 cup seeded raisins
½ cup nut meats
Toasted coconut or chopped nuts

Cover prunes with water and boil 10 minutes. Drain, cool and remove pits. Rinse figs and raisins, drain and dry thoroughly. Grind fruits and nuts fine. Blend thoroughly, divide and shape into rolls about 1½ inches in diameter. Roll in coconut or nuts. Chill before slicing. Makes about 50 pieces.

CHOCOLATE POPCORN BALLS

2 cups sugar
½ cup water
Pinch cream of tartar
1 teaspoon vanilla extract
½ teaspoon almond extract
8 cups popcorn
Melted coating chocolate

Cook the sugar, water, and cream of tartar to 260°, or to the hard-ball stage; then add the flavors. Pour a portion of the sirup over the popcorn and let the remainder stand in a warm place.
Form into small popcorn balls, then dip them into the remaining sirup, one at a time. Lay on waxed paper to become firm; then dip into melted chocolate.

PEANUT-BUTTER TAFFY

¾ cup sugar
1 cup maple sirup
½ cup corn sirup
¼ teaspoon salt
⅓ cup water
2 ounces (squares) chocolate, melted
¼ cup peanut butter

Cook sugar, sirups, salt and water over low heat, stirring constantly until sugar is dissolved. Cook to 288° or to soft-crack stage. Add chocolate, pour into greased pan. When cool enough to pull spread with peanut butter, fold over and pull enough to mix peanut butter thoroughly with candy. Cut into pieces and wrap each piece in waxed paper.

UNCOOKED FUDGE

2 ounces (squares) chocolate
¼ cup butter
3 tablespoons cream
2½ cups confectioners' sugar
1 egg, beaten
1 teaspoon vanilla
¼ cup chopped nuts
4 dates, chopped (optional)

Melt chocolate with butter. Add remaining ingredients and beat thoroughly Pour into buttered pan and chill 6 hours. Cut into squares. Makes 64 pieces.

EASTER EGGS

½ cup sweetened condensed milk
¼ cup brown sugar
½ teaspoon vanilla
1 cup sifted confectioners' sugar

Blend milk and brown sugar thoroughly. Cook over boiling water 4 minutes or until mixture thickens. Remove from heat and add vanilla and confectioners' sugar gradually. Blend thoroughly. Form into eggs and decorate with tiny candies and fruits. Makes 2.

Lunch Box

125 Ideas for Lunch Boxes and Picnics

THE GOOD LUNCH

Lunch is the most neglected meal of the day. Often women nibble at leftovers, men swallow a hasty cup of coffee and a sandwich, children buy something sweet, and these things constitute their "lunch". But good nutrition is not limited to just one meal a day. It encompasses all meals. A good lunch takes planning and preparation. This is especially true if the lunch is carried and has to be packed at home. Check your lunches against this list and see that your nutrition plans are carried out.

1. A good lunch is fresh. Your score is zero if you make up sandwiches the night before. Keep a plentiful supply of fresh fillings in covered jars in the icebox, other necessities on the pantry shelf, and use the mass production method of assembly.

2. A good lunch is attractive. Wrap sandwiches neatly in waxed paper or cellophane, use waxed cups for salads, fruits and desserts, thermos bottle for hot or cold liquids and glass screw-top jars for a hot stew or main dish (paper towels make a good insulation around jars).

3. All good lunches are balanced nutritionally. Check to see if your lunch contains each of the following: A serving of vegetables, raw or cooked, providing needed vitamins. This is accomplished by using lettuce, romaine, escarole, endive or watercress in the sandwiches or by using a vegetable filling. Vegetables can also be used in a variety of salads and as a relish such as celery curls, olives, radishes or carrot sticks. A serving of meat, fish, cheese or egg is essential.

The growing child, the laborer and the working girl require extra protein for tissue building. In a packed lunch, meat is ordinarily in the form of a sandwich filling, but there are many hot dishes that are suitable for carrying. They can add greatly to the variety and nutrition of the lunch. The daily fruit requirement can be included in an attractive salad or dessert. Whole fruit, raw or baked, and various fruit puddings are easy to prepare, nutritious and add a sweet satisfying finish to lunch. For a change and a surprise, tarts, fruit cakes, turnovers and dumplings travel well and have added attraction of being readily eaten. These too can fill some of the nutrition requirements instead of being just a sweet. As for the beverage, milk is necessary for children. However, for those reluctant milk drinkers, the milk requirement is easily camouflaged by packing flavored milk drinks, creamed soups, puddings, custards, scalloped dishes or creamed dishes. The adult too should have milk included even though it is not served as a beverage.

Lunches packed every day
Should be planned
To have them pay

PICNICS

For the picnic prepared at home, assemble in one place a thermos jug, basket, paper plates, cups, tablecloth, napkins, flatware, bottle opener and knife. If some cooking is to be done, add matches, long-handled skewers, hatchet, 2 kettles, dish towel and cloth, pot holders and old newspapers. It is best to carry your own wood and remember to douse your fire with water until you are sure it is completely out.

PLAN WELL

Prepare at home all foods needed for 4 people: 2 ham slices, 8 carrots, 1 stalk celery, 1 bunch radishes, 4 slices pineapple, 1 head lettuce, jar of mayonnaise, 8 rolls, apple pie, cheese, milk, cream, sugar, butter and coffee. Sister should clean all vegetables. Make carrot sticks, store with radishes in glass screw-top jar with chipped ice. Wrap cleaned celery in damp towel. Drain can of pineapple and place slices in a wide-mouthed paper jar.

Brother should fill small jars with cream, sugar and butter. Cover tops of salt and pepper shakers with waxed paper held by a rubber band. Wrap quart bottle of milk in heavy newspaper to keep. Dad will want to gather necessary utensils. Pack basket as foods are ready. Check items off. Mother has cooked ham slices (pack hot or cold), baked pie and cubed and wrapped the cheese. She makes coffee and pours into thermos jug. All should aid in straightening the kitchen and then off to the picnic where everyone will have a good care-free time.

Plan a picnic that will tick
Wind the Kebobs on a stick
Bacon burgers on a bun
Add relish as they're done

SOME NEW BREADS

BREAD-ON-A-STICK

1 recipe Baking Powder Biscuit

Prepare baking powder biscuit dough, using a little less liquid than is required for oven biscuits. Roll into 5x1-inch strips and wind around floured stick. (Be sure stick is long enough.) Hold over hot coals, turning frequently until bread can be removed from stick easily. Choose a green stick of hickory, apple, birch or maple. Makes 14 bread sticks.

CRUSTY PICNIC RING

1 cup lukewarm water
3 tablespoons melted shortening
2 teaspoons sugar
2 teaspoons salt, 1 cake yeast
1 egg, 3 cups flour

Combine as in Speedy Pan Rolls. Turn into greased 9-inch ring mold. Cut into 1-inch slices with well-greased knife. Let rise in warm place (80-85°F.) until light, about 45 minutes. Bake at 400°F. for 35 minutes.

SPEEDY PAN ROLLS

1 cup lukewarm water
1/3 cup melted shortening
1 tablespoon sugar
1½ teaspoons salt
2 cakes yeast
1 egg, beaten
3½ cups flour

Combine first 4 ingredients. Add yeast and mix well. Blend in beaten egg, add flour gradually. Mix until dough is blended but soft. Roll out on a well-floured board and fit into greased 8x12-inch pan. Cut dough with greased knife into 1x4-inch rectangles or 4-inch squares. Follow knife with brush dipped in melted butter, then brush tops. Let rise in warm place (80-85°F.) until double in bulk, about 30 minutes. Bake at 425°F. for 20 minutes. Makes 24 finger rolls or 6 square buns.

BUTTERSCOTCH BREAD

2 eggs, beaten
2 cups brown sugar
3 tablespoons melted shortening
4 cups sifted flour
1 teaspoon baking soda
1½ teaspoons baking powder
½ teaspoon salt
2 cups sour milk or buttermilk
1 cup chopped English walnuts

Beat eggs and beat in sugar gradually. Add shortening. Sift flour, soda, baking powder and salt together. Add to egg mixture alternately with milk. Add nuts, mixing only enough to dampen flour. Pour into greased loaf pan and bake in moderate oven (350°F.) 45 minutes, or until bread shrinks slightly from the sides of the pan. Makes 2 (1-pound) loaves.

A string shopper is a bright idea for carrying lunch in the morning and groceries at night

SANDWICH FILLINGS

Sandwiches, whether for picnic or lunch box, should be fresh, tasty, nutritious, well-filled and attractively wrapped. Remember that the sandwich must contribute to the day's good nutrition. Select and make fillings with care and keep a variety of them always on hand and fresh. Small screw-top jars for storage in refrigerator are handy. The supply can be replenished during morning cooking hours. Use wholegrain breads frequently in addition to other varieties. Pack lettuce or other greens in containers, waxed paper or cellophane, to be added to sandwiches at time of eating.

CHEESE

½ cup grated American cheese
¼ cup minced cooked bacon
6 drops onion juice
1 tablespoon minced pickles
3 tablespoons mayonnaise

1 cup grated American cheese
3 tablespoons tomato catchup
2 drops Tabasco sauce
1 teaspoon minced onion
2 tablespoons cream

½ cup grated American cheese
2 tablespoons chopped pimiento
1 tablespoon minced onion
2 tablespoons minced sweet pickle
2 hard-cooked eggs, chopped

¾ cup grated American cheese
5 tablespoons deviled ham
½ teaspoon Worcestershire sauce
4 tablespoons cream

1 cup grated cheese
4 tablespoons chopped sweet pickle
Mayonnaise to bind mixture

½ cup Camembert
8 slices cooked, drained and minced
  bacon

A sandwich assembly line saves time and effort

½ cup grated American cheese
8 small stuffed olives, chopped
1 hard-cooked egg, chopped
½ teaspoon minced onion
1 tablespoon melted butter
1 teaspoon lemon juice

¾ cup grated American cheese
¼ cup ground ham
¼ teaspoon Worcestershire sauce
2 tablespoons cream
2 tablespoons mayonnaise

½ cup ground boiled ham
½ cup ground American cheese
2 tablespoons ground pickle
½ teaspoon ground onion
Mayonnaise to moisten

⅔ cup Limburger cheese
⅓ cup chopped onion

½ cup cottage cheese
6 tablespoons minced celery
8 minced green olives
5 tablespoons minced green onion
Salt, pepper, paprika

4 ounces Limburger cheese
¼ cup butter
2 tablespoons grated onion
¼ teaspoon salt

CREAM CHEESE

½ cup cream cheese
½ cup apricot purée

½ cup cream cheese
½ cup Orange Marmalade

½ cup cream or cottage cheese
½ cup chopped cooked prunes

CREAM CHEESE—Cont.

½ cup cream cheese
1 minced orange
1 teaspoon grated onion
⅛ teaspoon salt

1 cup cream cheese
⅓ cup minced nut meats

½ cup cream cheese
¼ cup chopped olives
¼ cup chopped nut meats

3 ounces cream cheese
½ cup minced pimientos
6 tablespoons mayonnaise
½ cup minced nut meats
⅛ teaspoon salt

¼ cup cream cheese
½ cup peanut butter
¼ cup mayonnaise

¾ cup cream cheese
¼ cup grated uncooked carrot
4 drops lemon juice
Salt and pepper

1 cup cream cheese
2 tablespoons minced chives

6 ounces cream cheese
4 tablespoons butter
1 teaspoon onion juice
½ teaspoon sage
½ teaspoon savory
1 teaspoon celery salt
2 tablespoons lemon juice

3 ounces cream cheese
½ cup minced stuffed olives
¼ cup mayonnaise
1 tablespoon prepared mustard
1 teaspoon minced onion

CHICKEN

1 cup finely chopped chicken and
   giblets
½ cup chopped toasted almonds
1 teaspoon grated onion
½ teaspoon curry powder
½ cup mayonnaise

2 cups diced cooked chicken
½ cup chopped celery
½ cup diced cucumbers
2 tablespoons capers
¾ cup mayonnaise

*Variety in breads, shapes
and fillings adds interest*

CHICKEN—Cont.

¾ cup minced cooked chicken
⅓ cup crushed pineapple
3 tablespoons mayonnaise

1 cup ground cooked chicken
¼ cup cream
3 tablespoons sweet pickle relish

1 cup mashed cooked chicken livers
2 tablespoons minced cooked bacon
4 drops Tabasco sauce
1 tablespoon lemon juice

EGG

Hard-cooked eggs chopped and combined with:

Chopped boned sardines or anchovies, French dressing.
Chopped crisp bacon or boiled ham, mayonnaise.
Chopped olives, cooked salad dressing.
Chopped pickle, mayonnaise.
Diced cooked chicken, meat or fish, chopped pickles, mayonnaise.
Minced celery, pimiento, mayonnaise.
Minced onion, mayonnaise.
Minced pickle, minced cooked tongue, mayonnaise.
Minced pimientos, diced green pepper, chili sauce, mayonnaise.
Sliced tomato, salt, pepper, mayonnaise.

EGG AND VEGETABLE

4 hard-cooked eggs, mashed
Chopped watercress
Mayonnaise to moisten

3 slices peeled tomato, chopped
1 hard-cooked egg, chopped
2 tablespoons minced pickle
2 tablespoons minced onion
⅛ teaspoon salt, Dash pepper
2 tablespoons softened butter

2 hard-cooked eggs, chopped
1 cup chopped uncooked spinach
3 tablespoons mayonnaise

2 hard-cooked eggs, chopped
½ can condensed vegetable soup
1 teaspoon lemon juice
4 to 6 tablespoons mayonnaise
1 cup shredded carrots

MEAT

1 cup minced cooked ham
½ cup seedless raisins
1 teaspoon capers
Mayonnaise to moisten
Grind ingredients together:

1¼ cups chopped cooked lamb
½ teaspoon salt
¼ teaspoon pepper
½ tablespoon minced onion
1 teaspoon minced mint leaves
1 tablespoon lemon juice

¾ cup liver sausage
3 tablespoons minced pickle
1 teaspoon minced onion
3 tablespoons mayonnaise
¼ cup minced celery

1 cup chopped cooked veal
3 tablespoons minced celery
1 teaspoon lemon juice
½ teaspoon prepared mustard
Salt and pepper
2 tablespoons mayonnaise

½ cup mashed cooked Lima beans
¾ cup ground cooked meat
¼ cup minced pickle
Few drops Worcestershire sauce
Mayonnaise to moisten

PEANUT BUTTER

¾ cup peanut butter
¼ cup mayonnaise

½ cup peanut butter
⅓ cup mashed ripe banana
¼ cup mayonnaise

½ cup peanut butter
2 tablespoons chopped green pepper
1 teaspoon minced onion
2 tablespoons chopped celery
¼ cup mayonnaise

½ cup peanut butter
½ cup mayonnaise
3 tablespoons chopped pickle

½ cup peanut butter
½ cup ground raisins
3 tablespoons mayonnaise

⅔ cup chopped cooked prunes
⅓ cup peanut butter
1 tablespoon pickle relish

½ cup peanut butter
½ cup drained crushed pineapple

SEA FOOD

¾ cup flaked crab meat
1 tablespoon minced pimiento
2 tablespoons chopped cucumber
2 tablespoons mayonnaise
1 teaspoon minced chives

1 cup flaked salmon
4 tablespoons mayonnaise
3 tablespoons chopped sweet pickle
2 teaspoons salt, Dash pepper

1 cup mashed sardines
3 tablespoons mayonnaise
4 tablespoons chili sauce
5 tablespoons chopped pickled beets

1 cup cleaned cooked shrimp
¼ teaspoon salt
⅛ teaspoon cayenne
1 cup butter, softened
¼ cup lemon juice (or less)

½ cup mashed tuna or salmon
2 tablespoons mayonnaise
1 tablespoon lemon juice
2 tablespoons chopped stuffed olives
1 teaspoon Worcestershire sauce

VEGETABLES

¾ cup mashed baked beans
½ cup applesauce

1 cup mashed baked beans
¼ cup mayonnaise
2 tablespoons piccalilli
¼ cup minced celery

1 cup grated uncooked carrots
3 tablespoons mayonnaise
¼ teaspoon salt

1 cup minced celery
¼ cup mayonnaise
½ teaspoon salt

1 cup chopped cucumber
3 tablespoons mayonnaise
Salt

¾ cup sliced radishes
¼ cup watercress leaves, minced
3 tablespoons mayonnaise

Shredded cabbage, grated pineapple, mayonnaise.

STEAK IN SALT

5 pounds coarse salt
Water
1 (2-inch) steak

Wet salt thoroughly with water and place ⅓ of it in a large heavy paper bag. Place steak in bag and add remaining salt so that there will be a 1-inch layer all around meat. Bury filled bag in a bed of glowing coals. Roast 25 to 35 minutes. This makes a medium-rare steak. Break away salt crust and steak is ready to serve. The meat does not become salty. Allow ¾ to 1 pound steak per person.

If steak is to be roasted in an outdoor oven place filled bag in shallow pan in very hot oven. It is not advisable to roast steak by this method in a range oven.

Or wrap 1-inch cubes of steak with bacon. Alternate on skewers with apple slices, onion or tomato.

SAUSAGES AND SAUERKRAUT

1 (No. 2) can sauerkraut
1 (12-ounce) can sausages

Heat sauerkraut and sausages in Dutch oven in campfire 20 minutes. Serves 3 or 4.

CHEESE BOBS

6 (1-inch) cubes American cheese
6 strips bacon

Wrap each cheese cube with a strip of bacon and broil on the end of a stick or fork over coals until bacon is crisp and cheese melted. Serves 6.

Hot foods are sure to give added zest to appetizing lunch combinations

*Wrap your lunches neatly
and they will be easy to eat*

DEVILED-FRIED CHICKEN

3 to 3½-pound chicken
¾ cup flour
3 teaspoons dry mustard
3 teaspoons salt
¼ teaspoon black pepper
Milk for dipping
Lard for frying
1 clove garlic
1 tablespoon Worcestershire sauce

Prepare chicken for frying. Sift next 4 ingredients together. Dip chicken in milk and then in flour mixture. Fry in fat which has had garlic and sauce added to it. When golden brown and almost tender, drain and bake in uncovered dish at 350°F. for 20 minutes. Drain and cool.

FOLDOVERS

½ cup scalded milk
¼ cup shortening
2 teaspoons sugar
2 teaspoons salt
¼ cup water
1 cake yeast
2 eggs, beaten
3 cups flour

Combine first 5 ingredients, cool, proceed as in Speedy Pan Rolls. Roll ⅛ inch thick and cut with 5-inch round cutter. Place 2 tablespoons of meat, fruit or nut mixture on ½ of each round. Moisten edges, fold over, seal with fork, slash top and let rise in a warm place until double in bulk, about 1 hour. Bake at 425°F. for 12 minutes. Makes 12.

CAMP JAMBALAYA

1 cup rice
1 onion, chopped
2 tablespoons fat
8 frankfurters
¾ cup tomatoes
1 teaspoon minced parsley
1 cup boiling water
Salt

Wash rice and let soak 1 hour, then drain. Fry onion in fat until tender but not brown. Cut frankfurters into ¾-inch slices and brown in fat. Add tomatoes, parsley and water. When bubbling, stir in rice slowly. Cover tightly and cook slowly.

Omit frankfurters and add 1 cup 1 x 1-inch pieces smoked ham.

QUICK BAKED BEANS

1 (No. 2) can baked beans
3 tablespoons brown sugar
2 teaspoons butter
¼ teaspoon dry mustard
⅛ pound salt pork

Turn beans into baking dish. Add next 3 ingredients. Press pork into beans, rind side up. Bake at 350°F. 20 minutes.

PICNIC EGGS

4 hard-cooked eggs
¼ teaspoon salt
½ teaspoon dry mustard
Dash cayenne
1 teaspoon vinegar
1 tablespoon melted butter

Cut eggs into halves. Remove yolks and mash. Season yolks with salt, mustard, cayenne, vinegar and butter. Refill whites with mixture, press halves together and wrap each egg in a square of waxed paper; twist ends to keep the halves in place.

VARIATIONS

If desired, add 3 drops onion juice and 1 tablespoon mayonnaise or thousand island dressing.

Instead of seasoned yolks, use any of the following mixtures to fill egg whites:

Anchovies, minced parsley and egg yolks
Caviar with lemon juice
Chicken livers, sautéed
Chopped celery mixed with mayonnaise or salad dressing
Chopped stuffed or ripe olives and cheese
Chopped onions and mushrooms browned in butter
Crisp bacon, mashed egg yolk, minced parsley and mayonnaise
Egg yolk, chopped pickle and mayonnaise
Egg yolk, mayonnaise and Worcestershire sauce
Ground chicken or other meats
Ground seasoned fish
Green and red peppers, cheese and egg yolk
Liver sausage
Mashed cooked vegetables, as asparagus, peas, spinach and beets
Minced ham
Pâté de foie gras
Sardine paste

Picnic eggs are always a welcome treat for lunch or for camping out

SALAD SUGGESTIONS

Combine ingredients and add French dressing or mayonnaise as desired.

Drained crushed or cubed pineapple, shredded cabbage, chopped green pepper or pimiento, nut meats, French dressing or mayonnaise.

Pineapple wedges, chopped cranberries, tart apple cubes, mayonnaise or French dressing.

Pineapple wedges, seedless grapes, orange segments, mayonnaise or French dressing.

Sliced pineapple with sliced cucumbers — French dressing or Roquefort French dressing.

Chopped watercress or lettuce, sliced radishes, cucumbers, celery, chopped tomatoes, mayonnaise or French dressing.

Shredded carrots, sliced celery, mayonnaise.

Diced apples, sliced celery, chopped nut meats, mayonnaise.

Shredded carrots, raisins, French dressing or mayonnaise.

Avocado, tart apple and romaine.

Chicory, escarole and grapefruit.

Escarole, Chinese cabbage and watercress.

Chinese cabbage, tomato, radish and olives.

Endive, carrot sticks and grapefruit.

Shredded carrot, Chinese cabbage and romaine.

Orange, sweet onion and romaine.

Diced potato, celery, cucumber, green pepper and pimiento.

Green peas, mint leaves, lettuce.

Lettuce, fresh spinach, watercress, radishes, carrot sticks.

Cabbage, carrot sticks, diced apples, shredded green pepper.

Celery, carrots, peppers and peas are easily tossed together to make a healthful addition to any lunch box

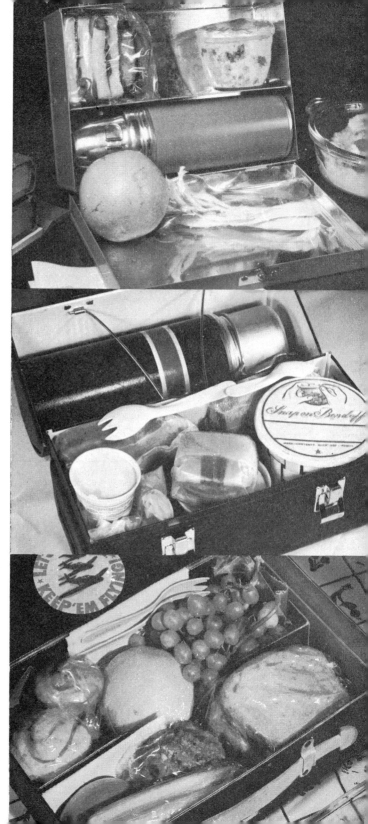

GRAHAM CRACKER CUSTARD

3 graham crackers, crushed
1½ cups scalded milk
2 eggs, slightly beaten
3 tablespoons sugar
Dash salt
½ teaspoon vanilla
9 marshmallows, quartered

Soften cracker crumbs in milk; add eggs, sugar, salt and vanilla. Fold in marshmallows. Pour into custard cups and bake at 350°F. 30 minutes. Chill. Serves 4.

STEWED DRIED FRUIT

Modern methods of processing dried fruits at the packing plants now make overnight soaking and long, slow simmering of dried fruits unnecessary. Count cooking time after water boils and keep at a brisk boil, adding more water if needed. It is usually best to add sugar only for last 5 minutes cooking.

STEWED APRICOTS AND PRUNES—Use ¼ pound prunes and ¼ pound apricots and cook 45 to 50 minutes.

STEWED PRUNES AND RAISINS—Use ½ cup raisins with ¼ pound prunes and cook 45 to 50 minutes.

DRIED FRUIT TIME TABLE

Dried apples and apricots require 40 minutes.
Dried figs—20 to 30 minutes.
Dried peaches—50 minutes.
Dried pears—40 minutes.
Dried prunes—45 to 50 minutes.
Dried raisins—10 minutes.

LINGONBERRY SAUCE

(Mountain Cranberries)
2 cups lingonberries
¾ cup sugar
¼ cup water

Wash berries, drain, pick over and wash again. Add sugar and water and heat to boiling. Simmer 10 minutes. Serve hot or cold. Makes about 2 cups.

SPICED PEACH BETTY

2 cups fresh diced peaches
1 cup brown sugar
1 cup sifted flour
⅛ teaspoon nutmeg
¼ teaspoon cinnamon
½ cup butter

Place peaches in greased baking dish. Mix dry ingredients together, cut in butter and sprinkle over peaches. Bake in moderate oven (350°F.) about 40 minutes. Serves 6.

MAPLE TAPIOCA CREAM

2 tablespoons butter
1 cup brown sugar
2 tablespoons quick-cooking tapioca
2 cups milk
2 eggs, separated
¼ teaspoon salt
1 teaspoon maple flavoring

Heat butter and ¼ cup sugar slowly. Stir until it boils and cook about 1 minute or until sugar is slightly caramelized. Add tapioca and milk. Cook until tapioca is clear, then pour slowly onto 2 egg yolks mixed with salt. Cook in double boiler and stir occasionally until thickened. Remove from heat and pour mixture over egg whites beaten until stiff with remaining brown sugar. Stir and add flavoring when slightly cool. Serves 8.

For lunch box, pour into jars before chilling. When cool cover tightly.

RAISIN CREAM TARTS

½ recipe Plain Pastry
2 eggs
1 cup sugar
1 teaspoon cinnamon
½ teaspoon allspice
¼ teaspoon salt
1 tablespoon flour
2 cups sour cream
1 cup seedless raisins

Line tart pans with pastry. Beat eggs slightly; combine sugar, spices, salt and flour; add cream, eggs and raisins. Pour into unbaked tart shells. Bake in hot oven (425°F.) 10 minutes, reduce temperature to moderate (350°F.) and bake 20 to 25 minutes longer or until filling is firm. Makes 6 tarts.

Fruits, tarts, and desserts in jars provide many needed vitamins

BLACK CHERRY COOLER

1 cup black pitted cherries
1 cup pineapple wedges
¼ cup pineapple sirup
1 tablespoon lime juice

Chill all ingredients and combine. Serves 4.
Use sweetened red cherries instead of black.

SCALLOPED APPLES

6 large tart apples
¼ teaspoon salt
4 tablespoons lemon juice
¾ pound peanut brittle, crushed fine

Pare apples, slice and add salt, lemon juice and peanut brittle. Place in greased casserole and bake in slow oven (325°F.) 1 hour. Serves 8.

WATERMELON STICKS

Cut melon into strips and pack in a cold container. Serve with salt and pieces of lemon. Eat with the fingers.

RAISIN AND NUT CLUSTERS

½ pound semisweet chocolate
⅛ teaspoon salt
1¼ cups seedless raisins
½ cup nut meats

Melt chocolate in top of double boiler. Remove from hot water. Let stand about 5 minutes to partially cool. Add salt, raisins and nut meats. Blend well. Drop from teaspoon onto a sheet of waxed paper. Makes 30 pieces.

For school, children will appreciate oranges, peaches, bananas and cherries

GRAPEFRUIT PUNCH

2 lemons
¾ cup sugar
2 cups water
2½ cups grapefruit juice
1½ cups Grape Juice

Slice lemons; boil with sugar and water 7 minutes; cool. Add grapefruit juice and grape juice. Chill. Makes about 1½ quarts.

SPICED PINEAPPLE CUP

2 cups pineapple juice
1 stick cinnamon
6 to 8 cloves

Combine ingredients, heat slowly to boiling, strain and serve hot or cold. Serves 2.

MIXED VEGETABLE JUICE

3 cups canned mixed vegetable juice
1 tablespoon lemon juice
¼ teaspoon salt
Dash cayenne or Worcestershire sauce

Combine all ingredients and chill thoroughly. Shake or stir well before serving. Serves 3.

TOMATO BEVERAGE

4 cups cooked tomatoes
1 teaspoon grated lemon rind
3 tablespoons lemon juice
½ teaspoon salt
Few drops Worcestershire sauce

Press tomatoes through sieve, add remaining ingredients and chill. Shake or stir well before serving. Serves 4 to 6.

Add 1 tablespoon tomato catchup instead of Worcestershire sauce.

Whether the beverage is hot or cold, a thermos will be handy as well as safe

Meals for Two

100 Menus and Recipes for Two

Off to a Good Start

COOKING EQUIP-MENT FOR TWO

Knives—2 case, 2 paring, 1 butcher, 1 bread, 1 chopping
Forks—1 large (2-tine), 2 small
Spatulas—1 narrow, 1 wide
Spoons—large (2 wooden, 1 metal), 1 slotted, 3 teaspoons, 2 sets measuring spoons
Standard measuring cups—2 or 3
French ball cutter, Egg slicer
Apple corer, Onion chopper
Kitchen shears, Knife sharpener
Long handled rubber scraper
Bottle opener, Corkscrew
Can opener, Pancake turner
Fruit reamer, Doughnut cutter
Cookie cutters—1 large, 1 small
Egg beaters—1 large, 1 small and 1 whisk, Cream whipper

Lure yourself into the kitchen with a shining array of practical equipment for mixing and baking

Pastry blender, Cutting board
Rolling pin, Food chopper
Flour sifter, small
Potato masher, Sieve
Strainers—1 large, 1 small
Salt and pepper shakers
Chopping bowl, small
Pastry canvas
Colander
Frying pans with covers (6-inch, 10-inch)
Griddle
Double boiler, 1-pint, 1-quart
Small teapot, Small teakettle
Tea ball
Small coffee-making equipment
Thermometers—oven, meat, deep-fat
Deep-fat frying kettle
Cake racks
Breadbox, Cakebox
Dutch oven, Top-of-stove oven
Toaster, Waffle baker
Waxed paper

Glass jars for keeping supplies and spices
Canister set
Pot holders
Grater
Mixing bowls, 1 large, 1 medium, 2 small, or nest
Custard cups, Small casserole
Piepans, 1 (6-inch), 1 (9-inch)
Loaf pans, deep (8x4 inch) 2
Cake pans, layer 2 (8-inch) Square shallow (8x8 inch)
Muffin pans, 2 sets of 6
Paper baking cups
Small spring-form pan
Tube pan (9-inch)
Small baking sheet
Small ring mold
Individual molds
Covered refrigerator dishes
Saucepans with covers, 3 sizes
Waterless saucepans, 1-quart, 2-quart, 3-quart
Small roasting pan

BUYING FOR TWO

FOOD	AMOUNT
BEEF	
Liver	¾ pound
Roast beef, rolled	1 rib
Chuck	1 pound
Round	1 pound
Sirloin Steak	1¼ pounds
Ground	¾ pound
LAMB	
Chops	2
Shanks	2
PORK	
Bacon	½ to 1 pound
Chops	2
Ham, slice	1 pound
VEAL	
Cutlets	1½ pounds
Kidneys	2
Chops	2
Shoulder	1 to 1½ pounds
POULTRY	
Broiler or fryer	1
Chicken breasts	2
Livers	¾ pound
FISH	1 to 1½ pounds
VEGETABLES, fresh	
Asparagus	1 pound
Beans, Lima	1 pound
Beans, string	1 pound
Broccoli	1½ pounds
Cabbage	1 small head
Carrots	1 bunch
Cauliflower	1 small head
Celery	1 bunch
Lettuce	1 small head
Mushrooms	½ pound
Onions	3 pounds
Peas	1 pound
Potatoes	5 pounds
Spinach	1 pound
Sweetpotatoes	2 pounds
Tomatoes	1 pound
Turnip, yellow	1 small
FRUIT	
Apples	2 pounds
Bananas	1½ pounds
Grapefruit	2
Oranges	12

COOKING TIME SAVERS

Cook enough cereal for 2 meals. Cover leftover cereal with a small amount of cold water and place in refrigerator. Stir and reheat for second meal; the flavor is as good as if freshly cooked.

Enough homemade soup may be cooked for several days and variety given by adding leftover vegetable waters and chopped vegetables or different soup accessories.

Cook sufficient dried fruit for several meals. Use part of it for sauces, for fruit whips, for desserts or for glazes on tarts.

Puddings made in quantities for 4 save time. Add chopped nuts and whipped cream the second time or serve with a sauce.

Bake at least 4 apples at a time. Use 2 for the evening's dessert, the remainder as a breakfast fruit.

Cook vegetables for more than 1 meal. Serve them the second time with a cream sauce or in salads.

Small roasts may be used if planned for 2 or more meals. At least once they may be served cold.

Liver and kidney should be served once or twice a week.

Chopped liver may be prepared for 2 meals. Serve it the second time in a casserole with noodles.

AMOUNTS PER SERVING

For soups, allow from ½ to 1 cup for each person, depending on kind of soup.

For desserts, allow from ½ to ¾ cup for each serving.

For creamed dishes, allow ⅔ cup for each serving and prepare enough to serve second portions.

STAPLE SUPPLIES

ACCESSORY FOODS

1 package unflavored gelatin
2 or more packages flavored gelatin
1 package tapioca
1 package cornstarch
1 bottle vanilla—2-ounce bottles are more economical than 1-ounce

BEVERAGES

Chocolate
1-pound can cocoa
Coffee
Tea—¼ to ½ pound tins

CANNED GOODS

Fish
Fruit
Evaporated milk
Soups, Vegetables

DRIED FRUITS

Apricots, Dates
Prunes, Raisins

FATS

Butter, Shortening

LEAVENING AGENTS

½-pound can baking powder
½-pound box baking soda

NUTS

Shelled pecans or walnuts

SPICES AND SEASONINGS

Allspice, ground
Basil, Bay leaves
Celery salt, Celery seed
Cinnamon—ground, stick
Cloves—ground, whole
Garlic salt, Ginger
Marjoram, Mustard
Nutmeg—ground

Your vegetable market will be one source of fresh and original buying ideas

Onion salt, Paprika
Pepper—black, white, cayenne
Sage, Salt
Tabasco sauce, Vinegar
Worcestershire sauce

SUGARS

Brown
Confectioners'
Granulated
Corn sirup, Honey
Molasses

VEGETABLES

Onions
Potatoes

NOTE: Where climate permits, buy cereals such as flour, all-purpose and cake; macaroni, rice, rolled oats and spaghetti; and vegetables such as dried Lima beans, navy beans, lentils and peas in larger quantities.

EMERGENCY SHELF

Keeping a well-stocked emergency shelf may be the secret of homemaker and hostess poise at all times. Package directions on the following list give good results:

Ready-to-mix piecrust, pancake flours, cake mixes and canned date and nut bread
Canned spaghetti, m a c a r o n i, baked beans
Canned meats, such as corned beef or spiced ham
Canned fish, such as salmon tuna, crab meat, shrimp
Chicken à la king
Chop suey vegetables
Condensed milk
Evaporated milk
Canned nuts
Anchovy paste
Corned beef hash
Pickles, Olives
Maraschino cherries

MEAL PLANNING

The modern homemaker knows that meal planning offers her a chance to use all her artistic ability and food knowledge to keep her family happy and healthy. Each day's meals should supply foods to build, repair and maintain the body, help prevent disease, furnish heat and energy as well as add to the joy of living. Modern standards require the following **musts** to be included in each day's menus:

MILK

Rich in vitamins A, B and D.
At least 1 pint for each adult, preferably 1 quart.

VEGETABLES AND FRUITS

Green leafy or yellow vegetables rich in vitamins A and C, 1 or more servings.
Tomatoes, oranges, grapefruit, and fresh cabbage, rich in vitamin C, 1 or more servings.
Potatoes, other vegetables or fruit, rich in vitamins A, B and C, 2 or more servings.

EGGS

Rich in vitamins A, B and D, 3 or 4 a week for each.

MEAT, FISH OR POULTRY

Lean meat, fish, poultry, rich in vitamin B, 1 or more servings. Liver or kidneys, rich in vitamins A and B, served at least once a week. Tripe is important for the same reason.

CEREALS AND BREAD

Whole-grain cereals and bread rich in vitamin B, at least 2 servings.

FATS

Fats eaten as butter and cream or cheese, rich in vitamin A.

SWEETS

Needed in small amounts.

Besides protecting health a good menu should take into account the contrasts in color, texture and flavor. The color of spinach is attractive with ham or tongue. Soft custard is a good texture to follow the crunchiness of raw carrots. A tart relish contrasts in flavor with sweet fritters.

Today's homemaker is well aware not only of the need of budgeting money, but also of budgeting her time and energy.

Meals planned for a week mean more efficient and economical purchasing, leftovers used to better advantage and simplified food preparation. Monotony is avoided when a record is kept of menus. One way to keep a menu record is in a loose-leaf notebook.

With whipped cream and a pastry tube turn a simple custard into an unusual New Year's novelty

Broil slices of Vienna sausage to border macaroni and cheese en casserole

DINNERS FOR GUESTS

Winter

Fruit Cocktail
Veal and Pork en Brochette, 902
Potatoes on the Half Shell
Broiled Mushrooms
Baking Powder Biscuits
Molded Cucumber Salad
Assorted Relishes
Coffee Pie
Coffee

Summer

Rolled Canapés
Chicken and Almond Mousse
Baked Tomatoes and Corn, 514
Parker House Rolls
Fresh Spinach Salad
Deep-dish Peach Pie
Iced Tea, Coffee or Punch

TOP-OF-THE-RANGE DINNERS

Winter

Hot Canapés
Beef Stew with Dumplings, 901
Cabbage Salad
Prune Whip
Coffee   Tea

Summer

Chilled Beet Soup
Breaded Veal Cutlet, 902
Sauerkraut
Salad Bowl
Sour Cream Spice Cookies
Strawberry Milk Mallobet
Iced Coffee

FISH DINNERS

Winter

French Onion Soup
Baked Fish, 314-317
Baked Potatoes
Broccoli with Hollandaise
Fruit Salad
Date and Nut Torte   Tea

Summer

Tomato Juice
Fish Cakes, 900
Spinach Ring
Buttered Peas
Strawberry Refrigerator Cake
Iced Coffee

BUSY DAY DINNERS

Winter

Jiffy Soup
Egg Frizzle, 287
Potato Pancakes
Buttered Spinach
Waldorf Salad
Apple Butter Refrigerator Roll
Coffee

Summer

Tomato Juice
Scrambled Eggs, 287-288
Anchovy Rolls
French Fried Potato Chips
Chicory Crown Salads
Strawberries and Cream

QUICK DINNERS

Winter

Broiled Steak, 901
Baked Rice Rings
Carrots and Peas
Lettuce Salad
Whipped Mayonnaise
Cherry Pie   Coffee

Summer

Frozen Sea Food Salad
Zucchini and Tomatoes
au Gratin, 519
Light Bran Muffins
Sliced Tomatoes
Stuffed Hard-cooked Eggs
Nut Toasties
Chocolate Coffee

BUFFET SUPPERS

Chicken Livers and
Mushrooms, 903
French Fried Shoestring Potatoes
Carrot Ring
Hard-cooked Eggs
Quick Nut Bread
Assorted Refrigerator Rolls
Balls on Picks
Sweet Pickles   Olives
Strawberry Shortcake
Mints
Iced Coffee   Punch

∨ ∨ ∨

Cold Meat and Cheese Platter
Salmon Salad
Deviled Eggs in Tomato Sauce, 308
Sourmilk Biscuits
Filled Pickles
Lettuce Cups
Sliced Tomatoes
Devil's Food Cake
Fresh Coconut Cream Frosting
Nuts   Candies
Coffee   Tea

OVEN DINNERS

Shepherd's Pie, 902
Spinach Soufflé
Hearts of Lettuce
French Dressing
Baked Custard
Coffee
∨ ∨ ∨
Jiffy Soup
Salmon Vegetable Casserole, 900
Filled Pickles
Vegetable Curls
Chocolate Refrigerator Cake
Milk   Coffee   Tea

DUTCH OVEN DINNER

Pot Roast with Vegetables, 353
Whole-wheat Muffins
Celery Curls
Sliced Tomatoes and Lettuce
Sour Cream Dressing
Pineapple Marlow
Delicate Butter Cookies
Tea   Coffee

PARTY LUNCHEONS

Fruit Cocktail
Sweetbreads with Mushrooms, 397
Cheese-Stuffed Pear Salad
Hot Rolls
Spongecake   Ice Cream
Coffee
∨ ∨ ∨
Cheese Fondue, 245
French Fried Potato Chips
Grapefruit and Almond Salad
Banana Bread
Lemon Chiffon Pie
Iced Tea

AFTERNOON TEA

Chicken Liver Canapés, 180,
214, 898
Candied Orange and
Grapefruit Peel
Nuts
Assorted Cookies
Tea   Coffee

*Bake pear halves with the
ham slice and fill the centers with crimson jelly*

FOR SUMMER

Lunches

Cheese Frankfurters, 245
Potato Salad
Olives   Radishes
Quick Chocolate Cake
Party Punch

∨ ∨ ∨

Baked Eggs in Tomato Cups, 293
Cheese Biscuits
Sliced Cucumbers
Leftover Cake Dessert
Milk   Buttermilk

Dinners

Skewered Lamb, 902
Buttered Spinach
Sliced Oranges on Lettuce
Sour Cream Dressing
Refrigerator Rolls
Peach Mousse
Iced Coffee

∨ ∨ ∨

Tomato Juice
Fried Chicken Breasts, 903
Mashed Potatoes
Cooked Cauliflower
Parker House Rolls
White Cake
Fresh Strawberries
Fruitade

FOR WINTER

Lunches

Scrambled Eggs, 287-288
Anchovy Rolls
Favorite Chocolate Cookies
Milk
∨ ∨ ∨
Potato Soup
Peanut-Butter Sandwiches with
Lettuce, 883
Orange Slices with Coconut
Tea

Dinners

Steak and Kidney Pie, 404
Carrots and Peas
Endive   French Dressing
Hot Rolls
Peach Pie
Tea
∨ ∨ ∨
Cheese Mushroom Soufflé, 306
Breaded Eggplant
Lettuce Salad, French Dressing
Nut Crisps
Milk   Tea
∨ ∨ ∨
Yellow Split Pea Soup
Liver Dumplings, 402
Stuffed Acorn Squash
Melba Toast
Cereal Flake Macaroons   Tea

CANAPÉ SUGGESTIONS

A canapé is an individual appetizer served either hot or cold. It is usually made of a small piece of attractively cut bread, toasted or fried on one side, spread with a highly seasoned food and attractively garnished. Spread toast rounds with anchovy butter. Cover with anchovy fillets and garnish with minced hard-cooked egg.

Spread toast strips with butter, then with cream cheese. Garnish with pimiento strips or sprinkle with sieved pimiento.

Spread toast squares with mixture of ¼ cup peanut butter, ¼ cup raspberry jam and 2 tablespoons butter.

Sauté 8 cooked cleaned shrimp in 2 tablespoons butter. Add ¼ teaspoon curry powder and ⅛ teaspoon dry mustard. Serve hot on small bread Croustades or packaged appetizer shells.

ANCHOVY BUTTER

Cream butter with anchovy paste. Use as a spread for canapés or as a filling for rolls.

Filled celery is a simple, succulent appetizer for the daily twosome dinner

ROLLED CANAPÉS

Remove crusts from bread.

Spread thin slices of bread with butter, then spread. Roll, fasten with toothpicks and toast under broiler. Fill as follows: ½ cup ground corned beef, seasoned with horse-radish and mixed with 4 tablespoons beaten egg.

3 ounces cream cheese, 1½ ounces Roquefort cheese, blend with ½ cup heavy cream, ⅛ teaspoon salt, fold in ½ cup whipped cream.

¼ pound Roquefort cheese, ¼ pound butter, 3 tablespoons brandy.

1 cup chopped broiled liver, 4 slices chopped broiled bacon, 1 tablespoon chopped onion, ½ teaspoon prepared mustard, 2 tablespoons catchup, ⅓ teaspoon salt, dash cayenne, 2 tablespoons mayonnaise.

1⅓ cups flaked crab meat, 2 teaspoons minced green pepper, 2 teaspoons Worcestershire sauce, 2 teaspoons chili sauce. Pile on tomato slices brushed with French dressing.

1 cup crab meat, 1 teaspoon capers, enough mayonnaise to bind mixture.

HOT CANAPÉS

HOT SWISS CHEESE CANAPÉS —Cover toast rounds with a thin slice of onion, then with mayonnaise and a circle of Swiss cheese. Melt cheese under broiler.

SMOKED SALMON CANAPÉS— Spread toast fingers with Lemon Butter. Place ¼-inch slice smoked salmon on toast. Cover with buttered crumbs and brown under broiler.

ANCHOVY ROLLS

2 round rolls
1 recipe Anchovy Butter

Cut thin slice from top of rolls; hollow out centers, toast and spread with anchovy butter. Serves 2.

FILLED CELERY

2 tablespoons nippy cheese
    or fish paste
1 teaspoon cream
6 small stalks celery

Mix cheese with cream; fill celery stalks. Chill. Serves 2.

FILLED PICKLES

Hollow out large sweet or dill pickles with apple corer and fill with seasoned cream cheese. Serve in slices.

Use softened Cheddar cheese instead of cream cheese.

POTATO SOUP

2¼ cups milk
2 large potatoes, boiled and cubed
¼ teaspoon salt
Dash pepper
½ tablespoon butter
¼ cup flour
1 egg, well beaten

Scald 2 cups milk, add potatoes, beat thoroughly and add seasonings. Blend butter and flour, add egg and remaining milk. Drop from teaspoon into hot soup. Cover pan and cook about 10 minutes. Serve at once. Serves 2.

CHILLED BEET SOUP

2 medium beets, cooked
1 quart boiling water
1 teaspoon salt
1 egg, beaten
2 teaspoons sugar
2 teaspoons lemon juice
⅓ cup sour cream

Remove beet skins. Chop beets fine and cook in boiling salted water until beets are soft. Add egg, sugar and lemon juice and mix. Chill. Top with sour cream. Serves 2.
Garnish with chopped chives.

JELLIED CHICKEN BOUILLON

1 tablespoon unflavored gelatin
¼ cup cold water
2 cups hot Chicken Stock
Salt
1 tablespoon chopped parsley

Soften gelatin in water 5 minutes and dissolve in hot stock. Season with salt and add parsley. Chill. When firm cut into cubes or beat slightly with a fork. Serve in cold bouillon cups. Serves 4. If the feet were used in making chicken stock, no gelatin need be added.

Add sliced cooked mushrooms, carrots, green beans and celery.

JIFFY SOUPS

Canned soups are especially adapted for cooking for two; variety is obtained by combining different kinds. Pages 125-6.
Cream of Mushroom and Chicken Noodle
Cream of Mushroom and Corn
Vegetable Beef and Celery
Celery and Oxtail
Tomato and Bouillon
Tomato and Clam
Chicken Gumbo and Clam
Consommé and Clam
Chicken and Celery
Chicken and Vegetable
Pea and Vegetable
Tomato and Pea

SOUP FROM CHICKEN FEET

Singe chicken feet, wash well, drop into scalding water and let stand 10 minutes. Skin; cover with cold water in a kettle; season and cook until they fall apart. Strain and use as chicken stock.

Cool, clear, sparkling jellied chicken bouillon with julienne vegetables and white glistening mushrooms

FISH CAKES

½ cup flaked cooked fish
½ teaspoon minced onion
½ teaspoon lemon juice
⅛ teaspoon salt
Dash pepper
1 egg, slightly beaten
½ cup cold mashed potatoes
1 tablespoon flour
2 tablespoons fat

Combine fish, onion, lemon juice, seasonings, egg and potatoes; mix thoroughly. Form into cakes, coat with flour and sauté in hot fat until browned on both sides.

SMOKED SALMON WITH SCRAMBLED EGGS

½ small onion, sliced
1 tablespoon butter
3 slices smoked salmon
2 eggs, scrambled without salt

Brown onion in butter. Add salmon slices; fry gently until heated. Serve on platter with border of scrambled eggs.

They are fun to catch, easy to fry and a joy to eat

FRIED FISH

Clean fish, leaving heads and tails on small fish. Cut large fish into 1-inch slices or fillets. Cook plain or dip into milk or egg mixed with 2 tablespoons water; then roll in salted flour, corn meal or fine dry crumbs. Place in hot frying pan containing ⅛-inch layer of melted fat; brown on one side, then turn and brown on other side, allowing 8 to 12 minutes total cooking time, depending on thickness of slice. Fish for frying are:

Bass	Haddock	Salmon
Butterfish	Halibut	Shad
Carp	Mackerel	Smelt
Catfish	Perch	Sunfish
Cod	Pickerel	Trout
Flounder	Pike	Weakfish

FRENCH FRIED FISH—Clean and coat fish as directed for fried fish. Fry in hot deep fat (365°F.) 5 to 7 minutes or until brown and tender. Drain on absorbent paper.
Serve fried fish with Maître d'Hotel Butter, Lemon Butter, Tartare Sauce or Hollandaise.

SALMON VEGETABLE CASSEROLE

½ cup diced potato
1½ carrots, sliced
⅓ cup peas
1 small onion, chopped
1½ tablespoons butter
1½ tablespoons flour
⅓ cup vegetable water
⅔ cup milk
¼ teaspoon salt
Dash pepper
1 teaspoon chopped parsley
½ pound can salmon, flaked
1 recipe Baking Powder Biscuit dough

Cook potato, carrots and peas together in a small amount of boiling salted water. Drain, saving ⅓ cup water for sauce. Cook onion in butter until tender; remove from heat. Add flour, stirring until smooth. Add vegetable water, milk, salt, pepper and parsley; cook until thickened, stirring constantly. Arrange alternate layers of vegetables and fish in greased casserole. Cover with sauce. Prepare baking powder biscuit dough and pat out to size of casserole; place over sauce. Cut small slits in dough or prick with a fork to allow steam to escape. Bake in very hot oven (450°F.) 30 minutes. Serves 2.

OYSTER STEW

2 cups milk
1 cup oysters (½ pint)
2 tablespoons butter
½ teaspoon salt
¼ teaspoon celery salt
Dash pepper

Scald milk; heat oysters in their own liquor about 5 minutes or until edges begin to curl. Add butter, seasonings and hot milk. Serve immediately. Serves 2.

STUFFED PORK CHOPS

2 double pork chops
½ cup bread crumbs
¼ teaspoon salt, Dash pepper
1 teaspoon minced parsley
⅛ teaspoon sage
1 teaspoon grated onion
¼ cup diced apple
3 tablespoons milk

Cut a pocket on the bone side of each chop. Combine next 8 ingredients and mix well. Stuff each chop with bread mixture. Place in shallow pan and bake in moderate oven (350°F.) about 1 hour or until tender.

STEWED KIDNEYS

3 lamb or pork kidneys
Salt and pepper
1 sprig parsley, chopped
¼ teaspoon thyme
1 bay leaf, chopped
1½ tablespoons drippings
1 cup water or consommé
1 teaspoon vinegar

Wash kidneys, slice very thin and season with salt and pepper. Cook with herbs in drippings until tender. Add water and vinegar, heat to boiling and serve.

BROILED STEAK

1 porterhouse or sirloin steak,
   1¼ pounds
Salt, Pepper, Butter

Preheat oven to 350°F about 10 minutes. Place meat on broiler rack 3 inches below moderate heat. Broil 5 to 6 minutes for rare steak or 8 for medium steak. Sprinkle with salt and pepper, turn and broil 5 to 8 minutes longer. Place on hot platter, Sprinkle with salt and pepper, and spread with soft butter. Broil filet mignon, club and rib steaks as above, allowing about 5 to 6 minutes for each side for rare steak and 8 minutes for medium steak.

BEEF STEW WITH DUMPLINGS

2 small onions, sliced
2 tablespoons fat
½ pound beef, in 1-inch pieces
1½ cups boiling water
½ teaspoon salt
½ teaspoon paprika
Dash pepper
½ cup tomatoes
2 potatoes, diced
¼ cup diced rutabaga
1 small carrot, sliced
¼ cup sliced celery

Brown onions in fat. Remove onions; brown meat thoroughly in same fat. Add water, seasonings and tomatoes. Cover and simmer until meat is tender, about 1 hour. After 25 minutes add remaining vegetables and cook until tender. When stew is ready, add small dumplings and cook 20 minutes without uncovering stew. Place meat on platter and surround with vegetables and dumplings Sprinkle with parsley.

DUMPLINGS

1 cup sifted flour
½ teaspoon salt
1½ teaspoons baking powder
½ tablespoon shortening
1 egg, beaten
6 tablespoons water or milk

Sift flour, salt and baking powder together. Cut in shortening with 2 knives or pastry blender. Add egg and liquid; blend. Drop from tablespoon on top of stew. Cover tightly and cook 20 minutes without uncovering.

PAN-BROILED VEAL CHOPS

1 tablespoon fat
4 veal chops
Salt and pepper

Heat fat in frying pan. Broil chops 15 minutes, season and broil on other side until browned.

Friend husband will say, "Ah, dumplings like Mother used to make"

Use lamb, veal or pork for the brochettes and tip them with stuffed olives for a clever and colorful effect

BREADED VEAL CUTLETS

2 veal cutlets, ½ to ¾ pound each
1 egg yolk
1 tablespoon cold water
⅓ cup bread or cracker crumbs
1 teaspoon salt
⅛ teaspoon pepper
½ onion, sliced
2 tablespoons fat

Wipe cutlets with a damp cloth; dip in mixture of egg yolk and water, then in crumbs. Add seasonings. Fry onion in fat until yellow; add breaded cutlets. Fry on both sides until browned. Cover and cook slowly 20 minutes.

CORNED BEEF AND POTATO CAKES

¼ pound cooked corned beef
1 cooked medium potato
1 egg
¼ teaspoon salt, Dash pepper

Chop corned beef and potato. Combine with egg and seasonings. Shape into cakes and brown.

VEAL AND PORK EN BROCHETTE

½ pound veal steak
⅛ pound pork shoulder
1 egg
½ cup fine crisp cereal crumbs
Fat
1 teaspoon salt
¼ cup water
¼ cup sour or sweet cream

Cut veal and pork into 1½-inch squares. Place 2 squares of pork and 2 of veal alternately on each of several skewers. Dip each into egg, then into crumbs and brown in fat. Season, add water, cover and simmer until tender, about 1 hour. Remove to hot platter and pour cream into pan. Heat to boiling and serve with meat. Serves 3 or 4.

BROILED LAMB CHOPS

4 lamb chops, 1½ inches thick
Salt and pepper

Broil chops for 9 minutes in a preheated broiler, 4 inches from heat. Season, turn and broil on other side for 9 minutes. Season. Serves 2.

SKEWERED LAMB

1 pound lamb steak (sliced ¾ inch thick)
1½ tablespoons cooking oil
3 tablespoons lemon juice
½ onion, minced, ½ teaspoon salt
¼ pound mushrooms

Cut lamb into 1-inch squares. Combine oil, lemon juice, onion and salt; pour over lamb and let stand several hours. Drain lamb and arrange on metal skewers alternately with mushroom caps. Place 4 inches below moderate broiler heat and broil about 12 to 15 minutes, turning several times. Serves 3.

SHEPHERD'S PIE

1 tablespoon fat
1 cup hot mashed potatoes
1 cup cubed cooked lamb
1 cup lamb gravy

Grease shallow baking dish and spread ½ inch thick with mashed potatoes. Fill with lamb and gravy and garnish top with mashed potatoes in large spoonfuls. Bake in moderate oven (375°F.) about 20 minutes.

BROILED CHICKEN

Singe and wash a young chicken (preferably under 4 months old). Split the chicken down the back with a sharp knife. Flatten out. Remove all loose or exposed bones. Sprinkle with salt and pepper, brush with butter or chicken fat and broil at moderate temperature (350°F.) in well-greased broiler for about 60 minutes, turning twice. Baste with butter when nearly done and serve with melted butter. Garnish with parsley. Allow ¾ pound per person.

CHICKEN LIVERS AND MUSHROOMS

2 slices bacon, cut small
4 chicken livers, diced
6 mushrooms, diced
½ teaspoon salt
Dash pepper
1 teaspoon flour
¼ cup cream
2 slices toast

Sauté bacon; add livers and mushrooms; season. Cook 5 minutes. Make sauce of flour and cream; add to livers. Serve on toast. Serves 2.

ROAST GUINEA HEN

1 guinea hen
¼ pound salt pork
Stuffing

Clean hen and lard with salt pork. The market will do this, if requested. Fill with stuffing. Close opening and truss. Place breast side down in uncovered roaster. Roast in moderate oven (350°F.) until tender, about 2 hours. Roast with breast down half of the time, turn and cook remaining time with breast up. Baste every ½ hour. Serves 2.

Chicken behaves better at the table if the breastbone is snapped out completely before broiling

CHICKEN AND ALMOND MOUSSE

1 tablespoon unflavored gelatin
1 cup Chicken Stock
2 egg yolks
½ teaspoon salt
⅛ teaspoon pepper
Dash cayenne
¼ cup finely chopped almonds
½ cup diced white meat of cooked chicken
¼ cup heavy cream, whipped

Soften gelatin in ½ cup cold stock for 5 minutes. Heat remaining stock; add slowly to beaten egg yolks and seasonings. Cook in double boiler until thickened, stirring constantly. Add gelatin, stir until dissolved and mix in almonds and chicken. Chill until mixture begins to thicken and fold in whipped cream. Pour into mold and chill until firm. Serve on crisp cold lettuce leaves, garnished with additional chopped nuts and Radish Roses. Serves 3. Add 2 tablespoons each sieved pimientos and minced celery. Remove centers from tomatoes and pour in mixture. Chill.

BABY CHICKEN BREASTS

2 breasts of chicken
½ teaspoon salt
1½ tablespoons flour
Fat for frying

FOR GRAVY—
2 tablespoons flour
½ cup Chicken Stock
1 cup cream or rich milk
1 egg yolk, slightly beaten

Remove breastbone from meat and split each breast into 2 fillets. Dip in seasoned flour. Fry slowly in greased skillet until tender and brown. Remove to hot serving dish. Remove all fat from skillet except 2 tablespoons, add flour and stir until well blended. Add stock and cream, stirring until thickened. Season. Add egg yolk just before serving, cook 1 or 2 minutes longer and add 2 tablespoons sherry if desired. Strain, if necessary, and pour over chicken breast. Serve on toast or on fried corn-meal slices. Garnish with sautéed mushroom caps. Serves 2.

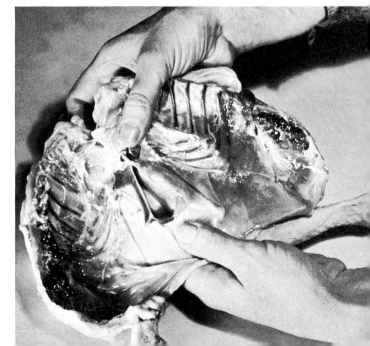

PEACH SHERBET

⅓ cup sweetened condensed milk
1 tablespoon lemon juice
1 tablespoon melted butter
¼ cup water
½ cup crushed fresh peaches
1 egg white

Blend condensed milk, lemon juice, melted butter and water. Add peaches and chill. Beat egg white until stiff and fold into chilled mixture. Pour into freezing tray of refrigerator and freeze. When mixture is about half frozen scrape from sides and bottom of tray, beat until smooth but not melted and freeze until firm. Serves 3.

CUSTARD FOR ICE CREAM

1 cup sugar, Dash salt
2½ tablespoons flour
2 cups milk, scalded

Mix sugar, salt and flour; add to milk. Cook in double boiler until thick, stirring often. Chill in refrigerator until needed. Makes 2½ cups custard base

VANILLA ICE CREAM—Fold ½ cup heavy cream, whipped, into 1 cup custard base; add 1½ teaspoons vanilla. Pour into refrigerator tray and freeze until firm, stirring 3 times. Makes 1 pint.

PINEAPPLE MARLOW

12 marshmallows
1 No. 1 can crushed pineapple
¾ cup evaporated milk, chilled
2 tablespoons lemon juice

Heat marshmallows and juice from pineapple in top of double boiler, folding over and over until marshmallows are half melted. Remove from heat, add pineapple and continue folding until mixture is smooth and spongy. Whip milk until stiff, add lemon juice slowly and whip until very stiff. Fold pineapple mixture into milk. Freeze in refrigerator until firm.

PEACH MOUSSE

2 to 3 medium peaches
¼ cup sugar
¾ cup evaporated milk, chilled
1 tablespoon lemon juice
Dash salt

Peel peaches, stone and mash enough to make ¾ cup pulp. Add sugar and stir occasionally until sugar is dissolved. Whip milk very stiff. Fold in lemon juice, salt and peach mixture. Freeze until firm. Makes 3 cups.
BANANA—Use mashed bananas instead of peaches. Increase lemon juice to 1½ tablespoons and add ½ teaspoon lemon rind.

STRAWBERRY MILK MALLOBET

16 marshmallows (¼ pound)
1 cup milk, chilled
¾ cup crushed, fresh strawberries
1 tablespoon lemon juice

Heat marshmallows and 2 tablespoons of milk slowly, folding over and over until marshmallows are half melted. Remove from heat and continue folding until mixture is smooth and spongy. Cool to lukewarm, then blend in remaining milk, crushed strawberries and lemon juice. Pour into freezing tray of refrigerator and freeze, stirring several times while freezing. Serves 2 or 3.

MAPLE MOUSSE

⅓ cup maple sirup
2 egg yolks, beaten
Dash salt
½ teaspoon vanilla
1 cup evaporated milk, chilled

Combine maple sirup, egg yolks and salt. Cook over boiling water until thickened, beat until cool, add vanilla and chill. Whip milk very stiff, fold in maple custard and freeze until firm.
MAPLE SUGAR—Melt ⅓ cup maple sugar and use as maple sirup.

STANDARD PARFAIT

⅓ cup sugar
2 tablespoons water
1 egg white
Dash salt
½ cup heavy cream, whipped
1 teaspoon vanilla

Cook sugar and water until it threads (238°F.). Beat egg white with salt until stiff but not dry. Pour sirup on slowly, beating constantly. Cool. Fold whipped cream into egg and sirup mixture and add vanilla. Freeze in refrigerator tray.

BURNT ALMOND—Add ¼ cup shredded toasted almonds and ⅛ teaspoon almond extract. Reduce vanilla to ½ teaspoon.

CHOCOLATE—Add 1½ tablespoons cocoa to the above sirup; combine as in standard parfait.

FRUIT—Add ⅓ cup fresh or cooked fruit purée to mixture. Serve in parfait glasses with whipped cream and nuts.

STRAWBERRY REFRIGERATOR CAKE

6 Ladyfingers or 1 small Sponge-cake
3 tablespoons sugar
1¼ cups crushed strawberries
⅓ cup heavy cream
¼ teaspoon vanilla
1 tablespoon chopped nuts

Line spring-form pan with split ladyfingers or sliced spongecake. Add sugar to strawberries. Whip cream with vanilla. Cover cake with berries and whipped cream. Repeat in layers until all material is used, saving part of cream for top of cake. Sprinkle with nuts. Chill 8 hours. Serves 2.

Quick Dinners for the Woman in a Hurry

50 Menus and
Recipes for Women
in a Hurry

Here's How
the woman in a hurry will be enabled to plan her time and food resources to meet the increasing tasks expected of her and still give herself and her family all the necessary variety and attractive service modern mealtime demands. The food manufacturer has helped in no small way with partially or fully prepared foods. Fresh frozen foods will be an additional time-saver. Breads and beverages have not been included in the menus but are left to free choice. Breads will not be made at home.

Dutch ovenettes for top stove baking and reheating, heavy metal pots for short period waterless cooking of vegetables and the small pressure saucepans that cook at high heat in 3-4 minutes will all add to the pleasure and the promptness with which food can be prepared.

If the mechanical refrigerator is defrosted over the week end, it is wise to rearrange, bringing leftovers forward where they cannot be forgotten. If you are really methodical a scratch list of the contents with a note of the amounts of staples, like butter and cream, can be pasted on the inside of the door. They can be scratched off as used and the list remade for the following week. This is the time, too, when space will be cleared for refrigerator desserts which will be conveniently made well ahead of time.

A number of small tricks will be picked up as speed is developed. Tomatoes, for instance, may be skinned by holding over a gas flame for a few seconds or allowing to freeze in the refrigerator instead of the scalding process. Experience will suggest other short cuts.

Pages 5-50 will give much additional information, helps and short cuts.

FOR YOUR INFORMATION

1. Check your refrigerator as a guide in meal planning.
2. Meal planning should be flexible enough to take advantage of market specials. For example, if broccoli is on the menu, but at the market, spinach is a bargain, spinach should be used.
3. Leftover meats and fish can be used in casseroles.
a. When using frozen vegetables, always cook entire package. Leftovers may be used in salads, creamed vegetables or soups.
b. Leftovers such as sour cream or milk may be used for pancakes, waffles, biscuits or cake.
c. Save juices of canned fruits, combine them and serve for breakfast, adding lemon juice if mixture is too sweet.
4. Milk, eggs and butter are not listed in the market order as they will be purchased in the usual quantities and be on hand.

5. French dressing, mayonnaise and salad dressing are not listed in market orders, but may be purchased as needed.
6. Use French dressing and mayonnaise as a base for other dressings such as blue (Roquefort) and Thousand Island.

STAPLE SUPPLIES

Macaroni, Rice, Flour
Unflavored gelatin
Cornstarch
Unsweetened chocolate, Cocoa
Coffee, Tea
Evaporated milk
Cooking oil, Shortening
Sugars
   Brown
   Confectioners'
   Granulated
Baking powder
Baking soda
Allspice—ground, Basil
Bay leaves, Cayenne
Celery seed
Cinnamon—ground
Cloves—ground, whole

Garlic
Ginger, Mustard
Nutmeg—ground
Paprika, Pepper, Sage
Salt, Tabasco sauce, Vinegar
Vanilla
Worcestershire sauce

EMERGENCY SHELF

Ready-to-mix piecrust, pancake flours, cake mixes
Canned date and nut bread
Canned fruits and vegetables
Canned meats, such as corned beef, spiced ham, corned beef hash
Canned fish, such as salmon, tuna, crab meat, shrimp, lobster
Chicken à la king
Canned soups—cream of mushroom, Madrilene consommé, chicken soup or your choice
Chop suey vegetables
Canned nuts
Anchovy paste
Pickles, Olives
Maraschino cherries
Maple sirup

DAILY MENUS AND RECIPES

For the woman who lives alone

WEEKLY MARKET LIST FOR 1

1 orange, 1 apple, 1 grapefruit, 1 lemon
1 pint strawberries
1 avocado, 1 tomato, 1 banana
1 bunch radishes, 1 artichoke
3 mild onions, 2 ears corn
1 pound potatoes, 1 head chicory
1 head lettuce
1 small pineapple
1 chicken breast
2 loin lamb chops
¼ pound beef liver
½ pound ground beef
2 perch fillets
7½-ounce can asparagus
2-ounce can mushrooms
7½-ounce can mixed vegetables
14-ounce can tomatoes
7½-ounce can beets
No. 2 can kidney beans
Small can sliced pineapple
1 can corned beef hash
Small can ripe olives
Coconut cupcake, Fudge squares
Meringue cup, ½ pound prunes
½ pint heavy cream
¼ pound American cheese
½ pound dried apricots
1 box chili powder
¼ pound walnuts
¼ pound vanilla wafers

SUNDAY

Pan-broiled Lamb Chops with Mushrooms
Mixed Vegetables
Chicory salad (p. 531)
Coconut Cupcake

HOW TO GO ABOUT IT
(Requires 25 minutes)

Open cans of mushrooms and mixed vegetables. Heat mixed vegetables in liquid.
Pan-broil lamb chops.
Set table; warm dinner plate by running hot water over it or by setting in warm place.
Wash chicory, arrange on salad plate. Serve with French dressing.
Remove chops to hot plate and heat mushrooms in skillet.
Drain and season vegetables.

PAN-BROILED LAMB CHOPS WITH MUSHROOMS

2 thick loin lamb chops
2-ounce can mushrooms
Salt and pepper

Place chops in hot skillet and brown on both sides, allowing about 10 minutes for chops 1 inch thick. Remove chops to a hot plate and empty mushrooms into skillet. Heat to boiling, drain and serve on chops. Sprinkle with salt and pepper.

MONDAY

Breast of Chicken on Toast
Buttered Asparagus
Radishes   Ripe Olives
Banana and Pineapple Salad

HOW TO GO ABOUT IT
(Requires 30 minutes)

Set table.
Prepare and fry chicken breast.
Wash chicory and radishes.
Arrange radishes with olives.
Open can of pineapple; drain 1 slice.
Open can asparagus and heat in liquid.
Peel banana and arrange salad. Chill in refrigerator.
Make gravy and toast for chicken.
Drain and season asparagus.

BANANA AND PINEAPPLE SALAD

1 banana
1 slice pineapple
3 sprays chicory
1½ tablespoons mayonnaise

Peel banana and cut into quarters lengthwise, then through center. Cut pineapple slice 8 times from outer edge toward center but not entirely through. Cut into halves. Place pineapple halves on chicory spreading the slits. Place a section of banana in the openings of pineapple. Garnish with mayonnaise.

BREAST OF CHICKEN

1 breast of chicken
½ teaspoon salt
2 tablespoons flour
Fat for frying
¾ cup milk
1 egg yolk, slightly beaten

Remove breastbone from the meat and split into 2 fillets. Dip into mixture of salt and 1 tablespoon flour. Fry slowly until tender and brown. Remove to hot serving dish. Remove all fat from skillet except 1 tablespoon, add remaining flour and stir until well blended. Add milk, stirring until thickened. Season. Add egg yolk just before serving and cook 1 or 2 minutes longer. Strain if necessary and pour over the chicken breast. Serve on toast. One tablespoon sherry may be added to sauce at the last.

The legs, thighs and wings may also be prepared by this method.

Pineapple and banana salad may be arranged in many attractive ways (page 907)

TUESDAY

Corned Beef Hash with
Poached Egg
Stewed Tomatoes
Pineapple Salad
Vanilla Wafers

HOW TO GO ABOUT IT
(*Requires 20 minutes*)

Scrub pineapple, cut a ½-inch slice from top. Keep this as a cover for remaining pineapple. Cut another ½-inch slice, pare and cut into small wedges. Arrange on chicory, pile 6 nut meats in center and garnish with mayonnaise on the edge. Separate wedges with slices of maraschino cherry or pimiento if desired. Open cans of tomatoes and corned beef hash. Save ½ cup tomatoes for chile con carne on Thursday. Set table.

Slice hash and brown slices in buttered skillet.
Season and heat tomatoes.
Poach egg and arrange on browned slice of hash.

WEDNESDAY

Sautéed Liver with Onions
Buttered Potato
Radish Roses
Grapefruit Salad
Fudge Squares (p. 692)

HOW TO GO ABOUT IT
(*Requires 30 minutes*)

Scrub 2 potatoes and cook, covered, in small amount of water. Pare grapefruit, cut out sections and arrange on lettuce. Add French dressing. Chill. Set table. Sauté liver and onions. Peel potato and reheat in butter. Keep other potato for Friday.

PREPARATION FOR THURSDAY
Cook apricots for whip. Rub through sieve, cover and place in refrigerator.

SAUTÉED LIVER WITH ONIONS

¼ pound beef liver, sliced
2 tablespoons cracker crumbs
¼ teaspoon salt
Dash pepper
3 tablespoons bacon fat
2 small onions, sliced

Wash liver and drain. Dip into crumbs; season. Fry liver slowly in bacon fat in preheated frying pan until browned on both sides. Add sliced onions and fry slowly until onions are tender.

THURSDAY

Chile Con Carne
Toast Strips
Head Lettuce with
French Dressing
Apricot Whip

HOW TO GO ABOUT IT
(Requires 30 minutes)

Prepare apricot whip and place in refrigerator to chill.

Open can of kidney beans and make chile con carne, using tomatoes left from Tuesday.

Set table.

Tear lettuce and mix with French dressing. Make toast.

CHILE CON CARNE

2 tablespoons diced onion
¼ pound ground beef
½ tablespoon fat
½ cup cooked tomatoes
½ cup cooked red kidney beans
⅛ teaspoon chili powder
¼ teaspoon salt

Brown onion and meat in fat, add remaining ingredients, cover and simmer 20 minutes. Add a very little water if mixture becomes too dry.

APRICOT WHIP

½ cup pulp from cooked dried apricots
Few grains salt
2 tablespoons sugar
1 egg white, beaten
½ tablespoon lemon juice

Heat fruit pulp, salt and sugar together until sugar is dissolved. Pour hot mixture slowly over stiffly beaten egg white, beating constantly. Add lemon juice. Pile into a parfait glass and chill. Use ¼ cup heavy cream, whipped, instead of egg white.

FRIDAY

Pan-Fried Perch (p. 900)
Cheese Potato
Sweet-Sour Beets
Artichoke
Strawberries in Meringue cup (p. 620)

HOW TO GO ABOUT IT
(Requires 30 minutes)

Prepare sweet-sour beets.
Cook artichoke.

Season fish, dip in corn meal or flour and fry in hot cooking oil, 4 to 6 minutes on each side.

Leaving skin on, cut cooked potato (left from Wednesday) lengthwise into halves.

Make several cuts in top of potato. Cover with grated cheese and heat under broiler until cheese is melted.

Wash strawberries. Whip cream. Arrange in meringue cup just before serving.

Set table.

PREPARATION FOR SATURDAY

Cook prunes for cream whip.

SWEET-SOUR BEETS

1 tablespoon butter
2 tablespoons vinegar
1 tablespoon water
¼ teaspoon salt
½ teaspoon sugar
½ cup diced cooked beets

Melt butter and add vinegar, water, salt and sugar. Mix with beets and heat slowly to boiling.

COOKED ARTICHOKE

1 artichoke
1 pint boiling water
½ teaspoon salt

Wash artichoke and cook in boiling salted water until the base of the outer leaves is tender. Serve with melted butter.

SATURDAY

Broiled Round Steak Patty
Broiled Tomato (p.513)
Corn on the Cob
Fruit Salad
Prune Cream Whip

HOW TO GO ABOUT IT
(Requires 30 minutes)

Prepare prune cream whip.

Wash orange, avocado and apple and prepare salad.
Husk corn and cook.
Wash tomato and cut into halves.
Season tomato. Perpare meat. Broil meat and tomato in broiler.
Set table.

CORN ON THE COB

2 ears sweet corn
2 cups boiling water
1 cup milk

Remove husks and silks from corn, place in kettle and cover with boiling water and milk. Cook 5 to 7 minutes. Drain. (Save liquid for cream soups.) Serve with butter and salt.

BROILED ROUND STEAK PATTY

¼ pound ground round steak
Salt and pepper

Sprinkle round steak with salt and pepper and form into a flat patty. Cook in broiler turning to brown both sides.

FRUIT SALAD

2 orange sections
2 slices avocado
2 slices apple
Chicory
French dressing

Pare orange and cut out sections, discarding seeds. Peel and slice avocado. Slice apple leaving peel intact. Arrange on chicory and add French dressing.

PRUNE CREAM WHIP

5 cooked prunes, drained
1 tablespoon confectioners' sugar
1 teaspoon orange juice
¼ cup heavy cream, whipped

Pit and cut prunes, mix with next 2 ingredients and chill. Whip cream, add chilled mixture and top with maraschino cherry if desired.

For the family of 3

WEEKLY MARKET LIST FOR 3

½ pound onions
3 potatoes
3 sweetpotatoes
¼ pound cranberries
1 head celery cabbage
5 large oranges, 1 lemon
3 tomatoes
1 bunch celery, 2 heads lettuce
1 green pepper
1 cucumber
1 bunch radishes
3 baking apples
¼ pound grapes
1 pineapple
13-ounce package frozen Brussels sprouts
4-pound roasting chicken
3 slices beef shank
1 pound liver
6 lamb kidneys
1 pound pork sausage
½ pound bacon
1-pound can asparagus tips
1 can julienne carrots
14-ounce can evaporated milk
15½-ounce can string beans
8-ounce can mushrooms
15-ounce can cream of corn soup
7-ounce can tuna
4-ounce jar stuffed olives
1-pound can sliced beets
1 No. 2 can shoestring potatoes
8-ounce can pineapple tidbits
8-ounce can sliced peaches
1 small can corn sirup
½ pint sour cream
1 package prepared cupcake mix
4-ounce package walnuts
4-ounce package pecans
1 package lime gelatin
3¼-ounce package vanilla wafers
¼ pound stick cinnamon
1 package prepared biscuit mix

SUNDAY

Roast Chicken (p. 412)
Baked Sweetpotatoes
Buttered Celery Cabbage
Asparagus Tip Salad
Baked Oranges

HOW TO GO ABOUT IT
(Requires 3 hours)

About 3 hours before dinner time prepare chicken and cook.
Prepare oranges and place in oven 2 hours before dinner time.
Drain asparagus tips, add French dressing and chill.
One hour before dinner time place potatoes in oven.
Set table.
Prepare and cook celery cabbage.
Cut 3 rings from green pepper and arrange asparagus in rings. Place on lettuce.

PREPARATION FOR MONDAY
(Requires 15 minutes)

Prepare mousse and freeze.
Marinate kidneys.

CELERY CABBAGE

Shred cabbage, drop in boiling salted water and cook rapidly, uncovered, for about 10 to 15 minutes. Drain, add butter, heat through, sprinkle with paprika.

BAKED ORANGES

3 large oranges
3 tablespoons sugar
3 teaspoons butter

Wash oranges and grate the skin of each slightly. Cover oranges with water and boil for 30 minutes. Drain and cool. When cool enough to handle, cut off a small slice at blossom end and remove core. Put 1 tablespoon of sugar and 1 teaspoon of butter in center of each orange. Place in shallow buttered baking dish, fill ⅔ full of water, cover dish and bake in 350°F. oven 2 hours.

MONDAY

Broiled Lamb Kidneys
Shoestring Potatoes
Broiled Tomatoes
Celery Curls
Butter Pecan Mousse

HOW TO GO ABOUT IT
(Requires 15 minutes)

Prepare kidneys and broil. Cut tomatoes into halves, add salt and pepper and broil.

Wash celery, scrape and cut into 2-inch lengths. Make several cuts in each end and almost to middle. Place in ice water. Open can of potatoes and heat. Make toast for kidneys. Pour melted butter over tomatoes. Set table.

BROILED LAMB KIDNEYS

6 lamb kidneys
1 cup French dressing
6 slices bacon

Clean kidneys and split into halves. Marinate in French dressing 12 hours. Drain kidneys and wrap each in half slice of bacon. Place 4 inches below moderate broiler heat and broil 12 to 15 minutes or until bacon is crisp and kidneys are tender. Serve on toast triangles.

BUTTER PECAN MOUSSE

1/2 teaspoon unflavored gelatin
2 teaspoons cold water
3/4 cup evaporated milk
1/4 cup finely chopped pecan meats
1/2 tablespoon butter
3 tablespoons sugar
1/2 tablespoon vanilla

Soften gelatin in water 5 minutes. Scald milk over boiling water, add softened gelatin and stir until dissolved. Chill. Brown pecan meats in butter and cool. Beat milk very stiff. Fold in nut meats, sugar and vanilla. Freeze until firm.

TUESDAY

Chicken Loaf with Mushrooms
String Bean Salad
Fresh Pineapple
Vanilla Wafers

HOW TO GO ABOUT IT
(Requires 50 minutes)

Prepare loaf, using chicken and gravy left from Sunday.

Open can of string beans, drain and add French dressing. Place in refrigerator.
Slice fresh pineapple, pare and cut out eyes. Cut into pieces, discarding core, add sugar and place in refrigerator.
Set table. Arrange salad.
Serve dinner.

PREPARATION FOR WEDNESDAY
(Requires about 15 minutes)

Make cupcakes, following directions on package.

CHICKEN LOAF

1 1/2 cups ground cooked chicken
1/2 onion, cut fine
1 stalk celery, diced
1/8 cup cracker crumbs
1/2 cup mushrooms
3/4 teaspoon salt
Dash pepper, 1 egg
1/4 cup gravy or liquid

Combine all ingredients except liquid. Pour into greased loaf pan, cover with liquid and bake in moderate oven (350° F.) about 40 minutes.

WEDNESDAY

Liver in Sour Cream (p. 401)
Buttered Brussels Sprouts
Orange Cranberry Relish
Cupcakes

HOW TO GO ABOUT IT
(Requires 70 minutes)

Prepare liver and bake.
Prepare relish.
Cook Brussels sprouts according to directions on package. Set table.
Drain and season Brussels sprouts.
Serve dinner.

PREPARATION FOR THURSDAY
(Requires 90 minutes)

Bake custard and chill.
Cook meat 1 1/2 hours. Cool and place in refrigerator.

CARAMEL CUSTARD

1/2 cup brown sugar, 3 eggs
1/4 cup granulated sugar
Dash salt, 2 cups milk, scalded
1/2 teaspoon vanilla

Sift brown sugar and place it in bottom of custard cups. Beat eggs and add granulated sugar, salt, milk and vanilla. Pour custard mixture into cups and place them in pan of hot water. Bake in moderate oven (350° F.) 30 to 35 minutes.

Serve with fresh strawberries, sliced peaches, fresh, tart cherries, hot wine pudding sauce, claret sauce or Hyannis sauce.

UNCOOKED ORANGE CRANBERRY RELISH

1/2 orange
1 cup washed cranberries
3/4 cup sugar
1/4 cup nuts, chopped

Cut orange peel into quarters and remove seeds and membrane from orange sections. Force orange peel, orange sections and cranberries through food chopper. Add sugar and nuts and place in covered jar. Chill until needed. Makes 1 cup relish.

CRANBERRY AND APPLE—Add 1/2 cored apple to cranberries and orange before chopping.

THURSDAY

Beef Shank Slices
Baked Potatoes
Julienne Carrots
Mixed Green Salad
Caramel Custard

HOW TO GO ABOUT IT
(Requires 50 minutes)

Place meat in oven to finish cooking.

Scrub potatoes and bake in hot oven (425° F.) 45 minutes.

Wash lettuce, cucumber, radishes and green pepper. Slice cucumber, radishes and onion. Shred a few leaves of lettuce and mix with sliced vegetables and French dressing. Place in bowl lined with rings cut from green pepper. Heat carrots in butter. Set table.

PREPARATION FOR FRIDAY
(Requires 20 minutes)

Prepare tuna salad and place in refrigerator.

BEEF SHANK SLICES

3 slices beef shank
Salt and pepper
Flour, Fat
½ cup hot water

Season meat with salt and pepper and dredge with flour. Brown on both sides in a little hot fat. Add water and cover tightly; simmer 2 hours. Or simmer only 1½ hours and finish cooking on the following day.

FRIDAY

Cream of Corn Soup
Molded Tuna Salad
Spiced Beets (p. 458)
Baked Apple Dumplings

HOW TO GO ABOUT IT

(Requires 45 minutes)

Make dumplings and start them baking.
Prepare spiced beets.
Set table.
Heat soup.
Unmold salad on lettuce.

PREPARATION FOR SATURDAY
(Requires 15 minutes)

Prepare fruit mold.

MOLDED TUNA SALAD

1 (7-ounce) can tuna
1 hard-cooked egg, chopped
¼ cup chopped stuffed olives
½ tablespoon minced onion
½ tablespoon unflavored gelatin
⅛ cup cold water
1 cup mayonnaise
Lettuce

Mince tuna with next 3 ingredients. Soften gelatin in cold water 5 minutes, dissolve over hot water and add to mayonnaise gradually, stirring constantly. Fold into fish mixture. Turn into mold and chill until firm. Unmold on lettuce and garnish with chicory.

BAKED APPLE DUMPLINGS

Baking Powder Biscuit dough
3 apples, pared and cored
4 tablespoons sugar
¼ teaspoon cinnamon
Butter, Juice of ½ lemon
¾ cup sugar
⅓ cup water
2 tablespoons corn sirup
1 tablespoon butter
¼ teaspoon vanilla

Mix biscuit dough using 2 cups of prepared biscuit mix. Place dough on floured board and roll about ⅛ inch thick. Cut into 6-inch squares. Place an apple in center of each square; fill center of apple with sugar, sprinkle with cinnamon and add small piece of butter. Pinch edges of dough together on top. Place in well-greased pan. Sprinkle with lemon juice. Bake in very hot oven (450°F.) 10 minutes. Combine last 5 ingredients and heat to boiling; cook 5 minutes. When dumplings have baked 10 minutes, pour sirup over them and reduce heat to moderate (350°F.); bake 25 minutes longer, basting occasionally with sirup. Serve with cream.

SATURDAY

Pecan Waffles
Sausage Patties
Sparkling Fruit Mold

SPARKLING FRUIT MOLD

HOW TO GO ABOUT IT
(Requires 20 minutes)

Set table.
Shape sausage into patties ¾ to 1 inch thick. Cook slowly 15 minutes, pouring off fat as it accumulates.
Mix waffle batter. Pour into pitcher and place on table near waffle iron. Heat waffle iron.
Serve dinner.

PECAN WAFFLES

2 cups sifted flour
3 teaspoons baking powder
½ teaspoon salt
2 teaspoons sugar
2 cups milk
2 eggs, separated
½ cup softened butter
½ cup chopped pecans

Mix and sift dry ingredients. Add milk to beaten egg yolks and butter. Add milk mixture to dry ingredients. Beat until smooth. Fold in beaten egg whites and chopped pecans. Pour about 4 tablespoons batter into preheated waffle iron and bake 3 minutes or until steam has ceased coming from the iron. Serve hot with butter and sirup. Makes 6 waffles.

SAUSAGE PATTIES

1 pound pork sausage

Shape into patties ¾ to 1 inch thick. Cook slowly 15 minutes, pouring off fat as it accumulates.

SPARKLING FRUIT MOLD

Recipe serving 8 may be found on page 545. Reduce the recipe accordingly.

Beverages

50 Beverages
for all
Occasions

BANANA MILK SHAKE

1 fully ripe banana
1 cup cold milk

Slice banana into a bowl and beat with rotary beater until creamy, or press banana through coarse sieve. Add milk, mix thoroughly and serve at once. Serve cold. Serves 2.
Add 1 large tablespoon vanilla ice cream.

BANANA PINEAPPLE EGGNOG — Add 1 beaten egg and 2 tablespoons pineapple juice to above.

BANANA CHOCOLATE MALTED MILK — Add 4 teaspoons chocolate malted milk and ¼ teaspoon vanilla.

FROSTED APRICOT MILK

1 cup cooked apricots and juice
3 cups milk
½ pint vanilla ice cream

Press apricots through a sieve. Mix apricot pulp and milk. Put ice cream in a pitcher. Pour milk mixture over ice cream. Stir until slightly mixed. Serves 4 to 6.

MAPLE FIZZ

¼ cup maple sirup
1 quart milk, Ginger ale

Add maple sirup to milk and mix well. Pour into tall glasses and fill with ginger ale. Serves 6.

ORANGE NOG

2 cups milk
1 tablespoon sugar
1 cup orange juice
2 teaspoons grated orange rind

Place milk and sugar in shaker or fruit jar. Shake well with ice. Add orange juice and rind and shake vigorously. If orange juice is very tart more sugar may be needed. Serves 4.

PINEAPPLE MINT PUNCH

3 cups cold milk
2 cups cold pineapple juice
¾ cup cream
¼ cup sugar
1½ teaspoons lemon juice
Dash salt
12 drops peppermint extract

Combine all ingredients and shake or beat until foamy. Pour into tall glasses, garnish with sprigs of mint and serve immediately. Serves 6.

PRUNE FLIP

3 cups chilled milk
1 cup prune pulp
Whipped cream

Beat milk into prune pulp with rotary beater or shake in shaker. Pour into glasses and top with whipped cream. For variety add a few gratings of lemon or orange rind. Serves 4.

RASPBERRY PUNCH

1 lemon
1 cup raspberries
1 cup currants
1 pint boiling water
1 cup sugar
1 cup tea infusion

Crush fruit and strain through a cloth. Without taking the pulp from the cloth, put it into another dish and pour the boiling water over it. Drain off, but do not squeeze or it will be muddy. Add the sugar to this liquid and stir until it is dissolved. Cool thoroughly before adding the fruit-juice and tea.

CHILLED GRAPE JUICE

Wash purple grapes and boil until skin, pulp and seeds separate. Press through jelly-bag and to every pint of juice add ½ cup sugar. Boil for 20 minutes, chill and serve with shaved ice.

STRAWBERRY MILK SHAKE

1 quart strawberries
5 cups milk, ½ cup cream
¾ cup sugar
¼ teaspoon salt
2½ teaspoons lemon juice

Crush strawberries and press through a coarse sieve; there should be at least 1⅔ cups purée. Combine with milk and cream, add remaining ingredients, and mix thoroughly. Chill well before serving. Top each glass with a spoonful of whipped cream. Serves 8 to 10.

STRAWBERRY FLOAT — Place 1 heaping tablespoon strawberry ice cream in each glass. Add ½ cup milk, mix well. Fill glass with carbonated water and top with more ice cream. One pint ice cream will serve 6.

MIXED FRUIT PUNCH

1 quart blue grape-juice
1 pint white grape-juice
Juice of 12 oranges
Juice of 12 lemons
Sugar or sirup to taste
2 quarts ginger ale
1 pint charged water

Mix fruit juices and sugar or, sirup. Add ginger ale and charged water and serve with chopped ice. Serves 25.

GINGER ALE PUNCH

Juice of 4 lemons
1 pint grape-juice
Sugar or sirup to taste
1 quart ginger ale

Mix fruit juices and sugar or sirup. Just before serving, add ginger ale.

GRAPE JUICE RICKEY

For each glass, mix juice of ½ lime with ½ glass grape juice and 2 tablespoons sugar. Shake in mixer with crushed ice. Fill glass with plain or charged water.

COFFEE

Use a grind of coffee suited to the type of coffee maker. Ingredients listed below will make coffee to serve 4.

6 (level) tablespoons ground coffee
3 (measuring) cups water

DRIP METHOD — Scald coffee-pot with boiling water. Set coffee compartment in place and measure coffee into it. Place water compartment on top and pour in freshly boiling water slowly. Place where coffee will keep hot but not boil and let stand until water has dripped through. Remove top compartment, cover and serve at once.

VACUUM METHOD — Measure water, either hot or cold, into lower bowl of coffee maker and heat to boiling. Adjust filter in upper bowl, measure coffee into it and place in lower bowl when water boils. Twist slightly to make an airtight seal. Reduce heat and allow water to rise into upper bowl until only a small amount remains in lower bowl. Remove from heat and stir well, taking care not to break seal between the two bowls. When coffee has returned to lower bowl, remove upper bowl and serve.

PERCOLATOR METHOD — Measure water, either hot or cold, into percolator, adjust basket and measure coffee into it. Cover and place over heat. When water begins to percolate, reduce heat and allow to percolate slowly 7 to 10 minutes. Remove from heat, take out coffee basket and replace cover. Serve at once.

ICED — Make coffee by any desired method, using twice as much coffee as usual. Pour hot coffee into tall glasses filled with ice cubes.

FRUITADE

½ cup sugar
1 quart water
Juice 1 orange
Juice 1 lemon
¼ teaspoon vanilla

Cook sugar and water together 10 minutes; cool. Add fruit juices and vanilla. Makes 1¼ quarts. Add leftover juices of cherry, pineapple, peach or other fruits.

PARTY PUNCH

1 quart sweet cider
1 cup orange juice
½ cup lemon juice
½ cup pineapple juice
1 (2-inch) stick cinnamon
½ teaspoon whole cloves
Sugar or honey as desired

Simmer all ingredients together 10 minutes. Strain and serve hot. Makes 6 cups punch.

CREAMY SABAYON

6 egg yolks
1½ cups confectioners' sugar
2 cups white wine
2 cups heavy cream, whipped

Beat egg yolks with sugar, add wine and cook in double boiler until thickened, stirring constantly. Chill. Fold in whipped cream and serve in glasses as a beverage or on puddings as a sauce. Serves 8.

CHOCOLATE COFFEE

¼ cup chocolate sirup
4 cups hot coffee
½ cup heavy cream, whipped

Mix chocolate sauce with coffee. Beat cream into chocolate-coffee Mixture. Serve hot. Serves 4

Level measurements are just as essential for good coffee as for good cake

CHOCOLATE MALTED MILK

Mix together 1 tablespoon each chocolate sirup and malted milk powder. Add 1 cup chilled milk and beat with a rotary beater or shake until frothy. For 1.

TEA

6 teaspoons tea leaves
6 cups boiling water

Place tea leaves in tea ball. Scald teapot with boiling water and place tea ball in it. Add boiling water and let stand 1 to 3 minutes. Remove tea ball. Serve with lemon or cream and sugar. Have a pot of boiling water ready to dilute tea for those who like it less strong. Serves 6.

ICED TEA

Prepare strong tea, using 1½ teaspoons leaves per cup of boiling water. Pour hot tea over cracked ice or ice cubes in tall glasses. Garnish with lemon.

COCOA

⅓ cup cocoa
6 tablespoons sugar
Dash salt
3½ cups hot water
1¾ cups evaporated milk

Mix cocoa, sugar and salt; stir in water gradually. Cook 5 minutes. Add milk and heat, but do not boil. Before serving, beat with egg beater. Add ¼ teaspoon vanilla if desired. Serve with whipped cream or marshmallows. Serves 6.

ORANGE JUICE WITH RASPBERRIES

Fill glasses with juice from chilled oranges; float a few raspberries on top as a garnish.

Aged coffee gathers no compliments; even iced coffee should be freshly made

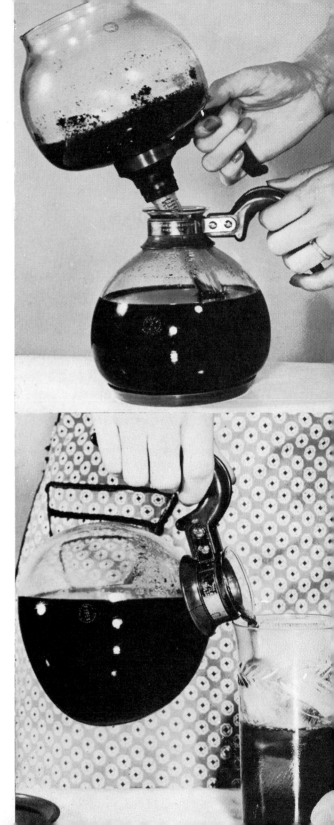

HOT CHOCOLATE

2 ounces (squares) chocolate
1 cup water
3 tablespoons sugar
Dash salt
3 cups milk

Cook chocolate and water over low heat until chocolate is melted. Add sugar and salt; boil 5 minutes, stirring constantly. Add milk gradually, stirring constantly and heat over boiling water. Beat until frothy before serving. Serves 6.

GRAPE JUICE SHAKE

1 cup grape juice
½ teaspoon lemon juice
¼ cup sugar
2 cups milk
⅛ teaspoon salt

Combine ingredients and beat with rotary beater. Serve at once. Serves 2.

The young lady who prepares the orange juice will be well rewarded with a refreshing beverage

APRICOT SHAKE

3 tablespoons sugar
¼ teaspoon salt
1 cup apricot juice
1 teaspoon lemon juice
2 cups cold milk

Dissolve sugar and salt in fruit juices. Chill. Before serving add to cold milk and mix well. Serves 2.

MULLED CIDER

2 quarts sweet apple cider
20 whole cloves
½ cup sugar
12 sticks cinnamon
14 whole allspice
¼ teaspoon salt

Combine ingredients in the order listed, heat to boiling and simmer 15 minutes. Allow to stand 12 hours. Strain and serve hot. Serves 8 to 10.

NUTMEG ALMOND FLOAT

⅓ cup sugar
¼ teaspoon nutmeg
Dash salt
1 teaspoon almond extract
½ teaspoon vanilla
1 quart cold milk
1 pint vanilla ice cream

Add sugar, nutmeg, salt and flavorings to milk and stir until sugar is dissolved. Pour into chilled glasses and top with ice cream. Serves 6.

EGGNOG

1 egg, beaten
1 tablespoon sugar or honey
Salt
¾ cup milk
¼ teaspoon vanilla
Dash nutmeg

Combine egg with sugar and salt, add milk and vanilla. Serve cold in tall glasses and sprinkle with nutmeg. For a fluffy eggnog separate egg, beat white until stiff, then fold into egg yolk mixture. May be served hot or cold, for 1.

CARAMEL—Add 1 teaspoon caramel sirup. Omit nutmeg.

CHOCOLATE—Add 2 tablespoons chocolate or cocoa sirup. Omit nutmeg. Top with whipped cream and grated chocolate.

CIDER—Use only 1 teaspoon sugar. Omit milk, vanilla and nutmeg. Add ¼ cup cider and ½ cup chipped ice. Shake all ingredients together very well.

COFFEE—Use equal parts milk and strong coffee and omit vanilla and nutmeg.

EASTER EGGNOG — Use sugar and cream instead of honey and milk. Omit vanilla and nutmeg and flavor each serving with 2 tablespoons brandy.

FRUIT JUICE—Use just tne egg yolk and pineapple or orange juice instead of milk. Omit vanilla and nutmeg.

HONOLULU—Use half pineapple juice and half cream. Omit vanilla.

MINT—Add crushed sprays of mint; omit vanilla and nutmeg.

SOUTHERN EGGNOGS — (A) Use only 2 teaspoons sugar and flavor each eggnog with ¼ cup brandy, rye or bourbon whisky. (B) **SHERRY**—Use ½ glass sherry and ½ cup milk. (C) **CHRISTMAS**—Use rum instead of brandy or whisky.

CREAM OF CHOCOLATE

¼ pound sweet chocolate
½ cup hot water
6 eggs, separated
1 teaspoon vanilla
Few grains salt
1 cup heavy cream, whipped
Brandy or sherry

Melt chocolate in top of double boiler. Add hot water to make a smooth paste. Beat egg yolks very light, add chocolate and fold in stiffly beaten egg whites, vanilla and salt. Chill thoroughly. Serve with whipped cream, flavored with brandy or sherry. Serves 8.

EGG LEMONADE

1 egg, beaten
3 tablespoons lemon juice
3 tablespoons sugar
1 tablespoon crushed fruit (pineapple, peaches or berries)
⅔ cup plain or carbonated water

Combine chilled ingredients and shake or beat thoroughly. For 1.

CHOCOLATE EGG FLUFF

1 egg, separated
3 tablespoons chocolate sirup
¾ cup milk
1 teaspoon sugar
Nutmeg

Beat egg yolk, sirup and milk together. Beat egg white and sugar together until stiff, fold into milk. Pour into a chilled glass and sprinkle with nutmeg. For 1.

FRUIT JUICE FLUFF

3 tablespoons orange juice
½ cup grape juice
1 egg white, stiffly beaten
2 teaspoons confectioners' sugar
Dash salt

Combine fruit juices. Beat egg white until frothy, add sugar and salt and beat until stiff. Stir egg white carefully into fruit juices. Serves 1.

Mothers with a "problem child" will find the chocolate eggnog an unexcelled disguise for milk

HONEY EGG MILK SHAKE

1 egg, well beaten
1 cup cold milk
2 tablespoons honey
Chipped ice, if desired

Combine all ingredients in a shaker or jar with a tight fitting cover. Shake until thoroughly mixed. Serves 1.

ICE CREAM PUFF

1 egg, beaten
4 tablespoons fruit sirup
1 scoop vanilla ice cream
½ cup carbonated water
Dash nutmeg

Combine chilled ingredients and shake or beat thoroughly. For 1.

Served hot in winter or cold in summer, zabaglione will give your party a "happy ending"

HOT EGG MALTED MILK

2 tablespoons malted milk
2 tablespoons boiling water
1 egg, beaten
⅔ cup hot milk
Dash grated nutmeg

Make a paste of malted milk and boiling water. Add beaten egg and milk. Beat until smooth. Serve with nutmeg. May be served cold. Serves 1.

ROOT BEER EGG SHAKE

1 egg, beaten
2 teaspoons sugar
½ teaspoon root beer extract
¼ teaspoon salt
2 tablespoons cream
3 tablespoons orange juice
1 cup milk

Combine chilled ingredients and shake or beat thoroughly. For 1.

SILVER FIZZ

1 egg white
2 tablespoons lemon juice
1 tablespoon sugar
Shaved ice
Carbonated water
Lemon peel
Maraschino cherries

Combine white of egg, lemon juice, sugar and shaved ice in a shaker. Mix thoroughly, fill glass with carbonated water and garnish with lemon peel and cherry. Serves 1.

STRAWBERRY SHAKE

1 egg, well beaten
½ cup crushed strawberries
1 tablespoon lemon juice
2 tablespoons sugar

Combine all ingredients and shake with chipped ice until thoroughly blended. Serve with candied mint leaves. Serves 1.

VERMONT FLUFF

2 eggs, separated
½ cup maple sirup
1½ cups milk

Beat yolks and 1 white, add ¼ cup sirup and milk. Chill. Boil remaining sirup 3 minutes, pour over stiffly beaten white; beat until cool and use as a topping on beverage. Serves 2.

ZABAGLIONE

4 egg yolks
3 tablespoons honey
2 tablespoons Marsala or sherry
Dash of cinnamon

Beat egg yolks with honey in top of double boiler until thick and lemon colored. Place over heat and add wine gradually, beating constantly until the consistency of heavy cream. Add cinnamon Serve hot or very cold as a drink or dessert sauce. Serves 2 or 3.

Omit wine and add ½ cup orange juice. Serve cold.

RASPBERRY VINEGAR

1 quart cider vinegar
6 quarts fresh raspberries
Sugar

Pour vinegar over 3 quarts raspberries, let stand 24 hours and strain. Pour liquor over 3 more quarts raspberries, let stand 24 hours longer and strain. Measure juice and for each pint add 1 pound sugar; boil 20 minutes; skim. Cool and bottle. To serve, allow 4 parts ice water for 1 part raspberry vinegar.

BLACKBERRY CORDIAL

1 gallon blackberry juice
4 pounds sugar
2 ounces ground nutmeg
2 ounces ground cinnamon
1 ounce ground allspice
1 ounce ground cloves
2 quarts French brandy

Wash berries and mash slightly, cover with water and cook until soft Strain Measure 1 gallon juice, add sugar and spices, boil and skim Cook until mixture begins to thicken, about 30 minutes Cool Add brandy or whisky, bottle and cork at once.

DANDELION FLOWER WINE

4 quarts dandelion flowers
4 quarts boiling water
1 cake yeast
3 pounds sugar
3 oranges, diced; 3 lemons, diced

Select fresh flowers being careful all the stems have been removed Pour boiling water over flowers and let stand 3 days. Strain, add remaining ingredients and let stand 3 weeks until fermented Strain, bottle and seal Makes 8 pints

Raspberry vinegar is a fine cooler for summer afternoons

MULBERRY WINE

Select mulberries changing from red to black. Spread on cloth; let stand 24 hours. Place in kettle, squeeze out all juice and drain. Boil 1 gallon water for each gallon juice and add a little cinnamon, slightly bruised. Add 6 ounces sugar to each gallon of cinnamon water. After it has settled skim, strain and add to mulberry juice. Add 1 pint white or Rhenish wine for each gallon of liquid. Let stand in a cask 5 to 6 days. Draw off wine and keep in cool place.

BLACK CHERRY BRANDY

Stone 8 pounds black cherries and combine with 1 gallon brandy. Bruise stones in a mortar and combine with mixture Cover and let stand 4 to 6 weeks. Pour off clear brandy and bottle.

CHEESE DISHES

50
Nourishing
Cheese
Dishes

ALPINE MUFFINS

2 eggs, well beaten
1 cup milk
2 cups sifted rye flour
¼ cup sugar
3 teaspoons baking powder
½ teaspoon salt
¼ cup melted butter
½ pound Swiss cheese

Blend eggs and milk thoroughly. Sift flour, sugar, baking powder and salt together. Add gradually to milk mixture, blending thoroughly. Blend in butter. Pour a thin layer of batter into greased muffin pans, cover with a thin slice of cheese and add more batter. Bake in hot oven (400°F.) 10 minutes, then reduce temperature to moderate (350°F.) and bake 15 minutes longer. Serve hot. Makes 24.

Add raisins or currants to cheese corn sticks for extra appeal and serve hot from the pans

CHEESE BISCUIT RING

1 recipe Baking Powder Biscuit dough
1 cup grated American cheese

Roll biscuit dough into an oblong sheet about ½-inch thick. Sprinkle generously with cheese. Roll up like a jelly roll and bring the two ends together to form a ring. Place on baking sheet. With sharp scissors, cut through roll about 2 inches apart from outside of ring, about ⅔ of the way toward inside. Turn each section over, placing cut side on baking sheet. Bake in hot oven, (400° F.) 30 minutes or until lightly browned. Serve hot. Serves 10.

ROLLED CHEESE BISCUITS—
Prepare ring as above. Cut crosswise into slices, place on greased baking sheet, cut side down and bake in hot oven (400°F.) 15 minutes. Serves 8.

CHEESE BUTTER LEAVES

1 cup milk, scalded
½ cup butter
1 teaspoon salt
¼ cup sugar
1 or 2 cakes yeast
3 eggs, beaten
4½ cups sifted flour
1 cup grated American cheese
2 tablespoons butter
2 tablespoons milk

Pour milk over butter, salt and sugar and let stand until cooled to lukewarm. Crumble yeast into mixture and let stand 5 minutes. Add eggs and mix well. Add flour, kneading until smooth. Let rise until doubled in bulk, knead down and store in refrigerator until wanted. Roll dough into a rectangle ¼ inch thick, or as thin as possible. Combine remaining ingredients and heat in double boiler until cheese melts. Spread ½ cheese over half the dough. Fold over. Spread half the dough again with remaining cheese mixture and fold again. Cut into 1½-inch squares. Place squares cut side down in greased muffin pans. Let rise until doubled in bulk. Bake in hot oven (400°F.) 25 minutes. Makes 18.

CHEESE CORN STICKS

1 cup sifted flour
1 tablespoon sugar
1½ teaspoons salt
2 teaspoons baking powder
1 egg
2½ cups whole-kernel corn
½ cup grated cheese
½ cup butter, melted

Sift flour, sugar, salt, and baking powder. Add corn, cheese and butter to well-beaten egg. Combine with dry ingredients. Spoon batter into hot, greased cornstick pan sections. Bake at 425° F. 10 to 15 minutes. Makes 12 sticks.

Kitchen Measurements

Kitchen Measurements

TEASPOONS

10 drops = dash
dash = less than $1/8$ tsp.
1 tsp. = 6 dashes
1 tsp. = 5 milliliters
3 tsp. = 1 Tbsp.
8 tsp. = 1 oz.

TABLESPOONS

1 Tbsp. = $1/8$ fluid oz.
1 Tbsp. = 15 milliliters
2 Tbsp. = 1 fluid oz.
4 Tbsp. = $1/4$ cup or 2 oz.
16 Tbsp. = 1 cup or 8 oz.

CUPS

$1/8$ cup = 1 oz.
$1/8$ cup = 2 Tbsp.
$3/8$ cup = 6 Tbsp.
$1/3$ cup = 5 Tbsp. + 1 tsp.
$1/2$ cup = 8 Tbsp. or 4 oz.
$1/2$ cup = 1 tea cup
1 cup = $1/2$ pint
1 cup = 240 milliliters
2 cups = 1 pound (16 oz.)
4 cups = 1 quart

DRY VOLUMES

2 cups = 1 pint
2 pints = 1 quart
4 quarts = 1 gallon
2 gallons = 1 peck
4 pecks = 1 bushel

LIQUID MEASURES

1 ounce = 28 grams
$1^1/2$ oz. = 1 jigger
1 quart = 2 pounds
1 Tbsp. = $1/2$ liquid oz. or 15 grams
1 cup = 8 oz. or 227 grams
1 quart (32 oz.) = 907 grams
1 quart = 64 Tbsp.
1 pound = 454 grams

BUTTER

1 lb. = 32 Tbsp.
1 lb. = 2 cups
$1/4$ lb. = 1 bar
1 bar = 4 oz., $1/2$ cup

CHEESE

1 lb. American or cheddar type =
    4 cups grated
1 lb. cottage cheese = 2 cups
$1/2$ lb. cream cheese = 1 cup (8 oz.)

EGGS

$1/2$ cup = 2 large
$1/2$ cup = 3 medium

ONE-POUND EQUIVALENTS

2 cups butter
4 cups all-purpose flour
2 cups granulated sugar
$3^1/2$ c. powdered sugar
$2^2/3$ cups brown sugar
2 cups milk

If you'd like to collect more recipes, please contact:
My Great Recipes, 11150 W. Olympic Blvd., Los Angeles, CA 90064

Lemon cheese sticks are even more attractive when dredged with minced nuts or coconut

LEMON CHEESE STICKS

3 cups sifted flour
1 teaspoon salt
1 cup shortening
1 egg, slightly beaten
3 tablespoons lemon juice
Ice water
1½ cups grated American cheese

Sift flour and salt together. Cut in shortening with 2 knives or pastry blender. Add egg combined with lemon juice; then just enough ice water to bind dough together. Roll dough ¼ inch thick; sprinkle half with grated cheese. Fold and pat edges together, fold again and roll to ¼-inch thickness. Repeat process twice, 4 times in all; cut into strips ¼ or ½ inch wide. Bake in hot oven (450°F.) until lightly browned, about 10 minutes. Makes 54 sticks (6¼ x ¼ in.).

NEW ENGLAND CHEESE PUFFS

1 cup sifted flour
1 teaspoon baking powder
½ teaspoon salt
¼ teaspoon paprika
¼ teaspoon dry mustard
2 eggs, separated
½ cup milk
1 cup grated American cheese

Sift dry ingredients together. Beat egg yolks and add milk. Stir into dry ingredients and mix well. Add cheese. Beat egg whites until stiff and fold into batter. Drop from spoon into hot deep fat (360°F.) and cook until brown. Drain on absorbent paper. Serves 6.
Caraway or poppy seeds may be added. Make small puffs and serve with soup.

CHEESE STRAWS

⅓ cup grated American cheese
1 tablespoon butter
1½ teaspoons milk
4 tablespoons flour
½ cup fresh bread crumbs
⅛ teaspoon salt
Dash paprika and dash cayenne

Cream cheese and butter together; add milk. Mix flour, crumbs and seasonings, and add to cheese mixture. Knead lightly until smooth. Roll ⅛ inch thick, cut into (6x¾-inch) strips and bake on buttered pans in 400°F. oven 10 minutes. Makes 12.

CHEESE GEMS

1 recipe Baking Powder Biscuit dough
1 cup grated American cheese

Roll dough ⅓ inch thick. Cover with grated cheese. Cut into strips 2 inches wide and place 4 strips one on top of the other. Cut this strip into pieces 1¾ inches wide. Place each of these pieces upright in buttered custard cup, so that cut edges are on top and bottom. Bake in hot oven (425°F.) about 20 minutes or until browned. Makes 12.

CHEESE ENTRÉES

APPLES BAKED WITH CHEESE AND SAUSAGES

12 link pork sausages
4 tablespoons flour
2 cups hot water
1 tablespoon vinegar
½ teaspoon salt
4 medium apples
2 tablespoons brown sugar
¼ pound cheese, sliced

Place sausages in cold skillet, heat and cook slowly until browned, then place in casserole. Remove all but ¼ cup fat from skillet, add flour and brown. Add water gradually and cook until thickened. Add vinegar and salt. Pare and core apples and cut into rings. Arrange on sausages, sprinkle with brown sugar and pour sauce over. Cover and bake in moderate oven (350°F.) 30 minutes or until apples are tender. Arrange cheese on top and return to oven, uncovered, to melt and brown cheese. Serves 4 to 6. Pork sausage patties may be fried and used instead of sausage.

CHEESE BROCHETTES

½ loaf white bread, sliced
1½ pounds Swiss cheese, sliced ¼ inch thick
1½ cups milk
⅓ cup flour
2 egg yolks
¼ teaspoon salt
1 tablespoon water
Tomato Sauce

Cut bread and cheese into small squares or triangles and spear alternately with a small skewer until skewer is filled. Dip into milk, roll in flour, then dip into a mixture of egg yolks, salt and water. Fry in hot deep fat (375°F.) until brown. Serve with tomato sauce. Serves 8.

Add 1 teaspoon Worcestershire sauce to milk, if desired. Any favorite bread and well-flavored cheese may be used.

For a glowing dish on blustery days try apples, cheese and sausages in a hot casserole

OYSTERS LOUISIANA

1 dozen oysters
3 tablespoons butter
2 tablespoons chopped sweet red pepper
2 teaspoons cut onion
3 tablespoons flour
Dash cayenne, salt and pepper
½ cup Parmesan cheese

Simmer oysters in their liquor until plump. Drain and save liquor. Place drained oysters in a casserole and keep hot. Melt butter and sauté red pepper and onion. Blend in flour and add oyster liquor with enough water added to make 1½ cups. Heat to boiling, stirring constantly. Season and pour over oysters. Add cheese and bake at 350°F. 15 minutes. Serves 2 or 3.

NOODLE AND CHEESE CASSEROLE

4 strips bacon, diced and cooked
1½ cups noodles, cooked
1 cup cottage cheese

Combine all ingredients in greased casserole. Bake at (325°F.) 30 minutes. Serves 4.

CHEESE CROQUETTES

1 egg white
¾ cup grated cheese
¼ teaspoon salt, dash pepper
1 egg, beaten, cracker crumbs

Combine egg white, cheese, salt and pepper and shape into small croquettes. Roll in egg and then in crumbs. Fry in hot deep fat (370°F.). Serves 3.

Serve with Tomato or Horse-radish Cheese Sauce.

CHEESE FONDUE

5 eggs, separated
1¼ cups milk
2 cups soft bread crumbs
¾ teaspoon salt
½ teaspoon dry mustard
½ pound cheese, shredded

Beat egg yolks and add next 5 ingredients. Fold in stiffly beaten whites. Pour into buttered baking dish; set in pan of hot water and bake in slow oven (325°F.) 30 to 45 minutes, or until firm. Serves 5 to 8.

CHEESE CREOLE

¾ cup minced onions
¾ cup chopped green peppers
3 tablespoons butter
¾ cup milk
¾ cup condensed tomato soup
1½ cups grated pimiento cheese
1½ cups grated American cheese
3 egg yolks, well beaten
Hot thin toast

Cook onions and green peppers in butter until tender. Add milk and soup and stir until thoroughly heated. Add cheese and stir until melted. Add to egg yolks, stirring constantly. Return to heat and cook 1 minute. Serve on hot toast. Serves 6.

Chopped olives or celery may be used in place of the peppers.

DRIED BEEF CREOLE—Shred beef. Cover with boiling water and let stand 5 minutes. Prepare cheese creole. Drain beef and add with milk and soup.

Bread slices arranged in pyramids browned in the baking are an added lure in this cheese luncheon dish

CHEESE LUNCHEON DISH

12 slices day-old bread
½ pound Cheddar cheese
4 eggs
2½ cups milk
½ teaspoon salt
Dash pepper

Remove crusts from bread. Arrange 6 slices of bread in bottom of baking dish, fitting them in so that the entire surface is covered. Spread bread with cheese (or slice it and cover the bread with it). Cover with remaining 6 slices of·bread. Beat eggs, add milk and seasonings and pour over bread and cheese. Let stand 1 hour. Bake in moderate oven (325°F.) about 50 minutes or until puffed up and browned. Serves 6.

For variety, reserve 6 slices bread to place upright in casserole. Lightly butter one side of each slice. Fold buttered side out and place side by side in casserole. Bake and garnish with parsley.

CHICKEN CASSEROLE

1 (4- to 5-pound) chicken, cut for
    fricasseeing
1 (12-ounce) package noodles
⅔ cup minced onion
½ cup diced green pepper
1 cup tomato juice
2½ tablespoons flour
Salt and pepper
1 cup sliced canned or fresh
    mushrooms
1 cup whole-kernel corn
1 cup stuffed olives, sliced
1 cup grated cheese

Cover chicken with water and
simmer until tender. Cook noodles in boiling salted water until
tender; drain. Remove chicken
from bones and measure 2½ cups
broth. Cook onion and green
pepper in a little chicken fat until lightly browned, then add
tomato juice and chicken meat.
Mix flour with small amount of
broth until smooth and combine
with remaining broth, then with
chicken mixture. Simmer, stirring gently, until thickened. Add
noodles. Season with salt and
pepper; add mushrooms, corn and
olives. Place half of mixture in
buttered casserole and sprinkle
with ½ cup cheese. Add remaining mixture and sprinkle
remaining cheese over top. Bake
in moderate oven (350°F.) about
1 hour. Serves 8.

CRUMB CHEESE CROQUETTES

1 cup bread crumbs
2 tablespoons melted butter
2 cups grated cheese
2 eggs, well beaten
½ teaspoon salt
Few grains pepper

Mix all ingredients thoroughly.
Shape into small balls and fry
in hot deep fat (370°F.). Drain
on unglazed paper and serve very
hot. Serves 6.

CRAB AND CHEESE FONDUE

1 (6½-ounce) can crab meat
1 cup chopped celery
3 tablespoons mayonnaise
1 tablespoon prepared mustard
¼ teaspoon salt
8 thin slices white bread
¾ pound American cheese
2 eggs
1 cup milk
1 teaspoon Worcestershire sauce

Mix crab meat and celery. Combine mayonnaise, mustard and
salt; mix well and add to crab
meat. Spread between slices of
bread. Cut sandwiches into
halves. Slice cheese thin. Arrange sandwiches and cheese in
alternate layers in buttered casserole. Beat eggs; add milk and
Worcestershire sauce. Pour into
casserole. Cover and let stand 30
minutes. Bake in moderate oven
(350°F.) 45 minutes. Serve immediately. Serves 4.

Deviled egg and shrimp
make a casserole ready for
the most important luncheon
guest

DEVILED EGG AND SHRIMP CASSEROLE

6 hard-cooked eggs
2 tablespoons mayonnaise
¼ teaspoon mustard
Few grains pepper
¾ teaspoon salt
1½ cups cooked shrimp
3 tablespoons butter
4 tablespoons flour
3 cups milk
¼ pound American cheese,
    grated
1 cup buttered crumbs

Cut eggs into halves and remove
yolks. Mash yolks and mix with
mayonnaise, mustard, pepper and
¼ teaspoon salt. Fill whites with
mixture and arrange with cleaned
shrimp in buttered baking dish.
Melt butter and add flour and
remaining salt. Add milk gradually and cook in double boiler until thickened, stirring constantly.
Add cheese and stir until melted.
Pour over eggs and shrimp and
cover with buttered crumbs. Bake
in moderate oven (350°F.) 35
minutes. Serves 8.

Garnish with 3 deviled eggs,
green pepper ring and parsley.

Versatile cottage cheese combines with noodles and ham to make a delectable and highly nutritious casserole dish

HAM AND NOODLE MEDLEY

1 cup medium noodles
2 tablespoons butter
¼ cup chopped green pepper
½ cup chopped celery
1 small onion, chopped
2 tablespoons flour
½ teaspoon salt
¼ teaspoon pepper
2 cups milk
1 cup diced cooked ham
1½ cups creamed cottage cheese

Cook noodles in boiling, salted water until tender. Rinse and drain. Melt butter in saucepan. Saute green pepper, celery, and onion in butter. Blend in flour and seasonings. Gradually add milk and mix until well blended. Cook, stirring constantly, until smooth and thickened. Remove from heat; add ham, cottage cheese and noodles. Pour into buttered 2 quart casserole and bake at 350°F. for 30 minutes, or until top is bubbly and brown. Serves 6.

MACARONI AND CHEESE SUPREME

1 8-ounce package elbow macaroni
¼ cup butter
1 teaspoon chopped onion
¼ cup flour
1 teaspoon salt
⅛ teaspoon pepper
2 cups milk
2 tablespoons chopped parsley
1 teaspoon dried sweet basil
1 pimiento, chopped
2 cups shredded sharp Cheddar cheese
6 eggs

Cook macaroni in boiling, salted water until tender. Rinse and drain. Melt butter in saucepan. Saute onion in butter; add flour, salt and pepper; mix well. Stir in milk gradually. Cook, stirring constantly, until sauce is smooth and thickened. Add parsley, basil, and pimiento. Add cheese, saving ½ cup to garnish top of casserole. Cook until cheese melts.

Mix macaroni and cheese sauce. Pour into 9-inch square baking dish. Make six depressions in the top of macaroni mixture and break an egg into each one. Sprinkle remaining cheese on top, leaving eggs uncovered. Bake at 350°F. for 30 minutes, or until eggs are firm. Serves 6.

COTTAGE SCRAMBLE

1 tablespoon butter
5 eggs, slightly beaten
4 tablespoons water
¾ teaspoon salt
Dash pepper
½ cup cottage cheese
Chives or parsley

Melt butter in top of double boiler. Add next 4 ingredients. Stir from bottom as eggs begin to thicken. Fold in cheese; continue stirring until cheese is melted. Garnish with chopped chives or sprigs of parsley. Serve at once. Serves 5.

SWISS CHEESE RAMEKINS

6 slices toast
4 egg yolks, ¼ cup cream
1½ cups grated Swiss cheese
⅛ teaspoon nutmeg
⅛ teaspoon salt
4 egg whites, stiffly beaten

Trim crusts from toast and cut each slice into 2 triangles. In the bottom of 6 individual buttered ramekins place 2 triangles. Add cream to beaten yolks and beat until blended. Stir in grated cheese, nutmeg, and salt. Gently fold in beaten egg whites and pour mixture into prepared ramekins. Bake at 375°F. for about 30 minutes, or until golden brown on top. Serves 6.

CHEESE STUFFED CHILIES

4 long green chili peppers
½ pound cheese, grated
½ teaspoon salt
¼ teaspoon pepper
1 egg, beaten, Olive oil
1½ cups Tomato Sauce

Wash chili peppers, shake in pan over heat until skins are blistered. Roll in wet towel and let steam a few minutes until skins may be easily rubbed off. Split down one side, remove seeds and stuff with cheese, seasoned with salt and pepper. Dip in egg and fry in hot olive oil until browned. Serve with tomato sauce. Serves 4.

MEXICAN PEPPERS

2 cups browned bread crumbs
1 cup diced cheese
1 cup chopped nuts
2 teaspoons minced parsley
2 tomatoes, chopped
2 small onions, chopped
½ teaspoon salt
⅛ teaspoon pepper
8 green peppers
½ cup Brown Stock or water
1 egg, beaten

Combine first 8 ingredients, and if too dry, moisten with a little tomato juice, stock or water. Cut tops from peppers and remove seeds. Place peppers upright in baking dish. Fill with mixture and pour stock around them. Bake in hot oven (400°F.) 30 minutes. Dip pepper tops into beaten egg and brown in hot deep fat. Place tops on peppers. Serves 8.

SURPRISE PEPPERS

6 medium green peppers
2 cups cooked celery root, diced
1 small onion, finely chopped
1 No. 2 can cream style corn
1 egg, well beaten
1 cup buttered cracker crumbs
½ cup grated American cheese
¾ teaspoon salt
Dash pepper, Buttered crumbs

Cut tops off peppers and remove seeds. Parboil 10 minutes. Drain and leave whole or cut into halves lengthwise. Mix remaining ingredients together, except buttered crumbs, and fill peppers with mixture. Sprinkle buttered crumbs over top. Place in buttered casserole and bake in moderate oven (350°F.) 25 to 30 minutes. Serves 6.

SPINACH CASSEROLE

2 cups cooked fine noodles
2 cups drained cooked spinach
½ teaspoon salt
¼ teaspoon pepper
½ pound American cheese, grated
2 cups Thin White Sauce

Place noodles and spinach in alternate layers in buttered baking dish, sprinkle with salt, pepper and cheese. Pour white sauce over spinach. Bake in moderate oven (350°F.) until browned. Serves 6.

Spinach with egg
Is sure to appeal
So try it with soufflé
For your very next meal

SPINACH AU GRATIN

1 quart spinach
2 tablespoons chopped parsley
4 tablespoons butter
4 eggs, well beaten
2 cups milk
1 cup grated Swiss cheese
1 teaspoon salt
½ teaspoon paprika

Wash and chop spinach. Add parsley and cook in butter 10 minutes. Add beaten eggs to milk and pour over spinach. Add cheese and seasonings, turn into buttered baking dish, place in pan of hot water and bake at (300°F.) 45 minutes. Serves 6.

Top with soufflé, if desired. Separate 2 eggs. Beat yolks. Add ½ cup Thick White Sauce. Fold in stiffly beaten whites. Cover spinach and bake

MOLDED FRUIT AND CAKE

1 square cake layer
1 package strawberry gelatin
1¾ cups boiling water
4 half pears, cooked
Green grapes or cherries
½ recipe Cream Cheese Frosting

Make a stiff paper collar 4 inches high all around cake. Fasten securely. Dissolve gelatin in boiling water. Cool. When gelatin begins to thicken, pour thin layer over cake inside collar. Arrange fruit on gelatin and chill. Pour remaining fluid gelatin over the fruit and chill until firmly set. Warm a knife in hot water and remove paper collar from gelatin. Frost cake with cream cheese frosting. Serves 12.

CHEESE CAKE

2 cups fine zwieback crumbs
1½ cups sugar
1 teaspoon cinnamon
½ cup melted butter, 4 eggs
⅛ teaspoon salt
1½ tablespoons lemon juice
1½ teaspoons grated lemon rind
1 cup cream or evaporated milk
1½ pounds cottage cheese
4 tablespoons flour
¼ cup chopped nuts

Mix zwieback with ½ cup sugar, cinnamon and butter. Set aside ¾ cup of mixture to sprinkle over the top; press remainder into 9-inch spring-form pan, lining bottom and sides. Beat eggs with remaining 1 cup sugar until light; add salt, lemon juice, rind, cream, cheese and flour; beat thoroughly and strain through a fine sieve. Pour into lined pan, sprinkle with remaining crumbs and nuts. ·Bake in moderate oven (350°F.) about 1 hour or until center is set. Turn off heat, open oven door, let stand in oven 1 hour or until cooled. Serves 10.

CHEESE PIE

½ cup butter
1 cup coarsely ground nuts
1¼ cups sugar
½ cup sifted flour
¼ teaspoon almond extract
¾ teaspoon vanilla
6 ounces cream cheese
4 eggs, separated
1 cup milk

Mix butter, nuts, ¼ cup sugar, flour, almond extract and ¼ teaspoon vanilla. Pat the mixture into a pie plate. Soften cheese and add slightly beaten egg yolks, milk and ½ cup sugar. Beat until smooth as cake batter. Add remaining vanilla and pour on top of nut mixture. Bake in moderate oven (350°F.) 45 to 60 minutes or until firm. Allow to cool in oven, then top with a meringue made from the stiffly beaten egg whites and remaining sugar. Brown meringue in slow oven (325°F.) 15 to 18 minutes. Makes 1 (9-inch) pie.

CHERRY CHEESE PIE

2 cups pitted fresh cherries
1½ tablespoons quick-cooking tapioca
¾ cup sugar
½ cup shortening
4 ounces cream cheese
1½ cups sifted flour
½ teaspoon salt

Combine cherries, tapioca and sugar and let stand 15 minutes. Blend shortening and cheese; cut into flour sifted with salt. Press into a firm ball and roll ½ the dough lightly on floured surface; line piepan with pastry. Fill with cherry mixture. Roll remaining pastry and cut into strips. Arrange strips crisscross on top of cherries. Bake in moderate oven (350°F.) 45 minutes. Makes 1 (9-inch) pie.

For one table of bridge nothing can quite match this decorative molded fruit dessert

HUNGARIAN PANCAKES

1 tablespoon butter
2 tablespoons sugar
4 eggs, separated
1 cup dry cottage cheese
2 tablespoons bread crumbs
1 tablespoon chopped sultana
   raisins
1 cup sour cream
Confectioners' sugar
1 recipe Thin Pancakes

Cream butter and sugar together. Add egg yolks, 1 at a time, beating well. Add cheese, crumbs, raisins and half the sour cream. Beat egg whites until stiff and fold into mixture. Bake thin pancakes, spread with cheese mixture and roll up. Place close together in buttered shallow baking dish and pour remaining cream over them. Bake in moderate oven (350°F.) about 30 minutes. Sprinkle with confectioners' sugar and serve at once. Serves 6.

Omit ½ cup sour cream. Spread pancakes with cheese and roll. Cover with preserved cherries and confectioners' sugar.

THIN PANCAKES

½ cup sifted flour
½ teaspoon salt
½ cup milk
4 eggs, well beaten
2 tablespoons shortening

Sift flour and salt together. Combine milk with eggs; add to flour slowly and beat until smooth. For each pancake, pour 1 teaspoon shortening on griddle; heat well, spreading shortening over entire surface. Pour few tablespoons batter and tilt griddle back and forth to spread batter. Fry until pancake is covered with bubbles, then turn and brown.

JELLY CHEESE DESSERT MOLDS

1 tablespoon unflavored gelatin
¼ cup cold water
½ teaspoon salt
¾ cup cream
2 cups drained cottage cheese
Red jelly

Soften gelatin in cold water 5 minutes and dissolve over hot water. Add salt, cream and cottage cheese. Line individual molds with mixture and chill until firm. Fill center with jelly and cover with remaining cheese mixture. Chill until firm. Unmold and serve with crackers or fresh fruit. Serves 4 to 6.

Make your pancake all in one. When it is done, fill in the cherries and cheese

CHEESE COOKIES

3 ounces cream cheese
½ cup butter
½ cup sugar, 1 egg yolk
½ teaspoon vanilla
1 cup sifted flour
¼ teaspoon salt
⅛ teaspoon nutmeg

Blend cheese and butter together, add sugar and egg yolk and cream together thoroughly. Add vanilla. Sift remaining ingredients together and add to cream mixture. Chill until firm enough to roll. Roll out on lightly floured board, cut with cookie cutter and place on greased baking sheet. Bake in moderate oven (375°F.) about 10 minutes. Makes 24 cookies.

FILLED CHEESE PASTRY

½ pound butter
¼ pound cream cheese
1 cup sifted flour

Cream butter well. Add cream cheese and blend well. Stir in flour and chill. Roll out dough, cut into squares or triangles and fill with jam, cooked prunes or any other cooked fruit, drained well of all juice. Fold dough and pinch edges together. Bake in moderate oven (350°F.) 10 minutes. Makes 8 to 10 squares.

Fine Art
of
Carving

Choose the carving set with care, and keep it protected, so the knife is not dulled or nicked. There are 3 styles: (1) full size, with the guard on the fork; (2) small steak set without a guard; and (3) the meat slicer with carver's helper. In any case, buy the steel for keeping the blade in condition, and use it as in this diagram.

The butcher will separate the back-bone from the rib on the standing rib roast. Remove it in the kitchen, after roasting. Use a platter that gives the carver plenty of serving space. Place the roast with large flat side down. With the fork in the left hand, guard up, remove each slice to the plate as carved.

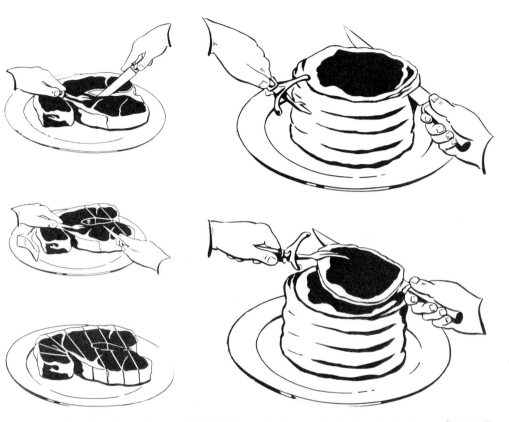

Use the steak set and insert fork at left of the **porterhouse steak** close to the bone. Slice with the fiber, not against it, as in other meats. As the bone is eliminated, move it to edge of plate. Rolled rib roast has ribs and backbone removed and is tied with heavy, clean cord. On a large platter, largest end down, carve it straight across, serving each slice as it comes.

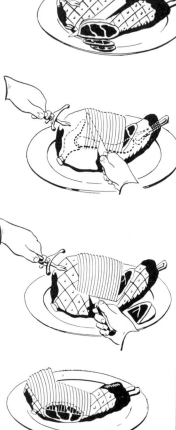

The butcher will separate the backbone from the ribs of the loin or candle roast, so that in the roasting, it can easily be removed before serving. Place the roast on the platter so the rib side faces the carver. This makes the rib an easy guide for slicing. A steak set does very well for use here, but care must be taken not to strike the sides of the ribs as the knife is inserted. If sliced even, there should be two boneless slices between two adjoining ribs.

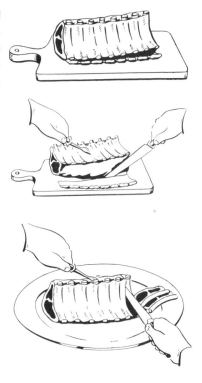

Place ham on a roomy platter, with the decorated side up, and the shank at the carver's right. A ham from the left leg will have the thick slices nearest the carver. Use the standard carving set with the fork's guard up. Or, if very tender, the meat slicer, and carver's helper. After the first thick slices are removed from the side begin to carve down the center, beginning at the second joint as in the illustrations.

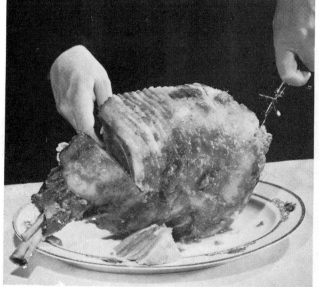

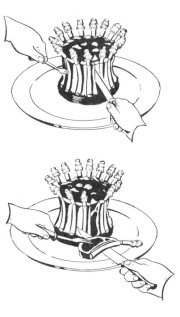

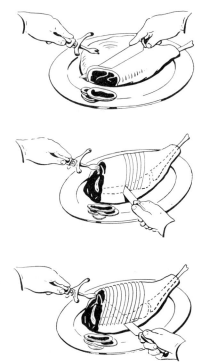

The crown roast is a loin roast rolled around the hand, and either tied or skewered together. It is carved exactly like the candle roast, except that if the center is filled with vegetables, they must be served as the carver proceeds.

A leg of lamb, like ham, should be placed on a roomy platter with the shank to the right of the carver. The carving is almost like ham. Slices are removed from the thick side, and then cross the grain, beginning at the second joint. The standard carving set is usually necessary.

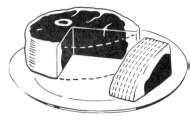

A blade pot roast is handled very much like the porterhouse steak except that often the bones are removed before the roast is served, and the meat is carved across the grain, since it is less tender than the porterhouse.

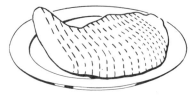

The center cut ham slice, beef tongue, picnic shoulder of pork, and beef brisket are carved according to the diagrams shown.

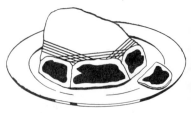

CARVING POULTRY

To carve poultry with ease and skill some information ought to be at hand about the bird and its bony structure, since most carving is done on the unboned bird. After roasting the ligaments between the joints are soft and pliable. By grasping the paper tip of the drum stick the joint can be found without trouble. Thrust the point of the knife into this spot and cut both ways. The joint will come away easily. If it is very thick as in the turkey, one or more slices may be cut from it. The fork is thrust into the second joint and when its joint at the body is located insert the point of the knife cutting both ways as before. Another method is to remove the whole leg at the body, then separate them on the serving plate. The wings come away from the body quite easily with the same technique. When both are removed slice the white meat parallel with the breastbone. This gives the largest slices and an even distribution. If there is a stuffing it is removed from the end of the body usually before the second leg is removed.

Turkey is carved in the same
way, fundamentally, as other
fowl except that the bird is so
well covered with meat that
there is more to slice. The
stuffing may be piled in a
mound and the slices piled on
it or the slices may be laid in
a tilted pile and the stuffing
served separately. The boned
fowl or the boned and rolled
turkey are sliced straight
through as in a rolled roast.
The procedure for boning of
chicken is on pages 410-411
and the boning and rolling of
turkey on pages 444-445.

Table Setting
and
Entertaining

FORMAL SERVICE

The modern homemaker has every opportunity to express the charm and cordiality of her household in her dining room. This room, with tastefully selected furniture and table appointments, can help give a house its aura of permanence and warm-hearted living. The table settings and food service can be so well chosen and smoothly executed that the personality and graciousness of the hostess will be clearly reflected to all present.

The clever hostess keeps her dining room and its appointments perpetually well groomed and always ready for the guest who just drops in. There should never be any feeling of a flurried rush to put things in order. The fragrance of well prepared food should not be mingled unpleasantly with the strong odor of furniture polish. The convenient arrangement of furniture and allowance of plenty of room for serving each guest can add a feeling of warm spaciousness to the already congenial room. The hostess should plan her table setting and food service well in advance. This means that she has checked her linen, china, glass, and silver to be sure of having appropriate, adequate service for all the guests.

LINEN

TABLECLOTHS—White damask is the classic table covering for the formal dinner. Linen and lace, embroidered linen or elaborate all-lace tablecloths are also correct and are used without a pad under them. The damask cloth is always laid over a pad or silence cloth which protects the table surface from damage and will help provide a noiseless service. Silence cloths are made of double cotton flannel and may be made at home by cutting them to fit exactly to the edge of your table. The pads are a heat-proof material cut and finished by the manufacturer to fit any table.

Lace is one of the correct cloths for lunch and while white damask is never used, the colored damask is appropriate. If you have an especially beautiful table, it can be attractively set with lace or other mats and damask napkins, leaving the rest of the table bare. A refectory table might be covered only with a runner in the center, dropping at both ends.

The tea table presents a good opportunity to use lovely embroidered or hemstitched tea cloths, a simple or elaborate lace cover, or a combination of linen and lace. The conventional tea cloth is white but a colored cloth may also be used in good taste.

The proper dinner cloth for the large table will hang evenly on all sides with a 15 to 18 inch drop. The cloth for the small table will have a drop of 12 inches on all sides while the lace cloth will usually have a longer drop. For dinners of 18 to 20 a tablecloth 6 yards long by 2½ yards wide or a 4 yard square may be utilized. Dinners of 10 to 12 require a tablecloth ranging from 2½ to 4 yards long and a cloth about 1½ yards square may be used for dinners being served at small tables. When purchasing linens the wise homemaker will measure the table top, allow for the drop, and keep in mind that the appropriate French hem should be from ¼ to ⅜ of an inch wide. The accepted size of doilies is 12 to 18 inches and many sets are used without runners to avoid an over-covered

Table decorations that match the linens with unadorned silver and china mark the formal table setting of taste and distinction

look on a bare table. Doilies should not overlap the runner.

NAPKINS—Dinners of 18 or more require a large dinner napkin measuring 30 by 36 inches or a square of approximately that size.

FORMAL SERVICE

The napkins that are 27 by 30 inches are appropriate for the tablecloth ranging from 2½ to 4 yards in length. Napkins should match the tablecloths and have hems of ⅛ to ¼ of an inch wide. When a lace tablecloth is used, dinner napkins of white damask may be used with it. Luncheon napkins are smaller than the dinner napkins, usually about 15 inches to 18 inches, and the tea napkin is 12 inches square. Napkins should be just as carefully laundered and precisely folded as the tablecloth they are being used with. Those with only one crease may be wound around a holder or laid in a drawer when not in use and later folded when needed.

Linen and organdy make a dainty table covering

MONOGRAMMING — A monogram must harmonize with the linen in type, design and size for perfect harmony and good taste. If there is no clear area on the cloth for the monogram, then the lettering should appear on the napkins alone.

For the large tablecloths the monogram is placed on either side of the center and midway between the center and edge of the table. Small yard-and-a-half tablecloths are marked at the corner, a foot from the center.

Square monograms look well on plain cloths and set in line with the table edge. More decorative monograms are better suited to elaborate cloths and are attractive when cross-cornered. The letters in a tablecloth monogram usually vary from 2 to 5 inches in height. The dinner napkin monogram is from 1 to 2 inches tall and monograms for the lunch or breakfast napkins are from ¾ to 1½ inches.

A large napkin has its monogram in the very center. It is folded into thirds lengthwise and thirds crosswise, making 9 thicknesses. With the edges turned under into a flattened roll, the monogram will show on the top. To have the monogram appear at the corner after folding, place the letters ½ inch from the right hand selvedge corner. Breakfast and luncheon napkins are folded once crosswise and once lengthwise, making 4 thicknesses, and the monogram appears on the top fold in the lower right-hand corner. When a napkin is folded so the edge is to the right, care should be taken that the monogram is on top.

CHINA

The greatest medium for bringing color and warmth to a formal table setting is the china. The stately dignity that a formal occasion demands can be mirrored in the dinner china and in the delicate patterns of the luncheon china. The homemaker can ac- cent the period setting of her room by selecting a china appropriate to that period or she can select different patterns and colors for the various courses, all of which blend harmoniously. Cups, saucers and little plates for tea service may be patterned, or a solid white or ivory, and used with service plates of china, silver or glass.

PLATES AND HOW USED— China producers have not agreed on measurement and standardization of plate sizes, giving rise to much confusion. The various trade sizes are often used to designate the same size plate, so, in the following list, measurements, in inches, are from rim to rim.

Service plate (also called a cover plate, place plate, or lay plate)— 10 to 11 inches, placed at each cover.

Dinner plate (roast plate)—10 inches, but seen as large as 10½ inches.

Entrée plate—8½ to 9½ inches. Used for serving salad, fish, the entrée, and the dessert when the finger bowl is brought in with the dessert silver.

Dessert plate—7½ to 8 inches. Used for desserts, salads, and as the cake plate at teas.

Bread-and-butter plate — 6 to 6½ inches. Used for all occasions except formal dinners. May be used for tea service to hold sandwiches, muffins, cakes and cups of tea.

Soup plate—8 to 8½ inches at rim, for the usual type of soup plate with the wide, flat rim. There is also a bowl soup plate, or coup soup, which has no rim.

Cream soup cup—4½ to 5 inches wide and about 2 inches deep. This low, broad cup, handled on both sides, is used for serving purées, bisques, cream soups, and clear soup at lunches and informal dinners.

Bouillon cup—this is the size of a tea cup but has 2 handles. Clear soups, consommés, and bouillons are served in it.

After-dinner coffee cup and saucer—these tiny cups and saucers are used for after-dinner coffee or demitasse. They come in sets, or a collection of various shapes and sizes may be used; thus they need not match.

GLASS

Clear, sparkling glass is the resplendent note on the formal table.

The king of the table glass, the long-stemmed goblet, is the preferred water glass for formal dinner use and is accompanied by not more than 3 other glasses, a glass for sherry, a glass for red or white wine and one for champagne. At banquet dinners, 4 glasses, in addition to the goblet, may be used.

The long-stemmed or short-stemmed goblet is correct to use for the formal lunch, and footed or plain tumblers and short-stemmed goblets are used for buffets or formal breakfasts.

For punch service use a large silver, china, or glass bowl, with its accompanying ladle and small cup-like glasses with handles.

GLASS MONOGRAMMING —

Personal taste is the only guide as to the kind and size of the monogram on glassware but it should be remembered that either all or none of the glassware should be marked. The monogram may be the single initial of the last name or all the initials. Glass for the dining table should be marked with the wife's initials while whisky or cocktail glasses are marked with the husband's initials.

SIZES AND USE— The shape, size and capacity of each glass differs with its use.

Goblet—capacity, 9 to 10 ounces. Usually from 7 to 8 inches high, the goblet has a flaring round bowl on a tall or short stem. The low goblet stem flares immediately into the foot and both types are used only for water. The goblet always has a foot, no matter how short the stem. It is the dominant member of the place-glass group and sets the style.

Large wineglass—capacity, 4 to 6 ounces. A duplicate of the goblet, the large wineglass used for dinner wines is the other regular member of the place glass group. The all-around wineglass holds about 5 ounces and is used throughout the entire meal.

Small wineglass—capacity, 2 to 3 ounces. Used for dessert, appetizer and heavier wines, at the table and away from it.

Cocktail glass — capacity, 2

ounces. Coming in countless shapes, the cocktail glass need not match the glass table service.

Brandy-inhaler — capacity, 5 ounces. This glass is recognized by its huge bowl in which is twirled 1 ounce of choice brandy for the development and enjoyment of the bouquet. This "snifter" may be 10, 14 or 16 ounces.

Liqueur glass—capacity less than 1 ounce. Used to serve brandies or liqueurs. This glass may resemble tumbler wine glass or parfait glass, but need not match the other glass.

Claret glass—capacity, 4 ounces. A round, bowl-shaped top on a tall stem and used for red and white wines.

Port glass—capacity, 3 ounces. Claret glass shaped.

Sherry glass—capacity, 4 to 5 ounces. Triangular in shape when viewed sideways and known as the "pipestem" glass.

Rhinewine glass—capacity, 4 to 5 ounces. This glass often has elaborate bowls and does not need to match the other place glass group. Used to serve Rhinewines and Moselles.

Champagne glasses—Glasses for champagne are of many varieties, should be of thin crystal and not over-decorated.

> *Coup*—This is a very shallow bowl on a tall, solid stem flared to a foot and is known as the "saucer" glass.

> *Trumpet*—This is a tall, slender glass, cornucopia shape, very narrow at base, and on a foot. The pointed bottom where it joins the foot aids the release of bubbles.

> *Hollow-stem*—This bowl of glass rests on a tubular stem and foot. The stem, open at the top, allows a rising fountain of bubbles.

Goblet—This is like a small water goblet.

Sherbet glass—capacity, 5 ounces. This glass has a medium depth, broad bowl on either a stem or a low foot and is used to serve ice cream, sherbet and frozen dessert.

Cocktail bowl with liner—This is a double bowl— a large bowl on a stem which holds cracked ice, and a small cup which contains the chilled sea-food, grapefruit or other cocktails. It is sometimes called a grapefruit bowl and comes in many sizes.

Finger bowl—The finger bowl is a low, broad bowl, round in shape and sometimes footed. It may come with matching under-plate, the use of which is optional.

Compote—This is a shallow bowl from 4 to 6 inches in width on a thick stem and foot and is used for candies and nuts.

METALS

Heirloom or collected antique pewter or silver, and the excellent copies of both made today in flatware and hollow ware, are much in demand, especially in the period dining room. A golden, solid metal alloy is comparatively new in the making of flatware and hollow ware, and is very attractive on the dining table.

SILVER

Whether sterling or plated, table silver is one of the proudest possessions of any hostess. The choice of sterling silver assures lasting beauty and lifetime wear, as does the very durable triple-plated (heavy-weight) silver. Plated silver may also be had in double-plated ware (medium weight), which has good wearing qualities and single-plated ware (light weight).

FLATWARE — A silver pattern should be chosen with great care and should harmonize with the furnishings and appointments of the dining room. Any of the classic silver patterns are always a wise selection for those who have no definite choice. Before purchasing, a check should be made to prevent buying a silver pattern which may soon be discontinued. The pieces of silver should be examined for size and shape. The handles should be comfortable to hold and well-balanced, and the tips of handles of the knives and forks should fit comfortably in the hand.

HOLLOW WARE PIECES—Some silver manufacturers make hollow ware for all the table service while others make only the more popular pieces. Silver hollow ware need not match the table flatware but special attractiveness is added to the table when it does.

After-dinner coffee set
Almond dish, Ash tray
Aspic tray, Beverage set
Bonbon dish, Bread tray
Bread-and-butter plate
Cake basket or tray
Candlesticks or candelabra

Card tray, Casserole
Cheese and cracker dish
Centerpiece dish
Chafing dish, Compotier
Coffee service, Cream pitcher
Cups, Entrée dish
Flower basket or dish
Fruit bowl or tray
Gravy boat and tray
Jam or jelly jar, Juice cup
Luncheon tray
Meat platter or tray, plain or with well and tree
Mayonnaise bowl
Match box holder
Muffin tray, Pepper and salt
Porringer, Pitcher
Punch bowl, Relish dish
Salad bowl, Sauce bowl
Sandwich plate
Service plate
Sugar bowl or basket
Sirup bowl and plate
Tea service
Vegetable bowl, covered or uncovered and with or without handles
Vegetable bowl, double or triple
Waiter tray

Silver hollow ware gives a regal accent to your table and with proper care will bring joy your life long

and are used for many desserts, cereals and fruits.
Angel cake cutter
Asparagus server
Berry spoon, Butter knife
Cake server
Carving sets, large size for roasts medium size for steaks
Cheese server
Cold meat fork
Entrée server, round and flat
Grape scissors, Gravy ladle
Ice tongs, Jelly server
Lemon fork, Melon knife
Olive spoon or olive fork
Pickle fork
Pie or ice cream server
Pierced server, used for serving many foods
Poultry shears, Poultry tongs
Preserve spoon
Salad dressing ladle
Salad fork and spoon
Sugar sifter, Sugar spoon
Sugar tongs, Tablespoon

Harmonize the design of monogram with the style and shape of your silver

PLACE AND SERVING PIECES—

Dinner knife and fork—used only for the meat course of a formal dinner and lunch.

Luncheon knife and fork—used at breakfast, lunch, buffets, and dinner, except for the meat course. May also be called the dessert knife and fork or entrée knife and fork.

Fish knife and fork—the knife has a dull, rounded blade and a notch on one side. The fork is shaped like a salad fork with the center tines longer at the bowl of the fork.

Tea knife and fork—used for pastries and for the spreading of jam on muffins at teas. They are smaller than the luncheon size knife and fork.

Cocktail fork—used for sea foods. It is a short, slender fork about ½ inch wide at the prong end of the fork.

Salad fork—used for salads and some desserts. It is a shorter handled fork with prongs that are also short, broad and widely spaced.

Teaspoon—used for many of the same purposes as the dessert spoon. It is used for all beverages served in cups.

Coffee spoon or five o'clock teaspoon—used for afternoon tea or coffee and is smaller than the teaspoon.

After-dinner coffee spoon—used in small cups. It is half the size of a teaspoon and need not match the table silver.

Orange spoon—used for halved oranges and other fruits. It has a round or eight-sided bowl with a pointed tip.

Dessert spoon—used for many kinds of dessert, fruit, cereal and soups. It is a medium spoon, a size between the teaspoon and the tablespoon. It is never used for soup in plates.

Saltspoon—used in individual salt dishes, it is 1½ inches long with a 5/16 inch bowl.

Soupspoon—there are 3 round and 3 oval soupspoons; the large round soupspoon, the round cream soupspoon and the round bouillon soupspoon. The large oval soupspoon is the tablespoon and is used as a serving spoon. The smaller oval soupspoon and the dessert spoon are interchangeable

MONOGRAMMING—Silver is traditional and a study of the design and period of the silverware and lettering combinations should be made before monogramming. One initial, or a combination of initials, may be engraved on both flat and hollow ware. When a single initial is used it is usually the initial of the husband's family name. The initials of the wife's maiden name, or the two initials of the wife and the initial of the husband's family name is preferred when three initials are used. Sometimes small initials of the first names of husband and wife are linked together with a plus sign along with the large initial of the husband's family name, or the initials of both the families' names are used. If the husband's family has a crest, this may be used as a monogram on the silver, but the wife's family crest is not used.

Candles on a formal lunch table are proper when there is no daylight

DECORATIONS

The centerpiece for formal meals can be of almost unlimited variety. An artistic arrangement of flowers in proportion to the flower container is most popular although dishes or ornaments of china, glass or silver, which need no flowers, are often used. Unusual effects may be obtained with formal arrangements of fruits and flowers, fruits alone, delicate figurines and other accessories.

The number of candles used on a formal dinner table depends on the size of the table and whether the dining room is otherwise lighted. There must be a candle for every person when candles are used alone to light the table and room and these should be of natural or white wax. The flame of the lighted candle should be well above eye level to avoid glare. The height of the candles should be in proportion to the candlestick and the candles should be lighted before the guests enter the dining room and allowed to burn until they leave.

Place cards are used at formal dinners and luncheons for convenience of seating the guests. They are usually plain, about the size of a visiting card, 1½ by 2 inches long.

Compotes in a variety of shapes and materials are placed on the formal table equally spaced and conveniently located. These hold fruits, nuts, candies and other edibles used more for their decorative appearance than as part of the menu.

Decorations for the formal luncheon are practically the same as for dinners. An overly large table may be decorated with several duplicate vases of flowers or other ornaments. Candles are never used on the formal luncheon or breakfast table except when the dining room is without daylight.

SETTING THE TABLE

A perfect table setting depends on artistic decision in the table decorations and mathematical precision in laying the carefully chosen table appointments. For the formal dinner the white damask tablecloth, with its one crease lengthwise, is laid precisely down the middle of the table. All edges of the cloth fall at equal distances from the floor, 15 to 18 inches below the edges of the table.

The centerpiece should be put in the center of the table next, along with the candles and compotes at equal distances from the center piece.

The cover is the place set for one person at the beginning of a meal. Place the necessary number of plates with the pattern right side up at equal distances on the table, allowing the guests enough room for elbow space and comfort, 24 inches from plate-center to plate-center is ideal.

After putting on the cover plate the silver is laid with the lower edge of the plate and the tips of the handles of the silver in exact line and all silver parallel to each other. To the right of the cover plate are placed all the knives in a straight parallel line with cutting edge toward the plate; the spoons are to the right of these. On the left are all the forks except the cocktail fork, which is laid to the extreme right of the knives when placed. The silver pieces are placed in convenient sequence for use, starting from the outside for the first course and working toward the plate. From left to right the usual arrangement is—fish fork, meat fork, salad fork, the cover plate, salad knife, meat knife, fish knife, soupspoon and cocktail fork or grapefruit spoon. If an entrée is to be served, the fork for this is placed between the fish fork and the meat fork, leaving the salad fork to be brought in later. Not more than 3 knives and 3 forks are placed on the table when it is set. All additional forks and knives are placed on the table during dinner, as courses are served. The dessert silver is either laid before dessert service or brought in on dessert plates. Every dish to be served should have the necessary silver serving pieces.

The water goblet is placed above the blade tip of the dinner knife with the champagne glass to the right, the claret glass in front between these 2 glasses, and the sherry glass in front or a little to the right of the claret glass. If burgundy is to be served, this glass should be in back between the goblet and champagne glass. The glasses may be set in one row diagonally from the goblet.

The napkin is folded and laid on the cover plate parallel with the silver. Fancy foldings are not in good taste but very large napkins may be folded to form a flattened roll. When food is on the plate before the guests are seated, the napkin is laid at the left of the forks with the open side facing the plate.

Salt-and-pepper shakers, or salt dishes and pepper pots, are placed between every 2 covers, or if there are only a few guests, the sets may be placed at the ends of the table.

Place cards and individual nut dishes are placed above the cover.

The after-dinner coffee tray should be large enough to hold the coffee pot, sugar bowl, cream pitcher and after-dinner coffee cups and saucers with the coffee spoons on them. If a silver urn or Russian samovar is to be used, it is carried in filled with hot coffee and placed on a tray that is already on a convenient serving table. The coffee is served from this table and the cups, saucers, spoons, sugar bowl and cream pitcher are on tray or table.

The table for formal luncheon is set with the places as for dinner, with the cover plate, 3 forks, 2 knives and a small spoon. The smaller lunch napkin, matching the table linen, is folded twice and the bread-and-butter plate with the butter spreader is part of the cover.

The formal tea table, unless of glass, is always covered with a tea cloth which may barely cover the table or hang ½ yard over each edge. A tray large enough to hold everything except the plates of food is placed on the table. This tray may be of silver, glass, aluminum or lacquered tin or wood and should hold the practical kettle, which has been filled with boiling water before being carried in, with a heating unit under it. Heat is applied after the tray is down on the table. On the tray also is an empty teapot, a full caddy, a tea strainer and drip bowl. A dish with lemon slices, bowls of sugar, cream, cups and saucers, little tea plates with a neatly folded napkin between each, flat silver suited to the menu, and dishes for the cakes, toast, muffins or sandwiches are all on the table.

Extra plates of food ready to be served may be placed on accessory furniture.

TABLE SERVICE

For the formal table, the Russian style of service is used. All food is served from the kitchen by servants, meat is carved in the kitchen and served individually or arranged for the guests to serve themselves, and vegetables are passed to each person and then returned to the kitchen. No food, except at formal breakfasts, is put on the dining table but the compotes containing candy and nuts.

Dishes are always presented at the left of the person served and are usually removed at the left, although, if more convenient, may be removed at the right. They are placed and removed one plate at a time, never stacked. They are presented flat on the palm with a folded napkin on the hand as a pad for hot dishes Glasses are filled and knives placed at the right and forks are placed at the left. A tray covered with a doily is used to pass several small articles such as silverware or sugar bowl and creamer

There must always be a plate before each guest until the table is cleared for dessert. The service plate is placed on the table when the covers are laid. The soup course and pre-soup course are set on top of the service plate and when the soup course is removed the service plate is removed also, and the plate for the next course is placed immediately. The service plate never reappears.

Rolls are passed at dinner when the soup is served, and guests take them with their fingers, laying the rolls on the tablecloth When the table is cleared for dessert, all plates, salts and peppers, wine glasses and dishes of nuts are removed and the table is crumbed at the left of each guest.

Then the dessert plate with the dessert silver, doily and finger bowl are brought in together. The guest then places the silver to the sides of the dessert plate and sets the finger bowl and doily on the table directly above the dessert plate. The dessert is then served and placed directly on this plate. Fruit may be served after ice cream followed by decorative candies.

After-dinner coffee is increasingly served in the drawing room, living room, library or garden. At very formal dinners, while the ladies are enjoying their coffee, cigarettes, and liqueurs in one room, the gentlemen have their coffee, cigars and liqueurs in another room. Increasingly, men and women now enjoy coffee together.

Coffee is served in several ways. An English silver, hot-water urn or Russian brass samovar with or without electrical connections, or a modern electric urn may be filled with freshly made coffee and served by a maid or the hostess. A tea cart or coffee table should be set with the necessary cups, saucers, teaspoons, napkins, sugar and creamer. The maid, hostess or each guest may pour the coffee. Cream and sugar, with the guest's consent, may be added at the time of pouring or placed on a small tray and served immediately.

THE FORMAL MENU

The dinner today, no matter how formal, consists of:

1. Soup; or oyster, melon, or clam cocktail
2. Fish or entrée
3. Roast with vegetables
4. Salad
5. Dessert
   After-dinner coffee

Formal dinners should be well-balanced, nutritious and simple. Good substantial food with well chosen flavors will give satisfaction to everyone and the servings should be generous.

The formal luncheon consists of not more than 5 courses and usually only 4. There are:

1. Fruit, or soup in cups
2. Eggs or shellfish
3. Fowl and vegetables
4. Salad
5. Dessert, Coffee

The fruit course is served thoroughly chilled as a fruit cocktail. Soup for luncheon is never served in soup plates but in two-handled cups, eaten with a teaspoon or bouillon spoon, or sipped from the cup. The kind of soup is limited to broth or bouillon, but many varieties of these are served. As at dinner, if one course is a very rich food, the other courses are quite simple. There must, of course, be one substantial course to satisfy the appetite. Omitting one course is possible when another course incorporates the same foods or is of large and sufficient amount, making the other course impractical. For example, a fruit salad may replace the salad and dessert courses.

The formal tea includes cake, sandwiches and hot bread. Each plate, however, may contain several varieties of these. Lemon slices as well as sugar and cream are served with tea.

This formal dinner table is properly set on a white linen and lace cloth. The tapers are tall, well above eye level, and the other appointments are appropriate

An informal party is the ideal time to use all the interesting ideas the homemaker has for table setting and food service.

LINEN

TABLECLOTHS AND NAPKINS—

Many hostesses prefer white, ivory or eggshell colored linens but today's market abounds with colored cloths and napkins which can be harmonized with any color scheme. Peach, grey and blue are very effective with silver and highly colored flowers, but any pastel shade can be used. Damask is always attractive; in solid color it can match the motif or strong color of the china or glass used, or repeat the wallpaper or upholstery pattern.

Net, appliqued with other fabric, and organdie, plain, printed, or embroidered make exquisite sheer cloths laid over the bare table. Any sheer fabric, dotted or embroidered swiss, rayon net, batiste, fine handkerchief linen, or lawn can be fashioned into lovely tablecloths. Dotted swiss should be slightly starched and laid with the dots face down to make a smooth surface for the glassware. Batiste, lawn, and linen may be embroidered or trimmed with a printed or contrasting colored border. Dining room motif or color can be applied to any cloth. Napkins of contrasting material and color may be used with any cloth for informal service, provided a basic harmony persists.

Novelty linens are innumerable—among them beautiful, hand-blocked peasant linens, with riotous colors in native designs, which enhance earthenware and pottery dishes; nautical designs in bright red, white and blue, for special occasions and hand-loomed cloths for alfresco lunching.

PLACE MATS—Place mats lead in popularity for table coverings on

Novelty linen with contrasting napkins add a festive touch to a gay party table

many occasions. They are easily laundered, less expensive than tablecloths and appropriate for luncheons, afternoons or snack events when the "bare table" effect is desired. A rectangular place mat, 12 by 18 inches is most convenient for the average table. Napkins and runners may be had in the same, or contrasting, color as the place mats, although when runner and mats are used together, care must be taken that they do not overlap.

The trend toward novelty place mats has brought a variety of ideas from the manufacturers which can be duplicated in the home, such as woven paper and cellophane mats, crepe paper mats for special parties, wallpaper and attractive magazine cover mats.

An ingenious homemaker can make unusual place mats from any material, printed, colored or plain. Woven raffia, straw, grass or rope, in plain or combined colors, make inexpensive mats.

Plastics are on the table today in painted all-over or border patterns, plain, or cut and trimmed to simulate lace. They can be cleaned with a damp cloth and are appropriate for dinner and luncheon service. For the sophisticated event there are mirrors or mirror mats, or squares of glass with patterns or designs pasted face-side up on the under-side of the glass.

Mats of copper or aluminum foil are attractive used with matching centerpiece or candlesticks for special table settings.

FOR COCKTAILS—A great variety of small square or oblong napkins are to be had and may be of fine linen with a delicate lace trim, embroidered pattern, or as sheer as a handkerchief. Many have embroidered or stamped motifs or mottos in cross stitch

Patterned earthenware makes an attractive table set on a solid-colored cloth

DISHES AND SERVING PIECES

CERAMICS—Ceramics consist of pottery, earthenware, semi-porcelain and porcelain. The difference is determined by ingredients and degrees of heat used in their manufacture.

POTTERY—Made from coarsely sieved clays which turn red or yellow when baked, pottery is opaque, uneven, and often only partially glazed. It can be used for serving fruit, nuts, candy and other similar food, and is very effective for decorative purposes. It is very porous, chips easily, and is not practical for daily use. Pottery is popularly accepted because of its bold coloring and patterns.

STONEWARE—Is a type of pottery also made of coarse clay, glazed and fired ,to a finish almost as hard, non-porous and non-absorbent as porcelain. It has a coarse texture and color and is used for baking as well as serving foods since it withstands heat.

EARTHENWARE—Comes in 2 qualities; coarse and fine. Coarse earthenware is opaque, porous, chips easily, and is very similar to pottery. The fine earthenware is less porous and more durable, being composed of a mixture of clays which yield a white body of fine texture. Both have a deep finish that is highly glossed and very attractive. Fine earthenware is durable enough for everyday use, and many potteries such as Spode and Wedgewood manufacture a superior grade of fine earthenware as well as porcelain.

SEMI - PORCELAIN OR SEMI-VITREOUS CHINA—Is very hard, usually thin, sometimes translucent, non-porous, and contains the combined properties of fine earthenware and porcelain. It is more resistant to chipping and breaking than pottery or earthenware and therefore most practical for everyday usage, though more expensive.

PORCELAIN OR CHINA—Is completely non-absorbent, non-porous, translucent, usually blue-white in color, and has a deep rich color and glass. It is tough and durable, and because of spe-

cial clays used in its construction, it is costly. The original porcelain is made with kaoline, a clay first found in China. England originated a porcelain called bone china, with bone ash (burned animal bones) in its composition and continues its manufacture almost exclusively.

Pottery, earthenware, and semi-porcelain have widespread use for informal service. Porcelain tableware may be used, but it is more popular for formal service. Although the peasant pottery used today is very soft in texture, its vivid native coloring and design compensate for its faults. Before the war, quantities of pottery were imported and the Portuguese and French pottery led in durability, followed by Italian, then Spanish, and lastly Mexican. Pottery now being made in the United States is more durable than any we have had before.

The shapes, colors and patterns of modern ceramic tableware and decorative pieces range from streamlined effects to accurate reproductions of antique ware in radically different textures. Earthenware dishes are made in leaf,

flower, and shell shapes, in delicate pastel tones or radiant colors. The homemaker should also discover the small potteries in her own vicinity where regional characteristics will be translated into ceramics to secure special pieces for informal entertaining.

Chop plates, sandwich trays, salad bowls, coffee and chocolate pots, and serving pieces are plentifully represented in pottery and earthenware, and may be used to introduce informality to the table setting.

WOOD — Emphasis has been placed on wood for table service at informal buffets, salad suppers, picnics or barbecues. Wooden dinner plates, salad bowls and serving dishes, plain or decorated set on an uncovered wooden table with or without place mats are very popular, especially for alfresco parties. Maple, oak, walnut, mahogany, teak and California redwood polished in natural color, lend themselves well to this type of service. Designed for convenience are the Lazy Susans, and the long sectional trays to serve relishes, cheese, etc.

METAL—Metallic wares have returned in recent years, and many beautiful pieces are available in pewter, copper, aluminum, stainless steel and other metal alloys. Whole table settings can be achieved in these materials. More popular than the whole setting in metal is the use of individual serving pieces and trays.

Beautiful stemware should be chosen as carefully as fine china and silver

GLASS—Setting the table completely with glass is not a new idea, but the glassware coming to market today is increasingly attractive. Sparkling clear glass is as popular for table service as always. Milk glass or blue glassware, looking very much like Grandmother's antiques, as well as Mexican glass are plentiful and practical. Serving trays and bowls of glass may be used to augment any dishware.

PLASTICS—Are beginning to make a substantial appearance in dishware, but as yet have not proved very resistant to heat. For picnic use multi-colored plastic plates are light, non-breakable and easy to clean, but beware of the effects of hot water on them.

STEMWARE

GLASS—Drinking vessels of glass are the most widely used and popularly accepted of all types and, because they are a large item in the budget, the homemaker will want to know about glass before she purchases. Table glassware is usually classified as handmade ("pot" glass) or machine made ("tank" glass), the difference being that one is hand produced, the ingredients processed in pots, and the other is turned out in large volume by machine after being processed in tanks. The basic ingredients are sand or another type of silica, an alkali such as soda ash, lime or potash, and in high quality glass, lead which gives glass clarity, brilliance and a bell-like tone when tapped. Thus, high quality glass is referred to as lead glass and is known as crystal, while less expensive glass, lacking lead, is called lime glass. Flint glass is the same as lead glass and bottle glass is a cheap grade of lime glass. By adding various chemicals to the ingredients, colored glass is obtained. Glass may often be classified according to its place of manufacture or its decoration.

Molten glass is shaped by blowing or pressing. Blowing entails gathering a mass of molten lead glass on the end of a blow pipe, lowering this into a mold, and blowing through the pipe until the glass has expanded to mold shape. Many decorative pieces are shaped entirely by blowing and molding by hand against a flat surface and are then called "hand blown." Pressing is a means of shaping molten glass by depositing it in a mold and pressing it to mold shape. This method is usually used in producing heavy pieces and is always executed in lime glass.

Glass may be decorated by: etching or acid burning a design into any type of glass; cutting (done on lead glass only) a design into glass by holding the piece against an abrasive wheel; carving the pattern by covering with tape all but the part of the glass to receive the design, then by means of compressed air, blowing an abrasive against the glass until a frosty design is carved into the uncovered area; or hand coloring a piece by painting enamel colors or gold on with a brush.

Cut glass may be imitated by pressing the cut design into molten lime glass.

When buying good glassware, the housewife should:

1) Feel the edges for smoothness.

2) Look for luster and clearness in color and pattern.

3) Listen for a clear musical ring when lead glass is tapped with the knuckle or fingernail. Pressed or lime glass, however, lack this ring.

4) Examine for defects in the glass itself as well as the shape and pattern.

Rock crystal is the term commonly applied to fine handmade glassware that has been cut and polished, but the only true rock crystal is natural quartz.

Stemware is preferred for formal service, but is also used for semi-formal occasions. For informal use, plain or footed tumblers, which are drinking glasses without stems, are the preferred drinking vessels, and usually appear in the following sizes:

4 ounce cocktail glass—for seafood cocktails or fruit cup.

5 ounce tumbler—for juices and parfaits, and informal wine service.

9 ounce tumbler—for water.

12 ounce tumbler—for iced coffee, tea, or ginger ale.

14 ounce tumbler—used for "tall" drinks that require room for ice cubes, orange or lemon slices or other garnishes.

16 ounce tumbler—same as above.

Tumblers appear on the modern informal table in many different colors and patterns; plain crystal glasses depend on their shape and quality for their popularity. Some glasses are painted with floral, animal, fruit or sport motifs. Highball glasses are often found with an engraved number on each glass as a means of identification, while others have a frosted space where a signature can be written. Often each glass in a matching set will have a different design.

Informal glassware may be monogrammed according to the taste of the hostess as long as the monogram is in accord with the style and size of the glass, and all pieces in the set are marked. The monogram may be a huge single letter down the entire length of the glass or a small three-lettered marking in the center of the glass.

Glass mugs, in lovely Mexican blue, are rapidly gaining popularity and are used for ales and other cold drinks. Mugs may be found in several types of heavy glass in colors ranging from clear to ruby red.

CERAMICS—Those who like everything to match will enjoy using ceramic tumblers that match the dish pattern.

Although they are not as cold-hot resistant as glass, they last long enough to be practical. Many pottery or earthenware tumblers are chosen to complement the color scheme with a matching or contrasting color. Equally attractive are ceramic mugs for beer, ale, chocolate or other beverages.

METAL—Drinking vessels such as highball or mint-julep tumblers and mugs appear in stainless steel, sterling or silver plate, copper, pewter, aluminum and other metals.

PAPER—A variety of colored and printed paper tumblers and mugs are available and are fine for alfresco and other informal occasions. They may be used to carry out a color scheme for a special event and their big advantage lies in the fact that they can be disposed of after use and are inexpensive.

FLATWARE

SILVER—STERLING AND PLATED—Both sterling and silver plated flatware are always appropriate and beautiful. Many silver sets appear with bone handles, or for those who specialize in steak dinners, it is practical and attractive to set the cover with steak sets, the knives of which have stainless steel blades. The steak sets may appear with bone handles or plain or patterned silver.

STAINLESS STEEL—One of the most popular metals for informal flatware is stainless steel, which is inexpensive, durable

TABLE SERVICE

For the informal table the type of service used depends on the requirements of the event and the availability of a maid or waitress to help serve. The hostess may serve in one of two styles or their modifications:

1) **Informal, Family, English or Hostess Alone Service.** In this type of service there are no servants at all and all food is placed on the table in large containers and served by the host, hostess or some other family member.

2) **Compromise, Mixed, Combination or American Service.** This type of service is a mixture of the formal European service and the informal service mentioned above. It requires some serving by host, hostess or family member and some service by maid. This service can be quite formal or can be modified to fit the particular needs of the event.

Usually the appetizer, salad, vegetables and dessert are served from a pantry or sideboard by the servant while the host carves the meat course and the hostess pours the coffee. The servant carries the plates of meat and cups of coffee to each guest and removes the dishes of each course at the appropriate time.

AT THE BREAKFAST TABLE—

The informal breakfast cover consists of an 8½ to 9½-inch plate in the center of the cover with a small fork at the left and a small knife at the right of the plate, followed by a cereal spoon, then a teaspoon for fruit. The water tumbler goes above the knife and the bread-and-butter plate. The butter knife either at the left of the fork or across the plate, is at the tip of the fork. The napkin is at the left of the plate if the fruit is at the place, but if no fruit is being served, the napkin is on the heated place plate. If the breakfast service is informal the food is placed on the table in large dishes and served by the host and hostess to the right. The coffee, teaspoons, cups, sugar and creamer are grouped at the hostess' place. She pours the coffee, places a teaspoon on the saucer to the right of the cup and passes a filled cup to each guest who then sets it to the right of his plate.

Compromise service for breakfast would find the food served and removed from the table by a maid. The coffee may be poured by the hostess or the maid may do all of the pouring from a sideboard. In either case, the servant carries the full cup to each guest. The host may serve the main course and have the maid carry it to each guest.

A country type of breakfast service has been adapted to fit our needs from the semi-buffet breakfast service long practiced in England. For this service the cover for each guest is set as usual and the fruit may or may not be in place. The guest serves himself from a hot buffet arranged on a separate table, with heating arrangements. Any course that is better prepared immediately before eating, is brought to the guest by the maid who also may pour the coffee and remove the dishes after each course. This type of service can be easily adapted to fit any family needs and is ideal for serving many people at various intervals.

In many households a breakfast tray is served to each person in his room, which is often more convenient for the servants and the household. The tray, which should be small, sturdy and have adjustable legs, is set with attractive linens and dishes and in the same order as the table breakfast cover. The hot food is usually placed on the place plate, covered, the fruit course at the right of the water glass, above the knives, and the cereal at the left above the forks. The coffee pot is placed at the right of the knives, near the cup, with the sugar and creamer, salt and pepper, and sometimes the napkin, at the top of the tray, above the place plate. There are no rigid rules for tray setting, only that the food, silver and dishware be conveniently placed and the tray meal attractive, appetizing and easy to manage.

Cheerful informality keynotes the breakfast table

AT THE LUNCH OR SUPPER TABLE—

The lunch cover is set with the salad fork at the left, next to the plate, and the meat fork at the left of the salad fork for any first course requiring one. A salad knife is at the right, next to the plate, followed by a meat knife, and a bouillon or fruit spoon. The water tumbler is at the tip of the knives, and the bread-and-butter plate at the tip of the forks. The napkin is laid on the place plate or at the left of the forks.

The cover for any meal can be arranged informally in a way most convenient to the service and the flatware set so that the piece used first is on the outside (knives to the right, forks to the left) and is removed with the course, leaving the next piece of appropriate flatware on the outside. The dessert silver is usually brought in immediately before or with the dessert service, or can be set on the table when the cover is laid. When no knives are used with the service the forks go to the right.

The first course of the lunch served in informal style would probably be in place when the guests are seated and all remaining courses would be served from large plates and bowls set in front of the hostess. The dishes can be removed after each course by the hostess or some other family member.

Compromise service would find the first course on the table or served by the maid when the guests were seated. The salad and dessert would also be served by her while the main dish might be served by the hostess and carried to each guest by the maid. **AT THE DINNER TABLE—** The cover is set as for lunch with the large dinner or cover plate in place and the flatware arranged in order of their use.

With the compromise service the host would carve at the table and the hostess would pour the after-dinner coffee while the remainder of the service would be carried on by the servant.

BUFFET SERVICE—The buffet party is one of the nicest ways to serve. It is convenient for the hostess and guests alike, with no waiting for the late-comers.

The table may be pushed back against a wall, after being opened to its full length, and the chairs removed or for a buffet dinner, place the extended dining table in the center of the room so that the guests walk around it easily and serve themselves. If a very large number of people are to be served, the table may be 2½ to 3 feet from the wall. This space gives the maid or maids enough room to serve, and at the same time keeps the line moving down just one side of the table. In choosing the proper table position, keep the path for your guests free from kitchen traffic. This precaution will increase the efficiency and pleasantness of your service and will also reduce the possibility of any embarrassing collisions.

The buffet table is spread attractively with the necessary serving pieces and dinner plates stacked at the convenient place for the guests. Low bowls of flowers and short thick candles are appropriate decoration. However, if your buffet table is small, omit all decoration and use flowers elsewhere on mantle, in windows, etc. A typical buffet menu consists of a roast or entrée, two vegetables, salad, dessert and coffee. Cocktails and hors d'oeuvres have been served as the guests assemble. There are several ways to serve the buffet dinner and all are equally correct. Guests may serve themselves or the maid may assist them. As each guest reaches the end of the table, he finds his place at one of the card tables. Place cards are used at a large dinner and may well be used at a small one.

Small tables are set for the guests with all the necessary silver, water tumblers, napkins, salts and peppers, and perhaps a small centerpiece.

Careful arrangement is the first requirement of a fine buffet

It is acceptable for the guests to return for second helpings and this opportunity should be made convenient.

The salad course may be on the buffet with the entrée and served to the guests at the same time or the maid may bring in a salad cart from which the guests select their own. It may also be served each guest directly from the pantry. If it is more convenient, the buffet is cleared and reset with the salad course. The guests then return to the main table and serve themselves.

Coffee may be served from the buffet with the entrée and/or with the dessert. However, it is correct to offer it only with the dessert. If the party is not too large and there are enough maids, the coffee may be served at the card tables. Creamers and sugars may be placed on each table or offered by the maid after she serves the coffee. Having the coffee served to each guest reduces the hazard of spilling.

Both the buffet and card tables are cleared before the dessert is served. Usually the maid serves

from the reset buffet with the accompanying silver.

Older people find this type of service slightly confusing and the perfect hostess will give them some extra attention. She may have someone take the guest around or serve at the table.

SMÖRGÅSBORD SERVICE—The smörgåsbord is a type of buffet service that has become very popular in recent years. The table is set as for regular buffet service and is bounteously spread with plates and bowls of hot and cold foods, meats, salads, relishes, sea foods chilled in bowls of cracked ice, sweets, desserts, cheese and fruit. The dishes are arranged in convenient order, the hot foods together, cold foods in a group, desserts at one end and the coffee at the table end. The guest serves himself from the table. Although it is a sumptuous way of entertaining, it can be done in a very simple way.

MAKE-IT-YOURSELF SERVICE— An extremely informal type of

buffet service which allows great freedom for hostess and guest alike is the make-it-yourself table. Ingredients can be assembled for making into salads and sandwiches and the guests may make their own. The table should include toasters, chafing dishes with raw materials for a hot dish, and may also include sandwich grills or broilers and a waffle iron with ingredients for waffles and pancakes. For a snack service, the hostess might furnish large bowls of chilled waffle batter and all the ingredients for variations and let the guests make their own. The beverages may accompany the dessert.

This method of entertaining is suitable only for small groups and menus must be simple and easily prepared. The hostess must plan carefully to avoid confusion and keep the service going smoothly.

TEA SERVICE—A tea may be a very informal gathering of 4 or 5 friends or it may be a semi-formal event with many guests invited. Hours are from 3 to 6 o'clock and tea may be served in the living

Smörgåsbord is a luxurious way of entertaining and easily done without a maid

room, dining room, porch or garden. The tea service is brought in on a tray or tea wagon and holds the teapot, sugar, cream, lemon, cups, small plates, silver and small napkins. If the tea is served in the dining room the table is set similarly to the buffet service. The hostess or a friend or both pour the beverage while the guests help themselves from the table or from plates passed by the hostess or a friend. Tea service in the living room is usually set on a low table and is served by the hostess. The proper tea menu consists of a choice of beverages, cookies, cakes, dainty sandwiches and hot breads. Since tea service is generally informal, there are no rigid rules of setting or service to limit the hostess.

COCKTAIL SERVICE—One of the easiest ways to entertain a large number of people is a cocktail party between the hours of 4 to 7 o'clock. If the group is small and the event really informal, cocktails mixed and served by the host in the presence of the guests are preferred. For a large group it is wise to have a well-trained person assume charge of mixing and serving the cocktails.

The small party can be served canapés and hors d'oeuvres from trays passed by the hostess or her friends and then help themselves from a small table in the living room or garden. Larger parties often require the services of a maid to serve.

A variety of cocktails should be served and the thoughtful hostess will always provide non-alcoholic drinks for those who prefer them.

ALFRESCO SERVICE— Eating in the open has become a very popular American custom in recent years and shows every prospect of remaining so. Climate, season and

location greatly influence outdoor eating, but every section of the country has a suitable season.

Outdoor meals may include breakfast, lunch, supper or dinner which may be served on a terrace or in the garden in the same manner as an indoor meal. The cover can be set for each person and the food brought outdoors on trays.

For the details of a carefree picnic see Pages 879-890.

GROUP SERVICE—An excellent means of entertaining a large number of people extemporaneously is to have each guest bring some contribution to the meal. The meal may be served buffet style or covers set around a large table for the guests.

The progressive dinner solves the problem of too much work for one hostess. In this type of service each course of a meal is eaten at a different house by the guests traveling in cars or on foot. The food is served buffet or sit-down style, according to needs of the group.

ENTERTAINING

SHOWERS—These are given for any special event such as the arrival of a new baby, the open-

A gay bon voyage party made festive with glass boat centerpiece and fish appetizer bowls

ing of a new house or to say goodby to a friend about to begin a trip.

The shower most often given centers around the prospective bride and is a popular way to honor her. If your garden is in bloom, set your table in its midst in colors harmonizing with the flowers and serve shower menus which may be selected from Page 70. Cover the table with a soft-colored cloth or place mats and let the centerpiece be a small doll dressed in bride's clothes, a wedding bell, or a decorated umbrella standing in a circle of leaves and flowers.

For indoor showers serve the Bride's Luncheon on Page 67.

Travel showers offer the greatest variety in table settings and menu selections. The traveler going southwest could be feted with the Mexican Supper on Page 82, on a table vivid with Mexican pottery atop hand-loomed placemats in native colors.

To decorate the table for a bon voyage party, "sail" a boat on a mirror or crushed blue paper. Carry a nautical theme on place cards and favors. Use blue napkins with a white cloth or place mats. A sea food menu is the appropriate one.

To bid farewell to those leaving by train, decorate the table with a miniature station, a child's train set, etc. as your imagination leads. Maps and toy automobile or plane also make attractive centerpieces.

BIRTHDAYS—Children look forward to the birthday party and the hostess has almost as much fun as they when she sets the table and plans the decorations.

For the younger set the Children's Party menus are on Pages 870-871. Color schemes and table decorations follow the season of the year, the age and activities of the child. For a Spring birthday, what child would not be thrilled with a circus party? Cover the table with a red and white candy-striped paper tablecloth and use white napkins made festive with animal stickers pasted on them. Paper cups decorated with tight-rope walkers, clowns, and other circus characters make gay additions to the table. The centerpiece might be a lion cage made from a bird cage or wire basket. Use toy lions, ladders and stools and arrange them as though the lions were going through their tricks. Dress a small doll in knee breeches and black boots to act as the lion tamer. Sandwiches can be transformed by cutting the bread with animal cutters and, of course, no circus party would be complete without ice cream and animal crackers.

The Teen-Age Party menu on Page 75 is what the hostess will want to serve to the teen-agers when they celebrate a birthday. The "sweet sixteen" birthday girl will enjoy her party if the table is set with a delicate pink cloth or organdie place mats and white or pastel dishes. With these use a low bowl of dainty pink or white flowers for the centerpiece and ribbon streamers ending at each place.

For adult birthday parties any of the Sunday Night Suppers on Pages 70, 76, 79 will add a festive touch to the event.

WEDDINGS—Whether the service is a breakfast, luncheon, supper or tea, the wedding tables require almost as much attention as the wedding ceremony.

The Small Wedding Breakfast menus on Pages 95-96 are served at a table covered with the best white or ivory cloth. The centerpiece may be the lavishly decorated bride's cake with low bowls of bridal flowers on both sides. Sparkling goblets, any lovely china and well-polished silver should be used. For the larger breakfast, buffet style is more convenient. The menu for a Large Wedding Breakfast will be found on Pages 95-96.

Lunch and supper service for a wedding is much the same as the breakfast. For supper, candles may be added to grace the already lovely table.

SPORTS PARTIES—With autumn harvest comes autumn sports which are often accompanied by sports parties. Entertain friends with one of the After-the-Game Suppers found on Page 82. Set the table with a dark brown or green tablecloth, pottery or wooden dishes, or both. Arrange a centerpiece by setting miniature goal posts on both sides of a football helmet. Place in the helmet a bowl filled with chrysanthemums. The Football Supper on Page 81 is the supper menu. Basketball and baseball games may be easily celebrated with any All-in-a-dish or Casserole Suppers, a Stag Supper, Page 83, or a Quick Dinner, Page 911. Set the table with school or game colors. Honor the successful fisherman with a lunch or supper of fish as in the Fisherman's Pride menu on Page 74, or the Outdoor Luncheon on Page 73. Start the hunters out with a Hunt Breakfast on Page 93, served buffet style featuring red in the table setting.

ANNIVERSARIES—Wedding anniversaries are important milestones and the hostess will want to celebrate with all charm and hospitality.

Celebrate the first or paper anniversary with any Buffet Suppers. Set the table with a colorful paper table cloth, paper dishes, cups, forks, spoons and napkins. The entire setting can be done in pastel colors. The centerpiece can be a huge bouquet of flowers fashioned from colored crepe paper. A wooden anniversary, the fifth, could be celebrated as a picnic with the Alfresco Luncheon menu on Page 76. Set the table with wooden eating utensils, bowls, plates, trays and mugs. A large wooden mixing bowl may serve as a centerpiece when filled with wild flowers.

The crystal, silver and golden wedding anniversaries should be celebrated in a more elaborate manner. The table is set with the hostess' nicest cloth, best dishes, glasses and silver. For these anniversaries it is well to serve a Wedding Supper, substituting an elaborately decorated cake or petits fours for the wedding cake. The Smörgåsbord menu on Page 64 or any of the Buffet Suppers are equally suitable. Set the crystal anniversary table with crystal accessories and use a crystal bowl filled with flowers. The silver anniversary table should be set with silver. As a centerpiece use a silver bowl filled with sweetheart roses.

For a fiftieth wedding anniversary use a soft gold colored tablecloth set with gold colored dishes and a centerpiece of yellow flowers. Flatware could be of metal that has a gold finish and the glassware banded with gold.

GRADUATION—For a centerpiece use a mortarboard and diploma set in the center of a circle of flowers. Small bowls of the same flowers or candles may be placed alongside. The Class Day Brunch menu on Page 94 is served with dainty place mats and a paper favor of a graduate in cap and gown at each place.

BRIDGE—Bridge parties, like teas, are among the most informal ways of entertaining. Decorations can take their theme from the season, a special event, or any idea the hostess has for entertaining. They can be the background for a shower, birthday, or farewell party and are a graceful means for meeting social obligations.

Clever cap and gown figures and a not-too-crowded table in college colors make a charming setting

Any of the Bridge Luncheons on Pages 57, 76, 79 would perfectly fit a bridge party.

CLUB—The centerpiece could feature the objectives or activities of the organization. For the annual meeting, a huge birthday cake decorated like a clock with hands set at the age of the club would be very appropriate. Especially planned for a small club affair served in the home, are the Club or PTA Brunch on Page 93. Tea service for the large group might take its decorative theme from a nation.

SNACK—After an evening at the theater the smart hostess will invite the gang for a Sunday Night Snack on Page 57. The table may be set in keeping with the evening, denoting the type of play, the season, the formality or informality of the event. Culminate a sophisticated evening by setting the table with a black cotton or linen cloth piped in white. Use white dishes and napkins and aluminum serving trays. For a centerpiece place a top hat filled with white chrysanthemums on a square of white.

Many hostesses make their guests welcome with a Pantry Shelf Supper. Cover the kitchen table with

a colorful red and white checked cloth using fruits or vegetables in a wooden bowl for the centerpiece. The Sunday Snack menu on Page 57 is another meal that can be quickly and easily prepared and served for any day of the week.

PARTIES FOR JANUARY—Start the year with a New Year's dinner or supper, menus on Pages 52, 53. Set the table to reflect all the gaiety of this event.

New Year's celebrations may also include breakfast and brunch menus on Pages 90-94. Serve breakfast or brunch on a blue cloth covered with icicle strips of white cellophane. In the center of the table place balloons repeating the blue and silvery white colors. Flank the balloons with silver bowls holding Christmas tree balls in the same colors. Use blue pottery dishes and silver serving pieces.

PARTIES FOR FEBRUARY—February calls for patriotic parties to commemorate the birthdays of Washington and Lincoln. Serve a Washington Birthday supper or dinner, Page 55. Cover the table with a blue paper cloth on which are pasted silver stars in groups

of 13 here and there over the cloth, with a large circle of 13 stars in the center. Fill the center circle with a red, toy drum and drumsticks tied together with a large red and white bow. Fill tiny blue and silver tri-cornered paper hats with red gumdrops and set these at each plate. The brunch menus on Pages 93, 94 can be set in the same manner.

Lincoln's birthday may be observed with a brunch, supper, or dinner menu on Page 55. Serve it on dark plaid or striped homespun cloth or mats, or use fringed squares of burlap, which comes in a variety of colors, and makes attractive place mats. Use candles in hurricane lamps made from cut-down tin cans, placed at either end of a centerpiece made of logs. At each place set a tiny log with a small hatchet embedded in it.

Celebrate St. Valentine's Day with dinner or luncheon menus on Pages 56, 57. Set the table with a cloth of white sprinkled with tiny red hearts held in place with small red satin bows. Have

Popcorn and suckers for the children's Fourth of July party and spell out their names in cinnamon drops

the florist fashion a heart of red carnations to be used as a centerpiece with a wide ruching of white lace or paper lace doilies. Or fill a bowl with indivdual nose-gays of early flowers, each with its own paper ruching, and tied with rose-colored ribbons, to be distributed among the guests at the end of the meal.

If breakfast or brunch service is desired, follow the menus on Pages 92-94.

PARTIES FOR MARCH—March brings St. Patrick's Day and an opportunity for the hostess to serve a colorful luncheon menu on Page 61. Invitations can be written in white ink on bright green paper shamrocks, or in green ink on small white note-paper with a shamrock sticker. For this party, set the table with emerald green mats and napkins. In the table center place a large patch of artificial shamrock. At each place set a small shamrock shaped piece of paper with a diminutive pig resting on it. Use white dishes trimmed with green and green glassware. For supper or lunch, set the table with a white cloth decorated with tiny shamrocks. Trim the sides and edges of the cloth with green ribbon hanging in scallops down the sides. Use vivid green pottery and glasses and place a large green carnation shamrock in the table center.

For a unique hors d'oeuvres server, in keeping with the spirit of St. Pat, make a green pig by coloring a grapefruit. Slit the rind in two places and turn back for ears. Use cloves for eyes, and attach a green olive for his snout. Use green matchsticks for legs. Cover his back with Green Balls on Picks, Page 22.

PARTIES FOR APRIL — Easter which may arrive in March or April is an occasion evoking both merriment and solemnity. Delight your guests with an Easter breakfast menu on Page 93, served on a pale yellow or lavender tablecloth. A large egg-shaped piece of cardboard painted to resemble an Easter egg with a gay face may be topped with an elaborate paper Easter bonnet and set in the center of the table on a bed of crinkled green paper. Paint faces on individual Easter eggs and place them at each plate. Pastel china is appropriate for this setting. The dinner or supper menus will be found on Page 58.

Or you can really let yourself go on an April Fool's party. There are no traditional decorations, so you might combine holly wreaths and American Flags, shamrocks, jack-o-lanterns, and Santa Clauses. Anything and everything will do, and the zanier the better, in keeping with the spirit of the day.

PARTIES FOR MAY—Serve May Day breakfast or brunch menus on Pages 90-94 on a delicate pink tablecloth with white or ivory china. In the center of the table place a large Maypole constructed of cardboard or peppermint stick candy with ribbons of pink. Surround the base of the Maypole with green leaves and white flowers. Place tiny baskets of flowers at each place and trim them with bows of ribbon matching the Maypole.

Mother's Day is certainly an occasion for a party. Nothing could be lovelier than serving Mother's favorite luncheon on a dainty white cloth. Use a gay set of china dishes with a floral pattern and arrange flowers in a low crystal bowl on top of a mirror

Memorial Day may be well remembered with a garden or porch gathering. Serve breakfast on Page 92 or a brunch on Page 94 with patriotic trimmings.

PARTIES FOR JUNE—Father's Day calls for masculine table settings and his favorite dinner on a plaid tablecloth with colored pottery dishes. Use Dad's favorite sport for a table decorating motif. If he likes golf, arrange a bowl of golf balls and colored tees in the center of the table.

PARTIES FOR JULY—Fourth of July offers possibilities for an outdoor party in the garden or on the porch and is an ideal way of serving the Fourth of July Brunch or Dinner on Page 72. Set the table with a white cloth extending to the floor and place a red, white and blue crepe paper runner in the center of the table, extending to both ends. A pleasantly colorful touch can be arrived at by the use of dark blue paper napkins and stainless steel cutlery with red plastic handles. Red, white and blue dishes may be used. If you use a red or blue tablecloth, serve the dinner on white dishes with colored napkins, rolled like firecrackers. For brunch service use a centerpiece made of a large imitation firecracker with many small firecrackers banked around it. For supper service use candles placed in empty tubes simulating lit firecrackers. Menus on Pages 71-73 may be served.

PARTIES FOR AUGUST — You will probably have difficulty keeping folks inside for a party during August, so why not go outdoors with them? Plan an outdoor grill in the back yard. Your menu should be extra-hearty—manageable food that can be cooked and served with dispatch and eaten in comfort. Grilled Hamburgers with Grilled Tomatoes and Mushrooms, French Bread, and a Tossed Green Salad might be used. And to top it off —a delicious Ice Cream Pie (Page 597).

PARTIES FOR SEPTEMBER—Labor Day parties may use the harvest or autumn as a theme. To enjoy the beauty of the outdoors at this season, the hostess may wish to serve the Labor Day picnic on Page 77. Set the picnic table with harvest colors, using a green, rust or burgundy paper tablecloth and napkins, along with paper plates, cups and eating utensils in a harmonizing color. A centerpiece may be arranged on the picnic site using a colorful branch of turning leaves on the table. To serve the Breakfast or Brunch menus on Pages 93, 94, set the table indoors or on the porch or lawn with a colorful block printed cloth featuring a leaf motif, or a solid cloth with leaves appliqued on it.

PARTIES FOR OCTOBER—After dark, fete your party guests with supper or dinner on Page 80, served in traditional Halloween manner. Use an orange or black tablecloth. If orange is used place a runner of black crepe paper down the length of the table. In the center of this place a huge pumpkin carved with a grinning face and lighted from the inside by a candle. Small pumpkins with similar carving and also holding candles may be set at each end of the table. Hollowed pumpkins filled with trailing green vines and bittersweet, flanked by paper figures of black cats and witches riding their broomsticks may be used as effectively. Smaller cat or witch figurines may be set at each plate for favors.

If you are fortunate enough to own a polished brass bowl, fill it with bittersweet or late fall flowers, and place it in the center of the table.

PARTIES FOR NOVEMBER—On Armistice Day serve brunch on a table set buffet style. Food may be eaten from tin pie plates and drinking cups to symbolize the soldier's mess kit.

Sadie Hawkins Day parties are very popular with the teen-age crowd. This is one occasion when the more rustic your decorations are, the better it is. The room should be decorated to look like a log cabin. Places should be set on a bare table with worn, red and blue bandanna handkerchiefs as napkins. Or you may use a tablecloth "mended" with many bright patches. Use stubby, burned down candles stuck in bottles, or on lids of tin cans, dried ears of corn, small kegs, old jugs, and dented tin plates to add to the Dogpatch atmosphere. A truly mountain menu might include Pork Chops, Turnips, Corn Bread, Green Salad, and a Sweetpotato Pie (Page 508), and cider. Embodying the spirit of Thanksgiving—the season of plenty—you might use a large wicker cornucopia filled to overflowing with apples, oranges, pomegranates, tangerines, plums, grapes, nuts, green baby squash, large white onions, carrots, sweetpotatoes, and red and green peppers, or anything you might have on hand. This may be banked with bright colored autumn leaves, or several smaller cornucopias filled with nuts and hard candies.

Thanksgiving always calls forth the hostess' best in entertaining. Serve guests the Thanksgiving

Dinner on Page 84 on the nicest tablecloth. A table set with earthenware dishes designed for turkey service is a change from traditional white. Decorate the center of the table with sprays of wheat laid on autumn leaves that extend to the table edges.

PARTIES FOR DECEMBER—The holiday season offers so many opportunities for parties that the difficulty lies in deciding what kind to have. Of first consideration is the Christmas Dinner on Page 86, with table decorations typical of the season. Spread the table with a white cloth and lay four bands of red ribbon lengthwise, to the table edge. In the center of the table place a holly wreath. In the middle of this circle set four thick red candles or a large novelty Santa Claus candle. Tiny wreaths and candles of the same design are placed at each place. Christmas Eve supper may be served buffet style on a table sparkling with white and silver. Christmas greens sprayed with white and sprinkled with snow powder may be banked around a generous group of white candles. Use those silver accessories you've been saving, and tie your napkins in rolls with silver ribbon. A Christmas Open-house will need to reflect all the warmth of your good wishes, so plan a gay, colorful table. Use a green cloth, red napkins, and red and white dishes. A cheerful centerpiece can be made of apples, candy canes, and sprigs of green from your tree or wreath. Your menu will be simple—sandwiches, appetizers, and sweets with punch or wine.

SEASONAL—To herald the advent of a new season is always an accepted reason for the hospitable homemaker to give a party.

Set the winter table with the warmest looking cloth you have, a dark green or tobacco brown cloth would be perfect. In the center of the table place a small decorative sleigh complete with tiny horses or reindeer pulling the sleigh through an avenue of banked cotton, which simulates snow. Serve a heavy winter breakfast from menu on Page 92.

Dinner might be served on tables pulled up close to the fireplace for cheery warmth and light. Set the table with a silvery white, or icy blue cloth and sprinkle it with shiny snow powder or paper icicle strips. Place a large novelty snowman in the center, surrounded by tiny snowballs. Serve an Oven or Dutch Oven Dinner selected from Page 897 or any other of the Winter Dinners on Pages 52, 55, 58. The Buffet Supper on Page 896 is equally appropriate.

A delightful seasonal event is the Eggnog Party. If the home is small, guests may be invited to arrive at various times. Preparations, as much as possible, should be made the night before, so the hostess will be free to greet her guests, who may be invited to help themselves. Cocktail napkins, plates, the punch bowl and cups, and a tray of canapes should be arranged on the table. A very gracious seasonal gesture is the use of your precious lace tablecloth with your best silver, and fragrant bayberry or pine candles to contribute to the air of quiet good will. The Eggnog recipe on Page 918, or its variations, multiplied according to the number of invitations issued, may be used.

Proclaim spring with one of the Party Luncheons found on Page 897. Set the table in spring garden colors whether the brunch is

indoors or out in the garden. Lovely pastel dishes in flower shapes would enhance the service if set on a pale green, yellow or blue cloth or mats. A large flower-shaped bowl, matching the dishes may be placed in the center of the table filled with fresh cut spring flowers or floating blooms. Serve the Class Day Brunch on Page 94. If lunch or supper service is preferred see the menus on Page 67. Introduce a cool note into summer by serving the Summer Dinner for Guests on Page 896. Cover the table with a fishnet or other coarse net cloth. Use cool coral colored dishes to correspond with the large piece of coral set on the table center in a very flat tray of white sand. Other suggested summer menus will be found on Pages 68, 71, 74.

A fix-it-yourself buffet table might be well adapted for an autumn event if the table is set in rusts, greens, and browns—the earthy harvest colors. A large horn of plenty with fruits and vegetables cascading down the length of the table suggests a bountiful harvest and helps set the autumn theme. Use pottery dishes decorated with a fall motif. Another fall party that would contribute much merriment to the participants is a Progressive Breakfast. Gather a few friends together and divide the breakfast preparation and service amongst four hostesses, each of whom will serve a course in her home. Each table may be decorated with the same or different autumn motifs. The business girl who is handicapped by a small apartment will find buffet service the answer to her problem. Service is simplified, great numbers can be accommodated, and the strain on the one hostess is greatly reduced.

Pressure Cookery

Recipes for Pressure Cooking

PROCEDURE

The pressure cooker can be a very useful addition to kitchen equipment if used properly. It may in time revolutionize the art of cooking, for it is already a boon to millions of homemakers and working wives. The pressure cooker operates on the principle of holding steam inside the utensil until it builds up pressure. Food is cooked at higher temperatures, with little water. Thus more healthful values are retained in the food.

Manufacturers of pressure cookers do not, as a rule, recommend the preparation of cereals, apple sauce, cranberries, or split peas in the pressure cooker. These foods froth and bubble as they cook, and may clog the steam vent.

SOUPS—Unless your recipe specifies otherwise, use 15-lbs. Standard Pressure for making soup. High pressure tends to extract all the flavorful juices, valuable vitamins and minerals from the meat and soup bone.

Have all soupbones cracked open so all the flavor is drawn into the soup stock.

Use a light hand in seasoning, as seasoning can be added before serving—less seasoning is needed for pressure cooked foods.

Do not fill your cooker more than half-full when making soup.

MEATS — Experience has proved that pressure cooking meats at 15-lbs. pressure has certain distinct disadvantages. Among these are the well-known "stewy" taste and fibrous texture which results from the driving out of the juices by the steam and pressure. Under low pressure, meats have a deli-

cious flavor and are subjected to less shrinkage. Low pressure is perfect for cheaper cuts of meat—the slower penetration of heat retains the juices and flavor and tenderizes the meat. Weight, size, and thickness of meats are considered, as well as the proportion of lean, fat, and bone. Also to be considered are the different cuts and grades of meat, and the degree of "doneness" the family prefers. In general, the larger the amount of fat and the smaller the amount of bone, the more minutes per pound pressure cooking are required.

FRUITS — It is difficult to pressure cook fruits at high pressure, as the least fraction of over-timing makes them mushy, pale in color, and unappetizing. Low pressure makes it possible to retain their firmness, delicate structure, color, and flavor.

FROZEN FOODS — Frozen vegetables need not be thawed before cooking. Be sure to break apart or separate vegetables before putting in pressure pan; otherwise the outer surface will be cooked while the center will remain frozen.

The time required to pressure cook roasts and chops from the hard frozen state is usually one-half to twice as long. If the meat is cooked in the frozen state, add more water for longer cooking.

VEGETABLES — Pressure cooking vegetables gives you all the advantages of waterless cooking plus pressure pan speed. The time required is so short there is practically no loss of vitamins or minerals. All the flavor is retained in the food and is not

lost in cooking water or vapor.

CLEANING AND CARE OF THE PRESSURE COOKER — The pressure control and dial gauge is a delicate mechanism that should be handled with care. To keep it in best condition, store it in a safe place when not in use. Be careful not to drop the dial gauge, and do not put it in water.

Before using your new pressure cooker for the first time, scour the inside thoroughly with steel wool pads. Then wash cooker, cover and rack in warm water and soap; rinse with hot water and dry thoroughly.

To make cleaning easy, pour warm water into the cooker as soon as you remove the food. Do not soak in dishwater. Clean the vent tube by using a very small brush or by forcing hot water through the vent tube to rinse it.

SUGGESTIONS:

Should you be called to the door or telephone while using the pressure cooker, turn off the heat or push cooker off the stove. Keep smooth edge of cooker free of nicks. Avoid hitting the rim of the cooker with a knife, spoon, or other utensil. A marred, uneven edge allows steam to escape. Keep the cover away from direct heat, such as burner, electric unit, or oven. Direct heat affects the gasket in such a way that it may not create a perfect seal and then pressure will not be built up in the cooker.

Perhaps the most important rule to remember is this. The manufacturer's directions should be read until thoroughly understood, then followed explicitly. Never attempt to change these rules. They are built into the cooker, and trouble is sure to follow if you tamper with them.

CEREALS

MACARONI

3¾ lbs. pressure 6 minutes
15 lbs. pressure 5 minutes

1 cup macaroni
3 cups boiling water
¼ teaspoon salt

Break macaroni into small pieces or hold over boiling water until macaroni bends. Bring water to boiling in the cooker and add macaroni and salt. Macaroni should be separated before placing cover on cooker. Pressure cook. Remove and strain. Combine with Cheese Sauce as a casserole dish or bake with layers of cheese in thin custard.

OATMEAL

3¾ lbs. pressure 5 minutes
15 lbs. pressure 2½ minutes

1½ cups oatmeal
3 cups boiling water
½ teaspoon salt

Stir oatmeal gradually into boiling salted water. Place cover on cooker. Allow steam to flow from vent pipe to release all air from cooker. Place indicator weight on vent pipe and pressure cook. Cool cooker at once.
STEEL-CUT OATS require 10 minutes to cook at 15 lbs. pressure, and 3 cups of water per cup of cereal should be used.

WHITE OR BROWN RICE

3¾ lbs. pressure 15 minutes
15 lbs. pressure 10 minutes

½ cup rice
2½ cups boiling water
1 teaspoon salt

Wash rice between the palms of your hands many times until the water loses all starchy appearance. Place rice in cooker, add water and salt. Pressure cook. Reduce pressure with cool water, then remove indicator and place cooker back on flame for 3 to 4 minutes. This will thoroughly dry out rice. Never fill cooker more than ⅔ full of water and rice.

SPANISH RICE

3¾ lbs. pressure 25 minutes
15 lbs. pressure 10 minutes

½ cup rice
1 cup onions, sliced
2 tablespoons fat or drippings
3 cups canned or fresh tomatoes
1 cup diced celery
1½ teaspoons salt
⅛ teaspoon pepper
1 teaspoon sugar
1 bay leaf (optional)
½ cup water

Wash rice and drain. Cook onions in melted fat in uncovered cooker until tender. Add remaining ingredients and mix. Pressure cook. Reduce pressure with cool water. Remove bay leaf. Add left-over meat if desired, or serve as meatless dish. Serves 4 to 6.

CREAM OF WHEAT

3¾ lbs. pressure 5 minutes
15 lbs. pressure 2 minutes

½ cup Cream of Wheat
3 cups boiling water
½ teaspoon salt

Bring water to boiling in cooker, stir in Cream of Wheat gradually, add salt. (Small cubes of dried fruit, such as apricots, prunes or peaches may be added if desired.) Pressure cook. Reduce pressure with cool water.

CHEESE CORN-MEAL SQUARES

3¾ lbs. pressure 15 minutes
15 lbs. pressure 10 minutes

1 cup corn meal
½ teaspoon salt
4 cups boiling water or scalded milk
1 cup grated American Cheese
3 tablespoons bacon drippings or fat

Mix corn meal and salt with boiling water in cooker. Pressure cook. Reduce pressure with cool water. Uncover. Stir in grated cheese, blending thoroughly. Turn mixture into greased 8-inch pan. When chilled, cut into serving squares. Heat corn meal serving squares in pan with bacon drippings or fat, turning to brown lightly. Serve hot with a spicy sauce. Serves 6 to 8.

FRIED CORN MEAL MUSH

3¾ lbs. pressure 15 minutes
15 lbs. pressure 10 minutes

1 cup yellow corn meal
½ teaspoon salt
1 cup cold water
3 cups boiling water
Bacon drippings

Mix corn meal and salt with cold water. Add to boiling water in cooker. Pressure cook. Reduce pressure with cool water. Pour mush into chilled loaf pan. Cover, chill until firm. Turn out of pan, slice, dip in flour and sauté in bacon drippings until crisp and browned. Serve hot with butter or margarine and honey, or with bacon, ham or sausages for lunch. Serves 4 to 6.

BROWN STOCK

3¾ lbs. pressure 50 minutes

15 lbs. pressure 30 minutes

2 pounds lean beef and marrow
1 quart boiling water
2 medium onions, sliced
1 carrot, diced
4 stalks celery, diced
1 bay leaf
3 cloves
Few peppercorns
2 tablespoons parsley
¼ teaspoon thyme
1½ teaspoons salt

Wash and cut meat into small pieces or 1-inch cubes. Brown meat in melted marrow in cooker. Place on rack, add boiling water and remaining ingredients. Cover and pressure cook. Reduce pressure with cool water. Uncover and strain. Serve as clear soup, bouillon, or refrigerate for soup stock. Makes 4 cups. After the stock is made, leftover vegetables, cereals, small pieces of meat, etc., may be diced or chopped and served in soup.

FRENCH ONION SOUP

3¾ lbs. pressure 6 to 8 minutes

15 lbs. pressure 4 minutes

4 cups thinly sliced onions
¼ cup butter or margarine
¼ teaspoon pepper
2 cups Brown Stock
4 rounds bread, toasted
4 tablespoons Parmesan cheese
1½ teaspoons salt

Saute onions in butter in cooker until rich, golden brown; sprinkle with pepper. Add Brown Stock and seasonings. Pressure cook. Reduce pressure with cool water. Serve with toast rounds topped with grated Parmesan cheese.

NAVY BEAN SOUP

3¾ lbs. pressure 50 minutes

15 lbs. pressure 45 minutes

1 cup dried navy beans
1½ quarts boiling water
1 teaspoon salt
¼ teaspoon black pepper
¼ cup finely minced onion
½ cup finely diced celery and tops
1 bay leaf
1 tablespoon butter or margarine
Milk, scalded, to thin mixture

Wash beans and soak overnight in water to cover. Drain. Place all ingredients except milk in cooker, cover and cook under pressure. Reduce pressure at room temperature; then under cool water. Strain mixture through a sieve, and thin to desired consistency with hot milk. Reheat to boiling point and serve. A ham bone adds to the flavor. Serves 6.

CREOLE GUMBO

3¾ lbs. pressure 25 minutes

15 lbs. pressure 15 minutes

2½ cups cut okra
3 tablespoons ham drippings or fat
1 large onion, chopped
2 garlic cloves, chopped
1 medium green pepper, chopped
1 8-oz. can tomato sauce
½ cup crab meat
1 teaspoon thyme
2 tablespoons flour
½ pint oysters with liquid
4 cups water
3 tablespoons ham, diced
2 medium bay leaves
1 teaspoon parsley, chopped fine
1 teaspoon salt
Dash pepper
½ teaspoon cayenne pepper

Heat cooker. Brown okra lightly in ham drippings in cooker. Combine remaining ingredients in cooker and mix well. Place cover on cooker. Allow steam to flow from vent pipe to release all air from cooker. Place indicator weight on vent pipe. Pressure cook. Reduce pressure with cool water.

Serve with whole-grain rice.

VEGETABLE SOUP

3¾ lbs. pressure 10 minutes

15 lbs. pressure 6 minutes

4 cups Meat Stock
½ cup cut green beans
½ cup chopped green pepper
½ cup diced carrots
½ cup shredded cabbage
½ cup diced celery
½ cup sliced onion
1 cup tomatoes, fresh or canned
Seasonings to taste

Combine all ingredients. Pressure cook. Reduce pressure with cool water. Serves 4 to 6.

LENTIL SOUP

3¾ lbs. pressure 45 minutes

15 lbs. pressure 30 minutes

2 cups dried lentils
2 quarts water
1 ham bone
½ cup diced celery
1 medium onion, cut fine
2 tablespoons flour
2 teaspoons salt
¼ teaspoon pepper

Soak washed lentils overnight in 1 quart water. Drain. Add remainder of water, ham bone, celery and onion. Pressure cook. Reduce pressure with cool water. Remove ham bone and skim fat from stock. Mix flour and seasonings to a paste with a little of the stock. Add to cooker for a few minutes over a low flame until smooth and thickened

CHICKEN SOUP

*3¾ lbs. pressure 90 min-
utes*
*15 lbs. pressure 25 to 30
minutes*

Wings, neck and back of a 4-to-
5 lb. stewing hen
1 quart water
1 sliced carrot
1 stalk celery, sliced
1 sliced onion
2 tablespoons rice
2 tablespoons minced parsley
1½ teaspoons salt
¼ teaspoon pepper

Pressure cook all ingredients. Reduce pressure with cool water.
Remove chicken from cooker.
Strain liquid. Remove skin and
bones from chicken, cut meat into pieces and add chicken meat
to stock. Return to cooker and
reheat. Serves 4.

SCOTCH BROTH

*3¾ lbs. pressure 25 min-
utes*
15 lbs. pressure 15 minutes

1½ lbs. neck of lamb
1 quart cold water
4 tablespoons whole barley
2 teaspoons salt
¼ teaspoon pepper
1 cup diced carrot
⅔ cup diced onion
1 tablespoon minced parsley

Cut excess fat from lamb. Place
in cooker with water, barley, and
seasonings. Pressure cook (12
minutes with 15 lbs. pressure;
20 minutes with 3¾ lbs. pressure). Reduce pressure with cool
water. Add carrot, onion, and
parsley and pressure cook again.
(3 minutes at 15 lbs. pressure;
5 minutes at 3¾ lbs. pressure.)
Reduce pressure with cool water.
Serves 4 to 6.

LIVER DUMPLING SOUP

*3¾ lbs. pressure 10 min-
utes*
15 lbs. pressure 8 minutes

½ lb. beef or calf's liver
1 cup bread or cracker crumbs
¼ cup boiling water
1 egg, slightly beaten
1 teaspoon salt
⅛ teaspoon pepper
½ teaspoon grated onion
2 cups Soup Stock heated to boiling

Skin liver and remove tough fiber.
Put through food chopper, followed by crumbs. Add water to
form a paste. Add remaining ingredients, mix thoroughly. Form
into balls the size of marbles.
Drop into boiling Soup Stock.
Pressure cook. Reduce pressure
with cool water. Serves 4.

CREAM OF ASPARAGUS SOUP

3¾ lbs. pressure 5 minutes
15 lbs. pressure 3 minutes

2 cups chopped asparagus
1½ cups boiling water
1 teaspoon salt
⅛ teaspoon pepper
½ teaspoon sugar
1 quart warm milk
2 tablespoons flour
2 tablespoons butter or margarine

Place asparagus in cooker with
water and seasonings. Pressure
cook. Reduce pressure with cool
water. Add milk and heat to
boiling. Blend flour and butter,
add a few tablespoons of the hot
soup and blend again. Stir into
the soup and cook until thickened. Serves 4 to 6.
CELERY. Put two cups diced celery through food chopper. Pressure cook as for Asparagus Soup.
Reduce pressure with cool water.

CORN CHOWDER

3¾ lbs. pressure 4 minutes
15 lbs. pressure 2 minutes

¼ cup sliced onion
2 tablespoons fat
1 cup cream style corn
1 cup diced potato
1 cup water
1 teaspoon salt
¼ teaspoon pepper
1 cup tomato juice
1 tablespoon flour
½ cup milk

Sauté onion in melted fat in
cooker until golden brown. Add
corn, potato, water, and seasoning. Pressure cook. Reduce pressure with cool water. Add tomato juice. Blend flour with milk
and add to chowder. Heat thoroughly. Serves 4 to 6.

CLAM CHOWDER

3¾ lbs. pressure 25 minutes
15 lbs. pressure 15 minutes

¼ cup diced salt pork
1 medium sized onion, chopped
2 cups soft shelled clams and
juice from clams
½ clove garlic, minced (optional)
2 cups water
¼ teaspoon thyme
2 tablespoons salt
⅛ teaspoon pepper
1 cup tomatoes, canned or fresh
1½ cups potatoes, cubed
1 cup diced fresh carrots
1 tablespoon butter
1 tablespoon flour

Fry pork and onions until crisp.
Halve clams, clean, separate soft
from hard parts. Mince hard sections, add to onions and pork.
Add garlic, water, seasonings,
vegetables, and strained clam
juice. Pressure cook. Reduce
pressure with cool water. Add
soft parts of clams, thicken with
blended butter and flour. Cook
uncovered until chowder boils two
minutes.

PORK CHOPS AND RICE

3¾ lbs. pressure 30 minutes
15 lbs. pressure 15 minutes

4 pork chops
1 tablespoon fat or drippings
4 tablespoons uncooked rice
4 slices onion
4 slices green pepper
2 cups canned tomatoes
1 teaspoon salt
½ teaspoon pepper

Brown chops well on both sides in cooker in melted drippings. Place rack under chops in cooker. On each chop put a tablespoon of rice, a slice of onion and green pepper, and a section of tomato. Add salt and pepper and cover with liquid from tomatoes. Pressure cook. Reduce pressure with cool water. Serves 4.

HAM AND SWEETS

3¾ lbs. pressure 12 to 20 minutes
15 lbs. pressure 10 to 15 minutes

Ham slice 1-inch thick
4 medium sweet potatoes, halved
½ cup pineapple juice
½ teaspoon cloves
½ teaspoon dry mustard
¼ cup brown sugar
4 slices pineapple
½ cup ginger ale
Flour or cornstarch

Brown ham slice on both sides in cooker. Place .potato halves on top of ham, pour in pineapple juice, sprinkle with spices and sugar. Pressure cook. Reduce pressure with cool water. Add ginger ale to gravy and thicken with a little cornstarch or flour blended with cold water. Serves 4.

PAPRIKA VEAL

3¾ lbs. pressure 20 minutes
15 lbs. pressure 15 minutes

2 lbs. veal round, ½-inch thick
1½ teaspoons paprika
2 teaspoons flour
2 tablespoons fat or drippings
¼ cup water
1 bay leaf (optional)
1½ teaspoons salt
¼ teaspoon pepper
1 cup mushrooms
1 cup sweet cream
Flour
1 tablespoon minced parsley

Cut veal into serving pieces. Sprinkle with paprika and flour. Brown in melted fat in cooker. Cool cooker few minutes before adding water to prevent evaporation. Add water and seasonings. Pressure cook. Reduce pressure with cool water. Remove meat. Add mushrooms and cream to gravy. Thicken with a little flour blended with cold water. Add veal and parsley. Serves 4 to 6.

MOCK DRUMSTICKS

3¾ lbs. pressure 20 minutes
15 lbs. pressure 15 minutes

¾ lb. veal steak, cut in 1-inch cubes
¾ lb. pork shoulder, cut in 1-inch cubes
1 egg, beaten
1 cup dry bread or cereal crumbs
3 tablespoons fat or drippings
2 teaspoons salt
⅛ teaspoon pepper
¼ cup water
½ cup sweet cream
2 tablespoons flour

Place cubes of veal and pork alternately on skewers. Dip each into egg, then into crumbs. Brown in melted fat, season. Cool cooker

a few minutes before adding water to prevent evaporation. Pressure cook. Reduce pressure with cool water. Remove meat. Mix flour with cream and heat with gravy in cooker. Serves 4.

KIDNEY STEW

3¾ lbs. pressure 12 minutes
15 lbs. pressure 8 minutes

1 lb. kidneys
½ cup water
¼ teaspoon salt
½ cup tomato
½ teaspoon meat condiment sauce

Remove skin, tubes and fat from kidneys. Cut in 1-inch cubes and soak in cold salt water ½ hour. Drain. Place kidneys, water and salt in cooker. Pressure cook. Reduce pressure with cool water. Add tomato juice and meat sauce. Thicken stew with a little flour blended with cold water.

BEEF RIB ROAST

3¾ lbs. pressure 5 to 20 minutes per lb.
15 lbs. pressure 12 to 20 minutes per lb.

1 beef rib roast, 4 to 5 lbs.
3 tablespoons fat or drippings
Salt and pepper to taste
2 tablespoons water

Wipe meat with damp cloth. Brown beef to a rich brown in cooker in melted drippings. Add seasonings. Cool cooker a few minutes before adding water to prevent evaporation. Add water to cooker. Pressure cook, the time per lb. depending on your family's preference for rare, medium, or well-done meat. Serves 6.

SWISS STEAK

3¾ lbs. pressure 30 to 35 minutes
15 lbs. pressure 20 to 25 minutes

¼ cup flour
1 teaspoon salt
Dash of pepper
1½ lbs. round, or rump beef, ¾-inch thick
3 tablespoons fat or drippings
1½ cups canned tomatoes
3 medium onions, sliced
1 cup diced celery
½ clove garlic, minced (optional)
1 tablespoon Worcestershire sauce

Combine flour, salt and pepper. Pound half the mixture with meat tenderizer into one side of beef, turn and pound remaining flour into other side. Cut beef into serving pieces. Brown meat on both sides in melted fat in cooker; add remaining ingredients. Pressure cook. Reduce pressure with cool water. If desired, simmer uncovered a few minutes to thicken sauce. Serves 4.

LAMB SHANKS AND LIMA BEANS

3¾ lbs. pressure 20 minutes
15 lbs. pressure 45 minutes

2 cups dried lima beans
½ cup diced onion
½ clove garlic, minced
¼ cup minced parsley
2 cups tomato puree
1 cup water
2 teaspoons salt
¼ teaspoon pepper
¼ teaspoon marjoram
¼ teaspoon mace
¼ teaspoon thyme
1 bay leaf
1 teaspoon sugar
4 small lamb shanks, split into halves
3 tablespoons fat or drippings

Soak washed beans overnight, or pour boiling water over them, cover, and allow to soak 1 hour. Drain, place soaked limas in cooker, add onion, garlic and parsley. Mix tomato puree, water and seasonings together and pour into cooker; mix well. Top with lamb shanks, browned well in melted fat. Pressure cook. Reduce pressure with cool water.

MEAT LOAVES

In making extra-moist, fluffy meat loaves it is suggested that the meat mixture be packed into a greased mold, placed on rack in cooker, water added, and pressure cooked. When cooking time is up, turn meat carefully out of mold. If desired, brown under broiler a few minutes. If mold is not used, chilling the loaf before cooking will help to prevent it from crumbling.

BEEF MEAT LOAF

3¾ lbs. pressure 20 minutes
15 lbs. pressure 15 minutes

1 lb. beef chuck, ground
2 eggs, slightly beaten
1 cup soft bread crumbs
⅓ cup minced onions
¼ cup minced green pepper
3 teaspoons horse-radish
2 teaspoons salt
½ teaspoon dry mustard
2 tablespoons milk
2 tablespoons catchup
3 tablespoons fat or drippings
¼ cup water

Fold in eggs with the ground beef. Add bread crumbs, onion, and green pepper, mixing gently. Stir in horse-radish, salt, mustard, milk, and catchup. Shape into loaf. Brown well on all sides in melted drippings in cooker. Brush top of loaf with additional catch-

up. Cool cooker a few minutes before adding water to prevent evaporation. Pressure cook. Reduce pressure with cool water.

HAM LOAF

3¾ lbs. pressure 40 minutes
15 lbs. pressure 30 minutes

1 lb. ground veal
1 lb. ground smoked ham
4 tablespoons catchup
2 tablespoons minced onion
3 tablespoons chopped green pepper
2 eggs beaten
1 cup dry bread crumbs
1 can cream of mushroom soup
3 tablespoons fat or drippings
⅛ cup water

Mix ingredients together in order given, except water. Shape into loaf and brown in cooker in melted drippings. Cool cooker for a few minutes before adding water to prevent evaporation. Add water to cooker and pressure cook. Reduce pressure with cool water. Serves 4 to 6.

HAM WITH ONION CAPS

3¾ lbs. pressure 22 minutes per lb.
15 lbs. pressure 20 minutes per lb.

4-5 lbs. fresh ham
2 tablespoons fat or drippings
Salt and pepper to taste
2 tablespoons water
Tiny peeled onions

Score ham in inch squares. Brown in melted drippings in cooker. Cool cooker a few minutes before adding water. Add seasonings and water. Pressure cook. Reduce pressure with cool water. Toothpick onions on scored sections of ham. Brown under broiler.

RABBIT

3¾ lbs. pressure 30 minutes
15 lbs. pressure 20 minutes

1 rabbit, cut in pieces
Flour
¼ cup fat or drippings
¼ cup minced onion
¼ cup diced green pepper
¼ cup flour
1 cup milk
1 cup water
2 teaspoons salt
½ teaspoon paprika
¼ teaspoon thyme
¼ teaspoon sage
¼ teaspoon garlic salt

Coat rabbit with flour and brown well in drippings in cooker. Remove. Sauté onions and green pepper in same drippings, add flour, then add the milk and water combined together and stir until the mixture thickens. Add seasonings. Place rabbit on rack in cooker, add gravy. Pressure cook. Reduce pressure with cool water. Serves 4 to 6.

SQUAB

3¾ lbs. pressure 12 minutes
15 lbs. pressure 8 minutes

4 or 5 squabs
1 tablespoon butter
Salt and pepper
1 recipe Raisin Dressing
1 tablespoon fat
2 tablespoons water

Season squabs. Prepare dressing and stuff squabs. Heat cooker; add fat and butter. Sear squabs golden brown on all sides. Add water. Place cover on cooker. Allow steam to flow from vent pipe to release all air from cooker. Place indicator weight on vent pipe and pressure cook. Reduce pressure under cool water. Squabs may be placed under broiler if crispness is desired. Serve with a tart jelly such as currant or grape.

FRIED CHICKEN

3¾ lbs. pressure 15 to 20 minutes
15 lbs. pressure 10 to 15 minutes

2½-pound broiler, cut in pieces
Flour
Salt and pepper
3 tablespoons fat or drippings

Roll chicken in seasoned flour and brown in cooker in drippings. Remove pieces to hot plate. Add rack and place chicken on rack. Add ¼ cup boiling water, cover and pressure cook. Reduce pressure with cool water. Remove chicken and rack from cooker and serve with country gravy made from drippings in cooker. Serves 4. Chicken may be dredged with seasoned corn meal, rolled corn flakes, bread or cracker crumbs.

COUNTRY GRAVY

4 tablespoons flour
4 tablespoons drippings
1 teaspoon salt
Dash pepper
2 cups milk

Blend flour in hot drippings, add seasonings and cook until light brown, while stirring. Add milk gradually, stirring constantly, and cook until gravy is smooth and thick. Makes 2 cups. For a richer gravy, use 1 cup milk and 1 cup cream and sprinkle with minced parsley. ¼ pound of mushrooms, sliced and sautéed, may be added.

CHICKEN WITH DUMPLINGS

3¾ lbs. pressure 50 minutes
15 lbs. pressure 40 minutes

4-pound stewing chicken, cut in pieces
2 cups water
2 teaspoons salt
Dash pepper
2 tablespoons minced parsley
1 cup diced celery
1 peeled medium onion, sliced
3 whole cloves
1 recipe Dumplings

Wash chicken and place on rack in cooker. Add all the other ingredients, cover and cook under pressure. Reduce pressure with cool water. Remove cover and rack, drop dumplings with a spoon into hot chicken and vegetables. Cover and cook, with pressure control lever open 5 minutes. Serves 6.

ROAST DUCK

3¾ lbs. pressure 15 minutes per lb.
15 lbs. pressure 10 to 12 minutes per lb.

1 4-lb. duck
1 recipe Stuffing
½ cup water

Clean, wash and dry the duck. Fill with stuffing, truss and weigh. Place on rack in cooker, add water. Pressure cook. Reduce pressure with cool water. Place on upper rack in hot oven (400°F.) or under broiler a few minutes to brown; baste with drippings. Serves 3 to 4.

STEAMED FISH

3¾ lbs. pressure 5 to 10 minutes
15 lbs. pressure 4 to 8 minutes

Cod, h a d d o c k , salmon, pike, trout, sole and other varieties of fish are suitable for steaming. Use fresh or quick frozen fish in ½-inch fillets or steaks, or cleaned whole small or medium fish.

Sprinkle fish with salt, pepper and a little lemon juice. Wrap in cheesecloth and place on rack in cooker. Add ¾ cup water, 1 teaspoon salt, and 1 tablespoon lemon juice or vinegar. Cover and cook under pressure, minutes depending on thickness of fish. Reduce pressure with cool water. If fish is to be served in individual portions, cut in serving pieces before steaming. Serve steamed fish with sauces, in scalloped dishes, croquettes, cold in salads, or in fish loaves.

STEAMED CLAMS

3¾ lbs. pressure 10 minutes
15 lbs. pressure 5 minutes

1 dozen hard-shelled clams
Cold water to cover
½ cup corn meal

Wash clams, cover with cold water, add corn meal. Let stand several hours or overnight. Wash well. Place clams on rack in cooker. Add 1 cup boiling water; cover and pressure cook. Reduce pressure with cool water. Open and separate clams from shell. Or remove rack and serve in cooker, clambake style, removing shells at the table. Serve individual cups of melted butter. Broth from clams may be served with the clams or separately.

TUNA LOAF

3¾ lbs. pressure 30 minutes
15 lbs. pressure 30 minutes

½ cup cooked rice
½ cups toasted bread crumbs mixed with 2 tablespoons melted butter
1 egg, beaten
½ teaspoon salt
½ teaspoon celery salt
Dash pepper
1 tablespoon chopped parsley
1 tablespoon chopped onion
1 tablespoon chopped pimiento
1 cup flaked canned tunafish
2 cups water

Combine ingredients in order given, except water, in greased mold. Pour water in cooker. Place mold in rack in cooker and pressure cook. Reduce pressure with cool water. Serves 4.

SHRIMP CREOLE

3¾ lbs. pressure 8 to 10 minutes
15 lbs. pressure 6 to 8 minutes

2 cups fresh shrimp
1 cup sliced onions
1 cup diced celery
¼ cup diced green pepper
1 garlic clove, minced
¼ cup fat or drippings
1 teaspoon salt
1 teaspoon granulated sugar
1 teaspoon chili powder
2 tablespoons flour
½ cup water
2½ cups canned or fresh tomatoes
1 tablespoon vinegar

Cook fresh shrimp under pressure in 3 cups water. Reduce pressure with cool water. Drain, remove shells and black vein running down back. While c l e a n i n g shrimp, cook in uncovered cooker sliced onion, celery, green pepper and garlic clove in melted fat until tender. Add salt, sugar, chili powder and flour blended in ½ cup water. Simmer over low heat for 15 minutes. Add tomatoes, vinegar and shrimp; heat t h o r o u g h l y and serve with browned rice. Serves 4.

STEAMED LOBSTER

Use only live baby lobster. Plunge it head first into boiling salted water to cover. Remove and place lobster on rack in cooker with two cups boiling salted water. Cover and cook under pressure 10 minutes. Reduce pressure with cool water. Remove lobster and serve as desired.
SALAD: Marinate for 1 hour, 2 cups of diced lobster. Drain, add 1 cup of diced celery and pile on lettuce. Cover with well seasoned mayonnaise.

LOBSTER À LA NEWBURG

2 cups diced, cooked lobster
¼ cup butter or margarine
¼ teaspoon paprika
1 teaspoon salt
Few grains nutmeg
1 tablespoon cooking sherry or lemon juice
4 egg yolks, beaten
1½ cups milk

Cook lobster according to directions for steamed lobster. Pick meat from shell and claws. Melt butter or margarine in top of double boiler; add lobster and cook uncovered over low heat for 3 minutes. Add seasonings and sherry. Beat egg yolks slightly, add milk and blend thoroughly. Add the mixture gradually to the lobster, while stirring. Cook until t h i c k e n e d , stirring constantly. Serve immediately on hot toast, in patty shells or t o a s t cups. Serves 4.

CARROT DRUMSTICKS

3¾ lbs. pressure 10 minutes
15 lbs. pressure 5 minutes

8 medium carrots
½ cup water
2 tablespoons melted butter
2 cups soft bread crumbs
1 egg, beaten
1 tablespoon minced onion
1 tablespoon chopped pimiento
1 teaspoon celery salt
1 teaspoon salt
Dash pepper
½ cup fine dry bread crumbs

Place carrots on rack in cooker, add water. Pressure cook. Reduce pressure with cool water. Drain carrots and mash. Mix butter, soft bread crumbs, egg, onion, pimiento and seasonings. Form in shape of drumsticks, inserting a wooden skewer in end of each. Roll in dry bread crumbs. Bake in 375°F. oven 15 minutes. Serves 4.

DEVILED GREEN BEANS

3¾ lbs. pressure 8 to 10 minutes
15 lbs. pressure 2 to 3 minutes

1 lb. cut green beans
½ cup water
1½ cup minced onions
2 tablespoons butter or margarine
1 tablespoon mustard
1 tablespoon horse-radish
½ teaspoon salt
Dash pepper

Place beans on rack in cooker, add water and pressure cook. Reduce pressure with cool water. Cook onions in fat until golden. Add to beans with remaining ingredients. Serves 4 to 6

WAX BEANS IN SOUR CREAM

3¾ lbs. pressure 6 to 8 minutes
15 lbs. pressure 2 to 3 minutes

1½ lbs. yellow wax beans
½ cup water
1 cup sour cream
1 egg, beaten
¼ teaspoon salt
Dash pepper

Place beans on rack, add water. Pressure cook. Reduce pressure with cool water. Drain beans. Add remaining ingredients to beans. Heat, but do not boil. Serves 4 to 6.

MINTED PEAS

3¾ lbs. pressure 4 minutes
15 lbs. pressure 1 minute

2 cups fresh peas
½ teaspoon salt
⅛ teaspoon pepper
⅓ cup water
2 tablespoons butter
2 teaspoons chopped parsley
1 teaspoon chopped mint

Place peas, salt, pepper and water in cooker. Pressure cook. Reduce pressure with cool water. Add butter, parsley and mint.

RED CABBAGE

3¾ lbs. pressure 6 to 7 minutes
15 lbs. pressure 2 minutes

1 medium head red cabbage cut in wedges
1 tablespoon minced onion
1 teaspoon salt
½ cup water
2 tablespoons butter
2 tablespoons vinegar
1 tablespoon brown sugar
¼ teaspoon cinnamon

Shred and crisp cabbage in cold water for 10 minutes. Drain, place in cooker, add onion, salt and water. Pressure cook. Reduce pressure with cool water. Add butter, vinegar, brown sugar and cinnamon. Cook a few minutes without pressure to blend sauce. Serves 4.

FRIED CABBAGE

3¾ lbs. pressure 5 to 6 minutes
15 lbs. pressure 2 minutes

4 cups coarsely cut cabbage
3 tablespoons butter or fat
½ teaspoon salt

Melt butter in cooker; add cabbage and salt. Mix well. Pressure cook. Reduce pressure with cool water. Serves 4.

BAKED POTATOES

Small
3¾ lbs. pressure 20 minutes
15 lbs. pressure 13 minutes
Medium
3¾ lbs. pressure 25 minutes
15 lbs. pressure 15 to 17 minutes
Large
3¾ lbs. pressure 45 minutes
15 lbs. pressure 23 to 25 minutes

Scrub desired number of potatoes. Cut a vertical and horizontal slit across top. Place on rack in cooker. Add ½ cup water. Pressure cook. Reduce pressure with cool water. Press potatoes toward center to burst open, fill opening with cube of butter and a dash of paprika.

VEGETABLE TIMBALES

3¾ lbs. pressure 15 minutes
15 lbs. pressure 15 minutes

2 tablespoons butter or margarine
2 tablespoons flour
¾ cup hot milk
1 teaspoon salt
Dash pepper
1 tablespoon minced onion
3 tablespoons grated cheese
2 eggs
2 cups cooked diced vegetables
1 cup water

Make a white sauce by melting the butter and mixing to a paste with the flour. Blend in milk and cook over low heat until smooth and thickened. Add seasonings, onion and cheese. Add eggs, one at a time, beating well after each addition. Fold in the vegetables. Pour the mixture into greased molds or pyrex custard cups. Cover molds with 3 thicknesses of waxed paper and fasten securely with string. Pour the water into cooker, place custard cups on rack in cooker. Pressure cook. Reduce pressure with cool water. Unmold timbales and serve with any favorite sauce. Serves 6.

CORN O'BRIEN

3¾ lbs. pressure 3 minutes
15 lbs. pressure 1 minute

½ cup shredded green pepper
2 tablespoons butter
2 cups cut corn
2 tablespoons chopped pimiento
½ teaspoon salt
⅛ teaspoon pepper
3 tablespoons water

Sauté green pepper in butter in cooker for 2 minutes. Add remaining ingredients, pressure cook. Reduce pressure with cool water. Serves 4.

SAVORY STUFFED ONIONS

3¾ lbs. pressure 15 to 20 minutes
15 lbs. pressure 12 to 15 minutes

4 large onions
½ cup water
3 tablespoons crumbs
1 tablespoon bacon drippings
2 tablespoons chopped crisp bacon
1 tablespoon minced parsley
1 egg, beaten
1 tablespoon butter
Salt and pepper to taste

Place onions on rack in cooker. Add water. Pressure cook. Reduce pressure with cool water. Drain and cool onions. Remove centers, leaving thick wall. Chop centers, add crumbs, drippings, bacon, parsley, egg, and mix well. Fill centers of onions, sprinkle top with additional crumbs, dot with butter, place in shallow baking dish and bake 10 minutes in 400°F. oven.

STUFFED ACORN SQUASH

3¾ lbs. pressure 18 minutes
15 lbs. pressure 10 minutes

½ lb. pork sausage meat
1 teaspoon salt
½ cup water
2 Acorn squash, halved and seeded

Make 4 sausages patties. · Fry till brown. Salt each half squash, place a patty in each and place on rack in cooker. Add water. Pressure cook. Reduce pressure with cool water. Serves 4.

SUMMER SQUASH DELICIOUS

3¾ lbs. pressure 5 to 6 minutes
15 lbs. pressure 2 to 3 minutes

2 medium crooked neck squash
½ cup water
½ teaspoon salt
2 tablespoons butter
2 tablespoons lemon juice
2 tablespoons minced parsley
¼ cup minced chives
⅛ teaspoon pepper

Cut squash into 1-inch slices. Place on rack in cooker, add water and salt. Pressure cook. Reduce pressure with cool water. Drain squash and mash. Mix in remaining ingredients. Serves 4 to 6.

BAKED BEANS

3¾ lbs. pressure 50 minutes
15 lbs. pressure 45 minutes

2 cups dried beans
⅓ pound salt pork, diced
3 tablespoons brown sugar
3 tablespoons molasses
1 teaspoon salt
½ teaspoon mustard
1 medium onion, diced or whole
2 tablespoons catchup
Water
    (Use 4-quart Cooker)

Soak beans overnight. Drain. Heat cooker and sear diced salt pork. Add beans, sugar, molasses, salt, mustard, onion, catchup and water enough to just cover beans. Place cover on cooker. Pressure cook. Reduce pressure with cool water. (If brown crust on beans is desired, place in casserole in hot oven or under broiler few minutes.)

CHILE CON CARNE

3¾ lbs. pressure 20 minutes

15 lbs. pressure 15 minutes

1½ lbs. ground beef
1 cup diced onion
½ cup diced green pepper
¼ cup fat or drippings
2 cups canned kidney beans
1 cup diced celery
1 No. 2½ can tomatoes
2 teaspoons salt
½ teaspoon pepper
1 teaspoon sugar
2 teaspoons chili powder
½ garlic clove, minced

Brown meat well in melted drippings in cooker. Add green pepper and onions and sauté. Mash 1 cup kidney beans and add to cooker with the cup of whole beans and remaining ingredients. Pressure cook. Reduce pressure with cool water. Allow to simmer without pressure a few minutes until d e s i r e d consistency is reached. Serves 4 to 6.

HUNGARIAN GOULASH

3¾ lbs. pressure 30 minutes

15 lbs. pressure 25 minutes

2 lbs. beef chuck or round, cut ¼-inch thick
4 tablespoons fat or drippings
2 teaspoons salt
2 teaspoons paprika
⅛ teaspoon allspice
2 bay leaves
6-oz. can tomato paste
1 cup water
4 medium onions, sliced
½ garlic clove, minced
½ cup diced green pepper

Cut meat into 1½-inch pieces. Brown well in melted fat in cooker. Add seasoning, spices, and tomato paste blended with water. Pressure cook (24 minutes at 3¾ lbs. pressure; 20 min-

utes at 15 lbs. pressure). Reduce pressure with cool water. Open cooker and add vegetables. Pressure cook (6 minutes at 3¾ lbs. pressure; 5 minutes at 15 lbs. pressure). Reduce pressure with cool water. Serves 4 to 6.

STUFFED GREEN PEPPERS

3¾ lbs. pressure 15 minutes

15 lbs. pressure 10 minutes

4 green peppers
¾ lb. ground beef
½ cup cooked rice
1 small egg
¼ cup water
1 tablespoon minced onion
1 teaspoon salt
¼ teaspoon pepper
1 cup tomato soup

Wash and clean peppers. Combine remaining ingredients, except t o m a t o soup, and mix thoroughly. Fill pepper shells lightly with meat mixture. Place on rack in cooker. Add soup. Pressure cook. Reduce pressure with cool water. Serves 4.

CHOP SUEY

3¾ lbs. pressure 12 minutes

15 lbs. pressure 10 minutes

1 lb. pork or veal cut in strips
2 tablespoons fat or drippings
¼ cup flour
1 cup water
2 tablespoons soy sauce
2 tablespoons molasses
2 teaspoons salt
¼ teaspoon pepper
½ cup diced green pepper
2 cups diced celery
1 cup sliced onion
1 cup sliced mushrooms
1½ cups canned bean sprouts

Brown meat well in melted drip-

pings in cooker. Add flour and blend. Add water, soy sauce, molasses and seasonings. Pressure cook (7 minutes at 3¾ lbs. pressure; 8 minutes at 15 lbs. pressure). Reduce pressure with cool water. Open cooker and add vegetables. Pressure cook again (5 minutes at 3¾ lbs. pressure; 2 minutes at 15 lbs. pressure). Reduce pressure with cool water. Serve with rice. Serves 4 to 6.

SAVORY BEEF STEW

3¾ lbs. pressure 30 minutes

15 lbs. pressure 25 minutes

2 tablespoons fat or drippings
2 pounds chuck, or rump beef, cut in 1-inch cubes
2 teaspoons salt
¼ teaspoon pepper
1 bay leaf
1 teaspoon condiment sauce
½ cup water
6 small onions, peeled
1 cup diced celery
4 medium potatoes, quartered
4 medium carrots, sliced
2 cups canned or fresh tomatoes
3 tablespoons flour
¼ cup water
2 tablespoons minced parsley

Melt fat in cooker, brown meat on all sides. Place on rack in cooker. Add seasonings and ½ cup water. Cover and cook under pressure (24 minutes at 3¾ lbs. pressure; 20 minutes at 15 lbs. pressure). Reduce pressure with cool water. Add vegetables, cover c o o k e r, and cook under pressure again (6 minutes at 3¾ lbs. pressure; 5 minutes at 15 lbs. pressure). Reduce pressure with cool water and remove stew and rack, blend flour and water, add to gravy, and cook (uncovered), while stirring until thickened. Add stew and minced parsley, heat through and serve.

DESSERTS

PRUNE MARMALADE WHIP

3¾ lbs. pressure 15 minutes
15 lbs. pressure 12 minutes

½ lb. dried prunes
½ cup water
¼ cup orange marmalade
1 teaspoon lemon juice
2 tablespoons sugar
2 egg whites
4 teaspoons chopped nuts

Pressure cook prunes and water together in cooker. Reduce pressure with cool water. Remove stones from prunes and mash the pulp. Add lemon juice, sugar and marmalade. Fold in stiffly beaten egg whites. Pile in dessert glasses and garnish with chopped nuts. Chill. Serves 4.

DATE CRUMB PUDDING

3¾ lbs. pressure 1 hr. 50 minutes
15 lbs. pressure 1 hr. 20 minutes
(Time includes steaming)

2½ cups toasted bread crumbs
¾ cup brown sugar, firmly packed
½ teaspoon soda
½ teaspoon baking powder
½ teaspoon cinnamon
⅛ teaspoon nutmeg
1 cup diced dates
1 egg, well beaten
¾ cup milk

Combine crumbs, sugar, soda, baking powder, cinnamon, nutmeg and dates. Combine egg and milk, add to crumb mixture and blend. Pour into greased 1-lb. coffee tin, or individual molds. Cover with lid or 3 thicknesses waxed paper, tied securely. Pour

2 cups water in cooker, place mold on rack in cooker. Steam 30 minutes without pressure, then pressure cook (80 minutes at 3¾ lbs. pressure; 50 minutes at 15 lbs. pressure). Reduce pressure with cool water. Serves 6.

VANILLA CUSTARD

3¾ lbs. pressure 8 minutes
15 lbs. pressure 4 minutes

2 cups milk
2 eggs
¼ cup sugar
¼ teaspoon salt
1 teaspoon vanilla
Nutmeg
½ cup boiling water

Scald milk. Beat eggs slightly. Add sugar and salt and blend. Add scalded milk to egg mixture, mix thoroughly. Add vanilla. Pour into 6 oiled pyrex cups. Cover tops with 3 thicknesses of waxed paper and tie with string. Pour the water into the cooker, place custard cups on rack in cooker. Pressure cook. Cool cooker at room temperature (5 minutes), then with cool water. Serves 6.

VARIATIONS

Caramel—Melt ¼ cup sugar in a skillet over low heat until it caramelizes, stirring constantly. Pour some of the caramel syrup immediately into each of the custard cups. Pour vanilla custard into each cup, and proceed as usual. Chill and unmold.
Chocolate—Use chocolate milk in place of regular milk, or add 1½ squares unsweetened chocolate to milk in top of double boiler and heat until melted. Beat with beater until blended.
Fruit—Arrange chilled, sliced bananas, pitted dates, prunes or other fresh or canned fruit in in-

dividual serving dishes. Pour vanilla custard into each cup or into large mold. Chill and serve.
Macaroon—Use recipe for vanilla custard, topping individual servings with crushed macaroons. Or place small macaroons in bottom of individual custard cups or line bottom of pint mold with crushed macaroons before filling with custard.
Maple—Omit sugar and vanilla. Substitute ⅓ cup maple syrup.

PLUM PUDDING

3¾ lbs. pressure 1¾ hours
15 lbs. pressure 1 hour

1 cup all purpose flour
1 teaspoon soda
1 teaspoon cinnamon
½ teaspoon cloves
½ teaspoon nutmeg
½ teaspoon salt
½ cup graham cracker crumbs
½ cup suet, ground fine
1 cup raisins
½ cup walnut meats
½ cup honey
½ cup fruit juice
1 egg, beaten

Triple sift dry ingredients. Add graham cracker crumbs, suet, raisins and nuts. Combine honey, fruit juice and egg with flour mixture and beat until smooth. Pour into a greased 1-lb. mold or individual molds. Cover with lid or waxed paper. Pour two cups water in cooker, place mold on rack in cooker. Steam 30 minutes without pressure, then pressure cook. Reduce pressure with cool water. Serves 6. Any of the following sauces may be served with this pudding: Hard Sauce, Brandy Sauce, Fluffy Brandy Sauce or Hot Rum Sauce. Pour ¼ cup brandy over pudding, light, and carry flaming to the table.

BANANA CARAMEL PIE

3¾ lbs. pressure 1½ hours
15 lbs. pressure 1 hour

1 can sweetened condensed milk, caramelized*
⅓ cup hot coffee (or hot water)
1 Crumb Pie Shell
Bananas

Cover bottom of pie shell with sliced bananas. Add hot coffee to can of caramelized milk and beat until smooth. Pour into pie shell, decorate with whipped cream or nuts.

To Caramelize Milk—Place unopened can of sweetened condensed milk on rack in cooker with 4 cups water. Pressure cook. Reduce pressure with cool water. Several cans may be caramelized at one time and chilled for future use. Caramelized milk can be used for pudding desserts, beaten until smooth with ½ cup hot coffee, water or fruit juices, and piled into sherbet glasses.

FRUIT RICE MOLD

3¾ lbs. pressure 2 minutes
15 lbs. pressure 1 minute

1 cup diced fresh fruit
¼ cup water
1¼ teaspoons unflavored gelatin
2 tablespoons water
2 tablespoons sugar
2 cups cooked rice
Dash salt
½ cup heavy whipped cream

Pressure cook the fruit in ¼ cup water. Reduce pressure with cool water. Soften gelatin in the 2 tablespoons water and dissolve in the hot fruit mixture. Add rice and salt, mixing well. Fold in whipped cream. Pour into mold and chill. When firm, unmold and garnish with whipped cream.

DRIED FRUIT COMPOTE

3¾ lbs. pressure 12 minutes
15 lbs. pressure 10 minutes

½ cup dried apricots
½ cup dried peaches
½ cup dried prunes
½ cup dried pears
¼ cup raisins
2 cups water
1 tablespoon cornstarch
½ cup sugar
⅛ teaspoon salt
¼ orange and rind, sliced thin
¼ lemon and rind, sliced thin
1 tablespoon red cinnamon candies

Pre-soak fruits only if extremely dry. Blend cornstarch with water. Combine all ingredients. Pressure cook. Reduce pressure with cool water. Chill. Serves 4 to 6.

BOSTON BROWN BREAD

3¾ lbs. pressure 60 minutes
15 lbs. pressure 45 minutes
(Time includes steaming)

½ cup whole-wheat flour
½ cup rye flour
½ cup corn meal
¾ teaspoon baking soda
¾ teaspoon salt
6 tablespoons molasses
1 cup sour milk or buttermilk
⅓ cup raisins

Combine dry ingredients. Stir in molasses and sour milk and blend. Add raisins, stirring to mix well. Fill two 1-pint greased molds ⅔ full and cover with 3 thicknesses of waxed paper. Add 2 cups boiling water to cooker. Place molds on rack. Cover cooker and steam 15 minutes with pressure control lever open. Then cook under pressure (45 minutes at 3¾ lbs. pressure; 30 minutes at 15 lbs. pres-

sure). Reduce pressure with cool water. Remove cover, run spatula between bread and mold to loosen, then invert on cake rack. Serve hot or cold. Makes 2 small loaves.

RHUBARB ORANGE PUDDING

3¾ lbs. pressure 2 minutes
15 lbs. pressure 1 minute

1 lb. rhubarb cut in 1-inch pieces
½ cup water
1 cup orange juice
Grated rind of 1 orange
¾ cup sugar
1 tablespoon cornstarch

Place rhubarb, water, orange juice, orange rind and sugar in cooker. Pressure cook. Reduce pressure with cool water. Mix cornstarch to a paste with 2 tablespoons water. Stir into rhubarb mixture and simmer a few minutes until pudding thickens. Serves 4.

PRESSURE COOKED CHOCOLATE FUDGE

3¾ lbs. pressure 10 minutes
15 lbs. pressure 5 minutes

1 can sweetened condensed milk
2 pkgs. (12 oz.) semi-sweet chocolate bits
½ cup chopped nuts
1 teaspoon vanilla

Place milk and chocolate bits in pyrex or metal dish, cover with waxed paper and tie securely. Pour 2 cups water in cooker, place dish on rack in cooker and pressure cook. Reduce pressure with cool water. Remove paper cover and stir mixture thoroughly, add nuts and vanilla. Drop by teaspoons onto waxed paper and allow to harden.

Index

X

L